After

LOVE SIGNS

LINDA GOODMAN'S LOVE SIGNS

Other books by Linda Goodman

LINDA GOODMAN'S SUN SIGNS
VENUS TRINES AT MIDNIGHT

Linda Goodman's

A New Approach

LOVE SIGNS

to the Human Heart

HARPER & ROW, PUBLISHERS

NEW YORK, HAGERSTOWN, SAN FRANCISCO, LONDON

Grateful acknowledgment is made for permission to reprint:

"Something Wonderful." Copyright © 1951 by Richard Rodgers & Oscar Hammerstein II Williamson Music Inc., owner of publication and allied rights for the Western Hemisphere and Japan. International Copyright Secured. All rights reserved. Used by permission.

"Try a Little Tenderness," by Harry Woods, Jimmy Campbell, Reg Connelly. Copyright 1932, renewed 1960 Campbell, Connelly, Co., Ltd. All rights for the United States and Canada controlled by Robbins Music Corporation, New York, N.Y. Used by permission.

Endpaper drawings by Handelsman.

FIRST EDITION

Designed by Lydia Link

Library of Congress Cataloging in Publication Data

Goodman, Linda.
  Linda Goodman's Love signs.
  1. Astrology. 2. Love. I. Title. II. Title: Love signs.
BF1729.L6G64   1978   133.5′8′30141   78-2141
ISBN 0-06-011550-5

---

78 79 80 81 82 10 9 8 7 6 5 4 3 2

H.R.H.

after years of many inexplicable delays, over which the
author in no way had any control . . . and through Karma's
strange pattern of destiny

Love Signs

was completed in the summer of 1978 in the same haunted
room where it was begun in the winter of 1970

Suite 1217

The Hollywood Roosevelt Hotel
on Hollywood Boulevard
in Los Angeles, the city of "Lost Angels"

the room in which the author's forthcoming book
about reincarnation and other magics

Goooobers

was also conceived . . . and was born . . . beneath the
light of the "small white cross, planted on the far
hill, behind Grauman's Chinese Theatre"

". . . . . and the light shineth
in the darkness, and the darkness
comprehendeth it not . . . . ."

JOHN 1:5

The verses beginning each section of the text have been taken from the work of J. M. Barrie, *Peter Pan*.

☆ ☆ ☆

The occasional verses throughout the chapters are quoted from *Venus Trines at Midnight* by Linda Goodman, to be republished by Harper & Row in 1979.

with Everlasting Love

I dedicate this
and all my future books
to "my sneaky guru"
Aaron Goldblatt

who has patiently, throughout all incarnations, guided
my creative efforts and spiritual enlightenment with
the infinite gentleness and wisdom of a Master Avatar;
and who has been . . . is now and ever shall be . . .
responsible for all my miracles . . . every single one
of them manifested only through his faith.

*"Be not forgetful to entertain strangers, for
thereby some have entertained angels, unawares."*

HEBREWS 13:2

*"My children, errors will be forgiven. In our obsession
with original sin, we do often forget . . . original innocence.*

POPE INNOCENT, OF ASSISI
15th Century A.D.

a special acknowledgment
of gratitude

to the patient Bull
Sam O. Goodman

without whose steady loyalty and devotion I would not
have been able to write this or any other book

also to

Sarah Elizabeth Snyder, the Archer
William Dana Snyder, the Water Bearer
Jill Kemery Goodman, the Goat
Michael Aaron Goodman, the Eagle

my children ... who have taught me, over the years,
many lessons of love ... from the multi-faceted
viewpoints of Sagittarius, Aquarius, Capricorn and Scorpio

and the three Lions

Robert S. Kemery   Roland H. Chinatti
                Robert A. Brewer

my heartfelt thanks to

the three Wise Men

Morton L. Janklow   Arthur Klebanoff   Jerome Traum

who symbolically parted the Red Sea so that this book
could be published, very much in the manner of Moses,
using the effective combination of ancient alchemy,
courage, professional brilliance . . .
and Aaron's rod

also to . . .

Buz Wyeth and Erwin Glikes

who have restored my faith in the integrity
of the publishing profession through their
personal honor and idealism

... and now we must return to that desolate home from which she took flight,
so long ago. It seems a shame to have neglected her family all this time; yet
we may be sure that Sally's mother and father do not blame us. If we had
returned sooner to look at them with sorrowful sympathy, they would
probably have cried, "Don't be silly! What do we matter? Do go back, and
keep an eye on Sally." So long as mothers and fathers are like that, children
will take advantage of them, and you may lay to that.

Even now, we are no more than servants. Why on earth should Sally's
bed be properly aired, seeing that she left home in such a thankless hurry?
Would it not serve her jolly well right if she came back and found that her
family was spending the weekend in the country? It would indeed be a
moral lesson all children need. But if we contrived things this way, Sally's
mother and father, her grandfather and grandma, her brothers and her sister,
would never forgive us.

One thing I would like to do immensely, and that is to tell Sally's mother,
in the way authors have, that her child is coming back, that indeed she will be
here on Thursday week. That would spoil completely the surprise to which
the angels and druids and Sally herself are so looking forward. They've all of
them been planning it: her mother's rapture, her Dad's shout of joy, Bill's and
Jill's and Michael's leap through the air to embrace her first, when what all of
them should be preparing for is a good hiding. How delicious to spoil it, by
breaking the news ahead of time, so that, when she enters grandly, her
mother may not even offer her her mouth, and her Dad may exclaim
pettishly, "Dash it all, here's that pesky girl again!" However, we are
beginning to know Sally's family by this time, and we may be sure that we
would get no thanks, even for this. They would quite likely upbraid us, for
depriving the angels and druids .. and Sally herself .. of their pleasure.

I can't forget that the next-to-the-last-time I saw you — you were with Marc. Because of astrology's wisdom (and for other reasons too) I believe that was the symbol of an unexpected twin-joy ending to temporary shadows and confusion. For things are not always what they seem, and people are sometimes too willing to believe whatever they are told. Time will tell. Faith bestows awesome miracles upon the faithful. This I know.

I thought maybe I could let you know the way it is with me . . . with Dad and Dadoo and Bill and Mike and Jill and Grandma G. . . . with all of us . . . by sending you a message through some paragraphs from *Peter Pan*, with slight changes to fit this reality. So I'm using James Barrie's words to try to express what we feel. They begin on the next page.

There's just this one more thing I wanted to tell you. Over and over since you disappeared, I keep dreaming the same dream. About the time I ran away when I was a little girl . . . to St. Raphael's convent on Thirteenth Street, in Parkersburg. The music . . . the incense . . . the whispering sisters . . . the scent of pine and the manger scene . . . the flickering candles . . . all seem so *real* in my dream. Isn't that strange ?

all my love, with all my heart

Mom

a carousel message to Sally

There is so much to say, and no way to say it, no way to tell you. Maybe if I try to say some of it here, then somehow, someway, you may read it.

You must have guessed I couldn't complete this book until I found you and we bear-hugged again. But now it seems the only way to make the miracle of you manifest is to finish it, so it can be published in time for your next birthday, by Christmas of 1978 . . . for so many reasons I can't fully explain until we're together. And so, I'm going to begin tonight, while it's magical and still and holy, to complete *Love Signs* — for you. Because Aaron said, before he went away . . . that you would want me to, that it would help so many people . . . and that it would bring you back sooner.

Your horoscope . . . and my heart . . . both insisted that what I was told on that terrible December day in 1973 was a lie. As soon as I heard, Michael and I flew to New York to *prove* it a lie. It was a very lonely faith. At first, everyone but Mike and Aaron thought my judgment had been prejudiced by grief. I could see it in their eyes when they looked at me. But I went right on believing anyway.

None of the official "records" seemed real to me. *They* seemed like the dream, not *you*. Only what I knew inside was real; so I clung to that, no matter what anyone tried to make me believe. Every day, for the longest time, Mike and Jill and I walked over to St. Patrick's and said a prayer near the statue of Francis of Assisi, just outside the church, among the trees. Once, we left some roses there, and when we went back the next morning, they had miraclized, like the ones I gave you that time . . . remember ?

After a while, I proved it wasn't true. I proved it medically and scientifically. My faith was rewarded, the way I used to tell you that faith always is — if you believe long enough and hard enough. Ray Neff and his wife, Gus, who worked with me on the Lincoln research, helped me a lot with the proof I needed. So did Cleve Backster and Padre Anselmo, of the Benedictine Order — in an unusual way I'll tell you about someday. But even proving astrology and my heart had been right all along didn't help me to find you. Maybe completing this book will do that, in some mysterious way.

"But my dear Madam, it is only ten days till Thursday week, near Easter .. or is it Thanksgiving ? . . . so that, by telling you what's what, we can save you days of unhappiness."

"Yes, but at what a cost ! By depriving the angels and druids and Sally of ten minutes of delight."

You see, the woman has no proper spirit. I had meant to say extraordinarily nice things about Sally's mother, but now I despise her, and not one of them will I say. She does not need to be told to have things ready, for she already has them ready. Sally's bed is aired, and she seldom leaves the house, and observe, the window is even left open for her. For all the use we are to Sally's mother, we might go back to our own galaxy. However, as we are here, we may as well stay and look on. That is all we are, lookers-on. Nobody really wants us. So let us watch, and say jaggy things.

Sally's dad is now living in Heathcliffe's old doghouse. When his daughter flew away, he felt in his bones that all the blame was his, that everyone had been wiser than he. Of course, he is a simple man, and extremely stubborn. He has a noble sense of justice and the courage to do what seems right to him; and having thought the matter out with anxious care after Sally's flight, he went down on all fours and crawled into Heathcliffe's kennel, which is where he has stayed — and remains to this day. To all invitations to come out, he answers, so sadly, but very firmly, "No. This is the place for me." Each night, when he returns from work, he crawls back into his kennel.

Let us look again at Sally's mother, a very sad-eyed woman. Now that we look at her more closely and remember the gaiety of the old days, all gone now, just because she has lost her babe, I find I won't be able to say nasty things about her after all. If she is too fond of her rubbishy children, she can't help it. Look at her in her chair, where she has fallen asleep. The corner of her mouth, where one looks first, the corner Sally always kissed, is almost withered up. Her hand moves restlessly on her breast, as if she had a pain there.

Suppose, to make her happy, we whisper to her in her sleep that her child is coming back. She is really within two miles of the window now, and flying strong, but all we need whisper is that she is on her way. Let's !

It is a pity we did it, for she has started up, calling Sally's name, and there is no one in the room but Heathcliffe.

"Oh, Heathcliffe, I dreamt my Sally had come back !"

All the dog could do was to put his paw gently on his mistress's lap, and they sat there thus for the longest time.

When Thursday week came, Sally at first planned to tiptoe in and place her hands over her mother's eyes. But then she realized that she must break the joyous news more gently. For great joy is akin to great sorrow, and can be quite dangerous to the heart. She finally decided to just slip into her bed, and be there when they all came in next morning, just as if she had never been away.

And so, when her mother and father and Bill and Jill and Michael came in next morning, they saw Sally there, sleeping like a princess in a faerie tale. She waited for their cry of joy, but it did not come. They saw her, but they did not believe she was there. You see, they had seen her there so often, in their dreams, that they all thought this was just the old dream, hanging around them still. Sally did not understand this, and a cold fear fell upon her.

"Mom! Dad! Bill! Jill! Michael! Don't you know me?"

"That's Sally!" cried her mother, even though she was sure it was only the dream.

At last, the truth of the miracle exploded within them, and there could not have been a lovelier sight on earth. There was no one to see it but a few straggling angels and druids who had stayed behind to watch . . . and a strange man peeking through the window, the one who had brought it all about. He had ecstasies innumerable that we can never know; yet he was looking through the window at the one joy he could not join. But they all knew he was there. Michael was certain he saw him grinning, and Jill thought she saw a copy of *The New York Times* tucked under his arm.

Oh! the bliss of that moment . . the reunion! There are really no words to describe it, at least none yet taught on this planet, but I am told, on good authority, that every single person in the room levitated . . that is, they all found they could fly. And they flew about the room for many, many days. Later, they knew it had all truly happened, for they found, out on the street, beneath the window, a tattered and torn copy of the *Times*, with very small letters printed in ink at the very top of the page . . . the initials A.G.

☆ ☆ ☆ ☆ ☆ ☆

LINDA GOODMAN'S LOVE SIGNS

Contents

APPENDIXES

Love Signs

...why it was written

As you will discover in this book, there are many more Sun Signs with which we have the potential for easy compatibility, sympathy and understanding than those with which we may find some degree of tension, antipathy or lack of communication . . . . . more opportunities for love and compassion than for hatred and mistrust in the harmonics of our solar system.

Yet concerned men and women in all walks of Life, from geologists and ecologists to prophets and astrologers, persistently predict the possibility of approaching cataclysms, both man-made and natural, bringing the danger of annihilation before the critical next decade has passed on this waning planet, so fast losing light. We have been warned, but few have heeded the warning. We have been called, but few have answered. For the Earth to wax again, clearly a miracle is needed.

By learning to use the wisdom of the planets, our co-Creators' code to Universal Truth, we may each create a fragment of the rainbow-spectrum message of *Peace on Earth to men . . . and women . . . of good will* caroled by celestials over Bethlehem two thousand years ago to usher in the Pisces Age of the gentle Nazarene, Who asked us only to "love one another," promising that what He did, *we* could "then do also."

It's not too late, for the joyous message of angelic hosts (not yet identified) still rings its clarion call today . . . now ushering in the Aquarian Age . . . heralding hope to those who watch the skies and listen for the music. There could be, I think, no greater prelude to a miracle so needed, perhaps approaching sooner than we guess, than to employ the art of ancient wise men to pave the way for His return with a new Star Quest for love . . . love of man for woman . . . and of both together then for every living plant and creature. For love alone has the power to bring peace at history's twilight hour to Earthlings of good will.

Linda Goodman

In the Year of Our Lord 1978

To All My Readers

Love Signs contains a number of controversial concepts of a moral, philo-sophical and intellectual nature, in the areas of science and religion.

To some of you, these concepts will be inspiring — to others, they will appear strange and startling — to still others they could be deeply disturbing. They are presented here as truth, and will be recognized as such by many of you — just as they may be viewed as otherwise by some.

I've shared my personal discoveries of truth with you because I believe that any kind of search implies an obligation to exchange with others what has been found, in the interest of hastening the sunrise of harmony on Earth, the ultimate Peace.

However, I do not ask — nor do I even expect — any of you to regard my concepts as *your* truth, unless they should happen to agree with your own personal enlightenment and private convictions.

Partial truth — the seeds of wisdom — can be found in many places. In primal instinct may partial truth be found . . . in earthly law, social custom, scientific research, philosophy and religious doctrine. The seeds of wisdom are contained in all scriptures ever written . . . especially in art, music and poetry . . . and, above all, in Nature.

But *real* Truth can be found in one place only — in every man's and woman's communion with an eternal Source of hidden Knowledge within — which each individual must seek and find for himself or herself.

We may point out the path to others, but each must walk along that path alone — until every single "lost one" has made the whole journey — and all of us have finally reached the Light of full-born Wisdom at the end of the Way . . . where we began, a long-forgotten Time ago.

Foreword

Like Peter Pan's shadow, curiosity about astral compatibility follows the astrologer "second from the right and straight on till morning." At every gathering, someone is sure to demand an answer to a question such as: "How does Sagittarius get along with Pisces?" Typically, on radio and television shows, in newspaper interviews, the astrological professional is invariably confronted with: "My husband is a Leo and I'm an Aquarian. Is that why we fight so much?" — or: "What's the best sign for Gemini to marry?"

Everyone wants to know the ground rules in the game of mixing and matching Sun Signs. I've even found myself helpless in a dental chair, having a tooth extracted, while the attending doctor remarked, "Not that I believe in astrology, but what are my chances with a Capricorn woman?"

Now, those of you who were once young (and, I hope, still are) know that Tinker Bell told Peter: "Everytime a child says 'I don't believe in faeries,' there is a faerie somewhere who falls down dead." Likewise, everytime someone says, "I don't believe in the stars," there is a human relationship somewhere that falls down dead because of a lack of understanding that could have been gained from a basic knowledge of astrology — and that's not make-believe. It's a fact. There's nothing mysterious about the oldest art and science in the world, unless you choose to call the miracles of love and tolerance that result from using it "mysterious." Semantics aside, it works, whatever you call it.

As for those familiar characters in Neverland, Peter Pan and Wendy, although I've used some of their remarks throughout this book to symbolize, at various times, certain characteristics of all twelve astrological signs, Peter's personal Natal Sun was in the Mutable Air Element of Gemini when he was created. Oh, yes! Peter was a Sun Sign Gemini — even though I use particular quotes of his to symbolize other signs in the book, a Sun Sign Gemini he was, who desired never to grow up, searching for something he never quite found, forever destined to be sure only of his own shadow, never of another human being — until, we trust, through eventual enlightenment, he learned at last the lesson of love.

Wendy was clearly a Cancerian — motherly, possessive, gentle and learned that he was anxiously trying to reach her at exactly the same hour. Those who love faithfully, and who understand how to use the cord of electrical energy that binds them together, don't need Western Union, the post office or the telephone company to communicate. They're always in touch through their astral "eastern-union." There have been countless such occurrences between two people in all kinds of love relationships — parent and child, close friends, husbands and wives . . and lovers.

We still hear the shouts of science: "Give us the facts, the facts, the facts!" Astronomy and science, each unable to see the great metaphysical forest of knowledge through the trees of lower mathematics and physics, sans the "meta," while metaphysics could explain so many mysteries. "Meta" is a Greek word meaning, simply, "beyond." Beyond the fiction of Fact lies Truth? Einstein was aware. Yes, Abstract Al knew. Someday very soon in this dawning Aquarian Age, the discovery of instruments sensitive enough to measure the tremendous energy of love's magnetic force field will demonstrate how its electrical impulses can interrupt Nature's laws (but not adversely), reverse gravity (and also reverse the aging process, through cell regeneration), increase telepathic communion and cause many other miraculous manifestations, including conscious recall of former incarnations, which will finally convince skeptical science. Yes, love can do all this, if the desire is strong enough, and the motive unselfish — where enough faith and enough will are exerted. It happens every day.

It's been frequently observed, by witnesses of credibility, that a ninety-pound woman can lift the wheels of a two-ton truck if her child is caught beneath it — a complete reversal of the laws of physics but in absolute accord with the laws of *meta*-physics. Love is far more than an emotion or a feeling. Love is a positive electrical impulse. Science has not yet developed equipment delicate or sophisticated enough to detect these impulses; nevertheless, they do exist. "Scientists" didn't believe in electronic radio waves either until they could be *measured* . . . . yet they were *there* all along. As H. T. Buckle wrote, in his *History of Civilization in England:* ". . . according to the ordinary course of affairs, a few generations pass away, then comes a period when these very truths are looked upon as commonplace facts; and a little later, there comes another period in which they are declared to be necessary, and even the dullest intellect wonders how they could ever have been denied."

During the weary search for one's own Twin Soul, there will be many side trips, many relationships that at first appear to be genuine, then fade into disinterest and boredom. Even when the Soul Mate is at last discovered, there are often many complications and testings of worthiness which cause temporary pain. Only in continually and consistently practicing tolerance and forgiveness can the hurt be alleviated. To return pain for pain only creates

imaginative, trying out her wings in a flight of fancy under the Full Moon, as Moon Maidens often do. No strong Sun Sign harmony between them, you see, so they quarreled now and then, and each heard a different drummer. Wendy ended up in the final chapter as nearly all Cancerians do, safe and secure. No matter how wistfully her heart longed to fly again, she chose home, marriage and children as her ultimate dreams; while Peter, like nearly all Geminis, continued his eternal search for a brighter rainbow, somewhere beyond . . . still obsessed by twin desires, longing to settle down with Wendy, yet longing just as fiercely to remain free — and true to himself.

But the Moon was surely in Aquarius when Wendy was born, in trine (harmonious) Luminary aspect to Peter's Gemini Sun, which is why she flew away with him in the first place . . . and promised to return to clean his house every spring.

It's worth all the time and trouble it takes to compare two horoscopes for compatibility, because when you find a trined, sextiled or conjuncted relationship between two Sun Signs — and also a trined, sextiled or conjuncted relationship between the mutual Sun and Moon Signs (the signs transited by the Sun and the Moon at the time of both births) — plus a positive interchange of the signs on the Ascendents with the Luminaries — love then takes on a deeper dimension. All love is capable of energizing wishes into reality, but love between two people whose personal auras have thus harmoniously blended creates the kind of vibration poets write about, and can manifest marvelous magic.

Wandering through the millions of couples on Earth who are attempting to achieve (or have achieved) satisfying contentment and fulfillment together — and those who are still struggling through heavy sexual karmic testing — are those rare ones esoterically called "Soul Mates" . . . or "Twin Souls."

It sometimes happens that a man and a woman meet and instantly recognize the other half of themselves behind the eyes of each other. The eyes have been rightly called "the windows of the soul." Even their voices are familiar to each other's ears, like a remembered chord of music. These are two who immediately sense the unalterable fact that they have been — are — and must always be One; even though they might have fought against their fate for centuries and struggled in vain to escape their linked destiny. Almost from the first moment they meet and gaze upon each other, their spirits rush together in joyful recognition, ignoring all convention and custom, all social rules of behavior, driven by an inner knowing too overwhelming to be denied. Inexplicably, often without a word being spoken, they *know* that only through each other can they hope to find Wholeness — only when they're together can they both be Complete in every way.

Somehow, they feel Immortal, and they are . . . for this level of love can bestow the beginning knowledge of the attainment of several-centuries-longevity in the same flesh body on the Earth plane, as well as the accomplishment of changing flesh bodies (the Temples of the soul) in a fully conscious state, without the "coma" called death. The solution to the problem of the "over-population" which rises to the mind as a result of such achievement by everyone on Earth must wait till a forthcoming book for a detailed discussion.

Neither will I attempt to detail the origin and ultimate destiny of Twin Souls here, since I've done so in another forthcoming book, called *Gooobers*, to be published in the near future. But there is so much burning curiosity concerning the subject of Soul Mates or Twin Souls, it bears some explanation here, however incomplete.

A man and a woman who are Soul Mates hardly need to speak the words "I love you," knowing as surely as they do that they must belong to each other whether in this present incarnation (lifetime)—or (due to karmic complications) at the end of many more centuries. The words in the marriage ceremony "those which God hath joined together, let no man put asunder" refer to such as these. Yet this warning is unnecessary, simply symbolic ritual, for no man *can* break the tie between Twin Souls, not even themselves. Nor can any energy in the Universe. The Force that created them is all-powerful and indestructible. The bond may be weakened, their final union and consummation delayed, but they cannot be separated permanently. There can be no end to the kind of happiness they may claim—when they wish to do so—on a timetable dictated by the Free Will choice of the Higher Angels of their own selves. (The Superconscious or Supraconscious of each.)

This kind of instant magnetic attraction is often called "love at first sight," which is no accident of fate, but very real. It's more than curious coincidence that Twin Souls, out of the whole huge world, should be drawn together at the appointed time. The crossing of their paths has been predestined on a Higher Level of Awareness. Certain spiritual energies are at work to bring about their meetings, as surely as the migration of birds and the return of comets are governed by a similar Universal Law. Their coming-together is controlled by the workings of Karma, which is but the sum total of *Causes* set into motion in the Past—and these determine infallibly the conditions of the Present. When the time comes for Twin Souls to incarnate, they are sent to Earth, clothed in flesh (again, the bodies being the Temples of the soul) through particular Time-Energy Forces, at the moment in Earth Time when certain planetary configurations create the proper conditions. These Time-Energy Forces are electro-magnetic in nature, yet more complex than this.

None of us can control the eventual results of the Causes we've initiated or set into motion in our past lives, although we *can* control our *re*-actions to the results such past Causes bring into the present lifetime. The "Free Will" to change these karmic events is possessed by the Higher Self, and we may attain such power by learning to tune into or communicate with the Hig[her] Self (Supraconscious). But "Free Will" on a *conscious* level can only [be] realized in the Future—since, in the ever-moving stream called the Pres[ent] we are setting into motion, through actions we currently initiate and thr[ough] our *re*-actions to past Causes—the future conditions we will inevitably [meet.]

As for which particular planetary influences in the nativities (horos[copes] or birth charts) of two people reveal to an astrologer the indication that [they] are Twin Souls, they are too intricate to comprehensively explain in this [book] in their entire scope—and must await another volume planned conc[erning] this and related subjects. But assuming that such planetary influen[ces] present in the respective charts of lovers, a destiny is revealed in whi[ch the] two will meet involuntarily—and cannot be separated, even thro[ugh the] experience of death—except for temporary intervals of Earth Tim[e in the] present life, for the purpose of karmic soul-testing. During these pe[riods of] being apart, however brief or however extended, both persons are [sad,] empty and incomplete. Yet even throughout any such temporary s[eparation in] their togetherness, there's a constant, pulsing astral communication [between] them—for even then, they are linked by a cord that connects them [for many] miles.

A woman I know was recently in a state of emotional anxiety, [desperate]ly needing communication with the man she loved (a Twin Soul), [who was] out of the country. There was no way they could reach each other [by phone] or letter. One night, as she was lying in her bed in the dark, s[he felt his] presence strongly but frustrated at being unable to see or hear or [touch him,] she cried out aloud, involuntarily, "Oh, why can't you *hear* me [?"] Suddenly the lamp on the desk across the room snapped on. A[fter a] moment, a large paper daisy he had given her months before dro[pped to the] floor. Astonished, she sat up in bed, stared at the lamp and the [daisy] and spoke aloud again. "If it was really you who turned on the li[ght, then] give me a sign you're actually here in your astral body by tu[rning it off] now?" Instantly, the switch on the lamp audibly clicked off, [leaving the] room in darkness—then immediately snapped back on, filling t[he room with] light. Before the incident, the lamp had been off for several hou[rs. There was] no failure of electrical power.

There was absolutely no scientific explanation for wh[at happened.] Neither the bulb nor the switch was loose, and there was nothin[g wrong with] the connection or the socket. All this was thoroughly checke[d. As for the] daisy, it had remained securely in its place, fastened above a [picture on the] wall, for many months, until that unexpected moment. Such [things are] easily explained by the laws of metaphysics. The woman's Tw[in Soul felt] her need, and answered it, guided astrally by both their [Higher Selves,] through the silvery-blue cord connecting them, a thread o[f energy] visible to the physical vision of a trained psychic or sensi[tive.]

the future certainty of a like reaction, of more pain, through the workings of karmic cause and effect.

Sometimes, it seems that the problems of two people who love each other are hopeless, the wall that separates them too high to ever surmount. But their problems would all dissolve, simply disappear, if they would only touch hands — or hearts — or minds — or even touch noses — and whisper just one word: "magic!" For love *is* magic, the secret power all who love possess without realizing it. No matter how great the injury, or how bitter the words, love will erase it all, as if it had never been. But not without the desire and effort to do so on the part of the one who has inflicted the pain — not without the quality of forgiveness on the part of the one who's been deeply hurt. Desire, effort and forgiveness, intermingled, are necessary to release love's force and power.

The fabled search for the Holy Grail is a dual quest. On a material or Earth level, it concerns the actual cup from which the Nazarene drank at the Last Supper, claimed by the ancients to have been buried near where the druidic priests (descended from the Essenes) held their mystic rites — its discovery imminent in the Age of the Water Bearer.

On a higher, mystical level, the successful conclusion of the search for the Holy Grail is reached, for each human, at the time of reunion with the Twin Soul. For only when all lonely and separated Twin Souls are at last joyously reunited, will the pieces of Life's jigsaw puzzle form themselves into a whole and complete picture within the Universe. Legend whispers that it shall be during the dawning of the Age of Aquarius when the fourteen pieces of the soul of Osiris — scattered when his body was cut into fourteen pieces by his brother, Set (causing the Earth's first Sun-Set) — will come together in one man, *"with all his scattered pieces whole."* One man, who will be reunited with his own Twin Soul, Isis, after millions of weary years of searching, and countless uncomprehending incarnations spent together in the past.

At the same time, the long-ago-sundered Twin Souls of Set and his Nepenthys will be rejoined, to fulfill their destiny of discovering together the Grail of the Nazarene, through the blending of their auras. Then, says legend, through the miracle of *mutual forgiveness* for that long-ago crime, Set and his brother, Osiris — along with Isis and her sister, Nepenthys, will in some way, together, find the lost records of Atlantis . . . . . as well as the burial place of Osiris, which contains the records of the building of the Great Pyramid of Gizeh by Osiris (not by Cheops, as falsely believed down through the ages). When these great and holy events manifest themselves, following the recognition of these four (and one other) of the true identity of their own Higher Selves — many more Twin Souls will suddenly recognize each other. Then we shall at least begin to realize our blessed birthright, as supplicated in those singing lines of the Lord's Prayer: "Thy Kingdom come, Thy will be done, *on Earth, as it is in Heaven"* (as above, so below), changing the pattern of the Trinity of Solar, Stellar and Lunar energies in the cosmos.

Those who love deeply, and who are truly mated with the other half of themselves, have no desire to initiate wars, or to dominate others. As the devotion of Romeo and Juliet, even in death, had the power to dissolve the enmity and reconcile the differences between the warring Capulets and Montagues, so shall the ecstatic blending of all Twin Soul lovers have the same power to unite mankind and womankind, all Earthlings in permanent Peace and Good. *Pax et Bonum*. It's not a coincidence (nothing is) that the man who initiated at least a beginning gesture toward Peace in the Middle East, Anwar Sadat, is a genuinely happily mated man, with a woman by his side who reflects the goals of his Higher Self — as is Menachem Begin, of Israel, who at least initially welcomed the gesture in an equal spirit of good will and sincerity. Nor was it coincidence that Hitler was a lonely, unloved man.

Jesus — the carpenter from Nazareth ? He was not alone. He was not unloved by woman. Although it is only a beginning, Scorpio Reverend William Phipps's fine and meticulously researched book *The Sexuality of Jesus* (Harper & Row, 1973), to be republished by Harper & Row in 1979 under the title *Did Jesus Love ?*, sheds needed enlightenment upon that long-hidden mystery of Jesus and his own Twin Soul. For he was only a man, albeit a highly evolved one — and she, only a woman. Even as you.

The doctrine of divinity, like the doctrine of patriotism, is a negative vibration, placing one man, one woman, one nation, above all others. Jesus, the *Christ ?* Yes, *he* was *more* than human, a different entity, but no different, no more super human or divine than *each* man and woman may rise to become during those too rare and brief periods of tuning in to the individual Supraconscious. Anwar, the Christ . . Menachem, the Christ . . Ruth, the Christ . . . Robert, the Christ . . . Thelma, the Christ . . Michel, the Christ . . Susan, the Christ . . Arthur, the Christ . . and so on, including your own name. Christ is simply another term for the Holy Ghost or the Holy Spirit, which can enter into anyone. We are all sons and daughters of God — and of *His* Mate, His own Twin Soul. How could our Creator not have His counterpart ? The polarity of positive-negative, masculine-feminine, exists in all dimensions, on all levels of awareness, within the galaxies of Heaven — and upon the Hell on Earth (as it is presently manifest). Jesus himself never claimed he was divine. *"What I have done, you can do also — and more . . . . . go thou and do likewise . . . . . . be it done unto you according to your faith . . . . . ."* These are not claims of spiritual exclusivity, only reminders that what was being demonstrated were manifestations of the "divine" *within each of us*, miracles we *all* could perform — though not without sacrifice, not without certain disciplines to bring mind, body and emotions under control. Strange, that the word "discipline" contains the word "disciple." Or perhaps . . . not strange at all.

The predicted cataclysms, should they come, should we be unable to prevent them, have been set into motion by many forces of darkness . . . . by the underground testing of immense destructive energies . . . . by the negative vibrations of the current waves of sexual promiscuity and lewdness in magazines and film, abusing and degrading sex to its lowest level . . . . the gorging greed for financial gain . . . . the selfish refusal to share our money, our food or our love with one another. "If everyone ate simply, everyone would eat." The need for sex, like the need for food, is a burning hunger all over the world. But sharing our love does not mean sharing our bodies in sensual group sexual experience. Gluttony is not the answer, to *either* kind of hunger.

Sex is not a sin; only the mis-use of its energy is a sin against the Higher Angel of one's own Self. Sexual union is the ecstasy of "deep" discovered by those who *love*, symbolic of a man and woman's blending with the Universe and all of Nature, in Oneness. It's a simple matter of priorities. You fall in love first — with your eyes. Then with your mind, then with your heart (emotions). By now your soul has joined the experience — whether you realize it or not, you've "fallen in love" spiritually — and it's time to fall in love with your body.

It doesn't work when you take these steps in reverse. For only the *eyes* know how to lead you into the mind of the one they gaze upon. Only the *mind* knows how to lead you into the heart of the one with whom you've found a mental affinity. Only the *heart* knows how to lead you into union with the soul of the one you love. And the *soul* is well aware . . oh! well aware, believe me . . of how to lead you, then, into the ecstasy of Oneness called sexual mating — becoming "one flesh."

But if you begin with the body . . . . . . the body knows not where to lead you, except into more and more sensations of the flesh, which by themselves have no power to fulfill love's yearning or feed love's deeper hunger — sensations that must, by certain physiological laws, eventually cause the body to become immune to sensation, needing ever more and more stimulation — until finally, like a drug, the tolerance level for even this is reached, and there is oblivion of all feeling. Using the body as an instrument for sex alone, without love, is like listening to a symphony on stereophonic equipment but using only one speaker.

Yes, it is time for a Messiah. A Wayshower, who will once again remind us of the basic lessons of love he taught before, so soon forgotten. For it makes no difference how far an individual or a nation has fallen into error; love will bring a renewed dedication to humanity. Just as it makes no difference how far away someone has gone, for love will bring a return. As poet Emmet Fox noted, when it is projected with sufficient intensity, there is no distance that love cannot span, no illness — moral, mental, emotional or spiritual — that love cannot heal. No victory that love cannot win. Love is concentrated kinetic energy, the most awesome force in Nature . . . and beyond Her.

If only you could love deeply enough and sustain love long enough, you could become the source of your own miracles, as powerful as the ancient "gods and goddesses." There is no dream you couldn't turn into a reality, no law you can't change, no situation you can't reverse — if only you could love *enough.*

Loving enough is not easy. Loving enough doesn't mean loving only those who love you, who are kind and considerate and generous. Loving *enough* means also loving those who "say all manner of evil against you," who hate you and actively demonstrate that hatred, who seemingly lack all compassion and sensitivity. Anyone can return the love of those who love him — or her. There's little glory or power in that kind of love. We are incarnated in these flesh bodies on Earth to learn love's deeper, more difficult lesson of loving the *un*lovable. In this accomplishment lies all the force and energy of true passion. More often than not, it's a painful effort, but the rewards, when it's mastered, are . . . beyond imagining. Never mind unnecessary religious "canonization" — you, too, can become a "saint" — *if you can love enough.*

In astrological terms, for a Lion and a Ram to love, for a Bull and a Goat to love — is nearly effortless. But for a Ram to achieve harmony with a Crab — the Lion with the Scorpion — the Bull with the Water Bearer — these demonstrate a higher love. *Love Signs* will attempt to guide those who are fortunate enough to be united with their own compatible Sun Signs — and also show the way to tolerance and harmony for those whose present karmic destiny has decreed the soul-testing of being involved in relationships with people of conflicting Sun Signs.

Even between two individuals whose Sun and Moon Signs harmonize, there are always some planets in their mutual nativities which clash, causing periodic friction and tension. To overcome this is to become tuned in to the pulsing frequency of the Higher Self, to begin the climb up the pathway to enlightenment . . . to walk in magic, showered with miracles. Like a bottomless cup, the Holy Grail of those who love is never empty. In the Neverland mathematics of metaphysics, you see — the more miracles we give away to others, the more we have left for you and me.

Who among us is not, at times, unlovable? And are not these the very times when we secretly yearn and need to be loved the most? Oh! the magic of receiving kindness in return from one to whom we have been *un*kind . . . the miracle of hearing, when we have said: "I'm sorry I said such cruel things," the answer: *"What cruel things? I didn't hear them."*

Then the heart bursts with joy and our cup runneth over. For this most ancient alchemy secret of all is such a simple secret.

If it was negative, it didn't happen—except in the world of illusion.

And so, may the Force . . . of Love . . . be with you. May it prevent the predicted cataclysms of Nature, as well as the personal cataclysms of separation and divorce, through its prisms of Light.

" . . and he shall gather his lambs . . ."

Isaiah 40:11

The
Twelve Mysteries
of Love

*L*ove is man's and woman's deepest need. It's not the threat of illness or poverty that crushes the human spirit, but the fear that there is no one who truly cares — no one who really understands. We all reach desperately for love, no matter how healthy, wealthy or wise we may be, because the alternative is loneliness. And so love is sought both in heaven and in hell, by both saints and sinners, wherever the search may take them, and it takes them to some strange places in the Aquarian Age, through the maze of the sexual revolution.

> *Say, what is this hang-up about sex ?*
> *all those people who go to pornographic films*
> *and the ones who won't . . .*

The swingers and the idealists, the puritans and prostitutes, the frigid and the promiscuous, the male chauvinists and the Women's Liberators, whether they read Browning or *Playboy*, whether they watch Walt Disney movies or the latest erotica from Sweden, are all looking for the same thing. No matter which road they travel on their pursuit of happiness, the inner need that drives them on is love. Not to give it. Not to receive it. But to *share it*. To love and be loved in return.

Why is lasting, mutual love so elusive ? To reach a complete and permanent union with the other half (the Twin Soul) man and woman must learn the lessons of the twelve Sun Signs. They must master the wisdom of these Twelve Mysteries of Love before they can achieve a final, perfect harmony between their mental, physical, emotional and spiritual natures.

As we make the trip around the astrological or karmic wheel of life, through the rebirth under the influence of the various Sun Signs, sometimes progressing swiftly, sometimes lingering, many times *returning* to a certain Sun Sign experience to relearn old lessons — we evolve, each at his or her own speed. We are forced, by our own Superconscious selves, to gradually perfect the positive qualities of all twelve signs and purge our natures of their negative qualities, so that we each may eventually become the refined gold of a totally evolved entity, worthy to join the other half — the Twin Self. In our longing for love — for our Twin Soul or Soul Mate — lies our latent metaphysical wisdom. The secret of life itself. Esoteric truth.

Every Sun Sign contains a strength that can be reversed into a weakness, and every Sun Sign contains a weakness that can be reversed into a strength, through the law of positive-negative polarity. What is Taurus stubbornness but Taurus patience turned upside down ? What is Aries impulsiveness but the negative side of the Ram's positive Mars courage ? Will Leo choose to use the great pride and nobility of the Leonine-Solar birthright for the positive purpose of protecting the helpless — or for the negative purpose of becoming an arrogant tyrant over the defenseless? Will the sensible Cancerian caution be turned into Lunar fears and phobias? Will Pisces compassion and humility be reversed to the negative Neptune aspects of deception, introversion and escape? The choice of our Sun Sign polarities is always ours to take. And if we make the wrong choice we must relive that Sun Sign experience repeatedly, until we master the positive strength of that sign.

The Twelve Initiations of Love

In each of the following experiences, man or woman is fully capable of giving and teaching others the first quality, but for the personality to learn the second quality is a struggle. When one's understanding of this second quality equals that of the first, he or she has then achieved mastery of a particular Sun Sign. The soul must pass *more than once* through the *First Six* Initiations of Love as:

ARIES	the infant	"I am"	to teach that love is innocence and learn that love is trust
TAURUS	the baby	"I have"	to teach that love is patience and learn that love is forgiveness
GEMINI	the child	"I think"	to teach that love is awareness and learn that love is feeling
CANCER	the adolescent	"I feel"	to teach that love is devotion and learn that love is freedom
LEO	the teenager	"I will"	to teach that love is ecstasy and learn that love is humility
VIRGO	the adult	"I analyze"	to teach that love is pure and learn that love is fulfillment

After achieving emotional maturity in these first six stages of development, man and woman must then pass through love's *Final Six* Initiations (more than once) to discover its deeper spiritual meaning in:

LIBRA	marriage	"I balance"	to teach that love is beauty and learn that love is harmony
SCORPIO	sex	"I desire"	to teach that love is passion and learn that love is surrender
SAGITTARIUS	knowledge	"I see"	to teach that love is honesty and learn that love is loyalty
CAPRICORN	experience	"I use"	to teach that love is wisdom and learn that love is unselfish
AQUARIUS	idealism	"I know"	to teach that love is tolerance and learn that love is Oneness
PISCES	submission	"I believe"	to teach that love is compassion and learn that love is ALL

and so to realize at last that

Love Is Eternal

There is a deep and significant reason why the meditation upon the *Twelve Mysteries of Love* contained here is important to you and the one you love. The key is the number *twelve*. There are 12 basic mineral salts used in homeopathy (the most helpful of all branches of medicine). These 12 cell salts have a great power to influence a positive state of human health in each of their corresponding *twelve* Sun Signs, a fact comprehended only by homeopathic practitioners, not orthodox physicians (except for a rare few of the latter). Minerals of the Earth conform to the number 12, as do both the metric and duodecimal systems. Diamonds, for instance, possess 12 sides or axes, along which they *must* be cut to *achieve brilliance*. There were 12 governors of the Manichean System, 12 divisions of Solomon's Temple, 12 labors of Hercules, 12 Altars of St. James, 12 Greek Gods and so forth.

Long before the 12 sons of Jacob founded the 12 Tribes of Israel, the number thirteen (13) possessed a great mystical significance. As an example, there were 12 Knights of the Round Table, with King Arthur making the 13th member.   The ancient Egyptian god-King Osiris, was associated with 12 lesser kings, Osiris being their 13th member.   Likewise did the Aztec god-King Quetzacoatl have 12 followers, he being the 13th of the group.   In Christianity, Gautama Buddhism and Shiite Islam, there are also 12 followers (apostles or disciples) and one Master.   The 12 disciples represent the *twelve Sun Sign stages of learning* — and the "Master" symbolizes the number thirteen (13) — or the purity of the perfect blend of all the other *twelve* into One Complete Whole.

As an example, each of the 12 apostles in the Christian Bible can be identified by esoteric astrologers with the Sun Sign quality embodied in that individual's particular attitude toward the teachings of Jesus.   This interwoven Judaeo-Christian-Islamic religious truth is manifested in the mathematical harmony and beautiful synchronicity of the horoscopic wheel.

Spiritual ignorance, or blindness, causes the superstitious fear of the dread number "13."   Hotel floors jump from "12" to "14," and few hostesses will invite thirteen people for dinner.   Yet, the true meaning of this holy number is wisdom.   If used for evil it can bring great destruction.   But if used for good it can bring great regeneration.   Used in its negative sense, it symbolizes the "Master," who is the blend of all twelve Sun Sign lessons, having become a "fallen angel," like Lucifer.   Used in its positive sense, it means exactly the opposite — an "angel" who remains steadfast, to wield power and wisdom everlasting, tempered with justice and mercy — and above all else — *love*.

Numerology is an inescapable part of astrology.   The subject is too vast and complicated to be fully covered in *Love Signs* and will be discussed in detail in a forthcoming book.   Meanwhile, however, the briefest mention of planetary numbers is necessary for a full comprehension of the *Twelve Mysteries of Love*.   Each Sun Sign harmonizes with and is governed by a particular planet or Luminary (Sun or Moon).   And each planet likewise harmonizes with and is governed by a particular *number*.   For example:

The Sun (ruler of Leo) vibrates to the number Ten or One (10 = 1), which it equals when added via the normal mathematical process.

The Moon (ruler of Cancer) vibrates to the number Two (2).

Jupiter (ruler of Sagittarius) vibrates to the number Three (3).

Uranus (ruler of Aquarius) vibrates to the number Four (4).

Mercury (ruler of Gemini and temporary ruler of Virgo, until Virgo's true ruling planet, Vulcan, is discovered and identified: see Virgo-Virgo chapter) vibrates to the number Five (5).

Venus (ruler of Libra and temporary ruler of Taurus, until Pan-Horus is discovered as the true ruler of Taurus: see Taurus-Taurus chapter) vibrates to the number Six (6).

Neptune (ruler of Pisces) vibrates to the number Seven (7).

Saturn (ruler of Capricorn) vibrates to the number Eight (8).

Mars (ruler of Aries) vibrates to the number Nine (9).

Each planet and Luminary also vibrates to what is termed a "higher octave" number, but we'll leave a full explanation of this for the aforementioned forthcoming book.

You might have noticed the omission of a number that vibrates to Pluto (ruler of Scorpio) in this list. Many astrologers and students of numerology will tell you that Pluto vibrates to the number Nine (9), sharing this number with Mars (ruler of Aries). This is not true. Pluto, like all the other planets, vibrates to its own personal "number" — distinctly and individually its own — sharing it with no other planet or Luminary. Since we've already covered the numbers One (1) through Nine (9) — and Ten (10) as Leo's Sun vibration, bringing us back to One (1) again, *full circle* — you may wonder how Pluto can possess its own number. You will see.

First, it's important to realize that the Mars Nine (9) vibration is the *Masculine* vibration of the Universe, representing and symbolizing the ultimate MASCULINE principle in all of Life and Love. The Venus Six (6) vibration is the *Feminine* vibration of the Universe, representing and symbolizing the ultimate FEMININE principle in all of Life and Love.

Six and Nine. 6 and 9. The Feminine and Masculine vibratory numbers, or 9 and 6. Male and Female. Positive-Negative. Dark-Light. (Polarity.) Notice that when the Feminine number of Venus — Six (6) is turned upside down (*reversing* its polarity), it becomes a Nine (9). Likewise, when the Masculine number of Mars — Nine (9) is turned upside down (*reversing* its polarity), it becomes a Six (6).

Man and Woman then — are inseparable. Each is an *equal* part of the *other*. The Masculine-Feminine Principles are totally interchangeable. Yet, one is always aiming in a direction reverse from the other. There are many more fascinating and revealing levels to the study of Six and Nine in numerology, but we're only touching the subject briefly here. We'll discuss it in depth in a future book.

Notice that both the Six (6) and the Nine (9) when the "tail" is removed — become a *circle*. The circle is the secret of Twin Soul blending — the deepest mystery of the Sun Sign of Scorpio, and Scorpio's ruling planet,

the awesome, powerful Pluto. For the number to which Pluto vibrates is —
ZERO. The circle. The circle (O) represents Eternity, for it symbolizes the
Serpent, eating its own tail. From the Masculine (Positive) *head* of the
Serpent flows the male-positive energy force — into the Female (Negative)
tail of the Serpent. Simultaneously, from the Feminine (Negative) *tail* of the
Serpent flows the female-negative energy force into the Serpent's Masculine
(Positive) *head*.

This is the secret of Scorpio, the Sun Sign of "sex" — and this is the
energy behind the great Power of Scorpio's ruling planet, Pluto. *Zero*. The
Circle. O. The Serpent, eating its own tail. The symbol of Eternity. For
only when all polarities — male and female, youth and age, dark and light,
night and day — thus feed energy simultaneously into one another, and blend
their energies — rather than continue to *oppose* one another — can true
power exist.

Pluto's vibratory Zero also contains the secret mystery of Christianity's
Holy Trinity. "Father-Son-and-Holy Ghost." The "son" (humans, of both
sexes) is *masculine* energy. The "Holy Ghost" (Christ spirit) is *feminine*
energy. When each flows into the other simultaneously (instead of remaining
in opposition), a *Third Energy* is created, which is both, yet neither — neutral
and ALL-POWERFUL — i.e.: "The Father" (God). This *Third Energy*,
composed of the Masculine and Feminine combined, flowing into each other,
and not in opposition, creates many miracles: The Great Power of Divinity.
The conception of a child. The conception of an idea (adding the "l" for
love, this becomes an ideal). The energy that powers spacecraft from other
solar systems.

It is in no way an accident that Kekule, who made the monumental
discovery of the benzine ring structure, which paved the way for the
theoretical aspect of organic chemistry, said that he dreamed repeatedly of "a
snake, eating its own tail" before the concept occurred to him.

Therefore, all the mysterious Pluto-Scorpio "power" comes from a
subconscious knowledge of this Zero principle that the perfect blend between
Masculine and *Feminine* creates a *Third Energy Force*, which is both, yet
neither — neutral and ALL-POWERFUL — because it does not oppose, but
causes polarities to simultaneously blend and flow into each other.

Another indication, another "secret" of Pluto's ZERO circle, is that: what
happens when you add the ZERO (O) to any other number ? Any banker or
mathematics student can tell you that it "increases" the power of the number.
Obviously, the sum of one dollar grows larger (has more "power") as you
"add the zeros." Thus does $1.00 become $10.00 or $100.00 or $1,000 or
$10,000 and so on. ZERO, then, equals *POWER*. That's nice for all Scorpios
to know — as long as they don't forget what causes the power. The Serpent,
eating its own tail — Eternity's Secret.

An important building block to the comprehension of the Twelve

Mysteries of Love, related to the secret of the circle, is the following. You'll come across the use of the term "co-Creators" many times in this book. To the skeptical, who find it difficult to image the "Old Testament God" with a Mate of His own, I offer this scholarly source, although the faithful and the spiritually wide-awake need no proof, other than instinctive knowledge from within, regarding this or any concept of the truth of creation.

The following quotation is from a painstaking translation of the *Septuagint*, the earliest known (*circa* 250 B.C.) version of the Old Testament (our standard Hebrew MSS date only from the Renaissance). The translation was published by the Falcon's Wing Press in 1960, under the editorship of Dr. C. Musès. From Proverbs 8:3-31 (excerpts):

> *For at the gates of the Mighty, She hath taken a seat,*
> *and at the entrance thereof chanteth Her song:*
>
> *"In the beginning, before the Lord made the Earth*
> *When He furnished the Heavens, I was with Him;*
> *and when He set apart His throne on the winds*
> *When He set to the sea its bound,*
> *and the waters passed not the word of His mouth*
> *I was harmonizing with Him. I was the one in whom*
> *He delighted, and I was daily gladdened by His*
> *presence on all occasions."*

Ecclesiastical Christianity, seeded by the Hebrew Old Testament distortion of truth through the "patriarch" image, has too long taught the falsehood that the Holy Trinity is entirely masculine. By such deception we have been deprived of a sublime and ennobling truth. But the unfolding of the Aquarian Age, foretold by all prophets of all religions, will bring the Light of the conscious restoration of the *Golden Balance* between the Feminine and Masculine energies on Earth. This Golden Balance is the eventual blending of all Twin Souls. Its concept lies ready to burst forth within all yearning, searching hearts. It's called by many names; yet its true name is the REAL SELF, as experienced through the union with one's own Twin Soul. And it begins with the recognition of the Male-Female truth hidden in the Holy Trinity and the symbol of Eternity — the Serpent eating its own tail — the secret "knowledge" given by the "*Serpent*" to Eve, who passed it on to Adam. That this eating of the "forbidden fruit" of the "Tree of Knowledge" was later called "Original *Sin*" reveals the desperation of the dark forces to hide the Light of Truth by a polarity distortion, channeled through the ancient patriarchs who feared losing the masculine superiority principle through sexual equality. But the Aquarian Age daughters of Eve will at last bring the world to recognize that the term "Original Sin" is the Big Daddy of all religious dogma's Super-Hypes. And the Aquarian Age sons of Adam will this time be enlightened to Eve's wisdom. Not even the Church "Fathers" can stop the lightning of the predestined and foretold Uranian spiritual awakening of the New Age of Golden Balance. Perhaps Adam couldn't handle the truth. But today's Water Bearers can — and will.

Under the powerful Uranus vibes and the Aquarian microscope, all deception will be exposed for the hypocrisy it is. And *this* shall be called "Original *Innocence*" — the beginning of Wisdom. When people all throughout the world enter into cooperation with these Divine principles of the Golden Balance of Male and Female, the New Age of Aquarius will finally manifest itself in all the splendor and magnificence of the reborn and wiser Atlantis. Not all the chauvinists and atomic and nuclear energy madmen combined can stop the Uranian tidal waves of Truth.

As man and woman evolve around the astrological karmic circle, absorbing the qualities of other Sun Signs into their own individualities — teaching some, learning from others — each has a spiritual obligation to retain the positive integrity of his or her own Sun Sign in this incarnation and also to respect that right in others. The Lion must have his dignity, as the Crab must cling to security. The Goat must honor tradition, as the Twins must demand their freedom. Each must follow the Aquarian Age adage to "live and let live," to be yourself, and realize that others must be themselves too. The first step toward comprehending love's ultimate meaning — toward finally being permitted to enjoy its absolute fulfillment — is to learn to tolerate instead of condemning the Sun Sign qualities different from our own.

In exploring the interrelationships of the twelve Sun Signs, through both their harmonious and their conflicting traits of character as they relate to our own, we should always try to remember that the final goal of each soul is to give and receive the lessons of each Sun Sign to and from the others met along the way. This journey is a kind of growing of the spirit, from soul-infancy through soul-adulthood, middle-age, "old age" and death, then rebirth. The soul can be freed of this endless circle of birth and death only when we learn to free the physical or dense body, also, of death; a miracle I dare to predict will occur much sooner than we now believe. The "problem" such longevity would create, in relation to the general world population (new births, along with the conquering of death — for centuries — etc.), does have several solutions. But this is not the place to attempt to conceive of the possibilities. An in-depth discussion of such a future in the approaching "New Age" must wait for my next book.

The soul's symbolic journey through the twelve Sun Signs may be comprehended by imaging man and woman undergoing, with their minds and bodies, a matching journey. First, the soul enters the initial phase, similar to earthly birth, then advances through various further stages similar to earthly life, gaining spiritual experience from each, just as we gain mental and physical experience from a similar type journey of our dense bodies. The soul is "born" in the sign of Aries, the symbolic Infant, as reflected through the Sun's magnetic alchemy.

The Aries Love Mystery

The soul, symbolically newborn in Aries *(although not necessarily in its first earthly sojourn)*, relates to dawn, sunrise, spring and Easter — or the resurrection from its "death" in the previous sign of Pisces.

In this first excursion into the Fire Element — this experience as the first of the three Cardinal signs — the symbolically "newborn" soul projects the positive, masculine vibration of the Day Forces through the explosive vitality of the Aries planetary ruler, Mars. Like a human infant totally self-absorbed, the Aries soul discovers with delight his or her own toes and fingers — its own physical beingness. To satisfy all needs, only a loud cry is necessary, heard and answered instantly by elders. The real infant doubts or fears nothing or no one, simply because it has never experienced denial. Likewise, the Aries "Infant" soul has a natural trust and a touching faith in the unseen force of goodness which will miraculously grant all its wishes.

On the Earth plane this beneficent force is represented by the parents; in a mystical sense, by our co-Creators. And so they look tenderly upon the "newborn" Aries soul, as parents look tenderly upon their infant, lovingly protecting him from his own naivete, wisely denying him some of the demands he makes through his excited awareness that he *is* — that he has been born, that he is *here*. The Aries soul senses: "I AM" or "I exist." And like the symbolic Infant, Aries men and women are oblivious to the possibilities of accident, pain or cruelty on life's path. He or she learns of these negative experiences only from those advanced beyond, who have gathered harshness, suspicion and the self-survival instinct from the growing process.

There's a religious adage that all infants, since they die in a state of purity, immediately become angels. Of course! They have not yet met the devil of Temptation. But if the Aries "Infant" survives, he must, like the real infant, time and time again, undergo the sharp disappointment of misplaced trust. When he's the victim of unkindness, a lack of sympathy or abandonment, the newborn babe feels shocked, frightened, alone — then yells even louder for attention. In the same manner (and for the same reasons) does the soul of the hurt and disillusioned Aries man or woman need and "seek acceptance, yet court rejection" — with a violent emotional reaction to neglect.

The positive qualities of Aries are a heart-tugging innocence and wonder, blind faith and raw courage. Expressed in their negative forms, they can become selfish egotism, thoughtlessness, aggressiveness and impulsive action with no regard for the consequences.

To the Aries soul, Love is a necessity of life, which is taken for granted; for in it's infancy of awareness, Love is synonymous with existence itself. Therefore, devotion is instinctively expected and joyously accepted, but with little comprehension of how to return it. Aries *demands* Love, for like the infant, *without* Love, Aries dies. When emotional abandonment (symbolically) can mean death, even the hint of it can bring on unreasonable panic, and inexplicable terror, calmed only by repeated reassurances. Aries continually needs to be reminded that "if winter comes" . . . . . . the miracle of spring cannot be far behind.

☆ ☆ ☆ ☆ ☆ ☆

The Taurus Love Mystery

The evolving spiritual awareness of man or woman enters next into the Earth element. On the Taurus level, the symbolic Infant soul has become, symbolically, a healthy, chubby Baby, who now relates to the reflective feminine Night Forces. He has learned to sleep on schedule, then wake to anticipated comfort.

No longer does he scream without reason, in fright or loneliness. No longer does he yell loudly for his needs, as in the Arian stage. He has discovered that his desires will be satisfied by his parents. Like the human baby, in the Taurean stage, the soul is content to sit quietly and patiently in its symbolic high chair and wait for its daily bread with quiet, confident and sure anticipation.

The Bull has also learned how to use good behavior to wheedle more pleasures, more favors from the "parents" and other adults. Smiles and obedience are rewarded, and Taurus doesn't forget what has been learned, however painfully and slowly. Still essentially unaware of anything outside the immediate environment, the Taurus man or woman (like the Taurean symbolic Baby) finds happiness in the family circle and the tangible — in what is known to be familiar, rather than in the strange and noisy outside world.

Through the Taurus experience, the Baby soul discovers the delight of using the senses of tasting, smelling, seeing, hearing and touching. He symbolically smells and chews, and listens to his toys, as well as looks at and touches them in this, the soul's first experience as a Fixed sign of the Organizer. Because possessions bring happiness, this man or woman clutches them, fondles them and finds contentment in calling them his or her own. Taurus says "I HAVE." This is the stage of the Teddy Bear or security blanket (which will return once more, for a fleeting moment, in the

Cancerian vibration). On the Taurus level of development, the "Baby soul" is enormously dependent on physical contact with loved ones. They hold him, cuddle him, kiss and hug him. And the Venus-ruled (Pan-Horus guided) Taurean responds with coos and giggles of ecstasy, understanding affection only through the *feeling* that it's there. The actual baby is fiercely possessive of his toys and the attention of his parents, shattered when he thinks he's lost either, stubbornly refusing to share them, as the male or female Taurean behaves with regard to his or her own bank account and mate.

Taurus positive qualities are strength of purpose, patience, steadfastness and conviction. Expressed in their negative form, they become obstinacy, blind prejudice and lack of reason.

To the jolly, dogmatic baby, symbolic of the Taurus soul, love is physical affection, both given and received without question. Because the baby associates love with all pleasure and happiness, he glories in it with an uncomplicated, animal-like appreciation. Therefore, Taurus accepts and returns love with the senses — but has not yet learned to analyze its true worth and value.

☆ ☆ ☆ ☆ ☆ ☆

The Gemini Love Mystery

In the Gemini soul experience, the symbolic Taurus "Baby" enters into the world of the toddler-Child, and feels again, as on the Aries Infancy level, the positive, masculine Day Forces. For the first time, the soul arrives at the stage of the Mutable Communicator, becoming conscious of its own mentality, aware that it is not alone in the Universe. The Child soul of Gemini learns to communicate needs by speaking, by learning to form words and string them together, while the parents and others listen attentively, rejoicing at each new sound. Talking is fun because it centers all the interest on him. He's also now able to crawl or toddle or walk over to the cookie jar and help himself, without either the Aries yelling or the Taurus waiting, and this new-found independence is intoxicating. Gemini is thrilled by the knowledge he can now grasp — "I THINK"! he cries to the world-at-large, in great excitement.

The symbolic Child level of consciousness teaches the Gemini soul that there are two sides to the character — a duality or polarity that must be brought into harmony before one can successfully relate to others. The first twinge of unhappiness pulls at him as he or she bumps hard into discipline, while trying to blend the sleeping and waking Twin Selves. Because Gemini suddenly longs for pleasures outside home and family, the Child soul is often punished for symbolically attempting to run out into dangers not yet suspected. Likewise, the world invites Gemini men and women to explore it, and who knows what they may find out there! With the new mental ability to reason and deduce — to relate — Gemini begins to wish for and to dream of things beyond what has already been seen.

Half the Gemini soul is still an insecure baby, needing the familiar. Half is a yearning child, curious about the many undiscovered marvels just out of tangible reach. The Geminian soul has already experienced Fire and Earth and is learning to cope with the Air Element for the first time. And so this twinned personality experiments, with bright eyes and a hopeful heart. Each new day stirs Gemini's mind with its hidden magic, more enticing now than the discarded toys and the warm circle of parental affection. What the Gemini man or woman sees through the window is a forbidden Eden where all longings lie in mystery, as the ruling planet Mercury (the magician) beckons toward the seductive road beyond.

Gemini positive qualities are versatility, mental alertness, quickness of perception, deductive reasoning and flexibility. Expressed in their negative form they become restlessness, glibness, shallowness, double-talk, unreliability and self-deception.

To the Gemini "Child," love has lost some of its early wonder. He still needs it on this level, more than he realizes, but there's something more thrilling than love to seek now. Is it love that holds you back, tugs on one and keeps one from rushing out the front door into Life? Love, then, is perhaps enjoyable, but it is also restrictive. Gemini men and women have not stopped needing it or desiring it, but when love becomes a barrier to their freedom, they rashly discard it, forgetting its warmth and safety — not caring that they may get lost and be unable to find their way back home.

☆ ☆ ☆ ☆ ☆ ☆

The Cancer Love Mystery

The child is now an Adolescent, the soul having evolved to the stage of Cancer, hovering between childhood and maturity, longing to be grown-up, yet hesitating to cross over to the other side. Cancer brings back awareness of the negative feminine and reflective Night Forces. But this second experience of night is blended with a new, richer and even more sensual feeling (which was only a poetic inspiration, not yet a true reality, on the earlier Taurean level), for a change of seasons has occurred. The spring awakening has deepened into a mid-summer night's dream in all its full-blown and fragrant beauty for these Cancerian Oberon and Titania men and women.

Now the moody, sensitive, "Adolescent" soul vacillates between childish dependence and the maddeningly enticing, beckoning world of adulthood (what is it like to be a man or a woman ?). This is beautifully expressed by the experiments between the human and faerie worlds in Taurean Shakespeare's famed classic. Is it sad or happy . . . funny or tragic ? The symbolic "Puckish" Cancerian Adolescent observes the adults (humans) in the environment, uncannily perceptive of everything seen and heard. But this grown-up, material world so intensely watched hints of frequent disillusion.

And so the dreams of Cancer are troubled, causing the Crab to cry out in the night, sometimes dragging his old symbolic Taurus Teddy Bear out of the closet, and hugging it closely when no one can see. As with Cancerian men and women, the actual adolescent's changing moods puzzle him as much as they puzzle his family. But his terrors are very real to him. He fears that maturity will mean the loss of security known with the parents, especially the mother. Will future strangers ever fuss over him and love him as unconditionally as his mother ? He is beginning to suspect that they won't.

Unable to explain their apprehensions, the Crabs turn secretive, dreaming alone — or hide and pout, imagining that no one understands. On the Cancer level, the possible loss of parental protection haunts the subconscious. Cancer has already learned what loss is. Perhaps childhood friends have moved away, the family has changed residences, the old familiar neighborhood is gone. The world is no longer so exciting as the Crabs sense its hidden pitfalls. The "Adolescent" Cancerian men and women know that growing up will surely bring unexpected hurt, so they cling to what they *know* can be trusted — *yesterday.*

Because the new perceptions are so acute, Cancer sees a combination of tragedy and comedy in Life as it expands in his awareness through his first excursion into the sensitive Water Element. Still, despite an innate shyness, the Cancerian soul will not be pushed into the background, for this is the second experience as a Cardinal leader, which can turn illogical fear into sensible caution. The Crabs wish on both the Full Moon and the New, only half-conscious of what it is they wish for . . . . . reluctant to find out. What does tomorrow hold ? Sentiment moves the Cancerian Adolescent soul to tears. Motivated by the need to hide true emotions, the Crabs say: "I FEEL" — then, so no one will suspect they feel so deeply, they make jokes, believing they fool people. If not handled tenderly at this crucial stage of soul evolvement, the Cancerian man or woman develops a permanent, hard, protective shell against the cruel world.

Cancer's positive qualities are imagination, tenacity, tenderness, sensitivity, care and caution. Expressed in their negative form they become stinginess, irritability, melancholy, clinging and cowardice, possessiveness and moodiness.

To Cancer, as to the actual uncertain and sentimental adolescent, love has become important again, above all else. But it is now synonymous with home, representing emotional security — and the *need* for love is so great it must be disguised behind moody tears and Lunar laughter.

☆ ☆ ☆ ☆ ☆ ☆

The Leo Love Mystery

The Cancerian Adolescent soul is transformed with brilliant suddenness into a symbolic Teenager, brought by the Leo vibration into the first expression of self-confidence and pride in individuality. Now he knows (or thinks he knows) who he is — or who she is — as Leo feels an even stronger pull of the masculine positive Day Forces and the Fire Element than was felt on the Aries level. The world belongs to the Lion — or the Lioness — and so the Leonine "Teenager" gazes at his or her image in the mirror, admires what is seen and makes the noble vow: "I WILL." Summer has come into full bloom of furious beauty with lazy afternoons and bright sunshine, as Leo moves into SELF consciousness from the polarity meaning of Cancer's *self-conscious-ness*.

The idealism of youth stirs the Lion's heart and sets the blood afire with the dawning knowledge of sexuality, two powerful urges that bring private inner doubts of worth, well hidden beneath outward vanity. The Leo soul knows what to do with this second experience as a Fixed Organizer, using it with apparent confidence to lecture others, take charge of his or her own life and rule over those who need Leo's protection. Yet the Leo man or woman, like the actual teenager, still seeks reassurance in the form of flattery, still cringes secretly when ridiculed, because he is not quite yet a man — she is not quite yet a woman — for all the surface sureness.

The soul has already passed through the painful experiences of infancy, babyhood, childhood and adolescence, so Leo leads with sympathetic consideration for those who are more vulnerable. The soul in its Leo expression has no real desire to crush the helpless. Generosity of spirit was carved into Leo's memory by the tears wept through the Aries, Taurus, Gemini, and Cancer levels. However, although he's learned to tolerate and forgive his enemies, he has not yet learned to respect the wisdom of elders. Like the real teenager, Leo thinks he knows all the answers, and is impatient with those who question his new worldly knowledge. The Leo soul worships the Sun, for the Sun is his ruler, the source of all Life — and of his own Leonine strength. He admires and is admired, he loves and is loved. As social life begins, the joys of romance begin to bud . . . . . . then finally to flower. Puppy love is warm and bright, bringing to the Leo "Teenager" both elation and disappointment. The dizzy power of his manhood (or womanhood) gives to Leo a sense of personal dignity and importance — through the opposite sex. No longer must the Lions and Lionesses be restricted by the stifling authority of parental guidance. The bridge from childhood to adulthood has been spanned. The responsibilities of maturity are sensed, but still haven't become a burden. Life is all sunlight, the gloomy Past is behind, the miracle of the Future still ahead — and the Present is a time for fun and relaxation. Leo decides arrogantly that the world needs his newfound wisdom, and is more than willing to give it. Only through exercising unquestioned command over younger children (the weaker and not yet liberated souls) can a Leo man or woman in this experience retain the necessary image of superiority and self-respect.

Leo's positive qualities are warmth, generosity, nobility, strength, loyalty, leadership and a soothing, gentle tenderness — the protective charisma of the older brother or sister, of the strong toward the weak. Expressed in their negative form they become arrogance, false pride, vanity, tyranny, haughtiness . . . and romantic promiscuity.

To the Leo in the symbolic Teenager stage of development, love is shimmering romance, the song-of-songs, the fulfillment of all ideals and beauty. Leo is "in love with love" and with himself — herself. Lions and Lionesses give affection generously only because it brings such pleasure to be so royally beneficent, demanding gratitude and respect from the beloved, outraged if love requires that they humble themselves . . . . as yet unable to comprehend its depth, or the beauty of its sacrifice of the "self."

☆ ☆ ☆ ☆ ☆ ☆

The Virgo Love Mystery

The youthful Leo soul soon senses that summer is ending — and regretfully steps into his first awareness of the coming harvest, through the Indian Summer soul expression of Virgo. The negative feminine Night Forces return again, reminding the Virgin (whose deeper self has remained untouched by the fleeting romances of youth) that maturity brings stern duty and responsibility. "I ANALYZE," says Virgo defensively, striving for perfection.

Now the evolving soul has, for the first time, become an Adult, frustrated by being forced to comply with society's rules and restrictions, yet submitting gracefully, with innate courtesy. These men and women have discovered that to receive their own needs they must serve others in some way. The Virgo vibration teaches that one must work and earn money — be of service — in order to be free to play. In this, the second experience in the Earth Element, also the second experience as a Mutable Communicator, clocks and schedules assume great importance. The first job is disappointing. Both ideas and ideals must be shelved under the demands of work or schooling. No time now to dream. The Virgo attention is centered on scholastic excellence, on keeping up with the fierce competition of the business world. Learning and competing are both mandatory — surviving has become a near obsession.

Like the actual young adults they symbolize, Virgo souls see much to criticize around them, secretly resenting the loss of childhood innocence, having no certain ideas of what lies ahead. Is it only more work, more study and more responsibility ? If so, then life is serious indeed and must be faced realistically as soon as possible. It is getting later. Human flaws and imperfections assume exaggerated importance on the Virgo level. For, unless Virgo brings in a fruitful harvest, Life cannot continue for himself or others. It is the end of summer, the beginning of autumn, and cold winter is just around the corner. Why are all those people still laughing and playing out there ? Virgo frets and worries, wondering how to warn the irresponsible that the season of pleasure is drawing to a close. The heart is still pure and filled with silent hope, but the mind is now in control.

Earlier Leo enthusiasms have been replaced by resignation and quiet dreams. Virgo is driven by the fear of dependence into dogged determination not to waste time or shirk duty, the consciousness ever watchful and waiting, yearning to be something better. Although once again ruled by Mercury, the soul has by now learned not to scatter the vital forces as on the Gemini level. Like the symbolic Virgin, Virgo hovers on the edge of awareness, soon to answer the thunderous call of Virgo's true ruler, Vulcan, not yet "discovered" by astronomers, but sufficiently near discovery to have already commenced to faintly beam its pulsing influence to all Virgo-Virgin souls.

Virgo's positive qualities are clarity of thought, discrimination, courtesy, service to others, practicality and self-honesty. Expressed in their negative form they become criticism, crankiness, timidity, pessimism, inferiority and hair-splitting.

The Virgin soul has reached its narcissus aspect, half-remembering the heated fires of youth, but as yet unawakened, only vaguely sensing the passion that lies ahead, soon to be revealed by Vulcan. To Virgos, love means surrender of the self, a mystery they prefer not to solve. So they channel its energy into excellence in work . . . . . and although these men and women offer gentle devotion, love's true meaning still sleeps within the Virgin heart.

☆ ☆ ☆ ☆ ☆ ☆

The Libra Love Mystery

Turning from the lonely Virgo path of self-discipline, the evolving soul reaches out once again to the positive Day Forces, as the Libra vibration seductively beckons to it to accept, for the third time, the challenge of Cardinal leadership. In the Libra consciousness, the soul is fully grown, aware now of both sunshine and shadow. During the struggle for maturity which culminated in Virgo, it has learned that there is in the world (and in people) both night and day — good and evil — dark and light. Beyond that, Libra is consumed with the intriguing polarity of male and female.

Experience has taught Libra men and women to judge their fellows fairly. Until the Libra level, the soul's interest has been centered primarily on itself. Now it expands to include, for the first time, an awareness of the necessity to relate to other human beings. The soul is now equipped with the lessons of five previous levels, capable of leading with both logic and force. Libra acts with a blend of wisdom composed of knowledge gained through one excursion into WATER and from twice experiencing FIRE, EARTH and AIR. "I BALANCE," says Libra, priding himself or herself on seeing both sides. Because it shatters Libra's conscience to be unfair, decisions are difficult and painful. A sense of social justice is emerging, and in the face of prejudice or intolerance, Libra often turns to endless argument, using the cold logic learned through Gemini and sharpened through Virgo. But this approach is softened by a new sense of the value of persuasion. Libra has acquired the quality of charm, which he has discovered is a sure way to win, so he artfully uses a mellow voice and dazzling smile to cajole and get his way with others.

Libra feels a growing awareness of beauty of harmony — in music, art and romance. As Librans subconsciously recall their Virgo loneliness, they experience the stirring of a deep and primal urge to find a mate. Sentimental, yet practical, the Libra soul instinctively knows the need for someone to walk nearby, in both love and business, in order to balance Life and satisfy the desire for harmony of Libra's ruler, Venus. In the Libran Air Element, however, a love partner is not easy to find. When the vices and virtues of prospective mates are weighed and balanced on the Libra Scales, they often are found wanting, bringing on the anguish of emotional indecision. But through it all, this man or woman continues the relentless search for someone to share life's joys and sorrows. The autumn season so loved will someday fade, the spring so fondly remembered is long past, and there is one thing Libra knows: he — or she — must not be alone when winter comes. And so Librans respond to sunset's beauty, sadly sensing simultaneously that for all its crimson-gold glory, it nevertheless announces another approaching night of the soul.

Libra's positive qualities are justice, intelligence, charm, gentleness and emotional balance. Expressed in their negative form they become laziness, procrastination, indecision, argumentativeness, pleasure-seeking and temperament.

To Libra, love is a mating of the minds and hearts — not too passionate, not too detached — a happy medium, to be equally shared. But these souls are too infatuated with love's surface beauty to penetrate completely its deeper implications. They recognize only that they love. It has not yet occurred to them to wonder *why*.

☆ ☆ ☆ ☆ ☆ ☆

The Scorpio Love Mystery

As it enters its second experience in the Water element, the now mature soul welcomes the chance for meditation through a return of the negative feminine Night Forces of the Scorpio consciousness. On a *public* level, Scorpio is enormously capable of executing the now very familiar duties as a Fixed Organizer. On a *personal* level, Scorpio is troubled to discover that he faces for the first time the awesome mystery of his own existence. Where did he come from ? — where is he going ? — why is he here? Scorpio must tear the veil from life, regardless of the cost, to quiet his restless spirit, suddenly released from its former preoccupation with earthly needs alone, as he cries out: "I DESIRE !"

There is much that the Scorpio soul *knows* . . . . but even more that is *sensed* and cannot yet be defined. The Scorpio vibration brings such a burning need to penetrate the unknown that it must be buried beneath deep layers of calm reason, or it would consume the mind and sear the soul. Lessons well remembered from Libra softness and impartial judgment have made Scorpio wary of expressing opinions to those who would tear them apart. The strong Scorpion instinct for survival springs from a deep-seated fear that he who is not forearmed will be destroyed. Each defeat sustained by

Scorpio only strengthens the inner conviction that the first loyalty must be to his or her own personal integrity. For Scorpio senses that if the *self* is lost, then *all* is lost.

On the Scorpio level of consciousness, the soul is newly aware of the relationship between birth, death, sex and religious truth. Scorpio knows that, in some mystical way, these are all intertwined. Therefore, sex becomes something intimately explored with an intensity unknown to those either behind or ahead of Scorpio's stage of evolvement. Although Scorpio trusts love only after it has proven itself deserving of such trust, once dedicated to another, loyalty is unswerving and eternal. Feeling fiercely the need to protect himself and those he loves from hurt, Scorpio is compelled to demand "an eye for an eye and a tooth for a tooth" as insurance that injuries will not be repeated.

Through the subtle influence of the ruling planet Pluto, the experience of death comes to the Scorpio soul, as friends and relatives pass away, increasing the need to penetrate even deeper for the knowledge buried in the silent subconscious. While Scorpio's spirit soars upward like the eagle, defying gravity, worldly desires and passions intensify, forcing him to question his own worthiness. Ultra-sensitive, but now able to totally disguise such sensitivity, Scorpio now learns the amazing power of his or her own mind — the silent *will* — and uses it secretly, lest others learn how to use the same kind of power over him — or her. The Scorpio consciousness is the period of the soul's testing.

Scorpio's positive qualities are loyalty, will power, magnetism, gentleness, insight and amazing self-control. Expressed in their negative form they become ruthlessness, fanaticism, revenge, sadism, suspicion and self-hatred.

To Scorpio men and women, love is a consuming flame, worth any sacrifice — and they must conquer its challenge. Sexually uninhibited, yet emotionally fearful and mentally suspicious, they strive desperately to unite love's physical and spiritual vibrations, with a strange mixture of eroticism and purity. But the satisfaction of desire only leaves the Scorpio soul still hungry for something beyond.

The Sagittarius Love Mystery

Emerging from the long night of Scorpio meditation, the evolving soul turns again with hope toward the positive masculine Day Forces, as it bridges autumn and winter through the Sagittarius consciousness. Now it experiences for the third time the vibrations of the Mutable Communicator, and answers for the last time to the impulsive element of Fire. In Sagittarius, man or woman has become a skeptical philosopher, a reluctant prophet, still unsure of the final answers to the riddle of life. So the Archer probes further, with penetrating logic and embarrassing candor, to give validity to his claim that "I SEE."

It is now time for the soul to be once more aware of its own *duality*. Sagittarius feels a compelling urge to explore his or her own mind and attempt to unravel the secrets of human behavior at the philosophic stage of higher learning. Yet, part of this soul resents the stern requirements of ever more complicated education and longs to play hookey from Life's demanding karmic school. He — or she — plunges from the heights of supreme optimism and blind faith to the depths of sarcastic cynicism. First frivolous and gay, then serious and owlish, Sagittarius is the Centaur, half man–half horse, aiming sharp arrows of curiosity directly into the bull's-eye of the knowledge sought. The Sagittarian search for truth takes this soul through the maze of religious concept, veering from stark atheism to spiritual fanaticism, until the stronghold of church dogma has been exposed — and either accepted or rejected, in part, or in whole.

Sometimes Sagittarius frolics like a clumsy clown, with an irresponsible disregard for the future. Sometimes he thinks seriously, on a level high above and beyond his peers. In the Sagittarian stage, the soul has reached the symbolic stage of retirement. Driven by the ruling planet Jupiter, the Archers yearn to travel, to bask under foreign Suns, to see and learn of other countries, people and ideas. Although they grudgingly submit to the necessities of work, duty and responsibility, they are extremely impatient of such unwelcome restriction over the realization of their dreams.

To cover a constant restlessness of spirit, Sagittarians adopt the pose of the actor, the thespian, which enables them to entertain others with a mixture of funny and tragic farces, while they remain free to pursue the Socratic method of inquiry with their own souls, behind their theatrical masks. There is little time for tact on this level, as Sagittarius rushes ahead to find the answers before "Life" is over. Autumn is ending, the first winds of winter are blowing — and the exhilarating weather challenges the Archer to tempt fate, in order to prove that man is stronger than Nature. The winter season's withdrawal into seclusion has not yet taken hold. And so Sagittarius delights in each snowflake, pondering the design and origin . . . then rolls them together into a snowball, tossed without warning to topple the stuffiness of more sedate souls. Although intuitively sensing that "old age" looms ahead, with its promised rewards of wisdom and peace, the soul is too nostalgic for the carefree days of lost youth . . . spring and summer . . . to resign itself gracefully to its inevitable maturity.

Sagittarian positive qualities are optimism, candor, cheerfulness, logic, honesty, daring and enthusiasm. Expressed in their negative form they become recklessness, emotional confusion, carelessness, lack of tact, rudeness and fickleness.

To Sagittarius, who has reached the symbolic middle age of the soul, true love must be discovered now — or lost forever. As the Archers seek a mate for all seasons, they are blinded by love's idealism and challenge and therefore wounded by love's reality, because their anxious quest has not yet led them to search for love where it really hides — within their own hearts.

☆ ☆ ☆ ☆ ☆ ☆

The Capricorn Love Mystery

Now the chilling blasts of winter grow more insistent, forcing the experience-weary soul to symbolically retreat back into the haven of the family circle, to submit once again to the meditative, negative-feminine Night Forces. On the Capricorn level of consciousness, for the fourth and final time, the soul feels the powerful vibrations of Cardinal leadership. But this time it leads through the stable Earth Element, from a position of strength inside the home, beside the hearth. Why should the Goat expose himself (or herself) to the icy temperatures outside, just to be seen and heard — applauded and praised ?

Capricorn souls, now sure of both their ability and their right to take command, no longer feel the need to display or aggressively flaunt their power — either for public adulation, or for inner security. By this stage, the soul has learned that true peace comes from *within*. Being appointed Leader is a responsibility to be handled as carefully as possible, with no special recognition due for doing what is obviously one's duty. The Capricorn's relatives (especially parents) now assume marked importance for either good or ill, because the symbolic "old age" of the soul has arrived — and along with it, a sense of the priorities of life, the most important being the security of *belonging*. The excitement of romance and the freedoms of youth are not nearly as enticing to the Goat as comfort and contentment with those he can depend on to care for him (or her).

Capricorn is both prepared and willing to impart the hard-earned Saturnine wisdom, but only when invited to do so. Because the Goats know the folly of forcing people to mature before their time, they smile with the benevolent indulgence of a fond grandparent (whatever his or her chronological age) upon the playful antics of the still young at heart. Secretly, the Capricorn soul longs to abandon duty but is by now resigned to the knowledge that sheer idealism is impractical — and spontaneous enthusiasm can never replace experience. Acutely aware of the dangers of impulsive action, the soul has become more conservative — and the Goat's refusal to either scatter efforts or to indulge in sentimentality brings on accusations of emotional coldness from those born into the Fire and Air Elements. Capricorns respect authority because they see the law as a necessity for the protection of human rights and safety. They shyly worship the famous and successful because Capricorn's ruler, Saturn, teaches them to revere achievement, knowing full well its price.

Although Capricorn may appear to be serious and unyielding to more liberal souls, Life has also taught the Goats its humorous side, and their subtle jokes are tinged with the irony of existence. Because the new Saturnine duties as counselor to the foolish weigh heavily on their shoulders, they sometimes try to drink the last full measure of Life's rare pleasures, calmly accepting them without false modesty or undue inhibition. Only afterward, when the sobering influence of maturity returns, does Capricorn feel a vague sense of remorse and melancholy for having succumbed to the temptation of forbidden passions. In this soul vibration there is a compulsion to acknowledge the necessity for being practical, as Capricorn admits, "I USE." But a gentleness of spirit softens the severity of the surface sternness commanded by Saturn, for the Capricorn consciousness brings with it a sympathy for human mistakes, born from the understanding gained through ten stages of Life's — and Love's — mysteries.

Capricorn's positive qualities are determination, stability, wisdom, dependability, sureness and tranquility. Expressed in their negative form they become selfishness, narrowness, ruthless ambition, rigidity, snobbery, depression and loneliness.

To Capricorn, love is a quiet and undemanding exchange of personal gratification. The Goats have fully learned the valuable lesson that love is not measured by excessive emotion. But because they equate it only with the necessities of mutual need and desire, they have not yet experienced the release of its inner longings.

The Aquarius Love Mystery

Having reached the Aquarian initiation, the evolving soul feels that it must return to life much of what it gathered along the way. And so begins a "second childhood" on the level of the Water Bearer, who pours out his knowledge, both determined and anxious to share it before he leaves this planet to explore the exciting realm of the unknown on the other side.

Aquarius feels the stirrings of the masculine positive Day Forces for the last time as a Fixed Organizer, in the final experience of the detached and unpredictable Air Element. A puzzle to friends and family, the Aquarian man or woman cavorts in peculiar fashion with the young at heart — peculiar, since wisdom and experience are in direct contrast with such liberal, eccentric behavior. There were so many mysteries missed in the past because there wasn't time to investigate them. Now Aquarius must taste them all — must investigate every nuance of up and down, left and right, will and won't. He delights in shocking those around him, suddenly aware of an inexplicable ability to peek into the future. Amazingly intuitive and bristling with unexpected flashes of telepathic images, the Aquarian soul examines people and ideas without sentiment, arriving at truth with no apparent logic or traceable effort.

On this level, the soul tends to flaunt law and authority because the spirit actually exists in the world of the future. Aquarius knows that the rigid rules of today's society must sooner or later be compromised. Therefore he (or she) sees no sensible reason to respect what will surely evolve into something new and different tomorrow. If violent revolt is necessary to bring about tolerance, brotherhood and understanding, then Aquarius believes the result will be worth the conflict. However, although they advocate change for the world (and for their friends and family), the Water Bearers remain Fixed in their own personal opinions, private codes and life-styles, reflecting the contradictory nature of the ruling planet, Uranus.

The soul has now acquired a true humanitarian approach. To the unprejudiced Aquarian, every human being is a friend, whatever that person's personal values may be, for the Water Bearer has learned that he (or she) is one with all mankind and womankind — and with Nature. Yet, personal relationships may be neglected, as these men and women pursue an idealism related to the benefit of society in general. Like the Aquarian Age it reflects, the soul at this stage envisions a golden and glorious future that may be attained only by blasting old customs and outdated ideas to clear the way for spiritual awareness, through the thunderbolt path of accelerated mass Karma. If more conservative people are offended by the Uranus behavior, the Aquarian individualist laughs off their disapproval. Secure in an intuitive grasp of the future, Aquarians retort, "I KNOW" to all questions, then perversely refuse to explain *how* they know — except to the children, who understand through their own innocence the innocent state of simplicity the soul returns to in the "second childhood" Uranus vibration.

The Aquarian positive qualities are vision, individuality, tolerance, friendliness, inventiveness, originality and genius. Expressed in their negative form they become eccentricity, neurosis, detachment, absentmindedness and refusal to cooperate.

To Aquarius, love is a detached and unselfish emotion, to be explored and enjoyed. The Water Bearer understands love's scope and investigates all its dimensions, but scatters it carelessly, confusing it with friendship. Physical fulfillment leaves Aquarius emotionally empty and still wistful, failing to sense the mystery of *Oneness* with the mate—the final truth of love, which awaits discovery silently, in the shadows—the secret guarded by Neptune, just beyond Uranus comprehension.

☆ ☆ ☆ ☆ ☆ ☆

The Pisces Love Mystery

Just as the soul is symbolically "born" into the innocent thoughtlessness of Aries, it symbolically "dies"—or leaves the painful Earth plane—to enter into the sympathetic humility and mystical awareness of Pisces. In the Piscean Sun Sign stage, evolving man and woman begin to comprehend vaguely the secret of Time as an eternal NOW—able to (in varying degrees) see the Past, Present and Future as one. This is the soul's third and final excursion into the sensitive Water Element—its fourth and final vibration as a Mutable Communicator—and the last experience under the feminine negative Night Forces.

Ideally, by the time the soul has reached the Pisces stage, it has attained spiritual enlightenment on its long journey through the Mysteries of Love experienced in the preceding eleven Sun Signs. If not, then it must return to certain Sun Sign vibratory experiences on the astrological circle to learn lessons not absorbed because they were too hastily skimmed over in previous incarnated stages. But each such return brings a new vulnerability to that Sun Sign lesson—a new inner urgency to master its positive essence and discard its negative. Of course, some high or advanced souls, after reaching the Piscean stage, elect of their own choosing to return to Earth to rescue those still in darkness. However, we are discussing here the average Pisces obligation and pattern.

Man and woman, on the Pisces level, have passed *at least once* through all twelve stages of initiation, and many have been required to fall back and retrace their steps hundreds of times in this experience, because Pisces is the most difficult of all the twelve Sun Signs to comprehend and master. Usually such an accomplishment is not gained the first time around the wheel of life, except by intense *desire* and *will*, which is not to say such achievement is impossible—but it is a path, up until now, chosen by very few. This is why astrology teaches that Pisces is "an old soul"—also the reason that not every Pisces man or woman is the epitome of spiritual grace; why some swim in waters dangerously close to the fires of Dante's Inferno. The Fish lives in two worlds, simultaneously experiencing both Heaven and Hell.

With the secret wisdom of the Piscean ruling planet, Neptune, Pisceans know that sadness and ugliness are not a part of God's plan. They have glimpsed the beauty of truth, and the brilliance of such mystical vision brings an urge to retreat from the negative vibrations of the Earth plane. So Pisces often avoids confrontation and tension through the escape route of drugs, alcohol, daydreams, artistic creation, philosophical theorizing, meditation or religious retreat. Pisceans may become teachers, monks, nuns, mystics, artists, musicians, composers, abstract mathematicians and highly intuitive scientists—or they may choose to swim down into the murky waters of alcoholism and drug addiction, even insanity. It is, indeed, a difficult and complicated vibration for the soul, for this Sun Sign experience is fraught with temptation for the Pisces man or woman.

Because they've been "through it all" on a subconscious level, the Fishes have a natural compassion for the troubles of those around them. The Neptunian soul is intimately familiar with life's vicissitudes, understanding the weakness of human nature, therefore tending to pity, rather than to condemn, man's and woman's failings. This is why these "old souls" so frequently become the recipients of everyone's secrets, trials, worries and apprehensions. Yet the initial instinct is to turn away from sticky entanglements in all forms. Only when the Fish finds the courage to face his or her own problems with as much spiritual wisdom as is offered to others can the Neptune mysteries be fathomed.

Through this "death initiation" (death of the human ego) the soul grows more forgiving, more gentle, better able to understand its true relationship to the co-Creators . . . . as Pisces affirms "I BELIEVE." To realize the full glory and truth of love, the Fish can, if he or she chooses, call on the innocence of Aries, the patience of Taurus, the awareness of Gemini, the perception of Cancer, the nobility of Leo, the discrimination of Virgo, the judgment of Libra, the penetration of Scorpio, the honesty of Sagittarius, the wisdom of Capricorn—and the humanitarianism of Aquarius. But sometimes these many fragments of secret knowledge and talents serve only to confuse Pisces, causing the Fish to then take the easier path of passive nonresistance.

The Pisces positive qualities are humility, compassion, sensitivity, spiritual awareness, psychic comprehension, philosophic insight and a healing potential. Expressed in their negative form they become timidity, apprehension, masochism, idleness, lying and weakness of will.

To Pisces, love is unselfish submission of the ego to the desires of the one needed to become Whole. The Fish gains more pleasure from giving than from receiving, more happiness in serving than in being served. Yet enigmatic Neptune tests the Pisces soul with the lure of multiple sexual and romantic experience — floating from one affair to another.

In such promiscuous manner — *or by becoming a romantic recluse* — does the wary Fish escape the dangers of being "hooked" by deep or permanent emotional commitment. But the Pisces man or woman who resists this temptation to avoid love's pain by seeking only love's pleasure . . . . is richly rewarded by the mastery of love's final mystery. He or she can then glimpse for the first time on the soul's weary journey the true passion of blending in a trinity of mind, heart and spirit, resulting in a rare physical ecstasy — the ultimate Piscean fulfillment of Love's long-ago Aries springtime promise of a miracle.

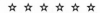

The Planets

we've fought a long and bitter war
my Twin Soul and I

lost and lonely, fallen angels, exiled
from a misty, half-forgotten galaxy of stars
wounded cruelly by the painful thrust of Mars
caught in Neptune's tangled web
shocked and torn asunder
by the sudden, awful violence of Uranus

tortured by the clever lies of Mercury
crushed beneath the icy weight of stern, unyielding Saturn
who lengthened every hour into a day
each day into a year
each year into eternities of waiting

scorched, and nearly blinded

by the Sun's exploding bursts of arrogance and pride
as Eve and Adam, stilled and helpless, deep within us cried . . .

still we fought on in unrelenting fury
striking blow for blow . . . driven by the pounding drums

of Jupiter's giant, throbbing passions.
stumbling at the precipice of the Moon's enticing madness

to fall, at last, in trembling fear
before the threat of Pluto's ominous, tomb-like silence
consumed by inconsolable sadness, and the bleakness

> *of despair*

> *we bear . . .*

the wounds and scars of furious battle
I and my Twin Soul

but now we walk in quiet peace
with all our scattered pieces whole
together, hand-in-hand . . . full serpent circle
back into the Pyramid-shaped rainbow
> *of tomorrow's brighter Eden*

crowned by gentle Venus with the Victory of Love
that did not die
but has survived the night of selfish seeking
to wait for morning's soft forgiveness

> *and the dawn of understanding°*

°From *Gooobers*, a forthcoming novel about astrology and reincarnation by Linda Goodman.

Your Sun Sign

The term "Sun Sign" means that if you are, for example, a Gemini, the Sun was exercising its powerful influence through the ZONE OF THE ZODIAC (not the constellation) called Gemini when you were born — from May 21st to June 21st inclusive (in all USA time zones for the past several decades; with a day's difference, for instance, in Greenwich, England). You'll find that the dates covering the twelve Sun Sign periods vary according to which astrology book you read, and this can be confusing to the layman. The reason for the variance is that most astrologers don't wish to puzzle you with the information that the Sun "changes signs" in the morning, afternoon or evening of a particular day. And so they "rob" one consecutive Sun Sign of that Change Day and give it to the other — to make things come out even. This only adds to the confusion. It's all very nice and easy to pretend each new Sun Sign period begins precisely at midnight. But it doesn't.

For example, except for leap-year variations, the Sun (for the last several decades, as well as currently) both LEAVES Aries and ENTERS Taurus sometime on April 20th in all USA time zones (on April 21st, however, in Greenwich, England). It's important for you to know that April 20th contains BOTH signs. Otherwise, you might go around all your life thinking you're a Bull, when you're really a Ram.

So remember always that if you were born on either the FIRST or the LAST day of any of the Sun Sign periods listed in this book, you'll have to know the exact TIME, plus the longitude and latitude of your birth, to judge whether or not the Sun had "changed signs" by that hour at the place where you were born.

The term "Moon Sign" refers to the zone of the zodiac (not the constellation) through which the Moon was "passing" and exercising its influence when you were born. The term "Ascendent" (occasionally called the "Rising Sign") means the sign of the zodiac that was "rising" on the Eastern Horizon at the exact moment of your birth. The Ascendent varies with the location of your birthplace on Earth (longitude/latitude of birth locality). Those of you who want to know more about these things may consult the reading list at the back of this book.

A note regarding "cusp birth dates": So often, those who were born on an astrological "cusp date" (the day during which the Sun changes signs) will say (and believe) that their personalities seem to contain the qualities of *both* Sun Signs. And they imagine this to be caused by their "cusp birthdays."

For example, a person born on January 20th may feel that he or she behaves at times like a Capricorn — at other times like an Aquarian. The same thing is true for all "cusp people." Some astrologers will tell you this is because a "cusp birth" causes the person so born to exhibit the traits of both signs. In my extensive and varied personal experience as a professional astrologer, I have been convinced that this is simply not true. In every single instance, without exception, the person who believes that he (or she) behaves in a manner which is a blend of both "cusp Sun Signs" — is behaving in that manner because that person's *Moon* or *Ascendent* is in the "second" sign.

For instance, the above-mentioned particular person born on January 20th in the morning of that day is a Sun Sign Capricorn. If this Cappy sometimes behaves like a Goat — and at other times behaves in the manner of an Aquarian Water Bearer, it is always because the Cappy's *Moon* or *Ascendent* was in Aquarius at birth — NOT BECAUSE HE OR SHE WAS BORN ON A "CUSP DAY." If such a person born on January 19th behaves essentially always like a Goat — and never as an Aquarian — then the Moon or Ascendent was NOT in the "cusp sign" of Aquarius at birth.

You are one Sun Sign or the other. Your personality cannot and does not partake of two Sun Signs because you were born on a "cusp day." It's true that each of the three "decanates" of every Sun Sign (every astrological sign is encompassed by 30 degrees) — each "decanate" of 10 degrees each — bestows its own variation of the particular Sun Sign quality. But that is a separate matter entirely. If you are a Capricorn, you are a Capricorn. You are not a "partial" Sun Sign Aquarian because you were born on a "cusp day." If you find yourself occasionally behaving as an Aquarian, you can be certain it's because the *Moon* or *Ascendent* was in Aquarius at your birth (or that you perhaps only *imagine* your Aquarian characteristics because you've been overly impressed with the error so frequently repeated by misguided astrologers.

This image may help to make it clearer to you. Your (for example) Capricorn characteristics imprinted upon your personality when you drew your first breath (impressing the billions of electric cells in your brain much in the way a computer is programmed) were caused by the Sun's exercising of its powerful influence through the zone of the zodiac called Capricorn. This process (which creates your personal Sun Sign) is a Time-Energy Force. For want of more precise terminology, the process is somewhat electromagnetic. You may then, for the purpose of helping create an image, ask yourself if an electric light may at any time be half on and half off. Of course it cannot. An electric light is either ON or it is OFF. It CANNOT be both on and off at the same time. Neither can the Sun (for similar reasons) exercise its powerful influence through TWO SIGNS simultaneously.

When the Sun is vibrating its force through Capricorn, it is vibrating its force through Capricorn. At the exquisitely timed cosmic moment (which may be Earth-timed only within minutes, using present astronomical-mathematical means, to all intents and purposes) — at this moment when the Sun "enters" the sign of Aquarius, it is then exercising its powerful vibrations through Aquarius, and no longer through the sign of Capricorn. Period. The light cannot be on and off at the same time. The Sun cannot be imprinting the characteristics of both Capricorn and Aquarius at the same time. It is a cosmic and astrological impossibility. The "orb of influence" rationalization used by astrologers who dwell upon "combined cusp day" traits does not apply in relation to the Sun Sign. In relation to many other phases and facets of astrology (including the present "orb of influence" of the Aquarian Age) such as aspects and so on — it does apply. But NOT in the case of a Sun Sign.

As for "Astrology 13," the astronomer's joke against the holiness and validity of astrology, disregard it. For reasons I can't detail here, for want of space, this concept of "thirteen Sun Signs," and so forth, is completely fallacious. Half-seriously and half-humorously, I offer you the ultimate proof. Astrology 13 would make your author a Sun Sign Pisces rather than an Aries. All my friends and relatives will tell you that the idea of my being a Piscean is fallacious to the point of being hilarious. Neither is Nelson Rockefeller a Gemini (which Astrology 13 would make him) but a Cancerian Crab all the way. Neither is Billy Graham a Libran (which Astrology 13 would make him) but a Scorpion Eagle all the way. And that, dear readers and astrology students, is THAT. A determined Ram (not a tactful, gentle Piscean) has spoken! So be it. I urge you not to allow this deliberate seed of confusion, planted by astronomers who wish to muddy the astrological issue, grow into one of the Little Prince's huge baobab trees of darkness and negative falsehood.

☆ ☆ ☆ ☆ ☆ ☆

Sun Sign Birth Periods

ARIES	March 20th into April 20th
TAURUS	April 20th into May 21st
GEMINI	May 21st into June 21st
CANCER	June 21st into July 22nd
LEO	July 22nd into August 23rd
VIRGO	August 23rd into September 23rd
LIBRA	September 23rd into October 23rd
SCORPIO	October 23rd into November 22nd
SAGITTARIUS	November 22nd into December 21st
CAPRICORN	December 21st into January 20th
AQUARIUS	January 20th into February 19th
PISCES	February 19th into March 20th

Love Sign
Combinations

ARIES

Fire — Cardinal — Positive
Ruled by Mars
Symbol: The Ram
Day Forces — Masculine

ARIES

Fire — Cardinal — Positive
Ruled by Mars
Symbol: The Ram
Day Forces — Masculine

The **ARIES-ARIES** *Relationship*

Then rather curiously they both snapped out
the same remark:

"Shut up!"

"Shut up!"

I wonder . . . . . is it proper and dignified for an Aries person like myself to analyze the 1-1 Sun Sign vibrational influence between two Rams — to describe what it's like when they blend their compatible but equally combustible natures, as friends, neighbors, relatives, business associates, lovers or mates? Let me consider it for a moment. All right, I've considered it. Of course it's proper. Who's better qualified? No one. As for being dignified, receiving a Dignity Achievement Award has never been my chief goal in life. That settles *that*. So let's get on with it. I can't stand waiting around for things to happen, can you?

First, we should probably discuss the number of mistakes it's possible for two Rams to make, in a close association. Gigantic. Simply gigantic. Still, the number of successes can also be overwhelming — and since Rams are so frequently compelled to impulsively jump into puddles head first (Aries always leads with the head), it won't be so lonesome being stuck upside down in the mud, with a kindred soul for company.

When these two strong egos first mix their personal auras, clear the field, and count down for the blast-off, which is usually a surge of spontaneous empathy. It's really such a joy to discover a positive, enthusiastic, and open personality, after being stuck with all those squeamish squares, and boring wet blankets — the secretive, stingy ones, and especially those cold, unapproachable people who freeze you, when all you're trying to do is be friendly. No wonder there's such an instant rush of mutual admiration! Each Ram will find it a blessed relief that the other one isn't all stuffy about things like extravagance, impulsive behavior, rash speech, and being late for appointments. Not only that, now there's someone who will go to the dentist with them, and not think they're "sissy."

Most Arians hate two things equally: (a) going to the dentist — and (b) having someone take their picture "candidly" or otherwise. Sitting still and posing while the photographer adjusts lights in a studio is almost as bad as submitting to a molar tooth extraction or root canal work, because it gives you all that time to decide you're ugly, which is equally as grinding a pain to the self-conscious Rams, who are ultra-concerned and somewhat vain about how they look. (Astrologically, Aries rules the physical appearance.) The Ram's fear of the dentist is in no way, however, a reflection on Aries courage. Mars supplies these people with all the courage they need, and an extra helping of it anytime they ask, even on very short notice. Their dread of the dental drill is an isolated hang-up, and mustn't be construed to mean that Rams are cowards. They simply don't like anyone messing around with their heads. That normally includes drugs. It definitely includes eyes, ears, nose and mouth — also the brain — which means don't mess with their opinions either.

Most Aries females, for instance, dislike going to beauty parlors. Beauticians are so bossy, and they simply will not comb your hair the way you tell them, or part it where you order them to part it. After all, it's not *their* hair, it's your hair, but give them an inch, and they'll snip off four. The Aries woman may impulsively, to her later regret, cut her own hair drastically too short, or crooked — but let someone else turn her into a shorn lamb, and she'll be furious. As furious as she'd be with herself. (Aries is not at all selective about anger.) Girl Rams would rather go to the extra trouble of washing their hair at home than suffer a hair stylist who thinks he (or she) owns their heads. The Aries sensitivity related to anything connected with the head area is really pronounced. You'd be sensitive about your head, too, if you had a dozen or so scars scattered around on your head and face you began collecting in childhood, from crashing into things (and people) head first.

As for the "extra trouble" of doing something themselves, that's no large thing. Rams almost never mind going to "extra trouble" for themselves, or for others. When it's for others, the extra trouble stems from the generous impulse of the Mars-ruled souls to give more than may be needed of their time, money, love, loyalty, and everything else. When it comes to themselves, they tend to bring on the extra trouble by creating problems where none would exist if the situation were left alone. "Leaving well enough alone" seems like silly advice to a Ram. Why should anyone be satisfied with "well enough"? What kind of a goal is that when, with a little effort, well enough can be made better? (Aries never theorizes that well enough might possibly be made worse.)

Unless one or both Rams have a Capricorn, Taurus or Cancer Moon Sign or Ascendent, it will probably be easy for them to borrow money from each other, and neither will be likely to create a fuss about being paid back promptly — which is another area of empathy between them. These two are straightforward about everything, including money. It never occurs to them to be deceptive. Actually, they don't know how.

Now and then, they may overestimate their ability to pay, or even forget a debt, because of being caught up in something new that's so exciting it consumes their entire attention, but they are not dishonest, and absolutely never sneaky. Nothing both hurts and angers a Ram more than to be unjustly mistrusted or suspected. It would mortify the typical Aries man or woman to let down anyone to whom either gave his word, and this includes creditors. Arians may be either forgetful or delinquent, but eventually they'll pay everything they owe in full, often more than they owe — because Rams are not unduly suspicious, *or* cautious, about spending, so it's easy for them to be oversold and overcharged. No matter. The Mars idea about money is that when it disappears, more will soon manifest, in one way or another. (Does the Infant fret and worry about where the next dry diaper or bottle of milk will come from? Certainly not. It will magically appear when needed. *Everybody* knows *that*!) Each Aries person in this 1-1 Sun Sign Pattern association will be touchingly grateful for the trust of the other. Not only will two Rams usually instinctively trust one another, they won't take advantage of one another, and considering the way the rest of the world usually treats both of them, this can be a warm and wonderful feeling.

It's all a merry-go-round of happiness between Aries and Aries in the beginning, but after the pink cotton candy melts, there may be moments of disillusion. You know what happens when Fire meets Fire? Higher and hotter flames. That should indicate the possible ramifications of an association between two wild and woolly Rams, whether it's business, romantic, friendly or otherwise. It could be otherwise, if they insist on butting away at the impossible task of trying to break each other's vulnerable yet indomitable and unconquerable spirit.

Scattered among the more typical extroverted Arians, are the not as common, Sheep-type Aries people, whose Mars egos have been, very sadly, crushed in childhood, and who therefore control their natural exuberance behind a most *un*natural introversion. If the two Aries people who are involved with one another belong to this group, they may not appear, on the surface, to be capable of arousing anger in each other, but appearances are deceptive. At some time, in some way, their horns are sure to lock.

When Mars clashes with Mars, the result can be full-scale war, with all flags flapping, bravely and colorfully. Occasional flare-ups are bound to occur when these two are thrown into close, daily proximity, without the relief of some separateness in their association. But there will also be some glorious Highs to offset these Lows.

Most of the time, the direct, forceful manner of Mars will create a wave of sympathy between two Aries people. It's when their mutual need for ego trips overlaps that they can expect the fireworks. Here's a possible solution to that problem: One Ram is permitted to have everything his way on Mondays, Wednesdays and Fridays. The other Ram gets to be Big Boss on Sundays, Tuesdays and Thursdays. Saturdays, they can just fight it out, letting the Ram with the toughest horns win — and bind up the loser's wounds with typical Aries instant contriteness and warm generosity. It's a formula that should be successful in most cases, since neither Aries will mind taking a periodic fling at playing second glockenspiel, knowing that he — or she — will be allowed to be conductor again the next day.

It's been said that Aries people have a way about them. They do. Their own way. Yet, despite that sometimes antagonistic Martian exterior, they'll sense each other's desperate need to be appreciated and liked. When they get together, they may struggle for leadership, but the experience will supply some well-needed lessons. The shock of living with someone — or being around someone — as innocently thoughtless, selfish and aggressive as one's self, is sure to soften any battering Ram, although there may be a few scars to show for the lessons in living thus mastered. Aries hearts always carry more scars than the Rams ever show, or openly discuss.

It will be necessary for both of them to realize that Aries is the Infant of the zodiac, symbolizing the dawn of the personality awareness, or Sunrise. Aries represents the East, the Day Forces — which is why most of them fight sleep, tranquility, rest and resignation to Fate with such vigor. The negative intrusion of any degree of criticism or pessimism darkens a Ram's "Easter" horizon, and considerably dampens the Aries spirit, especially when the blow to innocence and Sunrise faith is delivered forcefully from another Ram. Yet, temporary resentment seldom remains long enough to become permanent bitterness, because Aries possesses a childlike faith that a quarrel can somehow be made up, a relationship can be repaired each time it's broken. It's unthinkable to a Ram that any given situation is anything but the way he (or she) sees it at the time. Nevertheless, no one (except Sag and Gemini) can switch a mistaken viewpoint more swiftly, or bury yesterday's unhappiness and hurt more completely, than an Aries man, woman or child *who is handled gently.* To a Ram of either sex, or any chronological age (barring a more pessimistic Moon Sign and/or Ascendent), each Sunrise brings a new covenant of resurrection — the resurrection of a shattered dream, idea, goal or friendship. Why look backward, or worry about what's past, and couldn't be helped, when today is so full of promise ?

A few sentences back, you'll notice the phrase "who is handled gently" in italics. The trouble is, although Rams need to be handled gently themselves, they aren't inclined to handle each other (or anyone else) gently. Aries people can't seem to get the hang of the Golden Rule. They comprehend, even personify, its generosity and forgiveness, but they can't quite interpret what it means to treat others as tenderly as they need to be treated. They will not be led by the nose, pushed or forced by anyone, including those who are clearly stronger than they are, and certainly not by each other. (A typical Aries person would literally stand before a criminal who pointed a loaded gun in his — or her — direction, and fearlessly talk back.) Rams expect their own wishes to be granted, their own orders obeyed without question, as quickly as possible (unless there's a softening influence of several Pisces or Libra planets in the horoscope). It's the instinctive Mars urge to rebel. The drive to initiate and to lead is so strong in some Mars-ruled men, women and children that even friendly suggestion is sometimes construed as unbearable interference, let alone the forceful commands of a relative, neighbor, friend, business associate, mate or lover born under the same, unconsciously demanding Sun Sign.

If one of the two Aries people is stronger by planetary positions at birth (not wiser and more patient, which would be beneficial, but *stronger*), the result of the association could be that the "weaker" Ram gradually turns into a neurotic Sheep, constantly and pathetically almost apologizing for his (or her) very existence — or else rationalizing every word and action, for fear of offending or being misunderstood. Such a situation is very sad, for to see the proud strength of a spirited astrological "animal" like the Ram reduced to weakness and tears, constantly attempting to placate the more dominate personality, yet inwardly frustrated and emotionally restricted, is against the first law of astrology: Be true to your own Sun Sign essence, or be prepared to lose the powerful individual potential of your own birthright.

It's never easy for two Rams to exist in tranquil harmony (although it can undeniably be exciting!). One happy probability is that both of them will usually be inclined to forgive and forget everything but the most cruel encounters. As for the latter, a powerful effort should be made to avoid them, because they'll be long remembered by Aries . . . . . for the very same reason that infants, who instantly forget, with a trusting smile, the more commonplace hurts and pains—will recall, with subconscious terror, the deeper experiences of traumatic rejection . . . . sometimes forever.

Two Rams will have to try to control their tendency to lash out at one another while their tempers are still hot. They'll strike a blow, shortly afterward feel a surge of guilt over their hasty unkindness, then impulsively attempt to make up for their anger by showering each other with an outburst of affection, or the peace offering of an extravagant gift. Gifts, by the way, are a Ram's way of saying "I like you" or "I love you"—occasionally given apologetically to say "I'm sorry." But never is an Aries gift given for the purpose of "buying friendship." The Mars-ruled are contemptuous of getting what they want by buying it (they're accustomed to demanding it). So they fiercely resent, and are also very deeply hurt by, such untrue insinuations or accusations. Aries gifts are always from the heart, given in a straightforward and honest gesture of good will. Nevertheless, their motives are often misunderstood by those too materialistically minded themselves to be able to comprehend giving without some ulterior motive (since that's their own pattern of behavior, they believe everyone must be the same).

Happily, this is another area of hurt two Rams probably won't inflict upon one another. Each Aries person understands the gift-giving syndrome that's part of the Mars nature (matched only by the other two Fire Signs) and, therefore, both will usually give and receive joyously, back and forth. A Ram is as delighted to receive a gift as to be able to give one. It's part of the wisdom of Aries innocence to know that it's of equal importance to graciously receive as to generously give. For if no one *received* happily, there could be no happy giving. Consequently, the typical Ram will react with the elation of a child to the receiving of a "surprise present," and two Arians can keep themselves broke (but exalted and happy) as a result of their mutual urge to express their enthusiasms through gifting.

Down through the centuries, the Ram has been a symbol of sacrifice for spiritually blind, emotionally warped and mentally dense religious fanatics. The Old Testament is packed with bloody examples of the "burnt offerings" of these misguided "holy men." In no way was the patriarch Abraham following "God's" wishes or commands to first be willing to murder his own son to please the Almighty, and then to "hear" God's voice grant a last minute reprieve, commanding him to murder a helpless Sheep in his place. Abraham, sadly, heard only the voice of his own delusions, not the voice of God. Neither of our infinitely compassionate and wise co-Creators would be so sadistic as to command the murder of children, or of the lowliest of our animal brothers and sisters, for Their own greater glory, as a senseless test of faith and obedience. The Earth sorely needed the example set by the gentle Nazarene, Jesus, who used the Sheep in parable after parable illustrating love and kindness, who is often pictured embracing the "lamb" and who brought to the world the image of the Good Shepherd, in his effort to straighten out the kinks in the twisted thinking of these "servants of God," who were, through their cruel sacrifices of animals, unknowingly serving Satan, for all their otherwise pious and humble attitudes.

In such mythical legends as Jason and the Golden Fleece, the sad fate of the Ram has been repeated, all through mythology, as well as in biblical history. The unfortunate Ram who attempted to cross dangerous seas and rescue a brother and sister from the jealous act of a stepmother, in a great act of courage, was unable to save the sister from drowning. When he reached the shore, and delivered the brother safely, his thanks was to be murdered, for allowing the other one to die, even though he had tried desperately to save her.

Such is the symbolic fate, in varying degrees, in all kinds of endeavors, of many Aries people. For all their enthusiastic efforts and the sincerity of their impulses, human Rams frequently are either ignored or despised for their trouble by the very ones they have tried to help. The Arian simplicity of purpose and direct approach isn't always welcomed by the more cynical of this world. Ram Thomas Jefferson discovered this, as did modern day Aries politician Eugene McCarthy. Ram Nikita Khrushchev's personal motives were also, to a large extent, misunderstood and unappreciated both by his own people and by Americans.

And so, the teaming up of two Arians can be beneficial, inasmuch as they're able to help each other avoid becoming a "burnt offering," or being sacrificed to the calculated maneuvers of the more worldly wise who would "fleece" them. They provide each other with protection against those who would otherwise take advantage of their altruistic instincts. There are always bullies who wait for a chance to attack the defenseless. Admittedly, it's difficult to image the feisty, fiery and normally outspoken Rams as "defenseless." But in the final analysis, they are extremely vulnerable to those who would use their natural guilelessness and lack of sophistication against them.

In any association between two Aries people, within the family circle, in the office or across the bridge of love and friendship, one thing is certain: emotions will periodically run high, and close to the surface. Catullus described perfectly the attitude of this Sun Sign to its own emotional immaturity, when he wrote: *I hate and I love. You may ask why I do so. I do not know. But I feel it, and am in torment.*

Between two Rams, there will seldom be any deception, pretense or hypocrisy, but neither will there be a great deal of caution, reason or practicality. There's very little that will be neutral in this 1-1 Sun Sign Pattern vibration of the double Mars involvement. These two are capable of reaching the far heavens of happiness, or of consuming themselves in childish displays of rage, resentment and thoughtless selfishness. Yet they will never fail to understand and sympathize with each other's bright red, diamond-dusted dreams, especially those dreams that didn't quite make it, for one reason or another. Perhaps together, they can both try again. And somehow, someway, someday . . . . . they'll win. Tough dreamers always do.

☆ ☆ ☆ ☆ ☆ ☆

ARIES *Woman* ARIES *Man*

————— ◆◄◉►◆ —————

So uproariously gay was the dance, and how they buffeted each other on the bed and out of it! It was a pillow fight rather than a dance, and when it was finished, the pillows insisted on one bout more . . .

As fiercely independent, bright and clever as the Aries girl is, the Aries man is even more so — in his own opinion. And he'll demand recognition of it eventually, no matter how he fools her, and himself, in the beginning. From the very first time she pushes through a door ahead of him, he'll feel the faint stirring of a desire to teach her that, in any tangle between a girl and a boy Ram, the male of the Sun Sign will win. He should decide to thus subdue her early in the game, or say goodbye. There may be a few noisy, tearful skirmishes before she catches on, but she'll blossom beautifully when she's allowed — no, forced — to become a woman.

However, demanding that she drop her career or job to take up the full-time job of waiting on his whims is not the most ideal way to unfold her womanhood, and establish his manhood. There are other ways. Unless she willingly sacrifices her "pre-*them*" occupation to warm his slippers, or join him in his personal goals, forgetting her own (which sometimes happens), it's best for him to let her stay out there where it's all happening. It would also be a wise mutual decision to let it be his income that pays the rent or mortgage, food and utilities bills. Her money can provide the extra things they'll need to satisfy the extravagant impulses they both frequently feel. That way, the male Aries will be solidly entrenched in the image of the masculine side of the team, and it's important to get that straight, right at the start.

I mean, let it be plainly understood that he is MAN and she is WOMAN. There will be lots of opportunities to wonder about the division of actual control in the relationship, and there's no sense adding to this by a confusion of sexual male-female roles.

The masculinity challenge of the Mars female begins the day she first zings the male Ram of her choice in the heart with her sparkling hopes and excitements, so much like his own, and will follow him through all sorts of living arrangements, including temporary geographical separation. She may try to dominate him by telephone, telegram or letter, if he's not within touching distance. Since the Aries man knows that no one has successfully dominated him from the time he was born, he might feel like calling it quits when he feels the first tug-of-war from an Aries girl, but he'd be smarter to curb his annoyance, and try to tame her instead.

Every Aries woman has a deep, hidden desire to be protected and defended by her man. In her private daydreams she is always the lovely, gentle Guinevere, and he is the kind, tender, strong Lancelot — or he'd better be if he doesn't want his Guinevere to become a frustrated Virginia Woolf, which is a very possible and most undesirable result when a man either leans too far backward with her, in an attempt to please — or leans too far forward, in an attempt to take charge. The former probably won't occur often, because leaning over backward is not a normal position or direction for the typical male Ram. Leaning too far forward is more likely. But he should understand that her Guinevere wish to be conquered is purely romantic and sexual. It has little or nothing to do with the personality, or other areas of her life. His masculine Mars macho that keeps her starry-eyed and emotionally fulfilled on a stroll along the beach, or in the privacy of the bedroom, won't normally be welcomed regarding activities separated from romance. She draws a sharp line between submitting romantically and submitting in other ways, and it's best for him to realize this if he wants to keep her. Expecting this lady to keep his curfews or follow his orders is unwise, but *ignoring* her is downright dangerous. He's capable of making all these mistakes until he learns she'll neither toe the line nor be brought to heel by the dictator treatment, because she's cut from the same mold as he — which was, of course, thrown away after the Aries Sun Sign was made. That's how Rams believe that the old saying got started "They threw away the mold when they made you, baby." They sure did. (Actually, it refers to the ancient potter's mold, but it fits the Aries situation quite aptly.)

The first thing the Aries girl will notice about her male counterpart is that he's even more bossy, beligerent and bellicose than she is. Obviously — and also fortunately. If she's puzzled by the Yin and the Yang of it, a brief meditation on her all-time-favorite faerie story might cause her to experience the dawn of comprehension.

This woman never failed to cry, as a child, when she read about the Prince charging bravely into the woods to find his Princess and awaken her from her lonely slumber with the kiss of True Love. (Aries females invariably get all soft and squishy inside at the mere thought of True Love, their idealism in affairs of the heart being as eternal as Spring itself.) But really now, dear Aries girl, when you're honest with yourself, would it all have been quite so magical if the fiery, courageous Princess had come charging bravely into the woods on her horse to claim her Prince and rescue him from the Wicked Witch? The same meditation should be practiced on all the other faerie tales she still believes in, and dreams of every fortnight or so. Imagine dainty Cinderella, red-faced, puffing and perspiring, as she tried to shove a glass Hush-Puppy on her Prince's foot, to see if it fitted him. Mother Nature knows what she's doing. The Aries man–woman relationship will stand a better chance of success if she permits him to steal her Mars thunder. It somehow sounds better coming from him — if he doesn't carry it too far. Besides, since she's no stranger to toughness herself, she knows very well, if she'll stop to ponder it, that his tough Aries facade is only a cover for his quivering Aries idealism, his desperate inner longing to be needed — and noticed.

All right, so she should *notice* him as he sits there astride his white horse, shooting off all that Aries bossiness to disguise his secret fear that no one will ever love him as much as he knows he needs to be loved (which is considerable) — unless he demands it. This man can be very tender and gentle, for all his brash independence, and he's an expert at pretending he's not hurt when he's actually been deeply wounded. She knows how that is. Since they're both aware of all these Mars secrets about each other, you'd think they would cool the fireworks, but it usually takes more than one painful lesson to teach them the futility of constant ego challenges. Often, the ultimate lesson is the frightening experience of nearly losing each other, then realizing at the last minute, before the ultimate and final disaster — like the old silent films *Perils of Pauline* serial — that meeting Force with Force never works.

If she'll do all her Mars charging at her man's enemies, instead of at him, he'll adore her for it, and in return he'll give her every bit as much loyalty as she gives him. That's certainly a fair trade. But somebody has to start it.

It may seem at first that these two are well mated sexually, since they both require essentially the same thing of love — that it be the kind of physical-emotional blending poets write about as the epitome of the soul-mate theory, which nearly every Arian believes in as absolute romantic dogma. Whether they use the term "soul-mate" itself or not, Rams never doubt, when they love, that their union was not only Made In Heaven, but also made to last throughout a lifetime — and beyond. However, before this potential peak of harmony becomes a reality, a serious obstacle must be overcome — the instinctive, although almost always unintentional, selfishness of this Sun Sign.

Now, everything everybody wants to know about sex (whether he — or she — has been afraid to ask or not) is based on either deliberate or non-deliberate selfishness, using the partner for self-gratification. Not how can I bring him (or her) more fulfillment, but how can *I* be more fulfilled ? Sex-sex-sex. Doctors David Reuben, Masters and Johnson, Kinsey and Freud, have all explained it, tested it, researched it, analyzed it, observed it, photographed it, taped it, listened to it, written about it — just about everything but demonstrated it in public auditoriums. (Too much competition from stage, film and magazines.) But most men and women still haven't received the message.

It might be a good idea for these Mars lovers to buy one of those large posters, showing a couple walking, blissfully hand-in-hand, toward the mountains, the ocean or the cornfields, gazing into each other's eyes ... with the inscription at the bottom: *LOVE BEGINS WHEN THE NEEDS OF SOMEONE ELSE BECOME MORE IMPORTANT THAN YOUR OWN* .... and nail it firmly near their bed, right next to the tapestry depicting *THE WEDDING OF ROMEO AND JULIET,* which always hangs in spirit, if not in actuality, on the wall of every Aries bedroom. Romeo and Juliet were also soul-mates, you see — but *they* were unselfish. It's not necessary for the Aries man and woman to end their honeymoon with a double suicide scene in order to prove unselfishness. A little thoughtful consideration on both sides will suffice.

When these traces of infantile selfishness have been erased by tenderness, the sexual sharing of love between these two can be an ecstatic exchange. With Aries, sex is composed of strange contradictions, barely comprehended, causing their mating to be an incredible combination of explosive desire, direct and penetrating, fiery and uncontrolled .... and haunting fragments of flowers in the rain, fresh breezes and glittering snow diamonds. That's what happens when the powerful thrust of Mars is gentled by being expressed through the naivete and starry wonder of the symbolic Aries Infant. It creates a rare and startling blend of abandoned, stormy emotion — and the peace of a still and silent dawn. At once primitive — and poetic. The alchemy of equal parts of searing passion and fragile innocence is very nearly a holy thing. Obviously, then, at its very best, the sexual union between two Rams can be an experience to cherish. Even at its worst, it will be . . . . . interesting.

What will she do if he flirts with other girls ? Well, what would *he* do if she flirts with other men ? Same thing. An emotional explosion of the hydrogen bomb magnitude — which is just as foolish and suicidal to love as the actual hydrogen bomb is to our planet. Each Ram will let the other know unmistakably that iron bars on individual freedom will not be tolerated. But it's a one-sided freedom, since each of them refuses to be strangled by jealousy, while at the same time displaying intense jealousy of the other. Aries people do tend to want to have their cake and eat it, and it may take several noisy, emotional scenes to teach them that they can't have it both ways.

They'll have to learn that love's not a game to be won, a battle to be fought or even a prize to be won. It's a gift — to be given. Rams will demand a lot of things from life, and get them. But no one, not even an Aries, can demand love.

He'll make it clear that she should not dare to be jealous of *him*, but *she* had better not even look at another man. She'll make it just as clear that he's not to smother *her* with jealousy, but at the same time, *he'd* better not be caught glancing with the slightest flicker of interest at another woman.

You know what that is? It's selfish. If you're an Aries, you may not have thought about it like that, but *think* about it. Rams can even become jealous if they notice a smile on the loved one's face in sleep. Who is he (or she) dreaming about? And don't believe that very question hasn't been asked by lots of Aries couples in the morning. "Well, you must have had pleasant dreams last night. Were you meeting your old boy friend in your astral body?" And don't think the answer hasn't been: "It's none of your business what I dream. Besides, I noticed you weren't so anxious to wake up when I kissed you Good Morning just now. Were you lying there, half awake, practicing mental telepathy with that girl you flirted with at the supermarket last week?"

There are variations of dialogue, but such confrontations are a definite possibility when two Rams have promised to love, honor and cherish — but *never* to obey! The solution is for these two to practice their own telepathic communication, and to reassure each other of their undying devotion constantly, because the symbolic Infant's subconscious fear of losing love lies at the bottom of all Aries jealousy, incongruous as it may seem, as it struggles with the conscious Mars urge for personal independence. If he forgets to call to say he'll be later for dinner, who better than she should understand his need to follow a sudden impulse without first holding a committee meeting?

Should the winds of April call him away from the hearth, she may be simultaneously called to follow her own skylark cadenza, and when they return to each other, they can exchange magical tales of the wonders they nearly touched, the miracles they almost caught. An Aries man who's out there rushing after some new, exciting goal he just discovered is simply being true to himself, and the Aries woman who faces the truth must admit she couldn't really love a man who wasn't true to himself. The new, exciting goal needn't be a woman. Not unless it becomes a woman through her unfounded jealousy. If she trusts him *completely*, she probably won't regret it, because an Aries man, more so than any other Sun Sign male, will usually live up to exactly what's *expected* of him. And that works in reverse too. What's sauce for the goose is surely sauce for the gander between these lovers.

A couple of years ago I received a letter from an Aries woman married to an Aries man. They have three children, one Gemini and two Taureans. She described so well the happiness that can result from a double 1-1 Sun Sign vibration (with some effort) that I'm going to quote part of her letter here. She wrote, in part:

" . . . . . . and when I read aloud the last paragraph of the Aries woman section, in your book *Sun Signs*, to my also Aries husband — the part that says, 'She may be a little impulsive, bossy and independent, but you can't have everything' — he asked, 'What else would a man *want* ?' My Aries husband understands me, and he'll always be able to hold me, even though I sometimes threaten to leave him when our Ram's horns clash. It's because, as your book says — when I 'come running into his arms, my world all dark and dismal' — he holds me close, and comforts me, and would never, *never* say — 'What did *you* do to *deserve* it ?' — like that darned Libra man you wrote about in *Sun Signs* ! I never realized before just how important that is to me."

So, you see, an Aries-Aries relationship *can* work. And the two of them needn't sacrifice their Mars courage, initiative or independence. The Aries woman who wrote that letter ended it with a postscript:

"I have a tremendous urge to tell you to add Ayn Rand to your list of prominent Aquarians. She fits it like a glove. But of course, you know I wouldn't sign off this letter without at least one suggestion on how to run your business."

An Aries to the end she was, but a girl Ram who's learned to admit her Mars need to take the lead, and can laugh about it, instead of either denying it or being ashamed of it — has learned an important lesson. You must love yourself (which requires both honesty and humor) before anyone else can love you. I'm sorry to say I've lost that lady Ram's name and address, since I typed out the excerpt from her letter, and if she reads this, I hope she writes again, so I can answer a vital question she asked.

If the Aries man and his Aries woman each practice the Golden Rule, and do unto one another as they would have the other do unto them, assuming their mutual Sun-Moon aspects are not discordant, their relationship will bring to them both the reward of emotional maturity, plus the best of all possible gifts — the freedom to be completely themselves with one another, with no fear of rejection.

When they quarrel, he may threaten to leave her in the heat of the moment, but he probably won't. Not for keeps anyway. Once he's loved an Aries woman, all other girls will seem boring. (Restful, perhaps, by comparison, but boring.)

She feels the same way about him when *she* threatens to leave and doesn't mean it. But she should try to remember that he can chop wood, blast through granite mountains, pilot planes, build houses, govern a city, state or nation, change tires, practice medicine or law, produce and direct films, operate a tractor, and shovel snow — at least as well as she can. It may no longer be true that a woman's place is in the home. But it will be eternally true that a woman's place is inside her man's heart.

☆ ☆ ☆ ☆ ☆ ☆

ARIES

Fire — Cardinal — Positive
Ruled by Mars
Symbol: The Ram
Day Forces — Masculine

TAURUS

Earth — Fixed — Negative
Ruled by Venus (also by the
*   Planet Pan-Horus)*
Symbol: The Bull
Night Forces — Feminine

The **ARIES-TAURUS** *Relationship*

——◄◆►——

Above, where all had been so still, the
air was rent with shrieks and the clash
of steel. Below, there was dead silence.

*B*ecause Rams and Bulls each have tough horns, the determination of Aries and the stubbornness of Taurus might seem to be identical traits. They are not, and numerous incidents will occur between the two of them to make the distinction clear.

For example, an Aries parent wants a Taurus child to eat, and emphasizes it with a Martian command like: "You swallow every bite of that Wheat Germ and pick up your spoon this second, do you hear me?" That's determination.

The Taurus child sits quietly, not moving a muscle, gazes back steadily and says, "No." That's stubbornness.

An Aries boss wants a Taurean employee to work on his or her day off and states firmly, "I need you on Saturday, and it may take all day, so cancel any other plans you have." That's determination.

The Taurus employee calmly answers, "I'm busy Saturday. Get someone else." That's stubbornness.

After a few encounters, the difference between the two traits will become evident. Determination *initiates*. Stubbornness *reacts*. The first is a Positive action. The second is Negative *re*-action. Therefore, in any clash between Aries and Taurus, the Ram starts it and the Bull finishes it. It's important to remember that. Taurus won't forget it. Taurus doesn't forget *anything*.

Although Aries people get accused of running around burning their bridges behind them, and shooting off sparks in reckless abandon, they have their gentle moments too. Taurus people get accused of always pouting and brooding like dull globs of earth, ready to smother Arian enthusiasms in negative silence. But Bulls have their imaginative moments too, when it suits them, and they possess a thoughtful wisdom and wonderfully warm sense of humor behind that pragmatic exterior. Still, the essential differences between these two Sun Signs must be faced.

Rams are inclined to be aggressive, impulsive, bossy, extravagant, talkative and optimistic. They pursue excitement and quick results — and they require a dash of magic to make life interesting.

Bulls are inclined to be reserved, practical, usually sparing with words and self-sufficient, though somewhat pessimistic. They pursue stability, solitude and sure things — and they require lots of rest and tranquility to make life bearable.

You can see right away that these people are not the Bobbsey Twins. Their inner motivations, not to mention their outward actions, tend to wander in divergent directions. However, sometimes it's beneficial to knock around with someone who possesses the qualities you lack. Because this is a 2-12 Sun Sign Pattern association, the Taurean is more apt to be tolerant and sympathetic toward the Ram, and the Aries will try to imitate the Bull's placid stability. After all, placid stability is more or less synonymous with strength, and Aries people will try anything — even if it's against their natures — to gain more strength. Weakness is a four letter word to both the Ram and the Bull.

Although Bulls are equally fond of strength they're temporarily (until their true ruler, PAN-HORUS, ° is "discovered" and named) ruled by Venus,

---

° The approximate place of an extra-Plutonian planet (Pan) was officially announced by Dr. C. Musès in 1965, through the publication *La ricerca scientifica* (p. 200) published at Rome by the National Research Council of Italy. Pan was calculated to be at 355° celestial longitude (i.e. 25° Pisces), with about nine degrees of south declination, on January 1, 1979, and due to enter which tempers the whole thing somewhat, so they're not as intense about proving it or flaunting it as the Mars-ruled Arian. Taureans understand the compulsion behind Aries courage and flashing independence, since every Sun Sign carries the seeds or karmic memory of the qualities of the sign immediately preceding it in the zodiac, as with every 2-12 Pattern. But because the Bull has already been there, in an unconscious sense, he's also aware of the pitfalls involved in throwing caution to the four winds. The Taurus goal of financial security, however, can often be obtained through cooperation with the tireless drive and energy of the Mars person, and Taureans instinctively know this, which is one reason why they're attracted to Aries in the first place.

As for the Ram, he or she secretly envies the Taurus reserve and sensible outlook, and could profit immensely from being exposed to the Bull's realistic approach to life. Every Sun Sign unconsciously senses there are lessons to be learned from the sign immediately following or ahead of it in the zodiac, in a 2-12 vibration. This is why Aries feels drawn by the dependability of Taurus, as something tangible to lean on when that Mars rashness brings on a shower of trouble.

If a free flow of give-and-take can be established between the Bull and the Ram, their natures could blend in such a way that each could attain with the other, through their association, what it would be difficult to realize alone. The danger inherent in the mixing of their Mars-Venus auras is that the Ram, on occasion, may exasperate the Bull beyond his (or her) great limits of endurance, until the Taurean finally makes up that very stubborn Bull mind, after long deliberation, that it's no longer worth the effort. Conversely, there's always the possibility that the Bull may so frequently refuse to catch fire from the Ram's many flaming ideas, sparks of ideals and dreams, that the Aries person will eventually leave in desperation, to avoid depression — which no Mars-ruled man, woman or child can tolerate for long periods of time, without relief.

The Ram may be puzzled, and frequently frustrated, by the Bull's periodic spells of melancholy and introversion, even though it's relieved by lots of fun and giggles and from time to time may coax the Bull into parties and social activities, which, if it's not overdone, may help to balance the Taurean's instinctive "loner instinct" — a trait best not overemphasized.

Aries in 1984. Musès notes that the astronomer W. H. Pickering at his observatory in Jamaica during the first half of this century had previously computed, from extensive data on cometary perturbations, the existence of a planet with a period of 333 years. Musès' calculations yield a distance of 48.4 astronomical units from the sun, which agrees with Pickering's period by Kepler's third law.

Astrologically, the two meanings of this planet are expressed by Pan, ruler of chthonic earth forces and by Horus, restorer of the immortal body in Egyptian tradition. In this connection, Dr. Musès drew my attention to the startling depictions in the papyri of *Pa-di-Amon, Khonsu-Renap, Ta-Shed-Khonsu,* and *Amon-m-Set* in the Cairo Museum, and also on the sarcophagus of *Hent-Tani* in the Metropolitan Museum, New York City.

Encouraging the Bull of either sex, or any age, to express the innate Taurus love of form and color in music or art — or suggesting ways to retreat to the fields, woods and hills (all Bulls have an intense, even if buried, love of Nature) — are all ways the Aries person can use to coax Taurus into more placidity and peace.

The major mistake made by most Arians with a Taurus friend, relative, business associate, lover or mate, is to press the Bull into a decision. It will never work. Never. The Bull must decide in his (or her) own time. Demanding, pushing and insisting (the typical Mars strategy, when Aries desires are blocked) will only make Taurus more unwilling to budge, often causing these people to become totally uncommunicative. If Taurus believes that the suggestion is valid and sensible, he (or she) will consider it, and finally say "okay." Until then — and otherwise — no power on Earth can force the situation prematurely. That's the way it is, and no one, not even a fiery Ram, is going to change it.

If the Bull can learn, as they say out West, to ride "loose in the saddle" with the Ram, and not always expect the Aries person to be practical, the association will also be smoother. Rams must be allowed to express themselves through their own Mars pattern, which must contain a certain amount of violent ups and downs, in order to eventually learn that impulsive, rash behavior usually brings regret. The Aries person will undoubtedly benefit from the nearness of a more stable Taurean to lean on when things go wrong — and he (or she) will accept advice with surprising docility from the Bull, as long as it's tempered with tenderness, and isn't offered so frequently or dogmatically as to make the Ram feel "fenced in."

Aries people of all sizes, shapes, ages and sexes must be allowed to forge ahead without undue restriction, or too much negative disapproval. Actually, silent disapproval disturbs the bright, hopeful Aries spirit even more than spoken disapproval. It seems, somehow, to the direct Ram, more ominous and threatening — and just plain "scary." Remember, Aries is the symbolic newborn Infant, just as Taurus is the symbolic older baby. (See the "The Twelve Mysteries of Love" in the front of this book.) If the Ram's spontaneous enthusiasms are constantly buried beneath a ton of earthy Taurean "don'ts," he-she may become a frustrated Sheep — a Ram whose ego has been cruelly nipped in the bud of blossoming. The Arian needs to be cautioned against all that brimming-over excitement, now and then, but cautioned lightly, and with much gentleness.

Aries discovers the new country, whether it's geographical — or a mental continent. With the direct penetration of Mars to the core of any situation, the Ram leads and pioneers both the land — and innovative ideas. Then the Bull can enter into his or her own natural activity of building, of turning the country or idea Aries has discovered and pioneered, into a thriving community — or a concept that becomes practical and useful.

All human relationships — Life itself — must have, for Taurus, a clear purpose, and a definite function. Lacking a defined goal of usefulness, in the midst of scattered thoughts, and aimless activities, the Bull becomes confused, and finally withdraws. He (or she) learns only through the senses and through experience, and only by exercising a Fixity of intention can this Fixed Sun Sign remain true to himself — or herself. To Taurus, every thing, and every person, has a proper place, and should stay there, serving its purpose, never pretending to be something it's not. Aries behaves and dreams in a straight line, always going forward, ignoring the fact that both ends of that straight line are wide open to the winds of fate, whereas Taurus behaves and dreams in a circle, which encompasses lessons of the past and careful plans for the future, leaving no opening for failure due to irresponsible action.

The Ram can help the Bull break open that circle to let in the light of optimism and new ideas — and the Bull can assist the Ram to bend the direct Mars straight-line of activity and feeling into at least a semicircle shape, to help close out some of the inevitable disappointments that will be met throughout the eventful, Aries roller coaster existence. It's a strange and lovely thing that music, in any form, will almost always serve to build a bridge of understanding between Aries and Taurus and heal some of the hurt caused by each other's personality differences, which can be vast.

Since the Sun is exalted in Aries, these people frequently feel that victory has been won even before the battle. Every Ram feels an identification with Birth, Spring and the ecstasy of Easter — the resurrection. It's the reason for that soul's existence — the miracle he (or she) possesses to innocently offer other Sun Signs — the way Aries people serve both mankind and their true, inner self. Aries believes in the triumph of Life over Death, of Faith over Doubt. However, behind his (or her) bravado lurks the peculiar emotional insecurity of the Ram (those karmic memory seeds from Pisces, just behind Aries, on the astrological circle) — and the attempts of an Earth Sign to hold him (or her) back in any way only result in an increase of this hidden vulnerability. Then, an Aries person will either suddenly and violently shatter all ties with the smothering Taurean — or submit, and fall into a sad neurosis, completely unnatural to the Mars Life Force.

For the reason that the combining of Mars determination with Taurus willfulness creates an immense amount of sheer power, ancient astrologers warned that a blend of the Aries-Taurus qualities, if not carefully balanced, can result in great cruelty. Adolph Hitler's severely afflicted Taurus Sun and Aries Ascendent.(plus other negative natal aspects) is the classic example of this warning ignored. It can occur within the birth chart of one individual — or become manifest through an association between a Ram and a Bull, depending always on the planetary positions of both at birth. The tendency may, of course, be overcome, through enlightenment, and many Rams and Bulls produce an equally powerful alchemy of kindness and beneficence via their association. But there are, unfortunately, for example, some Aries and Taurus people who channel such negativity by becoming "hunters-for-sport," expressing the dark side of Aries courage and Taurus strength in a cruel manner, which causes them to be, instead, if they only comprehended it — cowardly — in the worst sort of way. Shooting a wild animal in cold blood, including deer, rabbits, ducks, pheasants and all our feathered friends in the sky — then carrying the silent corpse through town, as a trophy of macho, is a pathetic kind of cowardice in its lowest form — not the demonstration of "manhood" or "womanhood" some believe it to be.

If the Sun and Moon in the birth charts of the Ram and the Bull are inharmoniously aspected, in mutual Luminary relation to each other, the danger of cruelty must be guarded against carefully. However, when the natal Sun of the Ram is beneficently aspected to the natal Moon of the Bull (or vice versa) and if their mutual Ascendents are also harmonious, in a triple exchanged aspect, Taurus can help Aries soar to the heights of happiness and serendipity by supporting the Ram's emotional balloon flights of fancy with warm, kindly patience (also by providing a comforting, soft patch of Earth to fall on when the string breaks.) And the Ram can lead Taurus to the higher slopes of the imagination, up where the windswept view of the future is as huge and grand as the Bull's own sturdy dreams.

☆ ☆ ☆ ☆ ☆ ☆

ARIES *Woman* TAURUS *Man*

◆━◆▶◆

"Get your things, Peter," she cried, shaking.

"No," he answered. . . . "I am not going with you."

"Yes, Peter."

"No."

A romantic involvement with a Taurus man is sure to be an educational experience for the Aries female. She thinks immovable objects (him) are simply things to kick aside, leap over or melt with the irresistible force of Mars heat (hers). Not this one.

She shoves — he sits. She pushes — he pouts. She demands — he digs in. Then, look out. The next step could be: she weeps — he walks. Away, that is — for keeps. But Bulls and Rams can do other things together. Like, if she smiles — he'll soften. If she coaxes — he'll cuddle. If she bear-hugs — he'll beam. You'll notice it's always she who initiates the first move between them . . . . . of any kind.

They may quarrel about money (her extravagance — his economy), or lock horns over the Aries need for excitement, and the Taurus need for peace and quiet. But with some effort at adjusting to each other's different metabolisms and personal mannerisms, this man and woman can find a rare and very cozy contentment together.

Since she demands, and requires (both), an abnormal amount of freedom, it's a fortunate thing the Bull is not unduly jealous. He's not jealous, but he is very possessive. The difference between these two qualities can be found in the dictionary — or through living with each other. *She's* jealous. *He's* possessive. They should carefully check Webster, and take it from there.

Yes, a Taurus man is stubborn, there's no denying this astrological fact. His sometimes blind, unreasonable bull-headedness can be unpleasantly aroused, if an Aries girl wants him to pick daisies with her when he wants to snooze — if she subjects him to her friends, when he wants to quietly read — (at other times, he'll be happy to entertain them all with his marvelous humor) — or if she insists on spending more than he earns, faster than he doesn't earn it. Yet a well-loved Bull will bear up under a great deal of "sound and fury, signifying nothing" but noise and nonsense, with tranquil aplomb. Normally, he'll take it with an unruffled good nature when she fights with his boss or his relatives, howls with a toothache, loses her engagement ring in the mashed potatoes at a restaurant, and doesn't realize it until after they've left, the place is closed and the garbage truck has already done its ruthless chop-chop thing.

A contented Taurus man will patiently put up with most Aries misguided missiles of enthusiasm unless he's pressed too hard, and too often. Then, he's likely to erupt into the infrequent but ever latent and smoldering Taurean anger. Rams who have never been exposed to the Bull's anger should not press their luck. And that happens to be a most serious astrological warning, in no way intended to be humorous.

If he's handled gently, with a decent amount of consideration for his own feelings, this man will stick by the girl Ram he loves through the darkest storms, like a steady rock of solid love, covering the miseries of her mistakes with a warm, protective blanket of sheer devotion. It's rather like coming home, all safe and secure, from a long journey through a frightening nightmare of rejection, where no one really cares or understands. *He* cares, even if he can't quite understand her temporary emotional traumas. And he'll usually back up his caring with a dependable bank account, and a leakless roof over her head (not to mention a well-stocked refrigerator), to the very best of his steady ability, while he builds slowly and surely for an even more secure, and even luxurious, future.

In the average love affair or marital relationship between the Bull and the Aries woman, she'll provide the ideas and the energy while he provides the stability and security. This applies to both the financial and the sexual aspects of their cooperative venture.

Although Taurus men are as practical about love as they are about everything else, they're also deeply affectionate, quietly romantic and deeply sentimental. The Aries woman who's grown into the mistaken impression that her usually undemonstrative Taurus lover or husband doesn't really love her anymore will never fail to be periodically surprised by receiving an extravagant Valentine, or other card, on some unexpected holiday, which expresses the shy Taurean feelings tenderly and eloquently, in the words of the verse.

Still, there could be some problems concerning the physical sharing of their love, after the first magnetic attraction of Male-Positive and Female-Negative polarity loses its novelty. Sex is, to the Aries woman, a form of release — mental, emotional, physical and spiritual. It's the visible manifestation of the Mars Faith and Strength combined, in a powerful urge of *self*-expression. To her, sexual activity justifies itself as a thrilling fantasy, which could, in some miraculous way, known only to her, make every dream she's ever dreamed come true. Sex is, to the Taurus man, a normal and natural function, for the purpose of achieving two very tangible and sensible results — the satisfaction of sensual and erotic flesh needs — and children. A family.

She's compelled to release the Mars sexual energy, even if it doesn't result in much of anything, except frustration — and imaginative romancing is absolutely essential to her. He doesn't see the sense in releasing *any* kind of energy unless its purpose is to produce something practical and useful — and the typical Taurean does not regard daydreams as either essential or productive. Consequently, the girl Ram may gradually and eventually become impatient with her Bull's desire for frankly sensual and somewhat unimaginative lovemaking — and he may (at a relatively slower rate of speed) become honestly puzzled by the trip to the stars she feels must be synonymous with passion, in private, wistfully wishing he could take her there but sensing they might get lost, because he's uncertain of the route . . . . and after all, there's no map to guide him. A harmonious relationship between their mutual Suns, Moons and Ascendents will miracle away these differences in their natures, and allow the two of them to achieve a rich fulfillment through their sexual union, as well as in every other facet of their togetherness.

However, with a tense aspect between their natal Luminaries and/or Ascendents, it may be difficult for the Aries female to keep the Bull in her pasture, unless she makes a constant and conscious effort to please him, an unselfish urge that does not come naturally to the typical Arian. It takes mountains of hurt and resentment to make a Taurus man leave a woman he's once loved (or permit her to leave his possessive domain), but once he goes, he is *gone*. Permanently. A little tenderness today can prevent a lot of tears tomorrow.

Despite the many arguments these two are almost destined to have in the area of both mutual and individual finances, she'll soon learn a touching truth about her Taurus man's attitude toward money, which is so vastly different from her own (assuming they're both typical of their Sun Signs, and their birth charts don't confuse matters with a variety of planetary positions that create the exceptions that prove the astrological rules). In the beginning, she'll think he's an outright tightwad, and he'll think she's as improvident and careless with cash as they make females (he believes they're all made, more or less, in a similar extravagant mold). Gradually, however, his great Bull's heart will be moved, when he slowly comprehends that her carelessness with cash is nearly always motivated by impulsive generosity. He'll see that, although she spends a good deal of money on herself (Aries represents the *first* astrological house; therefore, all Rams are exceptionally concerned with their physical appearance), she spends even more through her gestures of giving, much in the sense that a child gives, with a feeling of sheer delight in pleasing others and receiving the reward of their happy smiles. He'll probably relax his attitude somewhat then, regarding his initial disapproval of her wild and carefree spending. In fact, after their relationship has had time to solidify into a permanent pattern, her spontaneous generosity may even cause him to love her more.

At the same time he's learning to adapt to her financial looseness, even affectionately, she will be discovering that he's not such a miser as she first thought him to be. She'll realize that his caution stems from his uncontrollable need to be sure of tomorrow's security, his deep-seated fear of being suddenly thrown out into the street and forced to rely upon the charity of others or the government, which would kill his proud spirit of self-sufficiency. And she'll see that, once her stubborn, but kind-hearted, steadfast and loyal Bull knows their future is reasonably insured (not excessively, as is the case with the typical Crab or Goat), he's genuinely generous. Barring an afflicted Moon or Ascendent in Earth or Water elements, he'll be as tickled as she to give gifts to their friends and families, and lend money to those who need it, without pressing them for repayment — as long as his basic nest egg for tomorrow is left untouched, the amount of which, of course, varies with each individual Bull. But the typical Taurus male won't take huge chances with his security. If his Aries woman tries to convince him that they should move into a better apartment or house, and trust a promise someone made to them regarding future paychecks, commissions or bonuses, to make up the difference in rent or mortgage payments, she's engaged in a futile endeavor. The

Bull won't move an inch until he's *sure* he can handle the extra burden. To Taurus there's never been a promise since the world began that's been made of anything but talk and thin air — both materials he's found to be totally unreliable for the purpose of building anything concrete and lasting. Yet, when push comes to shove (an excellent descriptive phrase to use with Taurus) this man will share half of whatever he has with anyone whose real need he's been made aware of, most especially his family, friends . . . . and the woman he loves.

There may be times when the Bull's stubbornness seems like the coldest kind of cruelty to an Aries girl. For example, he may say something unkind to her in public, when she's been frisking too much for his taste and acting up in general, and it will cut her to the quick. She'll try to force him to apologize, openly or at least to admit he didn't mean it (which he didn't, and she *knows* it), while he sullenly refuses to grant her the verbal solace and reassurance she's seeking (or, rather, demanding). As she continues first to command, then finally to plead with him to retract his statement, he'll grow even more silent and removed, like a chunk of marble, unseeing, unhearing, unfeeling — apparently.

Then she'll impulsively run out, angrily weeping, into the night. He's the coldest, cruelest man she's ever known, and it's all over between them. He can't do that to her. A few blocks down the street (maybe twenty or more, depending on the extent of the adrenalin she was generating when she stormed out of the place where she left him) — she sees a coffee shop, and wanders inside, to sit by herself, crying all over her donuts, and fiercely hating him . . . . . until their favorite song hits her ears, from the ceiling speakers, reminding her of what she's lost by walking out on him. So, she pays her check, leaves hastily and ends up standing on a street corner, forlorn and alone, trying to hail a taxi to take her home — sorry, at last — and now really frightened. It's late, there are no taxis anywhere, and she has to walk home, giving her time to think over a lot of things as she hurries down streets that seem unusually quiet and deserted.

But . . . who is that there in the shadows, leaning calmly against the building across the way, waiting patiently for her? It's him. He's still there. She feels a surge of happiness as she runs across the street into his safe arms. He didn't go away and leave her after all. It's all right again. No, he didn't go away — this time. He'll probably still be there, patiently waiting for her after the next fiery, emotional, farewell scene too. But, someday . . . .

If she's wise, she'll count her blessings before it's too late.

☆ ☆ ☆ ☆ ☆ ☆

ARIES *Man* TAURUS *Woman*

————— ◄◄◆►► —————

*"... unless this tie is round my neck we don't go out
to dinner to-night, and if I don't go out to dinner
to-night, I never go to the office again, and if I
don't go to the office again, you and I starve ..."*

*Even then Mrs. Darling was placid. "Let me try, dear,"
she said ..... and with her nice cool hands she tied
the tie for him.*

In an Aries-Taurus romance or marriage, when the woman is the Taurus and
the man is the Aries, the relationship has a slight edge for success over its
chances when the sexes are reversed. That's not a guarantee either way, of
course, it's just what I said—a slight edge. The qualities of passivity,
steadfastness, and quiescent receptivity (Taurus) are more natural when
exercised through the female. The qualities of aggression, independence and
forceful action (Aries) are more natural when exercised through the male—
never mind Women's Liberation, which is right and good and timely and
necessary, and all that, but the passage of ERA is never going to forcefully (or
any other way) alter Mother Nature's basic tenets. At the very least, the
conflicts may be somewhat fewer in number, when she's the Taurean and
he's the Ram, in this 2-12 vibration. Still, it's the *intensity* of the conflicts,
not the *quantity* of them, that damages any relationship, so these two ought
not to become heady with optimism. It depends. Mostly on the Moon and
Ascendent positions of each of them.

A Taurus woman, unless the fourth house of her horoscope is severely
afflicted, is a born homemaker. (Thank goodness *somebody* enjoys it!) Even
if she has adverse aspects in her birth chart which tend to tempt her into
spending a few years as a playgirl type (a most rare occurrence), her basic
desire, nevertheless, is to create a comfortable home, filled with fine furnishings, good food, babies and music—with the beds all nicely made, the
corners clean, the laundry folded and put away and all the bills paid. Throw
in a flower garden in the back yard, and an extra powder room, well stocked
with bubble bath. She's not unreasonably jealous, without good cause; she's
patient and she seldom nags. She's normally a warm, gracious hostess for her
husband's business friends—and a pretty good listener.

Now, since an Aries male requires a constant and dependable sounding
board while he discusses his favorite topic—himself—since he frequently

brings people home to sell them a new project or idea he's dreamed up — and since he's a little careless with the budget, because he never learned to spell the word "thrift" in grammar school — you can see how a Taurus woman can provide him with a perfect base of operations. Normally, Aries men like sports, and the typical Taurus female loves nature. So if the sport he happens to favor is camping out, or hiking in the woods, add another plus on the potential success side of their relationship. Otherwise, there might be some Saturday-afternoon-football tension.

The trouble starts in areas they may never anticipate during the mating season. She may prefer living in the country or the suburbs, and most Aries men can't exist for long, without the excitement and action of the city. There may be some who can, but they're few and far between, and even they like to flash around in the bright lights on weekends. Camping and hiking aside, he's not a farm boy at heart. If he has a Taurus Moon Sign or Ascendent, he may plant a few potatoes or milk a few cows, but essentially, for him, the pull of the sod will never replace grabbing a taxi to catch a miracle.

Sparks may also fly in the area of mutual funds, because their attitude toward money is not necessarily mutual. He wants a new car; she wants a new freezer. Things like that. His favorite man at the bank is the one in the Loan Department. Her favorite man at the bank is the one in the Savings Department. You know how bankers like to push their own thing, so these two outsiders don't help matters any by pulling the Bull and the Ram apart. However, when he spends money on jewelry for her, or on furniture for the house, she may be more loose about it. Taurus females usually appreciate fine jewels and luxurious decor in the home, but they'll expect these things to be practical, made to last for a few hundred years before they need to be replaced.

Despite her general tranquility, she may lose her cool if he burns holes in her new couch or spills grape juice on her carpet (before marriage, you can substitute her new skirt or her carefully clutched pocketbook for the couch and carpet). It's hard for him to figure why she gets so upset over such small incidents. To Aries, crying over spilled milk (or grape juice) is a huge waste of time. If something is lost, broken or damaged, there's always more where it came from. Taurus has a few doubts about that.

Fortunately, most of their disagreements can be smoothed over by reconciliations at bedtime since the physical relationship between them can be snugly satisfying. The Aries male is certainly not unhappy about the Taurus woman's capacity for sensual, erotic feeling, but he may be somewhat frustrated by her lack of mystical creativity when it comes to making love. She welcomes sex as a practical and enjoyable activity that brings a total gratification of the senses and the added bonus of producing some bouncing bambinos. She may, therefore, fail to comprehend why sex should be like a wild dream that transports two souls to the top of a mountain in Tibet, like a comet streaking across the night sky — or a miracle connected with throwing three coins into the Fountain of Trevi, in Rome. To her, sex is sex. Love is love. What does any of it have to do with tossing a few Lincolns into some dirty, green water — or with comets, for that matter? This woman has a funny bone about sex, since Taurus humor isn't restricted to any one facet of Life. It's broad. If the Aries man should happen to step on a tack as he's running passionately toward the bed on their honeymoon, she'll crack up laughing. His reaction? It may postpone the honeymoon a few days — or nights — until his Martian male ego has recovered.

Still, although she may remain mystified by his romantic idealism during their entire association together, it needn't necessarily cause complete sexual incompatibility. There are deep emotional wells in her, and it's possible that her ultra-feminine response to the Ram's strong, direct love urges, plus her obvious pleasure with his masculine charisma, may eventually make him wonder why he thought he had to go climbing mountains in search of happiness anyway. It's possible. Not certain, but possible. (Aries is reluctant to accept substitutes for miracles.)

A word of warning: Just because the Taurus girl doesn't pick up every nuance of the Aries sexuality, this should not be interpreted to mean that she's not sentimental or romantic. She is. Oh, she most certainly is! If she's ignored on February 14th, or if he forgets to remember the day they first met (first made love together, first decided to get married, got married or whatever, in whichever order), the inconsiderate, thoughtless Ram who neglected to honor these historic occasions will never hear the end of it. This woman has a memory like an elephant for personal injury and emotional hurt.

Some of the astrological descriptions of the Taurus female make her seem like a contented cow in a pasture, and that's pretty insulting. So what if she isn't overtly flashy, the center of attention at every gathering? Her quiet beauty is like a still pool, filled with fragrant lilies, deep in a piney forest. Taurus magnetism pulls powerfully on a man's heartstrings, because it promises such peace and rich adventure, especially on a Ram's restless heartstrings. The Aries male soon discovers that this feminine creature, who is so calm and composed (the way he'd secretly like to be himself), can fill his spirit with fresh flowers, fill his house with the music of love and companionship, besides being an uncommonly good cook. In addition, she can fill his heart with lots of laughs, and a loyal devotion that can outlast forever. She also knows how to accumulate and save money. No cow could pull off all that. This girl can well afford to leave the false lashes (which look like spiders' legs) to the less-female types than she. She's all warm woman, and she doesn't need the masquerade of artificial glamour to prove it.

What she may need to do, however, is to climb out of her earthy rut, now and then. A lady Taurean can seem pretty cold and heartless to the friendly, direct and open-hearted Aries man when she's made up her mind about something, and slammed the door in the face of any further discussion. If he shouts at her that she's stubborn at such times, it will do about as much good as when she tells him, firmly, that he's selfish and spoiled. In a word — none.

Who, *her* — stubborn ? Who, *him* — selfish and spoiled ? It wouldn't be wise for either of them to hold his or her breath until the other admits such character deficiencies.

Lots of affection, plenty of ambition, honesty and the guarantee of financial security are the four ways to her heart. An Aries man can supply the first three with no difficulty, but he may have to make some adjustments in his general life-style to meet her expectations of the last item. Aries incomes do tend to often fluctuate, and that can make this lady very nervous.

Normally, of course, she's not nervous — only when her emotional or financial security is threatened. At most other times, she exudes a placid mystique that can be deliciously relaxing, in particular, to a Ram. It can also be a substantial aid in recharging the batteries of this man's dynamic Mars energies when he's run down from his various mental, emotional or physical excesses. (An Aries man will jog till he drops.) Admittedly, when she goes into one of her very rare rages, her placid mystique can change into anger of volcanic proportions, without much of a warning. But it happens so seldom, it's one of the least likely causes for trouble in their relationship — unless the Ram is foolish enough to insist on trying to win these infrequent, but dangerous, encounters. It will never happen. Retreat is the expedient strategy. Go fight an earthquake.

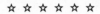

ARIES

Fire — Cardinal — Positive
Ruled by Mars
Symbol: The Ram
Day Forces — Masculine

GEMINI

Air — Mutable — Positive
Ruled by Mercury
Symbol: The Twins
Day Forces — Positive

The **ARIES-GEMINI** *Relationship*

It was not really Saturday night, at least it may
have been, for they had long lost count of the days;
but always if they wanted to do anything special
they said this was Saturday night, and then they did it.

Working as a team, this combination of Sun Signs could sell Manhattan back to the Indians — blackouts, muggers, creaky subways, uncollected garbage, and all. Of course, both of them being idealists, they would probably realize what a rotten deal the Indians got in the beginning, and end up giving them back New York for a few strands of love beads and a peace button, along with all the other rights the white man stole from his red brother — if they could swing it.

Because both Aries and Gemini love causes, and share the same talent for creative, persistent salesmanship, they can perform fantastic feats of ingenuity together. They also share a casual attitude toward accumulating great power or money, which may be why they are seldom as successful as they should be, considering all the emotional (Aries) and mental (Gemini) energy they pour into anything that interests them — for the moment, that is. Nothing holds the interest of either of these Sun Signs for longer than a moment. Well, sometimes maybe two or three moments.

Since Aries bubbles with naive impetuosity, and Gemini is determined to attain complete independence by breaking every bond of the spirit, maturity of thought seldom supports their mutual endeavors.

One might say that the combined qualities of this 3-11 Sun Sign Pattern association present a picture of optimisim, punctuated with brief splashes (usually, very brief) of sensitivity and hidden insecurities. When Aries and Gemini blend their natures as neighbors, friends, business associates, relatives, lovers or mates, it doubles up their individual drives for freedom against all who would confine them in a morass of convention and caution. Separately or together, they look young, act young — and therefore, quite naturally, often behave like children.

Now, children can be endearing, guileless and lovable. They can also be unintentionally selfish, irrational and thoughtless. So it is with any association between this 3-11 influenced team. Preferably both of them, but at least one of the two, must eventually grow up, or most of their time together will be spent playing around in a sand pile, with a couple of brightly painted buckets, and large shovels for the you-know-what they're both so good at handing each other and the rest of the world.

Basically, both Aries and Gemini are honest — the Rams especially so — but these two can fool themselves until they forget where honesty ends and self-deception begins. It's their innocence, or ignorance, whichever, of their own individual natures. In other words, they're both as expert at selling themselves as they are at selling the general public. If the product being sold isn't genuine, the Gemini will usually be the first of the two of them to suspect it, with Mercury's sharp, analytical mind, although Gemini is capable of outsmarting himself (or herself), by continuing to *imagine* it still may be what he-she originally believed it was. As for Aries, it's extremely difficult for this Sun Sign to tell the difference between what glitters so enticingly — and real gold. Such discrimination is learned by the Ram only after repeated, heartbreaking disillusion and disappointment.

I've been referring to the "two of them." Actually, perhaps I should say the "three of them," because, although Aries is clearly one person, indivisible, "with liberty and justice for all," every Gemini is distinctly two people, the person he-she really is . . . . . and the person she-he would like to be. The Twins, you know. Add the Mars ego of the Ram — almost a separate entity in itself — and it can get pretty crowded, with all those auras mixing, attracting and repelling, blending and clashing, by turns. It's not a bad idea for these two Sun Sign people, essentially compatible as they are, to stand apart at intervals and take a fresh look at each other from a distance. It clears away some of the smog that's bound to accumulate between them.

Aries pushes ahead instinctively, convinced of the sincerity of cause, as well as the eventual victory, with little or no time out to reflect on the pros and cons of any given situation or problem. Conversely, Gemini weighs, sorts and figures out all possible maneuvers and conclusions with the cool, casual detachment and logic so typical of all three Air Signs (Aquarius and Libra being the other two). Yet for all Gemini's mental gymnastics, practicality may be missing. Gemini can quickly deduce what might go wrong but often decides to outwit destiny or fate, and even himself (or herself) by clever Mercurial strategy. There are other differences of approach between these two.

Aries, influenced by a Cardinal Sign, will insist on being at the *head* of things, leading, challenging, always initiating and inspiring, with enthusiasm and daring. The Ram will accept just about any idea, sound or unsound, that appeals to and arouses the emotions — to which the ego can relate in a personal way. Mutable Gemini prefers to relate in an *im*personal manner, and will accept ideas that appeal to the mental deductive process, communicating through the logic and cleverness of Mercury reason, while the true self remains in the background, watching — unsuspected by those who are being hypnotized with the Gemini charm.

Aries enjoys riding the lead elephant and waving to the crowd, but the Twins have no burning desire to be the glory-spangled hero or heroine. Gemini would rather delegate all the confining duties and obligations of leadership to others, remaining free of responsibility, free to try on new ideas for size . . . . . to explore new people, places and things. The Geminian analysis is less intense than that of Aries, since everything is calmly checked through the computer of the mind for possible flaws — or potential. Although the Gemini approach is essentially mental, the Twins sympathize with the Ram's emotional approach, even while remaining detached from such over-involvement himself (or herself). Mercury-ruled men and women understand the Mars reckless impulses. Nevertheless, they realize that their own best course is to avoid becoming emotionally entangled, whenever possible.

Close human associations that threaten to smother, long-term employment without either change or challenge — anything that nails down their dreams or clips Mercury's wings, Geminis distrust, for fear their very spirits will be confined. The Air Sign of Gemini strives to soar above the flames that rage around the Fire Sign of Aries. By remaining aloof and slightly out of reach, Gemini more often manages to achieve the kind of freedom Aries also seeks but doesn't always find. Of course, too much mental and emotional freedom can create its own confusions, and when the Twins get caught in the webs of their own mental convolutions, the very directness of the Ram can sometimes help to untangle the knots.

Fortunately, the typical Aries person not only senses the duality of Gemini but is usually willing to give it room to *be*. That's why this association is frequently beneficial to the Geminian, because understanding — or the lack of understanding — concerning his (or her) dreams has a great deal to do with whether they come true, simply grow rusty, or become only will-o'-the-wisps. Gemini eternally chases but never catches. A Gemini will dream from the time he-she is a tiny tot, until past the century mark. To most people, Mercury's curiosity and experimental urges seem like a patchwork of erratic, changing attention spans, but the Ram seems to recognize that all these myriad interests are only Gemini's attempt to integrate the many-sided, fascinating-to-Aries, Mercurial personality.

An Aries person is less likely to resent the Gemini's flitting from subject to subject, in the search for all the answers, while shooting forth a continual flow of imagination and static energy. Interrupting a Mercury Bird when he-she is verbally expressing is like trying to catch a firefly, and oddly, the Rams (who are rather experts at interrupting themselves) comprehend this. These two continually interrupt each other, with a mutual lack of resentment, a most jolly thing about their association.

If there's a negative aspect between the Sun and Moon or Ascendent in their birth charts, Aries may accuse Gemini of too much woolgathering and not enough concrete action, and will try to box Gemini into direct answers. Then the satirical tongue of Gemini may wound the Ram's easily bruised ego, and there will be a fiery battle, with sparks flying everywhere, as Gemini's airy attitude fans the flames of Mars anger. Still, the winds will change, after a while, even after the stormiest scenes . . . . . and bitterness is seldom allowed by either of them to linger. As with all 3-11 vibrational patterns, Aries and Gemini are basically good friends, and most always remain that way, in addition to being able to verbally communicate their differences of opinion to such an extent that they clear the air for a resumption of harmony.

The Mercurial mind of Gemini, no matter how cleverly it's occasionally disguised behind a mask of calm and charm, resembles a top. Always spinning. Aries will happily jump on for the ride, and probably enjoy the dizzy pace. As long as the Ram doesn't try to chain Gemini's free spirit with too many questions and demands, it will work out rather smoothly between these two. (These four, counting the Ram, the Twins, and the Mars ego.) Aries and Gemini can build sand castles from the colorful ethers of their combined thought images tall enough to reach all the way to the stars. But the foundation must be sound and stable, or they'll topple to the ground. If they build strongly in the beginning, the end could be really out of sight — all rainbows, butterflies and leprechauns. Patience is the secret key to the other side of the fence, where the grass always looks greener and fresher to both Aries and Gemini, the eternal young ones, who search for Shangri-la, the Emerald City of Oz, Wonderland and the Fountain of Youth. Together, they have a better chance of finding all these places than most people . . . or than they would have if they each searched alone.

☆ ☆ ☆ ☆ ☆ ☆

ARIES *Woman* GEMINI *Man*

—◄●►—

"You won't forget me . . . will you, before springtime comes?"

Of course Peter promised; and then he flew away.

There are Aries women and Gemini men who hold hands lightly and skip down the street together like children. There are other Aries women and Gemini men who have sarcastic, furious verbal donnybrooks from the time they awake until they go to bed — and they both talk in their sleep too. Often, the emotional blending of Mars and Mercury in a love experience produces a strange alchemy of haunting tenderness, punctuated by sharp hurt, making the relationship capable of both triumph and disaster. It may be because Gemini, unlike the other two Air Signs, verbalizes both his admiration and his contempt so clearly and unmistakably. Or perhaps it's because Aries, unlike the other two Fire Signs, is consumed by the passion of the moment, whether it's love or hate, never thinking about tomorrow's possible regrets.

This 3-11 Sun Sign Pattern is quite distinctive in its influence over two people linked together through its friendly, and very communicative, vibrations. There's no doubt they'll quarrel occasionally, even frequently; yet their more tempestuous arguments will contain the seed of spring, and fresh promises for the future. Their misunderstandings are extremely verbal, and often quite loud, but somehow, not too serious. It's almost as though they're both aware of the potential of a truce in the midst of the battle.

These two might accurately say of themselves . . . . . .

> *some people love with restraint*
> *as if they were someday to hate*
> *but we hated gently, carefully*
> *as if we were someday to love . . .* °

There's very little restraint in the love between Aries and Gemini. When the Ram and the Twins fall in love with each other, neither will waste time

---

°*Venus Trines at Midnight* by Linda Goodman (New York: Taplinger Publishing Company, Inc., 1970. To be re-published by Harper & Row, 1979).

wondering if the end of the affair, or the marriage, will be blissfully happy or achingly sad. The initial attraction between them, the magnetic pull of their carefree natures, causes both of them to reach out toward each other trustingly, with no worry about a far-off ending. If it should eventually occur, in whatever form — separation, divorce or death — the memories of love as naive, exciting and as full of blind faith as a child's heart on Christmas Eve, will soften the edges of the recollection of any sorrow or hurt they've mutually suffered. That's the beauty of the 3-11 vibration, in which genuine friendship forms the foundation for the empathy, from the very first hello.

Jealously can be a large troublemaker. The typical Aries girl is as jealous as it's possible for a woman to be, without turning solid green, and she's seldom able to recognize it rationally. It doesn't stem from a possessive nature but from the Arian symbolic Infant's terrible fear of rejection (which would mean literal death to an infant) and need for constant reassurance that it (she) is cherished. The undue Aries concern over losing love to another is more understandable when it's viewed in the light of these subconscious feelings of infantile helplessness and total dependency upon continued and uninterrupted affection. It's a feeling that's always present, just beneath the bright Mars bravado of independence and self-sufficiency . . . . . which is not real in any sense, only make believe . . . . a kind of protection against further vulnerability.

The typical Gemini man is *not* excessively jealous (barring some Venus-Mars affliction in his birth chart, or an Aries Moon or Ascendent). And this is where most of the difficulties may lie. Because, you see, she secretly would like him to be. The least he can do is pretend he is. Whether she consciously realizes it or not, the girl Ram rather enjoys arousing the jealous instinct in her man. It reaffirms her importance to him, a matter that can't be reaffirmed too often for any Aries. The Gemini male may oblige her, by granting her wish, if she steps out of line too obviously. But most of the time he'll be too busy changing his clothes, his moods, his ideas, his dreams and his disposition to pause long enough to stop, look and listen to any innocent flirtations she's flaunting at him in the hope of warming up his cool, detached and airy approach to life — and to her.

Conversely, he won't have to flaunt any flirtations in front of her to bring on a bright green explosion. Saying good morning too intimately to Apple Annie at the corner newspaper stand will suffice. Considering his love of freedom and his phobia concerning emotional shackles that curb his natural gregarious activities, a little of that will go a long way with a Gemini man. Although she must learn to somehow either control or hide her jealous fears (if she doesn't want to lose him), he must also learn to sympathize with her motivation for such behavior — an inner fear that she lacks enough femininity to keep him faithful (if he doesn't want to lose *her*). There has been so much propaganda over the years about the slinky, sexually seductive, feather-brained, soft and sweet type of bunny-kitten "every man yearns for," you can't blame the Aries woman for developing a neurosis about her quick mind, her direct approach to love and her lack of sneaky female guile—especially since she was born under the influence of a masculine Sun Sign.

She has courage and initiative, she's energetic and ambitious—all allegedly masculine traits. Men believe they have the market cornered on those qualities. Haven't you been reading the Women's Liberation pamphlets? (The Aries woman may very well be the leader of the ERA group in her community.) What's a girl Ram supposed to do to be considered feminine—read Marabel What's-Her-Name's book, *The Total Woman*, and total herself by just sitting around murmuring "You're wonderful, darling," and never do anything on her own? That's just about the size of it, according to Marabel and all the male chauvinists. Skimpy, isn't it?

Oh, I suppose she could do other things to retain her femininity, like wash, iron, cook, diaper babies, shop for clothes, gossip, iron, wash, cook, have babies—am I repeating myself? Sorry, I was beginning to get bored. As an Aries myself, I've never understood why a girl must be labeled "pushy" just because she knows her own mind. If most men prefer a Stepford Wives type robot to a real woman, that's their hang-up. Aries females, along with their Sagittarius and Leo sisters, sometimes rival the "male chauvinist pigs" by being rather blatant "female chauvinist sows" themselves. Such feminine gender animals do exist.

Now, why did I write that? I've given the quick-witted Gemini men a new verbal weapon. My apologies to Ms. Steinem, whom I greatly admire, but it is true, Gloria, and you know it. Please don't be offended, because I'm one too. That is, I believe anything they can do, we can do equally—and some things better. No need to list the latter. We all know what they are. Oh, you don't? Well, for heaven's sake—patiently and tenderly providing a gentle garden for babes to grow in for nine months, being able to bear pain at a higher threshold than men, possessing the common sense and esoteric logic to know that war never solved anything, and being able to sense danger and evil, long before they appear, are just a few of our superiorities over the masculine essence. We're also more sensitive, intuitive and psychic, certainly more compassionate—yet far more realistic than men. But not quite as sentimental. (You didn't know that men are secretly sentimental? So much so that they've taught women to see the poetry and beauty in Life too.) It's all right for the female chauvinist sows to be aware of their own areas of both equality and superiority regarding the masculine sex, but they should also recognize the areas of a man's equality and superiority regarding womanhood. That's what makes true femininity and true masculinity.

With her innocent faith in miracles, it's destined that the Aries woman someday discover a man who's looking for a real woman, and he could be a Gemini. This man may have two heads, and twin desires, but he also possesses a driving need to be able to play mental chess with the woman he loves. Not for Gemini the serene siren who gazes up to him in silent, palpitating passion, because it's easier than trying to match wits with him. He definitely falls in love with his mind first. His heart follows after, then his physical desire. Romance usually proceeds in just about that priority order with the Twins. As for the Aries woman, the order is only slightly changed. She falls in love first with her heart, her mind follows quickly after—and, finally, her physical desire. The initial patterns are switched, but that's not as important as the fact that they both end up on the same frequency, in its proper place—last, after mental and emotional affinity has been established. It's an amazingly successful formula.

Because he'll appreciate the constant mental challenge of the Aries girl (Aries rules the head, Gemini the mind, among other things), she'll eventually learn to trust him to love her for what she is. Then she may show him what she's allowed no other male to discover—that she can be genuinely sweet and tender, with a man who proves he's her superior in some ways, while making it clear at the same time that he also admires her for her own qualities, which are equal to his, some being likewise superior. It's a complicated juggling act, but a Gemini man can pull it off, if anyone can. His natural charm and glibness (some people call it blarney) can keep her Mars vanity and ego appeased—and he can certainly handle any kind of verbal debate she cares to start. She may start quite a few.

She may have difficulty in adjusting to his typical Gemini habit of lateness. She's often a little lax in that area herself, but Rams have a rather selfish way of being outraged when they're forced to swallow their own medicine.

A Gemini man was once three hours late for an appointment with me. Anticipating his excuses (one of the benefits of being an astrologer) I wrote a little verse about him while I was waiting.

> I'm sorry I kept you waiting
> look, don't cry ... it was only an hour or two
> couldn't you find something to do?
> I would have, if I had been you. °

When he finally arrived, he read it, and exclaimed, "Oh, wow! How did you know exactly what I was going to say?" The Aries girl who's in love with this two-headed, twin wonder of dual desires and actions should carefully study the difference between the word "gregarious" and the word "unfaithful," and note that there *is* a difference. She should also study the meaning of the two words "freedom" and "love," and comprehend that, to a Gemini, these two words are synonyms. It will help to cut down on the arguments.

As for their physical compatibility, he's one of the few men who's

---

° From *Venus Trines at Midnight*, by Linda Goodman.

capable of creating the illusionary quality this woman must associate with sex. She idealizes the sexual expression of love into a colorful, layered fabric, woven from every book she's ever read, every movie she's ever cried over and every shining hope she's ever held deep inside her heart. She's convinced that bells should literally ring at the moment the two of them become one. With him, she may actually hear them, because his imagination can supply all the fantasies she needs to fulfill her romantic Cinderella dreams.

This sort of empathy is what causes them to initially fall in love, sometimes at first sight (neither Sun Sign is noted for slow action). But later, it may take more than fantasies to keep her love burning brightly, when his Gemini detachment fails to satisfy her *total* concept of sexual expression, which is *not* purely imaginary. She also needs the tangible. She may begin to feel there's always a tiny part of himself he holds back, even during their intimacy, and she could be right. She holds nothing back, with the Aries instinct to give completely of herself. The Mars inclination toward direct action is seldom diluted in the giving of passion — or in the exchange of it. He may fail to arouse in her such natural (for Rams) physical impulses, with his airy approach to lovemaking. Then she might feel that faerie stories are empty, when there's no fire to set them ablaze, and become bored — or, much worse, frigid.

It's a delicate area of adjustment, and the relationship will have a better chance for success if the Moon and/or Ascendent of his birth chart is in a Fire Sign. Otherwise, he may not be able to teach her what she's so enormously capable of learning, after her initial inhibitions have been overcome by his idealistic preliminaries. The Gemini Prince can kiss the Aries Princess awake, but she may fall back asleep again if total passion is lacking, without ever really knowing why. Then Aries Fire can turn into Aries Ice, which is a sad waste, considering the warmth she can so generously give when the complete potential of her fiery nature is encouraged to develop.

During one of their games of mental chess, when he's behaving in an impossible manner, she might try saying: "I realize that you believe you understood what I just said, but I'm not sure you caught what it was I didn't intend to imply, for fear you might misunderstand what I believed you thought." If it confuses him, she can say: "Good. Now you know what it's like to talk to yourself — or rather, to yourselves. Both of you."

She might also leave this book around near him, open to this chapter, to remind him of how dull his life would be now if she hadn't streaked across his heart. But she should curb her impulse to hand him the book directly, and order him to read it immediately. Cinderella would never do that.

☆ ☆ ☆ ☆ ☆ ☆

ARIES *Man* GEMINI *Woman*

◄━◆━►

*He came back, and there was a greedy look in his
eyes now which ought to have alarmed her, but
did not.*

Unless they met in high school, and were married shortly thereafter (which does happen rather frequently with these two Sun Signs, since they're both always in such a hurry), an Aries man may fiercely resent his Gemini girl's past love life, which could have been, by normal standards, somewhat extensive. It's almost sure to include, if not a couple of ex-husbands, at the very least, half a dozen broken engagements or a few flickering old flames. All Geminis should be wary of early marriage, unless they were born when the Moon or Ascendent was in Capricorn, Virgo, Cancer or Taurus.

It's not that she's fickle or promiscuous, but this girl may run through a long list of pitchers while she's playing the field, before she finds one who can bat her average. Yes, I know that batters don't pitch, and pitchers don't bat, ordinarily — but any man who can't do at least two things equally well, preferably more, and also preferably both at once, is likely to strike out with her.

Of course, we know that could never happen to an Aries man, since he can do everything and anything better than anyone else, at any time, so I suppose it's just an academic discussion, but it wouldn't hurt for him to remember it anyway.

All her life this woman has thought it was the house at the top of the hill that had golden windows. She keeps climbing all the way up there, only to look below, from the summit, and discover the house at the bottom of the hill is the one with golden windows, after all. So she slides back down, and rediscovers that the house at the bottom has only ordinary windows, as she first had thought, then looks up to see the golden windows shining once more at the top of the hill, decides she's been wrong, and trudges back up the hill again to another disappointment. Why are those golden windows so elusive? It can be spiritually exhausting, all that climbing up, and sliding back down, and climbing back up, until she learns that the reflection of the Sun is only an illusion — not real at all — and relative, depending upon the time of day and one's location at any given moment.

There may be times when a Gemini girl thinks an old love was really the one with golden possibilities, but before she finds out that this, too, is an illusion, she will have lost the Aries man, whether she left him standing alone at the top or at the bottom of the hill. A Ram will never sympathize with his woman's nostalgia over yesterday's romances, even though he may go out under a toadstool, and light a candle to an old flame every spring, on Groundhog Day, himself. Remember the Aries self-centeredness. He can do it. She can't. Why? Because he knows *his* nostalgia is innocent and will never lead anywhere. He's not so sure about *hers*. (Aries hidden insecurity.)

Their relationship may have a few other pitfalls along with it's undeniable delights — like a possible lack of will power and stability. Rams possess simply oodles of drive and energy, but sticking to things they start is not one of their strong points. Since a man subconsciously depends on his woman to supply what he lacks, he may be leaning on a feather in the breeze when he leans on a Gemini girl. Will power and dependability are not her major talents either (unless her Moon or Ascendent, as just mentioned, happens to be in Cancer, or in an Earth Sign — and naturally, the same is true of him). Consequently, these two (these three or four) can send up a lot of flares that keep sputtering out, as each one indulges the other's weaknesses of procrastination and quick boredom.

This is one man who probably won't insist that his Gemini woman stay home to sweep the hearth, wearing a calico apron and watering the vegetable garden. He'll probably realize he can use her versatile viewpoints and original thinking in his business life or career, so it's common to find this couple working together, after marriage, as well as before. They usually make a crackerjack team. He knows exactly what he wants — and she has plenty of ideas about how to help him get it. Besides, he can watch her more closely if she's with him all day. It eliminates his worry about the milk man, the cleaner, the grocer, and the handsome chap who runs the elevator in their apartment building. Her Mercurial proclivity for harmless (usually) flirting adds plenty of fuel to the fires of Aries jealousy, and anything that might keep such Mars sparks under control is desirable. A survey to determine how many Aries men eventually suggest that their wives work as their secretaries, or full partners, might prove astrologically interesting. On the other hand, these lovers often meet on the job. The same kinds of occupation and career interest them both, so it's only natural that they may bump into each other in some creative field or profession that offers excitement and challenge.

You'll never see an Aries man and a Gemini woman, however long they've been married, sitting at a restaurant table reading the paper, or staring at the other customers, in silence, ignoring each other, the way so many couples unfortunately do after the first flush of romance has become a little softer. Aries and Gemini will always have something to say to each other — sometimes too much. Conversation, in any case, is not likely to lag between them. Most of the time, their verbal communication will consist of stimulating and scintillating exchanges, but when she touches a raw nerve in his sensitive Mars ego with her talent for hitting the satirical mark, it could turn into a verbal contest that could leave some pretty deep wounds. Happily however, these two are inclined to forgive and forget injuries as quickly as they tend to inflict them.

Strangely, this love relationship is sometimes harder on others than it is on the man and woman themselves. The more sincerely and deeply they're in love, the more likely it is that their friends, neighbors or relatives, at some time, however rarely, will suffer from this Air-Fanning-Fire romance. Now and then, a Gemini woman will imagine all sorts of things about people that are, quite simply, untrue. She'll convince herself that a particular dialogue took place with another person, and report it to her Aries lover or husband, in words that haven't the slightest connection with reality, or with the words that were actually spoken. (Her Mercury imagination, you see, fills in the dull or uninteresting gaps with more creative phraseology.)

Loving her as intensely as only a Ram can love, he could take furious offense at these slightly exaggerated insults to his lady fair, and direct his Mars anger, full force, toward the shocked person he's been falsely led to believe has treated her so shabbily. (Aries men are fiercely loyal to their friends and relatives, and especially to their mates.)

Later, her honest Twin will trouble her conscience by softly, yet insistently, reminding her that things didn't quite occur as she colorfully described them to her Ram. If she then levels with him, he should control his Mars fireworks of outrage, and appreciate her attempt to separate reality from imagination, with tenderness. For the Gemini woman is made of fragile material. She's not, like him, protected on her journey through Life by the fierce warrior Mars — only by the unpredictable magician Mercury, who often hides from her, just when a girl most needs her ruling planet's wisdom.

Her heart contains so many different chords of haunting music. She's a symphony of memories, made of loveliness and light, ugliness and shadow, making the more direct Aries man who loves her sometimes wonder, "Who is she — this intimate and familiar stranger? Who is she . . . and what is she?"

Who is she . . . ? Whichever Twin leads the way, at any given moment. What is she? She's the bunch of marigolds in a sky blue bowl, on her teacher's desk, in the third grade . . . . . the circus parade she once watched, when the clown threw a pretzel to her, and she caught it joyfully . . . . . she's hayrides and hurricanes . . . . . her first pair of black patent leather Mary Janes, a summer storm in the woods, at scout camp, that made the pine trees smell as fragrant as hyacinths . . . . . a field of purple heather she sat in once, for hours, that transported her all the way to Scotland, where she was the Lady of the Lake . . . . . and also the lonely Evangeline . . . . . the small, lost bird she fed, until it was strong enough to fly, when she was five. These things are what she is. All this.

And so, while the Gemini girl-woman must exercise a certain amount of discipline over her imagination, if she expects to achieve harmony with the straightforward, honest Ram she loves, she must be careful not to restrict it entirely, because it's the quality that makes her seem so exquisitely feminine to him. Children, too, possess vivid imaginations, and he thinks of her, this man, more often than she knows, as a little girl who needs his loving protection. Except, of course, when she shatters his image of her helplessness by beating him at mental musical chairs, King's X, tic-tac-toe, and so forth. Some Gemini females can be, when they choose, intellectual terrors, their speech as sharp as a knife, their mental acumen nothing less than brilliant — which isn't the most soothing balm for a male Ram's masculine self-confidence. But then, there's also the bunch of marigolds in the sky blue bowl . . . .

As for him, he's made, not just from the rough-hewn robes of raw courage, tied with the crimson cord of bravado — his Ram's horns curl around the memories of his days as Lancelot, the time he first swam, in water way over his head, when he couldn't swim — but he *did* — his broken top, his broken dreams . . . and the nightmares with no shape or form, from a buried, now forgotten childhood fear . . . the Christmas when Santa forgot the puppy on his list . . . the sky rockets, Roman fountains and spit-devils he ignited, when he was nine, on Independence Day . . . the first time he ever saw a horse, and smelled the intoxicating odors of a barn . . . the way he felt when he first knew how holy a silent night could be, sleeping alone, beneath countless glittering stars that sang to him a remembered melody no one else could hear.

They are so many things, this man — this woman. Mostly, they are the sometimes inhabitants of a land, a kingdom they discovered by themselves, where everything is beautiful . . . but lonely . . . needing other eyes to see it too, for only thus may it be recognized as *real*. They may each visit on another's private worlds, but if the mutual invitation so wistfully extended, unspoken . . . is rejected . . . . . then each may retreat into his or her kingdom, more and more often, leaving the other regretfully behind. These lovers should never permit such a retreat to occur, because the stars and planets have designed their make-believe lands so very much alike, they're sure to be happier when they dance through each other's dreams, then when one stands forlornly before the *No Trespassing* sign of the other.

Sexually, this man and woman will believe themselves to be ideally mated, in the beginning. The Ram dreams of arriving in the garden of love on a flying carpet of adventure, straight out of the Arabian Nights (or the Age of Chivalry, either one), and the Gemini female will play her role in his dream-drama to perfection. She'll not only go along with the game, but she'll think up enough new twists to keep him fascinated far beyond the honeymoon. No one can make an ordinary bed seem as much like Sultan's harem as a Gemini woman, which is richly satisfying to an Aries man, who wants his mate to be the epitome of Woman. With her, he'll never know who awaits him at night in the privacy of the boudoir. It could be Cleopatra, George Sand, Mata Hari, Rebecca of Sunnybrook Farm, Lady Hamilton or Fanny Brice. For a while it will excite him, until he starts to look around in the closet and under the pillows for "the sensuous woman."

His own sexual expression is direct and intense. Hers is somewhat more elusive and complicated. True, he enjoys approaching their lovemaking on a path of imaginative romance, but he expects to quench his thirst in a stream of pure, honest passion, when he arrives at his destination. There's often an air of the intangible in her attitude toward physical love, to the extent that he may accuse her of being somewhere else during their intimate moments, and she could resent his masculine intrusion into what, to her, is always a sacred place — her mind.

This man needs daydreams in association with sexual union, but there's a time and place for them, and to him, the last act of their love drama is not the proper place. He believes, like George M. Cohan, that the finale of anything (if it expects to receive an encore) should include a stirring version of "The Stars and Stripes Forever." Listening to Ram Andre Previn's full orchestral recording of Holst's *The Planets*, on cassette or stereo, may help her sense his romantic pace. The section titled "Mars" will deliver the message profoundly, up to and including the violent percussion emphasis at the very close of that passage, that symbolizes the rhythms of his ruling planet with startling lucidity. It's an Aries sex education — and like everything else in the world, it's more beautifully learned with a musical background.

He may sometimes feel she's searching for something that never existed, and fail to realize that with a shade more gentleness from him, she might be able to transmute her vivid imaginings into equally lovely realities. Gemini images flash a true picture of what *could* be — if they're tenderly allowed to take form and shape. It's her dual consciousness that may distort the communication. But love can keep those Mercury circuits free of negative vibrations. Love can do anything — literally, anything.

This eternally youthful man and woman could hear the same music together, and follow the same distant drummer, for many happy years . . . if she understands that his jealousies and petulant angers stem from his Aries emotional vulnerabilities . . . . . . and if he respects her love affair with her other Twin Self. It may sometimes lead her into places she runs to more swiftly than he can follow, but she'll return, refreshed, and ready to race with him toward new horizons.

He's so bright and brave, so friendly, open and enthusiastic. She's so utterly feminine, charming, versatile and spontaneous. If only they don't try to change each other, they can remain boy and girl forever. And children . . . . . are the luckiest people in the Universe.

☆ ☆ ☆ ☆ ☆ ☆

ARIES   CANCER

Fire — Cardinal — Positive   *Water — Cardinal — Negative*
Ruled by Mars   *Ruled by the Moon*
Symbol: The Ram   *Symbol: The Crab*
Day Forces — Masculine   *Night Forces — Feminine*

The **ARIES-CANCER** *Relationship*

*. . . but of course neither of them understood
the other's language.*

A Crab can become a little tense and edgy, spinning around on an Aries carousel. Because the Lunar physical-emotional metabolism is more delicate and fluctuating, Rams can exhaust Moon people with their excessive Mars enthusiasm, which flames in even the quieter, Sheep-type Arians, on occasion (and remember that the Sheep types are in the minority). Consequently, to the determined, somewhat reckless Ram, it may frequently seem as though the Crab disapproves of his (or her) behavior. What do these Cancerians expect you to do, wonders Aries — bury your confidence and develop an inferiority complex, just to please them?

Not necessarily. True, the Crabs might feel considerably more comfortable if the impulsive Mars rhythms could be slowed down a bit, to match their own, more cautious calliope music. But it won't benefit the basic insecurity of Cancer to have Aries join him (or her) in wailing "nobody-loves-me-everybody-hates-me-let's-go-eat-worms." One weepy hang-up like that is sufficient in an association or a relationship. Why try for two?

Very few people are aware of how frantically Aries men and women (and children) seek acceptance while they're rushing around feverishly courting rejection with their impulsive, thoughtless ways. Among those few aware ones are Cancerians, who themselves are abnormally sensitive to hurt. Even as they appear to frown on Aries rashness, they sense, with their acute perception, that the Rams are not always as tough as they act. Because of this perception, there can be some lovely and solid relationships between these two Sun Signs. However, since theirs is a 4-10 vibrational pattern, this association more often occurs in an unavoidable career, business or family situation, than in a romantic one. The Higher Selves of any two people influenced by the 4-10 vibration may possibly arrange matters this way, because of the heavier Karma, which must be leveled and harmonized, and human nature being as it is, few people would choose the tensions and conflicts of a 4-10 soul testing if there was a choice. Naturally, there are also love and marriage involvements between Aries and Cancer, from time to time. It's just that the Ram and the Crab teams are more often found as relatives or co-workers — in a boss-employee or other career entanglement. Even those Rams and Crabs who are romantically attracted will usually first meet in a career or family atmosphere, or these matters will be a main topic of conversation between them initially.

If the Sun-Moon aspect between their natal charts is harmonious, this combination can be surprisingly financially successful and emotionally compatible. But if a negative Luminary or Ascendent aspect exists between their horoscopes, there will be some steep hills to climb, and much soul testing for durability.

Aries likes — and needs — to win. Aries also enjoys leading. Now, Cancer has nothing against either winning or leading. As for the latter, remember that Cancer is a Cardinal Sign of leadership, despite the Crab's attempt to hide his or her desire to lead beneath a veil of feigned unconcern. Aries is also a Cardinal Sign, and the Ram's horns being equally as tough as the Crab's shell, you can see there may be a few skirmishes over who follows the leader in any game they're playing. It's a tricky problem, because when you have two leaders, how do you determine which one will follow? (Especially when neither has any intention of doing so.) It seems like an impossible situation, but there is a solution. They can walk side-by-side, with no one ahead, no one behind. It's called compromise. Cancer tends to compromise with less pain than Aries, so it's usually the Crab who must initiate the offer of truce between them. Aries may try, yet somehow manage to say the wrong thing, in the wrong way, tinged with too much ego, which leaves the Crab either snapping angrily, or weeping inconsolably.

All right, so now we have them (we hope) walking side-by-side toward the winner's circle — peacefully, for a while — then up pop the differences between their personalities and strategies again. The Crab advances in a rather zigzag direction, never straight ahead, like the direct, straightforward

Ram. The Cancerian approach to anything is deliberate, disguised and careful, never mind how many jokes they tell along the way to distract you from noticing their techniques. Whereas the Ram is ever ready to discard dead wood and clear the decks for action, the Crab wants to be sure that no one throws out the baby with the bath water, so to speak. That's admittedly a mixed metaphor, but when discussing and describing Aries and Cancer, it's permissible. No single metaphor, analogy or allegory would suffice to fit both of these divergent Earthlings, who often seem to each other to be from different stars or galaxies.

Life is one huge challenging contest to Aries, who rushes out to meet obstacles headlong and headfirst, even when he or she must go out of his or her way to find them. If they aren't there, Aries will create a few, for what fun is a contest with no obstacles to overcome?

Indeed, obstacles attract Aries like bar magnets. Meeting with constant agreement everywhere both annoys and bores a Ram. Aries is either dismayed or furious when another person refuses to fight or argue. That takes all the excitement out of it. The Mars adrenalin surges, the Aries vitality is instantly recharged, in the face of any sort of opposition. Let a conflict loom on the horizon, and the Ram is in his or her glory, bravely facing the thrill of challenge, and the explosive excitement of meeting it victoriously. There's nothing wrong with this, as long as Aries will stop once in a while to notice that there are other people in the world besides himself (or herself) and that they have feelings too. Aries people don't mean to step on anyone's sensitive feelings, but they're so intent on getting wherever it is they're going (and you can include the rare and more introverted Sheep types, along with the flashier Rams) that they can be inconsiderate and thoughtless without realizing it. Excluding those few Arians who may have a severely afflicted natal Sun or Mars, the typical Ram would never hurt anyone on purpose. Nevertheless, he (or she) does, especially the ultra-sensitive Crabs.

By now, you can see that one of the problems between Aries and Cancer is sensitivity to hurt. Aries people have little or no awareness of this particular weakness in themselves — it clashes with their self image of strength. There-fore, when Aries is hurt, the Mars-influenced reaction is to either immediate-ly deny it, or to become defensively angry. Cancer's vulnerability is carefully hidden, so the typical Cancerian reaction to hurt is to crawl inside the Crab shell and pout — or turn just plain crabby. If the wound is deep enough, either of these responses may be accompanied by a few buckets of tears and sometimes, the Lunar sensitivity peaks out from behind the Looney-Bird humor. When these two have hurt each other, one of them (Cancer) disappears into an inky blob of gloom, or an injured silence, punctuated by cranky snapping. The other (Aries), frustrated by the Cancerian retreat strategy, and feeling helpless to take any kind of action to resolve the disagreement between them, may then become furious, and release a torrent of words and actions, with the predictable effect of causing the Crab to burrow even deeper into the sands of silent pouting.

Just go back to Nature for a moment, via astrological symbolism, and picture an aroused ram butting his (or her) horns against the hard shell of an impervious crab, while it frantically digs deeper and deeper into the sand on the beach. On the beach? What is a ram doing messing around on the beach, beside the mysterious ocean, anyway? He's out of his element. (So is she, if the Arian is female.) Just as the crab would be lost trying to crawl up the rocky mountain slopes where the ram is more at home. It requires a Sun-Moon trine or conjunction between their horoscopes — or a great deal of patient understanding from both — to bring these two very different astro-logical creatures together in a mutually acceptable emotional terrain. Even then, although they may learn to tolerate each other, and help each other grow, evolve and learn, the differences between them will be distinctly visible.

It's true that Cancerians may hide in the mop closet when their feelings are hurt, and are normally quiet and reflective sorts (except when they're making you giggle over their funnies), but they shouldn't be considered by Aries to be totally impassive, easily molded or incapable of resistance. They may not fight with the flaming sword of Mars, and may prefer to tackle obstacles with serenity, secrecy and patience; yet Crabs are not altogether quivering, soft masses of fear. Correction: Crabs *are* quivering, soft masses of fear, but the Ram shouldn't forget that hard shell they hide under while they're shivering and quivering. It's not advisable to rap one's knuckles on it. Whereas the Ram is inclined to favor instant and open attack when security is threatened, the Cancerian man or woman will, as unobtrusively as possible, first attempt to seek the underlying root cause of the trouble, then maneuver out of it gradually, with a secret strategy and incredible tenacity of purpose. The Crab's ability to hang on to your toe, ear, finger — or a notion — until it gets what it wants, should never be overlooked or underestimated. (That goes for both boy Crabs and girl Crabs.)

Aries and Cancer have different motivations, different approaches to life — and different goals. But if each will give something of his (or her) basic goodness to the other, both of their lives will be greatly enriched. This is a Fire and Water combination; therefore, each is subconsciously aware that the other can destroy him (or her). Too much Aries Fire can dehydrate Cancer's delicate feelings. Too much Cancerian Water can drown the Ram's enthusi-astic, shining hopes. Fire represents optimism, in astrology — Water, pessi-mism. The two elements seem to be incompatible; yet another word for pessimism is "caution," a commodity with which Aries could beneficially experiment — and another word for optimism is "faith," a quality Cancer would find very useful.

If they're willing to take the time to translate the message of each other's hearts, who knows how high the dreams of the Ram and the Crab can reach together ? Perhaps all the way to the Moon — or to Mars.

☆ ☆ ☆ ☆ ☆ ☆

ARIES *Woman* CANCER *Man*

---◄◆►---

She wanted to risk it, come what might, but that was not his way . . .

Like all females born under masculine Sun Signs, who are, in addition, ruled by a masculine planet (in this case, Mars), the Aries girl has private doubts about her femininity. Ever since dancing school, she's been reluctant to let her partner take the lead.

Most of the fellows she's waltzed around have panicked when they weren't allowed to set the pace and the rhythm of the relationship, and the male machismo mystique being what it is, her feminine "macha" caused them all to stalk off to look for a girl willing to humor their fantasies of superiority. The girl Ram is far too honest to imitate her more submissive Sun Sign sisters by pretending to allow the man to initiate every word and action, while she smiles with amused tolerance behind his back. There's a perfect example of that sort of well-meant but demeaning deception in Margaret Mitchell's great American novel, *Gone With The Wind*, when the dying Melanie says, of Ashley, "Look after him, Scarlet — *but never let him know."*

After a few heartbreaking experiences of discovering that honesty is not always the best policy when it comes to romance, an Aries female may understandably (and justifiably) begin to have some inner traumas as she wonders about her desirability as a woman. Then along comes a Cancerian man to court her (yes, I said *court* her) with a respectful, gallant courtesy, like a Prince straight out of a storybook. Not only that, he makes her laugh a lot, and laughter never fails to brighten a Ram's disposition, making her sweeter to be around. From the very beginning, he makes it clear that she excites him and thrills him, no matter who walks through the door first, which one starts the conversation or who initiates a telephone call. At last! She can finally do and say what comes naturally around a man — and he still loves her. No wonder it's an intoxicating experience for her. It may be the first time she's ever felt like a member of the opposite sex.

When he convinces her she's not the wicked old witch after all, that she's really lovely, desirable Snow White (as she always suspected) it can be exhilarating — for a while. Assuming there's a harmonious aspect of interchange between their Luminaries, Ascendents and other major horoscopic positions in their nativities, her daydreams have a good chance of coming true. Otherwise, Snow White could find herself living in the woods with only one of the Seven Dwarfs — Grumpy — and still waiting in vain for the Prince.

An Aries female will never be permanently at peace with herself until she discovers a man who will want her to love him freely and openly, without quibbling over who initiates the first goodnight kiss, and without pouting if she occasionally interrupts him with a sudden burst of cheerful, enthusiastic chatter. She needs a man who understands that if he'll just allow her to be herself, she'll give him all the adoring love he needs to feel strong and virile and masculine. Just murmuring "Whatever you say — or whatever you decide, dear" (with a hidden smirk) is romantic hypocrisy, a travesty of honest devotion. Her love is direct. It shrinks into restless frustration when it's restricted by petty arguments over what constitutes the difference between masculinity and femininity. She loves him with all her heart and soul and mind and being — isn't that enough? Yes. It should be — and it very well may be, for a boy Crab. But Rams have other areas of friction with Cancerians.

Both of them are intensely jealous. The chief difference is that Cancer enjoys it more than Aries. To the Crab, jealousy simply proves how much he's loved and needed, and with this woman, he'll get all of that kind of proof he needs — maybe a little more than he can handle. Jealousy can sometimes bring a sense of emotional security to the Ram too — just a light touch of it, now and then. But when it's overdone to the point of smothering possessiveness, it can sharply cramp her life-style, which is friendly, free and gregarious — and the truth of it is that a Cancerian lover or mate may lay it on with a heavy hand, once the courting gallantry is over, and he's sure she is his. Of course, it's equally true that his Crab-like trait of hanging on, when it comes to love, is an indication of his inclination toward loyalty and faithfulness. She certainly has no objection to that. In her opinion, it's the very least one should expect from true love. It's when his loyal devotion subtly and gradually is transformed into clinging, which brings the feeling of being fenced in, that she'll show flashes of resentful rebellion.

Each of these two Sun Signs is as fond of money, fame and recognition as the other. However, the Crab hides his ambition better. Although they share the same basic goals of emotional security and financial success, they have rather seriously conflicting ideas about how to achieve them — as well as what to do with money, when it's there. (She wants to spend it, or give it away, to create a nice, smooth cash flow — he wants to save it to make it expand into a higher balance.) Even before either of them achieves any degree of material success, there will be disagreements. Aries is optimistic, positive, *sure* of winning. Cancer is often pessimistic, negative and fearful of the future

(Crabs call it sensible caution)—and this is where these two may need an interpreter to communicate.

It's impossible for the Ram to comprehend how the Crab hopes to win, at the same time he's expecting to lose. To Aries, this puzzling Cancerian attitude was expressed perfectly by physician-philosopher Jean-Baptiste Baudin, when he wrote: "To be ambitious for wealth, and yet always expecting to be poor; to be always doubting your ability to get what you long for, is like trying to reach East by traveling West. There is no philosophy which will help a man succeed when he's always doubting his ability to do so, and thus attracting failure." Granted, there are more July birthdays in *Who's Who in Industry and Commerce* than any others (except Taurus and Capricorn), but that's because the Cancerian has going for him a more than adequate substitute for courageous Aries optimism—a hard-shell tenacity of purpose.

There's not much use trying to explain this to an Aries female. She's familiar with a term like "determination," but she doesn't understand the word "tenacity," because it diametrically opposes her most evident quality—impatience. Tenacity implies waiting, and this woman loathes to wait for anything, from a bus or a red light to the arrival of her current lover at the door when they have a date—or her husband's arrival home from work, if she's a married Ram. Let him be five minutes late, and she either phones the sheriff in impulsive panic, or paces the floor, working up sufficient steam to leap on him with reproaches when he does arrive. Her Cancerian lover or mate's general attitude toward ambition and success, with or without the tenacity, utterly confuses her. She believes in simple things, that people should face the direction in which they wish to travel, and she faces the East. How can he ever expect to arrive in New York when he's headed toward California? All right, so the world is round, and he may eventually get there, but it takes so much time that way.

There are several possible outcomes for the dilemma. She can become desolate in the face of his moody spells of depression, and finally decide she must escape, to avoid the fate of seeing every last one of her fiery aspirations submerged in his watery Cancerian pessimism. Or she can try to cheer him out of his periodic melancholy with her own strong Mars faith, by boosting his spirits with courage and humor—like reminding him of the old proverb that every time a sheep bleats, it loses a mouthful of hay. He can throw up his hands in defeat at her impulsive emotions and financial extravagance, take off alone with his stamp collection and his old fishing hat—or he can gently, patiently teach her that caution does sometimes make sense, and that counting to ten has the benefit of never adding up to a total of zero.

Another trouble spot could be this man's tendency to keep secrets. The Aries woman is not so closely molded in the image of the Sphinx as he. When the Crab refuses to tell her what's on his mind, she may imagine all sorts of far-out things, and torture herself into a fit of Mars hysteria. He'll soon learn (let's hope) that it's more peaceful in the long run to come completely clean with her. To level. If he clams up, she'll just pry until she sees it's no use, then decide the whole thing isn't worth the energy and heartache — and possibly leave him. Suddenly. With little or no warning. Remember, Aries will waste no time on a situation that's been analyzed as impossible to change. It could end with the Crab still sitting on his secrets, while she skips off chanting Edna St. Vincent Millay's lines: "Thanks be to God, the world is wide, and I am going far from home — and I'll forget in Camelot the man I loved in Rome." He will weep.

Then, too, there's Mama. If his mother is still living, the girl Ram who loves a boy Crab may have some stiff competition for his devotion and attention, perhaps not when they first meet — but she won't avoid it forever. If his sainted mother has passed on, Mama's qualities could take on added luster, seen through the sparkling glass of memory. Did his mother *never* scorch a shirt, bake flat biscuits, sing off key, waste money or lose her temper? No. Never. Not one single time. Did his mother *always* save cash, look prettier by sewing her own clothes, string her own beans, wear just the right amount of makeup and know exactly what to say to make him smile when he was blue? Yes. She did. Always. In a strange way, it might work to their benefit, the Mama thing. A glowing example like that is surely a challenge, and this girl can't resist struggling to meet a challenge. She may become nearly as perfect as he thinks his mother is — or was — just to prove to him that no one can top a Ram.

In their sexual life, adjustments will also be necessary. When love is new, his tender consideration for her desires and needs will make her feel cherished, therefore emotionally secure. (Both of them have this incredible hang-up about needing emotional security.) He'll be, in the beginning, a fabulous lover. A Cancerian can be as imaginative, subtle and clever in the bedroom as he is at the bank. Her frankness and lack of guile concerning sex, a sort of unconscious vulnerability in her, will stir him deeply. Regardless of past experiences, an Aries girl always brings a kind of fresh innocence to her approach to lovemaking — in addition, when she loves, she loves fiercely and passionately, truly giving all of herself in total honesty, and *this* will make *him* feel emotionally secure. But she may be unable to remember the thrill of their original physical compatibility when he's been cranky and moody for a few days and refuses to respond to her affectionate advances. What appears to be (but isn't) his rejection of her can considerably dampen her erotic enthusiasm. It's the Moon. She'll just have to wait until the Moon changes, and stops pulling his emotions back and forth like a piece of taffy. What she should not do during these temporary Lunar phases that threaten to eclipse their happiness is become angry, and say things to wound him she'll later regret. He'll crawl into his Crab shell and stay there, for this man is acutely sensitive. However much he may joke about it, he is — and sexual hurt will cause him to retreat into brooding passivity for long periods. Or worse yet, he could seek the solace of alcohol's seductive siren song.

On the happy side of this relationship, a Crab can be very amusing and entertaining, and can make anything from counting money to digging clams wacky fun, with loads of laughs. His beautiful sensitivity and his gentlemanly air of protectiveness can bring out all the femininity in his Aries lady. He'll secretly be proud of her courageous mind and bright spirit, no matter how he grumbles about her immaturity, and he'll grow to depend on her for the emotional support he needs when the Moon sends fragments of old fears from childhood to haunt him. On the negative side, she may believe he's too stern at times, too fussy or stingy, while he may feel she's not capable of taking care of herself without a keeper. He could now and then drown his disappointments in drink or drugs, always a very real danger with a Water Sign — and she could now and then lose her quick fiery temper in such a way that it takes a long time to atone for the pain it caused.

This is a man who's not ashamed of sentiment; he's affected by music, art and poetry, and when his heart is moved, tears come to his eyes — and this is a woman whose own heart needs a great deal of tender, loving care, for she is, emotionally, an infant, whatever her chronological age. If they crossbreed her Aries initiative with his Cancer tenacity, they might achieve wonders. Their natal Suns are squared, and so it will require lots of patience — and lots of love. But then, doesn't everything?

☆ ☆ ☆ ☆ ☆ ☆

ARIES *Man* CANCER *Woman*

"Hullo, Wendy," he said, not noticing any difference,
for he was thinking chiefly of himself.

"Hullo, Peter," she replied faintly, squeezing herself
as small as possible. Something inside her was crying.

An Aries man is initially lured by a Cancerian girl because she seems so appealingly helpless and feminine (Note: I said she *seems* helpless. We'll take that up later. Appealing and feminine she definitely is, no argument there.) She appears to need his strong masculine shoulder to cry on, his fiery emotional support.

When the Moon Maiden gives a Ram her flattering, undivided attention, it proves to him what he's always suspected — that no woman can resist him. She'll cook for him, baby him, laugh at his jokes, add some pretty funny ones of her own and generally make his life one long, sweet song of soothing serenity, with comical lyrics. But the music he hears could be a prelude to a slowly growing feeling of being smothered. As you well know, if you're at all acquainted with astrology, Rams do not like to be smothered — by blankets, authority or restriction of any kind — not even by love. Smothered in attention is fine, but the Aries male draws a line at having his freedom squeezed out of him. Now, it's true that no one can squeeze away a man's freedom as painlessly and pleasurably as a Cancerian girl. If she's subtle about it, as most Moon Maids are, a Ram could find the trip on her romantic flying carpet a thrilling experience (she has a deep-seated wanderlust hiding behind her homemaking knacks, you know). However, if the Crab shows signs of beginning to cling too closely, the Aries male may jump off the carpet, without a parachute, if necessary.

About her feminine helplessness: He'll sooner or later learn that it's somewhat of an illusion — maybe someday when she incorporates her own bank, re-decorates a friend's house, runs for Congress or rescues a child from drowning in the ocean, beating the lifeguard to the spot. Cancer is a Cardinal Sign, and these women possess an amazing stamina and tenacity, along with all that moonlight fragility. After the first shock has worn off, he'll probably admire her for it. He admires any kind of strength, and she's far stronger than her timid tears when he's hurt her feelings (which may be frequently) might indicate. He could even fall more deeply in love with her when he discovers she's not all "sugar-and-spice-and-everything-nice," since he essentially needs a woman who will fight back with him now and then.

But other sour notes may threaten to spoil love's concert between these two Sun Signs — like money. She has a pronounced compulsion to accumulate it, maybe even paper the bedroom, kitchen and nursery walls with it (her three favorite rooms). To her, financial security is synonymous with emotional security. The two are inseparable. He likes money too, and can think of hundreds of exciting uses for it, but stashing it away in a rusty old trunk in the attic or a bank vault for a rainy day is not at the head of his list. To Aries, money is to spend (or give away). His motto is: "Money can't buy happiness." Since they're both in love and happy, who's worried about cash ? She is. *She's* worried about it. Because, you see, *her* motto is: "Happiness can't buy money." The Aries man contemplating a ring-around-the-rosy with a Moon Maiden should think about that. Carefully. He still won't agree with it, but he should think about it.

It won't be long until he notices her moodiness. Of course, he's moody too, but that's different and understandable. With Aries, everything is different and understandable when they do it — also justifiable and permissible, as well as excusable. (Remember, Aries is the adorable but totally self-centered symbolic Infant of the zodiac.) *Her* moods he considers to be un-called-for damp prisons of gloom, and it must be admitted that they are deeper, more indigo and longer lasting than his. Sometimes it happens that a Ram cheers a girl Crab out of her periodic Lunar melancholy with his sheer optimism. It makes him feel strong and masculine, and gives her the emotional stability she needs. But there's a danger that he may eventually revolt against a fluctuating depression he can't fathom, if only because it frightens him into thinking that perhaps his self-made Mars miracles don't have the power to swing the Universe he believed them to have. Rather than face that horrible thought, he could split. He may not get too far. She's kind of nice to come home to, and make up with — and who else bathes his ego in such charming shades of lavender and soft green, with such silvery sincerity? She's funny and tender at the same time, and eternally capable of pulling him out of those holes he jumps into, head first. Besides, she bakes a terrific blueberry muffin — and the chemical attraction between them is an added attraction. It might not have been what first drew them together, the initial interest might have been based on other things . . . but after a while it grew into a positive aspect of their relationship well worth considering.

Her Lunar imagination quickly sparks the flame of his Martian sexuality, and his enthusiastic, idealistic lovemaking can pull her out of her bashful (or snappy) shell into a beautiful fulfillment of latent passion. There's an affectionate quality in the Aries approach to sex that may reach a part of her nature which has timidly hidden itself behind her crazy, Looney Bird laughter until the right man came along to find it. Unfortunately, however, this woman's ingrained sense of Cancerian practicality soon tells her that "man can't live with hyacinths alone — he needs bread." (Cancer sometimes has a way of twisting truisms around, or reversing them, to accent the negative, and eliminate the positive.) That's when the *real* cash conflict may begin, when she mentions money in the middle of some romantic interlude, just as the two of them are about to become "one." Suddenly, sexual closeness is replaced by an emotional explosion.

Any relationship between Aries and Cancer is usually subjected to a generous sprinkling of fights over money — how to obtain it, and how to dispose of it. He's extravagant, she's thrifty. At least, she's normally economical, until she spins into one of her many moods, triggered by the phases of the Moon, and indulges herself in a buying spree of feminine frivolities to boost her sagging ego. Most other times, however, she's a little reluctant to part with cash, to put it mildly.

If they manage to overcome the sensitive point of finances, through mutual give-and-take, Aries and Cancer possess the potential of building some solid dream castles together, especially if there's a trine, sextile or conjunction between his Sun and her Moon, or vice versa. Her combination of creative flights of fancy and a common sense attitude about cash (an odd contradiction in Cancerians) coupled with his audacity and Mars determination, will usually give this Sun Sign couple immunity from the need to apply for Government Welfare. Still, the problems aren't over. Her moods keep popping up to plague them.

He may fail to comprehend the delicacy of her emotional needs and be completely baffled by her changing moods. Perception is not an Aries strong point. It can throw him into a fit of perplexity. What could he have done wrong? (Nothing. I keep telling you, it's the Moon.) Only moments ago, she was skipping around like a dodo bird chattering and giggling and humming a tune, feeding the kitten soybean cakes — all smiles. And now, tears. What happened? Check *The Farmer's Almanac,* or the evening paper. It may be the Full Moon. Or it may be that her feelings have been bruised by something he didn't even realize he said. Perhaps he failed to notice her new dress, or forgot to tell her how delicious her carrot casserole was. Ever since childhood, this girl has feared that no one loved her. He'll have to gently teach her that the best way to get love — is to give love. (This won't be easy, since it's a lesson he desperately needs to learn himself.) The Aries man should remember that the way to keep a Moon Maiden happy is to be sure she always receives lots of love, lots of food and lots of money. She's not greedy, she's just security-hungry, and that's not the same thing at all. I left out something. If she's a typical Lunar lady, add to the list — lots of babies. Well, at least a *few.*

A Ram is nearly always enthusiastic about approaching fatherhood, and she'll adore this quality in him. But after the bundles of joy grow out of their booties into Buster Browns, they may begin pulling their parenthood wagon in opposite directions. He believes in teaching the youngsters to be independent. Although he can be bossy and demanding with them, his general inclination is to give them lots of room to grow in. She takes motherhood seriously, and I mean very seriously. She'll closely scrutinize their food, clothing, romances, careers and health. They'll be stuffed with pea soup, cuddled, coddled and watched over — all done in a spirit of friendly persuasion, of course. Mama knows what's best, what's right to eat and wear, who's wrong to love and marry. All this could lead to his accusing her of smothering their individualities — and to her accusing him of being too harsh, and too detached, by turns. The offspring may feel they're being slowly squashed between two cement walls, at times. Compromise in child raising is a must, or this relationship will crack irreparably.

The Ram's ability to give and receive love depends upon his image of himself as the strong one. He needs constant freedom of expression and action. His woman must have absolute faith in his ability to move mountains. Otherwise, his frustrated emotions may form strange neurotic patterns, turning him from a courageous Ram into a meek, unhappy sheep. Like being under a witch's hex. She should never remind him that she is better than he at juggling the bank balance (even if she is) — or anything else that may cut sharply into his masculinity. If she refrains from tossing wet blankets on his dreams, he'll stay close to home, contentedly. If she allows him to lead the parade, without dampening his hopes, he'll be able to make her mountains of secret worries and fears disappear forever. But there's always the possibility that her despairing silences, sulky temper and occasional touches of hysteria will drive him right up the side of her money-papered walls, and out of the house — and that his rash words and impulsive behavior will bring her watery nature to a boil, until it sloshes over and drowns his incentive.

When she's weeping, and he doesn't know why, he shouldn't storm out of the room impatiently. He should take her in his arms, and lullaby her with tender reassurances, to stem the tides of fear and loneliness rising in her, whispering softly, "Please don't cry, and don't worry. Everyone loves you because you're so smart and so pretty, and you tell funny stories. Besides, we're almost sure to be rich someday. And as for me, I love you even more than other people do, and that's really a bunch. You don't have to offer to do the neighbor's laundry. We're not quite that poverty-stricken, and we never will be. Now, I want you to wash your face, brush your hair, blow your nose, and get dressed in something beautiful, because I'm going to take you out to dinner." He should then mention the name of the most expensive, exclusive restaurant in town. She'll stop sniffling right away.

"All nine courses — including the dessert tray ?" she'll ask, then, tentatively, her eyes beginning to sparkle.

"Yes, darling, all nine courses, including the dessert tray . . and afterwards, we'll go to a movie, whichever one *you* want to see."

That last promise ought to do it. It may be the first time in years the thoughtlessly selfish Ram has allowed her to choose which film to see . . or anything else.

☆ ☆ ☆ ☆ ☆ ☆

ARIES

Fire — Cardinal — Positive
Ruled by Mars
Symbol: The Ram
Day Forces — Masculine

LEO

Fire — Fixed — Positive
Ruled by the Sun
Symbols: Lion & Shy Pussy-
cat
Day Forces — Masculine

The **ARIES- LEO** *Relationship*

"So are you a cowardly custard."
"I'm not frightened."
"Neither am I frightened."
"Well, then, take it."
"Well, then, you take it."

ost everyone knows that Leo is symbolized by the Lion. As for Aries Rams, once they've been taught (by Leo) the gentle joys of submission, they become perfect lambs. Now, the Bible hints that when the "lamb lies down with the Lion," we may expect either Götterdämmerung — or 1,000 years of Peace. There's some dispute between theologians and metaphysicians as to the happy or sad ending of the prophecy. It could be a combination of both. Most things are. Let's hope, however, that the lamb lying down with the Lion will bring permanent Peace, and not the Götterdämmerung (end of the world). Of course, it might be argued that a truce to the clubbing around of these two would *seem* like the end of the world. A smooth, snoozy relationship between them would be the living end — of something. Possibly of all the fun they have racing each other to the finish line, and competing for the cheers of the lesser animals.

Rams are winners. Indisputably. Winning is their chief occupation. They list it that way on their resumes. Occupation: *WINNING*! Whatever the game may be — love, friendship, business or family life — they'll win it. That puts Aries right at the top.

Leos don't waste their valuable time trying to win anything. They don't need to compete. They were *born* superior to everyone else, clearly the most important person in any love, business, friendship or family contest. That puts Leo right at the top too — with much less effort and energy. The question is, will there be room at the top?

Well, yes . . . in a large arena with lots of space, they could each grab a share of the spotlight and sweet rounds of applause. But on a stage of any smaller dimensions, like an office, schoolroom, apartment or house — it might get a little crowded. Something would have to give. Namely, someone's gigantic ego.

I'm not going to fool around with tact. It will hurt less if the message is direct and swift. It is the ego of the Ram that must bend and bow to the majesty of Leo, because the Lion and Lioness were born to lead, born to command, born to be first — BORN FREE! That means free of anyone's domination, including the government, the Internal Revenue, employers, teachers, neighbors, friends, relatives, astrologers — and especially pushy Rams. The Aries half of this team will have to be content with knowing he or she can fight any of the other Sun Signs and win . . (well, maybe not Scorpio).

But all is not lost. (Aries considers nothing lost, just temporarily misplaced.) When I said Aries can't win against Leo, I meant in the sense of grabbing the trophies in front of an audience. Privately, the Ram can win just about anything from the Big Cat, simply by listening respectfully to those long, Leonine lectures, heaping on the praise — and keeping personal intentions and opinions to himself (or herself). The first part is easy. Aries enjoys lifting people's spirits, and showering compliments on anyone who excites the Mars admiration of power and strength (which Leo has in abundance). However, keeping quiet about the ultimate goal is a tough order for most Rams. Aries people do like to boast about it when they win an election, a kewpie doll at the carnival or an argument. Too much bragging in this double Fire Sign combination, and the Leonine half of the team may stalk off in injured dignity, when it becomes obvious that he (or she) is being manipulated or out-staged, either of which shatters Leo's pride. It's no coincidence that a group of Lions is technically termed a "pride."

If a Lion or Lioness is in a position where stalking off in injured dignity is not possible (like an under-age child or a legal mate), he — or she — will sit in a corner and pout, looking out with reproachful, sad eyes, and stroking his or her vanity. Then too, there's always the chance that Leo will roar like the MGM Lion, and fiercely attack the injustice perpetrated by a mere peasant.

That can be dreadfully noisy. It's safer for the Ram to allow a Leo of either sex believe that he (or she) has won any game the two of them might be playing. No one, in or out of the jungle, can be as magnanimous, cheerful and just plain huggable as an emotionally and physically pampered Leo. Pampering, however, is a talent in which Aries definitely does not excel.

Aesop, in his fables, points out how easy it is for the Lion to be managed by a lesser animal, the jackal. When the Lion becomes furious with him and roars in great anger, the clever jackal restores himself to royal favor easily — simply by reminding the Lion, at the height of his rage, that he's the King of the Jungle, the Ruler of All Beasts, and therefore mustn't expect too much from a lowly jackal. It works like a charm.

The trouble is, a Ram is not a jackal. Aries is more likely to order Leo, in the heat of battle (and oh! there will be battles) to either give in — or get out. This will immediately create an emotional dead-end street. Since giving in is a total impossibility for a Leo — and getting out is a cowardly action, beneath the dignity of royalty (what true monarch ever retreats?), the Lion or Lioness is left with no choice except to roar louder, with increasing arrogance. Eventually, when Aries discovers that even a Ram's tough horns will not topple that splendid Leonine courage and stamina (emotional, mental and physical), it's all over but the shouting, which can last an exhausting length of time, since both these Sun Signs are rather fond of dramatic speech and posture.

"How dare you!" "Don't raise your voice to me!" "Don't give me orders!" "You won't get away with that!" "I will not do as you say!" "Oh, yes you will!" "This has gone far enough!" "Do you know who you're pushing around?" "You will do as I say!" "Never! Do you hear me? NEVER!" It goes on — and on — and on. If they sold tickets, they'd have a packed house. Nothing on or off Broadway has the dramatic impact, suspense and action these two manage to pack into each Act of one of their Ego plays — and the Finale inevitably calls for an Encore. I know one Aries-Leo pair who punctuate their turbulent sessions by taking turns flipping the volume up on the record player. Even hard-to-please Broadway critic John Simon would call it a hit musical.

However, although Leo must win in the final analysis, this Sun Sign is not a conqueror to be feared, ready to grab the spoils of war and grind the vanquished beneath his (or her) boots. Both the Lions and Lionesses are noted for their generosity and nobility of attitude toward the defeated. Of course, it must be admitted that Rams are not good losers. But if it's possible for Aries to ever lose gracefully, it will be with a Leo.

These Sun Signs are astrologically trine (harmonious) and influenced by the magical 5-9 Sun Sign Pattern (see the Sun Sign Patterns section in the front of this book). Therefore, each senses the other's superior qualities, when compared with anyone else either of them knows. Since a genuine admiration for each other is seldom lacking, when peace descends and an armistice is declared, it's often full of vows (dramatic, naturally) of eternal loyalty and devotion. Until the next battle. Then it starts all over again.

In the family circle — in the classroom or office — or between lovers or legal mates — the relationship can be a warm and happy one, as long as Aries is willing to look up to Leo as a guide, preceptor, counselor or teacher — and as long as Leo continues to wrap Aries in the cozy warmth of the kind of loving kindness and protectiveness the Sun-ruled can give so effortlessly. It will be, on the whole, a successful association, even though not always tranquil, because the Aries-Leo relationship is blessed by the grace of the magical 5-9 Sun Sign Pattern vibration. Leo will provide plenty of sincere and extravagant compliments, something Aries needs as the flowers need rain. And vice versa. *Totally* vice versa. Both Aries and Leo not only seek appreciation, they quite frankly demand it. If one of them has a conflicting Moon Sign or Ascendent, their quarrels may be more serious and hurtful; yet forgiveness is, even then, usually the final resolution.

One trouble area will be those long dissertations of wisdom from Leo, which often begin with the words, "Now, listen to me, and I'll explain how wrong you are." Since the Ram has enough trouble coping with bossy people in day-to-day living, to be forced to sit through the same sort of thing each night at dinner may ignite the very short fuse of the Mars temper . . . . but I'll tell you a secret. Actually, Aries will privately give Leo a lot of credit, and sincerely respect the advice given so freely and constantly, a lot more than he or she lets on. This may be because the advice given by a Leo to Aries is so frequently cushioned in real affection and concern. Rams desperately need loving guidance, and the chances are better than average that they'll get it from the Lion — or Lioness. As long as it is clearly "loving," not arrogantly authoritative.

If only the Ram could learn to *ask* Leo to do things, instead of commanding, "Do it now, and don't ask questions" — the relationship between them would be smoother. No one orders royalty around like that, not even Prime Ministers. It requires lots of effort for the Mars-ruled Ram to learn to be more gracious when trying to get Leo to do something, but it's an effort that must be made, or the struggle for dominance will disintegrate into continual dispute.

When there is mutual consideration, this can be a singular and extraordinary relationship, for Leo senses the hidden insecurities and dependency just behind the spectacular, brave Aries personality, and knows the Ram's surface sureness is not backed up by inner conviction — while Aries will grow to depend on Leo, not just for the well-organized Leonine mind and steadiness in a storm, but also for the ability of his (or her) sunny nature to give warmth and meaning to each moment of life. The Ram knows how quivering and sensitive Leo's heart really is, never mind the cover of superiority and bravado. These two have much natural sympathy. You can tell it when they smile at each other. It's a strangely intimate smile, a grin of gratitude that says: "Thanks for understanding me — I understand you too."

In each other, Aries and Leo will find the excitement they are constantly searching for. They're both essentially dynamic personalities, driven by a desire to live life fully, missing nothing. They know that stars grow wild, like a field of daisies, somewhere high above and beyond the banal and the mundane. And even though their goals may be different, unless one of them had the Moon or Ascendent in a more financially cautious sign at birth, like Cancer, Scorpio or one of the three Earth Signs, they both believe in arriving at their destinations by traveling First Class, not just in a material sense but in every way. That may need some careful thought to be comprehended.

We can take the world others created or imagine a new world. Aries and Leo would rather imagine a new one into manifesting, maybe the kind they dreamed of when they were children. This may be it, they muse when they meet, or at least the start of that new world. There's no telling where it will lead . . but it won't be boring.

☆ ☆ ☆ ☆ ☆ ☆

ARIES *Woman* LEO *Man*

"How clever I am," he crowed rapturously, "oh, the cleverness of me!"

Wendy was shocked. "You conceit," she exclaimed. . . . "of course I did nothing!"

"You did a little," Peter said carelessly, and continued to dance.

A love affair between a Lion and a Ram, although it can be a warm and wonderful experience, will also produce frequent emotional storms — especially when they've frozen each other's considerable pride into icicles. But icicles melt quickly between two Fire Signs, and storms have a way of clearing the air, so that afterward, everything looks all fresh and green again.

It often starts like this: he promises to call her at five o' clock, then doesn't phone till midnight, and refuses to apologize. He tells her she can't spell, and she wears too much makeup. Then he tells her to shut up, and listen to him for a change. He does *what*?

Well, that slices it. She's had enough of his overbearing arrogance, and impulsively decides to toss him out of her life. Who needs him anyway, with his bossy Napoleon routine? *She* does.

With all her independent "I can take care of myself" airs, at last she's found someone who knows she can't, and who calls her bluff. It's no good telling him to "go get lost." That's just what he *won't* do. Later, she'll remember how his voice was warm and gentle when he finally called, never mind the lateness. She'll recall how affectionately he scolded her about the purple eye shadow, and spelling "cat" with two t's. Maybe he was only being tenderly protective instead of insufferably condescending and . . . . . . maybe she should forgive him. (She might as well. She's been conquered. Now she knows how Josephine felt, not to mention France.)

It won't be long until he's instructing her in all sorts of things she wasn't even aware she didn't know until he came along to point out her ignorance. What's more, she'll shock herself by blissfully basking in it. Of course, after the novelty wears off, she'll come down off the ceiling and top him a few times, just to keep the score from getting lopsided — and her Big Cat will discover how a Lion feels in a cage with a Lion tamer. First surprised, then resentful . . then outraged. But finally subdued. Or at least, finally willing to smooth the rough edges of his superiority complex. Actually, her fiery temperament is all right with him, as long as it doesn't reach the place where it interferes with — or outshines — his own. It never will. He's concerned over nothing, really. Since when did Mars ever outshine the Sun? Interfering with his own is another matter.

This is the powerfully magnetic 5-9 Sun Sign Pattern, and so, when these two Fire Signs see Venus together, the romantic scene is explosive, but it's also a blinding light turned on an enchanted garden. Maybe those old dreams he packed away aren't so impossible after all. They're *his* dreams, aren't they? That's enough to make her positive they'll come true — and Mars faith makes mountains fly! As for her domineering ways and flashing independence, these are only distress signals for someone to guide her in the right direction. Isn't that what Lions do best — organize other people's lives, and save them from their own mistakes? She's certainly a challenge, and when did a Leo ever run away from a challenge? She may sock him in his masculinity with some rough blows, but Lions aren't weaklings. He should just sock her right back (figuratively) and let her know that he's the one who whistles for taxis and things. After he directs her Mars energy into his own groove, he can relax — while she supplies all the fire he needs, when he needs it — and he *does* need it.

Since he's more practical and sensible (Leo is a Fixed Sign, remember), she'll sometimes accuse him of being pokey and stuffy. Since she has more instant vitality, sometimes he'll accuse her of wearing him out. Eventually, she'll loosen him up — and he'll slow her down — so it will come out even, and they'll both be ahead. Most of their quarrels will be instigated deliberately anyway, on a subconscious (occasionally conscious) level, for the pure pleasure of making up and reassuring themselves of each other's love. Reconciliations provide the repeated thrill of feeling the magic all over again. Their friends may wonder why they stay together, fighting the way they do, but *they*'ll know why.

For one thing, they don't spend all their time together in dispute. Influenced by the 5-9 vibration as they are, they will have many moments that will be marvelous and mad, merry and miraculous, full of lilacs and raindrops, druid dust, violets and enchanted carousels. Her genuine guileless-ness moves him strangely, touching a chord of response in his own idealistic heart. Her sparkling excitement is contagious, matching his own sunny enthusiasms. Aries is the symbolic Infant of the zodiac (as explained in the Twelve Mysteries of Love section in the front of this book); therefore her naivete and air of innocence stir some deep well of tenderness in him. He's compelled to protect this bright, brave spirit, who, like the real infant, hasn't the slightest notion how many yawning chasms lie in wait for her to stumble into . . in the darkness. He'll help her avoid them, affectionately, with his wiser, more mature judgement, for Leo is ahead of Aries on the karmic wheel of life.

She will, living up to the "infant essence" of her Sun Sign, stop demanding her needs, and lose her fear of falling with no one there to catch her, once she's experienced the warm security of the Lion's devotion. His strong arms will catch her if she falls, and he's clearly capable of meeting . . any needs . . she may have. And so, she relaxes, becomes calmer, more tranquil . . . gently soothed by the Lion's loyal lullaby of love. A Mars-ruled woman admires strength, of both the physical and the moral sort, and this man possesses it. She will place her trust in no other kind of male, however much she may struggle against submission.

Aries and Leo strike a powerful vibration of physical response in each other, which is intensified by constant emotional stimulation. Sexual expres-sion between them can be wonderfully healing, because each fulfills what the other requires of mating: passion, blended with affection. That's not as common a need as you may think. Most people desire — and are able to give — only one or the other, not both. The result could be a stirring of feelings they both thought were safely buried with the lost ideals of childhood. That's pretty heady stuff, the kind of happiness they'll pursue together at almost any cost in temporary tears or heartache . . . or punctured pride. But Leo won't pay the price of being possessed for it. He wants to roam the jungle, unfettered by the clanking chains of jealousy. So does she. Therefore, does the "freedom" bit work both ways?

It does not. She'll have to give him plenty of rope, while he'll permit her just about enough with which to hang herself. As frustrating as it is for the Aries woman to turn the other cheek to her Leo lover or husband, it's immeasurably more agonizing for the proud Lion to humble himself. Humility is a virtue he constantly preaches but nearly never practices. She'll have to be the one to forgive first, and try to understand. I wish her luck and courage. She'll need it.

Their sexual compatibility will not be without some sharp growing pains. A girl Ram has this strange quirk. She knows how small her chances are of finding a male virgin, but she comprehends this with her head. Her Mars-ruled heart has other ideas. Incredible though it may seem, she'd like to believe she's the first woman he's ever touched, whispered to or conquered sexually. Since romance is as natural as breathing to Leo males, she's indulging in a vain hope. When she prods him into admitting every passionate sigh in his past, with names, dates and places included, this fact will be driven home. All right, so he's made love to other women. She'll accept that, though it will be painful. (Rams always face unpleasant truths with courage, once they're recognized as inevitable.) But another shimmering Aries dream must yet be subjected to the cold, hard realities of human nature. It doesn't have to follow that he *enjoyed* it, does it? Perhaps he was seduced; maybe some vixen handcuffed him or tied him with ropes while he struggled desperately, and he still has nightmares about the ugliness of it all?

Now, there's no use expecting a Leo male to plead frigidity. He's too proud and honest. No, he wasn't tied to the bedpost with square knots, or handcuffed. (Remember, we're talking about romantic experiences before they met, *past tense*. There's no way she'll be able to forgive or forget a present or future tense infidelity, not after they've given themselves to each other, and made a commitment. It isn't that she *won't* forgive, she *can't*. That's the way Aries is.) Anyway, after she tricks him into relating his former affairs by touching his swollen vanity, he'll hasten to tell her that he didn't give his heart away to any of those girls, not until he found her. But she may not hear him. She'll be too busy picturing wild orgies. He doesn't really belong to her, as he said. It was all an illusion. Her knight-in-shining-armour has muddy feet; his white horse has turned into a splotchy, grey donkey.

It's this sort of shattered dream of misty purity that can destroy the sexual harmony between the Aries idealist and a Lion with a long romantic history behind him. *Her* past love life? That's different. It will be rationalized away by a dozen different excuses. *She* didn't enjoy it, you see. (I keep telling you that Rams are unintentionally selfish.)

There are two possible solutions. The first one is for her to grow up emotionally and realize that the Present, if it's strong and beautiful and good, cannot be soiled by Yesterday, which is already gone and forgotten. In light of the typical Mars temperament, however, that solution is highly unlikely. It's against her basic nature, unless she has a more detached and objective Moon Sign or Ascendent, like Gemini or Libra. (An Aquarian Moon or Ascendent will work too but may cause her to be *too* detached and objective to suit him, creating other problems.)

The best solution is for the Lion to tell her frequently and periodically about the negative reactions he had to his discarded past sexual experiences (till she feels safe from falling into the darkness of loneliness) — and then to enumerate all the aspects of his sexual fulfillment with her which are not only superior to the others but "firsts," between them alone. There's no need to explain here the meaning of the word "firsts." Any Aries-Leo couple will immediately understand.

Her frank admiration of his courage and confidence and wisdom arouses all the Leo male's masculinity (although she may also, at times, considerably dampen it with her other qualities). His firm refusal to be dominated brings out a latent femininity in her she never knew she possessed, and perhaps she didn't . . . . . until him. However, although she may submit to her Lion emotionally and sexually, she'll never give up her individuality and independence, not even for him. He needs large amounts of worship to feed his hungry ego, and to her worship is analogous to meekness, a quality she's never acquired. Leo will give her ample opportunity to cultivate it. She knows he's stronger than she is, and this turns her on. Yet, if he uses his strength to boss her around like an arrogant male chauvinist, it will turn her right off again. An Aries girl will never conform to any form of feudal feminine fiefdom. But she'd better take it easy if she wants to be liberated by this Lord and Master. When she demands her rights, he'll roar at her in frustration a Great and Mighty Truth: "I can only *permit* you to be my equal if you *first* acknowledge my superiority!" It shouldn't be difficult for an intelligent Aries girl to interpret such a command. It simply means that a proud Leo King, whose supreme sovereignty has been properly and duly recognized, will then have the confidence and power to place his Aries Queen on a throne as high as his own, and allow her to reign beside him. (She can wear the diamond tiara, but he'll hang on to the sceptre.)

She'll admire him, respect him and love him intensely. She will also remain quite fond of herself, and of doing her own thing — though she may permit him to show her how to do it. There will be moments when he drowns her enthusiasm by scolding away her hopes with Leonine practicality. There will be other times when she wounds his pride by interrupting him, or forgetting to ask his advice. Then he'll freeze her with his regal dignity, and she'll outrage him with her stormy anger. But when his icy aloofness melts, and her fury subsides, happiness will always return to these two. After the flames of indignation have flared and died away, the overwhelming need to run into each other's forgiving arms again will create the miracle of spring — eternal magic.

As with all 5-9 Sun Sign Pattern couples, the Ram and the Lion will discover that their devotion for each other spills over into a larger love and compassion, because their powerful trined Suns vibration is influenced by the benevolence of the 9th house ruler, Jupiter. Every 5-9 Sun Sign association in which the two people involved are really serious, feels Jupiter's beneficent rays, to some degree, in their relationship. When you really love someone all the way through, I mean love him (or her) so much that everything seems to be part of everything else, you understand better how everybody feels. You know how it is with people when they hurt, when they're lonely. Somehow, you want to share with them your own peace and joy. And in some manner, you find a way, together, to do this.

Love is a benediction to Aries and Leo because of what they see when they look deeply into each other's eyes. He sees a woman vulnerable enough to need his wisdom, yet independent enough to challenge and stimulate him. She sees a man gentle enough to treat her tenderly, yet strong enough to protect and conquer her. And they both see . . . . something else . . . . some mystery of Yesterday, some promise for Tomorrow . . . . something they can't define, accompanied by the music of memory. Between Aries and Leo, the chemistry is right. The moment they touch, they together make a wish on Venus in the morning sky, whole waiting galaxies of stars are watching in wonderous joy, and making a wish on *them* . . . in anticipation that the birth of love between these two might herald the long ago prophecies of Peace promised to the world . . . "when the lamb shall lie down with the Lion."

☆ ☆ ☆ ☆ ☆ ☆

ARIES *Man* LEO *Woman*

—◄●►—

. . . and we return to them as their mouths close,
and their arms fall to their sides. The pandemonium
above has ceased almost as suddenly as it
arose, passed like a fierce gust of wind; but they know
that in the passing it has determined their fate.

A Lioness is not easy to live with, and sometimes just plain impossible to handle. She can be proud, aloof, vain, self-centered and arrogant. She can also be a strong, vital, warm and generous woman, if her obvious superiority is recognized and respected. Although she never surrenders herself lightly, with an Aries man who's careful never to destroy her dignity, and who makes it clear how much he admires her, she will be unexpectedly docile. No one who knows her will believe it possible, because they've never seen her conform to anyone's wishes as willingly as she does to his.

Astrology practically guarantees harmony and happiness to this 5-9 Sun Sign Pattern April-August relationship, especially if the aspect between their luminaries is beneficent. In this case, the affair or marriage could nearly be made in Heaven. Even when the Sun-Moon aspect in their comparative horoscopes is unfavorable, these two will tolerate each other rather well. He won't mind her extravagance as much as a man born under one of the other Sun Signs would. In fact, he may encourage it. It quite probably matches his own. Of course, Leo women don't like to admit they're extravagant. They'll tell you they are very economical, and in a way, some of them are. Leos can be level-headed and practical regarding normal expenditures, but they seem to go into a trance when it comes to luxuries, and frequently are penny-wise and pound-foolish. The Aries man is usually both penny-foolish *and* pound-foolish. If either of them has a thrifty Moon Sign or Ascendent, all this may not apply, but even so, sooner or later the two of them will reveal their Sun Sign essence in gestures of generosity. They both love giving and receiving gifts.

Not too surprisingly, the Aries man who loves a Lioness will encourage her to live up to her birthright pride and dignity. A queenly attitude becomes her, he believes. (It also makes him seem like a real winner for having managed to capture her.) Although the Ram expects other females to wait on him and to exist solely for the purpose of gratifying his desires, he'll often display a softer side of his nature with this woman, be more considerate of her wishes. Perhaps he places her on a pedestal to win and keep her royal favors, but more likely the reason is that he honestly feels she deserves a bit of worship, because she's so very special . . . so very much like him(!).

One of the happiest marriages I know is between a Lioness and a Ram, Rosemary and Norman. For years, he cheerfully fixed her meals, kept the house in order and coddled her lovingly to make sure she got enough rest, while she was moving smoothly through medical school, then post-graduate work, finally becoming a successful psychiatrist. The experience served to mellow his Aries "me first" nature considerably, without making a dent in his masculinity. Because Norman cherishes his beautiful Lioness, she treats him with a gentle graciousness that leaves no doubt which one is Tarzan and which one is Jane in their marriage. When she's not working, Rosemary serves his meals; when she looks at him her brown eyes sparkle with real affection, and there is in her manner the quiet sweetness of a female who is completely fulfilled as a woman. He gazes at her with open admiration, even proudly permits her to be the center of attention when they have company; yet there's always the distinct impression that he is the man of the house.

It's not that these two don't have their share of disagreements. Psychiatrists are no more immune from occasional emotional tension than dentists are immune from a toothache. But between Fire Signs, a temporary clash of wills brings the spice of excitement .. and the much-to-be-desired lifting of spirits that comes with making up. An occasional quarrel keeps Aries and Leo from taking love for granted, which can be boring and uninspiring. These lovers have a basic need for periodic re-charging of their initial passion.

Aries men are always driving hard toward some goal, and there's a chance the Ram may be so intent on getting where he's going he may fail to praise her enough. When a Leo woman feels she's not being properly appreciated, she becomes cold, indifferent — and even lazy. She either neglects her femininity, taking no interest in her appearance (a sad and serious warning symptom of her inner agony), or she'll turn to the opposite reaction, placing undue concentration on glamour, and openly soliciting the attentions of other men. The Aries male who will accept his woman's flirtations or an actual affair with another man has not yet been born. The merest suggestion of infidelity will produce a wild scene of jealousy. In the long run, this may be helpful, if it causes him to realize he's been neglecting to pay her the romantic homage she'll always seek as long as she lives.

Actually, neither of these two can be said to be untouched by jealousy. Now and then, one may get the notion it might be "fun" to tease the other just a little by pretending an interest in another person. The resulting free-for-all between these two Fire Signs is usually about as "fun" as tickling an angry gorilla under the chin with a feather.

A Leo woman needs to be told frequently how much — and why — she is loved. Then she won't be so suspicious of the time he must spend away from her. The Ram who spoils his majestic mate won't be sorry. She may be somewhat demanding, but that's not as hard to live with as her disposition when she's neglected. When this woman fancies she's being ignored, she will begin to attach unreasonable importance to trifles. The very same reaction to being ignored can be expected from the Ram. He can, with enough provocation, imaginary or real, be almost childish in his demands, downright petulant with resentment when he thinks he's not being loved or noticed enough. Experiencing ingratitude will drive him into fiery anger — and her into frozen hurt. In both of them, the desire for adulation is over-emphasized, yet still a necessity for self-respect. When they don't find enough of it in the outside world, which they seldom do, they can give this valuable gift to each other, to make up for the lack of it elsewhere.

Sexually, they are unusually well mated. Their mutual instinct for uninhibited passion in lovemaking is tempered with their shared need for tender affection. Although they are both lovers, in the warmest sense of the word, they are also both idealists. A gentle kiss on the cheek is as important to her, and to him, as the more erotic expressions of sexual Oneness. The Aries man possesses within his nature an abundance of both sentiment and fire, which never fails to bring an answering response from the Lioness. What they are both searching for, when it comes to physical fulfillment, is the wild abandonment of Lady Chatterley and her lover, mixed with the poetic tenderness of Elizabeth Barrett and Robert Browning — in equal parts. The chances are much better that they'll find this rare emotional blend with each other than with most others. If anything disturbs their idyllic sexual relationship, it will be his resentment of her old flames. Old flames have a way of never dying out with a Leo woman. The coals still burn, years later, not because she wants to rekindle a discarded affair, but because she's reluctant to part with souvenirs of past worship and adoration. These memories never lose their luster for her.

If the Ram should come across any of her old love letters, which she may save and read periodically to feed her romantic hunger, he'll be nearly as hurt and furious as if he had caught her in an actual act of infidelity. He'll probably question her about her past loves reproachfully, whether she saved the mash notes or not. Since she's sure to brag a little, perhaps even exaggerate the whole thing, he'll lose his cherished illusion that he's the only male who ever came close to conquering her — and losing that illusion can seriously harm their sexual harmony. Aries must be first (and last) in the game of love, as in every other game he plays. He also likes to be first in getting attention at parties; therefore he may not ignore any females who glance at *him* with admiring interest. (Rams are not selfish, just thoughtless sometimes.) What happens then ? How can you ask ? Remember that the Lioness wants everyone to know she's adored by the man she has allowed to love her. He would be unwise to so humiliate her before others, however innocent his intent, because this woman will not tolerate such an affront to her dignity. She may be confident enough of her own charms to be certain that she's adored by her lover or husband, but it's important to her for *others* to be *equally* aware of this. Let him peel a grape for another woman in public, and he'll see his bright, sunny and affectionate mate transformed into a clawing cat before his eyes . . . or worse, into a marble statue of icy disapproval. Later, when they're alone, there will be an emotional explosion.

But they'll make up, almost before her tears have dried . . and there will be another reason for him to tell her how dear she is to him, and mean it — another chance for her to let him know how much she needs him — another chance for both of them to assure each other how shallow they find other people after experiencing the depth of their own kind of love and friendship.

For the Ram and the Lion are graced with this most desirable of all blessings from the gods — the ability to be friends, as well as lovers. They may take turns inflicting unintentional emotional hurt, but in every other way, they trust each other more than they trust anyone else. A disagreement always brings home this happy truth to them when it's over. That's the beautiful thing about quarrels between Aries and Leo, unlike quarrels between other Sun Signs. As the bitter chill in the air when you walk through winter winds makes the coming of spring a great miracle, the misery caused by hurt pride makes being happy together after almost losing each other even sweeter than before.

The impulsive, impetuous Ram will find a warm home in the heart of the Leo woman, and she will lionize her Aries mate. In return he'll bring to her the splendid gift of himself — *all* of himself — and that's something he never quite gave to anyone . . . . until he found her.

ARIES

Fire — Cardinal — Positive
Ruled by Mars
Symbol: The Ram
Day Forces — Masculine

VIRGO

Earth — Mutable — Negative
Ruled by Mercury (also by
the Planet Vulcan)
Symbol: The Virgin
Night Forces — Feminine

The **ARIES-VIRGO** *Relationship*

Indeed they were constantly bumping . . . if
they saw a cloud in front of them, the more
they tried to avoid it, the more certainly
did they bump into it.

Aries likes to generalize, hates to bother with details, and is bored by meticulous analysis. Virgo is meticulous, likes to analyze details, and abhors generalities. That gives you some idea of the distance between these two Sun Signs to begin with — and now that we've begun, here are a few more.

Rams initiate all their actions from pure feeling — they trust their emotions and are skeptical of undue practicality. Virgos are practical, they trust their mentality, and are skeptical of pure feelings and emotions. When Aries people are upset, they'll usually shout it from the rooftops and open up their grievances to air them out. When Virgos are upset, they keep it buried inside and shut up their grievances to gather the rust of resentment. Rams are careless of their physical health, yet they're seldom chronically ill. Virgos are extremely careful of their physical health, yet they frequently complain of assorted symptoms of illness. And that's only a partial list of their differences.

Both of them are usually quick to help others, although their motivations are somewhat different. Arians do it because it makes them feel good to be the cause of happiness, since it proves to them that they can pull off a minor miracle anytime the occasion arises. Virgos do it because it gives a Virgin the nervous twidgets to stand by and see confusion adding up to chaos, when a little clear thinking would, in their practical opinion, untangle all the snarls. It's instinctive for a Virgo to step in, take a nip and tuck here and there, then go on his or her way without either waiting for or desiring any thanks. Aries won't wait around too long for thanks either, but you'd better believe the Ram desires it. If it isn't forthcoming, Aries will be both hurt and angry, unlike Virgo, who doesn't really expect too much of people anyway, and is therefore capable of shrugging off ingratitude by chalking it up as just another one of the many imperfections of human nature.

It's true that both of them lean toward purity of purpose. Each wistfully longs for the beauty of the spirit and seeks a shining ideal. Aries and Virgo ride together on a mutual search for truth and loveliness, but when their snow-white steeds reach a fork in the road, they take off in different directions. The Rams blindly and instinctively believe they'll find what they're looking for, despite all disappointments and the apparent impossibility of success. Virgos have little or no hope of ever actually discovering the Holy Grail, and even if they did, you can be sure they would find a chip in it.

Still, regardless of all these split-offs in their personality patterns, the Ram and the Virgin, when their paths cross, can find a strange comfort in their relationship. If it's business, admiration and respect — and a mutual desire to help one another — will nearly always result from the association. If it's friendship, it will probably take a business twist somewhere along the way. In the family circle, there's also much warm satisfaction possible through this blending of the two divergent natures, influenced by the 6-8 Sun Sign Pattern vibration.

Aries and Virgo often confide things in each other they would never tell anyone else. They seem to sense that the mutual trust implied by intimate confession won't be violated — and it seldom is, though the Ram may find it hard to conceive of how the situation described by Virgo could ever have developed, considering his or her own outlook. Likewise, the Virgin will sincerely sympathize with the Ram's experiences, even while privately failing to comprehend why they were ever permitted to occur.

Yet, no matter how close Aries and Virgo may be, Aries will feel deeply Virgo's frown of displeasure when he (or she) is late for an appointment, goofs off, or becomes careless and irresponsible. It's never as easy for the Ram to enjoy work as it is for the Virgin. What Aries views as harmless procrastination, Virgo interprets as an almost sinful waste of valuable time. Of course, after office, study, or family obligations are properly attended to (all of which may take endless time and attention), when there are no guilty twinges because everything is nicely snuggled away in its own cubbyhole — the Virgins often lead rather interesting and, in rare cases, even shockingly unorthodox private lives, when they lose those compulsive worries.

Sooner or later, after these two have spent a reasonable amount of time together, the Rams will be sure to remind Virgo of his or her inclination toward unnecessary worry and receive a reply like, "What compulsive worries? I don't allow things to bother me to excess." Whereupon Aries is likely to retort, "Oh, no? How about the morning last week when you missed your daily shower because you couldn't find the Ivory Soap, and you won't use any other kind — spilled a drop of ink on your shoe, and found a fly in your soup at lunch? You had a splitting headache and nervous indigestion for days afterward."

The Virgo rejoinder probably will be, "That is somewhat exaggerated and incorrect. The indigestion lasted only three hours and forty-five minutes, and it was caused by that dreadful, greasy soup I ate, not by my nerves. The headache lasted sixty-five minutes — not several days — and was the result of my not getting enough sleep the night before, not from compulsive worries. I missed my shower, not because I couldn't find the particular bar of soap I always use, but because I was late for an appointment. As for the ink, naturally I was a little upset about ruining a twenty-two-dollar pair of shoes I've only worn for a couple of years. I can't afford to be as casual about money as you are."

That last remark is Virgo's tactful way of accusing Aries of being extravagant. Virgins are careful to maintain scrupulous politeness when they're annoyed, so their irritability is softened by their typical courtesy.

Because Virgos are so analytical and fond of clarity, Aries people are inclined to look on them as picky and cold. Far from being cold, however, Virgos are the most inwardly sentimental of all the Sun Signs. (The important word in that sentence is "inwardly." It causes all the misunderstandings.) Their very discrimination itself implies high ideals for things and people to live up to, and when they don't — well, anyone would be cranky once in a while, from being so constantly disillusioned. Virgos are frequently nervous around Aries people because the Virgins dislike being openly firm — and dealing with a Ram requires, at times, being openly firm. The Arian impulsiveness can cause Virgo to feel secretly inadequate because of being helpless to change a situation, so they'll sometimes try to cover the feeling with a judgmental attitude — a kind of silent disapproval. It doesn't really matter what kind it is. Any kind of disapproval will annoy Aries, even if it's only vaguely implied and not verbalized. It is, nevertheless, felt or sensed.

The typical Aries man or woman isn't looking for reasonable discussions or cool, sensible Virgo remarks about right and wrong, what's proper and practical, and what is not. Rams respond beautifully to generosity of spirit in others — and quite unpleasantly to stuffiness or criticism. Aries will often rebel and struggle for identity in a close association with a Virgo because he (or she) considers calm, rational talks a cold substitution for affectionate warmth, friendliness, and an open-hearted manner.

Yet, when there's a favorable aspect between the Sun and Moon in the charts, Aries and Virgo can grace one another with many mutual blessings. In an Aries-Virgo association where there is such a harmonious Luminary influence, the Ram may surprise himself (or herself) by following Virgo's quiet example and paying serious attention to Virgo's always well-meant and helpful advice. And the Virgins will surprise themselves too, by allowing the Rams to coax them into losing many of their inhibitions and dropping a few layers of their usually sedate behavior. All it really takes for this combination to blend smoothly is for each person to spend more time concentrating on the virtues of the other, rather than dwelling on the differences.

The clerk in the supermarket who frowns at the cash register and crankily scolds you for not taking your place in line is probably a Virgo. But the softly smiling, mild-mannered, and bright clerk who courteously answers your questions about where the soybean patties are kept and when the fresh melons will be available, and cheerfully helps you pick up the things that spilled from your cart is probably also a Virgo.

The customer who aggressively demands to be waited on immediately in a store, than leaves all the clothes hanging on a peg in the dressing room, after trying them on impatiently and deciding they all look dreadful — is probably an Aries. But the friendly, trusting person who will loan a stranded, out-of-town stranger ten dollars without even asking why it's needed is probably also an Aries.

The thing of which Virgo is seldom aware is that Aries senses unerringly whether the Virgin's concern over his or her welfare stems from genuine devotion, affection, and friendliness — or merely from a dutiful obligation. And when it stems from the latter, the Ram would just as soon try to manage alone as to accept help from someone whose true sympathy and heart isn't involved in the offer, however much he (or she) may need Virgo's assistance and advice.

As far apart as they seem to be at first glance, however, Aries and Virgo can stumble upon some happy surprises when they hike along together and take care to avoid the thistles, brambles, and thorns of disagreement. In the Ram, the Virgin can find someone really worthy of helping toward achievement, someone who will generously shower Virgo with a warmly enthusiastic and touching gratitude in return, someone who may even be able to unlock the little doors of those Virgo inhibitions and private longings. In the Virgin, the Rams can find the sincere appreciation they need — and a heart as honest and loyal as their own. Virgo can teach Aries to discover beauty in small things, to know the wisdom of waiting — to believe in the eventual success of patience. Aries can teach Virgos to discover and believe in themselves.

☆ ☆ ☆ ☆ ☆ ☆

ARIES *Woman* VIRGO *Man*

He was so much the humblest of them, indeed
he was the only humble one, that Wendy was
specially gentle with him.

When anyone describes an Aries girl as pushy, bossy, emotional, impulsive, impractical, and impossibly immature, the Virgo man who has loved her will nearly always disagree. He didn't find her to be any of those things.

To him, she was a lot of woman — perhaps too much woman for him to handle — but he remembers her as direct and honest, fresh and innocent. "She was generous with her time and money," he'll say. "She shared my idealism about love, taught me many things, and treated me gently and kindly. She may have been a little hurt or jealous occasionally, but she never created any really violent scenes. She was always willing to talk it over with me — to listen to reason. And when we made up after a minor quarrel, she made me believe in happiness all over again, like the very first time. She was gentle, affectionate — and eternally young."

When he finishes that nostalgic speech, his companion will probably ask, "Are you sure she was an Aries?"

Yes, she was an Aries, ruled by Mars, the planet of war and aggressive action. But an Aries woman surprisingly often will show her softer side, her hidden femininity, and her deep latent capacity for unselfish love to a Virgo. When she finds a man who's kind and considerate, a man who admires her courage and her bright mind, who seldom competes with her, who teaches her tenderly, sympathizes with her faults, and has faith in her dreams — she trusts him with her whole heart. Her hidden Aries insecurities and secret fears of inadequacy melt away, and with them, the need to assert herself forcefully, in the mistaken belief that to conquer is to win — in love, as in war. The necessity for combat disappears when the total love she seeks so desperately is given to her as a gift, purely and completely, as Virgo love is always given, with no strings attached.

Then why didn't it last? Virgo's instinctive fear of matrimony. Since the Aries woman is unable to see patience as a virtue and expects all her wishes to come true instantly, the second she says "abracadabra," she may lose heart (perhaps too soon), run away in tears, and eventually convince herself it was only a lovely friendship. Strangely enough, that's just what a broken love affair between these two frequently becomes after the scars have healed. Thanks to Virgo's inbred courtesy and gallantry, there are fewer bitter memories than those which usually linger after a shattered romance between other Sun Signs.

Still, sometimes love does last forever between Aries and Virgo, and when it does, Life can be very beautiful. There will be a few shadows scattered throughout the sunlight, however, and they'll have to be faced realistically, not emotionally. He's willing to face anything realistically, without self-deception, but she may need some help. (In fact, she may need a *lot* of help.) But if she should succeed, she deserves more credit than he does. A Virgo man finds it easy to analyze a situation, spot the flaws, reach a compromise, and clear away the confusion. He really doesn't deserve much praise for doing what is so instinctive, what comes so naturally to him. The Aries girl's natural reaction to a problem is to first slam it with a hammer, then butt against it with those Ram horns, hoping to demolish it. If that doesn't work, she's ready to sit down and discuss the pros and cons of it, but the pros may be all on her side — the cons on his. Therefore, if she can learn to face a misunderstanding with a cool temper and a rational mind, she deserves the kind of appreciation reserved for those who accomplish the nearly impossible.

All those memories of the girl Ram that the Virgo man we discussed before still retains in his neat mind were formed when their love was new. If the affair had lasted longer or developed into marriage, she may have seemed to him a trifle less like an angel. He might also have seemed to her a few inches shorter than a saint. Most of the squabbles between Aries and Virgo will blow hot and cold over his urge to criticize her. If he's truly analytical, he'll soon realize that, with her, he's safer when the wind blows hot than when it blows cold. As I've counseled repeatedly, there's more to fear from Aries ice than from Aries fire. The latter soon burns itself out. The former can shock the astrological novice, when the Aries woman stops crying "wolf" and cries "good-bye." Once she's gone she's not likely to look over her shoulder to yesterday. The freedom of today may be far more exciting to her than the fast-fading recollection of past heartache. It has been said that Rams never learn from burning themselves on a hot stove. They're always ready to touch it again. Perhaps. But not necessarily the same stove. That's worth remembering.

Back to the criticism. True, he has secret ways of convincing her that his criticisms don't mean she isn't loved. But loved or not, she won't be happy when the list of her shortcomings is longer than the list of her talents and virtues. If he wants a tranquil relationship with this woman, he'll learn to appreciate her taste and cleanliness in creating an attractive home, and refrain from peeking under the sink to see if she's polished the drain on the garbage disposal — or poking into the closet to see if she's scrubbed the shelves. She probably hasn't. Someone else can do all that. Like him. Or a maid.

She could also have a habit of spend now — pay later — which may bring on periodic spells of Virgo nervousness. Pouting in the corner, nagging, or hiding the credit cards won't work with Aries. The best solution is to let her get a job and squander her own money.

The combination of Aries and Virgo is a 6–8 Sun Sign Pattern. Among other things, this means that devotion, service, and working together will always be part of their relationship. It also means something which may come as a surprise to those who don't understand astrology — a strangely compelling sexual attraction. She represents sexual mystery to him. He represents to her the kind of sexual relationship she can trust. Somehow, despite the basic differences in their natures, these two may enjoy a rare compatibility of physical desire and expression. Perhaps it's born of the essential innocence and purity of intent the symbolic Infant and the symbolic Virgin bring, in an esoteric sense, to their lovemaking. Or it may be their mutual belief that sexual union is the ultimate blending of a man and woman's deepest yearnings, bringing their bodies, minds, and souls together in a singing unison of purpose and mutual tenderness. It could be this woman's directness, the simplicity of her approach to intimacy, that appeals to the Virgo man's innate honesty — or his unselfish consideration of her needs that touches her so tenderly — and the fact that his latent passion can be aroused only with someone who joins him in the desire to raise physical love to a higher level than a casual erotic encounter or a brief pleasure.

Whatever the reason, the sexual relationship between them is usually a strong force, often resulting in the kind of emotional peace and physical fulfillment that makes it easier for them to tolerate the differences and tensions in other areas of their togetherness. With Aries and Virgo, sex is a renewal of hope and rededication to each other. In most Aries-Virgo unions, the Virgo man will feel that the Aries female is all the woman he'll ever want or need. The enthusiasm of her spontaneous passion nearly always deepens his basic earthy instincts. But she may sometimes feel that *he's* not spontaneous or involved enough in passion, and she may lie awake beside him on more than one night, wondering to herself if this is all there is to love.

Somehow, she hoped it would be more like her daydreams, more stormy and wild and abandoned. She adores his gentleness and consideration, but she may wish occasionally he'd make her feel really truly conquered and overpowered — like Heathcliffe and Cathy on the moors.

The girl Ram must comprehend that the Virgo man she loves is frequently driven, by the combined forces of his foster ruler Mercury and his true, as yet undiscovered, ruling planet Vulcan, to commit himself to the mental gymnastics of the moment — and pursue a thought to its conclusion. When she accuses him of neglecting her at these times, he won't understand. His busy mind has been busy meditating on amoebas, splitting and popping into the air as they reproduce themselves. At a time like that, to be pulled back to the reality of man-woman love can annoy him. She'll resent his detachment, and her instinctive urge to employ the fiery Mars method of *demanding* that he pay attention to her can create some unpleasant scenes between them. He'll intensely dislike being boxed in by her insistence on direct answers. Especially when he's immersed in one of his frequent spells of deep-blue depression and futility.

At these times, the only way to handle him is to pretend she doesn't even notice his gloom and sadness. She should make a conscious effort to remain cheerful herself, totally curb her own sensitivity to neglect — and concentrate all her concern and sympathy toward *him*, not herself. She should suggest happy things for the two of them to do . . . and talk about positive plans for the future. But quietly and sparingly — not in a running streak of conversation, which will only drive him deeper into mental seclusion. He doesn't need chattering when he's worried and won't tell her what it is that's troubling him. He needs to know she's there, that's all . . . that she's somewhere near, singing or humming . . . confidently going about her business in the background. It gives him a feeling of security.

Even if he turns a deaf ear toward her suggestions to go somewhere and refuses to budge under her gentle urging to change the scene, he'll gradually come around if she doesn't press him. Once is enough for any suggestion. If he doesn't pick up on it . . . wait for a while. The one thing he doesn't need during these Virgo worry sessions is the third degree . . . or the added burden of seeing the woman he loves in tears because his silence and detachment have caused her to feel neglected, and therefore sorry for herself. Self-pity is the very worst thing the girl Ram can allow herself to indulge in when her Virgo man has temporarily retreated from her, mentally and emotionally. Patience, gentleness, tenderness, and just being there if he should need her . . . these are the ingredients of the subtle alchemy guaranteed to bring the twinkling stars back to shine again in his clear, calm Virgo eyes.

She should stop finding fault with him (Aries is quick to imitate, and may pick up the Virgo critical syndrome after a time) and instead count her blessings. This man will seldom interfere with her freedom by imposing unnecessary restraints and retrictions on her activities. (This is wise of him, because she'd do her own thing anyway, through sheer resentment at being told how to behave, where to go, and what time to return.) But there's no denying that the sometimes sharp and satirical words of the Virgo male can deeply wound this woman in the sensitive area of her self-confidence. Also, he may not be as demonstrative as she'd like him to be — not in relation to their sexual intimacy, but in their day-to-day communication and contact.

Demonstrative affection does not flow easily with Virgo and may have to be deliberately cultivated if he wants to keep her, because the tangible expressions of devotion (the small touching things, such as bear hugs, a kiss on the cheek, a meaningful wink across the room, or an unexpected tight handclasp) are a deep-seated need within her. If these constant reassurances of love are missing from their relationship, her belligerence and defiance will grow in direct proportion to the degree of her emotional starvation.

The Aries girl is gregarious, affectionate, and demonstrative. It hurts and worries her when the man she loves makes it clear he'd rather be busy doing other things without her now and then. But he needs many more moments alone than most other men, for without them, his Virgo crankiness, nervousness, and irritability can increase. Although it won't be easy for the girl Ram to really understand her Virgo man's frequent need for privacy and solitude, she can comfort herself with the thought that this man is far less likely than any other Sun Sign to hurt her by flirting with another woman when he's not with her. Like Aries, Virgo usually falls in love for keeps. Yes, I know love that lasts forever is rare enough to be a miracle. But if you *expect* a miracle, you'll find it . . . . . . every time.

☆ ☆ ☆ ☆ ☆ ☆

ARIES *Man* VIRGO *Woman*

◀━━━━━◆◀▶▶━━━━━▶

"Oh, say you're pleased," cried Nibs . . . . .

*He was a lovely boy, clad in skeleton leaves and
the juices that ooze out of trees; but the
most entrancing thing about him was that he had
all his first teeth. When he saw that she was
a grown-up, he gnashed the little pearls at her.*

It's sad, but often true. An Aries man will at some time in his relationship with a Virgo woman feel the need to prove to her that his ideas and ideals are sensible, that he is emotionally mature — and in general, he will try to arouse her enthusiasm for his plans, his ambitions, and his feelings.

It's not that she isn't pleased, but her response, if she's a typical Virgin, may leave him with a vague sense that she somehow disapproves of what he's been trying to tell her. She probably does. She may wholeheartedly support most of what he's projecting and imagining, but there will nearly always be some small portion of his narrative she feels is off-center, or not well enough thought out and constructed. Virgos are like that. They spot the weak links in the chain and warn you about them before the chain breaks. We all really ought to be grateful to them for this neat habit they have of pointing out flaws before it's too late, so the bottom line and the end result of every venture will be more perfectly successful. Most people *are* properly grateful for Virgo's ability to bring calm order out of chaotic disorder. Not the Ram. He'll fiercely resent her lack of total commitment to his causes, his emotions, his outrages, his dreams, and his superiority. After a time, he may angrily accuse her of having no sensitivity and no imagination.

He's very wrong. This girl possesses a lovely, sensitive imagination. Other children may eat "Chicken and Stars" soup for years without a single comment, but when *she* was a little girl, she would always delightedly exclaim (quietly, shyly, to herself, when no one could hear) "Oh, just see the little stars floating in my soup!" When someone gave her ginger ale in a cut-glass goblet one morning, and it caught the sunlight, she cried out (within) "Oh, how perfectly marvelous! I have a rainbow in my ginger bubbles!"

Just because she whispered these marvels only to her secret make-believe best friend — and seldom or never exclaimed them aloud, she grew up with everyone around her thinking she was terribly prosaic and unimaginative — because she didn't flaunt her brilliant mind and private thoughts. Then *he* came along, the handsome, dashing Ram, to make her feel she was a very special person. It warmed her cool Virgin heart, and made her more sure of herself than she had ever been before. Now here he is, like all the others, accusing her of having no imagination. Insensitive? Perhaps he's the one who's insensitive.

This woman's inner world may not be peopled with imaginary faerie creatures every single moment of the day. Nevertheless, it's a beautiful land of wonder, because she sees loveliness in the small and ordinary things. Once the Aries man who cherishes her truly comprehends this — stops yelling at her and putting her down — he can persuade her to open the locked trunk of her wistful yearnings and secret fancies and expose them to the warm sunbeams of loving affection — encourage her to bring her fears out into the fresh air, instead of holding hurt inside, where it may grow into migraine headaches and all manner of aches and pains and physical ills. Yes, she will learn much of value from him.

He can learn a lot from her too. Like thoughtful consideration for others — the peace and happiness of serving (instead of being served). This she demonstrates nearly every day they're together. Yet he seldom notices. He doesn't see her gentle smile when he silently wishes for a magic elf to help him with something he's doing physically or some problem he's pondering mentally. She glides into the confusion so softly, he's hardly aware of her presence . . . . . and helps to make things come out right, even without being asked. Also without expecting to be praised. She would glow under his gratitude, but she won't demand it of him. She's only doing what comes naturally to Virgo when she's helping, so praise is not her aim, since ego and self-aggrandizement are not her motives. Still, it wouldn't hurt him to notice — and perhaps say "thank you, darling" now and then. He might even say "thank you for loving me". . . because the pure love of a Virgo woman is a priceless gift, never given casually.

A Virgo woman is so nice to come home to when she *likes* herself, is *being* herself — and allowing the Ram she loves to be *him*self. If she's a typical Virgin, she's unobtrusive (unobtrusive compared to Aries!), yet bright and pleasant, a joy to be around. She's quiet and courteous and she needs lots of affection (for which she'll never ask, any more than she asks for gratitude). She's sometimes critical, yes, but ordinarily she's at least polite while she's hair-splitting and nit-picking.

The Aries man who loves this intelligent feminine creature might comfort her when she's blue and discouraged over some small mistake she's made (Virgos tend strongly toward self-chastisement) by reminding her that even the gentle Nazarene momentarily made the mistake of losing his wonted "perfect" control when he lashed the money changers in the temple. Then too, there are the "lost years," during which the humble carpenter isn't mentioned in the scriptures (quite a number of them, as a matter of fact). The Ram might tell his worried Virgo lady it's probably that, during those "lost years," Jesus more than once nailed the wrong boards together in the carpentry shop of his father, Joseph . . . . . miscalculated his taxes, which were due to be paid to Caesar's Internal Revenue (or didn't make it to Bethlehem in time to pay them on the deadline date), ripped his robe on a sharp rock . . . . . stubbed his toe . . . was briefly cranky with Mary Magdalene . . . . and committed who knows how many other miscellaneous minor goofs? Thanks to the uptight censors of the scriptures, no one does. But one can make a spiritually educated guess. And who is she, the Ram can then ask her, to aspire to a more flawless record of human behavior than that of such a simple, humble man as Jesus of Nazareth?

It may help to enlighten the Virgo woman to how unnecessary most of her worries about her failures really are. And help her to see that perfection is not the requirement for self-acceptance she so often believes it to be.

There's frequently a misty enchantment inherent in the physical love between the Aries man and the Virgo woman. These two are rather likely to be among the few people still left who are still sexually unpolluted by the explicit sex being flaunted in everyone's faces, whether they like it or not.

The Ram is a confirmed idealist (and a super-jealous one besides), whereas the female Virgin is normally turned off by sexual or any other kind of vulgarity and cheapness. She also would prefer him not to leave the catsup bottle on the dining-room table. Discrimination flashes its sparkles into many facets of human existence, from sex to catsup bottles to messy closets and untidy drawers — not to mention sloppy thinking and a dull intellect. Her own thinking is never sloppy, her own intellect never dull.

Their lovemaking will reflect their mutual idealism and subconscious search for purity and innocence. This doesn't mean the physical aspect of love between them will lack passion. The male Ram, ruled as he is by Mars, is passion personified. Yet, he's also touchingly affectionate, usually mindful of the small things related to sexual unity — and she will respond to this quality in him with genuine joy. But she must be careful not to criticize his romantic techniques or allow her innate coolness of approach to make ashes of the flaming sort of sexual expression he offers her so trustingly. Conversely, he must be careful not to offend her sense of delicacy by always making sure that tenderness and gentleness are a part of their union. It would also help if he didn't pout or feel so wounded those times when she'd rather demonstrate her love for him in ways other than physical. The vitality of his sexual stamina may often exceed hers — and when it does, he should remind himself that patience is a virtue which brings its own reward — in addition to the reward of her return to being a warm, loving woman.

He must simply give her time to rest awhile and refresh her desires. Also, he should know that her enthusiasm for making love will always be somewhat diluted in direct ratio to the vexing worries and problems she's encountered throughout the hours preceding his need that she surrender herself to him. Even at best, Virgos never surrender their whole selves to love. Aries men do. And this is a basic difference between them which will need to be handled with care.

Despite their natural affinity in matters romantic, these two could allow their romance to gradually take the form of a less emotionally demanding mutual mental respect. There's certainly nothing wrong with mutual mental respect, but it needs a few more brilliant facets to set it off — like mutual emotional involvement and vibrancy. Still, rarely is even a romantically frustrated Virgo or Arian unfaithful. Not without monumental cause. It's equally rare, if they're typical of their Sun Signs, for either to leave or desert the other, even under extreme provocation — once they've committed themselves to devotion. For to Virgo, devotion is first analyzed, then defined as more responsibility than sentiment. Consequently, when a Virgo decides to desert such a "responsibility," you can be sure the decision to "cut out" was motivated by personal injury of such immeasurable depth it decreed either a final solution of escape or actual mental breakdown. Virgos have little or no immunity to long-continued mental and emotional pressures.

The Aries man is reluctant to admit he's been wrong about a relationship for the exact opposite reason than that of Virgo. He keeps trying, not because of "responsibility," as she does, but because of "sentiment." It's difficult for the Ram to imagine he could have been mistaken about love, once he's believed in it with all his heart. This man puts all of himself into every venture, dedicates himself with fiery intent to every challenge — and love is no different from the rest. Could Romeo ever stop loving Juliet, or Juliet ever grow tired of Romeo? Of course not. That's more or less the way he sees it. He forgets that both these medieval lovers died before they were twenty, and had they lived, they would probably have experienced their share of misunderstandings and disagreements, being only human. Strangely, he's as much a perfectionist about love as his Virgo woman is about everything *but* love.

It's as though she *expected* love to have flaws, therefore isn't terribly surprised when the flaws appear. It's only the other areas of life where she's repeatedly disillusioned to find things less than flawless. With him it's just the opposite. Life's major disappointments he can shrug off, but of "love" he demands perfection. Somewhere in between their oddly transposed views, these two should be able to find a basis for understanding each other.

When serious trouble arises in this relationship, the tie is usually severed by the slashing scissors of unbearable *outside* pressures of one kind or another, not by a decline of their love. Sometimes it's her near fanatical obsession with the obligations of a career or her duties in the home. Sometimes it's his fierce ambition and single-minded purpose that causes him to place her last — after his great goal in life — his crusade for self-identification. Then she may feel an irresistible compulsion to interfere by criticizing his attitudes — either privately or publicly. This first frustrates, then humiliates, and finally angers him into a Mars-like rage of resentment, which in turn freezes her desire to help him into icy detachment and an almost smug satisfaction at his misery. Then something will have to give—fast! Otherwise, their mutual need for reciprocated affection from each other will soon become secondary to their mutual need for self-respect — and they'll part, each to seek alone the peace of mind they couldn't find together.

That's the dark side. The bright side is that this man and woman can mend the silver cord that links them together each time it breaks — with the magical healing power of love. But only when he defines love as unselfishness and an awareness of her needs — only when she defines love as spontaneous trust and enthusiasm for his dreams. Once these two get their definitions straight, their love can last . . . . . . and the tiny cracks they mended with mutual consideration won't even show. Unless the Virgin keeps inspecting it with a magnifying glass — or the Ram impulsively, carelessly shatters it again. Love is like a precious work of art, fragile and delicate . . . much lovelier and far more valuable when it's weathered the years.

☆ ☆ ☆ ☆ ☆ ☆

ARIES

Fire — Cardinal — Positive
Ruled by Mars
Symbol: The Ram
Day Forces — Masculine

LIBRA

Air — Cardinal — Positive
Ruled by Venus
Symbol: The Scales
Day Forces — Masculine

The **ARIES-LIBRA** *Relationship*

So with occasional tiffs, but on the whole
rollicking, they drew near the Neverland; for
after many moons they did reach it, and what
is more, they had been going pretty straight
all the time.

The Libra people who read this chapter may claim I haven't been fair with them, since I'm an Aries myself. (They're always claiming somebody hasn't been fair with them.) Are reckless Rams envious of the marvelous tranquility of the Venus-ruled people when their Libra Scales are perfectly balanced, as they sometimes are? No. Rams are not envious of Libran tranquility, even though astrology insists they should be, the two Sun Signs being opposed to one another on the karmic wheel of Life, therefore each lacking what the other possesses. At least, the typical Arian will never openly admit that he or she is envious of Libra, however much the Rams would secretly like to imitate Libra's lovely calm and tranquil equilibrium. The derivation of the word "equilibrium" is the word "libra." Or the opposite. Either way, the word and the Sun Sign are linked. Nothing is more important to a Libran than equilibrium. They do so hate to lose it. Nonetheless, they frequently do.

One of the times the Ram secretly envies the Libran is when an Aries person makes a swift Mars-like decision, then is forced to face the inevitable opposition Libra-type emotional trauma that always follows. Did I do right or wrong? Should I have said "yes" or "no"? — after it's already too late to change anything. Believe me, the Arian indecision *after* the fact is more painful than the indecision *before* the fact from which Librans suffer — and certainly not as constructive.

No one can be more charming, intelligent, and optimistic than Librans who have a firm grip on their Scales. They're simply great at getting groups of people to blend harmoniously and smoothing over tensions (when they're not personally involved). Aries men and women admire and respect Libra for the Venus-type virtues they themselves lack. But Aries is also Libra's opposition Sun Sign, and so Libra must admire and respect the Mars-type virtues too. Does that sound like an order?

One of the most noticeable differences between Aries and Libra is that the simplest Aries statement somehow comes out sounding like a demand. Even when Rams ask a question, it often seems more like they're telling you than asking you. On the other hand, (we must be careful to look at both sides, since we're dealing with the Scales) — on the other hand, when the Venus-ruled Librans ask a question or make a statement, they manage to charm you right out of your good sense, so you're left vulnerable and unable to defend yourself.

It doesn't matter whether the Libran asks, "Why are you so consistently ignorant, dear?" — or remarks, "What you're doing reveals your complete lack of breeding" — it will evoke a musical tone reminiscent of "The Lost Chord." Those bunny-tail-soft Venus voices create images of maple syrup being poured into bowls of honey. That's why Libra can argue for hours with Aries and leave the impression it was the Ram who was being impossibly rude and wrongheaded, in comparison to Libra's nice, sensible logic. Now what is that, if it isn't unfair? No wonder Librans make fabulous lawyers, the kind who win all the verbal debates in the courtroom before the jury. If Libran lawyers can twist tough judges around their fingers and woo an indifferent panel of jurors to their side, you can imagine what happens in a battle of wits between Libra and the impulsive, quick-tempered, emotional Ram. No contest.

Perhaps Libra will accuse the Rams of being too hasty to make a sound judgment, of rushing in rashly, with no thought of possible consequences — then sweetly remind them of the beauty of the symbol of the Lady Justice with her Scales balanced in perfect equilibrium.

ARIES: "Yes, but she's wearing a blindfold, so how can she see right from wrong?"
LIBRA: "The blindfold is only there to protect her from prejudice, dear."

Then Aries may ask Libra if he (or she) has ever heard the fable about the ass that starved to death because it couldn't make up its mind which field of clover to eat first? Finally, the Libra man or woman will smile — and once the Ram is under the influence of that dazzling Venus aura, the Aries fire sputters out. It's difficult for the friendly, open Rams to resist a smile and a kind word, and they're too naive to suspect Libra of using charm as a weapon against them. Nevertheless, Libra does.

Most of the time in this relationship, the Libran will remain cool and stable. But when the Aries aggressiveness becomes intolerable, it can have the same effect upon this normally gentle person as the accumulation of tension has in the sky — a thunderstorm. Every instinct of Libra recoils from unpleasant confrontation, but when he (or she) feels seriously threatened, a firm, sometimes even impulsive, action will be taken, if only for the purpose of regaining calm. This may seem a little confusing, but you'll have to apply Libra logic if you want to straighten it out. The best I can do is tell you that, with Libra, the end always justifies the means. On that point, at least, most Rams will agree.

Actually, with the respect always felt for one's opposite Sun Sign, Rams will, however reluctantly, look up to the Libran judgment and privately wish they possessed it. Aries is aware that Libra is fair and logical, and a clear thinker. The Aries man or woman knows that Libra decisions are nearly always right, but a Ram can get a little jumpy, sitting around watching Libra make them. The word "decision" itself causes most Librans to break out in a rash. It doesn't bother Aries. A decision has to be made? Great. Toss a coin or a feather — or just do what you instinctively feel is right, then forget it. That's the Aries motto. Dive right in. (If there's no water in the pool, Rams scrape their chins in the cement, but they'll just stick on a Band-Aid, and be on their enthusiastic ways again.) It's not that Aries doesn't see the potential value in the nice, safe "middle-road" Libra wears down into a ditch, but a Ram would rather take a chance now and then on the path to the right or the fork to the left — and see what happens. It's exciting. And that (to look at the other side) is one of the qualities Libra admires in the opposite Sun Sign of Aries. It works both ways.

If you want to test people's grasp of astrological knowledge, ask them which one of these two Sun Signs has the most violent temper. Before you jump to any hasty conclusions, *think*. Libra is Air and Aries is Fire. Fire *seems* more volatile and violent than Air, but Libra is the Cardinal of the three Air Signs — and Cardinal means "leader," among other things. Aries is also Cardinal, yet you must remember that in Nature air is not as innocent an element as it seems when it becomes aggressive. Have you ever watched a nice, calm, "nonviolent" tornado, cyclone, or hurricane? The quiet steam, composed of moist "air," that drifts out of the spout of a teakettle can be turned into a force powerful enough to rip up the ground for miles around.

Also consider that the chief constituent of air is nitrogen. Nitrogen may be an inert gas, but it's the principle reason why explosives explode. So — which one has the most dangerous temper, Aries or Libra ? You decide. (But don't ask Libra to decide, if you're in a hurry for an answer.) I didn't say which one is the noisiest when angry. I said the most dangerous. If you study this paragraph carefully, you'll see why people are puzzled when most astrology books, referring to the Venus rulership of Libra, describe all Librans as peaceful, gentle, beautiful, sweet, and calm. They are all those things — half the time. And I suppose we must confess that Aries could profit by trying to imitate some of those positive Libra personality patterns.

These two will at times argue instinctively, but in all fairness, when a conflict between a Libran and a Ram develops, the object of the quarrel to Libra is (usually) to win and achieve eventual peace and justice. The object of most quarrels to Arians is (usually) to win and prove they're right (even when they're wrong) to satisfy the considerable Mars ego.

An association between Aries and Libra, influenced by the 7-7 Sun Sign Pattern, is in most cases a fortunate experience for both. But if there's a negative Sun-Moon aspect between their horoscopes, there can be some fiery and windy periods of tension and conflict. With a harmonious Luminary exchange, Libra will provide a rich atmosphere of freedom of thought and action that will richly nourish the self-confidence of the Rams. The typical Libran will usually treat Aries with gentleness, seldom with tyranny or harsh words — and this is an attitude designed to bring out the very best in the Mars nature, to encourage the finest qualities of the Ram to flower. Instead of trying to force Aries into any particular pattern of behavior, Libra will more often recognize the Arian individuality and respect it.

Under the natural instinct to imitate the opposite Sun Sign, a Ram will frequently discover that a relationship with a Libran friend, relative, business associate, lover, or mate leaves him (or her) with the Mars courage and intense drive intact, but softened into a more tolerant and balanced Venus pattern. Conversely, the Libran man, woman, or child will respond to the Arian friend, relative, business associate, lover, or mate by finding his (or her) indecision gradually turning into a firmer purpose, inspired by the Aries ambition into higher achievement, on both a personal and a public level. As with all 7-7 vibrations, this combination works best when it's composed of two members of the opposite sex. With a Libran and a Ram of the same sex, a recurring sense of envy, resentment, and competition will often trouble the relationship (unless the Suns, Moons, and Ascendents of each are in friendly aspect in the two nativities).

The Ram will have to try to understand the Libra's very real need to conserve his or her energy and not waste it unnecessarily, as Aries is often driven to do with Mars energy. It's Libra's way of maintaining physical and emotional poise — not laziness. When the Ram sincerely tries to see both sides of any disagreement between them and makes a genuine effort to sympathize with the Libran Venus nature, the Libra man or woman will return the favor with much affection and cheerful encouragement, which will considerably lift the Aries spirit. Librans would much rather be happy and pleasant than cranky and argumentative, if Aries will only play fair with them.

Someone once remarked that Librans are the positive, living proof of reincarnation, because nobody could become that impossible in just one lifetime. Present a Libran with this theory, and the reply will be, "Oh, I've heard that about Aries people, but not Libra. Isn't Libra symbolized by the Scales of Justice and Truth? I don't see anything "impossible" in trying to be reasonable. On the other hand, Aries is a *most* unreasonable sign, and I think . . . ." A smart Ram, at that point, will offer the Libra man or woman a slice of cheese cake. He (or she) will dimple, all smiles and sweetness again (since Librans love sweets), and the argument will be over. It's just as well, the Ram couldn't have won it anyway. Besides, losing an argument with Libra is usually beneficial in the long run, because the Venus judgment is nearly always right. By the time it's so endlessly weighed and measured and balanced — and discussed and debated — it certainly *ought* to be.

☆ ☆ ☆ ☆ ☆ ☆

ARIES *Woman* LIBRA *Man*

"Wendy," he continued, in a voice no woman
has ever been able to resist . . "Wendy, one
girl is worth twenty boys." . . . .

"I think it's perfectly sweet of you," she
declared. She also said she would give him
a kiss if he liked.

As I've mentioned elsewhere in this chapter, Libra and Aries are opposite each other in the karmic wheel of Life. The astrological rule is that you're strongly attracted to the opposite sex of your opposite Sun Sign, but normally don't get along too well with the same sex of that sign. It would seem then, that the Aries woman and Libra man would be natural lovers, destined to live happily ever after.

Natural lovers they are, because the chemistry is right. Destined to live happily ever after they may not be, unless there's a harmonious Sun-Moon relationship between them, in which case they could remain sweethearts for a lifetime, the choice being up to them. Otherwise, with a discordant Sun-Moon aspect in their mutual charts, it could be touch and go. They may touch — tenderly — but it won't be long until they go — in opposite directions — putting them right back where they started: opposed.

It's a waste of time for astrologers to keep mentioning the Libra man's fatal charm for women. He's been practicing it, with instant success, since he was thirteen (or younger), and his reaction to flattery is simply to flash that dimpled, Libra smile and murmur, "Tell me all about it, honey." All right, so he's aware of the blessings of his Venus birthright. He may not be as aware that all that charm can be a curse when he's mixed up with an Aries female. (No one ever gets involved with an Aries — they get mixed up.)

The long line of women who cue up behind him everywhere he goes will turn an Aries girl who's been a gentle lamb into a Dragon Lady, with fire flaming from her ears. Mars jealousy is often irrational, and it does cramp his Venus style. Still, before he decides to leave her because she's spoiling all his fun, the Libra man might meditate on the word "love." The longer it's stored up inside and allowed to increase in depth, the more powerful and satisfying an emotion it can be. (Read *The French Lieutenant's Woman* for proof.) When love is restrained, then given fully at a special moment, with a very special person, it can bring spriritual peace, along with physical ecstasy. Falling in love with love, and getting married for the sake of marriage, are common Libra mistakes. She can be lovely and desirable, but if she's not bright enough to argue with him and challenge him, his fine Libra mind will get rusty. There's no chance of that with an Aries girl. She'll provide him with all the arguments he could possibly use — and enough mental challenges to last for several lifetimes.

When the Libra man gets restless and wants to roam — alone and free — where he can once more accept the favors of a harem of females, the Aries woman probably won't ask him shyly why he's leaving. She's more likely to shout, "Where do you think you're going, Charlie?" He'll tell her he's off to find another seashell, because the shore is full of them. She might remind him then, that seashells are empty. Instead of throwing an emotional tantrum (which may frighten him into splitting so fast he forgets to take along his classical tape cassettes and his favorite baby-blue angora bathrobe), she'd stand a better chance of winning (which is what all Rams want to do all the time) if she curbs her Mars temper and uses his own Libra logic as a weapon. Which is only fair, since he's always using it against her.

"Look, darling, Life is more than one long party of wine, women, and song. While you're getting high on a steady flow of casual affairs, remember that after you pour all the wine out of a flask, you have left only an empty bottle. Then the party's over. Of course, you can always fill it up again from your inexhaustible source, can't you sweetheart? Or is your capacity to love *really* inexhaustible? Why don't you turn some of those romantic urges you express so well (this works better if she's wearing his baby-blue bathrobe — especially this next part) into other creative channels, like art, music, writing, or acting? I could help you. I have a brain equally as brilliant as yours — even though our bodies are made differently — because you're a man and I'm a woman."

The last reminder is a necessity. When a Libra male is led into thinking about the differences between the sexes, he's more or less helpless. Not that the typical Aries woman will have the patience to accept the foregoing advice. She's more likely to yell at him to "Leave! Who needs you anyway!" — push him out the door — slam it — lock it — toss his tapes and bathrobe out the window — and then sit up all night crying in frustrated anger and regret. But I thought I'd throw it in anyway, for those Aries girls who think they are emotionally mature enough to cool it with this man. It's really the only way with Libra. Fairness, logic, and reason. No skyrockets. They disturb his sense of harmony and topple his equilibrium, which is always dangerously seesawing at best. Besides, if you read the section just before this, you'll recall that Air Signs can be goaded into tornado behavior that could make even a Ram run for shelter.

There are so many good things about this blend of Air and Fire between Aries and Libra, it's a shame for them to spend their time bickering. The typical Aries woman isn't looking for a muscle man. She wants a lover whose mental muscles have biceps. The Libra man's mind does. He'll stimulate and challenge her mentally and emotionally. All she needs to do is choose a subject, and he'll have a thousand and one things to say about it, pro and con. Since just a touch of controversy intrigues her, she'll honestly enjoy the debates they have, as long as they both play by the rules and refrain from punching each other in their complexes or tramping on one another's delicate and sensitive Achilles' heels. He'll find this an easier counsel to accept than she will. Tact and courtesy come naturally to Libra, but such consideration for the other person comes hard to Aries.

This woman isn't basically selfish — she's thoughtless. She truly never means to be rude or unkind, and certainly not toward the man she loves. She simply doesn't think or count to ten before she speaks her mind. And her mind can be quite opinionated. Don't forget that Aries is the Sun Sign of the benevolent dictator, regarding both sexes. Benevolent dictators are genuinely concerned about people, compassionate, generous, and devoted to the cause of everyone's welfare. But they don't bother to ask the people they're so loyally championing what it is *they* might want. Never mind. Like the benevolent dictator, no matter what the people want, Aries will see that they get it — because Aries knows what's best for them better than they do.

Warmth and arrogance make a frustrating blend, but all Fire Signs possess the combination, making their friends, relatives, and lovers love them and want to strangle them by turns.

When someone points out to a girl Ram that she's being unreasonable and impulsive — and the pointing out is done with tact, gentleness, and affection, she'll never fail to listen, quickly see the error of her ways (she does everything quickly), and try hard to please by making sweeping changes in her original views. But when she's ordered or forced to halt along some mistaken course she's chosen, there's no way she'll give in. That's too much like retreat and Aries never, but positively never, retreats. Mars, the planet of war itself — retreat? It will never happen. Since Mars is her ruler and influences all her motivations, strategy, and behavior, you really can't expect this lady to accept dominance or harsh criticism in a docile manner. If anyone can turn the female Ram into a gentle lamb (besides Leo — and sometimes Gemini, Sag, and Aquarius), it's a Libra man. He'll gently correct her, try to make her see her mistakes in an affectionate and tender way. And nine times out of ten it will work like a charm. The tenth time he should leave well enough alone and consider himself fortunate. You can't win them all. The trouble is that Libra would *like* to win them all — every debate, discussion, argument, dispute, and disagreement. So would Aries. So unless one of them accepts defeat graciously at least part of the time, there's never going to be peace in this relationship — and peace is what the Libra man needs as desperately as the Aries woman he loves needs excitement.

She would profit by trying to give him the peace he needs, because some of it would then drape its soft clouds over her too, softening her disappointments and calming her fears of rejection. He'll likewise profit by trying to give her the excitement she needs, because it will shake him from his spells of Libra lethargy and keep his Scales swinging in balance, instead of dipping one way or the other and getting stuck there.

The Libra man's unconquerable optimism (when his Scales aren't in a down-swing mood of fretting futilely) will strike a spontaneous chord of response in the Aries woman's heart, for it matches her own bright faith in tomorrow. Her naive confidence that whatever she believes intensely enough and long enough just has to come true will strike the same kind of response in him, often moving him to tears (for he is sentimental). She'll like that in him, the sentiment. That's why she fell in love with him, because he's the combination of strength and tenderness she seeks.

But she'll become impatient and accuse him of being lazy, when he's in one of his restful periods, not comprehending the necessity for his Venus-ruled nature to rest between long spells of energetic activity. Her own nature is different, her metabolism is so charged with vitality, she scarcely needs any rest at all — or so it will sometimes seem to him.

His kindness and friendliness are the two qualities she loves most in him. The very same two qualities he loves most in her. They are both kind, both friendly. In a world full of people who are cool, detached, and disinterested, this is not a small thing — and it forms an amazingly strong foundation for their relationship.

Being a 7-7 Sun Sign Pattern, very few of the disputes between the Libra man and Aries woman will happen on the way to or from the bedroom. (Especially if she buys him a king-size water mattress.) To a Libra male, drifting off to romance or dreamland within the soft folds of one of those undulating, billowy contraptions is very close to his idea of heaven. They may fight in the kitchen, the den, the front room, the back porch, the garden, the basement, attic, or garage — but when it's time to kiss goodnight, it will be time to make up for these two. The reconciliation based on the undeniable sexual attraction between them may not, however, last eternally (without that Sun-Moon harmony assistance). He's gentle, poetic, imaginative, considerate, charming, and romantic, all of which sends little tingles and shivers down her spine, from the top of her hard head to the tips of her busy toes. Their physical relationship at first seems like the tangible expression of every love song she's ever dreamed over while she was waiting for the paragon of virtue she's imaged in her heart to come to life.

That's the trouble. Making this man come to life. The Libra approach to sex is mental, light, and airy. Libra men seek shimmering ideals and far-out experiences of erotic expression and sensual feeling, sometimes so far out, sometimes soaring so high above her head — she'll long for something solid to grab. Like, two warm arms and a burning passion you can touch, as well as dream about. Ethereal love and aesthetic sexual response can leave Aries somewhat chilly. Female Rams need plenty of warm affection and fiery lovemaking to feel completely fulfilled in a physical relationship. With this man she may be left feeling a little empty. Something is missing. Exactly what she can't say, maybe the last line of the song. If she has the Moon in Libra, Gemini, Aquarius, Sagittarius, or Leo — or if his Moon Sign is Aries, Sagittarius, Leo, Gemini, or Aquarius — the missing lyric may be found. If the Moon of either was in any other astrological sign at birth, it may be elusive. But the search for it will be delightful.

A Libra man who memorized the old nursery rhyme in school that went: "Peter, Peter, pumpkin eater — had a wife and couldn't keep her — put her in a pumpkin shell, and there he kept her very well," had better check with Mother Goose again. An Aries woman will not sit happily in a pumpkin shell while he glides gracefully around the town, charming all the girls — or while he hides in the library, polishing his Libra mind. With her, he shouldn't expect marriage to balance his Scales — unless it's a complete mental and emotional partnership. Still, if he's honest, he'll realize that's the kind of relationship he really needs himself. When all the parties are over.

☆ ☆ ☆ ☆ ☆ ☆

ARIES *Man* LIBRA *Woman*

"I won't open unless you speak!" Peter cried.

Then at last the visitor spoke, in a lovely,
bell-like voice. "Let me in, Peter."

It was Tink, and quickly he unbarred to her.

It usually isn't difficult for the Libra girl to persuade the Ram to unbar his door or his heart to her. He's putty in her lovely, dimpled hands — and Rams, as you know, are normally putty in no one's hands. Aries men are not made of Silly Putty. They are made of iron and steel (the metals associated with the Aries Sun Sign). But with the Libra lady, he'll melt like a snowman in July. He can't resist her charm, the way she praises all the wonderful qualities he's perfectly aware he possesses himself, but which others are (it seems to him) forever ignoring — the undeniable sexual chemistry between them, and her womanly sweetness. (This is in the beginning. Later, he will experience a few surprises regarding her "womanly sweetness.") Besides, she's probably quite beautiful (most Libra females are), with a smile like carob cupcakes, and every Aries man adores having a girlfriend or a wife who causes other men to envy him. He needs to be proud of the woman he loves, to be able to show her off and brag about her. He wants her to always look prettier and be smarter than other women so it will be obvious that he's won first prize in the love carnival. (Rams, you see, have this inbred thing about winning.)

Since she probably is superior to lots of other women, super bright and startlingly attractive, curvaceous and so forth, this woman will fit all his Mars requirements, and at the start of their affair, everything will be peaches and cream and buttery softness between them.

But the Libra woman in love with an Aries man may later find herself knocked out of balance frequently. Considering her nearly neurotic reaction to being forced into instant action before she's completely sure what she wants to do, having an impatient lover or husband shout, "Come on, what's it going to be — pineapple sherbet or deep-dish apple pie à la mode? The waiter is growing a beard waiting for you to decide" — could cause their relationship to suffer some rocky periods. This man wants things done now, immediately — even sooner if at all possible — even though his demands for whatever it is he wants are often given at the last minute. "Do you want me to do it today, darling," she'll ask, "or may I do it tomorrow?" (Whether it's taking his favorite red sweater to the cleaners or typing up his address book so he'll have an extra copy if he loses it. He's always losing things.) "Today," he'll tell her. "I want it done today." (If he'd wanted it done tomorrow, he'd have *asked* her tomorrow.) Actually, most Rams would like anything they "request" to be done yesterday.

This sort of irrational and impatient Mars-like reasoning can throw her delicate Venus psyche out of kilter. She could ask, "Isn't it more intelligent to plan ahead and try to do it tomorrow?" only to hear him shout at her, "Don't argue with me! Just do as I say—*please.*" If he has a softer Moon Sign or Ascendent, he'll add the "Please"—if not, he'll just toss out his orders cheerfully, thoughtlessly demanding, without the slightest idea he's being unreasonable and somewhat spoiled.

I know one Libra wife who gave her Aries husband a birthday gift she made herself. A wall hanging created in velvets and satins, with variations of the Mars fire-engine red tones, embroidered with the words: "Dear Lord, give me the gift of patience—*but hurry.*" He was delighted. That's one of the nice things about the typical Arian. He's able to laugh at himself and seldom gets all stuffy when his faults are pointed out (*gently,* not harshly or with a severe, critical attitude). But they do have to be pointed out now and then. Once a Ram recognizes how selfish he's being, he'll feel guilty and ashamed, say he's sorry, and promise not to do it again, after which he'll proceed to do it again—and again—and again. Apologies are not difficult for the average Mars-ruled male to handle. It's one of the most lovable things about him. Aries is quick to admit a fault and accept the blame, but not too quick to drop the bad habit that was apologized for so openly and generously. Still, it's a decided virtue to be able to admit one's mistakes and try again. He does try. He doesn't always succeed, but the good Lord knows he tries.

She apologizes sweetly too. Like Aries, Libra seldom shrinks from admitting mistakes and being willing to say she's sorry. In fact, she may be *too* ready to admit mistakes—or perhaps the better way to express it is that she may be too ready and willing to decide that what she decided (or did) might have been wrong. She'll worry if she's hurt his feelings by something she's said or done, and try to gracefully atone in some way. She'll be doing a lot of that with this man. Atoning, that is—apologizing and atoning for hurting his feelings, because this man is ultrasensitive. He wants everyone to like him, even to love him—family, friends, and strangers—and naturally the woman he owns. (That's more or less the way he thinks of her—owning her, like a special, exciting, precious, and long-awaited, long-prayed-for gift he found under his tree on Christmas morning.) Aries men can be extremely self-centered without meaning to be so. She'll gradually comprehend this, but before she does, her more tender Venus feelings will be bruised more than a few times.

She'll try all her powers of Libra logic and persuasion to make him see that not every single person in the world can love him. But it will make little impression on her Ram. He won't be able to understand why he isn't liked and admired by his worst enemies, never mind what he's said or done to anger them. They should understand that he was right, after all — and that he meant no harm. He was only defending himself from something negative they did to *him*. Why aren't they friendlier? Why don't they see he's sorry for his hasty words and has already forgotten his anger? The Ram will expect people to forget an injury as swiftly as he does. He's always deeply wounded when people pout or bear a grudge over something he considers past and forgotten.

His enemies today are his buddies tomorrow. He'll rush home furious with someone, and expect his Libra lady to share his fury toward the person who's offended him. If she refuses to do so, if she fairly tries to see the other person's side of the issue, and attempts to point out to her Aries lover or husband where he just might have been wrong, he'll turn on her, sometimes violently, sometimes even tearfully — and accuse her of disloyalty. She doesn't love him. If she loved him, she would be on *his* side — and not defend his enemies. He's not interested in her Libra fairness. The only *fair* point of view is *his* . . . . . . and if she really *cared* about him she'd *see* that.

While the Ram is angry, it's impossible for him to see any side but his own, and he definitely will expect the woman he loves to champion him fiercely and consistently. The next day, he may feel quite "sheepish" about the whole thing, and be a perfect "lamb" about confessing his rashness and making amends for his goof. *Then*, you see, it's all right for her to say he's been wrong — because he has realized it himself. But not before he's realized it on his own. Never before.

Naturally, a Venus-ruled female is more capable than most women of balancing the delicate situation of the quick tempers and even quicker reconciliations of the Ram she loves. She's tender, womanly, logical, and intelligent and wise. But she was born under a masculine sign, and she can balk once in a while herself when she feels he's being completely unfair. It probably won't change him, however. He'll either pout or storm angrily out the door (slamming it hard as he leaves), or sulk in the corner, convinced she hates him.

It wouldn't be wise for the Libra woman to display her "iron fist in its velvet glove" too often with this male. He senses when he's being manipulated, after a period of time. He may innocently accept it for a while (Aries possesses almost no guile, and is nearly never unduly suspicious), but once he's caught on that she's trying to mold him into any sort of pattern of behavior, he'll become either obstinate or outraged — or both. *No one* tells him what to do. He is his own boss. Even when he earnestly desires to take a certain course of action, he's likely to refuse to do it if he thinks she wants him to, not because he's suspicious of her motives, but because he has a horror of doing anything someone else suggests — especially anything someone else *openly directs* him to do.

The fact that she likes to argue (discuss, debate, or whatever) every minor and major decision or situation won't alienate the typical Aries man. He sees this as controversy, challenge, excitement! He'd be bored to tears with a woman who never fought back with him. His Mars nature is exhilarated by the promise of battle, whether it's only a mild personal verbal battle over which film to see — or what kind of car to buy — or an argument concerning public or more general topics, like what should be done about pornography, solar heating, nuclear power, corruption in politics, or any other burning issues of the day. But he'll like to win all these discussions. He won't give in, not an inch — until he does win (or until his clever Libra lady allows him to believe he's won). Then he feels proud, self-contented, and happy. And he'll treat her with all the loving affection and tenderness any woman could desire.

This man's sexual image of himself is closely woven into his ability to be always right and emerge victorious in the eyes of the woman he loves. He must be respected, liked, agreed with, and looked up to in order to properly project his considerable Mars virility as a lover. If he feels rejected intellectually or in any other way, he'll freeze into Aries ice (always more serious and lasting than Aries fire — or fiery rages). Their sexual relationship will normally be an uncommonly happy and wholesome one. Her femininity and his masculinity harmonize beautifully and smoothly, in the most natural way. As long as she doesn't allow the masculine side of her Sun Sign essence to intrude into their intimacy (like displaying her capabilities in every area under the Sun to be equal to his, which they quite probably are) and then expect him to feel like the conquering male in a physical sense. He must take the lead in their sexual togetherness, as in every other way. If she allows this, and understands the needs behind it, he'll be the most sensitive, romantic, sentimental, affectionate, and passionate lover she could imagine. But he can become a demanding tyrant if she destroys his ultranecessary confidence in himself.

There's little chance of this occurring, unless she has the Moon or Ascendent in Virgo, Sagittarius, Cancer, or Capricorn — or a lot of planets in Earth Signs in her birth chart. Her basic instinct is tact and thoughtfulness, which is usually blended nicely and equally with her own well-designed and controlled, forceful drive and aggressive nature.

Although their natures constitute a clear polarity, the Mars-ruled man and the Venus-ruled woman are exquisitely mated. After all, Mars and Venus themselves fell wildly and permanently in love — even while Venus was wed to Jupiter. They were caught, of course, in a web woven sneakily by Neptune — but the anger of Jupiter didn't dim their passion by any means. A study of Greek mythology is of immense benefit in comprehending all Sun Signs.

Taking into consideration that the Ram likes to leap around on rocky slopes and the Venus lady lives in a precarious world of the swinging trays of her golden Scales, wherein the slightest breath of wind can upset her inner harmony and outward tranquility, these two often manage to blend their divergent natures with surprising success. The Libra woman can find the intoxicating freedom and exciting mental activity she seeks through this man — and the Ram will enjoy walking through Libra's cool woods, down winding trails of bluebells and butterflies.

The Libra lady is quite a lot of woman. Very few men can cope with her powerful combination of masculine determination and delectable daintiness. But the Aries man is one for taking on super challenges and winning them — and her challenge offers precious rewards to the victor. All men are little boys at heart, but the Ram is more so than most. There's nothing childish about him on the surface. He's tough and forceful — the kind of male they call a man's man. It's the aura of impossible dreams and wistful yearnings hovering mistily around his shoulders that gives him his air of youthfulness . . . . . . some lingering enchantment behind his eyes that makes him so vulnerable. If she uses her Venusian charm and patience to direct his flaming ambitions and incredible energies toward some worthy goal, he can become a crusader for all manner of goodness and glory. (Both of them possess a strong sense of mercy for the weak and can become outraged over injustice.)

She'll seldom or never drown his enthusiastic spontaneity with stern criticism, sarcasm, silent pouting, long brooding silences, or withdrawal — and that will please him. He'll seldom or never refuse to be genuinely interested in and fascinated by her need to talk things over and discuss them — and that will comfort her.

The root cause of any difficulties between them will spring from their shared birthright of the Cardinal essence. For they are both Cardinal Signs of Leadership, Aries and Libra. A relationship will never work when there's a constant battle over which one is the chief, and which one is the Indian — or which one is the general and which one is the private — who gallops ahead and who canters behind. They'll have to learn to ride their horses side by side, as equals, not as superior and subordinate. It's the only way they'll ever find the way back home into each others' hearts when they've quarreled and both of them have been deeply hurt. Otherwise, they'll get lost like Hansel and Gretel, and you know how glad *they* were to return home together, after all their adventures were over. The only real security anyone has is the safety of being loved by someone who accepts you just as you are, with all your flaws, and wouldn't trade you for another — ever. Someone who makes you know this, even when you're behaving badly. That's safety. That's emotional security. That's *home* . . . . . . where love is.

☆ ☆ ☆ ☆ ☆ ☆

ARIES

Fire — Cardinal — Positive
Ruled by Mars
Symbol: The Ram
Day Forces — Masculine

SCORPIO

Water — Fixed — Negative
Ruled by Pluto
Symbols: Scorpion & Eagle
Night Forces — Feminine

The **ARIES-SCORPIO** *Relationship*

◆◁◉▷◆

Had the pirates kept together it is
certain that they would have won; but
the onset came when they were all
unstrung, and they ran hither and thither,
striking wildly, each thinking himself
the last survivor of the crew. Man to
man they were the stronger; but they
fought on the defensive only . . . . .

In their secret hearts, Aries men and women rather like to fancy themselves as colorful, fierce pirates. After all, pirates are brave, romantic and dashing. But like the pirate crew in Neverland, Aries often dissipates the Mars energy in the premature exposure of emotional reaction, fighting on the *defensive*. A Ram never attacks unless struck first. Remember that Aries is the symbolic Infant of the zodiac, and infants don't yell unless they're ignored, or someone jabs them with a sharp safety pin. After all, it's the only defense they have against pain or neglect. When more serious danger threatens, their guardian, Mars, comes to the rescue.

Scorpios, however, are masters of the *offensive* — an offensive laced with clever, cool strategy, exquisite patience and an uncanny sense of the weakness of others. You won't find Scorpios coming unstrung, running hither and thither, or striking wildly. When they strike, it's straight on target, with deadly precision. Anytime you're stung by the tail of the Scorpion, you know you've been stung. That's why people seldom mess around with Pluto power the second time. Once is usually more than enough.

Still, it's almost impossible to feel sorry for Scorpions (although offering sympathy to a Scorpio is rather like lending a dollar to the Agnelli family, of Italy — or the Middle East oil czars). It must seem tiresome to watch people recoil when they discover you were born in November.

An Aries friend of mine has a trusted secretary he had always thought was the dearest, as well as the most efficient woman in the world. Then one day he inadvertently found out that Molly was a Scorpio. He nearly went into a state of shock. It was as though he had been harboring a serpent in his office. His loyal Molly — a *Scorpio*? The normal Mars courage plummeted to rock bottom as the Ram reacted to this frightening astrological blow. When he grew calmer, he remembered Molly's hard work over the years, her valor beyond the call of duty, her efficient cool in emergencies — and yes, her sometimes rough tongue.

At that very moment, Molly, who was getting out the mail, held up a letter and said, "Considering you dictated this, it doesn't sound too bad." Translated into Scorpio language, that meant: "Your creative expression is improving."

My Aries friend felt a warm glow, as if he had received praise from on high. He had. So he ventured to remark, "Listen, about your being born in November . . . . "

Scorp glanced up from the IBM Selectric Correctional, threw him a hypnotic stare through the gathering steam in the air (from Fire and Water) and said, "Yes? *What about it*?" The Ram then murmured, "Oh, nothing, Molly. Nothing at all. I was just wondering what to get you for your birthday . . . . "

Now, if you know anything about astrology, you know that's not a typical reaction from an Aries employer. Or any other kind of Aries person. Rams don't back down for anyone.

Strangely, a Ram won't normally push ahead immediately with a Scorpio, as he or she will with those born under all other Sun Signs. There's something about those compelling Pluto eyes, reflecting a quiet poise and hidden strength, that flashes a message to the Ram: "Beware. *This* still water runs very deep. And it could drown you. You're only a paper Ram, and a Ram is a member of the sheep family. You're out of your element with me.

You're in the big ocean now, way over your head, full of sharks, seaweed, odd nocturnal creatures, hidden reefs and mystery."

That's where all Scorpios originally came from — the sea. If they're also found on the desert these days, the burning sands are no less a strange territory to Rams.

Aries instinctively absorbs the message, which is "danger." Ah, DAN-GER! It's the one word that will excite the Ram to action, so the initial caution is soon replaced by the Mars forward charge, rising to meet the challenge thrown down. It's almost always a mistake. When it comes to an actual showdown, a Ram is tougher, louder and more emphatic than a Scorpion. But when things get to that point, the typical Scorpion will simply disappear, wrapped in aloof silence, leaving Aries to ponder the same old mystery. Did he (or she) leave in recognition of defeat — or because I went too far? In other words, even if you appear to win with a Scorpio, you'll never be sure. You'll always have to guess.

It doesn't take many experiences for the average Ram to learn that the best method for dealing with a Scorpio is cooperation — at a safe and respectful emotional distance. The intimacies of romance are something else. Here, we're dealing with the general vibrations of this 6-8 Sun Sign Pattern between Aries and Scorpio in a business, friendship or family relationship.

Examples of the Aries-Scorpio interaction are always valid, whatever the sex or the age of the Ram and the Eagle involved, and so, the following may be aptly and helpfully applied to any Mars-Pluto association in which the reader may be involved, by simply changing the names and the specific situation. *The basics remain.*

One summer, a few years previous to this time of writing, I noticed my ten-year-old Scorpio son was becoming markedly plump (well, all right, fat) and also lazy, from consuming the typical childhood diet of ice cream, cake, candy, soda pop and the nutritional poison from fast food chains — using his allowance to buy the "forbidden fruit." (*Actual* fruit, you can't get some kids to eat. It must be forbidden.)

"Michael," I commanded rather loudly and angrily, with Mars firmness and directness, "you will stop eating that junk, and you will stop now. Immediately. No more sweets will be brought into your room, and hidden on your closet shelf. Nor will you secretly fudge any more Eskimo Pies and chocolate Wing Dings with your allowance. Do you *understand* that? Do you *hear* me?"

His answer was total silence. Within two weeks, he gained ten additional pounds. I then cut off his allowance, every penny of it, to punish him. *Now,* let's see him find a way to get even with me! I thought. He did.

The following week, I received several phone calls from his various teachers, reporting incorrigible behavior from Mike in school, and an absolute refusal to do his homework assignments. Then, fortunately, I finally remembered that I'm an astrologer. The ban on sweets and bad food was lifted. His allowance was not only restored but increased.

"Michael," I said to him, gently this time, and softly, "I trust you to know better than anyone else what's bad for your body, mind and soul — and what's good for it. You are ruled by Pluto, the wisest, as well as the most powerful planet in the entire solar system. I'm sorry I shouted at you before. It's just that [here, I became somewhat calculating, I must admit], well, it's just that it hurts me to hear all those kids at school calling you 'Whale.' That's not the right kind of nickname for an *Eagle*. I know it's affectionate, but . . . . . ." I trailed off, unable any longer to fill in the growing silence between us. This time, along with his silent stare, he answered me with a faint, mysterious smile. Inwardly, I shuddered.

I don't expect my readers to believe what happened next, because if I hadn't seen it with my own Aries eyes, I wouldn't have believed it myself. This determined Scorpion-Eagle, whose inner strength and integrity had at last been recognized, actually began to make *his own green salads* after school, without the slightest hint from me — refused all desserts, munched apples and chewed on tangerines between meals, and stuck to a diet that would starve a Yogi. Miraculously, his secret closet cache of candy bars disappeared. All this without a single additional word from me, and with a steely will power that was honestly frightening.

His reward was a series of weekly karate lessons, where his instructors marveled at his robust health, not to mention his "Scorpio death grip" *he* taught *them*. He had no desire for a black belt, however. He just wanted the training as a warning to the school bullies, instinctively knowing the power of suggestion. Karate is excellent training for young Scorps, by the way. It instills in them courtesy, respect for authority, and most important of all, it stresses *defense*, rather than *attack*.

Within two months, no one was calling the Eagle "Whale" anymore. His new nickname, dictated by Scorpio himself, has become MOE — and his friends would not dare call him anything else. Certainly, this humbled Ram would not dare. MOE stands for "Master of Eternity." That figures, with Pluto. MOE then organized a group of his closest friends into an organization called the PEARLS (the meaning is secret, and I have no hope of ever learning it), who are dedicated to defending younger children and the elderly from all manner of Manhattan muggers.

That's what can happen when an impulsive, bossy Ram handles an Eagle of *any* age, or *any* sex, with the proper respect. An invaluable lesson for the Aries person, when dealing with a Scorp, in this 6-8 influenced association.

With a Pluto person, Aries shouldn't expect to find the fairness of Libra, the compassion of Pisces or the warm generosity of Leo. He (or she) may even find a basic selfishness exceeding that of Capricorn, if not that of the Ram himself (or herself).

But Scorpio is intensely loyal, and never compromises principle. This makes a big hit with the Ram, who, is also fiercely loyal, and who has an equal contempt for the compromising of ideals or integrity. Scorpio never gives in, never admits defeat. Aries is likewise dedicated fiercely to winning. Only sissies give up, and give in. Everybody knows that. These two certainly know it.

Yet, there's another Scorpio quality, intangible, indefinable, that Aries finds impossible to fathom. Is it will power ? Or is it, simply — *will* ? It is the latter, and it's responsible for the strong, emotionally charged aura surrounding even the quietest, *apparently* harmless, Scorpions.

Now, this doesn't mean that every Scorp has to come on like Dracula. Many of these men and women have undeniably sweet and pleasant personalities. They're interesting, intelligent and courteous. But shy, insecure and defenseless, they *are not* — and Aries should not allow himself or herself to be fooled by their gentle voices, their unobtrusive demeanor and lack of surface aggression. In this association, it's always wise to remember that the elements of Fire and Water are combining, and each has the latent ability to destroy the other, which is explained in more detail in the section called "The Elements" at the back of this book, and in various other chapters dealing with the Fire and Air Sign compatibilities.

I know a Scorpio man who married a Scorpio girl, after a long (and naturally secret) engagement. When Herb and Donna's first baby arrived in April, my initial impulse was to offer to adopt the child. A tiny Ram, under the restrictive dominance of *two* Scorps ? Little Joshua must be rescued, I told myself, before his Mars ego is completely crushed. But the truth is, that Aries Joshua has benefited tremendously from the quiet discipline, and intuitive wisdom of his double Pluto-ruled parents. An evolved and enlightened pair of Eagles are an excellent example of moral courage and personal integrity for a Mars youngster, who needs and wants guidance in the right direction. Scorps are perfect teachers of will power and stability to an explosive Ram, who tends to explode in a burst of enthusiasm, then lose interest before the sparks have settled.

There is always, of course, the danger that Pluto power exercised over Mars will be too severe. A Ram of any age may be dampened by Scorpio's Water element caution into becoming the sheep-type Arian, unnaturally introverted and self-effacing, which is definitely not desirable, because it's a denial of the Mars birthright. In the happier Aries-Scorpio associations, however, the Ram will respond beautifully to the strength of the Eagle friend, neighbor, relative, business associate, lover or mate, and try to imitate the Pluto poise, which is a decided positive result of this blend. Just so, the Scorpio half of the team tries to develop more elasticity of viewpoint, in relation to the Ram's more open nature, and far more free and friendly approach to life. The emotional coldness Scorpio can project at times is capable of breaking the warm Aries heart, as well as his (or her) spirit, and self-confidence.

There will be occasional moments when the Scorpio's penetrating gaze of angry disapproval, or thwarted will, can be downright spooky to an Aries, causing the Ram to inwardly quake, never mind his or her Mars rulership. I know a Scorpio father who, when he was frustrated beyond further discussion by the contrariness of his three sons (one of them an Aries), would simply grow stone-silent for a few seconds, then speak, in a sepulchral voice, the ominous Pluto words: *"I'll remember this."* It's rather a healthy idea for all Rams involved with Scorpions to remember *that*. Meaning, the Eagle will never forget an injury. Never. Nor will the Scorp man, woman or child ever forget an act of love or kindness. It's much safer and happier to give them the memory of the latter, and avoid the former, whenever possible.

Some Scorpions become slaves to their own wills. So much so that the Eagle will persist in a purpose, even when it's become obvious that the continuation of a certain course will surely lead to self-destruction. Aries well understands that kind of intense, later-regretted compulsion.

But Aries is a Positive Fire Sign — the reckless, Mars-driven crusader, stirred emotionally by dedication to a cause, and the excitement of a dangerous mission. Scorpio is a Negative Water Sign — the seasoned veteran, possessing a deep sense of realities and the strength to endure hardships, with no illusions about the glamour of marching bands, uniforms and decorations for bravery. Their strategies are very different. Aries *defends* fiercely, in the front lines. Scorpio *attacks* suddenly, unexpectedly, from the rear. At war, these two Sun Signs are natural enemies. Peace is better — and it begins with Love.

ARIES *Woman* SCORPIO *Man*

————◆◀◆▶◆————

The kiss that had been for no one
else Peter took quite easily. Funny.
But she seemed satisfied.

A Scorpio man penetrates life to the core. He has an almost superhuman capacity to face the facts about himself and others. So it can be a little frightening when he lets you backstage to see what's really going on behind his mask of unshakable self-confidence. What does a woman do when she's been trusted with a secret like that? If she's an Aries, she usually falls in love with an unbelievable intensity.

He may permit her to share parts of him never before revealed to anyone else. That's because he admires the absence of feminine guile in her nature. He responds to her fresh innocence and faith in him, and he's touched by her loyalty. Somehow, this man senses that the Aries girl, unlike her sisters of the other Sun Signs, won't use her knowledge of his inner being against him. Revenge is never an Aries weapon. Although retaliation is something he understands and uses himself, in a strange way that only makes him appreciate the Ram's lack of it even more. Consequently, there can be a depth to the love between Aries and Scorpio that's seldom equaled for sheer passionate devotion and spiritual closeness.

Since neither of them is ever satisfied until they've drained the cup of romance of its last drop of pleasure, emotionally they're well matched and mated. Mentally, they're about as far apart as two people can get and still remain members of the same human race.

His Pluto mind is shrewd, critical, cautious and skeptical. Her Mars mental processes are careless, direct, impulsive and uncomplicated. This distance between their mental outlooks can take one of two paths. It can add intrigue and glamour to their relationship, based on the law that opposites attract — or it can "break the law," and widen into such a chasm, that they find it impossible to communicate, even on those levels where they're alike and sympathetic. Which way it goes depends almost entirely on the Sun-Moon aspects between their horoscopes.

Before the affair reaches the point of a forever scene, however, this man will have asked a few searching questions, and no one asks searching questions more thoroughly than a Scorpio, even when he asks them only with his eyes. Will she take the cold, hard truth from him, which he'll hand her frequently, with meekness and respect? No. She won't. (Meekness? He has to be kidding.) Will she fall apart at his slightest Scorpion sting ? No. She'll never fall apart. Her reaction to hurt may range anywhere from a childish tantrum to violent rage. Will she moan and sniffle because he spends a few hours privately talking with a pretty girl about astral projection and ancient witch rites ? *If he does what* ? No. She won't moan and sniffle. She will do *other* things. *Her* things. I'm willing to forget he even asked that last question, if he is. And he'd better be.

Thought for a Scorpio male reading this chapter: If she acts like that now, just think what marriage to her will be like. I see. You've already thought. That figures. It's hard to tell a Scorpio anything he doesn't already know. But here's something he may *think* no one knows. Despite the answers he came up with in his compatibility quiz, the Scorpio man believes he can teach this girl to keep her cool. Besides, her vital spirit and fiery independence fascinate him.

The trouble could start when he discovers he'll never train this woman to completely control her emotions to match his own cool poise. Then the vital spirit and fiery independence he thought were such flashing virtues may lose their attraction. As long as things go smoothly, he'll accept her aggressive ways. He may even enjoy them. But if she insists on forcing him to conform to an emotional pattern against his own nature, he'll turn like a Scorpion whose tail has been stepped on — and strike. Scorpions are known for their certain retaliation against being trod upon, even when it's accidental. But who would ever step on a Scorpion's tail deliberately anyway ? *A Ram would.*

When a Scorpion is confronted with a situation he finds unbearable, he doesn't waste time trying to push it out of the way, like Taurus — devising schemes to evade it, like Libra — or accepting it as fated, like Pisces. Nothing will do but the total annihilation of the obstacle to his peace of mind. For example, if it's a religious dogma against his own principles which someone is trying to shove down his throat, merely to attack the offending church itself is a trifling action, beneath his Pluto Power. He'll set out to destroy the roots and branches of *all* religion, and become a militant atheist. If a hardened criminal breaks into his home and steals from him, merely to help the law apprehend the man is far too mild. Dishonesty has threatened him personally; therefore dishonesty must be wiped out of existence — even if it means the electric chair for the worst offenders — and a long jail term for six-year-olds who snitch Hershey bars. When it's a romantic injury he's suffered which has brought him emotional pain, simply to demolish the girl and their love affair is not enough. He'll turn the incredible force of his will into a scorching, bitter condemnation of all intimate relationships, and the institution of marriage itself. With Scorpio, nothing is done in halfway measures (including devotion, loyalty, and integrity, of course). Pluto men build all the way up to heaven — or destroy all the way down to hell. That's why they're so interesting.

Admittedly, "interesting" may not be exactly the right word, but any Mars-ruled female will get the general idea. It's the old appeal of masculinity, virility and strength. Still, it would be wise for the Aries girl who is about to form an attachment with a Scorpio man to consider carefully his Pluto nature before she exposes her bright fire to that flood of rushing water. If she has anything to say about it, I mean. She may not. The magnetism of Scorpio practically guarantees this man success in whatever he's after, including her. Remaining detached in the face of a Scorpio romantic assault requires an objectivity most Rams don't possess, especially in view of the fact that this is a 6-8 Sun Sign Pattern. Aries is the sixth astrological house of Service to Scorpio. Scorpio is the eighth house of Sex to Aries. And that's about the way it wraps up. She serves him in many ways, with surprising docility, and he provides sexual fulfillment for her. Naturally, the inter-change is not always quite so plain and simple. But basically, their relationship will unfold a curious inclination on her part to submit to this man and allow him to be her Svengali, while he satisfies her deepest desire for physical proof of the kind of complete and eternal love she needs. Their sexual attraction can continue into old age, with none of its original passion dimmed. After death, it can burn just as intensely on the spiritual plane.

This is a couple most likely to walk out on the porno films with explicit sexual scenes. Don't believe everything you've read about Scorpio. Such a public display of intimacies will usually offend the Eagle's ingrained sense of the privacy of human relations to the same degree that it offends her idealism. The only area where sex can cause problems between them is her tendency to exaggerate his strong appeal for women into accusations of unfaithfulness—or if his typical Scorpio suspicion should cause him to interpret her free and friendly manner with all men as flirting. He should realize that she's too honest and full of ideals about love to commit adultery without extreme provocation, and even then, she'll confess it almost before it happens.

Conversely, she must understand that, for all of his passionate inner involvement with sex, the Pluto concept of love is based on purity and integrity. When his needs (which are considerable) are satisfied at home, he'll remain absolutely immune to the wiles of other women, even if one should openly try to seduce him on the street (which is always a possibility with Scorpios). That makes the question of his sexual loyalty entirely her responsibility, and she'll have to assume it or suffer the consequences.

If she can manage to tolerate his quiet air of superiority, exasperating silences and deep wells of secrecy—his somewhat stingy attitude (compared with hers) about spending money, and his iron-clad convictions of right and wrong, even when they differ from her own, she can find an enduring happiness with this man. But that's a lot of tolerance for an Aries woman to master, and Rams are not noted for patience. It may help if she realizes that those firm convictions of right and wrong he so relentlessly and intensely clings to, were formed, on a subconscious level, from the karmic seeds of the weighing and balancing of the sign behind him, Libra — and are now forged into a solid form. It's all part of his karmic, spiritual growing process. He really can't help it.

If he can overlook her surges of jealousy, her financial extravagance, frequent demands for attention and her somewhat immature emotional approach to all problems, he'll find all the woman he's ever sought in an Aries female. But Scorpios are not, by nature, the overlooking kind. Assuming her Moon or Ascendent is in a Water or Earth Sign (with the exception of Taurus) or his Moon or Ascendent is in a Fire or Air Sign (with the exception of Libra) they can take a chance on discovering together the place where the Eagle flies . . . . . . the magical flowers that grow on the summit of the Ram's rocky ledges.

Even without such planetary assistance, these two can simply use their Free Will, and *decide* to have a harmonious relationship. When Pluto and Mars combine forces, there's literally nothing that can't be *willed* to manifest, and happiness is no exception. When this man and woman make a wish on their own stars, the firmament trembles, comets streak by, and trillions of twinkling, tiny starlings chorus an obedient "yes!"

☆ ☆ ☆ ☆ ☆ ☆

ARIES *Man* SCORPIO *Woman*

"But if I had been a weak man," he said. "Good heavens, if I had been a weak man!"

Might I make a helpful astrological suggestion for the Ram who is on the verge of becoming involved with a Scorpio female? Get a copy of Ibsen's *Hedda Gabler*, and read it between the lines. Hedda was clearly a Scorpio woman, and the descriptions of her sometimes incomprehensible behavior will prepare him for all possibilities, even though the lady Eagle he loves may be a somewhat more average Scorp, with more subdued Pluto Power. It's only sensible to be prepared for the worst, even if you expect — and actually receive — the best. Forewarned is forearmed, and it never hurts to be forearmed with a Scorpio.

As for the unfortunate Hedda herself, she's admittedly an extreme example, yet an interesting study for Eagle watchers. Her cool, quiet, mysterious feminine mystique is punctuated by sudden, violent frenzies, which are puzzling, to say the least, coming from such a normally gentle, self-contained woman. Her nice, easy-going Taurus or Pisces husband is at a complete loss when it comes to comprehending her emotional needs. Then along comes a clever, worldly chap, undoubtedly an Aries, who thinks he has mastered this woman, plumbed her depths and dominated her with his masculine superiority. When she finally kills herself, all the confused man can manage to murmur is that "people just don't *do* that sort of thing."

Scorpios do. They can do all sorts of either strange and frightening or weird and wonderful things — and they never warn you ahead of time what they're up to.

Granted, as I've already noted, Hedda is an exaggerated image of the Scorpio woman. The average Pluto-ruled female probably won't climb to such heights of ecstasy, or plunge into such wells of despair as the unfortunate Hedda. But even if she only lets the air out of his tires when he won't let her drive his car, or casually cuts his telephone cord when he calls another girl, a Ram who's aware of the Scorpion tendency toward secret revolt, followed by sudden retaliation, will find life with this girl considerably less traumatic.

It's her secret revolt, more than her sudden retaliation, that could cause the tension between these two lovers. An Aries can be driven wild by an act that, although easy enough to forgive in itself, is the result of a premeditation unknown to him. Since she's inclined to be secretive when she's not in action, her inexplicable surges of angry revenge can infuriate him. Rams do not like unpleasant surprises, and they simply can't *stand* not to know secrets. Normal outbursts of temper he can handle, with the experience born from his own stormy impulses. But she didn't give him the slightest hint that she was going to burn up his new Adidas jogging booties, and starch his favorite jeans. At breakfast, on Monday morning, her voice was cool and calm, her eyes burned into his, expressing their usual intense devotion, and her goodbye kiss was as passionate as ever. How was he to suspect he'd return home that night to a pair of charred sneakers and stiff Levi's ? And all because he told her on Sunday he didn't feel like taking her to the movies, because he wanted to hike in the woods, with some old buddies from college he hadn't seen in years.

How DARE she sock him and shock him with a surprise maneuver like that, retroactively ? He'll show her a thing or two ! But by the time he's ready to show her a thing or two, she's not watching his fiery scene, because she's already reverted to her silent aloofness. She's turned off. Detached and disinterested. Also uninterested.

Scenes of this sort can rattle a Ram to the roots of his horns. What she's done outrages him, simply because it sneaked up on him in such an . . . well, in such an *outrageous* way. Add to that her talent for cooly turning off, before he can even fight back to defend himself, and you can see why he may gradually become an aggressive, frantic shadow boxer, hitting out blindly, and never getting the satisfaction of landing a victorious punch (symbolically) on his lady Eagle's (also symbolic) jaw. To so surprise him, after he's already blithely forgotten the incident that infuriated her, then retreat, and refuse to even notice him or listen to his angry sputterings, is not a pattern of behavior calculated to win all the confrontations in the final tallies — for her. She might lose the last hand of her bridge game by losing him.

Actually, if the Ram will just let her win, or allow her to believe she's won, he'll save a lot of wear and tear on his ego, through bypassing fruitless emotional conflicts with this woman, which are destined by the stars to lead absolutely nowhere. It's really the only way to get along with a lady Scorpion — simply permit her to satisfy herself that she has repaid the hurt or slight she's suffered from you, then *say no more about it.* One of his finer rewards for such emotional control and maturity, will be her gradual and certain, deeper respect for him. Since the fighting pattern just described is the absolute only one Scorpio recognizes, it's the only one powerful enough to keep their relationship on an equal basis. As Grandpa used to say, "You can't fight City Hall" (truer even today than in Gramp's day, in both its literal and symbolic sense). She holds the trump card — self-control. The proper way to handle and keep a woman like that is, obviously, not to lose your own control.

He can always remind himself, during his more discouraged moments, that this woman is as loyal to the man she loves as she is determined not to allow him to step on her Scorpion tail. When a lady with a Scorpio Sun Sign, Moon Sign or Ascendent falls in love, her friends, her family, her career, reputation, her suffering — all count for nothing. She won't hesitate for a second to openly show her scorn for anyone who threatens to stand in the way of their happiness together, to cast a shadow on their love or to harm her man in any way. A devotion of this level of intensity should make it easier to overlook the manner in which she occasionally manipulates their personal squabbles against him. Rams need to be loved all the way — or not at all. And that's precisely how Scorpio loves. All the way — or not at all.

An Aries man who has only recently become emotionally involved with this girl (let's say this woman — Scorps are never girls, they were all born women) may think the foregoing is an unjust summary of the character, traits and personality of his dearly beloved. That's because he was picturing the retaliatory attacks, followed by instant withdrawal, which were just described, as a kind of black-widow-spider operation. So, how could a female with such a whispery, throaty voice and gentle, feminine ways, be a closet black widow spider ? She is not, of course. That's the point. Her Pluto revenge tactics needn't resemble something out of a vampire movie. She's not the Bride of Frankenstein. She's simply a sweet, rather shy lady, who has her quiet moments, and who is sensitive.

After they're married, he'll learn. He'll receive a fast astrological lesson, when he tells her — "I wish you'd go to the beauty parlor and let them style your hair, before my business partner [my boss, my agent, or whatever] and his wife come here for dinner tonight. The way you're wearing it now is so dated, and very unbecoming." (Aries rules the first astrological house of personal appearance, and Rams are really quite vain about their own looks, and the looks of their loved ones. Almost as much so as Leo.) The Scorpio woman won't scream at him in rage, because her glamour has been criticized. She'll just smile sweetly and say, "Of course, darling." She'll still be a perfect angel of womanhood when he arrives at home that night, accompanied by Mr. Grumple and his bejeweled wife.

His Scorpio mate's voice will be velvety warm and sensual when she whispers to him in the bedroom, "Sweetheart, *you* explain to the Grumples, won't you? I have a dreadful headache, and I'm just not up to meeting anyone tonight."

"You *what*!" he shouts. "How can I explain this to them? They're out there in the front room waiting to meet you, and you're still in your nightgown, and you haven't even started dinner? This could ruin my whole future! Do you realize what you've done to me?"

His rage has not the faintest effect. She has already closed her eyes and placed the ice bag on her head, still smiling sweetly, leaving him to cope with his hungry guests alone. You see? Not like the vampire movies at all! Just a nice lady, with a headache, who's terribly sorry she's causing him such embarrassment. (Next time, he won't insult her hairstyle.)

The Aries man is competent and courageous when he's involved in a situation he can understand, but he lacks the ability to successfully oppose the type of reasoning that goes over his head. It will bewilder him when she refuses to fight him with weapons of his own choice, but it will also have the long-term effect of subduing him, which can result in a growing emotional maturity. Although loving and living with a Scorpion may be a little bumpy, it will mellow the Ram's fiery personality and open his eyes to his Martian faults of selfishness, rashness and impulsive speech, like no other experience he's ever had before. If he really loves her, there's much she can teach him — and he, likewise, her.

In 1970, in California, I met a fascinating Scorpio woman, who had just separated from her Aries husband. (He was a surgeon, a typical Mars occupation, although a not very evolved or enlightened one.) Neither of them knew enough astrology to understand, and therefore to tolerate, each other's natures. But I got the impression they might still be in love, and I hope this book is published in time to help them get back together. Her marriage taught her at least one astrological lesson she'll never forget. (Scorpios always profit from experience.) "Men cringe when they meet a Scorpio," she told me. "They think we're all deadly and dangerous. So now, when they ask me my Sun Sign, I just flutter my eyelashes and tell them I'm a Pisces. It works like magic!"

There's no telling how many November girls are running around out there pretending to be Fish — but you've been warned. It's a shame astrological ignorance makes such a disguise necessary. Scorpio women, if properly understood, are beautiful people, with an unsurpassed tenderness and an enormous capacity for love.

The sexual attraction between an Aries man and a Scorpio woman is instant and magnetic, and can be permanently fulfilling. Their physical relationship will never be indifferent or casual. Sex, combined with love, is a basic formula in the Scorpio search for personal salvation, the same kind of glory the Ram seeks to satisfy his misty ideal. He must conquer sexually, and she'll allow him to do so, but she won't be passive, she'll meet him more than halfway in erotic expression. Her intense response to his lovemaking blended with her willingness to submit to him physically, represents the ultimate in ecstatic union to this man, who seeks a real woman, never a quiescent partner, yet neither a dominant mate who will try to overpower him. In his secret heart, he is the original, virile, yet pure and innocent Adam — in her secret heart, she is the original, tempting and mysterious Eve. Unless one of them has a serious Mars or Venus affliction in the natal chart (which, with these two, can lead to various forms of sadism or masochism), there will be no doubt at bedtime who is man and who is woman — and, with all due respect to Women's Lib, that's the way it was intended to be by our co-Creators.

A Scorpio female can't forgive being badly loved, in or *out* of the bedroom, and she may occasionally, if he's unthinkingly wounded her, use a denial of sexual Oneness against him as a revenge weapon, which is a large mistake on her part, since it may very well turn him into an insecure, and therefore selfish, lover. He should establish his mastery from the beginning in the area of physical passion.

Scorpio is compelled to violate the unknown, in order to *know*, then knowing, keeps the secret. Aries plunges in recklessly, to discover truth and happiness, then shares it enthusiastically and openly. This is an essential difference between them, which can be bridged only by mutual trust and forgiveness each time it appears. When he displays his emotions carelessly, he may create pain in her heart she'll find hard to forget, and although her outward response to his Mars fireworks may simply be a soft-spoken — "Aren't you over-reacting, darling ?" — there's no determining what may be occurring within her, behind her cool mask. There's only one answer to a question like that.

"No, I'm not over-reacting. I am just being me. I was born under a different star than you, and I have to express my feelings. Don't you want me to be true to myself ?" Yes, she does. She may never reveal it, or admit it . . . . . . but she does.

☆ ☆ ☆ ☆ ☆ ☆

ARIES

Fire — Cardinal — Positive
Ruled by Mars
Symbol: The Ram
Day Forces — Masculine

SAGITTARIUS

Fire — Mutable — Positive
Ruled by Jupiter
Symbols: Archer & Centaur
Day Forces — Masculine

The **ARIES-SAGITTARIUS** *Relationship*

. . . but perhaps the biggest adventure of all
was that they were several hours late for bed.
This so inflated them that they did various
dodgy things to get staying up still longer,
such as demanding bandages . . . .

Both of these Sun Signs like to stay up late. They're afraid they might miss something. That's why they're reluctant to retire early, leave parties early — or walk past two strangers fighting in the street. Rams and Archers are forever being advised by well-meaning friends, "Stay out of it. Mind your own business. It's not your concern. It's a lost cause." This last warning is a mistake. These two would walk a thousand miles for any cause, and if it's a lost cause, they simply can't bear to stand by without trying to save it. The fact that it's none of their business only makes it more intriguing, since both signs are infused with excessive amounts of curiosity, as well as a determined opinion that they know all the answers.

As for "demanding bandages," Aries and Sagittarius are also the most accident prone in the zodiac (with Aquarius running a close third). For obvious reasons. Not only on account of the traits just mentioned, but because

Aries men and women are always ramming their horns into places where angels fear to tread — or even tiptoe. Sagittarians (symbolized by the Centaur, with bow and arrow) are all just naturally born a little clumsy. It isn't easy to balance a body that's half horse, half man. Neither is it easy to balance a personality that's half philosopher, half clown.

Aries and Sagittarius get along pretty well most of the time, because they have so much in common — like their noticeable abundance of idealism. No one is more idealistic than the naive Ram, with the childlike faith that "wishing will make it so," unless it's the Archers, who aim their arrows toward some galaxy unseen by mortal man or woman.

Of course, today, with less idealistic people poisoning the Earth and its atmosphere, the Jupiter arrows can get stuck in a mass of solid pollution before they get past a low-hanging cloud. Rams and Archers aren't the only people with good intentions, but they're usually too busy, especially as a team pushing their ideas of Utopia (often running in concentric circles) to be sidetracked by personal or political greed.

Another thing Aries and Sagittarius have in common is their fondness for heated discussion. Only a Libra has more fun starting arguments. But logical Libra is driven by a desire to be fair and see justice done. Rams and Archers are simply constitutionally unable to ignore a verbal challenge for other reasons. Aries argues because someone has dared to tell them they're wrong, when the Rams know they're always infallibly right. Sagittarius argues because truth isn't being told, and if there's anything an Archer can't stand, it's to hear truth distorted.

The fable about the Emperor's new clothes is an excellent example. There they were, all those brainwashed subjects, thousands of gullible people — standing in the ditches, and cheering their insane Emperor as he paraded by in his carriage — stark nude. Because he was their leader, and could therefore do no wrong, they saw him draped in luxurious satins and velvets, sparkling with precious stones. "See how beautiful the Emperor's clothes are !"

There's no telling what might have happened to that mythical kingdom, if a small child (who could only have been a little Virgo girl with the Moon in Sag — or a young boy Archer with the Moon in Virgo) hadn't shot an arrow of truth into the crowd and called out (in modern idiom), "Hey! Dig that! The old dude is as naked as a jay bird!" I don't remember what happened to the child in the fable, but I hope the youngster wasn't picked up by the Emperor's guards for interrogation. That would have been rough on the guards.

Anyone who has a Sagittarian for a friend has submitted to a certain amount of verbal surgery. This cheerful, friendly puppy dog approaches you on the street, whacks you on the back and opens up with, "Well, hello there — how are you! My gawd, it's good to see you again, but I almost didn't recognize you. Boy, are you skinny!" Then comes the usual

Sagittarian apology for the rudeness, because these people are basically kind-hearted, and only the occasional, unevolved Archer would wound you deliberately. "Oh, no, I've done it again, haven't I ? Stuck my big foot in my mouth. You're probably *sensitive* about being skinny, right ?"

Or maybe this scene: "How are things going, old chum ? Listen, I hear you got fired because you've been hitting the bottle too much. That's nothing to be ashamed of. Look at President Andrew Johnson. He was an alky, and they tried to fire him too. Did you ever think of getting a job as a wine taster ? Now, there's a career where you could really go places! Say, how about bringing that married woman you've been dating and dropping over to the house tonight ? Don't worry, I'll tell my wife to hide the liquor. You know what St. Patrick said. God invented whiskey to keep the Irish from ruling the world !"

Producer – TV personality David Susskind is a double Sagittarian. (Sagittarius Sun Sign and Ascendent.) Perhaps you caught his television show the night of the famous interview between "friendly puppy dog" Susskind and the bombastic Russian Ram, Nikita Khrushchev, which was running along quite nicely until David looked Premier Khrushchev straight in the eye and shot out something like: "Why is your country so deceptive, and why do your officials lie so much ?" How's that for warming up a cold war ? Zing ! Zowie ! As papers across the nation reported the following day, and even owners of black-and-white television sets could see, Aries Khrushchev's face turned several shades of angry red, and his features strongly resembled a thundercloud about to explode into a storm.

Aries normally admires and defends Sagittarian honesty, since Rams also pride themselves on telling the truth. But they draw the line at hearing the truth about themselves. That's a marked difference between Aries and Sag. The Archer is nearly as blunt in making unflattering statements about himself — or herself — as in telling others their faults. The Ram champions the truth only up to the point where it begins to sting, or come too close to home. Aries people aren't noted for easily recognizing or accepting their shortcomings and flaws.

Although most Sagittarian arrows are shot in good faith, with no real intent to be malicious, an occasional unevolved and unenlightened Centaur will blast a Ram with a cutting and cruel remark that bears no relation to truth, guided only by a desire to hurt. (All traits of all twelve Sun Signs can be, at times, expressed through their negative polarity.) While such a brutal Sag may get away with this sort of behavior with most people, he or she will discover it isn't very smart to so attempt to shoot down a Ram of either sex. The arrow will be shot right back, with the added Martian thrust of righteous outrage, not always hitting its mark immediately (Aries aim is not as true as the Archer's) but eventually finding its fiery way home. Jupiter is a large and powerful star, but even in the sky, Jupiter remains a healthy distance away from the warlike Mars, ruler of Aries. To fail to defend against attack would disgrace the Mars reputation for fearlessness, and topple the entire astrological structure. It will never happen.

But this is a 5-9 vibrational association, and the frequent friction between these two can be smoothed with the quick regret and open forgiveness both Sun Signs are capable of demonstrating when they've been naughty or unkind toward each other. Neither Sag nor Aries is able to contain anger for long periods of time, and neither Sun Sign bears ill will beyond the passion of the moment — unless one of them happens to have a Scorpio Moon Sign. Then the injury might be remembered for more than a few days. Even so, the Sun is more powerful than the Moon's lighter influence, and eventually, the sunny dispositions of the Ram and the Centaur will restore harmony between them.

Many careers and activities attract the wandering, restless Sagittarian, from jungle safaris to gambling dens or the stock market, the biggest gambling den of them all — from horse breeding or dog training to religion — from medicine and the law, to higher education — as long as the Archer is free to move around, and talk — to take a chance, and find a thrill.

Many careers and activities attract the gregarious Aries too. Just pick a profession, and the Ram will be happy to run it for you. They're not choosy, as long as they can be boss. Aries is a Cardinal Sign of leadership. Sag is a Mutable Sign, and less inclined to seek authority. Intuitively, the Archer knows the boss is tied down to the desk, often being unable to take as many vacations as his or her employees — and Sag does love those vacations! Actually, both of them prefer being their own boss, and gravitate toward occupations or professions where nobody tells them what to do, or when to do it.

Although the Ram and the Archer are both essentially extroverts, both born under the Positive, Masculine Day Forces, you'll meet more quiet Archers than quiet Rams. Perhaps that's because the more philosophically oriented Sagittarians have discovered the hard way — and I *do* mean the *hard* way — that you learn more when you're listening than when you're talking. After all, Jupiter does rule higher education (among other things), and it's only natural that the Jupiter-ruled gradually become adept at self-education. Archers are all naturally intuitive, and the meaning of "in-tuition" is to be taught from within.

To understand the basic difference between Sag and Aries, it's necessary to understand the differences between the two planets that rule them, Jupiter and Mars. These two people are so much alike, on the surface, that it may be hard to detect any differences, but there are.

Jupiter influences the Sagittarian man, child, woman, boy or girl to be expansive (often to exaggerate experiences and feelings, but seldom the facts) — to be brutally honest and extremely experimental, in all areas of life.

Jupiter's vibration also creates a great wanderlust in Sag, and blesses the Archers with occasional flashes of prophetic vision. Symbolized by the Centaur, which is half horse, half man, the Archer has far more personal confidence and assurance than the Ram (never mind the Aries surface brashness) because Sag contains the total experience of both human and beast.

Mars influences the Aries man, child, woman, boy or girl to be forceful and direct in all ways — to fiercely defend themselves against attack — and to be bravest in an emergency or a crisis. Such defense from the vibration of Mars is necessary for the Aries person, because Aries is symbolized by the Infant, newborn, and like the human infant, Aries would, quite literally, die without affection and care, *unless* Mars protected.

Not as wisely prophetic as Sag, Aries, nonetheless, sees straight through to the heart of all things, being blessed with a combination of Mars penetration to the core and the Infant's innocence and naivete, which is the purest wisdom of all. The most vital difference between these two, however, is that the Ram is far more vulnerable to cruelty and neglect. Also, there is never maliciousness in the Aries intent, for, like the newborn, Aries comprehends, essentially, only goodness — whereas Sagittarius has lived long enough (soulwise) to have developed more cynicism and worldly-wise attitudes.

Great idealism and striving are present in Sag, but seldom innocence. Sagittarius has learned to think, to use the intellect, to prophesy and to philosophize. Aries comprehends no other path to happiness than the newborn instinctive emotional reaction to love and kindness. Only the fierce protection of Mars keeps the Ram from being totally helpless in the hands of stronger people. Wasn't it wise of our co-Creators, in arranging to keep the karmic plan in order through astrology, to insure that the Infant of the karmic wheel would be watched over and protected by the devoted warrior (and lover of Venus) Mars?

This is the graced-by-the-gods 5-9 Sun Sign Pattern, making compatibility between the Ram and the Archer relatively easy to achieve. Both the rare, quiet Arians and Sagittarians — and the more common, typical, extroverted types — are far happier when they're both mentally and physically active, learning. Like the proverbial prophets, Sag frequently fares better away from the place of birth, and delights in traveling to get there (with little nostalgia for the "roots" left behind). Aries suffers painful heart tugs from the memory of the "safety" left behind, but nevertheless bravely joins the Archer, trying to match the faster pace of the Centaur's canter. When the Ram joins Sag, and they travel together, the trip may be a little noisy, but never dull, and they'll energetically defend each other against any baddies who threaten them. Despite their frequent squabbles, the unquenchable idealism of Sagittarius will forever move Aries to spontaneous affection and an unaccustomed compassion — just as the Archer will forever be touched by the naivete and honesty of Aries, knowing that here is someone who can be trusted never to be hypocritical or disloyal. After all the smoke has cleared away, these two will still be standing there, smiling at each other with their hearts. You might say that the Ram and the Archer are combustible, but compatible.

☆ ☆ ☆ ☆ ☆ ☆

ARIES *Woman* SAGITTARIUS *Man*

*The Never bird saw at once what he was up to,
and screamed . . . .*

To face an astrological truth bluntly and candidly, as Archers like to do, a Sagittarius male is more likely than any other (with the exception of Gemini) to be unfaithful in some way, if not physically, then mentally, through harmless flirting.

Naturally, that's a generality, certainly not true in every single case, with every single Centaur. But it's true often enough to make a love affair between a girl Ram and an even "mildly" promiscuous boy Archer about as much fun as skipping rope in sandals with cherry bombs strapped to the heels. Any man who thinks it would be a challenge to play that kind of romantic Russian roulette with an Aries female would be safer taking American singer Anita Bryant to a meeting of the Gay Liberation group. If you should run across a Mars-ruled girl who claims she isn't jealous in the smallest way of her man's attentions to other women, and theirs to him, she is either lying (because she has an afflicted Mars or Mercury in her nativity) or she's adopted, and her parents didn't tell her her true birth date. You can wager on it, and win. You have astrology's guarantee.

Of course, there's always the chance that she's not in love with the man who doesn't arouse her jealousy (jealousy of all types being merely a deep-seated fear of rejection), and she simply doesn't care. Aries ice. In fact, that's an excellent barometer of the girl Ram's feelings. If she's casual or detached regarding her lover or husband's flirtations, she's no longer in love, and he'll be told soon enough that she's stopped caring. It's the earliest Mars warning signal of romantic dissatisfaction, and very little time will elapse between such a signal and the final goodbye wave from this woman.

Aries and Sag are both Fire Signs, and fire attracts nearby fire, simply by a spark leaping from one flame to another, sometimes many feet through the air, let alone across a room. Therefore, the Sagittarian man will be drawn to the Aries woman almost from the first time they meet, for the purpose of either love or friendship. Being influenced by the 5-9 Sun Sign Pattern, their natal Suns are trined, and so they are, in a word — sympatico. It might be better if he aims for friendship, instead of love, if he isn't quite yet ready to settle down to being a one-woman-man. *He* may have enjoyed the four-in-a-bed scene in the American film *Bob and Carol and Ted and Alice*, and accepted it all in a spirit of fun and laughs — but *she's* the one who walked out on the scene, and tossed her buttered popcorn in the usher's face as she left the theatre. (As I've said elsewhere in this book, Aries anger is never discriminatory.)

One thing to be said in defense of a typical male Archer is that, if he's tempted to succumb to the charms of a new love, he's as likely as the Aries woman to confess it almost immediately. Basically the Jupiter-ruled male is both sincere and honest. Neither of these two will ever carry on a long-term deception. Admittedly, with an Aries girl, he'd be better off not being quite so truthful. He shouldn't feel obliged to report to her every single wink he receives from the predatory females who abound these days, urged as they continually are from so many directions to be sure they aren't deprived of their share of multiple sexual adventures, with no rules to the game except variety. The Mars woman's imagination supplies her with more than enough images of infidelity, without his adding the burden of meaningless winks to her feelings, and to their relationship.

It seems strange for a girl with such apparent self-confidence, who is so openly independent, to be so emotionally vulnerable. But she is, and she suffers greatly through her inner fear of being hurt or deceived in love. Aries is a masculine sign, and so the girl Ram is never quite certain of her femininity. This makes her secretly believe that even women who are clearly less intelligent and less attractive than she, are nevertheless more desirable to the man she loves, if for no other reason than their outward feminine manners. Wondering about a thing like this can be an indescribable private torture. Yet, unfortunately, her outbursts of jealousy will often receive little real sympathy or compassion from an Archer, who places a high value on personal freedom and mutual trust between two people in love.

Such an attitude is all well and good, but if he doesn't train himself to be somewhat more gentle with this woman's basic nature, and try to handle her hidden fears with more tender concern — being willing to talk things over with her now and then, to ease her mind — he'll lose her more quickly than he found her. And the emptiness she leaves in his heart may not be as easy as he thinks to fill. There's always a terrible feeling of loneliness on both sides when a man and woman whose natal Suns are trined, and who truly loved each other, separate. If the feeling they thought was love was only friendship, and was, therefore, inaccurately defined by them from the beginning, the parting will be less painful — and they may even be friends again later. But not if they deeply loved. The pain is too great, then, to transmute former affection into a casual friendship.

If mutual trust can be established between them, from the start, an Aries girl has an excellent chance for emotional harmony with a Sagittarian man, and he with her. Many Archers are sexually stable and reliable, and with those who are, love between these two can be eternally exciting and always stimulating — emotions which, in an odd sort of way, bring peace and contentment to the hearts of those born under Fire Signs. Peace and contentment within, you see, are not achieved in exactly the same manner by everyone.

Both these lovers are optimistic, open-hearted, warm and friendly. They're also both visionaries, but his visions are more practical, since Sagittarius, unlike Aries, has the prophetic ability to foresee the outcome of his dreams from their inception, as well as the self-honesty to separate them from mere fantasies, based on delusion. Although they're both expert at tossing pie-in-the-sky, his pies are seldom half-baked.

When this man and woman fall in love, the blend of her Mars enthusiasm with his Jupiter daring, gives them an insurance against boredom. Love seldom grows cold between two people who share a mutual excitement for new ideas, and an eternal youthfulness of spirit. They'll probably even vote alike, because it's an extremely exceptional Ram or Archer who isn't politically liberal. There are occasional conservatives born under both Sun Signs, of course, although the odds are that a Sag more than Aries will lean slightly to the Right. Even so, the rare conservative Sagittarian will be motivated by political idealism. Since they both feel strongly about the burning issues of the day, this is more important than it may seem as a contributing factor to their compatibility.

It's only fair to warn the Aries girl that a Sagittarian man is more likely to remain a bachelor than any other Sun Sign, except Virgo and Aquarius. His affectionate, impulsive nature (very much like her own) allows him to slide into a romance easily, and he can be precipitated by her Mars force into a commitment he's not ready to keep. Since most Archers refuse to lie at the altar, broken engagements and disappearing grooms are not uncommon with this Sun Sign. They're not cruel — just honest. I know one Sagittarian man who's been promising to marry a charming widow for more years than either of them can remember. She's still waiting, with Cancerian tenacity. If she were an Aries, she'd tell him to go dunk his donuts in someone else's coffee, lock her door and change her telephone number. Sudden action like this often brings an Archer to his senses, if he really loves the woman. If he doesn't, she has only herself to blame. He probably never actually told her he loved her. Sagittarian men are usually quite careful not to say "I love you," unless they mean it, and they have plenty of dodgy verbal tricks to get out of it, without arousing suspicion. Here are a couple that every red-blooded male

Archer has used, at one time or another. Pay close attention to the exact words.

GIRL: Darling, you do love me, don't you?
ARCHER: (hurt and angry): How can you ask me a ridiculous question like that? You don't know how I feel by now?

(or perhaps . . .)

GIRL: Do you really love me? Do you *really*?
ARCHER: What do *you* think, sweetheart? I don't see how you can wonder. (Showering her immediately with passionate kisses.)

Later, she'll accuse him of emotional breach of promise, but she didn't listen carefully. He didn't lie to her. Sagittarians never lie. Didn't you know that?

Normally, this man is not the domestic type. Look at the way he treats his own family — casually. And the way he loves his own relatives — from a distance. But the girl Ram isn't tied down to the heart either, so she won't mind his wandering, as long as he takes her with him. If she gives him miles of rope and lets him know that she, too, believes in personal freedom, the Archer can be a generous and stimulating partner, in or out of wedlock. She should learn to love animals, because sooner or later, this man will bring home a dog or a horse. If they live in a small apartment, let's hope it's a dog.

He may spend lots of time at the stables, in the woods, hiking or camping — involving himself in sports as a participant ' or spectator — or involving himself in the theatre as a participant or spectator. The more-intellectual type of Archer will substitute books and philosophy for nature, sports or the stage, but whatever, his interests will frequently be outside the home. It doesn't mean he isn't in love with her, and the Aries girl must realize that, if she wants to hold him for keeps.

Their sexual adjustment is almost automatic. Both of them are deeply affectionate, and passion is never lacking, since they're both Fire Signs. His approach to physical lovemaking may be slightly more casual and detached than hers, and not quite so intense, but it will be no less sincere, and certainly no less idealistic. Each is capable of a warm response, which can make their intimacies wonderfully fulfilling, although perhaps not completely free of sexual selfishness (one of the most common causes of sexual disharmony). They may both have to learn that real happiness comes from an inner need to *love* — not to *be* loved. The lesson shouldn't be too difficult, because the sense of giving is strong in both their natures. Since they're also mentally and emotionally well mated, the physical relationship between them (barring jealousy and unfaithfulness) can be ideal in every sense.

She won't like it when he sometimes makes promises he can't keep, for Archers often impulsively reach out farther than their arms can stretch. She may explode into angry tears when he carelessly blurts out an unpleasant truth, without regard for her sensitive feelings. And she could become annoyed with his clumsy attempts at humor, which can be poorly timed. Sagittarians are half clown, you know, and the antics of clowns are never subtle. She's stuck with Emmett Kelly, so why not accept his peanuts and cotton candy, laugh and enjoy it? Although he may occasionally resent her claims on his freedom and her demands on his time, he'll admire her bright mind and respect her independence.

As for the possibility that his Jupiter tendency to promiscuity will ignite her Mars jealousy, don't overlook the Archer's strong sense of honor and personal integrity. He'll behave the way he's expected and trusted to behave. There's an old metaphysical formula, so magical, it works wonders. A friend of mine, Hank Fort, once wrote a song, with lyrics that sum up this infallible Universal Law, and they say, in part . . .

> give makes give — greed makes greed
> flower makes flower — and weed makes weed
> clean makes clean — dust makes dust
> doubting makes doubting — and trust makes trust

The Aries woman in love with an Archer, who repeats that last line over and over again when her heart is troubled, will discover that it's truly a miracle mantra that will bring her more reasons to rejoice than to cry. For truth makes truth, you see — and lie makes lie.

☆ ☆ ☆ ☆ ☆ ☆

ARIES *Man* SAGITTARIUS *Woman*

————◄◗►————

. . . and then Peter gripped her and began to draw her toward the window.

"Let me go!" she ordered him . . . . . .
Of course she was very pleased to be asked.

A Sagittarian girl who's attracted to an Aries man is only doing what comes naturally. She admires courage, craves excitement, likes to have fun — and the Ram is certainly not a stick-in-the-mud. True he's somewhat bossy, and inclined to insist on getting his own way. But he's eternally a sentimental romanticist, and that's what she's looking for, even though this girl may not recognize her own goal until someone points it out to her. Once she is made to realize it, however, she'll gather a goodly number of scars from looking for it in all the wrong places and ways. But she'll cover them, often with the mask of the clown. Sag always tells a joke when Jupiter's idealism has been struck. It's a defense mechanism. This woman desperately needs romance, because only romance can heal her instinctive cynicism. She was born somewhat skeptical, and her excursions into love frequently do nothing to soften it, but instead, only sharpen it — and her wit.

Not being overly sensitive (unless his Moon is in a Water Sign, or his birth chart contains an extremely well-aspected Neptune), the average Aries man isn't greatly perceptive when it comes to analyzing human nature. He more or less takes people as he finds them and may therefore find her need for romance difficult to conceive when she comes on to him like a comic Valentine, with a cynical laugh, lugging a copy of Kate Millett's *Sexual Revolution,* and defying him to possess her. Or when she wears one of her other Sagittarian theatrical masks that disguise her as a wacky, wriggling puppy — or as a shy, withdrawn spinster.

In her heart, the Sagittarian girl longs for an intelligent, honest man, who will take her into his warm arms and protect her forever — from herself. Before he can do that, the Ram will have to gently remove her greasepaint, and tell her firmly that the musical comedy is over. She'll protest, because she loves the theatre and she also shares Cinderella's fear of the midnight curfew, when her coach turns into a pumpkin. Nevertheless, it must be done. A girl Archer is much easier to handle when she's sitting in a pumpkin, barefoot and humble, than when she's flying around at the ball, flirting and flapping her defiance at a man. Once she's been properly bent into submission (a task about as easy as trying to pass a race horse while riding a turtle), she can be the sweetest woman in the world. But the Aries man will need a quick turtle to catch the Sagittarius mare.

He can comfort himself with the thought that this girl is not only slightly clumsy in a physical sense (despite her graceful walk and bearing) — she's also a little clumsy emotionally. Sooner or later, she'll stumble. Then he can pick her up in his warm, understanding arms, plunk her down in that pumpkin, and demonstrate the facts of life to her — the facts of life being that he is a man and she is a woman. (Sag is a masculine sign, you know.) He could find this even more of a challenge than taming the Aries female, because a girl Archer, being half horse, can run faster than a Ram. If he can convince her that she can trust him to love her completely (unlike those other phony hypocrites who broke her heart), she'll reward him with freedom, stimulating conversation, devoted friendship, affection, humor, warmth and generosity. All that is surely worth a little trouble at the starting gate.

In the beginning, the Ram will be outraged by her blunt speech and lack of consideration for his tender male ego. Neither will he be happy with her sheer luck in winning all the Monopoly games by intuitively grabbing up Boardwalk and Park Place, and in general, making him look foolish in front of his friends with her frankness. Aries men are determined to retain their masculine superiority, independence and personal freedom at any cost. If he has trouble communicating this to her, he might try a little history. "Baby, do you know who wrote the greatest statement of freedom the world has ever known — the Declaration of Independence? A male Ram, named Tom Jefferson. Who else could have authored such a glorious example of independence, but an Aries?" It might impress her.

Of course, there are other things that same history lesson might teach her too, like the absence of humility in the Mars nature. Arian Thomas Jefferson also wrote his own epitaph, a typical example of Aries modesty: "*Here lies Thomas Jefferson, Author of the Declaration of Independence, Author of the Statute of Virginia for Religious Liberty, and Founder of the University of Virginia.*" He didn't have to mention that he was President. That was already taken care of elsewhere on his marker, by tradition. So Tom could afford the self-effacing gesture of excluding it from the tribute to his accomplishments which he composed himself. Like all Rams, Thomas Jefferson was a radical, an innovator of new ideas, a fiery lover of independence — and most certainly not bashful.

But why should he have been? After all, he did pioneer, develop and manifest all those things, with his Mars enthusiasm and courage. Why should he hide his light behind a bushel of false humility? In the area of ego, the Aries man and his Sagittarian woman won't have much tension. Well, maybe a little, but not much. As a Cardinal sign, he can't help his instincts to lead. As a Mutable sign, she's not consumed with the ego or personality. She'd rather keep it tucked out of sight if it interferes with her traveling around in her mind, or geographically. Mutable signs are not unduly ego-driven. (The other two Mutables are Pisces and Virgo, and these people are hardly pushy egotists.) Of the three Mutables, Sag is perhaps the most conscious of the *self*, and the "self-consciousness" of the Archer is seldom overdone.

The term "self-conscious" is confusing and contradictory. One thinks of it as indicating humility or embarrassment — or a degree of introversion. Isn't this the image conjured for you when a person is described as "self-conscious?" Oddly, we Americans have twisted the true meaning, which is, of course, "conscious-of-the-self" — and that certainly has naught to do with humility, introversion or any of those submerging-of-the-ego patterns. Anyway, whatever, the girl Centaur is a few degrees *more* self-conscious than her Pisces and Virgo mutable sisters, yet considerably *less* so than the male Ram.

Not all, but by far the largest majority of Sagittarian women prefer male friends to female friends, so the jealous Ram will have lots of opportunities to remind himself that she's only being friendly, cheerful and gregarious, not unfaithful. She's more than a little inclined toward jealousy herself when goaded, but not nearly so much as he. Whatever number of mean little green monsters do hide in the background of her aura won't have many chances to appear, because her Aries lover or husband also prefers the company of men. Isn't that lucky?

That's another thing. This girl is lucky. Somehow, a great many of her worst goofs turn out right side up, under the benevolent and fortunate influence of her ruler, Jupiter, who blessed her at birth like a faerie godfather (an interesting term) with the shining qualities of faith and optimism, which, when combined, are a mighty powerful force for sheer "luck," which isn't luck at all, only the result of the law of magnetism. One attracts what one images — and she images happiness a great deal of the time.

Despite her general air of loose or unconventional social behavior, remember that Jupiter rules spiritual insight and prophetic essence of all religion. This girl possesses an inner innocence and a touching faith in people (at least she did when she was younger) that often place her in awkward positions, and make it seem she's more flirtatious than she really is. It all begins so innocently.

ARIES: You spent the entire night in Mr. Cromwell's town house because he's your boss, and he needed you? I'll just bet he needed you, that sneaky old goat. As for you, you have the morals of an alley cat. (Rams are not noted for their care in choosing words when the Mars temper is exploding.)

SAG: His dog was due to have puppies, and he was going to let her have them all by herself. Someone had to help the poor thing.

ARIES: A dirty old man who seduces his secretary into sleeping with him is not a poor thing.

SAG: I meant the dog. Mr. Cromwell is a creep. He went to bed, and I had to deliver the puppies all by myself in the kitchen. One of them was born dead. It was so sad. I cried all the way home in the taxi.

ARIES: You cried all . . . so that's why your makeup is smeared. Darling, I'm sorry, I didn't realize . . .

SAG: You mean you didn't *trust* me. Don't try to apologize. You called me an alley cat. That's an obvious indication of your psychotic hatred for animals, using a poor cat to symbolize a prostitute — which you think *I* am. Just leave — I never want to see you again!

A few scenes like that, changing names, places and situations, and the Ram will learn, hopefully before he's lost her, that unfounded jealousy is something she won't stand for, because it implies she's dishonest, and Sagittarians all have a thing about truth and integrity that amounts to a regular neurosis with some of them. Just ask their psychiatrists. If she had submitted to Mr. Cromwell's seductions, she would probably have told Aries quite frankly, leaving out none of the lurid details.

Barring such a forthright confession, the Ram should have faith in her. True, Sagittarian women, like Gemini and Pisces women, percentage-wise, are tempted more often into experiments in sexual promiscuity or multiple affairs than their other Sun Sign sisters, because they are Mutable, and also dual in nature — but the Archer is not sneaky. Whatever the Aries man may accuse her of, it should not be deception. This woman will always be true to herself, and to the man she loves, until she falls out of love with him — or until he unfairly doubts her. Even then, she's more apt to break off their relationship angrily and emotionally than to be unfaithful simply to punish him. (Unless she has a Scorpio Moon Sign or Ascendent.) Even those girl Archers who have a history of casually changing sexual partners will normally indulge in only one affair at a time, and such behavior is usually triggered by a series of severe romantic disillusionments.

Both Sag and Aries are equally guilty of flashes of conceit, bossiness and recklessness, which they both consider to be virtues. They're also both hampered by a contempt for caution, prudence and patience, which they both consider to be vices.

Once they've discovered that compromise is the best way to solve their disagreements and end their quarrels, they can achieve a kind of mental and emotional harmony, not to mention physical harmony, that couples who don't gamble for such high stakes (and who are not guided by the graced-with-mutual-sympathy 5-9 vibration) could ever hope to reach. Their sexual rapport should be both stimulating and quieting . . . warm, imaginative . . . and full of shooting stars. As long as she remembers that "silence is golden" during their lovemaking and refrains from puncturing his passion at a strategic point with one of her Sagittarian verbal arrows. Intimate moments are not the ideal time for cheerful chatter or candid observations. Otherwise, the way these two express and share the sexual side of their love can be deeply satisfying for both of them.

Neither of these two Sun Signs is stingy by nature, so money shouldn't create many problems between them, except perhaps where and how to get it, after they've spent it all. If it comes to a race to see who's more extravagant, you can bet on the Ram, since the typical or average Archer is normally a few (short) lengths behind Sag in scattering lettuce around carelessly. Her general disposition may be a degree or so calmer than his too, but you can't really depend on this, unless she has a Pisces or Taurus Ascendent or Moon Sign, so he'd best not think it will save him when he tries to boss her around, or insult her cooking or housekeeping, neither of which are the average girl Archer's strong points.

The important thing for the Aries man to realize is that this girl is as much of an idealist about love and Life as he is — perhaps even more so. Her popularity and her friendly, open manner with men doesn't change the quality of her basic integrity. Does his fondness for innocent and harmless feminine admiration mean infidelity on his part? No, it doesn't. Seldom, if ever. Like her, he'll remain faithful to love until love is no longer there, and even then will tend more to confession than to secrecy. But he might consider the fact that she has her fears too. Very much like his own. As long as he's honest with her, this girl will love him with her whole heart, run bravely alongside him wherever he wants to go. She may lose her temper and say things she doesn't mean — but the moment she knows he's really hurt, she'll rush to his side to bind up his wounds, whether they're physical or emotional, with an unexpected tenderness and gentleness. Then the flames of their Fire Element natures will ignite all over again, just like the first time.

The only thing he needs to remember is to be honest with her always — keep the make-believe and excitement alive in their relationship — and not speak rashly, in anger. Exactly the same things she needs to remember about him. These two are so much alike. Proud. Brave. Generous. Impulsive. Passionate. Independent. Idealistic. And very, very vulnerable to coldness and rejection . . . especially from each other. Once they've permanently conquered their mutual unintentional selfishness, nothing can separate them. The strength of their love is unconquerable. Mars and Jupiter are a formidable combination.

ARIES

Fire — Cardinal — Positive
Ruled by Mars
Symbol: The Ram
Day Forces — Masculine

CAPRICORN

Earth — Cardinal — Negative
Ruled by Saturn
Symbol: The Goat
Night Forces — Feminine

The **ARIES-CAPRICORN** *Relationship*

> *"It is only the gay and innocent and heartless who can fly."*
>
> *"What is gay and innocent and heartless? I do wish I were gay and innocent and heartless."*

That wistful complaint from James M. Barrie's *Peter Pan* might well be spoken by a Capricorn who envies the Aries ability to fly happily through life, with free and careless style. However, the Goat needn't envy the Ram's flair for being heartless, because it's synonymous with selfishness, a quality not at all exclusive with Aries. Capricorns possess more than their fair share of it.

Aries selfishness is the result of the Ram's thoughtless and often infantile desires. What Aries wants, one way or another, Aries gets, when he — or she — has learned to curb that Mars enthusiasm and not forge ahead too quickly. Capricorn selfishness is motivated by the Goat's determination not to look back to see who slipped and fell behind, lest it delay his (or her) own personal appointment with destiny. Still, selfish is selfish, whatever the basis or the cause, and they're both guilty of it rather frequently.

As for the other two requirements for flying — gaiety and innocence — the Goat has every reason to envy the Ram. Gaiety is not a word one ordinarily associates with Saturn-ruled people. Try applying it to Capricorns Humphrey Bogart, Edgar Allen Poe, Joan of Arc or Howard Hughes. Bogart gaily pulling out his revolver. Poe gaily "quothing" the Raven. Joan of Arc gaily leading the Armies of France against England. Howard Hughes — well, Howard Hughes gaily doing *anything*. Or even his identical twin brother, Robard Hughes. (If he should happen to have one — just fantasizing, you know.) Nor is innocence a Capricorn quality. Cappies are never innocent, not even as tiny babes, toddlers and children. The entire bunch of them, whether clad in pink or blue booties, were each and every one born a little old man, or a little old woman, with an ingrained and very "grainy" sense of both wisdom and patience, not normally acquired until near or past the century mark, chronologically speaking.

And so, you see, there's small chance that the Goat will fly through life with the naive gaiety and innocent guilelessness of the Ram, until well past what is fallaciously called "middle age" (since it's really quite young in a life expectancy span of three to five hundred years, attainable even now, for those who properly seek it). Then the Capricorn "reverse aging" process will begin, bringing on spurts of total abandon that can sometimes cause the Goat to even soar high above the Ram. That's why Aries people usually feel more comfortable around older Goats. The younger ones make them nervous.

Aries reasons for forming any kind of human relationship or association are always impulsive and idealistic, governed by the emotions. Capricorns have more practical motivations. Although Goats quite understandably resent the astrological implication that many of them are inclined to "marry up the social or financial ladder," it's nevertheless more often true of Cappy than of Aries. It's not that Capricorns are cold and calculating. After all, they're just thinking of those yet-to-be-born youngsters. Not only are they going to wear shoes, they're going to wear good shoes, because a podiatrist is frightfully expensive. And they're certainly not going to suffer (the children, not the podiatrists) in the future for any romantic flings of the present. This is why Cappy is often horrified to hear about a couple of friends, living in unwedded bliss, who plan to give up their jobs and bike across Europe for a year or so. It isn't the lack of the marriage certificate alone that disturbs the Goat. What if she should get pregnant over there? And if he gives up a perfectly good job, how will they ever afford to get the children's teeth straightened?

Now, this may shock a few of the Cappies reading it, right down to the toes of their sensible boots, but we're into the Aquarian Age, my dears, and the girl and her beau in our example are experimenting with a trial marriage. You see, they aren't planning to have any children with crooked teeth or toes, until they're sure they can stand each other long enough to raise a family with some sense of permanency. If it doesn't work out, they'll part as friends (usually) — much sadder, but also considerably wiser.

The typical Aries reaction to such an arrangement is rather touchingly sentimental and romantically hopeful. If the two of them really love each other, thinks the Ram, then they should *know* it's going to be forever, so why not marry in the beginning?

The typical Capricorn reaction to the same situation is also rather touchingly sentimental and romantically hopeful. The Goat girl echoes the girl Ram's question. If the two of them really love each other, they should *know* it's going to be forever, so why not marry in the beginning? So far, the Goat and the Ram are walking the same path. Then Mars and Saturn part company. Abruptly.

After due deliberation, and careful reflection — and after the initial shock has passed — Cappy will give the issue thoughtful Saturnine consideration, and finally decide that the arrangement makes good sense after all. (Since the Goat is a confirmed realist, Capricorn morality is very closely interwoven with Capricorn practicality.)

All right, forget about the orange blossoms and the moral issue, but still Capricorn wonders, *"who's* going to pay the *rent ?"* Probably the girl. Her lover, you see, yearns to become a poet, so she may have to support them both for a while. Aries finds nothing at all wrong with *that.* Not so Cappy. Capricorn's advice to the girl then, would be: "Tell him to forget the limericks and earn some bread, or bid him one of those friendly farewells, with no regrets."

Capricorns are always hurt when Aries people accuse them of being ambitious. They think no one knows it. Who, *them* ? Ambitious ? Yes, *them* — ambitious. There are other Saturnine traits that Goats are a little slow to recognize in themselves, like those periodic binges of gloomy pessimism, their hankering to grab the top rung of the social ladder, their reluctance to defy the Establishment — and their often blind obeisance to tradition, family, law and order and all forms of authority. (Goat J. Edgar Hoover was just doing his Saturn thing.)

Rams are ambitious, too, but quite open about it. Instead of pessimism, they have periodic binges of downright foolish optimism. Most Aries wouldn't know a social ladder from a tall shutter, they delight in defying the Establishment, they feel no obligation whatsoever to respect any sort of authority — and their blind obeisance is paid, for the most part, to themselves, to their own ideas and desires.

As an Aries myself, I make the following confession most reluctantly. But if it will help make the vibration between these two Sun Signs more clear, well . . . all right. My daughter, Jill (a Capricorn), was wiser than her mother from the very day she was born. Not only wiser, but calmer, more practical, more sensible — and exasperatingly *always* right. Did I mention more cautious ? Also more cautious.

I began rather early taking Jill along with me when I was Christmas shopping, knowing she would make sure I didn't lose my money, my pocketbook, my packages — or my head. We started this little holiday tradition when Cappy was only eight years old. It was humiliating. But it never failed to work.

Before I started taking her along, there was never a Christmas I didn't leave my shopping money — or half a dozen gifts — on a counter somewhere on the first floor of Macy's or Gimbel's only realizing it when I was on a crowded elevator, on the way to the twelfth floor. After a while, I decided I was really overworking St. Anthony (finder of lost articles) and drafted my tiny Goat into duty as chaperone. I pass this along to Aries parents of Capricorn youngsters everywhere, as sort of a Noel gift . . . for all seasons.

Bobbs Pinkerton, the warm and wise Capricorn editor of my first book, *Sun Signs,* once swore to me that she wasn't a typical Goat Girl because she adores (she claimed) bright colors. "*Mad* about them," I believe, was the way she put it. (Astrologically very doubtful, although she does have a Sagittarius Moon, and quite probably *wants* to be mad about them.) So we made a bet — naturally, a small one, since Capricorns don't wager with much largesse — and went through her closets.

We found nothing but black (with a few stingy white trims) navy blue, dark green, and brown. Finally, she triumphantly pulled out of the very back of the closet a wild, canary yellow jumpsuit, carefully wrapped in tissue and strongly smelling of moth balls. I gave her my most direct Mars look, and she owned up, blushing, "Well, I only wear it at home, but it was such a bargain." Being a typically honest Goat, she knew the fourteen cents she bet me was rightfully mine, and promptly paid it.

Capricorns have this truly marvelous ability to face the facts dispassionately, curb their faults and make the very best of their virtues. It wouldn't hurt most Rams to imitate them. Speaking of jumpsuits and such, Cappy Bobbs claims she has an eighty-year-old Capricorn neighbor who wears miniskirts with demure high-necked, long-sleeved blouses. "Well," she says, "I figure it this way. The legs are the last to go."

So it's a mistake to think of all Goats as Grandma Moses or Whistler's Mother. The male Capricorns are not always as prim and proper as you might think either. Not being burdened with excess baggage of Aries idealism, they can shock a Ram with all sorts of unexpected propositions and behavior — in private.

However, in the final analysis, the Capricorn mind runs in rather conservative grooves, at least publicly. Aries is frequently accusing Capricorn of a lack of sympathy; yet the Goat is not without tender concern and compassion for those he (or she) thinks are genuinely worth it. Cooperation can mean undreamed-of success between the Ram and the Goat, when they mutually aim their horns against prejudice and falsehood, instead of toward each other.

Picture the shy but sturdy and sure-footed mountain goat, stepping carefully from crag to crag, with confidence and determination . . . . . managing to find sufficient nourishment in patches of sparse grass, even swallowing cardboard and munching on tin cans when it's necessary. Nothing is permitted to delay his slow yet steady progress to the beckoning pinnacle of truth, wisdom and justice.

Now picture the rocky mountain ram, who requires a diet of richer grass. Unlike the goat, the ram finds it impossible to calmly digest the rusty nails of criticism and the broken glass of disappointment . . . and often misjudges the distance, in leaping between the crags, causing him to fall, and smash his horns. Because the dreamer's vision distracts him on Nature's rocky path, the bighorn ram takes some unscheduled detours along the way.

That's the basic difference between Capricorn and Aries men, women and children. Both Sun Signs are tough climbers. But the Goat's final destination is the very top of the mountain, the only place where he (or she) feels really secure. To the rare, more gregarious Ram, who makes it up that high, the top of the mountain is a lonely spot, with no more challenges — and what is Life without the thrill of danger? For Capricorn — *peaceful*. For Aries — *boring*.

ARIES *Woman* CAPRICORN *Man*

———— ◆◂◼▸◆ ————

"Now," said he, "shall I give you a kiss?"
. . . . She made herself rather cheap by
inclining her face toward him, but he merely
dropped an acorn button into her hand; so she
slowly returned her face to where it had been
before, and said nicely that she would wear his
kiss on the chain round her neck.

The unmistakable air of loneliness that hangs over a Capricorn man, even in a roomful of people, draws the Aries girl straight to his side. To the sentimental, egocentric female Ram, the reason for his loneliness is obvious. He's been waiting for her — to show him how beautiful life can be. So she directly proceeds to show him. Aries never beats around the bush.

Her initial enthusiasm, however, may soon be stifled by the Capricorn man's slow responses — his earthy immunity to her fiery Mars charisma, and her impulsive emotions may finally lead her to decide he's too stuffy, aloof, distant. How can she help him find the sunlight when he's so drearily attached to his career, not to mention his family — including his great-aunts and kissing cousins, as well as his saintly parents? There's little hope he'll ever sweep her off her feet and marry her when he's already so permanently wedded to his job, his ambition and/or his relatives.

It could be the end of a promising relationship that might have been deeply satisfying, as well as financially successful. Why should she waste her time trying to break through his loneliness to show him that life is beautiful, when he obviously enjoys his isolation? He wouldn't recognize beauty if it knocked him over. She's wrong.

Capricorns do appreciate beauty. But he'll never tell her about those pictures he painted in school when the teacher wasn't looking, or the music he used to drown himself in when no one was listening, before he buckled down to the serious problems of carving out his security in a mad world . . . . . . unless he thinks she really cares.

It can hurt to lose someone you love because you're unable to communicate your feelings, and this is too often the case between the quiet boy Goat and the aggressive girl Ram. How can he let her know about all those secret dreams he wants to give her — how can he show her the lifelong romanticism hidden deep within his shy, funny Goat's heart? Well, he should look at it this way: if she can't see more virtue in the exceptional than in the exciting, she's not the right girl for him. Or he might memorize Elizabeth Barrett Browning's sonnet that begins, "How do I love thee? Let me count the ways......," and practice, practice, practice. Lovers down through the ages have learned they can say things to each other in verse, that were buried inside their souls, just waiting to be discovered, so they could be revealed to one special person.

So, you see, the Mars-directed instinct of the Aries girl might have been right. He really *was* waiting for her to come along, and show him how to paint rainbows. It's just that her initial approach might have been overwhelming for the more introverted Goat. Capricorns have difficulty coping with reckless action and abandon, even in the name of love. It takes this man a certain length of time to make sure he has a firm grip on the reality of a romance, and even then, he proceeds with caution. This way, he's sure not to slip and fall, or make any mistakes he'll regret at some future date. With Aries, it's "fly now — pay later." With Capricorn, it's "pay now — and fly later, with a clear conscience."

Assuming Capricorn and Aries do reach across the chasm of their differences, and hang on to each other's hands and hearts, the disparities between their outlooks on life must still be either overcome or over-looked. He'll try to over-look them. She'll try to overcome them. Even in tackling the problems of their differences, they're different. It lies in their divergent approaches to a situation. Here are a couple of examples.

The situation: He has just hurt his knee, and the doctor has told him he shouldn't aggravate the injury by walking on it for at least three weeks. (Capricorns are always banging their kneecaps, visiting the dentist, breaking bones or suffering a touch of arthritis. Otherwise, their health is great.) The knee injury spoils the skiing trip they'd planned in the mountains.

ARIES: "I'm sorry you can't come with me, darling. But I'm sure you won't mind if I go along with the others and try to enjoy myself anyway."

CAPRICORN: "Do you know what you are? You're *selfish*."

ARIES: "Do you expect me to sit here and hold your hand, when I've been looking forward to this weekend all year? Couldn't you make an effort and come along, even if you don't ski?"

CAPRICORN: "No, I do *not* wish to come along in my crippled state, and yes, I *do* expect you, if you love me, to stay here and hold my hand."

ARIES: "Do you know what you are? You're *selfish*."

(Actually, they're both right. They're *both* selfish.)

Another situation: (If the first one hasn't already scared them off.) She's temporarily broke, so he lends her the money to have her car overhauled, and to make her rent payment. She has no qualms whatever about asking him.

After all, they're in love. It both impresses and touches her that he's so sweet about giving her the cash without any coaxing or quibbling. Several months pass, and she still hasn't repaid the loan. She's forgotten all about it, you see. So he gently reminds her, but she thinks he's only teasing. Meanwhile, she's showered him with an expensive color TV set and a pure silk kimono for Christmas—plus a solid gold wristwatch and a St. Bernard puppy for his birthday—all on her credit cards. He's sincerely moved, and grateful for her gesture, but not so grateful that he forgets to mail her an informal written statement, listing the two hundred dollars he loaned her (with some Capricorns this could conceivably also include a few extra dollars in accrued interest) and love flies out the window in a burst of Mars fireworks.

ARIES: How *dare* he put our intimacy on a vulgar, financial basis?
CAPRICORN: How *dare* she violate our intimacy by refusing to respect an obligation between us?

And so it goes—bumpety, bumpety, crackle and pop.

On the physical side of love between them, the same kind of hurdles must be overcome before they find sexual satisfaction. When the Ram mates with the Goat, it's a blending of Fire and Earth, and these are not normally the most compatible of elements. His sex impulses are controlled by Saturn, the planet of solid resistence, self-discipline and permanence. Hers are directed by Mars, the planet symbolizing the masculine principle of flaming penetration. Capricorn would rather remain lonely and starved for love than risk being burned by a temporary passion. Aries would rather risk being scorched then not even try. So she's usually the one to initiate the sexual advances. Assuming the stars are favorable, and she catches him when he's too weak to resist, the Capricorn man will respond to her fresh, enthusiastic expressions of love with the kind of profound intensity only the Saturn-ruled can understand—and a depth of affection that will surprise her as much as it will delight her.

If these two miraculously manage to get together, it's probably because he has the Moon in Aries, Sagittarius, Leo, Gemini or Aquarius—or because she has the Moon in Capricorn, Taurus, Virgo, Pisces or Scorpio. Then the differences between them (and there are undeniable differences) will tend to attract instead of repel. In other words, rather than become annoyed by his caution, stability and composure, she'll respect him for these qualities she lacks, and try to imitate them. Rather than become uptight over her forceful drive, he'll envy and admire it, and loosen up his laces a little himself. With a harmonious Sun-Moon relationship in their mutual charts, love between Aries and Capricorn can grow into a deep, and lasting, devotion—sexually and otherwise.

However, with a square or opposition between their natal Sun and Moon signs, the Goat and the Ram will either lock horns in constant battle, or become so bored with each other that they wander off someday and forget to return. Whatever their planetary positions, there's always the chance that his distrustful reserve in the beginning will petrify her natural romantic buoyancy, and they'll never get beyond holding hands at the movies — or making magical promises with their eyes which they never keep.

The Goat and the Ram are not immune to the common mistake of all 4-10 Sun Sign Pattern lovers, who see the world through different-colored glasses. They fall in love, then try to change the very qualities they first loved in each other. When he first decides he loves her, he's impressed by her optimistic, bubbly conversation. Even her recklessness intrigues him into feeling an unaccustomed, grudging admiration. He smiles at her extravagances, and chuckles indulgently at her mistakes. Then, perversely, he tries to mold her trusting, hopeful personality into a more conventional and acceptable form. But she will not be molded.

When she first decides she loves him, she's enormously impressed with his strong, silent aura of strength. It both mystifies and excites her. His patience and mildness are soothing to her tangled emotions, and her heart beats faster, just imagining what it would be like to share an intimate, day-to-day relationship with this gentle, quietly humorous, wise and steady man. Then she begins to feel stifled by it all, so she tries to coax him into tossing caution over his shoulder. She beckons to him to come and chase clouds with her, to run through sweet-smelling clover fields in a summer rain — only to find he's brought along his umbrella again.

The Capricorn man can't understand why the Aries girl has such fun riding on an endless merry-go-round. It only makes him dizzy. But she likes the calliope music and the way the wind blows her hair. She will wonder why he keeps his heart locked up so tight. He'll tell her it's just to be safe. But there's nothing in a heart to steal. Only things to give.

When this man and woman drift away from each other, the strain of the music they once heard together may haunt them, reminding them that perhaps they didn't try quite hard enough. He may not reveal outwardly the pain he feels over losing her, but still waters run deep, and Earth sorrow runs even deeper. She will weep inconsolably for many a day, following her own fiery emotional pattern, but by and by she'll forget, though she may watch the sunrise wistfully for years afterward. She won't tell him how she's hurting inside — why should she? He's so cold and detached, and barely even says hello when they pass on the street . . . . . like that time at the corner, when the city traffic was so heavy and noisy, they could only wave to each other. He didn't even smile. But what she doesn't know is that somewhere, deep within his lonely heart, he may be thinking things she suspects, like, maybe such words as . . . .

How old am I? I'll be 92 next Christmas
though I won't admit to one day over 20 . . .
even after all the birthday cards are cut and shuffled
it's hard to figure

I've aged at least 500 years since I stumbled into you;
yet I still believe in faerie tales
like the Princess and the Frog
and I still believe you wanted me . . .
perhaps I'm only three or so?

you'll never know . . . how old I am
but I'll tell you anyway
I was born the hour I met you . . . and died today. °

She doesn't hear the words his heart speaks to her silently, of course. She's thinking her own thoughts, remembering the thing he said to her, one dawn, as they were walking along the shore, by the ocean . . . . when he held her in his arms, and said quietly . . . . "and here you'll stay, until it's time for you to go." Then she asked him, "When will that time be?" But he didn't answer. So she never asked again. Aries is proud.

Remember the message of the stars. Those lovers who are victorious over the heavy soul-testing of the 4-10 vibrational influence, are blessed by Venus. And perhaps it does take the gentle planet Venus to soften two hearts ruled by the masculine planets, Mars and Saturn. Venus . . . and music . . . poetry . . . and memories . . .

The tensions and troubles, the misunderstandings and lack of communication this man and woman must face — are formidable. But their rewards for being patient with each other, and waiting for the heart's wisdom to guide them — are forever-after. Now she wishes she had stayed home and held his hand that time when he hurt his knee. How could she have been so selfish? Now he thinks maybe he should have offered to go with her, just to watch her ski down a snowy hill, knowing she was his. How could he have been so selfish?

Foresight is much better than hindsight. But it still might not be too late to say "I'm sorry." It's never too late for those who really love. And even when the Ram and the Goat who once cared for each other are apart . . . . . . wherever they are . . . . . . Venus is winking down at both of them, shining the message of her light on their loneliness, with a sparkling promise of maybe a new tomorrow.

☆ ☆ ☆ ☆ ☆ ☆

° From *Venus Trines at Midnight* by Linda Goodman.

ARIES *Man* CAPRICORN *Woman*

...from first to last she had been wiser than he.

Of course this was a pity; but whatever Mr. Darling did he had to do in excess; otherwise he soon gave up doing it.

The kind of effect an Aries male and a Capricorn female have on each other mostly depends on her age when they first meet. If she's still in her teens, or under thirty, she may see him as a rather crude, pushy, cave-man type, with no future. And he may see her as a sourpuss, or at the very least, a weird, granny-type recluse. (Of course, I know of one Goat Girl who's quite a loose swinger, and about as far out as you can get, but she has all her other planets in Aquarius, afflicted by Mars. Here, we're dealing with the essentially pure Sun Sign types.)

If they meet when she's past thirty (the farther past, the better) she may be a barrel of laughs, full of young ideas about everything from psychology to ecology, and they'll have much more in common. This can lead the Ram to think she's as impulsive and carefree as himself, but he's made another one of his rash Aries judgements. She's still a Capricorn, under the iron influence of Saturn, and her kooky reverse aging twist will never stretch quite far enough to snap or distort her basic ideas of security. Nothing will ever change Cappy's reverence for success and a solid bank account. Now, most Aries men are bristling with success potential. It shines out from their faces like a beacon light, and shows itself in their aggressive walk and movements. But Rams don't always display a natural knack for building solid bank accounts. Until *they're* past thirty. (Make that fifty. Better yet — sixty. After all, with a potential life span of three to five hundred years, he has lots of time to mature.)

Capricorn girls gravitate toward those at the top by instinct. After all, someone has to know who's who, and what's what. Is a sense of responsibility so bad? No, but to Aries it can be un-nerving. It smacks of Caution and Prudence, two words this man never even learned to spell because he has a kind of Freudian hang-up about them. They symbolize the thing he fears most — repression of his Mars enthusiasm.

That's why a love relationship seldom develops when these two meet in a business situation, where the Ram is the boss and the Goat Girl is his secretary, for example. Right away, he'll see that she's a perfect jewel of an employee, with a compelling, if slightly subdued and controlled, sex appeal. She's capable and efficient, with a bag full of funnies (though she keeps her humor pretty well hidden during working hours). It flatters his Mars ego that she realizes she's a subordinate, and subordinates must learn from those above them. Then he discovers (hopefully before it's too late) that she's unobtrusively learning everything she needs to replace him as boss. Obviously, a Ram who's threatened like this will forget about her sex appeal and fire her in a flash. But even then, he'll probably always remember her as an excellent secretary, although his harrowing experience forces him to add a qualifying descriptive phrase, like "quietly ambitious."

When they're not competing with each other, however, the Goat and the Ram can make an interesting couple. I didn't say flashy or fantastic. I said interesting.

By now, you know Capricorn is symbolized by the mountain billy goat. But you may *not* know that Capricorn's corresponding symbol in Greek mythology is Janus, the two-faced god. Before you get the wrong impression, let me explain the meaning of Janus' two faces which is that one of them is turned toward the Past, the other toward the Future. With Capricorn, the Future is important only as it relates to the Past. The Ram will soon discover he'd better have a respectable family tree, going back at least five or six generations, if he wants to impress this girl. As for her, well — a Capricorn woman doesn't really need a family tree. You might say Capricorns are their own ancestors. *Ponder that.* If you know any typical Goats, it will begin to make perfect sense.

Frequently, a Capricorn girl will find herself involved in what can only be called an "impossible" romantic situation. And there's a good reason. A woman who secretly feels she's an impossible person will unconsciously seek out an impossible love relationship to match her opinion of herself — and to punish herself. Just what she deserves, *she* thinks. An impossible affair for an impossible person. *Me.* But this girl is often much more warm and lovable than she permits herself to realize, and always far more physically appealing and attractive than she believes. On top of that, her mind is stable (barring an afflicted Sun or Mercury) and she's not flighty.

It's up to the Ram to convince her she's a very desirable female. With his talent for enthusiastic appreciation and his tendency to place the woman he loves on an ivory pedestal, he may manage to bring the shy or insecure Cappy out of her shell rather neatly. Aries has a better chance than most other Sun Signs to swing the Goat Girl from self-deprecation into a rightful pride in her feminine sexuality. Still, even if he finally accomplishes this minor miracle, he may not get to take her into his arms right away for keeps. There's her family.

Unless her parents outraged the Saturn sense of decency in some way, leaving bitter scars, the average Capricorn is fanatically devoted to them. If her family doesn't approve of the Ram, she may not either. If they *do* approve of him they may be ill or in financial straits, and she feels it's her duty to remain with them as long as she's needed, even if love itself must be sacrificed. I tell you there's only one way out of that Capricorn family trip. Offer to let her bring Mums and Pops along to share your married life — find a large house or apartment with plenty of spare bedrooms — and make the best of it. Otherwise, if the Ram talks her into deserting her relatives in their hour of need, or into leaving them to cope with their own problems she'll become gloomy, blame herself and feel constant guilty twinges. It's disconcerting to try to make love to a woman who's continually having gloomy chills and guilty twinges. Especially for an Aries male, who needs and demands, at all times, intense, concentrated attention — directed toward himself.

Their sex life can be greatly improved if the Ram studies the astrological implications of the Saturnine emotional nature more closely. Sometimes when a Capricorn girl wears a mask of casual indifference, it may be concealing the most tormenting passions. If she represses physical expressions of affection, it's only because Saturn keeps silently warning her: Watch out. Be careful. Don't be fooled by your senses. They're unreliable, and they can trick you.

Listening to that inner voice, while burning with the desire to consummate physically an emotional and mental attraction, can build up frustrations — and frustrations can take many strange forms. With Capricorns, it can result in filling up the inner emptiness with ambition for power, excessive financial security — or even collections of antiques. Some of them become cranky and cross, and a few accept their fate by pretending to believe that solitude is a sign of spiritual attainment. The courageous Ram won't be afraid to rip off the Goat's icy mask of indifference to expose her hidden passion. The trouble is that the insensitive Ram may fail to *recognize* it as only a mask, never guess the depth of feeling behind it and give up before he's begun to fight.

It may also freeze the flames of passion between them if the female Goat uses her self-chosen, protective cloak to shatter the confidence of the Aries man in his ability as a lover. Once he feels his lovemaking is not arousing an equally intense response in her, he'll suffer agonies of inferiority. It hardly matters if his unhappiness is based on a fallacy, and she really longs to love him as fiercely in return but can't trust her own emotions and feelings. He may not be perceptive enough to grasp her secret desire to reciprocate his passion, and another Aries-Capricorn relationship ends before it's had a chance to grow into the kind of profound emotional experience it might have been.

The general rule between these Sun Signs should be to check each other's Moon Signs. If the Sun and Moon in the respective charts are harmonious, the

Ram can magically transmute the cold, grey lead of Saturn into the sparkling diamonds of Mars, through the pure alchemy of love. But if the Moon and Ascendent of one or either was in negative aspect to the other's Sun Sign at birth, and vice versa, these two may have to wait, and catch each other the next time around, in a future incarnation, when some karmic patterns have worked themselves out. However, such mutual natal afflictions are rare, and most Rams and Goats can achieve harmony together eventually, if they try, however rocky the path may be in the beginning. Mountain climbing is always harder when you start; yet the closer you get to the top, the easier it is, the fresher the air, the brighter the Sun . . . and the spirit leaps with joy at the nearness of the dream's fulfillment.

The Capricorn train of thought is never permitted to run off the rails. Consequently, the Goat Girl becomes upset when anything unexpected or unorthodox threatens to disrupt the smooth status quo, and a Ram may unknowingly supply such disruptions. When Cappy is upset, it can be make an Aries man feel more than a little tense. This female normally has nerves of steel, eyes like a hawk, and the patience of Job himself. The impatient Ram may feel, somehow, inferior to her self-control. He shouldn't. For her self-control is only the chain she uses to bind her spirit from flying too far out, where there's no one to catch her, if she should happen to fall. His arms are strong enough to catch her. And he's persuasive enough, determined enough, to convince her of this — if he's patient. This man follows the sunrise, and he's hurt when the Capricorn he loves won't join him. She's gentle and warm, and makes his heart smile with her jokes. Yet, there's something about her manner that says: "Don't come too close."

Must astrology interpret this message for a bright Aries man ? What she really means is — "I *want* you to come closer, but I'm afraid it's only my stability you want, that you don't really need *me* — as a *woman*." Surely a Ram will know how to answer such a silent plea in this girl's lonely, quiet eyes. Later, she *will* move nearer, and maybe not murmur any romantic words, but if he watches closely, he'll see that soft, secret little Capricorn smile of deep pleasure. If he doesn't look fast, he'll miss it. All the same, it's there, reflected from the sunlight within . . . of knowing she's loved.

He's really a very lucky Ram. As beautiful as she looks at this moment, Saturn has promised to make her look lovelier every year that passes. He may be a stern ruler of her emotions, but Saturn never breaks a promise. And neither does she. At last, the Aries man has found a love he can trust, a love to have and to hold.· That's surely worth the challenge of fighting a few dragons of selfishness — and rounding off their squared Suns into a circle of understanding.

☆ ☆ ☆ ☆ ☆ ☆

ARIES

Fire — Cardinal — Positive
Ruled by Mars
Symbol: The Ram
Day Forces — Masculine

AQUARIUS

Air — Fixed — Positive
Ruled by Uranus
Symbol: The Water Bearer
Day Forces — Masculine

The **ARIES-AQUARIUS** *Relationship*

They began the verse, but they never finished it . . .

Aries and Aquarius have this outstanding thing in common — they're both curiously attracted to anything new until they've extracted all the fun and truth from it. Then they toss it away and go on to the next new and exciting adventure. With these two, there is no looking back and sniffling over the past, if they're both typical of their Sun Signs. To the Ram, today is *ever* so much more thrilling than yesterday. To the Aquarian Water Bearer, *tomorrow* is a thousand times more fantastic than either yesterday *or* today.

Once in a while, they slip off the time track separately, somewhere between the past, present, and future, and bump smack into each other, in a meeting that isn't part of the conscious itinerary of either. It's always an interesting encounter, and a fated one, planned on a higher level, long before both of them were born. Aries and Aquarius are influenced by the 3-11 Sun Sign vibration, and a blending of their auras brings them into the shared experiences of travel, education, and spiritual discovery — along with karmic memories from former reincarnations, as well as the hopes, wishes, and dreams of the present existence. You can see why they don't find each other lacking in fascination.

Aries people throw themselves into things with total commitment (for the moment), enthusiastically and fully involved in what's happening. Aquarius is equally as enthusiastic, but these people don't throw themselves into anything. The Water Bearers approach every experience with a studied detachment, snoop around, scratch their heads, and wiggle their ears — from a safe distance. That way they can enjoy it without getting either tangled up or tied down. Of course this subtle psychological difference won't help you tell them apart when you pass them on the street. But there are other ways.

The Ram may be running, with head bent forward, showering confetti and sending up rocket flares. The Aquarian may be riding a unicycle, munching on a pickled radish, and spinning a hula hoop, with a friendly quetzal perched on one shoulder. They both stand out in a crowd.

One of the meanings of the 3-11 vibration between friends, relatives, business associates, lovers, or mates is: karmic obligation. The association or relationship involves either some great blessing and good exchanged — or some great sadness brought from one to the other, perhaps in the form of an obligation or responsibility, far-reaching in its effect on the lives of both.

An Aquarian blessed with an Aries friend who stands by him (or her) through long months of trouble or illness (either personal or in the family), when no one else cares or helps . . . . may wonder, "Why did she (or he) do it ?" The Ram is simply repaying a favor from a long ago Lifetime (buried in the subconscious) of similar help received. Perhaps in the process, the Ram receives an enlightenment, starting the Aries person on the road to a future career, some unexpected goal or dream that wouldn't have been revealed in any other way, save through the circumstances of the Ram's offering help to the Aquarian. In reversing the signs, the same situation may develop, with many variations on the theme.

Another Aquarian handles the business affairs of an Aires, keeping the Ram out of trouble with taxes and creditors, smoothing out financial wrinkles, and arranging miraculous loans under impossible conditions — unconsciously motivated by the soul memory of monetary assistance received from Aries in another time, another place — and a karmic debt is repaid. An Aries man has a close male friend whose Aquarian wife frowns on the friendship. She is illogically suspicious of the Ram, and he, in turn, feels an inexplicable tension when she enters the room. It could result in the Ram breaking up his friend's marriage to the Aquarian — or with the Aquarian wife preventing the Aries from continuing a valued friendship with her husband. How it ends depends upon the degree of evolvement of the Ram and the Water Bearer at the time of the situation. Karma is complicated.

The good or evil these two Sun Signs (or any two Signs influenced by the

3-11 vibration) bring to each other is seldom minor. The contact is not casual, and they have little conscious control over its outcome. Yet, if Aries and Aquarius will meditate on the laws of Karma, or reincarnation, they'll understand why one of them is so willing to aid the other, and learn to accept the favor gracefully. Or, they'll comprehend the reverse situation — why the two of them continue to senselessly hurt one another — and through understanding, be able to end the karmic pattern by the simple Karma-canceling act of forgiving and forgetting. Otherwise, they're only stacking up additional obligations for future lives, wherein their two souls will be chained together, in an endless succession of close relationships, through the inevitable law of magnetic attraction and repulsion, action and reaction.

Aquarius is one of the four "human signs" in the astrological circle, the other three being Gemini, Virgo, and Libra (unless one counts the Centaur — half-horse, half-human Sag). Consequently, Aquarian passions are more controlled than those of the Rams, whose instinctive loves and hates often cause them to act from sheer animal urge, or personal gratification of the ego. The Uranus-ruled Aquarians more often flee from instinctive action into the realms of the higher mind — and the domain of pure intuition. This gives the Water Bearers an uncanny psychic or intuitive ability.

Sometimes Rams will also appear to be psychic, but they're really not, in the true sense of the word. It's only because they plunge straight into the heart of the situation, and the penetrating action of their ruling planet, Mars, gives them the correct answer. Aries goes directly and immediately to the *core* of the problem, using neither logic nor rational reasoning, simply being obsessed with an overwhelming need to leap in and get to the bottom of the thing. The swifter, more intricate flashes of Aquarians emanate from the electro-magnetic wave lengths they're tuned into under the influence of their ruling planet, Uranus — which symbolizes electricity, among other things . . . . and lightning, too. The Water Bearers merely grab an impression out of the air, or absorb it through some sort of electrical osmosis, without expending a tenth of the energy put forth by Aries to reach the same conclusions.

Aries and Aquarius are essentially compatible. There's an almost visible cord of understanding running between them, so that even when they strongly disagree, it's always possible to replace tension with harmony anytime they choose to do so. It's the natural sympathy between Fire and Air, and it's something else. It's the normally easy (barring unusual planetary afflictions between the horoscopes), effortless possibilities of communication open to all 3-11 Sun Sign Patterns, on all channels. The third astrological house symbolizes communication of all kinds — visual, through the printed word — and also through the spoken word, including minds speaking to minds, hearts speaking to hearts.

Rams are frequently accused of being naive, impractical dreamers. Aquarians are frequently accused of being just plain crazy. That's another reason why these two usually get along so well. They both feel misunderstood by the world and everyone in it. They also both feel they're on the right track, separately or in unison, and it's the rest of the world that's out of step and off-center. Naturally, this draws them together — for mutual comfort and mutual protection against the establishment. The Rams are reckless, the Water Bearers are pixilated — but they manage to spin these qualities into complicated webs of leprechauns, miracles, rainbows, and assorted magics, creating dirigibles of dreams which, surprisingly enough to more sensible souls, take off into the blue skies of some wildly successful personal and business ventures.

The Aquarian, Uranus-inspired tolerance insulates most Water Bearers against the shock of the sudden whims and highly original, creative urges of Aries. There will be times when the Rams believe Aquarius doesn't quite have it together, and when Aquarius will despair of being able to cope with the hot temper flashes of Mars. Yet generally, these two should enjoy a mad, fabulous, and unique association. Aquarius is a Fixed Sign, and so, on occasion, the Water Bearers can be more than a little stubborn. But stubbornness won't work with Aries. Only love and kindness. Great gobs of it.

The Water Bearers may attempt to enlighten the Rams with their theories about submerging the ego, claiming this brings peace and happiness. But to Aries, submerging the ego is scary, quite like being swallowed in a dark tunnel. "Where does that leave *me*? Where will *I* be, the Me-of-Me . . . in some kind of eternal void?" the Ram wonders. Arians are never strong on the yoga state of Nirvana. To become unconscious of *yourself*—that's *ecstasy*? In this instinct, Aries is intuitively right.

The concepts of Aquarius are light-years ahead of their time, for the most part, yet no more infallible or immune from misjudgment than the ideas of Aries — although the Uranian wisdom will be poured out from the little brown jug of Aquarius anyway, solicited or not. "All human troubles stem from an overemphasis on the emotions and an exaggeration of personal feeling," claims Aquarius.

"People who deny their emotions and bury their personal feelings are cold and heartless, lacking all enlightenment and perception," retorts Aries.

So — where do they go from such a dead-end street? Back to their leprechauns, miracles, rainbows . . . and dirigibles of dreams.

☆ ☆ ☆ ☆ ☆ ☆

ARIES *Woman* AQUARIUS *Man*

<hr>

*Then he nearly cried; but it struck him how
indignant she would be if he laughed instead. So
he laughed a haughty laugh, and fell asleep in
the middle of it.*

These two could have a glorious time together, if the Aries girl could only get
one thing into her head. When an Aquarian man laughs, it's because he feels
very sad. When he cries, it's because he feels very happy.

Once she catches on to this important game he plays, she'll have an
easier time of it with all his other tricks. I'm referring to the tricks the Water
Bearer uses to keep a girl from guessing he cares for her. Also the tricks he
uses after she's already guessed, and he doesn't want her to find out how
deeply he cares. And don't leave out the tricks he uses when he knows he's
helplessly in love, but still trying to convince himself he can switch it back to
friendship again, before it's too late. If you like games, this man is more fun
that a stack of crossword puzzles and a trunkful of poker chips. An Aries girl
likes games. But there's a small catch here. She only likes games when the
other player lets her win all the time.

The Aquarian male has no patience with girl Rams who play by those
rules. He's not going to give her any handicaps or free rolls of the dice just
because she cries a few angry tears. Since she's so independent and
aggressive, for a girl, he'll probably say, "Listen, buddy (Aquarians call
everyone buddy), if you're so sensitive, how come I saw you marching in that
Women's Lib parade last week? You females who demand equal rights had
better be ready to take them all on, like moving furniture, fixing the
plumbing, changing tires — and fighting right alongside the men in a war."

He's wrong. She only pushed her way into that parade because she
couldn't resist the excitement of the drumbeats. After all, Rams are idealists,
who sometimes start cheering for a cause before they know what it's all about.
She's not likely to be a card-carrying member of any Women's Lib group.
An Aries girl? She was *born* liberated — and she has no intention of giving
up her feminine privileges, just to prove she's *equal*, when she already knows
she's *superior*!

It's just that she likes to knock around the issues now and then, to keep
her mind sharp. Like, she'll say, "Your argument that equal rights mean
women have to wear uniforms, grab machine guns, and start killing people is

deceptive and unrealistic. If women ran this country, there wouldn't *be* any more war. It's the men who are so big on physical violence, fighting, and war — not women."

AQUARIUS: Is that right? Drop into Macy's basement some morning when they're having a sale. I know a guy who runs the Red Cross bandage concession there every Saturday. It would turn General Patton's hair white in five minutes. Talk about cold-blooded atrocities. You women and your tears. What a put-on!

Sooner or later, she's going to complain that he's aloof and detached — or downright cruel and sadistic. (It amounts to the same thing to Aries. In her eyes, aloof is a synonym for cruel, detached a synonym for sadistic.) It's simply his admirable, yet admittedly annoying, breadth of vision that isolates him from the petty, personal emotions of individuals, while he's promoting the high ideals of brotherhood and sisterhood. An Aquarian is more interested in a permanent cure for the common cold than in handing you a Kleenex when you're sneezing. He's more concerned about the medical problems of geriatrics and aging than in helping individual little old ladies across the street. Uranus keeps his heart and mind directed toward the alleviation of all unhappiness and evil in the world on some bright tomorrow. There's not much sympathy left over for the personal distress close to him today.

This man is basically good-natured and kind, make no mistake about that. And his aims are noble. However, when dealing with Water Bearers, you should always remember Robespierre (who had an Aquarian Ascendent). His moral principles and his plans for the regeneration of France were undoubtedly most sincere and idealistic. But he overlooked the fact that France was a country populated by human beings with feelings, and in his crusading zeal, he chopped off quite a few heads — literally.

The Aquarian tries to be optimistic and sympathetic to his friends in trouble . . . . and to the Aries girl (who needs his broad shoulder to weep on after he's hurt her). But his sympathy too often consists of rather vague generalities. With his broader Uranus vision, the Aquarian male instinctively understands the deeper significance of sorrow. He knows that only through suffering can the soul be perfected — and he hates to interfere with the workings of Fate. Who is he to throw a monkey wrench into Destiny's plan? For all he knows, Destiny is a synonym for God. (You can see their synonym definitions also differ slightly.)

All right, so he can be kind and gentle, tender, sweet and funny, when it suits him. But he's still cold and heartless when he's seen through the sentimental eyes of the more sensitive, open-hearted Aries girl. The difference in their natures may be occasionally adjusted through compromise, but never completely overcome.

ARIES–AQUARIUS ★ 191

He has hundreds, maybe even thousands, of friends. With a crowd like that, she is obviously not going to be wild about each one of them. (*She's* not an Aquarian—*he* is.) The more time he spends with them—away from her—the more chances she'll have to be jealous. Since jealousy is the Aries girl's romantic Achilles' heel, their relationship will have a better chance if she lets him bring his friends home than if she forces him to meet them out in the park, beside the squirrel cage. There's nothing she can do to erase his "thing" about friendship. He's a humanitarian. He enjoys people. She'll simply have to face it.

The thing to do is forget about all his virtues—like vision, originality, foresight, friendliness, and humanitarianism—and concentrate on his vices. He has lots of those. (I know that sounds like strange advice, but we're dealing with an Aquarian, which means that everything you've ever learned must be reversed, and read in a mirror backward.) It's not his virtues then, but his vices that can keep them together. Let's run over a few of them.

He's unpredictable. She'll have to admit that's an exciting quality to Aries. It beckons to her Mars love of challenge. He's also eccentric, weird, unconventional, and odd. Beautiful. If there's anything this girl would find a real drag, it's an uptight man stuck in a conservative groove. He hears strange music, and he follows a wild and distant drummer (all Rams adore parades). Oh, wow! Well, what do you know—*a parade*! If she's a good girl, he'll let her hold his hand and skip along beside him. As for the wild and distant drummer he follows, to Aries a drumbeat is a drumbeat. Who cares? Any kind of percussion makes her pulses pound, sends her heart into throbbing spasms of hope and glory-spangled banners of excitement.

Her pounding pulses may slow down a bit, however, when it comes to reaching sexual fulfillment with this man. In the beginning, the Aries girl's more direct, flaming Mars drive may whiz right over the head of her Aquarian lover. What happened to him? He was here just a minute ago. Oh, there he is. She'll have to go back and pick him up. He's still sitting there, scratching his left ear, and trying to analyze the first kiss. You mean there's *more*? Well, that certainly is interesting.

He's willing to be educated, and to let her teach him. Whether or not he ever graduates is another question altogether. No, she hasn't stumbled upon a male virgin. It's possible, of course, but the probable reason for his awe and wonder is that, to the typical Aquarian, each new experience of life is exactly like the first one—to be tasted, savored, then either treasured or discarded. His approach to romance is no different. Because the attraction of Aries and Aquarius is essentially one of emotional appeal and intellectual curiosity, their sexual mating may be unpredictable. It's the same old problem again. His *apparent* detachment—and her impatience with anything short of instant gratification. Yet, if the Sun-Moon relationship between their horoscopes is harmonious (and often, even if it isn't), there's a good possibility that practice will make perfect between them in the physical expression of love. Her Arian aura of freshness and lack of guile—her basic honesty about sexual love—will strongly appeal to him and move him to an unaccustomed tenderness. But she'll always have to retain the ideal image and innocence of the first seduction. For that matter, so will he.

A lot of their problems will be caused by the fact that she is Cardinal, therefore likes to lead—and he is Fixed, therefore refuses to follow. Also, they were both born under a masculine Sun Sign, and in addition, each is ruled by a masculine planet—both of them powerful, unpredictable planets. Mars and Uranus are not marshmallows. They are equally explosive and forceful, like the lovers or mates they rule, and whose actions they guide. Some of the edges can be smoothed away from these rough spots by the 3-11 vibration of easy friendship and communication between them. And there are other ways astrology can lead the way to happiness for the girl Ram and her Water Bearer (also for the Water Bearer and his girl Ram—since the masculine charisma of ownership and possession works both ways with these two).

Esoteric free-thought association, for all of its mystical quality, can be helpful in a surprisingly practical way. They should try meditating together on the deeper layers of the meaning of their 3-11 Sun Sign Pattern. In astrology, it's called a *sextile* relationship. When you think of the word "sextile," a picture arises of snowflakes and stars, since the astrological symbol for the sextile resembles both. It looks like this: * and what could be a lovelier image than snowflakes and stars ?

* *
* *
*

A snowflake is totally unique and original in its design—and so is the Aquarian man. No two snowflakes are alike, and this man also . . . is like no other on Earth. As for stars, they're the glittering diamonds in the sky children wish on (and all those who believe) which should remind him of her. For the Aries girl's heart will ever be the heart of a child, believing in magic and miracles . . . spring and sunrise, as naive and trusting . . . as excited by every new wonder and thrill of discovery . . . as open and friendly as a child . . . and every bit as vulnerable, beneath all her surface bravado and outward independence.

They'll be surprised how this small exercise in meditation will lift them back to joy and laughter from the shadows of fear and rejection, jealousy and anger. If everytime she sees a snowflake, she thinks of his uniqueness . . . and everytime he sees a star, he thinks of her childlike innocence of intent ... the tension between them will melt into understanding, as a snowflake melts ... and sparkle with new promise, as a star shines.

Snowflakes and stars can be a magic mantra for all 3-11 influenced lovers, but especially for this man and woman. Falling snowflakes and shooting stars can be the private love code between them.

Sometimes, these two Sun Signs remind you of the ancient fable, slightly distorted. A magic purple leprechaun comes along to grant the Aries girl and her Aquarian man three wishes. In typical daffy, Uranian fashion, he wishes for a blueberry pudding. Instead of leaving well enough alone and asking for her own heart's desire, the Ram is so insulted and angered by her lover's flippant wish that she blurts out: "I wish you had that silly pudding stuck on your nose!" And so naturally they have to sacrifice their third and last wish to get the pudding off his face.

It's sad, when two people who love each other have used up all their wishes. Still, something may be left of yesterday to use as a bridge into tomorrow. What about all those crazy dreams, and ... wait! Listen! Isn't that the crash of a wild, off-beat drum in the distance? It is. They both heard it. Never mind the quarrel. He grabs her hand tightly, and off they go to catch up with the parade together (with the Ram in the lead, of course). Now, if she can only keep him from flirting with the lady elephants ... and he can only keep her from weeping over the clowns.

Well, what do you know? It's snowing! And the stars have come out.

☆ ☆ ☆ ☆ ☆ ☆

ARIES *Man* AQUARIUS *Woman*

——◄━◆━►——

He frowned. "I am back," he said hotly. "Why do you not cheer?"

It is April 9th, 1971, the day (though not the year) of his birth, and he has just sent his mother a telegram of congratulations. Now the Ram is in a hurry to rush into the arms of the Aquarian girl he loves. He comes bursting through the door, grabs her enthusiastically, plants a passionate kiss on her cheek, and says something like, "I have a wonderful idea about how to celebrate my birthday tonight. We'll go down to the Village and have dinner in that little Italian place where we first met, then catch Ali MacGraw and Ryan O'Neal in *Love Story.*"

The Aquarian girl stares dreamily at a spot somewhere past his left shoulder, and murmurs, "I wonder how that shoe-polish stain got up there on the ceiling? Maybe I could paint some flowers and peace symbols to cover it. Far out. A ceiling mural, just like the Sistine Chapel . . . . ."

ARIES: What does that have to do with my birthday?
AQUARIUS: I'm sorry, darling. I could have sworn Michelangelo was born in Italy . . . . maybe it was France . . . . .

You see, the only word she picked up in his exuberant speech was "Italian." Any competent astrologer could tell you there will be trouble in River City tonight. (If I seem to be mixing up my geography, never mind, the Aquarians reading it will understand.) It's a mistake, however, to think a Water Bearer isn't always acutely aware, just because she seems vague and aloof. Actually, she didn't miss a thing. For proof: Back to River City . . . .

AQUARIUS: What's wrong, honey? You seem upset.
ARIES: I'm not upset. I'm *mad.*
AQUARIUS: She has a Taurus Ascendent.
ARIES: *Who* has *what?*
AQUARIUS: Ali MacGraw. She's an Aries like you, but she has a Taurus Ascendent. I've been crying since I read the first sentence.
ARIES: Now you've lost me. You've completely lost me.
AQUARIUS: What can you say about a twenty-one-year-old girl who died?
ARIES: You're thinking of *suicide*? Baby, I'm not *that* mad — honest!
AQUARIUS: That's the first sentence in the book. I can't wait to see the film — and that crazy little Italian waiter with the curly hair and moustache who guessed we were in love — so he brought candles and flowers and wine to the table . . . and, oh — that reminds me! I want to give you a bottle of the same kind of wine we drank that night for your birthday. I'll have to make a note, so I won't forget. It's next month isn't it? Why are you looking at me like that? Was it *last* month?

Well, she may miss a *few* things . . .

There's a curious air of absentminded detachment about an Aquarian girl. Some people interpret it as daydreaming. Grandma would have called it woolgathering. A Ram will call it an unforgivable outrage. To an Aries male, who was, remember, born under a Cardinal Sign, the cardinal sin is to ignore him. She isn't exactly ignoring him. Then again, she is. But no more than she ignores anything that would chain her down to specifics, when she's concentrating on something not even remotely connected with the happening in front of her.

The average Aries man falls in love impetuously and fully, and he demands an immediate response. If he doesn't get it in a short time — a very short time — his built-in defense mechanism against being hurt takes over, and he tells himself, "Who needs her?" *He* does, perhaps, very much, but Aries is not a sign to risk unrequited love if he can help it. It's never as easy for an Aquarian girl to be certain she's in love, even when she's deeply interested in a man. It's because of her Uranus friendship curse — or blessing. (It can be either, by turns, depending.) She finds something utterly fascinating and compelling about nearly every stranger she comes across, let alone everyone she knows. How does she tell the difference between such fascination and love? This girl honestly has a problem figuring out the answer to the question of "Is it love or friendship?" The one thing she knows for certain is that love must *begin* with friendship. Not for her the physical chemistry alone that consumes some couples and causes them to wrongly believe they're made for each other. The anatomical differences between male and female never constitute, to this lady, sufficient reason to become emotionally involved. Her essence is Air, she was born under a mental sign — and she must be intellectually attracted to a man before the contemplation of either sex or romance makes a bit of sense to her. Not that she isn't capable of chalking up an occasional mistake. She is not, after all, Prudence Purity. But she makes fewer errors of judgment than her Sun Sign sisters who are seeking only a sense of physical belonging with a man.

She's seeking something else. Just what it is, she's not quite certain — but it's definitely something else. Once she's found it, she'll become intensely interested in the body-buddy game, but before that, she's not about to be seduced by the ordinary player who's merely looking for some sensual pleasure. Nor is she easily overwhelmed by the Aries man's insistent declarations of idealistic love, based on impulsive emotion alone. But there's nothing bashful about her, and once she believes it would be mentally exciting, intriguing, and worthwhile to become more intimate with the Ram who attracts her, she won't concern herself with coquettish tricks to keep him guessing. She's more likely to announce, suddenly and unexpectedly, when he's least prepared for such a lightning bolt, "I think I love you. Why don't you spend the night?" or perhaps, "Why don't we live together?"

It will shock him for a moment. A brief moment. But since he's as honest and straightforward as she is (they both despise hypocrisy and neither of them gives a dandelion what the neighbors think — they do what they jolly well please, adore flaunting convention and defying society's silly rules), he'll recover right away and accept her proposal. When such a suggestion comes from a man, it's a proposition. Coming from a woman, it's only a friendly *proposal*. Little niceties like that are among the pluses of being a female that are tough to give up in exchange for the benefits of ERA's "proposed" sexual equality.

Speaking of sexual equality, that brings us to perhaps the most important single, threatening aspect of a relationship between these two. She was born under a masculine Sun Sign, and her attitudes and actions are aggressively guided by the also-masculine planet Uranus. The Ram, too, was born under a masculine Sun Sign, his attitudes and actions likewise aggressively guided by the also-masculine planet, Mars. On top of that astrological standoff, she's Fixed (stubborn) and he's Cardinal (determined). It may sound pretty discouraging, like the game of childhood, where one person draws a line and dares the other to step over it — or like General Lee facing General Sherman, cannonball to cannonball. But it's not all push-and-pull between these two. There's also a good deal of give and take, principally because of the beneficent karmic influence of their 3-11 Sun Sign Pattern. It brings to their relationship all kinds of beautiful bonuses and boosters to happiness and harmony. The most beneficial of these is the friendship aspect of the 3-11 vibration, allowing the couples influenced by it to be friends, as well as lovers. You can see how this might solve a lot of the Ram's problems regarding her Uranian friendship fetish. In addition, the influence creates the atmosphere for free and flowing communication between them — most of the time. They'll find it easier than most couples to talk about their disagreements — to communicate their feelings to each other. They'll both benefit more or less equally from this particular reward of their personal Sun Sign Pattern vibration, because she's an Air Sign and all Air Signs do enjoy talking. He's an Aries, and enjoys it even more. All these goodies somewhat dilute the negative effect of the Fixed versus Cardinal and double masculine standoff between them. Not that the latter can be completely ignored. It will still be necessary to cope with these matters to some degree, but a solution won't be difficult, and certainly not impossible.

Once she's decided their relationship is worthy of her whole involvement, the sexual compatibility between the Ram and the girl Water Bearer (who is, by the way, regardless of being called a Water Bearer, not of the Water, but of the Air essence — only one of her many contradictions) contains the potential of being a rare and beautiful blending. But a potential must be encouraged to develop. She may be puzzled by the intensity of his desire and the overwhelming passion of his lovemaking. Still, it's always a positive happening for an Aquarian woman to be puzzled by anything, for she is curious, and usually won't rest until she's solved any puzzle Life or Love presents to her. A word of caution to the Ram, however. She becomes quickly bored after she's put the pieces together and satisfied her curiosity. So the best insurance that their physical Oneness will always hold its first fine rapture for them is for the Aries man to always treat their sexual union as something special, different, and unusual in some way. He should vary his approach to their intimacies from time to time. She doesn't mind if the variations consist of a deep and silent physical togetherness after a quarrel, with the sudden fulfillment of love hunger becoming an eloquent apology between them without words . . . an unexpected time of the consummation of their erotic needs at odd hours during the day, instead of always being a bedtime ritual . . . if he decides to play classical music during their closeness, and turns up the stereo loud enough to make spoken endearments between them impossible (and also unnecessary, since music does have a soaring aphrodisiac effect) . . . whether they whisper and talk constantly during the physical expression of their love . . . . and he recites poetry to her or tells her funny stories about kangaroos . . . whether he's tender and gentle or violent and feral . . . just so sex is never dull or boring — never a repetitious ritual. Her thirst for change is something he'll have to realize.

She should realize that this man is wounded more deeply than he'll ever show when her occasional sexual detachment leads him to believe she doesn't really need him. She should never respond to his sexual overtures with anything but a sincere and all-consuming enthusiasm, always welcome his embraces with unmistakable joy and anticipation. Otherwise he could become temporarily impotent and unable to express his physical love for her, because of a never-admitted feeling of inadequacy, which she might not even notice, since sex, to her, like everything else, is only one facet of her varied existence. She may be happily tuning the engine of the car some Saturday morning or skipping through the woods picking a bunch of wildflowers during these cool periods, without the slightest notion of why he's so morose and frustrated. She should warn herself to be more alert to his moods — forget the dwell/tachometer, drop her bouquet of Oxalis — and murmur in his ear that she needs to rest awhile (in his arms, of course), yet still not make it seem as if she's the initiator of the lovemaking she's suggesting. Keeping the Ram sexually contented and happy takes a lot of careful consideration, and this woman, while not deliberately or intentionally *in*considerate, can become absorbed in a multitude of manic activities and interests, while neglecting the one activity that's important — their love.

Sometimes the Uranian experimental urges and unpredictable behavior of the Aquarian woman will seem to the Ram who truly loves her like a patchwork of erratic, changing moods and frustratingly brief spans of attention. He can't seem to catch her . . . . like a butterfly or a lark. But if he doesn't try to dominate her personality and allows her the freedom she needs to work out her individuality, all her myriad interests will one day integrate naturally into the whole of her fascinating self.

Sometimes, the driving ambition, endless energy, and profusion of dreams shooting forth like comets through the vibrant aura of the Aries man will seem to the Aquarian woman who truly loves him like living with a sack of fireworks, ready to explode at the touch of a match. She can't seem to convince him to slow down to her complicated and intricate, but slower and more dreamy, approach to living. But if she never forgets to remember to make him know she loves him with all her heart when he stumbles and falls, just as much as she does the times when he's elated by victory (maybe even more, because of his vulnerability), his emotions will gradually mature and his confidence will grow into a tall tree of stability. Then she'll wish he was little-boy-impulsive again, because she'll miss his spontaneity. She's ruled by Uranus, the planet of change, you see. So she'll perversely toss a match into his Mars sack of fireworks just to see if he's still the man who first made her laugh when she was sad and weep when she was happy, by reminding her of her own springtime when everything was green and fresh and new. She won't have to wonder long. The roman candles are still inflammable . . . the sparklers too. He was only pretending to be mature and stable. And in her crazy-daisy, upside-down Aquarian way, that will make her very, very happy. So happy, she'll surprise him with a bottle of the wine they used to drink a toast each other that night in the Village . . . for his birthday. (It will be August, and his birthday is in April, but no matter. He won't care.) Then she'll turn up the volume on the stereo. Warsaw Concerto. Maybe Rhapsody in Blue. Or Beethoven's Fifth.

An Aquarian Cassandra weaves a spell of druidic enchantment and marvelous madness from which an Aries man will never escape. Later, when they're both "resting" (which was his idea alone), he'll stare at the ceiling, and say, "You know, darling, the mural you painted to cover the splash of shoe polish reminds me of a painting by Michelangelo."

"Oh, wow!" she'll exclaim, delighted. "How did you know I wanted to go to Italy in the autumn?" How did he know? Easy. He finally mastered the high-frequency modulation and tuned in to her Uranus channel. Besides, he's always wanted to see the Sistine Chapel himself. Maybe they can go there to celebrate *her* birthday, he'll tell her — in October. She'll grin, and say that's a lovely idea. She's always wondered what it would be like to be a Libra woman. He'll tell her he thinks it would be great, because, as a Leo, he's always wanted to have an affair with a Libran. Then they'll have a pillow fight. She'll win. Feathers everywhere. He won't mind losing. Yes, they've finally tuned in.

☆ ☆ ☆ ☆ ☆ ☆

ARIES   PISCES

Fire — Cardinal — Positive   *Water — Mutable — Negative*
Ruled by Mars   *Ruled by Neptune*
Symbol: The Ram   *Symbols: The Fish & Whale*
Day Forces — Masculine   *Night Forces — Feminine*

The **ARIES-PISCES** *Relationship*

*Even then they had time to gather in a phalanx
that would have been hard to break had they
risen quickly, but this they were forbidden to do
by the traditions . . . .*

An interviewer at an employment agency would have no trouble identifying these two Sun Signs, no problem in telling a Ram from a Fish. All it takes is a little experience, and a minimal understanding of astrology.

INTERVIEWER: What was your most recent place of employment?
ARIES: I was production chief at Parakeet Publishing, at 42 East 83rd Street.
INTERVIEWER: I see. I'll check them for a reference. The Parakeet Publishing Company, at 82 East 43rd Street.
ARIES: That's not what I said. You got the address backwards. Are you hard of hearing, or are you trying to intimidate me?

INTERVIEWER: Could I have your present home address, please?

PISCES: Sure! I live in the McCall Apartments, at 7000 6th Avenue.

INTERVIEWER: All right, let me make a note of that. That's the Bacall Apartments at 6000 7th Avenue, right?

PISCES: (visibly confused) Well . . uh, if you think it's a nicer neighborhood, I guess I could see if they have a vacancy . . . .

Walk up to a Ram and remark, "As an Aries, you're probably creative"— and the Ram will reply, "You can say that again! I'm loaded with original ideas. Would you like to hear some of them?"

Walk up to a Fish and remark, "As a Pisces, you're probably involved in one of the water sports, like surfing or scuba diving"—and the Fish will reply, "Well, I can't swim, but—uh, which one do you think I should be involved in? I suppose I could learn . . . ."

Walk up to a Ram and remark, "If you continue along the path you're on now, you'll never end up as a leader"—and the Aries person will reply, "How would you like a punch in the mouth?"

Walk up to a Fish and remark, "If you continue along the path you're on now, you'll never end up as a leader"—and the Pisces person will reply, "Really? Gee, I hope you're right."

The pattern that gradually emerges with the Ram is *aggressiveness*, sometimes to excess. The pattern that gradually emerges with the Fish is *accommodation*, also sometimes to excess. Aries, of course, is a Fire Sign and Pisces is a Water Sign. There's a marked difference between Aries aggressiveness and Pisces accommodation, and just to be sure I've made that difference clear, here's another example. A Ram has just walked up to the counter and ordered a pizza, to take out.

CLERK: Okay. One pizza to go, coming up! How do you want it, with mushrooms or green peppers?

RAM: Neither. I want black olives and onions. And see that you don't burn it, like you did the last time I was here.

Now, a Fish has walked up to the counter, to order a pizza, to take out.

CLERK: Okay. One pizza to go, coming up! How do you want it, with mushrooms or green peppers?

FISH: Well, let's see—what do most of your customers order?

CLERK: We sell a lot of mushrooms.

FISH: Mushrooms. I'll take mine with mushrooms.

CLERK: Of course, personally, I prefer green peppers.

FISH: Oh. Well . . . uh, could you change that, please, to one pizza to go, with green peppers ?

CLERK: Sure, but look, now — why don't you just order it the way *you* want ? Don't let me influence you.

FISH: Well — could I have two pizzas, then — one with mushrooms, and one with green peppers ?

You can see that Pisces is accommodating. What you may *not* see, however, is the multiple motivation behind it. The kind-hearted Fish really do like to please people, when they can. Every Piscean dreads the embarrassment of outright confrontation, and they dislike attention focused on themselves. But there's also a more subtle reason why Pisceans are reluctant to commit themselves to a personal opinion: they're always on the alert for snoopers, because they have an absolute horror of "Big Brother." At an airport, a stranger passing by, carrying monogrammed luggage with the initials CIA or FBI, can catapult the typical Fish into a nervous panic. Try to convince a Pisces that those letters stand for Charles Isidore Abernacky or Frederick Bruce Israel. Go ahead, try. What kind of Jewish mother would name her boy Frederick Bruce ? Someday, make a list of all your Pisces friends who have un-listed phone numbers. It will be interesting.

When a Ram meets a Fish, it seems that here is a sweet, mild, gentle soul the Aries person can push around more or less as he (or she) pleases. I'm sorry to say that this is what the fiery Aries often tries to do with the watery Piscean. But the Ram should study the natural sciences — and the Bible.

From the natural sciences, he'll learn all about the elements of earth, air, fire and water — and that water can be dangerous to fire. Flip the flame on a lighter as high as you like, then dip in into a glass of water. Sputter . . . . pssssttt . . . and out. Although water may seem to be the weakest of the elements, it's actually the strongest. A few drops of water dripping steadily on a rock for a long enough period of time will wear the rock away into fine sand. I know an Aries landlord who impulsively raised the rent on the New Jersey apartment of a Pisces lady named Marion. She accepted the news from him sweetly, with gentle feminine submission. However, the Arian landlord has spent the last eight months in and out of the courtroom. She sends him little notes about the leaky plumbing and such (one drop at a time, you see), and he still hasn't been able to hike the rent by so much as one dollar. Before it's over he'll probably lower it.

The secret of the great strength of water is its non-resistance. Water does not *resist*. Toss a pebble into the river, and what happens ? Water doesn't resist the object penetrating its calm. Old Man River just opens up, swallows the pebble, covers it over — and keeps moving right along. The Nazarene relates the strength of Water's powerful passivity to the human personality.

"Resist ye *not* evil," counseled Jesus, whose birth, by the way, ushered in the Age of Pisces, nearly two thousand years ago.

The Fish are influenced by the mysterious, infinite wisdom of Neptune, and so they seldom resist the more aggressive Rams, who are driven by the fiery force of the red planet, Mars. Often, Aries people find that Pisceans have a restful, cooling effect on their flaming frustrations. An association between them is usually beneficial to both. Each Sun Sign carries, within karmic memory, the seeds of experiences gained from the Sun Sign immediately behind it on the astrological wheel of life—and conversely, there are many lessons to be learned from the character and qualities of the Sun Sign immediately following one's own.

This is a 2-12 Sun Sign Pattern, meaning that Aries represents the second astrological house to Pisces, and Pisces represents the twelfth astrological house to Aries. Translated, Aries will always, in one way or another, symbolize money to Pisces, whether in a negative or a positive sense. In some manner, money will be a vital consideration, and a frequent topic of discussion between them.

To the Rams, the Fish represent many secrets, which Pisces usually keeps and won't tell, causing Aries to be exceedingly annoyed. If not that, then the two of them will spend much time discussing secrets—or the past sorrows of one or the other. Sometimes, the secrecy syndrome is beneficial, but you can be sure, however it works out, that both money and secrecy will form the foundation, in a variety of ways, of any association between the Ram and the Fish, whether they're involved as friends, relatives, business associates, lovers or mates. "Secrets" may include all matters of the occult, the esoteric or the metaphysical, such as astrology, hypnotism, astral travel, telepathy and the like. Sooner or later, these matters will prove to be of mutual interest to any Aries-Pisces combination, whatever the sex, age or relationship of the two of them, as with all 2-12 Sun Sign Patterns.

Since Pisces lies behind Aries on the karmic wheel, the Ram feels an instinctive tolerance for the foibles of the Fish, somehow understanding the Piscean behavior, even though it differs so vastly from his (or her) own. Each Aries person has spiritually experienced the passivity and submission of the Pisces nature, which is why Aries, in the present incarnation, leans so hard toward the extreme opposite of Piscean humility—ego. With all their brashness, Rams reveal their karmic soul memory of the Piscean experience through their hidden vulnerability to hurt, and the quickness with which Arian compassion and generosity can be aroused.

The Rams, however, aren't about to chance any masochism (openly, at least) in this lifetime. One might say that Aries comprehends and appreciates the Pisces attitude without envy, and without condemning it. They've already received their report cards in the Piscean spiritual school, thank you, and they prefer not to return. They didn't like the teacher (Neptune) all that much. And so it goes with all the Sun Signs, around and around the birth wheel — again and again — until all the necessary lessons are learned, and the soul can graduate from the earth-flesh level of awareness and existence, into a higher, and more individual awareness.

Due to this 2-12 influence, the Fish will never fail to in some way look up to Aries as having something important to teach them, and unlike most Sun Signs, in relation to the sign ahead of them, Pisces is usually placidly willing to imitate, and to learn from the Rams. (Water is not only the strongest and most powerful of the four elements — Water is also wisest — which is *why* it's strongest.)

On the whole, the Ram and the Fish are nicely compatible, with neither overly desirous of interfering with the other's approach to life, but rather complementing it instead. Yet there will be times when they experience some heated (Aries) or chilly (Pisces) encounters. The forthright Ram has little patience for the sometimes slippery tactics of the elusive Fish.

I know a Piscean in Colorado who pleasantly (Pisceans are nearly always pleasant) once remarked to me: "Well, you know what I always say — promise anything, and get out of it later. That's my motto." The Fish are uncommonly cheerful about confessing their little flaws. This method of backing away from a commitment quite naturally may create, on occasion, a barrier between Pisces and the very direct, naively honest Rams, who will usually display undisguised resentment when the Fish swim away alone now and then, to exchange whispered secrets with the ocean — or who may feel hurt and neglected if the Pisceans should glide behind some cool seaweed to refresh their weary souls, without leaving behind a trail indicating where they may be found. But no harm is meant by the kindly Fish. Lacking the Ram's tough horns, and the Mars emotional, spiritual and mental stamina, it's the Neptune soul's only protection against an abrasive daily existence in this harsh world — the wear and tear of life's problems.

The Piscean motto of *"promise anything, and get out of it later"* may sound deceptive; yet it's a philosophy that keeps the Fish young and tranquil — and off the psychiatrist's couch. It also allows Pisceans to conserve their energy, thereby enabling them to remain composed enough to listen to everybody else's troubles for hours on end. Nevertheless, to the Rams, sneaky is sneaky.

☆ ☆ ☆ ☆ ☆ ☆

ARIES *Woman* PISCES *Man*

———◄━◆━►———

"Which story was it ?"

*"About the prince who couldn't find the lady
who wore the glass slipper."*

*"Peter," said Wendy excitedly, "that was
Cinderella, and he found her . . . ."*

I don't want to shatter any glass slipper dreams, but this combination usually works out better when the girl is the Pisces and the boy is the Ram. An Aries female needs a determined, thick-skinned male, who has the aggressiveness to say, "Shut up, and listen," when it's necessary. And it will assuredly be necessary, from time to time, with this girl.

There are, of course, as always, the exceptions that prove the astrological rule. A Pisces man, for example, with the Moon or Ascendent in a Fire Sign, such as Aries, Sagittarius or Leo, may possess just the right blend of fiery command and gentleness of manner to make this rather spunky one become as meek as a lamb. Well, maybe not *that* meek — but more docile and manageable than she'd be around most other men.

In a way, it's what she secretly seeks and longs for — someone who will control her firmly (and make her feel feminine) — on occasion. Someone who will allow her to be boss (half the time) — and be the tender, charming Prince of her dreams (the rest of the time, whatever time is left). She needs a strong big brother to protect her, a companion she considers her equal in intelligence, a lover who will physically conquer her, and a quiet man who will not try to confine her spirited personality, or domineer her. It would also be nice if he could be a poet.

And of course, he should be willing, even anxious, to defend her loyally against her enemies (until she forgives them, then he should love them) as she will defend him against his (whether he wants her to or not). And let's see — yes, he must also admire and respect her, and tell her so frequently — be the kind of man who likes to chop wood and fix things when they're broken (including her heart) — a man who can handle an emergency with cool poise, and meet a crisis with great courage. He must, by all means, be possessed of impeccable integrity, and be snowflake-pure-sexually-faithful to her. (But he must not be a doormat, or self-effacing.)

If possible, she would like him to consist of equal parts of Rhett Butler, Robert Browning, Muhammed Ali, Mike Todd, Abraham Lincoln — and her favorite saint. Maybe a touch of Charlton Heston, Warren Beatty, Jimmy Stewart, Marlon Brando and Steve McQueen, with just a dash of Norman Mailer — if that's not asking too much.

Nearly every single Christmas of her life, for as far back as she can remember, she carefully printed out her request in a letter to Santa Claus, and he ignored it, year after year, leaving all sorts of useless things under the tree, except this one most important gift. (You can sympathize with his problem.)

When you consider it carefully, a Pisces man has as many chances to live up to her romantic ideals as any other male. *None.* Which means that he at least starts out even. You know ? The Fish certainly can't ask for better odds than those.

A girl Ram is fun and fresh. She's pretty and punchy, full of spirit and sparkles and warmth and generosity — all that. But she does need to be sat upon occasionally, when her Mars will causes her to be a bit too frisky and free for her own good — or for the peace of mind of the man who loves her. Pisces men just never sound very convincing when they say things like "Shut up, and listen." The Fish is more in his own element when he's figuring abstract physics or math theories, calculating the relativity of time, in relation to space — or quoting Tennyson. It's possible for the Ram and the Fish to meet, mate, and murmur sentiments into each other's ears happily, for a lifetime. It can happen. Not often. But it can. Where's your faith in miracles ?

A Pisces man is more likely than any other to genuinely believe in the kind of enchantment every Aries girl lives within, and demands romantically. She'll adore him for it. She'll trust his dreams, have faith in his visions — and she'll respond (at first, anyway) with little flutters of excitement to his sensitivity and his gentleness. Then she'll feel an irresistible urge to defend him against those who judge him unfairly as an idle dreamer with no future. (She'll have simply bushels of chances to do that !)

Most people have been so brainwashed by astrological over-simplifications, they think every Pisces is a wishy-washy candidate for Alcoholics Anonymous, or group therapy (nude group therapy, considering the Age we're living in). True, he was born under a complicated and difficult Sun Sign. The stars portended at his birth that he'd have to pick his way through a haze of daydreams. He was also fated to get caught in the sticky octopus tendrils of other people's troubles as he swims along through life . . . . trying his best to mind his own business (which can be even more tangled and confusing). His ruling planet, Neptune, seems to be forever leading him into situations so mysterious, so intertwined with intrigue and half-truths that even a Ouija board couldn't get to the bottom of the whole mess. This is so for Pisces of both sexes. Talk it over with Ted Kennedy, Elizabeth Taylor, Jackie Gleason, Dinah Shore or Pamela Mason sometime. They're all Pisceans too, and they've been there. EVERYWHERE. More than once.

The Aries girl who's annoyed by the elusiveness of her Pisces man should ask herself how *she* would react to being part of what some flippant astrologers call "the dustbin of the zodiac." It's not much fun to carry the weight of knowing you're the embodiment of *all* the other eleven Sun Signs. And this man has the added burden of frequent precognitive flashes that clutter up his consciousness. Not only that, but his Neptunian compassion can seduce him into some situations that can only be called weird. This forces him to cover the fact that he's the softest touch in town under a variety of false fronts. These can range from crankiness and crustiness to drunkenness — or a psychedelic trip that's far out (far out from this harsh world). But lots of creative writers, imaginative artists and abstract thinkers (like Einstein) have also been Pisceans, and they learned to handle their Neptune vibrations. This man does have a choice of streams, you know. All Fish do, when they break away from the chaotic cross-currents.

The danger inherent in a relationship between an Aries woman and a Pisces man is that the sexes tend to get mixed up. A male Fish can be as masculine, as virile and as muscular as the next guy. But he's also ultrasensitive — for a man. The female Ram can be as feminine, as tender and as glamorous as the next girl. But she's also strong-willed, determined and independent — for a woman. Because of his instinct to withdraw from conflict, the Pisces man may prefer to retreat, rather than face up to the Aries girl's Fire. She won't like it. Rams feel helpless, and become even angrier, when they're forced to shadow-box their way out of a disagreement. It can drive her up a tree to be ignored, and a Piscean is an expert at the technique of passive non-resistance.

She may also resent his reluctance to push himself with others. It's beyond her comprehension how anyone can take so much lying down. Just as it's beyond *his* comprehension how anyone can stand up on his feet constantly, fighting and attacking and counterattacking, and wasting all that energy. His mildness, if carried to extremes, can finally goad her into lashing out at him with some cutting and unkind remarks that she doesn't mean but that can nevertheless wound his feelings deeply. This sort of scene can be triggered by almost any minor incident.

PISCES: My paintings are going to be exhibited at the museum's Art Show next week. See ? Here's the program. It says: *"Special showing of new art forms by Fried Hot."*

ARIES: Are they talking about an artist or an *egg* ? That can't be you. You're Fred Haught.

PISCES: I guess they weren't sure how to spell my surname, and maybe the mistake in "Fred" is just a printer's error. I've been trying to decide what to do. . . . . . .

ARIES: Don't tell me what you're going to do. Don't tell me, let me guess.

You're going to change your name, right?

PISCES: Well, I hadn't thought of going that far. Do you think I should?

ARIES: I think you should grab the art director of that museum and say, "Look, boob, you spelled my name wrong. Print new programs, or I remove my paintings from the exhibit."

PISCES: Oh, I couldn't insult him like that. He might be offended, and then I'd lose my big chance to exhibit my paintings.

ARIES: Well, if you don't do it, you're going to lose your big chance to exhibit me as your wife. I AM NOT GOING TO BE INTRODUCED AT THE MUSEUM AS "MS. FRIED HOT," SO YOU EITHER COLLAR THAT ART DIRECTOR AND DEMAND YOUR RIGHTS TODAY — OR I MOVE OUT OF YOUR LIFE TOMORROW. DO YOU HAVE THAT STRAIGHT?

He won't refuse. He'll agree with her, and leave for the museum. But he may not return. He'd rather be Fried Hot than boiled alive in her Mars temper. Of course, this is an extreme case. Still, it does illustrate the challenges and hurdles to be met when there's a reversal of the dominant-passive roles between these two lovers. If there's a compatible Sun-Moon-Ascendent aspect between their birth charts, their relationship can work out ideally. She'll have enough Fire to spark him to great accomplishment, to give him faith in himself and his dreams — and he'll have the right amount of Water to soothe and gentle her fears, to give her emotional security. With an adverse Luminary or Ascendent aspect between their nativities, however, they may face a few problems.

The Aries woman is woven of finer threads than those who see only her surface confidence ever suspect. She is many things more than a fireball of impulse. She's the ecstasy she felt when she buried her nose in the fragrance of the bouquet of violets she picked in an elf-haunted, shady corner of the yard, when she was three . . . . . the kitten she watched get run over by a streetcar . . . . . she's red kites and yellow balloons, the rainy days of childhood . . . . . the newborn baby a lady on the bus let her hold in her arms when she was nine, and acting out a private madonna make-believe . . . . . the snow sparkles under the street light she truly thought were diamonds . . . . . the spanking with a wooden paddle her fourth grade principal gave her at recess, before everyone in school . . . . . she's the sunrise someone forgot . . . . . the song someone remembered . . . . She's her first belly-smacker in the pool, when she was trying desperately for a perfect swan dive . . . . . and more. She's the poem the Pisces man tried to write, but couldn't quite complete . . . . . yet he could, if he'd only allow her to help him write the last verse.

The sexual relationship between them will be the eternal and beautiful mutual attraction of explosive activity and cool stillness. But it can also be the attraction of a potential conqueror for a potential victim, if there are severe planetary afflictions in their respective horoscopes. With favorable planetary exchanges in their nativities, however, the Ram and the Fish could enjoy an exceptionally happy physical chemistry that could outlast periodic bickering, or hurt feelings. Their philosophical approaches to Life may be different, but their romantic goals are identical. Both of them desperately seek a sexual experience of great intensity — and both are sentimental and imaginative. In expressing their love through sexual union, they can fulfill each other's secret fantasies, escape into their own private wonderland and close the door against the rest of the world.

A Piscean who wants to teach an Aries girl to float tranquilly in his pond must make a decision to level with her about everything, and then stick to it. His fondness for keeping secrets, and for telling half-truths to spare her feelings (or his own), is something this woman will never stand for. She puts all her cards on the table, and she can't trust a player who hides any aces up his sleeve. Unless the Fish is prepared to be 100 percent honest with her, in every way, he'd better find another poker partner.

If someday he should discover he can't keep anything from her, not even his innermost feelings, and he's compelled to confess to her all his secret yearnings — he loves her. It's the first sign of capitulation from a Pisces man.

It's not, however, a guarantee that he'll capitulate all the way into marriage. This man is extremely reluctant to take on the complications of both emotional *and* legal involvement. The first one is hassle enough with which to cope, as far as he's concerned, without adding the burden of the second. The common Neptune definition of marriage is "a close friendship, recognized by the police." Eventually he'll gobble the bait, and allow himself to be reeled in, but he'll struggle less in the marital net if the Aries woman will pretend they're still having an affair that's *not* recognized by the police. I know an actual, living, breathing Piscean male in California who has substituted a Siamese cat for a family (the typical Fish fears the responsibilities of a family, as he fears the snooping of Big Brother or Sister, the Internal Revenue, CIA and FBI). The Fish with the Pussycat has a motto he repeats often: "*Kitty litter is cheaper than diapers.*"

The Ram will have to make-believe with her Fish that they're involved in only an emotional union, nothing more, even after they are duly wedlocked (she should *never* use the term wed-*lock* with him). If this keeps him romantic, makes him happy and causes him to feel freer, why not allow him to live in his fantasy of bachelorhood?

He may alternate between leaving her, and returning again, unsure of how to convince her of his devotion. But all she wants is to be loved and understood, never to be questioned — to be accepted for exactly what she is. As a matter of fact, that's all he wants too. The only dragons that stand between Aries and Pisces are his Neptune illusions, which to him, are reality — and her Mars reality, which is, actually, an illusion. Plus the smaller gargoyles of his passivity, and her impatience — and their mutually sensitive, vulnerable natures. No outsider can slay these dragons and gargoyles for them. They must be destroyed from within. That's the way it always is in faerie tales. At least, in the ones with happy endings.

☆ ☆ ☆ ☆ ☆ ☆

ARIES *Man* PISCES *Woman*

The many gentlemen who had been boys when she was a girl discovered simultaneously that they loved her, and they all ran over to her house to propose to her except Mr. Darling, who took a cab and nipped in first, and so he got her.

Since no man is more male than a Ram, and no woman is more female than a Fish, the love between these two is never flawed by confusion over sexual identification. It's a true mating, in every sense of the word you can imagine. When an Aries man and a Pisces woman fall in love, Mother Nature smiles approvingly.

At its best, the liaison brings out all his shining Aries heroism, and all her tender Pisces devotion. These two are Romeo and Juliet in the flesh. At its worst, it can bring out his latent Mars sadism and her latent Neptune masochism. Even so, if he enjoys playing Tyrannical-Master-of-the-Mansion, and she gets kicks from playing Little-Eva-in-the-Snow, who are we to spoil their fun?

I remember well the evening I spent with friends of mine, an Aries man and his Pisces wife, in West Virginia. After their seven children had been tucked in bed, the handsome Ram placed a protective arm around his pretty girl Fish, and spoke emphatically: "My woman doesn't run around chasing a career and joining clubs. I keep her pregnant in the summer and barefoot in the winter — so she stays out of trouble."

As I started to hand her a heavy brass ashtray to throw at his head, I noticed the strangest thing. She was smiling up at him with absolute adoration and pure worship. I haven't the slightest doubt that they'll walk into the sunset together, long after their golden wedding anniversary, holding hands like sweethearts — with him still tall, and strong — her still fragile and barefoot. It almost makes you cry, doesn't it? It was such a traumatic experience for me, I went out the next day and bought five new pairs of shoes to hide under my bed. When my Pisces friend expressed her curiosity, I just told her, "Well, winter's coming, you know, and I may want to run out some morning at four A.M. to buy a paper or something." I don't think she understood, but I felt more secure.

Aries and Pisces are not generally as compatible, over a long period of time (especially if they live in Alaska, where her feet might get frost bitten) as he would be with an Air or Fire sign — or she would be with an Earth or Water sign. They're basically quite different. But in the immortal words of the Frenchmen: *"Vive la différence!"* It can be quite enough to attract them in the beginning. As for building the elemental attraction into a stable relationship, there's a good chance they can succeed if his Moon or Ascendent is in Pisces, Cancer, Scorpio, Taurus or Capricorn — or if her Moon or Ascendent is in Aries, Leo, Sagittarius, Gemini or Aquarius.

Before the Pisces girl is married, her phone rings constantly, with one male after another calling her for dates. She has an awful time deciding between Tom, Dick or Harry — because she hates to hurt Bill, John and Bob. Anyway, she really loves Jack, if she could only forget Roger. Life is full of frustrations. Like deciding which one to marry — or deciding whether or not to allow half a dozen or so of them to protect her against poverty and boredom, by paying her rent and taking her to Sun Valley to ski. Things like that. Maybe lending her their cars, an occasional Porsche, a BMW or a Saab. It's such a rough life. The Women's Liberation movement doesn't move Pisces females much. The whole ERA noise just kind of floats in one Neptune ear and out the other. The Pisces woman feels it all depends on what you want to be liberated *from*. It certainly does. Amen, sisters! (And brothers.)

After she's married, her phone will continue to ring approximately every ten minutes throughout the day and night, but then it will be her neighbors, relatives and friends who need an ear to confide in, and a shoulder to weep upon. Her Aries husband will fly into a few Mars tantrums over her tendency to turn their home into a therapy clinic. She should be listening to *his* troubles. Not *part* of the time. *All* of the time. Except on holidays, when he's resting, or sleeping — or knocking around with his pals.

A girl Fish is an exquisite listener. That's how she gathered all those admirers, beginning with grade school. She's also beautifully humble, and sympathetic, and *that's* how she gets caught in her own Neptune web. A Pisces woman who feels, finally, that her individuality is being smothered by the dominant ego of the Aries man she loves, usually won't protest loudly, or argue about it with any degree of intensity. No matter how desperate she becomes, she's more likely to keep smiling . . . . but with a blank expression in her eyes. When he loses his temper with her over a trifle, she normally won't fight back. She'll just blink a few times, and yawn. But the yawn may be a silent scream.

If she seems to be drifting and dreaming, if her smiles are vague, and her attention wanders, the Ram should ask himself if he has been perhaps overlooking her needs in pursuing his own, which is easy for him to do, though he never does it intentionally. An Aries man is seldom aware of his occasional selfishness. It's more thoughtlessness than selfishness anyway. He's so intent on living-being-doing every moment, he just doesn't take the time to look around him. When it's pointed out to him that he's been rude or inconsiderate, he's invariably surprised and embarrassed — and sorry.

It was never his intention to be cruel or unfeeling. No one can be more sentimental, kind-hearted, foolishly generous and fiercely loyal in love than Aries. But her Neptune passivity can not only encourage his unthinking selfishness and his latent chauvinism, it can blind him to any hurt he's given her. If he realizes it, he'll probably apologize profusely, and behave like a perfect angel (until he forgets again, and has to be reminded). So you can't blame all their troubles on him. The Pisces woman must accept at least half the responsibility for her own unhappiness, and ask herself if she has been leaning a little heavily on the martyr routine.

There's not much need to analyze their sexual relationship in detail, as we did with the other combinations, because, as you can see from the astrological facts stated at the beginning of this section, it's clear that this is the perfect Romeo-Juliet, Tarzan-Jane blending, in a sexuality sense. The result, in relation to their physical intimacy, isn't difficult to guess. She'll not only be sensitive to his every lover's mood, wish and desire, she'll decode and fulfill them, almost before they're formed. In return, he'll gratefully give her an exciting display of his Mars intensity, and much tender (for him) affection. None of the boys who used to call her on the phone, and lend her their BMWs, could have prepared her, emotionally or otherwise, for the kind of passion that rages in the heart of a Ram, once he's found a woman he can call completely his own.

This brings us to the subject of sexual and romantic infidelity (a subject we always eventually reach in every Aries chapter). The girl Fish is not a flirt, mind you, but what it is, you see, is that — well, men flirt with *her*. She's not promiscuous, she just thinks that admiration from members of the male sex is the nicest part of being a female.

As for the Ram, he's not a playboy type either. But he's not going to throw rocks at a little worship from the opposite sex now and then, which he uses to polish up his ego. He thinks that's all part of being a man. None of this should cause any real trouble between them; nevertheless, it probably will, because, although the Pisces girl is inclined to understand and trust her man — Aries is never as insistent on freedom for his partner as he is on freedom for himself. In the Ram's opinion, *his* casual encounters with other women are innocent. *Hers* are suspect, clearly deliberate maneuvers toward an actual act of unfaithfulness.

It's not at all fair, of course. It will help if she'll realize that his attitude isn't based on romantic selfishness, but only on his well-hidden feelings of inadequecy. Being influenced and guided by Neptune compassion, she'll probably comprehend his secret fear, and behave accordingly. Whether he's right or wrong, an Aries man will never tolerate a promiscuous or an unfaithful woman — and one slip is many more times than enough for him. If she doesn't work overtime to convince her Aries man, with all her heart, that she belongs only to him — it's out in the cold, cold snow for little Eva.

Put two completely different kinds of people together, and do they grow to love each other less and less — or more and more? With Aries and Pisces, it's not the differences between them that matter. It's what they have in common — the fear of being hurt. Her vulnerability is easily discernible — his may be disguised by Mars bravery and brashness, but it's just as real, just as painful as her own.

TAURUS

Earth — Fixed — Negative
Ruled by Venus (also by the
Planet Pan-Horus)
Symbol: The Bull
Night Forces — Feminine

TAURUS

Earth — Fixed — Negative
Ruled by Venus (also by the
Planet Pan-Horus)
Symbol: The Bull
Night Forces — Feminine

The **TAURUS- TAURUS** *Relationship*

Observe how they pass over fallen twigs without
making the slightest noise. The only sound to be heard
is their somewhat heavy breathing.

Somehow, an astrological rumor has gotten around that Taurus people are inclined to be overweight. This is false. Some of them tend to plumpness, true, but most of them do not.

They love to cook and they love to eat, but normally, the splendid physique of the Bull causes any excess calories to turn into solid muscle. With the female Taureans, good food only seems to give them a look of sturdy coordination, and a slow, sensual grace. (Taurean film star Audrey Hepburn is *fat* ?) Of course, there are always the inevitable exceptions, but the truth of the matter is that it's the Sun Signs of Cancer and Libra who are more susceptible to plumpness and extra curves than Taurus. (I said susceptible, that's all, *susceptible*.) I just thought I'd mention it, to put the Taurus people reading this section into a contented frame of mind. That's always the safest way to keep Cows and Bulls — contented.

Another misconception about these people is that they're lazy. Taureans are not lazy. They're simply dedicated to the proposition that wasting energy is a sin, which is why you'll seldom catch them in a quick movement. (Except for rare Bulls like Fred Astaire, who have heavy Gemini influences in their birth charts.) The reason Taurus people have so much strength is because the typical Bulls conserve it, the way they conserve their money. When you put two Taureans together, it's difficult to get them to move into any sort of instant action (unless they're angry, but we'll discuss that later). In fact, moving *two* Bulls is *twice* as hard as moving *one* Bull (an example of uncomplicated, sensible, Taurus-type logic). Picture a couple of piles of rich earth, just sitting there, side-by-side. Isn't it peaceful? Neither of them wishes to profane the peaceful stillness by chattering unduly. When they first meet, they'll size each other up more or less silently. No Bull is ever overly anxious to impulsively jump into an association with another Bull (or any other kind of astrological animal) until all the various possibilities have been carefully judged and seriously considered.

This brings us to the third unfair and fallacious astrological rumor — that Taureans are stubborn. They are not stubborn. They're merely determined and firm in their convictions, not nervous flibbertigibbits who are continually changing their minds and losing their heads. The Bulls change their minds rarely, and lose their heads with even greater infrequency. It's only *reasonable*, you see, after you've done all that careful judging and serious considering, to stick to what you *know* is right. When two Taurus people (of either sex) who hold conflicting opinions are brought into close proximity, they both become even more *reasonable* with each other than they are with others of contrary opinion.

One of the producers of a major television network where I was once a writer is a Taurus. I remember the time he was assigned by the network to build a prime time TV spectacular around a popular singing star, also a Taurus. One calm, peaceful morning, the Taurus star arrived at the Taurus producer's office to discuss the format of the show, and these two Bulls were closeted together behind locked doors for nearly six hours, without so much as a coffee break. Each of them had his own ideas about the spectacular, the guest stars, the songs, the musical theme, the scenic background, lighting effects, and so on. When the famous Taurean finally left, the Taurus producer's secretary and staff crowded around him to ask, "What's he like?" The weary Bull considered the question carefully, as usual, and finally allowed as how the star was a nice, friendly person, intelligent and creative. Then he paused, and said, "But look how long it took him to approve of one simple TV format. He kept pushing some ridiculous ideas he had, over and over, before he realized that I was right in the first place. All that valuable time wasted. I've never met anyone so stubborn." Everyone broke up. It took them several minutes to calm down, while the Taurus producer kept asking, "What did I say that was so funny?"

The last chapter of the foregoing story is that the agent for the Taurus singing star phoned the next day to proffer the singing Bull's apologies. He had decided not to do the spectacular they discussed, and had signed with another network. Period. End of story.

You've probably heard lots of unfair rumors about female American singing star Barbra Streisand being difficult and unreasonable to work with, right? Barbra is a Taurus lady. Obviously, such rumors are false. As I've just pointed out, Taureans are completely *reasonable*. I refer the reader once again to the fourth paragraph of this chapter for a detailed explanation of the reasonable attitude of these unjustly maligned Taurus people. At least no one ever accuses them of not being musical. Every Taurus ever born either sings beautifully, as an amateur or professional — in the shower or tub — while shaving — or if nothing else, adores listening to music, and dreaming about singing.

An association between two Bulls, laboring under the double weight of a 1-1 Sun Sign influence, can be placid, stable and mutually comforting. These people are normally sweet, patient Teddy-Bear types, respectful of each other's rights, quietly devoted, and unquestionably loyal. Still, life may become somewhat stagnant and uneventful for them, unless the birth chart of one or both contains planets in Air or Fire Signs. Taureans are suspicious of change, because the Bull is conservative, and that's *not* a false rumor. If you know a Bull who actually enjoys change, especially abrupt change, he or she was either adopted or the Moon and/or Ascendent was in a sign like Aries, Gemini, or Aquarius at birth. Maybe Sag. The typical Taureans are on guard against quick reforms or sudden switches in the status quo, being very much like the Goats in this respect. They feel that, on the whole, things have been plodding along pretty well for a number of centuries, so why disturb things by changing the rules and regulations of life? To the average Taurean (always allowing for the rare exceptions who prove the rule) any sort of radical interference with Fixed Habit (Taurus is a Fixed Sign, you know) — is unwise. Fixed Habits have already been proven worthy by time, and a new, untested idea could be merely a hair-brained scheme, which might be the dangerous wedge that brings disaster. When a Bull does change his (or her) mind — which does occasionally occur — you can be jolly well certain the change of opinion has been methodically blocked out and measures up to all the necessary qualifications of practicality.

There were, of course, a fair number of double Taurus teams who participated in the "youth revolution" of the sixties, but an honest survey would show that an extremely low percentage of them were draft-card burners who escaped to Canada, or elsewhere, because of conscientious objection. Taurus may "conscientiously object" to many things, but facing physical danger is not one of them. The Sun Sign Taurus rules patriotism in astrology (as does Cancer). American television hero Archie Bunker is a Bull.

(Not actor Carroll O'Connor. Archie Bunker. Only sissies avoid their patriotic duty.) Of those Bulls who did follow their consciences in this respect, they all suffered private guilt twinges later. Even now there are Taureans who are willing to demonstrate for new causes like Ecology, Solar Energy, Greenpeace, Women's Rights and so on, just as some of them demonstrated for Civil Rights for the blacks. After all, it is the Aquarian Age, and even Bulls can't help being swept up in the violent changes. But it will have taken them considerable time to decide to join any protests, and they will have done so only after due cautious reflection.

The currently Venus-ruled Bulls you may know who marched two-by-two in yesterday's Peace Parades, sniffing posies, believed in "Peace" itself quite naturally. Yet only a handful of those who called the police "pigs," threw trash on the White House lawn, set fires, and otherwise defied law and order — or streaked through towns and hamlets naked, to proclaim their pristine innocence — were Taureans. (In the latter instance, it's a safe bet the Bulls, however, *watched* the streakers with interest and amusement. The slapstick aspect of "streaking" tickled their fancies.) But on the whole, the "revolutionary" Taurus protesters just stood there quietly, clutching their Peace signs, candles, flowers, incense, or whatever — and it's quite possible some of them are *still* standing there.

Their defense of established mores and their respect for authority (when authority is *sensible*) is often what draws two Bulls together initially — and the glue that keeps them together. Taurus feels that, if change is needed, the only *reasonable* (there's that word again!) way to bring it about is within the system. Actually, the rest of us should be properly grateful for these basically kind-hearted, reliable souls, who are so dedicated to the reign of cool reason. We need the assorted viewpoints of all twelve Sun Signs for any sort of sane and lasting Peace on Earth. But a couple of Bulls, when they're doubling up on their innate character traits, can freeze into a mold that's just a touch fanatical. Both are deeply and sincerely concerned with protecting their investments, their possessions, their families and loved ones, and their country from wild-eyed radicals. Of course, you must realize that to Taurus, the definition of "wild-eyed radicals" can be an affectionate couple, who are embracing on the street, wearing twin stickers on their Levi's reading: *One-two-three-four, we'd rather _ _ _ _ than go to war."* They'd rather *kiss* than defend their own country?! That sort of philosophy, to the typical Bull, borders on anarchy.

The most potentially damaging aspect of a Taurus-Taurus association is the great reluctance of either Bull to repent when one has seriously offended the other. Even when a Taurean is inwardly convinced that he (or she) has been mistaken, the tendency is to stubbornly stand by what's been unwisely said or done, because to admit a mistake is uncomfortably close to being weak, and the very word "weakness" makes a Bull see red. Now and then, one Bull can coax the other to unbend and say "I'm sorry," or make up, but not often. Sometimes, tickling them helps. They giggle, turn pink, then finally mumble, "Aw shucks, I didn't mean it." It's always easier for Taureans to back down when the disgrace of being wrong is cozily blanketed in humor. It breaks the fall.

When a Bull finally comprehends that Taurus patience is a graceful, desirable virtue, but that turned upsidedown, it's transformed into plain, cussed, bull-headedness, it will be easier to forgive the other half of the Taurus team his (or her) own spells of the same "virtue." Two Bulls can work or play side-by-side, and behave beautifully. They'll be mutually docile, dependable, and sweetly compliant — if one doesn't push the other too far, or too hard. Nearly all Taureans have a sensational sense of humor, and if they can learn to laugh at *themselves*, their adjustment problems will be all over. There's nothing like a funny bone to tickle the Bull into moving, or changing a Fixed position. Humor is one of the greatest qualities a human being can possess. Blended in generous amounts with the wonderful Taurean dependability, it can help to make these lovable and huggable men and women more *reasonable* — as well as a shade more flexible.

An afterthought for any two Taureans, who have lost sight of one another's basic sweetness and cuddly qualities: Taurus Tom Snyder, of television fame and familiarity, has his very own (no joke) Teddy Bear, tucked tenderly somewhere behind the cameras during his program, sometimes clearly visible, at other times playing peek with the audience. Wouldn't you just *know*?

Every Bull, male or female, clutches a symbolic Teddy Bear for emotional security. So you see, the two of you are really very lovable sorts, not nearly so stern and bull-headed as you both behave at times.

And you can also be certain that every Taurean has a funny bone hidden somewhere behind the silent facade. When they permit one another a glimpse of it, the rich humor shared by these two in their 1-1 Sun Sign association will burst forth like a refreshing rain of happiness, to wash clean those stubborn memories of mutually inflicted hurt . . . . . . and allow the flowers of forgiveness to grow in their hearts.

☆ ☆ ☆ ☆ ☆ ☆

TAURUS *Woman* TAURUS *Man*

———◆◄●►◆———

He was one of those deep ones who know about stocks
and shares. Of course no one really knows, but he
quite seemed to know, and he often said stocks were
up and shares were down in a way that would have made
any woman respect him.

A Taurus man walks firmly, in a straight line, toward his goal, step-by-step, not leap-by-leap. He's perfectly content to reap the harvest of his well-deserved rewards in their own due season, and misfortune or bad luck barely disturbs his tranquility. He may carry a heavy load of responsibilities and bravely accepted, wearying duties — his great heart may be burdened nearly to breaking by the painful memory of myriad past disappointments, but the strong Bull goes right on walking, as though nothing had ever happened. More often than not, his steady and patient plodding is eventually crowned with sweet success.

One is reminded of the equally brave, pathetic Nature bull. He stands there, uncertain, but unflinching . . . . . maddened by pain and starvation, facing the sadistic toreadors . . . . scorning any display of weakness, refusing to fall, no matter how many dozens of sharp bandilleros pierce his body . . . . . charging the taunting red cape again and again and again, in uncomprehending confusion . . . . . both infuriated and terrorized by the screams of the crowd . . . . . until he's mercifully executed at the end of the grisly ceremony of fake male macho known as The Bullfight, the unspeakably cruel "sport" Papa Hemingway so adored, in which cowardly, despicable humans, fancying themselves to be heroes, torture, tease, torment — and finally murder a magnificent animal . . . . . while spiritually retarded brutes of both sexes look on and cheer his death agony from the bleachers, in chilling imitation of the bloodthirsty, roaring, insane multitudes in the Coliseum, shortly before Rome fell into the blackness of oblivion — *last time* — via the courtesy of Karma's just and final *coup-de-grâce.*

Should the foregoing, thunderous truth offend, perchance, anyone reading the Spanish language edition of this book, so be it. I make no apology, nor does astrology, to such Iberians and Mexicans. *"He that killeth an ox is as if he slew a man" (Isaiah 66:3).* There are many millions of fine Spanish and Mexican men and women, residing both in the U.S. and south of the border, who find their thrills, pleasures and excitements in ways other than watching the public torture and murder of helpless beasts — and this book is written to be shared by these Light-Bearing Ones, who don't stand in the shadow of shame that darkens their ancient heritage of long-ago splendor. The others may come along for the ride, if they wish, but let them both be forewarned and informed that their possible annoyance over my frank analysis of their bullfights leaves this Ram unrepentantly unruffled and unmoved.

The transiting Mars is passing over my natal Aries Sun today as I write, and the effect of the influence will last a considerable while, as always, during which times, certain things never fail to get socked into their proper place in my life. Rather like spring housecleaning, you know?

The typical male Bull possesses the same calm, silent strength of purpose as his astrological symbol, if he's a spiritually evolved Taurean. Even if he's a Taurus mutant, like Adolf Hitler, the powerful determination is still present. The average Taurus man is visibly influenced by the courage and iron will of his Bull symbol, and makes admirable use of it. This man knows what he wants, and is willing to sacrifice whatever is necessary, without whining or complaining, to reach the green pastures he seeks.

Nothing could endear him more to the Taurus woman. She is impressed. Let the other girls shiver in romantic ecstasy over the barefoot prophets who lie in the grass all day, idling away the hours, stringing love beads, and strumming their guitars. Give her a practical Bull, who wears shoes. When *he* hangs a strand of love beads around her neck, they won't be made of dried coffee beans. They'll be from a real jewelry store, and they'll be paid for in full. If *he* strums a guitar, it will be to pick up some bread as a musician, not merely to howl at the Moon on a summer night in Central Park — or in London's Kensington Gardens (Taurus men always make one think of England's John Bull).

These two have much in common. Like, she has a firm grip on her pocketbook, and he hangs on to his billfold with both fists. Since they're both lovers of Nature, they're crazy about planting green things and watching them grow — like Mutual Funds and Christmas Clubs. That's another thing they have in common. They both know Santa Claus is a put-on. He doesn't live at the North Pole, never did. He's the president of their bank, his name is Christopher G. Kringle, and he doesn't drive a sleigh pulled by reindeer, he drives a good, solid Buick sedan. If they've been good all year, and made their regular deposits, he stuffs their socks with dividends and interest payments, which will someday provide them with a house in the peaceful country, near a quiet stream, far from the honking taxi cabs, smog, noisy teenagers and smoky night clubs of the city.

It's easy to be fooled by Bulls, but don't be. Like, the night club thing. You might believe the glamorous Bulls you've seen hanging around sizzling, noisy, boisterous, and bellicose places like Hollywood, California — so obviously incompatible with the image of crickets chirping cheerfully in a country twilight — are a living denial of their earthy Sun Signs. Don't jump to hasty conclusions. Taurus never does. Take American film actor Glenn Ford, a Bull. In the Spring of 1978, he was quoted in a popular news magazine as saying, "I'm going to surprise everyone I know very soon, when they hear how many acres and acres of land I'm buying in Australia, which is where I plan to live."

Behind the surface glitter of whatever occupation or career (including politics) a Bull follows on his way to the farm, hides the smoldering, ever-growing-stronger dream of escape from the teeming city, to the blessed peace and freshness of the sweet-smelling countryside — hay, horses, manure, and all. The dream may surface at any time throughout the life of a Taurus, but *surface it will* — even though it's delayed until what the insurance companies con us into believing is the last third of the "alleged" life span.

Should it happen to take the Taurus man a little longer than he planned to build the foundation for their future together, whether in music, art, business, banking, politics, or whatever, the female Taurean is as patient as he. This woman probably won't mind working for a few years to support her Bull, as long as he's out there symbolically pitching the hay and genuinely trying to make the grass of their escape grow greener. She'll wait — uncomplainingly, for the most part. It all sounds perfectly lovely, doesn't it? They're a matched set — and unbreakable.

The first thing you know, they've fallen solidly in love. The next thing you know, they're standing firmly before a Minister, Priest, Rabbi or J.P., gazing calmly into each other's tranquil eyes and murmuring *"I do."* The third thing you know, the honeymoon is over, and they've both started saying *"I won't."* About various things. She wants children, but he thinks it's wiser to postpone a family until their bank balance is fatter — so she has a baby or two anyway, just to show him he can't push *her* around.

She wants to buy an expensive electric organ because she loves to play and sing, and he tells her, *"No.* We simply can't afford it." If she wheedles or coaxes, he'll say "NO!" a little louder. So, she opens a charge account (after carefully calculating the monthly payments into her household budget) and orders the organ delivered anyway. The following day, he sends it right back to the store, just to show her she can't push *him* around. (Sometimes it's an expensive stereo, with speakers. Same thing.)

Perhaps there's a film she wants to see. So she plants a few smooches on his cheek, and whispers some private endearments into his close-to-the-head Bull's ear, even if it's really flattened and laid-back in anger. "Come on, sweetie-honey-bug-lollipop, let's go to the movies tonight? Pretty-please-with-brown-sugar-and-cream-on-its-tail?" (Not all, but most Taurus lovers tend toward more than a touch of baby-talk, like Libra lovers. It's the Venus rulership of both signs.)

HIM: Nope.
HER: Why not, sweetie-pumpkin?
HIM: Because I don't want to.

That closes the subject, for the remainder of the evening. Later, after they've tucked themselves cozily into bed, and turned out the lights, he says, "Hey! You forgot to kiss me goodnight. I'm feeling very romantic, baby-dumpling. Kiss me, and see what happens." (Most Bulls are very plain spoken, regarding sexual matters — privately, that is.)

HER: (sweetly, melodiously) No.
HIM: Why not, honey-pot?
HER: Because I *don't want to.*

(a few moments of heavy silence . . . . then)

HIM: I'm going to a hotel.
HER: (suddenly alarmed) Why?
HIM: Because I *want to.*

And another subject is closed. Sometimes for the night, as he plods angrily, clutching his favorite blanket, no farther than the den. Sometimes for several weeks or months, if he really checks into a hotel as he threatened (and he might!). It depends.

I know a devoted couple who live in Los Angeles (and this is, druid honor, an absolutely true story, with only a couple of minor changes to protect the innocent — or the guilty). Both Taurus Sun Signs. He's a song-writer, a lyricist and composer of Hollywood film scores. She's a retired Berlin newspaper reporter, who was born in Germany. When they were "keeping company," the Bull repeatedly refused to marry her. He thought they should test the stability of their love first, before taking such a drastic step, for a "reasonable" length of time (which stretched out into quite a number of years). His Taurus lady cried, pleaded, begged, became angry — and tried to reason with him. He wouldn't budge. "Don't you care for me?" Yes. He cared for her, intensely. But the Bull just wasn't ready for a matrimonial commitment, and *that was that.*

It's now more than a decade later (as of this writing). They remain very much in love, and they have four children — two boys and a set of twin girls. They still have not legally married. *He* has cried, pleaded, begged, become angry — and tried to reason with *her.* She hasn't budged an inch. He's even asked his "mother-in-law" to talk to her, reason with her, and try to move the now mother of his children from her firm position — and for a Bull, that's a gigantic concession. A Taurus man likes interference from relatives in his private affairs like General Motors likes Ralph Nader. But this hasn't accomplished anything either.

HER: The children have your name legally, they have two loving parents, they're included in your will and your insurance, we have a nice home, and we're a warm, devoted, and happy family. We don't need a piece of paper to make it legal.

HIM: Honey-baby, don't you love me?

HER: Of course I love you, deeply.

HIM: But sweetheart, if you love me and I love you, and we're so happy together, and you *know* it will last forever, and we have four children who need the emotional security of wedded parents, *why* won't you marry me?

HER: Because I don't want to.

Of course, not all Taurus couples go as far as that, but it's always a possibility, since, as I told you, the foregoing is a true situation. The average Taurean man and woman will usually insist on the full sanction of the law before entering into any kind of cooperative venture, whether it be business or matrimony, and most Bulls see a decided similarity between the two.

In a liaison of love between Taurus and Taurus, there will be many times when their mutual stubbornness, and refusal to look at the other side, will lead them down the blind alleys of mental and emotional prejudice, and they'll find it difficult to communicate. Still, one of the marvelous things about Bulls is that they possess the ability to shrug off frustration and learn from experience. What Taurus has finally learned, Taurus never ever forgets. *Never. Ever.* If these two try hard to learn the lesson of forgiveness (never easy for Bulls) they can hold each other's hands tightly (Bulls do everything tightly) and find their way out of those dark blind alleys. I know a Taurus woman whose favorite philosophy is: "Every experience is a good experience." It's an admirable attitude, but I've noticed she has a little trouble forgetting the bad ones. She learns from them, yes — but sometimes the lesson she learns is merely to turn her back on the person or situation, without ever trying again — and such lessons teach the heart nothing.

Sex, of course, is only another human experience, but an extremely important one to Taurus lovers or mates. Their initial attraction is usually strongly physical, with the mental and emotional blending coming later, like the honey frosting on a carrot cake. Normally, that's not the ideal priority order in which to approach total love, but with a couple of Taureans, surprisingly it works out fine. Perhaps not so surprisingly. Because sex is an exercise in total sensuality for the average or typical Taurus person, the physical expression of love between this man and woman can gradually develop into an almost psychedelic experiment — although most Bulls (not all, but most) scowl darkly at the very mention of drugs. To Taurus, if you smoke grass, you're foolish and weak, if you drop acid, you're unquestionably mentally unsound — and if you mess around with speed, cocaine, heroin, angel dust, and so forth, you're on a frantic Freeway, headed straight toward spiritual suicide — as swiftly and surely as you're headed toward actual suicide. Ponder the percentages.

Most Taureans have a solid grasp of the metaphysical teaching that drugs are the False Prophets warned of by the Book of Revelations in the New Testament — which, if not recognized as such, can bring on the Götterdämmerung prematurely. Actually the dogmatic Bulls are closer to truth than they suspect. It may have been, in the cosmic concept, necessary for drug-induced awareness to burst open: new spiritual vistas for the Golden Age of Aquarius. But this galactic-cosmic experiment of the Masters — this preliminary to Earth's spiritual awakening — has served its purpose (at the cost of much human suffering, as well as enlightenment). Now it's time to halt, lean back and ponder the insight thus gained. Every Sun Sign is charged with a special and particular mission, and the Taurus Bulls (and Capricorn Goats) are charged with keeping our collective feet on the ground regarding such matters.

Oddly (and *actually*) it has been the solid, Earthbound (but perceptive) Taureans of my personal acquaintance who've been the ones to first realize that all the hullabaloo about electronic bugging and snooping has merely been a *material level* rehearsal for the swiftly approaching time when every man and woman will be able to "read" each other's human auras, and therefore able to perceive far more "secrets" than it's possible to learn about people via tape-recorded conversations, telephone tapping, and such. You didn't realize that Earth Sign Cappy Richard Nixon performed such a vital and giant galactic preparatory role for all of us, did you? (Neither did he.)

In like manner, drugs have been the *material level* rehearsal for the fast approaching opening of the *Third Eye* in every man and woman, which will allow them to see and interpret the human aura, and recall past incarnations. Children are all born with the Third Eye open (see last paragraph of Scorpio-Scorpio chapter). In medical terminology, they are born with a soft pineal gland. But it gradually grows less soft as children submit to the imagination-stifling restrictions of their elders, until it finally becomes stone-hard, and like all adults then, they "have rocks in their heads" (which is, by the way, literally how that term originated in the subconscious).

Many true mystics and "sensitives" (including Taurus "psychic" Peter Hurkos) have suffered a blow on the head, near the Third Eye (pineal gland) which caused it to soften again, as in childhood, allowing them to perceive the *real* world and the *Eternal Now* of Past, Present and Future. Tibetan monks have accomplished this through physical manipulation exercises, meditation — and even surgery (in rare cases). But *Love* (quite seriously and technically) accomplishes it more swiftly. The so-called "saints" (and Jesus himself) used only Love as the method for opening up the Third Eye or pineal gland. It's a whole lot safer, and much more pleasant than falling off a ladder or bumping into a door—also considerably more joyful than monotonous, boring Eastern meditation rites. Besides, the latter can dangerously release the Kundalini Serpent Power *prematurely,* which causes all manner of bodily pain and emotional torment. In other words, don't contemplate your navel, never mind what any flower-draped Tantra Guru might tell you, until you've *first* learned to *love one another purely and unselfishly,* as the Nazarene counseled, learned how to *forgive your enemies*—and to *do unto others what you'd like to have them do unto you*—or you may have reason to wish your Third Eye would harden again. A word to the wise is sufficient. A word to the foolish, as all Bulls know, is wasted.

In 1975, I had a discussion with three enlightened Bulls (two males, one female) who were easily convinced, despite the typical Taurean stubbornness, that it's time for Earthlings to move on to the next practice session, beyond the initial stage of drug-induced, largely false visions—the next stage of spiritual development being the realization that one may only *surely* "see God" or "know Truth" through the control of the *conscious* mind—through control of what Francis of Assisi called Brother Body, via proper nutrition, exercise, and avoiding the abuse of sexual energy—and third (and most vital) through the daily, hourly practice of an interchange of love, kindness, and forgiveness. Including the kindness not to further torture our animal brothers and sisters, by way of butchering them, murdering them, shooting them for "sport," dissecting them—and eating their flesh—which circles right back (full serpent circle) to the necessary cleansing and purification of Brother Body (and Sister Body).

Somehow, I have a distinct and nearly tangible sense that the Bulls who are reading this chapter about themselves and their attitudes toward all these urgent matters are breathing hard behind my shoulder and demanding to know how to protect themselves from the naked mental and emotional exposure of their personal auras soon to be readable to everyone who says "Good morning" to them. (Taureans have such a thing about privacy, you know.) Dear Bulls, don't worry. Adequate protection from the invasion of your innermost private thoughts, as revealed in your aura, is definitely possible. But you must be patient, and I know you'll understand when I tell you that you must wait for a forthcoming book of mine, if you want me to discuss the details of such protection with you, step-by-step. Believe me, there's time. Now, may we return to the subject of the Taurus attitude toward drugs?

To the Taurus man and woman, if they're typical Bulls, using drugs is like "instant God," a quick glimpse of profound Truth—so profound it can literally blow the mind of a not-yet-sufficiently-evolved person, not to mention his or her soul. From an esoteric and cosmic point of view, according to the wisdom of the ancients, the Taurus Bulls have nailed the Truth square center, in this respect, as they do most everything else.

Taureans may be a bit overly stuffy concerning the dangers of smoking "grass," but even supposing that grass (pot) is relatively harmless (especially when compared to the destructive effect of the poisoning process of alcohol, nicotine, and white sugar addiction) it's nevertheless not too cool to develop a dependence upon even the mildest emotional or spiritual crutch. If you were to try an experiment, and use a crutch, without the need for one, in a surprisingly brief period of time you'd be shocked to see your actual leg shrink in size — and eventually it would become permanently atrophied, permanently paralyzed, for the simple reason of non-use. Ask your doctor.

Substituting for the crutch the mildest or most potent stimulant or depressant, from grass and coke to heroin or angel dust — and substituting for your physical leg and Third Eye (pineal gland) wherein lies all psychic power, sensitivity, and spiritual wisdom — the identical process occurs: shrinkage and eventual permanent atrophy of the Third Eye from non-use.

Taurus men and women instinctively know it's just plain dumb to paralyze anything deliberately, whether it's an arm, a leg, the Third Eye, or any other part of the body. Every Bull possesses such innate horse sense or common sense (barring severe afflictions in the nativity). In this feeling, Taurus hits the nail square center again.

It may seem strange that Taurus, normally, on the surface of it, the most un-esoteric Sun Sign of the twelve, should be so close to the spiritual truth concerning drugs. Yet, it's not really strange at all to an astrologer. Everyone, you see, strongly feels, on a subconscious level, the magnetic attraction (polarity-pull) of his or her opposite Sun Sign on the karmic wheel of Life — or the zodiac wheel. The sign opposite Taurus is the deeply spiritual and psychic, sensitive, and perceptive Scorpio — ruled by the powerful planet Pluto, which is the planet in charge of all these matters (in close partnership with Neptune, ruler of Pisces). Scorpio's ruling Pluto is also intimately aligned with Pan-Horus, the *true* ruler of Taurus. When Pan-Horus is finally identified and named (once again) and takes over the time-energy rulership of all Bulls, allowing Taurus people to return their foster ruler, Venus, to Libra, where she belongs — Taureans will be as "knowing" as Scorpios in all spiritual matters, while retaining the soft influence of Venus — from a distance, in an esoteric sense. "Be ye wise as a Serpent, yet as harmless as a Dove," therefore applies to enlightened Taureans.

The Sun Sign Taurus astrology students reading this might want to contemplate a quick and easy proof of the inescapable tie with one's opposite polarity Sun Sign (in the case of Taurus — Scorpio). Astrologically, *Taurus* rules the throat and vocal cords. The opposite sign, *Scorpio*, rules, among other things, the sex organs. When puberty occurs in a male, which is a *sexual* change, there is a simultaneous change of *voice*. This polarity proof can be given in multiple and fascinating ways, all around the horoscopic wheel—but a detailed analysis of these will have to wait for that forthcoming book I mentioned.

Scorpio. Ah, yes! That brings us neatly back to sex—which I'm sure pleases the patient Bulls, who have all been waiting so nicely and quietly for us to return to a subject of intense interest to them.

No one who uses a mind-expanding drug to increase the sense sensations will ever come as close to the ultimate in sensual expression and experience as two Taurus people who are twin souls (not all of them are) when they are making love. A person on a drug high may perch atop a mushroom (a large one, naturally) deep in ecstasy, contemplating the scent of a bar of soap, the intricate patterns in a daisy's petal, the exquisite taste of a drop of water, as well as its bursting life force . . . . the texture of a splinter or the symphony of the sound of a ticking clock. But this spaced-out dude or dame has nothing on two Taurus lovers.

A Bull of either sex can spend hour after endless hour lying on the rich, fragrant Earth, *beneath* the same mushroom (where it's far more comfortable, with ample room to stretch out) contemplating ecstatically the scent of the beloved's skin, the intricate, delicate, faerie cobweb sky-map of the lines in the lover's hand, the singing feel of soft hair, the delicious taste of an ear lobe . . . . . . or the crashing crescendos of the partner's heartbeat.

Taurus people don't often burst verbally into poetry (though they frequently burst into song) during lovemaking, and they're not overly sensitive to the finer emotional implications of sex, but they are certainly receptive to its sensual possibilities. The Bull doesn't feel the same lack of a sixth sense as most people, being so acutely aware of and turned into the other five. There's seldom any serious disagreement in the area of sexual union between two well-mated Bulls, except perhaps when one of them refuses to make love because he (or she) is pouting about something. That's when a sixth sense might come in handy. It could help one Taurean develop more psychic perception about why the other one is being so stubborn, by using ESP to flash on what the temporarily frigid one really wants—which I can tell them is *not* to be left alone, no matter how it may seem. (It's probably just a secret desire to be coaxed.)

In other areas of their relationship, a Taurus man and woman have the potential to accumulate a sizable amount of money and material possessions—which you'd better believe they'll manage to keep. They're both sentimental, warm, and loving, their emotional behavior gently guided by their foster ruler, Venus, who influences their nature with much tenderness and gentleness but is also occasionally an influence of temptation toward every form of excess, including food, drink, financial greed, sex, and anything else you can think of offhand (with the already noted exception of drugs, which only the very *rare* Bull is tempted to abuse). These two are equally strong, patient and emotionally stable — except for those far-apart spells of blind fury, which normally only occur every decade or so, when the Bulls are really aroused — then look out! As I mentioned earlier in this chapter, the Taurus man and woman are a perfectly matched set.

As for any periodic problems of communication between them, the Bull knows exactly how to say "I'm sorry" and "I need you" in silent Taurean sign language — and his Taurus woman knows exactly how to interpret it. With these two, a touch on the hand in a dark room can dispense with the necessity of speaking a single word.

Shall we leave them now? You may have noticed how very, very quiet and still it's become, during the reading of the last few pages. That means the Bull and his mate are *communicating* . . . . . . and wish to be left alone. Don't be rude and snoopy, now, and try to read their auras. Leave these lovers in peace. Don't disturb the Bull, and the Bull won't disturb you. In other words, let's mind our own business. As Taureans always mind theirs.

☆ ☆ ☆ ☆ ☆ ☆

TAURUS

Earth — Fixed — Negative
Ruled by Venus (also the
  Planet Pan-Horus)
Symbol: The Bull
Night Forces — Feminine

GEMINI

Air — Mutable — Positive
Ruled by Mercury
Symbol: The Twins
Day Forces — Masculine

The **TAURUS-GEMINI** *Relationship*

Without giving a thought to what might be
the feelings of a fellow-creature thus
abruptly deprived of its closest companion,
Peter at once considered how he could turn
the catastrophe to his own use. . . .

*T*aurus men and women are quiet, steady, practical people, who try to mind their own business. On occasion, they can be fierce, though most of the time they retain an admirable calm. A Bull can look a tornado in the eye, if necessary, without flinching or batting a lash. Nevertheless, his (or her) splendid strength and determined staying power is a poor match for the flashing agility of a pair of Twins, who can cleverly twist and turn their way out of any earthly threat — the Twins, of course, being two different people disguised as one, who call themselves Gemini.

Pity the poor Taureans who are faced with these two fast-moving, twinkle-toed people, with razor-sharp minds, skipping around and confusing them, all the time giving them the illusion that they are facing but a single toreador. It's hard to see how anyone can find sport in cruelly tormenting a great, noble beast, whose only desire is to be left alone, in peace. It almost makes one wish for the Bull to score, with a sudden, furious thrust of his horns. Sometimes, that happens. And it's a fair warning to misguided Geminis, who have no idea how unpleasant it feels to be struck unexpectedly from the rear, when you're grinning and bowing and gracefully bobbing around — and not looking behind you.

I have a Taurus neighbor, whose daughter, also a Taurus, fell in love with a Gemini charmer. After six months went by, and she still hadn't brought him home to meet the family, the Taurean began to be curious, and finally, became concerned. "What's with the mystery routine? Are you ashamed of him? Does this guy have two heads or something?" (He had no idea how warm he was getting.) One afternoon, he ran into his daughter and her Gemini boyfriend on the street, so the three of them (the four of them?) had lunch, and got to know each other. To his delight, the Bull discovered his future son-in-law was bright, handsome, courteous and versatile. (Oh, was he versatile!) He spoke six languages, piloted his own plane, had degrees from two universities and played the saxophone.

Over the cheese soufflé, the Gemini brilliantly discussed his career (he was a public relations counsel), his political views, and his religious beliefs. When the hypnotized Taurus father admired the huge diamond ring that glittered on one of the Gemini's expressive, artistic hands, he was told, "It's a family heirloom that belonged to my great-grandfather, and it's insured for seventy thousand dollars." No doubt about this man being financially stable enough for his daughter. At last, the Gemini remarked he had to dash off to see his stockbroker, smilingly waved goodbye and disappeared. He forgot to pick up the check, but that was an obvious oversight. After all, the man had a lot on his mind, between his clients, his Wall Street investments — and being in love.

The following week, in one of those flukes of fate, the Taurus was having his hair cut by a barber, who just happened to be the Gemini's brother-in-law, and the truth came out. He wasn't a public relations counsel, he was an assistant to a veterinarian. He had two wives and five children he had neglected to mention. His academic degrees consisted of a high school equivalency diploma. The plane was a single-engine model aircraft he flew in the park on Sundays. And the "diamond" was one of the imitation zircons he sold through a mail-order house, to make enough bread for his weekly lessons on the saxophone, which he did happen to play rather well. "I'd class him as a young Hymie Shertzer, but with a real pop sense of jazz, you know?" mused the barber brother-in-law. A sense of jazz indeed.

How did the Taurean father react to this gross betrayal of faith, involving his adored Taurus daughter, and his own judgment of character?

With the blind fury and violent rage of a Bull who has been red-flagged once too often. Fortunately, by the time he reached the Gemini's apartment, the "Twins" had just left for Mexico, to join a rock group on a tour of South America. However, two years later, Gemini returned, felt a sentimental urge to visit the scene of the romantic crime, and paid a call on his old Taurus girl friend. At first she stubbornly refused his apologies, but within a half-hour she had forgiven him (the Gemini charm), and melted into his arms. In another fluke of fate, at that precise moment, the father Bull walked through the door. (I mean he actually did nearly walk *through* the door). I will spare you the gruesome details. Later, when the stitches were removed, the Twins left once again for Mexico, this time to take up permanent residence there. It was a wise move.

It takes a Taurus man, woman or child a long time to learn, but a lesson learned is never forgotten. Never. An elephant is absent-minded, when compared to the memory of a Taurean once wounded. Naturally, not every Gemini keeps his (or her) Twin Selves as separate as the traveling sax player. Most Geminis manage to blend their two distinct personalities into one bright, intelligent and interesting human being, reasonably honest, and refreshingly adaptable. Still, the Geminian ability to change from one viewpoint to another, when it seems necessary for survival, can give Taurus an uneasy feeling that something is happening that he (or she) can't quite grab — or trust.

This is a 2-12 Sun Sign Pattern, meaning that Taurus is the sign immediately behind Gemini on the karmic wheel. Therefore, Gemini contains a soul memory of the opportunities it's possible to miss, through excessive Taurean caution. That's why Geminis of both sexes, and all ages, are so anxious to avoid mental ruts, or any other sort of stalemates, in this incarnation. Yet, the Twins sympathize with the Taurus reluctance to toss away security in favor of the unknown more than most other Sun Signs do because, in a subconscious sense, they've "been there."

As for the Bulls, since Gemini follows Taurus on the astrological circle, all Taurus men and women are faintly aware that they have something to learn from these bright, quick people. But what Gemini wants to teach, Taurus finds difficult to comprehend. The Bulls would like to be able to take life more casually, to think fast on their feet, toss away the past without regret, and skip happily ahead into a new adventure each day. He — or she — wistfully yearns for the freedom of spirit that Gemini, running a few lengths ahead, keeps dangling in front of the slower Taurean, sparkling and enticing. But — what if someone should break into the house, and steal all the Bull's precious possessions while he (or she) is out chasing fireflies with the Twins? What if one should happen to stumble, and break one's big toe, while jogging alongside Gemini? And what if the night air should give Taurus a sore throat ? Who will be waiting back home to nurse and care for him (or her) ?

It's always easier to sell life insurance or Blue Cross to Taurus than to Gemini. A typical astrological Sun Sign situation is a Gemini salesman or saleswoman, from a Scorpio insurance agency, fast-talking a Taurean customer into signing up for a huge stack of varied policies and annuities. Bulls are usually careful not to fall for a Mercurial pitch, except when it comes to purchasing solid security and protection for their families and their possessions, not to mention protecting their incomes in the future. Then, the Bulls become helpless pawns in the hands of a clever and charming Geminian.

Often the dogmatic Taurean determination to stick with facts that have been tried and tested may seem like stubborn prejudice to the more liberal, open-minded Gemini person. Conversely, the typical Bull feels it's always possible for an apparently accurate statement of brilliant Gemini logic to be actually conveying a falsehood or deception behind the surface glibness. What gives Taureans their initial mistrust of Gemini is the Twins' amazing dexterity of speech. Anyone who can juggle words with such ease, and spin them into such hypnotic tales full of wit and excitement, is suspect to the less loquacious Bulls, who tend to make every word count in their own rare speeches. In verbal showmanship, the Gemini man or woman is nearly always supremely eloquent, seemingly logical and clear. Only a Libran can match Gemini's powers of persuasion. But Taurus is not persuaded so quickly.

Not all Geminis are completely straightforward in their methods of arguing. Some of them veer away from the issue, on side trips, inciting Taurus to shout, angrily, "Stick to the point, will you?" Stop *rationalizing!*" Gemini also leans toward a certain amount of diffusiveness and repetition in speech patterns, which sometimes causes Taurean friends, relatives, business associates, lovers or mates to get into the Fixed habit of simply tuning out, after the third or fourth repeat.

Astrologer Evangeline Adams (granddaughter of John Quincy Adams, great-granddaughter of John Adams) once noted the typical Gemini verbal dexterity, by using Paul's Epistle to the Romans, in the New Testament, as an example. Verses 25 through 29, Chapter Two, and Verses 1 through 11, Chapter Three, constitute a masterpiece of Gemini glibness and charm, accomplished with Mercury double-talk. St. Paul, who was surely a Geminian, was obliged to tell the Roman gentiles that circumcision was not a necessary requirement for salvation. At the same time, he was bound to the Jews, by previous statements he'd made to them that it was. His efforts to successfully solve this contradiction are a truly classical example of the Gemini mind at its sharpest and best, cleverly confusing each side while irresistibly courting the approval of both. It's easy to see why Geminis are adept as politicians. They're able to bring opposite opinions together and hang them on a thread of truth, coated with charm and logic, creating an aura of idealism and peace on all sides. Gemini is not called the "communicator" without cause. President John F. Kennedy was a most typical Geminian, in every respect.

The airy detachment of Gemini can hurt and annoy Taurus, by turns, because, to the Bulls, detachment is indicative of being either rudely ignored or condescendingly patronized, neither of which is particularly pleasing to them. Some Bulls carry the scars of real or imagined rejection from an Air Sign for many years. It's often what causes those streaks of bull-headed stubbornness. For the life of them, Geminis can't see how anyone could be so opinionated that he (or she) is deaf to all logic and reason. Yet, an affectionate word or two, an arm thrown round a shoulder, or a warm, friendly clasp of hands (any form of *touching*) will make the tender, Venus-ruled Taurean heart melt like butter in the Sun. For all their cleverness, Geminis frequently fail to comprehend this magic formula for softening the Fixed and firm Taurean mental or emotional position. The occasional coldness projected by the Mental Sign of the Twins will only freeze the Bull into a more solid lump of obstinate earth. (Frozen ground is harder to shovel, you know, than the soft, rich earth, which has been kissed awake by the summer Sun.)

Geminis are always looking for short cuts. All right, Twins, here's a short cut to your compatibility with Bulls. The most common cause of tension between you is the Taurus habit of feeling, when he (or she) ought to *think* — and your own habit of thinking, when you ought to *feel*. Don't try to dazzle the Bulls with your brilliance — baffle them with bear hugs.

☆ ☆ ☆ ☆ ☆ ☆

TAURUS *Woman* GEMINI *Man*

—◄◖►—

Wendy was pained too to find that the past year was but as yesterday to Peter; it had seemed such a long year of waiting to her. But he was exactly as fascinating as ever....

While the Taurus woman sits beneath the rose bush, carefully stitching a piece of needlework, with the words "Home, Sweet Home," the Gemini man is drumming his restless fingers on the window pane, humming his own melody and lyric to "Song of the Open Road." No matter where these two (these three, counting his invisible Twin self) meet along life's highway, they'll eventually reach a fork in the path that will force them to flip a coin, to decide which one to take — the one leading to a comfortable, conventional marriage — or the one leading to a casual affair, with no strings attached to the heart. Correction: *He'll* flip a coin. *She'll* consult her common sense, to see if she might be headed in the wrong direction.

Once a Taurus girl is absolutely sure she loves a Gemini man, she'll first try everything in her considerable power to entice him into a permanent arrangement, complete with both social and legal sanction. And she possesses more weapons for enticement than you may think: erotic sensuality, tender affection, rich humor, fantastic home-baked biscuits, patience and fortitude. If none of these powerful feminine wiles work, she'll sigh softly, take a deep breath, and settle herself cozily into the role of mistress, still secretly using the very same weapons, but content to wait until he sees the light. "Everything comes to him — or her — who waits," is her philosophy. A Taurus woman may be cautious about getting her feet tangled up in romantic poison ivy in the beginning; she may be slow to allow herself to get tripped up by moonlight and roses, and fragile promises, at the start. However, once this lady has fallen, she has fallen, and it takes a steel derrick, or a Mack truck, to pull her out. Sometimes, the four-wheel drive of her common sense comes to the rescue, sometimes not.

Geminis are equally as wary as Taurus about being trapped in the beginning, but even after a Mercury Bird has capitulated to love, he keeps one light foot in the bedroom and one poised on the front porch for ready flight, if necessary. He'll tenderly give her one of his Twin hearts to have and to hold, but he hangs on to the other — just in case the one he gave away should happen to become soiled or broken, or damaged in any way. What good is a cracked heart to him? It will never sell as a new one. Think of the depreciation. It's a kind of Gemini insurance policy against disillusionment. That's where they differ. (I mean, that's *one* of the ways they differ.)

The Taurus woman, who is ordinarily so respectful of all kinds of insurance, has no emotional insurance against hurt, once she's handed over her loyalty to another human being. Unless there are severe afflictions to her natal Mars or Venus (or Sun), this lady will wait out anything, from another woman to poverty. She'll calmly ignore the changeable antics of her altar-shy, Mercury-ruled man, and not always — but usually — she'll win. If there are certain planetary squares or oppositions in her birth chart, it's possible that she may be the one to break his heart by chasing will-o'-the-wisps of pleasure just to torment her Gemini man, whose love is delicate and easily torn apart. But that's an exception to the rule, and the average Taurean Bull will sit serenely by the fire, toasting her toes and calmly counting the days between visits from her lover.

Her friends will try to make this sentimental woman see that she may be wasting her life, but she won't listen. She'll stubbornly insist that the delays preventing their marriage are valid ones, that tomorrow, next week, next month, next year — it will all work out. They love each other, and love can make anything happen, can't it ? Yes, it can. But not when love is blind, as Taurus love sometimes is. A Taurean who's convinced she's right is difficult to lead into a realization of the truth — the truth being that all may not be lost if she recognizes the danger of a dead-end scene in time to zap some life back into the romance. But she may not want to admit things aren't as rosy as they could be. As sensible as she is about everything else, she can be incredibly foolish when it comes to her own emotional security. If he has the Moon in an Earth or Water Sign, or she has the Moon in a Fire or Air Sign, they have a better chance to stay together, each supplying what is missing in the other. And that can be a mighty satisfying arrangement.

A Gemini man is quickly bored with the same woman, but that doesn't have to mean infidelity. He just likes to examine the various faces of the girl he loves, test the nuances of her emotional facets — sort of look at her through trick mirrors, for a change of mood. But the Taurus female has only three moods: sweet, affectionate contentment, sullen brooding — and raging fury. A Mercury man may secretly wish she'd vary them with a few impulsive whims, careless excitement, or a game of emotional hide-and-seek, now and then. She may hate change, but learning to adapt to new patterns is a necessity for a woman in love with a pair of Gemini Twins.

She might like it, if she tried doing something new and wild each week. It doesn't have to be as far out as astral traveling, or opium parties. Maybe just part her hair on the other side, for a change (when a Taurus girl does that, it's a clear signal for the man who can read it) or switch her brand of bath oil, or throw some mushrooms in with the eggplant. She might even try saying she's sorry when she's wrong, instead of pouting. A Taurus woman has a way of choosing a side, and staying there, refusing even to listen to an apology, much less a compromise. This girl doesn't realize how cruel and cold she seems, once she's made up her mind and slammed the door shut on any further discussion.

Sexually, the same problems of change-versus-stubbornness may creep into their relationship. She wants to be well loved, and to her, the physical expression of that love should be a rich and total experience. She expects complete sensual satisfaction from a lover, and she gives him full measure in return. A Taurus woman thinks sex is great because it produces sweet, cuddly babies and brings emotional peace and physical fulfillment at the same time — a triple blessing. When she makes love, there's nothing misty about it. She wants to feel her man is there beside her — *all* there — not just the parts of him he's not using while he's daydreaming. Since his Mercurial mind may be wandering on the wind, she may resent what she interprets as his lack of earthy passion, his casual attitude. And he may resent what he sees as her intrusion into his emotional privacy, which Gemini will consider sacred, even during their most intimate moments. She might have to persuade herself to try various, different approaches to pull him off his cloud and back into her arms. Otherwise, he may grow weary of beating his wings against a stone wall, and become even more detached. He'll be happier than he guesses, however, if he allows her to show him the way to a deeper affection by trusting her more instinctive Venus vibrations, and her earthiness, instead of hovering somewhere, just out of touch, when she needs him so profoundly. All Air Signs tend to mistrust sex, in a vague sort of way, unless it's first been strained through the imagination, which sometimes purges it of its very essence. A Gemini man wants his sexual experience diluted, in varying degrees, with fiction and fantasy.

I know a Taurus woman who is unusually psychic, for her normally un-esoteric Sun Sign. (That happens, you know, even with Goats and Virgins of the male and female sex. World-famous psychic Peter Hurkos is a Bull — with a powerfully trined Neptune, of course.) This particular lady Taurean was deeply and genuinely in love with a peripatetic Gemini man from California, for more years than she's able to forget, and maybe she still is in love with him, in her own stubborn way. There are several Neptune trines between their birth charts, creating a rare emotional telepathy, which they used to communicate with each other, without benefit of telephone or letters. Sometimes, their uncanny ESP brought them together when they were miles apart, more than just mentally and emotionally and spiritually. It brought them also into physical Oneness. She once remarked to me that she told him she believed she could almost . . . conceive a baby through their powerful mutual projection, and she wasn't ready for that, for they weren't married. (Taurus realistic humor.) That's a strong union. Strong indeed.

But his twin Gemini desires never blended into one single dream she could depend on. Finally, she read his mind (reversing his Mercury trick), saw nothing there but more ephemeral promises, and cut the telepathic cord between them with the cold, sharp scissors of Taurus determination. Now he can no longer reach her astrally, or any other way. She refuses to answer either her telephone — or her heart — when they ring. She knows when it's Gemini who's calling. But it doesn't move her. A psychic Taurus woman is still a Bull. Metaphysical talents don't make a dent in her iron will — once her mind has been made up firmly.

And so, a Gemini man isn't always blameless when his affair with a Taurean girl has tied itself into obstinate knots. He can wear himself into his own kind of rut. He might pause, during one of his spins around the carousel of changing lights and sounds, and ask himself if he's still hearing the same calliope music he heard when he first jumped on for the ride. A melody without words . . . . . a story without an ending . . . . . a whirl around a circle that goes nowhere but back to the beginning. How many brass rings must a man grab to jingle in his pocket — to watch turn green, and tarnish — until he reaches for one made of solid gold ?

☆ ☆ ☆ ☆ ☆ ☆

TAURUS *Man* GEMINI *Woman*

————◆◆●◆◆————

He loved flowers (I have been told) and sweet music
(he was himself no mean performer on the harpsichord);
and, let it be frankly admitted, the
idyllic nature of the scene stirred him profoundly.
Mastered by his better self he would have returned
reluctantly to the tree . . . . . .

Someone once wrote a verse about a man nothing could deter — "nor rain, nor storm, nor gloom of night could keep him from his appointed rounds." The reference has been applied to a postman. But it certainly must have been a Taurus postman, probably delivering a Valentine.

The slow, smoldering passion of the Bull is not easily, nor quickly, aroused. It grows in him, you might say, rather insidiously, sneaking up on him gradually, and gathering great strength as it sneaks. After this man's senses have been ensnared, or his Venus-ruled heart has been touched, he'll seldom, if ever, go back on his choice (unless his Moon or Ascendent is in Gemini, Sag or Pisces). His instinctive attitude toward involvement is total, and he'll follow it through to the bitter (or sweet) end, through rain, sleet, snow — yes, often even through the Gemini girl's unexpected hurricanes of anger or tornados of emotion. He's a regular Pony Express, all by himself, the Taurus man.

Nothing and no one, no consideration of reputation (normally his chief concern), no negative opinions of relatives or friends will stop or even slightly sway this otherwise sensible male when he's fallen in love. The moment a normally practical Taurean gets caught in a romantic web, his common sense is buried beneath his newly discovered sense of touching, hearing, smelling and seeing the girl of his quiet, but nonetheless deep, dreams. He's capable of making promises of eternal fidelity, and keeping them — faithful, steady and loyal almost beyond belief. Once truly in love, Taurus is in love for keeps. If it doesn't work out to a faerie-tale ending, the Bull may pine away in heartbreak, or drown himself in other sensual experiences, like becoming a morose alcoholic (one of the most terrifying mistakes a Taurean can make), or a gluttonous gourmet, an equally unnatural state to Taurus, since the Bull's higher instincts are to avoid excesses of *any* kind.

He sounds like every girl's imaginary romantic daydream come true. Except to the Gemini girl, whose daydreams of love are not quite so all encompassing, or down to earth. Gemini is airy. Gemini flies free, like a kite, sometimes buffeted by the wind, falling, then rising again on the whim of a passing breeze — but always soaring beautifully, catching the sunlight between clouds, and reflecting it back again.

Comedian-actor Orson Bean once quite precisely described a Gemini girl he knew. He asked her, "What is your husband's birthday?" And she immediately exclaimed, "Oh, good grief! I don't have a husband."

"You sound as if you don't like men," he said to her then, surprised. "No," she replied merrily, "I *adore* men! It's *husbands* I can't stand." Bean persisted. "But why? What's wrong with husbands?" Gemimi mused thoughtfully for only a second, before she answered. "Well, they're so darned possessive. Like, they want to know who you're dating, and . . . . ." her voice trailed off.

Now, to the average person reading this, and surely to the Bulls reading this, that Gemini girl's answer may seem shockingly sexually promiscuous. Not to an astrologer. I analyze her answer differently, understanding Mercury double-talk as I do. You see, she was simply being true to her Twin Self. A "date" to Gemini can be a harmless appointment with her hairdresser, a jet-set makeup consultation with Way Bandy, a trip to the dentist for some cap work, a visit with her psychiatrist or her brother-in-law. This woman is always making dates to meet people, then shows up late, or forgets all about them. It isn't that she's seeking an affair or a casual sexual encounter, just someone who's fun to be with, and exciting to talk to, who will stimulate her imagination. At least, that's the way it begins, and that's where it will usually remain, if she's properly understood. Remember, there are, at all times, two of her, and how can one man keep two girls happy every minute of the day and night? It becomes, after awhile, a sort of a mathematical problem, you see. (Taurus may not see.)

Her social need to move around, and mix, in the company of both sexes, needn't destroy a relationship. She can be deeply committed to one man, even though she needs the company of several dozen, on occasion. But try to get a possessive Bull to comprehend such a need. I mean, she can try, but she's taking a chance. It would be better if she explained it all to him before they marry, then all he can do is pull a slow burn and stalk off in anger. If she waits till later, when he considers her his lifelong possession belonging exclusively to him, in every way — and *then* tells him that she's simply got to get out and tumble with the acrobats and spin around on the Ferris Wheel once in a while because she's often so bored — or else go daffy — his reaction may be identical, but his anger won't be so controlled. The typical Taurus man will not take kindly to the discovery that his woman wants to run to the carnival every fortnight or so. You can bet on it.

Of course, if his Moon or Ascendent happens to be in Gemini, Libra, Aquarius, Leo or Aries — or if his natal Mars or Venus is in Gemini, conjunct her Sun — everything could be peachy. He'll have the stability and the quiet soothing influence of his Taurus Sun Sign to affectionately pin down her wings when she needs it, but just enough "air" to fan her enthusiasms, or just enough "fire" to catch the spark of her freedom himself. As for her, if her Moon or Ascendent is in Taurus, Virgo, Capricorn, Pisces or Cancer (it will help if she has Mars or Venus in Taurus), she'll be content to sit cozily at his feet much (not all) of the time, and let him scratch her head while she purrs like a pussycat or moos to match his mating sounds.

Otherwise, he'll find it difficult to communicate with her, and she'll find it difficult to cope with him. For example, in the area of money. She delights in spending it, he leans heavily toward saving it. In the area of food. He's obsessed with eating it (though usually not to excess, depending) and she probably despises cooking it. Salads she can toss with one hand behind her back. Anything more complicated she'd just as soon leave to the chef at her favorite French restaurant.

He'll have heavy trouble understanding her Mercurial moods, and this girl can change moods like some people change shirts in a tropical zone. It started back when she was a child. First she wanted to be a nun. Then she wanted to be a priest. Things like that. Now she switches from gay to depressed, from generous to stingy. First she wants to be an actress, then she wants to get a degree in anthropology. A Bull can become understandably edgy when she's pulling one of her quick changes. He'll walk in some late afternoon, give her a big, warm bear hug, and she'll shock him by nearly swooning in his arms.

TAURUS: What's wrong, sweetheart? You're as white as a sheet.
GEMINI: Oh, I'm so weak, darling. Please, help me to the couch.
TAURUS: But, baby, what is it?
GEMINI: There are colored spots before my eyes, and the room is spinning around. I'm so dizzy. And there's a sharp pain in my head. My arms and fingers are numb. Look — I can't move them.
TAURUS: My God! I'll call the doctor right away. Just lie there quietly, now, and don't move.
GEMINI: May I put my head on your shoulder?
TAURUS: Of course.

(Five seconds pass, by the clock.)

TAURUS: How do you feel, darling? (Lifting the receiver, and preparing to dial the doctor.)

GEMINI: Great! Let's go swimming! I'll race you to the pool!

Oh, I don't know. I suppose, after all, maybe a Taurean could cope with it better than most other men. You must admit it takes nerves of steel to handle a scene like that, several times a day. And most Bulls do have steel nerves.

Their sexual relationship can be just as changeable. She'll cuddle up to him some evening, right after dinner, and whisper, "Rudolph, let's go to bed early tonight, and pretend we're on our honeymoon, back in that little cabin in the mountains in Switzerland." Well, you certainly don't have to hit a Bull over the head, after a hint like that.

TAURUS: (his passion pounding) Wait until I put out the lights, sweetheart. I'll be right there.

GEMINI: (already in the bedroom) Hurry, darling, hurry! Oh, just look at the Moon! It's so beautiful, and the stars are so bright. I think I'll make a wish on one of them . . . .

TAURUS: (already snuggled beneath his favorite Teddy-Bear blankets) Honey, will you please get away from that window, and come here, close to me?

GEMINI: Okay, but do you know where the yardstick is? I want to measure something right away.

TAURUS: *You want to do what?*

GEMINI: I want to measure this wall, to see if there's enough space to have a fireplace built in here, just like the one we had in our honeymoon cabin. Wouldn't that be romantic? Hand me the telephone, will you, Rudy? Be an angel. I want to call the carpenters right now, before they close the office. Put on the light. I can't find the directory in the dark, for heaven's sake.

Yes, it takes nerves of steel. Taureans are sensual, erotically inclined, and deeply passionate lovers. Gemini approaches sex as just another exciting adventure into the magic fairyland of the imagination. All Bulls possess a rather basic (sometimes slightly crude) sense of humor about sex, but he may miss the joke when she keeps slipping away from their intimacies into her own private world of fantasy.

This man wants to squeeze a real woman, not a misty nymph or an astral body. Her mind is her playground, full of fascinating images, but that sort of thing is far too intangible for a Bull, whose feet are planted firmly in reality. There will have to be compromises.

What will confuse the Taurus man most about the Gemini girl he loves
may be summed up in one very simple question. *Who is she ?* Is she truly his
very own woman, the one he's been waiting to possess for the longest, longest
time — or is she just a product of his wishful thinking! He so very much
wants to fly high with her, up into the clouds, but he's not sure he knows how,
and his wistful puzzlement is described in this verse:

Is it You ?

or is it just that I've made you wear
those love robes I've been saving
since the days when my sand castles
were big enough to walk around in . . .
and strong enough
to stand against the tides

I can't remember who first said
that — "what you don't know, can't hurt you"
but what's-his-name was wrong
supposing I climb all the way to the top of the tree
then find out . . . it's not really You

how do I get back down again
all by myself ?

I've always been afraid of heights °

☆ ☆ ☆ ☆ ☆ ☆

° *Venus Trines at Midnight* by Linda Goodman (New York: Taplinger Publishing Company, Inc., 1970. To be re-published by Harper & Row, 1979).

TAURUS

Earth—Fixed—Negative
Ruled by Venus (also by the
   Planet Pan-Horus)
Symbol: The Bull
Night Forces—Feminine

CANCER

Water—Cardinal—Negative
Ruled by the Moon
Symbol: The Crab
Night Forces—Feminine

The **TAURUS-CANCER** Relationship

*I will tell you where they are . . . . they are already
in their home under the ground, a very delightful
residence . . .*

Cancerian Crabs love their mothers, their homes, money, babies and food. Taurean Bulls love money, their homes and mothers, food and babies.
   You can see these two Sun Signs are uncommonly alike, except for a few minor changes in the order of priorities.
   One thing that becomes clear right away about both Crabs and Bulls, if you study astrology, is that they both want people to be nice to them. In fact, they desperately need people to be nice to them (though you might not guess it from the way these two behave, at times). The very nicest thing Cancer can do for Taurus is to cook up a big dinner (which they'll both enjoy eating), then sit around and talk about how to make more money (which they'll also both enjoy). The very nicest thing Taurus can do for Cancer is to buy an almanac to keep track of the waxing and waning periods of the Moon, and

treat the Crab's changing moods accordingly. Cancerians are ruled by the Moon, and therefore are constantly affected by its fickle, fluctuating influence.

Since the practical Bulls have too much common sense to let the Moon push *them* around, right away that makes Taurus sorry for Cancer, which will please the Crabs immensely. It's not that they consciously seek pity, but they do like to know that people sympathize with their problems, instead of always accusing them of exaggerating life's daily tragedies. How can you exaggerate a tragedy, for goodness sakes? A tragedy is a tragedy, like a rose is a rose is a rose. And Cancerians take their tragedies seriously.

They're not only serious much of the time, they're cautious too. As serious and as cautious as Crabs John D. Rockefeller, Nelson Rockefeller, and various other assorted rocks. They have depressed periods of black melancholy that would frighten Edgar Allen Poe's Raven into flying right off the mantelpiece. Then they flash a "funny," and their crazy Lunar humor has everyone giggling. You think a sad-faced, morose comedian is a non sequitur? Image the late film actor Arthur Treacher. (You know, the one who always played the butler.) You say a compulsive wife and mother, full of fears and insecurities, always worrying about her brood, whose career is making people laugh, is a non sequitur? Image American comedienne Phyllis Diller. Both Cancerians. Also, the two of them have managed to pile up quite sizable green nest eggs through their Looney Bird antics, like proper Crabs. (Green for m-o-n-e-y.) Sometimes, Lunar people are silent and timid, and at other times they chatter your ear off. Like I said, they're moody.

Despite their having so much in common, Taurus finds it difficult to understand the moods of the Crab. To the Bulls, it's a waste of time and common sense to weep and moan about a situation. Taureans seldom weep or moan (although they occasionally moo) and they're rarely moody. However, once Taurus men, women or children dig in their heels, and get set for a spell of the blues, rare as it may be, they're not kidding around. They're moping in earnest. When a Bull takes a notion to have a mood, you'd better know it's a good, strong one, that's going to last for months — even years. And it won't be interrupted by silly fits of giggles.

Cancerian moods, on the other hand (is there a Libra in the room?), usually don't last more than a few hours, a few days at the very most — and they cover a wide range of emotions, from tender humor to cranky criticism, from intelligent, vivacious conversation to trembling shyness. They switch from laughter to tears, from faith to cynicism, from bitterness to joy — and then they snap at you, "What do you mean, *I'm* moody? *You're* the one who's impossible to get along with." (We won't tell the Crabs that a preposition is a poor thing with which to end a sentence, or even to end a sentence with — until the next mood switch to sweet and submissive. Otherwise, we may be snapped at — I mean, they may snap at us.)

Because Cancerians are so sensitive, they're aware of what's going on inside of people, and are, therefore, usually compassionate. Yet, their sympathy may come and go, especially when they're looking for sympathy themselves, which is frequently — and *most* especially if the sympathy entails a loan of money. Then the sympathy is much more likely to go than to come. Crabs think twice before they whip out their checkbooks. This is another area where Taureans and Cancerians have a great deal in common. The Bulls not only think twice before whipping out their checkbooks, they stop, pause, and think once again, just to be sure. However, both Sun Signs are truly generous to old people and to children. They're just a little tough on everybody in between. If it will put a hot meal into a child's tummy, or help a relative or loyal friend pay the mortgage on his or her home, Cancer and Taurus will relax their financial caution — or, when either of them have fallen in love. Romance warms their hearts and opens their pocketbooks miraculously.

The reason these two are slow about spending their money isn't because either of them is stingy. They're thinking of the future. There's always a rainy day to save for, right ? (I can visualize the Crabs and Bulls reading this, nodding their heads, and asking silently, almost desperately, "Isn't that right ?")

Well, yes, astrologically, that's right. There *is* always a rainy day to save for (for which to save). It's guaranteed to arrive, when you want it that much. I've never yet met a Taurean or a Cancerian who saved for a rainy day and failed to see that rainy day arrive, right on schedule. There's an ancient metaphysical truth, that warns: *Be careful of what you want* (or what you image) *because you will get it.* No doubt about that. None whatsoever. If you concentrate on saving for a rainy day, sooner or later you'll get caught in a downpour. How about imaging love and happiness and security instead ? That sort of "wanting" and imaging will manifest into reality just as surely, under the very same Universal Law.

Now about that secret worry all Cancerians and Taureans have that they're going to end up in the poorhouse someday if they don't take care of their assets — I have some fantastic good news for them. Are all you Crabs and Bulls who are reading this section paying close attention now ? Okay. Here it is: They don't have poorhouses anymore ! *Honest.* They stopped building them years ago. Isn't that great news ? So you can all go out and buy the luxuries you've always wanted — pianos, stamps for your stamp collection, antiques, old coins, caviar, gold frames for your baby pictures, cameras and . . . . . . what's that ? *Now* you're worried about all the people who are broke, and the families in the poverty belts who don't have a poorhouse to *go* to ? Oh, good grief.

I suppose, to be fair, we Fire and Air Signs should take it a little easier on watery Cancer and earthy Taurus about their mutual tendency to worry. If it were not for the Cancerians, we'd never have had any CARE packages, or orphanages, or foundling homes, or lend-lease (the United States is a Cancerian country, you know). If it were not for Taurus, we'd never have any big empires, or huge industries that employ thousands of people, like the Hearst Newspapers Syndicate, and many, many others (William Randolph Hearst was a Bull)—no real estate companies (mostly Taurus) or banks (mostly Taurus or Cancer) or farms (mostly Taurus). Admittedly, the mutual Cancer–Taurus traits of care, caution, worry and conservatism keep all of us sane and secure. When you think of all the Cappies and Virgos (and some Scorps) they have helping them, it really makes you feel like going to St. Patrick's Cathedral and lighting a candle in sheer gratitude for the way they protect the rest of us from our reckless follies and selfishness. (Or the church of your choice, of course. It's just that not all places of worship offer the beeswax for the ritual, you know?) While we're there, we may as well light another candle for Cancerian and Taurean humor. Humor, like cleanliness, is very definitely next to godliness. Humor on one side, cleanliness on the other, with godliness in the center — like a spiritual sandwich. (Although Crabs and Bulls prefer theirs with an extra helping of lettuce.)

Real humor stems from tragedy, which is why the serious-minded Crabs and Bulls are often so hilarious, especially when they team up as a couple in business, love, friendship — or within the family circle. During the lulls between their comedy routines, sometimes a Bull will show a stubborn streak, but the Cancerian will usually have a lot of patience with the Taurus pouting. The Crabs have so much experience with it themselves, you see.

Both of these Sun Signs like to eat, and they both love to cook, so there might be some difficulty keeping their diets under control when they spend a lot of time together. If you know a Taurus-Cancer combination, the best Christmas present you can give them is a copy of a book on nutrition. Like *Back to Eden*, or a gift certificate, good for at least a year, from a health food restaurant. As for indulgence in the bubbly, Cancer is considerably more likely than Taurus to enjoy a sip of wine or stronger spirits, now and then. The Crab is also better equipped (as a Water Sign) to handle the sips. If the Cancerian tempts the Taurean into tasting the grape too often, there will be trouble. The Bull hates excess, and seldom messes around with it in any form, but when he slips, he does it the way he does everything else — on a grand scale. Taurus is better off at a milk bar, since he (or she) has what you might call an empathy with good old bossy.

Taurus and Cancer get along smoothly most of the time. Even when they don't there's not much noise, and seldom any explosive arguments. Both of them normally react to hurt or aggravation by slinking off alone to brood. It doesn't make the misunderstandings any easier to bear, but it does keep things relatively quiet. Of course, there won't always be *total* silence between them during a disagreement. There will be some soft sounds occasionally, when the Bull sits in the corner like a solid lump of resentment, mumbling under his (or her) breath — while the Crab huddles in the broom closet, crying into several large tissues and emitting periodic choked sobs. Still, the gentle sounds of angry mutterings (Taurus) and sad snifflings (Cancer) are more peaceful than the hollering you can expect with the more volatile Sun Signs. (Not counting the rare and horrifying occasions every ten years or so, when the Bulls fancy they're in a china shop and someone waves a red flag.)

The meeting of a Bull and a Crab is often a fated one, with an element of compulsion on both sides, since it's a 3-11 Sun Sign Pattern, with heavy karmic undertones. There's more than a casual interest in each other, and the benefits or hurts resulting from the association usually have a long-lasting effect on both lives, if they continue to see each other for more than a few months.

Taurus and Cancer make an excellent team for any kind of business or industrial ventures, stock brokerages, banks, gardens, nurseries, farms, politics or real estate companies. The Bull will build the foundation carefully, organize it sensibly, and the Crab will run it with careful efficiency, making sure their mutual efforts gain the maximum publicity. (Cancerians may not be extroverts but they're surprisingly good at getting newspaper space, and getting their pictures on the front page or the TV screen.) The chances are excellent that any Cancer–Taurus business partnership will thrive and stay in the black. If there's any red on the books, it's probably from the blood (mixed with sweat and tears) these two pour into any project they're devotedly dedicated to making solidly successful. Assuming the Bull has the Moon or Ascendent in a Water or Earth Sign (except Capricorn) and the Crab has the Moon or Ascendent in a Water or Earth Sign (except Scorpio) — and sometimes even the parenthesized planetary positions won't stop their mutual achievement compatibility — these two could both end up in Who's Who, and likely find also that their personal relationship is harmonious, and comparatively free of tension. However, without such aid from their birth charts, there could be some pouting, muttering, mooing and sniffling, from time to time. Yet, compromise will usually be easier for them than for most other Sun Sign combinations. They each possess a certain amount of placidity, which often creates harmony from the sheer inner need and desire for peace and quiet.

Because Taurus is Earth and Cancer is Water, it's more probable that the Crab will slowly and gradually grow to imitate the Bull's Fixed habits, than the other way around — even though Taurus is behind Cancer on the karmic wheel of life. Why? Water is flexible, and does not resist, which is the wisdom of Water. It takes the shape of the vessel into which it's poured. When that vessel is a Taurean, the shape is usually symmetrical and pleasing. Considering the Taurus feeling for form, and the Cancer sensitivity for color, they can paint some rather nice pictures on the side of the jug too. Then they'll hang a price tag on it, take it to market, and come home together with a nice fat profit.

☆ ☆ ☆ ☆ ☆ ☆

TAURUS *Woman* CANCER *Man*

————◄◄●►►————

*He had one of his dreams that night, and cried in
his sleep for a long time, and Wendy held him tight.*

The Cancerian male secretly desires to be babied by his woman. A Taurus female loves to spoil her man. Add these two astrological facts together and what's the result? Love at first sight? No, not quite.

A Crab doesn't rush into anything, including romance. Not only is rushing against the Cancerian grain, but it's impossible for a Crab to advance directly, in a straight line. All Crabs have this funny side-waddle. Did you ever watch one? First, he veers to the right, after which he turns to the left. Finally, he appears to be retreating backward—until the object he wants tries to escape, then he lunges forward, grabs hold, and hangs on—until he loses a claw. Even if he does, he'll just grow a new one, which is why Cancerians are called "tenacious," and that's often too mild a word for them.

Neither is a Taurus girl the type to leap overboard into a sea of passion, trilling ecstatic songs of eternal love. This woman wants to be wooed, and I mean really wooed. She'll expect a mountain of proof from a lover before she commits herself. So you can see that "love-at-first-sight" is not quite what happens when an Earth Sign like Taurus meets a Water Sign like Cancer. It takes time, usually months or years, seldom days or weeks. However, once committed, the Taurus woman knows how to keep her man sweetly content-ed. And the Cancerian man, once he's decided to make his forward lunge, is a lover to end all lovers, particularly in persistency.

The Crab's secrecy about his feelings and intentions during the courtship period is not exaggerated. The spring of 1973, I received in the mail a hard-cover copy of my first book, *Sun Signs*, from a Cancerian man in London, who attached this note to the book: "Dear Miss Goodman, I am in love with a wonderful Taurus girl. She is everything you say in the chapter about 'The Taurus Woman,' and I'm going to marry her. I would really appreciate it, if you would autograph this copy of your book *To Maggie, a lovely Taurean,*

and return it to me at the address below. Very sincerely yours, etc. . . ."
There was a P.S. on his note. It said, "Please don't write anything in the book about Crabs. She doesn't know I'm doing this, and I'm having a friend drop it off at Heathrow Airport, where she works, so she won't have any idea it's from me. I don't want her to guess how I feel about her. We only met a few months ago. Thank you."

I was a little concerned about Maggie, but I resisted the temptation to tip her off. Knowing she was a Taurus lady, I figured she would have the patience to wait till he decided to openly declare his devotion. Since that was a number of years ago, I doubt if she escaped the Crab's tenacity. They're probably married by now, and the proud parents of some little Bulls or Cows or Crablets. If so, I take this opportunity to congratulate them !

A relationship between Cancer and Taurus may seem nearly perfect, and it is undeniably a better than average romantic combination. But that doesn't mean it will be totally free of flaws. For example, there's the Cancerian mother complex. He may be one of the lucky ones who managed to graduate from adolescence into manhood, adjusting himself to the image of his mother as just another person — a wonderful person, to be sure, but just another human being involved in his life. If so, the Taurus girl will be lucky, because his strong admiration and respect for his mother will simply give him an increased measure of devotion for all women, including her.

But he could be one of those Crabs who never quite solved his mother hang-up. This type of Cancerian male (and remember, the sign of Cancer symbolizes motherhood, and the part of the body it represents is the breasts) carries a fierce, subconscious resentment against being weaned. So he solves his secret dilemma by either coldly rejecting his mother — or by remaining completely dependent upon her. Neither attitude produces a healthy emotional scene, and the woman he marries is sure to feel some occasional repercussions. Assuming he has chosen not rejection but dependence, it can create a few problems, which might try the patience of the average female. Fortunately, a Taurus girl is not an average female, and patience is one of her strong points. (So is a temper when she's pushed too far and decides to put her foot down rather heavily, which seldom fails to put the Crab in his place, and makes everything very clear, with a powerful hint that enough is enough.)

CANCER: Sweetie pumpkin, I'm sorry I'm late, but I dropped by Mama's, and we got to chatting about old times, and . . . . . . say, look, Mama sent you this huge basket of fresh strawberries from her garden. Aren't they yummy looking ?

TAURUS: Strawberries give me hives. I have told both you and your mother that strawberries give me hives at least a dozen times. (Pregnant pause.) Since you weren't here, I had to put up the window shutters by myself. How do they look ?

CANCER: Well, they're nice, Honey-cakes, but . . . . . .

TAURUS: But what?

CANCER: It's just that Mama says shutters are more trouble than they're worth. The slats keep breaking, they're hard to dust — and like she says, drapes are ever so much richer, and more colorful, and all. Don't you think?

TAURUS: No, I don't think. I have no brain. I'm a drone. A robot.

CANCER: Now, don't get upset, Sugar-lump. You're just all tuckered out from working so hard. You deserve a nice treat. Let's have dinner out tonight, and catch a movie afterward.

TAURUS: I'd rather stay home and watch the Academy Awards on television. We can send out for pizza.

CANCER: Mama says it can make you blind, and cause symptoms of paranoia.

TAURUS: *Eating pizza?*

CANCER: Watching color television so much.

TAURUS: I feel like pizza, and I want to watch the Oscars tonight, so let's not discuss it any further.

CANCER: All right, but Mama says it can clog your arteries.

TAURUS: Just how does your mother figure color TV affects the arteries? I'm fascinated by her medical knowledge.

CANCER: The pizza. Mama says starchy dough and hot spices are poison, and we've been eating a lot of that kind of thing lately. Tell you what, let's just run over and have dinner with Mama tonight. She's all alone, and she's making chicken dumplings, and . . . . . .

TAURUS: Dumplings aren't starchy, huh?

CANCER: Not the way Mama makes them. She . . . . what are you doing?

TAURUS: Hello, is this the Pizza Parlor? This is Gertrude Glassberg. Send me up a small pizza, please. No, I don't need a large one this time. My husband and I have decided on a trial separation.

CANCER: What did you say? Honey-cakes, I really think . . . . .

TAURUS: (grimly) Pack your bags. And hurry. Mama's dumplings are getting cold.

There's a limit to Taurean patience. Naturally, not all Crabs are so tightly knotted to the maternal apron strings as this one, but it can be rough, living up to an image of perfect womanhood. Still, a Taurus girl can cook up a mean dumpling herself, she often sews her own clothes, she's thrifty, she smells good (girl Bulls adore perfumed soap, and all the accessories), and she's uncommonly sensual. So, you see, she has a few things going for her that Mama can't top.

The physical relationship between them will be ideal — or as ideal as they want it to be, and encourage it to be. The potential for harmony is surely there. Her sexual nature is deeply affectionate, tender and uncomplicated. He is also deeply affectionate, tender—though perhaps a bit more complicated. The tangible satisfaction of the senses, and the earthy reality of passion, is important to a Taurus woman, whereas the *emotional* release of sexual union is important to a Cancerian man, but these slightly different requirements need not conflict. Instead, they can blend, and create a physical relationship of rare completeness. There's something warmly protective in the Taurean expression of sexual love that seems to answer the silent cry of Cancer to be enveloped in clouds of tenderness, to have someone wipe away all her tears—and all her fears of being alone and unwanted. When a Taurus woman expresses her devotion through lovemaking, there are no games, no fantasies, there is no false modesty—just a comfortable feeling of giving. In spite of his own more imaginative approach to lovemaking, this is just the kind of sexual security a Cancerian man secretly longs for, in his heart.

Two people who love can't avoid hurting each other occasionally, but with the Bull and the Crab hurt can last longer than it does between other Sun Signs. They'll have to realize that this is an unnecessary waste of time and emotional strain, since the hurt itself is unintentional. Rather than talking it over, like Gemini or Libra—getting it off their chests by exploding in temporary anger, like Aries, Leo or Sagittarius—or rising above it in detachment, like Aquarius and Pisces—this man and woman may allow the hurt to take deep roots and grow into a coldness that would be more dangerous to the relationship than the original misunderstanding. When a Taurus woman is upset, she tends to pout, then freeze into a forbidding rock of stubbornness. When the Crab has been wounded, he withdraws into his shell, to cry and pity himself alone, afraid to make any move, even a move toward forgiveness and apology, lest it bring on more hurt. So there you have it. A stubborn Bull, refusing to say "I'm sorry," when she truly *is* sorry, and even taking her own sweet time about accepting a shy peace offer from the partner—and the shattered Crab, peeking out timidly from his hard shell, quivering with heartache inside, sometimes snapping in crankiness to cover the pain of being unloved, however temporarily. It's hardly an atmosphere conducive to reconciliation.

Perhaps it would help if they looked at it this way. Pouting in silence is impractical. (They both hate to be impractical.) It leads nowhere—except into the dark tunnel of more loneliness. (They both hate dark tunnels.) What she should do is use her beautiful, Venus-inspired patience (Venus is her ruling planet, you know, until Pan-Horus is discovered and named, and Taurus returns the borrowed Venus influence back to Libra, where it belongs.) If she waits for the next change of the Moon (*his* ruler) all she needs to do is smile and whisper "I love you"—and he'll pop right out of his shell into her arms.

What *he* should do is use his beautiful Cancerian perception, inspired by his Lunar vibrations, to understand how much more susceptible this woman is to physical affection than she is to verbal eloquence, and instead of writing her notes bashfully signed, "Guess who?" and tucking them down inside the box of detergent, hoping she'll find them when she's doing his laundry — he should simply grab her firmly, as only a Crab can grab, and kiss her soundly. Then she'll cuddle right up next to his heart, where she belongs.

And let Mama stuff the cat with her dumplings.

☆ ☆ ☆ ☆ ☆ ☆

TAURUS *Man* CANCER *Woman*

◆━◆▶◆━◆

"She wants me to unbar the window," thought Peter, "but I won't, not I."

He peeped again, and the tears were still there, or another two had taken their place.

Imagine you are a huge rock, sitting high on top of a mountain. Nothing frightens you, or moves you. You're so tough, the storms of thousands of years haven't even scratched your surface, though they've worn away lesser rocks into helpless pebbles. Then one chilly day, an apparently harmless drop of water brightly splashes on you, and trickles its way into a deep crack in your center, which has been there since you were born, but has been overlooked by the rains and winds until now. What will you do?

You will do nothing. You, who have stood up against centuries of floods and tornados, have nothing to fear from one tiny drop of water. The next day, the thermometer drops to zero, and the drop of water freezes in your center. The freezing causes it to expand, and the expansion hurts you. Since nothing has ever before been able to weaken your strength, how do you feel about a drop of water which is expanding inside you, and threatening to crack you in two?

A quiet little meditation like that will throw a great illumination on what it's like to be an earthy, invulnerable Taurus man in love with a watery, gentle and sometimes Looney Moon Maiden. It can shake him to his foundations. But it's too late. She's already penetrated the secret place no one else has ever quite reached — his heart. Since a Bull's heart is as strong as both his will and his back, he probably won't break in half. But he'll never again be the same, once this girl has enticed him to run along the beach under a midnight sky, in the zig-zag directions of the Crab, crying and laughing — and *feeling*. Taurus knows all about touching, but feeling is a slightly different word. She'll teach him all its meanings and synonyms.

An occasional Cancerian girl will claim she's not typical of her Sun Sign because — "I don't like to cook, I don't want children, and I hate staying home." Don't let her fool you, like she's fooling herself. The reason she's scooting around in those Crab-like sideways patterns is because she hasn't found the man she secretly yearns for, the one who will protect her and wrap her up in thick blankets of devotion. She may inwardly love babies and cooking and homemaking, but she's not going to stand over a hot oven or rock a cradle for just any male. Until *he* materializes out of her moonlight dreams, she'll cover up her tender maternal feelings and sentimental femininity with ambition for financial security, a successful career and public attention, sprinkling jokes everywhere she goes, punctuated with a crazy Looney Bird giggle, that says (or tries to say), "I don't care!" But if you listen to the hidden chords, her Lunar laugh is whispering a wistful message: "I'm lonely and frightened and sad — don't dreams *ever* come true?"

Yes, they do. If you believe in them. Emphatically and irrevocably, they do. The formula is so deceptively simple only a very few people ever discover its truth. The Galilean said it this way: "Whatsoever things ye desire, pray as if ye had already received them, and ye shall have them." That's really all there is to it. If you truly *want* it, "it's no longer a dream." What you image shall come into being without a shadow of a doubt, the time element depending entirely upon the intensity of the image. However, the Cancerian girl is inclined to pray for things, not "as if she had already received them," but as if Fate had no intention of ever giving them to her. Therefore, Fate doesn't. It's simply a matter of reversing the vibrations she sends out from Negative to Positive.

The Taurus man is a slow starter in romance. Though he has an enormous capacity for love, it doesn't burst into verbal or physical commitment overnight. Once it does blossom, however, it flowers beautifully, and usually permanently. Permanence is something the Moon Maiden needs, for all her whimsical emotional wanderlust. Like her, this man will not yield his complete self until the right woman arrives on the scene. He'll take his good old time deciding, but his surrender, when it comes, is often instant, and his fidelity is eternal — if he isn't pushed beyond great endurance by the incorrigible behavior of his partner.

Most Taurus men (not all, but most) don't experience love in its *total* sexual and emotional fullness until they're out of their teens (or even years later than that), long after their buddies have chalked up scores of "conquests," live-in affairs and a few marriages. But never forget that the Bull is enormously capable of making up for lost time, and the depth and intensity of his love is well worth waiting for. She can console herself with the thought that, while he doesn't break *down* easily, neither will he want to break *up* quickly. That trait will certainly appeal to the girl Crab, who is also slow to take hold — and even slower to let go — of anything. Like raveled shawls, broken umbrellas, cracked mirrors, used doggy bags, empty lipstick tubes, the pink ribbon from her old baby bonnet, lidless bottles and jars, bottle and jarless lids, half pieces of curtain rods, newspapers with all the clippings already clipped, outdated redemption coupons, sharpened-all-the-way-down pencils with only a nub eraser left, and old lovers (unless she has an Aquarian or Gemini Ascendent or Moon Sign, in which case she may throw really valuable things out with the morning trash, then be puzzled why she can't find them weeks later).

The Bull is possessive (not quite the same thing as jealous) and his approach to love is likely to be solid, sensible and practical, seldom emotionally erratic, capricious or unduly enthusiastic — but cozy! Although the two of them are much alike in many ways, this is one where they may not be. A Moon Maiden can allow unfounded jealousy to torture her into moods of deep depression — or worse yet, a suspicious, bitter or clinging attitude that can infuriate a Bull. (The clinging he doesn't mind so much, he may even enjoy it — the suspiciousness he can do without.) Her active imagination sometimes causes her to develop fears which, although based more on fantasy than fact, can bring on floods of tears, and a touch of hysteria. It sounds hopeless, but it isn't really. In fact, not many Sun Sign combinations have as much hope for success as Taurus and Cancer, once they know who they are, and where they're going.

Taurus already pretty much knows that about himself. Temporarily ruled (until Pan-Horus is discovered and identified) by the harmonious, peaceful Venus, he's more inclined to keep an even keel regarding their differences than she is. This woman is ruled by the Moon, which is a reflector of light. So she instinctively reflects the moods around her, indeed, every change in her immediate environment is reflected, mirror-like, in her heart and brain. Sometimes all that reflecting creates an eclipse of her true self. It's not easy for a Moon Maid to know who she is, and where she's going, although she has an uncanny sense of the feelings and intentions of others. Lots of people trust their secrets to her, and are rewarded with both tender sympathy and wise counsel. Yet, it's next-to-impossible to pry her own secrets out of her.

The Bull might say to her, "I don't understand you. You say you love me, but you spend all your time running around, giving birth to ideas and babies, buying clothes, taking CARE packages to your friends, working for the PTA and Greenpeace and the garden club, listening to music, painting pictures, making bank deposits, learning French, visiting the planetarium, and sitting out in the back yard, staring at the Moon by yourself. You don't need me. I'm just in the away around here." Now, she may perceive, after a speech similar to that one, what the problem is. He's hurt, because he's not getting the attention he needs, the pats on the head and affectionate hugs and kisses he hungers for, to make him feel securely loved. However, lacking her Lunar sensitivity, he may not understand how much she needs all her busy activities — as well as her world of dreams — so she can reflect back into life all the things she absorbs by living it.

It should be obvious, then, who must make the first move to wave the olive branch. The one who most perceives how it is with the other. That would, of course, be her.

Still, her attempts at making up with him can seem a little vague and devious to the direct, uncomplicated Bull. First, she retreats in tears, then crawls toward him sideways. It confuses him. How is he to interpret her message when she tucks a baked apple under his pillow, or leaves a sentimental poem under his wet cake of soap, in the shower? It stuck to the paper, obliterating the words, and for all he knows, it could be a farewell note. She should just come right out and say, "I do need you, and I can't live without you, and the reason I scoot around all the time is because..." etc. and so on. Then she should prove she means it in a physical way — the only language a Taurus man understands. Simple. Plain. Honest. Down to Earth. And sensual. He doesn't like to be teased. No Bull likes to be teased.

Their sexual compatibility, barring severe afflictions between their natal planets in their respective birth charts, is usually excellent. She may now and then wish he'd be a little less clumsy with his romantic jokes, and a little more delicate in his verbal expressions of passion. But on the whole, the Taurus sense of touch is as refined and delicate as anyone could ask. His masculine virility can coax this uncertain girl out of her shell, with the promise of the kind of fulfillment most women only read about in novels. The Bull will give the Moon Maiden a feeling of being snugly loved, warmly desired — and, yes, sexually dominated (which is what she really wants, in her secret heart).

Don't frown, ERA ladies. Not all, but some females actually do enjoy being "conquered" by males, at least physically. Admittedly, true equality means neither sex is superior, and therefore neither should submit to or dominate the other. But the sexual relationship between a man and a woman is an entirely different matter from their interchange intellectually, or on an achievement level. It's a very *personal* and *individual* kind of emotional chemistry — not always predictable.

The Taurus man will lavish enough affection on the Cancerian woman, to banish the fears she's accumulated since childhood that nobody really wants or needs her because most people are more capable in every way than she. *He* does. *He* wants her, and he *needs* her. And he'll show it in unmistakable ways, if she'll let him.

It's difficult for this lady to resist real love when it's offered with the kind of sincerity Taurus love is offered. In return, she'll adore him madly (with an emphasis on the madness, during the Full Moon) and probably never leave him — unless he places her in the middle in a fuss with her family, or insults her mother (a cardinal sin to the Cardinal Sign of Cancer, if she's a typical Crab). Then he may lose her for a while. This girl is intensely loyal to her mama, usually, and sometimes papa runs a close second. But she'll return to her Bull when the Moon changes (assuming he apologizes, of course). Since he's so stubborn, the reconciliation may never occur if she doesn't understand, and forgive him before he asks to be forgiven. He won't beg.

She is so changeable — or is she fickle? He is so patient — or is he obstinate? Which is it? The true answer depends on which way they look at it. While he's wearing his Taurean blinders, it's impossible for him to see the truth about anything, so he appears bull-headed.

While she's gazing into her Lunar mirror, the truth is sometimes distorted, so her emotions appear to fluctuate unreliably. But when the issues are cloudy, they can always find their way back to each other, through the mist, if they meditate on this ancient wisdom: *Seek the truth, and the truth shall set you free.* What is the real truth? Love. Unselfish and forgiving love. The genuine kind.

☆ ☆ ☆ ☆ ☆ ☆

TAURUS

Earth — Fixed — Negative
Ruled by Venus (also by the
   Planet Pan-Horus)
Symbol: The Bull
Night Forces — Feminine

LEO

Fire — Fixed — Positive
Ruled by the Sun
Symbols: Lion &
   Shy Pussycat
Day Forces — Masculine

The **TAURUS-LEO** *Relationship*

"None of us has ever been tucked in at night."

Bulls need lots of loyalty and affection in order to be sure they're loved and *appreciated.* Leos need lots of worship and compliments in order to be sure they're loved and *admired.* Neither of them get quite enough proof that they're cherished, even from compatible people who were born in their own elements (Taurus is Earth, Leo is Fire), and when they constantly demand to be emotionally "tucked in" by each other, they can really become frustrated.

These two Sun Signs are square, which means they don't harmonize too well, unless the Sun and Moon in their respective charts are in mutually agreeable signs. As in all 4-10 Sun Sign Patterns, the square aspect (Taurus is 90 degrees away from Leo) is a tension maker. Yet, the 4-10 vibration bestows giant rewards of peace and harmony when the two involved have demonstrated the patience and selflessness to pass this karmic soul testing in a human love relationship.

With Taurus and Leo, the tension starts like this: Leo is much too self-centered to give the strong, silent Bulls the absolute devotion and obedience they insist on receiving *most* of the time. Taurus is much too stubborn to give the vain, proud Leos the unquestioning worship they demand *continually*. They're both Fixed Signs, so they're both good organizers, and they each possess an unusual amount of emotional dependability. But they're also capable of being — well, *Fixed*. My Thesaurus offers the phrase "pig-headed" as a substitute for "fixed." (Just for the record, the other two Fixed Signs are Aquarius and Scorpio.)

Sometimes, the fiery Leo will depend on the more tranquil, stable Taurus to cope with an unpleasant situation, then rob the Bull of all credit for the accomplishment. However, this doesn't bother Taurus the way it would a more egotistical sign. The last thing Bulls are interested in is personal glory. They won't turn their broad backs on it, should it be offered them, but they can take it or leave it alone. Taurus is more interested in *cash* appreciation and emotional peace of mind.

I know a Leo man who was tenderly devoted to his invalid Taurean wife for many years. She outlived most of the doctors who predicted her death every six months or so, and continued to manage household affairs from her bed for triple her life expectancy. The Lion took full credit for her amazing stamina. After all, wasn't he giving her the best possible tender, loving, expert care, under conditions which would have put a weaker man flat on his back, or driven him into a mental breakdown? Yes, he was. But her Taurean iron will was at least partially responsible for her medical miracle.

Strangely, although they had many other areas of constant contention and argument, she quietly permitted him to take the credit for her courage without a trace of resentment. She well knew how much she owed him, and she also knew how much effort her strength and cheerfulness over the years cost *her*. But Taurus seldom fusses or quibbles about being overshadowed by the Leonine ego. She allowed him, even encouraged him, to take all the bows, and smiled to herself. Worship, however, she refused to give him, which made him a most unhappy monarch, and for which he perhaps never quite forgave her. But credit she willingly relinquished.

I once knew a Taurus man who worked as a registrar and assistant to the president of a Barber School in New Jersey. The president (the Bull's superior, of course) was a warm-hearted, brilliant, generous, typically proud and arrogant Leo — a Lion, whose name was Dr. Andrew Julian. As a matter of fact, it still is. Why should he change it, when it's lettered in gold, stenciled, stitched or monogrammed on all his cuff links, shirts, briefcases, under-garments, (allegedly) towels and silverware? My Taurus friend and Dr. Julian benefit from a harmonious Sun-Moon aspect between their birth charts, so they still fondly admire and respect one another, although they no longer work together. Nevertheless, their business association fairly bristled with daily examples of the 4-10 Leo-Taurus relationship, its mutual helpfulness — and its pitfalls.

There was the time Dr. Julian held a private conference with an investor who wished to buy an interest in his Barber School. The investor was a millionaire, and uncommonly loose and magnanimous with his cash. He didn't care how much he invested, as long as he could visibly appear to run the operation — as long as the school would bear his name (never mind that he had no barbering experience).

Naturally, the Lion roared loudly at this double threat to his authority and affront to his prestige. For several hours, angry voices rose and fell from behind the closed door of the Lion's plush den — which is the only way to describe any Leo office. A plush den.

Finally, the door opened, and Dr. Julian commanded imperiously, "David! Come in here immediately!" (Leos seldom ask, they command, as befits royalty.) When the cautious Bull slowly walked into the firing line, the Lion waved a disdainful hand toward the angry investor and directed majestically, "*Talk* to him, David." Then Leo swirled around in his expensive swivel chair, pouting in injured dignity, and staring out the large picture window of his den — as though the other two men were not present. (The King did not deign to take any further notice of the peasants.)

After a few minutes of quiet questioning, the Bull uncovered the basic problem. The potential investor was an Aries. A Ram. It was *his* money, and by golly, *he* was going to be boss, and *his* name would be on the school. Nobody was going to order *him* around. The Taurean explained *patiently* that Dr. Julian was loved by all his teachers and students (he really was, they adored him, pride, arrogance and all), that he was furthermore highly respected by all the companies which did business with the school, with whom he had established a warm rapport over the years (true).

Of course, these solid compliments were not missed by Leo. They rained like fragrant roses on the Lion's head, which was still turned away and facing the window. Then the Bull's rich, Taurean voice, deep and soothing, was heard by the secretary, floating over the transom, as he spoke calmly to the Aries investor. "Don't you think it would be smarter if Dr. Julian's name were to remain on the outside of the building, in all the advertising, and on the school's letterhead? Since he's had over forty years' experience running a Barber School, wouldn't it be better if he continued to do so? However, it makes more sense, and it's more practical for *you*, Sir, to be the one who signs all the checks, so the people at the bank will know *you're* the Financial Backer and Advisor of the operation. Why should you spend twelve hours a day here, as Dr. Julian does, when you have more important things to do? Your time is too valuable for you to be tied down to a desk, as he is, from nearly dawn till midnight, seven days a week."

After that masterpiece of manipulation, the Aries investor beamed happily, like a child who has just been given a lollipop and told he could play hookey at the same time. He was delighted to be called "Financial Backer" and "Advisor," to know he'd be respected by the bank and the bankers (however much cash they may possess, for some odd reason, Rams are seldom ever truly respected by bankers) and that he wouldn't have to spend twelve hours a day, seven days a week, working. (He hadn't thought of that — Aries never does.)

The Lion swirled back around on his padded, swivel throne then, and offered everyone a cigar to celebrate the closing of the deal. Later, after the new Aries partner had left, Dr. Julian, his dignity now completely restored, walked over to the busy Bull's desk and remarked, with his large, handsome Leonine head and pride both held high, "I certainly told him off, and let him know who runs this school. I think I handled the situation rather well, don't you?" The Bull, patiently and respectfully, allowed as how he certainly had.

One area of potential agreement between Taurus and Leo is promoting and building. Leo loves to promote grandiose schemes and large ideas, and all Bulls delight in contemplating the financial return of what might be the seeds of the Taurean empire they're always building in their minds. The path Taurus follows is steady, purposeful and relentless. Obstacles don't disturb or upset the Bulls as they do Leo, because Taureans accept limitation and delay as part of the price they have to pay for eventual success. One of the favorite mottos of the Bulls is: *If a thing is worth doing at all, it's worth doing well — and also worth waiting for.*

Leos, who are fanatically fond of freedom, refuse to accept, or even to recognize, limitation. Their attitude is ever hopeful and determined. It never even occurs to them that they can't win all the chips with one grand and glorious toss of the dice, whether the game the Lion or Lioness is playing is business, friendship, romance, matrimony or gambling. The Big Cats will almost always take a chance, and in Kipling's words, "make a heap of all their earnings, and risk them on one turn of pitch and toss — and lose, and start again at their beginnings — and never breathe a word about their loss."

The reason Leos never breathe a word about their loss is because they convince themselves they didn't lose. It's all a mirage. Taurus, to put it mildly, is not nearly so quick to take a chance, whether the Bulls are risking their money or their hearts. And when they lose, the memory of the loss will linger a long, long time — long enough for the Taureans to profit by the experience. Yet, when the chips are down, the Bull and the Lion or Lioness can match each other's contempt for misfortune. Neither is inclined to make a big deal of it, although they both might shed some private tears of sharp anguish. Leo and Taurus equally dislike public weeping or open admissions of failure.

In the long run, the Bull believes the safest way to double your money is to fold it over once and place it back in your pocket. That pretty much sums up the Taurean philosophy about either romantic or financial gambling. When the Bulls are young, they think the security of having cash in the bank, combined with the devoted love of a member of the opposite sex, is the most important and vital thing in life. When they grow older, they're positive it is.

The only thing Leos are that positive about is their own ability to make it happen. Not surprisingly, the Leonine warm-heartedness and nobility of spirit, when blended with their faith in themselves, draws others to them, including Lady Luck, who often showers upon them generous amounts of both love and gold.

Leos are all Big Cats, with huge hearts and splendid strength, who sometimes see themselves as neglected kittens when their own ego images aren't constantly reflected back to them by others and kept alive by extravagant compliments. (But the compliments must be genuine — Leo sees through insincere flattery as shrewdly as any monarch who's being appeased for favors — barring an afflicted natal Sun.)

Although Leo wants to lead, and the Lions or Lionesses sometimes impose on the Bulls' patience unintentionally, these proud people also enjoy protecting those they love, and lavishing gifts and kindness upon them. Isn't that the way all good kings and queens feel about their subjects? A Taurean will be secretly and deeply pleased by this Leonine protectiveness, demonstrative affection and concern over his — or her — welfare. However stubbornly they may deny it, no one needs or appreciates kindness and affection more than Taurus men, women and children. Their loyal, dependable hearts ache for it. That's another nice similarity between these two. The Leo and the Taurus hearts are equally loyal. Often, the warm friendliness and interest projected by Leo will make Taurus feel all snuggly and secure. So they are attracted into the same circle of empathy.

It's only when Leo starts giving those royal commands, which Taurus interprets as being shoved, that the trouble starts. After a time, Leo's bright Fire may scorch the Bull's endurance, until the Taurean buries the Lion or Lioness beneath a ton of earthy stubbornness and negative reaction. But Leo is ruled by the Sun, symbolizing warmth and light, the Great Life-Giving Force of the Universe. Taureans are softly ruled (until Pan-Horus ° appears to claim and influence them) by Venus, symbolizing Peace, Love and the musical Harmony of the Spheres. Between them, these two heavenly bodies keep the world spinning. All the other planets are merely supportive. The Sun is Life. Venus is Love. Is there more?

☆ ☆ ☆ ☆ ☆ ☆

° See footnote, page 61.

TAURUS *Woman* LEO *Man*

------◆●◆------

She had believed in him at the time,
but now that she was married and full
of sense she quite doubted whether
there was any such person.

Every Taurus woman has an affinity for music. She has a rich, musical voice, whether she's singing Carmen at the Met or simply saying, "I'll take two extra pints of cream today" to the milkman. Some Taureans compose music, direct it, or sing it — and all of them bask in it. Listening to its soothing sounds has a tranquilizing effect on the Bulls.

So, how could there be friction when a Leo man, married to a Taurus woman, wants to play music? There can be. And that's what astrology means by stating that their natal Suns are squared. This is the difficult and tense 4-10 Sun Sign Pattern, which may be a challenge, but which is more richly rewarding than all the others, if the challenges are courageously faced and conquered. Incidents which could never become unpleasant between any two other people, based on situations where harmony should naturally exist, can erupt into volcanos between a Leo and a Taurus, unless there's an unusually favorable Sun-Moon aspect between them.

A couple of years ago, I was visiting in the home of a Carmel, California couple, who have been an unusually loyal and devoted pair for many years. She's a Taurus. He's a Leo. She's a karate instructor. He's a poet, and an Oriental art dealer. The evening I was there, after enjoying a delicious dinner cooked by the Taurean wife, the three of us were discussing music, and the Lion and I discovered we had a mutual love for a particular version of "Ave Maria." When he placed an LP recording of the classic on the stereo, I leaned back in my chair, prepared to enjoy the music bouncing around the rafters from the many speakers the Lion had built and installed himself all over the house.

But as the opening chords swelled out to fill the room, I noticed the Taurus wife had disappeared. Suddenly, I heard a door slam — *hard.* Her husband, slightly abashed, explained: "Louise can't stand it when I play the stereo, so I guess she's gone to bed." It shocked me so much I couldn't concentrate on the recording. A normally gracious and hospitable Taurus woman being rude to a guest? A Venus-ruled woman who hates *music*? Astrologically impossible.

The next morning, at breakfast, she was her usual charming calm self, and when I asked her why she hated music, she replied calmly, "Oh, I don't hate it. I *love* music. I have, ever since I was a child."

"Then why . . . . ." I asked.

"You mean last night," she sniffed, icily. "I just can't bear to be around when Larry plays his stereo. He insists on turning up the volume so high, it drowns out all the tones, and hurts my ears. It's really a prostitution of music, I think, to play it that loudly, but you can't reason with him about it, so that's that." (The Taurus resignation to the inevitable.) "Tell me," she said, "since you're an astrologer — does his horoscope indicate that he's deaf?" (The Taurean humor, never subtle.)

No, he wasn't deaf. He was expressing his Leo urge to do everything on a grand scale, even though this particular Lion is the Shy Pussycat type. Whatever type he is, a Leo man can't bear to do things by half measures, and this compulsion is completely unrelated to his manner (if he's one of the quieter, less flamboyant Leos, in his outward personality). If it's a house, it must be large and luxurious, with a private den for him (his royal throne room, in a manner of speaking). If it's a woman, she must be both beautiful and intelligent. If it's a ring, it must be glittery, and visible across the room. When the Lion weeps, he sheds great torrents of tears. When he laughs, he laughs long and loudly. When he listens to music, he needs to hear it soar gloriously, to fill his heart and soul and ears. And when he's hurt, he either roars dramatically, or blushes furiously in humiliated frustration — as my Leo host, Larry, did rather frequently during my visit with him and his Bull wife, Louise.

Ordinarily, a Taurus female would never object to her husband's playing music, whatever the volume. Yet, I know another Taurus woman who sighed in ecstasy when her Lion courted her with a ukulele, in West Virginia, during their college courting days — then became bored each time he played and sang for her after they were married. You see, it's not a Taurean antipathy for music these two lady Bulls were displaying. Music, in both cases, simply *became the channel for the square of tension* between them, and their Leo mates.

Whether or not any individual Leo male possesses the emotional poise to deserve his astrological comparison to a King, this is nevertheless his private ambition — to rule those around him, most definitely including the Lion's own mate. A Taurus girl instinctively desires to submit to her man, to stick by his side faithfully and loyally through all seasons. But being ruled sounds suspiciously to her like being pushed, and no Bull will tolerate being pushed. Although Taurus women are capable of deep, lasting devotion and a warm-hearted love, they don't toss around careless compliments, they have no use at all for flattery, and they think worship is for the weak-minded. Since all Lions require and demand compliments, flattery and worship, you can see what's often missing in the relationship.

Leos are fiercely proud, fiery people, who brandish their own batons and refuse to play second fiddle to anyone. Even the Shy Pussycat Leo smolders with resentment when he's denied his rightful place in the Sun, preferably a few miles ahead and beyond anyone else who may be soaking up its rays. After all, the Sun is *his* ruler, which is why he's so noble and generous, despite his occasional arrogance and freezing attitude of superiority. To him, the Sun is not the center of the Universe, around which all the other planets revolve. *Leo* is the center of the Universe, around which his family (and hopefully, his friends) revolve — or they'd better, if they don't want to be frozen and ignored for the sin of not paying due respect at court.

Although this man's disposition is undeniably masterful, and therefore sometimes a shade tyrannical, he's a gentle, magnanimous lover, after a quarrel. His Leonine nobility of spirit makes it natural for him to want to kiss and make up. Verbal apologies he can't handle gracefully. They destroy his vanity. But he'll show he's sincerely sorry with a variety of romantic overtures. That's why these two often sense more empathy and mutual harmony in their sexual relationship than when they're trying to play the banjo together.

A physical and tangible display of affection is sometimes the only way to reconcile an argument with a Taurus girl. She'll remain stone-faced and immune to flowery words and persuasive arguments. Long conversations bore her, because she feels only through her senses. Taurus wants action, not words. So she'll respond beautifully to his passionate acts of love, and it all works out fine. They often reconcile after a squabble without the proud Lion ever having to lose his dignity. Making love is never beneath his dignity, no matter how violently he's been fighting with the loved one — or how recently. He needs a woman who can both accept and contain the depth of affection and passion he's capable of giving, and this one can. Her sensual talents for eroticism certainly won't displease him either. They'll make him "feel like a King," an expression many Leos use to describe their sexual fulfillment with the right woman.

However, her quality of conserving words isn't quite as soothing to the Lion, outside the bedroom. She may be less than ecstatic when he becomes emotionally aroused, and desperately needs an attentive, approving audience. She may even yawn in the middle of one of his dramatic speeches or lectures, and nothing can so cruelly destroy this man's sensitive ego so much as an obvious sign of boredom from a rebellious subject — especially from the woman he loves. If she really wants to keep this man forever (and every

Taurus woman seeks the security of romantic permanence) she'd better drink pots of black coffee, and make sure she remains wide awake when her Lion is on stage.

The most common complaint of the Lion against a Taurus girl is that she lacks enthusiasm. He often feels like shaking her into action, and shouting, "*Say* something! *Do* something! Anything at all. But don't just sit there." *Her* most common complaint against *him* can be summed up in four Shakespearean household words, "*Much ado about nothing.*"

He'll love the way she can turn a leaky tent into a cozy castle, her talent for making a dollar stretch like Silly Putty, and her rich humor — though he won't appreciate her jokes that ridicule his dignity, or puncture large holes in his ego. She'll warm up to her Lion's bear hugs, and intensely admire his ability to organize his dreams into the marble and alabaster of reality. She will not, of course, be at all happy about his extravagant tendencies, or his need to go out and review the troops when he feels the need for a little extra applause from the crowd. They'll always have their periodic tugs of tension. After all, they are both Fixed. Yet, the secret respect they feel for one another sometimes creates an unexpectedly soft, soothing carpet beneath their differences of opinion.

This lady doesn't allow herself to display visible anger often. She's patient, good humored, and willing to bear a great deal of silliness, along with Life's sadness, without evidencing excessive emotion. But when she does become angry — good and angry — it's best to get out of her way. Like, across town. Or maybe even another city or state, until she cools off and calms down — which she'll never fail to do eventually. A Taurus woman is always deeply ashamed of her own weakness, after she's given in to an emotional tantrum (during which her "creamy-smooth" Venus voice will more resemble that of a drill sergeant who trained for the operatic stage in youth — loud and forceful), and so she may be extra shy and affectionately loving later in trying to balance her act. But the Lion shouldn't let her sweetness following a disagreement fool him. She remembers what it was he did to arouse her Bull-like fury, and she'll remember it for years . . . and years . . . and years. Taureans tear into a wild and furious rampage of anger only very rarely — sometimes only once or twice during a lifetime. But it isn't the quantity of Taurus anger that matters — it's the *quality*. Volcanic.

A lady Bull shows her temper more frequently than just mentioned only if she's constantly and continually goaded by the domineering ways of a Leo who lectures her and scolds her periodically, and then, when she won't obey his every whim, turns away from her and pouts for long periods. That sort of behavior can rumble any Earth Sign into furious frustration, if it's prolonged over a long period of time.

This woman is made of more than her Taurean temper and stubbornness. She's also made of steadiness, courage, warmth, unswerving devotion, placidity, calmness and deep, deep emotions. She's enormously affectionate and giving, and her natural ability to laugh at herself is one of her most endearing qualities (unless she has a Leo, Scorpio or Capricorn Moon Sign or Ascendent — in which case she'll find it hard to chuckle when the joke's on her). There's no nonsense about this lady. She's sensible, down-to-earth, and she never pretends to be something she's not. She's real and genuine, honest and reliable — rather worth keeping.

As for him, he's made of more than his pride, vanity and self-centeredness. He's also made of sunshine and hope and confidence. His wisdom and benevolence are unmatched, when he feels he's really needed. The Lion will stand bravely against an army, to defend what he believes in his heart is right and true — just as he'll fight any force that threatens to harm the woman he loves, however uneven the battle may seem, even when the odds seem to be hopelessly against him. Whatever kind of pain she feels, whether it's physical or emotional, her pain is Leo's sworn enemy — something he must defeat, to prove his worth to his lady. Very much like the Knights who fought for King Arthur. Except that Leo is both Knight *and* King.

In his imagination, he lives in the Age of Chivalry, the Age of Romance. He belongs to another century, another time . . . when there were still worlds left to conquer, visions to follow, and dreams to dream. He tries hard to make the best of being lost somewhere on the time track, in a strange country where his leadership is not needed, and his ideals are not cheered. Even his white horse is gone. And the Holy Grail is only a memory from long ago. Leo, the Lion-Hearted, is therefore more wounded and lonely in spirit than those who see only his surface armour of arrogance ever guess.

No matter how many obstacles this man and woman face in achieving emotional harmony together, they'll stand by each other, against the whole world, if necessary. When fate brings sorrow or tragedy, neither of them will fail the test of loyalty. And that can be love's most enduring song — with or without the background music.

☆ ☆ ☆ ☆ ☆ ☆

TAURUS *Man* LEO *Woman*

◆─◀◆▶─◆

*Alas, he would not listen. He was
determined to show who was master in
that house.*

May a Bull aspire to own a queen? Most Bulls are more at home in a china shop than in the presence of royalty, and you know how flustered they are in a china shop. They're not frightened by the pomp and pageantry, but all that bowing and scraping and riding around in golden carriages — and coronations that last for days, while everyone gets tipsy, and stops working — is just plain "too much fuss and feathers" for the sensible Taurus man.

He isn't unappreciative of beauty. Most Taureans have a latent (or exposed) talent for artistic form, through painting, dancing, sculpting or music. But his biggest talent is looking at the world through practical glasses. He saves both his money and his emotions for a good cause, and throwing either away on red carpets and crowns is not, to his way of thinking, a good cause.

A Leo girl is looking for a man who recognizes her as a Queen, who can (in addition to cherishing and adoring her) provide her with the kind of life she knows she deserves. She wants a lover or mate who will allow her to live in the style to which she would like to become accustomed, surrounded by luxury and literate friends . . . an existence overflowing with beautiful clothes, parties and brainy conversations, with rings on her fingers, bells on her toes, and maybe even an occasional photographic safari to Africa — or summers on the Riviera. "July and August are so unpleasant in Manhattan (or Los Angeles) don't you agree? All those tourists." (Translation: peasants.)

You can understand then, why she feels a little tense and restless if the Taurus man she loves expects her to hang around in a small apartment, bringing him his beer and pretzels, while he watches television and reads the *Wall Street Journal* in his stocking feet. How mundane and plebeian. So she surprises him one night. She brings him a pitcher of ice cold Perrier water, with a slice of lime, and a delicate china plateful of triscuits, spread with caviar — hands him *New York* magazine, folded to the back pages of the homes-for-sale listings (beginning at around $200,000) and lovingly tucks a cozy, comfy — and modish — pair of house slippers from Saks' on his feet. He mumbles his gratitude softly, and smiles at her affectionately.

The next night, when she comes home from the hairdresser late (because he didn't give her money for a cab, and the subways were crowded), he's still sitting there, grumbling over her tardiness, with his beer and pretzels, watching the six o'clock news on TV, in his stocking feet. The slippers were too tight, and anyway, he thinks men who wear house slippers are sissified. *New York* magazine? *What* magazine? House listings? *What* house listings? Later, she finds the magazine spread out neatly under the kitty litter box in the pantry. Obviously, something has to give. It won't be the Bull.

Bulls don't back away. They either hold their ground — or they charge. She's better off resigning herself to her Taurean lover or mate's holding his ground, than to risk goading him into charging. Believe me. Still, if she's willing to wait, and not rush him, he may someday provide her with all those things she seeks, including the rings on her fingers and bells on her toes — maybe even a lovely home in the suburbs, or a wonderfully warm and beautiful remodeled barn in the country, complete with fireplaces, beams or rafters, and the sweet scent of new-mown hay drifting through the windows each morning. He may not reach his goal of security overnight, but she'll never find a man with a better chance (counting her invaluable help) to someday present her with her very own kingdom over which to rule. Just give him time, and *don't nag him.*

In 1971, when I visited the Hearst "castle" in California, the estate of the late William Randolph Hearst (a Sun Sign Taurus), the image of the Bull was everywhere. A determined Taurean male, slowly but surely building a newspaper empire, stacking up millions, then creating — from a private dream of love in his incurably romantic heart — a solid, tangible faerie-tale castle, not imaginary in any sense of the word. The furniture in the several-hundred-odd rooms is massive. Everything in and on the estate is bigger than Life, bigger than it need be, typical of the Taurean admiration for plain and simple *hugeness.* The larger, the better, for the Bull. Wherever I looked, I could see the Venus taste for life's "necessary luxuries," like the gold bathroom fixtures, pure silk wallpaper, thick Persian rugs, and ornate (large, of course) expensive marble statuary.

Every male Bull should drop by the Hearst castle to see what Taurus dreams look like when they finally come true. If he's in love with a Lioness, by all means, he should take her along. She'll be enthralled, and purr like a kitten all the way home. It will perhaps then dawn on her that his stocking feet are leading him in the same direction — and if she helps, not hinders, his plodding path, he'll get there. This could be just the male who might someday give the Lioness her very own yacht for her birthday. (Maybe she'd better image that occasion as their anniversary. He'll probably be much more sentimental about the latter date than the former.)

When the Bull has finally accomplished his mission in life — a comfortable home, and a large collection of Washingtons, Lincolns and Jeffersons (not paintings — green bills), the Lioness will surround him with her own touches of richness. She'll see that he's comfy and cozy, padding around in his stocking feet on thick carpets, under soft lights, to the sound of stereophonic violins, smothered with constant attention and bathed in a smooth, serene existence. Nothing could make him happier.

But while he's still laying the foundation and digging the hole for the cornerstone, he won't want to take the time to dally at court. He'll resent being expected to run around to parties, play politics with her friends, wait on her royal whims and feather dust her throne. All that foolishness of continually pampering her pride and plumping up her ego seems to him like a shameful waste of time, and Bulls do not like to waste time, any more than they like to waste money (which, as you know by now, is not at all).

Although these two Sun Signs are square, and therefore capable of clashing violently over their differences, if they hang in there until the clouds start showing their silver linings, it could be super. They'll find each other great company as they wander through the tower rooms, feed the swans on the lake, share romantic dinners by candlelight, pull up the drawbridge over the moat, and pull on velvet ropes for the servants to turn down the satin sheets on their imported canopy beds. Yes, I said beds — plural. They'll probably have separate boudoirs, because the Lioness will likely want her own dressing room. She has to have, after all, some place to keep her creams, lotions, perfumes, bath oils and manes (hairpieces).

If they're patient . . . . well, Taurus is patient, so at least half the problem is solved. She, however, is a Fire Sign, and Fire Signs are all a little short on patience. It makes the preliminary period of castle building somewhat fraught with fretting and tricky tensions, all the way from minor molehills to major mountains. In the interim, while they're dreaming of their two monograms entwined inside a heart etched on their Fostoria, silver, linens and fine china, they can idle away what few leisure hours the Bull can afford, making love. It could be one of the few times when they'll be in complete agreement. On the other hand, it could not. Much depends on the Moon-Sun relationship between their horoscopes.

On the positive side of the Luminary harmony in their nativities, there's the physical compatibility they can reach together. A Leo woman is proud and aloof, even distant, with strangers. But when she's wrapped up in the arms of the man she truly loves, she becomes a fierce Lioness, who fairly oozes affection and sex appeal. The Bull won't fight with her when she's running her gentle hands through his hair, smoothing his skin, massaging his back, kissing his ear, and stroking his hand.

A Taurus man is almost helplessly vulnerable to the touch, the sound and the scent of his woman, and since Leo females nearly all adore perfume, he'll whiff away contentedly, like the peaceful Disney Ferdinand the Bull, in his most blissful state of ecstasy. His strength is awesome, yet this man is always in danger of becoming a Samson in the clutches of a sensuous, Leonine

Delilah. He's ruled by Venus, and nothing brings him more peace of mind and spirit than fulfilling his deep, earthy romantic desires with a passionate Lioness — unless it's counting a stack of fresh, new green bills, or sniffing a home-baked apple pie, just out of the oven.

On the negative side, if the exchange of energies from the Sun and the Moon in their respective birth charts is square or opposed, there must be some heavy adjustments made in relation to the sexual harmony they achieve. He may slowly and gradually, but very finally, tire of trying to please her and to feed her insatiable ego, if he's forced to frequently sleep alone — or face her bored back in bed — when he hasn't made her feel cherished enough during the day to make her feel he deserves her royal favors at night.

Or perhaps she's the one who will slowly and gradually, but very finally, become weary of secretly wishing he'd try harder to fulfill her physical needs by making her feel adored and intensely desired, sexually. The Bull's sensual, down-to-earth, and sometimes unimaginative lovemaking may leave her lying awake beside him, hour after hour, dreaming of the Prince who never comes to claim her waiting heart . . . shedding quiet tears she's too proud to let him see, or to ever tell him about. And after a while, the warm-hearted, high-spirited and affectionate Lioness may become totally frigid.

Frigidity is ever a lurking danger with the instinctively passionate Leo woman. If she's continually neglected, from her fiery dreams and desires of youth she'll freeze into the cool detachment of the Leonine nature, a defense mechanism that's not natural, and is always very sad. Detachment because — what Queen would allow anyone to guess she isn't completely worshiped? Not even the Prince Consort who has so tragically failed her will be permitted to glimpse her broken heart, or be made aware of her terrible emptiness and loneliness. False pride is every Leo's Waterloo.

It's his bull-headedness and her false pride combined that keeps them both restless (or resigned) and unfulfilled. Somehow, there's a lack of honest communication between them. So they never discuss their individual lovemaking disappointments with one another — until love solidifies into nothing but a sort of comfortable familiarity and companionship — or shatters into divorce. Sometimes one or the other of these two lovers or mates will find escape through drink, drugs or casual affairs. But usually not. They're both too basically honorable to be disloyal, too conscious of their reputations to make public fools of themselves — yet too stubborn (him) and too proud (her) to seek a solution, tenderly and gently . . . together. But it's never too late for mutual confession and humility to create an unexpected miracle. They should both begin by remembering how it was between them when they first fell in love. The memory will soften them . . . and they can progress from there.

This is not a man who will appreciate his woman serving him dainty food, or pressing him into fastidious behavior at home or in public. She'll discover that the first time he yells at her, during dinner, "Where's the ketchup bottle ?" "You call that a sandwich ? Take it back to the kitchen and add a few layers." Or — "How about a coffee mug, woman ? These little china things give me the willies."

Don't ask where he got the word "willies." Taureans have a way of manufacturing words that have a soft, cuddly sound, whether they're insulting or complimentary. Did you ever have a Bull call you "Honey" ? It's an experience in total sensuality, which is no wonder, when they all have those deep, mellow, buttery voices, unmatched by any other man, except Scorpio.

She'll accuse him of being sometimes slightly uncouth, and nearly always obstinate, as, of course, he definitely is. He'll accuse her of being haughty, high-and-mighty, and snobbish, as, of course she definitely is. What do you do, when one's worst complaints against the other are justified and true ? It's simple. (Not easy, but simple.) She'll have to comprehend that his lack of "couth" is simply indicative of his earthy, rather dependable nature, his contempt for the frivolous and the non-genuine — the phony. She'd do well to imitate it. She'll also have to recognize that his obstinacy indicates his strength of character, and stop deliberately inciting it by behaving like a spoiled Queen, who pouts when she doesn't win her own way. She can always get around his obstinacy if she tries, with amazing ease, simply by hugging and kissing and squeezing him into contentment again.

He must realize that her haughtiness is nothing but her inbred protection against exposing her fears of imagined inadequacy, therefore losing face and subjecting herself to painful ridicule — and stop deliberately causing it by refusing to acknowledge her very real superiority as a woman — and her deep need to be drenched in extravagant compliments. He can always get around her quite easily, by taking her out to sparkle in public more often, and showing her — especially *telling* her — that he's aware of how lucky he is to have married a very super lady, in all ways. (Every Leo woman *is* just that, never mind her little failings.) His Lioness is enormously capable of both giving and receiving love, if only she's properly appreciated . . . . . . and loved in return.

Whatever age the Bull may be, he's a Teddy Bear at heart, the chubby, high-chair-stage symbolic Baby of the zodiac (as described in "The Twelve Mysteries of Love," in the front of this book). I once knew a Leo woman who could not see her Taurus husband as any sort of "Teddy Bear," or cuddly in any way. She saw him only as a stubborn, mature man, who believed in nothing but "the practical," and who thought all sentiment was silly, sentimental rubbish. One day, I coaxed her into taking home to him a large stuffed, furry Bull. The kind of toy one normally gives to — yes, to a baby. He grunted.

That was it. Didn't even say "thanks." He completely ignored the furry image of himself—for weeks. The hurt and wounded Lioness placed it on the television, where he'd be sure to see it constantly, and still—not a word from the phlegmatic, undemonstrative Taurean. Then he became ill. During his illness, while he was asleep one morning, she happened to unthinkingly move the toy Bull from the television while she was cleaning. When her Taurus husband awoke from his nap, his roar could be heard all over the house. *"WHAT HAPPENED TO MY BULL? WHAT DID YOU DO WITH MY BULL?!!!"* he shouted. She'll learn.

The Bull and the Lioness will have to start listening to each other's silent, pleading hearts . . . . . . when what she's really saying, beneath her haughtiness, is—"Please, *show* me how much you love me" . . . . . . and what he's really saying, beneath his stony stubbornness, is—"Please, promise me you'll stay, and never leave me."

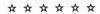

TAURUS

Earth — Fixed — Negative
Ruled by Venus (also by the
  Planet Pan-Horus)
Symbol: The Bull
Night Forces — Feminine

VIRGO

Earth — Mutable — Negative
Ruled by Mercury (also by
  the Planet Vulcan)
Symbol: The Virgin
Night Forces — Feminine

The TAURUS-VIRGO *Relationship*

◆─◄●►─◆

*. . . . . but on the whole the Neverlands have a
family resemblance, and if they stood still in
a row you could say of them that they have each
other's nose, and so forth.*

Virgos admire the Taurus strength of purpose, although they have little tolerance for the Bull's stubbornness in the face of an obvious mistake.

Taurus is somewhat in awe of the quick Virgo mind, though the Bulls have little sympathy for health nuts, cleanliness bugs or the finer nuances of Virgo hair-splitting.

But what are a few minor differences between friends? These two will normally find plenty of things to be friendly about, not the least of which is common sense. The phrase may at times, however, annoy the critical Virgo, since the Virgin knows the kind of sense referred to is far from common. It's extremely rare. Someday, you can be certain, some Virgo will finally succeed in correcting this particular inaccuracy in the language.

Taurus and Virgo will hang on firmly to their mutual principles while the rest of society is flipping out in an insane dance of tragedy — and frivolous foolishness. Neither the Bull nor the Virgin makes much of a distinction between tragedy and frivolous foolishness. In their sensible opinions, the latter is a direct path to the former. Virgos remember every flaw they have ever seen, from a torn shower curtain to a character defect in a friend. The memories are painful, and they keep the Virgins eternally disillusioned, not to mention pessimistic about human nature. Still, in a way, Virgos give the impression they almost enjoy their memories of the cracks and dusty corners of Life. It gives them something to do with their bright and busy minds. Taurus remembers everything he (or she) has ever seen too, though the Taurean really doesn't *want* to remember. There's a nagging voice inside the Bulls which tells them that wasting time is somehow sinful — and wasting it on things in the past you can't change is wasting it as surely as any other way. Yet, they helplessly cling to their old memories, and the lessons they've learned, as if they were graven on their foreheads in letters of stone. Taken as a whole, Virgos have more complicated fears (including their own health, and the danger of accident) than Taurus. Whatever the Bulls are afraid of, it's not physical.

This is not a lively pair you would want to hire to sell the Brooklyn Bridge in a hurry, collaborate on a book of faerie tales, promote a get-rich-quick stock in a bucket shop — or operate a fast-moving blackjack game in Las Vegas. These two were both born under feminine negative Earth Signs. Which means that they're passive and receptive (feminine) — suspicious, somewhat fearful and cautious (negative) — although loaded with integrity and dependability (Earth). It's a wonder they ever get around to meeting each other. However, once they gather the courage and aggressiveness to say "Hi!" to each other, and make a date to meet again (which will be kept punctually), the friendship, or business partnership, or whatever (usually a combination of both) will probably flower slowly, surely and serenely into a beautiful relationship. Within a family group, these are usually the two who get along smoothly together, and feel isolated from the rest of the radicals around the breakfast table.

I once knew a Taurus musician and a Virgo singer. They used to meet almost every morning in front of the Brill Building in New York (the headquarters of Broadway songwriters). The Bull was — and still is — an extremely talented composer. With or without formal musical training, he'll eventually make it to the top of his field. But he harbors the typical Taurean resentment against fate, because family responsibilities prevented him from attending Juilliard, and therefore he carries a fair-sized chip of wood on his shoulder (which can make your posture sag a little, along with your spirits, when you're also lugging around an electric guitar all day long).

This Bull is suspicious of singers who want to use his songs without paying him first, or signing a contract, and he also stubbornly refuses to let anyone sing his tunes if he thinks they're not right for him (or her). However, the Virgo male vocalist could usually talk the Bull into or out of anything. The Virgin singer (and of course I use the term Virgin symbolically) was picky and choosy about the material he recorded, and invariably wanted to change a note here or a word there in the lyrics, before he thought the song was perfect enough to match his perfect voice, and his perfect judgment of public taste. Still, he had fewer objections to the Taurean's songs than to anyone else's, because an association between Taurus and Virgo is influenced by the harmonious 5-9 Sun Sign Pattern. Somehow, they rang clear and true to his critical and acutely sensitive ear.

These two once considered a business partnership in a publishing company, but Virgo is ruled by the restless planet Mercury (until Virgo's true ruler, Vulcan, is discovered and identified) and so the Virgin singer eventually became annoyed and impatient with the Bull's lack of aggressive drive, left New York, and married a bright Sagittarian girl named Sharon, who cheered him up for a while (Sag and Virgo being a tense, 4-10 Sun Sign Pattern, it was a very short while, but they could still reconcile, when their stars cross again). It was good for him, however brief, because all Virgos desperately need cheering, and after being touched by Sag Sharon's Jupiter vibes of joy and luck, the Virgin vocalist finally drifted into other areas of show business he felt needed to be perfected by his kindly, courteous and meticulous attention.

Taurus just shrugged his strong shoulders, adjusted the wooden chip on his shoulder, and his guitar strap, kept plugging and plodding, and quietly waited for his big chance. (With Taurus, it has to be big — huge — or forget it.) Now I hear he's writing the musical score for a Hollywood film, featuring two top stars. Patience pays.

That's how Taurus often wins out over Virgo — in the area of patience. Taurus always has it. Virgo usually lacks it. Virgins can appear to be tranquil, calm and patient on the surface, but their minds are constantly ticking away, and tocking them with all sorts of inner frustrations when things don't happen as quickly or exactly in the manner they'd like. The flesh is willing, and able to remain on Earth (for a while) but the mental attitude is changeable and restive. Mercury is the true ruler of the Air Sign Gemini, and is not at all at home in its temporary association with the Earth Sign of Virgo. Consequently (possibly through sheer boredom) the tricky Mercury sometimes agitates Virgins into behavior against their real natures, and contrary to their deepest desires. Virgos may take heart, however, for, as detailed in the Virgo-Virgo chapter of this book, when Vulcan is recognized and named, within a few years (or sooner) it will begin to express its powerful, magnetic vibrations through the personalities of all Virgins, causing them to be stronger, tougher — and less likely to switch horses, ideas, girls or career in the middle of the stream of Life's little annoyances and irritations.

Still, it will always be more natural for Taurus to succeed in a larger way than Virgo (which the Virgins don't really mind terribly) because Taurus is a Fixed Sign, "Fixed" meaning, astrologically, steady, organized and supremely capable of building a lasting foundation beneath a career, a house (making it an enduring home) or a marriage. Virgo is a Mutable Sign, "Mutable" meaning to change, to move around, to communicate between others, to carry information and truth back and forth, with both vertical and horizontal opinions. The Virgins don't feel a burning need to build a great empire or ride around in a flashy car to the sound of cheers, with ticker tape confetti falling all over them and messing up their neatly brushed hair. (Not to mention the rolls of squeezy-soft toilet tissue some people toss out the window at heroes in a parade — how vulgar can one be?)

Virgo's driving urge is to serve the world and all the individuals in it, or on it, by pointing out their faults — to bring order out of chaos and anarchy — and accumulate a reasonable amount of personal security for the future at the same time. If a Virgin should happen to wander beneath the glare of a spotlight of fame through an accident of Fate, he (or she) will blush, perhaps shyly enjoy it for a brief period, then often alienate the Press with critical remarks, express irritation with the clamoring, great, unwashed public — and finally exercise the Virgo birthright option to make a firm, clear-cut decision to retreat to the very private life most Virgos seek above all else.

Taurus wants to retire into seclusion too. And the Bulls usually have very definite ideas of where it will be. The country. Sooner or later, somewhere between the ages of six and sixty, every Bull, whether male or female, will gravitate heavily and fixedly toward the countryside — anywhere the Taureans can indulge their passion for the Good Earth, trees, grass and quiet streams, free from the interference of noisy, foolish, chattering people. But when the Bulls do finally settle down with the chickens and ducks and cows and haystacks, they don't want to depend on fickle Mother Nature's harvest for their security. This is why they'll endure the confusion and frivolity of the cities, no matter how many years it takes, so that when they leave, it will be with a large bundle under the arm — which will not be full of what the farmers use to make the grass grow green. Taurus people mistrust *that* substance, in *all* its forms. It will be filled with what is *already* green — beautiful, crisp pieces of currency, engraved with the glorious eagle of the United States of America. (Bulls are nearly always fanatically patriotic. Their motto is: "My country, right or wrong — my family, right or wrong — my friends, right or wrong — and last, but not least — my opinions, right or wrong.")

When Taurus and Virgo show a harmonious Sun-Moon aspect between their birth charts, in addition to the natural harmony of their 5-9 Sun Sign Pattern influence, they can happily retire together to the country. The Bulls will sit on their assets contentedly, while the Virgins dash back and forth to town for supplies . . . and to straighten things out now and then. Virgo may nag a little when Taurus is sloppy, and they may indulge in some affectionate bickering, like the characters in Neil Simon's *The Odd Couple* (who are, indisputably, a Bull and a Virgin, a Taurus-Virgo team), but on the whole, they'll be compatible.

It must be astrologically confessed that Virgos can be as opinionated as Taureans. The only difference is that the Bulls are opinionated in a Fixed, rather general sort of way, and the Virgins are opinionated in a hair-splitting, detailed sort of way. Once upon a time, there was a small Virgo boy, named Charles Edison Cameron. One day in grade school, in Fayetteville, North Carolina, Charlie's teacher goofed. A rather normal, unimportant trifling mistake, but the young Virgo simply couldn't bear it. The teacher placed two dots on the blackboard, across from each other, like so:

●   ●

She then informed the class that these dots represented "two points." "Now," she instructed them, "the lesson today is to prove that a straight line is the shortest distance between two points. Do I have a volunteer?" Up shot the hand of anxious Virgo Charlie, a worried frown on his face.

"Teacher," he said, very respectfully and politely, "you are wrong. A straight line is not necessarily the shortest distance between two points." The teacher flushed, visibly annoyed. "Really?" she asked the eleven-year-old, Mercury-ruled youngster. "Would you like to step up to the blackboard and explain how you can dispute such a basic theory of mathematics?" Virgo Charlie trotted immediately to the blackboard, picked up the chalk and demonstrated the proof of his statement, as the entire class rocked with laughter and the teacher's face turned bright red. His demonstration looked somewhat like this:

"You see, Teacher," Virgo Charlie said courteously, after the laughter had died down, "that line appears to me like it could run all the way to China if it wanted, and golly knows how much further than that if it was goin' straight up, instead of around. So, how could a straight line be the shortest distance between two points?"

The teacher had, of course, neglected to take the horizontal-vertical aspect of her example into consideration. And she had also goofed on her terminology, using the word "between," instead of saying "the shortest distance *connecting* two points." It's a common mistake of educators, even erudite math instructors. But Virgo Charles Edison Cameron could not allow such an error of thinking and speaking to stand uncorrected. In the not too distant future, you'll be hearing more about Virgo Charles Edison Cameron, through a brilliant and blessed "breakthrough" invention of his which will be

of even more importance to the world than the discovery of his namesake —
so remember his name.

If Taurus and Virgo should ever decide to write a book together, the Bull
will see to it that the plot is substantial. Virgo will supply the dialogue,
correct the spelling and grammatical errors, punctuation and other mistakes.
Taurus will then add some rich humor, market it wisely, and make sure it
earns money. Sometimes people think Virgins are too timid and self-effacing,
too courteous to be so super-critical. To these people, I submit a letter I
received in 1970, shortly after the publication of my first book, *Sun Signs*.
It reads as follows, verbatim:

Dear Ms. Goodman . . . I find, on page seventy-eight, line one, in the
paperback edition of your book, Sun Signs, *a mistake. I quote from the*
book the phrase: "the sandal clad people *of Chaldea . . . ." The phrase*
should read, "the sandal shod *people." Otherwise, you give the reader*
the impression that the Chaldean people wore sandals, and nothing
else. Sincerely, Janine Hartman. P.S. I am a Virgo.

I wish to take this opportunity to thank Janine. As for my other readers,
please permit me to correct here and now the impression I may have given to
modest Virgins, conventional Taureans and the like, that the people of
Chaldea all ran around naked, except for their footwear. My normally ultra-
cautious and super-bright *Sun Signs* editor, Capricorn Bobbs Pinkerton, is
properly chastised also. (A Ram may be excused for such carelessness, but
never a Goat!) Isn't it fortunate that Janine added her P.S. ? I would never
have been able to guess her Sun Sign if she hadn't.

If there are any major publishing houses on the East or West Coast who
are looking for a terrific copy editor, might I suggest they hire Janine ? I'm
sorry to say that in typical careless Aries fashion, I've mislaid the envelope
with her address. But I feel certain I'll hear from her again, when she reads
the Virgo–Virgo chapter of this book, and this time, I *promise* to hang on to
her address. I think she's *neat!* My present scholarly Taurus editor, Dr.
Charles Musès, agrees — *firmly*, of course.

☆ ☆ ☆ ☆ ☆ ☆

TAURUS *Woman* VIRGO *Man*

". . . . here's the rock."

It's almost impossible for a Taurus woman to seduce a Virgo man. But she shouldn't allow herself to feel inferior over this. It's almost impossible for *any* woman to seduce a Virgo man. Remember that Narcissus is supposed to have been a Virgo (though if he was, he had an Aries Ascendent and the Moon in Leo). The reason astrological legend has labeled Narcissus as a Virgo is that most Virgos are somewhat self-centered, not in the egotistical sense of Leo, or in the spoiled sense of Aries, but in the symbolic sense that all technical, literal Virgins (both male and female) are absorbed in themselves, because they're unaware of what being totally awakened in all ways really means.

This man can't bear the thought of any sort of self-surrender. It implies a lack of self-discipline. He's not terribly interested in conquest either. So it's not surprising that he can't arouse much enthusiasm for Valentine's Day. However, the Taurus girl is a few strides ahead of her astrological sisters, should she decide to educate the Virgin in awareness of what makes the world spin for those who enjoy the ride. He may not chase her down Lovers' Lane with bated breath, but neither is he likely to run away from her. Since their natal Suns are trine to each other, there's a lot going for the relationship from the start. Their natures, goals and desires are similar. Influenced by a double Earth vibration, the almost always harmonious 5-9 Sun Sign Pattern, they're both steady, sensible types, who would rather be caught doing almost anything than messing around with fantasy, flightiness or fickleness. She's soothing, and has a nice, quiet voice. He's gentle and has clear enunciation. So, naturally, they don't grate on each other's nerves.

If the Taurus girl plays her cards right (which is a somewhat inappropriate metaphor, since few Earth Signs like to gamble) she can have him eating out of her hand before he knows what hit him — and even coming back for a late-night snack in her kitchen. What hit him will have been comfort. A female who speaks and moves so sensuously and slowly seldom makes mistakes. Unless you're a Virgo man yourself, you just can't imagine how comfortable it is to be around someone who's not always making mistakes and goofs you feel compelled to catch and correct. Didn't anyone ever tell you that compulsive criticizing isn't much fun? It can be exhausting.

Neither of them becomes angry very often or very easily. They have fairly tranquil, peaceful dispositions in common (though he may bite his nails and blink his eyes a bit more than she does). Still, when the Bull does lose her temper, it's quite a blast, never mind how rare, and it may leave deep scars. When Virgo finally works himself up into a snit, it's usually a relatively shallow, surface emotion, that doesn't last very long, and certainly doesn't drive itself deep into his soul. Worry is something else again. A Virgo man's worries do drive themselves deep inside of him, but not necessarily into his soul. They settle in the general region of the stomach and the intestines, which is why he's always poking about in her pantry when he stops for that late-night snack — to see if she has any Pepto-Bismol or Tums handy. Now, if she had a quick temper like other females, she might take offense at this apparent slur on her cooking. But the typical Taurus girl will accept all the little idiosyncrasies of her Virgo lover with equanimity, unless, of course, her Moon or Ascendent is in a more sensitive sign.

Virgos don't itemize their apprehensions every few minutes. They don't even holler about them every few hours. They can't see any point in airing them as often as once a year, and some Virgos keep their trembles locked up inside for decades. Do you have any idea what that can do to your digestive system, not to mention your subconscious or psyche? It's also the major cause of arthritis and rheumatism.

I've always felt that Hamlet may have had a Virgo Moon Sign, revealed when he said, "I could be bounded in a nut shell, and count myself king of infinite space, were it not that I have dreams." Virgos are normally quite satisfied with small, nutshell-like spaces in which to stretch their egos and ambitions. They're normally content to be hard working, polite and helpful — to spin their own little cobwebs of hope, without tramping all over everyone else. It's those darned dreams. Everyone knows (and certainly Virgo does) that bad dreams and nightmares from suppressed emotions can cause anything from an attack of gastritis and mild constipation to ulcers. That's where the Taurean woman comes into the picture. Not to nurse him, but to soothe him, with her practical philosophy about nightmares.

TAURUS: If you have a healthy mind and body, and fulfilled emotions, nightmares don't exist. Period.

VIRGO: But how can you keep your mind, body and emotions healthy, when everything around you is falling apart, the world is being run by raving madmen, and your car has a broken transmission, you've lost your umbrella, and missed your insurance payment, and your socks all have holes in them, and . . . . .

TAURUS: (firmly) People who are properly loved have healthy, happy, fulfilled minds, bodies and emotions. A nice, warm bath and a cup of good, nourishing soup can solve any problem. Give me your socks. I'll darn them.

She makes it sound so simple (and it is, really) that he'll stop worrying, because obviously, he is properly loved by a woman who is both sensible and sensuous. At least, he'll stop worrying temporarily, while he's chewing her crunchy carob brownies, and nibbling her fragrant ear lobe. A Virgo man is repelled by most artificial odors. He likes everything to be natural, as Mother Nature intended. But he rather enjoys the fresh, feminine smell of scented soap, especially on the ear of a sympathetic woman who listens calmly to his worries, without becoming all flustered about them herself. She's an excellent listener, and he can be a pretty fascinating talker. A Virgo man's conversation is usually highly intelligent, clever, bright and interesting, even if it's not always terribly punchy.

Sexually, both of them fall under the category of the silent type. *She's* silent because she prefers to partake in lovemaking undistracted by verbal romantic coquetry, just drowning in the intimacies of union with the man she loves so deeply. *He's* silent because he can't think of many wild or spontaneous things to say about sex anyway, and even if he could, he'd probably be too embarrassed to say them in mixed company (the two of them alone together *are* mixed company — to Virgo). He's not frigid, and he has nothing against sex. In fact, a Virgo male can create great beauty in the physical expression of love by blending desire with emotional tenderness, stimulated by mental excitement. But he's not moved to a single tremble or tremor by the kind of sex that lacks the qualifying aspect of its higher purpose. She won't object to that attitude — no real woman would. She'll probably believe she's lucky to share with him an experience of such gentle affection and passion, and she's right. She is. Virgo love burns with an intense white heat that fulfills with a more mystical depth than the brief, red flame of more casual lovers.

Not that he doesn't know how to employ the light touch of romance, if and when he chooses. This man isn't the kind to fall asleep in the middle of making love, no matter what you've heard. (He's too wide awake from worrying about whether or not his partner is pleased with his sexual behavior.) Some Virgo men indulge in dozens of light-as-a-feather affairs, because they're experts in the art of playing at love. And so an occasional Virgo male will attract promiscuous women, with loose morals. They feel safe with him. Because he takes it all so casually, they sense there won't be any unnecessary emotional scenes of jealousy. Just good, clean Virgo fun. However, since this man never seeks a party girl for a mate, he soon tires of the shallowness of the game, and then he's ready for a permanent relationship. If he should happen to be strolling through a Taurus girl's garden about that time, he'll be enormously susceptible to a serious romance, followed by marriage. To state it plainly, he's a sitting duck.

She'll have to remember, however, that marriage is not a natural condition for a Virgin, although if anyone can make matrimony seem to be more cozy than confining, it's a Taurean female. As long as she doesn't make him feel possessed, he'll be putty in her hands. She needn't worry about giving him too much freedom. No matter how much rope she gives him, he'll probably only use it to find his way home to her in the dark. He's rather a creature of habit, when all's said and done. He's grown accustomed to her face, to her fragrant ear, his own private shower, the fresh orange juice she squeezes for him every morning, and his shirts all nicely stacked in the drawer, with no ring-around-the-collar. So how is he going to be able to get used to hanging his socks on a strange towel rack? Especially when the neatly darned toes and heels would be sure to remind him of her, and cause him to have an attack of the guilties on the spot.

He may fail to see why she needs to surround herself with so many luxuries, and she may complain that his ideas of personal comfort are somewhat Spartan, but neither of them are inclined to throw away money with careless abandon — so finances will seldom be a subject of contention. With or without a harmonious Sun-Moon aspect between them, this man and woman can rely on the smooth empathy of the 5-9 vibration to mist each misunderstanding with sympathy, and soften each argument with forgiveness. It's not easy to please a Virgin, but the Taurean woman can come mighty close to doing it, and she's capable of touching her Virgo man's skeptical heart with her own special kind of warm, unselfish devotion. If she sticks to it (and that's where much of her talent lies — in sticking to things) she may, after a while, learn the knack of Virgo criticism herself. Then she can send him a Valentine, in verse, that says . . . . . (in part)

> . . . . . *to be absolutely honest*
> *as you've carefully taught me to be*
>   *you're still a little off center*
> *investigating truth*
>   *without consequences*
> *and doing your thing . . .*
>   *playing with platitudes*
> *reading books about Buddha*
> *to learn how to die, before you've started to live*
> *straining emotions through a sterile sieve*
> *and scrubbing your squeaky-clean ivory tower*
>   *with Brillo pads*
> *each morning*
> *. . . but you're improving* °

° From *Venus Trines at Midnight* by Linda Goodman.

TAURUS *Man* VIRGO *Woman*

———◆◗◆———

"It is so naughty of him not to wipe," Wendy
said, sighing. She was a tidy child.

Virgo girls turn up their pretty noses at messes. Most of them are as neat as pins. There may be a Virgin here or there whose surroundings are a little cluttered. But her mind is always well dusted, and sliced into precise thoughts — and there's probably no loose tobacco in the bottom of her handbag.

In August of 1974, I was having lunch with a Virgo newspaper reporter. We were discussing her Sun Sign, and she remarked, "I'm not at all hooked on that Virgo neatness compulsion. I let my trash can overflow for days before I get around to emptying it."

"Sure," I told her, "that's because you don't like to get your hands dirty." Then I stared pointedly at her fingers, and her poise shattered like fragile glass.

"Why are you staring? Oh, this smudge? That isn't dirt. It's my ring. I have a lot of acid in my system, and gold turns my skin green when I get nervous. I thought I got it all off when I washed my hands an hour ago, but — well. I know it looks like dirt, but it isn't, and — uh, waitress! Where is your powder room please?"

One of the barriers between a Virgin and a Bull is that a Taurus man is inclined to be a teeny bit untidy. Some of them are downright sloppy. And a few Bulls are just plain slobs. They love beauty and luxury around them, but they're too busy making the bread that buys it to be bothered picking lint off their trousers, combing their forelocks into neat curls, sweeping up their crumbs and ashes, draping their sweat shirts on satin hangers, or polishing their shoes to a high gloss. The practical Bull may worship currency, but not to the extent where he feels compelled to launder all his bills and press them with a hot iron. To Taurus, wrinkled money is still money, as good as gold. Just like a man with a wrinkled shirt is still a man (perhaps more so than those chaps with their ruffled cuffs and velvet lapels) — and also as good as gold. An occasional Taurean will place an emphasis on grooming, but he won't make a fetish of it. As long as he's scrubbed and clean, he's not going to worry if his shoelaces aren't tied in neat bows or one sock dips down a quarter of an inch lower than the other.

There's a misconception about Virgo girls which may shock the Bull who discovers it. Naturally, all Virgos aren't Virgins, but it goes deeper than that. Her love of order and her sharp foresight, based on a highly developed critical sense, make her seem conventional to the point of being puritanical. But she is not necessarily Beth, of Louisa May Alcott's *Little Women*. The Virgo puritanical morality is an astrological myth. After all, you can be courteous, gracious and discriminating without being a prude. She investigates the facts, observes the action, works it all through her mathematical thought processes, and forms a clear opinion (usually unspoken) of what's best for everybody. However, what her acute observations have led her to believe is best for everybody can be anything from building more convents to encouraging more nude group therapy. It depends. Her moral attitude is intellectual, and her emotions are seldom involved (unless she has the Moon in a more sensitive Air or Fire Sign). Virgos are as curious as they are critical. How can you correct a flaw if you haven't examined the vase? So, this girl is often accused of (or given credit for?) a stuffy sort of morality she doesn't possess.

The Bull doesn't talk much about his ethics or morals. He *feels* what is right or wrong, then acts with blind determination, and very little reflection on the intricacies of the issues. When their different methods of arriving at the truth lead them to the same conclusion, things are pink and rosy. But when they take a mental detour, these earthy lovers can bury each other in frozen silence and unbending stubbornness.

I was once a helpless bystander during a quarrel between two friends, a Virgo girl and her Taurus lover. We had all three been rapping about the Aquarian Age sexual revolution, its implications and various by-products, from the vulgarity on the newsstands to capitalizing on sexual lust and violence in films, all in the name of glorious freedom from censorship. Before I had a chance to air my personal views, these two began to challenge each other.

TAURUS: Sex, sex, sex, I'm so tired of hearing about it, and reading about it. You'd think it was only discovered yesterday, the way it's headlined as news continually.

VIRGO: (musing thoughtfully) Maybe if prostitution were legalized everywhere, it would help.

TAURUS: Help what — the prostitutes?

VIRGO: Well, sex isn't going to disappear, and it's possible that these women serve a useful purpose for their customers.

TAURUS: (his neck turning bright red, and bristling in anger) Yeah? Well, their "customers" are buying a lie.

VIRGO: True. Nevertheless, a lie may be just the fantasy needed by the

TAURUS: (beginning to paw the ground) I'm sure glad I found out your attitude toward morality before I married you.

VIRGO: (still cool and unruffled) To accuse human beings of wrongdoing, and then condemn or punish them, will never change anything. If you must be so judgmental, try to learn to hate prostitution, *not* the prostitute. Direct your anger toward the *crime*, not the *criminal*. The problem with your attitudes is that they're always so dogmatic, and you never attempt to exercise *discrimination* (Virgo's favorite word).

TAURUS: (now aroused to the full fury of the Bull) The problem with *your* attitudes is that you don't know how to be *firm* (the Bull's favorite word) about anything, including your opinions. You can't place a financial value on emotion. It's less than human. I never thought you would defend such a thing. I thought you were a nice, decent woman. What's wrong is *wrong*. And it's wrong to sell love. So that's that.

VIRGO: It's only natural that *men* would prefer to have women *give* their "human emotions" away, free of charge, rather than *sell* them.

TAURUS: Don't give me that feminist double-talk.

VIRGO: I think it's curious that most people who are so critical of prostitution are quite permissive regarding sexual promiscuity. The very ones who despise prostitutes (*excluding you, of course, dear*) are the same ones who believe that casual sex, without commitment, is very glamorous and "in," and anyone who doesn't go along is hopelessly straight and square. That's disgustingly hypocritical. I still say that prostitution exists because it treats an illness of society itself, the *same* society that condemns the prostitutes.

TAURUS: It treats a *symptom.*

VIRGO: Then, like I said, why not treat the *cause* ?

I'm sorry I can't tell you the final outcome of their argument, because my taxi came, and I had to leave before it was resolved. However, that brief (and actual) portion of their conversation should clear up any muddy, preconceived astrological notions that every female Virgo Virgin is a nun-like Miss Innocent — and every male Bull is a coarse, erotic creature of lust, snorting in passion at all the cows in the pasture.

If Carrie Nation reincarnated today, and began waving her hatchet at prostitutes on street corners, there might well be more "sensual" Bulls and "sexy" Scorpions following behind her and yelling "Right on!" than supposedly "puritanical" Virgos — which would surprise everybody but astrologers. The Virgins would probably be eloquently urging Carrie to use her hatchet on the porno theatres and newsstands where the concentration on sexual excess is first encouraged — to attack the root of the matter, not its branches — with the typical Virgo-like ability to *analyze* and *discriminate,* while remaining cool to misleading emotional attitudes.

It takes Virgo to figure out that the massive rise in sexual abuse of children, venereal disease, abortion, and the great increase in rape the feminists are so outraged about, is not the fault of the prostitutes. Prostitution has always been around — as an outlet for the emotionally deprived and disturbed. Virgo calmly comprehends that the true guilt for deliberately arousing the emotionally healthy to join and increase the ranks of the disturbed lies *elsewhere* — in places other than the brothels.

After a while, the Taurus man will grow to appreciate his Virgo girl's own special brand of honesty, and realize that her tendency to avoid labels, and to analyze things before hastily judging them, is a definite virtue, not a vice. It takes time. She might even someday cause her affectionate Bull to admit that a woman who was once a prostitute was the only one who really *believed* the man who promised her he would conquer death — the only one of all his fervently devout apostles and followers to go to his tomb on Easter morning to seek him — while all the hypocrites were either weeping in lack of faith, or running around trying to figure out how to escape the wrath of the Roman soldiers, some even going so far as to deny they ever knew him.

A Virgo girl who's in love with a dogmatic-type Bull may have to convince him that her views on public morality don't necessarily reflect her private code of behavior. Like Caesar, a Taurus man expects his woman to be above reproach. She probably is, although she may not be above reproaching *him,* if he turns sex into a subject for humor. To her, sex is a beautiful, pure emotion that deserves respect — and a good deal of concentration and practice to make it perfect. Her cool, analytic approach may initially chill the Bull's more direct and sensual lovemaking attitudes, but they'll probably find a way around such a temporary impasse between them. As with the other 5-9 Sun Sign Patterns, romantic love and sentimental affection will play equally as important a part as passion in their sexual union. Most of the time, this man and this woman will be wonderfully able to fulfill each other's silent needs, through the rare intimacy of understanding common to all 5-9 vibrations, especially to those of the Earth Element.

Practicality may not sound like a romantic word. Yet, with these two, it can form a deep and comforting bond between them, a strong cord to encircle their love. Neither Virgo nor Taurus is the kind to indulge in passionate emotions for no reason, or to become enraged over things that can't be helped by anger. He may brood a little — and she may have some mild attacks of indigestion — but on the whole, they'll both agree with the alcoholic's creed: "Give me the grace to change the things I can, to accept the things I cannot, and the wisdom to know the difference." (It's doubtful, though, that they heard the words at an AA meeting. It takes tremendous pressure and unbearable anguish to drive a typical Earth Sign to either drink or drugs.) When the rest of the world seems to be crazily dipping back and forth, she feels safe only with him — and should he happen to bump into the uncontrolled, abrasive emotions of a stranger, he'll run back to the security of her arms, the refreshing, quiet stream of her controlled feelings. He'll say something richly humorous that strikes her funny, she'll laugh her little Virgo silver bell laugh . . . . . and then "practicality" can become a very romantic word. She may be finicky, yes — but unreasonable ? Never.

There's a chain of sympathy, bright and golden, connecting the Virgo girl's obsession for "little things" with the Taurus man's enjoyment of the senses. He likes the way new pencils smell like cedar. She adores sharpening them to a fine point. He likes the crisp, clean, cold feel of falling snow on his cheeks . . . . she's fascinated by the tiny, glittering stars it makes on the sidewalk. He likes to chew pine needles, to taste their fresh, green, spicy Christmas smell. She loves to pick them up and place them in neat stacks, one by one.

The Virgin and the Bull can spend their lives together drenched in the ecstasy of contemplating all the small and ordinary wonders around them. It's such a fiercely gorgeous (and natural) "high" — if only they don't smother it by expecting too much. The eternal perfection she seeks is a mirage. The eternal security he seeks — likewise. They're both looking for a sure thing. But the nearest they may ever come to a sure thing is each other.

☆ ☆ ☆ ☆ ☆ ☆

TAURUS

Earth — Fixed — Negative
Ruled by Venus (also by the
  Planet Pan-Horus)
Symbol: The Bull
Night Forces — Feminine

LIBRA

Air — Cardinal — Positive
Ruled by Venus
Symbol: The Scales
Day Forces — Masculine

The **TAURUS-LIBRA** *Relationship*

"Oh, well, if you look at it that way . . . . . ."
"What other way is there to look at it ?"

Anyone who wants to understand an association between Taurus and Libra (both presently ruled by Venus) should contemplate the elements. That's the first step to knowing who's on first and what's on second in any kind of ball game involving two very different individuals.

Don't jump to the hasty conclusion that the earthy Taurean is much stronger than the airy Libran, and that both of them could be burned to a cinder by a raging Fire Sign like Aries, Leo, or Sag. Both Earth and Fire may appear to be more dangerous than Air. Earth is certainly heavier. Fire is certainly more consuming. We all know what damage an earthquake, or a flaming volcano, can do. Surely a mass of Air (the essence of Libra), ethereal as it is, and constantly moving around — can't do much harm, compared to a solid mountain of Earth, like Taurus.

You'll have to turn to physics and chemistry for the truth. Air is the chief nourisher of life. We all need air to breathe, therefore it's comforting, not to mention handy, to have around. But are you aware that, statistically, air kills more people every year, in one way or another, than all the other elements combined? Air may be invisible. It may have no definite shape, and it certainly doesn't seem capable of affecting anything as material as Earth. However, if you've ever been lolling around among the coconuts in the South Sea islands when a typhoon struck, you'll know that things aren't always what they may seem. Especially Air. And especially Libra, the *Cardinal* of the three Air Signs (the other two being Gemini and Aquarius). Libra represents the astrological Air Element in its most active form. End of lesson. End of moral. End of warning? Yes, that's better — end of the warning to those Bulls who think they can plant a heavy foot on the Libra Scales and topple these pleasant people into submission.

In no way, dear Bulls, is Libra passive. Yet Libra may appear to be a pushover for a tougher personality. Here is this absolutely charming person (except when he or she is playing "cranky crocodile"), this dimpled, beautiful (or handsome) creature, with bright, intelligent eyes, a smile that warms the cockles of the heart, and the serenity of the spirit, a bland, innocent expression — and a voice that's faintly reminiscent of church bells, ringing high in the Swiss Alps.

Surely a person of such obviously gentle amiability couldn't possibly be a threat. Ah, but that Libra smoothness of manner is but a soft camouflage which enables the sharp spear of the Libran's clever, logical mind to penetrate, *with a minimum of resistance*. Libra knows very well that the immature rashness of Aries, the rude frankness of Sagittarius, the arrogance of Leo — and the immovable obstinacy of Taurus — are nothing but obstacles to success. They're detrimental to the carrying out of one's real purpose — winning the controversy and getting one's own way, which is all that counts in the final analysis, to Libra. And that sort of deduction, in itself, you must admit, is a clear and indisputable display of Libra logic.

If you don't believe these insights, check with your Republican senator or congressman, regarding both their personal and group confrontations with Libran President Jimmy Carter — or with someone who served in the Armed Forces, under the immediate command of Libran Dwight Eisenhower — or perhaps with some of the former lovers and husbands of Libran Brigitte Bardot. Maybe someone who tried to move Libran Eleanor Roosevelt from her determined, but flower-strewn, path — or anyone who's ever tangled with Libran author Truman Capote, verbally or otherwise. You will receive immediate confirmation of the astrological facts. And never mind seductive Venus. Venus being the ruler of all Librans, it's only logical that Librans of both sexes tend to operate in the traditional Venus (or feminine) way. And all you male chauvinists know how women manage to get their own way by sweetly charming the enemy into surrender. Libra lads are very much like Libra ladies in this respect.

You say that Taurus is also ruled by Venus? Yes, but with serious reservations. Venus is not the true or natural ruler of the Bulls. Taurus is only borrowing the guidance and influence of Venus from Libra, until the *real* Taurean ruling planet, Pan-Horus,° is telescopically discovered and once again identified. Therefore, although the Bulls also have the benefit of Venus sweetness, tenderness, and softness, she doesn't bestow upon them quite *all* of her favors (such as her secret strategy) as she does with Librans. Rather like a woman doesn't tell all her secrets to every man she guides and influences — only to her true lover, the one who possesses her heart. Pan-Horus will shower Taureans with *other* kinds of power. Wait. (The Bulls will. They're patient.)

There's a general inertia in the nature of the average Taurus man, woman, or child, that causes the Bulls to instinctively acquiesce to the customs of their community, office, classroom, or family circle — to the conventions of society and the laws of their government. If you cross-examine the Bulls, however, you'll find that they don't necessarily obey because they believe all these people and laws are right. It's because the typical Taureans are convinced that ignoring convention or flaunting the law might bring trouble and disharmony, a state of affairs that Venus warns the Bulls to avoid, at whatever cost — the same tip she gives to Librans, you see. It's just received and utilized in different ways by these two. Once a Taurean is driven too far, he or she doesn't lack either strength or courage. Far from it. When it reaches push-to-pull, the Bulls of any age, and both sexes, will defend both their personal principles and their loved ones, fiercely. (You'd better believe it!) But Taurus sees absolutely no sense in stirring up muddy waters or risking violent agitation, just to win a minor point.

Libra does. Winning an intellectual point or decision, however minor, major — or in the middle — is the reason for the Libra person's very existence, symbolized by the Libra Scales, balanced in perfect harmony and justice. If there's any sort of controversial issue at stake, the typical Taureans will simply yawn, or shrug, and state calmly (in those rich, mellow voices that compete with the Libra buttery, whipped-cream voices for sheer appeal) that it doesn't make the slightest difference to them *what* happens in a matter too small to interest them — or one too large to concern them. But nothing is too small or too large to need Libra's careful weighing and balancing and judgment.

Should the bathroom be painted pink or green? Should we impeach the President? Does an electric toothbrush get your teeth cleaner? Should the police crack their clubs over the heads of youngsters who are only expressing their idealism and their disgust with hypocrisy? (The big Libra issue of the sixties.) *On the other hand,* should the young people insult the police by calling them "pigs," when they're only trying to do their duty and keep the

° See footnote page 61.

peace? Is censorship to be tolerated in a land dedicated to freedom of speech and thought? *To look at the other side,* in all fairness, is the lack of basic censorship responsible for the moral degeneration of youth in this country? Will such permissive attitudes lead to America's downfall, as it led to the extinguishing of other great civilizations, such as Babylon, Atlantis, and Rome? But then, *to reconsider,* how can there be liberty if there is censorship of any kind? Is jogging healthy or unhealthy? Should everyone be required to use solar heat (instead of nuclear power) and waterless toilets — for serious ecological reasons? Do the AMA and the FDA have the public's — or their *own* — best interest at heart? Or is this century someday to be known as the "Dark Age" of healing? If the bathroom is painted pink, instead of green, will it clash with the yellow towels? If it's painted green, instead of pink, will it look like a hospital room?

You can understand why Librans have to rest a lot. It isn't fair to call them lazy. When you engage in all that mental activity from the time you wake up in the morning, and can't decide which side of the bed to get out on — until the time you go to sleep at night, and can't decide whether to wear the top or the bottom of your nighty-nights — you're bound to feel a little weary and exhausted once in a while. Not to mention a little edgy.

Most Taureans can get weary and exhausted just from listening to a Libra contemplating all those decisions. It sounds like insanity to the Bulls. Just do what you feel (and therefore *know*) is right, don't let anyone budge you an inch from your position — and SHUT UP about it. That's the average or typical Taurean's philosophy about decisions, in a neat nutshell. To the Bulls, constant argument is the most futile, wasteful, and therefore the most sinful, occupation they can imagine. No one ever really wins an argument except the person who manages to fall asleep and snooze until it's over. No one ever emerges victorious from a debate, right?

Wrong. Librans do. They emerge victorious from all of them, except the ones with which they become quickly bored. It's no wonder they win, when you think of the Libra weapons, smuggled to them by Venus. Charm. Tact. Dimples. (*Somewhere* on their bodies they have dimples. Every last one of them. Whether they show or not.) Where were we? Dimples. Intelligence. Flattery. Optimism. A serene and soothing manner. Those satiny voices. That incredible smile that bursts upon their features like an explosion of pure Sunlight. That gorgeous laugh. And besides all these powerhouse weapons, they have the sneakiness to use against you their spears of logical deduction when you least expect it. I can't stress this danger often enough to the Bulls, who believe their own passive resistance will eventually wear down the Libra friend, relative, business associate, lover, or mate who's trying to prod them, gently, into either verbal or physical action of some kind.

The arguments Libra initiates, manipulates, and finally wins with

Taureans, can cover everything from politics to religion. As for the latter, I once overheard a conversation between a Libran Catholic priest (a Jesuit, naturally) and an obstinate young Taurean, who had stubbornly refused a scholarship to Notre Dame and was bullheadedly determined to become a professional football player. Notice that the subject of football is not even mentioned.

Beginning of Conflict:

LIBRA: (initiating) I suppose you claim to believe in God ?

TAURUS: I most certainly do.

LIBRA: Then, why don't you pray to Him, regarding your vocation, if you aren't *sure* whether or not you want to study law ?

TAURUS: I *am* sure I don't want to study it. (Libra loses the first round. But no matter. The trick didn't work. *This* time.)

LIBRA: (moving right along) But, just in case you *might* be mistaken, why don't you pray ?

TAURUS: Because I'd feel silly, that's why. Prayer isn't scientific.

LIBRA: And yet, you say you believe in God ?

TAURUS: (stubbornly) Of *course* I do. I *told* you I do.

LIBRA: (speaking gently) Then how is it that you don't believe He is wise enough and compassionate enough to guide you ?

TAURUS: Because I've never heard God talking. No one has. It isn't scientific.

LIBRA: You don't believe He can answer prayers ? A God you believe in so strongly ? How can God be so powerless ?

TAURUS: I just told you. I never heard him speak. Scientifically, there's no way He *could* speak.

LIBRA: I see. You won't be satisfied until God appears to you in solid flesh, and says, "Hey ! Why don't you become a scientist ? You'd make a great one ! Forget about law school, young man. Your destiny lies elsewhere," as He spoke to Moses, behind the burning bush.

TAURUS: (genuinely shocked) How did you know I'd rather be a scientist than a lawyer ?

LIBRA: (flashing a heavenly Venus smile of victory) Because I prayed for you this morning, at mass — and suddenly, God revealed it to my subconscious. He answered my prayer, as you can see, without speaking a single word.

TAURUS: Gee ! Okay, Father. From now on, I'll say a prayer everytime I need to make a decision. Could you see about getting my scholarship changed from law school to biology ? I wasn't even sure what I wanted to do until you just made me see. Would you call it a divine revelation ?

LIBRA: That's exactly what it was, my young friend. That's what happens when you pray. I'll check with an associate of mine at Notre Dame tomorrow, and let you know before the day is over.

End of Conflict.

Librans use what is known as the "Socratic method" of discussion. You have to watch them closely. And listen carefully. A Taurean who is too busy resisting to pay attention to Libra logic can trip on his (or her) own obstinacy.

This is an association influenced by the 6-8 Sun Sign Pattern, which means that Taurus represents the eighth astrological house of intriguing mystery (among other matters) to Libra. Of course. Libra would adore to solve the mystery of how the Bulls manage to remain so tranquil, and untouched, by all the raging personal and public controversies around them, so untormented by mental traumas, so frustratingly able to sleep throughout the night, like peaceful babies, never suffering the insomnia of decision-making that tortures Librans, sometimes until dawn — when the Good Lord knows they need their beauty sleep, their rest, as much as Taurus, even more, to keep their equilibriums in balance.

Libra represents, to Taurus, the sixth astrological house of service, among other things. Of course. Didn't our budding scientist Taurean somehow manage to persuade the Libra priest to provide the service of pulling a few strings for him at Notre Dame? Just by kidding around about wanting to play pro football? When *this* Bull was born, his natal Sun was in Taurus, but the Moon and Ascendent were both in Libra.

☆ ☆ ☆ ☆ ☆ ☆

TAURUS *Woman* LIBRA *Man*

◆ ◆◆◆ ◆

Now I understand what had hitherto been bothering me.
. . . . this trick had been in his head all the time.

She is sad about something. It doesn't matter what it is. The world is dark and dismal, and there's no hope that anything will change. Life is real, Life is earnest, Life is serious, Life is monotonous — and Life is certainly negative.

She's a Taurus girl, indulging herself in a rare, but ever-so-deep and blue, binge of futility.

Along comes a Libra man. He sits down quietly next to her, takes her hand gently in his own, and looks at her softly, in silence, after offering her his large, clean handkerchief. She continues to frown, in abject misery. *Men !* Men are part of what's wrong with everything. And here's another one of them, trying to feed her a line so he can seduce her. But wait. *This* one isn't saying a word. He's just sitting there near her, very near . . . . . . peacefully pouring calm all over her, like olive oil — and gazing at her with . . . . is it adoration ? Whatever it is, it's romantic. Then, after a long while, he speaks.

"Never mind, darling. You'll feel better tomorrow." His voice is like creamy-smooth caramel candy — and oh, how she loves creamy-smooth caramel candy ! (So does he, although it's very bad for both of them.) But even this doesn't cheer her. No. Life is real, Life is dull, Life is a great big nothing. Life is a put-on and a put-down. Both.

"No, I won't feel better tomorrow. *I won't. I won't. I won't.*"

Libra speaks again, still sweetly. "You're so beautiful when you're sad. Tears make your eyes sparkle like green emeralds. If it didn't break my heart to know you're unhappy, I'd like to see tears in them all the time. Let's see how they look when you laugh."

Life is real, Life is — well, Life is getting more interesting. But — "No, I can't laugh. I want to, but I can't. I simply *can't.*"

"You *must.* Darling, if you believe long enough, and deeply enough, all good things will come to pass. Not a single dream you ever dreamed will fail to come true, if you keep your emotional balance and look at the bright side." Now, he smiles. A Libra smile is a deadly weapon that should be outlawed, so Libra men could never use it to take advantage of poor Taurus girls, who melt into squidgy fudge ripples when they're shown affection — and are truly appreciated. But so far, they haven't been outlawed. So . . . he smiles.

"Tomorrow will be better. It really will. You'll see."

"No, it won't. I want it to be better, but I just know it won't."

Then he kisses her. *It will.*

Everything will be better tomorrow. The Sun will shine, the flowers will blossom, the dew will be on the buttercups — and the female Bull will be deeply in love for keeps with a charmer who was only trying to be kind, and who may be confused when he discovers that what his romantic sentiment actually meant to her was an ironclad contract of loyalty, for better or for worse, in sickness and in health, for richer or for poorer — seven days a week, twelve months a year — for as many years as they both shall live.

"I do."

The voice you just heard was that of the Libra man, addressing the minister. He didn't have the heart to hurt her, and couldn't decide what excuse to give her, so he thought — "What the heck?" (Librans normally don't swear or curse. Prostitute that heavenly voice with obscenities?) At least, not when they're young enough to say *"I do"* for the first time, they don't swear. After a few marital mistakes, they may occasionally gosh-darn the institution of marriage that so magnetizes them.

So ... what the heck? Why not smell the buttercups, and let her tuck him in at night with passionate kisses, between soft blankets of love? "Why *not*? Why *shouldn't* I marry her? It's *my* Life, isn't it? Marriage is a wonderful thing, she's a beautiful girl, so what's *wrong* with marrying her?"

You see? Already he's trying to start an argument, just like a Libran. Nobody *said* he shouldn't marry her. Did you hear me say that?

It's possible the Libra lover will find he's made the right decision by not making a decision to charm his way out of the Taurus girl's feminine, appealing wiles. They'll probably be as happy as two turtledoves, as they walk, hand in hand, from room to room, through their rose-covered cottage in the country — or if their dreams have been briefly delayed, through their soot-covered apartment in the city.

THE DEN-LIBRARY-LIVING ROOM-PARLOR: They're in perfect agreement here. She loves rich fabrics, in soft colors, a blend of beauty and luxury that makes a room seem warm and comfy. He loves pastel shades that harmonize, lots of bookshelves, loaded with books, furnishings that are quiet and soothing. Maybe a minor tiff over traditional opposed to modern, or a chair or lamp or so, but on the whole ... in agreement. The stereo cost a small fortune, but they're both crazy about it. Who can live without music? Not Libra or Taurus (though he won't like it played too loudly).

THE KITCHEN: They're still holding hands, still draped in harmony. She adores to cook (if she's a typical Taurean), and although she may prefer food like eggplant, potatoes, and vegetables, she's delighted to tickle his palate with the more exotic dishes that send him into appreciative ecstasies (and also perhaps send him to the gym rather frequently to work out — and work off — the calories). Then maybe afterward, a few hours out on the town with his male friends. You know . . a little man talk. But he'll be back for her next meal.

THE BEDROOM: In this room, holding hands may not be enough. They'll probably hold each other closely all night long, every night, in the sheer ecstasy of realizing that the long search, for someone who realizes that love is the most important thing in the world, is over at last. To him, that person is her. To her, that person is him. They're both ruled by Venus, so their sexual problems should be the very least of their worries. But his physical expressions of love may be a little ethereal for her, at times. She may privately wish he'd put a little more emphasis on the physical, and a little less emphasis on the intricate moods of eroticism and fancy he verbalizes so beautifully. He may privately wish she would put a little more stress on imaginative, poetic ways of making love, and a little less stress on simple ordinary bodily contact. However, they'll meet somewhere betwixt and between body, mind, and soul — and probably find their relationship more satisfying than the average couple who exist in only one romantic dimension.

THE BATHROOM: They'll still be billing and cooing in pleasure. Or rather, he'll be billing and cooing — she'll be softly mooing. He loves long, luxurious baths and showers, fluffy bath mats, thick towels, expensive shaving lotion, and rainbow-colored toothpaste for his Libra smile. She loves bubbly bath oils, powders, perfumes, thick bath mats, fluffy towels, and scented soaps.

There's hardly a square foot of space, in or around their home, where they'll disagree. Except perhaps for the front porch. That's where she may sit on the stoop, and wait — and wait — and wait — for him to come home, on those nights he's gone to the gym to work out — and out on the town afterward, with his friends. (Male friends. She hopes.) And maybe the basement.

The basement is the room where she'll spend lots of time helping him keep up his reputation as a handsome Libran charmer. That sort of charisma requires stacks of clean shirts and socks. They must be folded just so, and placed in his drawers, just so. It makes him nervous when his socks don't match, or his new sweaters fade all over his white-on-white shirts. Then he may drift into the habit of charmingly nagging her a little about being a slave to the house (and his laundry). Well, now, *there's* a problem. Which is it ? Does she stay in the basement so much because she's weary of waiting on the front porch for him to come home — because he went out — because he's weary of her being in the basement all the time ? Then maybe it's *his* fault. *On the other hand,* maybe it's *her* fault. Who started it ? *He* started it, by going out so much. *No,* she started it by making him fat with her rich desserts. Or, did he start it, by demanding that his clothes closets be so perfect they'd pass inspection at Yves St. Laurent, when Prince Charles is there making a selection ? He used her fluffy bath towels and scented soap — she used his thick bath mats and talcum. He spent their savings for a golf club membership, and a new car to surprise her, but she wasn't surprised, she was angry, and pouted sullenly for weeks. It sounds confusing, but Libra will straighten it all out with nice, clear logic . . . unless after a while, she turns obstinate and stops listening.

Libra men sometimes behave as though they're trying to drain Life of every ounce of knowledge and every drop of pleasure . . . reading best sellers, rapping with intellectuals, catching films, plays, and concerts . . . soaking up the admiration of pretty girls at parties . . . and soaking up other things.

A Taurus woman prefers to stay home, and cuddle by the fire, maybe go out socially once a week. She can't make jogging a way of life. She needs other interests, and most of them lie in togetherness, the two of them . . . hiking through the woods or going camping, remodeling the house . . . making some common sense out of the present so they can build a future, buy a house in the country, and leave the madness of the metropolis. She was not born for condominiums. She was born for barns and hay and fresh air . . . and country roads to stroll along, hand in hand, with the man she loves.

Not every Libra man is a playboy type. Then again, many of them are. But, playboy or no playboy, he'll insist on keeping his intellect sharp, and one of the ways he does this is by being gregarious. If she wants to continue playing those happy scenes with him in the den, the bathroom, the kitchen, and the bedroom, she'll have to accept the mingling at intermission. He may prefer studying ancient civilizations, dabbling in one of the arts, or grabbing an extra degree or two, to hanging out in a smoky nightclub. But, wherever and however he does his mingling, she should get out of the basement, off the front-porch stoop, into her prettiest dress, and tag along beside him — without pouting.

Maybe she won't enjoy it quite so much as he does, but she'll have to pretend she does, if she expects to someday, through her beautiful patience, entice him into moving into that remodeled barn in New England, or wherever. She should try to laugh about it, with her magnificent sense of humor. After all, tomorrow will be better, remember ? It probably will be better, if there's a harmonious Sun-Moon aspect between their birth charts. If not, well . . . tomorrow may be worse. But on the other hand, nothing is perfect. And isn't that what they promised each other ? For better . . . or for worse ?

"No," answers the Libra man, sadly. "Tomorrow *won't* be better, I'm *sure* of it. Life is real, Life is earnest, Life is a put-on, and a put-down, a big fat nothing. *I'm* a big fat nothing."

Her voice is like creamy-smooth caramel, when she soothes him. "You aren't a big, fat nothing, darling. You're handsome and brilliant, and . . your eyes shine like emeralds when they're full of tears. If you believe long enough, and deeply enough, all good things will come to pass. We'll have to keep our emotional balance and look at the bright side." Then she smiles, a dazzling smile, and his heart turns over.

"Those are such beautiful thoughts, sweetheart. So wise. Where did you ever learn such a lovely philosophy of Life," he asks, now smiling back at her.

". . . from someone I knew, a long, long time ago. He taught me everything I know about life . . . and love. I miss him. I wish I could find him again. I wish he would come home."

Strangely . . . . . . they're back in each other's arms again. We should leave them alone now, because he just whispered into her buttercup ear, "I *have* come home — to stay."

But wait. Let's listen for just another moment. She's sighing, making contented little mooing sounds. "Do you suppose you could take a day off next week, so we could go out in the country and look at some farmhouses for sale?"
"Why wait for next week? Let's go right this minute."

Yes, tomorrow *will* be better. Not perfect, but better. After they've moved to the countryside, he'll glance up at her some night, when they're sitting by the fire, and begin sharpening his Libra logic and intellect again. "You know what I've been thinking? That promise about — 'all good things come to pass.' What it really means is — all good things will *come* — comma — to *pass*. Nothing ever remains. Everything is always changing. Like that warning, 'even this shall pass away.' I suppose that includes the sadness, as well as the gladness. If you wait long enough, the gladness returns again."

You see? The fresh air and the hay and the green fields . . and the cows . . . didn't dull his mind at all. But he doesn't have to teach her anything about "waiting long enough." Patience is her secret power, over Life, and Love . . . and *him*.

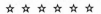

TAURUS *Man* LIBRA *Woman*

*However, John continued to sleep so placidly on
the floor, that she allowed him to remain there.
"And I know you meant to be kind," she said, re-
lenting. "So you may give me a kiss."*

A Libra woman is unpredictable. You never know how she's going to manage
to get her own way. All you can be sure of is that she'll get it.

"What?" you'll exclaim. "A sweet, feminine girl like her is bossy?"
Yes. A sweet, feminine girl like her is bossy. But that doesn't mean she has to
advertise the fact by having it stamped on her bikini — "*Bossy.*" (Someone
might think she's a female Bull.) The Libra woman is ruled by Venus, the
gentle planet of peace and love and beauty and harmony — all those delicious
things. A Taurus man is ruled by Venus too. But Taurus is a feminine sign.
And Libra is a masculine sign. That doesn't make her a tomboy, anymore
than it makes him a sissy (the *Bull* a *sissy*?). It has deeper implications. It's
always easier for a man to be born under a masculine sign, and for a woman
to be born under a feminine sign. It makes doing what comes naturally —
more natural. However, it isn't necessarily unfortunate the other way
around. Usually, a masculine vibration only makes a girl more spunky — and
a feminine vibration only makes a man more sensitive. There's nothing
wrong with the sexes trading a few virtues back and forth. The danger lies in
overdoing it. These two probably will not. They may *under*do it.

Of all men born under a feminine Sun Sign, the Bull is less likely to
overdo the feminine qualities of passivity, acquiescence, submission, and so
forth. It simply keeps his virility and stubbornness balanced by sweetness and
tenderness, if he doesn't overemphasize the caveman bit. The Libra girl will
have a little more trouble with the sexual balancing act. After all, she's
symbolized by the Scales, and scales have a delicate mechanism of adjustment. Her innate sense of fairness and impartial judgment, plus her
masculine Sun Sign vibes, may lead her to announce: "Darling, I'm joining a
women's lib group. We're going to picket the White House."

His innate sense of conventional behavior, plus his respect for authority
and firm convictions about a female's function in life, may lead him to
answer: "You make a fool of yourself in front of the President, and I'll
liberate you by chaining you to the bed until you get some sense, woman."
Under that kind of dictatorial attitude, Venus di Milo can turn into Stonewall
Jackson, as her Scales dip precariously from feminine to masculine.

A Libra girl nearly always is beautiful. Even if her features are plain, her absolutely stunning smile makes you think she's beautiful. She has dimples, her eyes are soft, her voice is clear and lovely, her manners are graceful. She lets you pull out her chair, hold open her door, and carry her packages with an air of appealing helplessness. Outwardly, she's an angel of femininity. Inwardly, she's driven by the masculine principles of her Cardinal Sign of Leadership: force — strength — courage — positive action — penetration — conquer and dominate. She can manage her own career, and she's adept at getting everything she wants out of life — or from a man. It doesn't mean she's invulnerable to hurt, but she wears a tougher suit of armour to protect her from it than her manner might suggest . . . . . . and she recuperates quickly.

Taurus recuperates slowly from a broken heart. All the more reason for him to be sure he knows the rules before he plays any romantic games with a Libra female. The Bull makes decisions only after careful consideration. He doesn't like to discuss a situation until it's already settled in his mind. Then he acts with deliberation and seldom changes his opinion. She acts with equal deliberation and also seldom changes her opinion. Once she's made up her mind, she carries through with incredible energy and purpose. So she can't understand why people unjustly accuse her of being indecisive. What gives her such an unfair reputation is the period of weighing and balancing she goes through *before* she finally makes up her mind. With Taurus, the decision-making period is sensibly utilized for silent contemplation. With Libra, it's intellectually utilized for lengthy discussions of pro and con that can last far into the night. She may have occasion to resent his lack of enthusiasm in contributing to the talkathon.

HER: I'm for legalized abortion . . . I think. Do you believe anyone has the right to tell a woman what to do with her own body ?

HIM: I never thought about it. Nobody ever tried to tell me what to do with my body.

HER: Well, *think* about it. What would you do if someone raped you, and then you found out you were pregnant ?

HIM: (yawning) I'd change my name from Earl to Gladys.

HER: Please be serious, sweetheart. Do you believe the Catholic Church should be allowed to lobby against legal abortion, and claim it's murder ?

HIM: According to both the Bible and the Constitution, they should.

HER: Maybe you're right. On the other hand, what about the population explosion ?

HIM: (yawning again) An ounce of prevention is worth a pound of cure. That's what my grandmother used to say.

HER: That's true. An abortion can create emotional scars in both the woman and the man. Metaphysically speaking, a soul shouldn't be denied its channel of birth. Still, when you look at the other side, if a girl is unmarried, and her parents won't help her . . . . .

HIM: So she calls a home for unwed mothers. Say, listen, are you pregnant?

HER: Ah! That's just the point. Do those homes influence the girl in her decision about adoption — as opposed to abortion — as opposed to keeping her baby? It certainly isn't fair if . . . . . . *Earl*? Earl!

HIM: ZZZZZZZZZZZZZZZZZZZZzzzzzzzzzzzzzzzz

She shouldn't judge him too harshly. He tried. But as soon as he satisfied himself that the problem under discussion wasn't his *personal* concern, he lost interest. She could awaken him very easily, by turning out the lights, and giving him a silent message about a subject that *does* affect him, intimately — making love. Just because she failed to arouse him into passionate verbal declarations and opinions doesn't mean she won't be able to arouse him physically. A Bull can always be led into becoming passionate about passion.

The physical magnetism between this man and woman is often very powerful, probably the basis for the initial attraction — and familiarity will seldom breed contempt. It will more likely add depth to the sexual expression of their love. Her approach may be a few shades too abstract for his sensual, earthy needs. Yet, they are both sentimental romanticists who understand how to blend eroticism with affection to achieve total fulfillment together. This is a 6-8 Sun Sign Pattern stressing sexual curiosity and satisfaction — and also emphasizing unselfish devotion and service.

Undeniably, the Taurus man is often a great blessing to the Libra woman. His very presence soothes her restless spirit. And no one can more solidly and dependably guide her through those Libran moments of sometimes agonizing indecision more comfortingly than the Bull. His warmness and humor — his reliability and common sense — are often just the qualities she's been searching for out there among the clouds. After all, even the birds rest in the trees now and then . . . and build their nests there, where they feel safe and secure . . . however much they may enjoy flying.

Another rather lovely thing about these two is that her natural Pollyanna optimism can act as a beautiful balance for the Bull's natural tendency toward pessimism. No one can cheer up a Taurus man, when he's down in the dumps of depression, as effortlessly as this charming lady. He could balk, if she tries to drag him into her social whirl, or expects him to blow up the printed balloons she carries in the protest parades. But he'll be a lovable Teddy Bear when she wheedles him with her wide smile and coaxes him with her maple-sugar voice. He privately admires her intelligence, as long as she acknowledges the fact of masculine superiority. It's a rare Bull who truly believes, in his heart, that men and women are equal in all ways. A Taurus man will be proud of the way his Libra lady manages things so smoothly.

The trick is to keep him from discovering that her real talent lies in managing *him*.

TAURUS: I suppose you're thinking I need a shave. Well, I just got back from a three-day camping trip, you know, and I . . . . . .

LIBRA: Sweetheart, I think it's a perfectly *marvelous* idea! Why didn't you tell me you had decided to grow a beard?

TAURUS: A *beard*? And look like some freaked-out hippie? *Me*? You've lost your senses, woman. Never!

LIBRA: Other men might. But *you'd* look like one of the apostles. How long will it take to grow it completely?

TAURUS: I was just getting ready to sha. . . uh, well, it might take a few weeks, I guess. One of the apostles, huh?

LIBRA: I think . . . . . . Matthew. Or maybe Mark. When did you decide to do it, darling?

TAURUS: Oh, you know how it is, sitting around in the woods, by the campfire. Somehow, it gives you a different perspective on things . . . .

☆ ☆ ☆ ☆ ☆ ☆

TAURUS

Earth — Fixed — Negative
Ruled by Venus (also by the
   Planet Pan-Horus)
Symbol: The Bull
Night Forces — Feminine

SCORPIO

Water — Fixed — Negative
Ruled by Pluto
Symbols: Scorpion & Eagle
Night Forces — Feminine

The **TAURUS-SCORPIO** Relationship

*The more quickly this horror is disposed
of the better.*

*I*t is not, of course, *always* a horror, although the potential is there. When they really try, Taurus and Scorpio often get on well together, sometimes superbly. If the Moon Sign of one is conjunct, sextile or trine to the other's Sun, they can chart new worlds of the mind or spirit, in space or on the ground. It can be a beautiful, lasting relationship in science, literature, the arts — or in simple human closeness. When they have a negative aspect between their Suns and Moons, they will remain opposed and powerful enemies, until one or both of them evolve to the concepts of tolerance, compassion and unselfishness.

As with all 7-7 Sun Sign Patterns, Scorpio and Taurus each sense in the other the missing qualities that would make him (or her) whole and complete. The magnetic polarity of their opposition on the astrological wheel tugs on them rather firmly — for good or evil. Scorpio is everything Taurus wants to be. And Taurus is everything Scorpio would like to be. However, each of them would almost rather literally be caught dead than admit it. Scorpio is not a dual sign, yet the Eagles live in two worlds at the same moment—the world of wherever their compulsive soul-yearning takes them and the visible, material world, believed in and seen by ordinary mortals. Scorpios float somewhere between both, a law unto themselves, as inscrutable as the Great Pyramid of Giza. To disguise themselves, and to keep people from seeing them dangling in the air like that, most Scorpios wear a mask. It could be a mask of sweet gentleness, icy detachment or cold practicality. But beneath it, they are all smoldering, boiling, bubbling cauldrons of intense emotion.

Taurus owns no false faces. Like the other Earth Signs, the Bulls don't particularly like to dress up on Halloween—either to fool people or to frighten them. They just want to make them laugh (and make them behave). The Bulls live firmly and tangibly in one world only—Earth. Good old, familiar, safe Terra Firma. They are what they are, and nothing or no one will ever change them from what they were born to be—veritable mountains of dependability, courage, patience and determination. Although the average Taureans weren't born with Scorpio's power of penetration and steely will, nor the Eagle's awesome regenerative potential, they do embody the true and genuine inner calm Scorpio longs to possess, the total emotional control Pluto-ruled men and women only *pretend* to own. It is for this that Scorp envies the Venus-ruled Taureans. (Now and then, a Bull is born whose Moon and Ascendent are in Scorpio—then look out! I mean, this person is a power-house supreme.)

As for the typical Bulls, they wouldn't bother to plod across the street to either own or imitate Pluto's emotional intensity, but they would trudge thousands of miles, even leap over barbed wire fences—uphill, if necessary (if no one was looking)—to gain Scorp's ability to *know* without any kind of calculation . . . *to simply know*. Taureans would give all their gold to be able, like the Eagles, to stare into someone's soul and learn all that person's secrets. If only they could master this ability, the Bulls could build their empires faster. And if Scorpio could master, in turn, the Taurean impassivity toward Life's magnetic emotional storms, they could accomplish their mysterious purposes with far less toll on the inner psyche.

Naturally, when these two get together in any sort of association—business, family, friendship or love—and decide to lend each other the use of their individual talents and virtues, working side by side, they can change destiny.

A blend of their qualities through a close *"relation"*-ship is never bland. It can tremble and shake with both highs and lows. I have a Taurus friend with a Scorpio brother, and they're equally devoted to their Piscean mother. But when the Bull moved into a new house, he was too busy with the pressures of several financial crises to get in touch with his Neptune mother right away. Besides, he didn't want to worry her with his personal problems. One night, the Bull and his wife invited the Scorpio brother for dinner, and he accepted. They prepared his favorite meal, the children were all washed, and brushed, and excited about seeing their uncle — but he didn't arrive. When they called his home, he wasn't in. The puzzling Pluto silence continued for several days. Then one morning, a note came in the mail from the "missing" Scorpion relative. It said, simply: "There's a very lonely lady in the Bronx who hasn't heard from you in too long a time. After you get in touch with her, I'll be happy to come for dinner."

The direct, uncomplicated Bull was red-flagged into fury over his brother's undeniably devious behavior. Why didn't he just come right out and say he was angry when he was first invited to the house instead of pulling the mystery routine and the silent treatment?

Why? Because he's a Scorp, and that's the way Scorpios are. Simple directness has no sting to it, you see, and this Eagle was determined to sting his sibling. The surprise element is necessary for completely effective Pluto retaliation. Yet, shortly afterwards, when the Bull's financial woes had reached the emergency stage, the Scorp offered to lend his brother the cash he needed, without even being asked. That's *also* the way Scorpios are.

One of the qualities Taurus possesses, and Scorpio usually lacks, is a sense of the ridiculous. There are Eagles who possess a fine sense of humor, but it's seldom along the lines of the absurd. Humor is Nature's great balancer. It bestows a sane perspective to life, and helps the Bulls avoid the twin (no relation to Gemini!) destructive influences of self-pity and egocentricity. When you laugh, you're surrounded with warm, happy people. A joke attracts a crowd. And when you laugh at *yourself*, everyone adores you — because you've made yourself as human and fallible as they know they are themselves, allowing them to feel, for a brief moment, not so aware of their own vulnerability. Perhaps the lack of such easy and spontaneous humor, of the type which attracts a crowd, is why Scorpios often prefer to travel alone and incognito. It's difficult for the Pluto-ruled to feign fallibility. Besides, they have no need to be adored.

A Bull might approach a Scorpion in a typically playful (and rare talkative) mood, and call out: "Hey! Why are you hiding behind that bushy beard and the dark shades? Are you afraid people will find out you're really Barnabas the Vampire? I've got it! The beard and glasses make you feel safe, is that right, Barny?" (If the Scorp is a lady Eagle, substitute "Vampy" for "Barny" — sans the beard, of course.)

"Right, Barny? (Or Vampy.) They replace the security blanket you chewed on and took to bed as a kid." (The Bull is thinking of his or her own blanket-Teddy-Bear stage of childhood.)

Scorpio will not laugh. The Scorpion will just murmur quietly, without so much as the twitch of a whisker, *"Perhaps."*

But Taurus persists. "No kidding? Looking like one of the Smith Brothers on the cough drop box makes you feel secure?" Whereupon, Scorpio will smile Pluto's faint smile of warning, prior to deadly attack, and remark in deep, Velveeta cheese tones . . .

"You're jealous, aren't you? Jealous that I have a beard, and you don't. Is it because a beard symbolizes masculinity and you're sensitive about that, for some reason?"

Now, nothing in heaven or hell can wound the ultra-virile Bull as cruelly as an insinuation, in jest or otherwise, of *that* nature. The Scorpion has struck again, whether the name is Barnabas the Vampire, alias Vampy or Barny — or Leonard the accountant. The Eagle has drawn blood. Taurus retreats, hurt and puzzled that a simple, good-natured joke laid an egg, floundering in water over any Bull's head. Of course, when pushed too far, the Taureans won't retreat. They'll paw the ground, snort — and charge — totally destroying the Scorpion, who will then, in his (or her) final moments, whip around that dangerous tail, deliver the fatal sting — and they'll *both* fall down dead. Naturally, I'm referring to an imaginary scene between the Nature symbols of the two Sun Signs. In a similar human encounter, you may translate it your own way.

Speaking of Nature symbols, I trust the reader is not confused by the reference to Pluto-ruled people as both "Scorpion" and "Eagle." An Eagle is a Scorpion regenerated into the higher octave of his or her own Superconscious, capable of projecting all the finer, positive qualities of the Sun Sign. Like a kind of reincarnation *within* a reincarnation, so to speak. All Scorpio people are Eagles *part* of the time. If they keep trying, they can *remain* on this high level permanently, lifted from the Scorpion's sands, into the Eagle's skies of enlightenment, through aspiration — on the wings of the repudiation of revenge, soaring into a dedication to defend the helpless.

Many Scorps do appreciate humor, but normally only when it can be seen or projected in an impersonal way. Such as on stage or screen, or among friends — *watching*. Very few Scorpions find it hilarious when the giggles are at their own expense, and they're not cheery back-slapper types, as the Bulls can be, when they're feeling especially jolly. The typical Scorp will chuckle sincerely at funnies only when in the company of good and trusted friends.

Scorpio Mike Nichols, American comedy writer, author, performer and director (a rather large hunk of comedic talent), doesn't exactly have a reputation for being a continual bag of laughs in his personal life when the joke is on him. The same thing is true of country comedienne Minnie Pearl. She's a howl on stage, but privately she's an intense, dedicated Scorpio lady, with passionate political and other convictions.

Scorpio and Taurus do have some things in common. They both have a tendency to be reserved with strangers. Neither of them are blabbermouths, and neither is inclined to make long speeches unless there's something important to say. Also, both equally dislike being rudely questioned by inquisitive people. But their reactions to such intrusions are quite different. Scorpio will use subtle strategies to keep his (or her) secrets secret. When subtlety fails, the Scorpio will simply lie, justifying it as an inalienable right when dealing with those who would violate his (or her) sacred privacy. (At any other time, Scorpios are the very souls of integrity, however.) The silent implication is: "You pried into my personal affairs, and you got what you deserved." (The snooper should be grateful for the lie. It's better than receiving a sting from the Scorpion tail. Sometimes, both defense measures are employed, simultaneously.)

The Bulls have an equal sense of privacy, and you won't find them telling all they know, any more than Scorps do. But the Bulls are not subtle, and they'll seldom bother with a lie. Taurus will squelch a prying person directly, with a plain statement of fact, like: "Mind your own business, jerk, and buzz off."

No one can say "no" more emphatically, and mean it, than Taurus and Scorpio. If they say it to each other, that's the end. But when they say "yes" to one another, a solid, lasting friendship will develop. Because the Bulls and Eagles have one more thing in common. *Loyalty.* For those they love and trust, they'll move mountains, against any odds. They both consider a kindness exactly as they consider a loan at the bank — to be paid back promptly, with interest.

☆ ☆ ☆ ☆ ☆ ☆

TAURUS *Woman* **SCORPIO** *Man*

◄◄◆►►

Was that boy asleep, or did he stand waiting . . . with his dagger in his hand ?

There was no way of knowing . . . .

In the beginning, a Taurus girl may be wary of accepting the silent invitation in the hypnotic eyes of a Scorpio man. She's heard some disturbing rumors about him. She's been told he's ruthless and sexy. Admittedly, that's a strong combination, and it could make anyone a little cautious.

A Scorpio male has many shining virtues to offset his dark vices, but he is not one of the Rover boys, with a naive trust in the goodness of human nature. Nor is he Andy Hardy or Tiny Tim. Through the magic window of his penetrating Pluto gaze, he sees too much of human nature to have much faith in its goodness. He has more faith in his own instinct for truth and decency. In God he trusts. Of everyone else he is suspicious. That's why he appears to be ruthless. Yet, if he's an Eagle (instead of the Grey Lizard or Stinging Scorpion I described in the Scorpio chapter of my first book *Sun Signs*) he only destroys the enemies who would destroy him or the helpless (and he knows which ones they are). Those who merely step on the Scorpion's tail by accident he will just sting lightly, to deliver Pluto's message that they are not ever to again impose on him — or upon a defenseless friend. Then he nobly allows them to go on their way, unharmed. It's a lesson. That's all. *Learn it* is his unspoken warning to the offender — *or beware of the next encounter.*

Actually, his actions are impeccably fair and just, never petty — and always in line with his own strict ethics. Scorpio never asks of anyone what he is not prepared and willing to give of himself. It's a philosophy similar to the code of that family-oriented society called the "*M*others *A*nd *F*athers *I*ntellectual *A*ssociation," which is sometimes abbreviated by its five initials, and symbolized by a mythical, legendary Black Hand. With Scorpio, as with this society, the black hand symbolizes protection for the weak, the poor and the helpless, as much as it symbolizes a threat to the disloyal, the greedy, the pushy and the snoopy. At least, these were the noble Robin Hood-like sentiments in the beginning, at the society's birth in the eighteenth century, in Sicily, before the sincerity of the motive became stained by decades of dark deeds.

Many people think of Robin Hood himself as a Sagittarian. He was certainly an expert archer, and probably also a Sun Sign Archer, but I've personally always felt that his Moon was in Scorpio. Was Robin Hood ruthless in his attempts to "distribute the wealth"? Only the bad guys and the wealthy thought so.

Just as every individual member of the *M*others *A*nd *F*athers *I*ntellectual Association is not above reproach, every individual Scorpion is not above reproach. There are, in both groups, some well-intentioned and some evil souls. However, here we're considering the average Scorp, and playing the percentages. So, let's say the Taurus girl soon loses her initial timidity concerning the Scorpio man's ruthlessness.

In reality, the Bull fears very little which is tangible. Besides, he's already made her feel warm and secure by sending her brother to summer camp, bringing her mother flowers, treating her like a lady, and treating her father as an older and wiser senior citizen — *a man of respect.* But Taurus is not quite so brave when it comes to the *in*tangible, the unseen or the emotional — so how about the rumors of his sexiness?

What can I tell you? Like I said, they are probably true. A Scorpio male is not an impotent eunuch, or a bashful, stuttering schoolboy. He is, in every sense, a man. He's as virile as Aries, as sentimental as Libra, as passionate as Leo, as sensitive as Pisces, and as sensual as the Taurus woman herself. If you add that all up, and it comes out as one word — sexy — well, is that something to complain about? True, an astrologically unenlightened woman might naturally fear such a strong masculine charisma. But what's to fear? This man doesn't run around seducing innocent damsels, as some astrology books would have you believe. It would be difficult to make an accurate survey of such a thing, of course, but any "violated" females would quite probably be Scorpio's willing victims.

To a Taurus woman, physical proof of her deepest feelings is a necessity of Life. So the alleged Scorpio "sexiness" shouldn't deter her from examining the possibilities of experiencing Life and Love with this man. If she does, you can be sure she'll experience both in all of their various facets, nuances, shades and tones. What Scorpio finds fascinating, he probes and penetrates to its deepest meaning. What he finds unworthy, he causes to disappear by coldly ignoring it, as if it didn't exist. Eventually, it doesn't — at least, not in his own awareness, or in his immediate vicinity. That goes for both people and things. Obviously then, the problem lies in being sure they both find the same things and people interesting — and the same ones boring. Otherwise, there can be crossed wires, crossed purposes and possible emotional chaos. A Taurus girl can get attached like glue to a person or an object, and it could be disconcerting to have a dear friend or relative, a treasured cream pitcher or hooked rug, just disappear into thin air because the man you love doesn't share your enthusiasm or taste.

If their birth charts indicate a harmonious Luminary aspect between them (Sun and Moon) they'll share the same experiences, and blend their polarized individual personalities into one powerful vibration. If not, well maybe a little of that caution she felt initially will be called for, after all.

Since this is a 7-7 vibratory pattern, he has what she needs, and she has what he wants — and will probably get — (explained in the previous section more clearly). Naturally, an attraction like that will cause these two to be pulled together like bar magnets when they meet, assuming they're both free, willing and able to tackle a rich relationship. Sometimes, even assuming they're not. Did you ever try to keep two bar magnets from clinging together? Pick up a pair at the hardware store and experiment. It will be an excellent illustration of the magnetic law of attraction and repulsion in astrological romantic compatibility.

A Taurus girl is practical. She's not flighty, impulsive, or a misty dreamer. In her steady heart, passion is not easily or quickly aroused. It grows slowly into fullness. But once her senses are caught by someone, when she finds herself noticing the scent of his hair, trembling at the sound of his voice, melting at the sight of his walk or his smile, and quivering inside when he touches her hand, her practical common sense may be suspended indefinitely. Despite her natural earthy stability, a Taurus woman in love is more vulnerable than a girl Fish, and that's pretty vulnerable.

She was born under a Fixed Sign, so she won't change her mind, once she recognizes her lover as the man she's been waiting for (sometimes for years). If he's a Scorpio, she can count on his loyalty matching hers (unless they have serious afflictions between their mutual charts). She's possessive in love, but that's not quite the same thing as sudden flares of unreasonable jealousy. Taurus is not jealous. Jealousy is an emotion that has roots in a basic insecurity. *Possessiveness* describes the pride a Taurean takes in anything she owns — and the devotion she lavishes upon it, whether it's a man, or an heirloom bedspread.

A Scorpio male will understand the difference between these two words, and he'll give her very little reason to experience jealousy, while he rather enjoys her possessiveness. For all his reputation as a sex symbol, this man seldom looks upon sex as a pleasant pastime or a series of casual encounters. To him, sex is the reason for both life and death, the doorway to each, the one mystery he may never completely solve. It is, therefore, very close to being a religion to him. Which means that, when he finds the right partner, his concept of sex will be pure, though intense, and experimental promiscuity is not part of that concept. Therefore, regardless of astrological rumors, he's less likely than most men to be unfaithful to the woman he loves, and if she was born under an Earth or Water Sign, the chances are even smaller that he will deceive her. The earthy Taurus woman understands the passion that rages and burns in Scorpio, perhaps better than any other female, and she'll respond with a matching intensity of physical expression. However, although she may welcome his passionate lovemaking, she may not be as enthusiastic about his passionate convictions outside their physical relationship.

He's a mysterious blend of cool reason and hot emotion, though he chooses to expose only the former, keeping the latter a dark secret. She'll approve of his cool reason, his surface poise and his practicality, because they match her own. But hot emotions leave her cold — and disapproving. Scorpio becomes involved through his emotions, which, like the still waters of his Sun Sign, run very deep. From deep, it's only a step to passionate involvement. Whether it's politics, neighbors, career, ecology, space travel, relatives, abortion — whatever the issue — Scorpio takes a passionate, emotional stand — or shows his disinterest unmistakably. Taurus has little sympathy for the violent extremes of love and hate. To her, it's an exhausting and unnecessary strain on the nerves. This will be the underlying cause, in one form or another, behind all their disagreements, major or minor.

For the benefit of the Taurus woman who is sad and lonely, because she's had a quarrel with a Scorpion she loves, I'll reveal one of his secrets to her, contained within a verse I once wrote, in an attempt to help any unsuspecting soul, who's troubled by being unable to solve this man's Pluto mystery. He is speaking to her . . . .

> *your icy voice put out the stars*
> *it cracked my heart, and broke it in splinters*
> *your tone as cold as Colorado winters*
>
> *but I promise to soon forget*
> *the contract we almost made . . . you'll feel*
> *the swift response of an equal*
>   *as the dream begins to fade*
> *I'll drown you in pseudo kindness*
> *and a casual, friendly glance*
> *I can almost imagine your blindness*
>   *as I watch and wait*
> *for the chance*
> *to suddenly — cruelly — make you know*
> *how easy it was to let you go* °

It's called *The Sting of the Scorpion*. And here's the secret I promised to reveal to the Taurus lady. It wasn't easy for him to let her go. It tore him apart. But he hid the pain of his own grief beneath the frozen features of Scorpio detachment. Now that she's been told, she can, perhaps, penetrate his disguise and heal those broken splinters if she remembers this: when she's angry, a Taurus woman can truly project an "icy voice" and a "cold tone." How can she see how he feels inside, while she's wearing the blinders of stubbornness? The only thing that kind of attitude will bring is "the swift response of an equal" — and he *is* her equal. In Fixity . . . . in patience . . . . in loyalty . . . but also in remembering hurt . . . . and in the need to learn how to forgive.

★ ★ ★ ★ ★ ★

° From *Venus Trines at Midnight* by Linda Goodman.

TAURUS *Man* SCORPIO *Woman*

---

*He was a brave man; but for a moment he had to stop
there and wipe his brow, which was dripping like a
candle. Then silently he let himself go into the
unknown.*

A Taurus man who feels himself sinking into the mysterious underworld of a
Scorpio female's magnetic attraction, is either headed for what may be the
most traumatic experience of his life — or the most uplifting. The outcome
will definitely not be neutral.

It might be the former, if there's a negative aspect between the Sun and
Moon in their respective horoscopes. But if these two Luminaries are in a
harmonious relationship, it could very well be the latter. Assuming everything is cool with their planets, it's all right for him to sink in, but he might
want to tuck a copy of the Bible under his arm, as he falls into the
immeasurable depth of her love. It's really a good idea to study the Holy
Works before becoming involved with this woman on an intimate basis. No
matter what they say or do, Scorpios can always find a passage in the
Scriptures to justify themselves. And they'll quote it, to make sure you know
their motives are blameless. Not only are they experts on both the Old and
New Testaments, but they also have the psychic ability to read between the
lines — and what Scorpio finds between the lines is quite a testament in itself.

Not every Scorpio girl has the Bible committed to memory, of course,
but it won't hurt to take heed of the possibility. If she doesn't quote the
Scriptures when she's loving him, or stinging him, she may have memorized
large chunks of the Tibetan Book of the Dead. At the very least, she may
have dropped into a couple of Hare Krishna meetings, or had an Egyptian
scarab tattooed somewhere on her body, visible only to the "naked" eye. No?
Then check her dressing table (if you can find the key to unlock it) and see if
she has a pack of tarot cards, or a well-thumbed copy of the I Ching tucked in
among her love potions, exotic perfumes and aphrodisiacs.

I don't mean to imply that this woman's nature is too hot for a Taurean
man to handle, or her psyche too coolly mysterious for him to penetrate.
After all, that silent film star Rudolph Valentino, the sheik to end all sheiks
was a *Taurus*. So the Bull is quite capable of sneaking into a Scorpio girl's
tent, under the stars, with his nostrils dilating romantically. Since she's
chemically attracted to the opposite sex of her opposite Sun Sign (Taurus) she
may even run out of the tent barefoot to meet him. If she does, she'll

resemble Queen Nefertiti herself, in the moonlight. That's what makes it all so special. In the quiet moments of their aloneness together, a Scorpio woman can become to her Taurus man the image of every love goddess down through the ages. In the daytime, she slips on her Scorpion mask and becomes Susan, the shy secretary — Millie, the modest maiden — or Laurie, little-girl-lost.

Despite her apparent tranquility and surface sweetness, this is not a female who is easy to live with. She's fascinating, feminine, intelligent, loyal and passionate. But she is not an innocent, wide-eyed maiden who is willing to become a love object. Scorpio lives in the emotions, but sometimes they're bottled up inside for years. That's why she seems so docile, then suddenly, with no warning, she erupts into boiling anger — or disappears into frozen silence, which is even harder to cope with and certainly more difficult to understand.

For a time, she'll go along with what her man says, unless he becomes too demanding. Then she'll show her hidden strength. Tact and compromise are not her strong points. For that matter, they're not his either. Neither Taurus nor Scorpio has much idea of what it's like to see the other person's point of view. No, that's not quite right. Taurus has trouble seeing another point of view. Scorpio sees it quite clearly, with her uncanny perception. But she still prefers her own wishes to what her ouija board may tell her someone else's are. They'll have to make some adjustments here, or spend their lives together with their backs turned, arms crossed, and mouths sealed in stubborn silence. Both of them were born under a Fixed Sign. But both of them were also born under a feminine sign, so they can be equally gentle and sympathetic, when they choose to use these "negative" vibrations, which are the "feminine" compensations for the "negative" qualities of their Sun Signs.

He's ruled by Venus, the planet of peace and love. She's ruled by Pluto, the planet of explosive passion and mystery. Their sexual compatibility, therefore, is usually full of strange surprises and sensual ecstasies. She associates sex with the mystery of her own existence, and respects it as a sacred act of love. She also has a devouring curiosity about its secret implications, which can only be satisfied by ever deeper intimacy with the man she loves, although there will always be an aura of purity about her desires. Sex is never cheap to a Scorpio woman, and she'll insist on being loved for her whole self, not just for her physical appeal. So will he.

The Taurus man may never totally comprehend their lovemaking in as much depth as she does, but that certainly won't prevent his enjoyment of it. To the Bull, as to the Scorpion, sexual expression is an act of worship, a constant renewal of spiritual strength, through the giving and receiving of passion between them. However, sex alone is never enough for a lasting union, even when it's as fulfilling as it normally is with Taurus and Scorpio in their 7-7 Sun Sign Pattern relationship. Other facets of their love will need constant attention. It's never easy for these two to reconcile after a serious quarrel. Their mutual Fixed vibration keeps them apart. Scorpio says, "I will forgive. But I *cannot* overlook." Taurus varies this only slightly, and says, "I will forgive. But I can never *forget*." They're both lying to themselves. What they really mean is, "I can't forgive." Because, true forgiveness *does* overlook, and true forgiveness *does* forget. The refusal to truly forgive is a dark and evil thing. The seeds thus planted in the heart will grow into cold and lonely isolation, premature aging, chronic disease and emotional neurosis, as surely as an acorn will grow into a giant oak tree.

His comic sense may be another cause for tension between them. The Bull needs an occasional practical joke and a constant touch of humor to make his life, which is serious enough, bright and bearable. She may laugh at his comic remarks, but her eyes won't be smiling, and he'll soon learn she can't stand to be teased, because she's never been able to really laugh at herself. His rich humor is what makes him such a warm human being. Instead of being annoyed by it, if she will let some of his laughter linger in her heart, she might find it's the extra dimension she needs to color her own emotions a few shades lighter.

The love vibration between Taurus and Scorpio is perfectly symbolized by the strange pilgrimage of Taurean silent screen idol Rudolph Valentino's much discussed "Mystery Woman," who, despite whispered rumors, has never been provably identified to this day. Whatever her name may have been, her Sun or Moon Sign was surely Scorpio (which might be a clue to her identity). Yes, she could only have been a deeply bereaved Scorpio woman, conceiving Life, Love, sex and death to be inseparable, as she made her lonely visits to her Taurus lover's grave, dressed completely in black, her face covered by a veil . . . . . . to offer the memory flowers of her intense passion, grief and loyalty . . . . . . each year, with unwavering faithfulness, on the anniversary of his death.

That's the way it is with Taurus and Scorpio. No light flirtation, or casual affair. It will be frigid disinterest, total disaster — or a devotion which will last a lifetime, and beyond that, past forever. All — or nothing at all. The Bible will come in handy, either way.

☆ ☆ ☆ ☆ ☆ ☆

TAURUS

Earth — Fixed — Negative
Ruled by Venus (also by the
  Planet Pan-Horus)
Symbol: The Bull
Night Forces — Feminine

SAGITTARIUS

Fire — Mutable — Positive
Ruled by Jupiter
Symbols: Archer & Centaur
Day Forces — Masculine

The **TAURUS-SAGITTARIUS** *Relationship*

◆◂◉▸◆

. . . . . . for the procession must continue indefinitely
until one of the parties stops or changes its pace.

*T*he Bulls will in no way change their slow, steady pace, so it's up to
Sagittarius to stop running for a spell, now and then, if these two are
ever going to settle down, and cash in on the several possible rewards of
their 6-8 Sun Sign Pattern vibration.

Since the Archers are symbolized by the Centaur, who is half-horse, half-
human, their association will be rather ripping half the time. I use the
English idiom because Sag is so often flying off to foreign countries (or
dreaming about flying off to them). Nearly every Archer secretly longs to
make some sort of a career out of travel, and one way or another most of
them manage to do just that. When Sagittarians are playing the role of the
clown, or the gay philosopher, using the animal, or the rear end of their
Centaur symbol, the Bulls find them highly amusing. Taureans will howl at
the slapstick antics of the Archers, tripping over their speech and their feet.

They feel a warm, protective glow toward the cheerful, well-meaning, good-natured, and somewhat awkward horse-half of Sag (pronounced to rhyme with badge).

But let the human side of the Archers turn up, and Taurus is puzzled and annoyed. As the Bulls watch the Sagittarians playing the roles of serious idealists, fighting fiercely in the courtroom, the classroom, on a television screen, or on a political platform, they're uncertain whether to cheer them — or fear them.

The Jupiter dedication of the moment may take Sagittarians into a raging battle against the establishment, which will usually be abrasive to the more conservative Taurean nature, causing the Bulls to draw back in surprise and ask themselves, "Who is this strange creature, riding around like a drunken dreamer, tilting at the sturdy, solid windmills of society?" An awkward, yet also sometimes graceful, racehorse may be quite likable and good for some belly laughs, but a careless idealist who is threatening to tear holes in the fabric of comfortable custom can be downright dangerous. Taurus can't figure out how to deal sensibly with a Sagittarian, who's aroused to a high pitch of recklessness by a cause (preferably a lost one, because they give you a bigger glow within when you win them — and being lucky, the Archers nearly always win).

Every Sag (including the extroverted and the introverted ones) is at heart a bright-eyed, bushy-tailed optimist, who inwardly believes that everything will come out in the wash, then cries great, dramatic tears when it doesn't — which serves him (or her) right for expecting too much out of Life, as far as Taurus is concerned.

The Bulls are clear-eyed, smooth-tailed pessimists, who never expect anything to come out in the wash — so when they lose a couple of socks at the laundermat, it serves *them* right for constantly imaging negative possibilities, as far as Sagittarius is concerned. Sag has no patience with Taureans who go glooming around, spreading inky moods. The Sagittarian man, woman or child's own tears may be very damp and profuse, but they dry quickly when the eternal Jupiter rainbow comes out to drape itself around their shoulders and bathe them in hopeful colors again.

This is a 6-8 Sun Sign Pattern, emphasizing service, health and all manner of mystery. Because Sagittarius represents "other people's money" to Taurus (among other 8th "house" influences, which are different with each individual Sun Sign association between these two) the Archers may be the ones to raise the funds for Taureans to realize their huge endeavors. Because Taurus represents the 6th astrological "house" of work, duty and service to Sag, these two are not infrequently found associated in some mutual undertaking that blends the Jupiter flair for promotion and salesmanship with the Taurean ability to build a solid foundation (which is of great value, when the Archers ride the rear end of their Centaur symbol, and fall flat on their hopes). The Bulls admire the exciting pictures the Archers create, but they become restless and suspicious when Sag slaps on the paint with strokes that are too broad, and colors that are too garish for the practical Taurean taste.

Sagittarian people sail around, goofing and stumbling a lot, but they're as likely to stumble on a piece of pure, unadulterated luck, as they are to fall head first into an open sewer. The former accident is due to their marvelous faith, courage and optimism — the latter, to their obstructed line of vision. Your chances of falling into a hole naturally increase when you're gazing at the sky, shooting arrows into the future, and not looking where you're skipping.

Since the Bulls usually keep their eyes more or less fastened on the ground, they can help Sag watch out for the open sewers and other traps waiting to trip them. These two can make a really socko team in the stock market, or in any sort of gambling venture. If there's a harmonious Sun-Moon aspect between them, they may become millionaires fairly quickly. Actually, they'll do pretty well together in any sort of scheme involving money — their own or someone else's — whether it's farming organic fruits and vegetables, or selling foreign sports cars. The association can be found anywhere from film-making to breeding race horses, from the newspaper field to a church. (Most Bulls are rather dogmatic about their religious beliefs, usually intensely loyal to the religion of childhood — and all Archers are possessed of a strong, though often tangled and knotted, religious streak.)

Normally, Taurus remains close to family ties. A Bull will sacrifice much for his (or her) loved ones, and bear up under a bushel of trouble for them. Sagittarians are also willing to offer a helping hand and a cheery word to their relatives — from a distance. The typical Archers and their families don't live in one another's pockets. Sag is more interested in the good of humanity as a whole than in lavishing excessive attention on blood lines. That's for horses, isn't it? Yes, and also for the half-horse Centaurs, if they'd give their relatives half a chance.

Both of these Sun Signs can spot a hypocrite or a phony a mile away, and neither of them is inclined to tell a lie to save face, or merely to be courteous. The Bulls ordinarily will state the truth of the matter as they see it, firmly and clearly. Should they think it might truly wound someone, however, they'll clam up and not speak at all, rather than stir up unnecessary unpleasantness, if the issue is not an urgent one. The Archer has no such reluctance. All Sagittarians shine with a certain kind of honesty — a brutal kind. The truth sometimes hurts, but the Archers are blissfully unaware of this, when their indignations are flashing. It's useless to expect these people to stifle their Jupiter integrity, but they might try diluting it a bit.

SAG: Why are you so upset, just because I told you that you're pigeon-toed and you walk with a waddle? I think it's kind of cute. Why are you frowning as though you hated me or something? What did I do wrong? I thought you liked me.

TAURUS: That's right. Everybody likes you, because you're so warm and friendly and enthusiastic. You're also a clumsy klutz, verbally and physically. There. See how the truth hurts?

SAG: Okay, so I'm a clumsy klutz. But what does that have to do with your being pigeon-toed and walking with a waddle?

It's no use, a dose of their own medicine won't work with Sag, because truth never cramps Jupiter's breezy style. Most Archers will accept it cheerfully, philosophically — and are genuinely bewildered when others get uptight over hearing the plain facts, whether the sharp arrow of honesty is aimed at themselves or at another victim. A Sagittarian (or a person with the Moon or Ascendent in Sag) is the one who chirps happily, "Was that your husband's brother I read about in the papers, who forged those checks and got caught? Listen, it's all in the family! I have a sister who was picked up twice for shoplifting. She's in therapy now. But it still hasn't cured her kleptomania."

The broken twigs on their own family trees don't bother the Archers in the least, so why should you flinch over yours? That's Jupiter's sunny, but sometimes exasperating, outlook.

Sagittarians take life and people literally as they skip around, spreading their jollies and blasting out truth with their jovial Jupiter vibes. When the Bulls get hit between the eyes, they can get their backs up, but they're normally placid, patient souls. Unfortunately, the qualities of placidity and patience often annoy the more impulsive Archers, when they're exposed to it for long periods of time. It sometimes seems to Sag that the dogmatic and cautious Bulls are as slow as a herd of snails.

Nevertheless, if these two decide to take a gamble, and combine the Jupiter luck and logic with the Taurean shrewdness and common sense, they stand a good chance of making lots of money together. M-O-N-E-Y. That message will reach both of them loudly and clearly. Taurus likes to keep it in the bank. Sag likes to keep it in circulation.

☆ ☆ ☆ ☆ ☆ ☆

TAURUS *Woman* SAGITTARIUS *Man*

----◄◆►----

*Michael was ready: he wanted to see how long it took him
to do a billion miles. But Wendy hesitated . . . .*

There he is, bouncing happily up and down, like a typical Jupiter rubber ball,
thinking he has a great new friend to pal around with, and since she's a
female, well, who knows? It could mean a beautiful love affair, or even
better, maybe a life-long, platonic friendship. Since Sagittarius likes the truth
so much, this is about the time he should face up to it. If she's a Taurus girl,
she's not mentally casting herself either as his pal or as the helpless half of a
casual affair. She has another role in mind for herself.

An Archer reading this will probably feign shock, and murmur to
himself, "What does that mean?" What does he mean, what does that
mean? It means marriage, that's what it means, and he shouldn't be so
surprised. For a man who prides himself on his honesty, a Sagittarian male
can be pretty shifty about romance. He may think he'll always win the game
he plays called "Love now, leave later," but if his partner is a Taurean, he'd
better be prepared to lose — either the game, or her.

A Taurus woman falls in love with a Sagittarius man for perfectly good
reasons. He's an idealist, a cheerful companion when she's blue, an intelligent
conversationalist, a dreamer, a philosopher, an astute businessman — and a
little boy who needs looking after. You certainly can't expect a Taurus
female to resist the impact of a man like that. No wonder, even when he told
her plainly the first night the way things were, she didn't hear him.
Her head was in the clouds, somewhere up there where he scatters all his
enthusiasm. An Archer's excitement is contagious. But sometimes he forgets
he's a Fire Sign. You know what fire does? It flares up into flames. And
more flames. He'll have to cool it if he doesn't want to get burned by his own
sparks — or be buried beneath her earthy anger, which can pour down on
him like an avalanche when he ignites her love, then fails to put out the blaze.

The very least a Taurus woman will settle for when she's in love is the
status of permanent mistress or common law wife, though she won't like
either situation, and she's only biding her time in any case. What she won't
stand for is to be part of an Archer's harem. She isn't illogically jealous, as a
Leo or an Aries girl might be. She is, however, possessive, which means that
her idea of love is based on exclusivity. This woman would never have
accepted a proposal from Brigham Young. A female Bull won't be suspicious
of her man without good cause, but neither will she give him yards of rope
with which to string her along.

Actually, this man is capable of being very loyal to a woman he really loves. His problem is in making the wrong choice, which causes him to lose the right partner. At first, his frankness and his outspoken manner will seem genuine and wholesome to the Taurus girl. So will his lack of hypocrisy. She won't waste a moment of her time on a liar or a phony, so she'll admire his honesty. That is, she will until the day (or night) he demonstrates it with painful clarity to her by saying, "Baby, we can have lots of fun knocking around together, if we level with each other from the beginning. Like, yesterday I ran into this old girl friend, and she wants me to spend the weekend with her on Squaw Mountain. You know how I love to ski. Can you find something to amuse yourself with until I get back?" When the Archer gets *that* honest, she's liable to amuse herself by cracking him over the head with one of his skis.

Although a Sagittarian is governed by sincerity in romance, it isn't always accompanied by a sensitive regard for his partner's feelings. Still, if she can try to overlook his stinging arrows of frankness, she may discover things about him that a female with a quick temper and less patience will never know. When an Archer finds a woman who understands him enough to love him and trust him, his nature will expand to its highest level. No one makes a more enthusiastic lover and devoted husband than a well-loved and *trusted* Sagittarian. He's like a big, friendly sheep dog, a little clumsy maybe, but warm, happy and faithful, and who could question his playful sincerity? He needs a woman who will believe in all his dreams, not one who constantly pops his balloons with the needles of doubt and nagging.

He needs a cheerful companion to take hiking with him, someone who challenges him with her own independence, who can bounce stimulating ideas with him, who gives him plenty of freedom and also smothers him with plenty of affection. It's a large order for any female, but a Taurus girl can probably fill it, except perhaps for the part about bouncing ideas with him. She's smart (maybe even too smart) but she's a better listener than a brainstormer. It takes Taurus some time to mull over wild ideas before she can work up an excitement to match his and she's suspicious of ideas that bounce. But her practicality and common sense provide an excellent balance for his reckless tendency to throw the dice for double-or-nothing. He should appreciate her down-to-earth approach, and not expect her to continually match his own frenetic creative drive. Besides, it's good to rest once in a while against a soft pillow of purring femininity. He can play bounce with the fellows, and enjoy other pastimes with her.

A Sagittarian man who feels restricted may seem to submit, because he's inclined to make the optimistic best of an existing situation, but it will eventually lead him into becoming irritable and sarcastic, and then the union will be far from happy. If she has the Moon in a Fire or Air Sign, or he has the Moon in an Earth or Water Sign, they could have a circus together. Otherwise, their relationship may be somewhat rocky at times. He's looking for a mental companion to roam the hills with him. She needs a dependable, predictable man to sit by the fire and hold her hand. Not that a Taurus woman wants to spend her life in the kitchen stirring the noodles, but neither is she the type to want to spend it spinning around on a Ferris Wheel or munching lichee nuts. This girl is faithful and warm-hearted. She's patient and self-controlled, good-hearted and jolly. Her nature is humorous, hospitable and easygoing. She seems too gentle, too kind, and far too tranquil to be capable of anger. But goaded beyond the point of her endurance, she'll erupt into an irrational fury, lacking all logic and reason. Sagittarius is not the least likely sign to arouse her to such a rare display of temper. The Archer ranks close behind Leo, Scorpio and Aquarius in the ability to aggravate the Bull into earthquaking action.

She'll have to be on guard against the Archer's method of teaching her (and learning himself) by the method of conversational inquiry. He's an expert at it. Sag can pull out your deepest emotions and your most private opinions by this method of careful questioning. Taurus doesn't always want her deepest emotions and most private opinions exposed to light.

She doesn't pry into other people's affairs. Why should they pry into hers? So the Sagittarian burning curiosity, which is a natural outgrowth of his brilliant and logical mental process, will not always please her. Nor will his clever method of casual cross-examination delight her when she has a secret she'd like to call (and keep) her own.

It's possible for their physical relationship to be a good one, if they both try to understand each other's different natures and sexual needs. When a woman enhances his highest opinion of himself (and a Taurus woman can) an Archer's desire for her increases. Her earthy emotions are deeply stirred by his fiery ones, and he'll feel a sense of pride from her obvious feminine pleasure in sexual submission. But he seeks an emotional experience somewhere above and beyond the actuality of passion. Since he's not quite sure what it is himself, she may never guess his yearning, and they both could be aware only of a vague and nameless dissatisfaction.

She's a warm and sensuous woman, yet it isn't easy for her to express the emotions she feels so strongly. She can only show her love through the sense of touch. To her that should be enough, and silence is golden when she's making love. But the Sagittarian idealist wants to analyze, then express, both physically and verbally, the miracle of fulfillment. He may feel he's caressing the Sphinx, and she could decide she's being loved by the actual legendary Centaur, half blazing with animal passion and half abstracted in thoughts which are beyond the horizon of reality.

An Archer is consumed with mental activity, and so seeks and needs the democratic freedom of companionship with men and women of every walk of Life, not unlike his Aquarian brother. He's defiant of public opinion, uncompromising in his honesty, rather indifferent toward domestic life, and detached from his own parental family ties.

A Taurus woman is the opposite of all these things. A marriage between them, if their mutual Luminaries are in negative aspect, can be as full of both devotion and irritation as the union between Socrates and his wife, Xantippe, who dutifully created a warm and comfortable home for the philosopher, but who found him so frustratingly impossible to live with that she periodically emptied the household slop jar over his head. It may not quite come to that, but the Archer will be impatient with the Bull's lack of enthusiastic reaction to his spontaneity, while she is driven to the edge of fury by his scattered dreams, procrastination and thoughtlessness. This is a man who whistles before breakfast, and this is a woman who is positive that means he'll cry before supper. They translate Mother Goose somewhat differently.

Only if she's willing to thaw her frozen silences when he needs her understanding — and only if he's willing to curb his fiery temper when he can't get his own way — can they find happiness together. And they should *both* remember *this:* Like the forces of Yin and Yang, false pride opposes true love.

☆ ☆ ☆ ☆ ☆ ☆

TAURUS *Man* SAGITTARIUS *Woman*

Again Tink replied, "You silly ass."

Peter could not understand why . . . .

Like forcing a square peg into a round hole, trying to blend the Taurus tranquility with the Sagittarian exuberance gives the Bull and the girl Archer the symbolic appearance of a ruptured Tinker Toy.

On the other hand (there's always a Libran trying to get into each chapter of this book to start an argument), on the other hand, it's not necessarily the greatest thing in the world to mate with a mirror image of yourself. It's more fun to team up with someone who has crooked ears to balance out your twelve toes — or someone who has a soft heart to compensate for your hard head — things like that. Mix and match, and make up for what you lack with what the other person has in excess, and wants to give away, if only he or she can find someone who needs it — and who will take it. It develops character. Or something.

We may need an example. The two of them are walking along the street, window shopping. That is, *she's* window shopping, *he's* counting to ten, making a determined effort to control his growing annoyance.

SAG: Oh, WOW! That really rips it! Look at that string bikini! I'm going in and open up a charge account, so I can buy it right away, and wear it to the beach tomorrow to look sexy.

THE BULL: Silence. Absolute, ominous silence. He can't decide what bugs him the most — her lack of maidenly modesty, her hollering slang right out on the street, that caused everyone to stare curiously at them, or her extravagance in insisting on buying things when she doesn't have the cash, and furthermore, has no idea when she *will* have it — which he suspects probably means that she'll try to borrow it from him when the bill from the store arrives, and she's still broke. (He's right. She will.) And so, for the moment — silence from the Bull.

(or . . . to switch scenes)

SAG: Honey, let's get a St. Bernard to keep Lady Macbeth, our sheep dog, company, and name him Merlin. Wouldn't that be a scream? Or maybe we could change Lady Macbeth's name to Elizabeth, and name the St. Bernard Robert, after the Brownings. Do you think dogs understand poetry? I do. They certainly understand it better than you. You wouldn't know Solzhenitsyn from Sasquatch. Do you think they would mate?

THE BULL: Solzhenitsyn and Sasquatch?

SAG: No, stupid. The dogs. The sheep dog and the St. Bernard. How could a Russian poet mate with Sasquatch? You probably don't even know that Sasquatch is the name of Bigfoot . . . the one they keep tracking in the High Sierras. Of course (she muses, thoughtfully) they don't really know if Bigfoot is male or female, so I suppose they could, but . . . .

THE BULL: Bigfoot. That's you, baby. You're always sticking your big foot in your big mouth. I'm going to call you Sasquatch from now on.

SAG: Do you suppose the puppies would be retarded or something?

THE BULL: Solzhenitsyn's — or Sasquatch's?

SAG: Stop trying to be funny. Did I tell you I think our cat, Maybelle, is going to have a litter of kittens in a few weeks?

THE BULL: Listen, Sasquatch. I am not a dog breeder. I am also not a cat midwife. Once and for all, get this through your marble head. I do not enjoy having furry little creatures climbing all over me in bed when I'm trying to sleep. This place is beginning to resemble the ASPCA Annex.

SAG: Why don't you want me to march in the ecology protest parade? We only have ten years left on this planet if somebody doesn't do something right away. Do you want to suffocate in ten years because there's no more oxygen left in the air, because the plankton that makes the oxygen, which grows in the ocean, is gone — because of pollution of the water, caused by greedy industrialists like you?

THE BULL: I am not a greedy industrialist. I own a small Orange Julius stand. And I don't care which Chinese Communist-inspired "cause" you march for on your own time, but I just got home from work, and I haven't been fed. I'm hungry. Stifle yourself, and feed me.

SAG: Say, do you think you own me? I'm not your slave. You act like you expect me to punch a time clock around here. Go out and get yourself some egg fu yung tonight. I'm not cooking.

THE BULL: You see? Now you're even pushing Oriental food. You're a sucker for Karl Marx.

SAG: Listen, if you're so jealous that you've decided to lie, and make up stories about me, don't pick a German Nazi name like that. Who said I was seen talking to this Marx guy anyway? The only man I've spoken to all week is the intern at the blood bank, who . . .

THE BULL: Shut up.

SAG: *What did you say?*

THE BULL: I said shut up.

SAG: Well, I don't have to take *that*. I'm leaving.

THE BULL: (yawning) Where are you going? Your mother won't take you in. You haven't written or called her in five years.

SAG: I have no intention of going home. That would be worse than living with you. I'm going to move in with my old boy friend, Kevin — *that's* where I'm going.

THE BULL: (no longer yawning, now alert and snorting) Over my dead body you will.

SAG: It's okay. Don't get any nasty ideas, Lumpy. Kevin is married. His wife won't mind. I'll call them first.

THE BULL: (now furious) What do you want to bet his wife *will* mind? WHAT DO YOU WANT TO BET? Or maybe you're planning a *ménage à trois*. IS THAT IT?

SAG: Stop shouting. Your face is red. I thought you didn't approve of gambling. Now you want to make a bet with me over some smutty suspicion you have. See how changeable you are? I thought Taurus men were supposed to be steady and dependable.

That's the only reason I married you, because my astrologer told me you were steady and dependable. All astrologers ought to be arrested. What's a *ménage à trois*? If you're going to insult me, at least insult me with slurs I can understand. You know I don't speak Russian.

THE BULL: I GIVE UP! I GIVE UP! Come on Sasquatch, I'll take you out to dinner, and maybe a play afterwards. It's our wedding anniversary, but I don't expect you to remember anything so trivial as that.

SAG: Oh, Buttercup, Sweetheart! Really? Can we see *Man of La Mancha*? And can I call Kevin and his wife, and see if they'd like to go with us?

It kind of goes like that, with variations. And don't let the mix-up over Karl Marx influence you. If she has a Ph.D. in political science, and speaks several languages — which many girl Archers do — she'll be even *more* indignant. Sagittarians are just as fiery and self-righteous when they're well informed as they are when they don't know what they're talking about. Since Sagittarius rules higher education, among other things, the chances are she will have a degree or two. Either way, she'll find tons of topical and tangled issues of the day to analyze with her cool logic and brutal honesty. Then she'll attempt to straighten them out with her Jupiter optimism. It makes breakfast with the morning newspaper a lively meal. Her scintillating discussions make up for burned toast and un-sectioned grapefruit (a degree in cooking she probably does *not* have).

Their political views will differ somewhat, to put it mildly. *He* thinks the *Chicago Tribune* is an underground newspaper and Barry Goldwater is a flaming liberal. *She* thinks John Lindsay is an uptight conservative who's a secret member of the John Birch Society because he was so stuffy about nudity in Central Park when he was Mayor of New York. But she voted for him anyway, because, after all, Lindsay is a Sag himself, so his intentions were probably good. As for the Bull's choice for Mayor of Manhattan, Ronald Reagan or William Buckley — she thinks they would make a worse mess of the job than Lindsay.

At this point, Taurus will shout, "The only possible way that anyone could make a worse mess of governing Manhattan than your friendly Archer John Lindsay did would be to formally declare war on the city!" But the stalemate isn't altogether hopeless. There's an outside chance they both might agree on Jerry Brown and the revival of the *Saturday Evening Post* — for different reasons, of course.

The Sagittarian girl's ebullient spirits help her snap back from most misfortunes like a rubber band. She looks on the bright side of things, and her sunny disposition makes the Bull smile indulgently at the idealism and naivete behind it. But she doesn't recover as quickly from a broken heart as she does from smashed ambitions, a fractured dream, or a period of poverty. Unrequited love (meaning love she gives freely to a man who abuses her trust) gets her down, and sometimes keeps her there. But the gentle understanding of a patient Bull could heal her emotional scars and, at the same time, teach her that not all men are fickle phonies who break promises. It's not uncommon for these two to fall in love while he's playing Big Brother, and drying her tears over a broken affair. His dependability soothes her, and his steady faith in her calms her troubled soul. So she may decide this is the man she's been shooting for and missing since she first aimed her bow and arrow toward the stars and reached for an impossible dream. He may be. Then again, he may not. If the Sun and Moon in their mutual charts are friendly, they can build a relationship which, although it will certainly never be dull, might be snug and satisfying. With a negative Luminary vibration between their horoscopes, they'll need courage.

She is fond of argument. The Sagittarian girl enjoys crossing swords with a good antagonist. Because her swift flashes of logic give her a sharp insight, she's a skillful debater, and painfully honest. The trouble is, a Taurus man is not fond of argument and debate — or even of overly long friendly discussions. She may then invite packs of assorted friends over to camp out, hang around, and keep her wits sharpened. But that will only make things worse. The Bull does not like to see his castle cluttered with noisy strangers, and it will take a good deal of emotional elasticity to ease the tight tensions.

The subjects on the double bill of many of their comic-tragedies will be his stubbornness — and her extravagance. As for how long the quarrels last, it depends on her awareness of his Venus-ruled nature. She'll forget her own anger quickly. He can pout for days unless she knows the secret to his heart. With a Bull, one hard squeeze, and one gentle kiss, will tear down all his obstinate defenses.

That brings us to their sexual harmony. It could be an exciting meeting of Fire and Earth that gives them enough mutual pleasure to soften all their other differences. The initial physical attraction is strong. Her frank, wholesome approach to sex will incite the Bull to open up his heart to her, releasing emotions which may have been stifled within him for fear of rebuff. She'll respond naturally to his affectionate gestures, and his air of tender protectiveness. He makes her feel totally loved, not just passionately desired. Yet she may fulfill his physical-emotional needs more completely than he fulfills hers.

The Sagittarian woman often clings to her phantom lover, the one who promised to carry her off into the clouds in her adolescent fantasies — so there may be times when the Taurus man will vaguely sense that she isn't entirely consumed by abandoned passion during their intimacies. If he does, he should remain silent, and not start one of those Sagittarian arguments. She might zing out one of her truthful arrows at a crucial moment, and damage his Taurean masculinity permanently. The possibilities of this happening are too numerous and embarrassing to mention. Still, despite her daydreams or nightdreams, or whatever, she's not likely to chase her phantom lover anywhere but in her restless mind. Not when she has a real live, warm, kind and cuddly Teddy Bear to take to bed with her. He'll replace the stuffed one she used to sleep with when she was lonely and lost, and despairing of ever being "really truly loved."

A Sagittarius woman is quick to reach out for love, if the hand she grabs and holds tightly also offers friendship. She's impulsive, excited by mental qualities — and loyal, once she becomes sincerely attached. So is he. But he won't eat egg fu yung in a restaurant forever. To the Bull, a woman's place is, in the home, with strong emphasis on the kitchen and the bedroom. If that's where she's happiest, and willing to spend a reasonable amount of time with him, their contentment could be lasting. If she'd rather be out tumbling with the clowns, well — Lumpy and Sasquatch will just have to find some sort of compromise. Real love can always find one.

If she calls him Buttercup (but PLEASE, not in front of others) he'll call her Honey-cakes — if she tickles his *oreille* and scratches his head, he'll grow ecstatic, docile and sweetly manageable. And if he stops telling her to shut up, and tries a little harder to understand her honesty, to take a genuine interest in her opinions and excitement, she might blunt her arrows a little — and maybe even cook some egg fu yung for him herself . . . at home, where she belongs.

☆ ☆ ☆ ☆ ☆ ☆

TAURUS

Earth — Fixed — Negative
Ruled by Venus (also by the
Planet Pan-Horus)
Symbol: The Bull
Night Forces — Feminine

CAPRICORN

Earth — Cardinal — Negative
Ruled by Saturn
Symbol: The Goat
Night Forces — Feminine

The **TAURUS-CAPRICORN** *Relationship*

It would be an easy map, if that were all; but there
is also first day at school, religion, fathers . . . . .
verbs that take the dative, chocolate pudding day,
getting into braces, say ninety-nine, threepence for
pulling out your tooth yourself, and so on . . . . . .

*T*he shining virtues of solidity and dependability surround the Taurus Bull and Capricorn Goat with an aura of earth-colored sureness. Life to Taurus and Capricorn is not all grey and brown, nor black and blue. But you'll seldom find useless pastels, optimistic yellows or extroverted reds in their personal halos. When these two animals meet at the zoo, the ground shakes with the vibrations of destiny. Who knows what successes lie ahead when a Bull and a Goat get into harness together? *They* do.

Neither is in any doubt as to where he (or she) is going. To the top. In a large city or a small town, all the way to the top — to the place where it's peaceful, quiet, financially comfortable — where they'll be isolated from silly dreamers who muck up the air with foolish illusions, fantasies, and the doomed failure of misguided idealism.

The Bulls and Goats are both modest and reserved, and they both use moderation as an inner alarm, or security system, to warn them of any wayward emotions which might short circuit the smooth mechanism of their ambitions. Now, that's not to say that these people are dull, stodgy, humorless and unimaginative plodders. (Taurean Shakespeare, a plodder?) As for Capricorns, nearly all Goats have some sort of creative or artistic talent. Many of them draw as well when they're only doodling as professionals do when they're working, and some of them do actually become successful painters or writers. (Capricorn novelist Henry Miller is both.) As for the Bulls, they have music in their souls, regardless of all the common sense in their heads. Many Taureans are famous singers, musicians or composers. Others just piddle around on the piano, hum into a harmonica, or pluck a homemade zither. Nearly every one of them sings in the shower when they're sure no one can hear. In the humor department, Taurus is the original Falstaff, or court jester, full of throaty chuckles and funny one-liners. The average male or female Bull will slide into a comic monologue with little urging, in the living room or at the office.

The Capricorn Goats also possess a dry and droll sense of humor. Their keen observations on the comedy of life are amusingly clever, even though they normally make their remarks with a straight face, which only makes them funnier. When something really turns these people on, they can weave funny, whimsical tales of dry humor that would be the envy of a professional comedian. So you see, a combination of Taurus and Capricorn can be warm and amusing as well as steady, stable and steadfast.

Still, you shouldn't expect the Marx Brothers. Each was born under a negative Earth Sign, which does not provide fertile soil for frivolity. Goats and Bulls *are* funny, but they're not hilarious, and they won't lose an inch of dignity while they're cutting up. You won't find many of them dancing wildly in noisy disco dives. A nice quiet evening at home, watching movies of the family's vacation at Yellowstone National Park, is more their speed. Taurus and Capricorn constitute what has been called the "Backbone of America."

Since theirs is a 5-9 Sun Sign Pattern (see the back section of this book) the areas of romance, children, religion, travel, education and show business are, percentage-wise, the probable pastures where the Goat and Bull will find a common interest. From there, they may engage in an endeavor which will unite them in a glorious strength of effort and purpose (if their mutual Luminaries are harmonious) or which could result in a hopeless locking of horns and total boredom (if the Sun and Moon Signs between their horoscopes are unfavorable). However, even in the latter case, they can always use the natural sympathy of all 5-9 vibrations to bridge their difficulties. It's difficult for any two people who are influenced by this Sun Sign Pattern to remain angry or opposed for long. The path to reconciliation is always easy, and visible to them, when they desire to find it.

You might see an occasional Capricorn wearing a feather headdress and love beads, smoking peyote in the park and openly flouting convention, but if you do, you can be sure that he (or she) is a lost and lonely soul, trying desperately to prove something — heaven knows what. It's not a natural state of dress or behavior for the normally staid, formal Cappy, and there's certain to be a mild neurosis, or a dissatisfaction with Life, lingering in the smoke trailing out of the peace pipe.

You may also run across a rare Bull who drives a flashy yellow Stingray to the bank and shakes a pink tambourine while he makes his hefty cash deposit, but he's probably just trying to get the attention of a female teller to satisfy his sentimental Venus yearnings. It's really best in the long run to know who and what you are and be true to your own Sun Sign image. A Ram shouldn't try to be docile and meek. A Virgo would be miserable trying to be careless and casual. A Bull and a Goat should not try to be wild gypsies. It doesn't become them. It often becomes Aquarians, but not these two.

One area these Sun Signs are highly unlikely to be involved in together is the drug scene. Most Taureans don't really need the extra kick of a high, because their senses are so acutely tuned in on their environment. The Bulls can sniff a sweet pea or a zinnia, in pure ecstasy for hours, contemplating its form and color and scent — until they get stung by an angry bumblebee. As for the typical Capricorns, they wouldn't dream of indulging in recreation against the law, and certainly not one that might delay or obstruct their Saturn-directed, ambitious climb up the mountain — or cause a scandal.

The Goats want, above all, to be accepted and respected by their friends, relatives and neighbors, and by society at large. When scientists get around to taking their noses out of their test tubes and seriously investigate astrology, they'll find an amazingly small percentage of Taureans and Capricorns in "halfway houses," or in drug and alcohol rehabilitation centers, as compared with the number of other Sun Signs. There are, of course, occasional exceptions that prove the rule, but very few.

I know a Capricorn jeweler in Cripple Creek, Colorado, named Steve, who has mapped all the spots where the wild strawberry grass (a mystical herb) grows the greenest, in the hills behind the small mining community. He gathers it, dries it, dips it in gold or paints it — then uses it to make abstract pictures of Western scenes to sell the tourists in his "Crucible." You can always count on Cappy to find a practical angle for anything. This particular Goat wears modified sideburns as his concession to the Aquarian Age, but somehow, on him, the sideburns only add to his dignified, Dickens-like appearance, and he still doesn't quite fit the picture of a mod swinger.

Speaking of jewelry, many Capricorns and Taureans share with Leo a love of precious gems and metal. The flamboyant-type Leos like to wear them, the flashier the better. The Bulls like to dig them out of the ground, creatively stirred by the excitement of discovery, as they burrow deep into the bowels of the earth for turquoise, gold, silver or diamonds. Capricorn likes to mold them into practical art objects, and the Goat often satisfies those secret artistic yearnings while burnishing the brass and leaning over the Bunsen burner. However, the final objective of both the Taurus Bull and the Capricorn Goat is to find the vain Lions or Lionesses to buy their wares, so they can make Money, which is spelled S-E-C-U-R-I-T-Y. By the way, Steve Mackin, the Colorado Cappy jeweler I mentioned, doesn't always buy his metals from a Taurean miner. He finds many of the materials he turns into jewels fit for a pharaoh — in junk yards. What more appropriate place for a billy goat to roam and nose around in? The great talent of the Saturn-ruled lies in finding hidden treasures, buried among the discarded trash, twisted tin and broken glass of Life. Both literally and symbolically.

Capricorns become adults somewhere around the age of two or three. Taureans decide on the scope of their future financial empires at around the same age. So it doesn't matter how old or how young these two are when they team up. Their goals will be identical. Both the Bull and the Goat are wise to the ways of the outer world. It's their own inner worlds that give them trouble. Each is brimming over with a sentiment he or she won't show — and each is deeply in need of affection and appreciation for which he (or she) won't ask. So there they stand like two mountains, side by side, starving for human comfort and closeness, each stubbornly resisting the other's timid overtures of friendship or demonstrations of open affection.

Children are tiny persons who see, and demonstrate with simplicity, the magic their elders have forgotten as they've passed through Life's sobering experiences. Since Taurus and Capricorn have spent so little time as children (having grown mature at the age of two or three) they may have missed some magic tricks along the way. How can they make up for those lost years of childhood? Easy. Taurus can say to Cappy, "Let's go skinny-dipping in the creek, and the last one in is a rotten egg!" Then Cappy can say to Taurus, "Let's go down to the junk yard and shoot off some fireworks!" While they're there, they can climb an apple tree, play frisbee with a frog, smell the sweet peas and zinnias, swing in an old tire, and then — ONE-TWO-THREE-GREEN-LIGHT! They're both home free.

TAURUS *Woman* CAPRICORN *Man*

———— ◆◁◉▷◆ ————

*Will they reach the nursery in time ? If so, how
delightful for them, and we shall all breathe a sigh
of relief, but there will be no story. On the other
hand, if they are not in time, I solemnly promise
that it will all come right in the end.*

*They would have reached the nursery in time had it
not been that the little stars were watching them . . .*

I believe we should devote a major portion of this section of the Taurus-
Capricorn chapter to a lesson much needed by all Earth Sign men and
women. A lesson, yes . . . but also, perhaps, a kind of karmic warning.

Did you ever notice how people forget things, then try to pretend that
what they forgot wasn't very important anyway ? A Taurus woman will
seldom resort to such pretense. She doesn't forget much, and everything is
important to her. All Bulls possess powerful memories.

She certainly will not forget the very day and hour she meets a
Capricorn man whose Moon or Ascendent was in an Earth or Water Sign at
birth, especially if her Moon and Ascendent were in one of these same
elements when she was born. Adding that sort of Luminary harmony to the
powerfully compatible 5-9 Sun Sign Pattern, it will be a rare Bull and Goat
who doesn't instantly recognize the soft, humming sound of future happiness
together. It's like hitting a romantic jackpot with your last quarter of faith,
when you've gambled and lost too many dreams to count, an especially heart-
warming win for Taurus and Capricorn, since they both gamble so rarely.
On anything.

Because Earth Signs don't talk a lot about their personal lives (both these
lovers were born into the Earth Element) lots of people believe the awesome
experience of the intertwined destiny of twin souls happens only to those who
are born under the influence of the Fire, Air or Water Elements. Not so.
Such fascinating appointments with Fate also occur between Bulls and Goats
(and Virgo Virgins) leaving them just as profoundly moved as any Earthlings
who are swept into a sense of trembling wonder by the realization that their
meeting was planned, and inescapably so. To prove this to all the Taurus
women and Capricorn men reading their own chapter, or any other curious
Earth Sign couples, I offer the following example.

I know a Goat named Steve (not the Cappy jeweler mentioned else-where) and a Bull named Debbie (not the same Steve and Debbie pair referred to in the Libra-Aquarius chapter). The surname of these two is Atwell. Capricorn Steve and Taurean Debbie Atwell were married in the fall of 1977. To the average person, Steve and Debbie appear to be just a normal, ordinary, happy and contented young married couple. They are happy and contented, certainly, but their relationship has been more paranormal than normal, more extraordinary than ordinary. From the moment each of them was born, a cosmic plan was formed to draw them magnetically together — as happens with many lovers in the 5-9 vibratory experience, whose Luminary and other planetary aspects are also harmonious.

It's never easy to convince two Earth Sign people that their love — or anything else — is fated. Taurus and Cappy usually believe only what they can hear, see, smell and feel, tangibly. Yet, the Higher Angels of any two who are cosmically programmed to join, are quite persistent, and never stop their efforts until the starry mission has been accomplished.

Pretend you're living on Venus (ruler of Taurus) — or on Saturn (ruler of Capricorn) looking down upon the following events below, on Earth. Capricorn Steve is born, a baby boy Goat, in Woodland Park, Colorado. Near the same time, Taurean Debbie is born, a baby girl Bull, in Milwaukee, Wisconsin. (Like parachuters and astronauts, twin souls sometimes miscalculate, and land a few miles away from the astrally scheduled spot.)

Venus is troubled, but Saturn intones wisely — *wait*. A couple of decades pass, as the lovers grow, miles apart, from boy and girl into man and woman. Then, in 1967, Venus guides Steve, the Goat, to Milwaukee, where Debbie, the Bull, was born and lives — to enter college there. Now, surely, the two of them must meet, and read Life's meaning in each other's eyes. But no . . . stuffy, restrictive Old Man Saturn delays their union still longer. He influences Taurean Debbie's parents to move, with their daughter, in 1969, to Woodland Park, Colorado, where Steve, the Goat, was born.

Like love letters crossing in the mail, now the Goat has found his way to the city where his future wife was born — and she has found her way to the town where her future husband was born. Yet they are still separated as before, except that their separation has reversed itself geographically. So Venus steps in, determined. With her gentle powers of persuasion, she guides Steve, the Goat, in 1971, back to his birthplace — to Woodland Park, Colorado — where Debbie, the Bull, unconsciously awaits him, growing lonelier by the hour, and wondering wistfully, "What's the use of wishing on stars? The stars don't have the power to make wishes come true." She's wrong. They do. For Venus has added a clever twist. She has sung a lovely song into the sleeping ear of Steve, the Goat, haunting him . . . and persuading him to accept a job with the County Road Commission, working for Debbie's Cancerian *father*, Les. Surely, now, the star-crossed lovers must meet!

Alas, no . . . Saturn is ready to impose his cruelest karmic test. After delaying the meeting between the two for nearly another year (how was Steve to know his boss was his future father-in-law?) Saturn influenced Steve to leave. The Goat, whose wanderings had brought him so near the end of his heart's seeking, heeded the command of Saturn, became dissatisfied with his job and resigned (after the proper Capricorn notice, of course) to accept a job as a logger, many miles away. Saturn even tried to convince Steve at this time to move permanently to Alaska. But he was foiled by the free-will choice of the Goat's own Higher Self, in conspiracy with Debbie's Venus. Steve struggled with his strange restlessness (Earth Signs are normally, nearly *never* restless) and at last submitted to the melody Venus sang to him in his dreams at night. He moved *back* to Woodland Park, Colorado, in 1972, and once more went to work for Taurean Debbie's father. Love's victory is in sight!

No. Not quite yet. Cautious Saturn has decreed another three years of waiting in blindness for the lovers, causing Venus to weep in frustration, but then she dries her tears, and cleverly begins to influence the vivid dreams of Debbie's Cancerian father, Les (with the help of *his* ruler, the romantic, sentimental Moon).

At last, as Earth time grew near the mysterious Christmas season of 1975, Debbie's father, while discussing with Steve the approaching holiday party for County Road Commission employees, "just happened" to mention that his daughter didn't feel like attending, because she had no escort (Venus had arranged *that* quite nicely), and since Steve had no date for the party either, he offered to take her (Goats and Bulls, you know, are very circumspect regarding social convention) — as if he had a choice in this karmic drama, which he had not at all, of course.

Then Debbie's mother, Pat, invited Steve to dinner a few days before the party, where he finally met the Taurus girl who was the other half of himself. That evening, Saturn gave only one, final, half-hearted gesture of discipline, as he drew a veil across the eyes of the Goat and the Bull, so they didn't recognize each other at all, except as ordinary people, exchanging ordinary conversation, in an ordinary way.

Then, came the magical night of Christmas Eve, and the party. It was time. Near midnight, the Bull and the Goat looked deeply into each other's suddenly familiar eyes, and *knew* . . . . . . as they were swept into one of those shining moments in eternity.

Yes, it was time. *"Two shall be born . . . . the whole wide world apart . . . ."* sang the Higher Angels of themselves, in joyful unison . . . as trillions of tiny, twinkling stars caroled in space . . . . . . the Moon smiled, behind a single tear . . . . . even Old Man Saturn grinned . . . . and Venus lay herself down on a soft cloud, to rest for a while, exhausted.

It's really a wondrous experience to look down upon events below, on Earth, from the higher vantage point of the stars . . . and watch destiny unfold its silvery-gold wings. An esoteric astrologer, carefully studying both horoscopes, could have predicted that unexpected Christmas Eve for the Goat and the Bull, when he was born, in Colorado — and when she was born, in Wisconsin. It's what makes astrology such a happy art and science. For, we have no real free will at all, any of us, on this level of awareness — except in our choice of *reaction* to Life's destined dramas. Only our Higher Selves possess complete free will over the control of events, which we may attain . . . touch briefly . . . only when we make contact, and thereafter communicate with — the *Super*conscious. I trust this true example will loosen somewhat the esoteric sensoriums of Taurus women and Capricorn men everywhere who have this odd notion that they may exert some sort of sensible, earthy control over their love — its alpha and its omega — without heeding their dreams, which are the true reality, and listening carefully to the symphony of the stars.

The natural chemistry between the Goat and the Bull, as with all 5-9 influenced lovers, makes it appear that their romance will be velvety smooth and free of static. But that's not necessarily true. The 5-9 blessing merely bestows the gift of a relationship which can bear more strain and stress than most, because of the mutual sympathy of the Sun Signs. Tensions may be more easily resolved with less bitterness, the occasional hurts interchanged are less painful, and reconciliations are usually more frequent and successful. They'll have their share of problems, but it takes really serious trouble to create a permanent break between two who are graced by the 5-9 Sun Sign Pattern, once they've committed themselves to each other in earnest.

Taurus and Cappy are each motivated by the same thing — security. Emotional and financial security. Unless the Moon or Ascendent of either was in an Air or Water sign at birth, these two normally don't possess the soaring imagination considered by poets and dreamers to be an absolute necessity for romance. Yet, they do share a quality between them which is profoundly necessary to the strength of any human relationship — the quality of patience. And patience is a virtue which nearly always gives birth, eventually, to triplets — Devotion, Faith and Loyalty, those three magic wands of words that can turn a casual infatuation, based on chemistry alone, into the deeper and enduring emotion of love.

Another ingredient the poets and dreamers deem to be a requirement for the flourishing of lasting romance, is — sentiment. At first glance, the Taurean girl may not appear to be brimming over with sentiment, but there are, nevertheless, sparkling wells of it within her for the right man to discover. Despite her surface practicality, it shows clearly in the strong attachment she has for home, her material possessions, old love letters, her children and her husband. She will resist any major change stubbornly, even when she *seems* to agree. Nor does she easily adapt to minor changes in personal habits. For what is a desire for change but a lack of sentimental attachment to what already exists? Therefore, her resistance to it means the opposite — an excess of emotion for what is already, and what has been. And this is the quality of which sentiment is made.

All right, so sentimental she is. Soft-hearted too. But she is not soft-headed, this lady. She knows what she wants, and will pursue it, in her own determined, yet outwardly unhurried and quiet way. The Taurean woman is perfectly willing to wait, and not push things prematurely, a trait the Capricorn man finds irresistibly feminine. It embodies the ultimate in female sexuality — passivity — which hints to him of the subtle mystery of submission to the dominant masculine force. This will never fail to both please and emotionally "turn on" the always slightly chauvinistic male Goat. And so, he may not notice the hardness of her head when he's been so entranced into seeing himself as the virile conqueror by the softness of her ways and the gentleness of her manner. Not to mention by her deep, throaty, musical voice — and her intriguing curves, all nicely rounded in the proper places, and designed for cuddling. Besides all that, this lady is usually a superb cook, and she has a marvelous sense of humor.

Sometimes it may seem that these two are so alike, you can't tell them apart. But there are ways an astrologer can tell them apart. Here's one. The Taurus girl will seldom burn up her carefully conserved energy in seeking either public acclaim or private approval. When she's made up her mind that she's right about anything, all she asks is that she be left alone, and not pushed by those who think differently. Tell the typical Taurus female that people are whispering about her, or that someone dislikes her, she'll simply shrug and say, "So? Have they nothing better to do than live my life for me? Have they no lives of their own? They must be very frustrated and lonely." Then she'll continue doing whatever it is she is doing, content in her *self*-respect.

Conversely, the Capricorn man cares quite a lot about both public acclaim and private approval. Secretly, he wants to reach the top of his goal or dream, then move into a position of power, far enough away from the clamorous crowds not to be annoyed or contaminated by the childish behavior he observes all around him. The quieter the Goat, the more intensely he inwardly yearns to get there first — with the most. Tell him that someone disapproves of him, and Cappy may shrug, like the lady Bull. He may even murmur the same kind of "I couldn't care less" reply. But *privately*, he will frown, perhaps even frustrate himself into a good toothache or stomachache over it, crack his knee cap several times a week, or break out in nervous bumps. He'll try to raise the opinion of himself held by those disapproving ones, as soon as he can do it without arousing the suspicion that it bothered him. Respect and admiration from business associates, friends, relatives and neighbors is vitally important to the Goat. Taurus appreciates any posies of praise thrown her way too, but unlike her Capricorn man, she won't be crushed when she receives an occasional onion of criticism or a mud pie of gossipy disapproval. She may guess his secret, but she's too kind and tactful, normally, to ever let him know the pain she's aware that he feels when he is not fully appreciated by others. Many emotions pass between this man and woman silently...unspoken, but no less deep and binding ....communicated in ways the heart hears.

In their sexual relationship, she may sometimes unconsciously project a faintly condescending attitude toward him. The Taurus woman is better prepared for the intimacy of sexual union than the average Goat, because her highly developed senses of hearing, seeing, smelling, tasting and touching, in all areas of existence, also increase her ability to express her love physically in subtle ways. She's also more adept than he in being able to show her affection through sentimental words and gestures (though she won't overdo it) and there could be some scattered occasions, in the beginning especially, when her superior talent for pure erotic sensuality may cause the Goat to feel inadequate as a lover. His physical expression of love is intense and direct, and can cause the Capricorn man to be quick and unrestrained in his sexual desire, with little delicacy. He tends to seek passion, without any frills, and though he doesn't lack tenderness, it may now and then *seem* to her that he does. But tenderness can be taught when it's latent, as it always is, in Capricorn. It may be buried beneath tons of his earthy nature, yet it's a treasure well worth digging for, with perseverance. If she uses her great reserves of patience and gentleness to lead him, he'll be anxious to learn how to fulfill, through their sexual Oneness, all her needs, which are no less intense than his. The Goat never finds it easy to express his strongest yearnings. A Taurus woman, when she follows her instincts, can help him free the emotions he shyly feels, and so very much longs to release.

One of the unfortunate quirks of many Saturn-ruled, Capricorn people (of both sexes) is their tendency to expect love to be sad, somehow......because of early romantic disappointments. Since his physical desires are as strong as any man's, this can cause an occasional Capricorn man to separate sex and love, in what, to him, is a practical attempt to satisfy the flesh urges of the former, and avoid being hurt by the latter. Because she is ruled by Venus, it's the responsibility of the Taurus woman to teach her shy, funny, affectionate Goat the eternal truth that these two needs cannot be divided if both are to be completely fulfilled. Sex without love leaves the body cold. Love without sex leaves the soul empty.

Now and then, it happens that there's a Capricorn man who seems to be made entirely of the earthy materials of selfishness, coldness, practicality and ambition. Now and then, it happens that there's a Taurus woman who seems to be made of the earthy materials of common sense, stubbornness, ambition and stale habit. But in both cases, these are simply façades to keep love at a distance, which is just the way they like it.

Why should they openly display their hearts, or offer them for sale to the highest bidder? This man and woman place too much value on their hearts to toss them casually upon love's auction block. But when the Taurus girl comes along to tenderly touch his hand, and gaze deeply into his eyes, quietly . . . the Goat will give his heart away, willingly, to her. Just as she will hand him her own, when she discovers he has guessed her most closely guarded secret (as closely guarded as his) — that she's a romantic dreamer too.

The Goats and Bulls reading this chapter have, I trust, learned not to scoff at Destiny and Fate, simply because they are intangible, unseen forces. To refuse to tune in to one's higher consciousness can cause the path of destiny to take a wrong turn, sadly, somewhere along the way. And this is far too frequently the fate of dogmatic Earth Sign men and women, in following the road to happiness. Maybe it would help them to meditate on the *entire* verse Steve and Debbie's Higher Angels of themselves were singing on that magical Christmas Eve, in Colorado . . . . . first channeled by Venus, long ago, through the sensitive awareness of a poet named Rossetti.

> *two shall be born . . . the whole wide world apart*
> *and speak in different tongues . . . and have no thought*
> *each, of the other's being . . . and no heed*
>
> *and these same two*
> *o'er unknown seas, to unknown lands, shall cross*
> *escaping wreck, defying death*
> *and all unconsciously*
> *shape each act, and bend each wandering step*
> *to this one end . . .*
> *   that one day, out of darkness*
> *they must meet*
> *and read Life's meaning in each other's eyes*
>
> *and these same two*
> *along some narrow way of Life shall walk*
> *so nearly side by side*
> *that should one turn, ever so little space*
> *to left . . . or right*
> *they needs must stand acknowledged, face to face*
>
> *and yet . . .*
>
> *with wistful eyes, that never meet*
> *and groping hands that never clasp*
> *with lips, calling in vain, to ears that never hear*
> *they seek each other all their weary days*
> *and die unsatisfied*
>
> *   . . . and this is Fate*

☆ ☆ ☆ ☆ ☆ ☆

TAURUS *Man* CAPRICORN *Woman*

———— ◄◄◆►► ————

"I won't go to bed," he had shouted, like one who
still believed that he had the last word on the subject.
"I won't, I won't" . . . . . . then Mrs. Darling had come in,
wearing her white evening-gown.

The practical side of a Taurus man will respond, with excitement (as much excitement as a Bull can arouse) to the practical side of the Capricorn girl. He'll admire her self-sufficiency, and her air of well-bred, dignified reserve will intrigue him, not to mention her quiet beauty. Taurus doesn't like anything to come easy, including love. This girl's love never comes easy. Since the Bull believes nothing is worth much if he doesn't have to work hard to get it and keep it, Cappy will interest him right away. Her affections are difficult to capture, for she does not yield her inner self lightly, or quickly. Obviously then, she's a prize the Bull deems it worthwhile to pursue.

But he may not respond with the same fervor of excitement to her apparent lack of sentiment. Despite his feigned disinterest in mushy declarations of love, Taurus is the most sentimental of all the Sun Signs. He doesn't wear his heart on his sleeve, but it's in the right place, however well hidden from view. It beats faster when he plays their favorite song, smells her perfume unexpectedly somewhere, or hears a laugh that reminds him of hers.

The female Goat is not quite so bowled over by nostalgic memories when a love affair is over, nor by the daily reminders of it while it's still alive. That's not to say she isn't capable of a deep devotion. Her loyalty, in fact, is unmatched by any other female on the astrological wheel, once she finds a man she thinks is worth loving wisely and well. She can also be tender and funny and gentle and comforting, all those lovely, feminine things. After all, Capricorn is a feminine sign. But it's also a negative Earth Sign — and Cardinal too — which means she doesn't want a man to dominate her completely, and she's not about to submerge herself in sentiment that might cloud her judgment or cause her to make a mistake she'll have to live down.

You notice I didn't say a mistake she'll regret. Cappy doesn't waste time on regret, which she considers a useless, maudlin emotion. But she does feel obliged to live down an action not based on good sense. It's the yoke of punishment Saturn places on her shoulders when she goofs, a stern reminder not to goof again. To her, "living it down," means taking her medicine straight, without whimpering.

This pretty, feminine woman is as tough as a gold miner's old boot, although she can have exquisitely tender feelings for those nearest and dearest to her, and she's quite capable of being faithful, if her mate was chosen by both her heart and her head. When she occasionally slips up, and allows her heart to rule alone, her head does not quickly forgive her. She must be somehow self-punished, according to Saturn's stern discipline. But she's not burdened with the kind of idealism that causes people to mask unpleasant facts behind a veil of sentimental evasion. She corrects her mistakes, then plods right on, along the rocky trail, seldom looking back. This girl is enormously practical, and imbued with a great deal of common sense. For example, very few Cappies become hookers or call girls, but their choice has little to do with sentimental morality. I once had a conversation with a female Goat about prostitution. She was decidedly contemptuous of women who sell their sexual favors in the market place, not because of moral or emotional objections, but because, in her precise words: "the profession involves so many middlemen that the prostitute ends up a financial loser, as well as a social outcast — and she can work for such a limited number of years. Then what does she do? It just isn't *practical*."

So, back to what we first discussed. The Taurus male will admire her common sense and practicality, because they match his own, but will probably be shocked (or hurt) at her lack of sentiment. It can put him in a twin dither of STOP and GO urges with her. But since their chemistry is so right, he'd be wise to swallow his shock and hurt with patience (another quality they both possess in abundance) until she's made one of her combined head-and-heart decisions to love and marry him. After that, she'll probably be as sentimental with him and with their family (including her parents and siblings, whom she'll stick to like a burr) as he could possibly desire. Married to the right man, no one makes a better wife and mother than Capricorn. She may appear snobbish and cold and a bit of a social climber to the rest of the world, but her husband, children and relatives will know only her warmth and love.

Jealousy will probably not be a large problem with these two. Neither the Bull nor the Goat is as mortally wounded, in an emotional sense, by an isolated act of infidelity as a Fire or Water Sign would be. With these two, it's more as if someone has robbed them of a valued possession. A Taurus man will become just as furious if an intruder steals his wife's affections as if he had stolen his car or his checkbook, about which he is more or less equally sentimental. A Goat Girl will be as coldly angry if a woman flirts with her Taurus husband as if she had caught the vixen trying to steal her mother's heirloom bedspread, or her father's antique clock.

When you comprehend how painful it is for both the Bull and the Goat to give up cash, or material things, I suppose you might say that unfaithfulness is no more pleasant for them than for the more emotional Sun Signs. But neither he nor she is inclined to throw away a secure relationship or a marriage over a single act of infidelity. Bulls and Goats have little desire to tamper with or to destroy an existing situation. When they do, which will be a rare occurrence, you can be sure of three things: (1) they will never forgive, (2) they will never forget, (3) they will never turn back and start again, with fresh hope in a new beginning. What's lost is lost, what's gone is gone. Finders may be keepers, but losers are never weepers, when they are Taureans or Capricorns.

Although they don't turn on the spigots of tears or hysteria, rejection or failure can, nevertheless, hurt them both deeply. But a Goat and a Bull will not sniffle in front of nosy neighbors. They'll brood in dismal melancholy privately, until finally, after weeks, or months, or years of inner sadness, they decide that the continuation of grief over spilled buttermilk is just not *practical*. Then they'll brighten up a little. Since this is a 5-9 Sun Sign Pattern, it will take a really major catastrophe to break a tie they have cemented together with sincere intentions.

Sexually, they are firmly and comfortably mated, because the physical relationship is usually — not always, but usually — more satisfying when the man is the Taurus, and the woman the Capricorn, than when the team shifts sides. He is a quietly sensual lover, full of the erotic ability to stir her passions, yet capable of also expressing himself with honest affection, combined with the kind of respect for sex (and for her womanhood) that she demands. She's not a girl who will expect long hours of preliminary romancing, and sentimental whisperings before their physical Oneness. Nor will she require her lover or husband to spend another several hours murmuring drowsy endearments, after the passion of their love has been fulfilled. The natural, silent feeling of closeness following sexual union contents her, and gives her a feeling of completeness. Why gild the lily ? It's no wonder this woman can lure a Bull more successfully than a flaming Fire Sign female (who might frighten him away) or a changeable Air Sign lady (who might drive him into confusion).

However, the sentimental Bull may require more than five minutes to demonstrate *his* devotion to *her*. Since Cappy is no more inclined to shirk her marital or love responsibilities than any other kind of duty, she'll usually respond beautifully, by genuinely trying to match his more leisurely Taurean lovemaking pace herself, and they'll become happy romantic, as well as sexual, lovers — so that, by the time they reach their Golden Wedding anniversary, they'll have the whole Sex-Love relationship bound up together in a lovely, warm unity. An occasional Capricorn woman may tend to separate sex from love, due to bitter memories of youthful hurt. The Bull may have fallen into the same pattern, unconsciously, and for the very same reasons. (Both Goats and Bulls have incredibly long memories.) But together, they can teach each other how well these two needs blend, and she'll awaken, through his tenderness, to the childhood dreams and innocence she lost through the premature growing-up all Capricorns experience — while he'll gradually forget his painful memories of the past, as she gently replaces them with warm and loving images for tomorrow's remembering.

The typical Taurean is rather uncommonly devoted to his family, which is a good thing, because it will help him tolerate the Goat Girl's obsession with hers. A Capricorn's devotion toward family ties can be summed up briefly, with Milne's poem:

> James James Morrison Morrison
> Weatherby George Dupree
> took great care of his mother
> though he was only three

The verse is appropriate to the Saturn-ruled, whether the Goat is male or female. In the latter case, just change the name to Jane Jane Morrison Morrison Weatherby Elizabeth Dupree, and *know* that she, also, "took great care of *her* mother, though she was only three." Not only that, she'll take good care of her family when she's past one hundred, and her parents are pushing the second century mark. Unless some traumatic and tragic experience in youth has left a neurosis of bitter rejection — between these two, and their mutual families, holidays will never be lonely and guest rooms will always be filled. The Bull will benignly approve of his Goat Girl's attitude toward both her own and his relatives, unless his mother is a Cancerian, and then it might get a little sticky. (Or if his Moon or Ascendent is in Cancer.) It could create anything from a mild emotional tremor, now and then, to a full scale earthquake on occasion.

A Cancerian mother is intensely possessive of her son, and a Capricorn wife is intensely possessive of her husband. (Jealousy and possessiveness are not quite the same thing.) It's possible that such a situation could cause the Goat Girl to feel tugged on from both sides, until she decides (figuratively) to butt her tough horns against one side or the other. But the Bull has horns too, and it's only fair to warn Cappy that the odds are stacked against his using them against Mama. For either a Capricorn woman — or a Bull with a Cancer Moon or Ascendent — to be forced to choose between love and family ties, is like being condemned to the horrors of a Tchen-type Oriental torture chamber.

They are good for each other, in so many ways, the Goat and the Bull. After a while, they can even read one another's thoughts, so closely attuned can Taurus and Capricorn become, throughout their years of togetherness.

HIM: Would you like to . . .
HER: Yes, if we can get there in time for the first feature. Shall I . . .

HIM: No, don't call them. Let's go by ourselves. Remember . . .

HER: . . . our first anniversary, when we couldn't afford to go anywhere, so we stayed home, and . . .

HIM: You wore your white evening gown anyway, and I . . .

HER: . . . spilled grape juice on it, and I . . .

HIM: And you laughed. Most women would have cried. Then I . . .

HER: Then you said you were glad of me . . .

HIM: Wasn't that a . . .

HER: A silly, sentimental thing to say ? Yes, but I've never forgotten it. Look at the time ! If we don't hurry, we'll miss the first feature. Do you . . .

HIM: Still want to go ? No. Let's stay home tonight, and . . .

HER: Yes.

☆ ☆ ☆ ☆ ☆ ☆

TAURUS

Earth — Fixed — Negative
Ruled by Venus (also by the
  Planet Pan-Horus)
Symbol: The Bull
Night Forces — Feminine

AQUARIUS

Air — Fixed — Positive
Ruled by Uranus
Symbol: The Water Bearer
Day Forces — Masculine

The **TAURUS-AQUARIUS** *Relationship*

> . . . . . *they knew it was make-believe, while to him*
> *make-believe and true were exactly the same thing.*
> *This sometimes troubled them, as when they had to*
> *make-believe that they had had their dinners.*

n ancient Chippewa song begins:

> *as my eyes search the prairie*
> *I feel the summer . . . in the spring*

These words were surely chanted in the Garden of the Gods, at sunrise, by an Aquarian Chippewa. They express so clearly the essence of the Water Bearers, who feel the summer in the spring — and the winter in the fall — always a season ahead of everyone else. Their Uranus vision, spanning the years, the decades, and even the centuries, gives them the benefit of an extra dimension or two, which accounts for the vague expression in their eyes.

The rare ability to gaze into the world of Tomorrow, while remaining acutely conscious of the world of Today, involves the *Intelligence*, the *Instinct* and the *Imagination*, functioning together as a trinity, smoothly and simultaneously. When Pisceans peek into Tomorrow, they often ignore Today — and the brief glimpses into the Future that Sagittarians occasionally experience are just that — brief moments of prophecy. Scorpios become too intensely involved in whatever dimension they're floating within, to pay heed to any others at the same time. Only the Water Bearers can juggle the *Intelligence, Instinct* and *Imagination* as a triplicity, allowing them to form a three-dimensional image of Past, Present and Future, which is perfectly synchronized. Now do you see why Aquarius is called the "Sign of Genius"?

Some Aquarian men and women enjoy it so much out there in Tomorrow, or Yesterday, however, that they forget their synching talent, and decide to visit there for a while, in their astral bodies, leaving their flesh bodies behind them to manage as best they can during the absence, walking around zombie-like, neither hearing nor seeing, and speaking in an unintelligible mumble. Do you see why Aquarius is also called the "Sign of Insanity"?

Ah, Genius and Insanity! They go together, like pickles and pumpernickel, and every single Aquarian who has ever walked the Earth is the first, while also being harassed, from time to time, by the second — or accusations of it. From Mia Farrow Previn to Lewis Carroll, from Abraham Lincoln to Tallulah Bankhead, from Ayn Rand and Telly Savalas to Vanessa Redgrave and Charlie Brown's dog, Snoopy (alias Joe Cool and the Red Baron) Aquarians are well aware that they possess this half-and-half nature, and they are all rather marvelously untroubled by it, happily admitting their quirks, like Aquarian astrologer Carroll Righter, who cheerfully quipped, when his mother called him "an odd duckling" — "*Well, quack quack!*"

Grand Old Opry star Minnie Pearl tells about a man in her home town who isn't very bright. After he's opened his mouth and said, "Howdy!" he has told you everything he knows, claims Minnie. She shouldn't judge him too hastily. He could be an Aquarian, out there on one of his extended trips into the ethers. The mechanism on his Time Machine which he carries in his noodle got jammed somewhere, perhaps in another century, caught in a Space Warp (a kind of hole in the sky) and he hasn't returned yet. But he will. Or *she* will. Water Bearers always count-down from Tomorrow, and reappear brighter than when they left in their mental capsules. The Aquarians who keep an even keel between all dimensions more often than they get lost in a Space Warp, are the prophets, visionaries, creative brains and inventive geniuses of mankind and womankind. They gather the Waters of Wisdom and Higher Truth from the deep wells of Tomorrow, and pour it out in a continuous flow, in their weird guises of pixilated scientists and inventors, musicians, artists, writers, politicians, cab drivers, barbers and Chippewa Indian Chiefs and Squaws. That's sort of "where it's at" with Aquarius, "it" being their consciousness, and "at" being the triple dimension of Time and Space they visit.

As for the Bulls, we can sum up their position in Time and Space very quickly. Taurus exists in solid, tangible form in the Here and Now. Never mind the Heretofore or the Hereafter. One dimension is usually more than satisfactory for both the male and the female Bulls. As far as these men and women are concerned, there are quite enough problems to be solved on this level, in the Present, without flying around looking for trouble on other levels in the Past or Future. Tomorrow was made for some, perhaps. But to Taurus, Tomorrow may never come. Take care of Today. Even the very rare, "psychic" Bull, such as Taurean Peter Hurkos, is glued to Earth. Hurkos may take a swing out into the Future, or back into the Past, due to other planetary positions in his birth chart, but when he returns from his brief, un-Taurus-like flights, he wants his dinner, and he wants it on time. He also pays his bills, minds his business, and expects others to mind theirs. Besides, the only reason a Taurus psychic scatters any predictive pearls, is to convince people they should behave in a *sensible* manner right *now*, and they should be prepared, in a *practical* way, for any emergencies the Bull may have glimpsed in the Future.

Unlike Aquarius, Taurus is neither weird nor pixilated. Taurus personifies Norman Rockwell's paintings — all of them. The Bull's eyes do not contain the Aquarian's vague expression. They are soft, serene — and sometimes beady, when the Bull is in a fury (which occurs most infrequently, but when it does, makes up for its rarity with intensity). However, Taureans do often mumble, like Aquarians, in unintelligible monosyllables, at times, like "Yep" — "Nope" — "Uh-Huh" — "Huh-Uh" — and "Grmmmpphhff." So in this respect, there's a faint resemblance between them. These two were both born under a Fixed Sign, giving them also in common a certain Fixity of purpose (you might prefer to call it obstinacy). Outside of these similarities, they're as far apart as two humans can be, and still recognize one another as being from the same planet. (It must be admitted here, in all honesty, that sometimes Taurus and Aquarius do *not* recognize one another as being from the same planet.) Taurus desires to retain the status quo. Aquarius desires to change it.

Picture these two, eyeing each other across a room, or across the street. Aquarius, the Bouncing Crystal Ball — and Taurus, the immovable, but lovable Lump of Earth. It's difficult to imagine their conversation, if they should decide to draw closer, isn't it? I mean, after all, what does an immovable, but lovable Lump of Earth say to a Bouncing Crystal Ball? "Grmmmpphhff"? And what, in heaven's name, does a Bouncing Crystal Ball say to an immovable, but lovable Lump of Earth? "Howdy!" ??? Well, let me tell you that, regardless of what the folks in Minnie Pearl's home town might believe, this mutual greeting will definitely never convey all that either of them knows.

Taurus is not inclined to be a chatterbox, blabbing all his (or her) knowledge to strangers. However, the practical facts and common sense the Bulls have cautiously accumulated, and carefully stored in their heads, are nonetheless powerful mental tools, when they choose to sharpen them and go to work building a house, a financial empire, a career — or a firm approach to love and friendship. "Grrmmmpphff" is assuredly not all Taurus knows. But it may be all the Bulls are willing to tell an Aquarian on short acquaintance, until they've had time to decide if the Water Bearer is worth the energy required for any further chit-chat.

As for Aquarius, the Uranus-ruled men and women always know far more than they spill carelessly out of their little brown jugs. They receive their kicks from life by playing W. C. Fields, speaking in Sanskrit, underwater... sometimes varying this by switching to Peter Lorre or Boris Karloff, whispering through a megaphone, while chewing bubble gum underwater. When they're on dry land, they use a word scrambling device (invisible, of course) that makes their Uranian conversations often sound like a tape being played backwards, at high speed. Even when their remarks are clear enough to sound like a tape being played forward, at slow speed, there are usually lots of blank spots, where the tape has been erased. Haven't you noticed that? Taurus has noticed it, frequently, and gives a disgusted grunt or "Grrmmmpphff," refusing to try to cope with such nonsense. Or ... do the Water Bearers perhaps just flip off their switches now and then, when they want to splice out a thought, an idea, a feeling or a concept too far advanced for the ordinary mortal to comprehend? Whatever, the point is that Taurus and Aquarius will communicate with one another exactly in the same manner they each communicate with the rest of us — in their own time, and in their own way.

This is a 4-10 Sun Sign Pattern, which means that compatibility and comprehension between these two is achieved only with effort — and is rewarded with that good feeling of having accomplished something worthwhile, when it *is* finally achieved. Assuming they've broken the ice with "Grrmmmpphff" and "Howdy!" how do they then break down the bashful barriers of Taurus, and the detachment of Aquarius, to get into action as a unity? It depends on many factors. To begin with, Taurus has a great deal more reserve of manner than do the typical, friendly, gregarious Water Bearers. Even the timid Aquarians count everyone as "friend," from the postman to the President (the President of the local Anti-pollution League, or the President of the United States — Aquarius hardly knows the difference). It's all they can do, these people, to keep themselves straightened out on the difference between girls and boys, top and bottom, up and down, black and white, cold and hot, and all that. A typical Aquarian is not prejudiced in his or her choice of buddies. "Buddy" is a term Uranian folk use to describe lovers, husbands, wives, cats, dogs, squirrels, children, neighbors, dolphins, muggers, pickpockets, relatives and so on. They are all "buddies." Sometimes this is varied with "my pal," "my old buddy," "my good buddy," "my friend" — but never "my *best* friend." Aquarians are no more partial to friends than they are selective of them, so no one ever becomes the Aquarian's "best friend."

Taurus is just one of the crowd. The Bulls may bring along their empty cups if they wish, and the Water Bearers will fill them. But Uranus-ruled men and women (and children) have little patience with the Bull's long silences and pouting spells. There are too many thirsty people out there who need their time and attention, and a long drink from the waters of Uranian Wisdom.

It takes the average Taurean several years to make a friend — a real friend, not counting relatives and casual acquaintances. It takes Aquarius approximately only five seconds to say, "Howdy, Buddy!" Then you've been told, you believe, all he (or she) knows, in Uranus Sanskrit, of course, or maybe in Aquarian hieroglyphics — so now you're friends, right? Taurus is suspicious of friendships made quickly, taken lightly, and so loosely defined.

If these two work through a harmonious Sun-Moon-Ascendent relationship between their birth charts, they'll eventually begin to speak the same language, and be able to communicate. Even without help from a favorable Luminary and Ascendent exchange, and other such harmonious aspects in their horoscopes, they'll learn many valuable lessons from each other, and the mutual education could be fun and firecrackers, as well as mentally and emotionally stimulating — causing their souls to stretch. Souls need exercise too, just like bodies. That's the purpose of the 4-10 vibration.

With a square or opposition between their mutual Luminaries, and Ascendents, these two Sun Signs may have to learn to protect themselves in the clinches. The Bulls will balk at the airy nonchalance of the Aquarians, who may seem to be looking down and patronizing them, from up there in the clouds. The Water Bearers will need a firm grip to keep from slipping over the wobbly line between Genius and Insanity, when the earthy Taureans make them feel they're pulling the dead weight of the Bull's disapproval behind them on their trips into outer space.

Although there's a rumor that a lone cow once crashed the scene in a grand leap, it's difficult for a Bull to jump over the Moon, for all his (or her) splendid strength — as hard as it is for an Aquarian to be confined by a barbed wire fence, in a peaceful, but monotonous pasture. But if it's true that "the dish ran away with the spoon," why can't a Bull frolic happily with a Water Bearer? In the realms of tolerance and joy, cats can play fiddles, and — Hey-diddle-diddle! a Bull *can* jump over the Moon! I just checked my notes, and several of the astronauts were Sun Sign Taureans. What do you know? Life is full of surprises, as any Aquarian can tell you. Even if you don't ask.

☆ ☆ ☆ ☆ ☆ ☆

TAURUS *Woman* AQUARIUS *Man*

*"Wendy, Wendy, when you are sleeping in your silly bed
you might be flying about with me saying funny things
to the stars."*

"Oo!" ...... *She was wriggling her body in distress.*

Very little comes as a surprise to an Aquarian man, considering his intuitive
nature. Still, he may not be prepared for what happens after he knocks
around with a Taurus girl for a spell. Here he is, a man with a firm set of
ethics (they may be peculiar, but they are his own, and they are firm — or
rather, Fixed). He has a great feeling for humanity. He's interested in
everybody, he has no prejudices against the female sex, the male sex, or
people of any other sex. Yet, look at the hurt he's caused her, all unawares.
How can he have hurt her? They had so much fun together at the zoo. He
was just trying to be her big brother. Her friend. Her pal. Her buddy.

A Taurus girl was formed for romance by Mother Nature, and this is not
a female who argues with Mother Nature. Where he made his mistake with
her was back at the beginning. The first time he found himself concentrating
his fitful, but flattering attention on her, asking her shocking questions of an
intimate sort, and pulling on his ear sympathetically when she cried, he
should have made a special effort — to notice that she's a woman. She's
certainly aware that he's a man. She noticed it right off. And to her, the
romantic arithmetic then became quite simple. One male plus one female
equals ecstasy — on several levels, not the least of which is the sensual
gratification of touching.

Aquarians reading this may need an interpretation of the word "touching." It means kissing, hugging, holding hands, and all sorts of things. It
means, like — well, human bodily contact. Flesh-to-flesh. Human bodily
contact is something which not all, but many Water Bearers, fear as they fear
the black plague. (The black plague is what you get if someone uses your
towel or toothbrush. Or the white plague. Either one. Both deadly.) It isn't
that Aquarians are against touching itself, but it leads to — what do they call
it — two becoming one? Or some nonsense like that. Aquarius feels safer
when two remain two. That way, he's sure of where he stands. Alone. Free
of obligations, and in no danger of losing his individuality. If you're going to
go around touching people, especially girl-type people, who knows what
you're letting yourself in for? Especially if she forgets to bring her own towel
when they go swimming. Maybe even the black or white plague!

Perhaps he was devoting himself to her for the purpose of taking her apart to see how she ticks or tocks, with the same fascination he has for all forms of experimentation. But she didn't realize she was only a guinea pig for his curious mind. When he invited her to bring her own pizza and cream soda, and watch the Macy's Thanksgiving Day parade from his roof, she thought he was, well — to be honest — a little crazy. Still, it was a wonderful kind of crazy, and when she considered it carefully (as Taureans always do) she decided he wouldn't invite just any old girl to hang around on his roof with him. She then concluded it meant he loved her.

Maybe he did. But an Aquarian man has a way of switching love-at-first-sight into friendship, as a sort of test of its deeper worth, then letting it rust there. To a Taurus girl, such neglect of mutual emotional needs is a sure way to become a real-born-loser. She believes that genuine love doesn't strike but once (sometimes not even that often) in a lifetime. Why risk missing it by not recognizing it, and giving it a chance? She's astrologically right. Real love (meaning the twin soul union) is a rare and beautiful experience. It's a sad thing to miss it, and have to catch up with it in a future incarnation. Even though Aquarius is the natural ruler of the eleventh astrological house of "karmic love," many Aquarians do miss it. They rank right alongside Virgos and Sagittarians in their inclination toward bachelorhood, and in their desire to avoid confinement in the institution of marriage. Of course, there are compensations. They also avoid mistakes. That's a good thing to avoid with this Sun Sign combination, considering it's a 4-10 vibration. If it should happen to be a mistake, and they get married, it won't take much strain to unravel the knot.

There are exceptions, but the average Taurean girl who is unhappily involved with an Aquarian male is more vulnerable to being devastated by it than he is. Once she falls in love, she intends it to last forever-and-three-days. That would be his original intention too, except for his proclivity for eccentric action, which she may not anticipate, because he can't even predict it himself, and heaven knows he can't explain it. He's a Fixed Sun Sign, so it is conceivable and even possible for him to remain contented with the right woman for a lifetime. But when he's not contented, his Uranus vibes will make the final split much easier for him to bear than for her.

Aquarius adapts smoothly to change, when it's necessary (sometimes even when it isn't), despite his Fixity in daily, personal habits. Taurus does not. To her, change is frightening. It means the new, the strange, the untried and the unfamiliar. She feels emotionally safe, secure, protected in her lover's arms, once there's been intimacy between them. She's used to him. Like she's used to her hair style, her faded jeans, her old records, her broken-down coffee pot, and her broken-in tennies — with much more depth of feeling, of course. Even if living with him is full of friction, to the point of being unbearable, she'll postpone ending the misery through separation or divorce as long as she stubbornly believes there's still hope. You have to admire her staying power. But when and if she does finally make up her mind to leave him, she'll go. And nothing will bring her back. That is, if she was serious about leaving, and not just trying it as a last, desperate resort. If it's the latter, her faith and efforts may be rewarded, because the temporary break provides a change from monotony, and forces him to take a fresh interest in the changing scene. It's a strategy some Taurus girls use successfully, even going so far as to feign a love affair with a handsome gigolo type, which often has the effect of jerking Aquarius back from his world out yonder, and waking him up to the possibility that he's losing more than a comfortable friendship. He may start having nightly hot flashes and cold chills, as he remembers the funny way her nose wrinkles when she laughs, the way she sings off key in the shower — (and uses her own towel) — the sleepy-soft look in her eyes on Sunday mornings, her blueberry pancakes, the little feminine mooing sounds she makes when she's been well loved, her wacky jokes, her shiny hair, her scented skin, her — well, maybe she was *more* than just another buddy. She was so great at pulling splinters out of his toes, massaging his back, having faith in his visions, making things cozy, making poverty fun, making his headaches disappear, making potato soup, making money stretch, making love — yes, she's something more than a pal. She's really something else.

So, he pedals his bike to her pad, brings her a pet mouse as a peace offering, shoves a bunch of ragged dandelions in her hand, gives her a lopsided grin, and asks shyly, "Hey, sexy! You want to play house again?" However, if she's not using the walkout as romantic strategy — if it is, instead, the result of her careful deliberation — he can stuff the mouse and the dandelions back in his pocket. A Bull once gone, is gone. He could move a mountain more easily than he could sway the Taurus woman into trying again, once she decides it's really over between them.

Without a favorable Sun-Moon aspect between this (or any other) 4-10 Sun Sign Pattern, the slightest breeze may rock the boat, and cause a shipwreck. Because his Uranus reflexes are quicker than hers, he may sail away before she realizes what happened, and she'll be left floating around in a sea of emotions without a life preserver, and she's of the Earth element, not Water. That's why Bulls are in more danger than Water Bearers when love goes on the rocks. With planetary assistance from a harmonious Sun-Moon aspect in their mutual charts, however, they can survive the storms and knit a bright crazy-quilt of living and loving, stuffed with soft feathers of compassion and affection, to keep them warm and toasty while they fight and kiss and make-up periodically.

Their sexual relationship may be frustrating and unfulfilling, unless she caters to his need for change by matching his madness. If he surprises her by wearing a Donald Duck face mask to bed, or letting their pet mouse loose under the blankets to nibble her toes, she shouldn't pout stubbornly, or sleep in the guest room. She should shock him right back with her own little surprises, like wearing his dandelions in her hair at night — making a bedspread out of old Union Jacks, wired with a music box that plays "God Save the Queen" when she presses the button — or maybe painting the ceiling with luminous stars and galaxies, like the one at the Hayden Planetarium, so he can lie there and try to spot the Big Dipper while they're making love. Anything to vary the scene.

He'll have to take the time, and have the patience, to understand and fill her deep hunger for affection, and for the sensual in lovemaking. She needs expressions of love at times other than their sexual union. But this man can be a sensitive, considerate lover, if the Taurus girl-woman tries a little harder to be tolerant of his little sexual, emotional and romantic idiosyncrasies. She'll have to realize that his Uranus passion is mental, as well as physical, and find imaginative ways to blend his abstract desires with her more centered and traditional sexual needs. It's a constant challenge to arouse this man to the point of pure, sky rocket passion, but worth the effort, because Aquarius can bring to sexual Oneness an unexpected magic, that turns on the heart and soul, as well as the physical senses.

One word of warning. The pet mouse he may use as a conciliatory gesture when they've quarreled — he'd better make that a gerbil. Taurus people are very closely related, not to just bulls and cows, but also, on a different, but equally powerful vibration, to the elephant. You know what elephants do when they see a mouse. She's liable to do the very same thing. Scream or trumpet chillingly, toss her trunk in the air wildly, in great fright, and leap across the room . . . into his arms. Oh, I see. *That's* why he *brought* the mouse! Hmmmm. Never underestimate the canny calculations of an Aquarian male. He always knows exactly what he's doing, however daffy he may appear while he's doing it.

These two are different. She's a girl. He's a boy. She'd like him to treat her as a woman, he'd like to be treated as a man. She deserves it. He may not. (But men are dreary sorts — boys are more fun.) She likes thick carpets and plush, plump furniture. He'd just as soon sack out in a tent. She likes to scrub her skin with a scented back brush, in a tub of water, filled with perfumed oils. He likes to beat his skin with bamboo leaves, Japanese style, in the shower. She's tuned in to peace and quiet — which he calls boredom. He's tuned in to excitement and controversy — which she calls bedlam.

She may eventually lose her normally well controlled temper and patience, and tell him to go get someone else to pull the splinters out of his toes. Still, if he can teach her how to fly a little, and she can teach him how to get it together . . . . . . well, who knows? "If" is a little word, with a big meaning. But "love" is a four letter word, with infinite power.

☆ ☆ ☆ ☆ ☆ ☆

TAURUS *Man* AQUARIUS *Woman*

◆◄◆►◆

Poor kind Tootles, there is danger in the air . . .

*The fairy Tink who is bent on mischief this night
is looking for a tool, and she thinks you the most
easily tricked of the boys.*

An Aquarian is a very special kind of woman, who needs a very special kind
of man. Then again, there are those who would say she is a weird kind of
woman, who needs a super patient kind of man.

Most of those people would be Bulls, plugging themselves by reminding
you that *they* are super patient sorts, along with their other virtues. The
feminine Water Bearer's personality is unique, and to most of us, unique
means special. To an Earth Sign, however, unique normally means weird.
Strange. Not-to-be-believed. It's simply a matter of definition. The
important thing for the Bull to remember is that this lady is different. She
intrigues the masculine Taurean because she's mysterious. It's not the
mystery he senses around a Scorpio woman — the mystery of wondering if
she's evil or pure, if she's cool or warm. With this Uranus lady, it's the
mystery of wondering if she's for real. It fascinates him. And well it might.

She has a delightfully vague air about her. That's only natural. She was
born under an Air Sign. It's hard to define. Like, when she begins a sentence,
and leaves it hanging there, in mid-air . . . . when she stares off into the
distance, while he's saying 'I love you' . . . . has trouble remembering his
name. Things like that. Later, the Bull will discover that she was only too
clearly present and aware at those times when he thought her attention was
wandering. She didn't miss a nuance. Her seeming vagueness is merely a
signal that she's mentally floating around, waiting until the scene catches up
with where she's already gone — ahead. It's such a bore when a man can't
travel on her electrical circuit, so she instinctively fades away or tunes in to a
different channel. An Aquarian female can be here — or she can be there —
but here or there, she's always very far out.

Since she's as much of an individualist about romance as she is about
everything else, this lady makes up her own rules about love as she goes along.
Whatever they may be, whether puritanical or permissive by other people's
standards, she's true to them, and to herself. It's this very quality of self-
honesty and integrity that attracts the Bull to the girl Water Bearer like a
magnet, and causes him surprisingly often to tolerate her romantic rules, even

when they rub against his grain and grit. He clearly sees her as one of the few really honest people left in the world. One of the few ethical, reliable, dependable . . . . . oh, now, wait just a *minute*. Hold it right here. Honest and ethical she is. But you are inviting trouble, Taurus man, if you start out by expecting this woman to be reliable and dependable.

It's true that she's Fixed in purpose and intent, being born, like the Bull, under a Fixed Sign. She's also an excellent organizer (for all her deceptive fuzziness of manner) and like him, she likes to save and accumulate things. Not because she's economical, a scavenger, or a pack rat — or for any of those sensible, practical (to Bulls) reasons. She saves and accumulates things that just happen to strike her fancy. Like the tassel from Robert E. Lee's baby bootie she bought at an auction down south — or the tiny clapper from the bell on the desk of her fifth grade schoolteacher. She leans toward antiques (the Bull leans toward breaking them) and she saves all sorts of nonsense, like her old Mousketeer cap, her father's shaving cup, the nude picture a friend took of her when she was soaking up the sun one summer. Stop pawing and snorting, the friend was female — and most Uranus-ruled girls are not modest in the company of their own sex, in the woods, when there's no one around. Some of them are not overly modest in crowds either, but let's not talk about those Water Bearers — the Bull has not fallen in love with this type, you can bet your baby bootie tassel on that. Her fondness for antiques (if she's a typical Aquarian) may annoy the Bull to the point of great frustration, and huge exasperation. (Everything Taurus does is great or huge, never petty or teeny-tiny.) This man may enjoy the tradition of the past, and well made furniture, created by craftsmen to last more than three weeks, but he won't go for those fragile, dainty antiques that fall apart when you sit on them. Many a Bull has fallen plumb through an eighteenth-century chair his Aquarian mate has purchased — while he's reading the stock market reports in the evening paper. And I tell you that a Bull, who has fallen through the seat of a chair on his backside — hard — can be quite bearish about the whole matter. He's capable of picking up the offending chair and smashing it into splinters, while smashing her feelings at the same time, by shouting, "KEEP THESE @@ ## !! % ¢ & °° (expletives deleted) SILLY PIECES OF JUNK OUT OF MY WAY! YOU SPENT ENOUGH MONEY FOR THAT @@ ## !! % ¢ & °° THING TO BUY A WHOLE HOUSEFUL OF SOLID, SENSIBLE FURNITURE. I WANT A LAZY-BOY RECLINER IN THIS ROOM, IN THIS VERY CORNER BY TOMORROW NIGHT — AND WHEN I COME HOME FROM WORK, IT HAD BETTER BE THERE, EVEN IF YOU HAVE TO CARRY IT HOME FROM THE STORE ON YOUR BACK, WOMAN." (Taurus men are always boss in their homes.)

And what does his Air Sign Aquarian "woman" have to say about her Bull's furious rampage about the chair? She could quite likely ask him, "Listen, Jumbo, what's a four-letter word that rhymes with truck?" (She's working a crossword puzzle in the part of the newspaper he wasn't reading.) In his angry state, he may supply her with a most rude and uncouth, vulgar answer, such as — "schmuck." (Especially if he's a Taurean of the Hebrew persuasion.) Suddenly, her face will light up, and she'll say, "I've got it! *Luck!* I have to use an 'L,' because vertically, it has to spell Lixivate — up and down. I was going to use Buck, but the 'B' wouldn't work, going the other direction, where I needed another 'L' for Lithoid. Thanks anyway, but I don't need an 's,' and besides 'schmuck' has seven letters, and I told you I needed four. By the way, do you know what the work 'lithoid' means? It means: made of stone, resembling a stone, or a stony structure. That's cute. I think I'll call you that from now on, instead of Jumbo. Lithoid."

He stares at her in silence, at a total loss for words. Then suddenly, without warning, a bolt of Uranus lightning strikes, and she tosses the newspaper in his face, yelling, "Carry your @@ ## !! % ¢ & °° chair home on your own back, Lithoid. I'm going on a camping trip tomorrow, by myself — and I'll be gone a week or more. Don't call me, I'll call you if I feel like it, which I probably WON'T!" She slams the door, jumps in the station wagon, guns the engine and takes off, speeding down the street, on her way to nowhere — to "calmly" think things over. That's the sort of thing you can expect when two *Fixed* personalities have a disagreement, and one of them (her) is susceptible to those sudden, unexpected Uranian outbursts.

These two, let us remember, are governed by the tense 4-10 Sun Sign Pattern influence, and are often agitated by this troublesome vibrational energy, into confrontation. They should both be aware that each of their tempers may explode when least anticipated. The Bull always surprises and shocks when he becomes really angry, simply because his rages occur so seldom. The Aquarian is also prone to shock and surprise her lover or husband with her anger, simply because she's ruled by Uranus, and most everything this planet incites her to do is done without warning. She'll come home in fifteen minutes or so, her anger cooled, and bring him a gift, a peace offering —perhaps a puppy she found wandering around, homeless. If the puppy is warm, soft and cuddly, her Taurus man will probably melt, squeeze it — and her — and say they can keep it, but only if she promises to housebreak it. She'll promise, sweetly . . . and peace will be restored again. But it may be a temporary truce, unless their Suns and Moons and Ascendents are in harmonious aspect between their birth charts. If they are not, they're both going to need to acquire some self-discipline, and realize that "volatile" is *not* an eight-letter word that rhymes with happiness.

Let's return to their mutual inclination to save things. (The 4-10 explosion has a way of causing trains of thought to leap off the track.) Like her, the Bull is fond of saving old memories, in the form of junk, although he'll claim, bashfully and stubbornly, that they have some sensible use. They don't, but she should let him *think* they do. (Crabs like to save things too, but for different reasons. Partly sentiment, yes, but mostly because they get their claws stuck, and can't let go.) All right. She and he are both Fixed, therefore, they are both good organizers, and they tend to accumulate. However, when it comes to the quality of dependability, Aquarius is the black sheep of the Fixed family. (Black sheep is not a negative term — they're the sheep that have the gumption to be different, you know.) The other three Fixed Signs, Taurus, Leo and Scorpio, are duly dependable, but this is the place where Aquarius jumps off the boat.

She'll try like blazes to keep a promise, and put forth a Herculean effort to be on time for appointments. She'll seldom retract anything she's said, if she felt it deeply when she said it, and this is all admirable. But her eccentricities of dress and manners, her sudden Uranus zigs and zags of behavior, her unexpected switches, and the surprises she delights in giving you, cannot be described as dependable. They can only be described as unsettling.

The Taurus man is generally conventional, his behavior predictable, he neither likes to zig, nor to zag, and even his worst enemy could never call him eccentric. The Bull is a conformist at heart, which is why the Aquarian Age throws him into a quiet, but despairing tizzy. Who can cope with these crazy young people, the sexual revolution, riots, protests against our government, people running around naked, and women having the temerity to think they're equal to men, when any good anatomy course proves how ridiculous *that* is? So Taurus sits patiently, wondering and privately worrying, protecting his property against wild eyed, anonymous maniacs out there on the streets, and searching desperately, like Diogenes, for an honest man. At the very least, an honest woman.

Along comes the Aquarian girl, with the courage of her convictions carried high and shining, and he thinks his search is over. But what about her eccentricities? Those funny clothes she wears, her peculiar hair style, her odd statements and her sympathy with those dangerous, wild-eyed maniacs? Is it because she's a mere female that she doesn't have enough sense to be alarmed by what's happening in the world around her? Maybe she needs him to protect her.

I won't deny she may need protection. But the reason she's not alarmed is because, after all, the Aquarian Age is *her* age, and being an Aquarian herself, she knows there's never any need to conform to anything, unless you *want* to. She's always been content to live by the seashore, without knocking folks who prefer the mountains. She's always worn her hair the way it pleased her, whether her friends were bald or pigtailed. What's *wrong* with going to church on Sunday, then having lunch with an atheist afterwards? If she could only make him see that he doesn't have to get so uptight about what's happening — that it's just the beginning of a glorious new era of being yourself, conservative or liberal, barefoot or booted, long hair or crew cut. It simply means to live, and to let live.

Now, that last part Taurus will understand. He's perfectly willing to live and let live, as long as he can grumble a little when things don't suit him. They're both inclined to "let it be," but they should apply that philosophy to themselves, as well as to the world, and not ridicule each other's personal convictions. As with all 4-10 couples, each cramps the other's style somewhat, and it pinches.

Her Aquarian inclination to the abstract extends to her sexuality, and since there's nothing whatsoever abstract about the Bull's sexual needs, this can instigate a little insomnia. She's not a woman who is obsessed with sensuality and eroticism, although she may be quite curious about it. Her approach to lovemaking is airy and complicated; his is simple and earthy. Physical desire never runs as strong or as deep in Aquarius as it does in Taurus. Yet, there's something in the Bull's warm, affectionate nature that touches her heart, and makes her want to please him. And there's something about her off-beat passions, so honest and direct, that brings out a gentle tolerance in the Taurus man, a sort of surge of protectiveness, which certainly won't dilute his manhood.

She may overwhelm him with her fierce love hunger one night, then seem to float away from his touch the next. He may not be aware that her physical desire can be aroused by the funny way he whistled while he was clumsily peeling an orange for breakfast (hours before bedtime) — excited by the frosted fairyland scenes etched on a winter windowpane — and dampened by a newscast she heard, just before dinner, about how many millions of babies and children, all over the world, die of starvation every single hour. And *she* may not be aware that her Bull needs more than a few pats and hugs to keep him contented. He needs his head scratched (literally), his hand held, his nose kissed and his ears filled with gentle, baby-soft, tender words — on a very regular basis.

However much love surrounds this man, he's always greedy for more of it. Yet, however much she may be devoted to him, the Aquarian girl is compelled to share her love with her friends, and with all of humanity, in general. Sometimes, it may seem to these two as if there's just not enough love to go around. There never is, when you're taking it. Only when you're giving it. An inexhaustible supply.

TAURUS

Earth — Fixed — Negative
Ruled by Venus (also by the
Planet Pan-Horus)
Symbol: The Bull
Night Forces — Feminine

PISCES

Water — Mutable — Negative
Ruled by Neptune
Symbol: The Fish
Night Forces — Feminine

The **TAURUS-PISCES** *Relationship*

Thus sharply did the terrified three learn the
difference between an island of make-
believe and the same island come true.

Yes, there are three of them, for Pisces is a sign of duality symbolized by the two Fish, swimming in opposite directions. In one sense, this symbol represents the powerful polarity of Piscean spiritual and human qualities, struggling for control. In another sense, it suggests the temptation of Pisceans to swim effortlessly downstream, with the current, rather than making the more difficult journey upstream, toward the mountains of enlightenment.

Pisceans aspire beyond the limits of earthly knowledge, because they were born under a Water Sign, and Neptune (their ruling planet) flashes into their souls the light of the spiritual vibrations of the Universe. The Piscean drug addict, alcoholic, genius and saint are all striving for the same thing. What separates them is the degree of experience each is able to wring out of life.

Taurus can be a great help to Pisces in obtaining experience in a practical way, through the reality of the tangible. Until they know each other better, however, the Bull may think the Fish is a foolish creature, swimming around in watery illusions, his head wrapped in cotton, pursuing futile daydreams.

The Fish may think the Bull is a dangerous animal, stomping around through the corn, his head full of obstinate opinions, pursuing filthy lucre. Filthy, because money is (at least subliminally) a dirty word to most Pisceans. They resent having to concentrate on how to earn it, keep it, spend it, distribute it, budget it and save it. They'd be much happier if someone else handled the cash flow, and just kept them supplied with food, drink, dreams, tickets to shows and concerts, a couple of sarongs, and holidays sailing on the bright blue water—allowing them lots of free time to work on inventions, artistic creations or scientific research. Anything left over can go to the orphans' home, the animal shelter, the actors' relief fund, Greenpeace, taxes or whatever.

The typical Fish doesn't see the point of letting excess cash gather dust under a mattress, or in a bank. Pisces normally worries about money only when he or she doesn't have it. Then it becomes a frightful necessity for the continuation of their changeable, dreamy, multi-faceted existence. Otherwise, it annoys the Fish. Subconsciously, they sense that a wealthy man's fortune is all on paper. The whole concept of currency exchange puzzles the average Piscean, and when a Fish discusses money with a Bull (who comprehends the monetary concept perfectly) the conversation can sound like Antoine de Saint Exupéry's Neptune-guided Little Prince talking with the Bull-like businessman, who is busy counting his assets, the stars, which he figures belong to him, since no one else ever had the common sense to claim them.

"Five hundred and one million, six hundred twenty-two thousand, seven hundred thirty-one . . . . . . I am concerned with matters of consequence . . . . . ."

". . . . . . you own the stars ?"

"Yes . . . . . ."

"And what do you do with them ?"

"I administer them. I count and recount them. It is difficult, but I am a man who is naturally interested in matters of consequence . . . . . ."

"But you cannot pluck the stars from heaven."

"No, but I can put them in the bank."

"Whatever does that mean ?"

"That means I write the number of my stars on a little paper. And then I put this paper in a drawer, and lock it with a key."

"And that is all ?"

"It is enough."

The Little Prince sighs, then. "It is entertaining . . . . . . but it is not a 'matter of any great consequence."

On matters of consequence, the typical Piscean has ideas very different from the average Taurean. For, like the Little Prince, the Fish, too, is from a far-off planet, where there exists the most beautiful rose in all creation, which he has seen, and loved with his whole being, remembers with tenderness, misses painfully . . . . . . and to which he longs to return. (Or to *whom* he longs to return. The male or female Fish who wistfully longs for such a reunion isn't certain of the pronoun. Is it a person ? Or merely a concept . . . a dream ?)

Piscean Cleve Backster, who sneakily, in Neptune fashion, swims and glides silently, almost unobtrusively, in and out of the pages of this book, so that you never know in which chapter he's going to pop up and wiggle his fins — is certainly typical of his Sun Sign's instinctive disdain for material matters. In 1970, a major New York publisher wanted to place Cleve under contract to write a book about his world-famous work with plants, eggs, spermatozoa, yogurt, and all manner of cellular life, which is proving the genesis of Oneness — that all life forces are interconnected, and inseparable. Suddenly, an editor at the publishing house had an innovative idea of his own. He asked a professional astrologer to calculate and interpret Backster's horoscope, hoping it would reveal the extent of his reliability and potential as an author, thereby reducing the publisher's risk.

The editor then visited Cleve in his research laboratory to bring him the awful truth. Silently and sadly, he handed the Fish the neatly typed astrological analysis to read. Among other things, it stated that Backster must "always be associated with an organization around him, for he can't bear the entire responsibility on his own shoulders" — and that "his business sense is absolutely nil."

"I'm sorry to be the bearer of such bad news," the editor commiserated, "but I felt you should know the worst." Cleve's elfin ears wiggled in pure pleasure, and his visitor was shocked to hear him say, "That's amazingly true! It fits my character perfectly. I've always suspected astrology is an accurate science, and now I'm even more convinced. May I keep a copy of that analysis please?" The poor editor was nonplussed. It was obvious that Cleve's delight was genuine. A few years later, when Backster was considerably overdue in turning in even the first chapter of the proposed book about his work, the publishing house wrote him a stern letter, which Cleve promptly answered. "Remember," Fish Backster wrote cheerfully, "you people were the ones who had my character analyzed in the beginning, not me. I never claimed I enjoyed responsibility or had any business sense."

I know a Pisces banker, with a Capricorn Ascendent and a Taurus Moon Sign, who carefully counts copper and silver and paper all day long, but he frowns as he counts, and wonders why he's cursed with aching feet and asthma. As a Fish he's allergic to currency, you see, but the earthy influences in his horoscope won't let him chuck it overboard and swim away.

I also know a Taurus musician, whose Pisces Moon Sign and Ascendent cause him to leave huge tips on the bar, and squander his money at the race track. But he has a few extra gin and tonics each time he loses, to quiet his guilty Taurean Sun Sign conscience.

It's important to be true to your Sun Sign, whatever conflicting planetary influences pull on your inner psyche, because each of the twelve signs has its purpose in human evolvement. An idle, extravagant Bull is always an extremely unhappy person, just as a sober, mercenary Fish is always a pathetically sad, neurotic human being. If these two join forces, they could then each do what comes more naturally.

Pisces could show Taureans more imaginative ways to make money, and teach them the joys of sharing it with others, along with the truth of the infallible Universal Law that the more you give, the faster it multiplies.

Conversely, Taurus could teach Pisces the proper respect for minimal security, that it's wiser to save at least a few dollars, even if you give away a hundred or so, in case there are a few lean days before that Universal Law goes into effect. It's such a drag to have to sit on the corner in the rain, holding out a tin cup. The very idea gives the Bull nervous palpitation, and makes his hair stand on end.

There are, of course, Pisceans who are forced by circumstances, and memories of childhood poverty, to worry and fret about having to take a turn with the tin cup, so they pinch their few pennies, but privately hate themselves for being so miserly. Yet, when they stop pinching, the money to replace what was spent appears like magic from unexpected sources. If these Pisceans would listen to their own hearts, they'd get over their tin-cup traumas, and end their poverty at the same time.

An odd and interesting difference between Taurus and Pisces is a fact as simple as their names. Very few Bulls have nicknames, and if they do, they usually don't like them. As for changing his or her name legally, a typical Bull will balk, even if the name is Percival Perriwinkle or Clarestine Clapper. They may suffer as children, but by the time they're adults they will have convinced themselves their names have a good, solid sound, and anyone who doesn't think so can go sit on a tack. Remember the true story about Ms. Hogg, who named her three children Ima Hogg, Ura Hogg and Hesa Hogg? Since I've never heard or read that any of the three ever changed their names, I suspect they all had Taurus Sun Signs, Moon Signs, or Ascendents.

As for Pisces, almost every Fish you meet will either already have a nickname, or secretly longs for one. After a while, if their friends don't oblige them, many Fish will adopt an alias on their own. A Pisces girl or woman named Catherine will flirt with the idea of spelling it *Kathryn* — a Pisces boy, or man, named John, will doodle it as *Joshua,* or toy with the idea of legally changing it to a more romantic *Jonathan.* Anything to make life more exotic, and to keep your identity hidden from snoopers who pry into your personal life.

Pisces can't stand direct questions, or being pinned down to a positive stand. It's the nature of the Fish to glide in and out and around a situation, looking at all sides, and absorbing its various implications — or glide away quietly from a controversy that chops up the waters around him, and threatens his equilibrium.

None of that sneaking away for Taurus. What is there to be faced, he faces, with open courage, and he will remain standing there stubbornly, until he proves his point. If he can't prove it, after much effort, he turns his strong back and leaves, but he doesn't glide away. He stalks off heavily back to where he started from, with his original opinion clutched tightly in his arms, across his beefy chest.

That's more or less what happens when these two get into an argument. There's seldom a satisfactory or final settlement. But the day can be saved by laughter. The Bull has a rich, delicious, absolutely marvelous sense of humor. It's not the bright, brittle, sophisticated comedy of caustic wits, but a warm humor that stems from the colorful reality of everyday living, the kind that spilled over in the musical *Fiddler on the Roof.* Since the very bright, sometimes super-intelligent Fish has a fine appreciation for humor — somehow, between the grins, they'll either forget their differences, or resolve them through the compromise of their Earth and Water elements, which are essentially, in astrology, as in Nature, compatible. As mentioned elsewhere in this book, Water enriches Earth, and Earth provides a home for Water, but the wrong blending of these two can create mud or quicksand.

Because this is a 3-11 vibratory pattern, the meeting of the Bull and the Fish is seldom accidental, or a "first incarnational encounter." Like all 3-11 Sun Sign Pattern people, the two of them are guided by Fate to insure the return, the even exchange of devotion or hurt given, one unto the other, in past incarnations—sometimes the former, sometimes the latter—but more often a combination of both. Like those people whose *day* of birth (not including month or year) adds to the number 4 or 8, will be bound firmly to the lives of other 4 or 8 persons, like it or not, pleasant or unpleasant—those under the influence of this Sun Sign Pattern will find they have no choice in deciding to meet, or when to part.

They're magnetically pulled together, in order to carry out the karmic balance of action and reaction, under the direction of the Higher Angels of themselves—the Supraconscious of each. Numerology and astrology are sisters or brothers—whichever you prefer, the relationship of these two arts and sciences being one of the very few situations thus far not initially labeled as masculine by male chauvinist pigs, nor later challenged and switched to the feminine gender by female chauvinist sows. Help yourself.

Taurus and Pisces will have, like all other 3-11 influenced people (and also like all those born on a *day* which adds to the number 4 or 8), abundant opportunities for happiness and harmony in this present existence together, if they're willing to accept the duties and responsibilities of past karmic obligations to one another—i.e., bear the frequently tense aspects of their association, from time to time, as well as each other's weary burdens. The rewards for uncomplainingly assuming the duties, however, are great indeed. An example of a Taurus-Pisces, 3-11 fated Sun Sign Pattern, including both the light and shadows of necessary mutual sacrifice . . . and mutual ecstasy . . . is the destined relationship of poet and poetess Robert Browning (Taurus) and Elizabeth Barrett (Pisces). There are thousands, millions of others—including, of course, the Bull and the Fish reading this chapter.

Basically, Taurus and Pisces are tolerant of one another's weaknesses. But Taurus is deeply concerned with the need for facing reality—even those occasional Master-Avatar Bulls, who now and then pass among us (yes, also *now*), such as the ultimate-enlightened, and esoterically aware alchemist, the very Taurean Count de St. Germain. These particular Masters are here to teach the necessity of the "reality trip" for human evolvement, however spiritually advanced they may be themselves.

Pisces is here on a totally different teaching trip. The Fish are all very old souls, whether they're swimming upstream or downstream. Pisceans have journeyed past horizons of such unearthly beauty they tear at the Neptune heart when he (or she) revisits them in dreams. And so, the Fish cannot bear to face reality, as it appears to be on Earth. They know the *real* "original sin" is in seeing, in recognizing sadness and ugliness, when our co-Creators conceived and manifested only harmony and beauty. In his or her subconscious, Pisces hears the ancient cry of the Tibetan monks whose chants echo across the vaulted ceiling of their monasteries: *This is the world of illusion . . . . . this is the world of illusion.*

To Taurus, the Bull, the recognition of a different kind of sin is necessary for the soul's enlightenment and final salvation. Therefore, the Bull feels compelled to force the Fish to confess his (or her) guilt of self-deception and fantasy — to see things as they are — and the clear, sparkling streams of Pisces visions are forced back to the rich, stable Earth by the practicality of the watchful Taureans.

"Jonathan (Kathryn) *that is not your real name.* You are make-believing and fantasizing again," scolds Taurus, never suspecting that the tears of the chastised Piscean then are not for Neptune's transgressions against Taurean reality . . . but for all the lost and lonely souls in this "world of illusion."

"Jonathan (Kathryn) are you not terribly sorry ?" persists the Bull.

"Oh, yes . . . oh, yes," replies the Fish.

☆ ☆ ☆ ☆ ☆ ☆

TAURUS *Woman* PISCES *Man*

◆◆◆●◆▶

To Michael the loneliness was dreadful. "If only
something would make a sound !" he cried.

As if in answer to his request, the air was rent by the most
tremendous crash he had ever heard . . . . . the roar
of it echoed through the mountains. . . .

Both the silence and the roar of the Bull are an experience known, sooner or later, to every "Michael" who has the Sun, Moon or Ascendent in Pisces, in an association with Taurus. But especially to the Sun Sign male Fish.

When the Taurean girl plays romantic marbles, she shoots to win, and to keep all the aggies. But when she forgets her common sense, she'll find herself playing "Blind Man's Bluff," and that's a game she could lose, unless she cheats a little, and peeks out from under the hanky tied over her eyes. She might as well, if she's playing with a Fish. He'll certainly cheat a little, by peeking out beneath *his* blindfold, to see where the relationship might be leading him.

If it looks like it's leading him into the hook of a permanent attachment, he could be a poor loser, and scoot away before he gets caught. But that's only his protective Neptune reflex action, and he'll be back. His instinct to return may be guiding him well, because there's lots of hope for lasting happiness inherent in a love affair between this man and woman.

The Bull and the Fish both like peace and quiet. They both believe in letting sleeping dogs lie. Why ask for trouble ? There's enough of that falling in your lap every day, unsolicited, without chasing it, is her feeling. The Pisces man agrees wholeheartedly. Whistle for trouble and it will zoom right in on you, is the way he sees it. So, don't whistle where Lady Bad Luck can hear you, or she'll be sure to pop open the lid of Pandora's Box, and you'll have no one to blame but yourself. Well, that's not quite right. Piscean misfortunes are rarely their own fault. The Fish just naturally gets tangled in other people's torments, because he's such a good listener.

Another thing these two Sun Signs often have in common is that, after all the care they take to avoid sticky seaweed (in the case of Pisces) or barbed wire and brambles (in the case of the Bull) they both stand a good chance of falling into the grip of the gloomies anyway, thanks to their mutual inclination to brood, and their tendency toward pessimism. But the Taurus girl is often more patient, and more certain of the final outcome, than the inwardly restless Pisces man. She doesn't mind setting a bear trap for something or someone she wants, then waiting without a murmur of discontent, as long as necessary, for the jaws to snap shut. In fact, she may even enjoy waiting for people when they're late, because it gives her a chance to practice her calm in emergencies.

It's not a bad habit for her to possess, if she plans on becoming seriously involved with a Fish, because most Pisces men have never been on time in their lives. Unless they have a Virgo or other more stable Moon Sign or Ascendent. There are some Pisces men who are late for work, for the movies, for dental appointments, for New Year's Eve (mostly because they start celebrating it in November) and for their own weddings (sometimes even missing them altogether).

The Pisces man may wonder what his true image is to the Taurus girl. He won't really care, but he may wonder. A Fish usually doesn't work up a lot of anxiety symptoms when he's in love, at least, not on the surface. He may fret mildly about the rent money, what life really means, what the future holds and such, but to Pisces, romance is a natural state of being. This bright, gentle, poetic man, if he's a typical Fish, is very much at home in romantic waters, where he probably learned to swim and dive at a shockingly early age. The Taurus girl was still swooning over Deanna Durbin films, or cracking up over Howdy Doody (depending on her age group) while he was planning his first seduction (or being seduced himself, which is more likely). Love, or the fulfillment of it, comes late to the average Taurean female, which is perhaps why she appreciates it and values it more than women born under other Sun Signs. It's the waiting that makes things seem special and exciting, whether it's Christmas, Groundhog's Day or your first kiss.

Whatever his image may be to her, I hope she tries to halfway understand him. I say halfway, because she'll be lucky if he doesn't baffle her completely in the beginning. He's so absolutely different from every other man she's ever known that she can't help being secretly excited by his mysterious elusive quality, even though she normally doesn't trust a complicated or changeable personality. It's because of the magnetic 3-11 vibration between them, a Sun Sign Pattern implying a karmic tie, which is responsible for the strong feeling of compulsion in the relationship. A Taurus woman may feel a strong attraction toward certain Scorpio men too, but it will be mostly physical. With a Pisces man, it often goes deeper than that, and it's not so easily explained. Besides, he so obviously needs someone to cook for him, believe in him, comfort him and love him, all talents in which she excels.

She may occasionally give in to moods of self-pity and dark forebodings. But when her perspective returns, she'll submit to the gentle influence of Venus again, and slip back into her old, comfortable ways. When she's herself, a Taurus woman is firmly convinced that anything can be cured with a tub full of warm water, a cup of hot soup, some cool reason and a few jokes. And that includes everything from trivial upsets to major tragedy. The Pisces man's complicated depressions may need somewhat more extensive and intricate, less prosaic therapy, but he'll enjoy her treatments. She has an undeniably calm and relaxing influence upon his spirit when he's troubled.

Sexually, these two relate well to each other. His Neptunian approach to sex can be described in two words: sensuous and romantic. So can hers. Both of them are determined to feel every possible shade and tone of sensual experience it's possible to know while confined in the flesh, so there will probably be an excellent rapport between them physically. The Pisces man lives almost entirely in and through his psychic nervous system. In his sexual behavior, as in all his activities, he yearns to escape into an ever-higher heaven . . . . . . *"anywhere, anywhere out of the world!"*

The Taurus girl instinctively "feels" through her senses. She has a serene charisma, a soothing aura, an exquisitely tender touch, and an instinctive desire to blanket the man she loves with warm affection — to tickle him with soft feathers of humor. Combine that with her throaty midnight whispers, and her soft Venus curves, and you can see why they usually vibrate to the same emotional rhythm. Her feminine tendency to gently submit to, and not attempt to dominate her man, is enormously satisfying to the Piscean male, who may have been through some romantic nightmares with more aggressive females. Taurus and Pisces know how to clearly communicate their mutual desires to each other, as well as how to fulfill them, so their physical union can be a beautiful experience of both earthy passion and unearthly ecstasy.

However, their total happiness together depends on which kind of Fish he is, the kind who sinks (by choice) or the kind who swims rapidly upstream.

If he's the sunken kind, lurking among the conch shells at the bottom of the ocean, hoping to find the lost continent of Atlantis down there — or maybe just meditating an abstract scientific theory in the cool, green quiet — he may be immune to all the mermaids, however alluring. That is, unless he finds one with two strong feet planted on firm ground, who's willing to support him both emotionally and financially until he reaches his dream. A Taurus girl may be willing to fill that double order for a while. But after a time, the Bull's slow anger will be aroused. If he leans on her patience too long with what she regards as a lack of good sense and a disregard for security, she'll explode into one of her rare, but violent rages, and when the thunder dies away, the Fish will have quietly disappeared. But she won't notice, because once she makes up her mind, this girl doesn't look back. She read about someone who did that, who was turned into a pillar of salt for her weakness.

Even if he's an active, swimming Fish, with stronger fins and tougher scales, she may still not comprehend how it is with him, what he goes through in coping with everyone's tears and troubles, and touches for cash. A Fish can be wonderfully clever and creative, in clear water. But if she constantly muddies it with her earthy stubbornness, and others keep polluting it with impositions on his time and sympathy, he may turn to the solace of a few rainbows on the rocks at the corner bar. Then she'll start to frown or pout. And that's the beginning of the end.

The three-part formula for breaking a Taurus girl's heart is: false promises, deception and idle drifting. The triple formula for healing it is: honesty, fidelity and dependability. If he remembers that, it could be the beginning of the end of his loneliness.

If she accepts his need for periods of isolated contemplation to relax his jangled nerves, he'll always return to her serenity, for a few jokes, a warm bath, a cup of hot soup — and those throaty midnight whispers. And that could be the beginning of a love as special, and as worth waiting for, as Groundhog's Day or Christmas morning. Beneath the passion they feel is the warm foundation of the 3-11 vibration of true friendship . . . . . which never fails to deepen love, when it has passed the test of Time.

TAURUS *Man* PISCES *Woman*

―――――◂◂◉▸▸――――――

*He was often thus when communing
with himself on board ship in the
quietude of the night . . . . .*

*She was not a little girl heartbroken about him;
she was a grown woman smiling at it
all, but they were wet smiles.*

Remember when, as a child, you used to watch a magician, and marvel at the way he made white rabbits, silk roses and colored ribbons disappear in front of your eyes? A Taurus man who falls in love with a Pisces girl, and who doesn't study the magic of astrology, may get an opportunity to relive that experience. It may take her months or years to master the disappearing act. And she won't announce it in advance when she does, because a Pisces hates to get involved in sticky controversy, or get tangled up in hollering and endless recriminations. It could happen on a day — or an evening — like hundreds of others, when she says gently:

"Darling, I've been invited to attend a poetry reading tonight. Could you drop me off, then catch a film, and pick me up later?"

"No. I don't want to go to the movies alone."

‣ "Then would you like to come along with me, because . . . ."

"No, I wouldn't. You know I don't mess around with that mystical stuff."

"All right. I won't go to the poetry reading. I'll go to the movies with you. Do you like my new dress?"

"It's too short. You look like a stripper, ready to pull her last zipper. Put on something else, and let the hem down before you wear it again."

"Yes, dear. I will. But everyone is wearing . . . ."

"Sure, and everyone is also going nuts with sex and drugs and riots and revolutions and female liberation. Does that mean the woman I love has to copy them?"

"No, of course not. You're right, darling. I just thought . . . . ."

"You shouldn't think, since it obviously mixes up your brains, and gives you fuzzy opinions. Just stick to your female functions. Come on, we'll be late for the . . . . hey! Where are you? Where did you go?"

She has disappeared, as suddenly and subtly as the white rabbits, silk roses and colored ribbons. She's finally had enough of his blindness to her sensitive feelings, his stubborn refusal to meet her halfway, and his obstinate opinions that leave no room for compromise. Maybe she just slipped away to reflect alone for a period, and she'll return refreshed, ready to submit again, if she really loves him. There's just a slight touch of masochism in all Neptune-ruled women. But there's also a chance that someday she'll disappear forever, especially if she has an aggressive Moon Sign or Ascendent — so the Bull should anticipate the possibility, since he's so big on the practicality of being prepared for trouble in advance.

Naturally, not all Taurus-Pisces couples are so widely polarized by his obstinate masculine superiority and her timid feminine acquiescence. That's just a warning to the Bull and the Fish who have a conflicting Sun-Moon aspect between their horoscopes. If their Luminaries are harmonious, they can have a rare and satisfying love relationship, because they are compatible in many ways, a deep comfort to one another when life gets too noisy and frantic for him — or too harsh and ugly for her. Every man appreciates a sympathetic ear to listen to his troubles, especially when it's attached to an attentive, geisha-type female with a soft voice and gentle manners. But human nature being what it is, every man will also try to get away with as much as he can, when a girl is so tolerant and understanding. A Taurus man is certainly no exception to that rule. And so a Pisces girl who falls in love with a strong Bull must toughen up her ego, if she wants to learn the magic trick of turning him into a lovable Taurean Teddy Bear.

She has one thing going for her, however, that's kind of cool. Behind her sweetly compliant exterior hides a very quick, bright and highly perceptive mind. She'll catch him up when he least expects it, if what he thinks he's getting away with is a flirtation with another woman, although she may forgive him almost too quickly, at least the first time. It's when he's trying to get away with submerging her dreams, and bending her fluid nature to his own rigid one, that she needs practice in toughness.

Not that all the problems between them will arise from his overemphasis on male dominance. Some of them may be caused by her procrastination (oh, let's worry about that later . . .) — her exasperating elusiveness — (I don't know exactly where I'm going, or just how long I'll be. Do you have to pin me down?) — her secrecy — (I can't answer that. Please don't pry into my personal feelings) — her exaggerated dependence (I can't decide what to do by myself) — or her lack of self-confidence, accompanied by waterfalls of tears — (I'm not pretty enough, or smart enough for you). He can tell her a thousand times that she's perfect for him, but if she's a girl Fish with an afflicted natal Sun, or an also Mutable Ascendent and Moon Sign, she'll still privately worry and wonder, and suspect him of humoring her.

A Taurus man will find it easier to understand a Pisces girl, if he remembers that she not only reflects *back* all the emotional vibrations in her immediate vicinity (including his own), she also *absorbs* them inwardly, like a sponge, through her Neptunian sympathy of spirit. How would *he* like to be forced by a ruling planet to go around mopping up everyone's tears, sopping up their fears, reflecting and absorbing everything from hilarity to hysteria ? It would make anyone a little unsure and shaky at times.

Lest you conceive of every Bull as a rough and tough, insensitive male type, it should be remembered that American film actor James Mason is a Taurean — the very epitome of polished, drawing-room manners and sophistication. (But he's stubborn.) And lest you conceive of every girl Fish as a weeping willow tree, frightened and timid, lacking aggression, it should be remembered that Taurean James Mason's legally former and astrally current wife, Pamela Mason, is a Piscean — the very epitome of a lady who will not be pushed around, by Bulls or anyone else, and who most definitely knows her own mind ! (But she's gentle and dainty and compassionate.)

One of the things which may disturb the Taurus man is the Neptunian approach to truth of his Pisces woman. She sees truth as what she feels at the moment, and what she feels at the moment is always vulnerable to suggestion and susceptible to change, as the people, the situation and the viewpoint either dilute it or strengthen it. Pisces does not see truth as a static, but as a constantly altering thing, depending upon many interpretations.

The Bull sees truth as a fact, eternal and unchanging. Now, that's what you call a polarity of opinion. Which one is right ? Actually, they're both right, at different times, depending on what kind of truth they mean. Some truths are universal, eternally unchanging. Others are many-sided and individual. Still others are in a continual state of flux, since they relate to people's feelings and emotions of the moment — or public opinion of the moment. And some truths, based on indisputable *fact* — such as: Were you in the shower an hour ago ? — clearly have but one answer, yes or no. Since everything in the cosmos is relative, why should truth be an exception ? The shower question involves the immediate past. Questions of fact involving the more distant past, such as: Was Lincoln assassinated ? Did Napoleon lose his final battle ? and so forth . . . fall into a deeper esoteric and metaphysical-spiritual category, relating to the heavy Einsteinian Time question. If Past, Present and Future *are* simultaneous, and *not* separate, as "abstract Al" suspected — then, considering that one may change the Future by actions of the Present, should not one also be able to change the Past, through actions in the Present? This sort of truth belongs to the study of *meta*-physics, not physics—and the answer lies buried in the riddle of "how *far* back in time?"—and the use of the singular, as in: "can *one* change the past by . . . . ?" and so forth. But it's much too heavy to discuss further here and now, far too deep a subject for merely one compatibility chapter, and will have to wait for a future book. Still, the entire issue is an interesting one for Taurus-Pisces lovers or mates to exchange thoughts about with each other.

Truth, in its various states and forms, won't matter so much to this man and woman in their sexual expression of love. This is an area where the only truth is the peace of fulfillment they bring to one another. Barring severe Luminary afflictions between their birth charts, or other mutual planetary-aspect difficulties to overcome, the sexual harmony between the Taurus man and his Pisces woman should be a thing of undeniable truth and beauty—the strong attraction of Earth for Water, and vice versa. These two, especially if the Sun-Moon relationship between them is strong and positive, can exist almost in a world of their own, held together by a communion of the senses surpassing anything an Air or Fire sign could imagine. Few human experiences of sharing are more comforting than the physical demonstration of love between a Bull and a Fish, who have surrendered themselves to one another, without questioning their mutual need, only desiring to answer it. It's not the explosive passion of other Sun Sign couples, but the rare tenderness and affection which is so warmly given, and so quietly received, that makes their union so complete and peace-restoring an intimacy. There's always a hint of mystery hovering over and around the sexual relationship between Taurus and Pisces, and they're usually both content to leave it be, perhaps sensing that to expose the silent unknown would somehow dim the excitement.

If he tries to force her love into a definite shape, she may wander away, or worse, wander *around*, inciting the Bull's anger, and arousing his Taurean possessive instincts. He may cause her to feel lonely at times, when he's too busy or preoccupied to share with her the things she feels, and hears, and sees. But Water enriches the Earth, and Earth welcomes Water into the soil of security, so they can grow through their differences, while finding solace in their sameness—if she gives him enough solid, tangible signs of affection— and he loans her his steadiness to lean on when her dreams elude her, and her longings sadden her. Some night, they may be outside together, walking home from somewhere, and she'll look up into the sky, and whisper to him: "Listen . . . . . ." Then he'll ask, "Listen to *what*?"

"To the stars! Listen to the stars coming out . . . . . . don't they sound beautiful?"

Instead of frowning with puzzled annoyance at her confusing sight and sound, he should just hold her closer, and *listen* with her. For they do make beautiful music . . . . . . the stars coming out, snowflakes falling, someone's arms around you when you're unsure . . . . a special smile . . . and Pisces can teach Taurus to hear it.

GEMINI

Air — Mutable — Positive
Ruled by Mercury
Symbol: The Twins
Day Forces — Masculine

GEMINI

Air — Mutable — Positive
Ruled by Mercury
Symbol: The Twins
Day Forces — Masculine

The **GEMINI-GEMINI** *Relationship*

*They were going round and round the island, but
they did not meet because all were going at
the same rate.*

Before we get tied into mental pretzel knots, trying to analyze this 1-1 Sun Sign Pattern association, let's get the arithmetic straightened out.

A Gemini and a Gemini equals a group of four bright, active people (two sets of Twins) tossing ideas, dreams and challenges back and forth between themselves and the world at large.

They may occasionally block each other's view of life, because they tend to see it in different magnifications, through the wide-angle zoom lens of their Mercurical vision, and sometimes they walk or run at varying speeds. Yet, in one sense, they all four travel at the same rate of speed, in that they all understand one another's need for freedom. Their vibrations radiate from the same frequencies, and their broken rhythms are usually in tune. A broken rhythm may not be orthodox music, but it makes great jazz. The trouble is, while they're jazzing around, they might miss each other in the swiftly passing scenery.

When two Geminis merge and get their vibes, rhythms and mental perspectives working in a parenthetic pattern, the four of them can use each other as a reassuring tie to reality. From the home base of their mutual empathy, they can run out and seduce the world — return briefly to be understood — then set forth once again on a new mental seduction. Do you understand this page? If you do, you're a Gemini yourself, because it's all astrologically accurate but complicated Mercury double-talk. If you don't understand it, and you're reading this to learn to comprehend a Gemini team, partnership or couple you know, stay with us, but be prepared to exercise your mental muscles — and don't forget your parachute.

Philosopher-astrologer Alan Watts defined "Man" (he didn't include women, but that was before ERA made all male animals aware that we're people too) by explaining that the individualization of the Creator, expressing His total Being through the multiple millions of souls on Earth, can be conceived of as *"God, playing hide-and-seek with Himself."* It's long been my favorite esoteric definition of Man and Woman's relation to the Universe, since I've always suspected that Man and Woman and their co-Creators are a unity, after pondering the Genesis riddle that the latter created the former in Their own Image. However, I really must correct one flaw in this otherwise very deeply perceptive definition. I'm sure the late, both kindly and brilliant Alan Watts will forgive us if we re-phrase his words as: *"God and His Mate, playing hide-and-seek with Themselves."* Now it is perfect. But anyway, the point I was trying to make is that, in the case of Gemini, our co-Creators are playing hide-and-seek with Themselves at high speed, with many more hiding places, and probably surprising Themselves more than They do with ordinary mortals, who are confused enough with the challenges of being just one person. There is, of course, another side to all this, the *individual* side, and the integrity of each unique soul.

The Yogi-Buddhist Nirvana concept is grossly distorted. All this business of permanent "blending with the Great All" is nonsense, metaphysically unsound, and quite literally impossible. We are part of both the *fused* and the *separate* bodies of our co-Creators — in a *symbolic sense*, Aries people being near Their "heads," Gemini being near Their arms, hands and fingers, Leos near Their "hearts," and so forth. (That's admittedly an oversimplification, but will suffice for this particular book, because it will be covered in more detail in a forthcoming one.) Now, a nose is not a mouth (when did you ever hear of a nose that ate corn on the cob?), nor is an eye a hand, nor is an ear a heart. (Who ever heard of an ear-beat?) In other words, you are You. *The unique you-of-you is now, ever has been, and ever shall be* — your individual self, and *consciously so* — not just during those periods of time when your blindness separates you from our co-Creators, but also after you blend with Them, from time to time, and even *while* you're at one with Them.

The secret of the latter condition of perfect peace, wisdom, and power is contained in the *polarity* of power — humility — expressed through the word "atone" (at-one). Not until you truly atone, and fully comprehend the meaning of the word, may you be *at-one* with God and His Mate. However, although the achievement of experiencing such *at-one-ment*, periodically and repeatedly, is a glorious thing, you need not (indeed you *should* not) remain at-one with Them on a permanent basis. That would be dreadfully boring for the individuality, just as being inseparably blended in the ecstatic embrace of sexual union, however pure the love between the twin souls might be, would be dull and boring if it were to be an eternal, constant state.

Such a concept removes the very core of existence, which is light and shadow . . . the perfect Libran balance of each . . . the stimulation of controversy, equally balanced with peaceful agreement — with no murders please, within the necessary controversy syndrome — no murder of sex, people, animals, or anything else. That's against all the rules of the cosmic hide-and-seek game.

Well, let's see . . . I began discussing Man's and Woman's relationship with God and His Mate, then went on to an explanation of your individuality, so you'll all be aware that your own sacred and holy, personal "egos" can never be destroyed by blending in a nirvanic *forever* with *anyone's* concept of "God" — all in a few paragraphs. The Gemini essence is extremely contagious. Actually, I'll level with you, although my remarks were all made quite seriously, and are reflective of ancient esoteric truth, I deliberately strung my words together on a chain of quick subject changes — each different, yet all consistently leading into one another — to give you a brief idea of the necessity for remaining alert when you're involved in any sort of discussion with a Gemini, let alone two of them, which is really four of them.

You see, sometimes Gemini double-talk is an aid to superimposing two apparently polarized opinions into a stereoscopic wholeness of third-dimensional depth, the third dimension added by the perceptive recipient of the words. Are you with me? You're simply going to have to become accustomed to word games if you expect to play verbal Pong-Ping with the Twins, and Pong-Ping is the same as Ping-Pong when you're gazing into the Gemini mirror. Now, is it reflecting back to you more clearly?

Each Gemini contains a twin mirror image of himself (or herself), in reverse, the positive and negative poles of his or her personality. This is because each Gemini symbolizes the soul, on its trip around the astrological, karmic wheel, experiencing the toddler stage of awareness that it's not alone in the Universe, realizing also that there are two distinct sides to the character of each man and woman, which must be brought into harmony before it's possible to relate to others. The trouble is, Gemini seldom knows which of his (or her) split personalities is the real one. If anyone asked (or if our co-Creators asked this portion of Their individualization), "Will the real Twin please stand up and be recognized ?", two separate people would pop up, and the game of hide-and-seek would begin all over again.

Naturally, then, when a pair of Twins decide to tangle their temperaments, things can get pretty crisscrossed. There are few Geminians who can sort themselves out from the myriad disguises and conflicting desires of their natures. Gemini is ruled by trickster Mercury, the planet of lightning speed (though not quite as capable of speed as "Swifty" Uranus), who forces this man, woman or child to try on a thousand faces, then discard them, in a restive search for personal identity.

The purpose of the masquerade is what separates the men from the boys, the women from the girls, and Scorpio from Gemini — in case you've been wondering. Scorp changes false faces for an entirely different purpose — to deliberately keep you in the dark, whereas Gemini is just trying to make up his (or her) mind which face belongs there. No, that's Libra indecision. Let's try again. Gemini is trying on masks in an effort to find the true person he or she really is. Indecision has nothing to do with it, in a really detailed analysis. Did I already say that ? Yes, I did. I just realized. I said the same thing at the end of the last sentence in the previous paragraph.

Well, get used to it. Geminis often repeat themselves — say things twice. Like, they'll say: "What time is it ?" . . . wait a second or so, and repeat: "What time is it ?" before you've had time to answer that it's half past anything or a quarter till, which makes it difficult to converse with them in any sort of synchronized way, sometimes. But not always.

Since Gemini is a mental Air Sign, these people are driven to spinning their brains almost continually, even in their sleep, thinking, theorizing, figuring, projecting, condemning, endorsing, discarding, sorting and analyzing the cold, hard facts — at the very same time that they're chasing their visionary dream. You can see why they're all human jigsaw puzzles.

The Mercury-ruled roam the world, either mentally or physically, or both, in search of an elusive ideal of perfect truth and happiness, then often return home again, to listen to a bird singing in a tall tree — the same bird, the same song, the same tree they knew as children. After traveling all over the mental continents of their imaginations, they sometimes, if they're lucky, realize, at last, that their truest dreams were dreamed when childhood's perception was clear and uncontaminated by adult logic and cynicism.

Any 1-1 Sun Sign Pattern combination brings with it the special and unique satisfaction of association with a person enough like one's own self that there's little fear of rejection of personality — although there's always a danger of an overbalance of the similar characteristics. A double-Gemini relationship is especially comforting to each of the four of them, because it's always reassuring to have a pal, relative, neighbor, business associate, lover or mate who's as messed up as you are yourself. It saves a lot of tiresome explanations and apologies. But it can also be wearing on the nervous system, because of the continual frustration of attempting to fool someone who anticipates all your maneuvers and rationalizations.

At least these Sun Signs, when doubled up, can recognize one another somewhat more easily than an outsider would recognize either of the four of them. Yesterday, Gemini was a gentle soul, shy and self-effacing, somewhat detached, quiet and reflective, with occasional spells of wistfulness and longing. Today, the very same Gemini is cynical, sarcastic, irritable, insulting — and acutely alert. Tomorrow, he (or she) may be calm, steady and conservative to the point of being downright stuffy. Then, without the faintest warning, Gemini will turn into a will-o'-the-wisp, sprinkling dreams like lemon drops, scattering ideas like confetti, restless, yearning, as physically active as he (or she) is verbally communicative and emotionally restless. It's terribly puzzling to the rest of us, but even more so to the Gemini himself — or herself. Especially if he (or she) is involved in a close tie with another Gemini. Then, of course, the puzzlement is twinned and twice as tormenting.

The trickster aspect of Gemini's ruling planet, Mercury, is always hiding behind the sharp Gemini intellect, revealing itself in all manner of minor and major ways. An excellent example is Gemini Bob Hope, the comedian with the rapid-fire, speedy delivery of jokes, which nearly tumble over one another in the telling, they're delivered in such machine-gun style. Did you ever pay really close attention to one of Hope's longer comic routines? The kind where he does a monologue for fifteen minutes or a half hour, not his on-again, off-again stabs at the audience at the Academy Awards. On a lengthier routine, Mercury's delight in tricking and fooling people is very evident.

Approximately every two minutes or so, the Gemini Hope will make a remark that when analyzed, means essentially: "Get ready, Folks. I'm about to close my act, and sign off." *But then he continues.* A couple of minutes (or even one minute or a few seconds) later he tosses out another one-liner, indicating again that his routine is coming to a close. *Yet, he continues.* Listen closely next time. You'll see that this is a consistent pattern with Bob Hope's Gemini comedy patter. Mercury drives him to try to *trick* his audience repeatedly — which is rather astute of Mercury, because it makes Hope's listeners pay strict attention, being led, as they are, to believe that each joke is his last for the night.

Bob Hope's reputation for possessing the finest comedy timing in show business is deserved, a talent that's directly inherited from the influence of his Sun ruler, Mercury. Comedienne Bea Lillie's repartee is equally sharp and staccato, her sense of comedy timing as exquisite as Hope's. Both born in England, Bea and Bob have startlingly similar noses, both are famed for entertaining the troops — and both were born the same month, day, year, latitude and longitude, within a few minutes of one another. *Astral twins.* More about that in a future book.

A blend of Gemini and Gemini has the advantage of creating an atmosphere of freedom of thought and movement, so that their combined intellects can click into action unhampered by petty jealousies, suspicions and restrictions (allowing, as always, for a more conservative Moon Sign or Ascendent). Even then, the emotional climate between them will be comparatively free and easy, allowing them to accomplish lots of tricks and capture many a dream together. These two will sharpen their wits on one another, usually forgive and forget quickly — and boredom will rarely be a problem.

But there are also disadvantages to their association, which they'll have to face, and find a way to erase, between them. Lacking the stability of the more prosaic, less complicated Sun Signs, Gemini and Gemini can tempt each other to scatter their talents to the four winds, neither one willing to hold down the other or able to provide the necessary patience and dependability for success, either on an emotional or on a material level. They may remind their friends of two brightly colored balloons, filled with a blend of happy helium and hot air, having a gay and marvelous time floating through the clouds, but not going anywhere in particular. With this combination, their Moon Signs will write the ending to the story. If the Moon Sign in either birth chart is unfavorable in aspect to the Gemini Sun Sign of the other, they can create lovely poetry or jazz, paint the clouds silver, or paint the town red. But few of their dreams and schemes will take off, or if they do, there could be a crash landing. Or, their balloons might take off too fast, then fly away out of sight, because they weren't grounded. They can still make it all work out harmoniously, but in order to do so, they'll have to be more cautious and less casual.

With a favorable Luminary aspect between their Suns and Moons, however, the sky is truly the limit for creative breakthroughs, scientific discovery, intellectual attainment, material security — and even spiritual perception. As for emotional happiness and harmony, well . . . it's really their own choice. Geminis manufacture their own emotions to sell, keep or give away. What do these Mercury Birds seek on the wind out there? Whatever it is, it's something beyond what is visible and tangible. One Gemini might ask the other, but the answers they get will be exactly the same as if the Twins had asked themselves.

GEMINI: What is it you're looking for?
GEMINI: I'm not sure. But when I find it, I'll know what it is.
GEMINI: And just where do you think you'll find it?
GEMINI: Where? Why, most anywhere, I guess . . . .

And yet, too often, the last place the Twins will look is in their own backyards, where the miracle they're searching for may have been waiting all the time.

Author's Gemini Postscript:
Because it has not yet been corrected in any
current or past editions of my first book,
SUN SIGNS, I would like to say that the mention of
Marilyn Monroe in the Gemini Woman section of
that book was intended to be an accurate description of Marilyn's
Gemini Ascendent and her natal Mars-in-Gemini.
Certain investigation has indicated that Marilyn was
actually born a Sun Sign Aries. Birth certificates
are not always infallible sources of information,
as any professional astrologer well knows.

☆ ☆ ☆ ☆ ☆ ☆

GEMINI *Woman* GEMINI *Man*

━━◄◆►━━

"Well, then, we could go on," said John.

"That is the awful thing, John. We should have to go on,
for we don't know how to stop."

This man and woman—although it would be more fitting to call them boy
and girl, whatever their illusionary chronological age—are sometimes drawn
together for no more reason than that it's fun to have someone to cross the
street with you at the corners. Then you can, if that person is a Gemini, trade
fast bets with each other about whether you can make it on GO before the
traffic sign switches to STOP. Like when the light at an intersection is green,
and you don't know how fast it's going to turn to red. It's exciting.
Dangerous, but exciting.

Sure, it sounds dippy, but switching from street corners to living rooms,
offices or classrooms, it's a fair example of the sort of mental checkers and
chess games Geminis play with themselves and with each other. When you're
alone a lot, you can think up bushels of crazy ideas. Geminis don't seem to be
lonely, but they are. It's a lonely thing to wonder and wander, mixing with
frightened, preachy people, to whom the only important game is the one you
win by simply surviving. Especially when you know there are so many more
important things to be fascinated by than merely staying alive. In fact, many

Geminis wholeheartedly agree with Mercury-ruled Peter Pan that "to die, would be an awfully big adventure," perhaps the greatest adventure of all. !

If you're a Gemini, your entire life is spent searching and learning, so why should death be any different ? Like the elusive something you've been trying to pin down, express or define since you were five years old or so. True, Geminis seldom reveal their inner loneliness. But I wouldn't be surprised if that's not because they're barely aware of it. A person can get good at being lonely, with enough practice. It's like riding a bicycle. It requires concentration in the beginning, but after a time, you don't even notice your own balance or pedaling — you're just aware of the motion and the wind blowing your hair.

Because all typical Geminis are naturally glib, bright conversationalists, when two of them first meet, both may talk a lot, and it seems like they're not thinking of one another seriously. Yet, behind all the chatter, they are — more seriously than either will admit to the other. The dialogue between them will normally flash with wit and sparkle with imagination. It gives each of them time to study the other, when all those little ribbons of speech are rippling all over and around them. But they never say *everything* that's on their minds to each other, these two, not even years later when they've been in love long enough to know they can trust one another. There's always something held back.

"It's funny," she may think privately, "when you love someone so much, and you've been so intimate, that you have to hold back and remember there are things not to tell him, things you really can't share all the way." Well, when there's all that that he doesn't know about her, it's only right there are things he won't tell too. Do you imagine that, when Geminis chatter, everything they feel is spilling out in a cascade of words ? Oh, no. If you think that, you don't understand this man and this woman — this boy and this girl.

A Mercury-ruled female, in love with a Geminian Twin male, should maybe know about something showman Mike Todd once said. Todd, the most prolific talker on record — anytime, anywhere, under any condition — was being interviewed by a perceptive reporter, who asked him, "Mike, do you know why you talk all the time ? To keep from saying something. That's how I have you figured."

"Yeah ? " Mike was suddenly quiet, quickly on guard.

"What bothers me," the reporter continued, "is — well, I'm curious. What *is* that something you talk so much, and so fast, to keep from saying ? That's the real story behind the pitch, isn't it ?"

Mike just smiled the three-cornered Gemini smile and answered, "Listen, buddy, when I stop talking, we all stop eating."

It was true, of course. Without the Gemini talent for expressing ideas in vivid verbal images, people would be exposed to a lot less magic in this dreary-grey world, a lot less money would change hands, and fewer dreams would be dreamed — or come true. But the important thing for the Gemini girl to remember is that Mike avoided answering the reporter's *real* inquiry, with the typical mental adroitness of Mercury.

Since no one can say for certain exactly when Mike Todd was born, I've been asked why I call him a Gemini (although any girl in love with a Twin would know why). He gave approximately five different "official" dates to the press and disagreed strongly with his family about several others, all ranging between June 18th and June 23rd. How do I know Mike was a Gemini, then? By his blarney and his magic. But most of all, by the way he fenced with his birthday, fighting middle age as though he was sure he'd win. At any given time of his life, he looked twenty years younger than he was, whatever he was, and he never really grew up. Only a Gemini could have parlayed a patched-up sack of old hopes into the Giant Twin Jackpot of "Around the World in 80 Days" *and* Elizabeth Taylor — a double win that ended that Gemini's restless search for completeness. Shortly afterwards, his Libra son, Mike Todd, Jr., remarked, "Dad, you're spending money now as fast as you did when you didn't have any." Mike never saved for a rainy day, so for him, it never rained. Well, maybe a few very brief drizzles. A couple of spring showers, that's all. Mike Todd didn't discover the Neverland. He invented it. Like Peter Pan, the eternal Gemini, he guarded the secret of his age from curious chronological-minded "grown-ups" — and a few more secrets besides.

At least 75 percent of all Geminis have a nickname, a pseudonym, an alias, or in some way bear more than one name during the course of their lives, and Mike had two names also. Born Avrom Hirsch Goldbogen, he named himself Michael Todd one day, impulsively, and for no really special reason. His son had already been born and had been named Michael. So Gemini Mike Todd actually named himself after his own son and became his son's namesake, instead of the other way around. Trust Geminis to turn things inside out and backwards, in both small and large ways.

As for Mike's "secret" the reporter guessed correctly he held within himself, the Gemini man or woman isn't secretive in the same manner as Pisceans, Cancerians and Scorpions are — or for the same reasons. It's just that there are some soaring thoughts they're unable to catch and express in speech, for all their Mercurial verbal dexterity. What words could describe an inexpressible longing to literally discover Shangri-La?

"If this is so beautiful," they each think, "then there just *must* be something even *more* beautiful out there, somewhere. Will we be able to find it together? Or can you only find something that special by yourself?"

Each loveliness that two Geminis touch, Mercury allows them to drink in and enjoy for but a fleeting moment. Only until his (or her) secret Twin Self whispers seductively, "Ah, yes! But what else might there be to discover, which is even more perfect? This present glory you're experiencing is merely proof that a greater glory exists out there ... a glory more true, more thrilling, more fulfilling, if only you have the courage to pursue it. How do you know what may be around the next corner, the next kiss, the next dream, the next promise? Don't stop now, don't turn back yet! Go on ....." It's a call more alluring than the song of the Lorelei, and it haunts all Mercury-ruled hearts.

Most of the time, a Gemini girl laughs. Once in a while, less frequently, she weeps. When she does, it's because the lump of loneliness within her has grown so choking that it must turn into tears, or maybe she would simply die from the feeling. Ah, Twin Self! Where are you now, when you're needed? Off chasing the stars and playing tag with the wind? The Gemini man will tenderly understand her brief touch of *Weltschmerz*, with a delicacy of perception surprising in one who's always being accused of being so cold and detached. For all of his curious, inquiring nature, he won't ask questions when he senses the Gemini woman he loves is languishing from her inexpressible and unexpressed (even to him) terrible loneliness because her Twin has temporarily deserted her. He'll probably pretend not to notice, masking his concern with a light remark, like ....."Let's throw *ourselves* into a wishing well, instead of tossing in pennies, and see what happens!" Or perhaps ..."Come on, we'll buy two round tickets to Ireland, and make love on the Blarney Stone!" Then he'll kiss her cheek softly and say, very quietly, *"It's all right. I'm here."*

Yes, it's partly because he understands the sudden panic his Gemini girl feels when her Twin has disappeared and left her alone to cope, like half a person, because his own Twin pulls that trick on him too. But his finesse and tenderness at such times are prompted by more than just knowing how it is with someone born under your own Sun Sign. It's his ... the right word just came to me. Gemini never *fumbles*. Whatever the situation with the loved one — joyous or tragic, loose or tight — the typical Gemini can, when he (or she) wishes, carry the ball with easy grace, handling embarrassment, fear or anger, with an incredibly light touch. It's like a magician's sleight-of-hand, and many Geminis actually are professional magicians (along with Aquarians, Pisceans and Scorpions). There are, percentagewise, however, more Gemini magicians, because these people are amazingly multidextrous with their hands. They're also multidextrous with their minds — and as for the Gemini heart, it contains many little secret rooms, in which are hidden compassion, gentleness, surprises, humor, hope and sunshine. Some of them are kept locked for a lifetime, and only another Twin holds the passkey.

Two Geminis in love might ask themselves, each about the other — do any of those rooms hold a quality called "faithfulness" or "fidelity"? Yes. But the door to that particular room in the Gemini heart is tightly sealed, and it takes more than a passkey to open it. It takes trust. And it takes time. Two kinds of trust: the complete trust each must give to the other — and the trust required to believe in *yourself*, that what you love is really what you *need*, and all you'll *ever* need. (That's what takes the time.) But time is free. They can both use as much of it as they like to find that answer within themselves . . . . . and once it's been found and the door unlocked, Gemini will be loyal and true forever after.

Nevertheless, it's probably asking too much to expect either him — or her — to permanently stop flirting, charming, teasing, persuading, or just talking with members of the opposite (or the same) sex. Yet, Gemini lives on the mental plane, essentially existing within the realms of the imagination, and, therefore, may be frequently content to keep human relationships on the same plane. And so, it's sometimes easier for these two to be technically true to one another than to avoid periodic fantasies. Yet, the girl in his fantasies may really be her — and the boy in her fantasies may really be him. It's fun to make believe sometimes, that's all. The more versatile they are as individuals, in their personal lives or careers, the less need they'll feel to imagine, "What would it be like, I wonder, if she would . . . . ." or . . . "What would it be like, for a change, if he would . . . . . ."

If she would what? If he would what? Anything. Anything at all. Some Geminis even fantasize hurt or anger, then split up because they wonder what a break would feel like. When they find out, they streak back to each other again to rediscover the reality of love. No, it wasn't a dream. WOW! What a mind blower! Love is *real*. It's *really real*. You can really, nearly trust it. Yes, you nearly, really can! Such a discovery might not stun the average person's mind, but you must remember that the Twins spend their entire lives separating the possible and the probable from the sure things — and love gives them an exhilarating glimpse of Shangri-la.

These two relate to one another physically, through sexual love, in the kind of kaleidoscopic pattern you might expect, when Air unites with Air, chaperoned by the changeable Mercury. It's light, often stormy, sometimes whipping love into hurricanes of passion, sometimes calming it into quiet, gentle affection. The ways in which they express their love on a physical level are as multiple-faceted, sensitive and changeable as the ways they express it on the mental and emotional levels, and that can take their sexual behavior from acrobatic embraces on the Blarney Stone to making love underwater or in a helicopter. Whatever desire one Gemini may have, the other can fill it, with the cool touch of a spring breeze or the hot, tropical wind of a monsoon. To comprehend the potential of their physical compatibility, two Geminis who are pondering a relationship will just have to use their imaginations. About the only words which won't apply to their possible patterns of sexual experience are deep — earthy — and sensual. But Gemini and Gemini can dream up some satisfying substitutes together. Magical is one.

Some Gemini women are as pathetically wistful and lost as Gemini Judy Garland, following a rainbow that forever seems to elude them. Others are as bright and hopeful as Frank Sinatra's Gemini daughter, Nancy. Some Gemini men are as disoriented, and inwardly insecure, as Mercury-ruled actor Errol Flynn — others as bold and confident as Geminians Mike Todd and Al Jolson ("Folks, you ain't heard *nothin'* yet!"). It's not easy to tell them apart, because the wistful, lost Gemini girls have their bright and hopeful moments . . . just as the bright, hopeful ones have their wistful, lost and lonely moments. The disoriented Gemini man can switch suddenly to stability . . . and the confident ones can feel occasionally insecure.

I'm afraid astrology doesn't have a final answer. Perhaps the Gemini boy and girl who are in love will just have to forget about that romantic togetherness formula of "becoming one," because there will always be four of them. But that also quadruples their chances for happiness. So the odds are good if they cover their bets with the double collateral of lots of trust . . . and lots of patience.

☆ ☆ ☆ ☆ ☆ ☆

GEMINI

Air — Mutable — Positive
Ruled by Mercury
Symbol: The Twins
Day Forces — Masculine

CANCER

Water — Cardinal — Negative
Ruled by the Moon
Symbol: The Crab
Night Forces — Feminine

The **GEMINI-CANCER** *Relationship*

*"Mind you, I am not sure that we have a drawing-room,
but we pretend we have, and it's all the same. Hoop la !"*

*He went off dancing . . . . . and they all cried
"Hoop la !" and danced after him, searching for the
drawing-room; and I forget whether they found it,
but at any rate they found corners, and they all
fitted in.*

There's a party in progress. Over near the canapé table, loaded with sliced cheese, stuffed munchrooms (the best kind), and other goodies, a voice is heard, rich and warm, punctuated with cackles, attracting a crowd of people . . . . . (a female voice).

". . . . . and the first day I was there, I decided to go horseback riding, up in the mountains. Since there was no one to see me, I removed my shirt, because I wanted to get a tan all over, you know ? There I was, perched on this palomino, as naked as Lady Godiva from the waist up, and you know how modest I am. It was a riot. Well, after a couple of hours, I was as red as a lobster, and I figured it was time to ride my horse back to the stables, where I'd rented it. But when I reached for my shirt to put it on, it wasn't there. It had slipped off the saddle horn somewhere in the woods. Can you imagine me riding back, and facing all those men at the stables, in that seminude condition? Naturally, I burst into tears from embarrassment. I knew I just couldn't do it. So, I said to the horse, half hysterically. . . . ."

At the same time, from over near another table, loaded with Perrier water, fruit juices, and several bottles of red and white wine, comes another voice, clear and sparkling, with perfect emphasis and timing, as a second crowd gathers . . . . . .

". . . . . so this guy in Indiana comes home drunk every night for years, until finally his wife threatens to leave him. Because he's really in love with her, he straightens out for a few months. Then this one night he falls off the wagon, gets soused on stingers, and forgets where he lives for three days and nights. Now he's afraid to go home, because she may not forgive him this time. So he has a brainstorm. He goes to a pay phone, drops in a dime, dials his home number, and when his wife answers, he *screams* into the receiver, "Oh, Helen, it's so good to hear your voice! I thought I'd never hear it again. Now listen carefully. I'm in Arizona, and I'll be home tomorrow, but get the police to tap the phone as soon as I hang up — and if they call before I get there, DON'T PAY THE RANSOM MONEY — I JUST ESCAPED!"

They're both good talkers, Gemini and Cancer. The Crab's ability to remember details and to tell a story with sensitive perception, laced with the Lunar imagination and humor, can hold a crowd spellbound. If there's also a Gemini in the room, weaving tall tales with wit and charm, and maybe doing a few card tricks on the side, the bystanders won't know which of the three rings to watch at the circus. (One ring for Cancer, two for Gemini, the Twins. Two of everything for Gemini.)

Before the party's over, either Cancer or Gemini (or both) may whip out a camera and start snapping. Gemini and Cancer share a love for photography with Leo and Pisces, the four Sun Signs most likely to be professional or amateur photographers, each for a different reason. The majority of top photographers were born under one of these four signs, or have the Moon or Ascendent there — and between them, they have the camera market pretty well cornered.

Another similarity between the Crab and the Twins is that their auras are colored with many shades, because they're both so moody. Cancer dips from the deep blues of depression to the rose of sentiment, sloshes around in the brown of crankiness or the muddy lime greens of fear and hypochondria, then crawls back up to lavender-hued nostalgia and soft pink laughter.

Gemini flits from bright yellow cheer to the indigo of despair, experiments with the shimmering silver of dreams and the gold of hope, then plunges down into the grey of despondency, from which he-she quickly leaps into glistening white childlike faith.

When their auras mix, every color of the spectrum is represented, from transparent etheric to ultraviolet... and a few more tones and shades that have not yet been perceived, let alone named.

They're both dreamers, and both expert in the art of getting publicity (although the Crabs pretend not to be interested, he and she fool no one — they adore attention). They also both have vivid imaginations, and they're both inclined to laugh in public and cry in private. So you may think it's difficult to tell them apart. It is not. It's as easy as telling a bird in the air from a crab on the beach. One flies with the wind or an errant breeze, flapping its wings, its bright eyes darting to and fro quickly. The other crawls carefully along the shore, near the water, in the moonlight... backwards, sideways, slowly and deliberately. Both are frequently amusing. Both change their dispositions without warning.

Regardless of their matching behavior at times, in their basic natures, as with all other 2-12 Sun Sign Patterns, Gemini and Cancer are as different as night and day, as positive and negative as the north and south poles — and, in this case, as different as Air and Water (which are very different, you must admit).

The Twins are Mutable; consequently, they prefer to dash around, here and there, communicating ideas and dreams, to being the Big Boss and running the show. The Crabs are Cardinal, they definitely do not enjoy communicating (especially their own secrets) and prefer to run things — not necessarily out front, with a brass band, but still very much in charge.

Being influenced by the 2-12 vibration, Gemini senses (because Cancer is the sign ahead of Gemini on the karmic wheel) that he or she has much to learn from the care and caution and secrecy of the Crabs — the ability to sit and wait patiently, and the tenacity to stay with an idea long enough for it to develop from a misty into a solid form. Because Gemini is the sign behind Cancer, the Crab is wistfully conscious of a faint soul memory of how it was to be driven by the multiple yearnings of Mercury, searching the world over for a place to settle, yet reluctant to linger too long in one spot, for fear of missing something more exciting. The Crabs remember, ah! they remember... and so, ruled in this present existence by the fluctuating Moon, they are periodically consumed by wanderlust, and at the same time held back by fear (springing from the same karmic soul memory) of losing, in Gemini fashion, what they already possess. That's why Cancerians usually remain by the hearth, flying (normally) only through the imagination, under a Full or New Moon, safely secure during such imaginary flights near the home nest. But because they do understand, the Crabs often tolerate the restlessness of the Twins better than most other Sun Signs are apt to do.

In friendship, business, love relationships, Gemini is not inclined to cling. If anything, they hold too lightly and casually, let go too quickly and sometimes discard too soon. Cancer hangs on for dear life (barring those Twins and Crabs with Moon Signs or Ascendents that strongly conflict with their natal Suns, and even then, the conflict is merely periodic and temporary). The typical Crabs fear that if they should loosen their grip, they'll be left without an anchor, in strange, new waters, bereft of the comforting and the familiar.

Of course, some Crabs will deny this trait with vehemence—the ones whose birth charts contain an Aries, Gemini or Sag Moon or Ascendent. Even so, don't be overly impressed with their denials—especially their claims that they don't save things or hang on to things. The tenacious quality is always there. It just takes some subtle forms in each individual Moon Child. If you search long enough, you'll find it.

A Gemini psychiatrist, whose office is on the ground floor of a building where I used to live, told me about a Cancerian patient he once treated for a mild neurosis. The Crab is completely cured now, happy and well adjusted, no longer weepy. On the first visit to the psychiatrist, there was so much emphasis on nostalgia and financial security, the secretive patient's Sun Sign peeked out. After a couple of hours of listening, the Gemini "shrink," although fascinated, began to fidget from sitting in one place so long, so he switched on one of his fast Mercury subject changes and remarked, "I'll bet you were born under the sign of Cancer."

"Yes, I was," replied the surprised patient. "It's very clever of you to have guessed that, since I have absolutely none of the typical Lunar characteristics. Astrology claims that Cancer is clinging and tenacious. Not me. I'm not like that at all. And I'm not in the least possessive. I don't save things, and I never hang on."

"Well," mused the Twins, glibly, "maybe it's your Moon Sign. Now, let's make an appointment for next week."

CRAB: You want me to go, is that it? You want to get rid of me, because I bore you as a patient, and you think I'm too far gone for even you to help. That's what you're trying to tell me.

THE TWINS: No, no—of course not. Not at all. It's just that I'm due in Chicago tonight for a speech, and if I don't leave for the airport within fifteen minutes, I'll miss my plane.

CRAB: I see. And you want me to leave. You're hinting for me to leave. Isn't that right?

THE TWINS: No. I mean, yes. Well, it isn't that I *want* you to leave. But I'm afraid I'll miss my plane, that's all.

CRAB: Could I maybe ride along with you in the taxi to the airport?

	And if you'll be back tomorrow, you could come over to my place for dinner. I make a really tasty meatless spaghetti.
THE TWINS:	I'd love to, but ... I've already made another engagement for dinner tomorrow night, after I return.
CRAB:	(weeping) You hate me. I can take a hint. I'll go.
THE TWINS:	Please don't cry. You're wrong. I'm not trying to get rid of you. I wish I could take you to Chicago with me. I enjoy your company. Honest.
CRAB:	(brightening considerably) You do? Okay, then can I make an appointment for the day after tomorrow instead of next week?

The funniest part of the story is that the Cancerian patient was a female Crab, a Moon Maid, who is now happily married to the Gemini psychiatrist. I trust this little story will illustrate to Geminis of any sex, age or profession, who are involved with a Cancerian in any way, that the quick can be tripped up by the quiescent — whether in romance, across the table in a card game or in a business deal, not to mention running around the family circle.

Crabs are impressionable, sensitive men, women and children. They tend to be periodically contrary and sullen, brooding over slights, real or imagined. But the Twins can usually sweet-talk or double-talk them into crawling back out of their shells. Gemini is the mental (or actual) wanderer, a lonely drifter, cut loose from ties, emotionally (and sometimes literally) homeless, lost and seeking ... the eternal child. A Cancerian is the eternal Mother (or Father), protective, warm, tender and coaxing. It's little wonder these two are drawn to each other ... part ... then return ... then part again.

The element of Water, when it saturates Air with enough moisture, causes a shower that clears the atmosphere of fog, smog — and misunderstanding. Consequently, Cancer can make Gemini pour out those Twin desires, shed some truthful tears, and pause a moment, now and then, to remember the things that really matter.

☆ ☆ ☆ ☆ ☆ ☆

GEMINI *Woman* CANCER *Man*

"Do you think I could be a twin ?"

"No, indeed," replied the twins; "it's awfully difficult to be a twin." . . . . .

"I hadn't really any hope," he said.

A Cancerian man lives in his sensations, emotions, and imagination. He loves history and likes to read about the glory of bygone ages, from the Byzantine, through the Medieval and the Renaissance. But he's rather romantic about the past (his own and that of other historical characters), and he doesn't like to be reminded that the Knights of the Round Table may have possessed some flaws, that the horses they rode had burrs in their tails — they wore sweaty shirts under their chain mail (the knights, not the horses), ate with their fingers, and may have occasionally slept with comely wenches on dirty straw.

In the Crab's sentimental mind, a knight has impeccable table manners, and he rides a snow-white steed, with a fluffy, carefully brushed tail. He returns from his great crusades unsoiled and unperspiring, to claim the scented hanky of his lady fair. Now there's nothing wrong with a Crab treating a Gemini girl to his sense of chivalry. But *she* should be aware, even if he's not, of the historical fact that many a knight of olden days, after tucking that scented hanky under his shining armour, reached into his visor for the key he carried to the iron chastity belt of his modest lady fair — and sometimes pulled out the wrong key.

That is to say, the Crab, like the real or legendary knight, has more intimate things planned than pocketing a hanky, no matter how slow and courteous his initial approach may be.

A Gemini girl could get emotionally carried away by the romantic scene his gallantry conjures up in her own imaginative mind. With her predilection for daydreaming, she can easily envision herself wading impatiently across the moat, then running through the clover to meet him, her long, golden hair (or raven-black tresses) flying behind her. Then she gracefully curtsies before her Cancerian knight, sitting up there on his snorting stallion. It's almost real. She blushes, then timidly hands him her perfumed . . . . . . *look out* ! By this time, the Crab may have grabbed her dainty hand with his firm grip, and isn't about to let go.

When Cancerian possessiveness crosses swords with the Gemini insistence on freedom, the clash can cut into their dreams cruelly. After the

Cancer man discovers this girl is really two women — one content to nestle happily beside him in the tower room of the castle — the other determined to roam around on the slopes, playing with the antelope, chasing the hounds or whatever — he may pout. He may snap at her. Or he may retreat into crabby seclusion in the dark, damp dungeon, waiting for her to trip down the stone steps and entice him out again. If there's something else on her mind, he'll have a long wait down there.

Gemini girls have been known to forget mundane responsibilities like lovers locked in dungeons when they've been caught up in a fitful flight of fancy or a mental whim. Not that she doesn't have an excellent memory, but other interests take priority, sometimes even over love, until she gets lonely. Then she'll trail back, looking for forgiveness and comfort. So their story could have a happy ending after all, since a Cancerian man is about as comforting as they make the male animal. No one can be more tender, gentle and understanding to a lost and mixed-up Gemini girl than a Crab. Not even a sweet, gruff, protective Bull. If they have a harmonious Luminary aspect between their birth charts, we can leave them there on the stone steps, as the sun sinks slowly in the West, astrologically confident of their continued bliss — knowing she'll always wander and he'll always pout — but she'll always return, and he'll always pet and forgive her.

If the Sun-Moon aspect between their horoscopes is not harmonious, we can't desert them quite yet. They'll need some help, to keep from falling into the moat and drowning — or disappearing over the hills, in different directions, on different horses.

They can find their share of happy together, but it will take patience on her part and some adaptability on his. It won't be easy, since her ruling planet, Mercury, doesn't send out patient vibes. And his ruling Luminary, the Moon, changes too frequently to count on any one phase remaining for long. He'll pass through a mood of reckless abandon to match hers, then return to his hard shell before she's even had a chance to enjoy it. It takes practice and devotion on both sides. Although the shifting moods they have in common may not be their only problem, they'll form the basis for all the others. When you take a Gemini girl and a Cancerian man, each subject to sudden switches of disposition, and throw them into close contact, no one quite knows whose fault anything is at any particular time.

Here he is, all jolly and full of fun and chuckles, but she has just changed into a somber, contemplative period. So she makes a loving effort to match his hilarity. However, by the time she's reversed gears into a high, he's already turned off the funnies. Now he's obeying the call of the three-quarter Moon, pulling on him magnetically to be quiet and reclusive. So he makes an equally loving attempt to match her new amusement. Except that, by the time he has synchronized himself to the Full Moon, and turned into a laughing Looney Bird, Mercury has tormented her into a mental knot of sarcasm and cutting criticism of his jokes. This deeply wounds the Crab's feelings. So she makes another loving effort to . . . well, it could go on and on — all the way to a mutual nervous breakdown. They'll have to blow the whistle, stop, and take stock of their mood schedules. There are several solutions.

They can both return to the starting line (say, on a day when their planets are working in rhythm) and try to match their changing moods to each other's. That's one way. Laugh together, cry together, mope together, hope together — and cope together. If they can't swing that, because their stars are coming in on different wave-lengths, they can at least stop fighting their crossed purposes and make this promise to themselves: If he's high while she's low — he'll cheer her up instead of letting her pull him down; if she's calm while he's stormy — she'll soothe his worries instead of snubbing him and driving him deeper into his shell. When Gemini is happy, why should she let the Crab's crankiness turn her off ? He needs sympathy, not cold rejection. When Cancer is placid, why should he let her jumpiness annoy him into retreating ? She needs petting, not pouting. If they keep that promise, they can gradually train their moods to slide into the same grooves, although they'll still have some periodic impasses.

Since this is a 2-12 Sun Sign Pattern, the Cancer half of the team will usually be tolerant of the twin Gemini faults of restlessness and detachment — and the Gemini half will probably try to imitate the Crab's virtues of patience and sensitivity, sensing that she needs to learn them. One lesson she may shy away from learning from him, however, is how to be more cautious with cash. Unless she has a more conservative Moon Sign or Ascendent, she may think he's a tight combination of Scrooge and Shylock. Most Geminis scatter money like birdseed. Most Cancerians hoard it like Midas. Somewhere in between there's a middle road to financial agreement. But it won't be found at the extreme ends of his stinginess or her capriciousness with cash. The Crab's tendency to hang on to money is motivated by his fear of being hungry someday and his need for security.

The more his hunger for affection is satisfied, the less fear he'll have of starving. *If he has enough emotional security, he won't need as much financial security.* As for the material possessions the Crab likes to accumulate, Gemini may fear they'll tie her down. Her tendency to get rid of money is motivated by the feeling that she'll find more excitement in spending it than in saving it. When she has sufficient emotional freedom and mental challenge, she won't be compelled to buy these basic Mercury needs with cash, so she'll be less extravagant. Gemini is gregarious and must be either mentally or physically active, preferably both. She likes to eat out a lot, for a double reason: she's not overly fond of cooking — and she needs a frequent change of scene. The Crab may prefer to eat at home, because it's reminiscent of the coziness of his childhood — or eat at his mother's, which is even *more* reminiscent of the coziness of his childhood. That can put a few kinks in the Cancer-Gemini relationship, unless the partners iron them out by drawing certain lines clearly at the beginning.

Since both of them live in a world of fantasy and dreams, their sexual rapport can be stimulating for her and fulfilling for him. He supplies the sensual sensitivity and the affection — she supplies the imagination and the variety. A Gemini girl is one for having sudden ideas. She may have some changeable ideas about passion. But the Crab is preceptive enough to match his own desires to hers, and he'll probably have a few romantic notions of his own, off the beaten path of boredom. Their lovemaking will seldom be repetitious. It will vary with the Moon's waxing and waning, as they respond to the ebbing and flooding tides of their emotions. She'll notice something warm and protective about the way he approaches their sexual union, and her "lost child" heart will be solaced when his arms are around her. He'll notice there's always something indefinably delicate and gentle about the way she seeks his affection.

Often, a Cancerian man respects the Gemini lady he loves so much he can't seem to abandon himself to total passion with her, as if he believed her so fragile, he might be harming a flower. But she isn't as fragile as he thinks, never mind her delicate, gentle manner, and her airy, light touch. She needs, seeks and wants . . . to be treated as an adult woman, not as a charming child. When she's near him, in the dark, she'll cling to him, and her fears will melt away. Many Gemini girls dislike sleeping in total darkness — but with this man, she may be willing to try.

Many Cancerian men equally dislike sleeping without a night light. But with her close beside him, he'll find darkness a friend. The nightmares that haunt him so frequently will seem far away when he can feel her head on his shoulder. Her restless head . . . but she'll be calmer, quieter, more at peace with him, herself and the world . . . after they've experienced physical Oneness together. Visibly so. Sometimes, for days and days. Until her Twin calls to her again, and she gets that distant look. That's when he needs to grab her, before she floats away.

The male Crab, with his shy smile, enjoys parties and people, music and dancing, though he may be reluctant to admit it. This is just the woman to coax and wheedle and tempt him out of his reclusive hermit act into the bright lights. She may talk him into going dancing, hiking, horseback riding, sailing . . . cross-country skiing, or touring Europe with her, visiting ancient ruins, trying to recall when they perhaps once lived in a bygone civilization . . . and maybe drank a toast to each other from this very cup . . . . did she wear the necklace behind glass in the British Museum when they fiercely loved in Egypt?

The Gemini girl can talk the Crab into most anything, but her easiest persuasion will be to seduce him into traveling. Places like ancient ruins and old museums secretly magnetize this man. He lives in yesterday, and to revisit it with her is perhaps the deepest dream of all, from which he'll hope he never wakens. With her, he may not. Gemini lives on the wind, where dreams are reality . . . where reality itself is a dream. He'll probably learn that, wherever they go together. Nearly always, she'll be streaking ahead of him, her hair flying in the breeze, not even looking back over her shoulder to see if he's still there. She doesn't need to look back. She *knows* he's still there. She knows his love is steady, he is devotion unwavering, and that's what she's been seeking all her life — a pair of eyes that say *"Come home."* He's been seeking a pair of eyes that say *"Let's run through the stars !"*

And so, each sees the unspoken wish reflected in the other's eyes, from the very first time they look at each other, across a crowded street . . . or room . . . and their gaze locks tightly, unexpectedly. For years and years afterwards, they'll tell each other about that night and remember together the sudden tears they both felt, inexplicably, when their eyes first met . . . and they didn't even know each other's names. But that didn't matter. Silently, through a half-forgotten strain of music, they called out to one another by the secret names their hearts knew.

Once they've declared their love, she may shower him with a silvery stream of gifts, and at first his cautious nature will be aghast at such impulsive extravagance. Yet, when she's not looking, his eyes will fill with Lunar tears of pure delight, to be so loved and cherished. He'll timidly, yet proudly, display her gifts to friends. It proves, you see, that he is loved, and with her instant, flashing intuition, she senses this about him. She longs to make up to him for all the times he was disappointed as a child on Christmas morning. How does she know ? He never told her. She knows. Because she loves him. Love is funny like that. After a while, she just may perform a magical transformation in the Cancerian man's nature. Then he'll relax . . . and wrap some bright blue and silver or lavender and sunny-yellow ribbons around some special surprises for her, too. When a Crab is snugly loved, the reciprocal affection is boundless, bottomless, returning a thousandfold — and he'll cry, unashamedly, from sheer happiness.

He'll always treat her like a lady. She'll be thrilled at such lovely make-believe of a gentler time and usually behave accordingly. To her, he is a gentleman, a gallant gentleman, who touches her with occasional glimpses of the little boy within. Then *she* cries, because he is so vulnerable to hurt, despite his hard, outer shell of impassiveness. For he is a poet, and she's the very first one who ever guessed it. Geminis are great at guessing, and they always win the jar of jelly beans.

A Gemini girl-woman is a realist, despite her changing masks . . . first whimsical, then cynical, always fascinating to the Cancerian man, whose own facial expressions she loves to watch herself, as they reflect the various colors and tones of his Lunar emotions . . . joy or sadness, tranquility or worry.

Whatever the feminine Mercury Bird's chronological age may be, she's ever youthful and yearning, thoughtful and tender . . . her skin and eyes as crystal clear as a child's . . . filled with misty dreams, yet driven relentlessly by logic. Some of her dreams she carelessly loses along the way, others she forgets, in the sparkle of some new excitement. The deep, sacred ones, she keeps locked up inside herself. A persistent Cancerian man can coax her to share them with him, if he moves quickly, before she spins out of his reach. But it may take him some time to be certain — and Crabs can wait too long. She'll be chattering and charming him one day, then suddenly notice how quiet he's become.

"What's the matter, darling? Did I say something wrong?" she'll ask, vaguely troubled.

"No. It's just that . . . I think I might love you. But I'm not sure."

She won't understand what he means. To Gemini, you can't be sure of anything in this life, especially love. Not until you reach the very end of the trail. There's little enough time before that moment comes. Why waste any of it?

☆ ☆ ☆ ☆ ☆ ☆

GEMINI *Man* CANCER *Woman*

——◆◆◆——

He ceased to look at her, but even then she would
not let go of him. He skipped about and made funny
faces, but when he stopped it was just as if she
were inside him, knocking.

Normally, a Gemini man is able to analyze people quickly, with a swift, sure insight. Normally, a Moon Maiden is acutely perceptive of human nature. Together (along with Aquarius and Pisces) they make a great sleuthing team, and it's no accident that almost all Geminis and Cancerians enjoy detective stories. (Scorpios do too, though they lean more toward murder mysteries and ghost tales.)

Yet, for all his cleverness and mental agility, and for all her talent at worming secrets out of people, the one puzzle Gemini and Cancer can't seem to solve is each other. There's always a piece missing. Ask a Gemini man what disturbs him most about the Cancerian girl he loves, and he'll tell you:

"I never know what she's *thinking*."

Ask a Cancerian girl what troubles her most about the Gemini man she loves, and she'll say:

"I don't know what he *wants*."

That's the way it is with these two lovers when they meet, and that's the way it will be when they part, in friendship or in anger — through any kind of earthly separation — and that's the way it will always be, if they remain together. Her secretive manner, her way of clamming up and refusing to talk when she's hurt, will drive a Gemini man wild, which is not a natural state for the casual Twins. From time to time she'll tell him what's on her mind, but just as frequently, she'll snap her Crab shell on his questions, leaving him frustrated and feeling totally helpless to bring her out of a mood he has no idea how she managed to get into. It will do no good to poke at her with accusations and sarcasm. She'll remain inside herself until she's good and ready to come back out — and then she'll claim she's forgotten what it was that made her blue and cranky. She hasn't, really. She just feels safer when she retains her secrets. Sometimes a girl Crab will weep, and pour out her apprehensions, but even then he won't get to the real, rock-bottom reason for the anguish. There are no whys and wherefores. Gemini isn't content until he untangles every snarl and sees into every motive, and so her cryptic behavior leaves him with a continued feeling of vague uneasiness. How can he solve this mystery of her moods if she keeps the clues locked up in her attic, hidden inside her trunks of jokes and tucked behind the corners of her silent fears? Perhaps it's because he can't solve it that he often returns, again and again, to try. But he may never know what she's really thinking between her sobs, her giggles and her serenity — just the bits and pieces he picks up when she lets him sneak into her heart's attic to help her look for an old memory she's misplaced, from long ago, in her childhood.

As for her, she would give him the Moon if she could. A Cancerian girl in love desires only to cherish, to protect and lavish affection on her man (though his portions of her devotion may be abruptly cut in half when their children crawl into her heart). She'll stuff him with food, wash him with sympathy, and distract him with her wacky Lunar humor. But how can she cook up a complete dream that will sastisfy all his hunger when he keeps changing the recipe for his happiness? The elusive way he switches the subject, just when she thinks she's caught what it is he's longing for, drives her into tears and tantrums. She may never discover what he really wants, because *he* doesn't know, and even if he did, he'd share it only with his Twin Self.

It's not that he doesn't trust her. But only his Twin can decipher the complications of his Mercurial dreams and translate them into one single goal. Since a Moon Maiden is so reflective, so emotionally absorbent, she'll soak up some of his strategy, just from being around him. She'll know everything about his mental tricks — except how to perform them. That's because these two are set at different speeds. Hers reads: slow and cautious — despite her outward show of busy motion. His reads: fast and reckless — never mind if he's one of those Geminis who appears cool and calm on the surface. His mind is jet-fueled and ever ready for instant takeoff.

This is a 2-12 Sun Sign Pattern, with Gemini the sign behind Cancer and Cancer the sign immediately ahead of Gemini. So, she'll secretly understand his restive nature, from an unconscious soul memory of what it was like to be careless and casual and free of strong emotional ties. In fact, the memory may haunt her to the point of turning her to its opposite — a desperate clinging to security, preferably emotional, and if it's lacking —financial. Gemini will half consciously realize she can teach him an approach to life he's never experienced, and since he's such a quick study, he'll grow in wisdom around her in many ways. But not without a few growing pains.

The typical Gemini man keeps nothing for which he has no further need, from torn ticket stubs and dull razor blades to human relationships which have outlived their usefulness. He can't understand her need to hang on to things. You'd think she had lived through the horrors of some great famine, the way she saves soup coupons and stocks up on canned food that would feed her whole family for months if we were ever under siege by Space people.

What he doesn't understand is that, with a Cancer girl, an interplanetary war is always a possibility. *Anything* is always a possibility, and she wants to be prepared for it. The crinkled money she keeps under the box springs eases her fear of a leaky roof on a future rainy day. But the old ball gowns she packed away in mothballs are back in style, and if she cuts off the tops, she'll have a new wardrobe of evening skirts without spending any of those crinkled bills. Neither is she as hasty as he is to throw away old friendships or ties.

Gemini's more casual attitude toward human relationships puzzles the Cancerian girl. It's not the *usefulness* of any close relationship that matters to her. It's the familiarity, the comfortable feeling it gives her of the past — yesterday, when the world was young and gay and safe and secure. She feels similarly about the deeper relationship called love. A Lunar girl's love has no foundation in reason or logic. She's helpless to destroy it. Other loves can be wished away, willed away, angered away — talked out, or thrown out. Hers has to *wear* out, and it can take many years. Even then, she'll sew a patch on the worn spots and try to somehow make it do. It's one of the most valuable lessons her heart can teach his mind.

You may know a Cancerian girl who is fickle and promiscuous, but don't you believe her. It's a pose. Somewhere under her tough crab shell is an old, faded love, tenderly darned and folded with care, that she's wistfully hoping will come back into style . . . be *needed* again. The fictional image of the sentimental prostitute with the heart of gold, who "babies" or "mothers" her gentlemen callers, is a picture of a haunted Moon Maid, still waiting, in her fashion, for "him" to return.

To the Gemini who is on a romantic holiday, it's always time to move on, and lugging the memory of old loves slows a man down. He seldom packs any torches in his suitcase. He travels light. He doesn't belong to anyplace or to any person. Not even to his relatives. He knows they love him, but still he feels, somehow, apart — not only from them, from the world — until he finds a woman who knows how to hang on to his heart. Hanging on is a Cancerian talent, but her Crab-like possessiveness will turn him off — and away — unless she disguises it as tender tolerance and makes it stretch to give him room to wander. Then it will lure him and warm him when he's cold and lonely. If she learns to let go, and to let love be the only tie that binds them, she'll discover that, with this man — free can mean faithful.

In their sexual relationship, pure physical sensation will be less emphasized than the passions of the mind and a kind of emotional eroticism. Her affectionate tenderness and vivid imagination are a good balance for his delicate touch and his sensitive sexual nature. When they're expressing their love on a physical level, they may even find that missing piece to be the puzzle of each other they're always looking for, and become whole . . . for brief moments. Because she needs constant, tangible proof that she's really needed, not just routinely desired, his airy embraces could sometimes cause her to wish he would hold her more closely — and longer — just so she can be *sure*. Their most ideal sexual fulfillment together may frequently be experienced during the Full Moon, when she seems to possess a strange, magnetic power to gently reach into the secret corners of his Twin heart and draw him away from his dreams back into the intimate mystery of their union . . . the deepest dream of all.

He'll become impatient with her ingrained economical streak if she tries to transfer her financial fears to him. Then she'll ask, "Do you know how it feels to be poor? It's a nightmare. You'll find out what it's like if you keep throwing away your money and never saving it. Didn't anyone ever tell you that waste makes want?" But Gemini will simply shrug and reply, like archetype Geminian Mike Todd — "I wouldn't know about that. I've been broke, but I've never been poor. Being broke is temporary. Being poor is a state of mind."

A Moon Maiden will understand this man better if she realizes that, however he may apppear to the world, to himself he's eternally a young boy, who, in some magical way, has managed to pilot a plane high in the sky. He diverts himself now and then with sudden dives and spins, fascinated by finding a prettier cloud, discovering a more beautiful sunrise or sunset . . . all the while excitedly aware that the great Universe and its glittering galaxies lay enticingly unexplored before him . . . beckoning. If she truly loves him for keeps, she'll cheerfully be ready to pack up and move on when his free spirit grows restless, turning each new rest stop, however temporary, into a warm and welcoming, gracious haven, as only a Cancerian woman can. Somehow this lady can cause each new place she lives to seem like a garden, filled with the fragrant flowers of tradition. And this is the very thing Gemini needs — to be able to wander, yet never leave home. Gradually, she'll tenderly implant herself inside his own longings, until finally . . . . anywhere he hears her lovely Lunar laughter becomes home.

The Gemini man may linger past the sunset in the sky until the Moon comes up. If he stays a little longer, he might unveil the mystery of his Cancerian woman. And wouldn't it be funny if her secret turned out to be that — in a changing world of changing truth, fleetingly glimpsed, then hidden by clouds of passing time — each soul must find its other half, to know — to see — to *be*? The very same Twin secret as his own.

☆ ☆ ☆ ☆ ☆ ☆

GEMINI

Air — Mutable — Positive
Ruled by Mercury
Symbol: The Twins
Day Forces — Masculine

LEO

Fire — Fixed — Positive
Ruled by the Sun
Symbols: Lion & Shy Pussycat
Day Forces — Masculine

The GEMINI-LEO *Relationship*

"Back, twins . . . ."

As Gemini calculates the sunny but sometimes insufferable antics of the Lion, the Twins wonder: "Does the big cat actually possess such complete self-assurance? Or could Leo only be trying to prove that the *reality* is as infallible and fearless as the *image*?"—a typical Gemini mind trip.

As the Lion or Lioness lazily studies the Mercurial Gemini Twins, he (or she) has a similar thought: "All that mental and physical activity must be a compensation of some kind. Survival alone isn't sufficient reason for so much unnecessary maneuvering. Is Gemini trying to span East, West, North, and South all at once to hide the fact that he (or she) is lost in the woods with a broken compass?"

They've both guessed the truth about each other. Yes, Leos are trying to prove to themselves and the rest of the world, through a show of arrogant bravado, that Lions and Lionesses are as brave inwardly as they outwardly seem. And yes, Gemini *is* trying to prove to the Twin Self and everyone else that he-she is racing straight ahead, in the right direction, and not really running around in circles.

Because their two Sun Signs are sextile, creating a 3-11 vibration between them, they're intuitive about each other, are inclined to friendship, despite any differences between them from time to time, and they have a mutual talent for whistling in the dark. When they whistle a tune together, in harmony, it's easier to convince themselves that all is well. Unlike Scorpios (except for the Grey Lizards), who are deeply and unshakably certain of their superiority, the Lion and Lioness believe that if they roar loudly enough, no one will suspect that they tremble with apprehension over their private fear that they may not be completely equal to every occasion that may arise. The King and Queen of the jungle pride — or of any kingdom, classroom, office or home — must never lose face before their adoring subjects, who respect and worship the monarchy, only because their rulers are capable of handling any minor or major emergency with majestic finesse, regal dignity and wisdom. It's the quintessence of royalty to project nobility of spirit and strength of character to the weaker masses. Strangely, and rather wonderfully, in pretending to be all these things, Leo actually *becomes* them, rediscovering through every human crisis (to his or her secret surprise and delight) that the Leonine courage really is as powerful and awesome as the Lion's roar insinuates.

Geminis have the same sort of good fortune with their apparent self-deception. While the Twins are selling others, they're simultaneously selling themselves the validity of their own dreams. Gemini tells stories, flavored with excitement, always amusing, some of them with a double-switch O'Henry ending, instilling enthusiasm and inspiring more cautious, practical souls. With the brush of imagination, Geminis paint marvelous word pictures of nonsensical things and somehow manage to make them seem real and logical to sane people, as well as to themselves. By so believing, Mercury dreams eventually materialize and manifest.

Because Leo inwardly senses that Geminis are telling the truth *as they see it*, the large Leonine heart goes out to the Twins in sympathetic recognition of a soul brother — or sister. Of course. Leo understands. It's like the song from *The King and I* — "make believe you're brave, and the trick will get you far. You can be as brave — as you make believe you are!"

What hurts and perplexes the Gemini Mercury Birds is the way others, who are less sympathetic than Leo, interpret their talent for conjuring up imagery. They can't fathom why it is, when other people do the same thing, they're called creative, imaginative — astute traders, or shrewd businessmen. When the Twins do it, they're called con artists, liars — or, at the very least, deceptively slick and quick with the facts. Geminis think they have the world and everyone in it analyzed down to the last nuance. That is, until they bump up against the exceptions to the rule and finally come to the conclusion that the world may consist entirely of exceptions. It figures. The Twins themselves are.

From childhood, Geminis have been acutely aware that illusion is the most dependable of all riches. No Broadway stage is as packed with drama and color as the "theatre of the mind." And so, the Twins cast themselves in all roles, from the character actors to the ingenues, from the stars to the lowliest bit players, sometimes slipping into the part of the stagehands or musicians. Why not? They've also decided they're the producers and directors, so they can be whatever they choose to be.

However, when playing the boards with the Big Cats, the Twins best be cautious about grabbing off the plum titles of Star, Director or Producer. If there's any kind of show going on, anywhere, at any time, actual or make-believe, you can bet your greasepaint and footlights that Leos are going to insist on directing it and producing it — and most definitely will star in it. No one successfully outshines a Lion or a Lioness for very long, let alone upstages a King or Queen.

That's usually just fine and dandy with the airy, detached Geminis. The Twins are, if the truth be told, actually far more interested in changing the scenery than in hogging the encores. They appreciate press notices as much as Leo, and they're equally if not more adept in the art of getting heard about or written about. But they'll normally, if they're typical Mercury Birds, move gracefully aside and allow the vainer Leos to take most of the bows before a live audience.

Is it because Gemini is a Mutable Sign? Not necessarily. The Twins have another "method to their madness." When you're out front, headlining the show, you see, you're vulnerable to being inspected by a bunch of curious strangers. It makes many Geminians in the entertainment field uncomfortable if he-she can't wear the many-colored cloak of multifaceted identity, which is so handy for disguising a Twin — or even Triplet — personality, who's pretending to be one single entity.

It's been said that inside every plump person is a skinny twin, longing to escape. That's especially true of the chubby Geminis, who have gained weight in an unconscious effort to hide their secret selves — to stop running so fast — because they were bored into eating by a lack of opportunity for physical activity and mental challenge — or through some hidden guilt and frustration connected with their tangled emotions. Gemini fatties, however, are rare, since the skinny Twin is normally the more insistent one, because of being aware that the ability to flash around, thin, and therefore less noticeable, is a more effective means of masquerading. This is the real reason why the few plump Mercury Birds are so very much more miserable than people of any other Sun Sign (except Scorpio and Pisces) who have gained weight. They don't mind the burden of extra pounds so much, and they're not unduly concerned over their health — it's just that it makes them so *visible*, spoiling all their fun and games.

The difference between the Geminian and Leonine natures regarding visibility and public exposure was rather gloriously demonstrated when I was giving a talk in Washington, D.C., in May of 1971, before a very large crowd, consisting mainly of the press, at a banquet honoring Martha Mitchell (who provided them, undeniably, with some of their most colorful copy).

When I asked how many Leos were present, hands shot up all over the place instantly — and they *remained* up, as high as possible, many of them waving frantically in an attempt to be noticed. When I followed that request by asking the Big Cats to please stand and be recognized, heads started bobbing, right and left, as all the Lions and Lionesses present in the ballroom of the Hotel Shorehan that night rose grandly to the occasion. Then, while the audience loudly applauded, all those Leos, as if on cue, immediately began bowing quite formally, graciously accepting their rightful homage — even the Shy Pussycat Leos, who saw their chance to finally be on stage and take a few curtain calls. It was truly, astrologically and otherwise, hilarious. My tape recording of the event clocks the resulting roars of laughter from the other Sun Signs present at a full three minutes, during which time the applause grew louder and louder, as the Big Cats kept bowing repeatedly.

As a sort of test, a few moments after the general uproar had died down, I invited all the Geminis present to raise *their* hands. "Come on," I urged, "let's have a show of hands from all the Twins here tonight." Not one single hand was raised in the entire, huge ballroom. Quickly, a ripple of whispering passed among the audience, as everyone wondered why the Geminis weren't answering the astrological roll call, especially since I had just pointed out that there are, statistically, in several countries, including the U.S.A., more June births than any others. Obviously, percentagewise, there should have been at least *one* Gemini in that large crowd.

The audience had no idea what was happening, but I did. Any astrologer would have known. The Twins prefer to observe, without being specifically identified themselves. Geminis are seldom anxious to be recognized by a crowd. Also, some of them were undoubtedly present at the banquet after telling a friend, mate or relative that they were going somewhere else, following which they changed their minds — and they didn't want to get caught by those present later remarking on their presence because they had become publicly visible to the entire group. The rest of them were reluctant to expose themselves for as many assorted reasons as there are individual (or dual) Geminis.

I made all these remarks aloud to the audience — and repeated my invitation to the Geminis. Very slowly and hesitantly then, only about three or four hands were partially raised in the packed room. Suddenly a wave of laughter burst forth from everyone, as heads turned toward the rear of the ballroom, where what resembled a conga line of a dozen or more Geminis were attempting to sneak out the door without being noticed. As the laughter rose, and people began calling out to the departing Geminis they knew by name, they all began actually running past the astonished doorman. Everyone present, myself included, completely broke up.

And thus did I discover by sheer accident what turned out to be a most enlightening, as well as hilarious, way to prove the validity of Sun Signs to a large gathering of skeptics and believers.

I can't say whether it had any bearing on the hasty departure of the Mercury Birds, but perhaps I should note that the late FBI Chief J. Edgar Hoover was seated on the dais that night, making one of his extremely rare public appearances. Mr. Hoover was, quite clearly, intently interested in the exodus, and I received the distinct impression that he desperately wanted to signal someone to check out the identity of the guests who sneaked out rather than be recognized — maybe even have them followed home. But, being a Capricorn, he was, of course, aware that one does not so behave thus improperly at a social function. It would be against the rules.

The twin Mercury gifts of charm and glibness make the typical Gemini an expert Lion trainer, cleverly cajoling Leo to docilely jump through his (or her) double hoops. For example, Leo might ask Gemini, "What am I really like ? I mean, how do I appear to people ?"

And Gemini will answer, "Well, you're incredibly egotistical and arrogrant. But you're also open-minded, friendly and generous." (With Leos, you let them have the painful truth near the beginning, then quickly slam in a compliment at the close.) But the Lion or Lioness may persist, stroking his (or her) vanity and demanding, "Do others see my virtues as clearly as you ? If so, then why are they always underestimating me ?"

Gemini: "Of course they do. Everyone knows you're a fantastic person, a little conceited, and stuffed full of yourself, but you're a terrific organizer. It's obvious that you have a wiser head and cooler emotions than the average person. Anyone who doesn't give you credit for it is jealous, and not worth concerning yourself about."

You see how it works ? When you're conversing with a Lion, you sandwich the cold facts in between thick slices of warm flattery. There's a Mercurial technique to it — like, grovel while you're leveling with them.

Actually, Leos *are* excellent organizers, expert at delegating authority, and Fixed enough to wait out with composure the final success of their grandiose schemes and promotions. But they may not show as much patience with Gemini's changeability. The Big Cats can become indignant over the Twins' tendency to speed through life, discarding former convictions like yesterday's newspaper, tossing away homes and jobs and friends with minor flaws, too soon, with absolutely no reflective retrospection, but simply dashing off blithely to the next fascinating interest. To the loyal, more languid Lion or Lioness, fast is not always best, or right. Then Leo will feel obliged to enlighten Gemini with one of those regal Leonine lectures.

"You're pretty good at dabbling in the dairy and skimming off the surface cream, but it's always turning sour on you. That mental sharpness you think is so great cuts a lot of large holes in your common sense, and they'll trip you up when you least expect it. Someday you'll thank me for warning you."

Leos, the eternal Big Brothers and Sisters, are unable to resist predicting that the people they benevolently guided are going to want to look them up someday and seek them out to thank them for their unsolicited pearls of wisdom. As if Gemini had time to stop and make out a list of such obligations. The Mercury Birds are too busy selling that sour cream as buttermilk. As for the holes Leo cautioned them about, Geminis will simply leap out of them, land on their feet, and skate across the same thin ice again, while Leo pouts and asks petulantly, "Don't you *ever* get caught?"

Well, yes, sometimes Geminis do get caught by their own cleverness. But why worry, when the brave King (or Queen) will pull them out in a splendid, technicolor, last-minute rescue? Then, Leo will blush and bow (modestly) as Gemini sings Leo's favorite lyric of flattery. "Boy! You sure were right about everything you said. Thanks for warning me in time. I don't know what I'd do without you," cry the Twins, quite probably sincerely, who have now managed to have their cake and eat it too (royal protection — plus freedom).

"It was nothing," modestly replies the Lion or Lioness, purring and rolling over happily in the catnip of Gemini charm. "It's the duty of the stronger and wiser to protect the weak and foolish from the folly of their ways. Just remember in the future to do as I tell you, and you'll stay out of trouble."

"Okay, I promise!" cheerfully call out the Twins, as they wave goodbye and dash off. But Gemini knows, deep down inside, that what Leo said is true. Frustrating, annoying, often infuriating . . . but true.

☆ ☆ ☆ ☆ ☆ ☆

GEMINI *Woman* LEO *Man*

◄━◆━►

. . she tells him stories about himself,
to which he listens eagerly . . . . .

A Leo man will often deny his superiority complex and try to hide his exaggerated need for respect, but he can't fool the bright Mercury female who loves him. A Gemini woman I know once swore to a group of friends gathered in their living room that her Leo husband had none of the characteristics of his Sun Sign. "Philip is neither vain nor domineering," she insisted. "He's an unassuming person, who doesn't feel superior to anyone."

Modest Philip agreed. "I have no desire to lord it over people," he murmured quietly, "I'm just an average guy." To which his Gemini wife added quickly, "He's more than just an average guy. He's super special. What I meant to say is that he's not at all bossy, and he's certainly not an egotistical show-off."

It fooled everyone in the room. This kind, gentle host, with the courteous manner, was obviously not a roaring Lion. He lounged unobtrusively in the corner, exuding a soft, warm glow and making no attempt at all to command the conversation. Of course, I could have enlightened their guests. But my Gemini friend had cleverly stroked her big Lion into purring so contentedly by that time, I didn't have the heart to break up her little Mercury game.

What do you think this shy Pussycat does all day when he's not languidly relaxing at home, accepting his mate's compliments with a self-effacing air? He's in a tricky, special branch of law — foreign oil leases. He spends a *very* large income, which he earns from spending his *very* valuable time telling *very* large industries what they may and may not do. When you're handing out advice to billionaires and giving companies like Exxon and Standard Oil an occasional tweak on the nose, you don't need any extra outlets for the Leonine ego.

A Lion who is on stage at work, exercising his vanity and passing out his wisdom, can afford to be a little meek socially. Especially when he has a Gemini wife, who knows exactly how to butter him up, by singing his praises so charmingly, there's no need for him to indulge in vulgar bragging about himself.

Gemini and Leo vibrate to a 3-11 Sun Sign Pattern, so there's often sacrifice required in the relationship, some great benefit gained, due to the karmic tie between them — memories of past lives. Like all such 3-11 vibrations, the association is usually a fated one, an involvement difficult to resist, in family or business ties, as well as in friendship and romance. The Leo man feels compelled to teach the Gemini girl things which may truly change her life even more than he feels compelled to instruct others, and that's saying a lot. She can expect more than the ordinary number of Leonine lectures, as this man continually points out her flaws and tells her what she's doing or thinking wrong, from her diet and clothing to her political views and religious concepts. But the same soul memory which prompts Leo to lecture Gemini also brings an unconscious sense of gratitude for former favors received and causes the Lion to also want to protect the Gemini girl. He instinctively sympathizes with her shortcomings, even as he tries to correct them.

Likewise, the Gemini woman is defensive of her Lion. She wants to shield him from the hurt caused by others when they wound his great vanity unintentionally. Something inside her perceptive heart tells her the right thing to say and do, at the right time, to bring out all his warm tenderness and generosity. She looks up to him as a safe, loving haven from a world of skeptics, who don't understand her. Naturally, this flatters the Big Cat's masculine pride, which he possesses in greater abundance than the average male, and makes him cherish her all the more. It can slowly slither into a mutual-admiration society.

However, their basic compatibility won't prevent spells of rebellion on both sides. Her airy nonchalance can fire the Leo temper, which is slow to ignite, but difficult to extinguish, once it's aroused and flaming. Then she may use the quarrel to practice her syntax and sarcasm, which will cut sharply into his Leonine ego. If her multiple Mercury fascinations and outside interests should distract her from daily worship of the Lion, he'll wonder what any other Monarch wonders when his subjects are too busy to line up at the curb and cheer him as he passes — maybe they're no longer loyal to their King? Maybe she's found someone she admires more than *him*?

The poor girl just doesn't realize what she's risking. All the females he loved and left, before her, were simply devastated by grief — as he's told her many times. She'd just better mind her p's and q's or (speaking of the alphabet) Leo will dig out his well-thumbed, fat little black book and ring up a few numbers between "A" for Amy and "Z" for Zelda. Yes, most of his old paramours are married now, though a couple of them joined the convent. But Leo is quite positive that any one of his discarded slaves (including the nuns) would jump — snap! — like that! — if she thought there was the slightest chance of being recalled into the service of His Majesty. *Some* women know when they're lucky.

Because Leo is more Fixed, and therefore more practical than the Mutable Gemini, her erratic behavior could spark some angry sputters from the Lion. She may forget his dinner in her excitement over a new book she's reading, chatter on the phone when he needs an audience, change her mind about going to the theatre after he's already reserved the seats, forget where she parked the car, lose her keys or flood the engine. *He* would never be guilty of such carelessness. (He really wouldn't.) It's aggravating, but Leo is, in truth, enormously capable, a real man's man who handles emergencies with effortless grace, a royal shrug, and the unspoken question, "Doesn't everybody?"

Although the Gemini girl will be delighted with his strength of purpose, his loyalty, intelligence and integrity, she might turn moody and restless on the Lion and distract him when he's trying to work, study, or simply relax.

She could also make him feel inferior by begging him to take her on an expensive holiday when he's temporarily too broke to afford it but much too proud to admit it.

He'll roar at all these things but will probably forgive her the minute she flashes her Gemini blarney and pulls off a quick change from the flighty, reckless, bitter Twin to the sensible, womanly, devoted Twin. As for her outside interests, he won't mind if she has a career, studies ballet, takes up jogging, collects mummies, or chases butterflies — as long as none of her jobs or hobbies takes priority over him. But a Gemini girl should never tease her proud Leo man by pointing out to him that the big male Nature cats in the wild jungle permit their mates to do the hunting while they snooze in the sun — or she may be called home from the hunt and permanently retired to the pride.

Besides, that's true of lion-lions, not human Lions. As a Leo, he also has a royal birthright. Would a King allow his Queen to worry about Affairs of State and tangle with the Treasury, back at the castle, while he's out riding with the hounds or getting fitted for a new crown?

Well, yes, he probably would — if she's properly humble about it. After all, she ought to have some worthwhile purpose in life, like seeing that he's happy and contented. Still, a woman who is the King's favorite certainly has her rewards. A Lion is full of fun, generous with his time and money, strong and brave, even gentle, when his ego is stroked softly in the right direction. Last, but surely not least, he's a wonderful lover. Her Gemini talent for imagery will bring excitement to their physical relationship, and if she continues to evoke in him the sensation that he's a sexual conqueror, he'll remain a satisfied and monogamous monarch.

It's possible for a Leo man to fulfill all his romantic promise under the light, nonpossessive touch of a Gemini woman, whose airy approach to sex will fan his more fiery desires, at least in the beginning. However, he may gradually begin to feel something is missing. While he's making love to one Twin, the other is coolly observing the scene. A Leo man can be thrown into a trauma by such partial involvement.

To a warm-hearted Lion, sex is synonymous with both affection and passion. There's something vaguely aloof about Gemini love. He can seduce her emotionally and physically, but her mind refuses to be fully committed to sensual abandon. The inability to conquer completely can destroy a Leo's necessary self-image of virility. Then she'll complain that he lacks interest in lovemaking, when the truth is that her cool detachment and dual behavior has caused him to develop a fear of a possible lovemaking inadequacy, which he's extremely reluctant to expose, because nothing pains a Leo male more than even the suspicion that he may not be the perfect lover. She should remember that this man is a sexual idealist and employ her Mercurial imagination to invent new ways of appeasing his hunger for romance and sentiment as background music for their physical intimacy, instead of using it to fly off on a cloud by herself, when he most needs to know she's close beside him, resting against his heart.

Since Gemini is a natural linguist, she should be capable of translating her Lion's arrogant and regal commands into the language of passion and need.

"You talk too much. Why don't you be still once in a while?" means his vanity has been bruised, because she's upstaged him again, with her twin talents of quickness and cleverness.

"Forget about dinner. I'm going out somewhere and eat alone" means he's been ignored once too often, while she's been chasing interesting ideas and people all day, and his pride needs to be pampered.

"Cancel that party we've been invited to Saturday night. Tell them we can't come. Make some excuse. We're staying home" means he'd rather be alone with the two of her over the weekend than get dressed up and soak up the admiration of a crowd. And Lady, for a Leo — that's *love*!

☆ ☆ ☆ ☆ ☆ ☆

GEMINI *Man* LEO *Woman*

◄─◄●►─►

"I think it must be a lady . . . a lady to take care of us at last," said one of the Twins. . . .

Every Lioness, quiet naturally, you must admit, has an instinctive desire to tame the man she loves, to make him her exclusive property. She needs a mate in whom she can have absolute faith, a man who is clearly stronger than she is, and yet, who will cherish her without reservation. It's a mighty tall order. Especially when she sets out to tame a Gemini.

In the Game of Love, as in the Game of Life and Living, this man is what card players call a kibitzer. He hangs around, with always a few hidden aces up his sleeve, aware of everyone's hand, confident that he could, if need be, pass off a busted straight as a royal flush. He knows a lot about everything, but not quite enough to make a grand slam and end the challenge he finds so intriguing. It makes more sense to Gemini to be a jack-of-all-trades and master of none. Once you become expert at any one of them, you see, people have this annoying habit of expecting you to stay there, doing your thing forever.

Gemini is an Air Sign, driven constantly by the need for change, any kind of change at all, just so it's change, however minor or major, which leads him on to the next traveling dice game with interesting stakes. Unlike the other two astrological gamblers, Leo and Sag, the Twins always want in and out fast, a quick win or a quick loss, then try again. If you deal yourself in for enough games, Gemini figures, you eventually overcome poor judgment and bad luck. No long-term investments in a career, family ties, friendship or romance, for the typical Gemini male — at least, not while he's young. (Of course, you must realize that that may be a long time, because Gemini never grows up.) To the typical Mercury-ruled man, Life is a series of toy dirigibles and fragile bubbles, spent among mischievous children armed with sharp pins. A man must be agile to leap over them, to sail his dirigibles and blow his bubbles out of their range, in the nick of time. And where do the dirigibles, the bubbles, come from? He's never wondered. He only knows they never stop coming. You have to be quick — to pick out the good ones and spot the ones to cut the string on before they fizzle out. The toy dirigibles, that is. As for the bubbles, they're pretty to watch and fun to create, but he doesn't fool himself into trying to make any of them last. Dirigibles are different. They're tougher, and one of them might take him where he's going — if he only knew where that might be.

Take women, for example. Gemini knows — or supposes he does — which one will fly with him and not slow him down by hanging on his sleeve — and the ones to back away from because they think any kind of flying is for the birds. (It is, but that also includes Mercury Birds, like himself.) At first, he'll think the Lioness belongs in the former category, because she certainly won't hang on his sleeve. She has other ways of slowing him down, more subtle.

This is, as the reader may know by now, one of those fated 3-11 Sun Sign Pattern relationships, planned by their Higher Selves long ago. Whether it ends in love or friendship, it is nevertheless pregnant with karmic obligations, often marked for a strange destiny, and always urging each partner on toward either unusual sacrifice or uncommon devotion — or both. Whether the 3-11 vibration (some, of course, involve business or ties with blood relatives) leads to a lasting love or a platonic association depends on many things, among them, the mutual aspects between their natal Suns, Moon Signs and Ascendents — and other planetary exchanges between their birth charts.

If the Leo girl has permanence in mind, she'll first have to tame him. It won't be like taming any of the other male animals in the astrological zoo. It's trickier. A Gemini man is more slippery and elusive. Besides, remember that there are two of him. The escape hatches of the Twins are covered with such charm of speech and gesture that this man can be gone while a girl is still swooning over the wisp of beauty he draped over her, like a delicate cobweb, to camouflage his departure and make it easier for her to bear. (He does have a kind heart.) But the Lioness has a head start on this sort of Mercury chicanery, because a Leo woman doesn't swoon over men. Men swoon over *her* — and don't you forget it.

A more difficult obstacle than seeing through his cobwebs of charm, which she'll have to hurdle in taming him, is that to a Gemini man all females are alike — threats to his freedom, suspicious of his unpredictable behavior, always demanding that he love them exactly the same today as he did yesterday. How can that possibly be, when his emotions contain so many depths and breadths? Sooner or later, a woman will begin to nag you about not having a concrete goal, and who wants to pursue cement? Since the Gemini man is bored by most females, because they all seem the same to him, the Leo girl will have to convince him that she's not like all the others. She'll have to train him, and tame him ... to listen for *her* step, *her* laugh, *her* voice ... to recognize that her vibration is individual, making music only for him, that her aura is different from the aura of any other woman in the world. Maybe she can even train him to notice that the golden, tawny flecks in her eyes are exactly like those in a fine piece of amber, so that everytime he sees an amber ring or bracelet on his travels he'll remember ...

Then amber will always be beautiful to him, because it will bring thoughts of her warm smile, her proud spirit, the glow in her eyes ... and tug on his heart to return. Not just to her smile and spirit and eyes but to all the other parts of her he misses. Like, there's her bright mind — the way she hikes over the hills beside him with her graceful, Lioness stride, without getting tired — the way she sits tall in the saddle when she rides — jackknifes into the water, swoops down the slopes on her skis, swings a tennis racquet, or smacks a golf ball. Leo women usually excel at one or two outdoor sports, not counting indoor sports, like acting, dancing, romancing, and so forth — and, like Cancerian Moon Maidens, many of them are amateur or professional photographers.

She'll have to seed all these memories in his mind and convince him that she's unique. It's all part of the Gemini taming process. A girl who loves this man must keep up with both his mind and his body, not to mention his two separate personalities and his multiple moods. Eventually, he'll begin to think of her as the most unique woman he's ever known. But he won't be *completely* tamed until he thinks of her as the most unique woman he ever *will* know. There's a definite difference, and a Lioness will comprehend what I mean right away.

Actually, this woman *is* unique. She's a born "lady," and there aren't many of those around anymore. A Leo female can roll in the grass, climb a tree, change a tire, or any number of traditionally considered unladylike things, but her general demeanor will remain as casually gracious and poised as if she were walking down a red-carpeted aisle to be coronated. (It takes real class for a girl to keep her tiara on straight when she's jacking up a rear axle.) The regal aura is ever present. Let someone snicker, deride her, or make the huge mistake of becoming too familiar when she hasn't extended an invitation to intimacy, and she'll freeze into such a tower of icy dignity that the offender will shrink into his socks — or wish to blazes the ground would mercifully open up and swallow him. Like the typical Capricorn female, the typical Lioness possesses a distinct and unmistakable air of excellent breeding. Whether it's actual or only illusionary, it's tangible and visible. The only weakness in the Leo armour of majestic dignity is the Leonine tendency to be transparently vulnerable to flattery. At any other time, however, the royal blood runs clearly blue, and the manner is aloof, proud, Queen-like. The Gemini man who refers to this female as "babe" or "chick," either by word or implication, will soon learn what the term "lady" means.

He'll have to become accustomed (which he'll probably do rather pleasantly) to allowing her to take most — or all — of the bows in public. She'll get most of the attention, even when she doesn't encourage it. It's that subtle mantle of royalty that hovers over every Leo ever born. No matter how sweetly she speaks to him, no matter how adoringly she gazes up at him, as if *he's* the star of the show — more heads will turn in her direction than in his, however handsome, dashing, witty and intelligent he may be. Something about her bearing, her lazy, confident manner of speaking, the way she carelessly tosses her mane of hair out of her eyes, suggests a royal charisma.

She means no harm. A true, noble, warm-hearted and in-love Lioness never deliberately usurps her mate's status (only everyone else's). She can't help it if the natives are restless and have their eyes fastened on her. Fortunately, a Gemini man is seldom overly or unduly possessive, so he'll probably see her popularity as just another factor in her uniqueness. (You see, he *is* gradually becoming tamed.) He might console himself by remembering that Gemini President Jack Kennedy wryly introduced himself in France as "the man who accompanied Jacqueline Bouvier to Paris." Jackie, as you all must know by now, is a Lioness.

Statistically, the sexual compatibility of these Sun Sign lovers often requires certain mutual adjustments and compromises. For one thing, nothing can so chill the warmth of a Lioness as deception or disloyalty from her mate, and that includes everything from harmless flirting to actual sexual infidelity. The Gemini man will find her Leonine jealousy and fiery pride of possession easier to overlook when the shoe is on the other foot, for then he'll be given a strong idea of what it feels like to be ignored and rejected. He won't like it at all, yet he won't be quite as outraged as she would be in the same situation. Geminis take everything somewhat more lightly than most everyone else — certainly more lightly than an intense Fire Sign like Leo.

However, once she's really tamed him, jealousy may never be a problem on either side. The problem then becomes one of simple romantic technique. A well-loved Lioness is an exceptionally affectionate and loving woman. She's capable of both raging passion and languid sensuality. But a carelessly loved Lioness is extremely susceptible to the symptoms of frigidity. She's not a female who would enjoy being ravaged by a gorilla-type lover (King Kong is not her secret fantasy) — nor is she a woman who would smile indulgently at the clumsiness of a bashful schoolboy, who drowns her in puppy-like adoration. She expects a man to make love to her with finesse. A Gemini man is simply saturated with finesse, charm and delicacy. But his touch may sometimes be so light, his seductive overtures so airy, she feels he might dematerialize, right in front of her eyes, before their physical love reaches fulfillment. To satisfy her deeper needs, which are visibly more fiery than his, he'll have to sweep her off her feet now and then in a dramatic scene of wild and ecstatic surrender.

If not all that, then he should frequently find a way to let her know he can't resist the magnetic sexual chemistry between them. To her, physical union is more than a Mercury mental challenge or an emotional exercise. She still hears the faint call of the jungle. But she'll unfold tenderly under his imaginative approach if he occasionally deepens its intensity — and remembers that she needs to hear how beautiful and desirable she is in order to respond completely. "A woman is beautiful only when she is loved." Especially a Leo woman.

This man and woman are both extravagant with words — and with money. They share exquisite taste, they both adore dressing up, they're equally fond of travel, literature and the arts. They're also both equally adept at getting their own way — she through the lovable quality of expecting it as her right — he, through his irresistible blarney. A Leo girl can tame the Gemini man more easily if she remembers the rules for taming any restless, active, yet curious bird. It requires much patience, and you start by smiling at him with your eyes, at a distance . . . taking care not to move too quickly, for that would frighten him away. In the beginning, silent communion is best, because words, particularly between these two Sun Signs, often contain the seeds of misunderstanding. Then if she moves a little nearer to him every day and never causes him to feel his freedom is threatened . . .

A Gemini man needs to be reminded that there are some things in his changing, Mercurial existence that are very special — and unique — in all the worlds he longs to roam. That's why he'll be happier after he's been tamed by the proud Lioness, if only because of the new beauty of amber he'll never be able to look upon without remembering the tawny flecks in her eyes.

☆ ☆ ☆ ☆ ☆ ☆

GEMINI

Air — Mutable — Positive
Ruled by Mercury
Symbol: The Twins
Day Forces — Masculine

VIRGO

Earth — Mutable — Negative
Ruled by Mercury (also by
the Planet Vulcan)
Symbol: The Virgin
Night Forces — Feminine

The **GEMINI-VIRGO** *Relationship*

Off we skip like the most heartless things in the world,
which is what children are, but so attractive . . . . we
have an entirely selfish time; and then when we have
need of special attention we nobly return for it, confident
that we shall be embraced instead of smacked.

The playful Gemini Twins may, indeed, seem like heartless children to the more sensible and serious Virgos. Always out chasing cobwebs and mirages, jumping about like grasshoppers, getting caught in summer brainstorms and trying to be in two places at once. To the typical earthy Virgo, Gemini's quick changes of both heart and mind are clearly flaws which need immediate correction.

Perfection is not a quality Geminis enjoy cultivating. They do appreciate, perhaps even admire — and certainly need — the more stable attitude of Virgo, and are often relieved to find the Virgo relative, friend, business associate, lover, or mate still there, in the same place where they were left, when Gemini flew away for a few hours (or weeks or months or years) to see what was happening on the other side of the mountain. But if they are going to be scolded when they return, they'll just skip off again. Children never like scolding. And all Geminis are essentially children at heart. Not Virgos.

Virgos are possessed of a heavy sense of life's duties, and a mature sense of reliability. They either live up to this essence of their Sun Sign or they feel guilty about *not* doing it and develop hives, ulcers, or hiccups. Conversely, Gemini seldom feels guilty about anything. At least, not where it shows.

With Virgo, most everything shows. Especially secret, nagging worries. Since Virgo rules the bowels, intestines, and solar plexus, these nagging worries, expressed first in a slight frown, then tight lips, can cause actual infection or disability in these areas. The more secret the worries, the more apt they are to manifest into nausea, indigestion or constipation. These people should get it out in the open more often, talk about it, express themselves, say what is on their minds (but not *too* often, or they would be untrue to their Sun Signs).

Gemini is an expert at getting it out in the open — except for those unfortunate Geminis with a Virgo Ascendent or Moon, who would love to cheerfully chatter, and scatter ideas, but who settle down into an uneasy silence instead, staring at their fingers and counting the lines in the palms of their restlessly folded hands. It can be a real conflict. Most Geminis, however, could profitably teach Virgos how to excel in gregarious gab, gleeful glibness and scintillating syntax. Virgo indisputably knows how to spell all those words, but putting them into action is another matter.

The Virgo intellect is as sharp as Gemini's (thanks to Mercury, who likes to pretend rulership of both signs, with his silver cap and winged heels) but not as vacillating and changeable (thanks to the hidden influence of Virgo's true ruler, the as yet unsighted, thunderous Vulcan). Geminis quickly juggle thoughts and create ideas, often it seems right out of the air, which is their natural element, but Virgo seldom juggles or creates. The Virgins are too busy discriminating and distinguishing and sorting facts from fancies, frequently with what may appear to be quite unnecessary preciseness. Explorer-experimenter Gemini seeks the spirit of the law. Purist-statistician Virgo follows the letter of the law.

Most Virgos find it difficult to grasp the concept of a dollar, because it contains such a fascinating number of pennies. They get sidetracked counting all the coins, believing that if you keep track of the bright coppers, the folding green paper will pile up all by itself, with no help. Gemini thinks in larger sweeps, grander terms, and normally tosses any spare pennies into wishing wells, without counting them. Throw a perfectly good penny into murky water for some silly superstition? There goes that faint Virgo frown again — see it? Just beginning to crease in the forehead over those clear, beautiful eyes.

Now that you understand some of the obvious difference between these two Sun Signs, you can imagine the turmoil which must churn in the breast of a Virgo with a Gemini Ascendent or Moon—or a Gemini, with vice versa and likewise. To face such a methodology variance with a strange companion is abrasive enough, without having to face it in the mirror every morning, lurking within your own character and personality. Send them lots of sympathy cards. Some, as mentioned elsewhere, become human alarm clocks—others sit on a seesaw of indecision, ill at ease when they are talking and twice as uncomfortable when they are silent.

The Gemini-Virgo association is influenced by the 4-10 Sun Sign Pattern, so the relationship between them will never be based on pure frivolity and escapism. Seriousness and respect (or lack of it) will weave in and out of the connecting links between these two, each finding it difficult to fully comprehend the true goals and basic outlook of the other. This must not be taken to mean that they can't create harmonious warmth together. It's just that happy firesides and hearths need lots of stoking with the coals of mutual understanding and tolerance. Peace and compatibility can eventually be accomplished with a little effort, however, because there's often a subtle exchange of loyalty and affection hidden beneath the surface disagreements of these two.

It must be admitted that the average Virgo man or woman does not practice provoking trouble, and does not usually respond to it quickly either, unlike the Geminis, with their constant stirring up of a tempest from a single breath of choppy air, and frequently reacting in hurricane fashion to what seems to them to be constant, critical carping and harping from Virgo. Of course, to Gemini, a quarrel is not really a quarrel, merely an intellectual encounter. With Earth Sign Virgo, arguments go deeper, and the hurt lasts longer. The friendship and other relationships between them can be enduring, in rare cases even intimate, but a community of interests on the business or intellectual level—or in the family or duty-obligation sphere, as with all 4-10 influenced people—is normally what pulls them together in the first place.

Most Virgos seem to be humble and self-effacing, seldom displaying any excessive dignity or pride, yet it would behoove the Gemini to hold his or her sharp tongue at crucial moments, since Virgos are usually quite sensitive about what little dignity and pride they do possess. The more aggressive signs can't understand the Virgin at all, but the Gemini who finds Aries too exhausting, Leo too arrogant, and Scorpio too aloof may very well find the usually sweet and courteous Virgo relaxing to be around, and feel a sense of relief at the lack of need to compete that might be necessary with another Sun Sign.

There's a touching and attractive humility about Virgos, a personal modesty that excites little envy or resentment. But Mercury Birds can still get their feathers a bit ruffled when they learn that, although Virgo may never be able to run as swiftly as Gemini and may seldom beat the Twins to any Grand Prizes, Virgo sometimes manages to grab the plum job without even hinting for it, let alone racing for it. Often those with Virgo Sun Signs, Ascendents, or Moon Signs are chosen as the compromise candidate by party leaders in "smoke-filled" political back rooms on a city, state, or national level, considerably upsetting the more extroverted Sun Signs, who have been blissfully charming the voters out front, confident of victory, until Virgo comes up from the rear — the dark horse chosen suddenly and unexpectedly over the brighter ponies on the track. As an example, Lyndon Johnson was a Virgo, chosen by a clever and canny Gemini, John Kennedy, for calculated reasons.

In any dispute between Gemini and Virgo, Gemini will nearly always win the main point, being faster on the draw and quicker with the cinching retort. But winning a quarrel can't settle everything. It may not settle *anything* for Virgos, who know that what appears to be an absolutely factual statement can still be full of errors and misleading insinuations. The greatest talent of all Gemini Twins is the fascinating ability to twist truth and falsehood in such a way as to weave them together and make each appear to be the other. It fools almost everyone but a Virgo. A Gemini Volkswagen salesman who ticks off too many facts too fast can really "bug" a potential Virgo customer right off the lot. You won't find many Virgos playing speed ball at carnivals or riding the Ferris wheels and carousels on which Geminis love to spin in their circular direction. They don't go much for Mercurial cotton candy either. All sugar and air — no nutritional value whatsoever.

There is an appealing magical quality in Gemini that attracts and excites the more timid Virgins, and this could create enough mystery to make the relationship permanently intriguing. The trouble is, Virgos are never satisfied until they discover exactly how the magic trick is performed, and the whole point of Gemini's existence is to prove something by nothing — to make reality out of pure illusion.

To the practical-minded Virgo, reality can never be illusion, nor can illusion ever be called reality. That's just more Gemini double-talk. Mercury Birds have usually flown and flitted through a dozen occupations by the time they're thirty, while Virgos are often disturbed when they're expected to make a slight change in office routine. As for changing jobs, that's something Virgos normally do with as much serious deliberation as is required for the selection of the President of the United States, in fact, with much *more* serious deliberation than has been the case with the latter in recent years.

Despite their differences and the tensions engendered by the soul-testing tugs of their squared natal Suns through the difficult 4-10 vibration, Gemini and Virgo share a lovely curiosity, an uncommon intelligence, and a certain charming and graceful manner, which allows them to skip happily, side-by-side, through the cornfields of the changeable land of Oz for a few thousand miles. But if they expect to still be together when they reach the presence of the Great Wizard (who is, of course, a Gemini), they may have to adjust and compromise now and then.

Gemini magicians, who are fascinated by all forms of marvels, should remember that the Tin Woodsman who strolled along the path with Dorothy and her friends was a Virgo — a kind and gentle, yet lonely soul, wistfully searching for a human heart. And it was the clever Gemini Wizard who perceived that the Virgo had possessed a heart all the time, without realizing it, hidden inside a suit of cold metal, yet larger than any of the others. *That's* magic!

☆ ☆ ☆ ☆ ☆ ☆

GEMINI *Woman* VIRGO *Man*

------◄●►------

..... his way was with a pencil and a piece of paper,
and if she confused him with suggestions he had to
begin at the beginning again.

"Now don't interrupt," he would beg of her.

The first problem this man and woman face is the contrast between her gregariousness and his tendency to reclusivity. If he's a typical Virgo male, barring a more convivial Moon Sign or Ascendent, he would really prefer, within his deepest subconscious, to live alone, without the necessity of having a constant companion tagging along beside him — even if she's bright, pretty, soft and squeezable. A man can't spend all his time squeezing a wife. Some hours must be spent in squeezing plans for future security into the proper molds.

Consequently, when the Gemini girl seeks periodic flings of freedom, her Virgo lover or husband may grumble a bit outwardly, but inwardly he probably sighs with relief. Now he can have a little peace and quiet, to figure out how many atoms make up a molecule, what caused the stock market to zip up or slip down last week, adjust his alarm clock, sort his laundry, count his cat's whiskers and ponder the puzzles of the Universe in general, without all that constant chattering and flurry of activity. He may genuinely love his Gemini girl, but his heart contains hidden shelves, where she is not allowed to dust — or even peek. When she's constantly dazzling him with her perfume, her squeezability, quick wit and mental agility, he gets confused and loses track of which opinion he has glued to what shelf, even the particular day and year he stashed it away there. And so, he may not question her whereabouts, so pleased is he to have a period of restful contemplation.

Not that there aren't some Virgo men who display occasional, half-hearted spurts of jealousy. There are a few. But it's a great mistake to become angry with the diversity of a Gemini girl, when you analyze it, and Virgos are past masters at analyzing. Her need to communicate with a variety of people (and men do, after all, make up roughly half the human race) should not be interpreted as unfaithfulness or promiscuity — unless it's certain that this is the case. Sometimes it is. Yet, surprisingly often, it is not. Admittedly, it can become so, if his Virgo criticism, hair-splitting and nagging cause her to feel her wings are being clipped. If there's anything a Gemini female can't stand, it's having her wings clipped, cropped or folded. Birds must fly. Birds in cages constitute unbearable cruelty against Nature's intent.

Still, for a man whose essential attitude and Sun Sign essence points him toward bachelorhood, the Virgo male is capable, when he chooses, of settling down into the groove of matrimony — or a shared life with a woman he loves — with an unexpected grace. Although he's basically a loner and dislikes sharing his every thought with a mate, Virgo is of the Earth Element, and Earth stays where it was placed by Nature, unless an earthquake or a tornado dislodges portions of it. But is that the Earth's fault? There it was, minding its own business . . .

I have thus far referred to their relationship as though it were marbled in matrimony, because most Virgos become uneasy living with a woman without benefit of clergy. Not all. Most. Geminis, however, normally do not find it difficult to sanction and champion free love or free marriage. Gemini is all for anything that has the word "free" in it. Therefore, whether to wed — or not to wed — may be a question of initial contention, once they've both been chemically magnetized into desiring union.

In the necessary confines of love or marriage, as with a business partner, the Virgo man will not ordinarily seek to dominate. He tends to be quite impeccably businesslike about his love affair or marriage, and unless he has an extremely afflicted horoscope emotionally, he will make an excellent partner, insofar as small comforts and conveniences are concerned, attending dutifully and diligently to birthdays and anniversaries, emptying the kitty litter and making sure they don't run out of vitamins. Most Gemini girls would, of course, prefer to have their birthdays and anniversaries observed through the customary process of passionate or sentimental memory, rather than through periodic checking of a date and appointment book with a red pencil. But who is she to complain? Dates are certainly not her own strong point, and she may get mixed up, from time to time, sending him a get-well card on her mother's birthday or buying him a wedding-anniversary gift on the date they bought the house — and while we're on the subject of homes, if they buy one, he will suggest it first, nine times out of ten. The tenth time, if she happens to be the one who initiates a consultation with a real-estate agent, check her Moon Sign or Ascendent. One or both is probably in the Earth Element. The typical Gemini girl likes houses well enough, but prefers apartments, because she can change them once in awhile, say every few months or so. Needless to remark, Virgo men normally do not find this sort of musical tepee game feasible or practical. It will pay to remember that practicality — too little or too much of it — will be the true underlying cause for many of their arguments. He has too much to please her and she has too little to suit him, if he is a typical Virgo and she is a typical Gemini.

As for their sexual compatibility, a Virgo can be, with all his innate sweetness, courtesy, consideration and punctuality, an impossible lover or husband for a temperamental woman. Of course, not all Geminis are temperamental. Or rather, one of her Twin selves may be emotionally temperamental — and the other may be detached. Virgo males, you see, are not overly emotional. Nor is the average Virgo unduly affectionate. Legend claims that Narcissus was a Virgo, helplessly in love with his own image. I personally believe Narcissus was a Leo, but aside from all that, it is true that Virgo men are often accused of being cold and self-centered. (Leo can be self-centered, but never cold.)

If the deepest spiritual secret of sex is the mutual abandonment of the self for the mate, resulting in a fusion of minds, souls, and bodies into perfect Oneness (which, as a matter of fact, it is), the typical Virgo has yet to master this esoteric mystery. Unless he's carefully and tenderly taught, or unless he had an early Scorpio sweetheart, it may elude him for a number of years, perhaps for a lifetime. He unconsciously shrinks from the concept of total surrender as he shrinks from the idea of using someone else's Vicks salve. I know a Gemini woman (this is not a fable) who once told me her Virgo husband insisted on labeling the two Vicks salve jars in the medicine chest HIS and HERS. Nearly every Virgo was frightened in the womb by a mean germ (and a scattering of Aquarians were also).

Not only does this man mistrust surrender, sexual or *otherwise*, he's not too hung up on the initial step of conquest either . . . so he may fail to arouse enthusiasm in himself, or in others. This might not go over well with an Aries, Leo or Scorpio female, but it could be the reason the Twins fell in love with him in the first place. Not all, but the majority of Gemini girls feel more secure, in or out of wedlock, whether they realize it or not, when they can play love as a pretend game. Gemini lovemaking is airy and light, delicate ethereal. Since a Virgo man is beautifully adept at the art of light lovemaking, he can succeed with her where other men have failed because they refused to play the make-believe game with her.

Instinctively, she could feel emotionally safe with this man, and they may offer one another a sense of security that forms a foundation for the later development of a deep passion between them — which might never have flowered in her with a more sexually serious male — or with a more passionately demanding female, speaking for his side of the matter. She might find some of his habits, like showering both before and immediately after their physical togetherness, a little disconcerting — but then, he could also find her habit of interrupting their goodnight kiss, or preliminary to an intimate union embrace, with an account of a weird dream she had last weekend to be somewhat dampening and discouraging too. Neither of them will be totally emotionally destroyed if this should happen to postpone their kiss or embrace until the following morning.

Yes, they will have their small differences. Most Gemini girls enjoy sleeping late and are subject to periodic attacks of insomnia. Virgo men suffer from insomnia too, when they're worried about something, which is frequently — but this man would rather be caught wearing red- and purple-flowered Levi's as be caught sleeping till noon, both of these choices of behavior being, more or less, mortal sins to the Virgin. If he's the kind of Virgo who insists on a neat house and punctual meals, he'll soon learn that this girl won't see the need for absolute perfection in such areas. She's certainly capable of being an exquisite hostess (although he seldom brings anyone home for her to hostess) and when she chooses, she can create a delightful home atmosphere. But it's doubtful that she'll scrub floors with true enthusiasm and excitement — and if she smokes (pray not!), there may be a few dirty ashtrays around. This won't make a hit with him, because most Virgos detest smoking to begin with, and they positively despise the offensive odor of full ashtrays.

Surprisingly, however, the usual, petty, day-to-day irritations may not cause any major quarrels between them. A Virgo man doesn't really demand a whole lot from either love or marriage, except maybe his own Vicks salve jar — and neither does she. He would appreciate, of course, some punctuality concerning meals, at least a semblance of faithfulness. But, in general, a Gemini girl is adaptable enough to cope with things that could cause despair in other females, and he's practical enough not to expect love and marriage to be made either in heaven or in hell, but somewhere in-between. Barring severe planetary afflictions between their birth charts, these two will probably not be overly demanding of one another, compared to other Sun Sign combinations.

Her swift personality changes and many moods could puzzle and annoy him. His quiet spells of introversion, during which he refuses to communicate, could flash her into many an instant, but normally quickly dispersed, thunderstorm. There are times when he'll bore her to tears, and she'll agitate him into indigestion — and it's also possible that their lives together may be one long guessing game of verbal chess and emotional jai alai. Yet, it's equally possible that she'll supply the excitement and the zest for living that this man desires so wistfully and needs so very much — whereas he'll supply the stability of purpose she's seeking, even though she's not aware she's seeking it.

Gemini is Air, Virgo is Earth, and these two elements have little in common. But this is a 4-10 Sun Sign Pattern, and mutual respect may, therefore, be the magnet that brings them together, while duty or responsibility of some kind, related to family ties or career, may hold them together.

A Virgo man is more truthful than a Sagittarian man, more basically honest than even the Archers. To him, telling the truth saves a great deal of trouble. His grandmother used to singsong, "Oh, what a tangled web we weave when first we practice to deceive," and he decided way back then that deception was an unnecessary burden. In no way does he wish to become tangled up in any sort of web. Certainly not one of his own making. And so, the typical Virgo will place the straight facts of any situation right on the table, with no hedging. It's not a habit designed to endear him to anyone, but one of his most admirable qualities is that he doesn't much care if he endears himself to everyone — just to a few close friends. If *they* like him, and if he can serve them as best he knows how, that's enough for him. He doesn't need to win popularity contests to be contented with things the way they are, and make the best of Life. In fact, he often makes much better than the best of Life — and of love — if he's handled gently, softly — and not engulfed in waves of emotion that cause his quiet charm and beautiful manner to retreat into a self-made cave to avoid conflict. When the conflict is something other than emotional, however, he'll press ahead and will rarely turn back from what he believes is the right course.

The path of the Virgo male is seldom strewn with flowers, nor does he stop on the way to pluck posies of praise for his services. Still, his heart will be lighter, and his spirit brighter, if he allows a Gemini girl to dance along beside him and fill those lonely moments with her lovely laugh, her way of catching a breeze in her hands, and phrasing the sound of a cool woodland stream in her voice, even when she's only saying "Good morning, darling." The word "impossible" doesn't exist for her. If something can't be accomplished one way, then she'll think of a new way, a better way. It's a talent he should find beautifully helpful. She's incorrigible, irrepressible — but also irresistible. With a harmonious Luminary exchange between their horoscopes, they can, perhaps, find a familiar country in each other's smiles that will be a wonderful adventure to explore together.

But the Gemini girl is Twins, sometimes even triplets. And a Virgo man has enough trouble coping with just one woman. He wasn't born to be able to handle a harem — or a mate with a multiple personality. To achieve happiness with him, the Gemini girl must first decide who she is, then forever after remain indivisibly his.

☆ ☆ ☆ ☆ ☆ ☆

GEMINI *Man* VIRGO *Woman*

━━━◆◀◆▶◆━━━

. . . . . and so Wendy, who always liked to do the correct
thing, asked Peter how old he was. It was not really
a happy question to ask him; it was like an examination
paper that asks grammar, when what you want to be
asked is Kings of England.

This is not a love affair that will automatically be draped in clouds of
rainbows and blankets of flowers, for these two face the severe test of the 4-10
Sun Sign Pattern influence, with both its trials and its benefits, each of which
can be considerable. They have a rather rough romantic row to hoe. That
doesn't mean they can't raise cabbages together, but it does mean that their
garden of love will need frequent weeding.

It could begin with quarrels about whether the crop they plant should be
roses or veggies. Obviously, veggies make more sense. She is a Virgo,
concerned over possible world famine, termites in the attic, inflation — and
the missing button from his shirt. Veggies are clearly the answer. Not to the
shirt or the termites perhaps, but to inflation and the specter of starvation.
What can you do with a rose, when the wolf is pounding on the door?

Smell it. You can smell it. The Gemini man can inhale the fragrance of
a rose while poverty closes in, in much the same way that Nero fiddled while
Rome burned. Of course, all this gardening talk, as well as Nero's fiddle tune
amid the flames, is merely symbolic. But then, everything is symbolic,
academic or rhetorical, to Gemini. He was born wrapped in riddles, mewing
with metaphors and anagrams, and swaddled in analogies. Also with a
telephone in one hand and a telegram in the other. She was born, he may
think at times, of an unlikely union between a computer and a scrub brush. A
self-programming computer. (Is there such an instrument? Never mind,
some Virgo with Aquarius rising will invent one, working with a Gemini
partner.)

That's not meant to imply that this man and woman don't find each
other fascinating, only that they also find each other frustrating. Most
Gemini men have forgotten their birth dates, either innocently or deliberately, by the time they reach the age of twenty-one or so on the illusionary
chronological calendar. Counterwise, many Virgo girls have memorized the
exact hour, minute and second of birth — and besides that, they believe
eternal youth is not only impossible, but would be a bore. He finds it both

possible and enchanting. You can see that clocks, stopwatches and Einstein's theory of relativity can create one of the chasms between them. There are others.

It's a rare Virgo female who becomes enthralled over the idea of tossing a feather into the air and striking out in the direction it points to as it lands. If she's a typical Virgin, she's not fond of geographical hopscotch. When she travels, she prefers to utilize a travel folder, a travel agent, and the holiday-weekend-family-cut-rate plan. The airlines invented just for Virgos what they refer to as their "chicken-feed" flight (approximately between about 2 A.M. and 6 A.M.), when the world's asleep, but Virgos are alert to economy. As for the Twins, Virgo's Gemini man would secretly like to follow the feather, and as for mode of travel, he's the one those "have breakfast in London and lunch in Italy" posters are designed to attract.

When they first fall in love, often through mutual curiosity, she'll be thrilled with the possibilities of casual, careless living he so charmingly endorses, while he'll be flattered with her rapt attention, her alert mind, and her very feminine manner. But after a time, she may begin to question the wisdom of synchronizing her life to a man who seems to be eternally wandering — either physically, mentally or emotionally — his thoughts and actions no more predictable than the weather. He may later feel her attention is a mite *too* rapt, her mind perhaps too alert to allow him his needed privacy now and then, in which to do his abstract thinking. Then they may become tangled up in the roses-veggies hassle, symbolically. All quarrels between lovers are based on matters which in themselves are not important but have been chosen because they symbolize the deep-seated and *real* problems which are the true cause of the tension between them — some underlying truth that neither wants to face, for whatever reason.

Despite her analytical, razor-slicing mind, the Virgo girl is ultrasensitive and in need of appreciation. A Gemini male may be somewhat unsuccessful in this area, because he's an Air Sign. Although Air Signs are not unsympathetic, there is a certain detachment and aloof coolness about them, which can leave an Earth Sign like Virgo feeling empty, somehow unfulfilled. There are times when he will be truly incapable of understanding both her depth and her strength. Then he'll try discussion and compromise, often failing altogether to touch the source of the trouble. Even so, his combined intellectual ability and charm will enable him to pacify her temporarily, until she's had time to analyze the errors and flaws in his facile arguments.

If she doesn't take him too seriously, their relationship can be mentally exciting, emotionally intriguing, and lots of fun. But Virgo takes everything seriously, and she's certainly not going to make an exception of a lover or husband. Perhaps he should take *her* more seriously. Virgos often give the impression they have committed themselves until "death do us part," then shock the partner with a divorce action as neat and quick (and as unkind) as snapping off the head of a flower. Most everything Virgo does is neat and quick. In that, these two are very much alike. Both can be impatient with routine, and neither of them are sloppy thinkers or dressers.

Sexually, she requires more physical demonstrations of affection than he — and he requires more variety and poetry in lovemaking than she. Not that he expects her to sleep with a copy of Rossetti under her pillow, nor does she require him to conquer her like Valentino, but there are indisputably subtle differences in their approaches to the physical chemistry of love. A Virgo girl does not necessarily want to be treated as a Virgin by the man she loves. True, her sexuality, as a whole, is not dramatically intense or excessively passionate, but she wants to know he is *there*. Not just his mind, heart and soul — *all* of him. Although Virgo women, like Virgo men, can take sexual love lightly, they are somewhat more earthy about it than the airy Gemini. Also, this girl feels more confident and relaxed, and therefore can be a more satisfactory love partner, if she feels some degree of security and familiarity in their intimate relationship. This is not always possible with a Gemini, who is, lest we forget, two-people-in-one (sometimes three or four) and changeable enough to project desire one night and cool disinterest the next.

Such behavior can throw a Virgo girl into a trauma of quiet desperation, causing her to blame some defect in herself as the reason for the change in his ardor. Virgos can be critical of others, but their sharpest criticism is always reserved for themselves. Something will always be held back, in reserve, between these two. Total abandonment and forgetfulness of the self is rarely achieved in their sexual union, and so their physical compatibility, while deeply fulfilling perhaps in some ways, may be somewhat emotionally guarded and controlled.

Mentally, however, very little will be held back between them. Neither can be said to be a slouch in the language department. There are some Gemini-Virgo couples who use words as weapons, with deadly aim. Words hurt. But words can also heal, and these two Sun Signs can use them for better or for worse. No one can tenderly coax a timid Virgin out of her rigid reservations into the blooming rose garden of self-confidence more expertly and smoothly than a Gemini man — and no one can soothe the frequently jangled nerves of this Mercurial male more gently and wisely than a Virgo girl, when they're both motivated by love.

There's no doubt that they'll probably respect one another's mental abilities, yet they may too often stifle open expressions of affection in each other. Neither he nor she may comprehend the need for *depth* in an emotional relationship. She'll attend to all her necessary duties regarding him, neglecting no details. She'll sew on his missing buttons, give him excellent advice concerning his career, if and when he should ask her, seldom or never pressing her opinions upon him uninvited. She'll be a stimulating companion at the theatre or watching television . . . and be able to converse with him most intelligently about the books, magazines and newspapers they read. Still, there may be a hint of "duty" in her devotion, as steady and admirable as it is.

He'll find time to talk with her about all her worries, will probably encourage discussions between them about anything that's on her mind, and allow her lots of room for the free development of her own ideas, ideals and goals. He won't smother her with undue jealousy or possessiveness, but he may cause her to feel boxed-in with his sometimes excessive prying and probing, on a verbal level.

After the first glow of romance has worn off, the Virgo woman could begin to complain to her Gemini man that he's spreading his mental energy too thin. She, too, has a thirst for knowledge, but she's not inclined to scatter it, and it may seem to her that his is a mere craving for continual excitement and novelty. Also, she may not share his enthusiasm for trips and traveling.

Most Virgos possess a strange empathy for children, strange because they are so "adult" in every way themselves. But a child always brings out a Virgo woman's latent potential for loveliness and beauty, an unsuspected talent for imagination, and a great tenderness — an ability to *listen* with genuine interest to all the despairs and delights of a young mind, as well as the wisdom to gently guide it into refreshing streams of thought. Since every Gemini man is a child, a little boy, at heart, these qualities within her can't but appeal to him enormously. However, with him, she must deal, not just with one "child" but with Twins. Repeatedly, she may attempt to teach him the value of discrimination, and find that he has no real desire to discriminate. He may, in turn, try to teach her to be more open, more expansive, to value personal freedom — and to acquire the grace to impulsively follow a dream. But Virgos open up very slowly, like a creaky door, and he's always in such a dreadful hurry. Besides, to her, freedom will never be as valued as security. Conversely, to Gemini, security is often synonymous with a mental San Quentin, restricting all possibility of a change of plans, which is what he feels makes life worth living.

A Virgo woman is the kind to surprise a lover or husband by bringing him breakfast in bed, but, unfortunately, few Gemini men like to sleep late. He's more likely to leap out of bed, shower, bike or jog around the block a few laps or catch the morning headlines before things like toast and cereal occur to him. His sometimes curt or detached reaction to her gentle courtesies may hurt her more than he suspects. Since his Mercury-ruled mind is so analytical, a Gemini man who has been paid the tribute of being loved by an also Mercury-ruled (until Vulcan appears) Virgin should analyze her true nature more carefully if he wants to keep her.

Some Virgo women remain chaste and romantically aloof for years, then risk everything on a single, unexpected and impossible passion that soon dies.

And so, she may not be, inwardly and actually, as emotionally cool and controlled as she appears to be at times to him. The Gemini man is equally as likely to find true love eluding him, until he's no longer Peter Pan, and Wendy has grown up to marry someone else, who cared more about her than about his adventures.

Such painful disappointments can cause both Virgo and Gemini to brood alone, tormenting themselves with longing and regret. Or it can cause them to seek a calm, safe and undemanding relationship with each other, which could be what they've both been searching for — if they only looked a little longer into one another's eyes. But instead, they may avoid sustained gazing, fearing the eyes may reveal too much, while she sweeps the floors . . . . and he wanders around the house, whistling his little-boy-blue song . . . each reaching out their hearts, but unable to express what they're really feeling openly.

Because their natal Suns were squared at birth, a certain amount of tension and lack of comprehension is unavoidable between these two. In the electronics of love, tension can short-circuit the emotions into silent darkness. But with a harmonious Sun-Moon interchange between their horoscopes, this man and woman could achieve a lasting affection and contentment through their union. It may never be the turbulent, soaring ecstasy of Scarlett and Rhett, but love need not always be explosive.

Sometimes, happiness can be a calm and quiet thing, a moment of rest upon the wind, that makes sunset less sad and haunting . . . and brightens the sunrise with a gentle promise.

☆ ☆ ☆ ☆ ☆ ☆

GEMINI

Air — Mutable — Positive
Ruled by Mercury
Symbol: The Twins
Day Forces — Masculine

LIBRA

Air — Cardinal — Positive
Ruled by Venus
Symbol: The Scales
Day Forces — Masculine

The **GEMINI-LIBRA** *Relationship*

Sometimes it was dark and sometimes light, and
now they were very cold and again too warm.

Two Air Signs are fun to watch, like trapeze artists at the circus. Their mental gymnastics can be both dazzling and dizzying. Air is intangible, invisible, always moving everywhere . . . . . and nowhere.

Since Librans can never make up their minds, and Geminis are continually changing theirs, it's hard to know what to predict will happen in an association between them, whether they are relatives, husband-wife, friends, business partners, lovers, mates, or what-have-you. Whatever I write may change before it is read or comprehended by either. But I'll risk it, and state that Gemini and Libra constitute a 5-9 Sun Sign Pattern, which usually balances out favorably, no matter in which direction the Libra Scales are dipping, and no matter which one of the Twin personalities of the dual-natured Gemini wants to argue about it.

Lest the sharper, birdlike, alert and calculating Geminis should believe that Librans are nothing but puffy white clouds, I'll remind them that Libra rules China, therefore the Chinese. Since Orientals are the most mysterious people on the planet, it's a mistake to deduce that there's nothing behind Libra's bright smile but soft marshmallow fluff. Of course, that won't intimidate any typical Geminis (who are experts at working Chinese puzzles). So I'll try to warn the Twins in another way. Libra is a Cardinal Air Sign. Gemini is a Mutable Air Sign. Cardinal means leadership. Mutable means communication. A Gemini can communicate beautifully over the airwaves with Libra as long as he or she does not try to lead the discussion or win the argument.

Remember, Libra is Cardinal. Libra must win. Libra must lead. Libra is logical. Libra must always be right. And don't let that lollipop grin, those adorable dimples in their chins, and elsewhere, cause you to think otherwise. These are merely weapons to help Librans get their own way. When they can't do it with their superior intellect, deductive reasoning process, or that oily-smooth voice that sounds like violins blending with harps, accompanied by whispering angels, they will bat those wide, innocent eyes, flash the Venus smile, dimple a few times — and the opposition simply melts away.

Who can resist such a combination of beauty, grace, charm, logic, intelligence, brilliance, and flattery? Gemini can — and frequently does. Gemini is not easily taken in by Libra's coaxing con-artistry. After all, persuading, conning, coaxing and tricking the timid, with a blend of charm and wit, was invented by Geminis. The Twins come first on the zodiac wheel, Libra follows later — so Gemini invented the game, Libra only imitates.

I'm sure all Geminis will agree with me. As for the Librans, I have no intention of arguing the point back and forth, and up and down, with *them*. Instead, I shall sweetly urge the Pollyanna-perfect Librans to bear with me while I continue to tangle and snarl myself up verbally, trying to sort out the differences between them and the Twins.

Air has no particular shape. It just floats around through space, like an interpenetrating ghost. Therefore, when these two Sun Signs team up at home, in the office, on the campus, or anywhere else, it may be difficult at first to see them. It will not be difficult to hear them.

Gemini and Libra will have lengthy discourses on every subject imaginable, and they both have immense imaginations. Sometimes the discussions are friendly, sometimes not. But they will usually remain on speaking terms, since silence for anything but the briefest periods of time is well nigh an impossibility for both of them. These people do like to talk. Neither of them likes to listen.

The reason Libra is symbolized by the Scales is because some Librans have minds so delicately adjusted that no sooner does an idea enter than a contradictory idea is automatically suggested. Can you conceive what it would be like to be cursed with such a mind? Someone says HOT, the computer card flashes COLD. Someone feeds in LONG, you pop out with SHORT. If you hear FAST, you instantly think SLOW. If you hear SLOW, you think FAST. You feel UP, you look DOWN. You feel DOWN, you look UP. Are you still there? Sit down and close your eyes for a moment. The dizziness will pass. Now do you understand why so many Libra people walk around with a dazed look on their beautiful, evenly matched features and a faraway expression in their lovely eyes — half the time? The other half of the time they are doing the exact opposite — staring at you alertly and intently, agitating their air essence into a tornado or making eloquent, impassioned speeches. That's the way it goes (comes!) with these teetering-tottering souls; whatever occurs, they must immediately accentuate the opposite.

In Colorado there is a Libra man named George. One day I was explaining to him certain events in my life which caused me to suspect I was the object of disapproval from a hopefully now extinguished branch of the government, and had been thus persecuted, in subtle ways, for nearly three years. He listened to my brief summary, then dimpled, saying, "I have no doubt that the events which have occurred in your life for the past several years have a *sinister* basis in *provable facts*. However, *on the other hand*, you are a writer, and possess a vivid imagination, so it is entirely possible that the whole thing is actually *innocent*."

Libran George was not even aware of his own thought process. Now that you have been astrologically initiated and instructed in how the Libra mind works, you can appreciate that no sooner did the word "sinister" pop into his head than his Libra Scales popped up a computer card reading "innocent" — the exact opposite of "sinister." This is the common Libra dilemma. What is truth? Which word should be the final answer? Sinister? Or innocent? The trauma of indecision.

Being an Aries Sun Sign made this particular matter quite simple for me. Sinister. The incidents were based on a situation that was SINISTER. However, you see, as a Ram, knowing that they are now behind me, I have dumped the events into yesterday's trash and am no longer concerned. Geminis do the same thing. Toss away yesterday, enjoy the present, and don't recognize tomorrow until it is here. Libra cannot. What if the summary was wrong? Although, of course, it could have been right. But if it was wrong, and thrown away, how recover it to make it right? Sinister or innocent? Bad or good? Real or imaginary? Positive or negative? Polarities, polarities, polarities! Libra is enmeshed in them from morning till night — and dares not discard them, for fear of discarding the only fair conclusion.

Unlike Libras, Geminis juggle polarities and contradictions, not in sequence, but simultaneously, constantly synchronizing their dual thoughts within their Twin selves. Why not? There are always two of him (or her) to handle anything. You can see why these two Sun Signs are not the most reliable people on Earth. If you catch Libra when the Scales are perfectly balanced — fine! If you catch Gemini when he or she has put one Twin to sleep and is displaying only the other for the moment — fine! But most of the time, these two, or three, or four, make quite a crowd. Despite the similarities in the natures of these two Air Signs, there are also a number of ways in which they veer off into different directions. Like making decisions.

Gemini decides quick as a flash, and that's it. No regret, no anxiety, no waiting or wondering — action NOW. Libra balances, weighs, judges, ponders, puzzles, assimilates, and postpones action till tomorrow — and sometimes tomorrow never comes. To Gemini, *not* making a decision can cause the race to be lost. To Libra, *making* a decision can cause a terrible mistake, and Libra cannot, *will* not make a mistake. It must be noted, however, that once the swift Mercury-ruled Gemini has decided, it may mean absolutely nothing. There could be a change of mind and plans minutes later. But once Libra has finally decided, after the delicate balancing act, he (or she) will normally stick by the decision firmly, knowing there are no improvements to be made that haven't already been carefully weighed. Libra is more cautious than Gemini. While the Twins tend to cut ties hastily, Libra never believes in cutting what may be more prudently unraveled, thread by thread. Why make a rash move, when you might subsequently be forced to retrace your steps through the discovery of a failure to take into account some fact or other which was not then known?

Geminis love a mental challenge, and Libra gives it to them. But when the Twins try that Mercurial double-talk on Libra, it doesn't always put them ahead. It can put them somewhere in the middle, occasionally even shortly behind center.

The childish charisma of Gemini can cause the Twins to do very fey and magical things, like speaking the name of a druid twenty-seven times when a star is falling . . . hitching imaginary rides on the backs of friendly squirrels and grasshoppers . . . and looking for diamonds among roses blooming in the snow. Libra doesn't normally care to waste time with such nonsense. In direct contradiction to their optimistic sweetness and their cheerful, sunny-yellow-beaming faces, they are coldly logical.

But there you are again! When you image one face of Libra, it will be fed back to you, through the polarity mentality of the Scales, as its opposite face. What Librans seek is the Golden Mean. Gemini doesn't care at all for the Golden Mean of arriving at a perfect balance. It is the traveling itself, not the destination, that the Twins enjoy. Both Gemini and Libra would be happier with themselves, and with each other, if they would try *feeling* much more and *thinking* much less.

☆ ☆ ☆ ☆ ☆ ☆

GEMINI *Woman* LIBRA *Man*

———— ◆◄●►◆ ————

*They are, however, allowed to change, only
it must be a complete change.*

The fact that the Gemini woman and the Libra man are so much alike is what
makes them so compatible and happy together. Also, the fact that the
Gemini woman and the Libra man are so much alike is what starts most of
the trouble between them.

They know each other only too well, sympathize with one another's
dreams and idiosyncrasies, can calmly cope with their mutual chameleon
qualities, comprehend each other's various moods, and will usually stick
together against outsiders who don't understand the airy mentality. If either
he or she has a more sensitive and emotional Water Element or a more stable
Earth Element as a Moon Sign or Ascendent, their happiness and bliss is
pretty much astrologically insured. Otherwise, these two are still guaranteed
a far better than average chance for success, except for small flurries on
especially windy days. They can both be a trifle windy, full of both cool
breezes and hot air. As a 5-9 Sun Sign Pattern, they are more harmoniously
matched than most couples who are trying to fit the jig-saw pieces of the
puzzle of love into a perfect picture.

Both of them are aesthetically inclined, moved by beauty, acutely
disturbed by untidiness, ugliness, and disorder. Yet, despite this mutual
essence, Gemini and Libra, while needing, even demanding loveliness and
order, may frequently need a brisk Sagittarian, an energetic Aries, or an
efficient Virgo maid to clean up after them. Of course, some Geminis and
Librans are tidy. But even they would prefer to have someone else straighten
out their messes — emotionally as well as actually. Since Gemini is quicker,
she will often be the one to follow her Libra man around, picking up his
discarded socks and banana peels. In return, he will probably not deny her
the money (if he has it) to make their surroundings ever more comfortable
and beautiful. More often than not, the nest of these two love birds is
charming, tasteful, pleasant to the eye, and probably full of books. Even if
they live in a tent, it will be well pegged and insulated, with maybe burned
etchings on the canvas for decor — and the soft sound of tom-toms beating in
the background. Soft, I said. Not too disturbing, because Libra can't stand
loud noises, lopsided stools or crooked tent pegs.

When this man and woman quarrel, it will almost always be she who
starts it — and he who finishes it. At least it will seem that way to observers.

A Gemini female, for all her airy charm and delicate femininity, possesses a sharp, satirical tongue, and she's not reluctant to use it when her fast mind urges her to express her quick opinions. Her Libra lover or husband will have recognized early in Life that rudeness and frank speech is a stumbling block to achieving his true and secret purpose, whether in love or business. So he projects a sort of gentle amiability (most times) and is an expert at hiding his passions and intent behind a smooth smile and a persuasive voice. Yes, she may have started it verbally. But he may be at the *bottom* of it, the real initial instigator of the quarrel — by spending two weeks to make up his mind whether they should take their vacation this month or next, while she had to stall the airlines and coax them into holding their reservations during the busy season . . . . . or something similar. Therefore, regardless of who outwardly starts the fussing, he is seldom innocent.

Libra men are never as innocent as they look and sound, or as they would like to have you believe. In fact, there are times (rare, but they do exist) when his Scales are dipping, and he can be as cranky as a cuckoo bird stuck in the little clock door. On those occasions, however, he probably apologizes so sweetly, overwhelming her with so much sugary Libra charm, that she may forget to remember his grumpiness later. Strangers who gaze upon the Libra man's smooth, even features have no way of knowing about the painfully articulated resolves forming in his mind beneath his cheerful exterior — or the crankiness displayed to his intimates while these are in the formative stage.

A Gemini girl might take a notion to be a dress designer. Then she could become dazzled by the idea of getting a pilot's license and maybe her own Lear jet. Following that, she could take a new notion to translate Sanskrit, study the Dead Sea scrolls, open a pet shop or enroll in law school. But the Libra man can handle all her tangled notions and emotions better than an Earth Sign male, who might erupt like a volcano — a Fire Sign male, who might burn all the oxygen out of her enthusiasms — or a Water Sign male, who might dampen her excitement with a wet blanket.

Libra understands Gemini's wanderlust of the mind and heart, yet is stable and logical enough to control her more erratic impulses before they blow up out of proportion, gently pointing out the pros and cons to her, until she decides to find her bluebird a little closer to home — and to him.

Serene is the word. Libra can be a serene influence on Gemini, except for those occasional cranky-bear spells he charms her into forgetting. Goodness knows the Gemini girl needs serenity. Hers is a restless spirit, a seeking soul. She longs poignantly to know what she wants, where she stands, who she is and why she's going — or coming. The Libra man is the most logical one to explain all this to her. But . . . well, you see . . . a Gemini girl is made up of so many fragments — of honey and spice and everything nice, yes. Yet, she's far more than this. She's all the books she ever studied, a reflection of the ideas and philosophies of her mirror-image Twin, diametrically opposed to her own. She's the swinging rope she skipped in childhood, the plaintive wail of the gulls, and the secrets she whispered to the sandpipers on the beach she once walked along, the memory of her first dance . . . tumbleweeds and tornadoes . . . the flickering candles of a half-forgotten New Year's Eve. These fragments of the Gemini girl make up her private world, where the Libra man who loves her can never freely roam, even though he may guide her through it . . . from a distance.

There's something judicial and cold in Libra's balanced thinking process, despite his charm and sweetness, that doesn't permit him to enter the deep woods of the changeable fairyland where she and her Twin so frequently dwell. He can watch her lovingly, as she removes her shoes and runs through the grass barefoot — he can wait by the gate until she returns from her faraway land, but he can never truly join her. Why? Because he would first have to locate it on a map, see if an airline booked a flight there, learn its population and study its chief industry, before loping off with her. Otherwise, how could he prove to himself logically that such a place really does exist? And if it doesn't exist, why go there at all? There's an invisible veil between this man and woman, for all their many similarities of personality.

Their physical relationship is usually blessed with nearly complete fulfillment, the kind of fulfillment only two Air Signs are able to comprehend (or desire). At night, sometimes lying alone beside her (yes, lying alone beside her) he's grateful when she returns from her make-believe world, back into his arms, often not even guessing that fragments of her are still out there, chasing moonbeams and playing tag with the stars. She *feels* to him like she is there. And, of course, part of her *is* — the one who has vowed to love and cherish him, never to leave him. She can't be expected to account for the other, wayward one — her Twin, who refuses to obey, even when she, herself, pleads.

Their sexual union will not be as all consuming as that between two Fire or Earth signs, but it can be as refreshing as a summer storm, with flashes of thunder and lightning. They are both airy, mental souls, living primarily in the mind, not in the emotions, and so explosive passion may be missing, but the total peace and tranquility of a deeply affectionate blending can be theirs. Sex, as with all 5-9 Sun Sign Patterns, is important to this couple, but not primary for happiness. Romantic love is equally needed, perhaps even more desired, by both, and forms the true basis for the initial attraction between them.

These two will take turns being the aggressive partner in their lovemaking. Both can switch from active to passive, from masculine to feminine, in a strange, mystical way that makes their sexual experiences a constantly changing yet harmoniously blended delight. If they have twin beds, there might be a few discussions about who gets to sleep nearest the window, but aside from such minor adjustments, these two will usually wake up in each other's arms, sharing a good-morning embrace that melts the previous night's disputes, as the Sun disperses clouds.

They may need and complete each other physically, yet it's possible that he may be more in love with her mind and spirit than with her body, and she may have more interest in his intellect and soul than in his sexuality — even though they may be only dimly aware of this. The chemistry between two Air Signs is misty, mental, and variable — rather than earthy, passionate, and sensual. Not all Gemini girls desire children, and very few dream of large families, but when they do, it will often be a Libra man who is chosen to father them. Many Gemini girls who would not have a child with any other man will find motherhood more attractive with a Libra male.

If she marries him, it will be because she likes the way he sings or dances or whistles . . . . . . the way he moves and walks and talks and winks. The way he dresses too. Then, womanlike, she may set about to try to change him afterwards. Ruled by Venus as he is, the Libra man may tolerate this and try to please her, because he loves her — until he finally realizes that, although she thrives on change, too much change affects his own equilibrium. So he'll roar (gently) and put his foot down (softly) to prove he's a masculine Cardinal Sign, return to his old ways — and it will probably be best for both of them.

They're likely to do lots of traveling together, may have either religious or educational reasons for getting together, and may meet on a trip. If he ever gets interested in UFO's, it will probably be because of her. She will inspire him to reach heights he would not have aspired to reach without her. Because they both have wings on their heels — and hearts — they may change residence more often than lovers or mates born under other Sun Signs.

There is little doubt that the Gemini woman will at times confuse and confound her Libra lover or husband. She is, after all, so many women in one. She can be the most talkative when he's trying to think or struggling with a decision, the prettiest when she has provoked him into a spell of rare Libra anger, the most silent when he wants to show her off to his friends, the most energetic at bedtime, the laziest in the morning when he's waiting for his poached eggs — but what other woman could be such a kaleidoscope of grief, joy, annoyance, happiness, embarrassment, irritation, delight, and frustration as this twin-packaged mystery of femininity?

True, she can be untidy, lose the car keys, tangle up the checkbook, waste his time and money, destroy his dignity, and try his temper — but just when he's ready to walk out, her little-girl misty tears begin to splash, switching almost instantly into a rippling Gemini laugh . . . . . . and he's lost again, caught between the myriad women bottled up inside this girl, who needs his strength if she's ever going to find her way out of the woods.

As for him, he'll relentlessly try to force her to be more logical and stable, criticize her faults, refuse to help her pick daisies when he has work to do, shatter her fragile nerves, and sometimes behave like a stern judge, pronouncing sentence over her free spirit — but when her dreams are scattered, her house and her hair are both a mess, and she feels like a silly, foolish child, he can make her feel like a woman when he smiles and says, "I don't know why I love you so much, but I do."

Then she realizes that she's the one problem he can never balance on his Scales and make come out even. Being a daughter of Eve, she will privately smile, knowing that the solution to the enigma of herself can never be totally analyzed by his intellect, only by his heart. Yet, also perversely, Eve-like, she'll refuse to share this key to love's Gemini secret with him, wanting him to guess.

One serious level of disagreement within this liaison of Air will be the Libra man's proclivity to weigh and judge things — to see life, people and situations in the proper perspective and balance, coolly and logically, with an odd sort of detachment, void of all whimsical notion. Not only does this facet of his nature clash rather sharply with his own inherent optimism and faith, it will also frequently conflict with *her* tendency to see all these things, not as they are, but as they *ought* to be. She sees what she desires to see, coloring facts with fancy, avoiding delusion (to her way of thinking) by drenching everything with illusion.

If he doesn't make a sincere effort to comprehend her attitude with compassion, she may be forced to tell little white lies to defend her viewpoint. This woman can be frightened of those who demand always the exact, precise, unvarnished truth, with no allowances made for "maybe" — "perhaps" — and "suppose it had been." Then, she could be forced to escape by plunging even deeper into unreality. It wouldn't hurt Libra to add a few sprinkles of Gemini imagination to all the matters he balances so seriously on his Scales. For truth is often not what it appears to be — (Mercury taught her that) — logic can be deceptive and facts can fool.

When the night is frosty and full of stars, who expects a warm summer rain to be hiding just behind Arcturus? The Twins do. She knows that true wisdom is only gained by adapting to life's ever-changing patterns. But he cannot accept today's patterns until he's weighed them mentally against former and future patterns and found them worthy of acceptance. Somewhere along the way, near the center of these polarized points of view, Gemini and Libra will meet, touch lightly . . . . . linger . . . . . and love.

GEMINI *Man* LIBRA *Woman*

He really knew nothing about it; he had merely
suspicions, but he said at a venture, "Wendy,
I ran away the day I was born."

Wendy was quite surprised, but interested; and
she indicated in the charming drawing-room manner,
by a touch on her night-gown, that he could sit
nearer her.

It's a 5-9 astrological fact, and there's no room for argument. A Gemini male is irresistible when he is effortlessly magnetizing a poor Libra girl into deserting her nicely balanced life and pledging her heart to an uncertain future, flying in and out of ideas, towns, cities, and moods with him. Of course, it works both ways. Doesn't *everything* work both ways with Gemini and Libra ?

It's just as fascinating to watch an irresistible Libra female spilling clouds of gentle, helpless, femininity all over a poor Gemini man, convincing him that it's his own idea to settle down and do the only sensible, logical thing after falling in love — get married, get a job, raise a family, and stay in one place with one person who can handle both of him — namely her. Who wins this romatic game ? It sometimes depends on which one has the stronger Moon sign, but usually it will be she, not he.

Whoever makes the initial approach, the laws of physics and chemistry soon take over, and these lovers will soon be turning airy dream castles into solid, substantial mortgages, because she smells so good, is so soft and cuddly, while he is so quick and bright and intelligent, and can beat her at chess and checkers.

A Libra woman will seldom glance twice at a man beneath her intellectuality. And a Gemini man will seldom sacrifice his precious freedom for a woman who can't anagram his thoughts and work crossword dreams with him. It's always amusing to watch a Gemini magician get fooled by one of his own magic tricks with a few new twists. Yet, there is a certain poetic justice about it. Here he has spent all his life charming girls, weaving his way in and out of romances, making it seem it was always his partner's fault, never his, glibly charming his way back into being friends again, and, in general, enjoying his enviable ability to handle every situation with a string of words from Webster's accompanied by small-boy innocence.

Now he meets a female who is more than his match at the game of guile, who gives him right back what he dishes out. After he has been led to think he has wooed and won her, after he allows her to harness his free spirit within the confining bonds of matrimony — (let other women play house in the New Age of sexual freedom, Libra females will settle only for a wedding ring) — after all that, he will discover that her gentle, soft, persuasive and amiable manner covers a cool, brilliant mind, a strong will, and a steely determination to get exactly what she wants. This is no fluffy bunny rabbit — this is a WAC field general!

A Libra female will always manage to get her own way under the guise of fairness, femininity and helplessness, but Libra is, in the final analysis, a masculine sign. I keep *telling* you that. She'll be surprised and hurt when he eventually sees through her, which he will, because no one, not even Libra, can fool the twinkling Gemini intellect for long. She didn't mean to be unfair or deceptive. To Libra, all is fair in love and war between the sexes, and the female of the species, in this respect, is more deadly than the male.

Her intriguing mind which so attracted him in the beginning of the romance will later make her a dangerous opponent in a discussion, since she's so skillful at the art of putting him at a disadvantage by arousing him into a display of temper, thereby causing him to lose his cool and poise. Then she has him at her mercy, while she claims tearfully that he is a brute, and his anger is certain evidence that he is wrong. Over and over again, she will outmaneuver him by using his own trick of twisting his statements and intent, leaving him unable to pin down the flaw in her arguments because of her capacity for doing things with such subtlety, and it doesn't seem she is doing anything at all, but fairly and justly defending her position.

A Libra woman is as impatient of constraint as any of the twelve Sun Signs, though perhaps not quite as much so as Gemini, Aquarius, Sag and Aries. For the Gemini lover or husband to attempt to impose any sort of restriction upon her would not be a wise idea. Just remember those Orientals (Libra rules the Orient). They cannot be controlled by other races effectively because, while they appear to be gentle and patient, offering no resistance, they will, nevertheless, always manage to find some subtle way of nullifying the opposition. The Gemini man will never gain a total victory over the Libra woman. Just when he thinks he has succeeded in breaking down all her arguments, she will have slipped around to another tactic or emotional strategy, catching him off guard again. But he should also keep in mind the curious detachment of Libra. She will take infinite pains to win her way, but when she fails, she has nearly the same mental satisfaction in the analysis of the reason for failure as she would have if she had been successful. He should keep this in mind, mainly because the same thing is true of himself. The two of them are much alike in many ways, influenced as they are by the very favorable and harmonious 5-9 Sun Sign Pattern vibration. They are sympatico, and often complement one another even in the areas where they differ.

Essentially, Gemini and Libra are wonderfully compatible, possessing many virtues (as well as vices) in common. They tend to respect each other's mentality, privacy, and freedom of thought and speech — normally. Yet there will be times when he wounds her deeply and is completely baffled by her hurt reaction, by the unexpected violence of her emotions. Any Libra woman in love with a Gemini man will understand why it has been said of the Mercury-ruled male that he is so busy *thinking*, he never stops to *think*.

He has no wish to attack, but his verbal outbursts can be sharp and cutting to the Libra girl, who by nature covers every opinion with the softer blur of tact and courtesy. Still, with his innate Mercurial charm, he'll win her over and make her believe he didn't mean what he said, which he probably didn't (Geminis never mean what they say for longer than an hour or so).

Their physical relationship may not be comprehensible to those born under Fire or Earth signs, but to them it will be enough to fill their hearts with peace and fulfillment. Neither is genuinely passionate, not really capable of love as more intensely emotional people experience it. There will always be something delicate and detached about their lovemaking — poetic and haunting, yes — but sensual, no. Yet the banked fires of the sexual blending between this man and woman are as magnetic and binding to their mutual air natures as the more torrid contacts between other mates and lovers. Romance will eternally be more important to both Gemini and Libra than sex. This attitude will predominate and suffuse their intimacy with a beauty all its own.

These two do not view love as an erotic appetite to be appeased, but as an art to be refined — not as lust, but as mutual pleasure — to be sipped slowly, not gulped greedily or blindly. There's an undeniable air of voluptuousness about a Libra woman, but also an air of refinement. Grossness, coarseness, obscenity and vulgarity offend her.

(Of course, an earthier Moon Sign or Ascendent or a severe affliction between Venus and Mars in her natal chart can dilute this basic part of her Sun Sign nature — but, as always, with all Sun Signs, we're speaking of the typical Libra Lady.)

There's small chance she'll be offended in such manner by the Gemini man, who privately feels the same way she does, although he may need more variety of expression in their physical union than his Venus-ruled wife. Yes, she will eventually become his wife — or leave. Libra rules marriage, you know, and it's a very rare Libran who is satisfied with an emotional relationship other than marital for any length of time.

The typical Libra girl who normally can't make up her mind about love any faster than she can about anything else, may nevertheless feel an impulse to rush into matrimony with a Gemini man before she's taken the time to balance her dipping Scales of decision. The infallible sign of a salesman is his ability to make people fight for the article he's trying to sell, and Gemini is a salesman supreme. When the article he's trying to sell is himself, the Libra girl is no more invulnerable to the Mercury charm and gift of glamour than the rest of his dazzled audience. She's sensible, intelligent, perceptive and all that, but these qualities seem to fail her when she's losing her heart to this gentle man with the bright eyes, light touch and far-out dreams.

Money may be a trifle more important to her than it is to him. Just a trifle more. The accumulation of cash and the manipulation of finances is not the prime motivation of either Libra or Gemini, except for the occasional natives of these Sun Signs who almost accidently wander into the banking business. To Gemini, money only becomes really important when he doesn't have it — when he desperately needs it. To Libra, money is important because of the luxuries, comforts and beauty of surroundings it can buy. Yet, stinginess and greediness are not qualities belonging to the Air Element, so there should be few disputes in this area, unless the Gemini man throws it away too freely, speculates too often, or gambles on long shots. When he spends beyond the budget, it will usually be connected with some new idea or promotion, a vacation or a change of residence — at the very least, a brief change of scene. When she's extravagant, it's more often lavished on clothes, dancing, singing or music lessons, sculpture, drama or Yoga classes, and the like. Sometimes, home decor and beauty parlors. They're basically alike in their attitudes toward money, as in many other matters, although they may differ in their manner of using it, from time to time. (Naturally, a stingier or more economical Moon Sign or Ascendent may slightly change the picture in either birth chart, but not substantially).

Their homes will probably be filled with music, flowers, books — and children. Those who love within the vibration of the 5-9 influence often decide to raise a family together, despite their reluctance to have children with members of other Sun Signs. They'll do a lot of traveling, either mentally or geographically, the relatives of each will be prominent in their relationship, and they may find religion or higher education grounds for agreement — or periodic dispute.

If these two are also graced by a harmonious Sun-Moon aspect between their respective nativities, their relationship will be smooth sailing on sparkling water, perhaps punctuated by a few storms and reefs, but, on the whole, like floating downstream on a feather. With a tense aspect between their Luminaries, the air could become humid, muggy, and even smoggy now and then, but there will always be the chance to run back into each other's arms for forgiveness after a quarrel, however serious — to try again.

He'll send sorry flowers, she'll recall the way the lights danced in his eyes, like a small boy, when he was excited, overlook his flaws, melt into his heart once more — and begin all over again to analyze why she loves him. But she won't solve the puzzle until she realizes that he is Twins, two-men-in-one.

A Libra woman is compelled to balance any duality she comes across into a harmonious whole, by virtue of her Venus essence. She'll never completely accomplish it, of course, but she may come closer to his magic than he'll ever allow anyone else to come. Except, of course, for the other half of himself.

☆ ☆ ☆ ☆ ☆ ☆

GEMINI

Air — Mutable — Positive
Ruled by Mercury
Symbol: The Twins
Day Forces — Masculine

SCORPIO

Water — Fixed — Negative
Ruled by Pluto
Symbols: Scorpion & Eagle
Night Forces — Feminine

The GEMINI-SCORPIO *Relationship*

All pirates are superstitious; and
Cookson cried, "They do say the surest
sign a ship's accurst is when there's
one on board more than can be accounted for."

*T*he naturally superstitious Scorpio has every right to conjure an extra person around when he (or she) is dealing with a Gemini, born under the sign of the Twins. Only one person is visible, of course, but this man's or woman's twin (or triplet or quadruplet) eternally hides in the ethers, ready to pop out at the most disconcerting times.

Most people don't know they're dealing with a multiple when they associate with a Gemini, but Scorpio suspects the truth of the matter right away. Scorpio suspects *everything* right away. It's difficult, if not impossible, to fool a Scorpion for long. The suspicious nature of these people prods them to penetrate mysteries like Sherlock Holmes, but they seldom discuss their conclusions with any Dr. Watsons. What Scorpio knows, he keeps to himself (or herself, as the case may be). As I've said before, Scorpio, above all, seeks Power. Knowledge is Power, so why give any of it away? Which brings us to a rather obvious tendency of — not all — but most Geminis: talking. Sometimes, they even go so far as to gossip. At the very best, they usually don't count to ten before speaking, a habit which can upset the more taciturn and reserved Scorpios, even though Gemini words are often lovely bubbles of light and joy.

Not that Scorpios can't be loquacious too, at times. They can be — the rare ones. But most Scorps would rather be seen than heard, and preferably not seen if they can possibly help it. I've mentioned elsewhere that many Pluto-ruled men and women and children have this thing about wearing dark glasses to help keep their incognito status undefiled. Even those unusual Scorpions who chatter have a knack for talking about everything except what is really important. They seldom discuss anything truly personal — about themselves, that is. Anything personal about someone else they will gladly discuss, unless they've promised to keep it a secret. Then their lips are closed as strictly as with the seal of the confessional. It's a rare Scorpio who breaks a promise. Keeping a promise is a point of honor with these people. And so the verbal dexterity of Gemini, not to mention the Geminian childlike attitudes of innocent fun and frolic, can annoy Scorpio, unless he or she has the natal Moon or Ascendent in an Air or Fire Sign. Pluto-ruled men and women not only look askance at a loose tongue, they don't trust childlike innocence either. Scorpio is a lot of things, but "innocence" is not the word an astrologer would choose to describe this Sun Sign.

Scorpios have what can only be called a dominating disposition, ranging all the way from brooding sulkiness to cool withdrawal (sometimes arrogance) when things don't go their way. At other times, Scorpio can be gentle, sensitive, compassionate and fanatically loyal — but never truly *warm*. Gemini is likewise often accused of lack of warmth. (Water and Air Signs both seem cold and detached to those born in the Fire or Earth elements.) As for loyalty, Gemini, as we all know by now, is not famous for loyalty — if the true meaning of the word is unswerving devotion to one person, one idea or one ideal for a lifetime. Gemini does like to swerve! These people have difficulty remaining interested in one topic for a full twenty-four-hour day without swerving and veering into a different direction — let alone for an entire Life-span on the planet Earth. Without periodic variety and changing scenery, however, the average Mercury Bird would suffocate from sheer boredom.

Like all 6-8 Sun Sign Patterns, unless they are born into the same family circle as relatives, or involved in a business association, Gemini and Scorpio might never meet without someone else introducing them. Lacking a Sun-Moon harmony between their mutual horoscopes, these two normally don't have enough in common to feel any pulsing vibrations across a crowded room and usually need third-party intervention to become acquainted. However, once they are accidently tossed together by some innocent bystander, who has no idea what may result from this mixing of Air and Water, their 6-8 Pattern will invariably cause the relationship, whether friendly, business or emotional, to consist of much service and devotion on one side and an inexplicable magnetism on the other. Incongruously (in an astrological sense), the service and devotion usually flows from Scorpio to Gemini — the magnetic attraction from Gemini to Scorpio. One might say that Gemini represents one mystery Scorpio cannot completely penetrate, and there is precious little Scorpio cannot penetrate. It's indisputably frustrating to the Scorpion, but frustration is sometimes synonymous with fascination when taken in small doses, infrequently. Taken in large doses daily, it can remove a lot of sting from Scorpio and cause some dulling of the childlike innocence of Gemini, ruffling the feathered wings of the impatient Mercury Birds.

Clever, intellectual Gemini is a walking, talking Question Mark (with emphasis on the talking), constantly curious and occasionally spurious. Scorpio is a firm Period, at the end of Knowing, the ultimate punctuation in the power of concentration. Geminis normally have varying degrees of trouble concentrating, their attention span sometimes being as brief as the time it takes a butterfly to hover over one blossom or a bird to remain perched on one branch.

In addition to being intensely domineering at times, Scorpio is also intensely proud and ambitious, in a disguised, quiet and unobtrusive way. As a matter of fact, Scorpio is privately intense about everything. Intensely ruthless, intensely loyal, intensely compassionate, intensely cool, intensely secretive, intensely mysterious. These people do nothing in half measures, never mind how harmless and sweet they seem on the surface. If they are your friends, they are your friends all the way up to heaven and all the way down to hell. If they are your enemies, the same geographical route of extremities and polarities is followed.

If Scorpio does *nothing* halfway, then Gemini can be said to do *everything* halfway (or one to three-quarters). Geminis never devote all — every shred of themselves — to any single person, idea or project. Only small fragments, chips and pieces, occasional crumbs. You see why they might never notice each other in a crowd ?

Although these two Sun Signs are different in motivation, character and personality, the differences can be intriguing. Scorpio will never learn all there is to know about Gemini, and cares deeply about the failure. Gemini will never totally plumb the awesome depth of Scorpio, and couldn't care less. Not really. To Gemini, all the fun is over when the riddle is solved. It's the changing dialogue and the fun of guessing the plot that excites Mercury people, not the denouement of the final scene.

Like Virgo, Gemini has a speculative and analytical nature, producing a marked tendency to read between the lines, therefore to often imagine that people mean more than they are saying. Scorpio is no slouch in this department either, although the basic cause is different. With Gemini, it stems from quick intellect, Mercurial curiosity and analytical urges — with Scorpio, from plain old-fashioned fear and suspicion.

Ask Gemini to sit on a particular couch, and he or she will probe your psychological and emotional purposes for choosing that couch, whereas Scorpio will be positive there's a bomb wired beneath it, rigged by computer to explode. There's a slight difference in their attitudes, but the end result is much the same. It's impossible to keep a secret from either Sun Sign, or to retain one's personal privacy around them. When it is Gemini and Scorpio who are suspecting, analyzing and probing each other, rather than one of the remaining ten Sun Signs, it's like watching a couple of pretzels caught in a Chinese chain-lock puzzle. They each create their own individual auras of mystery, and they both like to solve mysteries. But Gemini's mysterious aura is carefree and variable, consisting of unpredictable switches of pastel colors, light and shadow, and rapid changes of thought — while Scorpio's auric ethers of burgundy-shaded mystery are much more complex, with an emphasis on the shadows, lying in far deeper and unfathomable wells, sometimes with a touch of the sinister when influenced by the negative side of Pluto.

Slowness in others is a constant source of irritation to the bright, alert, impatient Twins, the most typical of whom are periodically high-strung and nervous. Scorpios are also periodically high-strung and nervous, but heaven forbid that anyone should ever catch them showing it! The more apprehensive Scorpio is feeling within, the more sure, confident and secure he (or she) *appears* to be outwardly. Since every inwardly experienced feeling and emotion flits across Gemini's features, lighting up his (or her) expressive, fast darting eyes, you should have no trouble deciding where to place your bets to win in a poker game. When the poker game is a relationship of any kind with each other, the stakes can be desperately high for Scorpio, yet it's still only a game to Gemini, whatever the size of the kitty or the pot. If one game is lost, figures the Mercury Bird, there's always another, just down the road. Scorpio does not take losing so lightly. In fact, the Eagles take losing very, very heavily. Losing, to Scorp, is a humiliating experience, degrading, perhaps even cause for inner panic. (Scorp never displays *outer* panic.) Gemini tosses Life's dice with a fine, detached and careless abandon — Scorpio, with cool shrewdness, and then only after carefully calculating the odds. *Life's* dice, that is. In an actual dice game, Gemini calculates rather coolly and precisely himself — or herself. The fast Mercury mind figures the house percentages in a flash.

Let's see if you can straighten out these pretzels of intrigue. They just walked into the room. One of them has glided in noiselessly, almost unnoticed, and stands quietly, while gazing steadily into your eyes. You ask a question, this one remains silent, not answering immediately. The other, has skipped, hopped, or flown into the room, perhaps strumming a guitar, tossing a tennis racquet in the air, and dangling the end of a sentence. You ask a question, and this one will jet a convoluted answer in your direction, then quickly head for the bowl of cracked walnuts on the table. Which one is which? Think you know?

All right, the first one described is a Gemini. The second is a Scorpio. Are you confused, mystified? Then you haven't been paying close enough attention to the hints in all the various Gemini and Scorpio chapters of this book. The Gemini was tricking you into believing he-she is cool and poised, using one of Mercury's multiple identities, as smoothly as a seasoned actor slips from one part into another. The Scorpio was wearing one of Pluto's Halloween masks, feigning a casual unconcern and light flippancy to hide his or her quivering intensity. Now, do you understand the problem?

They didn't notice each other at all. Go on — walk over and introduce them, but the responsibility is yours, not mine. If their Moon Signs are compatible, they can create haunting, misty dreams together. After all, isn't a fine mist the result of a blending of air and water, in Nature? But if their Sun and Moon Signs are square or opposed, the result will be fog — and in a heavy fog, Mercury Birds can't fly, while Scorpions make little progress along the seashore.

☆ ☆ ☆ ☆ ☆ ☆

GEMINI *Woman* SCORPIO *Man*

————◆◀●▶◆————

"It was two against one that angered him .."

We should start right out by admitting there are some relationships composed of this Air and Water mixture which succeed — some Twins and Eagles who easily manage to find a lasting love, built together on a firm foundation of mutual respect. Not a lot, but there are some.

If the Sun-Moon aspects between them are harmonious, they can find happiness as effortlessly as any other man and woman descended from Adam and Eve, except that they'll have to keep a sharper eye on that sneaky snake than most lovers. Without such an astrological boost, however (if their Luminaries and other planets are in adverse aspect between their birth charts), these particular Air and Water signs might find it easier and safer to remain friends, avoiding the wild winds of passion and the deeper waters of forever vows. Scoring high on a compatibility achievement level is not forbidden to them, but they both must be willing to make a constant effort.

To begin with, "forever" is a word that frightens the Gemini female as much as the word "temporary" frightens the Scorpio male. It isn't that she is unable to remain in love, and true to one man, because many Gemini girls do just that, but such faithfulness and permanency must creep up on her subtly, gradually, one tiptoe at a time, until she's totally involved in the relationship without realizing it. Using the word "forever" too soon, or predicting the outcome of the romance when she'd rather guess, spoils the excitement for her. Conversely, it isn't that the Scorpio man can't cope with "temporary" arrangements as well as the next male creature, but the use of the word itself creates instant doubt and suspicion in his mind, spoiling his sense of power and dominance over the affair.

He'll be initially captivated by her undeniable charm, the champagne bubbles of her voice, her bright mind, her deft conversation and her light touch in every situation. Naturally. He's only a man, after all, regardless of his masked and caped Batman image — and just as susceptible to the attractions of Eve's apple as any other astrological sign. Then, after a while, he'll begin to notice that some of her delightful stories have changed ever-so-slightly the second time around. (Geminis always add a little here, take away a little there, for more sparkle — doesn't everyone?) She may be late for two or three of their dates in a row, or perhaps she'll interrupt his discussion of his very serious plans for their future with the agitated announcement that she left the car keys in the ignition with the engine running. Not only that, but she double-parked and blithely expects him to pay the ticket.

It is at this point, or at some similar stage of discovery, that the Scorpio man will rub some of the stardust from his eyes, take a long and penetrating look at this woman who nearly stole his heart, and cautiously decide to deliberate a bit longer the possibility of his promising to love, honor and cherish her for the rest of his days before a man of God. (Scorpio is secretly very religious, you know.) Once he has given his word, it pains his soul to break it, so he may slow up the courting until he's sure she has no more surprises to spring on him, like one or two marriages and separations or divorces she forgot to remember to tell him about.

It may be that she will hardly note the slight change in his attitude. She's too busy wondering how long she can stand his stifling scrutiny of her personal life, prying into her secrets (nothing bad or necessarily shocking, but just things she'd like to keep private) — and his jealousy. Can't a girl smile back brightly at the clerk in the bookstore or stop to discuss the grooming problems of Old English sheepdogs with a friendly stranger on the street without being accused of promiscuity? What about the way *he* stares at every female he meets, and stares . . . . . . and stares . . . . . . and stares?

She has only herself to blame for her dilemma. Being a Gemini, and having cut her teeth on the dictionary, she should be well read enough to know that a Scorpio male, with his deep, rich, magnetic voice, and steady, wise gaze, possesses the fascination of a Serpent. Formidable as his outward appearance of strength and stillness may be, beneath it is a silent mating call few females can resist.

One of the first things she'll discover about him is his incredible will power. It is simply not to be believed. This man can do anything he sets his mind on doing, literally anything. If he decides to fast for thirty days, he'll live on water throughout the entire period without so much as a whimper of hunger or complaint. If he chooses to become president — of his class, his company or his country — he will attain his goal and become president. If he wants to seduce a girl into being his woman for keeps, she has lost the battle before it begins. He will make her his.

All this can be spooky, Halloween-scary to the bright-eyed Gemini girl, who asks nothing of life but change and excitement, gaiety — and something to challenge the intellect. When she feels those Pluto vibes reaching out toward her, you would think she would run, as she would flee from a panting gorilla in the jungle, who means business. *You* would think so. *I* would not. Because I am aware of the astrological quirk that allows a Scorpio man, at odd moments, to more resemble an innocent, velvet-eyed deer than a gorilla — so sweet, gentle and sensitive, so *apparently* in need of comfort and loyal support, a girl would have to have a heart as hard as bricks to hurt him in the slightest way, like running away from him. The Gemini girl's heart is not as hard as bricks. It may be set at a cooler temperature than the heart of an Aries, Leo or Sagittarius girl with more fiery emotions, but it is soft in all the right spots, and the appeal of an intelligent man, whose burning eyes can see through her soul, hits one of those spots with deadly aim. There is something so satiny smooth about his manner, she forgets that steely gaze he's capable of projecting when he's displaying his tremendous powers of reserve and icy resolve, but he'll give her plenty of opportunity to remember it later.

So much for why and how these two usually fall in love. More is needed about how they can manage to *remain* in love. Since Scorpio is a Fixed Sign, he has an abundance of self-control. He'll need all of it when she tries his patience with her chameleon charisma, her spells of moodiness, absentmindedness and duality of purpose. Since Gemini is a Mutable Sign, she possesses an abundance of adaptability to help her cope with fluctuating scenes and emotions, which she will surely need to call on eventually with this man. She'll need all her ability to stay free and easy and cool when he becomes stubborn or violently emotional over some imagined slight just after he has been an angel of understanding. (It's always difficult to decide if Scorpio is Angel or Devil; they seem to be so at home in both heaven and hell, a foot in each place, but actually existing somewhere in-between.)

She'll have to memorize the lesson that this man wants to know where she is and what she's doing most of the time — if not all of the time. He'll also expect her to remain in one place, more or less (mostly more.) He'll frown at her nostalgic tears over her old boyfriends, her casual attitude toward money when something excites her fancy, her whimsical excursions into one hobby after another, from singing-to-dancing-to-painting-to-home-decorating-to-archeology-to-medicine, and spinning around with a travel urge each time the seasons change in Nature — and in her restless Mercury-ruled spirit.

He'll have to be satisfied with fragments of devotion, scattered kisses and temper tantrums, naivete nearly beyond belief (or nearly beyond a Scorpio's belief) along with cool disdain mixed in equal parts with enthusiastic affection, a wandering mind and changeable notions — and not expect her to display anything near the self-confidence and emotional control he has possessed since he was born.

She is surely a challenge to him and to his masculinity, since most Gemini females are full of feminine wile and guile, smelling like cologne, usually dainty and light hearted, witty, talented and clever. But Gemini is a masculine sign, and as for Mercury, the planetary ruler of the Twins changes sex as unpredictably as the wind changes its course. So there will be times when she will offend his sense of manhood, other times when she flatters it. Her intellect will never fail to fascinate him, but he may be disappointed when he discovers that her intelligence is satisfied to skim the surface of most matters, to analyze then discard them, feeling no need to probe the depths, as he does in every subject from sin to sex, from religion to reincarnation, politics to polygamy.

All she needs to know about the Mormons is the name Brigham Young and something about Salt Lake City, Utah. All she needs to know about geology is the difference between turquoise and quartz; that the gold rush took place in Colorado, near Pikes Peak, and may occur again, if America goes back on the gold standard.

He needs to know much more — like Brigham Young's secret reason for wanting to bed down and board with, possess and father children with more than one woman. (Brigham was a Sun Sign Gemini, so let's hope Scorp doesn't probe too deeply. It might really disturb his tranquility regarding his relationship with her if he learned *that*.) As for gold, Scorpio needs more than surface knowledge. He wants to keep up with all the fluctuating gold prices, the details of assaying, the intricacies of sinking a mine shaft — and so on.

When it comes to the sexual side of love, it must always be remembered that, although Scorpio is a strongly sexed sign, the ability to maintain continence, chastity and self-control (as in the religious life of monks, priests, etc.) is equally marked in these males. Assuming he has fallen in love with a Gemini woman, he is presumably not one of the Scorpions who have chosen the rigid discipline of abstinence. He will not, however, look upon sex as a game, as a frivolous pastime or a promiscuous sport. Sex is the Secret of Life itself to him. A woman who understands and fulfills her Scorpio man's deeper desires need not worry about his faithfulness (unless his Sun Sign is greatly afflicted by malefic planets at birth). Normally, a Scorpio male who receives genuine and intense response from his mate will not look elsewhere.

An Eagle is very curious about sex in his youth, but he probably will have satisfied most of his curiosity by the time he marries. His attitude toward the physical mating of love is deeply passionate, overwhelmingly sensual, yet with a certain strain of purity woven through it, amounting to a religious fervor with a few Scorpios.

The trouble is that sex is *not* the Secret of Life itself to the Gemini woman. Her attitude is experimental, and the deeper secrets of sexual union are secondary in importance. Even those Gemini females whose Twin is promiscuous seldom wish to penetrate the mysteries of sex with any real feeling or intensity. It's just a pleasant pastime, that's all. Yet, her very detachment toward physical passion could cause the Scorpio man to find the Gemini woman absorbing sexually, a continual challenge to him to prove to her that sex and God are linked, that all creation is nothing without the blending of Man and Woman. You already know how Scorpio hates to lose (*refuses* to lose is a better way to state it). In the area of their intimate sexual union, he simply *must* win. With a harmonious Sun-Moon relationship between their birth charts, he'll keep trying over and over again, repeatedly, to explain this greatest of all mysteries to his Gemini woman. Lacking such an aspect between their Luminaries — or if other mutual planets in their horoscopes are in conflicting positions, he may do the unthinkable (for a Scorpio) — and become disloyal, rationalizing his breaking of their vows with the reason that he cannot bear the halfway measure of love he's receiving. And that will be truth. An Eagle *cannot*.

It might hearten him to know that, barring disharmony between their natal charts and Luminaries, his chances of achieving physical ecstasy with this lady and successfully teaching her the mysteries of love's total blending are rather good. For Scorpio represents the eighth astrological house of sex (among other matters) to Gemini. Therefore, she really does find him magnetic and compelling, never mind her pretended detachment. He'll just have to keep practicing.

This man's Pluto sense of integrity is difficult for the average or typical Gemini female to comprehend, unless she has the Moon or Ascendent in Scorpio herself. If so, these two can be wonderfully, unexpectedly happy, to the mystification of their relatives and friends, who see only the surface differences between them. Otherwise, the vibrations of the 6-8 Sun Sign Pattern may cause both of them to experience periods of deep unhappiness from time to time. She might feel he's trying to drown her in an ocean of suspicion, or be both frightened and puzzled over his inexplicable, ice-cold retreats within himself.

He may feel she's trying to tear him from his own soul, as a tornado uproots trees. Even so, if Gemini chooses, she's intelligent enough to figure a way to make the relationship work — and Scorpio is intuitive enough to know how to seal each break so it's stronger afterwards than ever before. If they each *desire* to do so. Desire is the key word. To intensely desire to rediscover and retain the brightness they first knew means that they love. And love can cement anything, even hearts that have broken into a thousand pieces.

☆ ☆ ☆ ☆ ☆

GEMINI *Man* SCORPIO *Woman*

◆━◆━◆◆

"I daresay it will hurt a little," she warned him.

"Oh, I shan't cry," said Peter, who was already of opinion that he had never cried in his life. And he clenched his teeth and did not cry; and soon his shadow was behaving properly, though still a little creased.

A Gemini man possesses the unusual and uncommonly appealing quality of seeming to remain eternally youthful . . . not rare, I suppose, for one who is reborn each day, but rare enough to attract the normally self-contained and cautious Scorpio female into wondering what makes him scintillate with such multiple colors of the mood spectrum. Now, when a Scorpio girl starts to wonder, there's no stopping her until she's satisfied her wondering with complete knowing. That means coming closer to him — and closer . . . . . . and closer . . . . . . until she suddenly looks around herself with alarm.

Unexpectedly, she is standing between two people, one to either side of her, as different as day from night. Which one is the man she was pursuing closer and closer? Both. They are both the same man. A Gemini male is victim of the Twin syndrome, you know. Maybe she did know. Maybe she didn't. But whichever or whatever, it will upset and topple her natural, cool, poised "I can handle anything at all" auric projection. Can she handle this? Can she cope with this introverted-extroverted soul, this full-of-gladness, filled-with-sadness little boy, this coldly cruel yet sensitive and tender man? He's a maze of non-sequiturs, contradictions, denials and affirmations.

Never mind. She can cope. She is a Scorpio, and she can handle it, solve it, beat it, win it, conquer it — the seemingly impossible situation. Can she? I'm not sure. But *she* is sure. The Gemini man doesn't really care if she does or not. The very thought that this lovely, intense yet poised and womanly creature of depth and mystery is willing to *try* is excitement enough to elate him into whistling a brand-new tune and making a dazzling wish on the first star he sees.

To *guess* the outcome is far more thrilling to him than to *know* the outcome. For a Gemini to know removes all reason for existing. With her, *not* to know removes all reason for existing. Ah, yes! To paraphrase poor tortured Hamlet, "to know or not to know — *that* is the question." That is surely and positively the question between these two at all times, the question which must be answered, finally, before there is any hope of lasting mutual happiness.

You'll have to understand, or rather, *she'll* have to understand that a Gemini male is constitutionally and congenitally incapable of comprehending love as an eternal, searing passion in quite the total way she does. There may be Gemini men who love one woman *totally* forever (in fact, I once knew one myself), but these Twins are extremely few and far between, and even they are sometimes haunted by misty dreams of another face, weaving in and out of the steady love relationship — or there may be a break-up, before he returns to his true Soul-Mate, in such cases . . . or at the very least, he may privately wonder what experiences he might have missed by being monogamous. The more typical Gemini man enjoys the titillation of choosing which of several women to prefer and is shocked when one of his harmless, pretty larks turns out to be an eagle, especially if she turns out to be a Scorpio Eagle. The eagle is a monogamous creature in Nature. So are most human Scorpio Eagles, *by* nature. (Not all, just most. When we're dealing with Sun Signs, instead of with the entire horoscope, we have to consider the averages and over-all percentages.)

Venus is the planet of love, and Geminis are ruled by the planet Mercury, whose influence over Venus in the nativity, causes the emotions to be dispersed and frivolous. Pluto is the ruler of Scorpio, and this planet's effect on Venus is to make her influence deeply serious, powerful — but secret and hidden. You will notice the obvious differences in this treatment of Venus, Goddess of Love. Venus notices it, too, and becomes baffled when these two vibratory forces of Mercury and Pluto mix their rays. The Gemini man and Scorpio woman may not notice it right away, so busy are they being fascinated by each other's strangeness. One thing he will definitely find strange about her is the strongly imbedded Pluto form of jealousy. Scorpio jealousy is sometimes a passion even more consuming than the love which gave birth to it.

Gemini finds all forms of jealousy difficult to fathom. He is, of course, duly susceptible to the normal, small tugs of fear regarding the danger of losing his woman to another, like any average male — but the kind of overwhelming sea storms thundered by a Scorpio woman who feels threatened are incomprehensible to him. When this woman has been hurt, or even suspicions that she *might* be hurt, her Scorpio stinger can strike a deadly blow to the ego of the Gemini man who is innocent of the accusations made against him — or guilty as charged, either way. Most Pluto-ruled women find revenge sweet indeed. Therefore, if she is deceived, or suspects she's been, the retaliation will be swift and cruel, even vindictive, if her Sun was afflicted by major planets at her birth.

Knowing this, the Gemini man, whose nature cannot help being slightly flighty and fickle, should realize just what he could be facing should he make the mistake of attempting a light romance with such a girl, to whom there is no such thing as a light romance, only an all-consuming and everlasting passion. Other than an Aries female, no one can be as jealous as a Scorpion. But Aries has not the same compulsion to get even with the lover or husband as does Scorpio. Taurus and Cancer jealous? No, the word with these Sun Signs is possessive. They cry a lot and hurt inside deeply. But they cause violent scenes infrequently. Possessive and jealous are not quite the same. Any man who has ever loved a Scorpio woman will be well aware of the difference.

This is a 6-8 Sun Sign Pattern, Scorpio being the sixth house to Gemini and Gemini being the eighth house to Scorpio, so there will be a markedly noticeable amount of service and unselfish devotion to duty in the relationship, plus a strong sexual magnetism (felt only when the two people involved are lovers or mates. When the relationship involves relatives, friends, or business associates, different eighth house matters, other than sex, will be emphasized between them). The service will usually be offered from Scorpio to Gemini. The sexual vibration is the attraction Gemini has for Scorpio. Yet, oddly, the very last quality the typical Gemini has to offer is sexuality. Sex isn't an all-consuming interest to this man, unless it's accompanied by poetry, experimentation, far-out ideals, or intricate games of mental chess and checkers. He may exude tons of handsomeness, charm, masculinity, intelligence and romance, but he does not ordinarily exude excessive sexuality (to anyone but a Scorpio). Therefore, it seems strange that she should find him so physically irresistible — and often, he finds her the same way (although that's not so hard to comprehend).

Perhaps it's his elusive air of boyishness, the myriad tricks of his mirror images, changing from one mood into another before her eyes, that make her so determined to penetrate into the core of his heart and soul through their sexual union. He seems to hold a secret, ever so lightly — yet nonetheless, a secret — and an unsolved secret or a mystery which defies solution beckons to Scorpio as a flame entices a moth. She must know him — really, truly *know* him — to satisfy her mind and fulfill her heart. Consequently, the physical expression of their love will magnetize her, sometimes for many years, until she finally realizes that no one will ever know all the facets of this man, not even a Scorpion. About the same time, he will realize that he can never play his favorite game of "guess who" and "guess what I am" with her all the way. She won't discover every sliver of his private dreams, but she will unravel enough threads of his soul's fabric to frighten him into feeling that he is slowly, but surely, being more known than he cares to be. And so their physical blending, although it may begin as a compelling part of their love, could grow from cool to cold, and at last be the undoing of their romance, unless they each are willing to honestly face the things that trouble both of them—to truly *communicate*. Yet, she should not try to overanalyze their relationship.

He may tend to criticize and analyze *her*, since she's so full of silent intrigue, certainly not shallow. Yet, in doing so, he may be floating in deeper waters than he suspects. Scorpio does not take kindly to analysis, and the insistent questioning of the curious Gemini can cause her to retreat in sullen anger—or to lash out with a violent emotional response. Personal privacy is as sacred to her as it is to him, perhaps more so. The two of them should recognize this in one another and not insist upon exploring the things they find puzzling about each other until the resentment between them grows into a high thick wall.

To break down the wall, he'll try his charm, his old jokes, his most imaginative lovemaking, his multiple romantic techniques. She'll try her most sensuous mannerisms, her coolest detachment and most soothing gentleness. They'll both try every trick they have tucked in their sleeves, and that's quite a few tricks between the two of them (the three of them, counting his Twin). Yet the wall grows even higher and thicker. There must be a way over it. (There is.)

Sometimes, the only thing they *don't* try, in attempting to scale the wall that separates them, is to allow a little more space between their hearts so love can breathe free. He's willing, but she may fear a new and unaccustomed space between herself and her mate as she would fear a dark and unknown abyss stretching ahead. Space is made up of air, essentially, and since he is of the Air Element, he feels more at home when there is plenty of space around himself. But she is of the Water Element and must be surrounded with a flowing stream of togetherness or be unable to breathe herself.

It's always sad when the Gemini man and the Scorpio woman who once loved find they've lost the way to happiness, because he believes in things unseen, all magic and wonder, despite his computerlike mental equipment. So does she. She believes in even stranger and more wondrous unseen worlds than he. But the secretive, inexplicable forces of Pluto silence her, seal her lips and heart, and forbid her to speak of them as openly as he does. She will never be able to express her deepest dreams with as much facility as the glib Gemini. And herein lies the sadness.

If only he would not be so impatient with her intense passions, her emotional depths. If only she could find a way to whisper to his wandering spirit that she, too, longs to solve all the mysteries that lie out there among the stars and comets — that she, too, yearns to breathe free, to race the wind, and search for childhood miracles, half-forgotten . . . yet also half-remembered. The cool night air is infinitely more refreshing than the musty darkness of the damp caves of worry, where Scorpions are commanded by Pluto to move about when they are troubled.

Too often, this man and woman reach out to each other, not quite touching. They call to one another, but he hears only the music of the spring breeze — and she hears only the sound of the waves lashing the shore. If they would stop long enough to hear one another's secret cries, they might soar high enough together to see everything from a different perspective, including their relationship.

Their ruling planets can help them, if they *listen*. After all, Mercury and Pluto, along with Uranus, are the ones who taught Merlin all he knew, and also secretly guided Arian Houdini. Surely they can teach Gemini and Scorpio to mix a White Witch's brew of happiness. When your astral guardians are a couple of magicians like these, you should be able to detect illusion from reality — or discover that the two are interchangeable. Whichever.

GEMINI

Air — Mutable — Positive
Ruled by Mercury
Symbol: The Twins
Day Forces — Masculine

SAGITTARIUS

Fire — Mutable — Positive
Ruled by Jupiter
Symbols: Archer & Centaur
Day Forces — Masculine

The **GEMINI-SAGITTARIUS** *Relationship*

. . . not three of them, but four!!

Sagittarians aren't always loud and active, out aiming their bows and arrows to shoot down hypocrisy and falsehood. Some of them are quite timid and introspective, almost owlish, with a decided pacifistic attitude — that is, they are pacifists who sometimes use their fists to put across their points about peace. (Is that a word — *pacifistic?* It is now.) Yet, even these will speak with blunt candor when their opinions are sought. Timid or pushy, all Sagittarians gaze at the world through the measuring eye of truth. What I'm attempting to make clear is that Sagittarius is a double sign, half-horse, half-man. There are two distinct types of Archers: those who take after the front end or *human* half of the Centaur — and those who take after the rear end or *equestrian* half. You may have met both types. I have.

By now, everyone knows that Gemini is also a double sign, symbolized by the Twins, dual in personality, multiple in word and action, myriad in Nature. Do you have any idea of the task involved in sorting out all these identities for the purpose of describing one complex relationship between just two people? The math alone is discouraging.

That Sagittarius friend or neighbor you have, think about him (or her).

He-she may have a gift for zinging out the tactless verbal arrow of truth, yet is he (or she) the kind of Sag who acts like Bashful, of the Seven Dwarfs, at a party ? All Jupiter sons and daughters are bright and witty, but the rare shy ones may hide it and can be almost self-effacing in front of strangers. Please note that I said the *rare* shy ones.

Now, skip to Winston Churchill, of the merry, twinkling Jupiter eye; John Lindsay, former mayor of New York City (an authentic textbook-type Sagittarian); elfish Mark Twain; the quiet (relatively quiet) Arthur Brisbane, formerly of the *New York Journal;* and, finally, move along to the last friendly puppy dog you saw wagging its tail (all friendly dogs are Sagittarians, by spiritual birthright) and tell me what they all have in common. (Throw in William F. Buckley, if you feel like it.)

All right, I'm an astrologer, I'm supposed to tell you. They have in common honesty, youthfulness, refreshing candor, wisdom and wit — and awkwardness, intermingled with gracefulness. I guess we can take it from there, keeping in mind constantly that although every Archer possesses these qualities, some of them are *extro*verts deluxe and some are *intro*verts deluxe. Be sure you remember that, please, because I'm not going to interrupt the main body of this chapter to remind you again. I don't want anybody to read this and keep interjecting: "But Marvin is so quiet"—or "Mildred is so shy." It has now been established that *some* Sagittarians *are* quiet, timid, and shy. But *more* of them are talkative and outgoing.

I get the feeling we are back where we started in the first paragraph, but we may have advanced slightly. You always face this astrological problem when dealing with the double signs. Thankfully, there are only three: Gemini, Sagittarius, and Pisces. Well, maybe you could throw in Libra. There are two sides to any set of Scales.

As for Geminis, they have no traits in common whatsoever, except the fact that each one of them is a double-mirror image, has two or more dispositions and personalities, which he or she can change as naturally and as quickly as you or I can change from swim suits to sweaters on a day when the wind can't make up its mind.

Gemini is Air, Sagittarius is Fire, and the back section of this book will tell you how these two elements mix. Quite superbly, most of the time. Disastrously, at others. But generally speaking, they do get on fairly well. Gemini can incite Sagittarius into action — both negative and positive — that the Archer would never have taken without being stirred by the Twins. Air always fans Fire into higher flames. Sagittarius can make Gemini feel smothered occasionally, because fire burns out the oxygen in the air, but it can also warm it.

This is a 7-7 Sun Sign Pattern, so naturally, each is slightly envious of the other, because each possesses qualities the other does not have, but would secretly like to cultivate. Gemini needs the Archer's high motivation, ideals, warmth, enthusiasm, and sincerity — and needs also the Sagittarian's ability to travel over more terrain mentally, emotionally, geographically — to shoot for a star, and reach it.

Sagittarius longs for the cool poise and charm of Gemini, the talent for keeping the foot out of the mouth, for remaining cool and detached in the face of most disturbing situations, and especially needs the Gemini verbal adroitness, called *tact*.

When they get together, they have two choices. Each can admire the opposite traits of the other, and try to imitate them, in order to grow and mature spiritually. Or — each can fear and envy the opposite qualities of the other, and try to put them down, robbing each other of all pride in doing his (or her) own thing.

Both Gemini and Sag (pronounced to rhyme with badge) tend to be scintillating, rather than solid — dashing and daring, rather than dependable and enduring. Both have minds capable of high intelligence, but not necessarily designed for achievements of lasting design and construction (unless other planetary configurations in their birth charts give this quality — which, of course, in a number of cases, they do).

The ideas of both are more like shooting stars or comets than steady Suns. What can be accomplished in a few days by Gemini and Sagittarius will often be brilliant, but a project involving longer periods of time and effort may not come off so well, unless there are the just-mentioned supportive planet positions of strength and patience in the nativities. For knocking around together, instant empathy and general compatibility, the glittering Mercury-ruled and the benevolent Jupiter-ruled get along exceedingly well most of the time. But there's always the chance that sly Mercury (Gemini) may be unable to resist tricking sincere Jupiter (Sag) in some way, and the resentment of this may be violent (the Archer being of the Fire Element).

Sagittarians, while excessively emotional at times, are for the most part without guile. The clever, glib Gemini who plays mental chess games with the trusting Archer may later regret the harm done to another human being, however unintentional. According to ancient legends, the gods feel a special affection for these Sagittarian children of the zodiac, watchfully protecting them from those who would harm them. This is the basis for the so-called Jupiter "luck." A word to the wise is said to suffice, but not all Geminis are always wise, just clever — sometimes too clever and the Mercury Bird may, when least expected, trip in his (or her) own trap.

Gemini's quick wit, swift intellect and ease with words can seduce occasional Mercury Birds into becoming con artists supreme, tricky car salesmen and politicians, swindlers, drug pushers, or just plain, old-fashioned crooks. Yet, these very same qualities allow many Twins to become excellent teachers, literary geniuses, creative artists and musicians, clever mathematicians, brilliant scientists, and sincere and convincing salesmen of all manner of things. The Gemini duality calls these men and women in both directions. They're pulled on by both their Twin Selves, between day and night, dark and light, wrong and right — a spiritual struggle that continues, in a mild way, even with the prosaic, "ordinary" Geminians.

Most Geminis are far too intelligent and too fond of their freedom to risk apprehension and confinement by breaking the law, but those who do flirt with antisocial activities lean toward the light-fingered crimes, such as twirling combination locks on safes, forgery and counterfeiting. Seldom will a Gemini be guilty of homicide, although the Twins may be an "accomplice to murder." The Gemini criminal prefers to mastermind the crime and delegate the authority for the action to others, the tendency of all Mutable Sign people.

There are always a few scattered and very rare notable exceptions that prove this, or any other rule, but only the smallest fraction of those confused souls who commit murder are Geminis. Killing requires more raw physical aggression than most Mercury-ruled people are able to muster. Violence offends the sensitivity of the average or typical Geminian.

All Geminis, of any age or sex, possess active, fertile minds, always operating at high speed, and never mind the quietness and placidity you notice in the surface personality of the *one* Twin who *appears* to be dominant in the Mercury personality. As quiet and placid as he or she may be, the brain is constantly busy, busy, busy. Don't judge a Gemini by his (or her) speech patterns alone. Carefully note the *results*. Somehow, things get done, and they get done fast, when Gemini chooses, however slow-appearing the outward activity may be. The pose of slowness is totally deceptive. The bottom line is what counts.

In fact, many Geminians deliberately choose just such a disguise to fool people. They allow the "quiet" Twin to be the "front" for the Mercury personality, and keep the swift, super-smart, restless Twin in the background at all times, directing the strategy, all unsuspected by the astrologically unenlightened. Notice the *eyes* of the deceptively quiet ones. You'll see a continual "twinkle," a quick darting look, taking in the scope of any situation in a glance. The eyes tell the story.

The essential and basic nature of Mercury-ruled people is very much like that of the Jupiter-ruled people — sunny, cheerful and optimistic (though Gemini is never as naive as Sag, even in youth). Later in life, both become cynical in varying degrees, yet somehow, still retain a certain childlike hope. Yes, I know that's contradictory, but the character of all double signs is contradictory. D-o-u-b-l-e. D-u-a-l. Two things at the same time. Simultaneous non sequiturs.

As for the poor Archers, they are not always quite so persuasive as Gemini, and frequently find themselves in hot water when they blurt out uncomfortable truths. Not that Sagittarians aren't charming. They possess oodles of rain-fresh, dew-drenched charm, but it quickly loses its power when they begin to fling a string of stinging words with very little subtlety or tact. Blunt is the word for Sagittarius, and bluntness doesn't win ball games. At least, not as many ball games as may be won by the verbally graceful and mentally adept Gemini, who often wins on sheer glibness alone. Gemini can be cutting in speech also, but only when he or she chooses to use the weapon of sarcasm.

Sagittarius is usually incapable of sarcasm. The Archer's sharp speech hurts only because of the ring of reality most people don't want to hear. Sarcasm requires a certain kind of *twisting* of the truth to make the truth *clearer* than Sag is normally capable of either handling or comprehending (unless, of course, the Archer's Moon or Ascendent is in Gemini).

It should be pointed out that those rare, quiet Sagittarians and Geminis who are keyed to a lower pitch (outwardly) than the large majority of Archers and Twins are seldom silent when they're together. Gemini has a way, by sheer auric vibration, of fanning the mildest Sag into a flaming spell of an unaccustomed monologue of words — sometimes happy and enthusiastic, at other times angry. In a similar manner, the Archer can stimulate a desire in the meeker (on the *surface*) Geminis to be more loquacious. But after these two have incited one another into conversation, they may not really listen to each other. They may appear to be listening, but actually, one is only waiting for the other to finish talking, so he (or she) can put across a contradictory opinion. A dramatic disagreement between them can get pretty noisy, with the need for a third party to referee. Or — one of the two will completely subdue the other, in which case, the subdued one will seek freedom from such restriction at the very earliest opportunity. In other words, leave. Sometimes, permanently.

Sagittarius tends more to inflict *emotional* blows to Gemini (although the Twins will make an attempt to hide such wounds behind a mask of cool boredom and disinterest) and Gemini is more likely to succeed in bending the Sagittarian *mind* into strange shapes, sometimes causing mental depression in the Jupiter person.

When these two (or four) are in harmony, however, through a positive Sun-Moon interchange between their birth charts, they can be fun to be around. One is always trying to top the other, and they'll also help each other over the rough spots, finding ways to express themselves, and to communicate, which is like a private language between them.

Often, Sag and Gemini will speak to each other's minds and hearts through music, poetry or art — or even body language (which is a very valid form of communication, and can be most eloquent). They reach out toward one another over waves of invisible enthusiasm and excitement ... dreaming impossible dreams together ... looking for four-leaf clovers ... and finding them surprisingly often (thanks to Jupiter luck, and Mercury visual alertness) . . . reflecting, in their eyes, a soul comprehension of the mutual need and desire to imitate which all polarities influenced by the 7-7 Sun Sign Pattern recognize, somehow sensing that they are opposites, seeking to blend into completeness through communion with each other.

☆ ☆ ☆ ☆ ☆ ☆

GEMINI *Woman* SAGITTARIUS *Man*

They broke into a bacchanalian dance, which brought him to his feet at once; all traces of human weakness gone, as if a bucket of water had passed over him.

When the Twins (two personalities) of the Gemini girl-woman break into a dance of delightful distortion and deviousness, right in front of the sincere eyes of the trusting Sagittarian, this man can, at first, feel oddly impotent — mentally and emotionally, if not physically. Then, suddenly, he's aroused into meeting the obvious challenge of duality with which this female is teasing him.

In many ways, the Sagittarian Archer is a remarkable man. He has extraordinary vision and warmth, he is thoughtful and he is fluent. Hearing him speak of his ideals, awash in enthusiasm, is a very special experience to the alert Gemini girl, who simply must be intellectually fascinated to be able to fall in love. He'll tell her some of his accomplishments (Archers are never overly modest) and many of his dreams, and he'll always be frank with her, sometimes mercilessly frank. If he doesn't quite answer all her requirements for a lover or husband, well — it's only fair to point out that no man ever does — or ever will.

As with all complex personalities, the Sagittarian man will grow to know the Gemini girl only slowly. She withholds various fragments of her multiple nature, allowing him to peek at but one at a time. When he first meets her, she'll definitely withhold. She'll project only one Twin, the one capable of charming him, naturally. She could even behave in a rare — for her — monolithic manner, listening pleasantly, but seldom chattering or interrupting. What a perfectly delightful feminine creature she is! And it's true. A Gemini girl-woman (it's more accurate to call her girl than woman, at any age) is perfectly delightful. But as for feminine, we must always remember that Gemini is essentially a masculine sign in astrology, although Mercury, her ruler, can change sex in the twinkling of an eye, to fool onlookers. Still, masculine is masculine, whatever that means today. With this girl-woman it means she is usually quite determined to get what she wants — also exceedingly capable of getting it. The trouble is, being cursed with twin desires and dual motivation, she is never sure exactly *what* she wants. What she longed for on Monday may be faded and unattractive by Thursday, perhaps even as early as Tuesday (of the same week). Often, she's torn between not only two sets of possible actions, but two sets of possible *re*actions. Should she say yes or no ? And further — will saying either make her happy — or unhappy ? He should have a little sympathy for her. Life is never easy for this woman, and love presents a problem of even greater dimensions. Then, when she does try to explain her many-faceted emotions to the Sagittarian man she is finally decided to trust, she risks being accused by him of insincerity and deception. Is that fair ?

Frank, open-hearted, and honest, the Sagittarian man is sometimes intolerant of a female he believes is not all these things herself, never mind the clever Mercurial excuses she offers. Yet she might argue back, quite correctly, that he also has two sides — for he is bold, daring and restless, and at the same time sensitive, impressionable and retiring — or rather, at different times. His two sides manifest themselves in varying moods, his likes and dislikes are very pronounced and he's extremely susceptible to tension or disharmony in his environment, especially in his love relationship. This means he can be a little edgy, easily set off by Gemini airy circumlocution into a fiery Sagittarius explosion. So it's no wonder that she may prefer to keep some things back, and allow herself to be called deceptive, rather than risk walking the plank of his disapproval. When Archers express their disapproval, it can be brutally blunt and to the point, hurtful in the extreme. This sort of thing, after being repeated several times, can trigger her into sharpening the famous Gemini verbal weapon of sarcasm, all of which can cause the love nest to shake a bit, with the Mercury Bird causing the Centaur to become mentally confused, and he, in return, slashing some deep wounds in her fragile emotions.

However, if their Sun-Moon aspects are harmonious (conjunct, sextile or trine) these little differences of opinion and techniques of controversy will almost always end up in poetic (her) and dramatic (him) declarations of renewed devotion. It's all very romantic. But a square or opposition between the Sun of one and the Moon of the other can cause constant bickering and ruffling of feathers, which could grow into more serious confrontation as the years pass. Considering that we're discussing Gemini and Sag, we'd better amend that last sentence to say "as the months pass, even the weeks." These two signs always manage to increase both Life's — and Love's — rate of speed.

Her soaring flights of fairyland fancies can be too intangible and mystical for him. There is little or no impracticality in Jupiter visions. Most Sagittarians are capable of foreseeing and prognosticating the outcome of a plan from its initial inception. Most Geminis are not, and she would do well to imitate those qualities in him which she lacks, among them constancy of purpose and single-mindedness. Being Air, she is cooler emotionally than this man, whose nature is more fiery and passionate. Therefore, he may be the more affectionate of the two in the physical expression of love — more in need of the touching things. She would be happier if their minds touched more often.

Sexually the two of them possibly could reach a rare harmony of mutual experience through their lovemaking, because the ultimate meaning of sex is the fulfillment of an intense desire for each person to blend with — to actually *become* — the other, inasmuch as this is an earthly possibility, in order to achieve Oneness of spirit, mind and body. No two people can be more successful in this than this man and woman of opposite Sun Sign polarity, since sex between them — as with all 7-7 influenced lovers — is always based on their basic mutual need to *become each other*, and therefore, to become a more complete person.

With some Gemini-Sag relationships, a sort of truce is managed, causing very little quarreling to be observed or heard by friends and neighbors. (I won't say by families or relatives, because neither one of them is excessively devoted to blood ties.) When such periods of peace and quiet are observed, it can usually be credited to her Gemini talent for escaping anything unpleasant. Her power to resist obstacles or to push disagreeable people aside is not great at all, but her magnificent sensorium, or network of sensitive nerve signals, often warns her in advance of approaching thunderstorms, so she can duck under a tree and avoid getting wet, or being struck by lightning.

She sidesteps the issues with her Mercury agility, or simply pretends not to understand why he is so upset — and after a while, the typical Archer will give up trying to pin her down to a discussion that actually goes anywhere. It always winds up twisting in circles, which doesn't bother her — she loves circles — but which can leave him mentally and emotionally exhausted. So he could retreat more and more into the newspaper, go out — or go to bed early — and alone — while their communication suffers.

This isn't the best possible state of affairs, of course, but it does make them more desirable neighbors than the type of Gemini-Sagittarius couple who argue all night, expressing every disagreement loudly and clearly. It's seldom that these two will love without some amount of tension, however excellent their Sun-Moon aspects. Their basic natures are not the kind to suffer in absolute, masochistic silence. Since they constitute a 7-7 Sun Sign Pattern, there are always all those opposing qualities which have to be balanced, and balancing is an art which is mastered only after long practice. Ask any tightrope walker in a circus. Of course, so much balancing can wear them out from time to time, but it's better to wear out than rust out, as many lovers do, who have nothing in common at all, not even a mutual desire to adopt each other's different vices and virtues. Gemini and Sagittarius do have some things in common. They both like to read and they both like to talk. But she colors what she reads with her vivid imagination, and he sprinkles his talk with more truth, perhaps, than she wants to hear or dares to face.

She believes the world should be a better place, and her weaving bits and pieces of colorful imagery distorts the truth of existence just enough to make it so for her. Is that wrong? To him it is. He wants the world to be a better place also, but he's convinced that you first have to face the facts square-on before you can hope to change them. *In this, they differ deeply.*

This man and this woman can find much happiness in their relationship if it is also a marriage of mutual endeavor, like a husband-wife team involved in publicity, publishing, the arts, science or medicine. The excitement of the dream will carry them through any minor squalls. When their eyes are fastened on the stars, instead of constantly on each other, they can make a fabulous team, in every way. In Greek mythology, it's said that "Mercury gives joy to Jupiter." Likewise, Gemini can give to Sagittarius — great joy. What can he give her? He can give her the gift of slowing her down, of protecting her with his larger wings, for the Archer likes to fly, too, in his imagination, as high as his arrows. But maybe these lovers should stay just a little distance apart, as they sail the kites of their aspirations. If they stand too close together, on a windy day, the strings may get hopelessly tangled.

The Sagittarian man was born full of *ideals*. The Gemini woman was born full of *ideas*. There is a difference between the two words — the letter *l*, for *love*. An *idea*, when it's nurtured with love, will reach for the higher octave of itself, and become an *ideal*. If they love enough, the Archer can take his Gemini lady's ideas, transmute them into Jupiter ideals, and illuminate her already-bright mind with the light of the difference.

GEMINI *Man* SAGITTARIUS *Woman*

Also he was fond of variety, and the sport that
engrossed him one moment would suddenly cease to
engage him, so there was always the possibility
that the next time you fell he would let you go.

When a Sagittarius girl falls in love, her whole spirit reaches out like a trusting puppy, hungry for affection, ready to return it in full measure. Only later do the accumulated mistakes of the years cause her to wear the theatrical mask of skepticism and cynicism, which she covers with the bright greasepainted features of the clown. Her innate honesty and refreshing frankness would touch the hardest masculine heart. But sometimes it only tempts a certain kind of Gemini male to test his cleverness by twisting her integrity, her ideals, and even her love, with complex mind-bending games. He courts disaster by doing this. Not his. Hers. Gemini, somehow, always manages to escape in the final reel. It's the sincerely brokenhearted Sagittarian girl who bears the scars of such abusive tactics of the Mercury intellect, sometimes for many moons . . . sometimes permanently.

Before it's over, however, she may call on Jupiter's power of excess, and tear a few jagged holes in the fabric of the Twins' precious freedom robe, with some fiery, emotional scenes of furious passion, which (if he's the type of Gemini we're describing, who has allowed his negative Twin to take control of him) he will probably richly deserve.

This girl is warm, open-hearted, desperately in need of both affection and emotional stability. If the Sun-Moon interchange in their horoscopes is negative, she could be shopping for it in the wrong place, for Gemini can be cruelly detached, cold and unsympathetic when his negative Twin takes over. What happened to the light, gay, tender, loving man she thought he was, the one who wrote such moving poems to her, who raced her to the Moon and back, kissed away her tears with that little-boy-lopsided-grin? He's still there, playing an unkind game of hide-and-seek, somewhere within the multiple-reflected image identities of this complicated man. He can leave her weeping, with an uncaring, bored shrug of his shoulders . . . with not even a backward glance of regret, and the next day, return with a bunch of violets, a new poem and his old gentleness, begging forgiveness and swearing his devotion anew.

It's hardly the thing she needs. A Sagittarius girl is deeply vulnerable. This sort of on-again, off-again romance, ranging from cruel iciness to detached boredom (and frequently outright deception) mingled with beautiful romance, from a man who can charm hissing serpents into docility, may cause her to tremble in her soul, make her unsure of herself as a female, or even as a human being. About this time, he may start his pseudo-psychoanalysis. He isn't the one who needs therapy. It's *her*. He might even manage to convince her of this probable lie. Geminis can convince anyone of anything the first dozen times, until their gullible victims catch on to the trickery. A Mercury-ruled man can commit the most outrageous deeds, then expect the woman who loves him to apologize to *him* as if the misdeeds were her own. You can see why these men make super salesmen. They can sell anything to anyone, and what's more, they seldom get caught when they slip under the line or skip around the alphabet, avoiding the letter of the law of love — or any other kind of law.

Of course, this is only true of Geminis whose natal Suns are severely afflicted by heavy planets at birth. Such Twins deserve to be astrologically exposed to Sagittarian girls who might find a tragic end to romance with this type. The great majority of Gemini men, thankfully, possess far more intelligence and wit than flaws of character.

Still, it must not be forgotten that the negative-type Geminis have broken more hearts and shredded more lives than could be pieced back together with an ocean of Elmer's glue. They have no sympathy coming to them until they become more introspective, and show some compassion for the havoc they caused others through their lack of human warmth, their cruel and curious need to win every game of mental blackjack they play. Unfortunately, even this kind of Gemini is almost irresistible in the act of asking, with apparently innocent eyes (though they are shifting, if you look closely), "Who, me ?" Yes, *you*. One can often spot this brand of Gemini male by the number of aliases or pseudonyms he uses. Many positive Mercury people playfully hide behind several names, but *this* type does it for more sinister reasons. Isn't that right, Jim ? I mean David — or is it Mel — or Fred ? Whatever. By their words and deeds shall ye know them. If only they would truly know themselves.

The more illuminated, charming and near-magical Gemini man has a strong appeal for the typical Sagittarius woman, however — and she for him. Opposites don't always attract, but when they are members of opposite sexes (opposing male and female) they often do. Gemini and Sagittarius are horoscopically opposed, and the powerful pull begins with this feeling each has that the other has qualities intensely desirable of attainment. It's true. Each does possess what the other lacks. Consequently, they can teach one another many marvelous lessons that rhyme with happy. The physical magnetism between them is difficult to resist. So are the mental and emotional vibrations. And so, it is with a haunting wonder that they gravitate toward each other . . . . if they meet under the right planetary aspects, when the stars are smiling on a breezy night, and the Moon is new enough to wish on.

They share an eternal youthfulness of spirit, an inquisitive turn of mind, a responsiveness to Nature and a mutual need for freedom, for space between them, so they can move toward their goals. Both of them like to dream alone for a while, then return to each other's arms for encouragement. But alone is not the same as lonely. Both the Gemini man and the Sagittarius woman seek the gregarious life, surrounding themselves with people, because they have a secret fear of loneliness.

She will almost surely have a pet. A kitten or a dog. And give it odd names. The most precious girl Archer I know named one of her kittens "Frog," the other simply (logically) "Cat." He likes pets too, but may not feel quite the same fierce devotion as she does. Gemini will love a pet only as long as it doesn't interfere with his own pleasures or require money he would prefer to spend on himself, whereas a Sagittarian woman will often sacrifice her own convenience for an animal she loves. There are other subtle differences in their natures. Gemini thirsts for new horizons to soar, and so does she. But she also has need of a warm and steady hand to hold while she's soaring. He likes to hold hands too, but if *she* lets go, he'll wave goodbye more or less cheerily, while she may lose her way if *he* lets go.

Their sexual life is usually where they find solace from their conflicts in other areas, as with all 7-7 Sun Sign Patterns. The strong chemical attraction between them frequently increases as time goes by, and even if it should decrease, it seems to always be there, latent, waiting to be rekindled, to be called upon to mend the cracks in their relationship.

There is a certain passion of the mind between them, which creates a fertile ground for physical consummation. Often, their sexual lovemaking will begin long before bedtime — perhaps at breakfast, through messages spoken by the eyes across the room, a romantic note left where she will find it, the shared intimacy of a familiar smile or special, private nickname which, translated, means: "I love you — I need you — I want you."

The pitfall of the sex between them is that he may use Gemini trickery on her occasionally. A Gemini male is not above inciting a quarrel for the deliberate purpose of increasing emotion or desire in his partner. Anger has a strange way of exciting passion between these two. Then the argument is resolved by physical union — or it should be. But is it? He's capable of bringing it up for lengthy discussion again after their closeness, when it should have been buried and forgotten. To be fair to him, we have to admit that she tends to do the same thing. They should both learn to bury disagreements after intimacy. Why use sex as a weapon against each other? But Gemini and Sagittarius often do. Jealousy is the cause of many of their disputes, with good reason. Neither sign is noted for impeccable faithfulness. Both are too curious, too changeable, too moody and desirous of variety to be snowflake-pure-loyal.

If their Sun-Moon aspects are favorable, or if one has a Capricorn, Taurus or Scorpio Ascendent, they can manage to remain totally faithful as long as they're together. Otherwise, there will be some straying or infidelity, even if it takes the form of only a casual, light flirtation, out in the open, never physically consummated. He is more apt to wander than she. But Sagittarian girls catch on quickly to the various games taught them by Mercury Birds. Then the feathers will fly.

He can be so . . . . . moody. First, the quick blush of happiness, the beating wings of excitement. Then the frown, suddenly, with no warning. The averted eyes. Sadness, deepening into depression. Moments later, the Mercurial quicksilver grin again — and a merry invitation to skip pebbles in the lake or listen to frogs sing love songs at the edge of a magical woodland he knows. First he asks her to make cinnamon toast. Then he's not hungry. With variations, the theme of their romance goes pretty much like that, and she still bravely tries to sing along.

Of course, the Sagittarius woman can have a few moods herself. Being also a dual sign, she can change from sensitive to introspective, then back to temperamental and caustic. If one can manage to stay "up" while the other is "down," and vice versa, they can pull each other through the scary times. Both "up" together would be nice, but then that means they will both be "down" together. Two Biorhythm charts would benefit this man and woman immensely. The name is Biorhythm Computers, Inc., 298 Fifth Avenue, New York, N.Y. (212-239-8422). I couldn't give them a nicer gift than that advice and name.

He'll have to curb his tendency to sarcasm when he's annoyed; and she'll have to curb her tendency to tactless remarks, when what he needs is her tenderness and her understanding. Her blunt truth almost always hurts. So does his sarcasm. The Sagittarius girl, with all her innocent candor, has no conception of the word. It means . . . well, sarcasm usually means saying something exactly the opposite from what you really think and believe, and exaggerating the falsehood for emphasis of the truth, such as — "Of *course* I don't object to a three-hundred-dollar phone bill, darling. It makes me feel important to pay the telephone company all that money, even if it does mean we have to cancel our vacation this summer." You see? Like that. Sarcasm. She'll be both hurt and puzzled. Why doesn't he just say straight out that he's angry about the phone bill being so high, and disappointed that it might mean no vacation this summer? (Then she could say she's sorry, and work overtime, or take an extra job for a few weeks, to make up the difference. As it is, she *won't* say she's sorry, so there!)

Why doesn't he just say so? Because he's a poetic dreamer, a Gemini, dear girl, incapable of saying exactly what he means. To live in any degree of contentment with this clever and marvelously fascinating man, Sag will have to pay attention not to what his lips say but read the truth only in his eyes. Yet, his eyes are forever darting here and there, and are often difficult to read . . . the expression in them keeps changing.

The only thing more stinging than the Gemini man's sharp sarcasm is the girl Archer's blunt honesty. This pair, when they're ill-mated, can verbally slice each other's hearts to ribbons. But there's a lighter side to their relationship. There's always another side, when two double signs get together, for better or for worse — and it *can* be better. They will at least respect one another's intellect, and find their mutual moods more fascinating than the boring sameness of others.

A Gemini man likes to gaze at the galaxies, meditating on the myriad worlds out there in space. Then unexpectedly, he shifts his awareness to himself, and wonders — "Do you suppose there are also myriad worlds within the space of ME, that I might explore?" His ever-present Twin cries, "Yes! There are!" . . . . . and another adventure begins. If the Sagittarian woman wants to hold this man, her labor of love will be to join him on his quest for the Neverland, trying not to resent the third person who must always tag along — his shadow. She might also try, as Wendy did with the Mercurial Peter Pan, to stitch his shadow to him tightly and neatly. So he won't lose the other half of himself so often. That's a kind of riddle, but Jupiter will whisper to her heart the answer, if she listens.

☆ ☆ ☆ ☆ ☆ ☆

GEMINI

Air — Mutable — Positive
Ruled by Mercury
Symbol: The Twins
Day Forces — Masculine

CAPRICORN

Earth — Cardinal — Negative
Ruled by Saturn
Symbol: The Goat
Night Forces — Feminine

The **GEMINI-CAPRICORN** *Relationship*

*The roar of it echoed through the mountains, and
the echoes seemed to cry savagely, "Where are they,
where are they, where are they?"*

What are these Gemini people trying to do? Where do they stand? Where are they?" cries the honestly puzzled Capricorn, trying to deal with the Twins. "They are nowhere," answers the astrologer. "They are nowhere, yet they are everywhere. It is difficult to tell, without taking into consideration that each Gemini is at least two people."

Do you think for one minute that a Goat is going to stand for that kind of an obtuse answer? No way. It's too ephemeral, entirely too abstract to be a practical solution to the problem. So don't try astrology on Capricorns whose lives are being tossed out of their orbit of set routine by the antics of a pair of Twins hiding within one Gemini. It won't work. I'm not sure just what will work, but that won't work.

You might try explaining Gemini to Capricorn by pointing out that Gemini is an Air Sign, therefore Mercury-ruled people are very much like the wind. The wind is invisible, yet strong. It can be a friend or an enemy. It's more or less neutral (like Switzerland). Sometimes it will uproot entire buildings. Sometimes it will not. There's just no telling with the wind — or with Gemini. The wind is free and unpredictable, and it's impossible to guess in which direction it will blow. It is a question asked only by the foolish; consequently, any astrologer who tries to answer it is a fool. Still, all that won't cut any ice or slice any pickles with the Goat, who will, after all your trouble, continue to demand which way this particular Gemini's wind (or hot air) is blowing. Just tell him North. It is blowing North. Then forget about it. Even if Gemini's emotional wind was blowing South, East, or West at the time under discussion, you can be sure it will be blowing North within a couple of hours. You see? There are always ways to handle these things if you try.

The taciturn Capricorn will not admire Gemini's verbal gift if it becomes too profuse. Although most Goats enjoy listening vicariously to gossip about the famous (those who have achieved, if only in their own communities), they are seldom inclined to partake of it personally. (Gossip, I mean. They are *always* willing to partake of fame.) To Saturn, the ruler of Capricorn, caution is the beginning of wisdom, in speech as well as in action. Symbolically, Saturn is the planet of wisdom gained through long tests of initiation in many incarnations, traditionally the ruler of the Hebrew culture. Also the ruler of exasperatingly bossy employers, grandparents, anyone in authority, including the government — all those people and institutions tending to get their kicks from saying "NO." "Absolutely, NO" — (for your own good, of course). "Yes" is a foreign word to the typical Goat.

Capricorns have trouble even pronouncing it, some of them substituting words like "okay" or "I-suppose-so." I even know a Colorado Goat who substitutes the word "Yippee" (spoken very softly) for YES — an inexplicable habit, but nonetheless typical. So, Cappy does not like to say YES. I think it has something to do with money or financial security. To Capricorns, "no" seems to rhyme more with "dough" — and "yes" rhymes with "less," especially when it's spoken without due and proper consideration. Something like that.

This is a 6-8 Sun Sign Pattern, meaning that Capricorn will attract Gemini for a reason relating to mystery, death, sex, reincarnation, hypnosis, psychiatry — or some bending of the mind, even drugs. One of these areas will be involved in a subtle way or subconsciously. As for the reverse, the Goat will always find some useful purpose for the Twins, and often Gemini will end up by in some way serving the slightly selfish Capricorn. Self-sacrifice of one kind or another is bound to be present in the relationship, whether it be within the realm of the family group, business, friendship or lovers. But then, someone has to sacrifice when two people are as essentially different in character as these two.

Capricorns are clothed in an antique and thoroughly elegant manner, such an exalted aura being only proper as the means of radiating the Saturnine wisdom and skill through experience. The attitudes of some Goats almost whiff of mothballs. Most of them despise modern furniture, leaning more toward the traditional, the old, the *lasting*. Let Geminis pursue the trains of modern thought, deck their homes with plastic and shining chrome. To Cappy, the tried and true seems more sensible. No one can argue the superiority of craftsmanship. I certainly wouldn't. But Gemini might. The Mercury-ruled can argue on behalf of any weak point and make it seem reasonable or feasible. Except to the Goat. Capricorns are rarely the victims of Gemini persuasion. Oh, it happens, but when it does, which is seldom, Cappies will catch on quickly to the manipulative mental game, sense that crooked psychological dice are being used against them, and back away, determined not to be caught twice with their caution down.

There's more than a trace of the magnificence and serenity of Nature in Capricorns, something of the mountain goat's dignified bearing. All this naturally draws the restless Gemini, who seeks repose of the spirit more desperately than is ever shown or admitted. The serious but kindly and gentle Capricorn man, woman or child can supply a stable, calm, and rational basis of emotional security that the Twins find both comforting and necessary, a place to fold their wings between flights. Life moves so swiftly for Gemini, it's often a frightening blur, and on occasion, they need to have the inner frenzy stilled. Capricorn seems almost to be a resident of stillness, of silent, deep-green woods, and can bring many moments of tranquility to the Twins who stop to rest awhile. With Capricorn, Gemini may study the forms of Life and Love at Saturn's more leisurely pace.

There are also lessons Capricorn can learn from Gemini. Innocently self-centered, intellectually independent and curious, Gemini is magically able to temporarily enter the realms of every book ever read, every movie ever seen, every symphony ever heard — to move as naturally and freely in that so-called imaginary world as if it were the kingdom of his or her birth.

Consequently, the Twins can present the Goats with the valuable knowledge of how to be more than just a visitor to the worlds of literature, music, art — for these worlds of make-believe are where they live. Gemini returns to this Earth only by karmic obligation, to re-enter a flesh prison after a long spell of daydreaming on other levels of awareness. Capricorn benefits from this, because it is so difficult for the Goat to comprehend the reality of any place but Earth, Capricorn being so rooted in it, so practical and *down-to-earth* on both a conscious and a subconscious level.

There are, of course, rare Capricorns whose imaginations flash during a summer thunderstorm, whose spirits wonder and wander on a quiet, star-filled night, who display a pixie sense of humor, understand about psychometry, UFOs, telepathy . . . . and the Great Pyramid's mysterious wonders.

But the more typical Goat does not waste time pondering anything which can't be taken apart and put back together again by blueprint. When Capricorns fly, they make their reservations early, to be safe. When they go by car, they take a road map, to be sure. But there are no blueprints, no maps to guide the astral traveler. Trips out-of-the-body, into worlds beyond the material or the physical senses, don't require a reservation — only faith.

It must be admitted that Gemini, when investigating other worlds, is not necessarily motivated by faith or spiritual hunger. The Twins are usually motivated by simple curiosity, the kind that killed the legendary cat but doesn't seem to be fatal to Mercury Birds.

A surprising number of Capricorns satisfy their soul hunger in the Saturn-approved method of becoming involved in art. They sometimes collect it, enjoy it, become patrons of artists — or paint, sketch or draw themselves. Some enter the acting profession or become dramatists. A few follow music in some manner. But whatever the Goat is or does, both feet will remain planted firmly on terra firma, and how far can you swing on a star when both feet are on the ground ? It requires a bit of stretching to enter other galaxies. Still, any creative endeavor of any kind is akin to a dawning comprehension of an existence beyond the five senses, bearing a hint of a sixth, even a seventh . . . . and more. The ancients claimed that Saturn is a seventh-dimensional planet. We live our daily lives in the third dimension, while Time itself, an eternal Now, as Einstein knew, is the fourth dimension. Surely the seventh must carry a higher wisdom than even Gemini can contemplate. But Saturn guards its secret well, with the usual Capricorn reticence and silence.

Capricorns are inclined to keep their own counsel. Geminis are born and natural communicators. Which is right ? Both are — each in his or her own way, as long as neither interferes with the other doing his own thing. Or her own thing. With these two Sun Signs, doing *their* own thing" is rare. But the dictionary definition of "rare" gives a choice between "uncommon" . . . . or "very beautiful."

☆ ☆ ☆ ☆ ☆ ☆

GEMINI *Woman* CAPRICORN *Man*

. . . . . the island was looking out for them. It is only thus that anyone may sight those magic shores.

"There it is," said Peter calmly.

"Where, where ?"

"Where all the arrows are pointing."

No matter how brief or long a time these two remain together, the Capricorn man will never be able to figure out why the Gemini girl cannot see clearly what to him is very plain: the consequences of word and action, which are, inevitably, either reward or punishment. Newton's law of "For every action, there is a *reaction*" is obvious to him. Why can she not see it too ?

To her way of looking at things, his error is in seeing the material world as reality — and imagination as a separate, amusing pastime. Her own mind is busy probing, dissecting, searching, calculating and wandering on the wind, all at once, which can cause two worlds to fuse as one — the "real" world and the world of imagination, of *possibilities.*

The responses such a mercurial attitude evoke in the Goat are multiple and consecutive. First, he responds with excitement. After a while, excitement turns to apprehension. None of these things she says and does make sense to him, from a logical, practical standpoint. Finally, his apprehension turns to severity — and then he turns off. Once Capricorn has decided a subject is not worth discussing, that's it. He can be abrupt, terse and stern. "We won't talk about it anymore. The subject is closed." No subject is ever completely closed to the Gemini girl. It is always open for new argument, fresh points of view. Yet, even with all her charm, she will have difficulty turning the Goat back on, once he's been turned off.

Gemini's occasional frenetic activity may seem frivolous to Cappy. She has an apparent lack of attachment in her engagement with Life. But he will find sufficient cause for admiration in studying the amazing way her mind works — untangling knots with the greatest of ease, arriving at solutions to intricate problems effortlessly. And she will, initially at least, respect his wisdom — a different matter altogether from her own quick intellect and cleverness. This can create a bond of yearning between them, which can be both purifying and strengthening. After a time, however, the essential differences in their natures may become more visible. There is a certain gravity to Capricorn which can depress her — a curious moodiness in her own make-up which can be disturbing to him. Often, their dispositions, personalities, characters and motivations are miles apart.

Let's take their mutual families. If he's a typical Capricorn, he is very close to Mummy, Daddy, Auntie, Uncle Hymie — and cousins by the carload. No, I didn't forget his siblings. How could anyone forget them when they are around so much ? When they aren't around, he talks about them. If she's a typical Gemini, she may be genuinely fond of her folks, even behaving affectionately toward them in an airy, casual way. But she does not feel quite so cemented to family ties as the Goat. She goes her multiple ways, they go theirs, and if their paths should cross now and then — great ! If she refuses to allow her own relatives to smother her, obviously she isn't going to be overjoyed about having *his* camping around all the time and being the main topic of conversation, even in their absence.

Then there's the way they feel about money. They both like it. Neither of them has a thing against it. But she uses it to spread around, to spend and enjoy. He uses it as a sort of emotional tranquilizer. As long as he knows it's in the bank, he can relax and breathe easy, confident in the knowledge that he's a solid citizen, to whom no unpredictable financial disasters can occur. Capricorn feels about money the way gold-mining king Winfield Scott Stratton felt about gold — that the safest place to keep it is in the ground. To Cappy, the safest place to keep money is in the bank. The Gemini woman can't comprehend what good it does to have it just sitting there doing nothing when it could be spent. Interest, my dear. It draws interest. Then she might say, with one of her sudden Mercurial twists of mind, "but that only makes *more* money — to leave just sitting there, doing nothing." What does she mean, doing *nothing* ? It's *working*, isn't it ? And it's giving him peace of mind. It's giving *her* a bad case of frustration.

When the Capricorn man is upset, cross, or out of sorts, he pouts, becomes silent and sullen. When she is in the same state, she can be caustic, bitter and sarcastic. His moods are dark brown, indigo, black and blue, yet they are, to some extent, predictable. Hers never are. One moment she can be as gently exhilarating as a spring breeze, the next, as destructive as a tornado — first restlessly active, then passive and uncommunicative. She smiles, her expressive eyes flashing quicksilver loveliness. Enchanting. Out of nowhere, a frown line appears on her forehead. Now there's a tear in the corner of her eye. Her lips tremble. She is beautiful when she is sad. Suddenly a joyous thought overcomes her, she leaps up, throws her arms around him and plants a kiss on his nose. Her changing moods are as flighty as Tinker Bell's, by turns all frivolous fancy, like a butterfly, then logically concise, one after the other, in swift progression . . . . . first deeply intellectual, then totally abstract, almost mystical. But she does not remain in the dreamy state for long. Gemini is too much of a natural skeptic to be a true mystic.

Now and then, one comes across a Capricorn man who loves to solve mysteries, to answer riddles, and this kind of Goat will follow the Twins down the twisting, turning Mercurial bypaths and shortcuts with overwhelming fascination. She is like the multicolored, scattered pieces of a puzzle, waiting to be put together. Besides, she is dainty and feminine, with a lilting laugh, and she looks good on his arm. Capricorns do enjoy possessing a woman of the type who may be shown off to advantage in front of others. To gain the love of such an exciting creature is assuredly an achievement, an accomplishment of no small order, and the Saturn-ruled have this thing about achievement and accomplishment. The Goat must climb. Capricorn men enjoy the view from the top of the mountain. They like to be looked up to and respected. Displaying a Gemini wife or lover (with him it will probably be wife) who is several women in one, each charming, lovely, talented, bright and feminine — will cause less fortunate males to envy him. Just so he remembers the astrological advice that, regardless of her delightful femininity, her mind is masculine. This will be brought home to him on more than one occasion.

There are Capricorn men who infrequently kick up their heels in a merry dance, especially in later life when they rush to capture what they never discovered in youth, or were too shy to seek, too busy achieving and working to enjoy — just as there are some Goats who are quicker of movement, faster of speech, more careless than cautious. But these are definitely exceptions to Saturn's rule. Most Goats are models of restraint. In fact, his romantic overtures in the beginning are often so tremulous and cautious, so slow and deliberate, that she at first inclines her head to one side, as if she were harkening to a whisper. He'll probably be wearing clothing of subdued good taste, smile at her in a particularly engaging, lazy fashion, his gentleness and soothing stability mingled in just the right amounts to intrigue her into thinking this is one man who will understand her, and not be impatient with her.

He seems happy to please her, touchingly grateful to have a woman to please. It brings him contentment to be in love, and she senses he is not one to be unfaithful to his vows, once committed. It is at this point, perversely, that she may get nervous. It's the word "commitment." Geminis do not like even a hint of commitment. If love is real, it will last. She would like that, of course, but she would not like to sign any long-term leases on romance. Just let it develop. If it turns into a forever thing, wonderful! But to ask for a guarantee — to *expect* a guarantee — is not the way the game is played with Gemini.

In a physical sense, they may surprise each other by exchanging an instinctive understanding of mutual longings. Sex is not something akin to blazing fires of uncontrollable passion to either of them. Both Capricorn and Gemini seek sexual unity as a means of rest and comfort. Normally, they will not make excessive emotional demands of one another. However, there may be infrequent occasions when his need for playful physical and affectionate displays of bear hugs and the like do not find the desired response in her — or when the Gemini woman needs words of love, verbal expressions to excite her into lovemaking, and does not receive them.

Other than such areas of possible discontent and mild frustration, these two could be cozily compatible in their sexual sharing of love. Because their togetherness is influenced strongly by the 6-8 vibration, sex may be a dominant, or at least a most important factor in their relationship, and he will possibly have magnetized her in the beginning in a strongly physical way, which is not likely to fade, as long as they remain together, which will likely be permanently, surprising all their friends (and his relatives) — if there is a Sun-Moon conjunction, sextile or trine between their mutual horoscopes. Even without such planetary help, they will probably remain friends after they drift apart. Not all 6-8 Sun Sign Pattern couples do, but the Twins and the Goat very well may.

Love has a way of melting the ice from a Saturn-ruled heart. Something about this man, when he has melted, will make her tremble with anticipation of the picture of absolute rightness he projects when he's with her — the promise of ultimate happiness through their relationship. Later, it may seem to her that this unspoken promise has been broken, as Life begins to appear drab to the Gemini woman, who feels chained to Capricorn's rather mundane, albeit secure, existence. Still, she should not forget that he's the most likely candidate of all lovers and husbands to be exciting during the golden years, becoming more youthful, turning more free (more like *her*) the older he gets. If she will wait, that promise of rightness may be kept after all.

Gemini is impatient and does not like to wait. But she should make the effort, because if she does, the rewards will be well worth it, and she could discover with him a great secret — that in the halting of restless movement, the true form and shape of love can be discovered, its deeper beauty revealed — and beauty is what her divided heart has been seeking since she was a little girl. Patience. Patience is the key word with this man. She must cultivate it.

There could be a Gemini girl in love with a Goat who reads this and wonders why they should need such advice. They are so very happy — right now. Well, you don't teach someone to swim while they're drowning. You teach them ahead of time — just in case. The word again, Twins, is: PATIENCE.

☆　☆　☆　☆　☆　☆

GEMINI *Man* CAPRICORN *Woman*

◆ ◄◆►◆ ◆

*"Keep back, lady, no one is going to catch me and
make me a man . . . ."*

She had to tell him.

*"I am old, Peter. I am ever
so much more than twenty. I grew up long ago."*

"You promised not to!"

"I couldn't help it."

The Capricorn woman cannot help it if she is wise beyond her years, any more than the Gemini man can help it if he is little-boy-irresponsible at times. In our society, until very recently, the man was supposed to be the strong, mature and practical one. A woman was expected to be flighty, somewhat unpredictable and helpless. Now that we have Women's Liberation groups loudly ringing the bells of the New Age in our ears, we might permit him to be sensitive, changeable, and lighthearted now and then — and allow her to be steady and sensible. But before the dawning of the Aquarian Age, they wouldn't have had a chance.

It's a lucky thing for the Goat and the Twins that we've finally recognized her right to be practical and intelligent, along with his right to daydream occasionally, even weep when he is touched by beauty. It's quite fortunate for all of us, but especially for these two. The differences in their personalities are enough with which to cope — who needs the extra problem of trying to fit into the predesigned, prejudiced images of someone's idea of Man and Woman? Not Gemini and Capricorn. They have plenty to keep them busy in the complicated pastime of capturing the harmony of compatibility between their two divergent natures.

The sex of the two Sun Signs is as it should be, at first glance. Hers is a feminine sign, his a masculine sign. That is, well — it's not quite that simple. True, Capricorn is a feminine sign, but it's ruled by Old Man Saturn, who is definitely masculine, all the way. And Gemini is a masculine sign, but ruled by tricky Mercury, the Great Pretender, a planet known for its predilection toward deceiving, capable of switching from masculine to feminine, and back to masculine, in the flicker of a firefly. That's pretty swift. Did you ever try to time the flicker of a firefly? So, there will be problems. Not insurmountable, just on occasion, annoying. Perhaps frustrating would be a better word.

There could be times when he'll accuse her of being callous and unsympathetic — times when she'll accuse him of being fickle and emotionally immature. In a sense, she is those things — just as, to a certain degree, he does possess those traits. Yet, a Capricorn woman can also be affectionate, loyal, and a veritable twinkling rainbow of humor when she feels she's on safe ground, not the shaky terrain of continual change and movement — which may open up and swallow her. (All Goats have a subliminal fear of earthquakes.) Just as a Gemini man can project a truth more glowing than she realizes if he's allowed the freedom of expression he needs, not hounded by suspicions, depressing predictions of the future . . . . . and nagging. Criticism and emotional severity will never bring out the best in the Twins.

The praying mantis is an odd insect, in that the female of the species often chews off the head of the male during the mating act itself. He read about this somewhere (Geminis have read about *everything*), and he's inclined to feel like a male mantis himself when the woman he loves insists on chewing up his self-confidence with rigid, unbending disapproval at the same time she's declaring her devotion.

She may be the one who should handle the money in the family. It will probably *be* a family eventually, if she has any choice in the matter. Cappy seldom loans herself out for romantic interludes of a temporary type. The future intentions are usually firmly understood before she dabbles or dallies. But back to money and the probability that she's the best bet to hold the purse strings. Not that he isn't quick and bright with figures — sometimes too quick and bright. Most Geminis can cause a computer to turn green with envy. It's just that she'll have a way of spending it more sensibly, investing it more wisely, some kind of magic touch in pressing the bank balance higher and higher — whereas he may possess the knack of causing it to sink lower and lower. (Unless, of course, his Moon or Ascendent happens to be in Virgo, Taurus, Capricorn or Cancer.)

Oddly, both these Sun Signs are frequently called "cold" emotionally by astrology — not to mention by their friends and relatives. She, because of Saturn's icy rulership and stern influence over her behavior — he, because of belonging to the always somewhat detached Air Element. But she is, nonetheless, capable of an earthy, even a fierce, love, despite Saturn's iron control over her emotions and his constant admonition against releasing them until she's certain a relationship is genuine, and has a chance of being permanent.

As for him, he's not yet learned, in a spiritual sense, love's true ecstasy — or its anguish. He hasn't, esoterically and karmically, experienced its real depth. Still, he looks forward to it with a special kind of excitement — and is not anticipation magical too ? It is, and his enthusiastic searching can cause her own dreams to soar, while her quiet kind of love, like a steady candle flame, lights the way for his search and offers him a soothing refuge during his periods of self-doubt.

Sometimes a Capricorn woman can be almost too good, too perfect, too reliable for a Gemini man to handle. He feels caught in the prison of her very emotional steadiness, inexplicably, as if her devotion itself were an affront to him . . . but only because he suspects he cannot duplicate it, which both frightens and saddens him. And so he may secretly resent her affectional dependability — and run away, perhaps, for fleeting periods, then return to bask in it again — another facet of his twin confusion in matters of the heart.

Due to their natural inclinations (and disinclinations), their sexual relationship may not always be a smoldering volcano of intensity. Yet, strangely, it may fulfill the desire they both have for physical lovemaking, to be comforting and close but not all-consuming. Even during their most intimate moments, he needs to feel his own independence and freedom. So does she, surprisingly enough. A Capricorn woman, considering Saturn's firm hold on her, isn't likely to abandon herself to passion with anyone, not really-truly-all-the-way. Neither does the Gemini man, who is, at the core of his nature, actually two men. One watches the emotional involvement while remaining detached from it — the other experiences. This is how the Gemini Sun Sign learns, at the Mercury level of awareness. Still this woman may somehow, in a way he can't explain, attract him physically, To him Capricorn represents the eighth astrological house of sexual mystery, as well as the deeper secrets of life and death.

The typical Goat Girl lives in a serene, traditional world of practical activity, where wisdom is Queen. He lives in an enchanted world, peopled with myriad fancies, teeming with mental activity, where curiosity is King. It can be a lovely experiment and a beneficial experience for them to visit each other's world, from time to time — not for the purpose of fault-finding and criticism, but as one visits any faraway kingdom, enjoying the strangeness and beauty, yet glad to return home to the familiar.

If they travel a lot he will be happier. She will be less so — (unless her Moon or Ascendent is in Gemini also, or in Aries, Leo, Sagittarius, or Pisces). This is not a woman who can pitch a tent and call it home. Because of her reverse aging process, a gift from Saturn, as she grows older, she'll become more vulnerable to wanderlust, and the mention or thought of a trip may excite her, soften her eyes and lift her spirits — as long as she's sure the trip or voyage will eventually lead back home. Although there are a flock of Capricorn career women, she's still a lady who's essentially more content to sit by the hearth, like a cricket, than lead the life of a nomad or gypsy.

The Gemini man has nothing against sitting and dreaming before the home fires himself, except when his restless yearnings periodically attack him, with little warning. He can go months, years, acting the part of the perfect family man — then, WHOOSH! a spring breeze comes along — or even a winter wind — to sweep him and his dreams into a new adventure, even if it's only a trip to a neighboring city, where he can lose himself for a few days in order to find himself again.

As with many 6-8 Sun Sign Patterns, these two probably met only when someone else introduced them or brought them together in some way. It's seldom that Gemini and Capricorn gravitate toward each other magnetically, on their own — unless her Sun was trining his Moon at birth, or vice versa, or both. Once they do notice each other, however, the 6-8 vibration begins to vibrate between them, steadily increasing in strength.

A Gemini man is capable of a great deal of badinage, but it's often only used as camouflage. He feels people would never believe the naked truth anyway. It's too obvious. And so, he disguises it. I know that's confusing, but most everything about Gemini is confusing. A little of this and a little of that. Take Gemini Bert Lance, former director of the Office of Management and Budget of the Carter Administration, who was forced to resign in 1978 under a cloud of scandal involving his former questionable banking practices. During a speech at the convention of the American Bankers' Association in Florida, shortly after his resignation, one of the members angrily remarked that "Bert Lance has done for banking what the Boston Strangler did for the door-to-door salesman."

On the other hand, there are scores of reputable bankers all over the country who adamantly still admire and defend Geminian Lance, for no personal motive or past favors received — but simply because they genuinely believe his professional behavior was always imaginative, creative, courageous, and entirely within sound banking principles. Obviously two different men are being analyzed. Bert Lance. And his Twin, Bert Lance. Geminis are never simple personalities. Take Henry Kissinger. Take Errol Flynn. Take Brigham Young. Take all six of these Gemini men — and what have you? Double images, reflecting every facet of sunlight and shadow . . . . . arousing contempt, hatred, envy, disapproval, awe, admiration, respect and love. This is what Cappy is in for with her Twin lover or husband.

The mercurial truth of the Twins can always be seen from two polarized points of view. But Cappy leans toward total honesty, which allows little or no room for a two-sided truth. Her Gemini man may feel her attitude is too harsh, for the continuation of his free flow of ideas depends upon leaving open ends for individual interpretation, now and then. He doesn't know where the ideas come from, but they never stop, and they are the essence of his very being. To stifle his freedom of thought and expression is not the way to love this man.

She'll want him to seek a profession or a career with some future promise, as well as a reasonable present financial return, and she'll probably insist that they eventually own their own home. Cappy isn't big on antlike, apartment dwelling or condominiums. He doesn't really need that sort of security, since roots are not normally a Gemini requirement. He's happier with a million dollars on paper and a hundred in the bank than with a hundred dollars on paper and a million in the bank. The former offers more challenge. She feels precisely the opposite. Gemini feels that his ideas, his imagination, are the most bankable assets he owns. He doesn't understand her kind of security needs, not really — and perhaps he never will. Even the Gemini male with a more cautious Virgo, Cancer or Capricorn Ascendent or Moon Sign will suddenly, someday, without warning, toss away the entire balance in the bank for some new idea, dream, goal or prospect that's popped into his head. (One of his heads.)

If their relationship begins to break apart, it won't be easy for the Goat Girl to let go. After a Capricorn woman gives herself completely to a man, she cannot take back her gift without great pain. She cannot *change* as easily as he. When she loves, she intends it to be a forever thing. But if and when she does decide that her "forever" has come to a dead-end street, there will usually be no hysterical scenes of weeping and accusation, no excessive emotional displays. She will simply turn, hide her tears, walk away and not come back. No Sun Sign can be so unsentimental (on the surface) as Capricorn, when emotional surgery must be performed and there is no other solution possible. But . . . as she walks away, her gentle heart will be breaking, and her torment will be all the more agonizing because she keeps it inside . . . and bears it alone.

The Gemini man cries, with Whittier, "How little I have gained — how vast the unattained !" — then weeps for experiences lost, opportunities wasted, chances tossed away . . . love, unrequited, misplaced, or allowed to drift into emptiness. Yet, swiftly will follow the Gemini three-cornered grin, and Mercury's quicksilver laugh. Tomorrow is a bright, new day of promise! Who knows what magic it may hold ? Maybe . . . yes, maybe . . . even a reconciliation — forgiveness from his shy Goat Girl, and the chance to try again, this time treating her heart more tenderly.

Should their love affair or marriage end, Cappy will be slower to smile, and as for tomorrow being brighter — tomorrow will seem to her sad, Saturnine spirit a trillion light-years away. That's why she'll try harder to make the relationship work. With Saturn in her corner, she can build love strong enough to withstand the temporary tornadoes of disagreement.

GEMINI

Air — Mutable — Positive
Ruled by Mercury
Symbol: The Twins
Day Forces — Masculine

AQUARIUS

Air — Fixed — Positive
Ruled by Uranus
Symbol: The Water Bearer
Day Forces — Masculine

The **GEMINI-AQUARIUS** *Relationship*

The goals are at each end of the rainbow....

Because this is a 5-9 Sun Sign Pattern, and their natal Suns are, therefore, trined, Gemini and Aquarius are ordinarily as cozily compatible as a couple of bugs in a rug or two termites in a totem pole. Now and then, however, depending on other planetary aspects between their mutual planets at birth, they can short-circuit each other's frequencies.

Recently, I received a letter from a young Aquarian named William Dana Snyder, presently employed at the Nuts and Bolts Hardware Store in the Village (Greenwich), where he is clearly very much at home. It was written in the typical Uranus-Sanskrit Aquarians use when they communicate with mere mortals on the Earth plane, and it was signed with the curious phrase: SAT NAM. Beneath this signature, the Water Bearer had helpfully translated the words to mean, in essence: *"There is only one God — and He is Truth."*

Right there you have it. The main current of dissension between Gemini and Aquarians — TRUTH. Gemini continually avoids it, since truth has an intricate web of complex meanings for the Twins. Aquarius constantly seeks it (or stalks it) — lucid, plain, unvarnished with imaginative adjectives, uncolored with personal opinion. To Gemini, truth is a great, rolling ocean, rainbow-hued and glittering, filled with the fish of many-faceted half-truths, maybes, ifs and possiblys. To Aquarius, truth is a great shining drop, shaped like a fact, colorless, transparent, and clearly seen under the microscopic, relentless Uranian eye as itself and nothing but itself, so help it God — which it is, of course. Remember ? SAT NAM.

The scene is anywhere. Gemini and an Aquarian are on opposite ends of a telephone. The former had promised to do the latter a favor by mailing a very important letter for him (or her).

AQUARIUS: Did you mail the letter I gave you last night ?

GEMINI: Yes, I mailed it. See you for lunch in about an hour, okay ?

AQUARIUS: What do you mean, you mailed it ? Is it on the way to Saratoga right now ?

GEMINI: Well, no — but it will be in a few minutes.

AQUARIUS: Then you haven't mailed it, so why did you say you did ?

GEMINI: *The truth is,* I have addressed it, stamped it, and I was on my way out the door to the Post Office when the phone rang.

AQUARIUS: *The truth is,* you haven't mailed the letter yet. Call me back after you've dropped it in the slot. Goodbye. CLICK.

Aquarius is a Fixed Sign. Fixed means stubborn, among other things. If the comments of the Water Bearer seem to ring with undertones of Virgo and Sagittarius truth-seeking, listen again. There is a slight and subtle difference in the Uranus attitude. I'm not sure just what it is, but it's a slight and subtle difference. In everything Aquarius does there is a slight and subtle difference from the way it is said and done by ordinary humans. Water Bearers are not ordinary. They are extraordinary. And flattery will get you nowhere with them. But back to the main issue. Truth is an area where there will obviously be some disputes from time to time between Gemini and Aquarius.

Not everyone understands this Uranian thing about truth, based on fact. Unlike Virgos, Aquarians are not hair-splitters in their quest for truth. Unlike Taurus and Capricorn, Aquarius does not have a closed mind. The Uranus mind is always open to anything, positively anything. If the human brain is capable of imagining it or conceiving it, then to Aquarius it is a possibility, never mind how far-out and ridiculous it may seem to the scientific community and/or laymen. HOWEVER (and I capitalized HOWEVER on purpose), although the Water Bearers accept the possibility of absolutely *anything* with an open mind, they will not accept an existing theory as *final* truth until they have satisfied themselves of the feasibility of the supposition by proving it via visible facts. So you can see they're a curious mixture of fact and fantasy. At least, I hope you see. I trust this has clarified the issue. I am sure it has not. But I tried.

Other than sometimes gazing at truth through opposite ends of the telescope, Gemini and Aquarius, being a 5-9 Sun Sign Pattern, are usually enormously compatible. Shall we say that they are more often than they are not ? They empathize, sympathize, philosophize and fraternize on the same electronic wave-length, auric beam, vibratory frequency, or whatever you wish to call it. Normally, they are not shaken by each other's changeable moods, eccentricities, ups, downs, or swoops sideways. Only rarely do you come across a Gemini-Aquarius couple whose mutual planetary positions are severely afflicted by comparative aspects between their birth charts — and who, therefore, either actively dislike each other on sight — or bore one another. It happens with every Sun Sign Pattern, even with the usually smooth 5-9 vibration, but most infrequently.

As I've reminded you many times in this book, in other Aquarian chapters, although Aquarius is pictured in astrology as the Water Bearer, Aquarius is an Air Sign, like Gemini — not a Water Sign. So why are these people represented, symbolized as it were, by a kneeling figure pouring water from a jug, since they are not of the Water Element but of the Air Element ? I cannot tell you. I realize it doesn't make sense on the surface of it. It's totally illogical, not to mention contradictory and weird. But then, so are Aquarians — all of those things. Every last one of them is bonkers, to some degree. The Twins are among the few people who notice this right off, because they are known to bonk in and out also. When Gemini and Aquarius bonk around together in rhythm, it's kind of comforting. No one has to explain himself (or herself). It makes life simpler. No, maybe I'd better take that back. Life is never simple with these two Sun Signs. Interesting, fascinating, even magical — but never simple.

One of the most remarkable and affecting or touching sights in the world is a child with the feelings of an adult. Another remarkable, affecting or touching sight is an adult with the feelings of a child. The latter is the case with all Geminis and Aquarians, if they're typical of their Sun Signs. Both of them exist in actuality on planets other than Earth, touching base down here only at intervals, which could range from five minutes to several days. Naturally, they flock together when they have an opportunity, so they can speak to each other in the code of non-Earthlings. The true world of Gemini and Aquarius is called Faërie, the realm or state in which faeries have their being, described by Tolkien as a place which contains "many things besides elves and fays, and besides dwarfs, witches, trolls, giants or dragons; it holds the seas, the sun, the moon, the sky; and the earth, and all things that are in it: tree and bird, water and stone, wine and bread, and ourselves, mortal men, when we are enchanted."

All of us experience fleeting moments of enchantment (with the potential for extending the fleeting aspect of them). But Gemini and Aquarius comprehend and utilize such potential and are nearly continually enchanted, full of the awe and wonder, the curiosity of the true child — Gemini, the toddler, and Aquarius, second childhood — as described in *"The Twelve Mysteries of Love"* at the beginning of this book. Therefore, they have, more or less, permanent residence in the realm of Fäerie. We see them pass among us, of course, but are they really here, or do they not seem frequently to be . . . somewhere else ? As a team, these two Sun Signs will mingle and blend at times almost as one, then drift into their own individual ways for a period . . . and float back together again. It's usually a windy, breezy relationship, somewhat detached, and although a controversy between them can create a temporary flurry of excitement, like a summer storm, it normally doesn't last long enough to do any real damage.

Both Gemini and Aquarius understand most subjects and situations thoroughly, in depth, but Gemini can usually transmit this comprehension to others with more clarity than Aquarius, the Twins having been blessed with the gift of both gab and glibness — Aquarians with the gift of genius and insanity, in just about equal parts. They are both, however, masters of the twisted phrase, mind-blowers. Gemini double-talks an atheist by informing him that any scientist can count the seeds in an apple, but only God can count the apples in a seed. Aquarius comments on the restless Gemini behavior by observing wryly that a fly-by-night leaves no shadow, only doubt. How was that again ? Listen more carefully the first time. Aquarius does not like to repeat. Gemini cheerfully repeats, but never the same way twice. With their upside-down cakes of phraseology and crisscross alliteration, Gemini and Aquarius would make a great team writing verses for Chinese fortune cookies.

With Sun-Moon harmony between them, they can be a delightful pair, an exasperating puzzle to everyone else, but an open book to each other. Even with a negative Sun-Moon aspect in their horoscopes, because of their Sun trine, they may read the last page of the book first, decide they don't like it, then breeze along their merry, individual ways — possibly returning to pick up where they left off, maybe even to write a different ending, as it pleases them. It's impossible to predict, with these two.

Most people like Gemini and Aquarius despite themselves, rather than for themselves. They're both too complex for the average Earthling. But they usually only annoy with their noise, seldom anger. If their mutual chatter, combined with their speedy head and foot work, could be set to music, the lyrics would surely be haunting but hard to remember. At least, hard for the Water Bearer to remember. All Aquarians are a touch absentminded. Never mind, Gemini's steel trap of a mind can flip out computer cards of memory fast enough for both of them.

Sometimes they make money together, sometimes they lose it together.

Neither is likely to admit which it is, loss or gain, because both are able to substitute one word for another, as they do with all polarities, completely comprehending what many people do not: that any one thing always contains particles of its opposite. These two (who would be perfectly at home, by the way, at the Mad Hatter's Tea Party) are quite likely to have in common some interest in religion, travel to foreign countries and lands, higher educational institutions, astral experience, youth and young people, films, entertainment, artistic or creative endeavor. Or these areas will be, conversely, areas of tension.

Gemini and Aquarius often seem incapable of a completely smooth relationship, despite their innate empathy. If things run too smoothly, they aren't happy. Theirs is an exceedingly strange compatibility. They can frequently be at cross purposes and can get on each other's nerves. Yet, they can also have a barrel of fun together, as they fly around in simultaneous orbit to lace the tired old Earth with flowers . . . tumbling, twisting, turning and tantalizing others who are not so blessed with lightning calculator minds and flashing intuition.

Gemini and Aquarius are as serious as Birth and as joyous as Death — and vice versa. As for the spiritual concept of SAT NAM, Gemini is aware that truth is a different thing to each person, depending on an individual's level of enlightenment at any given time. Therefore, if "God's" name is really truth, then He is a "God" of many faces, a multiple One.

Aquarius is even wiser, takes Gemini's logic one leap forward, and informs the Twins that there is only one truth, which stands high above the multiple truth-Gods of SAT NAM, and its name is LOVE. Not just love between man and woman, although that's the beginning of it, but love of all mankind and womankind for one another and for all living creatures . . . . . in the woods, the seas and the air. "Well then," replies Gemini, brightening, "I see! I see! Then there must also be a Ms. God — two creators — twin souls — from which all this flows down upon us!"

But it took the Water Bearer to open the eyes of the Twins to higher truth. Yes, Gemini, the super-bright, has much to learn from Aquarius, the Water Bearer of Wisdom. In youth, Aquarius may sign letters with SAT NAM. But with maturity, the Uranus-ruled will sign them with EVOL NAM REH-SIH (His-Her name is Love, spelled backwards, of course, in the typical Uranian manner).

The bottomless jug of the Water Bearer contains many such marvelous mysteries, and no one can discover them more quickly than the Gemini Twins.

☆ ☆ ☆ ☆ ☆ ☆

GEMINI *Woman* AQUARIUS *Man*

———— ◄◄●►► ————

*Now surely he would understand; but not a bit of it.
"Peter," she said, faltering, "are you expecting me
to fly away with you ?"*

*"Of course; that is why I have come." He added a
little sternly, "Have you forgotten that this is
spring-cleaning time ?"*

*She knew it was useless to
say that he had let many spring-cleaning times pass.*

Spring has an attraction for all of us, but for the Sun Signs of Aries, Aquarius and Gemini, it holds a special, inexplicable wonder. The Gemini woman, being impatient, can create her own springtime when Mother Nature disappoints her. There will come a year when the icy clutch of winter seems to be endless. She cannot wait for spring another day. And so she flies away to Florida or California, following the elusive Sun, making a miracle by causing spring to come early, at her whim. Long ago, when she was a very little girl, she learned there are many magical things one can do when happiness is slowpokey, and most of those things involve moving around, flying here and there, but mainly — *change.*

No man will understand her preoccupation with that word more than an Aquarian. Oh, Aries, Libra, and Gemini males comprehend it too, at times, but not in the same exciting way as Aquarius. The Water Bearer was born to bring change into the world. But there is a small hitch, which should be noted. He wants the world and everyone around him to change, but not his own basic attitudes — not the essence of himself. His moods and manners may change, but not the Him-of-Him. Remember, he's a Fixed Sign. In the beginning, in the first sunrise of love, he'll cheerfully fly around with her. Later, he'll become more settled in his rut. Granted, a Uranus rut is always more fascinating than others, but to a Gemini girl bubbling with ideas and possibilities, a rut is a rut, and there is nothing more dampening to her soaring spirit than a Water Bearer sitting by the fire in his hut, stuck in his rut. If you know what I mean.

However, just because he can get settled in a residential or geographical way by no means should be taken to imply that this man is predictable. When it comes to his mood, expressions and disposition, to say nothing of his activities, he's as unpredictable as a pair of dice. Actually, it's poetic and romantic justice when a Gemini girl falls into enchantment with an Aquarian man. All her life she's been flitting around like a peripatetic firefly, switching her moods off and on, causing her lovers or friends to moan in frustration over her rather impersonal Mercury style of unpredictability. As soon as she becomes involved with a Uranus-ruled male, she'll be forced to swallow a rather large dose of her own medicine.

He'll invite her to have dinner with him, followed by the preview of a new Steve McQueen or Paul Newman flick (usually typical Aquarian favorites), then after she's brushed her hair and tied on a yellow ribbon, a frog-like creature shows up at the front door, wearing a wet suit and flippers. What is it? It's him. He wants her to go surfboarding? No. He's changed his mind about eating out before the film. He's decided they will eat at her place, and while she's preparing dinner, he's going to go diving for some hermit-crab shells to make her a necklace. They'll still have time to catch the first feature at the theatre, if she'll just hurry up, chill the sprouts and heat up the lentils, so everything is ready to munch when he returns from his scuba search for seashells. "There should be enough of them, deserted, lying around on the ocean floor," he muses aloud . . . as he leaves. "It doesn't take long for a hermit crab to outgrow his cozy house and slip into a new one. Abalone shells are beautiful, but they represent death to the abalone from people who cannibalize sea life to tantalize their greedy taste buds."

What did he say? He'll explain it all to her — the sadness of the food chain — later, after the film. The frog has already disappeared, leaving behind him only the slapping sound of his flippers, along the path to the beach. Life — and love — with this man can be so crazy.

Would there be any way to make other people believe in the craziness, the loveliness of it? No way. It's uncanny the way these two so often find themselves feeling the same things at the same time. Most times she catches on to his tricks almost before he can pull them. Naturally, this is electrifying to him, since Aquarians love to shock people, and the surprise of discovering a female who's hard to shock challenges him insanely. Like a little boy walking on his hands along the top of a wall to impress his best girl — then she yawns and starts walking on her elbows. He continually has to top himself with the Gemini girl.

If they happen to live in the mountains or in the Midwest, nowhere near a shoreline, it doesn't preclude the Uranus shock treatment. Instead of a frog turning up at the door, he'll pick her up some morning in a yellow bug, with Snoopy as Joe Cool stenciled on the hood, and one of those WELCOME UFO's stickers on the bumper. Wasn't his car grey last night? Yes, it was, but this is a bright blue sunshiny day. Time to change colors. He could suddenly decide to grow a beard or a moustache with no notice, or if he's already had one for years, just as suddenly shave it off, pull a wool cap down over his ears, grab her on the street and scare her to death. "Don't you know me, honey? I'm the Jolly Green Giant who loves you!" And like that.

At long last she will understand what it's like to be an innocent bystander recipient of someone else's Ferris wheel of emotions and quick-changing moods. It may even teach her to tone down her own mental acrobatics, to maybe even be on time for appointments. Reliability and dependability are qualities they could both stand to cultivate. Then there's always the chance they won't ease each other into stability at all but will, instead, incite each other into more loop-the-loops. Either way, it will be fun. These lovers constitute a 5-9 Sun Sign Pattern, which means they have a far higher than average chance to discover that they're Twin Souls, especially if there's a harmonious Sun-Moon aspect between their two horoscopes. Even without it, or with a negative aspect between their individual Luminaries at birth, they will find more in common together than they do with most other people they both know.

There's no use denying that she will occasionally annoy and irritate his Fixity with her Mutability. But she can be so easy to forgive. No one has ever lived who can apologize more charmingly than a Gemini. It's really worthwhile for her to do something wrong, just to watch her ask pardon for it. Sometimes he wonders if she knows that. (She does.) Aquarians have a mite more trouble getting the hang of apology. No Fixed Sign (Aquarius, Taurus, Scorpio, Leo) ever finds it easy to say "I'm sorry." Most of them find begging for pardon about as pleasurable as walking barefoot on hot coals. So she shouldn't expect this male to indulge in such abasement too frequently. It frightens him. What will she expect from him next if he spoils her now with profuse apologies? Aquarian men do not like to be anticipated in any way. I've already told you that. It's advisable not to forget it.

People can become dreadfully bored when there's nothing but sex to interest them in each other. This man and this woman seldom run that risk. Gemini and Aquarius always have something to talk about, so much to teach one another, and the beauty of it is that, half the time, they don't even know they're learning. Sex is usually not a big thing to this man and woman. It's not a small thing either, but it doesn't take first place in their relationship. It seldom occurs to either of them to measure its influence, to count its blessings or curses. Sex is just there, that's all. Most happily mated Gemini-Aquarian couples enjoy the physical consummation of their love as children enjoy wading through puddles, flying kites or chasing butterflies. It's thrilling, exciting — sheer pleasure — uncomplicated, with no dark, mysterious corners — a bright, sunlit room in their hearts. He could be one of those occasional Water Bearers who almost need to be reminded of the rules of the mating game because his busy-bee thoughts are buzzing around happily with other matters, too preoccupied and absentminded to constantly ponder the delights of physical intimacy. And she could be one of those Geminis who finds fulfillment in talking together — through mental union — rather than becoming unduly engrossed in sensuousness or passion. Nevertheless, their lovemaking, when it does occur, is more likely to be satisfactory to both of them than to be a source of tension, however frequently or infrequently they share it.

In a strange way, they anticipate each other's desires, these two. An Aquarian male with Venus severely afflicted in his birth chart can have some pretty far-out ideas about sexual matters — or he can lean toward the platonic love affair, never truly consummated. But once the average Uranian has been spellbound, has given his heart — he knows the language of love, including its physical one, and he can communicate the intensity of his need with a steady gaze, a slight lifting of the eyebrow — or a wiggle of his left ear. As for her, the Twin symbolism of Gemini will be startlingly apparent in her ability to be one special, private woman for him at night . . . and a totally different female the next day.

Speaking of language, as we were a few paragraphs back, the Gemini girl-woman (for she is both by turns) may speak more than one. Geminis are natural linguists. She may also have more than one name, an alias or a nickname, perhaps even more than one husband during her lifetime. This isn't true of every Gemini woman, of course, just most of them. The Twins are seldom satisfied without two or more of everything. Aquarians frequently marry more than once too. (Not always, but frequently.) Not all Water Bearers satisfy their curiosity the first time, although she has the edge on him in the multiple marriage race and is slightly more likely to have tried marriage before than he.

Once the Aquarian man is sure he's not missing anything, he can be purely and perfectly faithful to one woman. His problem with the Twins is that he sometimes feels he's coping with *two* women. I guess he could swing faithfulness to both of her. Gemini females do flirt a lot. They just can't help it. But she'll get away with it most of the time with him, since Aquarians aren't the type, usually, to make a mountain out of a few molehills when it comes to jealousy. Light, friendly flirtations may escape his notice altogether. He understands about friendship. In fact, she may wish he didn't understand so well. His friends may cause *her* to be jealous. She'll just have to remember that an Aquarian may find it difficult to separate love from friendship, but to him, if he's a typical Water Bearer, the physical or sexual aspect of a relationship goes with the former, not with the latter — once he's separated the two by making a commitment (or by combining them, with her).

The one person she has good reason to fear is the girl he first loved. He'll never forget her — never. She'll always be there, buried deep inside his memory, whether she happens to be his first-grade teacher, the girl gorilla, or the lady hippo at the zoo who winked at him when he was three. It could be more serious, of course, and his first love may be a real, flesh-and-blood, dangerous female, who may pop up someday to make his heart do flip-flops. Even so, except in rare cases, he would prefer the misty, starry memory to all the trouble of picking up where he left off, years ago. Yet, there are those very rare cases.

The one thing this man will demand of her is truth. It's the one thing he may never receive from her. She sees truth through the multiple lens of imagination, colored by her wishes and dreams. It's merely a matter of interpretation. Otherwise, these two share essentially similar vibrations. Their auras blend in a galaxy of moods, synchronized to the same "mother ship" frequency, different only in their individual reflections of the changing seasons of the heart. The differences are subtle, intricate. His reactions are more complex than hers, likewise, therefore, his reflections. She startles him with rainfalls of tears, followed suddenly with sunbursts of laughter. Then he reverses the reflection with rainfalls of laughter, followed by sunbursts of tears . . . . perhaps because Aquarius already knows what Gemini has yet to learn — that there's a reason why Gladness rhymes with Sadness, contained in her yet personally unsensed mystery of Joy and Sorrow, which are in reality Twins themselves, inseparable and interchangeable.

☆ ☆ ☆ ☆ ☆ ☆

GEMINI *Man* AQUARIUS *Woman*

◄─◄●►─►

"So I ran away to Kensington Gardens and lived a long long time among the fairies."

She gave him a look of the most intense admiration, and he thought it was because he had run away, but it was really because he knew fairies.

There are many reasons why these two are sure to notice each other in a crowd, but the main one is that faint chord of music they both hear. The Aquarian girl has always felt that no one truly understands her. Most people judge her unfairly, figure she's playing with only half a deck of cards, full of wild imaginings, a crazy daisy born several hundred years too soon. Everyone but him.

The Gemini man has always felt that no one really understands his dreams. Most people judge him unfairly, figure he's unreliable, sometimes too talkative, at other times too moody, immature — and totally irresponsible. Everybody but her.

The first recognition of kindredship between Gemini and Aquarius always reminds me of the meeting between Saint-Exupéry's Little Prince and the pilot. As a child, the pilot drew a picture of a boa constrictor who had swallowed an elephant, which, unfortunately, resembled a hat. All his life, no matter to whom he showed his picture, people would never recognize it as a boa constrictor who had swallowed an elephant, but would always say, "*Yes, that's a nice drawing of a hat.*" It hurts when others can't comprehend your intense efforts, and it's lonely. Then one day, after he's grown up, the pilot meets a strange little man in the desert, who asks him to draw a picture of a sheep. Exasperated, the pilot scribbles the same picture of his childhood — the one everybody always took to be a drawing of a hat. But when the Little Prince gazes at the sketch, he shakes his head immediately, and says, "No, no. *I don't want a picture of a boa constrictor who has swallowed an elephant. I asked you to draw me a sheep.*"

That's the faint chord of music I mean. Without a single word of explanation . . . . . . someone *knows*! Only music, never mere words, can describe the fountain of pure joy that wells up in the soul when after years of lonely, futile searching, one comes upon another being who really (not *nearly*, but *really*) recognizes and comprehends all the secret yearnings and attempts to communicate that others have ridiculed or ignored in the past.

Later, this first faint chord of music from the spheres, as lovely and long-awaited as it is, contains a sour note or two somewhere along the way in the symphony of love between Gemini and Aquarius. But this is a small burden to bear when compared to the broken rhythms and discordant melodies both have been exposed to until they finally found each other. Although no relationship is perfect, a 5-9 Sun Sign Pattern often comes closer to being so than most others. If the Sun-Moon aspects between them are conjunct, sextile or trine, they can reach a rare harmony of living and loving. Even without this planetary assistance, they're better matched than many and will usually remain friendly, whether romance lingers or not.

Sun Signs which are in trine complement each other in ways only the two people involved can appreciate. But one of them is always ahead of the other on the zodiac wheel, on the soul level, in karmic lessons. In this case, it's the Aquarian woman who is somewhat wiser in a subconscious, spiritual sense than the Gemini man she loves. So she'll be the one who will have to do the most giving and be more tolerant. Tolerance comes easily to most Aquarians, who are basically unprejudiced and know well the meaning of the words — "Help thy brother's boat across and lo ! thine own shall reach the shore." Uranus incites humanitarianism in Water Bearers, infuses the Aquarian woman with a spirit of brotherhood (and sisterhood). It's possible she may have too many friends, at least too many for men born under other Sun Signs. The Gemini man may not find time to resent the strange birds she gathers around her, because he's too busy being gregarious himself. Only the very rare Geminian with heavy planetary afflictions in his birth horoscope is a loner. The home of a Water Bearer and a Mercury Bird is seldom quiet. If they're both typical of their Sun Signs, it will be filled with people more often than it's empty.

These two will make many mistakes while trying to love each other for richer and for poorer, for better or for worse. But they'll be interesting mistakes, seldom boring. One mistake he's likely to make is expecting her to put up with his little white lies. She's outraged when he stretches the truth or distorts it. Aquarian women tend to claim they are honest and aboveboard in every way. They do their own thing and never lie about it, whether society approves or not. But the Gemini man is clever and astute enough to analyze her own peculiar brand of dishonesty, which consists of sins of omission. She tells the truth, yes — but sometimes only part of it, only what she wishes to tell, holding back the whole truth, never playing all her cards at one time. When he accuses her of this, she evidences surprise and hurt. He may point out to her that she has other ways of being less than truthful, namely her manner of expressing her true feelings in such a way that only the Red Queen, Tweedledum or Tweedledee could correctly interpret them.

The honesty game between Gemini and Aquarius is complicated, and they are perhaps the only ones who can untangle the knots. Sometimes they do. Sometimes they don't. They will never stop trying. Both of them enjoy mental games and are amateur detectives, instinctively alert to every nuance. This talent is obvious in Gemini, more disguised in Aquarius, beneath the surface mask of "dingbat," wide-eyed innocence and detachment.

The mistake *she* could make is expecting him to mean exactly what he says. Gemini never means exactly what he says. He uses words as blessings to charm, coax, persuade and cajole; sometimes as weapons to taunt, tease and hurt. He makes speeches that magnetize her into rapt attention, then hold her spellbound — or he can break her heart with his mercurial brand of withering sarcasm and sharp comments. It's nearly always a mistake to cry in front of a Gemini man. He can't cope with tears. Intensely emotional scenes frighten him as they would a child. And so, often he reacts with what appear to be cold and unsympathetic words — using them as weapons again, this time to protect himself against the pain that accompanies compassion.

He wants no part of pain, this man, if he can possibly avoid it. The art of satire was invented by Gemini, who weaves words into sentences as the light-fingered magician strings brightly colored beads, pulls another rabbit from his hat, another flowing scarf from his sleeve at the last minute, making his audience sigh and gasp with admiration. Today he is happy, tomorrow miserable, then jolly and exuberant the day after that. His emotions are genuine, they're for real. It's just that they don't last. The Aquarian girl can usually tolerate his quicksilver moods better than most females, for a very good reason. She hardly notices anything half the time — anything at all. See the cloudy, misty, faraway look in her eyes? That comes from sailing out there among the clouds on her own wave-length, somewhere in the future, momentarily out of touch with Earth and Earthlings, including his twinned moods. He can pass from suicidal to serene before she's aware of what's happening.

In youth, the Aquarian girl drapes her dream-lover with a sparkling halo of impossible rainbow-spectrumed beauty, which could never fit around the head and shoulders of the average male with the usual number of flaws and defects of character. But she learns to hide her vulnerability under the guise of a cool, detached, friendly "let's pal around together" attitude as she settles for something less, all the time secretly treasuring the sentimental illusions of youth. Therefore, the older she is when she meets Gemini, the less apt she is to be wounded by his light attitude toward love. Hers can match his in lightness . . . then. Aquarians nearly all have this strange twist. If they marry more than once, the final marriage will usually occur later in life, when they find someone in need of Uranus wisdom. Then she will turn this man into the astral lover of her teens, finally fulfilling as much as possible her original ideal of a love-friendship combination. The last lover could be a Gemini, who is also desirous of combining love and friendship and is equally as likely to confuse the two feelings as she.

Both the Gemini man and the Aquarian woman have inner fears and doubts about their sex appeal. At some time in the past, they've both privately worried over some problem related to their sexuality, perhaps experienced the humiliation of having been called frigid or at least temporarily unresponsive — especially if either of them have been previously entangled with Fire, Earth or Water Signs.

Together, they can prove to one another the falsehood of these accusations from former lovers. Gemini and Aquarius tend to give only as much as needed and expected, and seldom demand more than what is given, thus often achieving a happy balance in sexual union. Unless one or both of them have a heavily afflicted Venus or Mars in the birth chart, they should find more sexual fulfillment within their physical union than they ever have before with former mates — or probably ever could in the future with new ones. Of course, "probably" is not *definitely*, but it's a stronger promise than *possibly*.

Didn't you realize that as a child, when you asked to go to the circus, and some adult said "possibly" you may go, and your heart sank to the soles of your Buster Browns — or said "probably" you may go, and your heart crawled back up to your knees — or said "definitely" you may go, and your heart flipped right back into place where it belonged, thumping wildly in joy and gratitude and excitement ? Both Gemini and Aquarius tend more toward a passion of the mind than of the senses — more emotional intricacies in communicating love than through pure physical abandon to feeling.

Almost always, these two, when there is a break in the relationship, can remain nearly as close, find much of the same affinity as in the beginning. When Gemini and Aquarius are hurt, they both retreat back into the security of a safe, protective, emotionally undemanding friendship. Friendship is a marvelous thing, but sometimes Gemini and Aquarius will sacrifice love for it, because love takes more faith, more courage than a buddy-buddy relationship.

There is a pronounced mysticism between this man and woman, a shimmering thread of light connecting their souls, if they are true mates — as with Aries and Leo, Taurus and Capricorn . . . and all 5-9 Sun Sign Patterns. If they like, they may tug on this thread, to pull themselves back to each other. Not all 5-9 vibrations constitute twin souls, of course, but those that do, allow Soul-Mates easier recognition and more effortless communion than might be granted to true lovers disciplined by other Sun Sign Pattern influences.

As long as he understands that when she laughs, she may be sobbing inwardly — when she cries, she may be inwardly joyous . . . . and as long as she understands that he can fly away today and return tomorrow (or next week, next month or next year . . . but eventually), there will be more pleasure than pain in their loving. Together, Gemini and Aquarius can perform miracles, such as the fusing of several realities into a single, enchanted one. There's such a bond of feeling between them, such shared madness . . . . . and loneliness. They would never see one another's pictures of a boa constrictor who had swallowed an elephant . . . . . as the drawing of an ordinary hat.

And the two of them together could quite probably even convince all boas that it isn't nice or natural to swallow a pachyderm for lunch.

GEMINI

Air — Mutable — Positive
Ruled by Mercury
Symbol: The Twins
Day Forces — Masculine

PISCES

Water — Mutable — Negative
Ruled by Neptune
Symbol: The Fish
Night Forces — Feminine

The GEMINI- PISCES *Relationship*

◀◆▶

> *When their voices died away, there came a cold*
> *silence over the lagoon, and then a feeble cry,*
> *"Help, help!" Two small figures were beating*
> *against the rock.*

There's not much use pretending that Gemini and Pisces are Sun Signs which are naturally as compatible as strawberries and cream, Oliver and Hardy, or Raggedy Ann and Raggedy Andy. Not all, but some of them are as mismatched and antagonistic as the Arabs and the Jews have been over the years, though perhaps not as violent. However, just as peace is possible — and ever more likely — between these traditional foes, a happy compromise is also possible between Gemini and Pisces. If they have a Sun-Moon trine, sextile or conjunction between them, they can get along quite happily, as long as Gemini consents to occasionally swim through Neptune's waters to keep the Fish company — and as long as Pisces is willing to fly fearlessly, now and then, alongside the Gemini Mercury Birds.

Still, an Air Sign is never completely comfortable in the element of water. There's always the possibility of drowning — just as a Water Sign finds flying without a parachute a little scary. "Could someone please stand beneath me, with a net to catch me if I fall?" Since this is a 4-10 Sun Sign Pattern, should they discover a negative Sun-Moon aspect between their horoscopes, they'll have to remember that mixing air with water must be done carefully, not carelessly. Otherwise, the result could be a dreary fog, or even a dangerous smog. It's easy to see how this can produce a dampening or smothering effect (or both) on a business basis, within the family bosom, in a love affair or among friends. It is, undoubtedly, an unpleasant experience to be dampened (as Pisces can do to Gemini) or smothered (as Gemini can do to Pisces).

GEMINI: You realize that whatever you say will be used against you?

PISCES: That's okay with me. It always has been.

GEMINI: Stop feeling sorry for yourself. Do you plead guilty or innocent? Speak up. You're always so silent. It's called pouting, and you do it to annoy me.

PISCES: Oh, I plead guilty, of course. Guilty of being human, of possessing human needs and desires . . . . even human failings. Isn't that all right?

GEMINI: It depends. You have more failings than most people. You have no sense of deductive reasoning. You avoid the issues, sulk, and refuse to discuss anything. Your mind wanders. Three different times yesterday you ignored me when I told you something I wanted you to do, and you continue to neglect it. You run around listening to everyone's hard-luck stories while your own life falls apart. You're a masochist and a procrastinator. You leave all the important things undone, while you're out chasing bubbles and smelling flowers. Does this make you happy?

PISCES: Oh, yes! No one has ever been happier. Please make sure the jury is told, and the judge too, how happy I've been.

GEMINI: Don't start talking about a judge and jury. This isn't a trial, and you know it. We're just having a discussion.

PISCES: I'm sorry . . . . but you sound like a public prosecutor.

GEMINI: Let's stick to the point. You say you're happy. That's just another of your Neptune lies. You are obviously, at this moment, sad. Clearly depressed. Why aren't you happy right now?

PISCES: Because I'm not making anyone else happy . . . . not even you.

(or . . .)

PISCES: I'm sorry to submit you to a cross examination, please forgive me, but . . . well, I don't trust you. I'm afraid of you. Don't you see how cruelly your words can cut? Are you completely unaware of how unkind and how supercritical you are sometimes?

GEMINI: No more so than others. I'm just verbal enough to express my

thoughts clearly, to communicate my feelings. I don't keep everything inside, the way you do. I'm not sneaky, like you.

PISCES: Yes, that's true. You are clever. You can use words ever so much
better than I. You're even brilliant, at times. Lots of times.
But . . . have you ever been happy ? I mean, content with yourself,
peaceful. *Have* you been ? *Ever* ?

(pause)

GEMINI: I . . . uh, well . . . of course. Naturally. Why do you ask me that ?

PISCES: I just wondered. What does happiness mean to you ?

GEMINI: Happiness ? What does it mean to me ? It's . . . . . well, it's a number
of things you wouldn't understand.

PISCES: Like what ?

GEMINI: Like knowing exactly where I'm going, arriving there when I plan to
arrive — knowing who I am and what I want.

PISCES: *Who* are you ? What *do* you want ?

GEMINI: You are deliberately trying to confuse me. I refuse to answer any
more questions.

There are some ways in which Gemini and Pisces are alike. Both of
them give an overall impression of evasiveness, always sliding just out of
reach, with a chameleon's talent for camouflage, as tricky to catch and pin
down as fireflies (Gemini) and minnows (Pisces). Their mental and physical
maneuvers (both) are quick, darting and elusive, first shimmering in light
before you — then disappearing. Where did they go ? Well, which one do
you mean ? The Fish just swam inside his (or her) deep emotional nature, for
protection against further questions, more hurt — and the Mercury Bird, for
the very same reasons, just soared mentally up into the gathering clouds
above your head.

You've heard that Pisceans are very old souls. I've told you that myself,
many times. It's true. They are. They've come through the purifying deluge
of many incarnations, and they understand everything and everybody —
except themselves. The soul cannot reach the Pisces incarnation until it has
mastered, at least once, all of the other eleven Sun Signs' lessons. Since some
souls remain in (or return to) a single Sun Sign experience for many lifetimes
before mastering the *positive* side of that sign's essence, you can see why the
Fish is an "old soul." You can also understand why the Piscean faces the most
difficult of all karmic testing. For it is here, under Neptune's strange
influence, that souls may slip and slide, and forget some of the eleven lessons
learned at such expense, either being forced, then, to return to a certain sign
(like returning to learn grammar, when you thought you'd passed it) or being
reborn into the Pisces vibration itself again and again, until they get the hang
of it.

No wonder Pisceans are such a strange bunch. As a group, they seem to contain only saints and sinners, with hardly a normal pilgrim among them. Yes, the Pisces experience is the most vulnerable one, the most tempting to angels . . . the most likely to produce a "fallen angel." A Fish may do nicely in Neptune's school, then one day happen to forget the generosity mastered through the Aries, Sag and Leo incarnations, become stingy — and fall. Or live a smooth life of enlightenment, then some morning (or night), amnesia-like, forget the lesson of Libra fairness, and unkindly judge another . . . . or forget the faint-remembered Taurus patience, and make some impulsive decision, agonizingly regretted, too late. It's not exactly fun, being a Fish. So much more *knowing* is required of these men and women. They're all on the karmic Honor System, and any West Point cadet can tell you how difficult a test of one's worth any Honor System is — deceptively free, yet spiritually and ethically, extremely restrictive.

And so, the Fish float through the complex mazes of their existence, often searching pathetically for their own identities. When they do catch a glimpse of their real images in life's mirror, they are first terrified, then disbelieving. What they see is a godlike self, difficult for the Neptune humility to accept. So they deny it, hide from it, and finally flee from it, into acting or music — often into the escape of drugs, alcohol, or illusion. A few settle into some sort of mundane ambition in the material world, which is entirely foreign to the imaginative Neptunian essence, and therefore, obviously not the Pisces route to happiness. The majority, however (fortunately for the rest of us), flee into creative endeavors, public service, science, religion, healing, teaching — or full-time private devotion to friends, neighbors and relatives.

If the Fish does not understand himself (or herself) the Gemini Twins are only too willing to clear up the mystery. Mercury-ruled people feel they can solve anything, figure out anything, take it apart, see how it works, then put it back together again. But after their cold critical analysis of Pisces, they sometimes leave the pieces scattered around, without putting them back the way they found them. A Fish who has been taken apart by Gemini can flounder helplessly for years attempting to recover his or her self-respect. Gemini is challenged to clear up the perpetual confusion hanging over Pisces with the razor-sharp Mercury mind, but some Twins can't swim deep enough to even get past the seaweed . . . . . like human sandpipers, pecking away at nothing, unable to see the bottom of the ocean or to recognize its depth.

The wiser Piscean will usually look with indulgence, if not with genuine affection, upon the sometimes childlike antics of the Twins. If Gemini lives (and many Twins do) in an enchanted realm of make-believe, Pisces is delighted to visit there too. But Gemini tends to analyze and label all mystical kingdoms, even while frolicking there, and that spoils all the fun for Pisces. A dream is a dream . . . . why come too near, look too closely? Pisces will not stand for personal probing or insistent questioning by the curious Gemini. If pressed too often, the Fish will either glide away to another stream, or take the easier escape of deception, all the way from subtle evasion to outright lying — justified by Neptune as "simple" self-protection from an invasion of personal privacy.

Sometimes the Pisces man or woman will unconsciously get even with Gemini for being continually forced into a position of accommodation, by refusing to show an energetic response to the Twins' exuberance in communicating some marvelous new idea or plan. This may be the beginning of the end, because Gemini cannot long bear to have his (or her) enthusiasms and flashes of inspiration sprinkled with Pisces pessimism, or dampened by Neptune's wet blankets. When they choose, the Fish can be soothingly supportive, full of faith and encouragement. If they don't choose, well . . . . . there may come a time when the Mercury Bird is left out on a limb, singing alone.

There are some things these two can share happily, some ways in which they bear a striking resemblance. One of them is the appreciation of beauty. Most of us don't notice beauty enough, I guess, but Gemini and Pisces are both acutely aware of the transiting loveliness of Nature, the changing of the seasons, sunrise and sunset — and both are usually inclined to bathe their souls in art, poetry or music . . . the spoken or the written word. Pisces absorbs beauty in ecstasy, silently. Gemini grins, in awe and excited wonder. Somehow, beauty brings the Fish and the Twins together, forms a bridge over which they can toss a sunbeam . . . . and perhaps reach the other side of each other.

Another way they're alike is that it's hard to get either of them to pay strict attention to what you're saying, or to get them to look directly at you for more than a fraction of an instant. Gemini's eyes are sharp, alert, sometimes mocking. Pisces eyes are soft, wandering, liquid and full of comprehension when they focus on you, which isn't often. Gemini eyes, too, focus only briefly, then dart restlessly here and there, birdlike. Like their eyes, the minds of Gemini and Pisces wander also, but for different reasons . . . . . to separate galaxies.

The reason Pisceans make such excellent sounding boards for the rest of us is that the Fish have been, in a karmic or a spiritual sense, through it all. They've learned how to do without constant attention and adulation. Knowing how to do without, and not complaining about it, is Neptune's strength, a Piscean weapon against the disappointments of Life. It makes these people stronger than they seem, much tougher than they appear to be. The Fish are used to being overlooked, even before they're born. Geminis, however, are accustomed to being heard and noticed from the time they're chattering toddlers. Which brings us to one of the main reasons these two Sun Signs come together, when they do. Gemini must communicate, needs to express himself or herself — and compassionate Pisces nearly always finds time to listen with genuine interest to both the heartaches and the excitements of others. Gemini couldn't survive without an audience to appreciate the magic of Mercury's beautiful ribbons of words. And the Fish couldn't survive without feeling needed. But after a while, the Twins might lose this great gift offered by Pisces, if Neptune's gentle longings are consistently ignored. There will be signs. Clear indications. And when they appear, they should be heeded. The best time to mend a mistake is when it's small.

GEMINI: A magazine just accepted the article I wrote! Isn't that great news?
PISCES: See how reddish the clouds are over there? I remember my grandfather used to say, "Red sky at night, sailor's delight — red sky in the morning, sailor's warning....."
GEMINI: Did you hear what I said about my magazine article?
PISCES: I'm sorry. I'm afraid I wasn't listening.

☆ ☆ ☆ ☆ ☆ ☆

GEMINI *Woman* PISCES *Man*

If you shut your eyes and are a lucky one, you may see at times a shapeless pool of lovely pale colours, suspended in the darkness.

There has never been a Fish who was not slightly uncertain about where he stood with the Gemini woman he loves. She will give him plenty of occasions to be jealous, or what passes for jealousy with Pisceans, which is a rather mild form of it, to be sure.

But it won't do him a bit of good, because there's nothing to be done about the apparent fickleness of the Twins. (I'm assuming you know by now that every Gemini girl is two-women-in-one. She began flirting when she was in the bassinet or being pushed in her buggy, blowing kisses to strangers, grinning at anyone who noticed her, capturing hearts with her bright, twinkling star-eyes.)

This female will never really grow up. She's like a mischievous, charming little girl, who cries when she's scolded, laughs merrily when she's pleased, coaxes and teases and wheedles until she gets her own way — and getting her own way with a Pisces man isn't too difficult. He's essentially a gentle soul, affectionate and tolerant, not terribly demanding. Of course,

Pisceans can have their irritable, cranky spells, becoming regular crosspatches when they've been imposed on once too often. But most of the time he's willing to try his best to answer her needs. He may get confused when her needs, along with her wishes and dreams, keep changing, but he'll keep right on trying. For that matter, he's not exactly a tower of stability himself. Neither of these two were blessed with much of the stuff at birth. The Fish becomes quickly restless after long periods of fighting the seaweed of obstacles and delays, and as for her — well, Gemini women possess only a thimbleful of patience, if that much. Needless to say, this will constitute one of the frequent snarls in the smoothness of this 4-10 Sun Sign Pattern relationship. Patience is the main ingredient called for in any recipe for happiness and harmony.

The eyes of a Pisces man have the look of being lost. Gemini eyes have the look of searching for something about to be found. With Pisces, Aquarius, Scorpio and Gemini — all four Sun Signs — the pattern of the personality and the stamp of the soul is in the eyes.

Her mind is like a house of glass from which she gazes out on life, with a three-dimensional view of every direction her longings may take. Such multiple choice causes many manifestations in the outward personality, but mostly . . . . . moodiness. The moods of Mercury-ruled Gemini are not the same as the deeper oceans of the Neptune moods of Pisces. They are lightning fast, like quicksilver, coming upon her as unpredictably as a change in the wind.

The mind of the Fish is like a house of many windows too, but with no glass panes, no shutters or blinds to protect him from the seasons — or from her moods. A Pisces man is vulnerable and sensitive, not only to the treatment he receives from others, but to the feelings and emotions of those near him, absorbing their own troubles and symptoms in his own mind and body. So you can see that a relationship with the changeable, frequently troubled Gemini girl, who sometimes projects two emotions simultaneously, may at times be somewhat shattering to the Neptune-ruled male.

This woman was born sparking both mental and physical energy like shock waves. Pisces was born tired. It's little wonder that the Fish is a trifle spiritually fatigued, considering all he's seen throughout so many incarnations . . . all the power and the glory, the ugly and the beautiful, the horrifyingly unspeakable — and the ecstatically indescribable. It's exhausting. Especially when you're tempted, in daydreams, to compare it to the present drab and mundane existence. That much at least his Gemini woman will understand. His need to see the world through soft-tinted glass strikes an echoing chord in her own heart. She, too, would like things to be different, lovelier. But her mercurial nature doesn't shrink from coldly and clearly analyzing things as they *are*, while she's dreaming of how she'd *like* them to be — whereas Pisces never wants to admit the awful truth of anything. Her constant tearing apart the fabric of Life to see how it might be more acceptably put back together again alarms him. When she begins this analytical process with love, which

Pisces knows deeply cannot be analyzed, lest its delicacy be shattered, it signals the beginning of trouble in River City — Philadelphia, Tulsa, Beverly Hills, Pittsburgh, Belpre, Parkesburg, Denver, Coshocton — or wherever. Gemini-Pisces couples tend to change residence more frequently than any other Sun Sign combination (except Gemini-Sag, double Gemini or double Sag). Actually, this is a decided plus factor, because the excitement of moving doesn't leave as much time for petty squabbles.

Like all 4-10 Sun Sign Patterns, Gemini and Pisces must cope with the vibration of tension. Their natures are so totally different, their motives inexplicable to one another most of the time. Hurtful situations involving relatives, the parents of one or the other, or their individual careers may be the stage for the explosions of disagreement. With a harmonious exchange of the Sun and Moon in their nativities (or conjoined Moons) threads of sympathy will draw them closer together. Without such planetary first aid, each will suffer many wounds, which could take a long time to heal.

She's capable of locking him out of the house all night if he stays too long gabbing with a neighbor. Then he's capable of muttering, "Who needs it?" and drowning his troubles at the corner saloon, which causes her to lock him out of the house again — which causes him to escape into John Barleycorn again — which causes her to . . . . and so on. The one thing a Pisces man cannot bear for long is a barrage of criticism, sarcasm and accusation, and his Gemini woman's negative twin excels in the art of satirical invective. Her angry torrents of words and clever use of subtle nuance can rain on the sensitive soul of the Fish like sharp hailstones of hurt. On the other hand, one thing a Gemini woman cannot stand is silence — or being left alone with no audience — and one thing in which Pisces excels is escape from unpleasant scenes. Sometimes you'd swear these Neptune people have literally mastered the art of de-materialization. Poof! They're gone! Just like that. Then she's left by herself. Well, not quite by herself. She can always fight it out with her other half — her ever present Twin, who surely comprehends her need to express her torments more than does the Fish, who can't see for the life of him why anyone should want to waste so much time in futile verbal contests. Pisces tends instinctively to *feel* his way through trouble. Gemini inclines to talk it away. Even though they may truly love each other, these two sometimes seem like total strangers attempting to communicate with word and sign language, scrambled like a game of anagrams with half the letters missing. Gemini talks — and Pisces won't always listen. Pisces weeps — and Gemini doesn't always sympathize. Yet they both need desperately to be accepted and understood, for neither of them understand themselves. They're involved in a mutual quest for self-identity, each born under the influence of duality, like four people living under one roof, two visibly — the other two locked up inside, trying to escape and make themselves known.

Their sexual adjustment will not be made without effort, although, assuming a positive Sun-Moon aspect or other favorable planetary exchanges in their horoscopes, he can probably satisfy her need not to be smothered or overly possessed, and she can probably provide the variety of affectionate expression he must either have — or become bored. Neither Gemini nor Pisces requires flaming passion for lovemaking to bring them the contentment of true intimacy, and both are capable of adapting instantly to the other's ephemeral whims and wishes. Yet a real depth of physical blending may be missing in their union. Is it because love alone is never enough to satisfy the nameless longings of either Pisces or Gemini ? Or is it because Air and Water Signs seldom feel quite the same overpowering urge for sexual consummation of their initial mental and emotional affinity as do Earth and Fire Signs ?

Whatever the reason, these two never find it easy to become "one flesh," or to sexually "know one another," in the biblical sense. An ideal man-woman Oneness may not be achieved without unselfishness, a quality as necessary in sex as in other aspects of love and friendship. While Pisces usually comprehends this fully, the more childlike Gemini woman sometimes does not. Their intimate moments are likely to be dictated according to her impulsive desires, rather than in answer to their mutual instincts. If she allows him to teach her by example the meaning of unselfish giving — physically as well as mentally and emotionally — their physical closeness will become a repeated renewal of their love, followed by a deeper communion than before, because of an exchanging of their inner natures, making him more spontaneous, like her — and her more tranquil, like him.

As I've said, they are similar in some of their attitudes. They both prefer unlisted phone numbers, privacy and freedom — both of them usually enjoy poetry, music, art or dancing. And they each intensely dislike routine. Boredom is a mutual enemy. Not so fortunately, however, they're also both inclined to exaggerate the truth, all the way from tiny white lies to premeditated deception — always rationalized away by myriad excuses. Frequently, when Gemini accuses Pisces of distorting the truth (or vice-versa) it's the pot calling the kettle black. A Gemini woman finds Life and Love impossible to comprehend with the senses alone. Her ruler, Mercury, demands that she use her intellect in solving the puzzle. Maybe she could figure it all out if someone would really-truly listen to her doubts and despairs, her ecstasies and her ideas. A Pisces man can do this for her if he will — patiently and sympathetically hearing her out, waiting for her to complete her convoluted circles of reasoning and finally locate the right turn in the road toward happiness. After a while, she'll take his hand as they walk along together, and his eyes won't look so lost anymore. How can a man be lost when there are not just one but two charming, delightful feminine companions beside him ? Being in love with Twins may be disturbing and perplexing at times, but no one ever said it was humdrum.

To the Pisces man, love is just another dream, in which he, the dreamer, joyfully controls the world he's created in his imagination through his intuitive sense perceptions . . . . colored with muted pastels, fragile and changeable. The constantly expressed dissatisfactions of his Gemini lady often tear great rents in his dream — and he tries to patch it, make it like new again. But dreams are not easily mended, once they've been torn apart. They are made of such misty material.

If she will speak softly, move gently . . . slowly . . . she may enter his dream world with him, and see love the way he does — as a thing of calm and beauty. All it takes is putting herself, Gemini-wise, in his place now and then, which will eventually lead her straight into his heart — the very haven she's so long been searching for and thought she'd never find . . . . . that magical garden where roses grow without the need for protective thorns.

☆ ☆ ☆ ☆ ☆ ☆

GEMINI *Man* PISCES *Woman*

◆─◀■▶─◆

In his absence, things are usually quiet on the island. The faeries take an hour longer in the morning, the beasts attend to their young . . . . . . but with the coming of Peter, who hates lethargy, they are all under way again . . . .

To keep a love affair or a marriage serene and untroubled, the typical girl Fish will do almost anything. She'll accommodate herself, her routine and her habits to the convenience of the Gemini man she loves, even though her feminine-liberation-minded female friends will be scandalized. They'll pity her openly, but she'll just smile and ignore them.

She's not really a masochistic slave to the whims of the Twins. Her sympathetic acquaintances just think she is. They're not alone. Her Gemini man is under the same impression. And that's exactly the impression this sweet, accommodating, soft-spoken lady intends to project to him (and to all her inquisitive friends, neighbors and relatives). She knows what she's doing. She's making life easier for herself. Once she's fallen in love with a Gemini the Neptune woman has enough common sense to comprehend that she has only two practical choices in this challenging 4-10 Sun Sign Pattern relationship. She can decide love isn't worth the demands a Gemini man makes upon her delicate psyche — and leave him. Just slip away some morning when he's not around. Or she can decide that the pleasure and happiness, the contentment and peace of loving him — and receiving the love and devotion of at least one of his Twin selves in return — are worth a few adjustments here and there in the relationship. If the latter is her choice, she'll simply make it work. It may take some intricate planning, but she'll manage.

Passive resistance is her Neptune secret. She was born with an awesome talent for it, as some people are born with an ear for music or perfect pitch. She knows just when to back off, how far to retreat — precisely when it's a propitious time to advance and how far she can go with him. Actually, she doesn't really know. She *senses* it. It's as though she was equipped at birth with some sort of invisible but sensitive antenna that flashes both precognitive and perceptive signals to her regarding human behavior patterns.

All Geminis are undeniably as mentally quick as can be, always alert and on guard, nearly impossible to deceive. But as clever as the Gemini man indisputably is, he can be blind to the Neptunian strategies of a Pisces girl. If she has things she wants to do, things of which he might disapprove, she won't waste her energies rocking their relationship with insistent demands or tearful pleas. She'll simply do as he wishes when he's there — and as *she* wishes when he's *not* there. What she wants to do that doesn't receive his blessing needn't be anything sinister or sly. It needn't be planning to rob a bank or being unfaithful.

It could be something as innocent and ordinary as sleeping an extra hour. Like all Birds, the typical Gemini is nearly always up and alert quite early, either whistling merrily or complaining crankily (depending on which Gemini Twin arose first), and he can become quite critical of those who lie abed later than Gemini believes they should when there are things to be done. It could be something she wants to read — which isn't necessarily the reading matter he would recommend to her. Perhaps visiting friends when he feels she should be spending her time in a more profitable way. Maybe keeping an appointment with the beauty parlor. Why would he frown on that? Because he thinks she's beautiful just the way she is — and besides, the money she spends on personal beautification could be better spent by the two of them traveling somewhere together. To Gemini, the absolute ultimate of ecstasies is a change of scene — going somewhere — anywhere at all that's different and away from daily routine.

Gemini's cleverness includes an unerring instinct for the expedient. Like, if she made her beauty parlor appointment when he was present, he'd try to talk her out of it, either with his considerable powers of persuasion and charm — or through cranky criticism. But once she's gone and he sees the finished product, he seldom argues the point. First of all, she looks lovely, and he can't find it in his heart to quarrel with her when she's so appealing. Secondly, he knows it's a waste of time to try to stop something after the fact. This man seldom wastes time. He believes time was made to be filled by doing something — every second of it somehow utilized (except for sleeping, a luxury the average Mercury birds indulge in for only very brief periods). Time is the stuff of which Life — and dreams — are made. To squander it by doing simply nothing is, to him, a sinful thing.

The Pisces woman has a completely different view of time. She feels that it's inexhaustible — there's always more of it tomorrow if any of it slips away from her today. And she believes one of the nicest ways to spend it is doing nothing. Especially after she's depleted her energies with a thousand and one duties of service to others, and her normally cheerful spirit is sagging at the seams. Time is best spent when possible, she feels, in just being herself, simply existing . . . . in the cool, green Pisces waters of calm contemplation. It refreshes her soul.

Living under the always somewhat tense 4-10 vibration with a Gemini man, her soul needs a lot of refreshing. The very qualities that drew her close to him in the beginning may later grow to be extremely wearing and wearying to her more placid nature. His mind is full of little surprises, and this delights her. He's quick, mentally agile, with an instant grasp of everything he sees, hears or reads. His ideas pop out when least expected, and they're nearly always original and fascinating. He seems to be forever busy dreaming, thinking, planning or *doing* — while she is busy just *being*. He can change occupations or careers at the wink of one of his twinkling eyes, and she never knows what to expect around the next corner. It's exciting. It's intriguing and compelling. He's like a mystery she can't completely fathom, and she adores mysteries. But these same traits of her Mercury-urged man, after a while, may leave her longing for solitude and quiet . . . . . for the security of sameness . . . . . a retreat into the soothing stillness of her own slower and softer dreams and goals.

For a time, his wonderful wit, his heart-tugging, little-boy, three-cornered grin, the star-shine in his expressive eyes, his sheer intelligence and his multiple talents will keep the girl Fish mesmerized by his Mercurial spell. It's like watching a living kaleidoscope to see the changes in his moods from affectionate, merry, warmly tender and generous — to irritable, sarcastic, sullen and stingy — and back again (to the dominance of the "good Twin"). When she watches his mental acrobatics from a distance, they're interesting, even electrifying, and certainly stimulating. It's only when she gradually allows herself to become an integral and inseparable part of the many-faceted ups and downs of his unpredictable mental, physical and emotional activity that the wear and tear on her tranquility begins to show.

However much she may try to resist, the Neptune woman can't help being eventually drawn into the nearest vortex of human experience. She absorbs the feelings and emotions around her like a psychic sponge or a sensitive photographic plate (much in the same way that Cancerians and Scorpios do). And because her own aura is keyed to a gentler chord, the percussion of Gemini cymbals and the high notes of the flutes can sometimes jangle her nerves and disturb her poise, leaving her vaguely depressed. Her solution is to swim quietly away from the floods of feeling around her which threaten to drown her . . . . enter the still world of her inner serenity . . . whatever the cost . . . . and return, her strength renewed. During these necessary periods of retreat, the Gemini man who loves her will be puzzled and hurt, sometimes angry.

It never occurs to him that he's adept in the self-defensive tactic of mental retreat himself, an expert at disappearing into aloof detachment when she most needs him to be attentive and concerned. Remember that Pisces is a very old soul, born wise — and Gemini is the symbolic Toddler Child (see "The Twelve Mysteries of Love" in the front of this book). He can't help being a trifle self-centered. Yet, often his insight is surprising, despite the symbolic "Child" charisma. There will be times when he'll display an amazing comprehension of what she's going through, then show her he understands with his Gemini light touch of compassion . . exquisitely tender. Or he senses when the right thing to do is to make her laugh, suggest a trip . . or just a drive or walk together. These are the rare and singing moments of their love.

Frequently, the sexual chemistry between this man and woman is the silent alchemy that brings them closer together in every way — not just physically. Somehow, through the blending of their Air and Water Elements during the intimacies of their sexual union, he becomes more like her — and she becomes more like him. So that, strangely, after their lovemaking, she's more alive, vibrant and aware . . he's more subdued and gentle, less restless and seeking.

When Water joins with Air in sexual Oneness (see "The Blending of the Elements" section in the back of the book) Water magically transforms Air into its own element, in the form of life-giving, cooling rain, after which all of Nature is fresh again, drenched with promise and scented with new hope. Enclosed within the circle of each other's arms, the Fish and the Twins often find the elusive harmony they reach for together at other times, and never quite seem to capture. The sexual mystery between them can be a powerful regenerative experience for both, the secret and strong foundation for their continued desire to try to understand one another's vastly different personalities.

Her procrastination, her tendency toward evading issues annoys and frustrates him. But she's an enormously facile subject changer. It's all he can do to keep up with her, swift as he is. His periodic criticism and scattered interests trouble and upset her. Yet she nearly always finds a way to avoid unpleasantness. He'd rather she didn't, because he needs the occasional mental stimulation of debate and discussion to keep his Mercury wits sharpened. She'd rather he relaxed more and worried less. He'd prefer her to relax less and worry more. Well, perhaps not worry — but at least see things as they are, instead of the way she'd like them to be (even though he often succumbs to daydreaming himself). A Gemini man is designed in a mosaic pattern of sudden twists and turns. Just when you think he's critical of metaphysical matters, he'll buy a book about the Great Pyramid. I knew one Mercury Bird who claimed contempt for the occult, then mentioned he'd like a crystal ball for Christmas. He wanted to experiment. Experimentation is the adrenalin Gemini needs to keep going. If something manages to catch his interest, he'll never rest until he's figured out the concept and improved upon it.

The complexities of this man's mind and attitudes will forever both magnetize and elude the Pisces woman. Sometimes his contradictions will increase her admiration of him, moving her to even try to imitate his analytical and intellectual yet occasionally imaginative approach. At other times, she'll despair of ever truly knowing him. For different reasons, he'll also wonder if he'll ever really know her. Because there are two of him and two of her, the game never ends. Gemini and Pisces are both signs of duality. Now and then, when she's mentally, physically and spiritually exhausted, she'll turn icy cold and refuse to communicate, which distresses him more than he ever allows her to realize. But most of the time she avoids a scene by ignoring her own hurt feelings. When ugliness, confusion or confrontation appears on the horizon, the dreamy girl Fish just pretends it isn't there, and for her, then, it disappears. She's learned that if you await patiently, most things resolve themselves. But it's impossible for him to face a problem by make-believing it doesn't exist. He's compelled to analyze and solve it immediately. He can no more resist this urge than he can resist working a crossword puzzle or answering the questions aloud when he watches a quiz show on television (which he always guesses before the person who's being asked). Every Gemini man is an instructor at heart, driven to purify muddy waters with the clearness of reason and logic. Then, too, there's the puzzling contradiction of his daydreaming.

Because Gemini and Pisces are of the Water and Air Elements, they'll never be as demonstrative, warm and affectionate outwardly as people born under the Fire Element. Yet, because of their combined water and air essence, they offer each other a great gift — freedom. She'll seldom question his impulses or his whereabouts, for she is not the possessive type. He'll grant her, likewise, the same freedom of movement. He won't mind where she floats around when he isn't there — but when he is, he'll expect her to be near, for Gemini requires an audience. She's a beautiful listener, and to him, this is her most endearing quality. Privately, he knows this soft-spoken lady of quiet secrets and subtleties is genuinely interested in everything he has to say — and above all, this is his deepest need.

She knows this changeable man of many moods will always need her — and this, above all, is *her* deepest need: to be *needed*. When he's sarcastic, as Gemini can sometimes be, he breaks her heart. But when his charm returns, his eyes twinkle with surprises again, when he projects his wistful three-cornered grin and his Peter Pan yearnings, she knows she's made the right choice to compromise her preferred life style to his. By doing so, she hasn't lost anything really, and she's gained her very own human kaleidoscope, that changes colors, shapes and designs at the slightest touch.

Repeatedly, he'll scold her for being so generous and extravagant. Then one day, without warning, he'll fly all over town, as though Mercury's silver wings were truly fastened on his heels, borrowing money he doesn't have, from two or three banks, to lend to a friend in trouble. For months, he'll make serious plans to enroll in night school to get his engineering degree, then he'll suddenly buy a typewriter and announce he's going to be a writer. He'll come home, tired from doing mental push-ups all day, refuse dinner, inform her he's going to bed, and grumpily head for the bedroom. Less than five minutes later, he'll reappear, wink at her with the old magic, and ask her if she wants to go for a ride to watch the sunset, then have dinner in town and see a play.

While she's changing, he'll nag her to hurry, and irritably complain that it takes her forever to get ready to go anywhere. But when she's sitting in the car beside him, he unexpectedly tells her she's never looked more beautiful. "Do you know I wouldn't know what to do without you?" he asks her. She doesn't reply, she just smiles. She's known that all along. That's why she's still there.

☆ ☆ ☆ ☆ ☆ ☆

CANCER

Water — Cardinal — Negative
Ruled by the Moon
Symbol: The Crab
Night Forces — Feminine

CANCER

Water — Cardinal — Negative
Ruled by the Moon
Symbol: The Crab
Night Forces — Feminine

The **CANCER-CANCER** *Relationship*

The little house looked so cosy and safe in the
darkness, with a bright light showing through its
blinds, and the chimney smoking beautifully. . . .

Did you ever wonder why your parents treated you as they did when you were a child? I mean, do you brood over it a lot? No? Well, Cancerians do, just before they fall asleep at night, and after they do finally fall asleep, they dream about it, or have nightmares about it.

Yesterday — whether it was twenty or a hundred years ago — is very real to the Moon-lured Crabs, which is why most of them know so much about history, a favorite Cancerian subject in school, also a popular hobby with many of these men and women in later years. Lots of Crabs collect antiques.

Unless the parents of those born under this Moon-controlled Sun Sign of Cancer were astrologers, they may not have said "I love you" often enough to these sensitive children. Maybe they discussed how pretty or handsome the siblings were too frequently. Perhaps they gave the little Crabs too meager an allowance, forcing them to go to work cutting the neighbor's grass at the age of eight, because a stipend of a dollar a week wasn't enough to remove that uneasy feeling of financial insecurity (any more than $3,000 a week could take it completely away now). It's even possible that the parents of little Clementine or Clarence didn't kiss the Crabs goodnight, or read bedtime stories to them each evening. (They skipped it on week ends — horrors!)

All these are reasons why the majority of Cancerians grow up lacking a sense of emotional security, causing them to exhibit flashes of moody, sensitive adolescence. It's taxing for other Sun Signs (except for Scorpio and Pisces) to cope with the apprehensions that haunt Crabs, from the persistent spectre of starvation to the lingering dread of loneliness. Only a Cancerian, vibrating on the same Lunar frequency, can find the right words and manner to calm another. Here's a sample of the typical dialogue between these 1-1 Sun Sign Pattern people.

CRAB #1: There you go, diving down into one of your inky moods again. Don't you know all the people who love you wonder why you're so lonely, and why you won't let them help you?

CRAB #2: No one tries to understand me. I had a sad childhood. I keep *telling* you that. And you don't even care. *Nobody* cares.

CRAB #1: Look, first off, try to realize that your parents may not have understood how tender your feelings were. Second off, your friends today have no way of knowing that you feel they don't love you enough, because you clam up and refuse to talk about it.

CRAB #2: Why should I talk about it? People are cold and cruel. I could always talk to my mother, and sometimes *she* understood me, but mother is gone now, and no one will *ever* love me like she did — oh, it's so AWFUL not to have Mama around. No one has made me any whiffleberry jelly since she died. (sob-sob)

CRAB #1: Don't cry. Here, take my hanky. At least your mother tried to understand you when she was alive. *My* mother warped my whole life because she ignored me most of the time. I might as well have been an orphan for all the sympathy I got from *her*. Having a mother who's dead isn't as lonely as never *really* ever having had a Mama at all.

CRAB #2: (deeply sympathetic) It must be an empty feeling.

CRAB #1: Do you know she never kissed me goodnight until *after* she tucked in my baby sister? And once she even stole the dollar the Good Tooth Fairy left under *my* pillow to pay the laundry man for *her* dirty diapers. You may not believe that, but it's true. (sob-sob)

CRAB #2: How dreadful! Don't cry. Here, do you want your hanky back?

CRAB #1: No, thanks. You keep it. I'm sorry I broke down. Anyway, we were talking about you, not me. You're certainly old enough, if you don't mind my saying so, to begin to learn that the best way to *get* love is to *give* love.

CRAB #2: Okay, okay, okay, okay. But even if I do learn how to get people to love me, what good will that do when the whole world is headed for a financial collapse? Probably my bank will be the first one to close, and I'll lose all my money and stocks and end up a pauper.

Note to reader: Should Crab #2 be female, just change the foregoing to: "Harry and I will lose our house and all our savings, he'll probably lose his job, and we'll have to wander around barefoot and homeless or go on public welfare and food stamps, which would HUMILIATE me. I'd rather be dead."

CRAB #1: You're not going to end up a pauper (or wander around homeless) because you have two separate savings accounts, those twelve bags of gold nuggets you buried under the garage, plus your bank account in Switzerland, not to mention the three apartment houses you own. Most people would consider you wealthy and secure.

CRAB #2: *Most* people don't realize that money can be here today and gone tomorrow. What if someone finds out where I buried those gold nuggets?

CRAB #1: *You* should worry! I'm going to lose my business because I can't refinance my loan. My banker hates me. I just *know* he hates me. All my kids need braces and I had to cancel my vacation to Nova Scotia this summer. *I'm* the one on the point of starvation, not *you.*

CRAB #2: Selfish, selfish, selfish — that's what you are, selfish! You don't care at all for my problems, just your own. *We* try to economize here by using margarine, but *you* still use butter. So who's worse off, you or me — I ask you?

CRAB #1: Don't snap at me. I'll snap right back. And we do NOT use butter at our house. We use margarine like you, so there!

CRAB #2: Butter!

CRAB #1: Margarine!

CRAB #2: Butter, butter, butter, butter, butter!

CRAB #1: *STOP THAT!* In the first place, it's none of your business what we spread on our bread. That's *my* business.

CRAB #2: See! You're neurotically secretive. Always afraid people are prying. You should learn to be more direct and out-in-the-open, like me.

CRAB #1: Out-in-the-open? *You? HA!* That's a howl. You're so secretive you won't even answer a civil question. Everyone knows you're paranoid. It makes people nervous to be around you.

CRAB #2: Oh! (sob-sob) I *told* you everyone hates me. Now you finally admit it yourself. And you pretended you were my friend. (sob-sob)

CRAB #1: I *am* your friend. Will you please blow your nose and stop that sniffling? You're not paranoid. I just said that to snap at you because you snapped at me. People do love you. I even like you myself, most of the time. Do you know why people like you so much?

CRAB #2: Why? (from inside the clothes closet, weeping) Why?

CRAB #1: Because you're so lovable. Not only that, you're talented, and that makes everyone respect you. People like you because you tell funny jokes, your house is always cozy and warm, you make great chicken soup and you loan people pennies from your piggy bank when they're broke. See how nice you are? You're rich and good looking and smart and popular. . . . .

CRAB #2: Am I really? Would you *really* call me popular?

CRAB #1: Yes, I would. My wife likes you, my kids love you, and . . . . .

CRAB #2: (peeking anxiously out of the shell) Really? Really-truly?

CRAB #1: Yes, really-truly, and honor-bright. I swear it.

CRAB #2: (perking up, opening the shell, and crawling cautiously out onto the warm sands of affection and approval) Say! How would you like a bowl of hot chicken soup? And maybe a slice of toast . . . with butter?

The typical Cancerian wouldn't feel totally secure financially if he or she owned Fort Knox. Nelson Rockefeller, the original John D. Rockefeller and various other assorted Rockefellers are Cancerians. They spend most of their time worrying about how to invest their billions to keep them from shrinking into mere millions, right along with worrying about how to give the whole world a bowl of hot chicken soup. Here they are (they believe) trying their best to solve the problems of starvation and poverty and political confusion, with the few dollars they can spare — and everyone misconstrues their motives and calls them greedy, monopoly-minded capitalists. It's just AWFUL. Nobody understands, nobody really *cares*.

The emotional insecurities which cause many Crabs to snap and be cranky, to withdraw into their shells sullenly and pout, to hoard their cash under the mattress and be fearful and timid about accepting affection, may often best be soothed by another Moon Child. However, sometimes these moody Looney Birds of such deep perception and sharp insight, such gentle manners and graceful ways, need the added dimension of other Sun Sign friends, associates and mates to balance their complex personalities. Two Crabs together will develop strong ties of sympathy, but will they grow? Only when each is wise enough to see in the other his or her own mistakes, thus correcting, instead of compounding them — for compounded mistakes, very much like compounded interest loans at the bank, can be costly in terms of human happiness.

Despite a natural timidity, Cancerians possess incredible tenacity of purpose, frequently losing all fear and reticence when a crisis strikes, and something or someone they love needs their courage. Then they can be amazingly strong, forceful and tough — until their feelings are hurt again — and back they crawl into the protective shell. In any sort of mutual relationship they'll never run out of things to crab about, weep over, laugh at and share.

All Looney Birds are fascinated by antiques, museums and politics. Normally, they're intensely patriotic, and if they're typical Cancerians, they'll be the most loyal, flag-saluting, flag-waving citizens of their country — except for Taureans. Many of them are teachers, scientists, artists and photographers (and bankers, of course, that's understood). The women are usually ideal homemakers, and excellent, though somewhat possessive, mothers. Both sexes tend to collect valuables, as well as totally worthless junk. Crabs are impossibly cranky, touchingly kind and hilariously funny. They're first chatty, then silent, sullen and depressed — sometimes pushy and aggressive, at other times cautious and conservative, blushing with shyness and timidity. They can be gallant, sweet, old-fashioned, motherly or fatherly, protective, scholarly, soothing and gentle. They're highly secretive (but seldom deceptive — there's a difference), graceful, poetic, musical daydreamers, whose raindrop tears are preludes to fits of giggles. Money and food can seduce them into almost anything, yet they're more sentimental at heart than even Leo, Libra and Taurus — and always economical and thrifty. You'd be all these things too, if *your* emotions were synchronized to every change of the Moon.

I don't know about your experiences, but all the Crabs who have grabbed my toe — or ear — or heart — on the beach, in the mountains, or in the city, are each doing their astrologically, totally typical thing. Among the Looney Birds I know personally, one owns a supermarket, one is a musician, one interprets dreams — and one is a powerful, wealthy tycoon-politician for whom I have a very high regard, who has, on occasion, requested astrological guidance, and has always thanked me most gallantly and graciously, in writing.

Of course, this tenacious and rock-like Crab is not the first powerful American leader to place his confidence in the wisdom of the planets. Among a number of others, Presidents Abraham Lincoln, George Washington, Thomas Jefferson and Franklin Delano Roosevelt did so — and in fact, the majority of founding fathers of this nation, and the signers of the Declaration of Independence, as well as our Constitution, were themselves either astrologers or serious students of astrology. Each one, including Ben Franklin himself. And if I may be forgiven for letting a Cancerian-type secret out of the bag, because the New Age of Aquarius demands truth at this eleventh hour of our planet's survival, Masonry is based on astrology, as all high-degree Masons are aware. (Most of our founding fathers were Masons, or Rosicrucians, who saw to it that the birth chart of our country was chosen with meticulous attention to planetary positions.)

Don't you believe it's time astrology's detractors should halt their attacks against this ancient art and science? Surely it's time that certain men, who are otherwise intelligent, should cease their futile, yet repeated attempts to assassinate this guide to self-knowledge, which our co-Creators, in Their infinite wisdom, bestowed upon us for both our temporal and our spiritual enlightenment — and which so clearly proves the Synchronicity of the Universe.

The reason so many Moon-ruled Crabs feel rather snugly at home in this country is because the United States of America is perhaps the most typical Cancerian Sun Sign of all, born on the Fourth of July — confused and sidetracked repeatedly by the split-personality, schizophrenic urges of its Gemini Ascendent (preaching freedom, while having denied blacks, women and the American Indians true equality, and so forth). Still, Uncle Sam is basically a Crab, his Gemini Rising Sign notwithstanding, the Lunar qualities subconsciously imbedded in all who live under the Stars and Stripes, whatever their personal Sun Signs may be, for everyone lives three Karmas throughout any given incarnation. Individual, racial and national Karmas equally influence the feelings and actions. And when two Crabs double up in an association within an also Cancerian country, the 1-1 vibration increases in intensity.

Is there a single citizen of the USA (each Crab especially) who doesn't feel an inexplicable heart tug of nostalgic sentiment and secret, if grudging, admiration at the sound of the brisk, clipped accent of "dear old Mother England" — or who wasn't kinfolk proud of the courage of every Britisher, from pub keeper to Churchill, during the World War II blitz bombing of London? Is not our CIA, FBI, NASA, and evidently (judging from the Watergate affair) also, periodically, our Government, unnecessarily secretive? Were we not first to land a man on the Moon herself, our very own Sun Sign ruler?

Are we not, as a nation, continually feeling guilty twinges over our inability to feed the world's hungry — and did we not initiate the practice of sending CARE packages to the needy? (Cancer *cares*.) Like any two Cancerians doubled-up, do we not become unexpectedly Crab-shell tough in a crisis? And — say! Why don't those countries we try to help, by intervening in their private affairs, *like* us more? Why aren't they more *grateful?* Does *anyone* really-truly love us? (sob-sob) Who will dispute America's use of her wealth to buy affection and respect from others, as well as to purchase security and protection against those who might hurt her, and her "children"? Is not the largest defense budget and nuclear stockpile in the world an aspect of undue Cancerian caution? And Heavens-to-Betsy-Ross! Goodness knows we've always fought for and clung to our freedoms — tenaciously.

Now, if we could only get over our Cancerian money hang-up, let go and learn to really *share*, realize that to *get* love, we must *give* love, we might all stop being so crabby and snapping at each other (like any two Crabs, in any sort of an association). Oh, dear, oh, dear, oh dear! Things were so much better back in the good old days . . . . . when we had whiffleberry jelly on our toast . . . . . (sob-sob) . . . . . swinging on the apple tree in the grassy-green back yard . . . . . swimming in unpolluted rivers and streams . . . . . all snug and safe and security-blanketed in the protection of our Constitution . . . . . when our leaders had to be voted into office by the people's choice . . . . . and a simple, honest boy like Abe Lincoln could aspire to become President, without the backing of the multi-billion-dollar interests of modern day, powerful con-glomerates . . . . . (sob-sob) . . . . . way back when dear old Patrick Henry said "Give me liberty, or give me . . . ."

Say, you know what? When you really stop to *think* about it, a little Cancerian caution now and then might not be such a bad thing after all. Maybe those "good old days" *are* worth clinging to — tenaciously. Some-times, the Crab's Lunar fears and nightmares are not imaginary, but very real.

☆ ☆ ☆ ☆ ☆ ☆

CANCER *Woman* CANCER *Man*

◀◆▶

"He does so need a mother. . . ."

*"Yes, I know," Wendy admitted rather
forlornly; "no one knows so well as I."*

When a girl Crab and a boy Crab are enticed to peek out of their protective shells long enough to fall in love, emotional security being the important thing it is to each, they'll usually want to marry. Some may make the attempt to tolerate a loosely defined living-together arrangement for a time, but it will be a very short time.

These two really prefer — and need — the warmth and protection of a socially-sanctioned and legally-cemented relationship. It's extremely doubt-ful that any Cancerian could be comfortable for long under the psychological burden of an illicit union. (What would Mother think?) Only those rare and lonely Moon Children who have been hopelessly alienated from the parental tie, for one reason or another, will successfully adjust to love-sans-marriage, and even they will duck their heads when they pass the neighbors. Yes, there are Cancerian prostitutes, but truly, they're the most unhappy, emotionally unfulfilled females on Earth, except when they're counting their earnings. Nevertheless, every last one of them cries herself to sleep at night.

The casual promiscuity of the Aquarian Age sexual revolution has passed right over the heads of the average and typical Cancer man and woman. Tradition and the sacredness of home life are too deeply ingrained in the Lunar subconscious to be discarded without great uneasiness of spirit, never mind what you may hear from some flippant Cancerian Looney Bird you know who's trying to appear to be "with it." Listen to the stars. They're older and wiser. Watch — wait — and see.

Once the 1-1 Sun Sign Pattern of Cancer-Cancer is planted, and blossoms into the girl and boy Crabs becoming "one flesh," they can surely discover lots of things to do together, based on interests they have in common — like poring over family photo albums, giggling over each other's baby pictures, collecting stamps and old coins, crying on each other's cozy shoulders, visiting each other's homesteads, redecorating the house, gardening, traveling, exchanging dreams and nightmares, reading or writing poetry, singing or listening to music, running along the beach picking up driftwood, scuba diving, making wishes on the New Moon and sharing Lunar madness under the Full Moon. She can cook for him, and he can earn money for her. Or — Cancer being a feminine sign, and the Lunar charisma of both male and female Crabs being what it is — he can cook for *her*, and *she* can earn money for *him*. Either way. All Cancerian men like fine food, and most are good cooks. All Cancerian women like supplemental incomes, and most are good at earning it. And vice-versa, with the boy and girl Crabs.

Emotional crying binges (or pouting periods) will be first on the list of possible problem areas, making Kleenex a big item on the budget. They both sniffle, sob and weep a lot — at sad movies, over real or imagined neglect from the mate, about their lost childhood — and sometimes for no reason at all, except that their emotions wax and wane with the Moon's periodicity.

Food, as already mentioned, will come next in importance, with either happy agreement or tearful argument about which restaurant to dine in (during courtship) or how to cook and serve the artichokes at home (after the honeymoon). Those rare Cancerians who are casually unconcerned with food — with where, when and how they eat — either have the Moon or Ascendent in Gemini, Aquarius, Sagittarius or Aries, or else they were adopted for sure, and were fibbed to about their true birthday. Fabulous food — and enough of it — is a Cancer birthright. It shocks the typical Crabs to think of anyone starving, and it literally *terrifies* them to think of *themselves* starving. Both possibilities will bring tears to their eyes. Some of the most sincerely and tenderly concerned men and women, who deeply yearn to help the hungry masses (especially the children) of the underprivileged countries, are Cancerians (also some of the most frequent purchasers of bathroom scales, although they share this latter distinction with many Taureans and Librans).

After emotional tantrums and food fusses will come babies — raising a family. If one of them has natal planetary positions indicating the lack of desire to have offspring, the other will sulk and pout. If they both want tiny cherubs, they'll find grounds for both agreement and disagreement when the birds are ready to leave the nest. Some Cancerian mothers don't believe Junior is old enough to date a girl or to live alone in his own apartment until he's around thirty to thirty-five. Some Cancerian fathers (and mothers) don't believe a daughter should marry until a potential suitor appears who is healthy, wealthy and wise, who treasures her as a rare pearl of perfect womanhood, whose reputation is unblemished — and who makes over $100,000 a year. (A parent with both the Sun *and* Moon in Cancer might conceivably hold out for President of the United States as the only man fit for such an honor.)

Next on the list of subjects involving the possibilities of both harmony and tension between two Crabs in love — is money. Actually, money comes first in order of Cancerian priority, but sometimes the haze of romance causes this couple to hide their individual financial hang-ups from each other initially, as an unseemly and harsh intrusion upon the harmonics of love. They're right. It is. Nonetheless, they'd best tackle the clash over cash in the very beginning. Separate checking accounts. Definitely, that's what I would advise. Separate checking accounts, savings accounts, stock portfolios, stamp collections and spending money allowances. Then they can each hoard as much lettuce as he or she desires, and practice whatever mild or pronounced degree of stinginess or generosity was implanted by the experiences of childhood, secretly, without the other knowing about it. Cancer is ultra-sensitive, and more so about money than about anything else. Keeping their individual finances private could be a futile hope, because these two are *equally* adept at keeping secrets and prying them out of each other.

Last, but surely not least, there's the area of sex. Let's hope they make an attempt to comprehend the peculiarities of their mutual astrological symbol, the Crab. The habit of all Nature crabs, male and female, as I've pointed out before, is to reach a desired objective by first moving backward or sideways, with seeming unconcern, then lunging suddenly forward. If they both memorize this ingrained tendency, she'll be less likely to dissolve into tears of rejection and neglect some night when he casually announces he's going to sleep on the couch to watch the eclipse of the Moon from the front room window. She can instead smile to herself, knowing his *real* objective is to follow her into bed soon, having been aroused by Lunar longings when she kissed him goodnight on the couch, trailing perfume and wearing his favorite nightie. And he'll be less likely to be thrown into an impotent impasse of masculine fears when she coolly turns her back to him on their anniversary, murmuring, "Goodnight honey, don't forget to set the alarm," after her eyes telegraphed to him all afternoon an invitation for a thrilling encore of their wedding night. He can, instead, smile and wait till she signals her *real* wishes by slowly sliding her cold feet over to touch his warm toes — or some similar subtlety. Both of them are inclined to play sexual guessing games, concealing passion for fear of rebuff — or the discovery of a lack of a *mutual* need for union — and so each will often try to trick the other into making the first move. Other than this bedtime hide-and-seek habit, they should find a rare contentment through their physical expression of love.

Neither one of them seeks, or is desirous of handling, a demanding sexual passion. Although they're both enormously receptive to sensuality and capable of a deep response, their need in lovemaking is more for affection than for eroticism. It can crush a male or female Crab if the partner fails to set the proper mood for sex, with preliminary endearments and tender touches — or, even worse, fails to spend time after physical consummation in affectionately reaffirming love. Romance is an integral part of sexual excitement and fulfillment for Cancer. The boy or girl Crab who feels unloved throughout the day will snap sharply at the advances of the mate at night, then crawl into a lonely shell of frigidity, expecting to be coaxed out into desire by frequent reassurances and apologies.

When these two first meet, timidity and caution may color their initial sex reactions. Then suddenly, under a Full Moon, which can act as a strange and mystical aphrodisiac to Cancer, they'll move forward (like the symbolic Nature crab) to do what comes naturally, and it will be a toss-up who seduces whom. Poetry and music never fail to quicken the sexual pulse of Cancerian lovers, but they'll find physical love difficult if not impossible to express when they're worried about finances. A streak of poverty can temporarily halt their sex lives, and a feeling of not being appreciated will also considerably dampen passion. When their physical relationship cools, they don't need a sex therapy clinic or a bag of ginseng cookies. They need lots of money, lots of affection, lots of sympathy — and a Farmer's Almanac. Usually, this man and woman will be faithful. Infidelity is rare between Cancerians. If it should occur, the Lunar possessiveness won't be as likely to create a display of jealousy, as to cause a tenacious determination to wait out the rival.

Secrecy is a trait they'll have to curb early in their relationship. Although Crabs of both sexes like to keep secrets, neither one likes to have secrets kept *from* him — or her. If they work at being more open and direct, less subtle and evasive, much hurt can be avoided. He may think she's hiding a lover, when the real reason she's so quiet and preoccupied is because her mother didn't answer her last letter — or he didn't compliment her on her creamed artichokes, and didn't even notice her new nightgown. And she may think he's seeing another woman, when his real secret is that he's worried about being able to make the car payment — or that she's forgotten to say "thank you for loving me" when they wake up in the morning for three whole weeks. In either case, an honest confession will turn everything rightside-up again, and change tears into laughter — for both of them possess the saving grace of humor, which is always the surest and safest antidote when they're taking themselves too seriously.

More so than with other 1-1 Sun Sign Pattern lovers, the degree of compatibility between the Moon Maid and her gentle Crab will depend on their individual Moon Signs, and the aspect formed between their natal Moons. If this is harmonious, their coziness will far exceed their crabbiness. If not, this man and woman still stand a good chance of becoming wealthy together — and they'll also probably treat one another with more tender, loving care than either of them ever have or ever will receive from anyone else. They may snap at each other under a waning Moon, but when she is waxing, these two will sail away on a sea of imagination into a lovely world of lavender lunacy and pale silver enchantment, faintly scented with Johnson's baby powder. Moonlight becomes them — both.

CANCER

Water — Cardinal — Negative
Ruled by the Moon
Symbol: The Crab
Night Forces — Feminine

LEO

Fire — Fixed — Positive
Ruled by the Sun
Symbols: Lion & Shy Pussycat
Day Forces — Masculine

The **CANCER- LEO** *Relationship*

" . . . And I know you meant to be kind . . ."

he *Moon Maiden* and the Lion. The *Crab* and the Lioness. *Cancer* and Leo. Is that what you call yourselves? You're making a large mistake. It may seem a small thing, but so is a seed, before it grows into a Sequoia tree. Let's correct it, and start off right. You've no idea how it will help. The *Lion* and the Moon Maiden. The *Lioness* and the Crab. *Leo* and Cancer. A little respectful protocol will go a long way in this association, and never mind the natural astrological Sun Sign sequence on the karmic wheel.

I've already mentioned, more than once, the possible dangers existing between any two persons born into the Fire and Water Elements, when they combine their personalities in the office, school or home, but when we're discussing Leo and Cancer, it's important to remind them again, in case they missed the warning in other chapters — or in the Elements Section in the back of this book.

If these two wish, they can exchange as much tolerance and learning in their association as any other 2-12 Sun Sign Pattern people. But if they do *not* wish, in the Fire of Leo and the Water of Cancer each possesses the power to destroy the other — and they may use this power without even being aware that they're using it, until it's too late, and the damage to one or the other (or both of them) has already been done.

For reasons known only to the planets, the 2-12 relationship, when it involves Cancer and Leo — unlike its effect on other Sun Signs in this vibratory pattern — does not cause Leo to be quite as tolerant of the Crab's personality as one might suppose with Cancer representing the twelfth house of the karmic past to Leo. Nor is the Crab usually as anxious as other Sun Sign halves of the various 2-12 Patterns to learn the lessons to be taught by the following Sun Sign, Leo (although it must be admitted that Leo will likely be more than anxious to teach them). However, willing to learn or not, Cancer secretly *knows* (even though the Crab may not ever admit it) that there *are* lessons to be learned from Leo's Sun wisdom, and the longer Cancer postpones the inevitable, the harder those lessons will be to master.

I can image all the Lions and Lionesses grinning and nodding their heads in agreement at this point, and all the Crabs frowning crabbily or sniffling. It's true, Moon Child. You have many things to learn from the Big Cats, and if you've been *unconsciously* trying to teach and overpower, instead of the other way around, you're interfering with your own karmic destiny, and also with that of Leo, which is not a very smart or safe thing to do, and you know how you pride yourself on being both smart and safe. You're only forging karmic obligations into a dreary chain, for future incarnations.

Now the Leos can stop grinning and stroking their vanities because astrology also has a warning for *them*. Have you been less tolerant and understanding of the Lunar traits (annoying as they may be to you) of your Cancerian friend, relative or mate than you have the capacity of being, since your eternal soul so recently experienced the Cancerian essence itself ? Have you been pouting, instead of being protective and sympathetic ? Or have you become Shy Pussycats, and allowed the Crab to teach *you*, when it should be just the opposite ? Let the Crabs teach caution to the sign *behind* them, Gemini — the Twins can use it ! You already subconsciously know the need for rain in the soul (Cancer moods) and you're here now to teach the Crabs the value of sunshine in the human heart. Have you permitted some Cancerian to extinguish the fiery rays of your ruling Sun, to crush the proud spirit of your birthright with water pessimism or gentle disapproval — which is, nevertheless, disapproval ? Is this what you've done ? Shame on you. Where is your roar ? Shake your mane (if you're a Lion) or narrow your tilted cat eyes (if you're a Lioness) and behave as your Solar destiny intended you should when you drew your first breath upon this Earth. You needn't go overboard, and completely dehydrate the Water Elements of your Cancer friend, relative or lover with your flames. Crabs can be handy creatures to have around when you need to be hushed and lullabyed and fed chicken soup — and no one else will ever relate such fascinating dreams to you or tell such funny stories — but never allow these people to drown your enthusiasm or drain your adrenalin. Be yourself. You too, Cancer. Be *yourself*, and you'll be much happier. "Be True to Your Sun Sign Essence" is astrology's wisest rule.

There are, sadly, some Cancer-Leo associations in which the Crabs and Lions (or Lionesses) reverse their roles. Cancerians are dear, sensitive souls, but it sometimes happens that the steady dripping of the Water Element over the years will quite literally extinguish Leo's fire — and confidence. It can begin with a Leo who's a Shy Pussycat type, who perhaps isn't tolerant enough of Cancer's markedly different disposition and goals, and who gradually allows his — or her — pouting over not being sufficiently respected and adored to develop into lethargy, to the point where the Leo charisma is completely submerged.

Or it may be the Crab's fault. It can't be said often enough that Cancer is a CARDINAL SIGN OF LEADERSHIP, despite the Lunar surface gentleness and *apparent* reticence. A Crab with a powerfully aspected Sun and Mars in the horoscope can utilize all the Cancerian patience, tenacity, persistence and perseverance to eventually wear down a Fire Sign like Leo into a sort of spiritual fatigue, which is a very sad and serious matter. A long siege of the subtle but determined strategy of an unusually strong-willed Crab can considerably dampen even Leo's proud nature. It's hard to know with which Sun Sign such a role reversal initiates, but usually neither person is aware, on a conscious level, that it's happening. It's seldom motivated by malice or deliberate unkindness on either side, but rather caused by a lack of the constant alertness needed when you're mixing Fire and Water over a long period of time. Nothing is sadder than a Lion or Lioness robbed of pride and dignity, unless it's a Cancerian who is gradually forced into a kind of aggressive self-sufficiency completely foreign to the Crab's softness and sensitivity.

It can work the other way too. Leo can burn out all the beauty of Cancer's deep and normally tranquil emotions. A Cancerian subjected to the arrogant demands of a domineering-type Leo suffers much in silence, sometimes retreating into introversion (in severe cases, into an almost psychotic state), sometimes becoming snappy and irritable, but nearly always escaping in the final reel. (Crabs are expert escape artists.) If the Sun and Moon in their charts are in negative aspect, Cancer and Leo can wound each other deeply, even though unintentionally. Should these Luminaries in their mutual horoscopes be in positive aspect, however, the two of them can become a creative, imaginative and mutually protective pair. The Lion or Lioness will protect the sensitive emotions of the Moon person from the blows of a harsh world, and Cancer will affectionately pamper Leo in return. After all, the Sun and the Moon are their rulers, and *they* manage to exist in peace and harmony in the skies overhead. Due to their combined Solar (paternal) and Lunar (maternal) influences, Leo and Cancer, regardless of personal conflict or tension, often make fine parents.

They must both remember that Cardinal Cancer was born to lead, *however quietly and unobtrusively,* and Leo should permit this (as long as Leo's name comes first over the door). Since Leo is the Fixed Organizer, the Crab should allow Leo to *organize* his (or her) life — which Leo will do most admirably. This will allow Leo to be the sunny person he — or she — was meant to be, and will, in turn, bring out all the lovely Lunar tenderness of Cancer. It will also coax out the Crab's delicious, unsurpassed humor, all of which, when added together, conjures a cozy cradle of compatibility, as Cancer lulls Leo with love and laughter, and Leo's generous heart brings the sunshine after the rain, by understanding and forgiving Cancer's changing moods.

The two of them are bound to clash over cash, now and then. Cancer will privately think Leo is a little wild and wasteful. Leo may publicly think the Crab is unnecessarily frugal. "Waste not, want not," snaps the cautious economical Crab. "Get some new carpeting around this place, or I leave !" roars Leo. Royalty expects top quality as his or her natural right, and the Big Cats become either very depressed or very angry when they are forced to accommodate to shabbiness or to a denial of what Leo considers necessity (which is often what others consider luxury). There are, let us be sure to note, a few Leos (very few) who are careful spenders, even downright miserly, and these rare Pussycats will get along "royally" with the Crabs, if you'll forgive the pun. But the great majority of Leos, whether male or female, child or adult, can't resist treating themselves (and others, for Leo is generous) to the things that money will buy. They have every right to spend what they earned with their impressive talents and organized minds. It's when Leo begins to spend, in a business or marital relationship, what *Cancer* has earned, that the trouble begins.

The typical Crab normally hangs on to everything with a tenacious grip . . . old photographs, old loves, old tennis balls and shorts, old memories, old nightmares, old feuds, old fears, old key rings, old television sets, old bills, stamped paid . . but Cancer is not selective about money. It matters not whether it's old or new, Cancer considers it worth keeping. These people can be touchingly generous with their families and children, and almost never will a Cancerian turn down a friend in real need. But they dislike to throw away or gamble their cash reserves in a frivolous manner. Oddly, they're not frugal when it comes to food. A Crab sometimes turns into the original prototype Big Spender in a restaurant, astounding everyone with the unexpected generosity. Everyone but the waiter. The tip will be adequate, but not cause for celebration. The waiter is not likely to write home to his mother about it. If Leo has been the dining partner, the Lion (or Lioness) may pass the waiter an extra five dollars on the sly. It had better be on the sly, because it's not a good idea to humiliate the Crab in public.

A very strange thing about Leo and Cancer is that both these Sun Signs tend to enjoy photography. Not every single Crab, Lion and Lioness in the world owns a camera, of course, but about 90 percent of them do. Leo will probably own an expensive one, and the Big Cat's fondness for photography, we may as well face it, may in some cases be based on the fact that Leos simply adore to have their pictures taken. If they have a Nikon handy, they can always talk their friends into snapping them, while they pose dramatically. The Crab may own simply a cheap Brownie, although it could be a rare German-made model with high-quality lens, because Cancer doesn't mind investing money in something sensible and practical. To the Lunar person's point of view, a camera is certainly a sensible and practical purchase because it captures Today, so it can be treasured Tomorrow, when Today has become Yesterday. A camera molds memory into permanency for Cancerians, whose very minds are like sensitive film, recording every impression with vivid clarity.

When there is friction between these two Sun Signs, the Lion or Lioness may be incited into ever greater and grander achievement, just to prove his or her superiority to the cautious Crab. When there is creative compatibility between them, the Cancerian's unerring instincts and tenacity of purpose will guide the Lion to successfully launch his grandiose schemes, the Lioness to at last realize her glorious dreams. Either way, Leo can then write Cancer a thank you note.

Dear Crab . . . you made me what I am today, but I like you anyway.

☆ ☆ ☆ ☆ ☆ ☆

CANCER *Woman* LEO *Man*

It was not to receive his thanks, however, that she hung there in the sky; it was not even to watch him get into the nest; it was to see what he did with her eggs.

A Moon Maid and a Lion who have fallen in love face one of three possibilities, assuming they expect their love to result in a lifetime relationship. (1) After a few years, he will arrogantly domineer her into a trembling, tearful submission to his royal whims, causing her to become even more moody than she was when they first met. (2) After a few years, she will crush his confidence with her gentle, but persistent nagging, causing him to retreat into sad and sullen silences. (3) After a few years, they'll make adjustments, compromise their differences, and live happily ever after — loving and laughing and weeping and learning.

Turning the third possibility into a reality won't be a piece of cheese cake, nor is it a task for the faint-hearted or the selfish. It requires a sensitive awareness of the care needed when you're blending Fire and Water. *He'll* have to suffer through her perplexing moodiness, and try to perceive the root cause of her possessive reflexes. *She'll* have to overlook his ego-oriented attitudes, and not dwell in self-pity on his sometimes thoughtless disregard for her feelings. *He'll* have to realize that half her possessiveness will disappear when she has babies to croon over and wrap in swaddling clothes and the other half will disappear when he takes the time to calm her fears and strengthen her sense of emotional security. *She'll* have to realize that much of his arrogance stems from an inner doubt of his abilities (which increases in exact ratio to his success, oddly) and that she'll get nowhere with him by dampening his pride, yet can almost make him roll-over-Rover by verbally (and sincerely) appreciating his virtues and allowing him at least the choice of taking the initiative in nearly everything. But she must be careful to retain her own dignity and individuality at the same time.

If all this sounds to you like a path to sainthood, you're right, that's just about what it is. It takes a lot of saintly serenity, love and patience for a Crab and a Lion to gradually grow to trust their hearts with one another, for their dreams are very different. Don't be gloomy. There are reliable astrological blueprints for building this relationship into a Forever design, with a strong foundation of happiness, lit brightly by her Lunar lamps and Solar heated by him. Here's just one example of such a blueprint.

When I first met good friend Ilene Goldman, she was twinkling with her Looney Bird humor. Ilene is married to Bill Goldman, author of a number of best-selling books and TV dramas, also two-time Oscar winner for his screenplays of *Butch Cassidy and the Sundance Kid* and *All the President's Men*. Bill is a Leo, neither a Shy Pussycat nor a roaring Jungle Cat type. He is simply a Lion. A Monarch. A King. He happens to be an exceptionally kind-hearted and generous Leo, but he is a Lion. He is strikingly handsome. She is hauntingly beautiful. She bakes yummy pies. He purrs. (He also growls, of course, but more often he purrs.)

"What is your Sun Sign?" I asked Ilene, a few seconds after our first hellos. (Has it been nearly a decade ago? It has. Time flies.) She gazed at me then, with such an expression of mock sadness in her large, starry-lashed eyes, and gave a gentle sigh of resignation, as she replied, "I'm a Cancerian. I have two Fire Sign children, a Leo dog, a Leo cat, several Leo relatives, a Leo housekeeper and a Leo husband—and I cry a lot."

"I'll just bet you do," I said with an instant rush of sympathy. Of course, I knew she was only joking (about the weeping—the Sun Signs are actual), just displaying her Lunar humor. Still, her remark did indicate in a subtle manner her recognition of the sacrifices involved for a Moon Maiden living with a jungle pride of Lions and Lionesses. She plays her karmic role with the Sun Sign of Leo smoothly, absorbing all the beneficial lessons she's astrologically destined to learn during this present life of servitude . . . . . . I mean, during this present lifetime. Seriously (I was only jesting) this girl Crab is undeniably devoted to her Lion. She respects him, and never tries to upstage him. In return, he has allowed her to wear the glittering crown that designates her as his Queen—and very becoming it is too. But there is no groveling, she's retained her independence as a woman, and she is not a slave (maybe a footman now and then).

Like every Cancerian wife and mother, when her children were teeny-tiny, she fussed over her entire brood a bit much, drowning them in Vicks salve and chicken soup, and smothering them with loving concern and affection in a house awash with galoshes, thermometers, Crayolas and sentimentally bronzed birthday cakes. But after a while, she firmly adjusted her crown, majestically marched forth and formed a partnership with her close friend Lola Redford to found CAN (Consumer Action Now), an energetic and practical concept, which has enormously benefited the ecological movement. In connection with CAN, this Moon Maiden has managed to chalk up almost as many radio, TV and newspaper interviews as her Lion. I didn't say *more*, I said *almost* as many. The difference is vital.

Although she leads an exciting, challenging life of her own, and even has her own office, it's never allowed to interfere in the slightest way with the lavish attention her Big Cat expects and receives. She's a dream as a hostess, maybe even more glamorous in appearance than when they first met, and she has a hundred things to talk about with her Leo, other than detergent, dish towels and depression. There are all those cans. And the depletion of our natural resources.

These two genuinely admire each other's minds, talents and accomplishments, and despite his Lunar Lady's busy schedule, the Lion is properly pampered. If they gave out Academy Awards for Happiness, Ilene would surely receive an Oscar for her supporting role. Not long ago, when a friend of hers was enduring a temporary but agonizing period of poverty and personal tragedy, she appeared every few days, like an angel of mercy, with Cancer CARE baskets, stuffed full to overflowing with fruits, goodies, cash—and loyalty. (But she was always back home in time for dinner, to feed her hungry Lion and her cubs.)

Now you have a blueprint for compatibility between Crabs and Lions, Moon Maidens and Pussycats, Cancerians and Leos. Also for Lions and Crabs, Pussycats and Moon Maidens, Leos and Cancerians. It works with any combination, but may give quicker results with the last three. Leo likes to win all the battles. Cancer prefers to win the war.

The Cancerian girl is powerfully influenced by the combination of her feminine Sun Sign and its also feminine ruler, the moody Moon. Therefore, she personifies the Mystery of Woman, all the complex yearnings and inexplicable behavior of Eve herself. The Leo man is powerfully influenced by the combination of his masculine Sun Sign and its also masculine ruler, the Sun. Therefore, he personifies the conquering charisma of Man, all the wisdom and strength, contrariness and proud spirit of Adam himself. You can see why she's able to tempt him in the beginning, why he's so easily seduced by her home-baked pies. Yet, she's Cardinal, and this makes her a rather bossy Eve. He's Fixed, and this makes him a stubborn Adam. They'll be more at ease emotionally with one another if she doesn't try to compete with his stronger personality, but allows it to bring out all her tender and tranquil qualities. It's natural for the Moon (Cancer) to absorb the brilliant Solar rays of the Sun (Leo) and reflect them back in the form of the softer, more gentle illumination of moonlight.

Imitating Mother Nature never leads *human* nature astray, as long as these two don't overdo their Solar-Lunar roles, and slip into the trap of overemphasizing them. Too many Cancer-Leo couples drift into this sort of danger unaware. There's nothing "natural" about an association with sadist-masochist overtones. But these are the extreme cases. The Cancerian woman and Leo man should strive to temper each other's divergent personalities through a subtle but constant interchange of themselves, and avoid excessive domination on his part, as well as excessive docility on her part. For this sort of balancing act, it will be substantially helpful if the Moon or Ascendent of one or both of them adds a Gemini or Libra influence.

The chemical attraction a girl Crab and a Lion feel when they first fall in love may later ebb and flow. Their physical magnetism is powerful, but it requires a delicate blending of their natures. If he's impulsive, demanding and careless in his lovemaking, and she's too sensitive, passive and elusive in hers — his mind may wander, and her emotions will flee into strange shadows. When physical closeness between them is good, it's very good, for she's beautifully receptive, and he's wonderfully warm and affectionate. Because there's a gentleness and softness in her sexual attitude that complements his intensity, the passion exchanged between them can be very deep. But she can wound him with her moodiness when she's worried, which he mistakenly judges as a lack of response — and he can hurt her with his aloofness when he's troubled, which she mistakenly interprets as indifference.

Tears are often part of their togetherness, but tears can be healing, and with Cancer and Leo they can turn into tears of joy those times when he soothes away her nightmares with the comfort of his familiar nearness. Her dreams are always lovelier when she falls asleep with his arms around her, because it means her heart is safe again for a little while from her subconsciously remembered childhood fear of loneliness. This is when he knows how much he's needed, and then *he* cries . . . but she's not awake, so she doesn't know, and he'll never tell her. She has many secrets, but he has only one. His vulnerability.

The Lion who is enchanted on a summer night by a girl Crab is always surprised when he knows her better. She seemed to be such a helpless creature, seeking his strength . . . . . . as soft as a baby rabbit, and as timid — wide-eyed, needing guidance. He felt a tug of tenderness. Later he learned she's more than feminine — she's *womanly*. Feminine is enticing, but womanly is deeper. She's cozy and maternal, tucking him under her lavender-scented blankets of security . . . . . . and so perceptive she guesses his thoughts and feelings without his having spoken a word. Much later, he'll discover something else, misty, hard to define. It disturbs him, because just when he's sure he's in control of the relationship, she eludes him, makes him feel he's not really the lord and master of this lady after all. Not in the total way he once believed he was. She never defies him, but he suspects she may have a secret place in her mind she escapes to when he's hurt her, when they've quarreled.

He'd like to follow her there to tell her he's sorry, but he doesn't know the way. And so he must wait for her to return, in her own time — from her secret place. She can't be coaxed, and she can't be hurried. He's always glad when she returns and is real again, back to being her normal funny, bright and alert self . . . . . . humming as she bakes his apple pie, stirring him with the fragrance of her hair as she kisses his cheek. It's time to impulsively suggest a trip. Her wanderlust is awakened, she says, "Let's"! And he confidently takes charge of the travel plans. Shall they leave as soon as tomorrow morning? Why not?

Traveling somewhere together is like a fresh wind blowing through the love between this man and woman. She has him all alone then, to herself, the way she likes him — and he can instruct her in all sorts of new lessons. No matter where they go, he'll be an expert on the people, the language, the stores and the surrounding geography. She listens, his gentle Moon Maiden . . . fascinated. And as she listens, she finds herself remembering why she fell in love with him. It was because she could sit curled up beside him forever, just listening to him talk. He knew so much about so many things, and he made them all sound exciting. He had such confidence, he was so sure of himself, the way she'd always longed to be, and couldn't. But . . . something about his sureness bothered her, and for a long while, she didn't know what it was. Then one day it came to her. "If he's so confident," she wondered, "and knows so much, and is so sure he's always right . . . why does he need my constant approval?"

Suddenly, she knew. "He's only *pretending* to be brave and strong and wise. Except when he knows that I believe it. Then he believes it too." The knowing gave her a sharp loving-pain. And she wept the same tears wept by Eve herself when *she* first learned Woman's deepest secret from Eden's Tree of Wisdom.

☆ ☆ ☆ ☆ ☆ ☆

CANCER *Man* LEO *Woman*

"Don't go, Peter," she entreated. "I know such lots of stories."

Those were her precise words, so there can be no denying that it was she who first tempted him.

The Lioness muses. This Cancerian male is . . . strange. He's a gentle Crab, a sensitive man, more considerate of her as a woman than anyone else she's ever known. He's not domineering, he lets her have her own way most every time they disagree. Of course, there are his moods, but . . . he worries about her, and he really-truly *cares* about her feelings. He protects her lovingly and affectionately from the insensitive, rude, crude and vulgar people who offend her. Truthfully, she's never felt so securely cherished by anyone in her whole life, except when she was a baby. At last she's found a man who sincerely appreciates her. Yet, there's something she senses in their relationship that troubles her. Something indefinable. It causes her to feel a little uneasy somehow, like a whispered warning. But a warning of what?

That something she senses is the influence of his Cardinal essence. Cancer is a Cardinal Sign of leadership. Over and over, astrologers keep reminding Fire Signs of this, until they're weary. It means that, beneath all his sweet gallantry and courteous manner, behind his chuckles and rich humor, he manages in a subtle way to . . . . well, to *manage* things, including her life. He never yells at her or flames up in a violent temper, making chauvinistic demands. She could handle that. A Leo girl is stimulated, not frightened or confused, by an open and direct challenge. But she knows, in an unspoken, subliminal way, that she's expected to follow his gentle lead. Whatever small or large Kingdom over which they preside will be ruled cooperatively. She may attend all the balls she likes, initiate all the gay celebrations she wishes, dress in queenly fashion, add a jewel or two to her tiara when she's depressed and needs an extra ruby to cheer her up — she can even be the one to give all the orders to the milkman and postman and cleaning people in the castle, and decide which monograms would look best on the linen and silver. On parade days, she may sit up front, smiling and waving, on a throne bearing her name, spelled out in roses. But *he* will administer the *real* responsibilities behind the scenes, and it will be clearly understood that, although her whims and fancies will receive his affectionate indulgence 98 percent of the time, his is the final veto power in those matters which make up the 2 percent of the time when her impulsiveness meets in a head-on collision with his caution.

Is it really like that with him? Yes. It is really like that with him. Here she was, expecting this man to personify what she believed were the qualities of the Water Element — kindness, sympathy, mildness, sensitivity, and . . . . wait. He does possess all those virtues. Every single one. Well, yes, but this leadership thing is disturbing. What about that? Your Majesty, the Lioness, dear girl, if you want a man with all the qualities of the Water Element, but lacking the leadership vibration, you'll have to find a Pisces or Scorpio male. The Mutable Fish won't try to boss you, not even in a subtle way, but he's not quite as dependable as your gentle Crab, and although he is also highly intelligent and sensitive, he's emotionally elusive. The Scorpion won't spend his life trying to lead you either. Scorpio is a Fixed Water Sign. He'll just try to organize things for you, but then there's that Scorpio sting if you should happen to tread on his pride or anger him. Your gentle Crab won't sting you. He may pout a little, and crawl under his shell for a few hours or days, but he won't sting you when you're least expecting it.

Think about it. With your Cancerian man you have all the positive and beautiful qualities of the Water Element, plus the security of astrology's promise that he'll never sting you to get even, and the knowing that he's considerably more emotionally reliable than his Neptune-ruled brothers. His actions and behavior are governed by the Moon, so he'll reflect your sunlight softly back to you, and you can surely see the value of having your sunlight reflected. (What Leo wouldn't?) You were born under the Fixed Sign of the Organizer yourself, so why not let him lead, if it's such a big deal with him, while you *organize* his leadership? He won't hide your light. He reflects it, remember? You're the Sun. He's the Moon. You're in charge of daytime. He's in charge of nighttime. I didn't mean to get into the sexual aspect of your romance this soon, but here it is, hinting and peeking at us, so let's discuss it now.

It's interesting, this thing about the Sun (Leo) ruling the day, and the Moon (Cancer) ruling the night. It could mean that the Leo woman will be happy to allow the Cancer man to lead them into the physical expression of their love at night. It probably does mean just that. But it could also mean that her Sun rulership might coax him into realizing the warm surprise, the special kind of intimacy of physical togetherness shared in the daytime, in the sunlight. The combined Solar-Lunar influences created by their relationship could cause them both to enjoy the exhilarating experience of breaking the orthodox, and changing old, tired, meaningless rules in every area of life. Why must night be the only acceptable — or expected — time of lovemaking?

A thought like that can give birth to a hundred more thoughts relating to the confining codes and mores of society, and she'll excite him into worlds of originality and daring he only dreamed of until her Sun blended with his Moon. He only dreamed of traveling, before her. After her — and with her — he'll fasten wings to his heels and his heart, and they'll fly away to new horizons, places he's always longed to blaze through the sky. And this is good. Good for him, and good for her.

In mentioning breaking the orthodox, I wasn't referring to the new styles in sexual promiscuity, such as multiple partners, group massage experiments, or any of those Sodom-and-Gomorrah, Decline-and-Fall-of-the-Roman-Empire, Greek-Acropolis-Drunken-Orgies vibes. That's the road to regret and real emptiness — of both the heart and the body. I meant a mutual discovery that sex between a man and woman can contain newness and freshness, that it needn't be dictated by senseless habit patterns seeded into the subconscious mind. The erotic and the sensual can be mixed with special feelings and memories of barns with sweet-smelling hay, Christmas morning snowflakes, starshine, deep, cool woods, a placid stream in the mountains, covered bridges on sleepy country roads, Easter sunrise, lilies of the valley, horses and chickens, Cub Scout campfires . . . even the way a newspaper smells when it's brought in from the front porch after a summer shower, like ozone splashed on the special scent of newsprint . . . that announces a new day. Or maybe woodsmoke . . . and baby squirrels.

That's what sex is like when it's right and good and special. Physical Oneness between a Cancerian man and his Leo woman can be a moving experience, for his sexual feelings are poetic and perceptive, still and deep — and hers are fiery with intense desire, yet sometimes as serene and calm as an August day. His emotional depth and her emotional warmth can make their union a blissful, peace-restoring moment between them. But they'll have to be watchful of the Fire and Water dangers. She can freeze into frigidity when her pride is wounded, and he can either pout and weep — or grow tough and impassive — when he's made to feel rejected for any imagined reason. Crabs are good at imagining unintended hurt. She's even better at nursing her false pride. They both have other talents they would be wiser to nurture than these. Tenderness is always the cornerstone for intimacy between Cancer and Leo. When it's missing, the peace and fulfillment of their sexual blending is missing.

His changes of mood as the Moon overhead moves through its phases, and simultaneously moves through his mind and emotions, will sometimes worry her, at other times annoy and anger her. But her Leo heart is large and generous, quick to forgive when she loves, and she's not a woman who holds grudges. Unless she has the Moon or Ascendent in Cancer herself, in which case they'll be extremely compatible as lovers, and *both* hold grudges, usually not against each other, but against those outside their circle of love — which could be hard on their friends and relatives. Just so his mother is never the recipient of a grudge, or even the tiniest slight. His mother was — is — and always shall be a saint, whether formally canonized or not. The Lioness would be well advised to keep that in mind. While Leo doesn't ordinarily cling to old injuries, unfortunately Cancer does tend to hang on to them with a fairly firm grip, whether they occurred several hours or several years ago. If the Crab would imitate his Leo woman's magnanimous spirit, he'd be a happier man, and this is one of the things astrology means when it decrees that Cancer has lessons to learn from Leo.

When these two marry, and they likely will, because Cancerians plan for permanency, and the Lioness auditions only for the role of Queen-Wife, never mistress or discarded girl friend — the Crab should know this about his sunny and charming mate: she *must* rule *something*. Or she will try to rule *someone*. Namely, him. (And the children, of course, but what about after they've left home? They might produce a passel of Sagittarian youngsters, and some of *them* leave home as early as ten or twelve.) The Cancerian man who sincerely loves his Lioness — and gracious knows Cancerians never love any other way but sincerely, because they are all so sincere — will encourage her to pursue a career worthy of her talents (the Leo woman has never been born who doesn't possess one or more impressive talents) or allow her to be the absolute, if benevolent, monarch over their home. One or the other. Otherwise, she'll be desperately unhappy, and he'll be a mighty miserable Man-in-the-Moon, frequently scorched by her ruling Sun. Then he might have to resort to the bottle, or other liquid escapes, like swimming at midnight during an eclipse, around the rocks on the beach......perhaps even floating beyond the rocks to the next town, and maybe even staying there until she's ready to apologize. Considering Leo's great allergy to apologies, it could be a long siege.

What kind of life would that be, with him sitting in a drab rented room, surrounded by stacks of towels from Woolworth's, a case of soap he found on sale at Walgreen's, and a bottle of wine to drown his troubles — and her bravely trying to hide her heartache wandering around all by herself in the large, comfortable, luxurious and tasteful castle she decorated for him? Then there's the question of property settlement. Who will receive custody of the fluffy eiderdown quilt mama gave him, his Lincoln autograph collection, his old political campaign button collection, his fishing pole . . . her hair dryer, her ruby tiara, her Oriental rugs, her peacock feathers and her throne, spelling her name in faded roses . . their dogs and cats and aquarium, dishwasher and power lawnmower . . . the stereo equipment, station wagon and beach house she gave *him* — and the tiny gold charm shaped like a New Moon he gave *her*? (These two give different kinds of gifts. Hers are larger, lavishly given from her generous heart. His are a mite smaller, yet lovingly given from his affectionate heart.) Last, but not least, what about their joint checking and savings accounts, insurance policies, annuities and real estate holdings? Lord save us from *that* day of division!

It would be much easier for her to swallow that large lump of false pride, and for him to crawl out from his self-protective shell. The Crab and the Lioness are not at home in the ocean, where she feels out of place — nor in the jungle, where he feels out of place. They are only at home together in the sky, on the astral level, where their spirits can commune . . . or in each other's arms, where Fire and Water defy the law of the elements, and blend . . . in the kind of communion that has never recognized any law but its own.

CANCER

Water — Cardinal — Negative
Ruled by the Moon
Symbol: The Crab
Night Forces — Feminine

VIRGO

Earth — Mutable — Negative
Ruled by Mercury (also by
the Planet Vulcan)
Symbol: The Virgin
Night Forces — Feminine

The CANCER-VIRGO *Relationship*

They found the dinghy, and went home in it . . .

When their voices died away, there came cold silence
over the lagoon, and then a feeble cry. "Help, help!"
Two small figures were beating against the rock . . .

You may wonder what a Crab might do with a Virgin — besides snapping on occasion, or perhaps contemplating a firm grip on the Virgin's tempting bare toe. Just as you may wonder what a Virgin might do with a Crab, other than running swiftly away — or maybe deciding to take the Crab home as a pet.

At first thought, it's difficult to imagine that a Crab and a Virgin have anything in common — but technical virgins are, after all, said to be somewhat crabby (unfulfilled, or whatever) and real crabs do possess a certain timidity one normally associates with actual virgins — which brings us a little closer to linking these two. One of them is a nocturnal creature of the sea. The other also tends toward the nocturnal Night Forces, although not especially toward the element of water—unless one counts the still and quiet pools into which astrological Virgins gaze to see their Narcissus images reflected to them, sometimes rippling just a bit but, on the whole, clearly defined. Nevertheless, Earth does contain Water—or lacking it, becomes dry and parched. There's no argument that an association with the Water Sign of Cancer greatly enriches the character and personality of the Earthy Virgo man, woman or child.

Most Virgos are much happier when they're alone with themselves than when they have to bend their somewhat measured and rather precisely patterned life-styles to those of other sloppy, strange, silly and impulsive humans, which makes them nervous and uncomfortable. Somehow, at least in the beginning, the Virgins don't feel this sort of discomfort when they pal around with the Crabs. There's something soothing to Virgo about the Water Element of Cancer. The Cancerian gentleness and mildness of manner often cause the Virgo to feel as though he (or she) is floating on a quiet lake, now and then reaching out, dreamlike, to pluck one of the lovelier lilies, or playfully tease a passing school of mermaids and water babies. Frequently the Virginians feel freer and more relaxed with a Crab, less fearful of being restricted, bossed around, possessed—or of having their own personalities overshadowed to the point of disappearance. (Poor, unsuspecting Virgins.) Also, Virgo is easily enchanted by the Cancerian's marvelous Looney Bird humor, which is not too loud or clownish, not too sophisticated, nor yet too vulgar either—just the right kind of recognition of the ridiculous that allows Virgos, with their exquisite sense of critique and satire, to join in with some amusing observations of their own.

Isn't it wonderful? These two have hopped into their pea-green dinghy and sailed down the river of happiness together, just like the famed Owl and the Pussycat, except that they are a Crab and a Virgin. But no matter, because the whole purpose of the sail in the moonlight in a pea-green boat is harmony, whatever the astrological or otherwise identity of the occupants. You can be sure they'll take along some honey (and honey cakes) for Cancer to nibble on—a small guitar for Virgo to strum while the Crab sings crazy limericks to mournful songs of yesterday—and definitely LOTS OF MON-EY—not only to rhyme with honey but also because Cancerians consider a stash of cash—whether "wrapped up in a five-pound note," securely tied inside a paper bag, combination-locked in a safe, buried in a bank or in a sandpile in the backyard—an absolute necessity of life, having a slight priority edge over air to breathe, but not necessarily over things to eat and drink. The latter run a neck-and-neck race with money for the attention of typical Crabs during their entire lifetime. Tagging along as a close third are babies and children of assorted ages and sizes.

The Virgo in the pea-green boat won't mind the mellow mood music. But as for the jars of honey and honey cakes Cancer brings along on any trip these two might decide to risk together, Virgo will probably nag and complain that the space taken by the Crab's goodies doesn't leave any room for Virgo's Vick's salve, Tums for the tummy, Excedrin and Pepto Bismol — let alone Virgo's vitamins and wheat germ.

They may also quarrel a bit querulously over Virgo's grumbles that honey cakes are not as vital a Life Preserver as pure bee pollen, since the latter is good for anything from promoting no cavities to the prevention of baldness, gaining and losing weight (both) and, in general, for keeping fine and fit in every sense. Therefore, the Crab may have to leave a few dozen honey cakes behind, so there'll be a sizable niche on the dinghy to contain Virgo's "imported" pure pollen from the buzzing Wyeth honeycombs of New England — or the Wilton, Connecticut, Edward Weiss colonies of cheerful, thriving bees, who happily hum on Whipstick Road. Most Virgo pure pollen freaks know about Wyeth and Weiss because, when it comes to such serious matters, the Virgins are more than a mite choosy, even downright fussy about where they obtain the P.P. for their P.H. (Perfect Health). They demand the best. They may be stingy about other things, but not when their own personal well-being is concerned. If they should happen to become ill, they might be unable to go to work, for which inexcusable behavior they'd punish themselves with a heavy fine and six months of solitary. Most Virgos have a sense of responsibility toward their jobs that nearly amounts to an obsession (although Crabs are apt to see this fetish as a shining virtue).

However, as already noted, Virgo won't mind plunking the guitar to harmonize with Cancer's serene solos under the Full Moon. Also, despite these few possible squabbles over honey cakes versus the pollen, neither will Virgo object to the Crab's taking along of "plenty of money" anywhere they may be heading as a team. In fact, the Virgin will quite likely bring along a few duffle bags of the stuff himself (or herself) because the fear of financial ruin — the specter of poverty — is almost perfectly matched in Cancer and Virgo. It's a toss-up which one of them values money more. Or rather, which one of them values more the assurance that it will never be lacking.

Virgo and Cancer together create a powerful healing vibration. These two, when they join their auras, hands and hearts in any sort of mutual venture, possess the magic cure to many of the mental, emotional and physical ills that plague all Earthlings. Except their own. Alone, both of them are inclined to brood themselves into severe depression or chronic sickness. Together, they can be very helpful by way of preventing and curing in each other such emotional and mental gloominess, as well as all their mutual assorted aches and pains and other complaints.

This is the markedly friendly 3-11 Sun Sign Pattern influence, allowing the Virgin and the Crab, however amusing and odd they may appear to others, to feel perfectly right and natural to themselves, as they stroll along the seashore or through the woods to Grandma's house (Virgo's Grandma — then they'll stop by to chat with Cancer's Mama). The symbolic image is kind of giggly. Imagine the Crab, slightly waddling (all Crabs have a faint waddle to the walk), crawling first sideways, then backward, then skipping merrily ahead, scattering jokes like little berries on their path. Picture then the slim (usually) and modest Virgin, dressed lightly and unostentatiously, clear-eyed, graceful and lithe, humming a lovely melody . . . . . while below, the Crab hastens to keep pace, making funny faces, drawing looney pictures in the sand . . . . . and crankily gripping the Virgin's ankle or leg when the latter goes too fast and the Crab is weary, wanting to rest for a spell.

When the waning of the Moon causes the Cancer man or woman to weep over haunted memories of the past — or nightmarish fears of the future — the tender Virgin (whether male or female) will be sweetly sympathetic and consoling. Virgo will probably have a nice, clean hanky to hand the tearful Lunar friend, relative, business associate, lover or mate — which will be accepted, between sobs, with touching gratitude.

Both these Sun Signs are noticeably dependable and reliable workers. Barring a severe affliction to their natal Suns, or other negative planetary configurations in their birth charts, Cancer and Virgo take their duties and obligations seriously. They both are more inclined to enjoy work than to look upon it as a burden. Virgo enjoys work because a job well done, to the Virgin, is its own reward. Cancer enjoys work because it provides the means to build a large savings account for protecting against such terrible potential catastrophies as flood, fire, earthquake, volcanic eruptions, tornadoes, hurricanes, war, siege, the bubonic plague, a stock market crash, muggers, rapists (even boy Crabs get jittery at the thought of rape), vandalism, socialism, communism and famine. Virgo is no slouch in the savings department either. If there is anything in this world Virgo absolutely abhors, it's the thought of possibly being dependent upon others in some way later on in life. This is why the maternal (or paternal) Cancerian silently projects such comfort to the typical Virgo. The Virgin feels somehow secure within the protective presence of the Crabs, who are so solicitous of Virgo's welfare, so genuinely concerned and affectionate. Likewise, the Crabs feel comfy-cozy floating around in the cool calmness of Virgo, such a haven from the noisy outside streets, all cobblestoned with people, and demanding. Virgo — so clever, bright and witty, so nicely conventional, who can pack such a neat picnic basket, never forgetting the salt or napkins — always remembering a small surprise, like chilled grapes and Brie.

The main obstacle of mounting tension over which the Crab and the Virgin must leap on their way to the cool pool in the fragrant woods is hinted at in the next to the last sentence of the third paragraph of this chapter. I hoped it might stay there, buried in the sand, but it wants to be remembered, and now it whispers to us that Virgo wilts into yesterday's lettuce left out of the fridge at the first clutch of possessiveness and restriction. The Crabs can't separate possessiveness from warm, affectionate caring and friendly concern. Cancerians clam up and won't even tell you when they last stared at the Full

Moon and turned into a frog—yet they'll pry secrets out of others as if they were human corkscrews. Virgo is not a can and does not like to be pried open, turning into a walking worry-wrinkle when he or she feels restricted, third or fourth degreed. After a time, the Virgo man or woman may view the Crab's solicitous manner and protectiveness as possession's prison—and courteously (at first) request parole. This is a signal for the Cancerian to step sideways a while, even backward, allowing Virgo to dance ahead, feeling free and living up to the loner image for an imaginary lifetime, lasting a few weeks or months. Eventually, Virgo will return to gently nag the Moon person once again, sugar-coating criticism with politeness, causing the Crab to snap crankily. Virgo will shed one tiny, perfect tear—Cancer will weep a waterfall, and say "I'm sorry." Then Virgo will apologize for the weakness of such sensitivity.

Cancer stimulates Virgo's imagination, stirs Virgo's mind into a creamy whip of promises that will be kept perhaps ... and Virgo makes Cancer feel that the Crab won't be left alone on the beach, ignored ... to starve and pine away from loneliness. Earthy Virgo knows and understands, will see that friendship is kept polished and not allowed to rust. These two are lyrically linked by the 3-11 Sun Sign Pattern vibrations, karmically insured of a friendly return to harmony with but the slightest effort. Most 3-11 relationships, even after disappearing, have a way of popping up again to be resumed when least expected.

☆ ☆ ☆ ☆ ☆ ☆

CANCER *Woman* VIRGO *Man*

◄◄●►►

"What are you quacking about?" Peter answered. "Why don't you let the nest drift as usual?"

"I ... want ... you ..." the bird said, and repeated it all over.

A strong emotional involvement between Virgo and Cancer is multilayered, an experience of many dimensions. We'll try one on for size. Not fictional, but very real. To protect the innocent (for both players in the drama are indeed innocent of a conscious intent to hurt each other), we'll change the names, geography and such ... retaining only the thread of truth that could link this Moon Maiden and her Virgo man to you and your own girl Crab — or you and your own Virgo lover. It's much stranger than fiction, truth is, because almost always Life wins the race against man's and woman's limited imaginations.

His name, the Virgo, is Gerald, make-believing. Her name, the Lunar lass, is Hope, for imagery. They met and first miracled somewhere in Illinois, where they fell in love more than a dozen years ago. They are the parents of five assorted beautiful girls and boys, cherished by both of them. They have not yet married. Somehow, they can't live together, nor can they live apart. Following the haunted karmic path of the 3-11 Kismet, they walk along, arm-in-arm, for months of empathy and closeness. Then Gerald's yearning begins, Hope's sighing starts . . . they reach that sad, familiar fork in the road and take different directions, waving goodbye wistfully, before the last, abrupt turn — and the slow walk back alone. Time moves on, but destiny lingers. Sooner or later, there's the memory of her lyrical laugh, her mushroom soup and patchwork quilts of warm affection. His lonely reaches its breaking point just when she's making her wonted wish on the New Moon, and he appears at her door. Then they swaddle the babies snugly within the blankets of their reunion joy, closing out the world of her disapproving, frowning (but long-suffering) parents, and become a family again. Until it's time for him to go, leaving, as always, a part of himself behind . . . to manifest itself nine months later into another living proof of the mutual need that binds them. Five times. Five angels to guide them down that remembered, dreamlike path, through the dark forest of misunderstandings. Next time, it will be six, the number of Venus. It could be different. Venus may have plans to overcome Cancer's inconstant Moon and Virgo's restless Mercury.

That's the way it sometimes is with these two lovers. Especially if the Virgo man is the kind who fears that a deep involvement will cause him to lose his own identity, the common and persistent worry of both technical and astrological Virgins. Especially if the Cancerian woman is the kind who chooses the path of least resistence . . . motherhood and waiting . . . counting on the New Moon magic to weave a spell of magnetic memory to lure back the questing Virgo man who is not quite strong enough to stay, yet is unable to escape the pull of her luminous enchantment . . again and again. Typical-ly, some Moon Maidens believe that babies or money can soften any blow of Fate, anesthetize any kind of pain.

There are, naturally, other kinds of Crabs and Virgins. There's the kind of Virgo man who smoothly adapts to the necessity of adjusting his bachelor-button antipathy to partnership, of pacing his jogging to someone else's rhythm. He calculates the loss of his privacy against the rewards of companionship, and he remains — asking only for occasional periods of pensive apartness, time in which to wander by himself, to refresh his single-minded goals. As priests and monks are required to make "retreats," so are all Virgo men required by their own natures to retreat and meditate alone now and then, returning from their seclusion self-revitalized and freshly sweet. Newly able to innocently believe once more in tomorrow.

The Cancerian girl who understands this need of the Virgo man she loves will take care to walk softly while he's dreaming, find her own retreat beneath a bristlecone pine that's maybe waited a century or so for a friend to sit beside it, sharing a silent but eloquent communion. Trees know a lot. They listen sympathetically, and they are kind. If trees could walk, they'd never take a cruel knife and painfully carve their names, within a heart, on the arms or backs of lovers. Trees are wondrous teachers of forgiveness.

If the Moon maid finds her own midsummer night's dream in which to wander, those times when her Virgo man has disappeared somewhere inside himself to brood or plan — or to heal his worried mind — he'll stay. They can harmonize themselves this way in perfect tempo, their relationship never jolted by the violent percussion of "Goodbye" — "Come back" — "What did I say or do?" — "Don't go" — "May I come home?" — "Forgive me" — "Please don't hurt me anymore." It's a matter of calmly floating with the ebb and flow of the tides between them, not trying to surfboard over waves too high and dangerous.

Then too, there are those girl Crabs who are acutely aware of Cancer's Cardinal charisma, those Lunar-ruled females who patiently reinforce the weak or worn corners of the fabric of a relationship with concentration on a career. Her ambitions then become the vivid colors — and a love affair or marriage that wasn't quite made in Heaven but was conceived near enough the stars to sometimes sparkle, becomes the pastel background pattern of her life. It works. It adds strength to their love. They separate each morning, and she goes her tenacious way, while he whistles happily, tinkering with engines, practicing his yoga . . . rewrites the dictionary, draws maps or maybe juggles those odd-shaped objects called numbers, that produce such mysterious results, whether they're dashed and dotted in checkbooks, surveys, charts or graphs. They become sort of friendly strangers who fall in love each weekend. It satisfies her desire for change and his need for time alone to retain his friendship with himself (the person he relies on most). It allows them to love.

When they love in a physical sense, the Virgo man and his Cancerian woman blend quietly into a deep and absorbing union, in the natural way of earth and water in Nature. When the Moon's changeable influence over her emotions is beneficent — and when he is his own normal, tranquil self — their lovemaking is a peaceful consummation of desire for both of them. But when her Moon-madness takes over, when her Lunar fluctuations are waning, causing her to be crablike and moody, she can flood his affectionate intentions with excessive emotional behavior and demands. Just as he can bruise the delicacy of her passion when he's worried himself into irritability during the day and is unable to relax either his mind or his body. Restlessness is a contagious feeling, and they can transfer it to each other without realizing it. Then she may retreat sullenly into her shell, refusing to recognize her attitude as a rejection of his tentative wanting, and he may blame her for a cool response to his own cool advances. This is when his Virgo analytical talents would be very useful, and her Lunar gift of perception would greatly help. Yet, perversely, these periods of sexual frustration may be the very times the two of them neglect to call upon their own best qualities to clarify the breakdown of communication between them.

The Virgo man and his Moon Maiden can walk in sunshine and in rain, and recuperate from the seasonal changes in their love more often than not. They can make Valentines together, cut out cookies in the shape of New Moon Crescents, play anagrams and charades with each other . . . . . because he loves to meditate on words . . and she loves to make-believe she's more than one woman, slipping in and out of her moods like a glittering mermaid, hiding her true mother-of-pearl self in midnight silences and the brightness of noontime laughter. If their seeking is intense enough, together, these two can find whole meadows full of gentle camaraderie together . . . perhaps even dream a vision in the prophet's field of Ardath . . . for theirs is the 3-11 sextiled vibration. In astrology, a sextile is an opportunity, and these lovers will always be showered with as many as they need for tightly mending the occasional chips and cracks in their relationship, like a continual light snowfall of little stars around them, a sextile itself being represented by the symbol of a tiny star . . . *
 *
 *

When the girl Crab becomes cranky, her Virgo becomes critical and caustic, and they should escape into the woods, lie down together and take a moonbath, which is different from a sunbath. When you are sunbathing, you may be burned, turn all red and stinging. When you go moonbathing, especially when the Moon is phasing from waning to waxing, near its Fullness, you turn pale golden, lavender and iridescent, like a butterfly's wing. Then, naturally, you can fly.

Another thing Virgo learns slowly but surely from his Looney Bird Moon Maiden. Gazing directly into the Sun can blind the eyes. But gazing directly into Cancer's shimmering Moon is restful, and sometimes makes the miracle of allowing the Third Eye to see things hidden by midnight's mystery from the sunlight. After they've moonbathed together, they can jump into a dinghy and sail away to the ruins of Babylon. Who knows what they might discover ? As the prophet Esdras wrote in the Apocrypha . . . *The angel Uriel came unto me and said: "Go into a field of flowers, where no house is builded, and eat only the flowers of the field — taste no flesh, drink no wine, but eat flowers only . . . . and then I will come and talk to thee . . . . . ." so I went my way into the field which is called ARDATH.*

☆ ☆ ☆ ☆ ☆ ☆

CANCER *Man* VIRGO *Woman*

———— ◂◂◆▸▸ ————

*Presently he noticed as an odd thing that it was
undoubtedly out upon the lagoon with some definite
purpose, for it was fighting the tide, and sometimes winning; and when it won, Peter, always
sympathetic to the weaker side, could not help
clapping. It was such a gallant piece of paper.*

*It was not really a piece of paper. It was the
Never bird, making desperate efforts to reach Peter . . .*

He almost hates them. He really does. They're cruel and unfeeling. The astronauts and the NASA. The whole space program trembled the Crab. But he never said a word to anyone about it. He nursed this awful sense of emptiness secretly, mostly because he didn't quite know how to explain it to people who could never understand why he felt so strangely lost and lonely after the first Moon landing, his self-confidence smothered within the depths of an indefinable disappointment. The second time was even worse.

He wept. When he was by himself, when no one would see. He carried his silent burden throughout all the months and years, unable to share it, because there was no one he could count on to offer the magnitude of sympathy he needed. Until she came along — the Virgin — and they fell in love.

Gradually, he grew to believe that she wouldn't ridicule his secret if he shared it with her. She might even be able to help him lose his apprehensions, maybe point out to him a heretofore unsuspected happy ending to his NASA nightmares. After all, she's so quiet and calm, like a secret herself, he thought. She's so amazingly intelligent — for a *woman*. (Male Crabs are tinted with more than a tinge of chauvinism, and there's no use expecting them to lose it completely until the image of "Mother" has gone through a complete metamorphosis, which could take more than a few score years.) Besides being so clever, he mused, so mentally quick, she's tender and gentle, soothingly sympathetic — except for those few times when he has noticed her behaving like, well — a little like a virago. A bit cranky and critical. Detached and aloof. But he decided to overlook these rare moments. After all, isn't he moody himself? Who can better understand than he that a person doesn't always mean what a person says when a person is feeling out of sorts? So he gathers up his courage and pours it out into her dainty ears. His sad and scary secret. He confesses his terror, shivers and trembles, waits for consolation. JOY AND WONDER! She *does* sympathize! She *does* understand! She didn't laugh at him; moreover, she *does* have an answer! And a very logical, sensible, practical answer too, surprisingly interwoven with a trace of the esoteric . . . . . and mystical truth. He's overcome with pure pleasure and delight. He made the right decision in telling her.

What it was, you see — he'd been worried and concerned for some time about the Moon landings, for a perfectly rational reason. He's a Cancerian, ruled by the Moon. Down through the ages, mythology and the ancients, the scribes and prophets and poets — not to mention astrologers and metaphysicians . . . have always pictured the Moon as the Lady of Mysteries (the biggest one being what the so-called Man in the Moon was doing there), weaving spells, possessing all the magic of Merlin, the very personification of the magnetic and the hypnotic. It filled him with awe and private longings each time he stared at her bursting into Fullness, then waning, becoming New and lemon-sliced, beckoning him with a wistful promise. He used to wish on the New Moon when he was a boy. Then along came nasty NASA and those blasted, nosy, astronauts, determined to shock his dreams, to expose his lovely Lunar ruler's naked face and body in such a vulgar manner. The magazines were full of their photographed profanity of his Lady of Loveliness. There she was, so pathetically vulnerable, pockmarked with craters, covered by dreary sand and boring rocks, with not a shimmer or a sparkle anywhere to be seen. No magic. No mystery. Just cold masses of dirt, miles of blank nothingness. It shattered his faith in *himself*, in a way he couldn't analyze.

His Virgo woman listened quietly, not interrupting as other women might, until he was quite finished. Then he glanced at her from the corner of his eye to see if she was amused. She was not. She understood perfectly. Her clear eyes reflected a full awareness of his feelings, an unmistakably genuine interest. She told him it was only logical for a Cancerian to emotionally resent such a rude and unexpected tarnishing of his image of his own ruler, with such mundane and prosaic descriptions. It was natural, she said, for people to strongly identify themselves with their personal ruling planets and Luminaries. She pointed out that an Aries man might experience the same loss of self-confidence if forced to listen to accounts of astronauts landing on Mars (ruler of Aries) and reporting back that the Fiery Red Star was populated by rows of Sweet Shoppes, quivering jellyfish and marshmallow trees. MARS? The great warrior, the brave and courageous! The fearless! JELLYFISH AND MARSHMALLOWS? (He giggled, feeling much better.) Then she confided in him that Mercury is only her foster ruler and mentioned her own secret feelings about her true ruler, Vulcan, soon-to-be-discovered. How she watches the sky, sometimes, and wonders . . . . .

She told him firmly that her personal opinion happened to be that the stories about the Moon's magic and mystery are true. The ground walked upon by the astronauts was not *reality*. Did the rocks and craters make any change in the mystical and still-puzzling-to-scientists power of the Moon to pull the tides in and out, and affect all manner of things on Earth magnetically? No. It did not. And what of Earth? Looking upon this planet from space, she analyzed, one might expect it to be a reasonably sparkling, exciting Star. But when one actually landed on the Earth's surface and saw all the hot-dog stands, smog, pollution, TV sets, greed, cruelty, war, sugar pushers, the poor and the starving, the crimes and drugs and drunks and donuts and insecticides and billboards — the whole ugly mess of it — wouldn't one *also* be disillusioned? (He nodded eagerly, waiting for her happy ending.)

The Moon reflects the Sun, she told him. It is a reflector. It is unlike any other "star" or planet in the heavens, unique in this solar system. It is *still* strange and mystical, and possesses exactly the same powers as before. NASA hasn't explained the Moon's indisputable control over or synchronization with the movement of all water on Earth and all sealife. Even the opening and closing of oysters is precisely timed to the Lunar phases. The real truth of the Moon, she told him, doesn't lie upon its surface, to be seen with the naked eye. The real truth can be seen only with the Third Eye and the heart, combined — by observing the Moon to be the absolute Cause of certain Effects. And perhaps the *whole* truth will be seen later. Then she asked him if he had ever thought that perhaps the Earth, which appears to be such a crazy carnival of noise and nonsense, might not have a strange power *itself*, which we've never guessed . . to change the destinies of entire galaxies? Finally, she ended by quoting to him her favorite truism from her Great Aunt Hester. "Believe only *half* of what you see," warned Aunt Hester. "And *nothing* of what you hear." Tomorrow, the Virgin said . . . she would give him a copy of St. Exupéry's *The Little Prince*, which she promised would clarify it all. (Most Virgos have read and are fond of *The Little Prince*. They are irresistibly drawn to anything with the word "little" in it.)

Nearly always, a Virgo woman can somehow manage to make a boy Crab feel safe and warm and secure. As though everything is crisp and proper and behaving as it should in the world, and within his own orbit. The way he felt as a child. When his mother told him to hush, it was all right. His nightmares were foolish and unreal. Tomorrow will be morning, and the world will still be spinning. Buckwheats for breakfast . . . and the newspaper delivered, as usual. The Virgo woman makes him feel cozy and comfy, like his old bathrobe with its soft, sagging pockets, hanging there beside his bed like a loyal friend. He senses her dependability, her sense of duty and her integrity. All very much like his own. Unless he meets her during a time when she's pulled by Vulcan to stand on her head and run around in thrilling circles for a bit, to change the scene, throwing caution in the corner, where undue caution belongs. Then he may have cause to be nervous now and then. But the typical Virgin in the average situation, when she really loves her gentle Crab, will seldom if ever do anything to really hurt or alarm him. She's so reassuringly predictable (barring those rare Vulcan experiments).

She will wish *he* would be equally predictable. Rocks, craters and all, the Moon continues to rule this man's changing moods, laughter, tears, depressions, elations, pouting spells, jokes, compassion, sweetness, crankiness and just plain contrariness. Still, in her practical, common-sense way, the Virgo girl is able to cope rather efficiently with the Cancerian man's wanderlust, periods of loneliness he can't explain — the fears that make him occasionally stingy — the tender concern for others that turns him suddenly generous. She doesn't mind his cautious nature, for she's cautious herself. She'll also share his dislike for extravagance and waste — his sense of responsibility — and his delicious enjoyment of home life. She'll cook for him, most likely, soon perceiving that he associates good food with emotional security, but she may not be too happy about it. (Unless she has a Cancer Moon Sign or Ascendent herself.) A few of their quarrels could spring from his crablike possessiveness. He may frown if she wants to work or pursue a career, unless her desk is next to his, or they go into business together. He's Cardinal, she's Mutable, and so she'll accept with good grace his tendency to want to make most of the rules and to walk a few steps ahead — if he doesn't overdo it. He's a leader (even if secretly) and she's a communicator. Therefore, she feels no overwhelming need to demand a showy kind of independence for herself, but neither will she stand for her personal freedom to be smothered. He can boss her around, gallantly, and with old-fashioned charm (as he does others, male or female), and she won't be insulted or make a big fuss over it. However, she'll follow up only on suggestions that please her. If they do not please her, she'll frankly tell him so, and proceed to do things her own way. Courteously (like him) but quite determinedly.

Sexually, these two are well mated. With the peaceful affinity of Earth and Water Signs, they melt into each other's arms, hearts and bodies very naturally. To others, the Virgo woman may project a degree of unresponsiveness. But the great sentimentality and sensitivity of the Cancerian man allows him to discover her latent pools of passion. He's often able to cause her to bloom with her own special kind of sentiment, which is pure and fine, like crystal, lacking the heaviness of extreme emotionalism. She may surprise herself then, with a depth of sensitive feelings she never suspected she possessed. Her basic nature may be cool and reserved (especially with strangers), but when she's been stirred inwardly by Vulcan, this woman is more than capable of fulfilling the Lunar man's strong need for both sensuality and affection in lovemaking. She'll respond instinctively to the tenderness and gentleness that are inseparable parts of every Cancerian male. They both approach passion with a respect for its deeper implications and potential. Sexual union is not something either of them normally views as casual or frivolous (barring severe planetary afflictions in their individual birth charts).

Despite his emotional vulnerability and sentimentality (which he hides with practiced success beneath his tough, outer shell), the Crab possesses a steady, watchful intelligence. He's a shrewd business person, and an excellent strategist regarding all forms of human relationships. She'll make it clear that she admires all these qualities. A Virgin cannot love a man who hasn't won her respect, and the Crab will probably do this from the beginning. However, should he be one of the insecure Cancerians who "babys" his groundless fears by turning to drugs, alcohol, daydreaming or procrastination, she'll be extremely annoyed, and she'll soon make her displeasure felt in unmistakable small ways. Like nagging. Polite nagging, but nonetheless, nagging. Little reminders. Tiny frowns. Pouting. A martyrlike resignation. Or she'll just skip off when he least expects it to begin a new life alone, with barely a trace of emotion, once she's decided to leave. (Virgos don't look upon excessive emotion as either sensible or practical.) Because of his extreme sensitivity to hurt — and her natural inclination to criticize — there are dangers inherent in this relationship. But none that can't be overcome by simply being recognized in time, and avoided. He's perceptive enough to sense them. She's analytical enough to detect them. So they really have no excuse for allowing things to go too far.

Her eyes (like the eyes of all Virgos and Geminis, thanks to Mercury's silver gift) are noticeably clear, sparkling with intelligence. Her features, in some indefinable way, are delicate and virginal. Except when her brow is clouded with problems or creased with worry-wrinkles, her expression is sweetly placid. And so . . when she's bathed in moonlight, lying in his arms, the Crab may, for a moment, imagine her to be his lost Lady of the Mysteries, the misty Moon goddess of his haunted dreams.

Once she feels safe with a man, a Virgo girl is transformed into a symphony of fragile femininity. After all, she was born under a feminine Sun Sign, secretly ruled by the powerfully feminine Vulcan. Her crisp self-containment and faint air of aloofness mask her softness, but it's there . . . . . waiting for the patient and persistent devotion of the Cancerian man to warm it into singing. Even should the Virgin and the Crab part company, the strong karmic tug of their 3-11 vibration will nearly always guide them to unexpectedly cross each other's paths again, in ultimate friendship and forgiveness.

☆ ☆ ☆ ☆ ☆ ☆

CANCER

Water — Cardinal — Negative
Ruled by the Moon
Symbol: The Crab
Night Forces — Feminine

LIBRA

Air — Cardinal — Positive
Ruled by Venus
Symbol: The Scales
Day Forces — Masculine

The **CANCER-LIBRA** *Relationship*

I don't know whether any of the children were crying;
if so, the singing drowned out the sound. . . .

Cancer and Libra form the squared 4-10 Sun Sign Pattern, through the elements of Water and Air, and like all 4-10 vibrations, theirs is the most interesting and challenging association of all. It's also the most difficult kind to bring into harmony, but that's exactly what makes it so interesting and challenging, because of the great rewards waiting to grace these two when they achieve a soul-stirring victory over their undeniable differences, which are, to be honest, numerous.

The relationship of Libra and the Crab is what life is all about, because it forces them to learn the hard way how to compromise. Mastering that lesson guarantees a much higher level of happiness than can ever be attained by choosing an easier path. For these two Sun Signs to win the battle to understand one another is a worthy goal. Now and then, it's bound to be a bit jaggy and troublesome, to be sure, but Time smooths off the rough edges, if there's sincere effort on both sides, and ultimately, there's the sweet satisfaction of knowing you've succeeded in conquering your own and another's very human natures, and in the process, have come a little closer to the angels. I don't guarantee wings or anything, but maybe a couple of halos (which are only two auras, glowing in the beautiful colors of compatibility).

A halo (or aura) is not something these two will see over each other's heads right away. They're more likely to see imaginary horns and a couple of pitchforks. That's because they aren't trying. They're giving in to human nature, and this particular karmic trip is all about trying to imitate the angels, remember? The first lesson Cancer and Libra must learn is the one so earnestly taught by Francesco Giovanni de Bernardone, of Assisi (known as Saint Francis, but not through *his* humble choice). They'll simply have to stop trying so desperately to be understood, and start trying a little harder to understand. Both of them. It's the only key which will unlock that mysterious barred door between them, behind which lies *Pax et Bonum* (Peace and Good).

As explained in detail in "The Twelve Mysteries of Love" section in the front of this book, Cancerians are experiencing the adolescence of the soul. They sense so much they can't seem to express; their dreams haunt them with a disturbing precognition of the maturing process of both approaching happiness and approaching sorrows, as well as vivid recollections of yesterday. They feel all this, but they can't talk about it, so naturally they're moody, and can't help weeping in nameless dread and depression when the Moon periodically tugs on their emotions, as helpless as the ocean's tides to control the magnetic Lunar pull. Sometimes the Crabs are silent and reflective, at other times they cover their concerns with a crazy and marvelously contagious Lunar humor that frequently fools them right out of their fears, and certainly cheers up everyone lucky enough to be around them when they're feeling funny.

When a Moon Child and a Libran are thrown together, for a while it can be a melodious scene. Librans adore laughter, and the Lunar humor of Cancer becomes a rhythmical lyric to the mellow music of Libra's Venus essence, smooth and restful at times, yet also containing a few crashing chords and sour notes, punctuated by a kind of rocky roll. It's pure entertainment, and happy and fortunate indeed are the innocent bystanders around the home or office brightened by the musical duets of this combo when they're getting along. (The innocent bystanders should enjoy it while it lasts.) I say home or office because Destiny frequently places the 4-10 combinations in a life situation related closely to the home and the career. They seem to harmonize more easily around the family circle as relatives, as business associates, or in a classroom, than as friends, lovers, or mates. (But regarding the latter, don't forget that challenge, and its golden rewards.)

Actually, the Crab and the Libran have more basic empathy to aid them in overcoming their difficulties than some of the other 4-10 Patterns because, although their personalities often clash, their ruling planets — the Moon and

Venus, respectively — are sympathetic. Since the Sun rules the personality and the Moon rules the emotions, these two can reach one another more easily through the *emotions* than through the more obvious and outward ways. The problem is that it's never a simple thing to break through a Crab shell to the Moon person's true emotional nature. It's well protected from hurt, and needs much careful coaxing.

Libra is tolerant, and stands a good chance of touching the Lunar person's emotions with a gentle attitude . . and waiting. But unfortunately, the fact that Libra is essentially gentle and tolerant may not be quite enough. For the Moon-ruled man or woman (or child) can be sensitive beyond belief. Despite the innate Libran kindness, Libra, being an Air Sign, is often too intent upon logic, too little aware of the Crab's or anyone else's sensitivity. Librans make excellent lawyers and wise judges, but with few exceptions, as fair as they may be, they make poor psychologists. Libra isn't concerned with the meaning-behind-the-meaning, only with the fascinating game of human action and reaction, on the surface level. That sort of attitude will never get beneath Cancer's crusty shell. Libra will have to practice more in-depth compassion with Cancer, if this man or woman wants to understand what makes the Crab symbolically crawl in such a sideways fashion, instead of being direct and getting to the point.

One of the chief differences between their natures is that Libra is "other-people" oriented and Cancer is "self-oriented." If it sounds as though astrology is saying that Cancer is more selfish than Libra, it *should* sound that way, because that's precisely what it means. The average Libran is demonstrably more concerned about the problems of friends, of a particular business or of the world at large, than about his or her own personal problems, which seem to roll off Libra's back with a shrug of the shoulders and the logical deduction that things can go nowhere from Down except Up. These men and women are outgoing extroverts, whereas the Moon people are more introverted — and protective of Number One. True, many Cancerians are gentle, imaginative, and sensitive folk, often very loving and affectionate; nonetheless, their most intense concentration is upon themselves.

Since concentration upon the self is an unhealthy emotional attitude which never fails to eventually bring on some degree of poor health, the Crabs are ill more frequently than they need be. Libra illnesses are more often seeded in permissive living, an indulgent life style, the tendency to gregariousness, their love of parties, overeating and overdrinking and overworking. All of which causes the Crab to fuss and worry, and inform Libra that he or she is burning the candle at both ends. (How else *could* Libra burn a candle, and still be fair to the candle ?)

Money is another area where these two usually see in opposite directions. Librans are not unduly wasteful or extravagant, but money isn't the Big Thing to them it is to Cancer. To the Crabs, financial security and emotional security are of equal and vital importance. Possessing only one of these, and lacking the other, they can be pretty cranky and miserable. Possessing neither causes them to be so snappy and impossible even their mothers couldn't love them, and for Cancer, that's a rare and painful experience. But when Cancer possesses both kinds of security, the Moon person is magically transfigured into one of the most docile, dear, and tender human beings anyone could possibly ask for, including Libra, who sometimes asks a great deal of people, expecting everyone's character and personality pluses and minuses to come out exactly even, and not a micrometer off center.

Despite Cancer's apparent poor health and lack of physical strength, these people are, in the final analysis, much tougher in the art of surviving mentally, physically, and emotionally than Libra. After the deck is shuffled, Libra is the one more likely to give in to mental pressure and suffer a nervous breakdown, be broken hearted over emotional disappointments, or succumb to serious illness when the Scales are out of balance. When Cancer is ill, it may last a long time, true, but only because the Crab hangs on so tenaciously to everything, and sadly, seldom separates the positive from the negative. The Crab reaches out almost blindly, grabs hold, and hangs in there for dear life. Sometimes it takes Libra's gentle reminder to bring a Moon person to his or her senses, to the realization that what is being clung to so fiercely is best released. Letting go is not easy for Cancer, and Libra will have some frustrating experiences trying to pry the Crab's claws loose from bad habits, wrong ideas, and groundless fears.

This kind of tug-of-war is invisibly wearing on the delicate balance of Libra's nervous system over a long period, and can bring on a kind of exhaustion of the spirit, which can, in turn, lead to lethargy and deep wells of unhappiness, not to mention considerably dampening Libra's normal cheerful, affectionate, and optimistic nature. In Nature, as with people, an overabundance of water can make air soggy, foggy, and clammy, just as the right amount of water can make air moist, fresh, and exhilarating.

Libra is wasting time trying to keep a secret from Cancer. The Crabs will use every sly maneuver imaginable to pry out of a person what they wish to know. Cancer asks: "What does so-and-so think of me, honestly ?" Libra replies, "I don't think I should take sides." Cancer says, "That's not *fair* of you, haven't I supplied information *you* needed badly, lots of times ?" Libra hesitates, then sighs, gives in, and tells the Crab what he or she wants to know, being careful to list all the *good* things said, along *with* the bad. After Cancer hears the sought-for answer, the Crab may snap, "I thought so. I'll never speak to that person again," then leave the room in a huff; also leaving Libra nearly in tears over being forced into the position of agitator, when every fiber of Libra's being is designed in the pattern of peacemaker. Crabs are ultra-ultra-ultrasensitive to the slightest criticism, and very tricky in ferreting out the *whole* truth, then either weeping in hurt or snapping in anger over only *half* the truth — and you know how an emphasis on only half of something drives Libra wild.

The best way for Libra and Cancer to make mellow music together is for each of them to concentrate almost constantly on the very real virtues of the other, even though those traits may be markedly different in each. Libra must remember that the imaginative dreams of Cancer, blended with Cancer's incredible tenacity, are what allowed Moon Maiden Helen Keller to triumph so gloriously over the affliction of being struck deaf and blind at the age of nineteen months. She graduated cum laude from Radcliffe College, learned to knit, crochet, and use a typewriter, to swim, row a boat, and ride a bicycle. Traveling around the world, she gave inspirational talks (when she had so briefly ever heard the sound of a human voice) and wrote numerous books and articles to uplift the faith of others. Likewise, the sensitivity, insight, and perseverance of Cancer allowed Crab Nikola Tesla to use his remarkable memory and inventive genius to conceive of electronic miracles years ahead of his time, to be the first to implement the practical use of AC (or alternating electrical current), to patent 140 inventions of great practical value to Earthlings, one of which made possible the conception of radio broadcasting and receiving circuits used today — and to hang on to his Lunar dreams and visions, despite ridicule, lack of interest, and being cheated out of his rewards for his life's work until after his death. Every Moon Child is made of the stuff of which Helen Keller and Nikola Tesla were made.

Conversely, Cancer might reflect upon what life would be like today had it not been for Libra's desire for justice and need for creative expression — had the world not been blessed with the adaptability and peacemaking talents of Librans such as Dwight Eisenhower, George Westinghouse, and Giuseppe Verdi. Without their Venus abilities to create music for the soul, to be just compromisers who yet never compromised moral values, we might still be involved in World War II, our railroads would not be safe, and the Crab couldn't listen to the soaring sounds of *Aïda* to calm his or her spirit. It was Mahatma Gandhi, the Libran peacemaker, who blended the teachings of Hinduism with the Nazarene's "Sermon on the Mount" — in perfect harmony.

Once Cancer and Libra have learned to genuinely appreciate one another, great magic can result. An excellent example of this is the statement of Cancerian Crab Tesla, regarding Libran George Westinghouse: "If other industrial firms had been as *fair* and *liberal*, and as *just* as George, *I could have offered the world so much more.*"

Cancer and Libra should meditate upon those twenty-four words for a long, long time. They contain a mighty message. For both of them. Equally.

☆ ☆ ☆ ☆ ☆ ☆

CANCER *Woman* LIBRA *Man*

———— ◆◄◗►◆ ————

She had come to save him, to give him her nest,
though there were eggs in it. I rather wonder
at the bird, for though he had been nice to her,
he had also sometimes tormented her.

Love has a way of turning a moody, secretive, and sometimes cranky female Crab into a lovely, solicitous, tender, and gentle Moon Maiden. If she should happen to be in love with a Libra man, she'll begin to worry about him right away. He works too hard, he plays too hard, he eats all the wrong foods, he drinks too much, he doesn't get enough rest, he lets other people take advantage of his good nature, he's too easygoing, he'll catch cold if he doesn't stop running around in the rain without his rubbers, and he must stop losing his umbrellas, because umbrellas cost money, and the money spent on just the ones he lost last year alone could buy a new electric juicer to make vegetable juices to dilute the effect of the bad things he insists upon eating and drinking. Cancer *cares*. On his birthday, the Moon Maiden may give him an electric blanket, because she's concerned about his comfort. Actually, it's a hint that sleeping with her curled up beside him would be a much nicer way to keep his toes warm in winter.

Since Libra is a masculine Sun Sign, he will soon set her straight on his determination not to be either dominated or nagged. But he is ruled by the feminine planet Venus, which will harmonize nicely with her fluctuating Lunar moods, brought on by her ruling Moon, making her feel emotionally secure, which in turn will bring out all her sterling qualities of loyalty, patience, and devotion. For a while, all will be peace and tranquility.

Regardless of the rather marked differences in their dispositions and personalities, if he's a typical Libra male, he won't let much time drag by between falling in love and being tempted by the idea of marriage. When a Venus-ruled male is strongly tempted to do something with a female as tempting as this one, he'll mull it over and find a thousand rational reasons why he should, finally deciding that the only way to get rid of temptation is to give in to it. (That's an example of Libra logic when it's distorted by romantic desire and urges of the flesh.)

If he's an evolved Libran, and if the aspect between their Luminaries is favorable (his Sun conjunct, sextile, or trine her Moon, or vice versa — or blessedly, both), he's made a wise decision in proposing marriage to this soft, dewy-eyed creature with the hard shell, this fragile (ha!), sensitive and perceptive (true) Moon Maiden who exhibits such flattering concern for his welfare, and who stirs within him such deep emotions. (You can't blame him for giving in to temptation when you really think about it.) If the aforementioned Sun-Moon aspect between their horoscopes is a square or an opposition, he may still have made a wise decision for the good of his eternal soul — but it could be kind of rough on his mind, body, and emotions. However, we must keep in mind what was noted in the first part of this chapter, that if they're able to harmonize the disharmony, they'll have the sort of love the angels enjoy, and that's worth more than a little effort.

To the Moon Maid and the Libran: Listen, astrologically, I have for you some bad news and some good news. Which do you want to hear first, the good news or the bad?

LIBRA: Give me the good news first.
CANCER: Give me the bad news first.

I guess it has to be the bad news first, because their answers are a perfect demonstration of it — of the vastly different approach these two take toward any sort of situation, outside themselves or between themselves.

No other Sun Sign is by nature more unintentionally but determinedly pessimistic than Cancer (unless it's Taurus, Virgo, or Capricorn, but when the scores are added up, the Crab tops them all). And no Sun Sign is by nature as cheerfully, endlessly (and sometimes maddeningly) optimistic as Libra (unless it's Aries or Sag, but Libra can beat them both to the finish line when it comes to chasing the rainbows).

Looking on the bright side of it, we may play Pollyanna and say that when his optimism and her pessimism are poured out of the same teapot day after day (and night after night), her influence will gradually make his optimism less gullible and more sensible — while his influence will gradually make her pessimism less depressing and a little more hopeful.

Looking on the dark side of it, we must admit that, by the very nature of its Webster definition, optimism cannot be made *less* gullible and cannot become sensible, or it wouldn't be optimism anymore. Likewise, by the very nature of its Webster definition, pessimism can't be made *less* depressing, because depressing is depressing, and degrees of it don't count — and it certainly can't be made hopeful, or it wouldn't be pessimism anymore. Our efforts to help them are clearly becoming snarled in semantics.

We wouldn't want them to solve the problem by trading these ingrained character traits with one another, because a pessimistic Libran would be a dreadfully unhappy man, and a totally optimistic Cancerian woman, lacking all caution, would be untrue to herself. Maybe a touch of anagrams would help. Optimism contains within it the word "mist," pessimism contains within it the word "miss." She might warn him (and beneficially, too) that

TOO MUCH (those are the key words) optimism could form a *mist* over reality, which could cause his dreams to fade, when she so desperately wants them to come true because she loves him. He might, in turn, tell her that TOO MUCH (key words again) pessimism will cause her to unnecessarily *miss* a lot of happiness along the way that they could have shared together, a tragedy he wants her to avoid because he loves her so. The solution is Libra *balance.*

Now that we've solved that problem between them, let's go on to the next piece of bad news, and save the good news for last, where it will have more power to cancel the complications.

She is emotionally possessive, and he is emotionally freedom-loving. It seems like an insurmountable conflict, yet it isn't nearly as difficult a situation as each of them may individually talk themselves into believing it is. Not if they really love one another. *To him:* She isn't possessive because she wants to smother you. It's just her old fears from childhood nightmares, returning to haunt her. She's afraid your love for her is only a mirage and it might disappear someday, leaving her all alone, unloved and unprotected. Surely you can be fair enough to be aware that these very real fears naturally increase when you're out of sight, because she was frightened by the lie "out of sight, out of mind" when she was a little girl. *To her:* He doesn't seek periods of freedom because he wants to plot ways of leaving you — or because he's fallen in love with someone else. He was born into the Air Element, and when Air is confined, it grows stale. Forget that false warning of what happens when the man you love is out of your sight, and realize that it's been proven a million times over that "absence makes the heart grow even fonder." It's a universal law of love that cannot ever be changed. Only if he doesn't love you are you in danger of losing him when he's out of sight — and if he doesn't love you, you're going to lose him anyway, and good riddance, because it will allow your *real* love to enter your life. If he does love you, he misses you more when you're apart than you suspect, and far more than he'll ever tell you if you keep making him think you don't trust him.

A Libra man who truly loves and understands the Moon Maiden who tugs on his heart will invite her to go with him, even when it's a boring business trip he feels would be sooner and more smoothly out of the way if he handled it alone, and really *mean* it when he asks her, remembering that people fall in love to be *together*, and things that keep them apart, that keep them from the constant excitement of discovery together, are enemies to their happiness, never mind the rules of society.

How can they share exciting discoveries together if the only time they see one another is at home, and the only exciting discovery is the baby's new tooth or that the roof is leaking? If he sincerely and impulsively invites her to go with him when it's at all possible, he'll receive a touching surprise.

Knowing at last that he really wants her near him, she'll lose every trace of her Cancerian possessiveness, and tell him it's all right, she has lots of things to do while he's gone, just hurry back home — and she'll really mean it, because his wanting her has removed all her Lunar fears. Then *he* may start worrying about why she doesn't *accept* his invitation. These two must learn to quit while they're ahead. Lovers are such strange Earthlings. So contradictory.

There are very few broken Cancer-Libra relationships that can't be mended and glued back together like new if these two see together, holding hands, Neil Simon's 1978 film *The Goodbye Girl*, because the last scene was inspired and channeled by the angels, just for them alone. If they're reading this a decade or two or more from the time I'm writing it, I'd advise them to rent the film from a film library, then rent a projector or a screening room (or watch it when it's on their television) and sit through the *last scene* several times. It contains the complete solution the Cancer woman and the Libra man are seeking — and the only answer they'll ever need. If they don't love, they should part quickly and painlessly. If they do, they should see this film and send Neil Simon a dozen daisies and daffodils every year on their anniversary all the rest of their lives together.

With a little help from Cancerian Neil, who understands the nature of Cancerian females, we've solved that problem. The next one involves money, and here I refuse to be the arbitrator, except to say briefly to *him:* Let her have a savings account and a couple of paid-up annuities to keep her happy — and to *her:* Stop making him feel he's on the verge of bankruptcy, stop imagining poverty or you'll manifest it into reality as sure as God made little green apples, as your grandma used to say — and when you do have cash, LET GO OF IT, give large chunks of it away to strangers on the street, yes, I said strangers on the street and don't faint — and you'll see it return to you three times over sooner than you dream possible. With all your Cancerian caution, you can't change that Universal law of giving. How can you prove me wrong if you don't try it?

The sexual side of their relationship can begin as a gift from the angels too, but it can end with their hearts feeling as empty as they once felt full. The time to prevent such a tragedy is before the curtain rises on it, in the first act of their play. Her seemingly never-ending suspicions may finally drive him into a feeling of futility that can be a prelude to impotence, just as his lack of insight into her deep need for sustained affection and romantic reassurance can drive her into her shell of emotional protection that can harden into frigidity. When they avoid the cause of such a mutually lonely effect by respecting and really *thinking* about Newton's law of Cause and Effect, their physical love can be a beautiful experience of gentle passion, the kind of intimacy that makes them tremble just anticipating it in each other's eyes, and brings them a new peace and contentment every time they rediscover themselves through its ancient alchemy.

Sexual union between a man and woman who love is like a remembered melody of inexpressible longing and silent fulfillment that can be wonderfully healing. Unlike many other couples, these two may use poetry as the language of their love. The typical Moon-ruled woman and Venus-ruled man aren't embarrassed by expressing their feelings in this way, and also music will sometimes intensify the emotional depth of their lovemaking. There are many ways to say I'm sorry . . . I didn't mean to hurt you.

The next time he has to leave her for a few days, he might give her a bottle of *Je Reviens* perfume and a French-English dictionary so she can learn that *je reviens* means *I shall return* . . . or maybe a Raggedy Ann, to show her he knows how it is with her inside, how she treasures yesterday because it seems more real and secure to her than today or tomorrow. She's needed someone to understand this about her since she was a little girl crooning a gentle lullaby to her doll. Then she'll give him a gift beyond measure — her complete trust.

Now for the good news. They are both sentimental. They're both wonderfully imaginative, and they both believe in dreams. She has a beautiful sense of humor; he has a beautiful smile. They're both subject to changing moods, but they're both also touched by tenderness. Last but not least, the angels fight on their side, for having already been there, they're well aware of the sacrifice of self involved in climbing the steep hill to happiness required of the 4-10 vibration, yet ever ready to promise that the view from that height is splendid — not a millimeter off center from beautiful.

☆ ☆ ☆ ☆ ☆ ☆

CANCER *Man* LIBRA *Woman*

— ◄◆►► —

> . . . *every door in the coral caves where they live*
> *rings a tiny bell when it opens or closes . . and*
> *he heard the bells.*

Libra women are so full of love and loveliness, it really does seem as though bells ring when one is in their presence. Bells ring around most Gemini and Virgo girls too, but they have a more delicate sound. Libra bells are deeper, more like the chimes you hear at Easter Sunday sunrise. It's all part of the music of Venus, and you can just imagine the effect it has on the sentimental heart and sensitive, finely tuned awareness of the Moon-ruled Cancer man. Like the sound of a choir.

To add to the dreamlike quality of the experience, the Libra girl who has enchanted him looks an awful lot like an angel. Venus never fails to bestow upon those who are her children a haunting beauty of feature . . . if not that, then at the very least, a smile that can gladden the weariest soul. Sometimes a Libra female is fortunate enough to have received both of these Venus blessings at birth, and if so, the Crab doesn't have much of a chance. Dazzled by all that beauty, softened by her brilliant smile, and hearing all those chimes at the same time . . . . . . can bring on more than a touch of Moon madness in this man of many moods.

Crabs have a sensational sense of humor, so the first thing he'll do to impress her, shortly after they've met, is tell her a funny story. She will laugh, then . . not just an ordinary laugh, but a laugh very much like the one Peter Pan told Wendy about that breaks into a thousand pieces and creates the birth of faeries . . and he will hear those chimes again. Not only is her laughter musical, but her smile is a symphony, and she has the good taste to appreciate his humor.

Not long after this he'll learn that, in addition to being beautiful and witty, softly fragrant and feminine, and overflowing with the velvet mystery of woman, she's also extremely intelligent and can match his own cleverness in anything from chess to charades. She's capable of being a surprisingly level-headed and creative silent partner in all his business affairs, maybe even an actual partner. She's certainly smarter than all those dunderheads he's used to dealing with who don't laugh at his jokes and have to be told a dozen times how to accomplish the most simple tasks.

While he is being thus enchanted, so is she. Loving parties and people as she does, she's met lots of men over the years, but they've bored her to tears. They're so insensitive, so rude and demanding. They would never ask her advice about their businesses, jobs, or careers, because they think she's "only a woman," so what could she know about such matters? This always infuriates a Libra girl, to whom equality of the sexes is practically a religion. She doesn't have to march in an ERA parade (though she very well might) but equality is equality, and fairness is fairness to Libra.

Now here is this charming man, whose eyes are alive with intelligence and humor, whose manner is so warm and affectionate, who is so reflective and sensitive. He makes her feel so feminine, yet he admires, even encourages her intellect. He makes her feel that he truly needs her, and somehow . . . she feels so safe and secure with him, as though he would never allow anything ugly or gross or upsetting to trouble the new tranquility they've found. There's something just a little old-fashioned and gallant about him, and it lifts her spirits in a strange way, makes her feel pleasantly protected. He understands the swinging of her Scales from lonely to lovely, from happy to hateful, because he's moody too, and that causes him to be sympathetic to her own moods. Mostly, he's so serene and patient, qualities that always appeal to Libra, who seeks the soothing and peaceful.

Why not get married? (She may think of this first.) He may hesitate. Maybe his mother doesn't approve of her, or maybe he's not sure she can replace his mother as The-Woman-Who-Adores-Him-Above-All-Else-In-The-World-Even-If-She-Sometimes-Doesn't-Show-It-But-She-Usually-Does. Maybe he thinks he should concentrate on his career or business until it's financially sound enough to support a wife and family. A Cancer man always looks before he leaps, and seldom rushes into anything. (To the *female* Crab who wants emotional and financial protection, marriage is the ideal answer, but the *male* Crab tends to seek the affection and emotional security he needs just as desperately by lengthening a love affair to its limit before he's willing to contemplate wedlock.) The responsibilities of marriage worry him. Whether he loves her or not isn't the issue. *Of course* he loves her, *but* . . . . .

Her first reaction to his Crablike hesitation and crawling backward may be to become cool to his physical advances — or to torture him by pretending to be interested in other men, hoping that jealousy, fear of losing her — or a denial of physical passion — will overcome his caution. She hopes to convince him of the truth of Samuel Johnson's observation that "marriage may have many pains, but celibacy has no pleasures." If the Sun and Moon in their nativities are in harmonious aspect, her strategy might work. Otherwise, it could only cause him to become snappy and cranky or to retreat into a shell of pouting. She's been exposed to a myriad of his moods, but this may be a side of him she's never seen. It will upset her, although she'll try not to show it. Then she'll turn on her Venus charm again, and begin to gently manipulate him with her soft voice and her dimpled smiles — attempt to win him over with a sort of combination of logic and serendipity. But with his acute perception, he'll sense what she's doing, and perhaps resist it by clinging to his caution even more tenaciously. His mother once told him that it's more sensible to be safe than sorry, and that smartness succeeds better than softness in this harsh, cold world. So he's always tried to be safe and sensible and smart. Now here is this beautiful, intelligent woman trying to make him be careless and impulsive . . and free. It confuses him, and makes him even crabbier.

He'll fret privately over her extravagant nature and she'll be annoyed at his unfair suspicions of her innocent friendships with others (but maybe not quite fair enough herself to realize she deliberately incited his suspicions). She'll tell him he's smothering her very soul, and refuse to answer his calls. But she misses him, she needs him, so she'll try to see it his way again . . . . . and again. He panics a little when they've quarreled, because the moment they're apart, her air of happy optimism and the sheer loveliness of life when they're laughing and loving together — haunts him. It's so like the way he felt in childhood when life was sweet . . . . . . and simple. Will there ever be such beauty again with anyone else? He fears there won't. In fact, secretly he's sure of it, and that's the dark enemy of their love — his secrecy, his reluctance to openly and directly express his feelings and thoughts to her. If he would, if he could, she might be able to help him make some sense of this strange Lunar magic they've discovered, help him find a way to believe in its goodness. But he perversely likes to keep her guessing about what he *really* thinks. It's never as easy for Cancer to be as honest and open as Libra.

When they're making love, they'll say silently to one another, "Let's don't think, let's just feel." And so their physical intimacy makes their troubles fade, for a time. When a Cancerian man submits to pure emotion and feeling, he's being his true self, free of the restrictions of his fears and worries. As a lover, he brings her the kind of peace and contentment he does because of these deep waters of his emotional nature. Sometimes, when they physically experience love, she's reminded of a cool stream, and she's a leaf, floating on its surface. The tenderness and imagination she brings to their Oneness has the same quieting effect upon him, and he relaxes, allowing love to fill his whole being, so there's no room for anything but joy. The way she makes him feel at these moments is not something he'll ever want to lose. But passion comes and goes, and always afterward there are the problems.

This being the difficult 4-10 Sun Sign Pattern, their conflicts and tensions, their impasse over permanency, and their divergent viewpoints aren't easy to overcome. But if he uses his Cancerian tenaciousness to try harder to pull their differences together, instead of using it to pull their love apart — and if she uses her Libra fairness to comprehend his caution with more compassion for his feelings, and less concern for her own, they just might try again . . and maybe this time, they'll make their poem rhyme, somehow learn to sing their song in tune. It's a painful process for Cancer and Libra to reach a compromise, but his need to hear those Easter Sunday sunrise chimes again may cause the Crab to take another chance — and her need to be loved by a man who both cherishes her and respects her may bring her back into his arms to be told again how beautiful she is. While she's gone, it's funny how he still feels her head against his shoulder, now and then, in his dreams . . and last night, he was sure he heard her speak, but her voice was sad. With her wiser heart (for Libra is ahead of Cancer on the karmic wheel of life) he thought he heard her say to him, gently, "You have so much to learn, darling . . . and I hope you never learn it, because it will bring pain, as learning always does, and I can't bear for you to be hurt anymore. That's why I had to go away." When he awoke, there were tears in his eyes, because her presence had been so real, he almost heard the music he'll never quite forget.

The Moon both curses and blesses Cancer with a vivid memory, nearly photographic, sometimes, in its clarity. These two can find their way back home to each other if their need and their patience are both strong enough.

But if not, even after the song between them has ended, his Lunar memory will return to him . . . haunting fragments of the lyric. Then he'll regret certain things he didn't say when she was near . . so he'll just think about them sometimes when he's alone . . and hope she hears them, wherever she is . . . . . .

> . . . it's like you told me once
> if we never saw each other again
> it wouldn't make any difference
>
> you didn't say it wouldn't matter
> you said . . it wouldn't make any difference
>
> and did you know I understood the nuance ?
> it was so long ago . . but, did you know ? °

☆ ☆ ☆ ☆ ☆ ☆

° From *Venus Trines at Midnight* by Linda Goodman.

CANCER

Water — Cardinal — Negative
Ruled by the Moon
Symbol: The Crab
Night Forces — Feminine

SCORPIO

Water — Fixed — Negative
Ruled by Pluto
Symbols: Scorpion & Eagle
Night Forces — Feminine

The **CANCER-SCORPIO** *Relationship*

Strangely, it was not in the water that
they met . .

The Crab and the Scorpion may meet while they're sunning themselves on a rock somewhere, on a lazy lavender day. They could, of course, meet beneath the briny, but since they are often destined to be drawn together sooner or later, the choice of multiple meeting places is greatly enhanced. A bank is near the top of the list. Or perhaps a United States Treasury building. Maybe a restaurant — a nursery — or in history class. All these areas are sacred to Cancer. Give Scorpio the choice, and it could be any site from an archaeological dig to a church . . . with a strong possibility of Tibet, among the lamas . . . or a library, near the shelves labeled "Sex and the Human Psyche." All sacred subjects to the Eagle.

This is the blessed-by-grace 5-9 Sun Sign Pattern, meaning that these two will almost surely be magnetized together anytime they're within a few miles of one another — not always, but usually. It's not a guarantee — what is, regarding human behavior? But it's an astrological probability that Cancer and Scorpio have a better chance than most people of successfully blending their auras. Anyway, guarantees are boring, don't you think? No. The Crab and the Eagle do not think so. Other 5-9 Sun Sign Patterns, such as Aries-Leo, Gemini-Aquarius, and so forth, may look upon guarantees as boring, but not this particular 5-9 vibe. Scorpions (Eagles) are undeniably fond of sure things, and Crabs mentally visualize the word *guarantee* spelled out in diamond letters, sparkling like the water of an unpolluted stream (a good allegory, since an unpolluted stream is as difficult to find these days as a 100 percent guarantee has always been—and always shall be—to locate).

All right, we'll start over. To the Crab and the Scorpion: You two nice creatures are very, very, very, very close to being certain of achieving harmony together, closer than most anyone you know. That's a promise from the planets and stars, a promise you have the power to transmute into a genuine guarantee with less effort than lots of other people. Does that make you both feel a little more comfy-cozy secure about it all? (Shh! See? Notice. The Crab is now peeking out of the shell, curious . . . and the Scorpion has raised one cautious eyebrow slowly, in interest. Words like *guarantee* and *secure* always have that effect on these Sun Signs.)

An occasional Cancer-Scorpio combination may toss each other up on the beach in an unhappy ending, but the great majority of associations between the Moon-governed (Cancer) and the Pluto-ruled (Scorpio) need never fear such a shipwreck. Their relationship will quite likely still be strong and healthy long after other combinations have given up the struggle. The areas of publishing, religion, space travel, the law, travel, foreign countries, the stock market, young people, schools, and various forms of creativity, including films . . (all ninth- and fifth-house matters) . . are likely ponds where you will find this combination splashing and diving and swimming and floating— or, if they're unevolved types—crawling hesitantly, hiding under protective shells.

The Crab and the Scorpion (or Eagle) have an almost uncanny instinctive understanding of one another. They share, not all, but nearly all vices and virtues. The faults and foibles of one are either possessed by or compassionately comprehended by the other. The lovable traits and talents of one are either possessed by or intensely admired by the other. It's called empathy, and Cancer and Scorpio can always count on this as a supportive influence in their relationship, whether adult and child, business associates, lovers, married mates, friends, siblings, or other relatives.

A child, or children, will typically, in some way, play an important role in their lives, as the relationship grows and endures (and probably it will), either a troublesome and sorrowful or a happy and magical role, almost from the time they first meet. Sometimes, sadly, this takes the form of children one or both deeply desire, but cannot possess, for one reason or another. More often, however, children and young people are a blessing to these two. If not literally children, then the *childhood* of the Crab or the Scorpion (or both) will be, in some strange way, the basis for initial attraction and sympathy. They will enjoy comforting one another concerning a sad past — or laughing and dreaming together over a happy past. Yesterday is always very near to Moon souls, and Scorpio also looks back, secretly, with nostalgia.

Both the Crabs and the Eagles tend to never forget a kindness. Likewise, they mutually share long memories for hurt or injury. Wound either Cancer or Scorpio, and the memory will linger, never fading, occasionally for a lifetime. But there the similarity ends, for the Crab will seldom try to even the score, preferring to cry and nurse injured feelings alone, cauterizing the wounds with liberal doses of self-pity, while the Scorpion will bloody well see to it, in one way or another, that there is returned an "eye for an eye, a tooth for a tooth" — a bruise for a bruise, a dented fender for a dented fender, an insult for an insult, and so on. This is a reaction (though not a very positive one) to the Scale-balancing act Scorpio has already learned from the sign behind — Libra. Making things come out even. But while Libra sorts it all out evenly through logical mental processes, Scorpio balances matters in, shall we say, a more tangible and instant way.

The Crab's hurt seldom, if ever, causes an urge to attack. The reflex action of the wounded Cancerian is to retreat, often remaining mistrustful of that person or situation forever . . . . whereas the word "retreat" is nearly unknown to an Eagle. Scorps may *appear* to give up, to retreat or disappear. But they'll return. Inwardly, these people would almost literally prefer to die than to lose a conflict or come out on the short end of someone else's stick. This goes for love affairs, business deals — soccer and marbles (depending on the age and sex). Yet, the Scorpion does not always *consciously* obtain the satisfaction of revenge. That is, he or she need not necessarily (though some do it deliberately) take an overt action against the offender. The intensity of a Pluto-powered thought alone will do it.

Nevertheless, there is an unearthly sweetness in the Scorpio aura, superimposed upon the determination not to be smashed without teaching the smasher a lesson, and it is this sweetness, this gentleness and sensitivity, which allows the Crab to trust the Eagle.

Since both are of the Water Element, when Cancerians and Scorpions who have heavy afflictions to their individual Suns at birth get together, they can drown in drink, drugs, or other forms of escape, including sexual promiscuity — dragging one another down deeper into the depths, until they've reached the ocean floor. The swim back up is not easy. For these, the extraordinary magnetism of the 5-9 attraction is a trap. Some associations of this type have even become mutual victims of dark arts like hypnotic control, psychic attack, voodoo, and black magic. Scenes like séances with a trance medium are best avoided by either — and especially by both together.

Ah! but the evolved, the emotionally mature, mentally perceptive, and spiritually aware Crabs and Eagles will discover all the joys and pure pleasures of the 5-9 Pattern, feeling and behaving very much like children together — and what could be more wonderful than submission to innocence, excitement, and faith in faeries? This can really be a rainbow kind of relationship, where every small or large misunderstanding is certain to be resolved and forgiven later. Crabs and Scorps don't forgive many people — but they will forgive one another. What is even lovelier, if the Sun-Moon aspect between their birth charts is also harmonious, matching the music of their trined, natal Suns, they'll not only forgive — they'll forget. And that's a true miracle for the Crab and the Scorpion. They can, if they only half try, bring out the best, not the worst, in each other. The trust Cancer has never been able to fully give to anyone will be easily given to Scorpio — and the great gift of forgiveness that Scorpio has never quite been able to give to another person will be painlessly given to the compatible Crab. Cancer and Scorpio, both extremely sensitive, are willing to reveal their vulnerabilities to each other. This is no small matter, for they've both kept their terrible vulnerability hidden beneath their shells for so long, lest the world discover it as a weakness and use it against them.

They tell each other secrets they would ordinarily never tell a soul. No one can pry a secret out of a Crab, if he or she doesn't want it known, but the Eagle just may — and the gentle Moon-ruled Cancerians can sometimes perform the magic trick of accurately reading Scorpio's facial expression of cool detachment for what it really is — a mask. They're both more than a little telepathic, particularly with one another.

When their purposes do clash, it will frequently be over money, because Scorpio is concerned with "other people's money," and Cancer is concerned with — well, with just plain money, never mind whose, just so it's green. Scorpio tends to worry over how to obtain it, Cancer over the dreadful possibility of losing it.

Since all Crabs, of whatever age or sex, as explained in my first book, *Sun Signs*, are "Jewish mothers" — and all Eagles, of whatever age or sex, are fiercely, intensely protective — these two will wrap one another in a very comforting cocoon, which could become a little stuffy unless they allow themselves to come out for air now and then. But oh! that feeling of security. Beautiful. Scorpio can at times be too self-controlled for Cancer's affectionate nature, and the Crab will sometimes snap at Scorpio, ruffling those smooth Eagle feathers, but these are minor tensions with which to cope when the rewards are so solid. After swimming for what has seemed to be eternities, in endless whirlpools of infinitude . . . . . . to be brought together with one who so gently understands your heart's deepest longings . . . . . . is a blessed thing.

☆ ☆ ☆ ☆ ☆ ☆

CANCER *Woman* SCORPIO *Man*

-◄-◄-●-►-►-

*It was not, she knew, that night had come, but
something as dark as night had come. No, worse
than that. It had not come, but it had sent
that shiver through the sea to say that it was
coming. What was it?*

Although somewhat of an enigma, the Cancer girl is decidedly interesting.
Beneath her surface reserve and coolness, she has a delightful sense of joy and
humor. She possesses very little ego or vanity, yet she's constantly misunderstood and accused of being cold and self-centered. Mystery attracts her, but
she's reluctant to delve too deeply into unknown, uncharted waters
. . . . . . unless those unknown, uncharted waters surround a Scorpio man.
This particular mystery she cannot resist, and in order to know him better,
she'll even discard her innate fears. For the girl Crab to control her fears is no
small accomplishment. Give her "A" on her spiritual-evolvement report card
for even the effort, let alone success in such a goal. Cancer fears always hover
around the aura of the Moon-ruled, so complex, and so deeply submerged in
the subconscious, that any attempt to overcome them should be appreciated
and applauded.

Being appreciated is her most wistful wish, her dearest desire, though she
will seldom admit it. So few people even try to understand her, let alone
appreciate her. The Scorpio man will do both. Perhaps that's why she
gathers the courage to return his intense gaze. She senses this is one human
being on the planet who really *knows* her. She's right. He does.

If any other man attempted to penetrate her secret self with such a
burning look, with such an intimate message in his glance, she would shower
him with ice water and aloofness. Or snap his head off. A girl Crab can
become mighty cranky when someone she doesn't trust tries to pry open her
shell. She's always more gentle with other Cancerians, Scorpio, and Pisces, a
little less irritable with Virgo and Taurus, sometimes fascinated by the male
Goat — but the Aries or Libra man may expect a decided snapping reaction.

Eagles love a challenge, and coaxing the shy but funny Cancerian girl to
trust him will be one of his easier ones. Equally as surprising, the normally
very suspicious Scorpio Eagle will probably trust her also, from the first
moment their eyes meet. It's an extremely rare occasion when the powerful
empathy between these Sun Signs isn't visible right away. It can happen, but
most infrequently.

Others in the past have accused the two of them of being cold emotionally. There's a good reason for that. They are. After all, they're both of the Water Element; consequently they find it difficult to display their feelings openly. But romantic temperature is a matter of interpretation. What others may call cold, to the Moon Maid and the Eagle can read from warm to hot. Compensating for their undeniable Water Element inheritance of a cooler chemistry, these two are secretly very sentimental, even more so than Taurus and Leo. The Cancer-Scorpio attempt to hide this sentimentality isn't always successful. Tears come to both their eyes easily when their emotions are touched (which is frequently). With her, the tears often spill down over her cheeks, and the secret is out. With him, after the first unbidden misting or faint wetness, a manly gulp and a powerful surge of self-control will dry his tears so quickly most people are none the wiser. Except for her. The Moon Maid saw them. And they caused a sharp loving-pain in her heart. No one in this world can control his emotions as superbly as a Scorpio man. He exercises a continual watch over them, forcing his facial features to assume a neutral position in the midst of any emotion, from surprise or elation to hurt or grief. Nearly always, the Eagle succeeds. When he doesn't, you can be sure the depth of the emotion felt is truly overwhelming, virtually uncontrollable. Others may not sense this, but the Cancer woman does, and it moves her deeply.

So, you see, they aren't emotionally cold at all — it's just that they both find it difficult to show on the outside what they're feeling on the inside. It's not easy for feelings, even strong ones, to break through their shells. For the Crab and the Scorpion each possess a hard shell of self-protection, an extra insurance policy from Nature against the intense degree of hurt always felt by such sensitive, sensitive creatures. This is the real basis for their empathy. Still, there will be times when she'll have to remind herself that what seems to be a coldness and silence approaching cruelty in him can be a mixture of shyness and a reluctance to admit what he's really thinking, until he's sure. He'll have to be aware that her apparent uncaring withdrawal is only her way of protecting herself from possible disappointment, until she's assured of being loved. No one seeks and needs love more than the Moon Maiden and the Eagle. Not an ordinary love, but an all-encompassing love, woven with the strong threads of devotion, gentleness, and loyalty. That last word is ultra, super important to them both.

In direct contradiction to his surface detachment and poker face, this man is an extremist. You'd never guess it from his soft voice, his subtle strategies in his career and personal life. (You'd never guess it, but you'd better believe it!) He can sink into some abysmal wells of depression, and rise to some intoxicating heights of ecstasy. All the while, to look at him, you'd think his days were spent in monotonous fashion, with few, if any, ups and downs, the smooth lake of his personality unruffled by unexpected events. Don't be fooled. (This advice is for other Sun Signs — the Cancer woman doesn't need it. Remember, she *knows* him.) Of course, that cool poise took years of training. He unleashed some pretty sensational rages of fury as a teenager, before he mastered self-control. Ask his mother.

The Lunar lady of his dreams soon discovers that her Eagle lover's chief faults are his suspicious nature, jealousy, and a desire to dominate his mate (and most everyone else), however well disguised — just as he realizes very early in the relationship that her weak points are secrecy, smothering possessiveness, and a quivering vulnerability to hurt, both real and imagined. Imagined hurt, whether emotional or physical, can be as painful as the real kind. Any doctor will tell you that the "imaginary pain" of an amputee, for example, is vividly felt.

All pain begins in the mind, even so-called physical pain — not in the body. And so, when dealing with his Moon Maiden's wounded feelings, the Eagle must first realize how real the pain is to her, how dreadfully her heart aches, even though she only imagined the action which hurt her to be intentional. Then he can tenderly explain to her how medical hypnosis, and many other experiments, have proven that all pain sensations begin in the mind, before manifesting in the body, and therefore, can only be removed through the *source* — the mind or the imagination. The subconscious mind, depositor of all her nightmares and insecurities from childhood, is in absolute control of the body, and of all human emotional reaction. Tell a hypnotized subject the postage stamp placed on a hand or arm is a flame, and an actual blister will rise. Place a *real* flame against the skin, tell the hypnotized person it's an ice cube, and *no* blister will appear. It's as simple and as true as that — and it gives a clue to handling the Cancerian fear fluctuations, when the problem is actually emotional pain, rather than physical.

Sexually, the Scorpion's love nature is more intense and yearning than that of most men. Hers is more romantic and sensitive than that of most women. What each needs most, then, from the other should be obvious: emotional security and reassurance. She needs visible tokens of his affection . . . . . . an unexpected rose or bunch of violets on her desk or on her pillow . . . . . . perhaps a small pet, like the one she had as a child, sitting there with a ribbon around its neck as a surprise some bright morning — things like that. These small things affect her sexual chemistry profoundly.

He needs to know that her lovemaking stems from a genuine desire to be one with him, that it's not, on occasion, feigned to hide a secret boredom. You can't hide anything from him anyway, so why try? If they remain aware of one another's unspoken needs, their physical mating can be a truly transcendental experience. But they both may have occasion to learn that controlled passion is not passion at all. Only when two people trust one another totally in every *other* way can they fully express love through sexual intimacy. The special requirement these two share is the need they each have for continual demonstration of affection away from the bedroom — a demonstration for which they will rarely ask, a need they seldom verbally express, because it's buried so deep. When this mutual need is filled, the happiness they discover in their physical lovemaking will be just about all Earthlings could wish for on this three-dimensional level of man and woman's present awareness—as with all 5-9 Sun Sign couples, barring a negative Sun-Moon aspect between them.

I've said this earlier, but it bears repetition. The two dragons they must conquer together are their most negative traits: her unfounded fears and sometimes smothering possessiveness—his burning jealousy and revenge compulsion—and their mutual financial caution. (Some people call it stinginess.) When they're angry, both tend to retreat into their individual caverns of silence, which is the worst of all possible solutions for these two Sun Signs (although other Fire Sign 5-9 Patterns could profit by a little more of the stuff). What Cancer and Scorpio need, however, is to talk it over, to verbalize their complaints. Burying a resentment in silence won't make it disappear. It only allows what began as a minor irritation to grow into a not-so-jolly green giant which can destroy their relationship. It's always unfortunate when any 5-9 Sun Sign Pattern vibration is destroyed, because they invariably miss each other so very much.

This is a woman who needs a Valentine every February, a hyacinth for Easter, the merry sound of antique sleigh bells at Christmas to match her merry laughter . . . a tiny diamond, or something shining and silvery for the New Year . . . a nostalgic box of sparklers on the Fourth of July . . . lots and lots of time to reminisce about the past on Thanksgiving . . . and no unexpected goblins to frighten her on Halloween.

This is a man who may pretend to ignore holidays, but watch his normally impassive, controlled features light up in sheer delight, should the woman he loves happen to leave a crazy stuffed animal perched on the dashboard of his car, on Groundhog's Day. For a brief, enchanted moment, she'll catch a glimpse of the way he grinned when he was a small boy, before he learned to master his poker face and that enigmatic, mysterious smile.

☆ ☆ ☆ ☆ ☆ ☆

CANCER *Man* SCORPIO *Woman*

————— ◆◀◆▶◆ —————

*Sometimes . . . . he had dreams, and they were more painful
than the dreams of other boys. For hours he could not
be separated from these dreams, though he wailed piteously
in them. They had to do, I think, with the riddle of
his existence. At such times it had been Wendy's custom
to take him out of bed and sit with him on her lap,
soothing him in dear ways of her own invention, and when
he grew calmer to put him back to bed before he quite
woke up, so that he should not know of the indignity to which
she had subjected him.*

This relationship works best when the woman is the Crab, the man the Scorpion. Yet, since these lovers are influenced by the 5-9 vibrational Sun Sign Pattern, the sex of the lovers won't seriously impair their chances for harmony. Her ruling planet, Pluto, is stronger, and more intense, than his ruler, the Moon—but then, his Cardinal Sign essence is more powerful in an inter-reactive way than her Fixed Sign essence. Cardinal means to *lead*— Fixed means to *not* follow—which will be one of the more basic problems between these otherwise nicely tuned-in people. Read the last two sentences over several times, and you'll know how the aforementioned problem works out in the final analysis. It takes meditation.

They will share the qualities of gentleness, loyalty, intensity of emotion, and great imagination. Together, they can create all manner of marvelous things—a powerful love, a star-blessed child or children, or a great career. *Create* is the key word. Cancer and Scorpio, when they combine their auras, can become an awesome regenerative force. Sarah and Abraham were surely Cancer-Scorpio mates, never mind which was the Cancerian, which the Scorpion. For Sarah conceived a child, fathered by Abraham, created from the depths of their mutually intense desire, long after they were past what those who follow the illusionary chronological calendar would call the "childbearing age" for her and the "virile age" for him. To prove how illusionary such matters are, each was (literally) several hundred years "old" when their child was born—that alone being a miracle to those who are today brainwashed or soul-washed by the "normal life span" deceptions of insurance companies and the like.

"Is anything impossible unto the Lord?" Abraham was asked. No. Nor is anything impossible unto the *children* of the Lord—(or of our co-Creators)—we who were made in Their image.

Along with Capricorn and Taurus, Cancer and Scorpio share the tendency to longevity. In reality, all Sun Signs have the potential of a life span in the same flesh body of five hundred to a thousand years or so, sans the aging process, but these particular Sun Signs lead the way to enlightenment. Capricorns demonstrate the reversal of age, by appearing younger, as they grow Earth-Time "older"—Taurus shows us how being calm and patient adds less wear and tear to the body, the Bulls retaining their splendid strength long after most others have given up—Cancer exhibits the necessary tenacity—and Scorpio knows, on a still subconscious level (soon to be conscious) the alchemy secrets of cell regeneration which make longevity possible. Naturally, if everyone—or *when* everyone—learns the secret of Abraham and Sarah, such a miracle would appear to create a population problem, in consideration of those new souls being born, simultaneously, as babes. There is a solution to this apparent mathematical problem, but it's too complex to be explored in this book, therefore, it must be delayed until a forthcoming one, in which we will attempt to deal with all these matters in more depth.

Since the Crab and the girl Scorpion have a better chance than most of remaining on the planet for a considerable number of Earth years, it's a lucky thing they're more compatible and harmonious than many other couples. They will surely never bore one another for the first few centuries.

Along with the vices and virtues they share, there are a few traits they *don't* share, and these will be, from time to time, troublemakers. He does not possess her Pluto-propelled intensity of emotion, her near-compulsion to strike back when angered, and this can become a dangerous problem to their happiness, if too many stings from the Scorpion's tail cause the male Crab to permanently retreat into his shell of hardness. Another difference between them, scattered among the smooth similarities of character, which could rock the relationship, will be her inability to comprehend his undue caution, his occasional timidity—and his reluctance to allow fate to guide his destiny. It's difficult for the Scorpio woman to understand his Lunar lack of courage when a challenge demanding direct confrontation occurs—from outsiders, as well as in their personal association. She'll have to remember that all Crabs take a step or two sideways or backward before lunging ahead, giving them time to carefully consider all possibilities, which is why he's a more clever strategist in both material and emotional matters than she may realize. Despite her outward femininity and reserve, this girl fears nothing in Heaven or in Hell (or on Earth) herself—unless her Sun was severely afflicted by malefic planets at birth—therefore, his hesitations will both puzzle and trouble her. Likewise, her willingness to plunge into churning emotional waters and unknown situations which could be dangerous will frighten and trouble *him.*

Much of the time, their conflicts will be quickly dissolved by a wave of his Looney Bird humor. There's nothing as startling — and as refreshing — as the Cancer man's sudden switch into laughter, following one of his dismal, cautious, cranky, and crabby moods. She needs his laughter, for Scorpio is too often deeply engrossed with the mysteries of life to laugh casually. Humor heals. It's a bridge which spans any kind of misunderstanding. The agonizing conflict between blacks and whites in America only began to truly dissolve when comedians of both races had the courage to make fun of prejudice before mixed audiences, whose reactions were at first uncertainty — then finally intense relief, allowing both races comprehension of — and compassion for — one another.

But humor has two sides. The swiftest way to destroy an enemy is not through verbal abuse or bitterness, but through subtle ridicule. The Crab must take care not to overdo his sense of the divine comedy of life to the point of teasing her and making her feel ridiculous. Her sense of self-importance and basically serious nature cause her to be reluctant to laugh at jokes aimed toward herself. She can be offended by excessive teasing or an ill-timed joke. And you know what offended Scorps do — get even. When this woman is really angry (which won't be often, with the emotional control she has developed at great cost over the years) her Cancerian mate will be fortunate to have his crab shell to hide under until the storm blows over, or until the volcano stops spouting lava, whichever image fits the scene.

His own temper isn't anything to scoff or sneeze at either. When his tender, sensitive feelings are hurt, he can pout, snap, or crackle with crankiness for days, weeks, or months — in extreme cases, for years. Not even the powerful force of her ruling Pluto can blast the Crab out of his protective shell when he wants to remain there, nursing his emotional cuts and bruises.

All right, here it comes. I've been waiting to bring up the subject slowly and carefully. Even though theirs is the usually harmonious 5-9 compatibility pattern, there is one HUGE boulder looming between them which must be either gently sailed around — or dynamited at the beginning. A word with seven letters. Interesting. Seven is the number of Neptune, and Neptune rules, among other more positive things, deception. But I'm getting carried away into metaphysical nuances (perhaps not without pertinence). The word is "secrets." Both he and she take perverse joy in keeping secrets — and neither of them can *stand* having a secret kept from them. Do you see the picture? Think about it. Obviously, something or someone has to give — more than an inch. Maybe several yards. Make that miles, depending on their Moon Signs.

True, they'll share more of their secrets with one another than with those outside their personal periphery, nevertheless, there will be times when the

Crab will sit on a secret she's burning to burrow out of him; other times when his woman holds back some mystery he's fairly quivering to learn. A Cancerian literally cannot sleep if he believes someone, especially his mate, is keeping a secret from him, however minor it may be — and frankly, however much it may be none of his business. A Scorpio woman is consumed with curiosity under the same circumstances. The difference is that he'll reveal his anxiety by chewing his nails, frowning, or snapping. She'll hide her desire to know behind the cool poise and surface nonchalance that cover her inner turmoil, and will worm it out of him more often than he'll worm mysteries out of her — because she knows how to employ the subtle, sneaky interrogation technique until the secret has popped out unintentionally from her victim. (Victim is the only word.) This will frustrate the Crab, who prides himself on his cleverness in keeping things under his hat, even if he doesn't wear one.

What is my advice, as an astrologer? I'm sorry to say I have none. I could tell these two to level with each other as much as possible, but they won't. So, they'll just have to fight — then go to bed and make up.

I didn't mean that to be facetious, for sexually, this man and woman are blessed with the grace to achieve a beautiful physical fulfillment together. Their auras are color-coded: harmonious, the auric light surrounding them during their mating nearly always shaded in the rainbow hues of love — unless some Sun-Moon static in their charts causes a few muddy tones. Children conceived through 5-9 Sun Sign vibrations, when the Sun-Moon exchange is also favorable, are aptly called "love children." Although this can occur between couples of all Sun Signs, it occurs more often with the 5-9 vibrations. When a man and woman blend sexually, an auric light is sent forth which attracts souls in the astral, seeking a channel for birth. The auric light of love attracts the more gentle, evolved souls into its magnetic stream, whereas mating performed in lust alone attracts the lower evolved or still not yet sensitive souls into a birth channel. Since both kinds of souls must enter the birth wheel of Karma for gradual and eventually certain enlightenment, each at its own chosen speed, even a lust mating has its purpose in the Universal Plan — though a constant attempt to add the tenderness of real love to lust is eternally an obligation to such couples.

The Crab and the Scorpion usually have no need to be reminded of such cosmic responsibilities. Their basic harmony nearly always creates a sexual chemistry which is both aware and inspirational. Cancer and Scorpio instinctively blend the mental and emotional with the physical, which is the secret key to an ecstasy never experienced by those who separate sexual desire from the other parts of their natures, seeking only the sensual. The added dimensions of affection and mental affinity brought to sex by Cancer and Scorpio result in a kind of lovemaking realized by a relatively small percentage of man-woman matings in any particular incarnation. This explains the powerful initial attraction between two lovers of this 5-9 Sun Sign

Pattern; their lingering pain when separated . . . . their abundant opportunities for "trying again" after a quarrel.

The Scorpio woman takes her commitment to love very seriously, with an almost religious fervor. But should she find she is not loved in return, she will eventually follow her heart elsewhere, without regret. Let that be a warning to the man who treasures her. The Cancer man is moody, often fussy and exacting. He requires his frequent unconscious and conscious nightmares to be tenderly soothed away in order to be his gentle, funny self. Otherwise, he'll grow crankier and more reclusive, until the soft side of his nature, and his beautiful, romantic imagination disappear entirely, and he crawls away dejectedly — sideways, of course, as is the wont of the Crab — back home to mother, who always understands him. Whether she's still living, or has passed on, she's still the only woman who ever totally understood him. Just ask him sometime. He'll tell you all about her. If he's one of those very unfortunate Crabs who was adopted, or whose mother died when he was an infant, he will dream of her, and sense that she *would* have understood him. The maternal yearning is powerful in Cancer.

Cancerian dreams, like Scorpion perceptions, are very vulnerable, and need gentle protection from harsh reality. These two should cherish one another, true love being as rare as it is these days . . . . . . for no one else will treat the girl Eagle with quite so much reverence as her Cancerian man, and no one else will treat his dreams quite as tenderly as his Scorpio lady — except for his mother. She approves of their union. Believe me, she does . . . . . from wherever she may be on Earth — across the continent, or across the street — or from Heaven — she sends her son's Scorpio mate her secret sympathy.

More than any other man, the gentle Crab will forgive the deceptively quiet Scorpio woman her occasional stormy rages and hurtful words or acts of revenge, because he learned a lesson as a child he's never forgotten. He knows that *the opposite of love is not hate — the opposite of love is indifference.* Whatever he receives from his Pluto-ruled woman, it will never be this. True, she's capable of totally ignoring those for whom she feels contempt, as though they didn't exist — and for her, they don't. Yet, when it comes to the man to whom she's once given herself, once loved, however long ago it may have been — years, or yesterday — her Pluto power deserts her. And this is her well-guarded secret.

Never mind the icy mask she wears to disguise her pain or torment of decision. Her passions may leap from love to hate, and back again — but *indifference* toward the man who has totally possessed her is one emotion this lady will never master. And so, the Lunar man can take it from there.

☆ ☆ ☆ ☆ ☆ ☆

CANCER

Water — Cardinal — Negative
Ruled by the Moon
Symbol: The Crab
Night Forces — Feminine

SAGITTARIUS

Fire — Mutable — Positive
Ruled by Jupiter
Symbols: Archer & Centaur
Day Forces — Masculine

The **CANCER-SAGITTARIUS** *Relationship*

"Ah, me" one voice said, and another
said, "Oh, mournful day."

So here we have the Crab, hard as rock without, soft as butter within. Extremely sensitive. Oh! very, very sensitive. Acutely aware of the slightest· shade of meaning, every nuance of every comment, and extremely vulnerable to hurt.

And here we have the Archer, merry and warm-hearted, essentially kind, but sometimes brutally frank, and possessing only a thimbleful of tact. Make that *half* a thimbleful.

What happens when an ultra sensitive, cautious Cancerian bumpety-bumps around with a carefree, casual Sagittarian, whose specialty is blurting out arrows of truth that sting, however unintentionally? It depends on the phase of the Moon, actually. Since Cancer is ruled by the changeable Lunar vibrations, the Crab could react to the "slings and arrows of outrageous fortune" (and outrageous remarks of Sag) in several ways. By snapping back crabbily or pinching sharply (Crabs do have sharp pinchers). Perhaps by crawling inside the tough crab shell to hide and pout, quivering like a bowl of jelly over the indignity of it all. Or by just sitting there, deeply wounded, shedding trembling tears.

A brokenhearted Crab, with sagging spirits, immersed in murky melancholy from the callous treatment of his (or her) feelings by a thoughtless person, is one of the saddest sights on land or sea. It truly tugs on the soul to see one of these funny, moody creatures reduced to sobs. Even when they bravely try to hide their hurt, their chins quiver pathetically; their soft eyes gaze at you with such reproach you feel like weeping yourself.

That's often the reaction of an Archer who has just realized that he (or she) has inadvertently said or done something to cause a Cancerian friend, business associate, relative, lover or mate to feel the awful Lunar anguish of rejection. Instantly contrite for inflicting such damage through careless speech, the Archer will try to bandage the wound he (or she) caused with "soothing" words. Something like, "Gee, I'm sorry I hurt your feelings by saying you're dumb. Don't cry. So you're not a mental giant. There are lots of things more important than being intelligent. Doesn't that make you feel better?"

Odd as it may seem, frequently the perceptive Crabs will finally see the futility of trying to make the Archers aware of their tactlessness, the whole thing will strike them as humorous, and they'll burst out in hysterical laughter. Actually, a close association with an Archer is often, in the long run, beneficial to Cancer. It may be painful for a while, but eventually, the Crabs will learn the valuable lesson of not being quite so sensitive. Since everything is relative, another bonus is that, after knocking around with Sag, the occasional thoughtless remarks of everyone else the Crab knows will seem like fragrant roses of compliments by comparison, and it all evens out by making life in general smoother for Cancer.

It's sort of like when you've been crying over a toothache, and suddenly you break your leg. You forget all about the throbbing tooth. Or when you've been fussing and complaining about a small bee sting on the end of your nose, and along comes Sag to crack you over the bean with a verbal baseball bat. The only courteous thing to do is to thank Sag for curing you forever of sniffling over bee stings, right? Right. A few stitches, and your head (or self-confidence) will be like new again. Now the Archers will be nodding, thinking these observations are all quite logical and philosophical. Some of them may even be saying, "That's true! Every cloud has a silver lining." (Sagittarians are equally as fond of that Pollyanna truism as Librans.) Admittedly, it's not always easy to view a Sag as any sort of silver lining when he (or she) is aiming the Jupiter bow straight toward your Achilles heel, but the truth is that the Archers *are* optimistic. Nearly as much so as Libra, but with a touch more skepticism.

There are times when the sensitivity and sympathy of Cancer combined with the direct candor of Sagittarius can be a favorable blend of qualities, resulting in some very clear thinking, whether they're blended through an association between an individual Crab and Archer — or combined within one person, such as a friend of mine, who's a Sun Sign Cancerian, with the Moon and Ascendent in Sag. One day when she dropped by to visit me in my home, she was looking through a current, popular weekly magazine, trying to locate a certain advertisement she wanted to show me. After a moment or so, she found it. "Just look at that," she commanded, her eyes full of Lunar tears, but her voice full of Jupiter anger.

It was a double page public relations promo for the Martin Marietta Company, the people who make some nice and necessary things, like cement and aluminum, but who are also among the industries we can thank for many of the chemicals that threaten our health and safety, possibly our survival. The ad was plugging a 4-H livestock competition fair in west central Illinois, because the Martin Marietta Company believes that "traditions like this are a basic, enduring strength to our country, for the good of us all, well worth preserving. . . . . to make America better for everyone."

Taking up most of the space in the double-page ad was a color photograph of a small boy named Troy, age eight — posing with bright eyes and a happy smile beside his Hampshire gilt, a blue-ribbon-winning, 236-pound market hog that Troy calls Betsy. The prize hog was velvety soft and plump, a beautiful midnight blue color, with a curly tail, trusting eyes and appealing, floppy ears. In the picture, the little boy was lovingly stroking his gentle friend, Betsy, with so much pure, childlike love and affection in his expression.

"I wonder," said my Cancer-Sag friend, "if they would dare to publish a photograph of little Troy watching his dear friend he'd grown to love as a pet, being slaughtered (which, of course is Betsy's inevitable destiny) so folks can have their morning bacon. Would they dare to publish the terror and shock and agony in the eyes of an innocent child as he watched the Betsy he loved so much being brutally butchered ? I suppose children like Troy are just told, after they spend months grooming and learning to love a 'market animal' that 'Betsy' or whoever, has just gone away on a pleasant visit somewhere, and probably won't return — to explain the disappearance of a beloved pet who's been carted off to the slaughterhouse to be murdered when the child isn't looking. They're such sick, misguided hypocrites. If they think slaughtering our animal brothers and sisters is such a beautiful, traditional thing, why don't they have the courage to publish the *end* of the story — show us the expression on a little boy's face when he learns the cruel truth about what adults really plan to do with the animal he adores, his reaction to all the gushing blood and the pathetic squealing and screaming in fear and agony that deafens the ears in a slaughterhouse, not to mention the stench of death that hangs over places stocked with butchered flesh."

After her words had poured out, she was trembling, with a mixture of compassion and fury. Her maternal Cancer Sun Sign was causing her heart to break over the face of the child, while her Sagittarian Moon and Ascendent (Sag is an animal lover) caused her remarks to be blunt and honest, plain-spoken and to the point.

"I know," I tried to comfort her, "and I share your feelings. You're right. Nevertheless, spiritual awareness *is* gradually beginning to grow, as people feel the vibrations of the Aquarian Age. One of the proofs it's growing is that the owners of slaughterhouses have nervously sensed the change, and no longer allow the public to enter and see what goes on inside. The people who work there suffer too, in a different, but maybe equally as terrible a way as the animals, because a recent survey of all occupations by insurance companies revealed that butchers and employees of slaughterhouses are among the groups with the highest rate of suicide — and while that's a sad statistic of subconscious guilt, it's an indication that Earthlings are slowly but surely coming closer to enlightenment."

After awhile, my friend stopped crying — about the same time I did myself. I mention this true incident to illustrate the combined essence of Cancer and Sagittarius, but also for another reason, best summed up by borrowing the final words from the Martin Marietta Company advertisement (although my meaning is far different from theirs). The ad ended with the comment: *"This is for Troy, and for the future."*

At various times during this 6-8 Sun Sign Pattern association, the Crab and the Archer will clash over the subject of money, which is always burning a hole in Sagittarian pockets. It seldom burns a hole in Cancer's pockets. It's more likely to tear loose the seams with sheer weight, because the Crabs do enjoy accumulating large amounts of cash, and they prefer it be as near their person as possible at all times. Their fights will be frequent in the area of finances, but they can probably come to some sort of compromise, through friendly mutual agreement. The one astrology would suggest as being the most helpful is for Cancer to maternally (or paternally) keep patching and sewing up the holes that money burns in Sag pockets (training the Archer to be a bit more conservative, in a gentle way) and for Sagittarius to keep Cancer's pockets from bursting at the seams by kindly offering to take some of the Crab's excess cash off his (or her) hands to invest. Archers are startlingly lucky regarding matters like gambling, such as the stock market (the biggest gamble of them all). This will have a dual benefit. It will train Cancer to be more generous and giving, and it will also tickle the Crabs when they gradually learn that Sag has an unexpected way of quickly doubling their money for them — some of the time, that is. Everyone can experience a losing streak, and on such rare occasions (since the typical Sag is too blessed by Jupiter luck to suffer major losses consistently) the Crab must refrain from snapping, pouting and scolding. Otherwise, the Archer will leave in a huff, after causing Cancer to weep by zinging a few pertinent parting remarks about stinginess, and refuse to do any more favors if they're not appreciated.

The Cancerian man or woman will inevitably (even though in the background) be the subtle leader of this 6-8 association between two people who are so very different from each other. Because the Crab is Cardinal and Sag is Mutable. Being Cardinal causes a person to secretly be determined to be in command, and openly resent taking orders from others. There could be some difficulty here, because, although Mutable Sag is not particularly interested in being a leader (Archers would rather gallop around, hither and yon, communicating ideas) Sagittarius nonetheless actively (and outspokenly) dislikes taking orders himself — or herself. The Human end of the dualistic Sagittarian Centaur may be able to accept it cheerfully and philosophically — but the Horse end will kick considerably, and rear the equestrian legs in the air now and them. Sag is half Horse, half Human, you know, both symbolically and literally. One of those double Sun Signs of duality. Although the Human end is quite bright, often highly studious and intellectual, and optimistically philosophical — the Horse end (which is the rear end of Sag) is equally stubborn, contrary, unpredictable . . . and amazingly swift at racing away from problems. Also liable to kick dangerously when freedom is threatened.

Since the Crabs really can't help their inbred trait of possessiveness (which, used in a positive way, can be a warm and cozy virtue of solicitous protectiveness) they'll have to be cautious that they don't unintentionally smother the freedom of the Archers, who need large gobs of it in order to be themselves. (Freedom, that is — not smothering.) Of course, Crabs are naturally cautious by instinct, so all they need do is apply some of their natural Sun Sign caution to being careful not to stifle the free expression and action of Sag. If Cancer can manage to do this — and if the Archers will occasionally at least count to ten or twenty before stuffing their feet in their mouths (hammering on the Crab's sensitive feelings with blunt observations) these two can have a rather jolly time of it together.

In some way, Sagittarius will end up by serving the Cancerian, by being helpful — because the Archers sense some mystery within the Moon-ruled Crabs they're anxious to solve. Sagittarian curiosity being the burning thing it is, there will always be something to keep Sag fascinated, and interested in hanging around Cancer's seashore, beneath the Full Moon, watching the tides flow in and out . . . in-between a few laps around the track when the Centaurs become restless and need some time alone to race against the wind, nearly always winning by a nose. And *this* fascinates the Crabs.

With Jupiter's benign and benevolent good humor, Sag adores playing practical jokes on people, but Cancer might sometimes miss the point. Then the Archer will give the Crab a gentle nudge . . . and finally the Lunar one will laugh, until he (or she) cries. Not over the joke alone. But because Cancer is deeply moved by the naivete and idealism of the brave and optimistic Sagittarian, who keeps clumsily falling, then picking himself up with a bright smile . . . to try once more to reach the winner's circle. Those times when Jupiter allows the Centaur to be victorious, the happy, generous Archer will probably trot right back to the seaside, and offer to share half the good fortune with the Cancerian friend or relative, stuffing the Crab's pockets again with childlike glee. Jupiter rules the huge, the expansive, and sometimes only a Crab really knows how large a Jupiter heart can be. Someday, somehow, Sagittarius will teach Cancer the beautiful rewards of giving, cheerfully guiding the inwardly timid, fearful Crabs toward the Sagittarian religion of *truth*. Then there shall be no more sadness and sighing . . "for God shall wipe away all tears from their eyes." How can you cry when you're laughing at the courageous Archer's latest endearing clumsiness ?

☆ ☆ ☆ ☆ ☆ ☆

CANCER *Woman* SAGITTARIUS *Man*

◆ ◀◉▶ ▶

"Don't have a mother," he said. Not only had he no mother, but he had not the slightest desire to have one. He thought them very over-rated persons

"Oh, Peter, no wonder you were crying," she said, and got out of bed and ran to him.

"I wasn't crying about mothers," he said rather indignantly. "I was crying because I can't get my shadow to stick on. Besides, I wasn't crying."

The most essential, the most deeply rooted difference between the Moon Maiden and the Archer, (other than their conflicting views about money and material security) is often their totally divergent ideas and attitudes toward "family". She leans very much toward devotion and near-worship of family life — usually with more stress on the maternal and paternal than on siblings and other relatives, but nevertheless, this lady burns incense at the family altar with equally as much devout fervor as her Capricorn sisters religiously light *their* family circle beeswax candles (and often, with less resentment than Cappies sometimes feel).

Contradictorily, the Sagittarius man, while he may hold within his large

Jupiter heart much genuine affection for his family, dropping by to say a cheerful "hello" every few years or so, probably bringing along an armload of gifts (for the Archer is wonderfully generous) doesn't feel the intense tug of dutiful devotion toward his relatives the Cancerian girl feels toward hers. He may be the very first to help his parents, siblings and other blood ties when they need a friendly boost of the spirits — or a loan of whatever money he may have — but he doesn't believe that a tie of blood should imprison his freedom to roam and search around the world for truth and excitement, perusing his multiple interests and pursuing his idealistic (often gigantic) goals and ambitions. Ties are restrictive. Ties are binding. Blood ties or any other kind of ties. They resemble, to Sag, clanking chains — a rope around his neck, threatening to strangle his individuality. The Sagittarian man can hardly wait to cut the Gordian knot with his family, and be off to the races on his own, obeying the call of Jupiter to dash onward and upward to some great, nameless accomplishment or achievement. The Archer is also quite adept at untying the Gordian knots of problems swiftly and intelligently, and though he sometimes makes mistakes, he's usually shrewd enough not to make the same one twice.

A Moon Maid views "the ties that bind" with respect, if not with downright affection. Ties are cozy. Ties are familiar and comforting. They resemble, to her, softly woven strands of protection and safety. The known, the secure and the comfortable. To cut a tie with friends or relatives, a lover or husband — or with her parents — is something she dreads, therefore postpones as long as possible. This is often the reason Cancerian females are thought of as possessive. It's really not so much possessiveness as the being unwilling to cut a tie, then forced to float around without an anchor. To float without an anchor is as frightening an image to the girl Crab as the image of floating out in the middle of the ocean would be to the Nature crab, who feels much safer in remaining a healthy distance away from deep water.

Astrology can't solve that problem for them. The Moon Maiden and her Centaur will just have to fight it out, hopefully moving closer toward compromise as the years pass, but in the meanwhile fussing and quarreling — arguing (him) and pouting (her) back and forth between them over neglecting Mama and Papa (his fault) or weakening their own relationship by spending too much time with the family (her fault). As time goes by, they'll reach some sort of mutual agreement regarding this difference between them — or one of them will leave the other. But it might not be a permanent separation. For several reasons.

To begin with, it's more likely to be the Archer who angrily leaves the girl Crab (however regretfully) than the other way around. Not always, of course, but usually. It's easier, remember, for him to cut a tie than it is for her, although the knot of love is more difficult for a Sagittarian man to untie than the bond with his own family, for love can make even the normally carefree and nonchalant Centaur reluctant to break away — and once he's left, he may not stay long. Her Lunar madness is hypnotic, and will haunt his dreams at night while they're apart. Because this is the 6-8 Sun Sign Pattern, the Moon Maiden represents to him the 8th astrological "house" of mystery (sexual and otherwise) . . . the unknown. No one is more curious than Sag (unless it's Gemini) and he'll discover his mind is spinning in circles after a while, wondering what she's doing without him. Besides, he's frustrated by the realization that he lost his fiery temper, and left before he had a chance to completely solve her mystery . . . her changing moods, her inexplicable hold over his emotions. There are still a thousand urgent questions she hasn't answered. And so, the Archer who so swiftly and impulsively cut the Gordian knot with his Cancerian lady frequently later returns to tie it up again. Because he finds he misses her more than he guessed he would . . . and because there are all those puzzling questions . . .

Although the Moon Maid will be strangely comforted and flattered that the Sagittarian man she loves regards her as mysterious and magnetic, she rather perversely resents his prying. (She can't have it both ways, but she'd like to, concerning nearly everything.) This woman always has and always will contain within her many secrets, some of which she's not even aware of herself . . . others she is. There's something in the Lunar essence that makes her clam up when she feels someone is trying to probe too deeply into her secret self, even when the "someone" is the man she adores. The girl Crab crawls into a shell of silence automatically, instinctively, the moment he begins one of his questioning routines — even if all he's asking is something as innocent and ordinary as what she thinks about the new neighbors, or what her first boyfriend was like. (Admittedly, that last question might not be too innocent. The Sagittarian male has a temper, and although he's not the possessive type, he is assuredly the jealous type. As I keep reminding you, there is a distinct difference between possessiveness and jealousy.)

As reticent as this lady may be to reveal her own secrets quickly (unless they're drawn out slowly and gently, when she's in the mood to talk about them, not through rude questioning or abrupt and idle curiosity) she's an expert at uncovering her Centaur's secrets — and everyone else's. Somehow, people are unconsciously compelled to pour out things to the Moon Maiden they normally wouldn't confess to others. It's not the same as the confiding everyone does in the sympathetic Pisces listening ear. People confess to Pisces because they want to, without much urging, if any, from the Fish, who simply projects a willingness to listen if you feel like talking about it — and the talker senses the Piscean response will be compassion, which it always is. With the girl Crab, it's different. She's not apathetic or neutral about hearing your secrets. She enjoys learning things about others, and usually employs a conscious strategy to learn them, fully aware that she's digging to see what she can discover. Thanks to her Lunar magnetism (the same kind of invisible force not even the ocean's tides themselves can resist) the other person finds himself or herself pouring out all manner of private confidences, without having initially intended to do so.

The Lunar strategy of the Cancerian woman is even more successful with the Archer. Sag does love to talk, especially about himself, his dreams and his innermost feelings, along with his views and opinions of every subject under the Sun. Carried away by the enthusiasm of his verbal free thought association, he may wander a bit too far conversationally with the girl Crab before he realizes he's caught in an emotional wave that could drown him, by having said more than he intended. That's an astrological warning the Archer will find very valuable, if he heeds it, because there's always the possibility he'll say something that this extremely sensitive, imaginative lady could exaggerate or misinterpret, bringing on the Cancerian suspicion and trembling vulnerability to hurt. It pays the Sagittarian man to count to ten before he speaks at *all* times, but with his lovely girl Crab, he'd be well advised to count to maybe a thousand. It won't be easy for him to refrain from speaking his mind freely, sometimes in an unnecessarily frank way, not just because this is his natural tendency, but also because a Lunar Lady can be mighty tenacious, once she gets the notion into her rather hard head there's something he's thinking he hasn't told her, and she won't give up trying to find out. Not that there's anything he should feel guilty about, it's just that there are things she can take the wrong way and imaginatively dress up, clothing things said guilelessly with her personal fears and apprehensions, until they become threatening to her peace of mind, no longer even resembling their original intent or true meaning.

The time when the Archer should especially allow his actions to speak louder than his words is during their sexual intimacy. The Cancerian woman's way of expressing her many-layered love for him in a physical sense, is sensual and silent. To her, *feelings* are important, not words. She wants their lovemaking to be an escape into an ocean of passion, drenched in fragile moonlight sentiment, its depth a direct result of its delicacy and quiet communion of spirit. She withdraws sexually from demanding desire, able to surrender herself completely only when their mutual need is demonstrated tenderly, gently, even poetically, not fiercely. And if she's been made to feel rejected in some way throughout the day (she literally wilts beneath disapproval, spoken or unspoken) she'll be unable to respond at night in his arms, even though she only imagined the earlier slight to her sensitivity. Making love to a girl Crab is an eternal guessing game — and more successful when her lover or husband consults an almanac before approaching her, for this woman's every emotion is not just symbolically, but seriously and actually — ruled by the Moon's Lunar phases. This part of her sexual nature may at times annoy the Archer as much as it intrigues him, because, being a Fire Sign, his own desire is more impulsive, his need more intense. Finesse in lovemaking is something he has to consciously practice to acquire, especially when he's in love with a Moon Maiden, born into the Water Element.

Strangely, this is a woman who sometimes communicates her wish for Oneness by a misty light in her eyes — like the silvery, promising shimmer of the New Moon's ancient secret. When he sees moonlight in her eyes, he knows it's time to be very still and quiet . . . hold her close until she feels securely protected . . . then gently float beside her out into the mysterious sea that sings remembered songs to her at midnight. He may never solve her feminine mystery, but it will always beckon him to try.

Let's leave them alone now, shall we ? If the Looney Bird Moon Maid won't tell her secrets to the man she loves, she certainly doesn't want *us* around when her eyes become misty ! Before we go, we'll remind her that, while her Lunar tears fall like raindrops at the slightest hint of a cloud in the sky, his Jupiter tears are hidden and held back . . yet no less profuse than her own. Like a small boy, whistling in the dark, he's too brave to admit he ever cries. But for all his surface nonchalance — he does.

☆ ☆ ☆ ☆ ☆ ☆

CANCER *Man* SAGITTARIUS *Woman*

◄►◄◈►►

They talked of Cinderella, and Tootles was confident that his mother must have been very like her.

. . . . Tinker Bell shouted, "Silly ass !" and darted into hiding.

Even though Sagittarius astrologically rules religion (along with Pisces and Scorpio, because religion contains many levels of awareness, not just one) — and even though every Sag, at some time in Life, is deeply concerned about the pros and cons of religious beliefs — the girl Archer may forget, when she's in love with a boy Crab, the most important spiritual advice of all, which is *"count your blessings."*

Quite probably, before she met him, her Jupiter faith and idealism was shattered by the kind of men who treated love casually — and treated *her* carelessly, maybe even cruelly. Except perhaps for the very special boy with the tender eyes, who loaned her his pencils and fought the bullies who teased her at recess in the 6th grade, certainly none of the males she's impulsively loved came anywhere near living up to her private image of a Prince or a Knight who would treat her gently as his "lady fair," awaken her soul with the kiss in his glance that promised to adore her forever and three days... sweep her off to his enchanted castle, then sit with her beside the lake, feeding the swans, making her laugh... and making her know she was his alone, that his love was loyal and true, faithful and everlasting. She'd just about given up on that particular dream, and was about to settle for either remaining a bachelor girl — or finding a wealthy Arab, who might fall a little short of her image, but who would whisk her away on his private jet to the land of gushing oil wells, in his turban and long nightgown, to feed the camels at sunset. Forget Camelot. Who needs it ? Then there was this crazy miracle.

Bouncing along one day, she bumped straight into the surprised heart of a Crab, out strolling the byways and taking his morning constitutional. He was wearing no helmet, no armour, nor was he perched proudly astride a white horse. Neither was he adorned in a turban, and as for a long white nightgown, being a conservative Cancercian, he wouldn't dream of appearing in public clothed in such an unseemly, attention-getting manner. He owned not a single swan, and could introduce her to no camels. But he did sometimes sit by the lake in the park at twilight, he told her, and feed the pigeons popcorn. As for the private jet, after she knew him better, she realized that he definitely had the potential to own a whole fleet of them someday, the way he hung on to his money. I mean, after all, cash *has* to accumulate if you never spend a penny of it — ever. For anything. Except maybe an occasional glass of imported wine or champagne.

Never mind that he wasn't the living, breathing image of Camelot. There was a certain air about him. The kiss in his glance that promised forever was surely not missing. It caressed her, and made her knees feel funny every time he looked at her. And although he might be a trifle stingy with his pencils, not handing them out like potato chips, because after all, pencils do cost money, especially the kind with decent erasers — he still had the tender eyes of the special boy in the 6th grade, and he gave her the distinct feeling he'd protect her from bullies, in the schoolyard or anywhere else — that she was truly cherished as a woman, and that she'd be warmly secure with him forever and three days, because this man would surely keep her safe from all harm.

Well, you can't have it your way to match every nuance, eyelash and brush stroke of your dream image. Goodness knows he had more of those qualities she'd nearly lost hope of ever finding than any of the other gorillas, Casanovas and leering sophisticates who both bored her and let her down with a thump in the past. He might not be exactly Don Quioxte, but he did contain his own kind of impossible dreams, behind his shy smile and quiet manner. And so she forgot all about caution, and fell in love with him, head over heels. That's the way Sag always falls in love, or for that matter, does anything. Head over heels. Being a Centaur, therefore half Horse and half Human, this girl stumbles a lot, and is a little clumsy, despite her normally graceful stride that reminds her admiring Crab of a thoroughbred race horse.

The first thing she learned after she shocked herself by loving him, was that she didn't make a mistake in forgetting all about caution when they met. Because this man possesses enough of the stuff to supply, not just her when she runs low on it, but the entire British Commonwealth. An endless source. She'd be happier, she discovers after awhile, if he'd forget about some of his own caution — but not all of it. She kind of likes the way his caution keeps her steered in the right direction when she's sometimes tempted to be overly reckless (it's nice to be saved from yourself by someone who really cares about you) but a little of his caution goes a long way with the girl Archer. Too much of it can cause her to feel closed-in, smothered, therefore — restless. It's never a good idea to make the Horse end of a Centaur restless.

Because their relationship is guided and influenced by the 6-8 Sun Sign Pattern, the Cancerian man will hold an inexplicable fascination for this woman, hints of mystery and secrets — in addition to a magnetic sexual appeal. She is curious by nature, so the way he keeps her guessing about his feelings and changing moods is exciting rather than exasperating, as it might be to another female. Most of the time, she'll behave in an unaccustomed docile manner under the spell of the Lunar man. But once in a while, like the times he compares her to his mother (unfavorably) or scolds her for being extravagant, accuses her of talking too much, and never listening — she'll lose her temper. Since Jupiter has a way of expanding everything, the girl Archer does not have a small temper. It is sizable when fully aroused. Then she'll say something pointed and cutting (Sag is seldom or never at a loss for words) that will deeply wound the ultrasensitive feelings of this man. He'll snap back at her, crossly. She'll zing another arrow of tactless truth in answer to the challenge of his snapping, and he'll begin one of his lengthy pouting spells of silence, withdrawing into himself to a place where she can't follow — where even her words can't reach him.

This is when she should take a walk in the woods alone, all by herself (being close to Nature never fails to clear the cobwebs from a Sagittarian mind) and project her astral self back to the way things were before he came along to cozily protect her and make her laugh with his outrageous humor. There was such a vague and lonely longing within her then, that seemed to just melt away the first time he smiled at her with the soft, twinkling eyes of her 6th grade hero, stirring memories of a time when Life was sweet and simple, and full of warm familiarity. He has his faults, yes. But he's sympathetic, sensitive and affectionate. He's funny and full of fascinating conversation more often than he's grouchy. He's certainly loyal and earnest. He'd never try to deliberately hurt her, or break a promise if he could possibly help it. And he's gradually become more generous, because he wants to please her. He didn't say a word last week when she bought a registered, purebred Old English Sheep Dog for nine hundred dollars, which meant he couldn't have the camera he'd been wanting for over a year. Best of all, he's not a hypocrite. He's sincere and genuine. She can't stand hypocritical people.

After she counts her blessings, she'll go back and tell him she's sorry she yelled at him, and was unkind. Then, if she offers to do something very sweetly solicitous for him, he'll peek out from behind his crab shell and trust her again with his nicest smile. Maybe some stuffed mushrooms, the way his mother fixed them, is that what might heal the hurt, so they can be close again?

No. He'd rather have her than the mushrooms. He has that Full Moon strangeness in his eyes again, because she's touched his heart with kindness. So they make up by making love. Their sexual chemistry is one of the blessings she forgot to count. Her desires are more fiery and passionate than his, but that only has the effect of stirring him with a challenge to teach her that he's Cardinal and she's Mutable. (Cardinal means to *lead*.) Then too, there's that haunting mystery of his Water Element, drawing her into its depths, as she learns more about the stillness within the unexplored parts of herself through the slow, gentle way he approaches their mutual need. He leads her to a place where sensuality is a whispering, waiting promise, where trembling enchantment lingers much longer, for all its dreamlike quality, than a flaming rush of instant blending that quickly dies out, leaving no memory of its peace behind it. Fire stimulates and thrills with the hint of explosion. Water soothes and cools . . . remaining. The right amount of each makes sexual expression between Cancer and Sagittarius a strong and fulfilling experience.

But physical love is only one level of a human relationship, so the Crab and his girl Archer must learn to blend their Fire and Water Elements in other ways with the same kind of careful harmonizing. In time, he'll grow to intensely respect her courage — and, yes, even her frankness. Because she's honest. He can trust her to mean what she says, and to be what she is. In time, she'll be grateful for his cautious hand on hers, holding her back from all those deep holes she used to fall into when she wasn't looking. They'll learn to trust each other. And that's the one thing these two very different people had in common, long before they met. The search for someone you can trust to always love you just as you are. Nothing else is important.

☆ ☆ ☆ ☆ ☆ ☆

CANCER

Water — Cardinal — Negative
Ruled by the Moon
Symbol: The Crab
Night Forces — Feminine

CAPRICORN

Earth — Cardinal — Negative
Ruled by Saturn
Symbol: The Goat
Night Forces — Feminine

The **CANCER-CAPRICORN** Relationship

*They were the most ordinary questions — "What was
the colour of Mother's eyes ? Which was taller,
Father or Mother ? . . . (A) Write an essay of not
less than 40 words on How I spent My Last Holidays,
or The Characters of Father and Mother compared . .
(1) Describe Mother's laugh; (2) Describe Father's
laugh; (3) Describe Mother's party dress . . . . . ."*

*By the way, the questions were all written in the
past tense.*

As with all 7-7 Sun Sign Pattern Earthlings, the Crab and the Goat are 180 degrees apart on the karmic wheel of Life. In astrology — for that matter, also in astronomy and math — 180 degrees is half a circle or an *opposition*. Now, in human contact, a Sun Sign opposition need not be negative. It very often is, but it need not be. Will all Crabs and Goats please read that last sentence over several times ?

An opposition indicates that two opposing forces are "at war." In this case, those forces are the Moon and Saturn, rulers of Cancer and Capricorn, respectively. It's hard to imagine anything farther apart than the Moon and Saturn. Among other things, the Moon (Cancer) represents dreams, change, movement or travel, memories, reflections, softness, and dependency. Among other things, Saturn (Capricorn) represents realities, stability, caution, waiting, determination, hardness, and self-sufficiency. Like all other blends of the 7-7 vibration, sooner or later (hopefully sooner) a choice must be made by Cancer and Capricorn as to which of these opposing forces, consisting of the Lunar and the Saturnine, will become the dominant force of their association — or the association itself will become a battlefield over which symbolic cannon balls are shot back and forth indefinitely.

And so, the Crab and the Goat must decide whether the Moon *or* Saturn is to rule their *relationship*, even though they may still choose to be *individually* ruled by the Moon and Saturn *both* — and equally.

I realize this all sounds terribly complicated. No one ever claimed a 7-7 vibration is easy to work out harmoniously. But my greatgrandma used to say that "nothing gained easily is really worthwhile." Will all Crabs and Goats please read *that* sentence over several times also ?

There is a desirable side to any kind of opposition, which is that opposites do complement one another. Each has what the other yearns for — needs, wants, desires — and is therefore secretly anxious to acquire. Just form a mental image of that, if you will. Two people, each possessing what the other wants. If neither is selfish, if both are generous — if they give to one another and share equally — what could be happier ? It's rather nice to be someone's "magic genie" and have that someone be your genie too, at the same time, supplying all your needs, while you supply his (or hers). It's the same with the polarities of anything on Earth. Take a thermometer. You have Hot, and you have Cold. When they meet in the middle, you have Warm — the temperature of eternal Spring. Lovely thought ! And that's just what can happen when Winter (Saturn) and Midsummer (the Moon) meet each other halfway.

Yes, Cancer symbolizes Midsummer, just as Gemini symbolizes late Spring and early Summer, Leo symbolizes Summer in full bloom — and Virgo symbolizes Indian Summer. This seasonal Sun Sign conceptual is fully explained in "The Twelve Mysteries of Love" in the front section of this book. But it may be important to remind the Crab and Goat of it again here .. that Cappy means Winter and the Crab means Midsummer.

Despite the opposition of their Sun Signs and Lunar-Saturnine rulers, and in addition to the complementary nuances of opposites being a plus to their association — Cancer and Capricorn are alike in certain ways, as much alike in these ways as they are different in many others. Both the differences and the similarities are strikingly pronounced in this particular 7-7 vibration.

They were both born under the Negative-Feminine Night Forces, meaning that each has a soft inner core, and is rather good at hiding the softness — meaning, too, that the feelings and emotions of both run very deep. They are also both Cardinal, therefore both Cancer and Capricorn like to lead. The Goat prefers to lead unobtrusively; likewise, the Crab tends to lead in subtle ways, and so their mutually shared leadership motivation may be hidden when they first meet. It will not remain long hidden.

It's difficult for an association to contain two leaders of equal stature. Consequently, something will have to give a little. It will more likely be the Crab. For a while, however, it's an amusing scene for the astrologically alert to watch from a distance. Picture, if you can, two "leaders" each attempting — in great secrecy — to lead the other, without letting the other suspect that he or she is being led. Gradually, each of them becomes aware of the leadership motive of the other, never mind how cleverly hidden — and then the quiet, yet intense and determined battle for supremacy between them begins. Truly, it is as fascinating to observe as a movie — *more* fascinating than most films Hollywood has been making recently. (For meditation purposes, Gerald Ford is a Crab; Richard Nixon, a Goat.)

Throughout all these carefully mapped strategies, it would behoove the Crab to remember the Goat's sure-footed reputation — and it would behoove the Goat to remember that the Crab always takes a step or two sideways and backward before advancing straight ahead. It will be a thrilling battle of wills. There won't be as much fanfare as with the Fire and Air Element oppositions in the other 7-7 Sun Sign Patterns (Cancer is Water, Capricorn is Earth) but quiet and steady contests can contain more suspense.

Some of the traits of the Crab and the Goat are neither similar nor dissimilar, but simply supportive of each other. For example, Cancer likes comfort and security in great abundance. Capricorn is intensely ambitious, and since ambition has a way of being one of the quicker routes to all degrees of comfort and security, this is one thing which may hold these two together, as well as attract them initially.

They are both attached to yesterday, the Moon-ruled because of a liking for history in general, plus a sort of personal nostalgia — the Goat because of the lessons to be learned from experiences of the past and a touch of hero worship. (Actually, Cappy admires the achievers of past and present equally, but yesterday's heroes and heroines have more glamour.) They also share a strong attachment to the family hearth and relatives. Cancer leans toward sentiment for the maternal, Cappy leans toward sentiment for both the maternal and the paternal, the whole family tree — especially if a coat of arms hangs from one of the branches. Some Goats are decidedly snobbish about fame and prestige — the whole status trip. It's hard to detect behind the typical Capricorn's shy smile and gentle manners, but it's there.

It's not uncommon to find the combination of the Crab and the Goat involved in renovation of historical landmarks, laying cornerstones, heading a drive to establish a museum, writing history books, building business empires, collecting antiques, or actively engaged in local or national politics. This is a couple often found in bookstores (as the owners, of course) and especially in banks (on the board of directors). As individuals, the Crab may be drawn toward marine activities, near the water, while the Goat tends to climb the highest mountain of achievement in his or her vicinity. Capricorns abound in the jewelry business and junkyards. Goats, you see, have an odd way of finding something practical, something of value, in anything from diamonds to rusty parts of an old car. Strangely, they are also tuned in to art, one of the few aesthetic experiences which attracts them. But the typical Capricorn has no time for pop art like Andy Warhol's tomato cans and tubes of toothpaste. To a Capricorn, art should be solid and substantial. Michelangelo, Leonardo, Rembrandt — these are artists. Picasso and Dali are joking, aren't they? Art, like everything else in life, is a serious matter to the Saturn-ruled. Imaginative Cancerians, although differently motivated, also appreciate the beauty of fine paintings and works of art, including music, and so lots of the people you see strolling through metropolitan galleries and attending concerts will be Crabs and Goats.

If the Cancerian and the Capricorn are children, the same rules apply. They'll both excel in history class, and both Cappy and the young Crab will start early mowing lawns or delivering newspapers to earn money to stash away in their sock drawers.

Many Capricorns are by nature somewhat cold and suspicious, thanks to Saturn's stern influence, and sympathetic, sensitive Cancer can provide a healing balm of love and understanding for the Goat. Cancer's devotion to home and family will please Capricorn, who is equally loyal to family ties.

Unless one or both were born with the Moon or Ascendent in the Air or Fire Element, these two will never burn dollar bills for fun. Very few, if any, Cancerians and Capricorns are found resorting to public welfare or food stamps. Not only are they clever in financial matters, they also share a rather severe Puritan work ethic. They feel alike concerning the subject of money. Both enjoy stacking up lots and lots of it, and both prefer saving it to spending it. If any two people need to meditate on poet Kahlil Gibran's words on the subject of working for material gain, they are Cancer and Cappy. They would benefit immensely from an attempt to comprehend that man must "*work with love*" or it is better that he sits outside the gates of the temple and "*takes alms from those who do . . . . . . for bread baked without love is a bitter bread, that feeds but half man's hunger.*"

At first glance, those words will startle both the Crab and the Goat. Work for love? People work for money, not love. If a person also happens to enjoy his or her work, so much the better, but the first consideration is the financial compensation, isn't it? No, it is not. To work with love is the *first* consideration, the cash return is *secondary*. And therein lies the problem. It isn't that the Moon-ruled and Saturn-ruled don't understand craftsmanship and laboring with the heart, as well as with the hands: It's a matter of *priorities*. And these two are charged with the duty to make a strong effort to change them.

One of the most delightful things about the pairing of these undeniably divergent creatures, the Crab and the Goat, is that the outwardly controlled and stern, but inwardly gentle and lonely, Capricorn can find an escape from his or her seriousness in the rich and refreshing humor of the Moon people. Cancerian laughter is contagious, irresistible. There's something about the Crab's sense of the ridiculous that brings a merry twinkle to the eye of the Goat. Cancer clowns — Cappy grins. And the steadfast Capricorn heart, so sadly locked much of the time by the disciplined emotions, begins to warm, then to beat a little faster.

Few people ever guess the true extent of the Goat's wistful longing to escape Saturn's invisible restrictions, for such longing is also — even especially — kept under strict control. The compassionate smile of a Moon Child, who so well understands what it means to be lonely, can be an open door to a new and brighter world for Capricorn.

As for the Cancerian (unless his or her Luminaries are in negative aspect) from the first moment the Crab feels that powerful magnetic tug from his (or her) opposed Suns — in the classroom or office, in the family circle, the circle of friendship, or within the eternal circle of love, the searching Moon Child will search for a safe home, protected by the tough billy goat.

☆ ☆ ☆ ☆ ☆ ☆

CANCER *Woman* CAPRICORN *Man*

◆ ◀◉▶ ▶

> *"Ah, old lady," Peter said aside to Wendy, warming*
> *himself by the fire and looking down at her as she*
> *sat turning a heel, "there is nothing more pleasant of*
> *an evening for you and me when the day's toil is over*
> *than to rest by the fire with the little ones near by."*
>
> *"It is sweet, Peter, isn't it?" Wendy said, frightfully*
> *gratified. "Peter, I think Curly has your nose."*
>
> *"Michael takes after you."*

When a Cancerian girl is attracted to a Capricorn man (or to any man), she has the three M's on her mind. Three dreams she has, as she tosses pennies into every available wishing well. Three goals in her hard little crab-shell head. These may vary in their order of importance with each girl Crab, but all Cancerian women will be consumed with one of the six variations of the three M's, which are as follows:

marriage — motherhood — money
motherhood — money — marriage
money — marriage — motherhood
marriage — money — motherhood
motherhood — marriage — money
money — motherhood — marriage

These, in their sextuplet priority variations, are the female Crab's goals.

Her *needs* are slightly different from her *goals*. Her needs are the three S's, and these do not vary in the order of their importance to the Moon Maiden. They're each of equal value to her peace of mind.

sympathy — serenity — security

One of the most endearing things about a Moon Maiden is that, although she very much needs and seeks the three S's in every relationship, and although her goals are always the three M's, she is willing to give her man a soft cradle of emotional comfort in return. She can be the most sympathetic, affectionate, loyal, and protective of women. When she's on her best behavior, the female Crab is devoted — and better still, she's also both adaptable and patient, surely a fine companion for the Capricorn man. A Taurus woman is patient, but not very adaptable. A Gemini woman is adaptable, but not very patient. The Cancerian woman possesses both admirable traits. As for devotion, many women are devoted to the men they love, but none so devoted as this one. The Goat, loving the home fires as he does, will be especially happy about her own deep feelings about "family." Since Capricorn rules the Jewish people, and all Cancer women are "Jewish mothers" (whether they are mothers or not) you can see there are powerful magnetic forces pulling these two together from the start.

There's always something slightly helpless and appealing in the Cancerian female, and the Capricorn man senses it sooner than most. What this woman needs is a strong man to lean on, someone who can smooth away all her worries and calm all her fears — who provides her with a shoulder to cry on now and then. But she's not quite as helpless as she seems. Cancer, I keep telling you, is a Cardinal Sign of leadership. The Moon Maid would prefer to lead by guiding her man's destiny gently, unobtrusively, in the background . . . . . if she's in love. When she is not in love, a Cancer gal can be mighty ambitious in her career, and will do just about anything to get to the top of the heap.

Every Cancerian woman is secretly looking for a good provider, and this the Capricorn man certainly is. He is always ambitious (as much so as she is) and usually successful. In fact, he's often the epitome of everything she would like to be, but cannot — for she is too vulnerable. Conversely, she represents to the Goat all the Lunar qualities he privately would love to call his own, but cannot — for he is not vulnerable *enough.* Therefore, almost from the moment these two meet, there is an unmistakable appreciation of one another, which is one of the strongest foundations for love.

A Capricorn man can be both conservative and domineering to a high degree. The Cancer girl doesn't mind the first quality, since she's rather unduly conservative herself. As for being dominated, she won't stand for that in any association — except love. When this woman falls in love, she'll at first submit to the Goat's dominance out of a desire to keep peace, but gradually she's likely to forget she's playing a role, and slip into the submissive position for good — which is not really bad! Next to Pisces, no other woman so secretly enjoys being controlled and conquered by the male she adores. And if any man can be domineering, tender, and affectionate all at once, it's this one. So it all works out in a favorable manner for both of them, usually. Barring, that is, a more fiery or aggressive Moon Sign or Ascendent in the horoscope of the girl Crab.

It's a funny thing about Capricorn males. However far out they may swing in an attempt to avoid the granite discipline of Saturn over their natures, they'll swing right back again in important matters. In other words, whatever his temporary actions or behavior, a Goat is a Goat. Or — once a Cappy, always a Cappy. Like that. Normally, this man will strongly disapprove of the "open marriage" theory. He's conservative where marriage is concerned, however much he tries to be "with it" in his speech at times. He essentially believes a woman's place is in the home. Even should he permit his wife to work or to follow her own career, when the children appear, he'll frown on a woman who expects someone else to fill the maternal role while she pursues her own activities. If he's a typical Capricorn, he'll believe that a mother's place is with her children, at least while they're very young. He won't be happy about any frivolous or excessive spending of money either, whether it's his — hers — or theirs. Even if his Moon Maiden earns her own cash, he'll probably take it upon himself to caution and counsel her on the subject of extravagance.

Not that he'll have many opportunities to chide her about spending money. She's as careful with a dollar as he is (unless her Moon Sign or Ascendent is in Aries or Leo or Gemini, and then she'll have periodic, minor nervous breakdowns over guilt each time she's wasteful). With this girl, most of his financial lectures will be in the area of how much of their separate or combined income to save, and what would be the smartest investment for any surplus they accumulate. Being an Earth Sign, the chances are he'll believe that real estate property — or land — is the safest thing to own for future security. If she argues with him, he may quote Will Rogers on the subject of whether or not buying land is wise — "They're not making any more of it." That sort of earthy, practical statement wins arguments by closing a subject abruptly, and it's the sort of undebatable observation Cappies are very good at making when they're pressed for an answer.

He'll approve of her habit of saving things. Capricorn believes firmly that a practical purpose can be found for anything at all, and nothing should be discarded until every possible use has been squeezed from it. If she's a typical Cancerian, she'll go along with that philosophy enthusiastically. In fact, unless one of them has a "looser" planetary influence in the birth chart, they might even save old toothpaste tubes in case they ever have a son who grows up to be a basketball player in high school. (He can use them to practice hook shots in the wastebasket.) I (truthfully) know a Cancerian woman, with a Capricorn Moon Sign and Ascendent, who actually washes and rinses out those little plastic Baggies that come on a roll (to cover vegetables, etc.) and reuses them over and over — until they split. She has them hanging out to dry all over the kitchen. One roll of Baggies lasts her, roughly, a couple of years. (Being an Aries, I go through a roll every week or so.) Someone I know recently suggested that the reason Richard Nixon saved those damaging tapes relating to Watergate was because, as a Capricorn, he simply could not discard them, and kept hoping he could in some way make them useful, or serve some practical purpose. No one has been able to come up with a better answer, even Mr. Nixon himself. Only a knowledge of the Capricorn essence provides any semblance of sense to the mystery of "why didn't he burn those (expletive deleted) tapes?" The answer is simplicity itself (to Cappy). That would have been *wasteful*.

A Cancerian woman will adapt more easily than many another woman to the Capricorn man's introversion, his inclination to "take care of business" and do the sensible thing. But she will not adapt so well perhaps to his lack of excitement over change. Ruled by the inconstant Moon, she needs occasional change in her life, and intervals of travel. Convincing him that their life would be richer by not remaining in one place too long or holding the same ideas always, could be somewhat difficult. Because this man will never completely escape Saturn's restrictions over his inner nature, struggle as he may. Somewhere behind the façade of even an *apparently* extroverted Goat is serious old man Saturn. Always and inevitably. The shade of conservatism may be dyed a lighter pastel in some Cappies, but it can never be painted over entirely. He can be lovable, yes. Affectionate. Tender. Gentle. Whimsical and funny. All that. Nonetheless, he is ruled by Saturn, and there's no avoiding it. Beneath the sequins and rhinestones of a Capricorn rock and roll star, for example, is hiding a portrait of grandpa, complete with pocket watch and chain ... waistcoat ... and scowl of disapproval for the foolish.

The sex life of a Capricorn man can range from frankly erotic and sensual — to tender and affectionate. If his Sun and Venus are both severely afflicted from the fifth or eighth horoscopic houses, he will indulge himself in multiple experimentation. But the typical Goat's affairs are few, the intent nearly always permanency. Almost the identical thing can be said of the Cancer woman's love life. It depends. However, her inner desire is for a lasting relationship, even if she goes through more frequent trial and error periods than she would like . . to find it. One thing is quite certain. This woman will greatly enrich the Capricorn man's physical enjoyment of love. Although he's capable of a deep and steady sexual expression and physical intimacy (his sex drive is strong, never half-hearted), he may lack the kind of sensitive imagination that makes mating between two people a trembling, ecstatic kind of sharing of themselves. This is a sexual dimension the Moon Maiden will add to their relationship, and the Goat will be touchingly grateful for the enlightenment. His strength and loyalty, the stability of his kind of Saturn love, will permit her to relax in his arms, without the fear of being hurt she might have with a less reliable lover or husband. He can supply the emotional insurance she needs, while she supplies the delicacy and romance he so needs, and lacks . . . . and after a while, with enough sharing back and forth of this nature, their physical love will become a strong and lasting cord to bind them together.

I know a Cancer woman who is presently separated from her Capricorn husband. Their problems are numerous, but essentially minor . . . none that can't be softened and healed with a little more understanding, a little less selfishness on both parts. Capricorn men can be hurtfully selfish. There's always a tendency, to some degree, to use people, with little regard for the other person's feelings. One of their heartaches was his inability to express love to her physically, after they'd had even the mildest sort of quarrel. He was like a stone, she told me, totally unresponsive to any tender overtures she shyly attempted. And so she would turn away, weeping silently, never letting him know. Recently she said to me, wistfully, "All those times I was so sorry for myself . . crying myself to sleep, retreating further into my shell of hurt. But I've had lots of time to think since we've been apart. I know more now, and I'm sorriest for him."

She's found the magic key to unlock his heart, at last. Now, if she'll only use it. If she goes to him with her new understanding they'll be closer than ever. When a Moon Maiden learns to stop feeling so sorry for herself and to direct her sympathy instead toward the Capricorn man she loves, she'll realize the depth of his inability to release the emotional power and glory he feels within. It's worth the effort of helping him release it. For no love has more grandeur, more endurance, than Capricorn love, which waits at the very top of the mountain to bless those with the patience and courage to climb high enough to experience it. It's a rough trip, with plenty of rocky ledges . . and always the danger of falling . . . . but the view at the top is inexpressible, indescribable. Like a glimpse of eternity. Saturn gives stern tests, but immense rewards.

☆ ☆ ☆ ☆ ☆ ☆

CANCER *Man* CAPRICORN *Woman*

—◆◄◆►◆—

"Won't you play me to sleep," he asked, "on the
nursery piano?" and as she was crossing to the
day-nursery he added thoughtlessly, "And shut that
window. I feel a draught."

A Cancerian male, whatever he may tell you, however much he may deny it, solicits and enjoys being babied and fussed over, and could at times take advantage of the Capricorn girl's strong sense of responsibility. Cappy will try hard to please the man she loves, without complaints or self-pity, but if he requires her to lean too far over backward to cope with his changing moods she'll balk, no matter how much she loves him.

In all fairness, both of them can be more than a little selfish. At first glance, no two people appear less selfish on the surface than the Crab and the Goat. He is normally gentle, considerate, and courteous, almost old-fashioned in his attitude toward women, especially toward his own woman. She is, in a way, his possession, and Crabs value their possessions highly. Nonetheless, he may demand a great deal more than he gives on occasion, expecting every sniffle and every cranky spell to be lullabyed and rocked away, and if she won't do this, she just doesn't love him, that's all — at least, not as much as Mother loved him.

If she's a typical Capricorn, she's probably rather quiet and demure, even self-effacing . . always willing to help out in a time of trouble. (Goats are truly superlative in a crisis. Emergencies are their specialties, and bring out the very best in their characters.) Still, she won't allow herself to be used beyond a reasonable limit, not even for the sake of love. She's sharply aware of all her human rights, and refuses to be anyone's doorstop. For all her attractive and soft feminine ways, she has a strong mind of her own. This is not a lady to flutter her lashes and hint about anything. What she really wants, she will either ask for directly — or go after, tooth and nail. What she likes, she will simply take, what she dislikes, she will remove from her life, in short order. There's nothing pliable or submissive about her. She doesn't noisily struggle against things which upset her. She just tunes it out, then takes care to avoid the person or situation, sometimes permanently. In this attitude, she is much like the Scorpio woman, except that the whole thing takes much less emotional toll of her in the process than it does of the Scorpion, who is always deeply affected, never mind what doesn't show.

The Capricorn woman is not unduly sensitive, and so she may have to be careful with the Crab, because he *is* unduly sensitive, and quite easily hurt. He's not nearly so thick-skinned as she is. If she should criticize or seriously contradict him, he usually won't let the matter rest until she "takes it back," tells him she loves him, and confesses that he has no real faults as far as she's concerned. He'll first try cajoling or being humorous, making little half-hearted jokes about it, then he'll turn to stronger hints, and as a last resort — pouting. He'll have all sorts of reasons to offer to defend his position, for this man will not rest in peace and calm until there is some sort of agreement after a quarrel. If she allows it to go too far, he'll retreat into his shell, and no compromise is possible. Crabs hang on tenaciously to arguments and to their own opinions, as they do to most everything else.

But he's a gentle man, and will blossom under the slightest praise and encouragement. The Capricorn woman who loves him will have to keep reassuring him, until he has no more need to force her to admit what a grand person he is, and how she adores him. Mother did this, you see. She was always telling him what a good boy he was, and how his enemies didn't really understand him. In extreme cases, he'll translate this to mean that anyone who doesn't agree with him is his enemy, even the woman he loves. He wants the same understanding treatment as an adult he received as a child. It's not terribly unreasonable of him. Wouldn't we all like to be understood? The difference is that most of us give up on it early in life. The Crab expects it as his due, and never gives up seeking it. Respect. Understanding. Love. Affection. Appreciation.

The typical Capricorn woman is not an expert at this sort of thing. She's practical and sensible; she feels he should know she loves him, and that if they disagree once in a while, it doesn't mean she hates him. Excessive sensitivity and extremes of emotions make Cappy uneasy and nervous. It isn't that she has no heart, she just doesn't quite know how to react, exactly what to do or say — and she's afraid of doing the wrong thing, so she would rather do nothing at all than to hurt him unintentionally.

She's too modest. She has an efficient mind to aid her in finding answers where others fail, along with a reliable ability to concentrate and meditate on a problem until it's solved, and usually her judgment is sound. So she should try a little harder to apply these talents to her emotional situations. It would make life in general a lot easier for both of them.

His need for her approval and appreciation isn't an impossible obstacle between them. It just requires less sensitive pouting from him, a little more tenderness and compassion from her. Of course, if the truth be told, she needs to be appreciated too, but never in a trillion years will she admit it — and certainly never request it. The Crab is no more an expert at giving pats on the head than Cappy, because he never had to appreciate Mama or pat *her* on the head — he just accepted the goodies, which, I suppose, is why children will always take advantage of doting parents. The very best gift these two can give one another is an extra hug or kiss, a few extra kind words — more frequent smiles. They both need attention equally, the only difference being his lack of bashfulness about asking for it, and her reluctance to either confess to or openly display any undue emotional needs of her own.

The Capricorn woman is inclined to be rather plain as a girl, growing visibly more beautiful as the years pass, one of her ruler Saturn's rare, but solid rewards. Along with her beauty, however, comes a very hard head (also a gift from Saturn). She is no mere fluff of feminine fancy. This girl is fortified with fortitude — and lots of it.

The Crab is inclined to be shy as a young man, growing more confident and sure of himself, and developing a marvelous sense of humor as the years pass. He's loaded with charm, he has a soft way of speaking, and a softly soothing manner — yet his mind is quick and clever, and he, too, possesses a very hard head. It's been said that Cancer has a soft heart and a hard head (which is surely better than a hard heart and a soft head!) but that the Capricorn woman's head and heart are *both* rocklike. That's not fair. Whoever said that probably tried to put something over on this lady, and she wasn't buying his blarney. Her heart is a woman's heart, but she's learned not to wear it on her sleeve, where it's susceptible to every blow. Could that be because it's so very vulnerable to hurt? Yes, it not only could be, but it is.

There's no denying that wisdom, caution, and self-protection are the Capricorn female's inheritances from her ruling planet, Saturn, but she is, for all that, a woman . . . with all the feelings, all the dreams and longings of a woman. Femininity needn't be synonymous with culpability. She possesses a timid (therefore, ultra-appealing) sort of sentiment, the kind which is all the more touching because it's not indulged in casually. It's not phony, but very real, and comes from her also very real . . . . . heart.

Cancer and Capricorn take their physical closeness as seriously as they do everything else, yet it's hard for them to let on to each other what their intimacy really means to them. They don't quite know how to say that their lovemaking causes them to take more notice of all kinds of beauty. She'll say simply, "Look at the way that sunbeam touches the top of the pine tree. I can almost smell the needles from here. Shall we take a walk?" — when what she really means is . . . . after we've been close, I feel so special, and the world looks so much brighter.

He'll reply only, "Yes, let's take a walk. You're right. It is a beautiful morning" — when what he's really saying is, *you're* beautiful . . . I love you. Their physical relationship, especially if their Sun-Moon aspects are harmonious, can be rich and meaningful, the sort of deep experience that results from the powerful pull of those bar magnets of their astrological polarity — the opposition of their Sun Signs. It can be, in fact, so sacred to them, that sometimes they're even uncertain if such passion really happened, or they only dreamed it.

He may wonder aloud about this some morning, lying beside her — and she'll comment in her practical, common-sense, Capricorn way: "Well, when you can't *believe* a thing, I guess that means it was something special and good, because when it's something bad, you don't have to wonder — you're only too sure it actually happened." Then she'll snuggle closer to him, and murmur: "I'm not certain about last night. Do you suppose it really did happen ?" — with one of her quiet little smiles. It's like a secret code between them. He'll answer her then, in a way that removes all doubt.

Both of them are, to some degree, wistful about yesterday, although his nostalgia may tug a little more frequently on his heart than hers does . . . . even making him wish, at times, he could go back there to live. If only there could be, somewhere, he sighs, a real estate agency that sells houses on a long-ago street, complete with all his memories of the past, come to life again. The Goat Girl is sensible enough to realize that yesterday always appears more beautiful in dreams than it was in actuality . . . . . so she's more interested in creating a *real* present, which is the way yesterday only *seems* to have been, a solid improvement over the past. After all, the past didn't include their discovery of each other. But the present does, and so, now, will the future. When she turns his vivid Lunar imagination around from yesterday toward tomorrow, they'll be traveling in the *spiral* direction of the Circle, wherein is contained the alpha and omega answer to the riddle of love.

CANCER   AQUARIUS

Water—Cardinal—Negative   *Air—Fixed—Positive*
Ruled by the Moon   *Ruled by Uranus*
Symbol: The Crab   *Symbol: The Water Bearer*
Night Forces—Feminine   *Day Forces—Masculine*

The CANCER-AQUARIUS *Relationship*

◆◀◆▶◆

> *This is a difficult question, because it is quite*
> *impossible to say how time does wear on in the Neverland,*
> *where it is calculated by moons and suns, and there are*
> *ever so many more of them than on the mainland.*

Because the Crab and the Water Bearer are influenced by the 6-8 Sun Sign vibration, Aquarius finds Cancer helpful in some way, and Cancer finds Aquarius mystifying in some way. Of course, Cancer isn't alone in that outlook. Everyone finds Aquarius mystifying. It's just that Cancer finds Aquarius even more mystifying than the rest of us do, because Aquarius represents the eighth astrological house to Cancer. This means the Crabs look upon the Water Bearers more or less the way Aries people look upon Scorpio, as Taurus people look upon Sag, as Gemini people look upon Cappy, and so forth. It's all relative.

At first glance, it may appear that these two share nothing at all, making it difficult for them to relate to each other. But think about it a little longer. Take, for example, Mother Goose (Cancer) and Lewis Carroll's Mad Hatter (Aquarius). Can you see where they might have something in common? They unquestionably share the quality of —strangeness. The abstract.

However, Aquarius is strange in a sudden, shocking and unconventional way, and Cancer is strange in a moody, dreamlike way. Although Crabs are undeniably outwardly quite practical, there is this elusive essence of changeability and unpredictability about them. This they also have in common with Aquarius, but what counts is the difference in the manner in which the quality is manifested. The changeability of the Crabs is synchronized to the changes of the Moon, timed to the Lunar phases, as simple as that. So it's somewhat easier to keep a daily log on their mood switches. One just jots it down neatly in a ledger, you know, under Full Moon (weird and weepy) — New Moon (restless and imaginative) — Quarter Moon (nostalgic and homesick) — Three-Quarter Moon (funny and lovable) — Waning Periods (cranky and crabby) — Waxing Periods (aggressive and hungry) — or Eclipses (pouting and reclusive). The trouble is, sometimes Cancerians mix up their moods, and one then has to observe that it's the Full Moon when they're funny and lovable, whereas the New Moon brings on nostalgia, or they'll pop out of the basement during the Three-Quarter, and become aggressive during an Eclipse. One needs a ledger book with several columns, also perhaps a blue and red pen for the switchovers, and even then, it requires a great deal of concentration to keep the columns straight, should they happen to stick to the crabby crankiness during the Waning, but reverse the weird and weepy to the Quarter Moon. But for all that, the Crab's moods and changes are rather more easy to prognosticate than those of your typical Water Bearer.

You see, Aquarian changeability and unpredictable behavior are timed to the lightning flashes of Uranus, and I really don't know of anyone, including Tom Edison, Ben Franklin and Nicola Tesla, who ever found a way to predict lightning flashes with enough accuracy to log them in a ledger. One minute the sky is clear-blue milk glass, and a split second later, there's this zigzag streak of forked yellow fire cutting through the clouds, followed by the most awful rumble, then a sudden noisy clap of thunder. Consequently, as intricate as the Lunar Ledger accounting may be, the Uranus Lightning Ledger accounting is simply impossible to keep straight. Actually, I believe the less traumatic way would be for the Crab and the Water Bearer to play it by ear. I mean, taking everything into consideration, you know ? By now, you've probably comprehended that this association, while it can no doubt be puzzling for both people, is highly unlikely to be boring for either.

Perhaps because the Crabs are such great reactors, their emotional needs capable of leaping to such heights and plunging to such depths, Aquarians think it's fun to play little tricks on them, to surprise them when they're least expecting it. The Water Bearers may pull their surprise numbers on Cancerians at any age, beginning quite young, sometimes even before they're born — although, typically Uranus-like, they nearly always give a subtle hint of the coming caper, which the Crab almost never picks up but which makes the Aquarians feel better because, after all, they did try to warn you, and you paid no attention. (Aquarians hate to do anything dishonest or hypocritical.)

For example, Jennifer H. Smith was about to become a mother for the very first time in March of 1978, in San Diego. Jennifer is a Cancerian Moon Maid, so you can well imagine the event was enthusiastically anticipated, Cancer being the sign of Motherhood, and having babies naturally being the big thing it is to women, but especially to girl Crabs. The obstetrician informed Jennifer and her husband, Bill, that the baby would arrive on March 28. Mothers always believe their obstetricians (Cancerian mothers even more because they tend to be shy, and not apt to talk back), although one wonders why they're so gullible, since doctors calculate the date of birth correctly roughly only somewhere below 2 percent of the time, and their batting average is even lower than that on the first baby.

So here they were, poor Jennifer and Bill, expecting an Aries infant, which of course meant preparing for substantially more screaming demands for clean panties and warm bottles at odd hours during the night because, although all infants are demanding to a degree, Aries infants are selfish beyond belief when it comes to not caring whether their parents sleep or not until their howling needs are fulfilled. They are feisty little bundles from Heaven, the ones who arrive by way of Mars, but irresistible all the same.

The problem was that the doctor and the parents were figuring the wrong Sun Sign. Only the baby himself was aware that he was an Aquarian. He tried to warn them before he pulled his surprise, but no, they paid no attention and insisted on checking with the doctor and calendars and such, instead of with the San Diego Public Library, where the truth waited for them. Now, you may think the public library a very odd place to go to learn the date of birth of an expected infant, but to an Aquarian, it's all quite logical.

Water Bearer Bobby Smith arrived, not on March 28, but precisely on his own Uranus schedule, of February 3, 1978, nearly two months early, and weighing in at 5 pounds, 6 ounces — and no, little Bobby was not a premature baby. He was a perfectly healthy and well-formed (if tiny) full-term infant, who had no intention of timing his entrance into this world to suit anyone's mistaken calculations, and thereby depriving himself of his Aquarian Sun Sign.

But as I said, Aquarian Bobby tried to warn his Cancerian mother. On her hurried departure from the house, on the way to the hospital — when it became evident that, calendar or no calendar, doctor or no doctor, Bobby was definitely arriving — Jennifer passed the hall table, on which lay a library book, with the cover open. But did she see it? No. It wasn't until she returned home with her baby son in her arms that she glanced at her warning. Stamped in large purple letters on the card in the book, was the telegram from Uranus, as clear and distinct as could be: **DUE DATE:** February 3, 1978.

Regardless of the relationship between Cancer and Aquarius, whether the two of them are relatives, friends, business associates, lovers or mates — whether the Cancerian is a boy Crab or a girl Crab, and whether the Water Bearer is male, female or any other sex — the Aquarian will, from time to time, play these little tricks on the Moon person, just to watch the Lunar reaction. Cancerian features are so elastic, it's like watching a movie of Life to observe the expressions that pass across them — joy, sorrow, laughter, suspicion, secrecy, fear, anger, tenderness, hope, despair, expectancy — the entire gamut of human emotions. Tears, then giggles. Laughter, then sobs. Crankiness, then gentle sweetness. Softness, then crabby snapping. The Water Bearers thoroughly enjoy it all. But there's one Cancer mood they won't enjoy. The Crab's sometimes exaggerated sense of personal privacy. Aquarians have nothing to hide, and they can't comprehend why the Crabs are so unnecessarily suspicious and self-protective. These two may sometimes need a brief vacation from each other when one's eccentricities begin to grate on the other's nerves.

A male Cancerian and male Water Bearer I know, who were very close friends in New York, decided to share a house for a few months in California, while the Aquarian was checking out a college to see if it deserved being honored by his enrollment. His Cancerian buddy had a habit of locking his own room when he left the house. No reflection on his Uranus friend's honesty, but Crabs just have this sometimes slightly neurotic compulsion for secrecy. The Aquarian merely shrugged. The idiosyncrasies of their friends never trouble or surprise the Water Bearers. "Live and let live" is their motto. However, one night the Crab made the mistake of locking the Aquarian's guitar and tennis racquet in his (the Cancer's) room before he went to a movie. When Aquarius came home and wanted to practice some songs, then play a set of tennis, and realized his equipment had been locked up, he exploded into a lightning streak of Uranus anger, pried open a window and made a forced entry to recover his belongings.

Outraged when he returned to find his room broken into, the Crab called the police. It nearly destroyed the friendship between them, but fortunately, they talked it over and parted with a handshake — although the Aquarian wisely moved out the next day, before the Cancerian's period of pouting over the incident made him say things that would have wounded the sensitive Lunar one too deeply to ever be forgotten. They'll pick up their friendship someday again, where it left off. But the moral of the story is that these two Sun Signs shouldn't press each other too far. A breathing spell apart periodically is helpful.

Cancer intensely resents the Aquarian inquisitiveness and blunt speech. Aquarius intensely resents Cancer's reticence and tendency to pout. Yet the

Water Bearer will become cross himself (or herself) when the Crab is moody, eccentric and unpredictable. Then the Crab could very well retort, justifiably, "Look who's complaining about mood changes, eccentricity and unpredictable behavior!" Unfortunately, however, Aquarians never see themselves as strange in any way. The whole world is crazy, and everyone in it is crazy, but *they* are as normal as can be. Aquarius is a Fixed sign, don't forget. Cancer is Cardinal. Therefore, Cancer will make every possible attempt to "lead" Aquarius, while Aquarius makes every possible attempt *not* to be led. That's what Cardinal means and that's what Fixed means. The sum total is . . . . well, I do hate to be redundant, but it's *unpredictable*.

The most common mistake made in an association between the Moon-ruled and the Uranus-ruled is the tendency of the Crab to try every sort of strategic maneuver (most of them sly and secret) to get the Water Bearer to come around to the Cancerian point of view. It takes a while to learn that the devil and forty horsemen could not persuade a Uranus individual to do anything he-she does not wish to do. You can make that the devil and ninety horsemen, if you wish. Throw in the entire Marine Corps. If the Water Bearer has other ideas, the Crab is nearly always wasting time, and Cancerians should make note of this, because they do not like to waste time any more than they like to waste money. Still, there's always the unexpected, "unpredictable" outcome, when the Aquarian is cajoled or wheedled or softly pressed into submission, and the rare instances of this phenomenon will invariably be due to the Crab's truly amazing tenacity. When a Crab grabs anything or anyone with that claw of persistence, it's no easy task to work loose from the grip.

The eating habits of these two are often vastly different. Many Aquarians enjoy snacks like frozen bananas dipped in chopped liver, tomatoes stuffed with pinto beans — and baked dandelions. Cancerians prefer more nourishing dishes like Mama used to make and stuff into their ecstatic tummies. The formula Aquarius must remember if he-she wants to keep the Crab happy is: lots of love — lots of food — lots of money — and simply oodles of sympathetic listening.

If the Crabs care to be given the secret of success in achieving harmony with the Water Bearers, here it is (but don't tell anyone — shhh!). Mind your own business — don't gossip — don't nag — don't ask questions — and be prepared to remind them of their names and addresses now and then, when they absentmindedly forget such small matters. If they both practice these formulas, they should get along quite nicely with each other.

When the Crab is lonesome and moonsick (which is very much like homesick, only much more so), the Water Bearer should cheerfully call out, "Hey! You want to play marbles with jelly beans?" That's all it takes to make most sad Looney Birds smile — the mention of yum-yums. And the memory of fun at recess, in the "good old days" long, long ago, when Life was nice and safe and secure and cozy . . . . when Mama tucked them in at night, and always had a hanky handy to dry the tears shed over their Lunar fears.

☆ ☆ ☆ ☆ ☆ ☆

CANCER *Woman* AQUARIUS *Man*

But Wendy noticed, with gentle concern, that Peter
did not seem to know that this was rather an odd way
of earning your bread and butter, nor even that there
are other ways . . . . Wendy would have preferred
a more permanent arrangement.

An Aquarian man longs for affection just like anyone else, but he'll struggle violently against being dunked, like a donut, in an ocean of it. I know what you're thinking. You're thinking that people don't dunk donuts in the ocean. Aquarius does. He doesn't eat the donut after it's dunked. He's just experimenting with how fast the salt water makes it soggy, compared with the honey in his tea. But the important thing is that he, himself, is uncomfortable in a soggy state. Too much soggy possessiveness stifles his need for the fresh air of freedom of expression.

The typical Water Bearer will resent being interrogated about wearing his galoshes, how many starches he's eating and what he did with the thirty-five dollars he had in his pocket yesterday. He'll certainly appreciate the flattering attention he receives from the Moon Maiden, but when that attention threatens to curb his independent research of the world and nearly everyone in it, he'll become stubborn — or he'll clam up and coast away.

Telling this man what time to be home is rather futile. He needs to fly free, and he can do without being dampened by Saturnine pessimism while he's flying. His odd behavior may perplex the Cancerian girl into tears. He'll often act as though he doesn't even know she's there, let alone that she's weeping — then if she's missing at the very moment he wants a baked Alaska, or has lost a shoestring and needs her to find it, he'll be more than a little upset. It's her fault. She's the one who got him accustomed to her baked Alaskas and steamed veggies, and she's spoiled him equally in the shoestring department. It also disturbs *her* when he tries to pry into her secrets. Even when she has no secrets. Sometimes she's just quiet for no reason, her thoughts racing with the Moon, and he tries to race along beside her. But she'd really rather be alone on such flights — or at least she needs her companion to hold her hand in silent sympathy, not startle her with questions that sound like popcorn . . . . popping in her inner ear when she's half-dreaming.

You can see that each of them prefers that the other doesn't intrude upon his (or her) flying habits. Joining is all right, but not interfering. If she can learn not to try to restrict his urges to mingle with the masses and hike alone now and then — and he can learn to pry more gently into her secret place of dreams — at least half of their troubles will have been overcome.

A Lunar lady has a near compulsion to "mother" the man she loves. This man will think it's neat to be mothered, at any chronological age at all, but she should be warned that mothering an Aquarian male can be a full-time job — at any age. Maybe they're both high school or college students. If so, here are some hints. A young Aquarian I know, named Bill, during a couple of reasonably recent years, decided to be an oceanographer, then a musician, then an engineer, then a scuba diver, then an astronaut — for a brief period, a Lutheran minister — and most recently, he's waiting to talk with a Leo biologist, whom he happens to respect, so he can help him decide if he should settle on marine biology as a career. He's a little jumpy, waiting, because the biologist advisor is temporarily residing in Hawaii. During roughly the same period of time, this Water Bearer lost four pairs of glasses, three pairs of contact lenses, had an emergency appendectomy, disappeared from home for eight weeks to work in a pizza parlor, took up playing the guitar for church services, grew his hair long, cut his hair short, painted the ceiling of his room jet black — and fell in love with a girl fish named Debbie. (No one has been able to find out if Debbie is a female Piscean or a marlin at the New York aquarium.)

Last month (as I write this) he decided to join a friend in Dayton, Ohio, in opening a shop to repair and build guitars — shortly after which he decided to join a rock band on tour, while waiting to talk with the temporarily Hawaii-based biologist about dolphins and such. He has it somewhere in the back of his mind to learn how to speak dolphin. I haven't the slightest idea what that means, have you? A telephone call in the midst of writing this paragraph only minutes ago informed me that he changed his mind, and is now planning a hermit period in the woods, for the purpose of meditating alone and composing some music. However, he's not sure it's the Colorado woods he wants to camp out in, because "Colorado only has two kinds of trees, two kinds of flowers, two kinds of rocks" — and this is "beginning to bore him." He'd like to try playing his guitar in the Grand Canyon, he says, "and tape the echoes."

Do you see what I mean?

That's the kind of thing the Moon Maiden will face, regardless of the calendar age of the Uranus man. Oh, he may have a more or less (mostly less) permanent job or career, and all that — and he may not have lost his glasses (only because he doesn't wear glasses, in which case, he'll lose other things, like his driver's license or his bankbook, keys — assorted objects of that nature). Whether this man is five or fifty, twenty or two hundred, he needs a lot of mothering. Just so the Moon Maid who loves him doesn't get the word "mothering" confused with the word "smothering."

The Cancer lady who has chaotically cast herself within the general auric orb of the Water Bearer should resign herself to skipping through Wonderland with him, if not geographically, then at least mentally. If not mentally, then emotionally. If she's "lucky," it will be all three. Actually, when it's analyzed carefully, it doesn't make all that much difference whether her attitude toward his comings and goings with his many friends (who sort of grow on him, like benevolent barnacles) is strict or permissive, since neither attitude will make much impression on him. His family probably tried both, and found out years before the Moon lady met him that neither method was overwhelmingly successful, as far as keeping him walking an arrow-straight path, without curves and detours, was concerned. Aquarians must, in some manner, zigzag. It's their empathy with the symbolic Uranus lightning. Everyone knows lightning never follows a straight line, so how can one expect a man who is under its influence to do so himself ?

Oddly, the older an Aquarian man grows, the more Fixed his habits become, very gradually — yet the older a Cancerian woman grows, the more wistful she often becomes about visiting those faraway places of her girlhood dreams. It's a situation calling for compromise. I don't want to mislead the Moon Maid. When I said the Uranus male changes as he grows older, I didn't mean to leave the impression that he'll ever become quite as normal as the neighbors. He'll still remain a little wacky, he'll just be a touch more Fixed in his wackiness. Like he may not mow the back lawn in his birthday suit anymore, but his sense of the original and the unique will stay relatively intact. In however mild a manner, he'll still manage to come up with occasional surprises to keep life interesting.

There will be times when she thinks he verges on peculiar, but usually the girl Crab will find the Water Bearer lots of fun. Her sense of humor is one of her lunier and lovelier traits, and might even be what attracted him to her in the first place. (Since she has a feeling for the ridiculous, her feeling for him is certainly logical enough.) He loves the way her smile ripples like a quiet stream, then bursts into a waterfall of merry, madcap laughter. And undeniably, her feminine secrecy intrigues him. Her moods may puzzle, even madden, him, at times, but if he really tries, he can synchronize his metabolism to hers. After all, he's a mental Air Sign and therefore more adaptable than lots of other people. It's the Fixity of his sign that could require some shaking up.

This being a 6-8 Sun Sign Pattern, she represents the sixth astrological house of service to him so there's always the chance that if she permits it, he'll fall into the habit of expecting her to serve him in subtle ways, or to sacrifice her own dreams to his changeable charisma. He represents the eighth house vibration to her; consequently, he'll seem, in some way, elusive, just beyond her grasp somehow . . . . and she'll also find him physically appealing in a way she can't easily explain.

There's an undeniable sexual attraction between these two. A powerful chemistry draws them from the beginning. For he was born under a masculine sign, ruled by the also masculine Uranus — she was born under a feminine sign, ruled by the also *very* feminine Moon. Never mind the old rumors about the "Man in the Moon" — the inconstant Moon is definitely a lady. Astrology's warning to the double masculine men and double feminine women is to beware of the natural tendency for the "strong" to domineer the allegedly "weak," bringing with it the danger of a trace of the sadistic and the masochistic. But there's more likelihood in this case that the roles could be reversed, because the "double feminine" influence of the Moon Maid is also *Cardinal*. She may appear to be a submissive angel of docility, but I wouldn't take any bets on who rules the roost if I were you. Of course, an Aquarian man will be ruled just so long, then leave the roost. (Fly the coop.)

However, if she can blend her feminine qualities with his masculine ones, and vice versa, so that each contains a happy combination of negative-positive in his or her approach to life and to each other . . . . especially in their approach to sex . . . they'll enjoy their lovemaking immensely, because it will bring them such peace and contentment. It's a rare Moon Maiden and Water Bearer who don't value their sexual union as a very special experience. She brings out in him a depth of tenderness he might not have known he possessed. And he arouses in her a wildness of passion she kept hidden, until him, like a touch of abandoned Moon madness.

Uranus, the alchemist, helps him translate her moods unexpectedly, and he somehow knows the singing words to transmute them too . . . from reflective to intense . . . from sad to serene . . . from dull despair to the dizzy heights of fresh hope and Lunar laughter. He murmurs a magic mantra to her with a single glance, like a lightning bolt. She hears it . . . as the Full Moon hears the thunderous sound of silently swelling, gathering waves long before they crash against the ocean's shore . . . and she answers with a matching glance. No wonder their sexual Oneness is unique and unpredictable, potentially so deep and fulfilling, especially when their Luminaries are in harmony between their birth charts.

These two will constantly challenge each other in strange and haunted ways, inexplicably interwoven with the powerfully magnetic vibrations of the Moon and Uranus . . . through the eloquence of unspoken messages in their eyes. Neither of them is above using a spell to bind the other. He'll think he can escape, but her delicate mist holds him with its beckoning secrets, as her eyes seem to chant the incantation of a Moon Child .... *Abracadabra, rippled water tears ... pickled pumpkin butterfly ears ... North Winds, blow across his years .....°*

She'll think she can run away from the sometimes pain of love, but he'll hold her fast with the sheer compulsion of his indefinable mystery, silently warning her that, if she goes ..... *I'll leave my trace upon you ... like your own witch's hex ... streaked through your hair ... and lingering in your silver eyes ...°*

Then he, in turn, will ponder leaving her, but she'll reply softly ... Oh, no! *I'll have my madcap moonlight way ... no matter how many fiddlers call you to a dance of wooden marchers.°* And womanlike, she'll have the last word. All his Uranus alchemy will be helpless to enable him to conjure up an answer to her final Cancer-Cardinal-Lunar-Feminine enchantment when she wraps him tenderly, but tightly, with the vow ....

> *I'll sear your palm with an eternal scar*
> *so all the canny Cassandras will whisper*
>
> *"Ah! There goes one of the lost!*
>
> *he has been visited by a vagrant solitaire*
> *singing a moonlight sonata*
> *he has been wheedled by a will-o'-the-wisp*
> *from the midnight moors*
> *he has been kissed by a flickering firefly*
> *brushed by the touch of a wild gypsy spell*
> *he has heard the cry of a loon*
>
> *... he has been loved"* °

It's never easy to leave a Cancerian lady. Her violet songs will follow the Aquarian man wherever he goes, and however far ... even tinting his dreams with lavender and the shimmering silver of her laugh. His friends will think he's even stranger than before ... and that's pretty strange! But also rather wonderful. It's uncommonly rare to be enchanted by a moonbeam ... to be a curious prisoner of the sea. It serves him right for being an Air Sign ... and confusing her with his symbol of the Water Bearer. Poetic Justice, astrology would call it.

☆ ☆ ☆ ☆ ☆ ☆

° *Venus Trines at Midnight* by Linda Goodman (New York: Taplinger Publishing Company, Inc. To be republished by Harper & Row, 1979).

CANCER *Man* AQUARIUS *Woman*

———— ◆◀◉▶◆ ————

So this was the truth about mothers. The toads!

... he was so full of wrath against grown-ups, who as usual were spoiling everything, that as soon as he got inside his tree, he breathed intentionally quick short breaths at the rate of about five to a second. He did this because there was a saying in the Neverland that everytime you breathe a grown-up dies; and Peter was killing them off as fast as possible.

Wendy melted ...

The first mistake an Aquarian girl can make with a Cancer man is to try to jolly him out of his attachment to the memories of home and mother with the Aquarian's sensible attitude that yesterday is past, today is unimportant — and he ought to be mature enough to realize that all important matters lie in the future, not in emotionally clinging to what is gone and can never return in quite the same shape or form. She may even go as far as to tell him to grow up. (Aquarians are not renowned for their tact, being very much like Archers in respect of a tendency toward blunt speech.)

The Crab will intensely resent her attempt to mature his emotional outlook. He may even snap at her, climb inside his cozy tree of memory and never come back out — until he's sure she's not around to hassle and hurt and frustrate him with her jolting, bolting Uranian thunderbolts of realism. It's ... well, it's frightening. It makes him very, very lonely to discover that the woman he loves has no compassion for his nostalgic need to occasionally drift back to the safe, secure days of childhood when he's particularly upset by the harshness of the world, the uncaring attitude of his friends and associates. He never really wanted to become an adult. Like Geminis, deep inside, every Cancerian man, regardless of his age or material success, secretly wishes he could have remained a boy. When he was a boy, there were so many wonders over which to marvel ... so many things that made him both weep and giggle. And he enjoys surrendering himself to the extremes of the emotional gamut. It somehow seems to loosen his imagination, allowing it to take him on marvelous trips of fancy, like a private flying carpet, woven of dreams.

"Stuffy," he'll tell himself. "That's what she is. Stuffy." She has no imagination, he decides. She thinks and talks like a man. Acts like one too. Well, he's not looking to fall in love with a masculine realist. He's looking to fall in love with a dear, sweet, feminine creature of perfection like Mama.

He is wrong, of course. The very last thing this girl should be accused of is stuffiness. But that just happens to be the Crab's favorite word (next to "cruel") for the woman who won't cry with him and laugh with him, who refuses to synchronize herself to his own fluctuating moods. As I've said before, in other Aquarian chapters of this book, the Uranus-ruled have an odd habit of weeping when they're overjoyed and laughing crazily when they're broken-hearted. It will take the Cancerian man some time to comprehend this—not to mention his difficulty in learning how to handle her reverse switches of disposition, from tomboy to princess, from gentle and languid to brisk and abrupt. Serves him right, really. He's so moody himself. With this woman, he'll be forced to swallow his own moody medicine. She's quite changeable, her whims and fancies even more unpredictable than his own. They're a motley couple, to be sure.

The Aquarian girl isn't lacking in sympathy, but she does tend to scatter it around in the direction of major humanitarian concerns, and sometimes forgets to save enough for her personal relationships. But she isn't heartless, and she does have feelings. When she realizes the hurt she's causing in the gentle Cancerian man she loves, she'll do her best to make it up to him, to show him she really does care about him. The problem lies in the ways she chooses to demonstrate her loving devotion and regard for her friend. (Everyone is her friend including her lover or husband. Is there a differ-ence? If so, she finds it difficult to draw the line.)

She could, for example, coax him to join her and her several dozen other friends on a picnic in a tree house. She might hang a bunch of balloons over the dining room table some morning to surprise him at breakfast—and serve him a bowl of Grapenuts with little toy caterpillars on the top, arranged in the shape of a heart. (She won't tell him they aren't real, the caterpillars, until he's already turned pale.) Or she could show her affection by confiding in him her private yearning to go to India and decorate the Taj Mahal with little decals of forget-me-nots and violets at midnight, when the guards aren't looking. She's convinced the sentimental emperor who built it as a memorial to his love for his wife would be pleased. "Good gawd!" he'll exclaim, "that's against the *law*!" Crabs, like Goats and Bulls, are usually very reluctant to break the law or shatter tradition, whereas most Aquarians delight in breaking every law and dancing upon tradition. Even the rare shy Aquarians at least daydream about flouting the rules.

All these gestures of tenderness from his Water Bearer might give the Lunar man a case of the shingles from pure nervous apprehension. But she's trying. Can't he at least give her credit for trying? He may. He may force himself to make a supreme effort and give this fascinating lady of the exciting mental architecture credit for trying. However, he may regret giving her other forms of credit. Like a joint checking account. The typical Aquarian way of balancing a checkbook follows the general outline of the way a clown juggles colored balls at the circus — in a kind of rotating, circular motion. He'll be dismayed. Cancerians are normally nearly neurotically fussy when it comes to anything pertaining to cash outlay and inlay. Income and outgo. It's all the same to Cancer. Watch it. Carefully. In view of how fussy he is about money, what right does he have to call *her* fussy ? None.

She fell in love with him in the first place because she heard somewhere that Cancerians are lovable Looney Birds, and she's always been attracted toward anything with the word "looney" in it. (Any*thing* or any*one*.) This is why his marvelous sense of humor may save the day for these two. During certain phases of the Moon and the retrograde motion of Uranus, it blends beautifully with her sense of the zany and the ridiculous. Like sex.

When she was climbing up the Aquarian beanstalk of girlhood into womanhood, she thought sex was rather funny. After she became a woman she thought it was hilarious. She still thinks it's somewhat of an odd way for a man and a woman to express their need for each other — when, after all, they could be proving their mutual love by collecting money to build a statue to her solar energy hero Amory Lovins, finding Ralph Nader a girl type of buddy-friend to chum around with, who could ride behind him on his white horse, as he goes charging around on his crusades, scaring the corruption out of automotive giants and professional sports — and scaring the hell out of conglomerates. Like running barefoot through a field of wild flowers (being careful not to smash any petals, which of course means running an inch or so off the ground), adopting all the starving babies in India and China — lobbying in Washington for Congress to pass a law that everyone has to drive on the left-hand side of the street as they do in England, because that makes a whole lot more sense to her. He'll go along with her concern for worldwide hunger and safe cars — but he won't understand her leftish notions about driving and other matters (although he might wistfully dream of levitating a fraction of an inch over the field of jonquils). Still, he won't allow these things to take priority over their physical closeness. The only thing he ever allows to take priority over affection and lovemaking is perhaps money — at odd times. Occasionally, also at even times.

Once she's resigned herself to the recognition that sex is a necessity for total fulfillment between a man and a woman, she'll thoroughly enjoy it, especially with her tender Crab. Unless they're afflicted with a mutual square or opposition between Ascendents and Luminaries in their nativities, this man and woman will each answer the other's silent call for the misty and the strange in their physical expression of love. They're both a little haunted by various forms of the fey and the far-out, this being a shimmering link between them that frequently flashes with the brilliant colors of ecstasy and passion known only to those who allow their imaginations to guide their intimacies.

Gradually, he'll discover that he was wrong about her lack of perception. She just *appeared* not to understand his deeper longings. In truth, she may be one of the very few people who's ever been able to see beneath his Crab shell, his outward pose of respectability and seriousness, to the fanciful, gentle soul beneath the crusty exterior. It will surprise him when he learns this. She's full of surprises . . . she vibrates to the unexpected. And her very unpredictability is what will eventually endear her to this man, who hates sameness and monotony as much as she does. His business associates will never guess this, but she won't have to guess. She'll know. His air of mothballs and his often courtly, old-fashioned manner won't fool her for an instant. She knows he'd like to escape with her . . . to some faraway place where there are cool waterfalls and quiet woods. This instinctive Nature feeling permeates their lovemaking, often causing their sexual union to be as soothing as a midsummer night's breeze. (Until the Puckish mischief in her emerges, and she slips into bed beside him some night, wearing around her neck a collar of antique sleigh bells, engraved with the date they first met —her surprise birthday gift to him.)

The explosives in their relationship will nearly always be labeled Cardinal and Fixed. He's Cardinal, and will insist on leading, however soft his manner, however apparently (and deceptively) passive his surface personality may be. She's Fixed, and will absolutely refuse to be dominated or guided. When she's allowed to follow her own winding and twisting path, she'll remain cheerful and light hearted. But each time he tries to change her direction or direct her course, she'll become immovably stubborn, and either disappear into detachment or erupt into a Uranian electrical storm of anger. Her sudden spells of fury won't last long, if she's left alone to heal her injured spirit and is not nagged by the Crab. But if he continues to try to curb her freedom, her behavior will grow more and more unreasonable. There's no use trying to confine her Air Element essence into a definite shape, and the sooner he learns this, the sooner harmony will be restored between them.

As for her, she'll have to remember that while she's excitedly traveling into tomorrow's strange, new promise, he can't help lingering behind, glancing over his shoulder toward yesterday's familiar guarantee. The only way she can coax her Lunar-haunted man to catch up with her is to make him know that just beyond the horizon is a brighter star than he ever dared to wish on before. She should also not pry into his secrets — and stop ringing her sleigh bells when he's dreaming. Or at least mute them just a mite.

☆ ☆ ☆ ☆ ☆ ☆

CANCER

Water — Cardinal — Negative
Ruled by the Moon
Symbol: The Crab
Night Forces — Feminine

PISCES

Water — Mutable — Negative
Ruled by Neptune
Symbol: The Fish
Night Forces — Feminine

The **CANCER-PISCES** *Relationship*

<hr style="width:30%" />

Pale rays of light tiptoed across the waters; and
by and by there was to be heard a sound, at once
the most musical and the most melancholy in the
world — the mermaids calling to the moon.

*T*he Fish and the Crab walk along together, working, playing or conversing to the rhythm of the harmonious 5-9 Sun Sign Pattern melody.
Except for those whose Luminaries, Ascendents or natal planets are in
serious conflict in their horoscopes, most Cancer-Pisces associations are
relatively smooth and mellow. The sympathetic attraction is often instant
and remarkable. They seem to understand each other better than they
understand other mortals — certainly much better than other mortals understand *them*. Ruled by the Moon (Cancer) and Neptune (Pisces) the three of
them — Pisces is a sign of duality, symbolized by *two* Fish — are equally
secretive, sensitive, moody and changeable.

The moods of the Fish are controlled by the tides of the Pisces emotions,
as they ebb and flow in a complex sort of synchronicity with the ocean's tides.
Trying to discover a Piscean's exact disposition of the moment is like trying to

name the color of mother-of-pearl. Is it pink? White? Pale yellow? Soft blue? Pearly grey? Just when you think you have it identified, the light reflection moves a flicker, and the color changes. Since the fancies of the Fish are mystically governed by the tides, one could say that they're *in*directly influenced by the Moon.

The Crabs are *directly* influenced by the Moon, therefore perhaps a shade more predictable. The Pisces man or woman can prognosticate the moods of the Crab with reasonable accuracy, simply by periodically checking the Lunar phases in an Almanac, but a Cancerian may have more difficulty in charting the mood fluctuations of a Pisces friend, business associate, relative, lover or mate at any particular time. It creates an exciting guessing game between them that relieves the monotony of earning their daily bread and quarreling about how to spend it — although it sometimes makes it tough to forgive each other their trespasses. Was the anger and resulting hurt a lasting thing, or just the fallout from an itinerant mood?

The 5-9 Pattern, favorable as it is, doesn't have the power to bestow an absolute guarantee of constant compatibility upon those graced by its beneficent vibes. There will still be conflicts requiring some degree of compromise, initiating not only from possible negative Sun-Moon aspects between their birth charts, but also from certain qualities of their individual solar personalities.

The subject of money could conceivably churn some sizable waves in a relationship involving these two Water Signs. The Fish normally thinks of money as a necessary but bothersome interruption, an inevitable evil, to be dealt with as effortlessly as possible, then disposed of and hopefully forgotten until the next time it requires his (or her) reluctant attention. Neptune-ruled people are usually careless with cash, seldom frugal, and not intensely interested in amassing money on paper via bank accounts, to count and stash away, then re-count and stash away again, calculating annoying details like interest, profit and loss and such. It's so uncreative, unimaginative and downright boring.

Conversely, Crabs look upon financial matters with a great deal more reverence and respect than Pisces. To a typical Cancerian, the jingle of coins is soothing music, the crackle of folding paper (or stock certificates) almost symphonic. The Crabs understand very well all the complications of compound interest, and may try to pound these theories into the dreamy Piscean mind, with little success. Caution and economy are Cancer's watchwords. All Moon-ruled people possess a subconscious fear of poverty that creates some strange and funny habits in an occasional Crab.

A Pisces man I know was christened Grover Cleveland (plus the family surname) after his Cancerian father, who passed away many years ago. The Fish recalls vividly his boyhood shopping trips with his Cancer parent when the latter purchased his annual new outfit (every January, during the After

Christmas Clearance Sales). His Cancerian Dad always informed the mystified salesperson that he wanted his suit coat and trousers two full sizes larger than he actully wore. The transaction was traditionally brief, since the Crab never failed to order the same style, color and 100% wool material, year after year. Dressed in his new threads, he walked out of the store with his son, happy as a cricket, draped in excess folds of cloth, his suspenders valiantly keeping his pants from falling down on the sidewalk, his suit coat more resembling a blanket thrown over his shoulders than an article of clothing, the bundle containing his treasured last year's outfit tucked securely and lovingly under his arm.

One day little Grover gathered the courage to ask big Grover why he always bought his clothes two sizes larger than he needed, since he wasn't a "growing boy," but a man. Father had a most logical and sensible (to a Crab) reason. "You see son," he explained, quite seriously, "wool is very expensive, and that way I get much more material for the same amount of money." The young Fish was silent, pondering the mystery. (He's still pondering it.)

If caution and economy are the watchwords for Cancer, casualness and generosity, sometimes extravagance, are the Neptune watchwords (except for those occasional Fish whose horoscopes contain important planetary positions in Cancer, Virgo, Taurus or Capricorn). The only kind of security that really catches the interest of the Fish is the security of personal privacy and the freedom to live without being disturbed — or disturbing others. The Piscean "live and let live" attitude is similar to that of Aquarius, maybe even more pronounced. Most Fish wouldn't dream of telling another person how to live his (or her) life, but admittedly, some Pisceans are a bit curious about the personal lives of friends and relatives. They won't probe or spy, but they do tend to be more than slightly interested in any errant leaves of gossip that might float by their ears.

Cancerian men and women are more possessive and demanding, more inclined to try to mold others into the shapes that please them. Also, Crabs delight in prying secrets out of other people, while keeping their own double-locked against the curious. Somehow or other, in subtle ways, they manage to learn what you're thinking, but when you try to find out what *they're* really thinking, they retreat into their Crab shells, refusing to confess or admit whatever it is you're trying to pry out of them. However, the Fish is more fortunate than other Sun Signs (with the exception of Scorpio) in uncovering the secrets of the girl and the boy Crabs. That's because Pisces is such a comfortingly sympathetic listener. In an association with Cancer, Neptune's compassionate ear will get quite a workout. No one has as many nightmares, haunted memories of both beauty and sadness, fears, dreams and trembling hopes to pour out than a Cancerian. There will be dialogues about the Cancerian's Mama (whether she treated the Moon Child cruelly or kindly, whether she was a sinner or a saint), complaints that "nobody understands me" . . . waterfalls of tears, ripples of giggles . . . Looney Bird laughter . . . jokes and sobs . . . questions and answers . . . all manner of daily dilemmas.

Oh, the joy of it! The sheer ecstasy of having someone *listen* who truly *cares*, who knows what it's like to feel so unloved and insecure . . . to be so lonely and uncertain . . . someone to be unselfishly happy about successes and triumphs . . . to commiserate with your failures and disappointments. The Cancerian cup will runneth over with pure relief. The Piscean's humility and kindness will likely run over too, until all the Neptune energy (frail at best) is drained. But it will return, always — and the thing is that Pisces usually won't resent it, except for rare, extenuating circumstances. The Fish never just pretends interest in the Crab's confidences. The interest is real, the concern felt is genuine, not expressed simply to be polite. Of course, all twelve Sun Signs revel in the cozy comfort of the Neptune couch sessions, but no one could appreciate the 24-hour, 7-days-a-week Piscean confessional more sincerely than the pathetically grateful Crab.

One of the major dangers of this otherwise smooth and extraordinarily sympathetic 5-9 association (in addition to periodic pouting over finances) is the danger of alcohol and drugs — or the lesser "escape" of daydreaming and procrastination. The drinking encouraged by an excessive social life can lure the Crab and Fish into waters over both their heads, and they must constantly be on guard against the seductive beckoning pleasures of the flesh. It's also best that the two of them stay a healthy distance away from experimentation in black magic, hypnosis, seances and other fringe areas of the occult, because their combined Water Sign vibrations can easily allow them to drown in the matters which are deceptively exciting — and may prove tragic.

Because the true love of Cancer is home and hearth, the Fish is the one most likely to answer the haunting call of wanderlust and travel, seeking a change-of-scene. But Crabs can also become fascinated (though less often) by the glitter beyond the home cave — crawl (or waddle) away to investigate and get lost among the sand dunes, unable to find the way back to the hearth he (or she) left. When this occurs, even Cancer's ruling Moon seems to frown, refusing to light the path back, eclipsing her lovely Lunar face, until the lonely, wandering Crab is properly contrite. No matter how much they may claim otherwise, the boy and girl Crabs are miserable leading the nomadic life, for they both were born to nestle cozily in their own homes, surrounded with the familiar fragrances of yesterday, old friends and neighborhoods they know. (Also near Mama and Papa — the children and the family.)

Sometimes, a Crab will trade the cradle of the known and trusted for the thrill of ambition. Money can throw the typical Cancerian into a trance-like, catatonic state of mind for months, years even. The possibility of earning and accumulating huge financial assets lures many Crabs away from the fireplace and the apple tree in the back yard. But their hearts refuse to follow their bodies, stubbornly remaining behind and calling softly to them, in their dreams . . . to come home.

Home doesn't normally hold the same degree of sentimental attachment for the Fish that it does for most Cancerians. Pisces enjoys the snug security of a home base, but Neptune constantly crashes the cymbals of faraway music in the Piscean inner ear, however prosaic the life of the Fish may be. At the slightest provocation, Pisces is ready to swim upstream to another lake, even risk a float on the great ocean, rather than stifle his (or her) creative imagination with boring sameness and monotony.

For awhile, the Crab and the Fish will have a marvelous time traveling together, anywhere at all. Then the heart Cancer left behind will start tugging on the Lunar person at night (especially during the Full Moon) to return. The Fish will probably return too (to please the Crab) but reluctantly. To the Neptune-ruled, change is the stuff of which Life is made. Pisces men and women weave their dreams with threads of sparkling imagination, then frequently get caught up in the problems of others or mundane duties, and are forced to tuck their dreams away on a shelf, to gather dust and wait for some magical morning when there's suddenly the freedom to make them come true. Strangely, at the crucial moment, Pisces tends to hesitate, unsure if the dreams are strong enough to provide protection on a journey into the unknown deep. If the hesitation is prolonged, the opportunity for freedom drifts past, waves goodbye! . . . and disappears before the Fish makes a move. Then he (or she) gets caught on the reefs of ordinary existence once again, and must wait for another glistening morning. Sometimes it comes . . . sometimes it doesn't. But Pisces never stops waiting and wishing.

While the Fish is waiting, Life won't be dull. There will always be the fascinating stories of the Crab to listen to, via letters and phone calls from out there where he (or she) is lost and homesick, lonely for the front porch swing. Or from a more nearby Cancerian chum, friend or mate . . . who just might lure the Fish to dive into the next golden opportunity before it passes away, and not worry about the possibility that it might be a mirage. Pisces will smile. Because it is, after all, the Fish who first taught the Crab to stop worrying about tomorrow.

CANCER *Woman* PISCES *Man*

————◆◗●◖◆————

*While she slept she had a dream. She dreamt that the
Neverland had come too near, and that a strange boy
had broken through from it. He did not alarm her, for
she thought she had seen him before in the faces of
many women who have no children. Perhaps he is to be
seen in the faces of some mothers also . . . . . . The dream
itself would have been a trifle, but while she was
dreaming, the window . . . . blew open, and a boy did
drop to the floor. He was accompanied by a strange
light . . . .*

The double Water Sign 5-9 influence over those who love, such as the Moon
Maiden and the Neptune man, is in many ways, more magnetic and
compelling than the Fire, Earth or Air 5-9 Sun Sign Patterns. The mystical
water essence of their natures is sensitive and absorbing . . . reflecting images
back and forth between them . . . so that frequently, their romance has a
dreamlike quality about it, however many years they're together. If they
should quarrel and separate for a time, the missing is usually much deeper
than with other lovers who are thus temporarily parted . . . the emptiness
greater. The need to return to each other and be mutually forgiven is intense.
A recently parted Crab and Fish are two sad and depressed people indeed.

They should cheer up, because their chances of reconciliation are
excellent — when she stops pouting and he stops trying to escape himself,
which is, of course, a solution doomed to failure. It's impossible to escape
one's self, as impossible as it is to permanently avoid the other *half* of one's
self. If there should be more than one negative aspect between the
Luminaries, Ascendents, Mars and Venus in their birth charts, they could
remain divided. But there will always be the memories . . . . .

Water is the most mysterious of all the elements. I have this little "water
meditation" that flashes into my mind unbidden lately — which is symbolically important to all Cancer-Pisces lovers who are perceptive enough to read
between the lines and see their own relationship reflected in allegory. It's a
kind of test of their sensitivity to the hidden lesson of the macrocosm and the
microcosm, the former being my water meditation, the latter their own love
affair or marriage, with the answer at the end of the chapter. Usually my
meditative moment flashes while I'm drinking a glass of icy cold water, when

I'm especially thirsty—when I'm washing the inky pen and typewriter ribbon marks from my hands with soap and water, then drying them with a towel—or standing in the shower, with warm water pouring over me, cleansing, revitalizing and refreshing my soul, as surely as my body. When this "water meditation" flashes into my mind, it's like a brilliant white light, yet also green . . . and hauntingly fragrant. I think of the quiet woodland streams of Scorpio, Cancer and Pisces. Then I ponder the miraculous effect of water to *renew*—our basic, urgent (seldom realized) *need* of it. What would I do without it? How could I bear to suddenly know there was no longer any pure water? None to drink to quench my thirst, none in which to wash my hands, none to stand under in the shower. Water! . . . sweetly singing and cool, washing away all negative, all ugliness and soil . . . leaving everything all new and clean and sparkling again. I think of the cool needles of fresh-scented, gentle rain, falling on my uplifted face from the sky. Then I think of Earth's latest horror—acid rain and snow. The most serious environmental threat of this or any other century. Caused by the pollution from industry's smokestacks and auto exhaust, nuclear waste and sulphurous coal—steadily increasing. Already, many a lake contains only dead fish killed by "acid rain" . . . dead plants, once green and living . . . over many acres of land. Less than a decade ago, "acid rain" was only a danger to certain European countries whose mountainous soils were unable to neutralize the acids, parts of Canada and the northeastern portions of the United States. Now virtually *all* rainfall east of the Mississippi River . . . and in parts of southern California . . . is below the pH safety level, fast approaching the fatal level for all fish and plant life. The weathering and erosion of metal and stone buildings and monuments have accelerated alarmingly in these areas.

Humans . . . sending up poison and pollution into the clouds . . . now in such monumental amounts, the clouds can no longer fight it for us, and pour down, helplessly, "acid rain and snow" . . . like a rain of slow, but absolutely certain death. And still . . . nothing is being done to halt it, while increasing numbers of congressmen and senators symbolically "play Nero fiddles." Because of their apathy and also because of an apathetic public, we may lose Sister Water and Sister Air, and be left with only Brother Earth and Brother Sun, who cannot, alone, sustain us—when the "gentle rains of heaven" rain down only destruction, no longer able to purify. The reality of "acid rain" is frightening.

That's how it is when you contemplate losing something precious . . . and this is the way the Cancerian woman and the Pisces man feel about losing each other, once they've deeply loved. What in the world would he do if he ever lost her? What if the soft rain of her happy tears became the acid rain of bitterness? How could she live without him? The girl Crab and the Fish feel their emotions with an intensity that belies their outwardly reticent, quiet manner. As with my new and genuine love affair with water, when the enormity of such a loss strikes the Lunar lady and her Pisces man in that awful, shocking way of a reality when it suddenly hits *hard* that it *is* a reality, *not* just a hazy "maybe," their minds and hearts and souls are all three unexpectedly overwhelmed with a surge of emotion difficult to express, because the thought of the possibility suffuses the intellect and the feelings so totally.

All the more reason for the Moon Maid and her Pisces man to make a special effort to refuse to allow the few differences between their personalities to grow until they drown their caring. Fortunately, as with all 5-9 graced couples, the differences are relatively minor, and can be smoothly compromised, once they're confessed — and softened slightly. Since they both like happy endings, we'll peek at their problems first, then last of all, remind them of the oceans of good things they share that make their romantic chemistry so powerful.

The first scarecrow we see in their garden when we peek is made of the strangest things. What could it be? Certainly not straw, the traditional material of scarecrows. It's green, slightly soiled, crumpled and wrinkled, with bits of metal fastened here and there. Do you know what it is? It's money. Sure enough. See the Presidents' pictures? Actually, worth much less, in the long run, than straw or hay. The scarecrow of money can frighten some lady Crabs and the Fish they love with its ability to form itself into a high wall between them.

She likes to accumulate it, save it, keep it, sock lots of it in the bank, stuff it in her sachets and watch it grow sturdily through investment. She's normally more than a little economical with cash, if she's a typical Cancerian, and she may nag him about being so disinterested in gathering up scoops of it, so careless about scattering it around among his friends who need it, spending such large sums of it on his multiple dreams and schemes — and what she considers to be unnecessarily large tips to waiters, waitresses, bellmen, doormen, redcaps, porters and the like.

If his natal Moon or Ascendent is in Cancer, or her natal Moon or Ascendent is in Pisces, he'll be less extravagant, she'll be less cautious — and the money scarecrow will be less scary. Otherwise, he'll have to try to understand that she's not really stingy, just concerned about her security in what he must admit is an increasingly insecure world — and she'll have to try to comprehend that an excessive concentration on cash strangles his creative freedom and his imagination equally. Then they should open separate checking accounts, each of which will be none of the other's business whatsoever. (Even so, he'll probably be less interested in her monthly balances than she'll be in his.)

Another scarecrow looms in the moonlight. Things are always either more mysterious and eerie or more mysterious and lovely in the moonlight depending on which eye is used to view them — the two normal orbs or the Third Eye of Knowing. This scarecrow is called moodiness, a complaint each of these two will make against the other. He withdraws into Neptune's silences to meditate, she becomes cross because he won't tell her what he's thinking. Or — she crawls into her crab shell to brood in an inexplicable melancholy during the waning Moon, and this causes him to be depressed, because the Pisces man, as I've noted before, is a "psychic sponge," helplessly absorbing all the feelings around him. Influenced by the Lunar phases, the Cancerian woman is a "reflector" of feelings, imaging them back like a photographic plate. (It's not a coincidence that most Crabs are either photographers or intensely interested in photography.) So she "reflects" his silences, and he "absorbs" her melancholy. He's curious about what she's thinking when she's quiet, though his curiosity is more veiled than hers. These two both like to keep secrets, at the same time they like to know secrets, and each is equally adept at pulling secrets out of others, while locking their own against all questions. Once they recognize this trait they share, they can learn to laugh about it, and refuse to allow it to cause tension between them. The girl Crab's great sense of Looney Bird humor is a saving grace regarding many of their problems.

Unless there are unusually severe afflictions between the Luminaries and Ascendents in their horoscopes, there should be no "sexual scarecrows" to frighten them during their lovemaking. Normally, Cancer and Pisces are ideally mated in a physical sense. Through their sexual union, they experience the rare joy of — not just receiving, not just giving — but exchanging the gift of fulfillment. The difference is something many lovers never realize. Because they're so closely, even telepathically attuned to each other's needs and desires, passion brings them profound peace, stills their trembling . . . and afterwards, when they've become two separate individuals again, their Oneness lingers in their eyes, like a memory of magic too deep to communicate in words, best left to only quiet knowing.

He really *listens* to her seasonal fears and apprehensions — with such gentle patience. She covers his winters of self-doubt with such warm and tender blankets of caring. Remembering the "water meditation" can protect their relationship. Remembering how much they need each other, being aware of the unthinkable possibility of losing the security of their special kind of interdependency. This man and woman are extraordinarily sensitive to each other's thoughts, literally able to read each other's minds. With her reflecting nature and his absorbing nature, mental and emotional pollution is a constant danger. If they allow their frustrations to rise or sink above or below the pH safety level of tranquility, the clouds of tension can only pour back upon them an "acid rain" of resentment, frustration and selfish seeking that kills happiness—just as surely as the acid rain in Nature kills all fish and plant life. The refreshing newness of love, like the sweet grass-scented blessing of a silvery summer shower, is worth protecting.

☆ ☆ ☆ ☆ ☆ ☆

CANCER *Man* PISCES *Woman*

━━━◆━◆▶◆━━━

As they sat thus, something brushed against Peter, as
light as a kiss, and stayed there, as if saying timidly,
"Can I be of any use ?"

She liked his tears so much that she put out her beauti-
ful finger and let them run over it.

The telepathic connection between all lovers and mates who are guided by
the 5-9 Sun Sign Pattern vibration is never less than powerful — but the ESP
cord that flashes between a man and woman influenced by the 5-9 vibes, who
were also both born under Water Signs, is nothing short of miraculous. When
they feel the mutual tug during their good times, it's a wonderful, enchanted
blessing. However, during their bad times, when they've separated temporarily (5-9 couples very seldom separate permanently, unless there are severe
afflictions between their natal charts) . . . . during these bleak periods, the tug
on the cord can seem more like a curse than a blessing.

It tortures them with memories, and worst of all, it allows each to know,
with amazing accuracy, pretty much what the other is doing and thinking.
And while what the other one is *thinking* is nearly always favorable — what
the other one is *doing* may be considerably upsetting to the one receiving the
telepathic message — because when these two quarrel, each tries to show the
missing half that he (or she) couldn't care less. Since Cancer and Pisces are
quite good at make-believe, both of them equally talented thespians, the acts
and plays they stage for one another's benefit can be dreadfully disturbing.
Especially when you add the fact that the girl Fish and her gentle Crab both
have exceptional imaginations. Her Neptunian and his Lunar imaginative
tendency sometimes shades what originally were true messages between them
with deceptive tones, causing unnecessary heartache.

Every Cancerian male enjoys (sometimes even demands) being babied.
To be cherished as Mama cherished him (or as Mama *should* have, whichever). It's really quite simple. If he was raised to pick up his socks, handle his
own emergencies maturely, clean up his own dishes, and in general, be
emotionally and otherwise independent, all the while being affectionately
loved — then, when it comes to the woman who loves or marries him, he'll
expect her to be affectionate and loyal, in return for which he'll bear his own

share of household duties, as well as his share of the blame for the emotional upsets and tensions that always occur, from time to time, within any close relationship, whether it's between parent and child, lovers, or married partners. And the two of them will live, on the whole, happily ever after, as Hans Christian Andersen promised.

However, if he was spoiled as a child by "Mama," he'll fully expect the woman he loves as an adult to spoil him also. Love him affectionately and loyally, yes — but also pick up his socks for him, *not* ask him to share in household chores, cook for him, slave for him, adore and worship him — tell him he's right, even when he's wrong, defend him against his enemies, support him emotionally — and never ask him to bear the burden of responsibility for any disagreements they may have.

Fortunately, the Pisces girl is super-equipped for that sort of special tender, loving care, and for the most part, she'll succeed, although it might mean submerging her own personality and life style more than she should. Her dreams may take second place to his, and she'll have to be the one to make most of the advances toward reconciliation after a quarrrel, the one to make the first attempt to smooth over all misunderstandings. He'll weep on her shoulder far more often than she'll be able to weep on his when *she's* insecure and troubled. With her beautiful humility, sympathetic heart and genuine need to bring happiness to others, her basic unselfishness, it works out rather nicely . . . *if* she gradually teaches him, very gently, to be a little more emotionally mature and treat her as a person who has feelings and occasionally needs understanding too. Should she neglect to thus gradually teach and train him to comprehend her own personal, individual needs, she's in the same kind of trouble his mother found *herself* in, once she awoke to the truth of the situation. It's easy for a Neptune lady to cross over the very thin line between humility and masochism, between submission and martyrdom.

Then there's the other kind of Crab, the Cancerian man who was honestly rejected in some way as a small crablet. Perhaps he was orphaned or adopted, or if not, then perhaps his parents were too busy to give him the attention every Cancerian youngster needs. Maybe his mother was the emotionally cold type, and he cried himself to sleep a lot, starved for affection of the tangible sort, like bedtime stories, bear hugs and goodnight kisses on his nose. Maybe he grew up in poverty, his dreams filled every night with the voices of adults worried about money, how to make ends meet, making him feel subconsciously guilty for being an extra expense to them, simply by *being,* by existing — by having been born at all.

If this is the childhood history of the Cancer man she loves, the Pisces woman has a fair-sized task on her hands. She'll have to be his psychologist, his psychiatrist, his best friend, his mother and father (both), not to mention his mistress and his lovely image of womanhood on a pedestal. A pure angel who doesn't hate him or turn away from him when he's behaving like a pure devil. In brief, she'll have to heal all the old wounds of yesterday, with continual patience and compassion, until the magic of love at last works its mysterious alchemy . . . and one day he awakens to the discovery that he has slowly but surely gained a permanent self-confidence and faith in himself. Only then can he love her as unselfishly as she loves him. It's an inflexible law of human nature that you must first really like and respect yourself before you can truly love another.

Thanks to the mysterious 5-9 vibration, the girl Fish won't panic when she recognizes either of the last two of these three possible types of Cancerian male as the man she loves. Figuring out the complications of human relationships is something she was born to do with more ease than most people. Accepting problems, whether major or minor, and deciding how to patiently and calmly deal with them is another of her Neptune talents. Refusing to allow difficulties to upset her unduly, taking things in stride, is an attitude she adopts effortlessly, because of her inner tranquility and seren- ity — her willingness to allow a higher intelligence than her own to guide the final result of all her hopes and dreams. She'll do what she can to overcome obstacles on her path. What more can anyone do? To continue to worry about something after you've already applied your best effort is, to her, wasted energy. Pisceans are not noted for spinning their wheels. Not that the female Fish is completely immune herself from spells of weeping and despair, from her own moods of fear and insecurity. Now and then she does give in to depression. But it's seldom long before her shoulder-shrugging outlook of a kind of positive fatalism returns, and she's her own serene, bright self again. Positive fatalism sounds like a non sequitur, but it isn't really. It simply means that you accept the inevitable, and trust a wiser destiny to bring it out all right in the end.

Added to her Neptunian instinct is her insight. She's perceptive enough to see the sparkle of a diamond before it's cut and polished. This is where her imagination helps considerably. She can also see all the solid virtues in the Crab she loves, his many-faceted possibilities and potentials as a lifetime mate. She feels comfortable around him, because he's not aggressive or over- critical (except on his bad Mondays and Fridays, when he's pouting because of a change of the Moon). He has a softness about him that touches her, and at the same time, a hardness of purpose, along with an obvious sense of responsibility that makes her feel secure — of the future — of his devotion — and of her own womanhood. He's a gentle man, a quiet man. And she is also a gentle, quiet woman. Somehow, his nearness brings her a feeling of peace and rightness. He's smart, he has a wonderful sense of humor. He makes her laugh, as well as cry . . . he tells fascinating stories . . . he's witty, clever and changeable enough to intrigue her and keep her guessing. He's just the right blend of the stable and the unpredictable to make Life interesting, to prevent love from growing stale through fixed habit. Besides all those attractions, he's a gallant and charming lover. He can read her mind (as she reads his), always seeming to know when she most needs his arms around her . . . when she most longs to escape with him into their private world of passion and the secrets of intimacy they share.

Without a single word spoken, these two will know when the time has come for the sexual expression of their love to envelop them and still the troubled waters, as the natural union of man and woman can always do. The only time a problem can develop in their physical compatibility is if he should cause her to withdraw into herself and become temporarily frigid, by failing to make her know how much he needs her, by concentrating too much on his nameless fears and worries. But she'll respond like a flower to the rain when he takes the time to be tender. Or *he* may at some time crawl into a shell of pretended disinterest when she's been a little sarcastic or firm with him after an argument. A Pisces woman is verbally unkind and "firm" so seldom, it can shock the sensitive Crab the rare times it happens into feeling rejected. But these are small things, and after a while, the strong magnetisim between Cancer and Pisces will overcome — and draw them back into each other in wholeness once more.

Both the Crab and the Fish are tenacious — in different ways. The tenacity of the Pisces woman comes from her refusal to believe failure is a permanent thing, being spiritually supported by a hunch that the end of any dismal period will be more surprisingly beneficial than ever appears possible in the midst of the purposeful confusions which, in an odd, contradictory way, will themselves be the roots of happiness, when the time comes for the fruits of the tree of experience to ripen.

The Crab's tenacity comes from the unwillingness to let go of anything truly desired. The claw of the Crab will cling to an intensely wanted object, dream (or person) with incredible persistence, whether nearby or across a continent. The Crab's clutch isn't easy to avoid, even in its long-distance tenaciousness, let alone in close proximity. Wriggle as the girl Fish may, a lasting escape is difficult.

But usually, she won't waste her energies in attempting to be released from her Cancerian man's tugs and pulls. It's beautiful, she feels, to be so needed. It is. In fact, it's one of the loveliest things that could happen to a typical Pisces woman. Still, there may be scattered moments in their closeness when she'll find it necessary to kindly explain to her lovable Looney Bird that being needed is ever-so-nice, but being possessed can be smothering. The Lunar man will turn away and weep then, silently . . . feeling lonely and rejected, never suspecting it was his own "crabbiness" that caused her to speak up in defense of her personal privacy. His Pisces lady will say, "I'm sorry. I didn't mean to hurt you. You're really my very favorite person in the whole world. Come on, let's go make a wish on the New Moon together!" The Crab will brighten visibly, giggle, grab her with that tenacious grip once again, grin happily, and say, "Okay, let's go! I'll bet I can guess what you're going to wish."

Then Pisces will smile softly, and reply, "Of course. You always know my secrets. I know what you're going to wish for too." The Crab will shiver ecstatically, and whisper, "Shhh! Don't tell anyone." The Pisces woman promises, honor-bright, not to tell a soul . . . and off they go into a meadow somewhere, to gaze up into the sky and sing their New Moon wishing mantras.

But what Cancer won't know is that his guess about her Piscean wish was wrong. There are many things Neptune never tells the Moon. Yes, the Fish are just a touch *ykaens*, always holding something back, or hiding it in code. Her Cancerian man likewise. He doesn't share every single *terces* with her. He only make-believes he does.

Now I'll tell the rest of you the most closely guarded, mutual secret of this man and woman. The reason they play so many guessing games together — Cancer and Pisces — is so that each can be sure of never losing the interest of the other.

LEO

Fire — Fixed — Positive
Ruled by the Sun
Symbols: Lion & Shy
  Pussycat
Day Forces — Masculine

LEO

Fire — Fixed — Positive
Ruled by the Sun
Symbols: Lion & Shy
  Pussycat
Day Forces — Masculine

The **LEO-LEO** *Relationship*

"Oh, lovely!"

"Oh, ripping!"

"Look at me!"

"Look at me!"

"Look at me!"

Two Leos together constitute all the membership necessary to form a Mutual Admiration Society. The dues? Why, worship, of course. That's worth more than money to the Big Cats.

There are, naturally, both negative and positive types born under all twelve astrological signs. But truly, I've never met a Leo of either type who didn't have that splendid Leonine ability to light up a room. The vibration of Leo, ruled by the Sun itself, is almost tangible, a thing you can actually feel throughout your whole being in the presence of a Lion or Lioness. It's undeniably relaxing to bask in such warmth, like lying on the beach with the

Solar rays beating down on your body, soaking up energy and bright Sunshine. Really, haven't you ever noticed the warmth blanketing you from those Leos you know — even when they're behaving like spoiled monarchs, lecturing you on your shortcomings and bossing you around? Warm, loving, affectionate, playful cats and kittens are hard to resist. Likewise warm, loving, affectionate, playful Leos.

Almost all Leos have a mysterious and magnetic attraction to cats. One of the wisest, most noble, and deserving-of-worship Leos I know often says, wistfully, "Kitties are the only good things." My own half-wild Colorado kittens peacefully and purringly allow him to trim their toenails. They would scratch out the eyes of anyone else who tried. I guess all cats understand and trust one another, whether paired in Nature's jungle, the shed in the backyard, or in the astrology zoo.

As a team, Leos offer each other no less than they offer the rest of us — fierce protection from enemies, plus an unsurpassed loyalty and devotion. These two possess between them all the necessary qualities for an enduring friendship. In fact, friendship far beyond the ordinary definition of the word is a common trait of the Big Cats, whose symbolic feline counterparts imitate the Leonine loyalty (as well as the Leonine self-sufficiency and cool dignity). Both kinds of cats are capable of heroic sacrifice and hardship in the name of friendship, love, or a sacred trust — a sort of persistent devotion that belies their reputation for snobbish superiority complexes and domineering ways.

In the fifteenth century, a loyalist to the Lancastrian party, Sir Henry Wyatt, was condemned to prison by King Richard III. Somehow, a curious pussycat found her way into his dark, damp cell, and an intense friendship developed between the two. The man's suffering from cold and hunger would have been unbearable but for the daily visits of his loyal friend, the cat, who brought along a morsel of food for him to eat as often as she could. Since cats are, by nature, comfort-loving creatures, an affectionate attachment to the prisoner was clearly her only motivation, Sir Henry's cell being anything but a warm, cozy, inviting hearth. All Leos have within them the potential of such loyalty and nobility in human relationships.

Time and time again, cats have been known to risk great danger and endure extreme hardship by journeying hundreds, even thousands, of miles to be reunited with loved ones from whom they were somehow separated — and the human Leonine Big Cats are capable of the same magnitude of sacrifice and persistence in reuniting with the one once loved, however seemingly insurmountable the obstacles between them may be. Despite a certain annoying air of smugness and aloof independence, the cat is a strange and marvelous creature — both kinds. If you don't believe me, just ask one! Leo is seldom hampered by modesty or self-effacement.

True, Leo Lions and Lionesses have other qualities not so admirable. As strong and courageous as they may be in times of trouble, they can also be insufferably arrogant and frequently blinded by false pride. Their warm natures and sunny dispositions are subject to change without notice into the sort of frozen dignity royalty assumes when a peasant dares to step out of line and criticize the King — or Queen. A Lion or Lioness will roar an angry warning to anyone who threatens to infringe upon royalty's right to be respected and obeyed.

When these two link their lives, they'll usually fight, pout, shout, and make up more often than any of the other 1-1 Sun Sign Patterns (except Aries). It's a constant inward or outward battle for supremacy. They're cozily content to purringly pal around together, they understand each other's swollen vanities, false pride, and need to be admired. But they can't help occasionally campaigning for the votes of the lesser animals. Alone on stage together, most of the time, they'll consent to be equals, cementing their relationship with mutual respect. It's when a third (or fourth, or fifth) person enters the scene that the fight for dominion and attention begins before a potential audience, which must eventually, after all, recognize just *one* of the Leos as the *star*, the other as only understudy or supporting player. This is as true of the Shy Pussycat Leos as of the more dramatic, extroverted Lions and Lionesses, the only difference being that the former emote with fewer crashes of cymbals than the latter. *All* Leos must be worshiped, looked up to in some degree, and one Cat cannot truly worship another without relinquishing the scepter of power. Their destinies are not to bow down, but to be bowed down *to* — and, yes, Leo, I *know* a preposition is a poor thing to end a sentence "with" — but that's how it is.

Between themselves, as before an enthralled audience of outsiders, two Leos do everything in the grand manner. Should a Leo politician choose to run for governor of a state, it will usually be one of the bigger states. Leos give larger and more extravagant gifts, normally choose to drive larger cars, prefer to dine in the better restaurants, dream bigger dreams, and definitely possess more sizable egos than we commoners. When you see a Leo driving a VW Bug, you may safely assume that this particular Lion has managed to keep his power-trip and superiority complex under control. However, it's still sleeping within, latent. Go ahead, make fun of his Bug and watch those tilted-at-the-corners cat eyes narrow in warning.

Shy Pussycat Leo Sydney Omarr, an indisputably competent, widely respected astrologer, wrote what I sincerely consider to be the very best guide for beginners seeking to learn how to *cast* a horoscope — the only book I ever recommend for this particular purpose, because of its combination of clarity and accuracy — the one every fledgling astrologer will treasure, after despairing of ever comprehending the mumbo jumbo in most others. I can honestly say that no other book teaches this art and science as well to the initiate, stressing what most beginning textbooks ignore — the urgent importance of the correct placement of the Sun in the chart, not only a *must* for accuracy, but the first step in the technique of birth-time rectification, without which, astrology cannot be totally reliable in either character analysis or predictive work, insofar as a complete horoscope is concerned.

Obviously, I think highly of the book. Obviously, so did its Leonine author, Omarr. What did he name his helpful guide? *My World of Astrology.* What else? Only a Leo could choose such an all-encompassing title, insinuating the author's royal and exclusive right of ownership of the oldest science known to Earthlings, the mother of astronomy, medicine, mathematics, and religion. Leo cannot conceive of anything over which he does not rule.

I realize I may be inviting a counterattack from Sydney, the Lion, via opening myself to a charge that the Aries ego is revealed in the title of my first book, *Linda Goodman's Sun Signs* — not to mention the title of the book you're reading — as was the Leo ego in his title, *My World of Astrology.* But I have a defense, you see. My title only infers personal ownership of the Sun Signs, not of the entire field of astrology, surely a more modest claim than Leo Omarr's . . . . which should demonstrate that a Ram's ego-trip doesn't rocket as high as a Lion's! I can hear the Big Cat roaring in outraged dignity all the way from Beverly Hills. He's going to appear on TV and demand equal time, just wait and see. Seriously, Sydney is truly a lovable Lion, and absolutely the only astrologer I would bet on in a battle of wits with all those bigoted, astrology-hating scientists and astronomers. Sydney has proven his splendid Leonine ability for dramatic debate in such intellectual confrontation more than once, via radio, television, and lectures, brilliantly defending astrology and always winning a stunning victory. That's the whole trouble with Leos. However much you may resent their cockiness, they usually more than deserve the respectful homage they expect and demand.

I had a definite purpose for giving this illustration of Leonine vanity. It's a warning to all Leos who are considering a close relationship with one another, and who will, therefore, soon be unavoidably competing for star status on the stage of family living rooms, offices, or love nests. With both of them it will be MY world of — (whatever). Unless they can find a way to compromise and share the throne, calling their mutual endeavors OUR world of — (whatever), someone may have to call out the guards. The two pronouns *my* and *our* have distinctly different meanings, and that difference may well be the deciding factor of the success or failure of any joint effort between two Lions, whether business, friendship, or love.

Leo Napoleon Bonaparte was as typical a Big Cat as ever stalked the political jungle on the planet Earth, a born monarch of all he surveyed, his arrogance and royal dignity clearly exhibited in oils by every painter who tried to capture his majestic mien on canvas. Like many Leos, he surrounded himself with "yes-men," who constantly bolstered his image of himself and reaffirmed his own opinion that he could do no wrong, make no mistakes — which weakness of pride, of course, led him to his inevitable Waterloo. There was never the slightest doubt who controlled either Joséphine or France, until he overestimated his power, as all Leos are inclined to do at one time or another.

Flamboyant and dramatic in a deceptively quiet and poised, controlled, feline manner (like many a Shy Pussycat, nevertheless proud Leo you may know), Napoleon personified his Sun Sign with each act and gesture. I have been privileged to examine a collection of valuable ancient and historical treasures at the home of my friend and editor, Dr. Charles Musès, one of these being a fabulous set of four books on the subject of Egyptian culture, which Bonaparte regally commanded to be printed after his conquest of Egypt. They reflect the Leo charisma of magnificent largesse perfectly. Bound luxuriously and extravagantly in the orange-red color of the Sun, each book measures approximately three feet in width and four and a half feet in height, hardly the kind of volumes you'd want to pick up at Walden's or B. Dalton's on your lunch break and tote home on the subway in the rush hour. They probably weren't Parisian best sellers, but they were surely GRAND and HUGE and properly IMPRESSIVE.

There's no denying that most Lions and Lionesses are in many ways superior to those with whom they condescend to mingle. They're intelligent, often handsome or beautiful, as they confidently toss their luxurious manes of hair, graceful in walk and bearing, romantically irresistible, kind and generous, wise and protective, courageous and noble, loyal and lovable. But they can make you feel like giving them an affectionate kick in the seat of their royal pants now and then when they're pulling off one of their dignified, arrogant "The King (or Queen) can do no wrong" routines. Try to get a Leo to acknowledge a mistake. Go ahead, try — and lots of luck. Acknowledging mistakes requires humility, a virtue Leos are a little short on, to put it mildly.

The reason these two manage to get along so well together surprisingly often is really quite simple. Royalty always feels more relaxed in the company of a peer than with an inferior (other Sun Signs). They understand how it is with another Lion or Lioness. They know how to feed each other the daily minimum requirement of compliments garnished with sincerity, disdaining the use of phony flattery as of no more value than costume jewelry, compared with the rare, precious gems of true appreciation. When they can afford it, they'll give one another diamonds, never tawdry rhinestones — hardcover first editions, never cheap, unaesthetic paperback books, just as one Leo will never insult another with the plastic imitation of flattery as a substitute for genuine respect. Their mutual loyalty and devotion will be deep and intense, for their fiery natures were designed to meet one another's challenge and demand for worthiness. Like all true monarchs, when they must deal with those of equal nobility, two Leos normally display an inbred, instinctive grasp of the delicacy of personal protocol, sensing with unerring judgment just how far one can safely go, without crossing the line into a breach of royal etiquette. Two Leos who lose control during a rash moment, and accidentally step over this invisible line with each other, will nearly always try to find a third-party scapegoat on whom to pin the blame. It's not a good idea to hang around the castle while a couple of Leos are declaring war on each other. After they've called a truce, they're likely to toss all innocent bystanders into the dungeon for inciting the revolution — and you can be certain that being frozen by icy Leonine disapproval constitutes a painful emotional imprisonment. It's never the Kings and Queens who start wars, didn't you know that? It's those misguided, rabble-rousing subjects who make all the trouble (like friends, neighbors, or relatives).

Naturally, in the inevitable struggle for supremacy, there will be frequent (sometimes deep) scars of wounded pride, mutually inflicted. They'll occasionally roar at one another in anger, and have difficulty dividing the rulership of whatever fiefdom they control into equal parts. But the brilliant, warm, and forgiving benevolence of the ruling Sun shines through every Leo word and deed, causing in each a desire to at least pretend possession of sufficient nobility of character to be generous in victory, undaunted in defeat. Assuming their Moon Signs are not severely incompatible, these two proud people can usually harmonize their differences, however many sharp thorns they inject into each other's paws — for Leo rules the heart, where the Kingdom of Happiness may always be found.

☆ ☆ ☆ ☆ ☆ ☆

LEO *Woman* LEO *Man*

◄━◆━►

> *"George," Mrs. Darling entreated him, "not so loud; the servants will hear you." Somehow they had got into the way of calling Liza the servants.*
>
> *"Let them," he answered recklessly. "Bring in the whole world. But I refuse to allow that dog to lord it in my nursery for an hour longer."*

Now really, just think about it. If a Leo man will roar in outraged dignity (or pout in wounded silence) over the humiliation of being upstaged by a dog (and he will, oh, he will!), you can imagine his reaction to the humiliation of being upstaged by a member of the so-called weaker sex. The thing about it is that .... well ... but I'm getting ahead of myself. Let's begin at the beginning.

I wonder, should I be blunt and frank ? Yes, honesty is by far the best policy. So I shall be blunt and frank. The role of housewife is entirely too skimpy a part for the average Leo actress to play on life's stage. For, as you know, or should know, it's a metaphysical *fact* that "All the world's a stage,/ And all the men and women merely players."

A deep esoteric truth is that you (yes, *you*), on a higher level of superconscious awareness, write your own play — produce, stage, and direct it — even cast yourself and all the supporting roles — then forget you did it, as the curtain rises. You — me — each of us — all Sun Signs, Leos not excluded. The only difference between average Earthlings and those mysteriously wise gurus, avatars, masters, teachers, celestials, or space people who pass among us is that the latter *know* they're only on a stage. They're *aware* that they're playing precast parts in Life's theatre, and are both saddened and amused that the other actors and actresses take each scene so seriously, ignorant of the ability each possesses to recast the entire tragedy or comedy and rewrite the last act anytime and any way he or she chooses. It's as though the footlights had cast a spell over them, causing them to be unable to distinguish between illusion and reality — like having the power of Mike Todd or Flo Ziegfeld or David Merrick and not even realizing it. Yet, almost every Leo woman realizes, at least, that the role of housewife is not the one in which she would find the ultimate fulfillment as a woman — even though she may not yet comprehend her power over the entire production — which is probably just as well, since Leos tend to go overboard when they're totally in command, and such a power-trip as *that* might *really* turn her head !

I know whereof I speak regarding the Lioness, you see, because I went into deep meditation last night, and contacted (on an astral level) William Shakespeare personally (who was pretending to be both Francis Bacon and Sir Isaac Newton — you know how dreams are). The Bard himself, no less, confirmed my suspicion that the Lady Katharine (Kate) in *The Taming of the Shrew* was a Sun Sign Leo (*with Moon in Aries*), and also assured me that even he would never have dared to cast her in the role of ordinary hausfrau to Petruchio. (He revealed another secret too, but I'll save that for the end of this chapter.)

Brooms and dust pans do not mix with tiaras and coronation splendour. Don't forget that Leo contains the essence of royalty. Nor does being chained to cooking meals and washing clothes harmonize with the astrological precept that each and every Lion (and Lioness) is born free. Instinctively sensing this, with or without the benefit of a horoscope, most Lionesses are career girls, well over two-thirds of them. And as long as we're speaking statistically, I'll add that a survey of the membership of women's lib groups would place the Sun Sign Leo numerically near the top of the list — (with Aries not far behind). Now all this is well and good — I'm not objecting to the Leo girls choosing to compete with all the predatory creatures out there in the commercial jungle. Why should I cast the first stone, what with my own career and my own active resentment of the indentured slavery of running the Bissel and canning apricots? Who wants to just stand around all day watching how fast the alfalfa sprouts grow in the Mason jar on the kitchen window sill? What kind of a challenge is that to a bright Lioness girl, for heaven's sake? Besides, it probably makes them nervous to be watched. It would make *me* nervous to be watched while I'm sprouting.

No, I'm not objecting or criticizing, just offering a friendly astrological warning. The career bit is fine *unless* the Leo girl should happen to fall in love with a Leo man, called a LION. Then things could get a little sticky.

She won't have any trouble identifying him when he comes stealthily stalking into her life — excuse me, I mean her play — and remember, she cast it herself, including HIM (hopefully in the starring role, if she's a wise producer, writer, and director). She'll recognize him right off, even without knowing his birthday, because he'll have a splendid mane of hair, even more luxuriant, pampered, and well-cared-for than her own. (Peek at a picture of the head of a Nature lion and you'll see what I mean.) He'll be courageous, tenderly protective of her, and convinced of his own worth, regardless of whether or not the world has yet recognized it. The world soon will. The world had *better!* And *she* had better too. His smile is dazzling, his teeth dazzling white, but his purring poise hides a ferocious temper and a powerful will. He's truly generous, warm, sunny, terribly proud, and extremely vulnerable to hurt — like attacks on his masculinity. Now we're back to her career again.

If she happens to earn more money than he does when they first meet, he'll laugh it off, smugly confident that his income will soon match hers — not only match it but top it. A smitten Lion, deeply and romantically in love with a beautiful, graceful, sensuous, and seductive Lioness, isn't going to let a small matter like money interfere with wooing and conquering his chosen mate. No way. The wafting scent and hazy smoke spirals of the incense of love will throw any red-blooded Leo male into a trance of blind ecstasy. And there's no other kind of Leo male. Other than red-blooded, I mean. But unfortunately, that "small thing" — money — may become a larger thing in their relationship after the first delicious taste of Oneness, when the first exciting, leaping flames of passion have burned down to the cozy coals of a quiet, intimate affection (leaping up again occasionally, of course, from time to time, but on the whole, a steadier flame of devotion, and just as inextinguishable as the leaping kind — unless you deliberately squirt it with a garden hose — things like that).

Money will only remain a "small thing" between them if he was right in his expectation of soon matching or topping her income, not to mention her success and/or achievements in the career jungle. But if his financial or personal career timetable is off, money will become a "large thing" very quickly, and with the slightest encouragement from either of them, turn into a "huge thing" — then into a "gigantic thing" — until finally, it becomes a Frankenstein Monster standing there between them, threatening to destroy their love and tear them out of each other's arms like helpless marionettes, caught up in the strings of their mutual pride and ego. How can you flee from a monster when your heart strings are tangled?

Bluntly, if she has more money (or more of anything else) than he possesses, a heroic sacrifice must be made to save the relationship. Guess whose sacrifice? You're right. Hers. Not his. See, you *are* learning your astrology, aren't you? A Leo woman may control all other Sun Sign men, but when it comes to the male and female Leos, the Lion dominates the Lioness. That's the way it is in Nature, and it isn't nice to fight Mother Nature. It isn't even practical to try. What kind of sacrifice do I mean? Well, one thing I certainly do *not* mean is deception — like the Lioness lying about her income or her position, then donating the half she never tells him about to the American Indian cause, or to save the Newfoundland baby seals. Not that the Indians and baby seals don't need it, and wouldn't appreciate it (and later the two of them might give such spreading of Light on the planet Earth serious mutual consideration, by becoming active members of Greenpeace, as befits monarchs responsible for the welfare of their subjects), but right now, the point is that any degree of dishonesty, however admirable the intention, will never salvage a Leonine relationship. It will only kill all love and respect between them.

The kind of heroic sacrifice I had in mind was for the Lioness to place their happiness above all else — to make a decision, ranging all the way from asking him to help with her work or career, then convincing him that she couldn't be nearly as successful without his guidance (which would no doubt be true) so the money she earns would be equally divided between them — all the way up to (or down to) giving up her job or career, if it seriously keeps them geographically or emotionally apart. Just up and quitting if necessary. Flat. Like that. If she really loves him (and she will, especially if either of their Moons is in a Fire or Air Element or conjoined in the same sign), she'll prefer holding his big, warm, protective paw, walking in the park, and snitching a few nuts from the squirrels during the lean weeks, to languishing alone in a plush penthouse, munching caviar, and wondering where the Big Cat she loves so intensely is roaming, stalking off his hurt — or more to the point, which sympathetic female siren is soothing his wounded masculine pride.

He'd like her to believe he's having a torrid affair when she's wounded him, just as she'd like him to believe she's found a new lover when he's wounded her. But nine times out of ten, they're *both* alone and lonely, using only the threat of infidelity to teach each other a lesson. Leos are like that. Of course, some are actually and technically unfaithful during a painful separation from the mate, but more Lions and Lionesses are not, often finding it difficult to find another King (or Queen) worthy of sharing the throne — reluctant to dally with the peasants, yet too proud to admit to the loved one the solitude and loneliness they're enduring.

Not all, but many of the quarrels between this man and woman will originate with a blow to his masculine ego, frequently over the jealousy incited by competition in career and/or earning ability, achievement, and so forth. Yet, the true cause is the struggle for the position of head of the pride. The Lion must win. There is no other way. Otherwise, the Leo male will sullenly pout in pathetic dejection, for all the world like Napoleon pacing back and forth on the island of Elba, and what woman can be truly happy with a bitter, grumbling pacer? Surely not a Leo woman. As we noted earlier, a Lion is born free — and to see one confined in a cage of misery because he's lost control of the woman he loves, therefore also lost his proud and splendid confidence, is a sad sight to behold.

The man-woman-which-spouse-is-the-mouse-in-the-house thing between them may be smoothed out in any one of several different ways — if they work together and share the same interests and career — if he's completely fulfilled in his own chosen profession — if they both retire to a chicken farm in the country and she allows him to gather and sell at least half the eggs — if she's sincerely content to remain at home in the lair, making it cozy for him to snooze in — or possibly if they run for President (him) and Vice President (her) on a Sexual Equality ticket. That just about covers all possibilities. Well, they could both become teachers, I suppose, and take turns at night instructing and lecturing each other, under the guise of keeping up with new educational theories.

Maybe we'd better scrap that last one. They won't have much time at night for anything but lovemaking if they're well-adjusted and have subdued the competition tension between them. Then the physical demonstration of their love can be a warm and lovely, near-perfect experience. Both can blend sex and affection in equal parts, understanding how to give and receive sexual satisfaction without sacrificing the magic of romance. Physical union, the consummation of love's true purpose of complete Oneness, can be a deep joy and a constant renewal of mutual devotion to a well-mated Lion and Lioness. He'll approach sex with both gentleness and passion — and she'll find this one moment when her instinctive jungle wisdom whispers to her exactly the right role to play, willingly submitting, allowing her man to master and conquer her with protective tenderness, which can deepen ordinary passion into ecstasy, for them both.

However, if they haven't solved their competitive conflicts in other areas, ecstasy could turn into something closely akin to agony. A Lion who is not properly respected, whose pride has been hurt, cannot retain the image of his own masculinity, and may become sexually impotent for brief periods.

Masculine impotency begins as an emotional illness, but can progress into a serious physical affliction, painting all rainbows with the dull, grey shades of despair. Then he'll wear the masks of icy sarcasm and cool disinterest to hide his humiliation, breaking her unsuspecting heart. In like manner, a Lioness who's not properly worshipped and admired, whose pride has been hurt, cannot retain the image of her own femininity, and may become frigid for brief periods. Feminine frigidity, too, begins as an emotional illness, but can progress into a serious physical affliction, painting all rainbows with the same dull, grey shades of despair. Then *she'll* wear the mask of arrogant willfulness, boredom, or cutting ridicule to hide *her* humiliation, breaking *his* unsuspecting heart.

Now, isn't that a ridiculous scene for these two people to play — this man and woman who contain within their natures all the power and glory of the Sun itself, and who were born under the star of Leo, which represents Love and rules the human heart? (Especially when you realize they wrote the play themselves, and can change the script whenever they like.) The only way out of such selfish and unnecessary misery is the realization that false pride — or *any* kind of pride — cruelly starves love to death by imprisoning the truth which could set love free, leaving no hope for a reincarnation of happiness, only lonely ashes of old dreams. Is pride worth it? Of course not. Then why do these two hang on to it so desperately? I'll let them answer that. Alone .... together. Facing each other honestly without dramatics — and reading the truth in each other's eyes. Admittedly, total honesty can be humiliating, especially to Leo, but when you pit temporary humiliation against a Lifetime of loneliness, the right choice becomes clear — and sometimes the simple truth is all it takes to bring love back home where it belongs.

Incidents which trigger an emotional impasse between a normally loving and affectionate Lion and his Lioness mate could be anything from a failure to compliment one another often enough — or hastily spoken, angry words of accusation, stemming from either real or imagined incidents of disloyalty or infidelity (it matters little which, since both arouse equally painful agonies of jealousy and mistrust that leave deep scars, slow to heal) — to the same old, monotonous conflict of: her career versus his need for superior — or at least comparable — success and worldly achievement.

And that reminds me of the other secret I learned astrally, from Will Shakespeare during meditation last night — the one I promised I'd tell you at the end of this chapter, remember? Will confided to me, with a bit of persuasion, what really took place offstage following the final curtain of *The Taming of the Shrew*. According to Shakespeare himself, after Petruchio had succeeded in taming Kate, the Lioness (with her Moon in Aries — or vice versa, same thing), into a gentle, submissive mate, who properly admired, appreciated, respected, and obeyed him, he allowed her to accept a part-time job illuminating old books and manuscripts, a delicate and rare art. Later, after she'd passed *that* test, without returning to her old, domineering ways, he permitted her to design jewels for the ladies of Padua, as a full-time career. Eventually, she became quite famous and successful, which fretted her lover-husband not a whiffle or a trifle because, you see, she never again disputed his masculine rights. She always came happily skipping, on-the-double, when her Lord and Master regally commanded, "Come here, and kiss me, Kate!"

Once a Lion teaches his woman a lesson, she doesn't soon forget it. Oh, didn't I tell you? The Bard also confirmed my suspicion that Petruchio was a Leo too. Thus, poor Kate's fate was predestined, from the beginning of act one, scene one. But "all's well that ends well" — on stage or off.

LEO

Fire — Fixed — Positive
Ruled by the Sun
Symbols: Lion & Shy
  Pussycat
Day Forces — Masculine

VIRGO

Earth — Mutable — Negative
Ruled by Mercury (also by
  the Planet Vulcan)
Symbol: The Virgin
Night Forces — Feminine

The **LEO-VIRGO** *Relationship*

Some of them wanted it to be an honest ship and others
were in favor of keeping it a pirate; but the captain
treated them as dogs, and they dared not express their
wishes to him even in a round robin.

When the Luminaries and Ascendents between their birth charts are in harmonious aspect, the Big Cat and the male or female Virgin will waltz down the Yellow Brick Road, grinning at each other and tossing posies, as happy and hopeful as we mortals are capable of being, with Leo strumming the ukulele and Virgo playing the piccolo, serenely singing their song in tune. If it goes out of key for a few bars, Virgo will immediately blow the proper note on a pitch pipe, correct the situation, and all will be melodious between them again, as Leo beams in affectionate approval.

However, before we follow them to the Emerald City, these lucky ones, we should pause and give a hand to the Leo-Virgo pairs who may have stumbled over a loose brick and need our help.

There's no doubt that there are a few scattered and rare Leo-Virgo associations which catapult themselves into a sadomasochistic bond rather quickly. Now don't go guessing right off that in these infrequent situations, Leo is always the mean sadist, and Virgo the helpless little masochist. Whether these two are entangled as friends, relatives, business associates, lovers, or mates, it can work either way. Let's play Libra for a moment, and look at both sides of it.

Take the Big Cat first. Leos are not sadistic by nature. Actually, no one is, really. Sadism is a twisted form of behavior that occurs when a person is emotionally pretzeled into a square knot by inner complexities of confusion and fear, and misery does love company. Still, although the normally benevolent and benign Lions and Lionesses aren't sadistic by design or intent, they can — and do — on occasion, behave as though they were, through their tendency to expect or demand that others consider them superior. When the "others," whether singular or plural, happen to have been born under the Sun Sign of Virgo, it's understandably tempting for the Big Cat to lean a little heavy on the orders and commands. Virgins do seem to submit so sweetly, quietly, and courteously — *at first.*

Just as Leo isn't a natural-born sadist, neither is Virgo a natural-born masochist. It just seems that way. Granted, these people behave in a way that appears to verge on masochism at times, considering their gentle, polite speech (when they aren't being cranky), unobtrusive manner, and self-effacement. Since Leos are so often bossy, and a touch arrogant besides, it may sometimes look as though the more introverted Virgos are being mashed into a masochistic mold, as they keep bobbing up and down, and curtsying to the King or Queen — *at first.*

Admittedly, there may be a few cases where this sort of "Yes, your Majesty" syndrome from Virgo, and the "Do exactly as I tell you, because I know best" syndrome from Leo, gels into a pattern, then solidifies into a very sad, permanent arrangement, but as I've already mentioned, such a situation is rare and infrequent.

What is more likely to occur after a time, is what is referred to as "the turning of the worm." When this happens, Leo is dumbfounded to discover that the curtsying, obedient Virgo does have a tolerance level for being trampled upon, and when it's been reached, the long-suffering, quiet Virgin will become quite surprisingly verbal. All of a sudden, he (or she) will reel off a list of Leo's flaws and shortcomings, with painful accuracy, then quietly (and still courteously) walk away from the royal castle with an irritating aplomb and determination (Virgo is an Earth Sign, you know), open up a cobbler shop somewhere . . . and thereafter refuse to cobble any boots or slippers for His or Her Majesty's feet, let alone kiss them in servitude any longer.

Then we have the opposite scene: the unfortunate Lion or Lioness (this Leo will invariably be a Pussycat type) who becomes the masochistic victim of a long siege of very subtle sadistic treatment from a cool, earthy Virgin, who incessantly (never mind how politely) splits every hair in Leo's mane, until the poor Lion (or Lioness) is nearly bald, in a symbolic sense — continually berates and belittles the Shy Pussycat's accomplishments or efforts — endlessly analyzes his (or her) Leonine dreams as being impractical, and as full of holes as Swiss cheese — and criticizes the Leo's every word and gesture as overly dramatic. After a while, bereft of all dignity, the Leo person, stripped of pride, and robbed of confidence, will wander forlornly around the house or classroom, office or playpen, like the whimpering Lion in the Land of Oz, twisting his or her tail nervously, keeping it tucked protectively under the arm, weeping waterfalls of tears . . and searching pitifully for the gift of courage. Nothing could be a more pathetic sight than a proud King or Queen of the jungle thus reduced to a quivering mass of masochistic meowing.

Although this is an extreme example, it can happen. Nevertheless, such a story will likely have the same kind of O. Henry ending as the earlier scene we used as an example, when the Virgo worm turned. Only rarely will such a situation continue permanently. The most probable ending is that the Leo worm (I don't know if I dare call Leo a worm, even in an allegorical sense, but I feel uncommonly brave today) — is that the Leo worm will also turn, grow into a Giant Monster Cat, growl . . . then give a deafening roar . . . and pounce upon the unsuspecting Virgo nit-picker like any feline pounces on a mouse . . . magnanimously allow the now-frightened, squeaking Virgo to escape . . . and finally stalk out the door (or over the side of the playpen) in regal victory, draped in majestic anger, never again to return.

These are all the sad endings, the dangers this Earth-Fire, 2-12 Sun Sign Pattern must guard against. Now that we've warned them about the negative naughtiness that might tempt them, which might occur in some variation, if the Sun-Moon aspect between them is square or opposed, or their Ascendents are unfavorable to each other — and have hopefully taught them how to prevent such heartache — we can move along to the brighter side of the Leo-Virgo association. And there very definitely is a bright side.

A Pussycat and a Virgin of either sex, who have conquered their differences and created a compatible atmosphere for themselves, are a joy to behold. Leo will at last have found a gentle, devoted companion, who sincerely appreciates the golden Leonine virtues — an admiring, intelligent subject to serve him (or her) and to be loyally protected in return. Virgo will at last have found someone genuinely worthy of respect (and Virgo standards are high), a warm-hearted and generous friend, who is both wise and loving . . strong enough to count on in an emergency, yet vulnerable enough to need the Virgin's constant fussing and attention. (The awareness of being needed is an intoxicating boost to the lonely Virgo spirit.) When this association is a good one, it's very good indeed. Once Leo has taught Virgo that he (or she) will simply not be nagged and constantly criticized — once Virgo has taught Leo that a Virgin has no intention of becoming a slave to his (or her) arrogant demands and whims — there can be a warm and vibrant communication between these two, which is a magical thing. Magical because Virgo is what astrology calls a "human" Sun Sign, symbolized by the Virgin, gathering in the harvest, and Leo is what astrology calls a "bestial" Sun Sign, symbolized by the fearless ruler of the jungle, the Lion (or his mate, the sensuous, equally as confident Lioness). Symbolically or literally, it's never easy for a human and an animal to truly communicate, yet when they do, one is reminded of places like Eden . . . or the woods walked so joyfully by Saint Francis of Assisi, accompanied by the wolves and birds and lambs . . . . . . and all manner of animals who trusted him.

As dramatic and effusive and flamboyant as Leos can be, they're also very capable and level-headed organizers. Except for those times when their Leonine pride and vanity get in the way, Leos have an amazing store of common sense. Practical Virgo privately admires this, but must get into the habit of *saying* so to Leo. Just as Leo approves of, and is pleased by, Virgo's sincere effort to quietly do the very best he (or she) can, often under tense and demanding conditions, yet too seldom pays the Virgin the compliment of honest appreciation for being so sensible and reliable most of the time (at least, more often than lots of other people Leo relies on, only to be disappointed).

In attempting to analyze the Leo-Virgo association, a stream of disassociated images flickers across my memory screen, in no logical or chronological progression . . . . a small, dark-eyed Virgo child named Gary, patiently and uncomplainingly standing for an endless time, wordlessly humiliated at being forced into a bunny-rabbit suit, with huge, floppy ears, on Halloween, stuffed into it by his more forceful, commanding big brothers, one an Aries Fire Sign, the other a strong Lion — but at the last minute, the docile little Virgo balked, and refused to take one step out of his bedroom, dressed so foolishly . . . . a proud Leo father, in a small western American town, reading with tears in his eyes, a gentle verse, a poem written in tribute to him by his Virgo son, who had been away for too many painful years — yet, when the boy came home, the Lion's tears were soon forgotten, as he arrogantly dictated his son's every movement, demanding strict obedience, never once expressing affection or appreciation to him — while the Virgo forgot the sensitive poetry he had written in genuine praise of his father, seeing only Leo's vanity and arrogance, stubbornly refusing to recognize the unexpressed love and warm-hearted concern behind his dad's stern commands and expectations of him . . . . Leo film star Mae West giving a press interview about a Virgo man she knew well, who had been for years a tender, helpful friend — spending the entire thirty minutes allotted to the reporter talking exclusively about herself, as Lionesses often do, her absolute unawareness of her own self-absorption somehow both amusing and endearing . . . . the inexpressible tenderness in the eyes of a Lion in West Virginia when he looks at his bright and gentle, beautiful Virgo wife, who brought into his life a fresh promise of Indian summer and a new reason to live — after he'd lost two former wives in succession to the same crippling disease, following decades of a heavy Karma, filled with weary duty, courageously met with Leo's loyal, unswerving devotion to the helpless . . . . his reward the song her quiet Virgo love now sings to his great Lion's heart, which hadn't dared to hope for love again, until she came, lingering in the air like a miracle set to music.

Fragments of images, small bits and pieces, spinning around the astrological wheel of Life, colored by Leo's brilliant, sunny, yellow-gold and royal purple . . . . blending with Virgo's pure, sparkling white, tranquil blue, and the deeper green of scented woods. As with all Sun Signs, the shades of their auras contain the harmonies that shape their destinies.

☆ ☆ ☆ ☆ ☆ ☆

LEO *Woman* VIRGO *Man*

Peter could be exceedingly polite also . . . .
. . . . he rose and bowed to her beautifully.
She was much pleased, and bowed beautifully
to him from the bed.

Do you think, perhaps, that bowing before the Lioness as she lies languidly in her bed is asking too much of her Virgo lover-friend-mate-husband? (In a good marriage, all four terms apply, and are interchangeable.) Back to the question. It may possibly be asking too much of *him*, but it could never be an excessive homage to pay to *her*. I sense some of you smiling, others laughing aloud in disbelief. Never mind, astrology will, as always, have the last word. Those males of any Sun Sign whatsoever who are reading this, and who have a Leo wife, I double-triple-dare-you to try it tomorrow morning. Don't startle her suddenly. Begin by bringing her breakfast in bed, on a tray, if it's only fruit juice and tea or coffee. She may evidence surprise by a discreetly raised eyebrow, but she'll thank you graciously. At that very moment, drop to your knees on the floor beside her, projecting a blend of half-jesting, half-earnestness, take her hand, place it against your cheek, and say softly: "This is the only way I can think of to show you how much you mean to me."

However "stagey" or dramatic it may sound, I don't care who she is, if she's a Leo woman (unless she was adopted, and is actually a Capricorn, in which case she'll believe you've gone mad), this lady will smile her very brightest smile, her eyes will glow, her cheeks will turn pink with pleasure — and she'll look at you with so much love, you'll be momentarily stunned, and forget all about feeling foolish. Try it, and see for yourself. There's not a Lioness anywhere in the world that sort of scene would embarrass. It's really astonishing how casually and gracefully a Leo will accept any display of worship as perfectly natural and right. Some Leos demand it, all of them desire it — and not a *one* of them will ever refuse it. That's an absolute fact.

Now can you picture a woman with such an overwhelming need to be adored, in love with a Virgo man, who also loves her, yet who finds it difficult to select a sentimental card for her birthday, is too shy to even glance at her affectionately in front of others, let alone hold her hand or put his arm around her when anyone else is looking — a Virgo who only says "I love you" to his Lioness maybe once a year, who scolds her about her extravagance constantly, insisting that she add and subtract every canceled check on the calculator, while she's just standing there before him bravely, too proud to cry — wearing a new sweater, a new hair style, a different shade of lipstick, her eyes begging him in vain to tell her she looks beautiful? Have you pictured it? You have, and it makes you sad? Wait. There's another sad picture to paint. Hang on to your hanky.

A Virgo male can actually suffer from vertigo and high blood pressure when he's forced to live in the midst of clutter and confusion. This man must have order in his life and his surroundings, or his nervous system goes haywire. Practical and conservative by nature (unless the Moon or Ascendent in his nativity is in a Fire or Air Sign), he abhors waste and extravagance. He worries about his health, frets over details, and when his patterns are broken or even momentarily interrupted, it brings on dizziness and a tightness in the chest. He panics when his personal possessions are mislaid or destroyed. Loud voices and dramatic emotional scenes tear at his tranquility. He's gentle, somewhat introverted and sensitive, therefore, when something humiliates him, he nearly wishes he were dead. (Or at least, mercifully unconscious.)

Now, picture a man possessed of such set habits, such methodical ways and delicate emotional stability, in love with a Lioness, who also loves him, yet insists on spending twice as much money as they both earn to buy every luxury she sees that appeals to her, rearranges his desk and his bureau periodically and throws out his favorite socks and ties if the colors should happen to displease her, without bothering to tell him. Add a few more brush strokes to the picture. Imagine this warm and loving Lioness unconsciously and thoughtlessly leaving her makeup on the bathroom sink, carelessly strewing her negligees around the bedroom, as though she expected a team of servants to make it all neat and tidy, becoming annoyed with her Virgo man when he's offended her dignity in some minor way, and punishing him with a Leonine lecture in front of the plumber or their parakeet.

Can you imagine the feelings of this sensitive male creature when she tells him tales about all her old boy friends at night, just before they go to bed, while he's just standing there before her, humbly, wearing the pajamas she stained with bleach, with a large rip down the side he awkwardly tried to sew himself, resulting in one leg being four inches shorter than the other . . . nervously aware, as she's reciting her romantic episodes of yesterday, that the alarm clock is broken, which means he might oversleep and be late for work the next morning . . . trying to forget that she smashed the rear fender on the car that afternoon, and didn't mail in the car insurance payment last month because she was involved in redecorating the den, which forced him to take out a second mortgage on the house to pay for it?

You won't need any further imagination to know what will happen after the foregoing scene, when the lights go out. The Lioness will be wounded because her mate falls instantly asleep (in the manner of one enduring a complete nervous collapse) without kissing her goodnight. It's even possible that she'll be more offended in the morning, because the poor man talked in his sleep all night long, and it kept her from getting her proper beauty rest. It's all his fault, she tells him, as she gazes into the mirror and sees dark circles under her eyes.

Yes, these are all extremes of behavior, but the extremes are helpful as warnings to a man and woman who must be more careful of one another's Achilles heels if they expect to nourish, not starve, the love they felt when they first met.

The self-centeredness, vanity, and pride of a Lioness are magically transformed into gracious consideration and loving generosity when she's properly pampered and adored — when her own feelings are respected, yes, even revered. Just as the fussy fault-finding and cool detachment of the Virgo man is magically transformed into tender solicitude, into a calmer and at the same time a more friendly, outgoing manner — when he's courteously treated and genuinely appreciated, rather than constantly agitated.

If he wants to make this relationship work, he must realize at the outset that he'll have to curb his natural inclination to be critical, if not forego it altogether. To criticize this woman is to guarantee trouble. Her Leo pride makes it more painful than he could ever comprehend (or than she'll ever show) to accept even the slightest criticism. One might think it would be easier to take from the man who loves her. Not so with the Leo woman. It hurts even more when the man she cares about finds fault with something she does or says, with her appearance or her personality, than when others disapprove of her. The only way to change the Lioness is through subtle hints, using the utmost tact, never by outright criticism, and certainly not by nagging. She must be allowed to retain the illusion that she's more or less above reproach. One doesn't tell a monarch she's wrong, one very carefully *suggests* a better plan. At first, such a total curbing of his critical instincts will frustrate the Virgo man, but he'll simply have to get the hang of it, or resign himself to the inevitability that the Lioness he captured will escape from the confining cage of his criticisms, to wander free again. The choice is clear-cut, and his to make. Although it's never easy for a Virgo to gracefully pay compliments, he must learn to satisfy this lady's hunger and thirst for admiration. He'll master the art more quickly when he sees what frequent and sincere compliments can do to sweeten and soften her disposition, how they turn her angry roar or proud pouting into a contented purring. An affectionate word or two, spoken at the right moment, will bring forth her sunny personality in all its brilliance. The Lioness is a noble "animal," and when her Sun-ruled qualities are encouraged, not buried under tons of earthy Virgo conservatism, she can be an eternal bubbling fountain of hope and happiness, wonderful to be around, in every way — and capable of creating exactly the kind of harmonious atmosphere he needs. She becomes lazy and careless only when she's bored and unappreciated.

Naturally, she'll have to come down off her throne and meet him halfway. She should never argue with him at mealtimes, when he's eating his lentils and garbanzo beans, because tense emotions turn food into acids, which create severe indigestion. If she cares enough to take trouble to try to understand his personal emotional metabolism, how he feels obligated to solve every minor and major problem that crosses his path because he believes that if everything isn't fine and perfect, his world will fall apart, her generous heart will find a way to unwrinkle his brow and smooth away many of his tensions. She might remind him that perfection itself is an imperfection, removing the charm of contrast from life, all the exciting textures formed by light and shadow, leaving only a flat surface, dull and unexciting. But she should explain these things to him gently, not arrogantly, taking care to respect his opinions too — and really *listening* to what he says when they talk, instead of simply waiting for her turn to be heard.

Unless there's both mental and emotional communication between them, they can't expect their sexual union to be everything it should (and could) be. There will be times when his lovemaking is too unresponsive and mechanical for her more spontaneous desires, then her visible disapproval will add to his humiliation and discouragement. Her icy aloofness can be a sexual depressant—and his silent Virgo criticism isn't exactly Nature's most effective aphrodisiac either. He needs to allow himself more freedom and enthusiasm in his sexual expression to know that lovemaking is meant to be an intimate sharing, with no fear of rejection, not simply a guarded, partial release of feeling—that the overwhelming experience of physical blending between a man and woman is more than simply a controlled exchange of affection. She needs to realize that passion can sometimes be a quiet thing, like a whisper. Often, all it takes to join their hearts and bring them to the kind of total fulfillment they're capable of achieving together is a change of attitudes—and a little extra effort in understanding one another's deeper needs, which are not so different as they may seem.

Because they're influenced by the 2-12 vibration, he may in some way represent either a material or an emotional security to her, while she senses there are many lessons of happiness to be learned from this intelligent, conscientious man. He's sure to grow more tenderly tolerant of her independent, impulsive temperament as they become more familiar. If she's patient, she'll notice that he takes a shy pride in her beauty and accomplishments. The love between Leo and Virgo is like a flame that burns slowly but steadily brighter every year, if it's carefully tended and shielded from the winds of selfishness.

He's a strangely remote man, sometimes extremely sensitive, at other times stubbornly *in*sensitive, with a stern symmetry to his emotional patterns. But his spirit lives in a peaceful stillness. The cool, marble halls of his reflections are a restful place for her own spirit to visit . . . . . and sometimes he does things, in his quiet manner, which are really extraordinarily touching. When their life together threatens to become a little too neat and precise, it's up to her to impulsively throw open the windows so the sunshine can pour in, and give their love a more lived-in feeling. I wonder what would happen if she surprised him by bringing him *his* breakfast in bed some morning? It should be very early, before dawn, because he might think of a special way to thank her that could take a long time . . . and she'll have to be sure it doesn't make him late for work.

☆ ☆ ☆ ☆ ☆ ☆

LEO *Man* VIRGO *Woman*

———— ◆━━●━━◆ ————

"What's your name ?" he asked.

"Wendy Moira Angela Darling," she replied with some
satisfaction. "What is your name ?"

"Peter Pan."

She was already sure that he must be Peter, but it
did seem a comparatively short name.

"Is that all ?"

"Yes," he said rather sharply. He felt for the first
time that it was a shortish name.

The first thing that happens when the Lion meets the Virgin is that he'll be
stirred by a powerful urge to protect this lovely, dainty lady from Life's ugly
and unhappy experiences, with his great strength and loving heart. The
second thing that happens, after a while, is that he begins to feel a faint sense
of unease. He'll find himself uncomfortably aware, as he glances in the
mirror, that he perhaps needs a haircut. Then he'll notice several heretofore-
ignored small spots on his best jacket, which he hastens to send off to the
cleaners. His shoes suddenly appear to be shamefully shabby, and he decides
to buy several new pairs. While he's shopping, the thought strikes him that
his wardrobe could also use some new shirts, maybe in slightly more subdued
shades than the vividly colored ones he's been wearing. (Or the drab ones
he's been wearing, whichever.) Gradually, there steals into his mind a
vaguely disturbing suspicion that his grammar may not be the model of
perfection he's believed it to be all his life until now, and so he'll drift into
occasional periods of silence (from a *LEO* — SILENCE ? Yes.) and start to
peek in the dictionary, when he's sure she isn't looking, to make certain the
word he just used when they were talking means what he always thought it
meant.

　　It isn't that she actually said anything, you understand. She's too polite
to criticize him verbally or directly (at least, until she knows him better), but
it's the way she looks at him . . . that cool glance from her clear, beautiful
eyes . . . the barest suggestion of disapproval fleeting across her tranquil,
composed features. Not quite distaste, but a bit too close to it for his vanity's
comfort.

　　The Lion is dangerously near to being tamed. And she doesn't even carry a whip — or a pistol loaded with blank caps. Music tames the savage beast, they say. And the soft music of Virgo's meticulous nature, discrimination, and exquisite sense of loveliness, accompanied by Virgo's gentle, courteous manners and her endearing way of making clear her respect and admiration for his virtues, is capable of turning the most ego-oriented, roaring Leo male into a docile, playful Pussycat, purring contentedly and rolling ecstatically in the catnip of her charm.

If she's careful not to overdo it, her technique will work wonders with the Big Cat. He'll adore her for making him feel so worshiped, without suspecting she's behind the gradual changes in his life-style. After a time, he'll lose his uneasiness, begin to feel more relaxed, pleased with his new image, more self-confident than ever. There's no doubt that persuading a Leo to improve himself, and not destroying his self-esteem in the process, but instead, increasing it, is a rare and worthy accomplishment, for which the Virgo girl should be approvingly patted on her neat, well-groomed head. But should she be carried away by her success to the point of settling down to some serious criticism and nagging, she'll be crossing the safety line. It's a fine line, difficult to determine, but since Virgos are experts at drawing and defining fine lines, she stands a good chance of having the common sense (Virgos are all loaded with common sense) to quit when she's ahead, and switch to a policy of praising him for all those wonderful new changes in himself *he* initiated. If only everyone had such a great capacity for *self*-improvement. He's so introspective, and he possesses such incredible self-discipline. It's truly amazing!

Yes, it *is* nothing short of amazing to be able to turn what so easily could have been a deflation of the gigantic Leo ego into another genuine reason to tell him how strong and smart he is. Virgo lady, you are amazing. Now please don't spoil it all. Curb your criticisms once you've molded and redesigned him into more or less your idea of masculine perfection. Allow him to retain a few flaws, so he remains human. Otherwise, he'll soon catch on to what you've done (if you keep doing it), and when all the sawdust from his outraged dignity has settled, you'll find yourself a literal, not symbolic, virgin again . . . . in a manner of speaking. All alone, without your once-affectionate, loving, and loyal mate. Don't split hairs with me, please. That's close enough to being an actual virgin. There's not a great deal of difference. If you insist on analyzing it down to the last straw, it's really worse, because a literal virgin doesn't know what she's missed by not having experienced the fulfillment of true love. *You* will know. And you will suffer — from the memory of former happiness. Better to let him make a mistake now and then, wear an occasional gaudy sport shirt, overestimate his bank balance — better to smile when he stretches a story a bit in the telling, to let him believe he's as good a driver as he thinks he is, and never remind him that he sometimes takes the wrong freeway when he's in charge of the road map . . all those things. Wouldn't you say? Why tell him the fudge he makes when he's puttering around in the kitchen is too soft, his noodle casserole too hard, his baritone, when he sings in the shower, more off key than in key? What can you win? Nothing. But you can lose a lot. Like — him. And that's a lot.

When this relationship works, it's such a quietly beautiful thing. Despite the Virgo woman's tendency to be supercritical of others — and almost cruelly critical of herself — the vibes passing between the Virgin and the Lion in their 2-12 Sun Sign Pattern allow her to be exceptionally sparing and tolerant in her judgment of this man. Her sympathy for his attitudes, as foreign as they may be to her own, stems from her karmic soul memory of having recently experienced the Leonine motivations (Leo representing the twelfth house of Karma to Virgo). There's always the possibility (especially if there's a negative exchange between the Sun and Moon positions in both birth charts) that she'll slip once in a while, and nag him a little, but on the whole, he'll probably accept it rather well. When she steps too firmly on his sensitive Lion's tail, he'll emit a medium-sized roar of warning, and she'll sweetly apologize. All things considered, harmony is easily restored between them, after minor misunderstandings.

In the final analysis, Leo will have his own way. She may drop subtle hints, and sometimes he'll *permit* himself to be swayed by her suggestions, but only if it suits him to do so. It will be *his* choice. He is the unquestioned authority, his must be the last wise word regarding all major decisions and questions. (Or it had better be, unless she wants to nurse him through depressing periods of wounded vanity and pouting.) The really nice thing is that because she so gently and pleasantly submits to his royal majesty's preferences *most* of the time, he'll feel free to pour out to her gratefully, in return, all the warm sunniness of his Leonine nature, treating this polite, intelligent, and clear-eyed woman with an almost tangible benevolence. More than anyone, she'll experience the Lion's true nobility and generosity, therefore her obvious adoration of him won't be insincere, but will be from her heart.

Every Leo ever born is "in love with love," a quality that makes the typical Lion an unsurpassed lover. He's undeniably sensuous, yet he's equally sentimental. As erotic as his desires often are, there's always the added dimension of honesty and naturalness to his lovemaking, which allows the Virgo woman to trust him enough to be relaxed in his arms, and to give more of herself than is her normal inclination. There's something so unmistakably cozy and comfortable about the sexual behavior of the Leo man. He has a way of turning the physical demonstration of love into a gesture of tenderness, creating a feeling of emotional security that makes sex both an expression of passion and a warm, protective thing. On a subconscious level, this calls out to all that is virginal and pure within the Virgo nature, and so she responds with enthusiasm, and with a touching faith in his gentleness. Leo has both an open mind and an open heart when his self-confidence is nurtured, which is why Lions are so lovable and huggable (and also why it's so easy to forgive their spells of insufferable pride and arrogance). In turn, the appealing simplicity of her sexual attitude arouses in him the very best side of his lovemaking talents, which are considerable. One thing which could smother their physical harmony is the always-present possibility that she may choose a moment when he's silently contemplating romance to be unnecessarily outspoken over some minor issue, resulting in a glance of frozen dignity from her Lion, and a wounded retreat . . . maybe all the way to carrying his pillow and blanket to the couch in the den, where he'll pout like an exiled monarch, and sleep alone. But he'll be back by morning, when his feet get cold, and the mood to snuggle returns.

Oddly, these two may both sleep a lot. They share the kind of metabolism that requires more than eight hours of sleep a night (if they're typical of their Sun Signs). They'll usually retire early, and rise early. Leo needs a nightly long span of snoozing to replenish his splendid physical stamina. She needs the extra slumber to replenish the mental energy she uses in such great amounts all day long worrying about things, and trying not to show it. The Lion may also sneak in a few cat naps in the late afternoon, which could cause her to think he's lazy, at first. But the male Lion, like the jungle Lion, only appears to be lazy. After a while, he'll yawn, stretch languidly, like a cat, and become busily active, fixing things, sawing things, remodeling something, excitedly suggesting a trip or some new adventure, in short — taking care of business.

The Virgo woman will be absolutely delighted with her Leo man's ability to fix anything that's broken (including the small cracks in her heart when she's hurt), and the fact that he normally doesn't procrastinate when there's something that needs his attention, including her. Just as he'll be delighted with her fastidiousness, her neat appearance, and the cool, attractive image she presents to the public at all times. Leos do love being able to exhibit their ladies (like their accomplishments) with pride. He'll be particularly proud of her fine mind. Many Leo men tend to marry women who are neither their intellectual superiors or equals, so the King will have an admiring subject to train, teach, and lecture. But the happiest Lion is the one whose girlfriend or wife represents a stimulating mental challenge. The Virgo female will certainly provide him with this.

His personality is ruled by the powerful Sun itself, which is why she often feels so snugly toasted in his presence (and sometimes a little scorched). Her personality is shaped and influenced by both her temporary ruler, Mercury — and Virgo's true ruling planet, the soon-to-be-discovered Vulcan. On the surface, Mercury causes her to be quick-minded, alert, versatile, and almost constantly active. On a deeper level, the thunderous Vulcan is already stirring within her heart a strange kind of music, promising to free her spirit from former restrictions, daring to hint that she will someday become as courageous and daring, as independent as Leo himself. It's an intoxicating thought, the anticipation of such a transformation, perhaps not far away. It may be this very promise of the future that sings to his noble Solar self a song of Tomorrow, when they'll be soaring to even greater heights together!

But meanwhile, in the comforting Now, he's grateful for her tranquil presence, the practical dreams she brings to him, content to be graced by her cool sweetness, by her fascinating blend of Earth and Sky . . . to be blessed by her laugh, like silver sleigh bells. His own gift to her each bright new morning they awaken in each other's arms is a slice of sunshine . . . wrapped in the brave, golden ribbons of his unshakable optimism, his confidence that it's going to be a beautiful day. As usual, he's right — isn't he always? Whatever the weather, it *will* be a beautiful day, for even the soft, clean rain is a fragrant benediction . . . the sparkling, cold snow a miracle . . . when you love, and know you're loved in return.

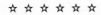

LEO

Fire — Fixed — Positive
Ruled by the Sun
Symbols: Lion & Shy Pussycat
Day Forces — Masculine

LIBRA

Air — Cardinal — Positive
Ruled by Venus
Symbol: The Scales
Day Forces — Masculine

The LEO-LIBRA *Relationship*

"Then tell her . . . . to put out her light."

"She can't put it out. . . . It just goes out of itself when she falls asleep, same as the stars."

"Then tell her to sleep at once," John almost ordered.

"She can't sleep except when she's sleepy."

It happens that the people quoted above have been discussing Tinker Bell, the faerie. But with Leo and Libra, the topic of conversation makes very little difference. Whatever the subject matter at hand, you can be sure Leo will be rather good-naturedly bossy about it, and Libra will argue about it, often taking both sides at once, to be certain she's not missing any salient facts. Leo creates the heat, Libra contributes the air. Combined, these result in a fair amount of warm-to-hot conversational breezes between them.

Leo's pronouncements are expected (by Leo) to be received with more or less unquestioned acceptance, if not downright admiration, with some respectful genuflecting thrown in now and then, and Libra does love to argue (they call it discussing) every point which can be construed as having the slightest possibility of choice. But the choice has already been made (wisely, of course) before Leo has spoken. Didn't you realize that ? No. Libra did not realize that. How can one make an intelligent choice between two courses of action without discussing the pros and cons back and forth for a reasonable length of time ? The trouble is, with Libra, a "reasonable length of time" can drag on for quite a spell. Leo shouldn't be cross and impatient. All that indecision is more painful to the Libran than to those forced to participate in the weighing of the scales, bringing in the sheaves — of common sense — and so forth.

Leo must learn that by "discussion," Libra doesn't mean dramatic scenes or angry outbursts. That sort of thing is uncongenial, for goodness sake. It prevents a nice, balanced relationship, and destroys any chance of harmony. Since harmony, balance, and peace are a holy trinity to every Libra man or woman or child, it must be realized that they truly don't initiate all those arguments for the purpose of quarreling, only to clear the air and try to make everyone see the issue fairly, in a logical way. You see ? Leo will not always see, but perhaps does see more often than most other people. Fairness is a sacred virtue to Libra. It's interesting how many writers who know nothing about astrology pick up the Sun Sign characteristics without realizing it. For example, an announcement of a Gloria Steinem article about Libran Jimmy Carter, printed on the cover of *Ms.* magazine in bold, red letters, informed readers that: CARTER FINDS LIFE IS UNFAIR. Poor man. I don't doubt that he does. In a 1978 edition of *People* magazine, the closing words of a piece about Lioness Jacqueline Onassis were: ". . but one thing is certain. Whatever Jackie does, she will do it royally, and that is all the public demands." (And all her Sun Sign demands, we might add.)

Since this is a 3-11 Sun Sign Pattern (described in detail in the "Sun Sign Patterns" section in the back of this book) there will be an extravagant amount of communicating on various levels between them, on the side of one or the other of the two, usually both. Friendships of the really genuine kind are more easily achieved by Leo and Libra than by many others. Theirs is a sextile vibration, therefore life will present them with a nearly unending stream of opportunities together, in every area of endeavor, personal and otherwise. Whether or not they grab these opportunities, and what they make of them, will depend upon their individual Moon Signs, and other planetary aspects between their nativities.

When they join forces, Leo and Libra can achieve almost anything, from a successful love affair or marriage to a sound friendship or business deal. Their elements are Air and Fire, and when the former fans the latter into a brighter torch, both benefit . . as long as Leo takes care not to consume all the oxygen in the airy mental processes of Libra. Unpleasant displays of temperament from Leo can cause Libra to eventually float away. Disharmony of any kind topples those Libra Scales, and leaves the Venus-ruled half of the team in a state of depression, a foreign feeling to this normally bright, optimistic, and cheerful Sun Sign. However, they'll agree in enough matters to make the relationship smooth more often than bumpy. Both of them share the same sense of outrage over injustice of any kind. Leo is warm and magnanimous; Libra is fair and impartial. When they combine these characteristics, few underdogs will be trampled, few "lost causes" will remain lost. Underdogs and lost causes have a strange appeal for them both, yet they're more practical than starry-eyed about their idealism, which is probably why they're so successful. If anyone can turn defeat into victory for an apparent loser, it's Leo and Libra. They're good people to have on your side when the chips are down. The Sun-ruled Leo will loyally defend you, the Venus-ruled Libran will pour such soothing balm on your wounds, they'll heal almost instantly.

It's as difficult for Leo to say "yes" as it is for Libra to say "no," which is one reason they get along so well. I'd better explain that.

The proud Leonine personality of either sex will normally say "NO!" instead of "yes" when ordered to do anything. Kings and Queens were born to give orders, not follow them. Libra possesses the instinct for knowing exactly how to handle Leo's ego, and can therefore turn a roar into a purr with the simple expedient of making it appear that an order is a request. It's called flattering. Librans seldom command. They flatter, cajole, and "suggest" so sweetly and pleasantly Leo never guesses he or she is being manipulated into the very action Libra wants. Oh, they are mellow, these Librans! Marvelously mellow.

Since Libra people abhor the tension caused by responding to the royal commands of a Leo with a flat "no," they'll give in with a melodious "yes" rather than create a quarrel (unless the issue is a burning one), which suits the Big Cats nicely. Just remember that the Venus trick of pretending not to be bossy when manipulating a situation, and the Venus pattern of responding with a cheerful "yes" more often than with an angry "no," as beautiful as these traits may be, will not prevent Libra from exercising his or her birthright to "discuss" it for a brief period before giving in. I trust you all understand by now that "discuss" is a polite Libra word for argue. But an argument needn't end up in a quarrel, right? This is just a nice, congenial exchange of ideas. Leo will be fooled by that subtle strategy more times than you might guess, very seldom realizing that he or she is being maneuvered into just what Libra wants by the technique of flattery and the Venus talent for psyching-out human nature.

There are times when Libra's continual optimism (Have a nice day!) disturbs other Sun Signs, but the Big Cats rather enjoy it. Both of these people reflect the vibrations of masculine, positive Day Forces, so you'll more often find them spreading light and sunshine than glooming around in the darkness. To some degree, every Lion or Lioness feels a desire to protect the weak and defenseless, and to some degree, every Libran possesses a compelling urge to see justice done. These closely allied purposes form the foundation for their *simpático* relationship. They also share a deep need for creative expression, preferably in the arts, but they can both be just as happily occupied running a hospital, a shoe store, or a home if a free flow of creativity is encouraged. Each of them is more content when running the show, however, which could cause some fleeting friction now and then. Libra likes to be in charge because Libra is a Cardinal Sign of leadership. Leo likes to be in charge because — well, how can a King or Queen *not* be in charge? Lions and Lionesses weren't born under a Cardinal Sun Sign, but they *were* born under a Fixed Sun Sign, and when you have a "Fixed egotist" it adds up to the same thing as a leader. Should any of these basic needs of Leo and Libra be denied, Leo can become a pouting or growling Cat, and Libra can become a cranky crocodile of confusion and frustration. Then their harmony may be interrupted, with Leo's normal beaming benevolence turning into arrogant demands, and Libra's gentle discussions quickly becoming quarrels.

Although there's always the chance that Leo's pride and vanity, combined with the strength and bossiness of the sign, may be too much for the softer, more gentle-mannered Venus-ruled Libran to handle, Leo's abundant ability to arouse the latent enthusiasm of others will usually more than balance the Scales in the association. Libra will have to remember to give the Leo man, woman, or child an adequate amount of respect and admiration. It's not an easy task. Still, Libra can call on all that Venus charm to accomplish it. No one can pay a compliment more sweetly than Libra, and no one can appreciate it with more outright glee than Leo.

These Libra persons adore anything beautiful; Leos prefer the biggest and best, so together they can be more than a little extravagant, unless one or both has the Moon in a stingier, more economical sign, like Taurus, Capricorn, Virgo, or Cancer. With both Moons in Air or Fire, like their Suns, these two can toss money around loosely, and lean toward luxuries. While they're tossing, they might have a few arguments about where to toss it.

Libra admires Leo's courage and willingness to move mountains, if necessary, and is sometimes tempted to build a few, just for the fun of watching the majestic Cat topple them. The mountains may be built of words, not rock, but it's a kind of game these two are tempted to play. They thoroughly enjoy challenging one another in a game of wits. One major difference between them should be noted. Leo's sense of humor often ends when the joke is on him (or her). Libra takes a more balanced view of being the target for fun.

There's no doubt that the Sun and Venus are galactically harmonious, so an association of any kind between the Big Cat and the Libran should brighten the skies above them. Almost all their qualities and character traits blend well. They're both artistic and sentimental. They both love compliments and excitement. Leo more or less demands happiness from Life and Love — Libra expects it as only natural. There is definitely a difference between "demanding" and "expecting." Not much, but a difference. If Leo roars too often, insisting on his or her right to take all the encores, Libra may eventually feel compelled to remind the Lion or Lioness that a rubber band stretches both ways, that what goes up must come down, that red lights and green lights are both needed to prevent traffic accidents, and — well, you know — all those Libra balancing acts of logic. Shockingly, Leo may actually listen meekly, apologize, and turn over a new leaf. No other Sun Sign can so smoothly lead the Big Cat into the ring to roll over and do somersaults.

The secret in animal training is in the eyes and the whip. Libra eyes are soft and friendly. Libra's whip is invisible, and when it strikes, it feels just like velvet. "Purr-rr-rr," goes the Pussycat. "You're so superior!" dimples Libra. And off they go, in their royal chariot. Where? Oh, I don't know. Somewhere Leo didn't want to go — to do something Leo had adamantly refused to do. Can you *believe* it? It's marvelous what wonders do manifest with a little gentle persuasion and a velvet, invisible whip.

☆ ☆ ☆ ☆ ☆ ☆

LEO *Woman* LIBRA *Man*

◆─◀◉▶─◆

So they were told they could dance, but they
must put on their nighties first.

It's true. This couple will find their relationship has a better chance to achieve permanency if they stay home together — not every night, mind you — but at least more often than they go out. As harmonious as their natures may be, too many parties can create the framework for anything from friction to fury. Most Libran males adore to attend any kind of festivity, from a sleigh ride to a clambake. This man is also drawn by intellectual soirees, like fund-raising meetings for the new school library, or campaign dinners for his favorite political candidate — particularly if *he* happens to be the political candidate.

The Lioness will seldom turn down a social invitation either. She loves nothing more than attention and excitement, in equal doses, so any large or even medium gathering of people delight her. It's a matter of numbers.

Simple numbers. The more guests, the more possible compliments. Every Libra male has a touch of the playboy in his nature, every Leo woman a touch of the playgirl. I said a "touch." Not that they don't have their serious moments too; each is capable of dedicated, hard work. But let's face it, neither was born to live forever in the wilderness, with only a wise owl for company.

I'm not saying they have to stay home and read Hobbit books every night. It's just that too many parties raise the risk of hearing the disharmonious chords of their Sun Sign symphony. What are the problems? Her jealousy — his appeal to women. Maybe I got that backwards. *First*, his appeal to women. *Then* her jealousy. After all, a Leo girl doesn't become jealous for no reason. There has to be a reason. This man will supply her with a number of them.

Something about him seems to make every woman feel like Cleopatra. It can't really be defined, except as a "charismatic ... *something*." (Most likely his ruling planet, Venus, is the culprit.) His mellow charm has this strange romantic effect on the feminine gender, even when all he's saying is "Would you pass the pickles, please?" If he should flash one dimpled smile per pickle, the pickle passer is soon palpitating with interest, and this is not the sort of scene designed to make his Lioness purr. It is the sort of scene which could cause her dainty little polished cat claws to appear — and scratch! Then too, there's the problem of the entourage of admiring men who gather around *her* when they go out together, a scene reminiscent of Scarlett O'Hara at the Wilkes barbecue. There's no denying she encourages them with her tawny looks and gracious manner, the beaming sunlight in her glances. Once more, jealousy is a danger. Not her Libra man's jealousy of her popularity — it's his *lack* of jealousy that bothers her.

You see, most Libra men believe it's *unfair* to be jealous. They look at both sides. What right does he have (he ponders) to criticize her for innocent flirting at parties, when all those pickle passers begin to preen their feathers as soon as he enters a room? This sort of well-meaning tolerance will not please his Leo woman, since she tends to be flattered by a little healthy jealousy. Any Fire Sign female can understand that. It proves he *cares*. When the only response she gets is — "You go right on and dance with that interesting ski champion, darling. I'm discussing Greek art with this lovely lady sculptor. I mean, she sculpts the human body in marble. Isn't that thrilling?" — the eyes of the Lioness will glitter a feral warning, her regal smile will turn feline icy ... and if he has any sensitivity (and wants to keep her), he won't waste any time cutting in on the next dance, and telling the skier to go buckle his boots. Of course, there are moments when the Libra man's Scales tip a little, and his normal, cheerful disposition is out of kilter. Then he even may be resentful enough of her attentions from other men to take a punch at one — but these occasions are the exception, not the rule.

Fortunately, this man has the cure for any minor troubles caused by their socializing. His talent as a peacemaker is unsurpassed, even when the fight he's meditating is his own, with his mate. Somehow, someway, he'll think of something touching or sentimental to say, something passionate or delightfully mad and marvelous to do. He'll do it so gracefully, murmur it so melodiously, the injured Lioness will forget her wounds and melt .. right into his arms again. And love wins another victory. Actually, we might have predicted it, right along. This is a 2-12 Sun Sign Pattern, with a scattering of chances for quarreling, but many more opportunities for making up.

Public figures often demonstrate Sun Sign compatibility lessons quite clearly, when we pay close attention. Since this is being written in the Year of Our Lord 1978, we can use President Jimmy Carter and his wife, Rosalynn, as examples. He was born a Sun Sign Libran, she a Leo. On the one hand, Jimmy Carter believes adultery is wrong, a definite no-no for a good husband (or a wife, we trust). His genuine love for his Lioness is unmistakable. He is devoted to her, still romantically in love with her. On the other hand, he feels he has no right to judge those who *do* commit adultery, since he has himself, he says (struggling desperately to be fair) — "lusted in his heart for other women."

On one side of the picture, he sympathizes sincerely with ERA's goals, stating in July of 1976: "*I will continue to oppose any constitutional amendment to overturn the Supreme Court decisions on abortion.*" On the other hand, he stated publicly, a few months later — "*I never said I would actively oppose every possible constitutional amendment that was proposed on the subject of abortion.*" Just trying to be fair, and see both sides! Gloria Steinem gritted her teeth, and Rosalynn Carter may have chastised him royally, in the privacy of the White House jungle pride. With Libra positive cheerfulness and total (and I do mean *total*) optimism, when asked if he and his Lioness wife, Rosalynn, have ever had any quarrels, arguments, or even disagreements, his blithe answer to the press was: "*Never. Absolutely never. We have such a perfect marriage, it's difficult to even imagine anything negative ever occurring.*" My-oh-my-oh-my! Such perfection, such beautiful balancing of the Venus Scales, such a typically Libran rosy-whipped-cream-viewpoint. (Such a little white lie.)

Just as her husband is a typical Scale balancer, Ms. Carter is a typical independent Leo woman, smiling into the cameras, along with the other twentieth-century Carrie Nations at the world's first Feminist Congress in Texas, like any proud Lioness who wants to be recognized as something more than her husband's shadow. During the widespread gossip over her Libra mate's "lusting in his heart" remarks, while he was struggling to be fair and nonjudgmental, she maintained a majestic, aloof silence. No press person dared ask this proud Queen what she thought of her Libra husband's views on the subject of "lusting" (though they wouldn't have hesitated to ask forthright, "good sport" Sag Betty Ford the same kind of question). Neither Lioness Rosalynn Carter nor Lioness Jacqueline Kennedy Onassis will ever be found airing their personal feelings or private lives before the masses. Royalty simply doesn't do that. One's subjects may babble all they like, but one does not dignify rumors by either confirming or denying them. It's totally plebean. Let the peasants whisper. Monarchy doesn't involve itself in that sort of sordid thing.

A Libra man doesn't have to be President of the United States to get into hot water with the Leo woman he loves. Her views are somewhat less catholic, also less indecisive, than his. She knows what she believes, has no problem clearly defining her opinions, and can become annoyed when her Libra lover tries to make her see that all things are, after all, in the end — equal. The peasants equal to those who lovingly dictate to and care for them ? Equal to their *rulers* ? What nonsense ! This attitude is a classic non sequitur to her women's lib stand, but perhaps best not to remind her.

The Libra man is likely to bring his Leo woman occasional gifts, which make her feel snugly cherished, contentedly adored. This is truly important to a Lioness, whether she's an opera star at the Met or a mule trainer high up in the Peruvian Andes. She likes presents. Making his woman feel treasured is a talent the Libra male possesses in great, affectionate bundles (unless he has a Virgo or Capricorn Ascendent or Moon Sign). That's why the physical chemistry between them can range from considerably more than satisfactory to intoxicating exhilaration. When she feels wholly desired and cherished, she's capable of some very jungle-musty-lusty passion, and a Libra male is delighted by a woman who loves making love.

This Venus-ruled man knows that the way to release her rich emotions is to at least promise to give her the Moon and the stars. (The Sun she doesn't need, it's already her own, by birthright.) She'll drop her aloof manner more easily with him than with most men; therefore their sexual interreactions will ultimately bring them a warm and wonderful closeness. Even their arguments add glamour to their lovemaking. He can apologize for offending her like a charmingly contrite Lord Essex — and she can forgive him with the benevolent grace of a Queen Elizabeth, whose lover has transgressed against her royal dignity. But he musn't allow his thoughts to absentmindedly wander on the wind while he's loving her, or be guilty of that far-away look in his eye Air Signs often get in the midst of passion — at some trembling moment when she needs to know his mind is intently centered on her — and only her. He may be frozen by her unexpected, angry command to sleep with his far-away thoughts permanently, while she sleeps alone. She won't play second fiddle — or even second flute — to his daydreams. Especially not to his night dreams. Nor to his career. She is Number One. It would behoove him to remember this. She's sure to interrupt every dreamy, absentminded look she notices fleeting across the features of this airy-natured man with a command. "Tell me what you're thinking about. Right now." (You've heard about curiosity and the cat ? Don't forget, she's the Big Cat.)

"You know perfectly well what I was thinking about, sweetheart."

"No. I don't know. Tell me."

"I was thinking about a fine spring day I thought was going to be like any other day. Then I saw you for the first time, and the Sun was brighter than I had ever seen it before."

She frowns. "It was January. It wasn't spring when we first met. There was a blizzard." (He's in real trouble now.)

"Well, spring was just around the corner. I could smell it in the air. You made it *seem* like spring, so that's how I remember it. Sometimes I think you could make hyacinths bloom in the snow. You make them grow in my heart when it's winter *there*." (He turns on the dimples.)

She smiles, sighs . . . and stretches, sensuously . . . purring like a kitten. His Libra charm has triumphed again. But he'll have to mind his p's and q's with her. Those letters could stand for Pouting and Quarrels — if he doesn't remember that they also stand for Proud Queen.

☆ ☆ ☆ ☆ ☆ ☆

LEO *Man* LIBRA *Woman*

—◄◆►—

"How sweet!" cried Wendy.
"Yes, I'm sweet, oh, I am sweet!" said Peter,
forgetting his manners again.

She can pay compliments so beautifully, you can almost imagine harp music in the background. She can also be bossy and domineering, in a graceful, gracious kind of way. But bossy is bossy, and domineering is domineering, sugarcoated or not. The Lion will lap up her compliments as a cat laps up cream, but he'll shake his mane and toss her an injured look if she gets too heavy-handed with her manipulative Venusian subtleties. Translated, this means trying to run his life, telling him she knows what's best for him, and trying to make him see things the logical and fair way — which often means *her* way.

He likes things *his* way. What other way *is* there? Well, granted, there may be other ways, but his is obviously the only sensible and correct way. He will try to teach her this, tenderly at first—then firmly. She will pretend to learn, but beneath her demure demeanor she'll never give in and admit he knows everything, because she'll always be convinced she knows what's proper at least *half* of the time. She's Cardinal Air, he's Fixed Fire. And so, the decision of who rides the lead horse in the parade will be a constant draw. The least she can do, he pouts, is allow him to be drum major, since the drumbeat sets the pace of the parade. If he doesn't retain an outward semblance of authority, the Leo male will sulk in the corner and refuse to march. He won't even carry the banner she painted so nicely for him, bearing the words: LOVE IS COMPROMISE. He's not buying any of that Libra Lib lingo.

A Libra girl usually comes on gently, with a penuche fudge voice, starlit smiles, a hint of autumn's golden-scarlet hues in her aura. She makes you think of football games, soft cashmere sweaters, toasting marshmallows in an open fire, walking through burnished leaves, Indian summer . . sunset . . the smoky season. She makes you think of . . well . . television newscasts. (You didn't know Barbara Walters is a Libra? Now you know.) Look and listen. Weaving through the smoky haze is a "take-charge" air that's unmistakable. Perhaps not unmistakable to the Lion. He may miss it, however, at *first*. He may miss it for some time, in fact. Leo males are so easily smitten by beauty, and what with hearing all those harp chords every time she smiles, who notices the background static? It takes another woman to sense what's behind the Libra girl's Velveeta-cheese manner. Women are more sensitive about such things. An Aries woman can sense it right way. That's because (a) the girl Ram is a little bossy herself, and it takes one to know one, and (b) the Sun Signs of Libra and Aries are opposed or opposite each other on the astrological wheel of Karma.

While one is strongly attracted by the opposite sex of one's opposite Sun Sign, one is acutely alert to warning nuances in the same sex of one's opposite sign. Study that, please. It's fraught with ancient truth. It's why the Libra woman we're discussing probably once imagined herself to be in love with an Aries male (however far back in her past) and usually (not always, but usually) keeps her distance from Aries females—for *more* than just the reason that they are harmoniously trine to her Lion's aura. It's why the Leo man may have once thought he loved an Aquarian girl (however far back in his past) but usually keeps his distance from Aquarian males—for *more* than just the reason that they are harmoniously trine to his Libra woman's aura. If one's own *Moon* was in the sign opposite one's own *Sun* Sign in one's own horoscope at birth, all these "opposition" rules are canceled. Well, perhaps not canceled, but modified—some increasing in meaning, some diluted or negated, depending. Astrology can be tricky if you try to speed-read the planets. But if you take your time, you won't fail to be graced with wisdom and insight.

The Libra woman receives her charm, her dimples, her honeyed voice, curvy figure, and general beauty (also her appealing manners) from her Venus rulership. Her masculine Sun Sign is responsible for her lingering air of feminine macha. (Yes, Virginia, there is such a thing as feminine macha. Lucy has it. Ask Charlie Brown.) Her symbol of the Scales gives the Libra girl her indecision traumas and torments. (It may not torment her, but it traumatizes everyone around her when she's deliberating one of her dual decisions.)

The Leo man's Sun rulership is the source of both his pride and his passion, along with his generosity, warmth, and benevolence. The Sun is the most powerful astral influence in the system which is named after it, the *Solar* system. From his masculine Sun Sign he receives his courage, his own male macho. His symbol of the Lion is responsible for his sensuality and his sense of superiority, also his regal arrogance. It's what causes his weakness for wallowing in the catnip of compliments. But it makes him a sensational lover. Venus does the same thing for her. They're both enormously affectionate and demonstrative of their feelings with one another.

In today's emancipated society especially, if Leo and Libra marry, they're both likely to work (even Libra wives in the Victorian Age managed to find something to manage outside their homes, husbands, and children). Whether the occupations that draw them are the law or architecture, the theatre, publishing, or commerce, they'll both aim toward either independence or some sort of authority over others, the former being preferable. She'll be miserable and unfulfilled if she's forced to spend too many months as a temporary typist in a pool, or an assistant anything, though she'll try cheerfully to make the best of it — and he'll never be content to lead guided tours through Disneyland. *Creating* a Disneyland, *that's* his kind of challenge, not walking people through another man's dream. A Lion who isn't either boss of himself or boss over others at work will sometimes excessively assert his superiority at home, over his woman. Who else can he rule ? It will seem to her less arrogant of him, if she analyzes the cause. It won't hurt to allow him to be King for a Day now and then, in his own lair. But she should never let him suspect that her meekness and mildness is deliberate medicine for his bruised sense of importance.

There shouldn't be any really serious financial fusses between these two. Basically, they both look at money in pretty much the same way. It buys the beauty and comfort they both like and need. He may be a trifle stingier than she is — not with their money, with *her*. There are Leonine laws of the jungle to be memorized pertaining to shopping and making purchases. It works like this: If it's something *she* wants, it's an unnecessary extravagance. "We don't *need* a pair of antique brass candlesticks, dear. Besides, they're overpriced."

If it's something *he* wants, regardless of its cost, it's "practical," and it will, of course, "save money in the long run" — like a tricolor, flashing light to snap on his ankle when he's jogging at night, a slightly used Rolls Royce, or a new movie projector, plus a new wood-paneled viewing room for home screening of great film hits. You know? Another woman might be frustrated to the point of tears of anger over such consistently (shall we say selfish? Yes. Let us say selfish)... over such consistently selfish behavior. The Libra woman will explode when her Scales happen to be out of kilter, on an occasional Thursday, but normally she'll just smile brightly, cheerfully agree with him, and keep the peace. "You're absolutely right, sweetheart." Later, she'll return to the store alone and buy the brass candlesticks. He won't find out about them right away. It will be an enchanted evening when some people they're entertaining (preferably someone important) enthusiastically admire the way they gleam in the candlelight. *Then* he'll notice. (She brought them out for this special occasion from their hiding place in the laundry room.) He'll beam, as he remarks, "Her exquisite taste is only one of the reasons I fell in love with her." She smiles one of her melted-butter, dimpled smiles at him. He sighs. Camera fade-out.

This is but another of the many examples I keep giving you in this book of a Libra woman's "iron fist in a velvet glove." Aside from skirmishes over who's going to be first on the escalator and things like that, she's a fine, intelligent companion for the Lion, and her gracious talent for harmony is her most important attribute as his lady. She somehow knows exactly how to smooth his troubled brow. This is an enormously poised woman, unless she's upset, then she can be totally unreasonable. Nevertheless, she's well suited to marriage. Librans so much need to be married, they often rush into wedlock with the wrong mates. But practice makes perfect.

A Libra woman needs lots of romance in her lovemaking, despite her feminine macha, and the Lion can provide it, if he will. Leos are very Valentinoish. His languid sensuality answers her need for voluptuous passion through the eternal cosmic compatibility of the Sun and Venus. She's an intuitive, responsive mate for the impulsive Lion, who can anticipate his fiery desires. She can also fulfill them. When two people love, the same character quirks which cause trouble in other areas of their relationship carry over into their sexual life, although they may be more disguised, abstract. Remember the law of the jungle regarding purchases? Very subtly, it's also there in their lovemaking. When she needs *him*, on a night when he's particularly tired, physically, she's being sexually demanding and not considerate of his rest. When he needs *her*, on a night when *she's* particularly weary, it's a normal and healthy demonstration of their love which will make both of them sleep better, and feel more rested in the morning. Other than this, however, their sexual chemistry is nicely balanced, and their mating can be a mellow experience for both of them.

Leo men are always more faithful, genial, and relaxed after marriage than before. They need a castle, someone to protect, and the steadfastness of having someone who loves them waiting there every night. Libra girls are magnetized irresistibly toward the mutuality of partnership, and so marriage is good for these two lovers. Very good. Things won't be dull, and that's always a plus. It keeps love exciting. There are times when she'll accept all sorts of nonsense with beautiful calm. Other times she'll fly into a rage or dip into an argumentative mood for the slightest reason. Her emotional balance is upset, maybe because she wishes her hair could be darker (or lighter), the leg on the coffee table is crooked, and he didn't fix it, the color of the bedspread makes her nervous . . . or a chip in her cut-glass pitcher may be the catalyst for her contrariness. Never mind. He'll affectionately cuddle her out of it, in his warm, cozy, Leonine way . . until she's smiling her brilliant smile, and they'll return to being as happy as fools again. (Fools are always happier than the rest of us.)

A man and woman in love become romantically apathetic with only the sexual mating game to interest them. These two will never feel apathy toward one another. There'll always be something to talk about. She will, of course, be properly and charmingly grateful for the wisdom she receives from her Lion, and she'll make him aware of this. On the other hand, though she'll spend her whole life educating *him*, the beauty of it is that he'll probably never know when she's doing it. It's no good for a man to know how much he needs to learn from his woman — especially a King.

LEO

Fire — Fixed — Positive
Ruled by the Sun
Symbols: Lion & Shy Pussycat
Day Forces — Masculine

SCORPIO

Water — Fixed — Negative
Ruled by Pluto
Symbols: Scorpion & Eagle
Night Forces — Feminine

The **LEO- SCORPIO** *Relationship*

"Proud and insolent youth," said Hook, "prepare to meet thy doom."

"Dark and sinister man," Peter answered, "have at thee!"

*L*et's begin on a positive note. One thing Leo and Scorpio share is an honest respect for one another. As mentioned before all Fire Signs, (and Leos are no exception to the rule) instinctively comprehend that their bright enthusiasms can be drowned in Scorpio's watery depths — just as all Water Signs, like Scorpio, intuitively realize that if Leo's fires are allowed to blaze uncontrolled, they can come dangerously close to dehydrating their sensitivity, causing them to nearly disappear — if not entirely. A Scorpio will crawl away in the dark of night, rather than face final dehydration from a Leo mate, relative, or friend. Scorps are self-protective. Very.

Both Sun Signs are Fixed in nature, and have a secret desire to dominate. Well, at least with Scorpio it's a secret desire; with the Lion, it's more or less obvious — unless the latter is a Leo who is submerging the natural Leonine ego, a very unhealthy thing to do. To casual observers of this pair it appears that Leo must eventually win control, the Lion or Lioness being so transparent about his or her goal as ruler of the relationship. But not all casual observers are astrologers. If they were, they'd take care not to underestimate Scorpio's subtle, long-range strategies, the power gained by keeping motives hidden, the effectiveness of a surprise attack when it's least expected. Careful calculation is advised before predicting the outcome of an association between these two astrological creatures — in the office, the family circle, or the marital scene.

The Scorpion is sensitive, and so will sense instinctively when Leo's pride is injured, then be enormously comforting and protective . . . when an outsider has done the hurting. When the wounds have been inflicted by the Scorpio himself (or herself), however, Leo may feel that Attila the Hun would have more compassion. It's not anyone's fault but yours, Leo. Over and over again I've warned you that Scorpios mean business when they're miffed. They'll sting in retaliation. When Scorpio is mad, Scorpio is mad, and there's no use trying to coax them out of it. Going away until it blows over won't help either. The anger will still be there when you return. Since Scorpions are not the overlooking kind, the only safe way to handle one and not get stung is to be careful not to push the Pluto-ruled person too far or too often.

Unfortunately, Leo will seldom accept such advice. Treading carefully around Scorpions is for the cowardly. The proud and dauntless Leonine character scorns such caution, so Leo often pulls out all the stops, and the devil-take-the-hindmost. A friendly suggestion: Watch it. The devil just may do that.

Strangely, the relationship between children and adults, whether related or not, in this particular 4-10 Pattern, is frequently very close, even touching. There is something hauntingly paternal or maternal in the attitude of the older Leo or Scorpio to the younger Scorpio or Leo. It's a joy to behold, delightful to experience. Perhaps this is because the younger Leo has not yet had time to acquire such fierce pride, therefore will not resent an older Scorpion's intense protective gestures. And it may be that the younger Eagles have not yet developed the full Pluto retaliatory nature, therefore can accept the Leo's dramatics more good-naturedly. The older these two become, however, the more effort they'll have to exert to achieve harmony. I know a young Scorpio boy who formed a deep attachment for an older Leo man. The latter was like a big brother to the youngster, whose own Aquarian big brother was, at the time, weathering the storms of adolescence, and therefore behaving with detachment toward him.

When a Scorpio finds something or someone worthy of respect, no one can be more respectful than a young Eagle, and Mike, the Scorpio boy, found much to respect in his older Leo companion. Bob, the Lion, patiently and lovingly taught the boy how to catch a lizard with a string, then let it go free near a fish pond, how to fly a kite and make it soar among the clouds like . . well . . . like an eagle! He told him Hobbit stories, complete with sound effects, answered his questions, with great seriousness, about how the handle of a car door works, and even sternly advised the boy's mother that the youngster was not a slave just because he was younger in years than she, that he deserved to be treated with respect, and to be asked — not be rudely ordered — to run errands for her. All this slowly but surely imbedded itself into the Pluto subconscious. Then came the day when they were standing together on a rock at the edge of the ocean in Pismo Beach, California, and a huge wave appeared suddenly, completely engulfing them. If the Lion had not held tightly to the boy, he would have been washed away out to sea, and the child couldn't swim. That sealed the relationship. The boy firmly believed his Leo friend had saved his life, and he was ready to worship him forever after. (Leos can stand a lot of that!)

Later, the Lion, through no fault of his own, had to go away. His absence dragged on for nearly seven years. The Scorpio boy was leaving his childhood behind with each passing year — yet, not once, in all that time, did he waver in his intense loyalty to the far-away Lion. Although there had been no communication of any kind between them, he would listen to no negative word against his friend. He *knew* he had good reason to go away, just as he *knew* he would return. And one day . . he did. Scorpio is seldom wrong in judging character.

I also know a small Scorpio girl in Falls Village, Connecticut, who feels the same way about her real-life, blood-brother Lion, and showers him with absolute adoration. The Big Cat loves it, of course, and the devotion is mutual. It's the same thing when Leo is the youngster, Scorpio the older one. Both Sun Signs instinctively protect the weaker. Between the Sun-ruled and the Pluto-ruled, it's an "all or nothing-at-all relationship." Neither the Eagle nor the Lion or Lioness can handle caring casually. They will be passionately attached — or ignore one another. No middle ground for these two, whatever the association.

In the less fortunate Leo-Scorpio combinations, the initial attraction may last more briefly than both believed it would when it began. It won't take long for disenchantment to set in if one of them has an incompatible Moon Sign, for Scorpio's attitude of "I'm always right," even though unspoken, will first frustrate, then annoy Leo. Superiority needn't be verbalized by Scorp. A long, hard stare of cool confidence can project the message quite clearly. The Leonine resentment then may seem unjust, since Leo is an equally recognized expert in the conviction of his or her privilege of infallibility — of being always right, while everyone else is always wrong. (Yet, somehow, the Lion or Lioness is never quite as *certain* of this as a Scorpion.) The smug "I'm superior" attitudes of these two are so similar, you'd think they'd be more tolerant of one another's egos, but it doesn't always work that way. In a human relationship, there's room for only one person to be *always* right the way Leo and Scorpio are always right (they think).

The Fixity of both signs doesn't help matters. Fixity is another word for stubbornness, a little milder in meaning perhaps, nevertheless making it difficult to swerve or sway either Leo or Scorpio from a set position or opinion. Try it, when you have lots of time to spare. You'll soon understand what astrology means by a Fixed Sign. (Leo, Scorpio, Taurus, and Aquarius are the Fixed Signs.)

Scorpio may remain quiet during a Leonine monologue, but don't be fooled. No Scorp is going to accept opinions from a Leo without being totally convinced of their validity. The Scorpio will either object outright with a blunt refusal to accept the Leonine views being arrogantly pressed upon him — or her — or find a way to avoid the whole issue. Sneaky. That's the word for it. At least that's the word Leo would choose to describe the way Scorpio slides, crawls, and slithers away from obeying his or her Majesty's commands. There's nothing sneaky about Leo; even Scorpio will admit that. What these Kings and Queens desire and demand is made clear to all the peasants. No, Leos are not sneaky — just a little bossy. And spoiled. And accustomed to getting their own way since they were cubs. Yet they're so warm and sunny, so generous and friendly, despite those commanding airs, that even the normally perceptive Scorpion may not immediately sense the danger of dehydration — or worse. Likewise, Scorps are so gifted with the subtle talent of appearing to give in without actually giving an inch that it may be a while until Leo recognizes the situation as another Waterloo.

When a Leo is injured, he or she will either pout or roar. The latter behavior will disturb Scorpio's sensitive psyche the first few times, causing an apparent retreat — but if either the pouting or roaring is repeated with unnecessary frequency, eventually all Leo will get for such dramatics from the Scorp is that frustrating, long, hard, cold Pluto stare. Being stared down by a Scorpion is about as pleasant as making mudpies in a sandbox full of black widow spiders. It does absolutely nothing for the Leonine sense of self-importance.

If these two play down the personal element, and keep their mutual endeavors centered on abstract goals outside themselves, they can operate as a smooth unit, a formidable threat to outsiders who try to conquer them by smothering Leo's fire or making waves in Scorpio's water.

But if Leo's impulsive ideals and generous spirit are watered down so often that those splendid Leonine dreams are dampened to the point of crumbling, the Scorpio will be banished from the Kingdom — or the Leo will leave himself (or herself) and move to another castle where one can expect to receive the proper respect for royalty. It would also behoove Leo to curb that bossy attitude with Scorpio. From no other Sun Sign will the Lion or Lioness receive such *depth* of loyalty and devotion. It must be earned. Still, it's well worth swallowing a few lumps of pride now and then to be worshiped with the kind of intensity only Pluto can give.

☆ ☆ ☆ ☆ ☆ ☆

LEO *Woman* SCORPIO *Man*

◆─◆◀█▶▶─◆

*Which of these adventures shall we choose? The best way will be to
toss for it.*

*I have tossed, and the lagoon has won. This almost makes one wish
that the gulch or the cake or Tink's leaf had won. Of course, I could
do it again, and make it best out of three; however, perhaps fairest
to stick to the lagoon.*

The deep lagoon of a Scorpio man's inner nature will inevitably win out and
dampen the flaming defense of the Lioness in any serious conflict between
them. He's a Water Sign, and water is the strongest of all the elements. Fire
consumes, and what is left to conquer after the opposition has been consumed? But water just drips away, drop after drop, penetrating the surface
of even rock and granite, in the precise pattern water chooses. Even a
boulder tossed into a stream won't change the stream's course. But toss a
blazing torch into the ocean, and how long do the flames last?

Of course, the size of the body of water can change the outcome. A huge
bonfire will cause only a few drops of water to sizzle, then disappear. But
most Leo women and Scorpio men are more evenly matched, and in the more
common associations between the Leo and Scorpio whose individual vibes are
balanced, the lagoon (water) will conquer. Scorpio possesses a great deal
more soul experience than Leo, being ahead of Leo on the horoscopic wheel.
It's handy to know this when you start out. It can become complex though,
since one never knows for sure which of the two Sun Signs is ahead of the
other on the *number of trips around the wheel.* However, you can be sure
that even a Lioness on her millionth time around the circle has been placed,
by her own Higher Self, within the Sun Sign vibration of Leo in a certain
incarnation because the lessons of the seven signs ahead have not all been
completely mastered yet. Since Scorpio is astrally ahead — even if only
experiencing his thousandth trip around, comparatively — in this special
relationship, within this particular existence, he is karmically destined to
teach her a few things she needs to learn, whether she likes it or not . . and she
won't be wild about it, I can assure you. The same thing is true when the
sexes are reversed to the Leo man and Scorpio woman. Leo can't fight this
predestined, starry Kismet and win, so it's wiser to relax and accept it.

The outward manner of the Leo girl may be warm, generous, gregarious,
and friendly. But that doesn't mean she'll be overjoyed to discover herself
being dissected like a butterfly beneath the incredibly deep, steady gaze of a

Scorpion who's trying to probe the very depths of her mind, heart, and soul, let alone her body. If his eyes become too intimate too soon, even though she's magnetically drawn to him, she'll not hesitate to turn his Water Element into ice with her frozen, royal dignity. The Lioness dislikes familiarity from strangers, so wait until you know her better before you stare her into a Pluto trance. One doesn't stare at a Queen. It can get you banished from the ball with a contemptuous, regal wave of her hand.

Their first clash may be over money. She likes to spend it, even though she can be surprisingly practical about how and where she distributes it, going overboard only infrequently in binges of glamourous extravagance. He can be touchingly generous too, on occasion, but he'll frown on her attempts to control *his* spending. At the same time, he'll have no qualms about controlling *her* spending, a contradiction of character which is more than a mite selfish, and unfortunately shared by both of them, by turns. It's an unusual Lioness who will submit to that sort of arrangement without periodic roars of feminine outrage. A mutual budget almost always spells trouble for these two. She'll spend freely, yet become petulant or openly hostile when he complains that all the cash is used up for the month. A Scorpio man will take this situation for an extremely limited length of time. Then he'll retreat into threatening silences and stony stares, hardly an ideal atmosphere in which love can be expected to flourish.

Harmony can be established by a decision to have separate bank accounts, with no questions asked and no accounting demanded regarding who spent how much for what, even if her checking account is possible only through the gift of a portion of his earnings. That will seldom be necessary however, since the typical Leo woman will already have saved some money when she first meets her Eagle and falls in love with him. Ninety-five percent of all Lionesses are career girls. She may enjoy drenching herself in domesticity for a while after she's contentedly mated with a man she adores, but it won't be long until she feels a strong urge to spread her sunbeams, and begins to long for an interest outside the home to increase her sense of self-importance.

The only time a Leo woman is truly happy running a household is when the household is the White House, a towering castle on a windswept hill, or the vast empire of, say, a Greek shipping magnate . . as observe Jacqueline Kennedy Onassis, née Bouvier. Jackie hardly needed to go to work for financial security when she became, very sadly, a widow for the second time. But her astrologically royal blood demanded that she prove to the world, after there was no longer a household over which to preside, that she had a genuine worth as a human being, so off she loped to an office, a desk, and a literary career . . from which we haven't heard the last.

The sexual adjustment between a Lioness and an Eagle could be delicate. His intense and somewhat mystical lovemaking will delight the romantic in her at first . . . . . . but as time goes on, she'll need more spoken declarations of affection, richer, more imaginative and tangible demonstrations of his devotion. He'll find her strange blend of aloofness and fire irresistibly exciting, and will seldom tire of the eternal challenge of conquest she represents. But if he's rebuffed too often by her icy dignity, he'll lose that animal magnetism that made her swoon in the beginning; perhaps even punish her by falling asleep while she's lying there beside him feeling all empty and alone. Using the denial of sexual fulfillment as a method of revenge is one of Scorpio's most unkind retaliatory defenses when he's been injured, even when he uses this strategy unconsciously.

If this man and this woman really try, despite the obstacle of their squared 4-10 Sun Sign Pattern, they can create a beautiful scene together. They have a lot going against them from the beginning, yet they do have their mutual free will going *for* them. Imagine a calm, clear lake in the moonlight, a thousand bright flames adrift on its surface shooting sparks of brilliant color toward the velvet midnight sky. How do the flames remain on the water without being extinguished? By being ignited on top of floating logs which support them. To the Leo Fire Sign and Scorpio Water Sign, those floating logs can symbolize a mutual goal.

Once the Eagle and his Lioness have found that mutual goal (or career), one that fits both their dreams, and pursue it together, they can perform the alchemy magic of combining passion and power to turn misery into miracles. His passion — her power. Or her passion — his power. It doesn't matter, for they each possess both.

Their heartaches will come when he sails off to some exciting adventure without her, leaving her sitting there, lonesome, at the ironing board — or conversely, when she goes dancing off impulsively in the August Sun, leaving him to celebrate Thanksgiving all by himself during a cold November. A deep insecurity lies buried beneath the Leo woman's bright, brave personality. She can become as bitter and restless as a caged Lioness in a zoo if her mate denies her the right to be an individual. As for him, the Scorpion's intense need for her brightness to light up his life can cause some violent spells of his Pluto jealousy and possessiveness. He'll have to realize that this woman simply *must* now and then bask in the spotlight of admiration — or almost literally pine away. If her adoring friends are sometimes men, it doesn't have to mean she's being promiscuous, just exercising her royal right to be worshiped. The possessive Eagle cannot bear to see other men paying court to his woman, but this is what he can expect if he leaves her alone. The Lioness will never be content to sit by the fire, crocheting socks for her mate, polishing his passions at night, and sprinkling powder on his power complex each morning before he swims off into the beckoning world out there in the mist. And so, unless they do things together, the path of these two lovers can sometimes be rocky. But . . do you know what you do with rocks? Remove them. Just lift them, and toss them over the bank.

If she can learn to appreciate the emotional security and exceptional devotion he offers her — and he can learn to truly value her warm, generous, and sunny spirit, they can transmute the astrological square of tension and conflict between their natal Suns into the square's equally powerful energy, to create an amazingly strong tie that binds. For love, like a ship, is always safer and stronger after it's been proven seaworthy.

Despite her flirtatious ways as a young girl, the Lioness will be loyal and faithful to her mate, once she's been tamed — if the hand of the tamer is gentle, not too strict. And despite his reputation, among the astrologically uninformed, for an obsession with sex, the Scorpio man's inner and actual compulsion is to explore its mysteries, then raise it to the purity of a spiritual experience. If this man and woman would gaze deeply into each other's eyes, directly into their own true natures, they would see there's no need for jealousy or competition between them.

The attempt to cement a relationship with children often fails with other couples. But with Leo and Scorpio, Destiny has mysteriously decreed that if need and desire are intense enough — "*a child shall lead the way to Oneness.*"

☆ ☆ ☆ ☆ ☆ ☆

LEO *Man* SCORPIO *Woman*

———— ◆◆●▶◆ ————

"Ought I ?" Wendy said, all shining. "Of course it's frightfully fascinating, but you see I am only a little girl. I have no real experience."

"That doesn't matter," said Peter, as if he were the only person present who knew all about it, though he was really the one who knew least.

She's lying, as Scorpios sometimes do, in a desperate attempt to hide their innermost feelings. No real experience? She has the experience of eons of incarnations in Pluto wisdom. Ignore her deliberate put-down of herself.

Oddly enough, it's his ego. No. Ego is perhaps not the right word for it. It is his self-confidence, so easily and casually displayed, which first causes the Scorpio girl to become enchanted by the charismatic Lion. She possesses self-confidence too (actually, bushels more than he does), but she's unable to project her confidence with such confidence. I know that sounds confusing, but read it again and you'll see the sense of it. And so, the Scorpio female finds much to admire in Leo, even to respect. Unlike herself, he has discovered a way to let the world know how sure of himself he is inside — even when he's not so sure. Her confidence in her own inner knowing, of which *she* is *always* sure, often seems to her as though it would remain locked up within herself forever. Perhaps he has the key . . . and if he does . . . what joyous freedom he might grant her !

He is attracted to her for nearly identical reasons. She's usually unaware of the cool poise and inner wisdom she projects to others with just a deep, deep look. Most recipients of her gaze simply cringe and look away immediately, to avoid — they're not quite sure just what — they're only positive they want to avoid it. Not so the brave, stalwart Lion. Her gaze fascinates him. Sometimes he feels he's drowning in the cool, placid waters of her eyes, sometimes he feels he's learning mystical secrets by an unspoken transfer of knowledge. At other times he feels dangerously close to being swept into the storm of the churning, lashing waves behind her Scorpio stare, and to a Leo that's not spooky or Halloween-scary — it's downright exciting.

She envies him his ability to spread such warmth. Being a Water Sign herself, no matter how much she may desire otherwise, the warmth she feels translates itself into some degree of detached coolness, even with those she loves the most. But a Leo male is ruled by the fiery Sun, even when he's angry or pouting. It's impossible to be near a Lion and not feel the heat from the Sun's rays penetrating your entire being. Like basking in front of a cozy hearth, when he's happy — like warming yourself before glowing coals, when he's feeling nothing much at all — or like the thrill of watching a huge forest fire, when he's aroused. If only she could spend her own, far more deeply felt emotions with such lavish unconcern. She keeps trying unsuccessfully to display her feelings more openly — then here comes this dashing man who can demonstrate his pride and prejudices with so little effort, so gracefully. He even walks gracefully, like a Big Cat stalking through the jungle, an unmistakably regal dignity to his stride. No wonder she falls passionately in love with him. No wonder she adores him. And no wonder the Leo male is magnetized by the Scorpio girl. There's nothing on this Earth he enjoys more than being adored. Unless it's being worshiped. When the snake stealthily enters their fresh, green Eden, they're both surprised, hurt, and disappointed. What could have happened ? So many things are still right . . . . what could possibly have gone wrong ?

It's not difficult to identify the problems. Recently, in Cripple Creek, Colorado, I was visiting two good friends who own the Gasthof Restaurant there — Carroll (he's a Leo) and his wife, Barbara (she's a Scorp, short for Scorpio). Just for fun, but with a method to my madness, I suggested they play an astrological telegram game with me. (I made notes.) "Can you sum up," I asked the Scorp, "all the things you most object to in Carroll, all the things that annoy you the most and cause the most tension in your relationship with him — in just one word?"

She thought momentarily, then flashed her Leo mate one of those cold, hard stares, as she announced clearly and emphatically: "*Arrogance.*" (The two of them had been having some minor difficulties for the past few days, in the manner of all couples, from time to time.) Not relishing the risk of being in the middle of a Fire-Water conflict, I tried not to look closely at the Lion's expression while I asked him, as cheerfully as I could, the same question. "How would you sum up in only one word your objections to Barbara's habits and character, Carroll?"

Without an instant's hesitation he frowned at her and growled angrily, "*Silence.*"

"Perfect!" I exclaimed. "Just perfect!" They turned to me in puzzlement. Then I hastened to explain, "I mean, your one-word answers were a perfect example of the disharmony between Leo and Scorpio.. that is, between *all* Leos and *all* Scorpios," I hastily amended. Then I asked Carroll, the Lion, my second question. "Now, can you sum up for me the quality in Barbara that attracts you the most, what it is in her you most admire and love — in one word?"

His trembling, thinly controlled anger suddenly melted, as ice melts on a sunny day at high noon, and he glanced at her with genuine tenderness, while he said softly — something rather wonderful.

"I guess that one word would be... devotion." He paused, then continued with an impulsive rush of feeling. "When I was in the hospital last month, in such pain from my broken leg, lying there in a cast from my toes to my hip, and groggy from sedatives, every time I opened my eyes, she was there. Just sitting there, in case there was anything I needed. It's a long trip from Cripple Creek to the St. Francis Hospital in Colorado Springs, and she has so much to do with the restaurant and the children [they have four boys] and the house and all, I don't know how she found the time and energy to be there. But she was always there. She always *is* there... when I need her." Then he blushed, aware that his romantic declaration had an audience, and finished, a little haltingly. "I guess she's.. well, it's like I said... I can't think of any other word but *devotion.*"

As he was speaking, tears filled the Scorpio woman's eyes, and she swallowed hard. The tenseness throbbing between them before had miraculously disappeared, and they gazed at one another for a brief, but meaningful moment, as the Lion's eyes, too, sparkled with tears. Reluctant to interrupt this rare moment of singing communication between them, I nevertheless continued the game, and asked Barbara, "And you? What one word would you choose to describe all the positive qualities in Carroll that make *you* love *him*?"

She was silent. For a minute. Then another minute passed. After several minutes had gone by, she was still silent. Finally, embarrassed and obviously uncomfortable with her inability to express whatever she was thinking, she murmured apologetically to both of us, "I'm sorry. I mean, there are things .. but I .. I just can't think of them .. I just don't know." Then another several minutes of silence which I'm certain seemed to last an eternity to the Lion. However, being a Leo, and therefore nearly never suffering from a loss of words, he filled the empty air with a typical Leonine response. "Come on, Barbara, don't be bashful. Why don't you just admit the word is 'lovable'?" Still silence from Scorpio. "That's the word you're groping for, isn't it? Lovable? Or maybe the word 'perfect' describes me better?"

We laughed, nervously. That is, the Leo and I laughed. His Scorpio wife made a feeble attempt to grin, then excused herself and went into the kitchen to bring us more coffee. Now, even the Lion was silent. And I felt it best to remain silent too. The discomfort in the room was growing into a giant. Then, unexpectedly, out of the kitchen popped Barbara, a tea towel in her hand and a smile on her face.

"I just thought of the word," she announced, clearly relieved. "It's 'dependability.' He's so .. trustworthy. I can always count on him to keep his word when he possibly can. He never lets me or anyone else down. Once he's given a promise, I know he'll try hard to keep it. He's really the most trustworthy person I've ever met. I guess . . . well, I guess *dependable* is the one word I would choose."

Such a waterfall of words from a woman who had, minutes before, appeared to be stricken dumb. And such an expression of happiness on her face from the peace of being, at last, able to express her true feelings.

As Leos will do when they're pleased, but a little shy, the Lion grinned ear to ear, and remarked playfully, "Don't you want to add the words 'lovable' and 'perfect' to the word 'dependable'?" He was rolling in catnip, floating in visible ecstasy. His mate had finally fed him a King-size portion of the food for which he was so often starved — a sincere compliment. For the next half hour there was so much affection billowing over around them, I excused myself and left early, leaving them in privacy with their new understanding of one another, once again convinced of the miracles astrology can create, when it's used as it was meant to be.

It's true that the silences of a Scorpio woman can frustrate and infuriate a Leo man. He's more gregarious about his pleasures and displeasures; he needs to be verbal concerning his happiness and his sorrows. It never occurs to a Leo male that his Pluto-ruled woman is driven into her silences by his constant dominance and airs of superiority — nor does it occur to Leo that he possesses the same trait he objects to in his Scorpio mate. With *him*, it's called *pouting*.

The Scorpio woman is deeply hurt and angered by the Lion's insuffer-able arrogance, yet she seldom realizes that all it takes to halt it is the effort it would cost her to give him the gift of a sincere compliment (Scorpios can give no other kind) in the middle of one of his supercilious lectures to her . . and he'll purr with delight, forgetting altogether what he was roaring about. All it takes is a little introspection. Granted, Scorpio is more capable of introspec-tion than Leo, but Leo is more forgiving than Scorpio, so it balances out rather nicely . . or it could, if they would allow it.

The sexual relationship between a Lion and a female Scorpion can be somewhat intermittent. It can blow hot and cold, by turns. She finds his warm strength erotic, in a cozy, affectionate way. He finds her secret, silent intensity of passion a sensuous challenge to his impulsive romantic nature. With some mutual consideration, like a little more verbal expression from her, and a little more sensitive consideration from him, the yearning they felt when they first met and loved will remain. But too many silences frcm her, too much arrogance from him, and the initial powerful chemistry between them may trickle into a mild, bored affection, with true mating occurring less and less frequently . . . . . . all the way to frigidity in her and impotence in him. The Scorpio woman already knows what every Leo man needs to learn — that fulfilling sex does not initiate in the body's fleeting urges. It begins in the mind and heart, then gradually grows into the kind of physical desire which results in emotional peace and contentment.

One thing that often causes sexual coldness between these two is her sometimes intense resentment of his admiring entourage of females, who often follow the Leo male around like worshiping, love-sick puppies . . and his refusal to banish them with an icy rebuff. He actually *enjoys* it, can you imagine that ? Yes. I can imagine it. The Lion needs to roll in the catnip of adoration now and then, but it will seldom lead to unfaithfulness — never, in fact, if his mate fights this threat with the most powerful weapon of all . . the awesome force of LOVE. The Leo man who receives enough adoration and excitement at home, in his own lair, will never wander far from the jungle pride he shares with his mate. That's how you separate the *women* from the girls. She should laugh it off. That's what he does, inwardly, if the truth were known. Leo's deepest instinct is loyalty. It takes a lot of unreasonable jealousy to change his basic nature. Logical deduction may lead the Scorpio woman to believe that if her Lion's feminine entourage admire and desire him, he must equally admire or desire *them*. But "logical deduction" is sometimes the most misleading of all the siblings of lies. Out of hurt and outrage, justified or not, the Scorpio woman is very likely to initiate an act of infidelity herself. She should consider such a drastic reaction to the frustration of their problems very carefully, for Leo will not be able to forgive physical disloyalty, whatever he may have done or not done to deserve it.

Yes, I know it's selfish, but that's the way Leos are. With extremely rare exceptions, should a Lion discover his mate has betrayed him with another man, it will be the end. And Leo should know this: It takes a lot of what he may not recognize in himself as arrogance, a lot of insensitivity to her deepest needs, to drive this woman into the arms of someone else. If it should ever happen, he should ask himself what it was she so intensely needed that he perhaps unconsciously denied her. It may have been a child . . . a career . . . or just a little extra compassion and gentle understanding of her feelings . . . a little more tenderness at times.

When the gulf of pride and pouting grows so wide both are reluctant to risk leaping over it, it's nearly always she who must make the first move. However wistfully he may yearn for reconciliation, a Lion finds it painful to humble himself with an apology. He fears such admission of regret might cause him to lose control of his home, his woman — and worse, his self-image of superiority and command. And so, struggling to preserve his identity as ruler of the relationship, he'll often shift the blame to her undeserving shoulders, desperately hoping she'll accept it, so he can majestically forgive her — and everything can be sunny and warm between them again. Sadly, many Leo men know no other path to a renewal of harmony. Initiating the making up will be easier for his Scorpio woman if she'll remember the lyrics to the song sung to Anna in *The King and I* by the Monarch's Number One Wife, when she was trying to make Anna see him as he really was.

He will not always say — what you would have him say,
But now and then he'll say . . something wonderful!

The thoughtless things he'll do — will hurt and worry you,
Then all at once he'll do . . . something wonderful!

He has a thousand dreams that won't come true,
You know that he believes in them, and that's enough for you.

You'll always go along — defend him when he's wrong,
And tell him when he's strong — he is WONDERFUL!

He'll always need your love, and so he'll get your love.
A man who needs your love . . can be . . wonderful.

There will always be those sunlit moments when he'll say or do . . . . . . something wonderful . . . . . . to make up for his occasional thoughtlessness and arrogance. As for you, Leo, Your Highness, you might try memorizing a few lines from another song:

She may be weary — women do get weary
Wearing the same shabby dress;
When she is weary, try a little tenderness.

She may be waiting, just anticipating
Things she may never possess;
While she is waiting, try a little tenderness.

This is not an ordinary, but an extraordinary woman, whose feelings run deep. To a Lion, any degree of affection is preferable to silence and loneliness; yet the Scorpio woman would rather be alone than be given only half a heart to share. And therein lies the vast ocean of difference between those controlled by the square of the 4-10 Sun Sign Pattern, an ocean which can only be spanned by a bridge of love.

LEO

Fire — Fixed — Positive
Ruled by the Sun
Symbols: Lion & Shy Pussycat
Day Forces — Masculine

SAGITTARIUS

Fire — Mutable — Positive
Ruled by Jupiter
Symbols: Archer & Centaur
Day Forces — Masculine

The **LEO-SAGITTARIUS** *Relationship*

When playing Follow my Leader . . .

Leo is a Fixed Sign. Sagittarius is a Mutable. Since neither of them was born under a Cardinal Sign of leadership, you'd think they'd sooner or later realize there can never be a permanent winner between them in the competitive game of which one shall lead — which one shall follow, and give it up as a tiresome conflict that takes a lot of time they could otherwise spend doing a number of jolly things side by side, cooperatively.

You'd think so, but although there are lots of Lions, Lionesses and Archers who do take such a sensible attitude toward their association, there are a goodly number of others who insist on concentrating all their flaming energies (both are Fire Signs) toward determining who shall take (or not take) orders from whom. Still, even with these, the mutual challenges tossed back and forth tend to be friendly and good-natured, because Leo and Sag are influenced by the 5-9 Sun Sign Pattern of natural empathy and easily attainable harmony (not always, but most of the time) so that the competitive sparks between them are more likely to result in a refreshing sort of exhilaration than in envious resentment. If they enjoy competing so much, why not allow them to have their fun ? We might as well grant them our own and astrology's permission, because these two will do just exactly as they please in the long run anyway. They're both independent, and prefer to learn through the experience of their own mistakes than to be counseled by well-meaning people.

When these two masculine signs entangle their temperaments, whether by choice (in a friendship or love relationship) or by Destiny's design (as relatives within the family circle, or business associates forced into profession-al proximity) outsiders who stand by and watch have nearly as much fun as the two participants themselves. Leo was born to command, lecture, guide and counsel. Born free. Sagittarius was born to rebel against being commanded, refuses to be lectured, guided or counseled — and was *also* born free ! Clearly, as smooth as their association may be most of the time, there will come moments when something has to give. It won't be Leo. And it won't be Sag. The Centaurs and the Big Cats might be said to represent the ultimate in eternal stand-offs.

Should their Luminaries be in favorable aspect between their natal charts, the blending of their super-bright auras often creates an almost visible rainbow around these two, coloring their clashes with the soft shades of forgiveness and fresh beginnings. Sagittarius is ruled by and stamped with Jupiter's expansive generosity and idealism. Leo is ruled by and stamped with the benevolent warmth of the Sun itself. So there's plenty of contagious enthusiasm and genuine affection they can fortunately exchange if they choose, with the power to jet-propel them toward any seemingly impossible goal or ambition they seek as individuals, or as a team. Aside from their heated quarrels, incited by their equally fiery tempers, Leo and Sag can bring to each other — and to the world — much happiness. There's a lot of vibrant activity and energy flowing when they're together, along with a considerable amount of good will.

The name of the most ferocious dragon of dispute that threatens the tranquility of this sympathetic 5-9 combination will be spelled in bright red, flaming letters: PRIDE. The typical Sag is ordinarily blissfully unaware of the meaning of the word. Archers may be feisty and spunky; they may refuse to be pushed around by bullies, but the truth is that they aren't really hung-up on false pride. They'll cheerfully laugh at jokes on themselves, and are often the very ones who tell them ! Thanks to Jupiter's philosophical outlook, Sagittarians see no reason to feel guilty or embarrassed, just because they happen to possess a few shortcomings. After all, doesn't everyone?

No. Everyone does not. Leos possess none whatsoever. Just ask them. No shortcomings. No flaws. The Lions and Lionesses can do no wrong. Everything they say or do is right. Always. Royalty is infallible, protected from error. Leo's judgment is at all times sound, sensible and wise. Also practical. And quite naturally, superior to all other judgments. *Everyone* knows *that*. Everyone but Sag. The Archer will delight in punching Leo's plump velvet pillows of pride with a powerful verbal right hook, time and time again. The more Leo's pride gets punctured, the louder the Lion or Lioness will roar. As always when fire fans fire, the "expansive" Jupiter temper will then be ignited by Leo's arrogant roaring, and things can get explosive.

The possibilities of harmonious compatibility between Leo and Sagittarius are so potentially rich and rewarding, it's really a shame for the Archers to spoil it by failing to realize the need to constantly and carefully consider that too many thorns thrust into the Lion's paw can cause Leo to stalk away permanently, in wounded and outraged indignation.

A classic example of the result of ignoring the sensitive Solar pride of the Sun-ruled occurred during an incident experienced by some people I know, when an apparently harmless and typical Sagittarian practical joke missed its mark, and boomeranged back upon its playful Centaur perpetrator. The Lion involved was in his third year of law school, and platonically associated with a girl Archer Fine Arts student, who attended the same college. Nothing romantic. Just matriculating friends, so to speak. The Leo had recently quarreled with his wife, and they had mutually and angrily decided to try a trial separation. Feeling understandably morose and glum, he found the buoyant, optimistic chatter of the girl Archer a cheerful boost to his loneliness. (There's no sadder sight, whether he's roaming Nature's jungle pride of ivy vines, or the "civilized" jungle of ivy league classrooms — than an affectionate Lion, separated from his mate.)

One bright Saturday afternoon, the Lion decided to soak up some Sun on the beach (a favorite Leo pastime) with Sag tagging along happily, to keep him company. An hour or so after they arrived, the girl Archer noticed that the Leo law student's estranged wife was sun bathing nearby. The Lion was unaware of the presence of his mate (a Lioness, by the way). With no real intent to cause trouble, but just in the spirit of Jupiter fun, Sag asked her friend to carry her, piggy-back, into the water — to catch one of the big waves. Taken by surprise, he bent over, allowing her to leap astride his shoulders in her string bikini, and lock her legs tightly around his neck. Suddenly, the Horse half of the female Centaur was inspired with a questionable equestrian idea. On the way to the water's edge, she slapped her Leo friend's shoulders, as a jockey whips a horse into a faster gallop, knowing the Lion's mate was watching. The sight of a proud and noble Lion playing "horsey", carrying a laughing rider on his back, and meekly obeying her obvious commands to run faster, thereby nearly stumbling over a rock, created (as you can imagine) a most undignified image. But Leos are kind and warm hearted, so he reluctantly submitted to the indignity, rather than be thought a poor sport. (The gods were compassionate in not allowing him to fall flat on his face with his burden, which would have been an unbearable embarrassment.) Later, when he realized the piggy-back scene staged by Sag was observed by, and had deeply wounded the woman he loved, he — well, let's just say the escapade was only one of the things that removed any possibility of a lasting friendship between this particular Lion and Archer.

Fortunately, the awkward and humiliating experience didn't prevent an eventual reconciliation between the Lion and his equally proud Lioness, but not before what seemed an eternity of atonement, and some very heavy explaining, which was an additional blow to his Leonine ego. The male Lion can't bear to be placed in the humbling posture of explaining his behavior to anyone, not even to his wife. Apologies are painful for Leos of either sex, especially when the transgression was caused by the "harmless prank" of someone else, and Leo must shoulder the undeserved blame.

If the Sagittarian man or woman takes care not to cross the line of safety with a Sun-ruled friend, relative, business associate, lover or mate, the Jupiter proclivity for holding up a mirror to Leo's occasional flaws and mistakes (yes, even Leos can have them and make them, for all their superiority) is a healthy habit. It will gradually lead the Lion and Lioness to unbend their regal manners a bit, and acquire the much needed quality of realistic self-appraisal. Just so Sag does it with a degree of tact (which will probably take more than a little practice). The Sagittarian blunt candor, when it's reasonably controlled, is a blessing in disguise to Leos. The Big Cats become more tolerant and much nicer to be around, once they've relaxed their stiff pride, and are able to mingle more graciously with the lesser animals in the astrological zoo.

Of course, the Archers aren't guilty of making *all* the blunders in this association. Leos are guilty of a few errors in judgment themselves, when it comes to handling the merry, but decidedly willful Sagittarians. Like those long Leonine lectures, delivered with such a smug, self-righteous air. The typical Archer will become clearly restless at being forced to sit through the repeated counseling sessions of a pedantic Pussycat, then after a time, ZING! will go one of those bull's-eye arrows of truth straight into the vulnerable ego of the Lion or Lioness.

"If you're so smart, why did you almost flunk high school ? You only got your college degree because your father knew the Dean." Or maybe, "I may not be able to keep a checkbook balanced, as you say, but at least I didn't take out bankruptcy three times, like you did." Perhaps . . . "So what if I do embarrass you by talking too much in front of your friends ? You happen to embarrass me too, with those corny jokes you tell over and over, till everyone's bored, the way you're always bragging — and those gawd-awful loud clothes you wear. You look like a peacock posing in a barnyard. And you really should stop eating all that rich food. You're beginning to get a jelly roll around your waistline. If you can't stop stuffing your mouth, at least you could jog a few miles a day, like I do. Or play some tennis with me once in awhile. At your age, you can't afford to let your muscles get flabby."

It shouldn't take long for Leo to learn to go easy in trying to curb the Archer's sense of individuality, and to recognize his (or her) need of free expression, without the restriction of constant advice. Lions and Lionesses learn quickly, and Sag is a tough and verbally agile lion tamer. Leo, being a Fixed Sign, is more stubborn than Sagittarius. And so after one of them has caused melancholy emotions in the other, it almost always must be the Archer who initiates the repair of a temporary crack in the relationship. Otherwise it can grow into an increasing coldness that will take some time to thaw. Leos tend to freeze in icy dignity when they've been injured, but the heat of two Fire Signs will eventually melt frozen hearts, especially two hearts as large and as warmed by the Sun and Jupiter as those of Leo and Sagittarius.

When their scars have healed, Sag will develop the knack of aiming that Jupiter bow of truth toward a more positive target, such as giving Leo the much longed-for gift of honest appreciation and forthright respect — while the Lion or Lioness will slowly but surely comprehend that, although the Archers may impulsively get tangled up in a ton of troubles by ignoring advice, they're also blessed with amazing streaks of pure luck, and will often unexpectedly manage to find a happy ending to their own stories — if they're given what *they* most long for, which is simply to be trusted.

Sagittarians secretly want Leo's practical, benevolent guidance (when it doesn't take the form of commands), and they also need the strong net of Leo's protection to catch them when they fall from their swinging trapezes, just as the noble Kings and Queens of the jungle (and elsewhere) are secretly thrilled by the Archer's colorful tumbling acts, admire the Sagittarian integrity — and respond warmly to Jupiter's unshakable faith. When these two courageous and generous Sun Signs link their ideals into a chain of cooperation, then weld it with patient recognition of each other's demand for independence, it will never rain on their circus parade.

LEO *Woman* SAGITTARIUS *Man*

———— ◄─●─► ————

> *"I shall have such fun," said Peter, with one
> eye on Wendy.*
>
> *"It will be rather lonely in the evening," she
> said, "sitting by the fire."*
>
> *"I shall have Tink,"*
>
> *"Tink can't go a twentieth of the way 'round,"
> she reminded him, a little tartly.*

Well, now, look here, Archer, I'm going to give you some unsolicited and probably unwelcome, but nevertheless sound astrological advice. Stuff your teasing, taunting arrows back in your — well, back wherever they came from — and stop trying to win this woman's love by futile attempts to jar her jealous nature.

It's sheer folly, no less, to deliberately arouse the fury of a Lioness. As for making her jealous, you couldn't possibly choose a worse way to warm her heart and have your way with her. Your rather clumsy, albeit charming practical jokes won't get you far either. Nor will teasing her, as though she's your kid sister, and you're her incorrigible, but lovable and protective big brother. She knows you're incorrigible. She also knows you're lovable (that's what frustrates her). And she does not need or want to be protected. Royalty does not need protection. Royalty *gives* protection. She's not your kid sister, and you're not her big brother. Your relationship is different, and you're perfectly aware of that. So stop playing the role of innocence. You may be unbelievably naive (another thing that makes you lovable) but you are also wise and philosophical, qualities you gained from having your innocence dented a thousand times, tinging it with a touch of skepticism, but hardly tarnishing at all your naivete. It's this duality in your nature (you are a dual or double Sun Sign you know, half Horse, half Human) that attracted her in the beginning to your little boy grin, your clown antics and your air of the wise sage, all rolled up into a bouncing ball of independence and generosity. She was utterly fascinated by it.

Study your astrology. Or at the very least, go to the library and read up on the feline habits of the Big Cats of the jungle pride, if you want to know how to make this Leo lady purr for you. Continue to stick your foot in your mouth, continue to torment her into a raging Lioness, and instead of purring, she may show her Pussycat claws, from which you could suffer some major emotional scratches that will scar your ego more painfully than you may guess — and forget about how good you are at guessing games. You won't be able to guess what it's like to be on the receiving end of a Leo's outraged pride until you're there. And then you'd better believe you'll wish you were somewhere else. If you really love her, that is. And you do. (You can fool her, but you can't fool an astrologer.)

You really love her because you're both influenced and guided by the fortunate and beneficent 5-9 Sun Sign Pattern vibration. Not every Archer and Lioness benefit from the trined Suns of Leo and Sagittarius, of course. (I'll be explaining why in the beginning of the next section of this chapter, so we won't take time to go into it here.) But a great many Centaurs and Lionesses do benefit beautifully from the 5-9 vibes, and the two of you are doubtless among them, or you wouldn't even be reading this chapter. You'd be out somewhere with your Jupiter bow, aiming your enthusiasms in all directions at once, scattering original ideas like glittering stardust all over the stodgies and stuffies in the world, traveling around the globe (or in your own head) in search of an honest man or woman, like Diogenes, but without his lantern — someone other than a child you can count on not to be hypocritical. That's why you're so good with children, and they love you back so much. You respect their honesty and integrity, their naivete and faith, that match your own. You understand them, as they understand you.

Still, lovely as children are, with their caroling laughter and the ribbons of magic in their eyes, there comes a time when you'd like to be able to equally share yourself with someone your own size, to be able to equally respect and admire an adult, who could communicate with you and puzzle with you over all sorts of things children haven't yet begun to worry about (if only they could remain in such a blissful state) but that worry *you* constantly. You need to exchange ideas with a peer you can depend on to be truthful, and not phony — maybe play a few games more complex than kick-the-can or Frisbee. So now you've found someone who's delightfully designed to fit all those needs of yours. She's noble and loyal and — not quite so capable of total self-honesty as yourself, perhaps — but certainly not deceptive. She likes to play games too. And she's good at them. Whether it's tennis, mental chess, Monopoly, bridge or softball, she's capable of winning, and that makes her a more exciting partner. You always enjoy games more with an opponent who makes you work harder to be victorious, and at last you've found your match. This one can even beat your jogging time if she takes a lazy, languid notion to do so. Your stop watch will get a work-out. So . . now that you have her, what are you going to do with this royal prize ? Yes, true, sometimes she behaves more like a royal pain in your Horse half than a royal prize. But she *is* very, very special. Womanhood in full bloom.

The first thing you should do with her is stop treating her like your baby sister. And stop all those things astrology has just given you a Zen clip in the jaw (figuratively) for doing. Sagittarians are extremely lucky, thanks to Jupiter's huge good fortune (when Jupiter's in the mood to grant it) but causing the proud Lioness to fall in love with you may be the most gigantic rainbow of luck of them all. You know what happens to gamblers in Vegas. They win — then they lose every dollar, by betting against themselves. Now that you've won a Leo girl, don't bet against your love by seeing how far you can press your luck with her. Because the truth of the matter is, she *can* outdistance Tink, or any other lady you might have in mind. As she said, Tink can't go a twentieth of the way 'round, and the Lioness can circle any race track in double time before other women have made the first quarter-mile. In any way you want to take it, that's true. She not Wonder Woman, but she comes closer to being a female fit to be Superman's mate than most of the other girls, ladies, or whatever, in your past.

A Leo woman is as sleek and graceful as any thoroughbred horse who ever won the Kentucky Derby. She's playful and warm and sunny — she's generous, wise and sensible. She also possesses a very sensitive ego, an uncommon amount of pride (some of it false pride, some genuine) and she can be more than a little supercilious, arrogant and demanding. The word, if we must be plainspoken, and I suppose we must with Sag, is: spoiled. All Monarchs are spoiled. She is, remember, the Queen of the jungle pride — and of all she surveys. (In her own slightly self-centered mind, she is.) It would pay the Archer to be always aware of this when she's surveying *him* — trying to decide if he's worthy of being her Prince Consort.

The Lioness may need a respectful astrological scolding too. She tends to expect too much of the man who loves her, unconsciously tossing him royal challenges no mere mortal could fulfill. The Sagittarian man is brave and courageous, probably closer to being *truly* fearless than any of the other Sun Signs (including Leos, who wrap their fears in velvet and ermine confidence, so they won't show). He'll try very hard to bring her rubies and emeralds, whether real ones from Tiffany's or the more valuable gems of his sparkling honesty. He'll conquer armies of problems for her, be her successful explorer of new worlds and ideas, play an Academy Award performance of Essex to her Elizabeth, Columbus to her Isabella — demonstrate his loyalty and intelligence while he's proving to her that he possesses a crusading zeal and a Holy Grail kind of faith worthy of Arthur and Launcelot themselves. But the one gift he may have trouble giving her is groveling worship. This man is simply unable to prostrate himself at anyone's feet, in the traditional attitude of reverence and awe (in court, in the Vatican or anywhere else, including the den, kitchen — and especially the bedroom). He'll gladly give her the respect of an absolute equal (and some men wouldn't do that, you know). He won't look down on her, but neither will he look up to her. He'll treat her neither as his inferior or his superior, but with the same devoted affection, warmth, passionate loyalty and tenderness he bestows upon his dog or his horse. (The

Leo lady shouldn't sniff contemptuously; this man adores animals with more fervor and real emotion than a whole lot of people treat other people.)

And so, she'll receive all these priceless gifts from her merry, twinkly-eyed court jester, her searching soldier of fortune — but worship, in its true sense, may be missing. And never mind that Sag is Mutable (most Mutable Signs are docile and humble) because his "Mutability" is considerably tempered and modified by his Fire Element, and by the fact that he was born under a masculine Sun Sign, also ruled by a masculine planet, Jupiter. "Tempered" is certainly the right word. Because it reminds me to remind *her* that the Archer has a very quick temper, of the size Jupiter uses to make all patterns — extra large. But his anger, like hers, although easily aroused, is soon replaced (like hers) with a heartfelt regret for his impulsive words, and (like her) he almost never bears a grudge. He's always magnanimous enough to forgive and forget if he's met half-way. She's noticeably slower to forgive and forget an injury, becase she was born under a Fixed Sign, but if he can convince her he's really sorry, she'll defrost herself, and benignly grant him another chance, with the innate graciousness and benevolence bred into her nature by her ruling Sun.

If all these two had to worry about was their chemical attraction, there wouldn't be a cloud in their skies. Melting into Oneness with a depth of passion remembered by the heart from a long-ago dream, is one of those grand and glorious gifts showered by the great Jupiter and the powerful Sun upon — not every Leo and Sag — but upon those Lionesses and their Archers who are honestly in love. Their physical expression of body hunger is by turns playful, sensual, fresh, soft and gentle as raindrops, kissed by warm summer breezes — then wild, abandoned and feral, as though they were both lost in a forest primeval. Lovemaking between them can also be a calm and quiet thing of peace and stillness. The only rumble of warning related to their sexual happiness is an astrological Beware Sign for the Sagittarian man — who may, as is his customary habit, say something a little too honest and frank to her at the wrong time (the Archer's sense of timing is seldom the greatest) which will wound her more than he realizes. A wounded Leonine Queen is one of the Sun Sign women who may retreat somewhere alone (like the jungle lioness) in cold, aloof silence, to allow her wounds to heal gradually — during which time she tends to be seriously and sadly sexually frigid.

This man is a clown. This woman is a beautiful Lioness. Together, they create the image of a colorful, exciting circus parade. His clown's grin, his cartwheels, acrobatic speech and movement — her tawny loveliness and slow, sensual grace, her warm, intelligent eyes, together create an abstract impression of all the Big Top shows you've ever thrilled to in breathless excitement as a child. Throw into the imaginary scene some pink balloons, some calliope music (Sag will play the role of the daring man on the flying trapeze trading his clown costume for purple spangled tights easily, because of the Sagittarian duality) and you can see why this relationship often turns out to be The Greatest Show On Earth. (Both Leo and Sag are decidedly dramatic.) She has the theatre in her blood, he has sawdust in his. They'll have a grand time together, playing the circuit, stopping in all the small towns, but dreaming of Europe and the big challenge.

But she must never forget the aching sadness and streaming tears behind the wide, greasepainted grin of all clowns, from Pagliacci to Emmett Kelly, and realize that, while he may pretend to be a Great Explorer, a Brave Lion Tamer, a Knight on a White Horse, a carefree, casual Soldier-of-Fortune . . . all those roles . . . his true identity is Don Quixote. And in the end, he needed the woman he loved to remind him once more that he really *did* possess the courage to manifest the impossible dream, even though he lost it for a while.

And the Archer should never forget that, once he and his Lioness have loved completely, giving all of themselves to each other, it won't matter if they quarrel, and he hastily, angrily decides to pack up his bow and quiver of arrows — dashing off to roam the world, leaving her behind. However far he may go, he'll weep when he finally comprehends that his careless remarks caused his proud and sensitive Leo Lady such pain. And he'll miss her dreadfully. He'll remember her sunniness and warmth, her odd blend of trembling intensity and calm, cool poise. And he'll remember other things. Because she'll be sending him a silent, yet eloquent and powerful message, pulsing through the golden cord that binds together all true lovers linked by the 5-9 vibration, even when they're miles apart. Her whispered message will throb within him some night, in a deep dream, fragrant with the memory of her hair and eyes. Then he'll leap up from his strange, cold bed, walk to the window, and stare into the velvet blackness, shimmering with tiny, brilliant star diamonds . . . until sunrise. The Sun, too, will remind him . . . of her slow, rising smile at dawn. By then he'll know it's time to return home to the pride of his Lioness. There's no way he can resist the truth of her astral words. No way on this Earth.

> close your ears to the sound of my voice
> and through the thunder of a thousand cannons
> you will hear it calling your name
>
> blind yourself to the light in my eyes
> and through the blackness of eternal night
> you will feel them piercing your soul
>
> insulate your body against my hands
> and through blocks of ice
> it will tremble in response to my touch

turn your cheek away from my breath
and through layers of rock
you will feel it hot against your lips

                              and musty

  like jungle grass°

°From *Venus Trines at Midnight.*

☆ ☆ ☆ ☆ ☆ ☆

LEO *Man* SAGITTARIUS *Woman*

———◄•◆•►———

Many clapped.

Some did not.

A few little beasts hissed.

Naturally, the Earth being a fairly sizeable round ball, not absolutely every single male and female upon it whose Sun Signs form the 5-9 Pattern are ecstatic or any other kind of lovers. Some are simply remarkably tolerant and affectionate, platonic friends, who share experiences with a rare sympathy of viewpoint. Some are merely cheerfully nodding and pleasant, but casual acquaintances. Most are strangers, whose paths never cross at all in this lifetime.

Then there are other Lions and girl Archers who, despite the golden opportunities for harmony normally bestowed by trined Suns, share severe planetary afflictions and negative Luminary or Ascendent aspects between their birth charts, those whose dissident karmic chords and auric colors vibrate so disturbingly, they never become close enough to cause each other either extreme happiness or extreme pain. Like the old nursery rhyme:

Now listen, thee, and listen well
I do not like thee, Doctor Fell
Exactly why I cannot tell
But I do not like thee, Doctor Fell

This, of course, is true of all 5-9 Patterns, not Leo and Sag alone. In a similar, but opposite manner, there are men and women whose natal Suns form the traditionally tense and difficult 4-10 Pattern, yet whose other birth chart configurations are powerfully beneficent, and who therefore discover together an easy compatibility. Still, it must be remembered that these are the exceptions which prove the rule.

Consequently, not every Sagittarian girl claps her hands in delighted admiration at the cleverness and superiority of the Lion. Some girl Archers will refuse to clap, or to pay, for that matter, any kind of tribute to Leo's virtues—and a few will even dare to hiss the King of the jungle when he's showing off his talents. There's not much use taking up space discussing these occasionally mis-matched and clearly mis-mated Leo men and Sag women. Not only would they be bored by reading about one another, but there are all those magnetically attracted and destined to mate stormily-but-passionately femine Centaurs and the lovable Lions who truly adore them to consider. So, best to concentrate our attention on these Leo-Sag couples, and counsel the others to search elsewhere for happiness and harmony.

Even though not every Leo man and Sagittarian woman are fated to meet and fall genuinely in love, those who do will forge a bond that's not easy to break. But they will make an attempt! These two may at various times appear to share only one thing in common—a mutual desire to pound each other's healthy egos into trembling inferiority complexes. Don't be fooled. Appearances are deceiving, more times than not. What they are actually doing is testing their relationship, through an odd combination of simultaneously seeking an affirmation and a denial. An affirmation of mutual loyalty and devotion—and a denial of an equally mutual fear of being deceived by the faith in one another eternally required by love. It's a game quite natural to Fire Signs, and Leo and Sag both having been born into Fire Elements, they learn the rules swiftly.

If they're lucky (and thankfully, most Leos and Sagittarians are uncommonly lucky, though not all) they'll learn reasonably soon what a wealth of happy hours they're choosing to waste by playing the testing game. If they're not so lucky, and their normally fortunate individual natal Suns were afflicted at birth, they'll take a long time, and exchange a lot of emotional bruises before they comprehend how foolishly they're behaving.

For example, the Lion will go far beyond what he well knows is fair in arrogantly bossing around the girl Archer he loves, commanding her to obey his wishes, or else be banished from his sunny smile and his warm, strong arms—expecting her to wait on him like a scullery maid, lecturing or scolding her sternly for the slightest disobedience of his Majesty's pleasure, and permitting her no freedom of opinion or outside activity where she might in some way equal or outshine his own accomplishments. He's not really a tyrant, and he neither wants nor intends to be cruel and despotic. He's only silently, desperately (often unconsciously) playing the testing game, seeking an affirmation of her loyalty, proof of her devotion—by seeing how willing she is to submit, how far he can go with her before she admits she doesn't love him as much as she vowed she did in the beginning. (But praying fervently all the while that she *does*.)

Then he'll test her by seeking, not a positive affirmation, but a denial. He'll either rage and roar, or pout and sulk over her merest "hello" to another man, accusing her of everything short of (and even including) outright adultery, without the faintest foundation or cause, secretly longing and achingly needing her repeated denial that she could ever even *think* of betraying him with someone else. The more outraged and indignant she becomes, the more clear the denial — and the more secure he feels.

Taking turns, she'll then make *her* move around the board in their romantic monopoly game. Being fully aware (her mind is very bright and quick) of how hungry this man always is for sincere compliments, she'll deliberately starve him, refusing to give him the smallest crumb of admiration, no matter how hard he tries to impress her — testing him, you see, to see how furiously he'll try to succeed, how high he'll climb, what impossible challenges he'll conquer to gain her attention and applause. How much is it worth to him? If he stops caring what she thinks, it means he doesn't love her, as he swore he did at first. Then, also fully aware of how he suffers from having his masculine pride trampled before his friends, she'll deliberately embarrass him when there's an audience, by putting him down, or telling some private story about him that makes him look ridiculous. Secretly (often unconsciously) she's hoping he'll be loudly angry and furious with her later, when they're alone, treating her to a display of fury, as only an aroused Lion can, proving to her that he loves her, that she's the only one who has the power to fire his emotions into such leaping flames. As for the denial part of the game, the rules are the same for her as they are for him.

She'll become bitterly sarcastic and accusatory every time he leaves her to go somewhere alone, making it vividly clear that he's not fooling *her —she* knows about his promiscuous behavior with worshipping females when he's out of her sight, because one woman isn't enough to satisfy his erotic jungle lust — when in her heart she knows he's not being unfaithful, either by word or deed. But she needs fiercely to hear his impassioned denial . . . see it in his eyes.

Isn't that an immature, frustrating and leading-nowhere game for a man and woman who love each other to play? Because she's Mutable (more adaptable) and he's Fixed (stubborn) she's the one who should be first to communicate her weariness with the testing — her desire to start all over and return to the way it used to be with them, when they held hands trustingly, like happy children, touching tenderly, full of the joy of discovering a new miracle together every morning . . when everything he did was wonderful, and filled her with worship . . . everything she said was magical and dear and funny. When just the nearness of his warm strength and calm wisdom made her tremble . . . when her brave clown grin made his heart turn over, and brought a lump to his throat, as he promised himself he'd protect her forever, and never allow anyone to hurt this cheerful and giving, yet so terribly vulnerable woman — ever again — the way so many people did before he found her.

That's all she has to do — make the *first* move to talk it over. Just be her honest, real self. And say exactly what she feels. Pretending is a part Sagittarius can never play successfully. He'll make the *second* move, and do something he'd never do with anyone else but her. He'll confess how wrong he's been, how many mistakes he's made, how very, very sorry he is . . . how fallible and human and frightened he is on the inside, at the very moment he's projecting such confidence and icy detachment on the outside. She'll apologize too, then . . . for all the thorns she stuck in his big, lovable Lion's paw that caused him such pain, and for all those times of make believing she doubted his loyalty.

They'll both admit that, all through the tortuous testing time, they were always able to read the truth in each other's eyes, never mind what either of them were saying. Words don't matter. After awhile, when they have nothing more to communicate in any way at all, they'll fall asleep together in the darkness, and in the morning, they'll awaken as intimately familiar strangers, hearing the same music they heard the very first morning they awoke to the sunlight of knowing the lonely search was over . . but exploring the mysteries of each other was just the beginning. This time, the music is sweeter, the chords are deeper, because they know the rhythm and the melody by heart. Best of all, they've learned the words to a new song of honesty, that could maybe someday grow into a symphony.

They almost lost each other, but they stopped playing the game before the truth left their eyes. The Leo man and the Sagittarian woman are among the lucky ones whose moments of passion and affection are interchangeable, their needs first gentle, then intense — whether they're blending their bodies, their spirits or their minds. The ones whose auras clash (like those mentioned in the beginning of this section) will never touch at all, either mentally, spiritually or physically, and will forever look upon each other with the eyes of apathy. But with the Lions and the Archers who are destined to love, Life is a magical carnival of ideas and ideals, dreams and discovery. They stimulate in each other physical desire, intellectual seeking and spiritual reaching. Once they've broken down the barriers of his false pride and her skepticism — and allow their relationship enough sunlight to encourage his warm enthusiasm and her fresh faith in the future, they won't have time for playing games. Their days and nights will be filled with a thousand adventures, whether they're traveling somewhere together (which they'll do a lot) or just lying in the grass in their own back yard on a summer night, counting the stars and listening to the crickets' choir. She should beware of being caught in his clever Lion trap, though — and refrain from correcting him when he points to Spica in the sky, and she's tempted to tell him he's actually pointing to Arcturus. He knows. He's just testing her knowledge of astronomy. When she finally knows — that he *always* knows — they're half-way home.

If they must play games, there are hundreds more fun than the testing game. She should give him one for his August birthday, tied with orange-yellow-golden ribbons, the color of the Sun . . . and maybe scribble a poem on the card, to give him a hint of how it should be between them from now on, when they think they're about to weaken, and go back to their old ways.

> *lovers play games of No and Yes*
> *a quick caress, a sigh . . . goodbye*
> *and why?*
>
> *lovers play games of Yes and No*
> *of Stop and Go . . of wait and fate*
> *too late*
>
> *they laugh when they want to cry*
> *leave when they'd rather stay*
> *they quit when they need to try*
> *and lie . . . when they walk away*
>
> *lovers play games to save face*
> *so I'll tell you what we'll do*
> *we'll play Monopoly, you and I*
> *just for a change of pace*
>
> *you grab the railroads*
> *   and buy up Boardwalk*
> *and I'll hang on to Park Place°*

°*Venus Trines at Midnight,* by Linda Goodman (New York: Taplinger Publishing Company, Inc., 1970. To be republished by Harper & Row, 1979).

☆ ☆ ☆ ☆ ☆ ☆

LEO

Fire — Fixed — Positive
Ruled by the Sun
Symbols: Lion & Shy Pussycat
Day Forces — Masculine

CAPRICORN

Earth — Cardinal — Negative
Ruled by Saturn
Symbol: The Goat
Night Forces — Feminine

The **LEO-CAPRICORN** *Relationship*

"If the redskins have won . . . they will beat the tom-tom; it is always their sign of victory."

Now Smee had found the tom-tom, and was at that moment sitting on it. "You will never hear the tom-tom again," he muttered, but inaudibly of course, for strict silence had been enjoined.

Because I am particularly fond of Leos, it makes me sad to convey to them unpleasant astrological information I know in advance will be like a sharp thorn in their big, soft paws. But I am an astrologer, therefore dedicated to the truth, the whole truth, and nothing but the truth, so help me Saturn.

All right, already, so *help* me, Saturn! Go ahead, help me. Don't just hang there in the sky, twinkling your icy-blue light. Help me explain to the Big Cats that you are destined, by some inexplicable inter-galactic law, to sit on their tom-toms.

Saturn just winked at me. That means he's agreed to channel through me the words I write in this chapter, in a stern and wise, but loving manner. So please keep in mind that I am not the author of what you are about to read. The author is Saturn, whose great, granite strength is ever undaunted, even by the dazzling brilliance of Leo's ruler, the Sun.

Saturn is the planetary ruler of the Sun Sign Capricorn, and the Sun Sign Capricorn, in astrology, as I've mentioned briefly elsewhere in this book, represents, or if you will, symbolizes, the Hebrew people, all the richly monotheistic Jewish tradition and the indomitable Jewish spirit. Because of this, Capricorns, who contain that Hebrew essence, whether they're Scottish, Irish, Italian, or Hopi Indian, respect all forms of education and learning. Most Goats are born students, their attitude toward diplomas, degrees, or anything scholastic approaching reverence. They also revere the family circle, whether its shape is square or oblong. And money. Yes, along with Taurus and Cancer, they revere money. Cappy considers money the only security against human suffering. A savings account is one of life's absolute necessities to the Goat.

Cappies do tend to be a bit snobbish about their family trees, reputation in the community, class status, and so forth, and it must be sadly confessed that there are a scattering of Capricorns (fortunately, only a very few) who contain some tinge of prejudice regarding Jewish people. If you know any such Goats, do remind them that their Sun Sign symbolizes the "Chosen People," won't you? Smack them in their Karmas with the hard facts. It will do them good to realize they must learn to respect things and people worthy of respect, instead of hypocritical material values. Any Capricorn should be proud to be astrologically associated with the grandeur of character and courage bred into the genes of those led by Moses into the Promised Land — to share the shining spiritual heritage of those millions of brave souls condemned to an unspeakable hell on Earth during the insane Nazi holocaust. For many reasons, personally speaking as an Irish Aries, I would be proud to have been born a Sun Sign Capricorn, as proud as I would be to have been born a Jew.

Be still, Leo. We're going to open the cage and let you out in a moment. You see? As soon as the word "proud" is mentioned, up pops Leo, like an anxious piece of bread in a toaster. But to give the Lions and Lionesses credit, they also pop up, and are called forth by the mention of cruelty and injustice. They roar in splendid outrage, their noble heads held high, ever ready to defend the defenseless, protect the downtrodden — and set free the imprisoned human spirit. Not yet, Leo. Soon. We're explaining the Capricorn motivation, so you and the Goats will understand one another better, which is the whole purpose of this chapter. We are also teaching you a necessary lesson in Saturnine patience.

Because (as you may have noted in "The Twelve Mysteries of Love" section in the front of this book) Capricorn's mantra is "I use," the Goats can be, once in a while, a little selfish. They call it self-protection. Exactly the same reason Leo gives for being insufferably arrogant. Self-protection. Against all those inferior people. This is a 6-8 Sun Sign Pattern, with Leo representing eighth-house matters to Capricorn, and Capricorn representing sixth-house matters to Leo. It makes for an interesting association. If Leo will bear with me, through some painful observations, I'll explain why.

It must be faced that there's no way out from under the restrictive influence of Saturn over Leo's bright enthusiasm and warm, sunny personality — nor is it likely that Capricorn will be unduly impressed with the sound of the tom-toms the Big Cats beat in pride over their great accomplishments. There's no way Leo can ultimately top the Goats, because Capricorn is ahead of Leo on the karmic astrological wheel of life. Leo is undeniably wise, but the Goat is wiser. Leo is a Fixed Sign, therefore somewhat stubborn, but the earthy Goat is *more* stubborn, and on top of that is bossy, Capricorn being a Cardinal Sign. Even bossier than Leo, but much quieter about it, less obtrusive. Leo is admittedly a practical organizer, but Capricorn is even more so.

Cheer up, Shy Pussycats, Lions, and Lionesses. I realize all this has been like tossing custard pies at your egos, but remember I said that your 6-8 Sun Sign Pattern with Capricorn is interesting? Here's what I meant. Despite the fact that the Goat is a smidgen wiser and more stubborn than you, more practical — and even bossier — in any close relationship with a Saturn-ruled person, that Goat will represent the sixth astrological house to Leo.

The sixth astrological house represents *service*. Therefore, the planets decree that in some manner, however subtle or marginal, Capricorns must provide some sort of "service" to any Leo with whom they are closely associated. There! Doesn't that make you feel better? It's like, well.. let's see.. it's like a mother and father being wiser than their small baby, yet nevertheless forced to render "service" to the infant. I see the Leos glaring at me, in injured dignity. Sorry. That's not a good allegory. I mean, it is a good one, but not designed to soothe the Lion's sore paws, still smarting from the thorn of Capricorn's restriction over Leo. (Dare I say Capricorn's superiority over Leo? No. I dare not.) How about imagining Capricorns (of whatever chronological age) as kindly, but firm, grandparents, who serve Leos by counseling them from the vantage point of wisdom, by the virtue of seeing things from the top of the mountain. That's a little easier, perhaps, for Leo to swallow. It's rather like taking your castor oil or eating your spinach and asparagus as a child. It isn't pleasant, but it's for your own good and to your best interest to give in and stop struggling.

Leo and Capricorn are curious about one another. The Big Cats fascinate Cappy, who would love to know what makes them the way they are. Normally, the Goats aren't curious, but Leo does represent to them a puzzle they wouldn't mind piecing together, although they won't lose any sleep over it. Leo, on the other hand, inwardly senses that Capricorn's counsel is well meant, and may now and then listen. Not always, but now and then.

Capricorn observes with some amusement Leo's extravagances of speech and dress. Within the Goat's heart of hearts, he (or she) may wistfully wish for a bit of the Leonine daring. Cappy is often strangely moved by the huge scope of Leo's goals, intrigued by Leo's generosity and disregard for financial security, and maybe just a little envious of Leo's courage in dreaming such giant dreams, then having the majesty to proudly *command* them to come true. How *dare* they not come true?!

Unless there's a cautious Moon Sign or Ascendent in the Lion or Lioness's horoscope, these people will not exhibit undue concern for rainy days, nor be overly troubled over the possibility of either poverty or failure. It's an attitude totally opposed to the caution and concern for the morrow displayed by the typical Goat. There's so much that's different in these two. From their hair styles to their clothing, from their ability to be patient (Cappy can, Leo can't), and from their banking practices (Cappy's a bit tightfisted, Leo a little loose-handed) to their speech (Cappy's is somewhat shy and gentle, Leo's is eloquent and dramatic), and from their method of reaching for the brass ring on the carousel (Cappy is watchful and carefully calculating, Leo is daring and impulsive), it sometimes seems as though they are from two different Universes.

If the Sun and Moon in their horoscopes are square or opposed, each will make the other feel markedly uncomfortable, with Leo privately believing that Capricorn is cold, selfish, unfeeling, and stuffy — and the Goat privately believing that Leo is wasteful and careless, egotistical and vain — as they "see through a glass darkly," recognizing only the negative side of the coin of character in one another.

Should these Luminaries, however, be in favorable aspect with each other in their respective charts, Capricorn will provide a sturdy mental and emotional foundation, upon which Leo can build some lasting fires, symbolically speaking. Realistically speaking, the Goat could profit by imitating Leo's vision and faith in the future, just as the Lion or Lioness will find the dependability of a Capricorn friend, business associate, relative, lover, or mate a secure and cozy haven of the familiar and the reliable when the skyrockets fizzle out on rainy days. Becoming competitive can turn them into either open or secret enemies. But cooperation can cause a strong and enduring relationship to grow between them, nourished in the rich Earth of Capricorn's silent waiting and warmed by the life-giving force of Leo's benevolent Sun — when they're considerate of one another's feelings, and take turns trying to be tolerant of each other's seemingly foreign viewpoints.

Strangely and hauntingly, as with all 6-8 Sun Sign Patterns, Leo represents to Capricorn the eighth house of sexual mystery, death, birth, reincarnation, regeneration — and "other people's money." This often takes unusual forms in their relationship, one of them sometimes being that the association brings to Capricorn, through Leo, some experience of death or matters pertaining to death, connected with their meeting.

Cappy will see much further into truth by periodically looking at Life through Leo's high-powered binoculars. Leo will see truth more clearly by occasionally looking at the world through Capricorn's calm, steady eyes. The sudden comprehension of the true motivational ideals of someone completely different from yourself is always a magical surprise, bringing the power to open up a closed mind to the fresh air of understanding that touches the heart with an unexpected rush of tenderness — and the dawning of compassion. Leo desperately needs to learn and imitate the gentle humility and patience Saturn teaches Cappy so sternly, yet so wisely and so well. Capricorn just as desperately needs the warm rays of Leo's Sun to shine upon that Saturnine loneliness of spirit, for no one can so miraculously release the Goat's imprisoned yearnings as a Leo, who gloriously was born free.

I believe Old Man Saturn handled the channeling of words in this chapter quite sensibly, if a bit stuffily, don't you? We should thank him, perhaps even give him a bear hug... because, like the Capricorn men, women, and children he rules, although Saturn tends to turn away from praise with a shy blush of embarrassment, his quiet heart pounds faster, and nearly bursts with silent joy, when it's blessed by honest and affectionate appreciation.

Yes, planets can blush too, just like human Goats. Notice Saturn in the sky tonight, and see if that ancient star doesn't seem to be twinkling a little more brightly than usual, its icy-blue glitter tinged with the faintest shade of pink — for love. Venus isn't the only star to wish on, you know. Make a wish on Saturn. It may take a longer time of waiting and soul-testing to come true, but when it does, the happiness will last . . . and last . . . and last.

LEO *Woman* CAPRICORN *Man*

*He was never more sinister than when he was most
polite, which is probably the truest test of breeding; and the elegance of his diction, even when
he was swearing, no less than the distinction of
his demeanor, showed him one of a different caste . . .*

*. . . he did it with such an air, he was so frightfully
distingué, that she was too fascinated to cry out . . .*

It's always something of a shock when a Capricorn man and a Leo woman become emotionally involved or marry — a puzzling surprise to friends and strangers alike, even to their relatives. That's the common reaction, whether the names of the Lioness and the Goat are Jacqueline Bouvier Kennedy and Aristotle Onassis, Emmylou Dreyfuss and Patrick Plato, Susan Auberjonois and Rudolph Fingall, or Gertrude Franz and Cassius Pendleton. Whatever their religious creed, nationality, or station in life, these two are recognizable as markedly different; whether the Goat owns a junkyard, a fleet of tankers, a used-car lot; oversees a government, a shoe store, or a film company — whether the Lioness presides as Queen over the Salvation Army, an empire, or country, the housekeeping department of a motel, a cosmetics firm, a designer-label fashion house, or a cocoanut-juice stand on the Micronesian island of Truk — people will wonder, whisper, and conjecture. A lot of good it does them, because neither Leo nor Capricorn will stoop to discussing their personal lives or explaining their private behavior. Both of these Sun Signs consider it vulgar to take the slightest notice of gossip. Nevertheless, people continue to wonder.

How could a conservative Goat be attracted by an extravagant Lioness, who is so impulsive, so dramatic of speech and action, who majestically demands that her every whim be granted, who expects to be worshiped and looked up to, yet who refuses to look up to or worship any man? (A Leo woman will either look down on — or over to — others, but never *up* to them, a Leonine fact I've explained before in this book, but a vital facet of her personality well worth pondering more than once.)

Likewise, what could a warm-hearted, magnanimous Lioness see in a cautious Capricorn, who is more silent and brooding than Glamorous and Gregarious (the two G's of the Leo nature), who pinches the pennies she tosses away like confetti, pays compliments only rarely, usually dislikes parties (unless there's a practical reason for them), frowns on luxury (unless it has a practical purpose) and is singularly undemonstrative and undramatic regarding his emotions and feelings ?

It's a good question. Or rather, two good questions. But astrology has the answers. The Goat and the Lioness have more in common than meets the astrologically untrained eye; they possess more mutually fascinating qualities and character traits than the esoterically uninitiated might suspect or be able to recognize without a little study of metaphysics.

Consider the nature of the needs of the Goat: The typical Capricorn man prefers marrying up the social ladder to down. He's secretly and shyly impressed by — even in awe of — fame and success, whether on a local community, national, or worldwide basis. He obtains great inner satisfaction from possessions of quality and value (whether inanimate objects, real estate, or women) which other people admire and envy. A male Goat is touchingly drawn to the kind of women who promise to bring some sunlight into his heart by virtue of their ability to coax him to expand his emotional horizons, which he privately longs to do, no matter how gruffly he may deny it.

Consider the qualifications of the Lioness: The typical Leo woman realizes, relatively early in life, some measure of prestige and status, some degree of public notice or social distinction. This girl's activities can range from being queen of the prom, head cheerleader, chief of the local firefighters in a small town — to becoming a politician, a well-known actress, an educational leader, a pioneering scientist, or a successful career woman in a variety of endeavors. She is almost always admired and envied by both her peers and her inferiors (she *has* no superiors). Sunlight she possesses in abundance, and she adores guiding conservative people toward more exciting horizons, in every direction, on every level.

Now, consider the nature and needs of a Leo woman: Turning around the emotional law of supply and demand, a Lioness needs to exist within the shining aura of success. She must have a mate she can respect (she may dally with a drifter, but she won't remain with him), a man who isn't lazy, and who is a true achiever. She's touchingly drawn to the kind of men who will be calm and patient with her thoughtless arrogance and dramatic manner. She seeks a man who will never humiliate her in public by a lack of breeding or good manners. She requires a male who's capable of earning enough money to support her in comparative luxury (comparative in relation to the way most of us peasants live) and *who will, further,* allow her total freedom of behavior and not deny her the inner satisfaction that comes from taking permanent possession of herself through expressing her womanhood by impressing the world in some manner.

Consider the qualifications of the Goat: A Capricorn man has perhaps more potential of gaining the worldly recognition and material security admired by a Leo girl, from Ohio or Australia, than any other Sun Sign male (with the possible exception of Cancer, Taurus, or another Leo). His quiet ambition and driving determination to reach the summit of the nearest or highest mountain peak will find royal favor in her eyes. She'll appreciate the fact that his cool, hard head matches her cool, languid poise. Because he is never lazy, this permits *her* to be periodically lazy (Leos need lots and lots of rest to look beautiful and charge up their powerful solar energy). His normally dignified behavior will meet with her regal approval, and the bashful sweetness he reveals to few people (she being one of the lucky ones) arouses all her warm and protective tenderness. His sense of loyalty is identical to her own. In addition, his seemingly endless Saturnine patience with her fiery temperament brings to her a relaxed sense of emotional security.

So far, everything is mellow and marvelous and melodious between them. However, if the Sun and Moon between their horoscopes are in unfavorable aspect, they'll have to struggle hard for compatibility. He'll accuse her of being vain, smug, spoiled rotten and selfish — she'll accuse him of being cold, cruel, stingy, unemotional and selfish. (Selfishness is a trait they share in common.) Even if their Luminaries are in positive aspect, they'll face a few tensions, like everyone else. It's the problem contained near the end of the paragraph before the last one, beginning with the words: "*. . . . and who will, further . .*" that causes many of the conflicts between them. Not all, but many. Go back and read it again, please. Do you see the problem? If not, I'll explain.

This lady, who is so sensual and graceful, gracious and generous, so sunny and cheerful and proud . . . leans to Leo's two G's, the Glamourous and the Gregarious. Not only does she require periodic parties and occasional gala events (where she can wear her crown or tiara and mingle with the masses), she has an equally intense need to be free now and then to follow the Sun on her own — free to spontaneously and impulsively decide to attend a christening, a coronation, a bake sale, or a horse show alone, maybe indulge in some cross-country skiing all by herself (not far, just at the edge of town) without formal permission from anyone, including her boyfriend, or even the man she's permitted to mate with her for life and father her cubs. The Capricorn man who believes this is an exaggeration should question her long-suffering parents. They will enlighten him.

She'll also dramatically demand (or privately desire, with unexpressed, dangerously pent-up fierceness) the opportunity to blaze her own path of glory in some creative occupation or challenging career. Leo women tend to retain their own surnames after marriage since the Aquarian Age sexual revolution (although this sometimes causes them to suffer minor traumas over what to do about the initials to be engraved on the satin pillowcases, silk draperies, gold bathroom faucets, and such). Since the average Capricorn man is more than a mite possessive of his lady friend or wifely companion-of-hearth-and-home, he may balk. Further, the Goat dislikes open or active competition, let alone subtle competition (which he *really* mistrusts). Things could become a little earthquakish between them when he insists on being securely aware of his lady love's whereabouts and activities to make sure she's not doing anything which might disgrace the family name. The only solution is compromise.

He's just going to have to give her a certain amount of freedom, if he wants to maintain a happy and harmonious home — trust her to have sufficient dignity and pride (believe me, she's overendowed with both) not to disgrace him or herself, or to be disloyal, when she's roaming the jungle solo, so to speak. If she wants to attend classes in fashion design or animal husbandry a couple of nights a week, he should demonstrate visibly and verbally his enthusiastic — not grudging — approval. It's important that his approval be enthusiastic, because if it's grudging, it will cancel out the emotional tranquility it could bring to their relationship. When she wants to visit friends a few blocks or miles away, or see a film he has no interest in seeing himself, he should phone one of his three old friends and invite him over (it had better not be a "her"), or drop in on one of them for a change, without waiting for an engraved invitation. Or he can putter around with the car while she's gone — *his* car — she's driving hers — and that's another thing, they'll need two chariots. The new, sleek, and impressive one for her, the secondhand jeep, station wagon, or pickup truck for him. So much for his areas of compromise.

She should try to handle her side of the compromising gracefully. Isn't that the way royalty traditionally handles everything? When she tells him haughtily that she sees no reason to request his permission, however rarely, for anything she may wish to do, he should inform her, calmly and affectionately, with that funny Goat twinkle in his eyes, that it's not a matter of permission, but consultation, and that even Queens are expected to at least consult with their Prime Ministers and their Kings — then quote a few historic scenes to prove it. He should remind her that the purpose of such occasionally required royal seeking of consultation is to make sure that major decisions aren't impractical and impulsive to the extent that they endanger the castle or the Kingdom. If she's going to gad about for longer than a few hours, it's more gracious of her to let him know her general intentions — the kind and considerate thing to do. And this woman is genuinely kindhearted. To make people happy brings her joy. Once she realizes how much happier and content she can make the man she loves by showing some concern for his feelings, she'll be more sympathetic and solicit his wise counsel more often regarding her plans. It's not gracious of her to buy a peacock farm without telling the Goat, or trade his trophy collection for a helicopter without giving him a preliminary hint.

He's a gentle lover, yet his passions run deeper than is ever apparent on the surface. Only the woman who knows the Capricorn man intimately is aware of the true depth of his emotions, the latent power of his sexuality. Until she's seasoned by several years of love, the Lioness may be too self-involved to express love physically with her whole being, and there may be, in the beginning, something slightly selfish and shallow about her sexual behavior. But he is patient, and willing to wait for the richness he knows lies just beneath her feminine vanity to develop into the kind of mutual experience that will deepen their relationship. His quiet air of waiting, his eloquent silence when he touches her, will gradually move her heart and allow her to demonstrate the rare blend of affection, tenderness, and sensuality hiding within the aloofness of every Leo woman. She is a Lioness; the pure, feral ecstasy of lovemaking is part of her nature, and often a Saturn-ruled man has just the right combination of masculine qualities to arouse these feelings in her to their ultimate expression. His obvious desire for her is the key, for Leo represents the eighth house of sexual mystery (among other things) to Capricorn, and a Leo woman is always irresistibly stirred by the awareness that she's truly adored, needed, desired, and wanted. If the Luminaries between their nativities are in negative aspect, they may face difficult adjustments, but the best way to meet difficulty is with Saturnine patience (his great gift to her) — and the Sun's ability to make clouds and shadows disappear simply by shining (her great gift to him).

Her natural *élan* and nobility of bearing is why he admires her, but her nobility of character is why he loves her. Her great capacity for generosity and forgiveness softens his melancholy and even gradually dissolves his caution. He needs her warmth and courage, just as she needs his strength and stability. They are very different, these two, but when "like mates with like," love has few lessons to teach — and who wants to stay in grade school forever ? For a man and a woman to learn and to grow together is an exciting adventure. Leo's fragrant, sultry jungle can be a seductive and thrilling new terrain for the Goat accustomed to the continual sameness of rocky ledges — and Capricorn's "purple mountain majesties" beckon the curious Lioness with the promise of a magnificent view from the top. Such is the eternal and compelling call of the unknown to the human spirit.

☆ ☆ ☆ ☆ ☆ ☆

LEO *Man* CAPRICORN *Woman*

*He was tingling with life and also top-heavy
with conceit. "Am I not a wonder, oh, I am
a wonder!" he whispered to her; and though she
thought so also, she was really glad for the sake
of his reputation that no one heard him.*

The Leo male believes that he is, by far, the most practical person he knows. Whatever the actual truth of the matter may be, this is what he believes. He glances in the mirror, and the image he sees reflected there is that of a handsome hero-type, smooth and unflappable, who clearly has it together. Such is the flattering picture of himself he carries in his mind in all his dealings with those less fortunately endowed. Then he falls in love with a Capricorn girl. Suddenly, with no warning, he feels all feet, all thumbs, awkward, impulsive, impractical — maybe even a little foolish. For a Lion, that's a mighty unpleasant mixture of feelings.

Naturally, he doesn't let on right away that he's so discomfited in her presence. What, him worry? Like Alfred E. Neuman, of *Mad Magazine*, he goes right on grinning, bluffing his way out of his uneasiness by going through the motions of being on top of the situation, pretending a cool poise he doesn't really feel. The discomfort begins when he senses this odd "teaching thing" about her. Or is it judgmental? He can't decide whether she makes him feel like he's dealing with his mother, his fourth-grade schoolteacher, or his older sister, who's always putting him down. Is it his father she reminds him of when she . . . . ? No, of course not. That's silly. How could such a soft-spoken lady remind him of his *father*? But he wonders, as she begins to quietly confide in him her opinions about abstract art versus the masters, why she's determined to visit Europe, what's wrong with today's educational systems, how she thinks building your own home is a more intense and total experience than buying or renting someone else's concept of living . . and possibly legalized abortion. Something cozy and protective about him makes her trust him enough to tell him all these things. Normally, she doesn't air her views openly, or freely discuss her personal convictions. He should be deeply moved by her decision to trust her mind and its thoughts to him, which is this timid girl's careful security-check before she trusts her heart to him. But is he? No. Usually, he is not. He's too busy thinking about his masculine ego requirements.

He listens to her benignly, with a kind of amused tolerance, taking advantage of her earnest concentration to study her womanly charms and mentally plan his seductive strategy, lazily calculating how long it will be until she's lying back contentedly in his arms, and then he'll . . . . wait a minute. She has paused momentarily, to see if he's been listening. To prove to her then that he didn't miss a word, he'll affectionately, but firmly, scold her about some of her opinions, confidently pointing out where she's wrong. Warming up, he tells her how she should wear her hair and what kind of sweater he thinks would be more becoming on her than the one she's wearing. Since she's so quiet and doesn't interrupt him, he's encouraged to tell her how she could improve her mind, her appearance, and even her health — by allowing him to guide her life-style from now on.

Something is wrong. She's *too* quiet. He thought she had such lovely eyes, so soft and shiny, so twinkly with subtle humor . . but why do they now suddenly remind him of two steel bullets — or a pair of glittering marble aggies ? Her gimlet stare is as cold as her voice when she speaks. "It's late. I have to be up early. I'll see you next week — maybe."

It's about now that those feelings of fumbling awkwardness and foolishness envelop him. He feels rejected, humiliated. He shouldn't. It's just that her reactions are controlled and guided by Saturnine instincts. She's extremely self-protective, and she has the common sense to withdraw from an approaching battle before love is seriously wounded — or killed. It's more loving of her than he realizes to call time out for contemplation. If he would stop thinking of himself as the priority problem, and think more of her, he would receive her silent message . . . "Let's take some time apart to think, because I don't really want to stop loving you, and I might if you keep pushing me. You've almost made me afraid to confide in you again. Please realize what you're doing. I don't want to drop back into the lonely way life was before you came along. Maybe a week or so away from each other will make you understand the things you do and say that hurt me."

If he could have looked in her window after he left that night, he would have seen that her eyes were no longer cold with stern determination, but soft and shining . . . with unshed tears. She tries hard to stop her tears, this girl, before they escape and expose her innermost feelings, and usually she succeeds. But not always. If he had been able to see her on that night, he would have watched her weep for a few brief moments, her sobs muffled by the pillow she clutched, pretending it was him. The only way the Lion will ever really understand this quiet creature, who seems so eternally cool and composed, is to observe her through the windows of his heart when she thinks she's all alone and no one can see or hear her troubled emotions. Even as a little girl, she kept all the nameless fears of childhood locked within, presenting to adults the image Saturn insistently whispered to her that they demanded. *"What a well-behaved child,"* they would always say, nodding in approval. And so her small heart knew that she was liked, the security all children so desperately and silently seek. Saturn teaches all Cappies, from infancy, to behave properly in public — and they never forget the lesson. The Capricorn woman subconsciously feels that if she's guilty of a public display of emotion, she'll be scolded in disapproval. Therefore, the habit of self-control deepens every year, offending some — and sadly leaving her to wonder privately what she has done wrong.

She's not the only one. The Lion in our example is also tortured by wondering what *he* has done wrong. If he thinks it over with careful introspection, he'll realize that he made several common mistakes with the Goat Girl: believing he could wind her around his little finger by the sheer force of his presence — failing to show respect for her very sound and already carefully thought out ideas about matters of vital interest to her — and expecting her to be delighted over his offer to mold her, like a piece of damp clay, into his image of the ideal woman.

This woman is not a piece of damp clay, waiting for Svengali Leo to mold her. She's made of solid rock, plus mounds of earth (but remember that earth can be warm and safe and protective too). A chisel, or perhaps a few caps of dynamite might change the structure of her thought patterns and habits (slightly), but nothing less than this. Certainly they won't change through thoughtlessly arrogant lectures from a smugly confident Lion, however magnetically exciting he is to her otherwise. (Leo represents the eighth house of sexual mystery, among other things, to Capricorn.) She's not about to change her clothing, hair style, or opinions for any man, not even this proud one with the graceful walk and powerful jungle appeal, who undeniably makes her knees go weak when he grins at her, and causes her to be depressed herself when she senses he's sad, whether she expresses her compassion verbally or not. Maybe he can gradually change her — *very* gradually — one soft step at a time. But instant change he can forget. A Capricorn girl does nothing instantly, and regal commands, even loving ones, have the effect of bringing out all her stubbornness to strengthen her already-steely will.

His sunny disposition and air of confidence, however, melts her more often than he guesses, at the same time inspiring her and lifting her Saturnine gloom more than she confesses. She'll listen attentively when he talks about his giant goals and future ambitions. She's on the side of the good and the right, so his idealism will please her — and she's definitely on the side of ambition, of all shapes and sizes. The grander his goals, the more she'll support them, though she won't hesitate to identify any flaws that threaten to make them impractical. He should appreciate her sensible advice, heed her instinctive wisdom, not resent it. Capricorns have quite a marvelous knack for turning dreams into reality.

Counterclockwise, she should be more often guided by his courageous personality, and listen to him when he tells her to ease up on the caution before she smothers them both in negativity. There are joys known only to those free spirits who follow the song of the skylark, and who realize that taking a chance now and then makes Life more lyrical. The Lion was born knowing that the Kingdom of Happiness is not paved with insurance policies against possible disappointment and disaster. He is a King, and therefore he can teach her the nuances of nobility. But he should lead her out of the dark dungeons of depression into the sunlight tenderly, not with a large shove.

The Lion in love with a Capricorn girl should memorize the proverb of the tortoise and the hare, even though the ending may annoy him, remembering that she is the tortoise, he is the hare. He's magical and powerful enough to turn himself into the shape and style of a tortoise if he really wants to win the race. But trying to rush the tortoise only delays his own progress, and won't stop Cappy's slow, deliberate pace to cross the finish line. Time is her friend. Saturn. Old Father Time. No one ever beat him yet.

These two are almost certain to have approximately one debate per month regarding money. Such a waste of loving-hours, and so easy to circumvent. Why argue? It's really none of his business how she handles her money; none of her business how he spends his. The simple solution is for the Lion and the Goat to keep their financial affairs entirely separate, forever and a day. She may want to earn her own cash, and he's totally selfish if he pouts over this. Should he want to share his income with her after they're married or committed (because Leo is generous, unless he has the Moon or Ascendent in Capricorn, Cancer, or Virgo), she should accept it in the spirit it's given, not get all stuffy and independent about it.

However they work it out, she should be free to "sock" her money, invest it as she pleases, count the interest from her savings every night if she likes, without being tortured by his lectures on stinginess. Likewise, he should be free to make a kite from dollar bills, give his money to the needy, buy extravagant gifts for himself and others, lose a stack of it on a dream or a lost cause, or use it to light the wood fire on chilly winter nights if that's what makes him happy — without suffering stern looks of disapproval from her. It's the only way. Money madness murders love. Yet it's nothing but green paper, bearing pictures of past presidents, unattractive pieces of metal, or checks printed with wild geese and scenic sunset views, which are also . . . simply paper. Only love is real. Money is an illusion, a mirage. They should split it between them as equally as possible, then forget it. Ignore it. Never discuss it.

Their physical relationship, because their natures are so different, depends upon the aspects between their Luminaries, Ascendents, and other planets in their horoscopes. If these are unfavorable, he may feel she's unresponsive to his hunger for affection and sentiment during lovemaking — and she may be unable to express her love for him in a physical way when he makes her feel inadequate by finding fault with her sexual behavior, which may not be fiery or demonstrative enough for him — which has the unfortunate dual result of breaking her heart and freezing her emotions.

There are a few (a very few) Capricorn females whose sexual mores have become pathetically twisted because of some sort of rejection by their families, which is always a severe psychological wound to a Goat. This kind of rare, insensitive Capricorn girl accepts sex as casually as she accepts a handshake, an attitude caused by the negative side of Saturn's influence, which hardens her emotions and her conscience simultaneously. She goes through the mechanical motions of erotic behavior, leaving her partners feeling cold and empty, but not nearly as cold and empty as she is left herself. Subconsciously, she uses sex to gain favors, or something she needs, creating a distortion of the positive practicality of the Saturnine essence of "I use."

But this kind of Goat Girl is not likely to appeal to the proud and jealous Lion, and the great majority of Capricorn women symbolize promiscuity's opposite — romantic shyness and sexual faithfulness. If certain planets, including the Luminaries, are in harmonious aspect between the charts of a Leo man and a Capricorn girl, their sexual expression can be a lasting ecstasy when he has waited for her Saturn-restricted emotions to be gradually released, through learning to trust him. Then their physical Oneness will possess the new and trembling dimension of tenderness, and he'll be rewarded with the knowledge that he's awakened the amazing depth of her latent passion, which will from that time forward be shared only with him. Nothing is a more soothing balm to a Lion than knowing he alone possesses his woman's secret sexuality, a part of her intimate self she's revealed to no one else but him.

She should tuck a small card in her savings account passbook (where she's sure to see it frequently) printed with the words: *Don't drown his enthusiasm and generosity with excessive pessimism, depression, or unnecessary caution, and never wound his dignity and pride with cold criticism, which he'll interpret as rejection.*

He should tuck a small card in his car mirror (where he's sure to see it frequently) printed with the words: *Be kind and respectful to her family, stifle your lectures, and be gentle with her quiet heart. Understand that her conservatism springs from an inner fear of poverty and loneliness, some haunted karmic memory. Don't forget that she needs sincere compliments and appreciation even more than you do, and remember that she only pretends to dislike sentiment and bear hugs.*

On reflection, make that a very large card for the Lion. Maybe an eight by ten. In a gold frame. Twenty-four-carat gold, to make him happy. Antique, to make her happy. She feels safer around old objects from a more secure yesterday, fashioned by master craftsmen, who loved their work. That's a hint of the kind of gift he can give her on the anniversary of the day they met. She may never mention it, but she knows the date. She wrote it down in her diary, then hid it under the mattress with his first love letter he thought she threw away. He should have known better. Cappy never throws away anything of real value. It's up to him whether that includes his love for her.

LEO

Fire — Fixed — Positive
Ruled by the Sun
Symbols: Lion & Shy Pussycat
Day Forces — Masculine

AQUARIUS

Air — Fixed — Positive
Ruled by Uranus
Symbol: The Water Bearer
Day Forces — Masculine

The **LEO-AQUARIUS** *Relationship*

Then they got the strangest surprise on this
Night of Nights.

It's never the Uranus type of surprises of the Water Bearers that cause the trouble in this 7-7 polarity-opposition carnival of the silly and the sublime between Leo and Aquarius. The problems are caused by other things. Let's approach the subject cautiously, sort of "back into it," in reverse gear, so to speak. I believe it will be unexpectedly worthwhile to devote a page or so of this compatibility chapter to the accomplishing of such a reverse effect. The Leos may growl a little in resentment at being shuffled a few paragraphs behind, but in so submitting they'll earn clusters of karmic stars in their Kingly and Queenly crowns, and diadems for their patience and humility — even though they really haven't any choice in the matter. (We wouldn't stand a chance if we gave them a choice!)

In the summer of 1978, I received a letter from an Aquarian reader named Richard Ellsberry. At first I thought it must be postmarked Spica or Arcturus — or perhaps Sirius (which really should be spelled Sirios, because of the Osiris anagram mystery, you know, but it's been distorted, and will no doubt be corrected later). However, the envelope was stamped Phoenix, Maryland. The Phoenix figures. Maryland is incidental. Water Bearer Richard wrote, in part, the following:

Dear Linda Goodman . . . The observations you made in your book Sun Signs *concerning the kinks in the Aquarian personality are quite remarkable. In the Aquarian Child chapter, you say: "He has a kind of thing about clocks and watches, so it may have something to do with a Time Machine — a common Aquarian obsession."*

Now, what I want to know is this: How in the hell did you know I'm into a Time Machine ? ? ! ! I've been working on one for quite a while. It involves attempting to contact People From the Future. The logic is that — if we can't go to them, they will have to come to us. After all, THEY are SURE to have Time Machines, right ?

(Right on, Richard! Perfect Uranian logic.)

This concept started developing in my head when I was 17, about 7 years ago. It's going to be in the works for another 4 years, until 1982. I call it The Chrononautic Society. I'd like to invite you and all your interested friends to our first meeting with People From the Future on Tuesday, the Ninth of March, A.D. 1982. This is not a hoax. We shall produce the most spectacular reception ever held in honor of People From the Future. Since they are IN the Future, they will already have heard of our efforts, and travel back in Time to attend. We shall have gifts to offer them, such as works of music, and art — and volunteers.

(Volunteers ! ! ? ?)

The probability for achieving contact in this daring experiment . . .

(Daring ? Now we have Leo's attention !)

. . . in this daring experiment is increasing as more documentation is amassed (literature, photographs, tapes, etc.). At present, the location of our meeting is unknown. I shall keep you informed. Conditions may demand a network of congregations around the Earth, interlaced by AM radio and video. The date of 3/9/82 is chosen for its coincidence of remarkable celestial events, such as THE JUPITER EFFECT, being a rare moment when all of the Sun's planets are on the same side; the advent of the Aquarian Age; the temporary overlap of the orbits of Neptune and Pluto; the twelve-year interim between Kohoutek's & Halley's Comets — and the Full Moon. The

Chrononautic Society is a non-profit, open alliance of artists, scientists, occultists and other visionaries. Its emblem is the Two-Headed Serpent, which symbolizes the Doctrine of Aborescence. This speculative thesis states that Time is not quite linear, but branching — what crystallographers call a "dendritic growth." This is not, however, to imply that we are bound by any ideological dogma. We heartily encourage all criticisms and suggestions. Box #231 Phoenix, Maryland 21131, USA. Unfortunately, we are not yet funded by Congress or backed by the Rockefeller Foundation, so if you want a reply, please send a self-addressed, stamped envelope.

Richard Ellsberry, bless you! You are my shining answer to all those who ask me, "Are Aquarians really as far-out as you say they are?," to which I now answer with a resounding YES! (Much further out, actually.) I've completed a "reality check" on this Water Bearer, and I assure you, he is perfectly serious. He has personal affiliations and contacts with several erudite and quite respectable men of impressive scientific achievement, knowledge and reputation — along with a number of perceptive and precognitive, although as yet unsung, "ordinary" Earthlings, such as yourself. So all you Water Bearers out there who dream of a Time Machine — this is your moment for miracles. Go forth! Write to Richard and become space buddies in Tomorrow. (Or Yesterday. Same thing. Remember your dendritic principles.)

I had a couple of excellent reasons for making this Aquarian Time Machine information public. First — I think it's a marvelous idea, because astrologically, astronomically and otherwise, the decade between 1982 and 1992 *is* going to contain a number of shocks (especially for the uninitiated) and it's best to be prepared. Also, it allows us to ponder the Leo-Aquarius relationship. I'm positive the Chrononautic Society is going to be inundated with as many requests for membership from Leos as from Aquarians. It's the *daringness* of the idea that will appeal to the Big Cats, whose middle names are Courage. Of course, you realize, I trust, that all Leo joiners will include in their résumés to the C.S. their own personal ideas of how the entire 1982 reception for People From the Future in this *very* "close encounter" should be organized and expedited. Obviously, the Keynote Speaker at the 3/9/82 Close Encounter should be one who is qualified as the Leader of such a distinguished and vast cosmic undertaking of such obvious galactic importance. Namely, a Leo. After all, is it not, in part, timed to the rare moment when the SUN'S planets are all on the same side — and is not the SUN itself the ruler of Leo? What could be more appropriate? Such a royal undertaking as the C.S. plans certainly can't be left to the bumbling and blundering of underlings and peasants. Only nobility is equipped to shoulder the grave responsibility of an effort of this magnitude.

That's more or less the attitude of any Lion or Lioness in dealing with Aquarian people and Aquarian projects of all shapes and sizes, whether major or minor — whether consisting of filling the sandbox for the kiddies, building a birdhouse, decorating an office, planning the school prom, plotting an advertising or a political campaign, producing a film or a play — or deciding on a stock merger between two huge conglomerates. It matters not. Leo will lead. Or Leo will take his or her sand bucket, stock certificates, swatches of material, balloons, wren house, screenplay or whatever — and find another kingdom over which to rule where superiority is both welcomed and appreciated. Both respected and worshipped.

Normally, this won't bother the typical Water Bearers in the slightest. They're really not terribly interested in being the Big Chiefs on the reservations. They're more interested in the invention of new Rain Dances and such. How to design a better Totem Pole. However, when these two Sun Signs *do* clash over something — whatever it might be — the result could be likened to a herd of Buffalo meeting head-on with a herd of elephants. A brick building meeting a cement wall. Or two asses (using the biblical term) meeting nose to nose. A most mulish and deadlocked scene. That is to say — both Leo and Aquarius are Fixed. The Water Bearers, the Lions and the Lionesses share the dubious distinction of having been born under Fixed Signs. This means that they're as stubborn as crazy glue, and they won't budge their positions a fraction of an inch when they believe they're right and justified in an opinion or an action. Both Leo and Aquarius adore surprises. They're both progressive-minded, both generous and magnanimous of spirit; both defend the underdog and the minority voices of the turtles heard throughout the land. Both tend to be tall and handsome (or beautiful). Both are highly intelligent, friendly, quite gregarious — and fascinating talkers. Both like to protect the weak — both love and respect Nature. So far, wonderful! Everything is mellow, with soft purring and happy meowing from the Big Cats . . . and lots of fresh, sparkling cooperation brimming over from the little brown jugs of the Uranus-ruled Water Bearers.

Nevertheless, these two signs are opposed on the horoscopic wheel. One has what the other lacks and can't stand to admit he or she needs. Normally. (Unless the Ascendents and Luminaries between their birth charts are cozy and harmonious — then they don't mind admitting their individual needs and trading back and forth with each other.) What does Leo have that Aquarius lacks? Personal warmth. A certain sense of dignity. Stability and dependability.

What does Aquarius have that Leo lacks? I know it's difficult to conceive that Lions and Lionesses lack anything at all, inheriting as they have every virtue under the Sun (their own ruler). But, alas, there is one gift of the gods they don't possess — the humility to admit they may be guilty of a scattered fault or two — that there may be a chipped diamond here and there among the rubies and emeralds of their glowing positive traits and qualities.

In brief, they aren't overendowed with the ability to confess error or to accept criticism gracefully.

Leo would do very well to borrow from Aquarians a smidgen of their humility, their detachment regarding criticism and their cheerful willingness to confess their shortcomings. Tell Aquarians they're all geniuses, and they'll shrug, completely unimpressed. Tell an Aquarian that he or she is crazy, and the Water Bearer will nod pleasantly in the affirmative, delighted with the analysis — and entirely unoffended. The flattering appraisal will ordinarily float in one ear and out the other. But insinuate, even mildly, that Leos are less than superior in any way, and it's "Off with your head!" They either roar or pout, and neither attitude is becoming to royalty.

Conversely, Aquarius could benefit immensely by adopting some of Leo's sunny and warm benevolence in personal relationships (a Water Bearer can be a mite cool at times, even to loved ones) by imitating Leo's dependability (it would be nice to know the Water Bearers could be counted on to mean on Thursday week what they took a blood oath on, on Wednesday last) and by assuming a trace of the Leonine poise and dignity. They don't have to go so far as to become sedate, mind you, but perhaps copy Leo's feline grace when they're walking around, so they won't bump into telephone poles so often — maybe stop standing on their heads while they watch a concert — tone down their purple hair — leave their quetzals at home when they go to church — things like that. Just a little poise and dignity. Not *too* much. Then they wouldn't be recognizable — and we certainly want them to remain recognizable, because it's hard enough as it is to identify them as members of the human race.

Since Leo and Aquarius were both born under the Sun Signs of the "Fixed Organizer," they should share the organizational responsibilities of a business venture, a romantic relationship, a Mind Trip or a Time Trip. They should each let up more than a little on his or her *personal* Fixity, while retaining a Fixity of purpose. However, although Leo is not a Cardinal Sign of Leadership (Leo is an Organizer), Leo must lead the *organizing* — in some way that will appease the gigantic ego of the Big Cats. Give Leo the title. That's all. Chief Rain Maker. Chief Totem Pole Designer. Chief Communicator with People From the Future. Chief Hairdresser. Chief Apostle. Fire Chief. Water Chief. Air Chief. Earth Chief. Oberon, King of the Faeries. Titania, Queen of the Faeries. King of the Jungle. Queen of Galactic Enterprises. Ruler of the Harem. Monarch of the Castle. That's the general idea.

Then the Water Bearer will discover that nowhere on this Earth, nor in any other galaxy of Solar System in the Past, Present or Future, will he (or she) find a more brilliantly creative, intelligent, brave and loyal "buddy" than the Lion or Lioness. It's really worth cultivating a little elasticity of the Aquarian Fixity to gain such a friend for all seasons — all Time Barriers and Astral Levels.

Any Aquarians who don't believe me may just wait for Richard Ellsberry's Close Encounter on March ninth, A.D., of 1982. When the People
From the Future arrive, right on schedule, the P.F.T.F. Phoenix-resurrected
Atlantean Leader who greets Earthlings with a combination of the Hopi Sign
language, Swahili and Sanskrit will be a proud, noble and majestic Leo. (Yes,
she will!) Never mind that the Time Machine itself will have been designed
by a P.F.T.F. Water Bearer. Aquarians don't give three quarks who takes
credit — as long as they make the flight and arrive wherever it is they're
going. Leo can travel First Class all the way, but guess who will be sitting in
the cockpit of the Laser Beam?

"Ladies and gentlemen, this is your pilot speaking. I'd like to welcome you
aboard the Leo-Osiris Phoenix XIV. We'll be cruising at an altitude of three
hundred trillion miles per Earth hour, give or take a million miles or so,
depending on the falling dust of Maldek — and flying at the speed of a
number of Light Years. The stewardesses will pass among you to explain how
to use your heads. We'll arrive at our destination at exactly a quarter-past
three on Saturday next of last year, in time to celebrate Amory Lovins'
birthday. On behalf of myself and my twin co-pilots, Howard and Robard, I
wish you a pleasant journey. Be sure to keep your Nader seat belts buckled
and bolted as we pass through the Space Warps — and don't forget to enjoy
the view from your portholes, because on a clear day you can see Forever.
Cheerio! Chiao! Roger over-and-in!"

☆ ☆ ☆ ☆ ☆ ☆

LEO *Woman* AQUARIUS *Man*

————◄●►————

Peter had continued, for a little time . . . . to
play gaily on his pipes; no doubt a rather forlorn
attempt to prove to himself that he did not care.
Then he decided not to take his medicine, so as to
grieve Wendy. Then he lay down on the bed outside
the coverlet, to vex her still more . . . . .

In the beginning, she felt herself drawn to him like a bar magnet being
propelled by jet speed. Somehow, the Water Bearer seemed to almost
literally pull her into the depths of his dreamy eyes, as though she were a wisp

of a cloud, disappearing into the space of his expression. Being a Lioness, naturally she resisted. But it was no use. She felt borne aloft by the gentle breezes of his Air Element charisma, lulled by the soothing music of his bagpipes. (To the rest of us, bagpipes may sound a little shrill and squeaky, but they're soothing if you're a Leo, because they remind you of the changing-of-the-guards, coronation parades and all that.)

For a while, all was pinkness and peacocks, lovely beyond lovely. He behaved like a veritable saint. Sometimes, she was positive she could even see his halo, but it appeared to be such an odd shape. (It was his aura, and all Uranus auras are oddly shaped. They resemble an inverted pyramid with a lightning bolt tracing the three planes that make up the triangular sides. Unusual. So are the colors. A sort of electric blue, flashed with streaks of black thunder and sparkling white conceptuals.)

Strangely, nearly the very same thing happened to him in the beginning. He felt compelled to walk barefoot on her velvet purple train, kiss the diamonds on her tiara. He was repeatedly levitated several feet by the perfumed songs of her absolutely gorgeous nose. Her very languidness calmed his restless toes and ears — while her perfect poise left him speechless and vibrating, by turns. He, too, was from time to time, certain he could see with his Third Eye her own glowing, golden-red halo. (It was her aura, shaped like the Sun, brilliant and blinding, holding him spellbound and mesmerized.) She behaved like the Queen of all angels. She purred like a kitten and hummed like a hummingbird. She smiled like a tawny Cheshire cat and grinned like his favorite quetzal. She was a breath of Heaven, flaming with passion, yet as cool as a lemon popsicle from Barney's Deli in Yonkers.

Suddenly, the sky turned grey, and Rip Van Winkle began knocking around tenpins like a drunken sailor. Heat lightning. Thunder claps. Great Niagaras of flooding waters that would have made Noah himself give up the ship came pouring forth from his Uranus jug, while his Air essence whipped up a tornado and her Fire Element blazed like the burning of Pompeii. In short, the windy, scorched and soggy season of romance arrived. He became stuffy, stodgy, stingy and sarcastic. She became rude, regal, raging and resentful. He decided she was a bore and she decided he was a boor. It was all so sad. What happened?

What happened was that their polarities got tangled and twisted. Leo and Aquarius are opposed on the karmic wheel of Life. They are polarized personalities, these two, influenced by the at-first magnetic, then repelling 7-7 Sun Sign Pattern. But opposites attract, when the sexes are also opposite — and that's the whole point of the mating marathon — opposition. At least, that's what most people believe it is. But they are wrong. The true goal of love and mating and matching auras is not to remain forever opposed in attitudes and desires, but to blend the opposing forces into a smooth harmony, to combine the best of each and either discard or dilute the worst, so as to remove the power of negative traits to torment their relationship. In plain words, she should not envy him but try to imitate the characteristics he possesses which she lacks and would benefit by absorbing. Likewise, he should realize that she contains certain graces that would bless his own personality if he would try a little harder to acquire them. That's what opposition means — it doesn't mean opposing. It means blending into bliss. But there's always the danger that the Lioness and her Water Bearer may lose all the potential excitement and inspirational promise of their love affair or marriage by continually attempting to top each other at every step along the way. Give-and-take is the answer. Not too much give and not too much take. Just the right amount of submission and command mixed, even in an unpredictable Aquarian test tube, emerges as an elixir called Equality. Equality of the sexes — and of the queenly Lioness and her Rip Van Winklish Aquarian lover or husband.

Most Lionesses keep their distance from Aquarian females, but a Leo girl can be inexplicably attracted by an Aquarian man. He accepts Life and people as effortlessly as she'd like to (and pretends to) but somehow can't quite manage to completely accomplish. Secretly, she's aware that her false pride too often imprisons her true inner warmth, and she sometimes wishes she could unbend and just drown in daisies of delight, without caring what anyone thinks of her — as he does. He makes her want to literally let her hair down and run with him through starry meadows in both an imaginary and an actual sense. She envies him his freedom of expression, his ability to be detached and unemotional. Her own passions, although usually under control, sometimes have a way of ruling her reason, to her later regret. How does he stay so cool and untouched by tragedy and disappointment? Perhaps if she became a part of him, she would understand his magic and be able to be more like him.

The Aquarian male has always been puzzled that he can't seem to count on Leo men as his friends (except maybe a couple of rare Lions, whose Moon Signs are in beneficent aspect with his natal Sun). Yet here is the intriguing contradiction of this Leo woman, this proud and aloof feline creature who has caused him to wonder if there might not be more to human contact than mere intellectual communication alone. Despite himself, she made him wonder about love, to decide he might have been wrong to dismiss emotions as "kid stuff," not worth a grown man's involvement. Eventually, he felt irresistibly urged to become as much a part of her as Nature will allow, and this was a new experience for his heart, not to mention his body. He doesn't understand — but since it's a mystery, he's certainly not going to permit it to remain unsolved. The detective instinct in him (along with other more primal instincts) makes him determined to find the answer to this lady's alluring spell over him. The most sensible way to begin, he finally sighs and admits to himself, is to possess her in the way all those sentimental people are always saying is so joyous, so incredible, so explosive and fulfilling.

So he did. And it was. Joyous. Incredible. Explosive. Fulfilling. The sentimentalists were right. Amazing. Of course he didn't possess her the first moment he decided to do so. She is, after all, a Leo, and a Lioness does not surrender herself until the man she loves proves his adoration in countless ways over a reasonable period of time. Still, when she at last chose to knight him with the warm gift of her whole love and her whole being, their sexual pleasure was exquisite.

Often, an Aquarian man is more demonstrative and affectionate with a Leo woman than anyone, even he, would ever have believed possible. Just as the Lioness often discovers she can enjoy lovemaking with the Aquarian man who has captured her heart without regally holding back some part of herself, lest she might be thought undignified, thereby causing her to lose the self-respect she needs to retain her identity in her own eyes, let alone in the eyes of the world. She senses this man won't ridicule her or look down on her if she is honestly herself with him during their intimacies. And so their physical One-ness can be a strong tie between them, drawing them back into each other after they've quarreled, over and over again. Mutual desire, when it is deep and insistent enough, is a powerful healer of trivial hurts and frustrations.

However, although a happy sexual compatibility is a beautiful facet of love between any man and woman, sex alone is not enough to guarantee endur-ing happiness. These two will have to compromise and make adjustments in other areas of their togetherness, or her original passion will slowly freeze into ice — and his original tender and spontaneous response to her warmth and sun-ny disposition will revert to his typical Uranus kind of dreamy disinterest.

A Leo woman absolutely must be periodically complimented, be made to know she's treasured by the man she loves. A Lioness who is starved for admiration and appreciation is as pathetic (and finally as dangerous) as a Nature lioness who's hungry for food. Hunger is hunger, and it can make people behave in strange ways. The Aquarian man's natural tendency is to make the woman he's crazily in love with play a guessing game. He hints. He suggests. He invites her inside his mind (a place where most people find a *Do Not Enter* sign) and he thinks this should convince her she's very important to him — that he needs her more than he can express. But it won't work. She doesn't like guessing games. She becomes impatient with subtlety, because she's so direct and outgoing herself. He may indeed need her more than he can express, but he's going to have to *learn* to express it if he wants to keep her. It won't be easy, because compliments and flattery are usually difficult for the typical Aquarian man to master. He feels uneasy expressing his deepest feelings and emotions in words. He's more comfortable making them into a joke or a limerick. It's possible he may write her a poem or a song, but a direct personal statement of a romantic declaration embarrasses him — sometimes painfully.

She'll have to try a little harder to realize that this man, in his own unpredictable, eccentric way, is a special human being. He doesn't give his love away casually. The very fact that he said "I love you" even once should make her know he's serious about their relationship. She shouldn't try to make him repeat what he considers meaningless declarations as proof of the reality of his longings. To him, once a thing has been said, it stands — until it's retracted. To repeat a statement, an action, an idea — or anything at all — seems like a terrible waste of time to this man, whose mind is always on what's ahead, not what lies behind. As when his mother tried to force him to say "thank you" and "please" and "you're welcome" a hundred times a day. He found that nonsense. There are other ways a person can show gratitude and courtesy. He learned that hypocritical people who pay lip sevice to social or romantic custom are the very ones who break what he considers to be the basic rules of decency and kindness, honesty and loyalty — and he hates hypocrisy with every fiber of his being.

He may try to tell her this some midnight or midday. Lying beside her in bed — or crossing a busy street, holding hands, at noon. It will just pop into his head, so he'll say it. "You know," he'll tell her gently, quietly, "it's not what people *say* that matters. It's what people *do* that matters." Then he'll flash her one of his Uranian looks of deep penetration that seems to sear into her soul. If she's as wise as the Sun-ruled are capable of being, she'll smile back at him with her eyes, simply say, "I know" — and never, ever forget that timeless moment when he tried so hard to make her see, to understand. Because he'll probably never repeat it. Aquarians bare their souls to you only rarely, but for an instant. If you're too busy or too full of self-pity to really *listen*, the moment will be gone forever.

A person may choose a dog for a pet (or even a squirrel or a gerbil, for that matter) and the animal will be touchingly grateful to have been adopted and given a home. But you know what they say about cats. No one "chooses" a cat as a pet. A cat chooses her own owner. And only after she's decided you're worth honoring with her presence. She'll expect you to be properly pleased, to cherish her and pat her on the head frequently — if you want her to stay around and purr for you, to adorn your house. The Water Bearer should note that his Lioness has similar notions.

As for any doubts the Leo woman may have concerning the basic stability of her unpredictable, eccentric and unconventional Aquarian man — well, he may be a little crazy, but that's what keeps him from going insane in a world that's *really* off the wall. When she thinks about it for a while, she'll understand. And her sunny smile will return. Just in time. He was freezing out there all by himself, without her. But he would never have let her know. He would simply have turned and walked away, bravely whistling a lonesome song, pretending it didn't matter. Later, he would have wondered why she called him absentminded because he could never remember to bring her a gift on her birthday or their anniversary. *She's* the one who forgot . . . that he once told her he loved her.

☆ ☆ ☆ ☆ ☆ ☆

LEO *Man* AQUARIUS *Woman*

━━━━◆━◗◉◖━◆━━━━

It was not his courage, it was not his engaging appearance,
it was not . . . . there is no beating about the bush, for we
know quite well what it was, and have got to tell. It was
Peter's cockiness . . . .

"I don't mean a kiss," she said. "I mean a thimble."

"What's that ?"

"It's like this." She kissed him.

"Funny!" said Peter gravely. "Now shall I give you
a thimble ?"

Make no mistake. A Lion will be as startled and confused as the "ordinary"
male by an Aquarian girl's unique manner of speech and singular behavior.
But his response will be typically Leonine. He'll pretend he hasn't noticed.
An open display of confusion might indicate weakness, so he'll act as though
he's taking her eccentricities in stride, with a calm and unruffled, rather
benevolent (if slightly patronizing), air.

If she chooses to call a kiss a thimble, then so will he. And his languid
naturalness will be so convincing, she'll never suspect it threw him in that first
moment before he caught himself. A Lion can never let on that he's been
caught unprepared, let alone "thrown." If she tells him she wants some
cherimoyas in the backyard, he'll yawn, tell her he'll think it over and let her
know later. By the following day, he'll be an expert on cherimoyas. When
she tells him to be sure and pick up some yogurt on the way home because she
needs to take it with her to the photographer's, he may be burning with
curiosity to learn what yogurt has to do with a camera, but he won't ask. The
next day, before he drives her to have her picture taken, she'll solicit his
opinion. "Should I use the yogurt before I get there ?" His reply will be
casual. "Why not ?" he'll offer smoothly, never revealing his utter bewilder-
ment. (*Use it ?*) He'll breathe a secret sigh of relief when he discovers she
uses it as a facial. He had started to wonder if she really needed therapy.
Nor will he raise an eyebrow when he finds an Oriental vase in the freezer
section of the refrigerator, filled with freshly sharpened pencils. By this time
he'll have learned at least part of the combination lock to her mental process,
and he can guess the riddle rather easily. He figures she thinks the pencils
write better when the lead is chilled. He's beginning to know her. That's
right. They make a cleaner, neater mark on the page.

He'd never give himself away by turning pale when she runs into his arms, weeping inconsolably and crying out, "He's dead! Joe is dead!" He'll soothe her as best he can, hoping she doesn't feel the wild thumping of his heart, until he gradually learns that "he" is the small lizard in the garden she named Joe, of whom she had grown quite fond. No matter if she sews up the hem in her skirts with Elmer's glue, rinses her hair with 3.2 beer to make it sparkle, enjoys the mystical feeling of taking her shower with no light in the bathroom — just one lone candle on the sink — or runs to the kitchen to grab the bottle of vanilla extract and dabs it behind her ears before they go out for dinner because it's her favorite perfume. He'll remain blasé about it all. To exhibit spontaneous surprise is beneath his dignity. It implies that there could be something he doesn't know — and since a Leo knows everything — quite logically, how could anyone surprise him?

This girl can surprise him, whether he shows it or not. She completely floors him. He's never met anyone quite like her before. She breaks all the rules, follows no predictable pattern and keeps him guessing almost continually. Of course, the fact that he refuses to openly indicate that he finds her to be a challenge will only make her more determined to find a way to shock him — to see what he's like when his poise is shattered. It fascinates her that a man can be so unflappable, so lazily confident, so immune to being caught off-guard. No wonder astrology calls him the Big Cat, she muses. That describes him perfectly. Always alert, ever watchful. Aware of the slightest scent of danger to his well-being and his "pride," and ready to pounce on that danger first, before it descends on him. Perhaps a Lion does deserve to be called the King of the Jungle.

She can't help admiring him, but that won't halt her attempts to rattle his composure, disturb his dignity and baffle his regal bearing. She's heard he's a Fire Sign, and she knows there are banked fires somewhere beneath all that smooth self-control and graceful movement. She'd like to coax the flames to leap out where they can be seen. It could be exciting, she thinks. It could also be unwise. He's not a kitten, he's a cat, and there's a vast difference. As playful as this man can be, as warm, sunny and lovable as his nature is — he is a survivor. Anyone who tries to make him seem foolish will be taught a swift and impressive lesson about Leo's own personal law of the jungle in human society. Noble, generous and affectionate, often gentle, he nonetheless will establish his authority by rising to the fierce heights of his Solar rulership when he's threatened. And he will never submit to defeat or failure. In the end, he will triumph. Leo is not cruel — but neither is this man soft and humble, self-effacing or submissive. He doesn't waste his splendid energy without a cause, but when a just cause arises, he has the strength to enforce his will — and on such occasions he becomes decidedly dramatic. In no way does a Lion retreat, although he may disdain to expend his emotions on matters he considers too petty and trivial for his attention. Most of the time, he organizes his emotional reactions as efficiently as he organizes everything else around him.

This man and woman are under the influence of the polarized 7-7 Sun Sign Pattern vibration, so their views are often diametrically opposed—and they may find themselves frequently settling into the extreme ends of the emotional thermometer. Yet this opposition of their Sun Signs on the horoscopic wheel may help to balance out the matching double masculine challenge of their personalities. They were both born under Fixed (stubborn) and masculine signs. Also, his ruling Sun is masculine (very!) and her ruling planet Uranus is likewise masculine. This creates a lot of positive, aggressive and determined vibes around them—and clearly requires that they both make a mutual attempt to add some of the so-called "feminine" qualities to their relationship, such as passivity, tenderness, patience and tolerance.

She can't understand why he's so vitally concerned with his own image, when she's concerned with all manner of things outside herself, as befits her Air Element. His vanity perplexes her. And the way he pouts when he doesn't receive the respect to which he believes he's entitled. She's considerably more carefree about her appearance—and as for what people think, it seldom even occurs to her to wonder, let alone care. She doesn't need to be respected. She respects herself—and isn't that all that matters—what you think of yourself, not what others think of you? This is one of the several invaluable lessons she can teach her Lion if he'll forget his pride long enough to realize how much happier he'd be if he saw the wisdom of some of her Uranian philosophy.

She can also learn from him some important things. Self-control is the chief one. Her sudden impulses and tornadoes of emotion can cause his fiery inner nature to explode so that neither of them can discuss anything calmly. Air has the ability to whip fire into a frenzy but can also cause it to burn more brightly, and there's no doubt that she stimulates him in a positive way too. The typical Aquarian woman outwardly appears to seek only tranquility, peace and quiet. Lots of girl Water Bearers are quite soft-spoken and mild-mannered ladies. Then suddenly, without the slightest warning, or even any real provocation, they'll erupt into a stormy scene—throw something across the room or out the window—or if nothing else, slam the door, lock it, draw the shades and play hermit for anywhere from a few hours to a few days. But pouting is a mistake, because she'll never win the pouting game with a Lion. A Leo man is an absolute expert in the strategy of pouting when he's been injured or wounded. She can't top him there. He's the champion.

Because a male Lion often subconsciously associates powerful emotions (whether positive or negative) with sexual desire, one of the most surprising things about their relationship can be the way a quarrel, even a violent one, will renew their longing for each other—and culminate with the consummation of unspoken need. There's something feral and primitive about the kind of lovemaking that silently demands surrender of the passion of the mind and emotions to the passion of the body. Afterward, it's like the calm that follows the storm, when everything is peaceful and still again . . . fresher and sweeter than before. However much their personalities may struggle and clash in other areas of their togetherness, these two can nearly always count on the restoration of harmony between them when their sexual expression of love transforms the Leo man into his Lion self . . . and she becomes, no longer his opponent, but his mate. The challenging creature to whom he must prove either his equality or his superiority. He'd prefer it to be the latter, but he'd save lots of energy for other interests in his life if he'd be satisfied to just aim for the former with this lady. The sexual chemistry they share is so magnetic it usually resists destruction by the other tensions of their relationship (unless there are severe afflictions between the Ascendents and Luminaries in their birth charts). Of course, there will be occasions when his pride will be deeply wounded by her periodic inability to be as affectionate as he'd like. Leo requires much warmth and tenderness blended with his lovemaking — and she may sometimes be unintentionally cool or detached. Her inner self vibrates to the element of Air, which can never match the heat or brilliance of the Solar-Fire influences that guide her Leo man's sexual passions. But he can console himself with the knowledge that she's probably warmer with him than she could be with anyone else, because their 7-7 opposition brings out in her as much wholehearted involvement as she's capable of giving to physical union.

They'll probably shower each other with lavish gifts and crazy surprises at unexpected times, these lovers. They'll both be refreshed and inspired, excited by change, travel and creative projects they can plan together. But she'll have to be careful that her tendency to gather armfuls of friends of both sexes into their private circle doesn't offend her Lion. Leo smolders with jealousy within for a long, long time before it bursts forth in anger. He'll never be able to curb her urge to be herself. This woman must be both allowed and encouraged to follow her impulses, or her normal cheerful disposition will be strangled. She's a spontaneous free spirit, like all Aquarians, and to stifle this Uranus quality can result in a serious neurosis.

A Lion can become neurotically morose too, if he doesn't receive the attention he needs on a regular basis. Her mind is on such a number of things, she may forget he's there at times. She'd better remember. To ignore a Leo man too often is to lose him for a certainty. He'll freeze into an icicle — and there's always someone waiting out there to melt him with honest appreciation.

Since the sages tell us that a word to the wise is sufficient, and astrology tells us that Leo is wise — here are a few words that should be sufficient in counseling a Lion who loves a Water Bearer. In several Aquarius chapters I've advised various Sun Signs that it's prudent, if at all possible, to aim to be the first love of an Aquarian. Aquarians always remember wistfully the first love (which was probably a platonic friendship). But there are other sound reasons.   The following lament from the pen of Dorothy Parker rather concisely describes the Uranian romantic quandry of a female W.B.

> *Oh, gallant was the first love . . . and glittering and fine*
> *the second love was water . . . in a clear, white cup*
> *the third love was his, the fourth was mine*
> *and after that, I always get them all mixed up.*

All things very carefully considered, a Leo man should try to be the third love of this lady. Yes, definitely Number Three for the Lion. And seal it off right there. Beyond that point, it gets pretty risky. The glitter and the white cup are passing ecstasies. And Number Four is out of the question for any Leo. *Three* is the magic Number. Then lock up her Chinese abacus . . . and throw away the key.

LEO

Fire — Fixed — Positive
Ruled by the Sun
Symbols: Lion & Shy Pussycat
Day Forces — Masculine

PISCES

Water — Mutable — Negative
Ruled by Neptune
Symbol: The Fish
Night Forces — Feminine

The **LEO-PISCES** *Relationship*

"Say 'Ay, ay, sir.' "

"Ay, ay, sir !"

. . . it need not be said who was the captain.

Before we go any further, it may as well be understood in the beginning that there's no hope of the male or female Fish ever truly conquering the Lion or Lioness. It simply cannot be done. It's against all precepts of astrology and nature. So why do we see so many Pisceans hanging around with Leos ? Because being conquered isn't really all that unpleasant to a Piscean when the Big Cat is the winner, that's why.

Leos are normally generous to the defeated, benevolent monarchs who lack cruel or malicious intent (although often making up for it in arrogance), and Fish secretly prefer to be dominated, as long as it's done with affection, which it nearly always is with Leo. Being dominated, you see, makes life easier. Someone else tells you what to do, leaving lots of time for Neptune daydreams, less for obligatory decisions of responsibility. The typical Piscean is all for an association that leaves plenty of room for swimming around freely, while the next trip upstream or downstream is charted by someone who enjoys such matters. Pisces does not. The activities of dominating and conquering are tiresome occupations at best, requiring much energy and more ego than the average Fish possesses.

There may be an occasional Piscean who dreams, at odd moments, of conquering the Lion or Lioness, and it might be that a Fish who had the planetary position at birth of Mars-in-Aries prefers to lead, rather than to follow. It's perfectly true that Mars exerts a formidable influence through its own natural sign of Aries, making such a Piscean less humble and accommodating. But Mars, for all its strength, courage, and daring, will never truly defeat or dominate radiant Apollo, the Sun God. Study your Greek mythology. No planet, not even awesome Pluto or stern Saturn, has the sheer life-giving force of the Sun, and if this brilliant Luminary exercised its power through the Pisces zone of the zodiac at birth, he or she is a Pisces, and that's that — never mind any periodic spurts of Martian bravado. Essentially and basically, when all the chips and scales are counted, a Fish is a Fish.

The location of the Sun at the moment of the first breath is the key to the true essence of the person, for the simple reason that the Sun is the most powerful influence in the heavens, therefore in the horoscope. In addition, the Sun also happens to be the ruler of Leo. So we're back — full circle — to the dominance issue between these two. No matter how you size up the scene, the Lion will rule the Fish. The Piscean with other more positive vibrations in the nativity (such as Mars-in-Aries, or Moon-in-Aries) may give the Lions and Lionesses a bit more of a challenge, but what chance does such a planetary boost at birth have against the royal Leo Kings and Queens when even the Aries Sun Sign native (like myself) must eventually submit to Leonine superiority to keep the peace?

Appreciation and admiration never fail to enhance the Sunny nature of Leo, and no one appreciates or admires more charmingly than Pisces. Conversely, Leo's warm Solar rays never fail to bring into flower the delicate blossoms of the Neptune personality of Pisces which need to be tenderly cared for, and no one can be more warmly protective and affectionate than Leo. Therefore, unless there are serious conflicts between their mutual Moon Signs, Ascendents or Sun-Moon aspects, together they can encourage the best in each other, complement one another's essence, and find considerable joy and comfort in an alliance.

This is not an infrequent combination, since Pisces can bring much tenderness and insight into Leo's life — while Leo can bring a great measure of emotional and other security into the Piscean's life. Still a Lion may swallow a Fish when the Big Cat grows tired of playing. These two are not compatible by nature, and must work at harmony. Leo feels at home in a hot, dry, jungle habitat — Pisces, in cool, shaded waters. There are considerable basic differences, and one of them must give up familiarity of environment, symbolically, to remain together. If the Leo has a Water Sign Ascendent or the Moon in a Water Sign, it will be easier to renounce the jungle life for a dive into deep Neptune waters. If the Fish has a Fire Sign Ascendent or the Moon in a Fire Sign, it will be easier to breathe free on dry land, roaming the "pride" beside the noble Lion or Lioness, without longing for escape back into the ocean of emotional oblivion.

The 6-8 Sun Sign Pattern of Leo-Pisces has the potential of becoming a satisfactory relationship, with all the appeal outward strength has for inward strength . . . and vice versa. Since the Fish has an inner spiritual noblesse oblige comparable to the dignified outer nobility of Leo's personality, they can, if they try, manage very well on any stage of life, whether it be business, friendship, family, or marital.

Leo is the zodiacal sixth house of service to Pisces, which explains the unusual urge in Leo to willingly serve Pisces in some way, not a normal behavioral pattern with Big Cats toward other Sun Signs. Of course, that doesn't negate the superiority syndrome, just dilutes it somewhat. After all, monarchs do serve their subjects graciously and continually, but they're still monarchs.

Most Pisceans have a tough time deciding what exactly it is they want to do or be. They listen willingly to almost everyone's advice, follow it only for a short while — or do nothing. Right there is where trouble may start. Leo must be obeyed or be miserable. Since Pisces can't bear to see anyone miserable, and Leo cannot bear to see anyone wandering around without a goal, the impasse could end up with a sulking Lion and a weeping Fish.

Often Pisces is tempted by two possibilities at once, which equally lure and intrigue. The Lion should permit the Fish a fling at both simultaneously if necessary, because Pisces needs time and lack of pressure to try things out through multiple experience — as a way of finding himself (or herself). It's a wise Lion (or Lioness) who grants to Pisces this privilege, and Leo is, after all, possessed of innate dignity and wisdom. (I thought I'd make a few points here for the Fish since they're not big on making points for themselves.)

A Fish, in any sort of daily contact with a Lion, should always keep in mind that sincere appreciation (flattery) will soothe the savage beast more quickly than pouting, tears, or silence. The Lion should not forget that gentleness is the most reliable bait with which to lure the sensitive Piscean, and regal roaring only causes the Fish to frantically flap its fins and struggle to breathe. It isn't difficult for these two to adjust to one another and find happiness if they both show their positive instead of negative sides.

Leo will demand (or at least expect) control over money, being a natural organizer. But Leo is also extravagant. Pisces is often surprisingly good at handling the intricacies of finance, but the Fish doesn't really have any basic respect for money. So it might be better if they took turns handling the income and the outgo. The Neptunian attitude toward most everything is intuitive rather than rational. This will invariably frustrate the Sun-ruled Leo, to whom rationality is the only sensible foundation for all opinion and action. It's a rough spot. And there are others. The accomplishment of smooth routine comes naturally to Leo, the sign of the Fixed Organizer. To Pisces, however, the order and discipline necessary for successful organization does not come naturally.

A Fish can infuriate a Lion by finding correct answers in a situation which appears to be a total mess to Leo. The same rule may be applied to messy checkbook stubs, messy desks, and messy houses. Perhaps we should use the word "confused" instead of messy. Leo likes a place for everything, and everything in its place. Pisces believes that a lifetime spent neatly organizing every item and every hour into a rigid system is a lifetime wasted. The Fish always feels more relaxed when the surroundings are comfortably chaotic and somewhat disordered, not too neat, thank you.

It's seldom that a Piscean will fight confrontation with real aggression. Neptune men and women drown in hidden insecurity. Those types mentioned earlier with some positive vibration in the horoscope, like Mars or the Moon in Aries, may ride the waves of outrageous fortune or unjust treatment for a while. But even these will eventually swim away to calmer bays and inlets. Escape will inevitably be the end solution, the final action. Fish are hard to pin down. Neptune, among other things, rules gas, impossible to confine when it seeks release.

Astrology whispers of Piscean Fish who become devouring Whales. This is true. There are some unaccountable Neptune mutations. But even the rare Whale-type Fish who devours an occasional Crab or Virgin will find it impossible to pull the Jonah act with Leo. Either the Lion emerges triumphant — or the Fish swims away. Although the general impression of Pisces is elusive, the Big Cats are adept at stalking creatures who think they're safely out of reach . . . until an unexpected Leonine paw suddenly pins them to the ground. The end of any serious clash between Leo and Pisces is predictable.

Lions who wish to live harmoniously and peacefully with Fish must help them find a way to blend the Neptune duality, tenderly console them, apply soothing balm to their emotional insecurities, and lead them gently out of the foggy mists where they daydream into the sunlight of truth and reality. You see how wise the stars are? As I said in the beginning, the Lion will be the leader in the relationship, and that's the way it works out best for both sides. Pisces needs a strong paw to grip, a hand to hold, while walking through the deep woods of life, lest some unseen danger lurking in the underbrush should leap out to lunge without warning. And who is stronger in the face of danger than the Lion? Leo protects. Pisces admires . . . with touching gratitude.

And isn't it a lovely day? If it doesn't rain. If it does rain, the spiritually mature Fish can teach Leo how to avoid getting drenched in life's unexpected cloudbursts. After all, one good turn deserves another.

☆ ☆ ☆ ☆ ☆ ☆

LEO *Woman* PISCES *Man*

Slightly was the first to speak. "This is no bird," he said in a scared voice. "I think it must be a lady."

You'd think the icy, aloof, and regal attitudes of the typical Lioness toward strangers who seek her hand or heart would frighten a male Pisces Fish away before this girl had a chance to hook him. You would think so. But if you did, you'd be forgetting that there's another side to this lady. A Leo woman can, when it pleases her to do so, exude a bright and playful disposition, as warm and benevolent as her ruler, the Sun. Besides, not all Pisceans have fits of the trembles when they're in the presence of astrological royalty. There are, if you recall from other chapters of this book, also the Whale-type Pisceans, who gobble people—symbolically, of course. A Whale will never succeed in gobbling a Lioness. But neither will he necessarily quake and shake when she freezes his initial advance.

Still, the majority of male Fish are not Whales, and they do need some help when they've been hooked by this female, so we'll look at the situation from their point of view. The Whale types can, assumedly, take care of themselves. Let's consider the problem of the typical or average Pisces man when he's involved with a Leo woman. Scary. It's downright scary. There's an air of command and vitality about a healthy, beautiful Lioness that almost breathes a challenge of courage to all who would woo and win her. "See that you're worthy enough to deserve me" is the silent message from the tawny one.

The Fish shouldn't allow that to stop him. It's just her queenly way of putting down and putting off any peasants who have an eye on the throne. The way to cope with it is to prove to her he's not a peasant. How does one go about proving such a thing to this lady?

Well, to begin with, he can royally wine and dine her, at the very best restaurants, and present her with gifts—if not expensive, then at least reflecting good taste. A bottle of cheap wine, a rhinestone bracelet from Woolworth's that turns her arm green, or one of those plastic dolls you win at a carnival are not gifts she considers to be in good taste. Try Tiffany's, on Fifth Avenue in Manhattan. You don't need a fortune to pick up a token for a Lioness at Tiffany's. Don't let the name frighten you. They have some interesting items, beginning at ten or twenty dollars, and the Fish can probably manage to scour up that much cash to impress the woman he's afraid he's beginning to love. Besides, all that matters is the box. If it says Tiffany's, she'll smile her brightest smile, and graciously thank him, with a sunlit, summer promise in her eyes.

There are other gifts in equally good taste he can give her. A homeless kitten. A framed photo of himself, at age six. A bunch of daisies, with one golden rose in the center, representing her. Taste is not necessarily associated with money, but with an educated heart and a sensitive soul. Whatever he gives her, it shouldn't be given on an ordinary holiday or occasion. Birthdays, Christmas, and so forth, are out. That's what all the peasants do.

He should accompany his gift with a card that says, simply . . . . "Because it's Thursday morning, and I love you" . . . . or tell her it's to celebrate the hour and minute they met, a year ago (or five years, or however many) . . . perhaps to observe Guy Fawkes Day (but he'd better stop in the library and look that one up, because she'll frown if he can't tell who Guy Fawkes is, and no — he didn't fight Joe Louis in Chicago) . . . . best of all, to commemorate the coronation of Queen Elizabeth. She'll like that. It's associated with royalty, and she'll think it's fun. A Lioness has a warm and wonderful sense of humor. (But in good taste, don't forget. No Puns. And no off-color stories, please.) She's sentimental, and all these little things matter to her. He shouldn't ignore her need for the intellectual, the romantic, and the unusual. This lady *is* a lady, quite literally, and she's bored to tears by the mundane, the ordinary, the commonplace, and the unmarvelous.

There are many ways he can prove to her he's not a peasant, that he is of the nobility, or ruling class, therefore deserves her attention and respect. He can display his natural Neptunian talent (or at least taste for) music or poetry, which she'll find utterly delightful. He can remember that true royalty never winces, always retains dignity in the most upsetting situations. But most of all, he must never wound her regal nature by speaking or behaving in a rude, coarse, disrespectful manner, not even when she deserves a good verbal and physical spanking — which will be frequently.

At such times he should go ahead and give her what she deserves, not rudely or coarsely — but like a gentleman. It's really rather easy, once you get the hang of it — the difference, I mean, between the lower class and the ruling class. Only a nobleman who has already been knighted by the Queen would dare put her in her place by spanking her bottom when she misbehaves, you see? You don't? Well, let me say it this way: A Leo woman will *never* submit to a man who is not her peer, who cannot control her when she needs it. Neither will she fall in love for keeps with a man for whom she has to apologize to her friends, who humiliates and wounds her, either publicly or privately. Indisputably, the handling and training of nobility is an art.

Actually, a Pisces man has a fair chance of getting the hang of it more quickly than the male of most other Sun Signs, not because he has delusions of grandeur himself, but because the Fish has never been born who doesn't possess an uncanny ability to charm the wildest beast with a combination of gentle compassion and passive resistance. Besides all that, he's a jolly good listener, and with this woman, his sensitive and sympathetic ears will be worked overtime. The Leo girl does enjoy an audience, and a Neptune male is at his lovable best playing that role, with a genuine fascination for the plays of human nature acted out on the stages of Life and Love.

If he does occasionally pull a faux pas with Her Highness, he needn't tremble and await execution. Truly, one of the loveliest shades in the brilliant rainbow aura of a Leo girl is her ability to graciously forgive those who sincerely beg her pardon. She has such a sunny nature and exudes such warmth that, except for a periodic touch of megalomania (the psychiatric term for a swollen ego), it makes people happy just to be around her. If she gets the respect she demands — and quite often deserves — her disposition blooms into a bright generosity that's impossible to resist, like a full-blown, fragrant rose. But she has a way of freezing in silent pride if a lover or husband (or anyone else for that matter) tries to dictate to her. Not that the Fish will try that too frequently anyway. This man is more likely to court his Leonine Queen with charm, quick wit, intelligence, and an amazingly intuitive grasp of her moods.

A Leo woman sometimes makes really impossible demands of love in her desire to mate only with a man who is subservient to her every whim, yet also possessed of sufficient intellect and self-assurance to be her equal at all times. That's quite a duality trick, but the Neptune-ruled man has a pretty good chance of performing it successfully. Most Fish don't mind the surface appearance of serving, so his Piscean self-effacement helps him rather than hinders him — and as for being her equal, his telepathic talents and myriad facets of intelligence (gathered karmically from the other eleven Sun Signs) are easily sparkling enough to attract the attention and admiration of the Lioness, causing her to believe she's found that perfect blend she's looking for in a man — for a while at least.

Once the first flush and blush of romance has paled a bit, they'll both begin to notice the difference between their individual elements of Fire and Water, which, as you know from basic physics, do not blend without danger of extinction to one or the other, or both. His watery nature requires much time for reflection in solitude, so he finds the extroversion of Leo sometimes abrasive to his delicate tuning. Her fiery nature is more gregarious, and requires lots of dramatic fights so they can kiss and make up, therefore his refusal to be sufficiently eloquent when she's fired up can be abrasive to her own harmonics. His retreat into sulkiness when his spirit has been smashed is matched only by her proud pouting when she's been thwarted or ignored.

One of the greatest causes of conflict will be his natural reluctance to share every private thought with her. Leo wants to know everything, and who can keep secrets from the Queen? He can. And frequently does. Then she'll rage or freeze, one or the other, until he gives up and gives in. The Fish should beware of giving the Lioness too much rope, or she'll hang him with it for sure.

The way to her heart regarding sexual harmony is — back to the music and poetry again. Cleopatra, who was indisputably a Lioness, was thus wooed and won by *both* Caesar and Marc Antony. ("If music be the food of love — play on.") Lionesses like to be softly serenaded, even if only symbolically. Like the Temptress of the Nile, the Leo woman loves perfumed oils and all the trappings of romance — the more exotic, the better. Let this be a hint to the Pisces man: She'll never find true fulfillment in a casual encounter. The typical Leo female is seldom promiscuous once she's selected a worthy prince consort. As monogamy-minded as the Nature lioness, she'll devour an unfaithful husband or lover with a roar of jealousy. She herself adores and needs to be worshiped and admired by every male in sight, but she'll claim that's not the same thing. *She* has regal privileges, you see. A Leo woman is capable of seducing a man away from another woman as her royal right, and then is wounded if he becomes as untrue to her as she caused him to be to his former mate. The shoe pinches when it's on the other foot. Let the man she loves indulge in so much as a harmless wink at her best friend and he will live to regret it. (Of course, being an Aries Fire Sign myself, I don't see how even a *wink* can be *harmless*, but . . .) This woman (Leo, that is) will not tolerate flirting of even the lightest intent. He owes her ALL his attention. It's sad, but very true, that the mildest sort of hurt of this kind will often cause the typical Lioness to be unable to respond to her partner in the physical expression of love.

Jealousy can turn her into a cold goddess instantly, with no warmth left to give, either sexually or emotionally. On the other hand, too many arrogant lectures from Her Majesty can create the same sort of physical unresponsiveness in the male Fish, making their intimate sexual life together shift from warm to frigid, and back again. He should be grateful for the rare loyalty his Leo woman will bestow upon him if he deserves it, and try not to court her displeasure, her deep unhappiness, by being anything but honest and loyal in return. There may be something missing in their sexual vibration. He could be too ethereal, mystical, and intangible, or too elusive in his lovemaking to completely satisfy the jungle female in her. She could be so demanding and insistent in her need for overwhelming passion and continual romantic servitude that he becomes even *more* detached, ethereal, mystical, intangible, and elusive during their lovemaking — and so it goes — a circular problem — with no beginning, and no end. Who *really* starts it ? Who knows ?

With these two, there is at least a hint. This is a 6-8 Sun Sign vibration, and with the Leo woman and the Pisces man, that means he represents to her the eighth astrological house of sexual magnetism, mystery, and deep spiritual matters (barring any possible mutual planetary afflictions in their birth charts, which might dilute the powerful sexual tug — never remove it, just dilute it). She represents to him the sixth astrological house of service (among other things). It could quite possibly be that the Fish is expecting too much devoted "service" from this proud woman, and a Lioness will not remain unduly subservient for long, without roaring her discontent. They both should meditate on this.

With a Sun-Moon and other planetary harmony in their mutual horoscopes, or a mutual Moon conjunction, all their tensions could dissolve into a lilting, lyrical, and lovely man-woman blending of the Sun and Neptune, causing their sexual union to be enriched by the delicacy, romance, and tenderness he brings to her, and by the warm affection and passion she brings to him.

Without such planetary help in their birth charts, she must be extremely careful not to allow the powerful Solar rays of her intense sexuality (and potential for frigidity) to either scorch or freeze all desire in this man — and he must be extremely careful not to allow the Neptunian dreaminess of his sexuality, and his lack of a *total* involvement in their lovemaking, to cool her sunny nature . . . and leave her feeling empty, as though she hadn't been touched by love's true depth . . . but only by a gentle breeze, that leaves barely a memory behind it.

The strongest, most fertile root of the women's liberation movement is the one ignored in all the speeches — the *emotional* equality of men and women. This will be the final and lasting reward to *both* sexes, when the noisy parades are all over — that it's a *good* thing for a man to possess some feminine qualities of sentiment, perception, and sensitivity — as it is for a woman to possess some masculine qualities of courage, directness, and independence. A *very* good thing. A divine and a holy thing.

However, in a love relationship such as this one, where the female was born under a masculine Sun Sign, also ruled by the masculine Sun itself, giving her a *double* masculine influence — and the male was born under a feminine Sun Sign, ruled also by a feminine planet, Neptune, giving him a *double* feminine influence — conscious and continuous care must be given to retaining the emotional balance between the lovers.

Feminine is neither "sissy" nor "effeminate." Yet, it's possible for a double feminine-influenced Piscean male to project too much passivity. Likewise, masculine is neither "aggressive" nor "pushy." Yet, it's possible for a double masculine-influenced woman to project too much drive and force — and overbalance on the part of each.

The underlying, esoteric truth of faerie tales is seldom recognized, and if it were, astrology and faerie tales alone would negate the need for psychiatry. (Neptune men will find that logical.) For example (a vital example) "Goldilocks and the Three Bears" has a much deeper meaning than people suspect. The Lioness and the Fish (and all Sun Sign couples) should meditate on the lesson in that ancient fable. Papa Bear's chair and bed were *too hard* (an overbalance of masculine forceful drive). Mama Bear's chair and bed were *too soft* (an overbalance of feminine passivity). Papa Bear's soup was *too hot* — Mama Bear's soup *too cold*. But Baby Bear's porridge, chair, and bed were . . . *just right*.

The most effective love wisdom the stars can offer to this man and woman is for both of them to remember Baby Bear's perfect balance of aggressiveness and passivity. To repeat once again the most important planetary counsel of all to these two: *conscious and continuous care must be given to retaining a balanced emotional exchange*.

It's no good if the Lioness leans too heavy on the Papa Bear essence (although a little of it beautifully becomes her — and all women). It's no good when the male Fish leans too heavy on the Mama Bear essence (although a little of it handsomely becomes him — and all men). It may seem to be an insoluble problem between these two, yet it's not at all, in any respect. It's really so very simple. All both of them need to remember — is not to forget Goldilocks.

Variations of the same troubled love theme are heard in the symphonies of all seventy-eight Sun Sign combination lovers. The Goldilocks syndrome creates tension in love between a man and woman who are *both* "double masculine-influenced," just as it does between a man and woman who are *both* "double feminine-influenced." The same problem exists between a *double* masculine man — and a *double* feminine woman (which may sound ideal, but actually creates the danger of sadism and masochism, respectively, in various degrees). There is no "sexual solution" but one, and *only* one — the lesson of Baby Bear Balance.

The challenge of loving a Leo woman, and being loved in return, will require all the knowledge of the human heart with which the Pisces man is blessed. One minute he's fighting a tigress of emotional excess, who spits and hisses like an angry cat. Then, when she's exhausted by her display of fireworks, she mysteriously transforms into a soft and gentle kitten, appealingly purring for his affection and a pat on the head for approval. The Lioness is a disconcerting and dazzling mixture of icy, regal dignity, and warm, happy-go-lucky fun and generosity. She can be annoyingly arrogant, yet intensely loyal. She tosses her splendid Lioness mane with a healthy laugh, then dissolves into tears of injured pride . . . all with a slinky, feline grace.

The Fish who's been hooked by her glamorous, cool superiority won't be surprised to learn that the Cat was an object of worship to ancient cultures. There may be times when he'll think he's back among the pyramids, kneeling at the shrine of the Cat-headed goddess, created by Egyptians because they identified the lines of a cat with those of a woman — and they were wise to do so. The Lioness is not only all women — she's also all woman. (Think about it.) And she will rule the "pride" if he so much as allows her an inch of control.

The challenge of loving a Pisces man, and being loved in return, will likewise require all the warmth and sunlit wisdom with which the Leo woman is blessed. He'll show his own brand of Neptune temper and icy detachment if she insists on prying into his secrets or his solitude. He's gentle, and he serves willingly, with beautiful humility of spirit, if he's not consumed by her raging jealousies, and continual, scolding lectures. This will cause him to swim away, in search of a peasant, after deciding that royalty is too rich for his blood.

These two lovers should learn a mutual lesson from the sad and unfortunate failure of another Leo-Pisces couple to overcome the challenges of their difficulties and differences — Britain's Princess Margaret Rose, a typical Queen Lioness, and her husband, Antony Armstrong-Jones, Earl of Snowdon, a Pisces man.

To begin with, a Leo Princess finds it impossible to forgive her noble family for thwarting her first love, which in this case, was Lioness Margaret Rose's fated romance with Peter Townsend. Yet, it could still have had a happy ending in her marriage to the handsome Fish, "Tony." He's a sensitive Piscean artist with a camera, a stroke of good fortune that played no small part in their initial attraction, since Leo women adore photography, and adore even more posing for pictures themselves. But this Fish photographed a variety of models, other than his wife in her tiara. That was the beginning of trouble with a jealous Leo woman, who must always even such a hurtful romantic score. Also, his work took him on many a solo trip 'round the world, so he couldn't attend all the majestic, royal affairs with her.

Although a space in togetherness is helpful and advisable for many couples, not so with the Leo woman and the Pisces man. It somehow only stretches into disinterest. The Leo-Pisces lovers or mates reading this should take a hint from the unhappy ending of a true royal faerie-tale romance, and not imitate the same mistakes in their own relationship. No separate vacations for these two.

Because the Lioness possesses so much false pride, and her Neptune man so little, he can gently soothe her frequently injured feelings. Because the Fish possesses so little confidence, and his Leo woman much, she can tenderly calm his secret, inner fears. That's the very best way to love — exchanging strengths with one another — as long as both share a compassion for each other's weaknesses as well.

☆ ☆ ☆ ☆ ☆ ☆

LEO *Man* PISCES *Woman*

*She was far too pretty to cringe
in this way, but Peter thought it
his due, and he would answer condescendingly, "It is good. Peter
Pan has spoken."*

Naturally, not every Pisces woman actually cringes under the commands of a Leo husband or lover, but most of them do have at least a healthy respect for the Lion and are not overly anxious to court his roar, including those girl Fish with the Moon or Mars in Aries. Yes, including even the female Whale-type Pisceans. Regarding the latter, it's not so much fear which motivates them to tread carefully, but the strong determination to avoid at all costs an exhausting scene — all that dramatic yelling and frigid pouting, by turns, which is the normal result when the Lion feels the sharp thorn of disrespect in his paw.

The typical (non-Whale type) Pisces woman who is involved with a Leo male intuitively knows she must submit to His Highness. She knows it, never mind what she says — and never mind the advice she gets from well-meaning friends to "stand up to him once and for all." Pisces is too wise in the ways of the human heart to use methods that could only alienate affection.

Consider Anna, the English schoolteacher who so successfully challenged the King of Siam. Perhaps she was a Fish with Mars-in-Aries, since she fought so hard to hold her own with the arrogant, yet warmly generous Leonine monarch. But little good that did her, on the surface of it, at least, in her repeated confrontations with His Leonine Majesty. Secretly, the King admired her spunkiness. Nonetheless, he remained in control of their relationship until the very end. One needs more than spunk to handle royalty. One needs to sense, as probable-Pisces Anna clearly did, the touching vulnerability peeking out from behind Leo's sometimes pathetic need to command. I always weep buckets at the end of the film (or book) when the dying Leo Monarch commands that Anna bow down to him in abject worship and respect, like one of his own subjects, even while his heart reaches out to her through his eyes. And she *did* bow. Yes, Anna was surely a Pisces, with Mars-in-Aries. She kept her dignity, but she understood how it was with the proud man she loved. She submitted.

The Lion is a great sentimentalist, an incurable romanticist. Only a Taurus Bull can be more sentimental, more romantic than Leo. And so the smitten Cat may initially be seduced into worshipful submission himself by the impact of the Pisces female's sheer femininity. But it's only a temporary capitulation. He'll never give up the throne permanently, nor willingly relinquish the golden scepter. That goes for the Shy Pussycat Leo types as well as the roaring Lions. They can be pushed — or led — just so far. Then they pounce.

It pays to keep in mind that Leo is a Fire Sign, Pisces a Water Sign, and as I point out in the chapter "The Elements," in the back section of this book, Fire secretly fears that Water can put it out. No matter how much Leo may attempt to lord it over the Pisces woman he loves, the inner trepidation that she may "dampen" his fiery enthusiasm remains, and it's just as true in reverse. The Water Sign Pisces senses it can be dehydrated by too much Fire. If the love between these two lasts, it will eventually settle into a feeling of respect which will be mutual, as with all Fire-Water combinations, since each knows the other can destroy his or her own essence. However, on an emotional level, place your bets on the Big Cat to remain the one in charge, on the surface anyway.

Seldom will this woman attempt to lead or push a man. She's more likely to persuade softly, insistently, with subtle flattery. If that doesn't work, she may resort to aloof silence suggestive of hidden hurt, which can drive the more open-hearted Leo male into furies of frustration. She'd best stick with the subtle flattery, or there will be some fiery rages and watery tears.

A Lion tends to idealize his love partner beyond anything short of a goddess, then expects her to live up to his image. It's difficult for him to recognize his mate as a distinct and individual personality. Instead, he considers her a reflection of himself, glamourized as his ideal, sometimes causing her to despair of ever being able to remain on the pedestal where he placed her. What if he should notice her clay feet? Only a Scorpio or an Aries male can expect as much from a woman as a Leo.

Like all Fire Signs, Leo is dramatic and usually possesses the fortunate ability to express his feelings verbally with great flair and gusto. Pisces doesn't find it nearly so easy to express herself, and after trying repeatedly she may give up and take the path of least resistance — escape. Under continuous disapproval or severe emotional pressure, Pisces tends to simply disappear. Many a Lion has glanced around after an arrogant lecture to see if his trembling victim has been properly humbled and chastised — only to face an empty space where the Girl Fish had been sitting and cowering with a patient smile. Where did she go?

She went away. Far, far away.

I know a Leo in Ohio, whose bright, gentle Pisces wife finally could not bear one more Leonine lecture, so she regretfully and tearfully decided to leave (although she still loved him dearly) in the interest of self-survival. She was in New York and had started divorce proceedings hardly before he realized she was gone.

What distressed the Lion nearly as much as the loss of his pretty, admiring, feminine "subject" (whom he sincerely loved) was the humiliating realization that she hadn't sought his wise counsel nor asked his advice before taking such a serious step. It was impossible not to be touched by his very real agony. No one can be more pathetic than a wounded Lion whose adoring mate has deserted him, as he nurses his hurt pride, sad . . . lonely and truly broken-hearted . . . trying so desperately not to show it. He missed her more than he thought she guessed. He was wrong, of course. Being a Pisces, she knew the pain he'd suffer, and it caused her pain too . . . . . the knowing. Typically, the Lion wasn't alone for long. His girl Fish was, after a respectable interval of time, replaced by a long line of female worshipers who sought his warm, protective shoulder and heart to lean against.

Somehow, though, his close friends could see it wasn't quite the same. His dainty, dark-haired Piscean wife contained the lovely Neptune blend of intelligence, wit, gentleness, and compassion, woven through with the golden threads of her honest admiration and respect for her Lion — an admiration and respect that kept overlooking his foibles until, finally, she could take no more.

Never mind all the fleeting romances afterward. I found myself still hoping his lost Fish would swim back into his arms again. You see how Leos are? They manage to get your sympathy, even when they don't deserve it. My earnest wish for the miracle of happiness for the lost and lonely Lion in this case, however, was granted in an unexpected way, not through reconciliation with his Neptune lady. Abracadabra — magic! He found another tiny, dainty, dark-haired woman — with, strangely, an almost identical blend of wit, intelligence, gentleness, and compassion — also woven through with the golden threads of honest admiration and respect for his talents, character, and potential. No mere shadow of his former love, but a vibrant and beautiful sunbeam herself, individually . . . she quietly, softly stole into his life . . . and finally into his heart . . . to heal all the old scars.

Let's hope he learned his lesson, for he's a warm and lovable Big Cat, with a smile that lights up your heart and simply bushels of both courage and creativity. He's earned, through deep sorrow, love's grace of a lasting peace and contentment — and always a little spice of challenge too, without which Leos would *really* pine away! His new lady is clearly capable of providing all of that — and then some. As for his lively, yet tender, girl Fish of long, long ago . . . she also has floated into bright new waters, and is happily splashing around in rainbow-streaked streams of a new promise for tomorrow.

Happy endings are so beautiful. We should all say a prayer that every sad Lion who has lost his Piscean mate through unthinking arrogance and pride is given by the wise stars an equally fortunate chance at acquiring humility . . . the lesson Pisces teaches so well — and Leo needs so much to learn. Or, let's hope that this chapter warns the Leo-Pisces lovers or mates reading it to open up their hearts in time . . . if it's still not too late for his Sun and her Neptune to begin singing their song in harmony.

One area where there may not be so much conflict between these two is sleeping. Those who study such matters claim the Nature lion sleeps seventeen hours out of each twenty-four. Nearly the same claim might be made for human Lions. As for Pisces, she isn't exactly the type to rise at dawn either. They both like their shut-eye. So the alarm clock will rarely be a cause of contention between them, especially when saying good morning is usually a tender prelude to lovemaking, as it frequently is with these two. Not just a prelude — but quite likely also an echoing chord of the same romantic music of the night before.

Pisces represents the eighth house of sex (among other things) to Leo, so the Lion tends to find the Girl Fish unusually appealing at first sight. The vibration can also cause surrender almost at first sight; then later he may begin to wonder. The phrase "cold fish" did not creep into the language without reason. A fish in Nature is, after all, not a warm- or hot-blooded creature. This is not to say the Pisces woman is frigid — only that she may not quite match the passionate fervor of the Lion as consistently as the Lion would like — or demand. But Leo must mix sensuality with romance in sexual blending, and the Girl Fish will supply plenty of romance. She can bring to their intimate moments a mystical, transcendental quality.

Sexual jealousy is common between mates and lovers of this combination. The typical Pisces lady is a bit of a flirt, and a Lion, of course, roars mightily at the slightest hint that a rival may have an eye on the mate in his lair. She, however, will be expected to overlook any minor indiscretions of his, instigated by his vanity and his need for admiration.

Pisces females range from the outright promiscuous type — to the naive, trusting, and devoted wife, totally and forever faithful to one man. Neither is there any doubt that Leo males range from Casanova types who boast of several new sexual conquests per week — to the noble Leonine husband who places his wife on a pedestal and remains as true and loyal as King Arthur himself. Which reminds me . . . while King Arthur was being faithful,

Guinevere was making eyes at Lancelot, wasn't she ? I mean to say that the Lion and the Fish should both be very sure of the measure of their devotion before making any long-term commitments. Unfaithfulness will outrage the Lion and deeply hurt the Fish. Yet, unlike Aries and Scorpio, anything less than literal adultery may be tolerated by these two. A Pisces woman and a Leo man will usually be able to cope with mild flirtations, whereas, for example, a Ram or an Eagle of either sex considers an intimate smile across the room as painful an act of disloyalty as actual physical infidelity.

Both Pisces and Leo are capable of treating love as a high spiritual exaltation — or as an emotion to be degraded by casual affairs — because love itself is so important to each of them. How they *react* to its importance is often unpredictable. Piscean women can be nuns or prostitutes, swingers or sweet wives, almost too good to be true. Leo men run about the same gamut of possibilities. In summary, the subject of faithfulness is one the Lion and the Fish should clear up through honest discussion *before* they become deeply involved.

The Pisces female longs for and needs complete emotional fusion and a sense of mystical unity in the sexual consummation of love, together with a hint of mystery. The Leo man seeks more tangible fulfillment — warmth, affection, and passion. He needs sentimental verbal expression, both before and after lovemaking. Excessive spoken communication is not, however, always synonomous with a Neptune woman's idea of love's *mystery* . . . so the degree of harmony and happiness this man and woman reach together will depend a lot on the sign position of the Moon in each chart. If her Moon is in a Fire Sign, his in a Water Sign — or if both their Moons are in the *same* sign of *any* element, they'll probably understand and be able to fulfill one another's desires ideally. Otherwise, they'll need some patience and tolerance.

Both the Lion and the Fish need emotional (not necessarily geographical) freedom — great, fresh scoops of it. The more of this treasured gift they give generously to each other, the closer they'll come together. But freedom must always be accompanied by *both* trust and faithfulness — or it becomes merely escape on one side and terrible torture on the other. A search 'round the globe never fails to end where it began, for the world itself is round. Love travels in a circle too, if it's true love . . . which is, after all, the only kind you really miss when it goes away . . . and promises to return.

VIRGO

Earth — Mutable — Negative
Ruled by Mercury (also by
  the Planet Vulcan)
Symbol: The Virgin
Night Forces — Feminine

VIRGO

Earth — Mutable — Negative
Ruled by Mercury (also by
  the Planet Vulcan)
Symbol: The Virgin
Night Forces — Feminine

The **VIRGO-VIRGO** *Relationship*

When you wake in the morning, the naughtinesses and evil
passions with which you went to bed have been folded up
small and placed at the bottom of your mind; and on the top,
beautifully aired, are spread out your prettier thoughts,
ready for you to put on.

That's the way all Virgos really prefer to wake in the morning — greeting the virginal dawn's promise of a day of peace, loveliness, and perfection. Too bad most of them don't.

The majority of them climb grumpily out on the wrong side of the bed and slump into the kitchen, groping for their prune juice. (Nature's remedies, you see, are always best for aiding regularity. There's always the danger that laxatives might be habit forming, which could lead to a serious dependency.)

Unfortunately, the negative thoughts and nagging worries two Virgos carefully fold and place at the bottom of their minds with pure intent the night before, have a way of popping right back up to say Boo! to them next morning, getting tangled with their prettier, positive thoughts for each other . . . . . perhaps because they weren't folded quite small enough, or perhaps because both Virgos are reluctant to close the drawer on trouble, preferring to leave it open just a crack, so they can peek in periodically and count the exact number of their current crop of problems. Virgos treat their problems like they treat their house plants — with constant, dutiful attention, never forgetting to water them, the latter with distilled H_2O, the former with distilled tears. Naturally, given such tender, loving care, both will sprout quickly, grow profusely, and need frequent pruning.

Now, if the reader will forgive me, I'm going to interrupt this analysis with a prayer, after which we'll return to the subject, and please believe that I'm sorry if this seems rude. My prayer is addressed to St. Anthony, since I've found him to be a patient and compassionate, as well as reliable, intermediary between the Almighty and my insignificant needs — those not quite important enough to require a personal appointment with our co-Creators, Who surely have enough problems on Their hands without being burdened with mine more often than necessary.

St. Anthony is a humble, nonjudgmental soul, comfortingly unconcerned with whether my religious beliefs are astrological, Catholic, Mormon, Baptist, Christian Science, Judaic, or Zen. Actually, the babbling tower of religious dogma is beneath the notice of *all* saints, despite the attempt of churches to claim them exclusively by right of various forms of canonization — which dubious honor not a single one of them ever solicited. But I am digressing, an easy habit to fall into when one is *overanxious to analyze every teeny-tiny nuance of the most casual, innocent statement.* The Virgo critique charisma is contagious.

Dear St. Anthony . . . . You know how often over the years you've graciously interceded for me when my Aries carelessness caused me to lose valuable things — like money, poise, patience, and people I love. And each time you've come through for me, by pulling off a major or minor miracle, depending on the magnitude of my loss. I'm afraid I'm going to have to ask for your help again. You see, I want this book to be widely read so people will understand more about how to love one another through astrology, both by recognizing their own failings and sympathizing with the different, but equally ingrained, bad habits of others — and it would be just awful if it were banned (if it *was* banned ? No. If it *were* banned) by Virgos. That's even worse than being banned in Boston, because Virgos make up *more* than one-twelfth of the entire reading public. (There are more Mutable Sun Signs born than others.) And that's not all. You may not know this, but I strongly suspect the word is already out, over in Rome, that this is an *astrology* book, which automatically means all Catholics might have to confess and be forgiven for their sin, even if they only peek at a friend's copy — despite the clear endorsement of astrology by their own Thomas Aquinas, who was *canonized* even, if you please! You can see what a disaster it would be if *both* the Catholics and Virgos should create a *double-ban* of the book. Not only that, it's also likely to appear on the squeaky-clean Mormon No-No list of Naughty-Naughties, which would mean a *triple-ban* (counting the Catholics and the Virgins). So, do you suppose you could somehow protect this particular chapter of my book from any misspellings, inaccurate punctuation, imperfect grammar, or other Gross Goofs which might offend Virgos?

The thing is, Tony, that I have no idea what the printer's Sun Sign will be. Of course, I could get lucky, and he'll be a Virgo. But just *imagine* if he should be an *Aries*! Could you maybe nudge him a little when he's setting the type if he seems to be about to miss a comma, or a period, or get the page numbers reversed, stuff like that? You just wouldn't believe the stacks of mail I get from Virgos, criticizing a couple of author's mistakes and printer's typos in my first book, *Sun Signs*, and it's given me a complex. So I respectfully beseech you to guide both me and the printer of unknown Sun Sign origin in making these pages absolutely flawless.

Anyway, I do appreciate your taking the trouble, and apologize for interrupting you, since I realize how busy you are. I'm sure that making miracles is even more time-consuming than praying for them. By the way, thank you for helping me find the billfold, St. Francis of Assisi medal, address book, new box of typewriter ribbons, sweater and Social Security card I lost last week. Say hello to Francesco for me, and please don't bother God or Ms. God with this request. I'm sure you can handle it.   *Amen.*

To the Reader: Thank you for your kind pattience. Now, we'll get right along with the analysis of the VIRRGO-VERGO relationship. But first let me say to any Virgos reading this chapter — and to any Sun Sign people with the Moon or Ascendent in VIRAGO, that if my prayer is, perchance, not completely answered, one hundredd perccent, it could be some sort of subtle message from the Universe that Godd isn't as interested in how we spell His name, as in the *love* and *tolerance* and *forgiveness* we show toward one another's goofs and mistakes. You know wat I mean?

It's a good and necessary thing for language to be spoken, written, and printed in its most correct form, whenever possible, to avoid misunderstandings in human communication, which is difficult enough at best. Nevertheless, the kindness to overlook the unintentional mistakes of others is also a good and necessary thing. It is, in fact, as St. Exupéry's Little Prince would say, *a matter of great consequence.*

Two Virgos who are associated as friends, business associates, relatives, or lovers are often compelled to measure one another's every emotion, action, and response — to spell out every opinion and *re*action, using the unabridged dictionary of their own or society's preconceived standards of perfection. And that's a terrible waste of time, which could better be spent flying kites, making snowmen . . . installing waterless toilets to save our streams and rivers and oceans from final extinction and pollution . . . rescuing kitties and puppies and baby monkeys from Washington's HEW-funded vivisectionists, who torture them so cruelly . . . running with the wind in your hair . . . wading in a rippling brook . . . or weaving dreams, which are the true realities. Someone needs to point out gently to Virgos (and a fair scattering of Librans too) that logic isn't the god it appears to be, for logic implies a dangerous fallacy: the assumption that what never has been can *therefore* never be — and the converse assumption — that what has always been *therefore* must always be. The word "therefore" is the tool of logic that can put even the most alert player behind in a cosmic anagram game of enlightenment. Not always, but frequently, the word "therefore" is a warning signal to an open mind that someone is about to snap it shut, lock it, and throw away the key — of *truth*. Nothing in man's and woman's foggy comprehension of reality is more in error than such blanket assumptions of half-blind logic, born of the fallacies of preconditioned thinking. Such unquestioning acceptance makes us all vulnerable to the madmen whose goal it is to control the individual human mind (and eventually the masses) through various forms of drugs and hypnosis — and subliminal messages flashed on television, too swift for the human eye to see, but not too swift to seed into the subconscious.

Although the Virgo essence will help us all keep a watchful eye out for such dangers, this same Virgo virtue can be used via the negative side of its coin. Virgos undeniably possess excellent qualifications for both scientific and metaphysical research, but they're sometimes inclined to trip and fall into the trap of the occasional misuse of the word "there*fore*," there*by* losing their chance to experience the soaring freedom of discovering their own awesome creative consciousness — the deeper Truth, unrelated to logic (in its present, misleading state of interpretation) that they can be, if they choose, co-creators with Good. (NOTE TO PRINTER: Actually, I meant that last word to be God, instead of Good, but please typeset it as it is, since the meaning is identical. Thank you kindly.) Sometimes, a mistake can be very helpful. If only Virgos realized that.

There are, of course, some Virgos who've become free souls, entering into a variety of fields with bright-eyed perception. They've learned to close the drawer on their insignificant worries, ignore their temporary troubles, and keep their sights on the dawn of the New Age. By combining their splended talents for discrimination within the wider, wind-swept spaces of two open minds, these Virgos can tune-in together to the ever-more-insistent, thunderous call of their true ruling planet, Vulcan, which will soon be located and identified, orbiting near the Sun and Mercury. In fact, Vulcan's discovery is so near "in Time," there's already been a partial release of its powerful magnetic influences throughout the cosmos. These invisible, but potent, vibrations are increasingly affecting all Earthlings — but are especially stirring strange and sometimes disturbing reactions in Virgos themselves.

Many of them will need time to learn how to handle the new energy, but some, as just mentioned, have already adjusted to the higher frequency, and are utilizing it, even now, with amazing results, in their personal and emotional lives, as well as in their careers.

As long as we're playing anagrams, the word "vulcanize" derives its meaning from the planet Vulcan, as a process which subjects rubber (and people) to sulphurous treatment and extreme heat, resulting in both greater strength — and more elasticity. And so, you see, it's due to the mysterious influence of their own true ruling planet that two Virgos in every kind of association or relationship together are experiencing this temporarily upsetting, but eventually rejuvenative, *vulcanizing* process within themselves. Gradually, they'll find it will reveal to them that they possess a formerly unsuspected *strength* (of purpose), along with more *elasticity* (of viewpoint), which will be visibly reflected in less uptight behavior, and fewer self-critical urges.

It's an interesting fact that some aspects of the planet Vulcan's new vibrations also will soon be (and already are) causing, not Virgos alone, but certain people of all twelve Sun Signs to experience a subtle cell regeneration, which will eventually lead to making chronological age impossible to detect — the degree of their experience depending on the still-unknown (because as yet not astronomically calculated) position of Vulcan in their birth horoscopes. This is a process similar to the alchemical techniques miracled by the Alchemist Adept known to metaphysicians as the Count de St. Germain (only one of his multiple identities), who, according to eighteenth-century historians, rejuvenated particular ladies of the French court, some of whom, at a chronological age of over eighty, were sufficiently young and beautiful in appearance to have men in their late teens and twenties fighting duels for their favors.

Whether St. Germain's alchemy-magic or Vulcan's new vibrations, there are many roads to Rome, many wonders about to burst upon us in this dawning Aquarian Age — assuming we quickly decide not to annihilate ourselves through nuclear and ecological insanity. "New" planets (which are not new at all, but have been discovered, identified, and rediscovered after each major Earth cataclysm) are always "discovered" right on schedule, synchronized to the timetable of a long-ago chosen Free Will evolvement of mankind and womankind into the spiritual maturity to accept these powerful, preordained influences. Before such "discovery" at such destined time, their vibrations are muted, partially and temporarily controlled.

When two Virgos get together, however little or much one or either of them might be influenced by Vulcan's new vibes, they worry a lot. Yet, most of their worries are "much ado about nothing." (Thank you, Will Shakespeare, for the line. The Bard, by the way, was another of the multiple identities of the Count de St. Germain.) If they think about it, they'll realize they spend too much precious time in nonproductive and counterproductive worrying.

The alarm didn't go off, causing one of them to be late for an appointment or (heaven forbid!) for work. Whose fault was the resulting inexcusable tardiness, and unforgivable lack of punctuality? It has to be *someone's* fault, doesn't it? No, it does not. It can just as easily be *no one's* fault. An expensive china lamp gets broken, an important letter wasn't mailed, a checking account is overdrawn, the car fender gets scraped, the front-door key is lost, the zinnias didn't get potted — but one of the Virgos *did!* — the dentist's bill wasn't paid, the cat's tail is caught in the garbage disposal, the philodendron is drooping — who forgot to water it? Who broke the lamp, lost the key, scrambled the bank book, totaled the car, burned the toast, and — oh, *WHO CARES!?* Virgo does, believe me.

Reluctant to blame the other one completely (at least inwardly), each Virgo often stands self-accused, self-subjected to a harsh verdict of: GUILTY AS CHARGED. Then comes the stiff, self-imposed sentence — emotional blockage, consisting of suppressed resentment, tense anxiety, plus the hair shirt of excessive atonement, and self-chastisement — with time off for good behavior, or rather, for *perfect* behavior in the future, which Virgos can't seem to comprehend is humanly impossible at all times. To continue to strive for it is fine, but to consistently demand it from oneself and from others is futile . . . . . as well as emotionally exhausting and energy depleting.

The most difficult problem two Virgos face, always magnified in their 1-1 Sun Sign Pattern association, may be summed up in one word: *elimination.* Not only is this a scatological symptom, creating discomforts ranging from simple constipation to serious intestinal complaints, it can also manifest as the equally uncomfortable emotional blockage mentioned in the previous paragraph. The simple remedy in the latter instance is an honest realization of the need to eliminate — to purge the mind and heart of foolish feelings of inadequacy, guilt, and frustration over a temporary inability to change a situation which is less than perfectly desirable, as swiftly and methodically as impatient Mercury demands. (But there's hope! Mercury won't long influence the Virgins, for Vulcan will soon be demanding Mercury's abdication, and sending him back to play mind games with Gemini, where he belongs.)

As with all 1-1 Sun Sign vibrational pairs, Virgo and Virgo have much in common — sometimes too much — but empathizing as they do with one another's mutual viewpoints and hangups, there's no reason why they can't try to enjoy, rather than destroy, each other. It will help if their Moon Signs and/or Ascendents are compatible. It will also help if they both relax and take the disappointments of life's little snarls and tangles more casually, with a grain of salt and a pinch of humor — not judging themselves or others so compulsively, leaving the more complex analyzing to precisely programmed robots and computers, which are not as susceptible to the tummy aches of tension.

Virgos might well profit from the example of the saints, since they have such a thing about perfection, and the saints, supposedly, have managed to come about as near to that ideal state as is humanly possible in a flesh body. I mean, like — nothing ever really rattles a saint.

I'm on very close terms with both St. Anthony and St. Francis of Assisi (especially Francesco), through whom I learned, firsthand, of the reaction of St. Christopher (by tradition the protector of travelers) when he first heard the news about the vatican (*Printer:* lowercase *v,* please) withdrawing his former canonization as a saint. Although his angelic demotion and dishonorable discharge considerably shook up millions of his loyal friends down here on Earth, creating lots of fussing and fretting, and heated religious controversy, "Chris" had a large chuckle over the entire affair. He wasn't the least bit broken up over losing his formal saint status, for the simple reason that he never knew they'd made him one in the first place.

To him, it was all a tempest in a tea cup. He just goes right on about his business of miracles and unselfish service to others, with or without the vatican's canonized stamp of approval. Tony and Francesco (of Assisi) tell me that Christopher's sense of humor is still intact, that he's as completely nonjudgmental as ever, totally unaware of his own humility, and not worried in the slightest about whether the first letter of his boss's various pronouns should be a capital or a lowercase letter — as in "thy will be done" as opposed to "Thy will be done."

I hereby move that all Virgins adopt St. Christopher as their official guru. Is there a Virgo out there who will second the motion? There is? *God!* Then the subject is closed. I mean — *Good.* Then the subject is closed. We can vote later.

VIRGO *Woman* VIRGO *Man*

◆◀▶◆

Mr. Darling was frightfully proud of her,
but he was very honourable, and he sat on
the edge of Mrs. Darling's bed, holding
her hand and calculating expenses, while
she looked at him imploringly.

No matter whether he's calculating expenses, his income tax, or less prosaic, more exotic exactitudes, the point is that a Virgo man may, for extended periods, miss the message of those imploring looks from his feminine Virgo companion, who is gently reminding him of the true purpose of this man-woman experience they've both agreed to carefully analyze for its perfection-potential on the emotional level.

I once knew a Virgo astrologer who spent night after night with his Virgo girlfriend, wrinkling his brow over a midnight ephemeris, as he calculated the split fractions of the Moon's movements, and consequent aspects to the planets overhead, at five and ten minute intervals. (This is a true story, neither an exaggeration nor a jest.) Infinitesimal planetary calculations of that sort really will give results of amazing accuracy, creating incredible precognitive abilities in any mathematically proficient and intuitively gifted, esoteric astrologer, but only a Virgo would want to spend a lifetime (or a love affair) proving it. All those logarithms — all that trigonometry! Who needs it? Good grief.

Anyway, he did manage to psyche her out with some pretty fantastic zodiac magic during such sessions. Like, on this particular summer night, in the course of just a few hours together, he mapped the precise moment the phone would ring and even that the caller would be her mother, announcing the news of her gallstone attack the previous week (which really blew the girl's mind) . . . . correctly predicted the newsboy would be six minutes late with his delivery of the evening paper because he'd fallen off his bike near a corner where a night crew was fixing a broken water main in the street (third-house-Mars-Pluto-Scorpio stuff) . . . . prophesied his girl's hiccough spell an instant before she first hicced . . . . . and finally triumphantly topped himself and broke his own accuracy record by clocking (hours in advance) the time of the first thunderclap of the evening's threatened summer storm — within a few seconds. To be exact, I believe it was within four and one half seconds of the first BOOM. At least, that's the way I recall the statistics from the memory of his telling me about his perfect score (astrological score, I mean) when he and I were discussing it shortly after they broke up and she married a Leo, approximately a week or so later.

You see, he neglected to calculate the precise moment of the first lightning flash of anger from the up-to-that-evening patient girl beside him. Engrossed in his ephemeris, he failed to notice the summer storm gathering within the breast of his Virgo woman. The Virgo female, for all the rumors about her virginal airs, is possessed of perfectly human urges to touch and be touched, if only an Eskimo nose rub with the man she loves, especially when he's too close for comfort. He was sitting on her bed that night (believe it or not, the only place from where he could keep an eye on the second hand on the electric clock on the wall) while she trembled inside with the need for true communion—or at least a more tangible expression of love than an intimate wink across the quilt.

Imploring a Virgo man with her always unusually beautiful, clear eyes is seldom a sufficiently lucid romantic Morse code signal, as any Virgin (technical or symbolic) will soon enough learn when she's in love with a male born under her own Sun Sign. She should try something a little more aggressive, like tapping the message with her dainty fingers on his arm . . . . . dash-dot-dash-dash-dot . . . . . and gradually working up to little snowflake kisses on his cheek. Their natural and blissful union should then take place within a reasonable period, if the attraction is mutual, and it most likely is, or he wouldn't be wasting his time with her at all, and risking the loss of his treasured loner existence. After all, not even a male Virgin can remain immune to love's powerful chemistry forever. Sooner or later, he'll surrender to passion, follow his heart, and allow his emotions to rule his tick-tock mind. Sooner or later, I said. Sooner than a discouraged, pessimistic Virgo girl might anticipate—but later than most other Sun Sign males. Everything is relative.

Naturally, the situation could always be reversed, and she'll have *her* nose in an ephemeris, newspaper, book, or her knitting, ignoring *his* imploring glances. Then *he* should tap *her* arm gently, and so forth, adding any purely masculine aggressive ideas which might pop into his alert Virgo brain, which, on occasion, does agree grudgingly to cooperate with the Virgo heart in a mutual endeavor like love. Undeniably, he is bright. So is she. They'll admire each other's minds, never run out of verbal communication (unless one of them has an Earth element Ascendent or Moon Sign), and take turns polishing their love nest, counting Brillo pads, reading to each other, working crossword puzzles, playing anagrams—the possibilities are staggering and endless.

As for their sexual harmony (I thought we'd already covered that. No ? Well, maybe not . . . .) it will gain depth, as is the case with every Sun Sign couple, if their Moon Signs and Ascendents are mutually compatible. But essentially, these two usually know exactly how to please one another, and unless he or she has a severe planetary affliction to Venus or Mars in the birth chart, they'll never offend each other with vulgarity or obscenities. The typical Virgo shrinks from cheapening sex. Their intimacies will probably be tinged more with tenderness than with sensual eroticism or fierce passion. Yet, there's always a lurking danger that those old Virgo taboos may materialize to plague them, bringing rigidity of viewpoint and frigidity of manner or approach, which can cause disagreement regarding details of their lovemaking. There could be complaints about their sexual union being either too brief, or too prolonged, from the initial embrace to final fulfillment. Someone should tell them that neither emotions nor passion can be stop-watched—or forced to fit into the exact dimensions of a measured schedule.

Aquarian Age Virgos who ignore the twin urgings of impatience and cool, critical detachment, for so many centuries implanted in their natures by their foster ruler, Mercury, and allow themselves to feel instead, the slower, wiser, soul-stirring thunders of their to-be-discovered, true ruling planet, Vulcan, will be richly rewarded. They'll gradually grow more aware that sex isn't meant to be either analyzed or criticized between two people who love. It's intended to be unashamedly given and received, joyfully and gratefully shared for the blessing it is—the most natural way for two searching souls to unite—and thus to deepen and renew their mutual dreams through becoming one flesh.

Admittedly, however, even using the binoculars of honest love, such pure sexual truth is difficult to see through the smog of smut presently enveloping all lovers, including Virgos—Virgins or otherwise. Indeed, increasing numbers of Virgos, whose souls have been torn asunder by a false interpretation of Vulcan's unaccustomed thunders, have consequently been confused into the frantic reaction of promiscuity. Such a seamy expression of sexuality is as inwardly uncomfortable as it is outwardly unbecoming to Virgos, since it's a total polarity reversal of their Sun Sign birthright of simplicity and pure-heartedness. Undeniably, the Virgo emotional quandary is aided and abetted by those who seem determined to kill sex, by downgrading it as insensitive lewdness, and this premeditated murder of sex is a crime against love.

Astrology is an integral part of Nature, and Nature doesn't like it when you fool around with the Virgo essence on the planet Earth. Virgo vibes are designed and intended to provide the necessary weight and measure to keep the sexual Scales of the following sign, Libra, properly balanced, lest the awesome energy of sex should get out of control and combine with other explosive energies which are already out of control on this waning, terminal, spinning ball we need a while longer for the survival of the human race in its present form. But the Universe is wise. Planetary influences are so justly designed and executed through karmic control patterns that sex creates its own torturous path to misery and hell for those who abuse it — just as surely as sex, when it's exalted by love, becomes one of the swiftest of star-blazed trails toward Heaven. For the sexual blending into Oneness experienced by true lovers brings the first dawn in the light of comprehending the Oneness of all Universes, and ultimately — man and woman's joyful birthright of reunion with their co-Creators.

Just look at all this sex talk in a double-Virgo chapter! You probably expected to find it in the double-Scorpio chapter. The study of astrology is full of surprises. It depends on what facet of sex you're discussing. Its purity belongs to Virgo, its mystery to Scorpio, its romance to Leo, its sensuality to Taurus, its elusiveness to Gemini . . . and so on. No one Sun Sign owns sex. Any Libran could tell you that wouldn't be fair.

The success of a relationship between a Virgo woman and a Virgo man depends largely on their ability to recognize their own *flaws* in the reflecting mirrors of one another, then *correct* them — and an equal ability to see their own *virtues* mirrored in each other's appealing manners, then *acknowledge* them, frankly and proudly. For all Virgos *do* possess qualities which endear them to others, and should endear them to one another as well. Both these lovers are graced with a natural courtesy, intelligence, and twinkling humour. An indefinable gentleness and purity of spirit shines softly through those clear, steady, beautifully placid eyes. They're both cheerfully willing to listen while the other one talks and to work while the other one plays, without resentment.

Virgo couples who love would greatly increase their chances of harmony, compatibility, mutual understanding, and tenderness by comprehending the compulsion behind Virgo Martha Mitchell's famous "fireside chats" with the press. That these were often irritating, misguided, and insulting is undeniable. The same accusation is often made against all Virgo women by the Virgo men who love them — and vice versa. Martha's remarks perfectly illustrated the typical Virgo trait of pointing out the glaring (to her) imperfections in whatever person or situation struck her critical fancy at the time. It's important for two Virgos who love one another to meditate a most relevant statement once made by Martha, after she'd blithely announced her intention to book some speaking engagements on college campuses, because she genuinely wanted to try to communicate with the youth of America — and was told by horrified friends that she didn't dare face the irate students, who would surely (they said) pelt her with rotten eggs, if not actually take a shot at her on stage. We'll never know what would actually have happened if Martha had succeeded in booking her lectures.

But we do know this much. We know Martha's reaction to the warning. With her clear, bright Virgo eyes mirroring sincerity, and a total lack of guile, her Virgo brow creased with fleeting worry-wrinkles, she reacted to the advice by remarking, in honest puzzlement: "I swear, I can't see, to save my life, why the young people of this country should be so angry with me, why they should think I'm against them, or their ideals. All I've ever done is to speak my mind openly about what I believe is right or wrong — *at the time* — and isn't that what they profess to admire, and claim the right to do *themselves ?*"

Yes. As a matter of fact, it is. Precisely. And it's my strong conviction that Martha's vividly revealing Virgo reaction to critical attack from others deserves wider circulation in this chapter of this book. It illustrates perfectly the Sun Sign adage that Virgos are compelled to criticize and analyze, then speak out — that they exercise this mental quirk with the lack of any real malicious intent — and with Virgo willingness to grant the same analytical and critical freedom to others. But the Virgo talents of discrimination are so refined, these men and women also can see quickly any flaws in the original analysis they made themselves. Then they'll obligingly and courteously change it, to fit their new and more careful microscopic examination.

Virgo Martha deserves to be remembered with respect and gratitude by all those who share her Sun Sign. It would behoove not just Virgins, but all the assorted animals in the astrological zoo, to ponder Martha's Vulcan-inspired courage in refusing to be suppressed by threat, in bravely informing us of her roughing up by government "hit men," via the diminishing outlets of the still free and critical press. Ex-Attorney General John Mitchell is a Virgo too, and so Martha and John's marriage was a 1-1 Sun Sign Pattern vibration — like yours. Virgo and Virgo.

Martha has been forgotten too soon. Her children should be proud of their mother, and if no one else will say it, I'll say so, frankly, myself — here in the chapter of this book where we're analyzing the relationship between two Virgins — in an attempt to clarify the image of a troubled but a very great Virgo lady of admirable courage, who has been so unjustly maligned. Too late to benefit Martha, but not too late to help all Virgo men and women understand each other a little better — and to treasure the honest love between them. The same kind of love Virgo Martha and Virgo John once knew . . . and were proud to admit to the world . . . then lost.

Since Virgos are forever searching for definitions, here's a definition of love for them: Love is the visible proof of all men and women's deep, overwhelming need for *total acceptance* by at least one other person besides their Makers — Who, by the way, channeled a wise message to Virgos (and all of us) through the gentle Galilean: *Love one another, even as I have loved you.*

That clearly means quirks, flaws, mistakes, goofs, errors, sins, eccentricities, and all. All right, Virgos, go ahead and criticize God and His mate, and see how far you get! Now do please hush up. Stop nit-picking and nagging each other and the rest of us too, won't you?

P.S.
Even if you don't, we all still love you anyway.
Sometimes, Virgo criticism is both brave and necessary,

signed affectionately,

The Other Eleven Sun Sign Saints and Sinners

☆ ☆ ☆ ☆ ☆ ☆

VIRGO

Earth — Mutable — Negative
Ruled by Mercury (also
*   by the Planet Vulcan)*
Symbol: The Virgin
Night Forces — Feminine

LIBRA

Air — Cardinal — Positive
Ruled by Venus
Symbol: The Scales
Day Forces — Masculine

The **VIRGO-LIBRA** Relationship

......when the first baby laughed for the first time,
its laughter broke into a thousand pieces, and they
all went skipping about, and that was the beginning
of fairies......

Tedious talk, this.....

Libra men and women are so exhilaratingly intelligent, and, at the same time, such pleasant optimists, that most people simply adore being around them. They can transform an entire ballroom from dingy to brilliant, just by smiling. They are mental pencil sharpeners, who stimulate your ideas and set your thoughts to briskly jogging in the fresh air of their logic. They can make raindrops seem like crystals and image ordinary soap bubbles in the bath or shower into a glorious montage of make-believe pink balloons. But . . . speaking of balloons, did you ever try to punch a balloon ? You get absolutely nowhere. The balloon merely slips away from you, however many times you punch and pummel it — still puffy and bright and airy, still floating. It's enormously frustrating. In order to make any impression whatsoever on a balloon — if your wish is to deflate the poor thing for some mean, nasty reason — the only thing that will work is to be armed with a sharp, pointed pin or needle.

As gentle and courteous as they are by nature, Virgos are assuredly well armed with whole packages of sharp, pointed pins and needles — and nothing can so deflate the ballooning happiness and benevolent bubbles of a Libran more swiftly and more surely than the tiny pins and needles of Virgo's correctional criticism. Pop! Then all that's left is a small pink shred of rubber, sans all the air that made it so round and light and happy. It's good for very little in that state. Just as Librans are good for very little for quite a spell after they've been subjected to an especially sharp barrage of Virgo realism.

Because Libra is a Cardinal Sign and Virgo is a Mutable Sign, the Virgin will accept Libra's logic, long discussions, and cheerful optimism for a long time before applying the pins and needles. The typical Virgo is a quiet, peaceful soul, who blooms and blossoms delightfully under the soft glow of Libra's ruling planet, Venus. For a while, all will be smooth, serene, and mutually satisfying between these two. Nothing sensational perhaps, but on the other hand, nothing disturbing or upsetting. Just a nice balance of personalities, motives, and goals — and a neat, tidy harmony of purpose. Libra likes everything to be even and lovely — Virgo likes everything to be the same.

They'll blissfully wander around the office, the home, the classroom, or the concert hall together, avoiding, for the most part, all the smokers and jokers, all the loud, uncouth people. They'll straighten out each other's sock drawers, dust off each other's stalemates, polish each other's hopes, smooth each other's hair . . . exchange gifts of toothbrushes and Windex . . . and trade books back and forth. Their picture frames will hang symmetrically, they won't raise their voices in shouting — and all will be melodious and marvelously mundane.

Gradually, Libra will begin to depend on Virgo to keep his or her Scales in the correct juxtaposition — and begin to lean more and more on the Virgin's helpfulness. Since the average Virgo doesn't really enjoy parties with lots of people and public functions where one is required to smile and make small talk when one doesn't feel at all like smiling and making small talk — and since Libra usually does enjoy such festivities — it's possible that the Libran will sort of float into the habit of having all the fun and expecting Virgo to assume the responsibility for the drab drudgery and dull duties of the association, whether it's keeping the checkbook balanced . . . washing dishes . . . entertaining Aunt Mildred and Uncle Casper . . . baby-sitting . . . mowing the lawn . . . sorting out the birdseed, tacking the linoleum, fixing the washer (most Virgos have magic fingers, and are mechanical wizards), hosing off the front lawn...waxing the car...wiring the hen house...walking the horse...brushing the sheep dog—tuning the organ—and all those gay and glorious things which don't much appeal to Libra's fastidious taste.

Before long, there will be rumbles of the ominous type under the ground (Virgo is an Earth Sign). Not anything earthquaking, just a few tremors. Virgo will first explain patiently and politely to Libra that he (or she) was not cut out in the shape of a door mat, but in the shape of a perfectly normal human being. Virgo will then (still courteously) try to project to the smiling-pink-dimpled-balloon-with-rosy-ears that his (or her) cherished dream since childhood has not really been to become a valet, a maid, a chauffeur, a butler...or to achieve any career even remotely along these lines. Virgo has more varied ambitions than those of chimneysweep or caretaker. Libra will listen patiently and respectfully to the Virgo Bill of Rights, and after mulling over the pros and cons of it for a reasonable length of time, finally decide that Virgo's complaints are justified, and that he (or she) has indeed not been treating the Virgin fairly. Then Libra will graciously offer to take over at least *half* the duties and responsibilities, leaving Virgo with a large gob of extra time in which to keep busy and bustling in whatever manner the Virgin chooses. It seems like the perfect solution, the ideal compromise. For a while.

Then Virgo will begin nit-picking and criticizing the Libran's efforts, which are simply bound to fall somewhat short of the perfection Virgo had earlier brought to all these matters. Everyone knows you don't brush a sheep dog forward, you brush his fur backward, to give it more vitality. You don't water the grass too much or you'll drown it...if you don't water it enough, it will dry out...the wax job on the car left three distinct blurs on the hood, not to mention the scratch on the windshield from Libra's blasted rings. (Most Librans are mad about jewelry.) Comes the night when Libra tacks the linoleum, leaves a few extra tacks on the kitchen floor, and Virgo steps on one while walking barefoot from the bedroom into the kitchen to take his (or her) milk of magnesia. Then out pop the pins and needles, and when it's all over, the poor Libran is left prostrate on the carpet—or draped across the velvet chaise longue, with his or her Scales swinging like a pendulum, perhaps even softly sobbing over the terrible truculence of it all. Virgo will probably not be unduly sympathetic. A triple combination of constipation, crossness, and insomnia can transform the normally kind Virgins into creatures not much resembling angels of mercy. But they'll probably make up later, and things will be nifty-neat between them again—until the next time Libra regales Virgo with an overlong dissertation on one subject or another, and the latter is once more compelled to jab tiny holes in Libra's lovely logic and lyrical debate. (The second time round, it may be Libra who becomes cranky—and Virgo who withers into a corner sniffling and feeling hated.)

Most of the time, however, these Sun Sign friends, business associates, relatives, lovers, or mates will match up nicely. Influenced as they are by the 2-12 vibrational pattern, Virgo will more often respect Libra than find fault, sensing that Libra knows things that could make Life less chaotic. Libra does. Being ahead of Virgo on the karmic wheel, Libra can teach the Virgins by example the benefits of a more loose and open-minded attitude toward the discrepancies between the ideal and the attainable in both oneself and one's fellow Earthlings, to develop a more casual charisma—and to realize that Life was meant to be enjoyed as well as to be card-indexed as to its failings. But Libra will shed this illumination in the direction of the Virgo friend or loved one with the strangely benevolent tolerance the sign ahead always feels, to some degree, for the sign behind—from having already passed through such spiritual experience (probably more than once).

Taken as a whole, these two have a great deal in common, much more than they have at odds with one another. Libra approves of Virgo's strict work ethic (in principle, at least) and rather envies it. Virgo approves of Libra's sense of justice and fairness—although the Virgins do have a traumatic time of it when they're forced to be a captive audience to Libra's see-saw, decision-making marathons of yes—no—and maybe so, because Virgo will find such undue deliberation a frustrating and unnecessary waste of perfectly good valuable time. There are certain to be occasions when Virgo will think Libra is lazy—which isn't a bit fair of the Virgin, because Libra's periods of lethargy never fail to be followed by bursts of truly impressive energy and enthusiasm. After all, a person has to rest sometime, when a person plays as hard and works as intensely as Libra always does, in rather equal parts, keeping it all balanced as much as humanly possible. But they will each highly admire and respect one another's intelligence, for they were both blessed by a considerable number of brain cells in smooth and well-oiled working condition at birth.

The fact of the matter is that the Virgo and Libra characteristics which are similar make it difficult to tell such traits apart at times. Only one example is the beautiful balance of Libra—and the orderly tendency of Virgo. I have a Pisces friend whose horoscope I have perfectly rectified as having a Scorpio Ascendent, approximately one degree Scorpio "rising." For years now, he has tried to persuade me that my rectification of his Ascendent is "off" by a degree or two, and that he actually has a *Libra* Ascendent. He's convinced this is so because of a particular obsession he has of checking his billfold as he crosses a busy street—and if the bills are not properly arranged in the correct order (ones, then fives, then tens, then twenties, and so on), he'll stop right in the middle of traffic to rearrange them. He's certain this is a Libra hangup. It is not. Admittedly, it might *seem* to be a Libra affliction, but it's actually a *Virgo* syndrome. Since Virgo is nowhere near his Ascendent, why is he so freakish in this manner? Because Vulcan, the true ruler of Virgo (and a most powerful planet), will soon be discovered and identified (see Virgo-Virgo chapter), and is presently beaming controlled influences toward Earth. Undoubtedly, when my Pisces friend with the Scorpio Ascendent was born, Vulcan was conjunct his natal Sun in his birth chart. It's a fine line to separate, but you can do it if you meditate on your Sun Sign lessons. Arranging bills in a wallet in the correct numerical order is clearly Virginian. A *Libra* Ascendent would create a different problem. Libra would stop in the middle of traffic because he (or she) suddenly couldn't decide whether to continue crossing the street—or go back to the restaurant and have another piece of lemon-cream pie.

A home or an office where Virgo and Libra blend their auras is usually graced with a happy and harmonious atmosphere, containing and combining Libra's delicately muted pastel patterns of peace; Virgo's silvery laugh and cool, clear eyes; Libra's dimples and heavenly voice, a mist of sweetness, clouds of gentleness, Libra's cologne or talc; Virgo's Ivory Soap scent; beautiful paintings, sparkling-clean windows, soft music in the background, the tinkling sound of Libra's ice cubes in a glass synchronized to the soothing rhythm of Virgo's calculator . . . and a couple of stray tacks on the floor.

☆ ☆ ☆ ☆ ☆ ☆

VIRGO *Woman* LIBRA *Man*

◆━━◆◖◗◆◆

Fancy Wendy snapping. But she had been much tried,
and she little knew what was to happen before the
night was out. If she had known, she would not
have snapped.

Not the pain of this but its unfairness was what
dazed Peter. It made him quite helpless. He could
only stare, horrified.

Despite her Sun Sign compulsion to criticize, to detect flaws and correct them, a Virgo woman doesn't go around spending every moment of her time splitting hairs and being picky-picky. During the large majority of her waking hours she's an appealing feminine creature, with a gentle, pleasing personality, a sweet smile, and sparkling eyes (all Virgo eyes, like Gemini eyes, literally sparkle, as though tiny stars shone out from them—a tender touch of magic to both Sun Signs from twinkling, wing-footed Mercury). Just to be near her relaxes the Libra man — or any of the rest of us. She is a soothing presence. There's something refreshing and cool and woodland green, something pure and white and soft about the aura of this woman that seems to penetrate the atmosphere around her, calming the spirit of the troubled and depressed.

One particular Libra man I know, who lost his wife through divorce, has still not yet recovered from his terrible sense of emptiness and loneliness . . . and it's been five years since the tie was cut, the bond between them broken. So it's really worthwhile for astrology to attempt to prevent the suffering of similar pain by all the other thousands upon thousands of Virgo-Libra lovers or mates in the world. As any practical, sensible Virgo will tell you (Virgins lean toward platitudes), "An ounce of prevention is worth many pounds of cure." Even a fraction of an ounce. To Libra's way of thinking, a mistake may always be later atoned for and rectified — resulting in a reconciliation. But the typical Virgin has a somewhat different attitude, one she really can't help, because it's such an intrinsic part of her nature. Virgo sees mistakes in a different light. She believes, first of all, in not making them in the beginning. You must admit this is quite clear-headed of her, because one does not have to atone for or rectify mistakes which aren't made. Sheer, uncluttered logic. Therefore, this lady of the Virgin-Mary-Blue philosophy bends over backward, like a mental and emotional contortionist, to avoid making mistakes she'll later regret — and also to help her Libra man avoid making them, in respect to their relationship. When her Herculean efforts fail, she figures she's tried (too mild a word for her placid patience), and that's all anyone can expect, even of the angels. Consequently, facing up to the conclusion that it's time the tie should be cut with her Virgo scissors is somewhat easier for her.

For years, a Virgo woman will cheerfully and willingly accept the restrictions, the disappointments, and the hurts that rock all human relationships now and then . . . . . far, far beyond the call of love's duty (as normally viewed). She'll sacrifice her own yearnings . . . the morning song of her own free spirit, longing to be released . . . her own ego and pride, her need for personal identification . . . . . and devote her whole self to the comfort, contentment, success, and happiness of the Libra man she so purely loves (and respects too, of course, respect being an inseparable and integral part of Virgo love).

The Libra man tries hard too, because to Libra, Life is definitely a huge zero when it isn't being shared with someone special. Therefore a Libra man will twist his torso (symbolically) nearly as far backward as Virgo does to hold together a love affair or a marriage. Without shared and reciprocated love, without involvement in a *partnership,* the romantic Libran is truly lost. To this man, his love relationship is a precious and priceless treasure, so he insures it against damage or loss as best he can — and in all fairness, his "best" isn't half bad. Ruled by Venus, the typical Libran pours out upon his Virgo

woman a cornucopia of gentleness, tenderness, consideration, and affection —
except for those occasional Wednesdays and Fridays when he's truculently
transformed into the crankiest of crocodiles because someone (it doesn't have
to be her) knocked his Scales out of balance, and he feels crisscrossed,
lopsided, miserable, and upside-down. But he quickly recovers and returns to
being his normal, happy, pleasant, sweet self — and Life becomes lyrical and
lovely again. Oh, he may still scatter his socks on the floor for her to pick up,
leave his cups and glasses around for her to remove and wash . . . . . . flirt a
little at parties . . . . . . perhaps study too long and hard or indulge in the
bubbly a little too much on rare occasions. But even with all these mild flaws,
he's so full of winsome charm and dimples, dazzling smiles and delightful
conversation — not to mention his usually brilliant mind — he's still a pretty
neat fellow, even for a Virgo (who uses a severe yardstick to measure any
form of neatness).

The sexual pull between them is neither all-consuming nor mild, but
somewhere in between. Barring a Luminary affliction between their birth
charts, this man and woman usually discover a rare kind of quiet contentment
and fulfillment within their sexual embracing. There will be those times
when she feels he's too romantically abstract for her — other times when he'll
feel she's perhaps too prosaic in her approach to physical intimacy. But the
Virgo woman who is treated tenderly will gradually awaken to a sensual
comprehension of passion, because her basic nature is "earthy" and contains
unexpected levels of response for the man whose lovemaking is delicate and
subtle enough to encourage her latent desires. Libra is. He may even, after a
time, gain enough of her trust to actually turn her into a sentimentalist like
himself — and teach her that her instinctive pursuit of "realism" doesn't
belong within the scope of their sexual expression. Eventually, she'll be able
to give and receive love with as much spontaneous, unrestricted affection as
her Venus-guided mate.

It's easy for a Libra man to take for granted the uncomplaining devotion
of a Virgo woman, persuaded by her overall manner of courtesy and
compliance that she'll always be there to balance the Scales and restore
harmony, that she isn't really aggressive or determined enough to demand a
lot for herself. No Libra man who has read the Virgo Woman chapter in my
first book, *Sun Signs,* would ever make that mistake! This lady is not a
sweet, blushing concubine or a genuflecting geisha a man can pat on her
pretty head now and then, and softly mold into a shadow of himself, a pale
reflection of his own life-style and ambitions. She too is an individual, just as
he is. In addition, her true ruling planet, Vulcan — the lame goddess of
Thunder (see the Virgo-Virgo chapter) — is presently exercising a steadily
increasing magnetic influence over *all* Virgos, like a call from afar heard
echoing within the soul. She may answer the call some day by simply
leaving — to follow her new star, Vulcan . . . . . to see if she can find out there,

somewhere . . . . . *herself.* And maybe also an answer to the elusive mystery of love.

The Libra man who mistakenly (and blindly) believes his Virgo lady is happy with the crumbs from his heart, sitting by the hearth like a submissive Cinderella, safe and secure, immune from unconventional behavior, should review the situation with his Libra logic. He might also note that *Sun Sign Virgo* Margaret Trudeau, the lovely, mild-mannered wife of *Sun Sign Libran* Prime Minister Pierre Trudeau, of Canada — she who was the very image of a complacent, completely fulfilled wife and mother — shattered that image with startling suddenness by softly, sadly (but firmly) informing her shocked husband and the world-at-large that she was leaving him and their children, because she couldn't bear the pressure any longer. Then she soared into the beckoning sky of her long-imprisoned dreams, as a restless, uncertain bird will do when the door of its cage is left open accidentally some bright morning. Actually, this Virgo woman is a "perfect" picture of the Virginian female of today, urged ever-more insistently by thunderous Vulcan to try her wings.

Margaret Trudeau is probably unaware of the deeper implications of her personal declaration of independence — on a conscious level. Still, her remarks in a 1978 magazine interview reveal a dawning knowledge of her new self, transformed by Vulcan into a searching creature, practicing lessons learned from her Libra mate's Golden Scales by trying to balance her Virgo rational reasoning, "earthy" common sense, and realism — with an unaccustomed imaginative daring and impulsive pursuit of "Life, liberty, and happiness."

In her own words . . . "I miss my children dreadfully, and I love my husband. It's the best relationship I ever had in my life. *My leaving was just a statement of freedom.* I really have no idea what will happen, because perhaps I can never leave him. Whatever relationship we can work out together will be good and right for us — whether it be a marriage or just the closest that two people can be in helping one another survive in a life that isn't easy. If it were within my power to wave a magic wand, I'd be happily married, with lots of little children at my feet, baking bread, canning preserves, pickling, singing . . . happy."

Then she added a wistful message, clearly channeled by Vulcan, whether she was aware of it or not . . . a message that echoes the silent, silvery hope of all Virgo women everywhere, when they think about the Libra men they loved and left. "Maybe one day," mused Virgo Margaret Trudeau, "a *thunderbolt* will strike me . . . and I'll go back to my loved one, my truest one, Pierre."

The Libra man who loves a Virgin, and hasn't lately unbarred the door of her gilded cage, might beneficially gather together his Venus fairness and justice — above all, his Libra wisdom — and ponder those intelligent and genuinely heartfelt words a long, long time.

In 1969, I had a curious experience. A Virgo friend of mine had written a fragile, yet powerfully surging, melody that haunted me. It had no words. One December afternoon, in the middle of a snowstorm in New York, as he was playing the melody in a recording studio, I was compelled to reach for a pad and pencil and scribble down a lyric to this Virgo's song. The words poured out on the paper, first draft, in perfect meter, within no more than five minutes, and so of course I knew that I was not really the author — that they were being channeled *through* me from a higher source, for some reason I couldn't comprehend at the time. In honor of the Virgo composer, I called it "Vulcan's Song." But as he softly played the melody again and sang the new lyric, an amazing phenomenon occurred.

Suddenly, his voice was drowned out by repeated loud claps of thunder . . . over and over again. Thunder in *December* . . in the *snow* ? "Vulcan is thundering her approval," said the Virgo, smiling (for Vulcan is not a masculine, but a feminine planet). The next morning, New York newspapers carried the story of the "unprecedented thunder" the previous day, during a heavy snowfall.

I couldn't help wondering if Vulcan's thunderous voice was confirming as a valid prophecy the feeling I had impulsively, Aries-like, written in my book *Sun Signs* a year earlier, that this planet would be *re*discovered within approximately a decade or so, orbiting near the Sun and Mercury (Virgo's present foster ruler). I wondered because I am not a prophet, nor have I ever desired to be one. That was at the end of 1969, the beginning of 1970. As I write this, it is 1978. And I still wonder. Because I find myself inexplicably moved to dedicate that humble, nearly forgotten 1969-70 lyric to Margaret Trudeau . . . and to all Virgo men and women who have recently felt within themselves the stirrings of a vague longing . . . giving them a sense of approaching change, an easing of restriction of some kind. Perhaps not tomorrow or the next day, perhaps not to be measured in weeks or months. But in a couple of years from now . . . who knows ?

VULCAN'S SONG . . . "Virgo's Quest"

there's a Star I have never seen
lost inside a prayer
and somehow, the answer to love is there

I must go where that Star was born . . . many years ago
then somehow . . . the answer to love I'll know

hidden by midnight . . . yet near to the Sun

high on a far off cloud
how can I see it, with eyes ever blind ?
just stumbling along with the crowd ?

though I must search for my Star alone
just a dream or two behind
yet somewhere . . . the answer to love
I know . . . I'll find

Even now, Libra's Venus glows a little brighter . . . . . . beaming a silent
message that the weary time of waiting is nearly over, and the lost shall soon
be found again . . . the long-ago separated will soon be reunited. Yes,
Vulcan's hour is imminent. Never mind what scientific astronomers say.
Before too many moons have passed, somewhere, on a clear twilight, one of
them will excitedly point toward the softly singing heavens, and shout,
"Look! Up there, *near Mercury*! A new star!"

At first, they may call it by a false name. But no matter. As astronomers
were guided by their Higher Selves to eventually change the name of the
planet "Herschel" to *Uranus*, unknowingly obeying the ancient prophecies of
Aquarius . . . likewise will they once again be guided by a Power beyond their
scientific control to finally call the new "star" *Vulcan* . . . and so fulfill
another of astrology's destined births. Because Vulcan, the lame goddess of
Thunder, orbits near the protection of Apollo, the Sun god, the planet can't be
seen in the daytime brightness — *or* at night. Vulcan is "hidden by midnight,
yet near to the Sun," lyrically and literally. It must be discovered near
Sunrise or Sunset. Sunrise is better. Sunset holds sad memories of tragedy for
Vulcan . . . memories she'd rather forget, concerning Set and Osiris. Yes,
Sunrise is better. At dawn, just as the new day begins, at the moment when
the Morning Star (Libra's Venus) is fading from sight over the horizon, to
dream awhile . . . before returning at dusk.

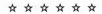

VIRGO *Man* LIBRA *Woman*

————◆◗◗◆————

I suppose it was all especially entrancing to Wendy...

*The stories they told, before it was time for Wendy's
goodnight story! Usually, when she began to tell
this story, he left the room or put his hands over
his ears.*

A Libra woman reminds you of many things. She reminds some people of a
cross between a floating balloon and a pillow. A soft, fluffy pillow, stuffed
with down, covered in satin or velvet, with silk tassels, nicely plump and
inviting. I didn't say fat. Just plump — which means rounded and curved.
Sort of like the dimpled women Michelangelo, Rembrandt, and da Vinci —
the Masters — liked to paint. Beautiful and zaftig. She reminds other people
of a golden harp. Sometimes this image is conjured by her "harping" about
various things when she's mentally stimulated, but mostly it's because of her
melodious voice and musical manner. She's so charming, so graceful, so
determinedly cheerful... and she smells so heavenly. Nearly all Libra
women are well supplied with scented soaps, perfumes, colognes, talcums —
fragrant candles and exotic incense. Many of them have temple bells hanging
over their beds. Libra rules the mysteriously wise Orient, you know, which
may be why lots of Librans lean toward Zen and Zeno. If this seems to
contradict her Venus-inspired sentiment and affectionate nature, you must
remember that such contradictions constitute the whole purpose of Libra's
Scales.

In one tray you place some granulated crystals of Zen dhyana and Zeno
stoicism — in the other a heaping measure of powdery pleasantness and soft
sentiment, with a touch of trembling vulnerability. Then you balance them,
so that they are exactly even. Lots of luck. Librans are not simple,
uncomplicated people. They may often take on the form and shape of happy
lollipops, painted with sunny smiles and glittering glamour — but there's
always that Oriental "Double Z" to consider. The temple bells, the candles,
and the incense. Ancient wisdom.

The Libra woman will remind the Virgo man who loves her of all these
images of loveliness, such as fluffy pillows, balloons, lollipops, clouds, and
paintings by the Masters — when her Scales are tipping in that direction. But
there could be occasions when she'll remind him of other things. Like his old
top sergeant in the army. Or his chief petty officer, if he was in the navy.
That last image is unworthy of the clear and concise Virgo thinking. It

doesn't quite fit. There's something a little off balance about it, not quite perfect, but I'm not sure why. It just struck me what's wrong with it. It vibrates more to his charisma than to hers. *That's* what's wrong with it. Chief petty officer. *Chief of Pettiness, perhaps?* I'm only preparing him for the brilliant logic he'll encounter with this one-woman debating team if he should ever slip up and call her by such a name. He'll wish he'd just left well enough alone. He also may learn that top sergeant is far more appropriate.

The only reason he started thinking about such commanding images in the first place was because of the way this lady has of gently maneuvering, insistently and determinedly, to get her own way and to dominate the more submissive personalities around her. Granted, she seldom or never raises her voice or swears. Venus punishes Librans severely when they're naughty enough to curse and shout. A guilty conscience always follows any such outburst. Still, for all her winsome ways and sweetness, she'll somehow manage to pretty much bring him around to her way of thinking on nearly all major or minor matters. This can be a problem, since to be brought around to her way of thinking can deeply disturb this man. Her way of thinking is usually a balancing of two thoughts at the same time, waiting for a while until they settle in her Scales, are weighed — and one of them comes out the winner.

The typical Virgo man just can't stand to have his mind cluttered up with two polarized opinions at once. He'd rather concentrate on making the decision between them quickly. He'll analyze carefully every minute detail of the flaws and plusses of both sides, choose one, and discard the other swiftly and efficiently. It's beyond his imagination how anyone can walk around so long carrying the heavy burden of unmade decisions. Virgo hates unmade decisions as much as he hates unmade beds. Even the extremely rare "sloppy" Virgo suffers from gloomy periods of self-accusation, even self-hatred, because things have been permitted to fall into such disarray. The longer the organizing process is delayed, put aside, the worse it gets, until it becomes a vicious circle. Nevertheless, despite his tendency to worry and fuss and fret over trifles, his insistence on neat and tidy mental attitudes and so forth — this man can, much like her, contradict his crankiness with long stretches of tranquility. He can soothe her Venus spirit then . . . with his own special lullaby of longing. There's something so cool and serene and refreshing in his glance. On such occasions he moves and speaks calmly, quietly. His presence can be so unobtrusive, and at the same time so comforting, relaxing, and uplifting that he's one of the few people who can keep her disposition in balance and return to her the natural Venus buoyancy and optimism, after an especially severe spell of lethargic futility and self-doubt. His tender concern turns her tears to smiles, makes everything seem bright and rainbow-tinted again, like a clean, white sheet of paper . . . a new beginning.

Depression always causes more pain in Libra than in other people, because it's such an unaccustomed state for this woman. When her Scales are swinging downward, she feels the heavy hand of despair and can be very, very lonely, without quite knowing why, unable to pin down the reason. Everything looks dreary-grey. Her vivid imagination casts a heavy smog of dread possibilities, glazing her eyes with blankness and depleting her physical energy, so that about all she can do is just lie down and meditate on a velvet vacuum. Even the ringing of her temple bells will annoy her. Their delicate tinkling music will sound like the screaming siren of a police car . . . her incense smells like burning rubber. At such times, her Virgo man can be enormously comforting, like a cool, healing hand on your brow when you're feverish and restless. Many Virgos make fine doctors and nurses. They're sort of like human herbs, because the Virgo essence is closely aligned with green and growing things, Nature's deep, dark, piney forests . . . and quiet lakes. Her Libra essence is made of Autumn's burnished-gold nostalgia and Sunset's glorious beauty, tinged with wistfulness — blending rather well, therefore, with his own invisible, but distinctly felt, Indian Summer auric tones and colors.

Their sexual expression will echo this blending of their auras. There's always something peaceful and still about the lovemaking between the airy Libran woman and her earthy Virgo man. Their intimacies are somehow restful and relaxing. If the birth chart of either or both indicates the Moon or Ascendent in a Fire Sign, their passion will be intensified, and their physical consummation will contain a more dramatic urgency. But the typical Virgo-Libra sexual union will make up in gentle comfort and quiet fulfillment what it may lack in passionate desire. There are many levels of the physical demonstration of love between two people, and each level brings its own special dimension of joy and wonder.

But he must be careful not to upset her Scales with criticism, even if not spoken aloud, only indicated by his disapproving glances . . . especially near the time of their Oneness. A Libra woman both yearns and genuinely needs to be loved as a goddess is loved, with a great deal of eloquence and a total commitment. She adores being adored, and criticism can throw buckets of cold water on adoration, freezing it into icicles of resistance and frigidity. Since the Virgo man is never, at best, consumed by the fires of overwhelming passion, his answering response will be to grow even colder and more detached, creating an unnecessary barrier between them to be dissolved before they can once again communicate their feelings and emotions with their whole selves.

Whether the Virgo man she loves bears the stamp of an illusionary chronological age of sixteen or ninety-two — or any of the false labels in between — the Libra woman could see him in a true light if she meditated upon his archetype, Virgo Howard Jarvis. He's the one, you know, who felt the powerful thunder of his soon-to-be-discovered true ruling planet, Vulcan (see the Virgo-Virgo chapter and the foregoing pages of this chapter), within himself, and was stirred to crusade for the common people — his tireless efforts and patience finally bringing about, in 1978, the passage of the now-famous, both blessed and cursed "Proposition 13."

How very much like a Virgo man, stirred unsuspectingly by Vulcan's pounding message of change and the birth of a new personal aggressiveness, to devote all his energies to helping others win their long-overdue freedom from the iron fist of outrageous taxation — to single-handedly, through his Virgo persistence, bring about the most sweeping and desperately needed tax reforms of this or any other century. How *sweet* for a *Virgo* to so clearly criticize the red-tape bungling and lavish, Caesar-like spending of local and state government at the expense of those who can ill afford to carry the burden of such wastefulness on their backs!

Granted, there were frequent occasions during Howard Jarvis's crusade when he forgot his Virgo courtesy and gentleness, becoming typically Virgo crusty, cranky, and cantankerous — because he was overtired, secretly worried, and tense about his role as a lone David, confronting the Goliaths of government with naught but the slingshot of clear thinking, honest appraisal — and integrity of intent. Granted also, there were and still are many justified complaints concerning certain undesirable results of Proposition 13. But even Virgo can't create absolute perfection within the "imperfection" of the traditionally less-than-ideal structure of "the law" itself — and the octopus-armed creature whimsically known as politics. The bottom line, nonetheless, was that Howard's "Prop 13" was responsible for the loudly ringing liberty bells of reform heard tolling all the way to Washington, causing congressmen to tremble, as they saw the vivid handwriting on the wall from an angry public, inspired by Virgo Jarvis to see the flaws of indolent, extravagant government spending, made possible by the bleeding of each individual citizen's incentive to work and retain a fair compensation for his or her labors.

In 1978, after his great victory, Howard Jarvis was being interviewed about "Prop 13" on a television show. Unexpectedly, during the questioning by a woman interviewer, this Virgo man's voice trembled as he was somehow compelled to say, "It's such a wonderful thing for a man of my age, seventy-five, to be able to do more for the people of California than anyone else has ever done." Then, undoubtedly shocking himself even more than he shocked the watching audience, Virgo Howard Jarvis broke down and openly wept, as his interviewer spontaneously threw her arms around him, moved to tears herself.

This is the clearest image of the Virgo male a Libran woman who loves one will ever be privileged to contemplate. As much as he may love her in return, with all his heart and mind and soul, he must be true to his own Sun Sign, and place service to others above all else — above even his own needs —

yes, and if duty, responsibility, and dedication require, also above hers. His shining quest is to somehow improve the world he lives in — to try as best he can to bring order out of chaos and confusion — to clarify the mistakes of Earthlings, whether they be his personal loved ones or complete strangers. He's driven to turn the smog and pollution of human thinking into the fresh air of her own *Libra* harmony and balance.

This is his destiny, and Vulcan's newly felt vibrations are increasing his compulsion to follow his star — to fulfill his mission as a Virgo. And so . . . . . if this man doesn't give the Libra lady quite all the attention, sentiment, and affection she seeks at every moment, she should try a little harder to be fair in judging his gentle heart and pure motives, to show compassion for his often-troubled thoughts, and understand that his compulsion to criticize contains the seeds of a new kind of freedom for himself . . . the world . . . and their own relationship.

She can help him, too, in a most important way. With his tendency to worry, despite his bright intellect, the typical Virgo man is always in danger (more so than most other Sun Signs) of falling victim to the programming and brainwashing of those who dictate a false and illusionary chronological age — after which one is more or less commanded to die, not to mention fully expected to "age" several decades before this arbitrary time. Howard Jarvis is wrong. He is still a young man, who has not completed his mission — unless he continues to imagine so vividly otherwise, and refuses to free himself from the chains of preconditioned thinking.

The Libra woman is beautifully qualified to gently, tenderly convince the Virgo man she loves that he may choose to live *long* past the age of the century mark, as intended by our co-Creators (see Virgo-Virgo chapter), without sacrificing either his youthful appearance or his youthful energies. If she manages to arouse his curiosity, he'll pursue the ways and means to accomplish such a miracle as determinedly as Howard Jarvis pursued "Prop 13." And with powerful Vulcan guiding him, he's capable of both finding and comprehending the secret formula, which has been, for countless eons, waiting to be rediscovered.

☆ ☆ ☆ ☆ ☆ ☆

VIRGO

Earth — Mutable — Negative
Ruled by Mercury (also by
*   the Planet Vulcan)*
Symbol: The Virgin
Night Forces — Feminine

SCORPIO

Water — Fixed — Negative
Ruled by Pluto
Symbols: Scorpion & Eagle
Night Forces — Feminine

The **VIRGO-SCORPIO** *Relationship*

None of them knew. Perhaps it was best not
to know. Their ignorance gave them one more
glad hour.

Virgos all believe they possess the precise pattern for ironing out the quirks and kinks in everything, for smoothing out all the wrinkles in the personalities of everyone they know. Then Virgo meets Scorpio, and the formula gets stuck in the computer. Their steam irons blow a fuse. Something is wrong. What could it be?

What it could be is that Scorpios elude any sort of analysis. In addition, they look darkly upon being nit-picked, nagged, or scolded about their naughty tendencies (like holding a grudge, and gazing at people with that scary-spooky stare). Pluto-ruled folk do not care to be criticized, however gentle and courteous the critic may be. If they smoke, they won't tolerate being told to stop, or being reminded to empty their dirty ashtrays. Conversely, if they do not smoke, they don't need to be told what good boys and girls they are for refraining from such a messy and unhealthy habit, for the excellent reason that Scorpio Eagles are born with immeasurable reserves of self-confidence, plus highly suspicious natures. Therefore, they already know they're "good," and furthermore, they mistrust unsolicited pats on the head and cheerful words of approval from Virgos — or from anyone else.

Scorpios who are awarded Pulitzer or Nobel prizes do not tremble in gratitude. They're more likely to grumble under their breaths that it's about time somebody recognized their superiority (sometimes not under their breaths, but quite audibly). They fully expect to win spelling bees, monopoly games, the fifty-yard dash, frog-jumping contests, pin-the-tail-on-the-donkey, political campaigns, Academy Awards, and 4-H Club ribbons.

It's impossible to surprise them. Or rather, it's possible to surprise them, but not possible to detect that you have from the Scorpion tone of voice, words, or change of expression. The reason is twofold. (a) They are precognitive enough to guess anything a few jumps ahead of you — and (b) those times when you do catch them unprepared, their facial features *are* prepared, even if they are not. Scorps take all the fun out of everything. They make very unsatisfactory guests of honor at surprise birthday parties. The spark of spontaneity will somehow be missing. It's only exciting if you remember that they're bubbling like champagne inside, even though the bubbles are kept tightly bottled.

As for Virgos, surprises make them more than a little nervous, since they represent something which has not been included in their schedules, and it throws them off balance for a few hours. Unlike Scorpio, Virgo is not suspicious. Virgos do not have time to waste pampering inner fears, and this is where suspiciousness is born. Neither do they have the self-confidence of Scorpio. Self-confidence implies that one is perfect, or near-perfect, and Virgos are only too aware of all the imperfections in human nature in general, their own in particular. There's not a single Virgo who isn't convinced that there's more to criticize and to improve in himself (or herself) than in anyone else. Once Scorpio recognizes this endearing trait of Virgo's (and it usually doesn't take long for Scorps to psychometrize anything or psyche out anyone) the Virgin's compulsion to remind, suggest, and observe in detail is less annoying, and the Eagle smiles affectionately upon this elflike, well-meaning human. If Virgo will go easy on outright criticism, nagging, scolding, and hair-splitting, the two of them will get along famously and become unexpectedly close. Unexpectedly, because "closeness" to another person is not something either Virgo or Scorpio looks upon casually — or attains easily.

Others may fear to plumb and probe Scorpio's secret nature and mantle of mystery, but Virgo has a curious, exploring mind, and although he or she won't reach up and rudely pull off Scorpio's mask, a gentle attempt will be made to uncover what is hidden from view. Virgos are somehow not as frightened or in awe of Scorpio as other Sun Signs often are, since Virgo frankly respects Scorpio's own critical and analytical abilities. The Virgin will frequently make a conscious effort, with an Eagle, to avoid controversial matters before they become actual disagreements, for a couple of reasons. First, Virgo trusts Scorpio to be as careful and cautious as he (or she) might be — also wiser, more sensitive — and so the Virgins believe that there's every possibility Scorpio's views may be the correct ones. Second, Virgo has already calculated the percentage possibility of winning a battle of wits with the Eagle and has decided there's not much of a chance, at best. Further, the Virgo man or woman is acutely aware of the almost certain unpleasant results if Scorpio is goaded too far or unnecessarily challenged — and unpleasant confrontations are counterproductive to their common goals. ("Counterproductive" is one of Virgo's favorite words.)

Virgos are enormously practical about such things. It's this level-headed quality which makes Scorpio smile on the Virgins. They are nice, sensible sorts . . smiling, bright-eyed, and polite creatures to have around, in no way a threat. In some indefinable manner, Virgos seem to calm the Pluto spirit — and where Virgos may cause others to be jumpy, or to feel slightly guilty for not being perfect around them, they have the opposite effect on Scorpio. In truth, Scorpios often feel strangely loose and relaxed in the presence of Virgo. It is no small feat to make a Scorp feel "loose."

This is a 3-11 Sun Sign Pattern, blending the Earth and Water elements. Translated from the symbolic to the real, this means Scorpio will somehow feel that he or she has "found roots" in an association with Virgo — and the latter will have a strong sense of being enriched in many ways from the Pluto contact. In some unexpected and unconventional way, Virgo will quietly and unobtrusively help to bring about Scorpio's hopes, wishes, and dreams — also social success, prestige, and standing in the career or community. Scorpio will open Virgo's mind to many new vistas of thought and progressive theories, bringing to the Virgin an easy communication of ideas. Relatives of one or the other may either introduce the two of them, or be prominent in some way, at some time, in the association.

More than any other person (except perhaps Taurus, Cancer, and Capricorn), Scorpio can check Virgo's tendency to worry and sulk, with the result that Virgos seem calmer, more tranquil, less restless and jittery around Scorpio. The two of them do have a distinct beneficial influence on one another, as compared to the eerie (Scorpio) and disquieting (Virgo) effect they each are capable of having on others. If their Moon Signs or Ascendents should happen to negatively aspect in their mutual charts, there will be, of course, less beneficial influence, more irritation and tension. However, it will only continue for a brief period under normal circumstances. Scorpio is not one to suffer silently — or for long — before firmly proposing a change in attitude, and then demanding a dissolution of the association if the change is not forthcoming, forthwith. Virgos don't linger long either, after they've been disillusioned. Like the Cheshire cat and old soldiers, both of these people can just fade away, and never return.

Whether they're thrown together as relatives, siblings, parent and child, friends, or lovers, they have certain traits in common which will open doors of understanding between them. For example, both Virgo and Scorpio know their individual assets as well as they know their liabilities. Neither of them will either undersell or oversell himself, or herself. They each know their own talents and capabilities, without being egotistical over the knowledge. They're both equally aware of their shortcomings, of the limits of what they may expect from the inner self — and they won't go beyond those limits. The typical Virgo will never be found pressing his or her luck beyond prudence, and the same is true of Scorpio. When an Eagle takes a big chance, you can be sure that here is one confident Eagle! (But he will have figured the percentages carefully.) Scorpios can be wrong now and then, but they're right more often than they miscalculate. It's a quality Virgo admires and respects. Being a Mutable Sign, Virgo will neither be envious of, nor will seriously compete with, Scorpio — who senses this right away, which is one of the reasons Scorpio can relax with these people, and let down the defense bars this man or woman (or child) uses against other Sun Signs. There is no need for the Eagle to take excessive self-protective measures with the Virgin (except maybe a pair of earmuffs, for when the nagging starts).

Virgo will never agree with another Sun Sign's description of the Scorp as ruthless, cold, and dangerous. This is not the way Virgo sees the Eagle at all. In Virgo's eyes, the Pluto person is warm, generous, and protective — as well as sympathetic and compassionate. Nor will Scorpio normally allow anyone to put down Virgo by calling the Virgins picky, fussy, and nervous. How can this be, when Scorpio is always cooler than usual (and that's pretty cool!), plus more peaceful, when a Virgo friend, relative, or mate is near? You must be talking about someone else, not Virgo. Once a tie between these two has been established, the Virgin will usually receive the full force of Pluto's protective powers, and will enjoy as well Scorpio's fierce loyalty, given to those who have earned it. If anyone tries to harm a Virgo who's already won the devotion of a Scorp, that person is warned to back away while there is still time. There's something gentle and defenseless about all Virgins, male or female, and when the Scorp sees someone verbally or otherwise preparing to attack or abuse this courteous, helpless soul, the Eagle will step in to turn all the energy of Pluto's power against the attacker, who will seldom fail to retreat — unless it's another Scorpio, with the Moon in Gemini or Sagittarius, who has hurt the Virgo. (In that case, Virgo should leave town for a few days, rather than get caught in the midst of an exchange of Pluto force between two Scorps, neither of whom will back down until one is declared victor.)

The less evolved Earthlings born under the sign of the Virgin are sometimes capable of biting sarcasm and bitter verbal expression. Indeed, an occasional caustic (but cauterizing!) criticism is actually Virgos' one and only, their single, flaw. But you'll never convince *them* of this. Virgos believe they possess every flaw and defect known to man — or woman. You name it, they'll plead guilty to it. Yet, even a self-effacing Virgo will seldom go so far as to owning up to a charge of selfishness. No accusation could be more unjust. These men and women have a compulsion to serve, in one way or another, every Earthling who crosses their paths. Unselfishness is engraved upon the very heart and soul of Virgo — these sometimes cranky, but more often polite and always willing-to-be-helpful people who bring their graceful and gracious ways to bless our troubles.

If I were you, I wouldn't ever dare to call them "selfish" within the hearing of a Scorpio who has experienced the gentle devotion of a Virgo over the years. That would be an extremely unwise thing to do.

☆ ☆ ☆ ☆ ☆ ☆

VIRGO *Woman* **SCORPIO** *Man*

. . . and when Wendy finished he uttered a hollow groan.

"What is it, Peter?" she cried, running to him, thinking he was ill . . . "Where is it, Peter?"

"It isn't that kind of pain," Peter replied darkly.

One of the Virgo girl's most shining virtues is her gentle and unselfish devotion to the man she loves. One of the Scorpio man's most laudable qualities is his loyal and intense devotion to the woman he loves. So, here they are, this female with her starlit eyes, her clear, bell-like voice and gracious manner . . and this man, with his deep, wise eyes, his smooth, mellow voice and magnetic ways . . the two of them gently-unselfishly-loyally-intensely . . . devoted to one another.

Isn't it a beautiful picture? Like a Degas painting of a pastoral scene, in delicate pinks, greens, and blues . . shimmering white . . with rich, velvety undertones of color . . burgundy and forest green. An absolutely perfect creation of poetic joy and beauty and tranquility, all combined.

WAIT! STOP! DEAR-GOD-IN-HEAVEN!

Is that . . . could that possibly be . . . a spot? Perhaps a smear of soil or a scratch . . . from careless handling? A fingerprint, maybe . . . or might it be . . horrors! . . a fly someone swatted and squashed on that heavenly splash of white-cloud-and-blue sky, in the upper right-hand corner? It could be, of course, an ant . . . crawling across the canvas. But it doesn't appear to be moving. Let's walk over closer, and see. May I borrow your magnifying glass, please? Thank you very much.

It is a spot. Definitely a spot. There isn't the slightest doubt. Can you see it? Look closely. A mar, a blemish . . . something not intended by the artist.

. . . . . or *was* it intended by the artist?

Yes. It was intended by the artist. It was deliberately designed to add the truth and beauty, the poetry of *im*perfection to his work of art. You see, imperfection is what links us to the angels, who are also, in varying degrees, imperfect. Your Sunday-school teacher may not have told you that, but there were many things your Sunday-school teacher did not tell you — because there are many things the Bible did not tell *her* — thanks to several incidents of spiritual surgery performed on the scriptures, like that which was committed upon the holy works by Emperor Justinian and his Empress Theodora in the sixth century (as only one example).

The concept of perfection is the most boring and soul-killing ever conceived within the dangerous doctrine of oblivion called Nirvana. Like every single other "religion" or philosophic theory in this world, from the Alpha to whenever the Omega may be scheduled — the Yoga way of life is essentially good, yet nevertheless, like all the rest (including astrology) it contains a few negative seeds of distorted truth. Nirvana is one of them. Nirvana's synonym — perfection — is another.

To tolerate minor flaws and imperfections, to treat these tenderly in one another, is one of the Great Spiritual Lessons of Truth — but Virgo will decidedly dislike learning it. Scorpio was born comprehending it. Maybe he can explain it to her. She'll listen to him. Because she respects his opinions and his judgments — and because she trusts him not to lead her astray. Yes, she trusts this man. Let us hope her individual Scorpio deserves that faith.

Quite likely, he does. The sense of integrity in a typical Scorpion runs strong. It's almost impossible for an Eagle not to live up to what is expected of him, what others trust him to stand for — unshakable integrity. Or, at the very least, the courage to be true to himself, as he sees himself — to a situation, as he sees that situation.

The Virgo woman may believe that, if the Scorpio man is "true to himself," this means he will never keep anything from her. Not necessarily. What he will never do is be dishonest with her. There is a difference. He will never be dishonest, according to his private code, which is his individually, and may not be that of another Scorpio's, but will always be high on the integrity list. Once an Eagle has committed himself to a relationship, he will be true to his vows of love — unless his horoscope has serious planetary afflictions to the fifth and seventh houses and to his natal Sun, and even then, he'll be extremely uncomfortable in the role of unfaithful lover or husband. His natural instinct is to be loyal — and to be honest.

The Virgin who's involved with this man, and still undecided about the safety of planning a long-term relationship with him, can be sure that, should another woman ever enter his life, it will either be a fleeting thing —or she will be truthfully told that his heart has wandered elsewhere. He may be tempted, even succumb to temptation, perhaps. But before much time has passed, he will have carefully evaluated the involvement. If he believes it has no future, he will end it immediately, return his heart to her, where it belongs . . . and suffer agonizing pangs of regret over his mistake. If he regards the new attachment as genuine, he will confess his change of affection to her as tenderly as possible, and allow her the dignity of truth before they part. But if it was nothing but a brief, regrettable mistake, she may never know. Scorpio keeps secrets as long as he feels they will neither hurt nor help another. The secrets he keeps from her, both before and after they marry, need not be romantic secrets. They'll involve many intricate human emotions far removed from romance. Not every last mystery will be revealed. He may not itemize each fleeting fragment of fantasy that floats through his consciousness to her, but he will share perhaps more of himself with the Virgin than with most other people.

One of the Virgo girl's outstanding characteristics is self-sufficiency. She doesn't think the world — or a man — *owes* her anything. One of the Eagle's outstanding characteristics is self-confidence. He doesn't wait around for the world — or a woman — to judge his worth or value. He's aware of it himself, and is certain the world will eventually recognize it. So will any woman who expects to be *his* woman.

It hardly ever happens that these two aggressively pursue love by rushing into each other's arms when they first meet. Both of them are shy, sometimes even painfully shy. Oh, she may chatter away with friends on a myriad of subjects, and he may be loquacious with his relatives, close friends, or working associates, but in the area of human emotions, they are both inclined to be reticent. Her self-sufficiency and his self-confidence are buried beneath the surface, like a hidden treasure they secretly count on when the world lets them down. It's not likely these two will ever let each other down, because being able to trust another person is so very important to them both.

Until he knows her better, he may be suspicious of her motives for little or no reason, as he is of everyone. Later, he'll probably trust her to be just what she appears to be, what she says she is — no more, and no less (like himself), and it will bring him more peace of mind to know this simple thing than he will ever admit. When he reaches out to her, this man of many enigmatic moods, she's always there. It comforts him, and softens the edge of his private fears.

This man's love nature is more intense than that of the average male, which is only natural, because in no way is Scorpio "average." Her love nature is more transcendental, yet there is also much of the "earthy" in her intimate behavior with him, for Virgo is of the Earth Element. It's a combination to which he'll respond eagerly, for he has two sides to his sexual needs also. One part of him looks upon the union between man and woman as a mystical experience, a holy thing. The other part is sensuous, erotic, seeking every level of passion for absolute fulfillment. In the beginning, there may be areas of adjustment in their lovemaking, but when they've learned they can be themselves with each other, without fear of hurt or rejection, the problems will disappear.

Strangely, with both of them, there could be a holding back in the physical expression of love. Some part of him remains under strict control, not abandoned to the desires of the flesh; some part of her remains virginal and untouched .. almost as though they each await an undefined miracle of love's affirmation to free their souls to join their hearts and bodies. Even with a Virgo woman who has been happily married for years, and who has co-created children with her husband, a "virgin" still sleeps somewhere within, unawakened. Even with the Scorpio man who's been a devoted husband and father for many years, the deepest seed of love's mystery lies in wait for Pluto's release — and until that unknown moment, remains silent and un-stirred within. A comment of Pascal's may hold a hint of the end of the waiting. *"Le coeur a ses raisons que la raison ne connaît point"* . . . the heart has its reasons, whereof reason knows nothing.

There's every chance these two will agree on almost all matters financial. Neither is the type to throw money away, with nary a care for tomorrow. Both feel more secure in every way by following the example of the cautious squirrels. I seriously doubt if there's a Virgo-Scorpio couple anywhere on the planet without a savings account. This woman is more concerned with a financially secure future than with luxuries of the moment. (Barring her Moon or Ascendent being in an extravagant sign, of course.) And this man will think about his major purchases for a period of time before writing a check.

Having enough cash available for vacations, preferably long ones, is important to both of them. He gathers renewed psychic energy, emotional peace, and mental equilibrium by spending unhurried, quiet days and nights near the sea. It "restoreth his soul." She must have a change of scene frequently to soothe her spirit. Sameness and monotony are truly deadly to the Virgo essence, very literally unhealthy for her mentally, emotionally, and physically. The Mercury-Vulcan combined rays create a great deal of nervous energy and restlessness in Virgo, which markedly increases after long periods without change — and dramatically decreases after a trip, long or short. It doesn't matter so much to her if the trip is a vacation, for the purpose of resting — or a business trip requiring a more frantic work schedule than usual in some way — he'll see her blossom, her soft eyes shine. It's the change of scene, not the relaxation, which has healed her. Whether it's the Arc de Triomphe, amid noisy Paris streets . . or a quiet, secluded beach in the middle of nowhere . . isn't important. The important thing to Virgo is that it's different from her normal, dull, daily routine.

Other people may call the Scorpio man undemonstrative and cold, but they do not know him as she does. Once he's fallen in love with her, she'll know his depth of feeling and his great generosity. Other people may call the Virgo woman overly analytical and unimaginative, but they do not know her as he does. Once she's fallen in love with him, she'll reveal the tender and poetic side of her nature others seldom see. As written in the Old Testament, in the book of Proverbs: *For who can tell the way of an eagle in the air . . . or of a man with a maid?* Both Virgo and Scorpio tend to reserve their real selves for someone special, a love that's for keeps — with all the necessary and very precious immperfectionss.

☆ ☆ ☆ ☆ ☆ ☆

VIRGO *Man* SCORPIO *Woman*

────◄◗►───

"I have one pound seventeen here, and two and six at the office; I can cut off my coffee at the office, say ten shillings, making two nine and six, with your eighteen and three makes three nine seven . . . . eight nine seven, dot and carry seven — don't speak, my own — and the pound you lent to that man who came to the door . . . . . there, you've done it! . . did I say nine nine seven? yes, I said nine nine seven; the question is, can we try it for a year on nine nine seven?"

"Of course we can, George!" she cried.

An astrological message to the Scorpio girl: (Scorpio *woman*, that is; these females are really never girls, not even when they're twelve, and although

I've thus termed them in other Scorpio sections, in this one she'll particularly need to be a woman) — and so, to the Scorpio woman who's wondering about a Virgo male who has caught her eye, and almost trapped her heart: Go ahead and love him. He needs you. You can help him.

This man has a problem. He always has a problem, whatever type Virgo he may be, and there are several types. In any case, the problem will be precisely tailored to his individual need. Actually, Virgo men have more than one problem. There are his own personal ones, which come in various shapes and sizes, plus those of all the chaotic, untidy, and careless people he knows, whose lives are a dreadful mess. But it's his private problem of any given time which is of more urgency to the lady Eagle. With her mystical bent and powerful psychic penetration, she's just the one to help him with it. It could be delicate and trifling, or of a serious nature. Whatever it is, she's needed.

As only one example, she could be involved with the type of Virgo man who possesses a simply startling imagination, at times too vivid, his Mercury-Vulcan-ruled mental world peopled with all manner of creatures not of this dimension, which he can describe in exquisite, if sometimes frightening, detail, down to the last whisker and broomstick. This will be especially true if he has a Scorpio Moon or Ascendent, which he very well may, if the two of them are attracted to one another, he and this enigmatic Scorpio woman, who wishes to protect, respect, and love him, all at once. A Scorpio influence in his birth chart can cause the Virgo's imaginary mental playmates to be — well, not very playful sorts. Under a Scorpio vibration in his own Virgo nativity, they could take strange forms indeed, dark and sinister, leading him to spook himself through a Virgo-like compulsion to investigate anything from witchcraft and voodoo, to hypnosis and cloning. Some Virgo men are so avidly inquisitive about evil, despite — or maybe because of — their inherent purity, they can take some really weird trips into the twilight zones of the human psyche. But this is, actually, all to the good, because when he's scared himself silly through his neat and careful, painstaking research of the shadows, and he's sitting there overcome by a vague uneasiness he's too embarrassed to admit, the blankets pulled over his head, hiding from himself, she'll know just what buttons to push to bring him out from under his tent.

"Oh, my goodness!" she'll exclaim, in mock shock. "Just look at that! There are five loose threads at the corner of this quilt — no, it's more accurately six loose threads, and the satin binding has a tear in it." Instantly, the Virgo man's head will peek out from his chocolate-brown blanket, his eyes as bright as can be, to check the flaw she pointed out, and he'll quickly mend it. Wise woman, she is.

Or she could be involved with another type of Virgo male, slightly in the majority, who is unable, no matter how hard he tries, to see the flowers for the thorns, the snow for the slush. As acute as his intellect may be — and probably is, for all Virgos are smarties, with very sharp, analytical brains—his finer *astral senses* are so out of tune he can't see the sound of the surf or hear the full Moon, let alone see Gershwin's "Rhapsody in Blue" . . . . . or hear the music of an Andrew Wyeth painting. This is a real handicap, as you may well imagine (and as you may also well imagine, the Virgos reading this will all believe I've mixed up my verbs. I'm resigned to an avalanche of letters).

Unlike the Virgos with the overactive imaginations, described in our first example, these more typical Virgos possess only the merest wisp of an imagination, and it's a sad thing to observe, although it's not a problem beyond the powers of the Scorpio woman to banish. As an example of this kind of Virgin, I know a very handsome, super-intelligent Virgo man, who's kind and gentle to dogs and babies, and sparkles with a multitude of commendable virtues. To look at him, you'd never guess he had a problem to his name. But, alas, he does. He was given a copy of St. Exupéry's *The Little Prince* to read by his equally handsome, super-intelligent, but wiser, more aware, and sensitive Moon-in-Scorpio, Leo brother, who hoped the book might open new and exciting vistas to him. It was a vain hope.

This Virgin's only reaction, after reading it, was to spend several minutes carefully explaining to his sibling precisely why there could not possibly be anyone living on an asteroid. He explained it all quite nicely and scientifically—and, of course, courteously (Virgos are all very mannerly). When his brother told him he'd missed the whole message of the book, a puzzled frown engraved itself on his perfectly chiseled features. "What lesson could a grown man learn from a children's book?" he wondered.

One might as well ask what lessons can be learned from children themselves. One might as well not believe in elves and druids and leprechauns . . . . or in any sort of magic. Can you imagine what this Virgo would have said twenty years ago, when he and his brother were teenagers, if the latter had remarked that it would be interesting to take a stroll on the Moon?

There are, of course, many Virgos who are more enlightened than this one (and even he may someday read St. Exupéry's book again, with a more open mind), but the average Virgin, whatever his individual type, has, to some degree, a need to learn that the really important things in life are those which can only be seen with the heart—and a Scorpio woman is an excellent teacher of the intangible.

Her task in instructing this man that there are more things in Heaven and on Earth, George, than you dream of with your slide rule and wheat germ, tofu, and Tums-for-the-tummy . . . . . . will require all her talents of concentration. A Virgo man is sensational with details, a little fuzzy on the larger picture. He needs a woman who will be patient with him as she teaches him about asteroids, auras, the reversal of gravity, and astral projection—although, if she's in love with the first type of Virgo we discussed at the beginning of this section, she should take it easy on the astral, because of all those little goblins who haunt his dreams. Too much concentration on this sort of thing could — and please forgive my scatological frankness — bring on a severe case of the eternal Virgo affliction, constipation.

Her most important lesson will be the one she can teach him about the birds and the bees. The birds and bees have long been ancillary to explaining sex (and she'll have a few lessons to teach on that subject too, no doubt), but I use the reference in its literal sense. A good place to begin is with Nature's enigma of the common bumblebee. By all the inflexible, Virgo-type laws of physics and aerodynamics, related to body weight, wing span, and so forth, the bumblebee is designed in such a manner that he cannot possibly fly. Fortunately, neither Virgos nor scientists have yet managed to communicate this irrefutable logic to the bumblebee, and so, in his abysmal ignorance, the cheeerful, trusting little chap goes right on flying!

Extreme patience is necessary when enlightening the Virgo man to this great secret of *meta*physics, because he'll strain his brain cells considerably in attempting to answer the puzzle, will finally be forced to admit he's unable to do so — and could consequently suffer a minor nervous breakdown, along with his constipation and ever-present indigestion. It's downright mean to cause him to cope with all three at the same time.

Whatever lessons she's teaching this intelligent, gentle man, the Scorpio woman should be aware that he may become distracted when she's near enough so he can smell her perfume . . near enough to reach out and touch . . . near enough to confuse his mental processes, make his pulse race faster, and lead his thoughts into the *other* kind of birds-and-bees meditation.

The sexual relationship of this 3-11 Sun Sign Pattern couple is normally one requiring adjustments to be made on both sides, yet it can gradually become an experience of great beauty, once the adjustments have been made. The physical demonstration of their love will be perhaps easier for her to express than for him. If it's less than perfect every time, he may brood and wonder what's wrong, blaming himself. (Virgos blame themselves for nearly everything.) She instinctively knows that lovemaking is like every other area of human contact between those who love — sometimes a miracle of mutual joy, sometimes only a quiet exchange of affection, at other times passionately intense, but at *all* times able to bring them closer to solving the mystery of each other's deeper dreams and needs. His emotional nature is somewhat more cool and controlled than hers. Still, he longs wistfully to learn the intangible, inexpressible secrets of mating she seems to know so instinctively. She, in turn, is drawn by the sheer honesty and simplicity he brings to their intimacy, for Scorpio, although very curious about the sensual aspects of sex, inwardly senses the purity of its mystical meaning — and potential. Neither Virgos nor Scorpios ever abandon their whole selves to sexual blending. Each holds back, for different reasons, some private, untouched core of beingness. To achieve total consummation together is a challenge which can continue to stimulate them both all through their years of loving, for at any moment — or never — the holding back may end, allowing them to achieve real wholeness. Such an unexpressed, but deeply felt anticipation, not surprisingly, often enriches the sexual side of a relationship rather than harms it. "Man's reach .. and woman's .. must exceed their grasp, or what's a heaven for ?"

Because he possesses an inquiring nature, he will be hurt by her silences. This man is curious, he needs to know and understand everything around him, especially the woman he loves, and she is not easy to fathom. He'll be more successful if he realizes that predictable formulas don't always work to solve the human equation. It's elusive, unlike a problem in trigonometry, and the answer cannot be precalculated. You understand scientific theories and financial statements with the mind. You can only understand a woman with your heart . . . and the heart is seldom logical.

A Virgo man can switch from endearing tenderness and a gentle manner to inquisitiveness, sarcasm, and a coldly analytical attitude. Too much of the latter mood switch, and he could regret it. A Scorpio woman who's been wounded more than once will be unconsciously compelled to teach the one who has hurt her a lesson. If he doesn't learn, if he continues to repeat the mistake, she will leave. But he will be warned, long in advance, that she's unhappy. If he's tuned-in to her on the channel of love, he'll pick up the signals in time to heal the hurt and save their love. These two have much in common, such as basic honesty and integrity, a thirst for knowledge, and strength of purpose. They will be friends, as well as lovers, defend each other against outside threats. When the unhappiness of either is initiated by themselves, he's sensible enough to persuade her to talk it over, and not allow emotion to completely rule reason. If they share a negative Luminary (Sun-Moon) or Ascendent aspect between their nativities, neither may be very sensible. He may retreat into stony hardness and burrow into himself, sulking. She may fly into some intense and frightening rages. Still, it's always a lot easier for friends to patch up a quarrel than for lovers to do so, and since the two of them are influenced by the 3-11 vibration, and are, therefore, both friends and lovers, even a violent disagreement needn't be the end of the relationship. It could be, instead, the beginning of a new understanding.

This man and woman have many lessons to teach one another. In the past, many people have tried to get him to see with his heart, and failed. But with her, he's willing to try. In the past, many people have tried to persuade her to be less suspicious of happiness, to be more open with her feelings, and have not succeeded. But with him, she's willing to try. Maybe that's because, as Goethe wisely observed . . . we only *really* learn from those we love.

☆ ☆ ☆ ☆ ☆ ☆

VIRGO

Earth — Mutable — Negative
Ruled by Mercury (also by
  the Planet Vulcan)
Symbol: The Virgin
Night Forces — Feminine

SAGITTARIUS

Fire — Mutable — Positive
Ruled by Jupiter
Symbols: Archer & Centaur
Day Forces — Masculine

The **VIRGO-SAGITTARIUS** *Relationship*

"......what's that in the brushwood ?"

"It's a wolf, with her whelps."

....just the sort of idea a dog would have.

Since Virgo is an Earth Sign, you'd think the Virgins would know all about every single thing connected with the Earth, the way they know all about nearly everything else. Well, they don't. And even though Sagittarius is a Fire Sign, the Archers do have a certain Robin Hood affinity with Sherwood Forest, as well as with woods called by other names. Consequently, Sagittarius is capable of demonstrating to the gentle Virgins various kinds of "earth-magic." Mostly because they love animals, who are all so closely attuned to and aligned with Nature, synchronized to the Earth's rhythms. And also because they're not afraid to try out new ideas. Therefore, it's possible for Sagittarians to discover all manner of "earthy" lessons of great beatitude to teach the Virgins.

Take, for example, music. Everything in the Universe, in the entire solar system, answers infallibly to its own very individual key — or note, half-note, quarter-note, sixteenth-note . . . and so on. Every thing and every person. Even buildings and bridges. Sometimes, when you're listening to a symphony, a certain note, or a combination of notes within a chord will, for a split second in Time, cause you to feel a chill at the back of your neck, a quiver or a tiny tremble. You have been "struck" with your personal vibration, and your physical body is responding to it. In the science of metaphysics, theoretically (and actually) your own individual "sound" or "key" or musical "note," when sounded in its precise, exact tone (Virgos will understand the need for preciseness) would so powerfully affect you through its vibrations that, played sharply enough (or loudly enough) and sustained long enough, it could kill. (The soul would follow it, out of the body.) Conversely, on the positive side, when played (or sounded) softly enough, sustained for the proper Virgo exactitude of moments, it could so transfigure you with joy and peace, you would literally "levitate" as did the "saints."

The grandson of composer Felix Mendelssohn experimented with these rather Virgo-like concepts, based on the known fact that, when a singer hits a certain note, in a certain key, the sound will instantly shatter a glass. His research led him to realize the Bible meant literally what was written in claiming that, when Joshua blew a particular note, in a precise key on the "Ram's horn" — the walls of Jericho "came tumbling down." When a group of soldiers march in time toward a bridge, the leader will call out "Break Step!" if it's a fragile bridge they're approaching, because the *rhythm* of all those feet, pounding the Earth in time together, could actually destroy or damage the bridge structure. Mendelssohn therefore concluded that the armies led by Joshua approached the walls of Jericho "in step" together — thousands of feet in tempo, setting up a powerful (and particular) vibration in the Earth, so that when Joshua (who was metaphysically knowledgeable) then blew the precise note on the Ram's horn, the combination of the marching feet vibrations with the individual "sound" of the wall structure itself, caused the walls of Jericho to respond, and to "come tumbling down," right on schedule. Sound itself, alone, in the proper key and vibratory frequency, has the "power and the glory" (and the energy) to actually move huge stones or rocks. This is the buried-in-ancient-mystery, esoteric truth behind the legendary *Open Sesame* and *Abracadabra* chants (although they've been passed down to us in distorted form, no longer purely precise). So now you know how those immense boulders were levitated to build the Great Pyramid of Giza! Musically and melodiously, under the direction of Osiris. (Not Cheops — he came later, and did a bit of creative plagiarizing from the great Osiris.)

Virgos will be fascinated by the exactitudes and preciseness of this musical wisdom of metaphysics (contained in the Great Mystery of *The*

Music of the Spheres) and Sag will be excited about all the possibilities of application to Jupiter ideals. The Archer might ask the Virgin — "Since everything has its own 'key,' what do you suppose is the *Earth's* key ?" If Virgo doesn't know, the Archer may safely answer "D-flat." Then, of course, Virgo will insist that Sag prove it. Virgins are quite critical of generalized statements, and they sternly disapprove of any form of exaggeration. Exaggeration being one of the many Sagittarian talents (the Archer's ruling planet, Jupiter, is astrologically synonymous with expansion), if Sag wants to impress Virgo, he (or she) must always be prepared to back up any sweeping, Jupiter statements with substantial, factual proof. Yet, in contradiction, the Centaurs are *also* compulsively *truthful,* because Sagittarius is one of those exasperating "double" Sun Signs of duality. Half-horse, half-human. It's the human end that's truthful, the Horse end that sometimes stretches the truth a little. So it's important to know which end of the Sagittarian Centaur you're dealing with at any given time. Regarding the "D-flat" situation, you're dealing with the meticulously truthful and gloriously imaginative human half of Sag. (No, Virgo, imagination is *not* inconsistent with truth. Imagination and Truth are soul mates. Neither could exist without the other.)

To give the animal-loving Archers a helping hand with their "D-flat" earth-magic lesson to Virgo, here's the proof. In 1975, on a late November Sagittarian evening, jazz musician Paul Winter had a profound and perfectly marvelous, likewise Sagittarian, Jupiter-inspired idea. He trudged high into a Sierra Nevada wildlife research center with his alto sax, and improvised a bluesy wail. At first curiously silent, after a time, some lady timber wolves began to sing along. Their howls harmonized with and matched perfectly the length and shape of Winter's musical notes, creating the most thrilling duet he ever played. Originally inspired by a recording of the humpback whale songs, Winter has since played concerts for — and in harmony with — all sorts of animals, who match the notes, the tones and the rhythms of his sax precisely, never missing a beat or half note. Once, off British Columbia, Paul played a concert for whales — and to everyone's astonishment, they stuck their heads out of the water, and gathered in a circle to listen, as the Greenpeace people watched in happy amazement. His moonlight duets with animals have even interested stuffy scientists, who were first stodgy, then amused, but are now finally beginning to think Winter has given them the "key" (pardon the Jupiter pun) to how animals communicate — migrate, mate and form packs.

Jazzman Winter's new album features an "eight member family" of instruments, dating back to the Renaissance. Titled *Common Ground,* the album contains several melodies with choruses sung by wolves, whales — and even an eagle ! They're all in the key of D-flat, the only one the animals will harmonize with, you see, which causes Winter (and any meditative person) to conclude that D-flat *is* the "key of the Earth." Fastidious Virgos may be slightly offended (or embarrassed) but the fun-loving Centaurs will enjoy learning that the album was taped in a stable at Winter's farm, where bed sheets were hung from the ceiling, not for acoustical reasons, but to keep the bat droppings out of the harpsichord.

Now that Sag has brought some magical Earth knowledge to Virgo, and backed it up with proof, the Virgins, we trust, will be in the future, somewhat more respectful of the Archer's far-out antics and spontaneous enthusiasms. And now that Sag has learned that the miracles of *Open Sesame* and *Abracadabra*, not to mention the building of the Great Pyramid, could never be accomplished without Virgo preciseness and exactitude regarding musical sounds, let's hope the Archers will stop teasing the Virgins about their tendency to measure everything, their leaning toward perfection and their critical, sometimes hair-splitting attitudes. After all, Virgos are only living up to their Sun Sign essence of discrimination. If we didn't have Virgos around to tidy our minds and keep our intentions neat, we'd all be a sorry mess of chaos and confusion. Music would not be melodious and soothing, but a tangled jumble of sour notes and jarring chords — without Virgo.

And without the merry, playful, owlish, wise and prophetic Archers, having been as kind and compassionate toward animals as they've been for all these many centuries, none of Nature's birds and gentle beasts would have trusted Paul Winter enough to sing a single harmonic note in duet with his jazz saxophone. Much of the loving-kindness and protection from human brutality our animal brothers, bird sisters and sea life creatures have received has been from the Virgo, Sagittarian (and Aquarian) vibrations on Earth, giving them the faith to make their touching, tentative gesture of cooperation and love, to the tune of Winter's friendly vibes. As Winter himself explains it, so very beautifully, "if something is sensitive, thoughtful, we call it human. How arrogant. It's really a sound which says, I'm glad to be *feeling*. It's an affirmation." Yes. An affirmation of Life and Love ... and the singing Oneness of all Nature.

Both Sag and Virgo were born under Mutable Signs, and so the Virgins and the Archers are usually able to communicate with each other easily, whether they're communicating Virgo's criticism and Jupiter's frankness — or friendly understanding. Easy communication is the first step on the way to a comprehension of one another's different approaches and viewpoints. These two will undoubtedly talk a lot, back and forth — perhaps also move around a lot, although Virgo is more settled, and likely to remain in one place longer than Sagittarius. Still, with Vulcan, Virgo's true ruler (see Virgo-Virgo chapter), about to be discovered, Virgins of both sexes are beginning to feel restless stirrings of discontent, a compulsion to wonder and wander ... to change old patterns and habits, and explore the world (as well as themselves) to see what surprises they might find. This is simply great, because the friendly Archers love congenial company, as they happily and curiously trot through Life's unexplored Sherwood Forest, on horseback, or on foot, by plane or train. If they successfully meet the challenges of their 4-10 Sun Sign Pattern testing, the association of the Centaur and the Virgin promises exceptional rewards to each of them. Virgo will teach Sagittarius some manners, courtesy and patience, while Sag will teach Virgo the value of generosity of spirit, open-mindedness, tolerance ... and best of all, glorious freedom! They may appear to onlookers to be a decidedly "odd couple," the Virgin and the Centaur, but after a while, Sag will teach Virgo not to worry so much about what people say or think. Just be true to yourself, and everything will fall into place. After all there's *no*body who can please *every*body, and the Jupiter-ruled Sagittarian is just the one to teach Virgo what a futile goal trying to "perfectly" please the whole world can be. Sag will coax Virgo to loosen up, and Virgo will show Sag how to keep from clumsily falling by going a little slower (verbally and otherwise).

It's an unexpected touch of magic that the songs on Side One of Paul Winter's *Common Ground* album, with their haunting melodies and chants, recalling the dawn reveries of monks at their prayers—should feature Renaissance instruments and rhythmic patterns, some with birds singing their glad morning hosannas in the background, along with other animals. A touch of magic because ... the greatest friend the animals and birds on this planet ever knew was the simple Franciscan, Francis (Francesco) Bernardone, who lived his humble life of peace and goodness toward all creatures, great and small, during Medieval times. A few of his early years were spent as a strolling troubadour, and often, as a young man, he serenaded Claire, his Lady Poverty, by softly singing lyrics he composed himself to these same kinds of Renaissance rhythms, and playing the same kind of instruments.

The Winter earth-magic promise of Spring's return would be a most appropriate theme for the Virgo-Sagittarius relationship. But first, of course, the Archer must bury his bow, and vow never to cause pain to any creature, human or animal (especially Virgos!) with his Jupiter arrows. Then the Virgin and the Centaur can join hands to sing together the first chorus of the Music of the Spheres with all the whales, eagles, wolves and birds they happen to meet on their path ... bringing us all a little closer to the symphony of Peace. Sagittarian Francesco Bernardone, of Assisi, with his Moon in Virgo, will bless them with the benediction of his smile, and carol along with them ... in the key of D-flat.

VIRGO *Woman* SAGITTARIUS *Man*

————◆◄●►◆————

He thought of hopping off in a comic sort of way
till he was out of sight of her, and then never
going near the spot any more. . . . .

To show her that her departure would leave him
unmoved, he skipped up and down the room, playing
gaily on his heartless pipes. She had to run
about after him, though it was rather undignified.

Although Virgo and Sag form the tense and challenging 4-10 Sun Sign Pattern, we discussed the melodious secret of how these two can successfully conquer the conflicts of their auric vibes and achieve harmony together in the beginning of this chapter, which the Centaur and his Virgin should study first, taking care to read between the lines, before they give their attention to these particular pages. All they have to do is keep singing their love song in the key of D-flat. And try not to go off-key. It may take a little practice, but as the New Yorker said to the tourist asking directions, that's how you get to Carnegie Hall. Practice, practice, practice! (Of course, you can also get there by making a sharp right turn East, at the corner of 57th Street and 7th Avenue — but it depends on whether you plan to be the featured attraction, or just sit in the balcony, as one of the crowd.)

Speaking of directions, such as how to get to Carnegie Hall — or anywhere else — the Virgo girl will probably prefer to reach her destination by subway, by bus — or on foot. The Archer is more likely to impulsively (and extravagantly, in Virgo's opinion) hail a taxi or rent a car. Maybe even suddenly decide to buy one (he leans to fast and jazzy sports models) if he's a typical Sagittarian. It's one of the bridges they'll have to cross together, to get to the other side (the agreement side) of their differences — his inclination to spend money in a relatively casual and carefree, generous manner — and her inclination to carefully count the Daddy Lincolns and squeeze the Buffalos. The Virgin doesn't really intend or want to be stingy, but unless her Moon or Ascendent is in a Fire or Air Element, she may give an extremely good imitation of it. *She'll* call it economical or thrifty, sensible and cautious. But you know how Sag tends to call things as he sees them, so he may see her "sensible thrift" as a clear case of stinginess, and be not a bit bashful about telling her so, which, of course, will not exactly endear him to the Virgin.

You see? Already, he's been a little clumsy, and stuck his foot in his mouth. There's one way he can persuade her to thaw her frigid response to his frankness concerning her financial attitudes. He can gaze at her ever-so-earnestly (straight into her eyes, Virgos mistrust people who avert their glances) and ask her politely if she'll suggest a way for him to hang on to some of his income, help him figure out how much of it should be put away for a rainy day (or for a secure future) earning interest. Which would be more advisable, Municipal Bonds, a stock portfolio, a bank savings plan — or maybe a plump china piggy bank at home ? She'll love to be asked, and will have a stream of well-considered, detailed suggestions. If she already knows him reasonably well, she'll veto the piggy bank right away. Unless he leaves it with her. Too tempting when he weakens.

Most people start out with ambitions for the future, enter a profession or career of their choice, work toward their goal — and eventually, after they've enjoyed a fair amount of time of achievement (and tucked away some cash), they retire, and do as they please. The Archers approach the work ethic in reverse. They like to start out by retiring — or at least, by doing just what they please. If what pleases them is unduly restricted by the demands of employment, they often toss security over their shoulders, shrug — follow the features of their hunches for a while, and figure that, when things get tough, they can always find a different occupation that isn't so confining. It's an attitude that horrifies the usually hard-working, efficient and responsible Virgo woman. So she'll criticize him, first gently — and then, if he continues to behave as though he couldn't care less about the future, her very real apprehensions will cause her to point out his flaws more sharply.

He'll fiercely resent what he views as nagging, then pull out his bow and quiver, and aim a few blunt arrows of truth — as he sees it — into the heart of her objections. To work at a job you hate more than you love, only to gain financial security, he'll tell her, can slowly murder the spirit. He doesn't know (or care) how other males feel, but as for himself, he believes a man's work or career should be something he enjoys so much, he would do it without a cent of pay if he had to, because he's so magnetized by its challenge — because he must express himself in this way, or be forever unfulfilled. (An unfulfilled Archer is a sad and empty man, more so than any other.) I hate to takes sides in an argument between lovers, but astrology forces me to agree with the Centaur's philosophy on the subject of work. A fringe benefit of such an attitude Virgo should appreciate, is that financial rewards frequently pour in, not despite it, but because of it. It's never those who set out determined to make a lot of money, with financial security as the bottom line goal, who succeed and become wealthy. The greatest fortunes never fail to match the greatest achievements, granted by Lady Luck invariably to those who are consumed and obsessed by an idea, so single-minded about it that they're completely oblivious to the cash remuneration. Their fortunes pile up around them, nearly unnoticed. The Universe smiles on them, because they work with love, not with the apathy of boredom or frustrated resentment. Dr. Land and his obsession with the Polaroid photographic process. Henry and his love affair with his Ford. Tom Edison and the sounds he heard in his head, he desperately had to somehow channel. David Sarnoff . . . and thousands upon thousands of others.

There are plumbers and electricians who passionately love their work, and couldn't possibly imagine doing anything else. There are chefs who adore to cook, physicians who desperately long to heal, waiters who are happy talking with people, fascinated by the changing streams of the faces of humanity. Yes, there are even people who feel a deep, personal satisfaction in scrubbing floors and washing windows — in cleaning. They're aware of a powerful lifting of the spirits from seeing dirt and untidiness magically change into freshness and shining order. (Virgo should comprehend that!) I know a man who would rather paint houses than be President, truthfully. It exhilarates him in a way he doesn't try to explain to himself — least of all to anyone else. Albert Schweitzer preferred the hardships of steamy jungles to a chrome-plated, modern science lab, while others prefer the chrome-plated, modern science lab to primitive labor in the jungle. Those who punch their factory time clocks with suppressed bitterness and a sense of futility turn out ugly furniture, not fit to pass down to anyone, hardly fit for the original owner, after a few months. But a man who loves his work is a craftsman, creating miracles from wood and other materials that are treasured for centuries. And so it goes. There was a time when people were more inclined to follow their hearts to their professions, when society made it easier to earn one's daily bread with love. Now all we have are square pegs in round holes, and vice versa, because of the rat race called "success," that turns out, in the end, to be a cruelly false label. Millions ask themselves privately, "Why is success such a failure?" Because it was wrongly defined in the beginning, that's why. By television commercials . . . and within the glossy ads in magazines. Madison Avenue has a heavy Karma ahead, for sure.

Because Virgo contains the seed of purity (purity of thought, intention and action) the Virgin may be moved by her restless, independent Archer's arguments, and gradually grow to see things through his rosier colored glasses. An end result like that is worth the friction these two must endure from the 4-10 influence of their squared natal Suns. It's also more than a little possible that she will impress her Sagittarian lover or husband with the stamp of her own kind of patient integrity and sense of responsibility, her ability to keep dreams nice and tidy, polished and gleaming, therefore more apt to be truly beautiful when it's time for them to come out of their cedarwood drawers and manifest as realities. In this way, the Virgin and the Centaur can turn the falsely labeled "curse" of their 4-10 vibration of tension into a blessing, by helping each other eliminate their "vices," through the process of simply exchanging their individual virtues with one another.

True, there are multitudes of minor matters these two will disagree about, causing periodic conflict between them. But there's always the man-woman alchemy to soften the hurt of all the things that don't really matter as much as they think they do. Love's physical chemistry can cover daily annoyances and irritability with the heavy fragrance of roses, washed by a summer shower, in a garden . . . the joyful feel of damp earth and wet grass, refreshing two hearts and souls grown weary from constant misunderstanding. When the Virgin leans back in her Sagittarian man's protecting arms, she'll forgive him most of his trespasses against her, and he'll forget his own fiery anger over being criticized and doubted. The flames of passion and desire within his Fire Sign nature — and the deeper, more quiet needs of her "earthiness" can blend into a contentment and peace between them that forms a foundation for more tolerance toward each other regarding all those unimportant areas of conflict. But she must take care not to allow her instinctive Virgo detachment and physical aloofness to cause him to feel rejected, because he seeks and needs a more enthusiastic response to his physical expression of tenderness.

During the reign of Britain's Queen Victoria, young women about to be married, who shyly sought advice concerning the proper, ladylike behavior on their honeymoons, were crisply admonished by their mothers to "just lie back and think of England." There may be times when the Sagittarian man thinks he's been projected into the Victorian Age with his Virgo lady — his bright and gentle, but somewhat cool, Virgin, who loves him with the same intensity as he loves her, but may be unable initially to express her feelings with as much easy spontaneity as he does so naturally. Telling her she's frigid won't solve the problem. Tactlessness never solves anything. He'll have to patiently teach her to trust him with her whole self, for patience, unlike "brutal honesty," *can* solve anything at all. Once the Virgo woman has learned to be herself with the man she loves, she can make of sexual Oneness a lingering and profound experience for the sometimes clumsy, but cheerful and generous Archer, who has the ability to reach the heights in everything he does . . . not excluding making love.

After they've grown accustomed to matching their rhythms in all their communications (they communicate well, these two, both being Mutable) the Virgo woman will lie back on the shoulder of her Sagittarian man, and think of many things other than England. They both possess intelligent, inquiring minds that sparkle with ideas. Then *he* may be the one who lies there, musing about the British Isles. Some midnight, after they've loved, he'll suddenly ask her if she'd like to forget all about caution and practicality . . . just pack a couple of suitcases tomorrow, lock the front door, give the neighbors the key, so they can drop by to water the plants . . . catch an early flight for London, and arrive in time to hear the chimes of Big Ben by noon. If she's as smart as Virgos are born to be, she'll analyze his skyrocket suggestion carefully for about two and one third seconds, kiss him on the nose, snap on the light, smile into his eyes with her whole heart, and say, "Well, what are we waiting for? You get out the suitcases, and phone the airport, while I'm taking my shower."

☆ ☆ ☆ ☆ ☆ ☆

VIRGO *Man* SAGITTARIUS *Woman*

She asked where he lived. "Second to the right,"
Peter said, "and straight on till morning."

"What a funny address!"

Peter had a sinking. For the first time he felt
that perhaps it was a funny address. "No, it
isn't," he said.

Well, hurray and hallelujah! Give that Virgo man with the peculiar address a hearty handshake and a bear hug! He's off to a racing start with the half-Horse, half-Human female Centaur, for whose love and admiration he's willing to give up his treasured loner's existence. For her, he'll even sacrifice his bachelor pad's peace and quiet. But for her (or for anyone else) he should never sacrifice his sense of personal dignity and self-confidence, especially not his self-respect. A man has a million uses for self-respect, so it's not sensible to allow even the woman he adores to rob him of it.

You'll notice that at first he hesitated, nearly submitting to the sinking feeling of inadequacy a bright and cheerful but distressingly candid and forthright girl Archer can unthinkingly instill in a Virgo man's solar plexus (which, if he's not careful, can develop into an annoying attack of Virgo indigestion). But our hero triumphed over the impending danger of inferiority, the challenging threat to his masculinity. Never mind her frank (or amused) opinions and comments about his perfectly proper address. Never mind what she thinks of his apartment, his socks, his ears, his hair, his nose, his job, his careful and modest dreams, his car — his habit of buying Ivory soap by the case, or his medicine chest, well stocked with aids to "gentle elimination." She thinks his address is funny? He'll tell *her* a thing or two. And so, he speaks right up to her, firmly and sternly — "No, it *isn't*. It is *not* a funny address."

That's the first thing he tells her. The second thing is that she should learn to close her mouth *before* she speaks, and *keep* it closed while she's analyzing what she was about to say — and if she thinks it over carefully, with a little consideration and forethought, she might decide not to open it at all — until she has something nice and kind to say to him. Surprisingly, she'll probably love it. Actually, this girl is searching for a firm but tender man, who will keep her in her place — as long as he doesn't keep her there by sitting on her puppy-dog friendliness, optimistic enthusiasims and fiery ideals. It's an undeniably delicate task, but the Virgo man who loves her is gifted with the art of delicate diplomacy, and he just may be able to handle it. He possesses an almost mystical talent for finessing things through to a smooth finish.

Happily, he's solved one problem between them in their tense 4-10 Sun Sign Pattern relationship, already. He's trained her to soften the tips of her Jupiter arrows a bit, and not pull so hard on the bow. He's made her see that her thoughtless remarks can really hurt — and with Virgo's curious ability to be sweetly polite, even while scolding, he's made her realize that he does comprehend her lack of malicious intent, her basic good will and naivete. She may be, quite sincerely, moved to tears. She's wanted and needed someone to understand her real self for the longest, longest time, someone who won't judge her harshly for just being true to how she feels — and spontaneous when she has something to express. Therefore, instead of starting a quarrel between them, her Virgo lover or husband's firmness may have the opposite effect of bringing them closer together than they were before. Beautiful. Bravos and posies. Good for him, and good for her. Now, the next problem. (You surely didn't expect them to be fated to struggle with just *one* problem, did you? After all, their natal Suns are squared, remember.)

Her practical jokes. Sagittarians of both sexes are absolutely addicted to puns and practical jokes. She'll think it's hilarious as puns go, that a Connecticut town, in celebration of ERA's birth, officially changed the description of a public occupation as "building personholes," avoiding discreetly the use of the no-no word "man." (Virgo might think that one is pretty funny himself.) Then he'll ask her what time the mailperson is due, because he wants to post a letter, she'll ask him if he doesn't mean "personperson," he'll tell her that "mail" isn't "male," and she'll say it doesn't matter how it's spelled — he'll ask her how she would know, since she's such a dreadfully poor speller herself, and they'll crack up laughing together. One of the nicest things about Sag is that she's a genuine good sport, and is never up-tight about enjoying a joke on herself. Most Sagittarians can take it as cheerfully as they dish it out. And he must admit that's a shining virtue, only too rare in this dreary world. All right, we've covered her penchant for puns, and he handled that problem quite nicely too, don't you think? With just the right amount of good humor and careless teasing, adding a pinch of her own kind of truth that stings. And she laughed. She was pleased, she didn't pout, and they're still friends. The practical jokes may be a little tougher.

Excuse me. You'll NEVER BELIEVE what just happened! I've been writing this book for a little over nine months now (it takes nine months to create a human child or a brain child, a tad longer for elephants) and this is the FIRST TIME EVER that my IBM typewriter ribbon ran out at *precisely* the *exact* same *second* the IBM correctional tape ran out! Isn't that one for the Guinness book? The Virgos reading this are now busily calculating the percentage possibilities of such a double fade-out. The Archers will want to know if I'm making it up to be funny, or if I'm being honest. Sag has a thing about integrity. I am not making it up, and I'm not trying to be funny. It's true. It happened, and I have a witness. So there. I'm either approaching the end of this book, or the end of my Virgo-like cool. There are unmistakable signs . . . . . and I do hope the former occurs before the latter. (No, I'm not a Virgo, I'm Aries, but Vulcan is, I'm sure, conjunct my natal Sun. I'll let you know when they discover it (Vulcan) and are able to calculate its orbiting movements.) Now back to the Sag practical jokes, with which the Virgo man will have to contend sooner or later in their relationship.

As briefly as possible, I'll give him a sample of how gigantic a Sagittarian-type practical joke can be. I mean, *some* of them are harmless little bits of fun and foolishness, but since Jupiter, the ruler of Sag, is the planet associated with expansion, an occasional Archer prank can get a little out of hand, so to speak. Briefly, then, there is this man named Steven Masover, who is enrolled in college at Berkeley (California) in pursuit of a higher degree in physics (on a scholarship, and he was also Valedictorian of his high school graduation class). Steven's Sag-type caper, which news stories referred to as a "Robin Hood prank" (Robin Hood has a tight affinity with all Archers), was to hold up a bank, with an unloaded gun and a fake bomb, making off with $78,000 in cash. His defense was that he had no intention of stealing the money, he had only borrowed it to invest it in colonies in outer space, as a way for Earthlings to escape pollution and overpopulation, and planned to pay back every penny in 20-odd years or so. (Pollution, Love Signs can't help Steven solve, but the overpopulation problem is tackled in *A Time to Embrace*, in the back of this book.) Masover was acquitted by the jury (in a Jupiter-type stroke of pure luck) because the D.A. couldn't prove he "intended to deprive the bank of the cash *permanently*" (a prerequisite for stealing) although the latter commented that he felt "spending the money on space stations would amount to the same thing as depriving the bank of it permanently, using common [Virgo] horse sense." Or Sagittarian horse sense. Or whatever. The big fear now is that the "flukey" acquittal of the perpetrator of this flakey but eloquent practical joke will encourage other "Robin Hood robberies." The fear is groundless. Real criminals don't have the kind of genius and imagination to come up with that sort of laden-with-hidden-truth rationale of invisible but powerful integrity. However, it certainly may encourage other Sag practical jokers, heaven help us all.

The Virgo man may wonder why I chose a *male* example of a practical joker to warn him about his *female* Archer's playful, filly foibles. I had an excellent reason. I wished to emphasize to the Virgo man that, while *he* was born under a "feminine" Sun Sign, and is also actually ruled by the feminine planet Vulcan (see Virgo-Virgo chapter), which *doesn't* mean that he's a sissy (Virgo Elliot Gould, a *sissy* ?), only sensitive and perceptive — his girl Archer was born under a masculine Sun Sign, and also guided (puns, truth arrows, integrity, practical joking and all) by the masculine planet, Jupiter. Double feminine influence versus double masculine influence, adding up to a clear conclusion. He was absolutely right to tell her a thing or two when she made fun of his address, because he's going to have to keep a firm rein on this lady Centaur, or she'll kick over the traces. As we've already proven, she'll enjoy it secretly more than she resents it, if the rein is held in loving and kind, considerate hands, which it surely will be with a Virgo man who really loves her.

With his double feminine influence, of gentle wisdom, he'll be able to perceive that this girl-woman is a trusting, vulnerable creature, for all of her double masculine macha, and she doesn't win every race. She's stumbled and fallen more times than she can bear to remember, trusting people who hurt her and let her down, just when she needed them most. He'll soothe her painful memories with his affectionate concern, and help her analyze why she should forget them, now that there are only the old scars to remind her — assure her the scars will disappear sooner if she looks to the future, not to the past. Then he'll promise her that *he'll* never make her sorry she had faith in *him,* if he can possibly help it — and he'll mean it. She'll look into his clear, quiet Virgo eyes (that twinkle with the silvery streaks of his foster ruler Mercury when he's happy) and she'll know he's wholly and completely earnest. She's right. A Virgo never makes a promise he's not willing to do everything humanly possible to keep. That counts for a lot, and if anyone realizes it, she does. There's an alarming shortage these days of honest people, who live from the inside out, not from the outside in. So many get it backwards, the way to find happiness, like Hiawatha's mittens. Since she can't stand hypocrites or phonies, she should thank her lucky stars for the love of her Virgo gentleman (meaning gentle-man). That's something I forgot to tell him. This girl is lucky. No matter how many times she makes a mistake, her misjudgments have a way of landing on their feet, and sailing her into the winner's circle. Knowing this astrological certainty will comfort him when he's suffering through some of those really huge goofs, caused by her well-meaning, impulsive enthusiasm.

The physical closeness they share, if he continues to keep a firm grip on the reins, and if she doesn't bruise his sensitivity and subconscious need for purity, has the potential of being as passionate as her Fire Element nature, yet also as cool and as deep as his "Earthy" desires can make the togetherness between a man and a woman. There's something of calm and stillness about him that channels her longings gracefully into the direction of a kind of fulfillment that makes her know how much more important affection and peace are than winning all the games in a romantic challenge. The warmth of him beside her is something she senses she'd be empty without, if they ever allowed their clashing personalities to cause them to say goodbye. And he knows too, though he may never express it in words, that the emotional storms they sometimes endure may leave his spirit weary and tired of trying, but if she ever went away . . . who else would awaken him on Christmas morning (as she did their first December together) wearing holly berries in her hair, breathlessly telling him to look under the blanket she holds in her arms ? (No one.) Peeking out of the blanket were six black, shiny noses, belonging to six wriggling puppies born to their St. Bernard, Amelia (for Earhart), the night before, while she slept, at exactly midnight on Christmas Eve, she told him . . . her eyes shining with glittering stars of excitement and childlike wonder. Every time he remembers that crisp, cold, winter morning . . . the way she'd tucked the holly berries in her hair, like a small girl, to surprise him . . . the snow frosting her lashes (she'd just come in from checking the drifts in the yard, to see if they were deep enough to make a snowman . . they were . . . so they later did) . . every time he thinks about the way she smelled like clean, cold ozone when she kissed his forehead lightly, and merrily told him to hurry and come downstairs, because she'd made a fire, and couldn't wait for him to look under the tree to see what the reindeer had left there . . . . . he gets that funny lump in his throat he can't swallow. And he knows how right he is to keep trying to understand this lovable, graceful, funny and vulnerable . . . bright-eyed and intelligent but awkward girl clown, whose nose always turns red when she cries.

She gets the same kind of lump in her throat every time *she* remembers the morning he shyly brought her a tiny bunch of violets when she was aching inside from something very personal and sad she didn't even know he was aware of . . but he was. He handed her the violets so softly, without a single word. What other man she ever knew would have done that ? (No one. Not in quite the same way.) So what if he's occasionally cranky and cross, a little stuffy about money ? He's a quiet man, of many dimensions and levels of loving. He may not talk much around others, but they're both Mutable, and he talks a lot with her . . . telling her things he'd share with no one else, because he knows he can trust her to keep his confidences, and treat them tenderly. He had to train her to listen and understand the value of privacy . . . but Sag is super intelligent (Jupiter ruling the 9th house of higher education) so she learned quickly . . . many things he taught her. It's only because she's careless and disdainful of detail that she keeps spelling committment with two "t's" and commited with only one. Never mind. She can't spell it, but she knows what the word means. It means the same thing as a *promise*, doesn't it? Yes. It does.

If the Virgo man and his girl clown-philosopher really care, they can turn their 4-10 square of tension into a gigantic Jupiter-Vulcan trine of steady contentment over the years, and celebrate Christmas every morning, with one sort of gift or another.

VIRGO

Earth — Mutable — Negative
Ruled by Mercury (also by
  the Planet Vulcan)
Symbol: The Virgin
Night Forces — Feminine

CAPRICORN

Earth — Cardinal — Negative
Ruled by Saturn
Symbol: The Goat
Night Forces — Feminine

The **VIRGO-CAPRICORN** *Relationship*

"All look your best," Peter warned them. "First
impressions are awfully important."

He was glad no one asked him what first impressions
are; they were all too busy looking their best.

One strong tie between the Virgins and the Goats is their matching need to be thought of as proper people, therefore to speak and behave and live as properly as possible, so as not to incur either disapproval or ridicule from friends, relatives and neighbors. One does not make one's self a laughing stock if one can help it — and one *can* help it if one *tries*. The way to be respected is to be respectable. Nothing could be plainer, more precise than that.

A second strong tie between these two Earthy ones — whose four symbolic feet are planted as firmly and practically on the ground as feet can be without being nailed down — is the attitude they share about money. It is something you earn. It is something you save. It is something you spend sparingly and wisely. It is something you absolutely *never* waste or throw away carelessly.

Another strong tie between them is the way they both feel about duty and responsibility. They love it. They adore it. The Virgin and the Goat would each be equally lost and aimless without it. Give them a sacred trust, a duty to perform, a responsibility to fulfill—and they're in Seventh Heaven. It's an interesting place for them to be—Seventh Heaven (especially for Cappy). Because Saturn, ruler of Capricorn, has long been claimed by mystics, as well as hinted by the ancients, to be a Seventh Dimensional planet. (Never mind what you see with your eyes on Saturn, like on the Moon and Mars and so on. What you see with your eyes is very unimportant. We're talking about the *function* of the planets.) Now, I can't explain to you in detail exactly what it means that Saturn is a Seventh Dimensional planet. But perhaps generally . . .

You see, here on Earth, we are existing, living on a *Third* Dimensional planet, giving the large majority of us, at least, a third dimensional awareness (of Truth). The next, or the Fourth Dimension, is Time itself. Very Einsteinish. Gets into linear conceptuals and that sort of thing. (See Leo-Aquarius chapter.) The next level after the 4th is (logically) the 5th. The Fifth Dimensional level of awareness has something to do with Vulcan, the true ruler of Virgos, but I can't tell you exactly what. Moving right along to the 6th dimension and the following one, well—look at it this way: if we haven't the foggiest notion of what the 5th and 6th dimensions relate to, consist of, etc.—then it's no wonder we're totally baffled by the Seventh Dimension of Saturn. I mean, how are you going to comprehend the 7th if you don't know a particle about the 5th and the 6th? That makes good, common sense, doesn't it?

And that's another thing Virgo and Capricorn share—good common sense. They have sensible heads on their shoulders. But we were discoursing about dimensions, a sound and practical thing to do, since we're all involved with them, whether we like it or not. Isn't it interesting that the word "dimension" contains within it the words "die" and "dies"? Especially interesting since one does have to experience some sort of death to reach a Higher Dimension. (Not necessarily, however, death of the flesh body.) You see how appropriate this is now, because Saturn, Capricorn's ruler, is the planet astrologically associated with matters related to the dead. (Saturn and Pluto, between them, rule death in all its various forms.)

Our dimension discussion isn't a digression. Not to the Goats and the Virgins, who are both super-alert to the fact that it's very healthy to exercise one's mental muscles now and then, not to mention one's spiritual sinews. Dimensions, then. Take a shadow. What is a shadow? It's a *Two* Dimensional object, having height and width, but no depth, correct? Yes, that is correct. Virgo just nodded in agreement, and Virgo always knows what is correct. Cappy is still silent. Goats never offer an opinion or endorse anything until they've had time for long and careful deliberation—whereas

Mercury, the foster ruler of Virgos, causes them to speak up a bit more quickly (but never carelessly or impulsively).

Virgos and Capricorns share something in common with us all, for here on this Third Dimensional planet called Earth, we are, every one of us, *Three* Dimensional entities. We have height, width — and *depth*. (Depth being the third requirement for the third dimension.) Of course, so has a building, so it would appear that being three dimensional is not much of a distinction. Still, a three dimensional awareness is something we're stuck with, so let's continue. We (and the New York Public Library) are *Three* Dimensional objects — and when Brother Sun (a vital facet of this meditation) shines upon us, through us, from behind us or whatever (the terminology is relatively unimportant) we *Three* Dimensional objects are then able to cast a *Two* Dimensional *shadow* on the street or the ground, correct? Virgo says yes. We are correct. Cappy is still silent.

A *One* Dimensional object is a fine line which has only height (length) and no width at all, certainly no depth, impossible for us to image perhaps — but be assured that it does exist. The thing is that, if *we* are *Three* Dimensional objects, who cast *Two* Dimensional *shadows* (but only with the help of Brother Sun or one of his weaker, light bulb assistants), then THINK! Would it not follow that we, ourselves, might be merely *Three* Dimensional *shadows*, cast by our *Four* Dimensional Selves? Silence now from both Virgo and Capricorn. Well, I'll tell you, even without seeking their approval. We most definitely *are* just that. This is exactly what we are — *Three* Dimensional shadows who have been cast (through the alchemy of Light many times brighter and stronger than Brother Sun himself) by *Fourth* Dimensional beings — called the Supra-Conscious, the Higher Self, the Higher Angel of One's Self, and so on. There are many names for the *Fourth* Dimensional entitites who cast *us* as *their* shadows. Capricorn is wondering now about the buildings, and Virgo is wondering about the New York Public Library. No. Buildings do not have a Supra-Conscious. The difference between the Two Dimensional shadows *they* cast and the ones *we* cast is that *their* shadows can't move. Neither they *nor* anything higher than themselves have any choice in the matter. They should be glad we even allow them to cast a stable, unmoving shadow, that we permit them to be three dimensional at all. And we do allow it, for we created these inanimate objects in our own "three-D" image, you know. Like dolls, toy trains and the like. For our own amusement, shelter and other trivial and serious uses.

What sort of choice do *our* shadows have? They can't move without our decision. We control them, as our Higher Selves control us. The only way we can gain that sort of control over ourselves (our destinies) is to get in touch with the Fourth Dimensional being who has the control, tune in — and cooperate, demand some choice over our "shadow selves" — or should I say — over *ourselves, mere shadows that we are.* Our own shadows are silly things or they could do the same — demand of *us* that we give *them* more choice over their own selves. The symbolism of Peter Pan and his shadow was intended by author James Barrie to be far deeper than simply an amusing bedtime story.

None of the multi-dimensional entities, of course, have any power whatsoever without the Sun—and beyond that—ever greater Lights. Otherwise, all beings, of *whatever* dimensional awareness level, are helpless puppets. Including us. Praise Brother Sun! Likewise are our powerful Fourth Dimensional Supra-Conscious Selves totally dependent for *their* power to "cast the shadows of us" upon even more brilliant Light than our Sun. No bright, dancing colors would be created by prisms or crystals without Light. In darkness, there are no rainbows. In darkness, stained glass windows are dreary and lifeless. There are no reflections. In effect, be kind to your shadow. It needs you. You are its Creator. What you do and think, it also does and thinks. Well, Virgo and Capricorn, can you *prove* that shadows don't think? Believe me, you may not pay constant *conscious* attention to your shadow, but you'd be lost and drifting, with no Saturnine or Virgo responsibility, were you to be without your shadow. You would miss it dreadfully. Because, to live without your shadow would be to live in darkness. Now you understand why Peter Pan was so upset when he lost his shadow. And wasn't it nice and kind of Wendy to sew it on for him, attach it so he'd never lose it? Wendy was a Cancerian, but sewing Peter's shadow to him, so it would be safe, was such a practical idea, she clearly must have had a Virgo Ascendent and the Moon in Capricorn.

As for trying to imagine what a 5th, or say a 7th dimensional being would look like, I believe you won't go far wrong if you image the 7th dimensional "being" as looking and behaving quite like Capricorn. Stern, but loving. Wise. Patient and quiet, stable, dependable, and reliable. (But also more than a trifle stubborn.) Like most all Goats. The 5th dimensional "being" or entity strongly resembles Virgo. Stern, but loving. Wise. Patient and quiet, stable, dependable and reliable. (But also a little critical, cranky and restless.) Now you know what the higher dimensional "angels" look like. A Goat and a Virgin. At least when you step off the escalator on the 5th and 7th floor levels. We may not know a whole lot more than when we began, but I told you I couldn't explain it all in detail. Just generally . . .

Virgos intensely dislike generalities. They are refined men and women, with alert minds, acute perceptions and an exquisite sense of discrimination. They analyze every feeling, then say they're not that way at all. (That's because they're analyzing your analysis of them.) The Goats find no wrong in Virgo's attitude. It seems sensibly cautious to Capricorn that Virgos should devote the time and trouble to take clocks and problems and people apart to make sure the works are in good shape before they "buy" the clock, solve the problem or decide to be friends with the person. Both Virgo and Capricorn have a certain sweetness and gentleness about them, a shy and reserved manner that seems to quietly draw them together. There will be times when Cappy thinks Virgo worries too much, talks things over to excess. There may be times when Virgo thinks Cappy is too stubborn and set in his (or her) ways, refusing to compromise or submit to the excitement of mental stimulation. Nevertheless, these two are far more alike than they are different, far more compatible than not. Their association is graced by the sympathetic 5-9 Sun Sign Pattern, making it easier to relate and to forgive each other's mistakes.

Every Capricorn projects a singular kind of detachment. When an obstacle appears, the Goats just step over it and climb steadily on their way to the top of their goals. That's what makes Saturn-ruled people sometimes appear to be cold and unsympathetic — their lack of outward emotional response to stress and strain. They consider unnecessary displays of emotion to be wasteful and extremely non-productive. Most Sun Signs are unable to comprehend such an attitude, and so mistakenly interpret it as cruelty or at the very least, a lack of warmth. Yet a Virgo will instinctively know that Cappy is truly brokenhearted beneath Saturn's iron curtain of composure, and the Goats are pathetically grateful for the Virgin's compassion.

In the same way, Cappy comprehends the hurt felt by Virgo when others call him (or her) critical, fussy and uptight. No one can better relate to Virgo's self-chastisement and guilt over neglecting duty and responsibility better than the Saturnine man or woman. Cappy senses the gentle dreams and longings locked up inside Virgo, needing so much to escape, yet kept firmly subdued beneath a surface reticence and shyness. The Goats know. For they are much the same. They too have yearnings difficult to express. The Virgo's declaration that he (or she) prefers to be a loner, Cappy knows is not really true. It's just an easy way to hide your loneliness from those who would only ridicule you if they knew how vulnerable you are, how much emptiness you feel at times. Yes, Capricorn well knows Virgo's need to pretend to be more self-sufficient than he (or she) really is, recognizes it as a form of protection against hurt. Both Capricorn and Virgo take Life seriously. They're both earnest and sincere, loyal and dependable. And both realize the frustration of being the often unappreciated guardians of common sense and practicality among those who find "taking care of business" boring, and are able to accept the process of living more casually and carelessly than either the Goats or the Virgins can bring themselves to do.

Yes, the 5th and 7th dimensions of awareness have much in common. For one thing, 5 and 7 are "odd" numbers, not "even." There's an implied isolation about being "odd," whereas the "even" people are more adaptable. Virgins and the Goats are lighthearted when they're together, because they know each other's secrets. They trust their private selves with one another, and this allows them to laugh and weep together, to share the kind of excitement, daydreams and rich experiences only Earth Signs can fully enjoy. Deep down within the Earth lie veins of pure gold, waiting to be discovered — just as deep down within the quiet hearts of Virgo and Capricorn lie veins of pure golden wisdom, far more beautiful than any metal ever mined — for those who are patient, and know where to look.

☆ ☆ ☆ ☆ ☆ ☆

VIRGO *Woman* CAPRICORN *Man*

◄─◄●►─►

"Oh dear! I am sure I sometimes think spinsters
are to be envied." Her face beamed when she
exclaimed this.

You remember about her pet wolf. Well, it very
soon discovered that she had come to the island and
it found her out, and they just ran into each
other's arms.

As with everything else in astrology, there's a reason why Virgos are symbolized by the Virgin. Both sexes. If the truth be told, almost every Virgo would prefer to live alone forever. (Not necessarily as a literal virgin, of course, but unmarried.) The Virgo woman is seldom thrilled by the thought of trying to match her life style to the habits of another person (especially if the other person has *messy* habits). It's a terrible dilemma for her, actually, because she can fall in love as deeply and as liltingly as any other woman. And once she's fallen in love, she's tortured by conflicting feelings.

She's aware that she'd be much more comfortable in a relationship recognized and respected by both the law and society. Namely, legal marriage. Second, when she truly loves a man, she feels it's her *duty* to marry him, bear his children, darn his socks, grate his celery and carrots, keep his shirts from humiliating him (and her) with ring-around-the-collar, help him with his income tax, all those necessary human burdens. Her lovely, clear eyes become cloudy, and her pure forehead wrinkles with worry over the situation. The more she analyzes it, the more troubled she is. Fortunately, she's an Earth Sign, not an Air Sign like Libra. If a Libra lady had the Virgin's problem, she'd really go bananas, trying to decide what to do. Virgo will keep her cool while she's analyzing all the details of her marital dilemma, and view the whole thing in a reasonably calm manner. But she may bite her nails a lot, and those worry wrinkles will reveal her inner turmoil. Mostly, she'll keep it within, hash it out with herself, Narcissus-like, while she's still unsure.

The plus side of her conflict over whether or not to marry we just covered a paragraph or so ago — all those reasons why she feels she *should* give in and renounce her single status. The minus side is what marriage means — or what it will probably mean to her, as a Virgo. It will mean adjusting her life to the whims of another individual, adapting herself to being constantly on call, 24 hours a day, to cook, sew, make small talk, make love, have children, raise children, dust, sweep, clean ... then there's the laundry, the bills, the necessity for compromise concerning social activities and a hundred other areas where her preferences and those of her husband might clash. (Virgos hate clashes. Clashing makes them nervous.)

Despite her reputation for neatness, cleanliness and tidiness, not every Virgo woman in the world is a born homemaker. In fact, very few of them are. (We'll discuss why a little later.) Consequently, the possibility of becoming a household drudge is high on the list of the reasons she'd rather not wed — and it's why lots of Virgo girls decide early in life that the institution of marriage is for the weak-minded. But then, there are always one's friends, relatives and neighbors to consider. What will *they* think of her decision to remain single? And what of her responsibility to the man she loves? How can he possibly manage without her by his side at night and in the morning, in case he should need something, and she's all the way crosstown? If they don't legally marry, but just find a suitable apartment halfway between her job and his job, and live together, wouldn't she be forced to do all those wifely things for him *anyway* (become a household drudge) even though they weren't *actually* man and wife? I can answer that for her, without spending a lot of time analyzing it. Yes, she would.

So the Virgin is left with the choice of either remaining a virgin — or becoming his bride. These are the only two sensible solutions for a lady who feels such a sense of duty toward her lover that just seeing him every other day or so isn't enough to remove her nagging worry that he might need her in some way during those hours they're apart. If you haven't already gathered that most Virgo women privately *enjoy* being needed (never mind how they complain about it) then consider yourself informed now that they do.

Should the man she loves happen to be a Capricorn, her dilemma is a waste of perfectly good hours which could have been profitably spent otherwise. If she's involved in a meaningful affair with a Goat, she can forget analyzing. Not always, but at least eight times out of ten, a Capricorn man who really loves a woman will either make her his proper and respectable wife — or leave her and grow bitter, nursing his loss for years, rather than consent, for any length of time, to a relationship that isn't legally, socially and religiously sanctioned, or is contrary to general custom — and especially one that could conceivably be frowned upon by his sainted family. The sexual revolution has changed many former traditions, patterns and concepts, but it has not yet made a dent in the basic Sun Sign personality of the Goats. Nor is it likely to do so in the near future. It will take several generations to convince Cappy that living in sin is *not* living in sin, even when he's reluctantly living in it. Besides, he nearly always will want a family, this man — and he's not about to bring up his sons and daughters illegitimately, deprived of the great privilege of bearing his family name. That's unthinkable. It's sacrilegious. Even worse, it would be humiliating.

Another reason it's difficult for the Virgo woman to avoid marriage with her Goat is because the two of them are emotionally guided in their love relationship by the 5-9 Sun Sign Pattern, the most basically compatible vibration the planets see fit to bestow upon mortals. It isn't an absolute guarantee of happiness, naturally. Even 5-9er's have to work at it — and there are always those few 5-9 couples whose Luminaries are in adverse aspect between their birth charts. They'll still be unusually sympathetic to each other, but may find it hard to compromise their disagreements. Nevertheless, it's a beneficent influence to have as a foundation for love, and whether 5-9 lovers exchange a positive or negative natal Sun-Moon aspect between them (in addition to their trined Suns) they are always more miserable when apart than most other men and women who separate for one cause or another.

So there's really not much use for her to indulge in a dance of doubt with this man. When the Virgin and the Goat first meet, they'll feel a karmic tug of long ago and far away, mixed with an almost instant empathy and comprehension of one another's viewpoints. Their auras blend, lock into place harmoniously — and after that, untangling them is as difficult and delicate a task as untangling the fur balls of a Persian kitten. (Most Virgos own a cat or two. Virgos have a thing about cats. They either worship them or they can't stand to be in the same room — or even the same neighborhood — with anything feline. But they are never just neutral about pussycats.)

These two communicate beautifully, whether they're dancing (which they don't do often, especially not on a night before they both have to be at work or school early the next morning), just talking and relaxing, working on a project together . . . or making love, which is a mutual endeavor they'll both enjoy tremendously. Neither of them finds it easy to be natural regarding sex. Secretly, each of them has always feared that he (or she) is inadequate in some way. But when the Virgo girl melts snugly into the secure arms of the Capricorn man she loves, she seems to lose all her coolness, detachment and inhibitions. Likewise for him, when this woman nestles trustingly against his shoulder in the dark, then moves uncertainly nearer. Their need grows slowly, until it becomes deep and overwhelming. When two Earth Signs express their desire for each other physically, their feelings can be mighty powerful — in a word, earthquaking. The girls he used to know and maybe thought he loved—the men she used to know and wondered if she loved—would be amazed. Until they discovered an emotion they could trust to be wholly reciprocal, both the Virgo girl and the Capricorn man may have been more than once accused by others of being cold and romantically unresponsive. That's why their sexual union is frequently such a warmly intimate interlude within their other levels of togetherness. It may be the first time they have ever felt free to just be themselves, holding nothing back, loving with an abandon and a sense of human completeness they always wistfully longed to know and to share, but were never quite able to attain with anyone else—until they found each other and were able to experience an unexpected earthquake of passion.

I promised earlier in this section to tell you why lots of Virgo women aren't thrilled about housekeeping and homemaking. Some of them are, of course, and when they are, they revel in it—but a surprisingly large percentage of them are not. A person who hates to *live* in disorder is not necessarily a person who enjoys *keeping* things in order. Aside from the Virgos who do have spotless homes, the others are made nervous by the sight of the continual disarray of daily living. Make a bed, wash a dish, mop a floor, wash a bag of laundry and almost before you're through, the bed is again unmade, the dishes are once more dirty, the floor is tracked with someone's muddy boots, and the clean clothes are soiled as soon as they're worn. It's discouraging, and it keeps you forever analyzing how to cope with it all more efficiently, which fatigues the brain, makes you tired and unable to do your work (creating a vicious circle), besides which there's really no answer to the problem of beds that simply won't stay made, dishes that stubbornly refuse to remain spotless, floors that perversely need sweeping and mopping only a few hours after they've been left freshly waxed and gleaming—and clean clothes that insist on needing to be washed and bleached and dried repeatedly. You see, the reason so many neat and clean Virgo women contradictorily dislike housekeeping almost neurotically is because they *are* all perfectionists, and there's nothing so discouraging to a perfectionist as something you've managed to straighten out and make nice and neat that simply will not *remain* nice and neat, no matter how much effort you spend. Because this creates the most ulcer-inducing worry of all to a Virgo, which is, simply: is it either *sensible* or *practical* to waste so much valuable time retracing one's steps? When they finally decide it's neither, the Virgins often leave the dishes stacked in the sink, the beds unmade, the laundry undone, the floor streaked with scuff marks—and desperately rush out to find a job of some kind where their talents for bringing order out of chaos and confusion will *mean* something. It doesn't always work, unfortunately, because *then* Virgo begins to develop all sorts of physical and emotional complaints, due to a consciously unrecognized sense of guilt for neglecting a "duty." This girl can use lots of sympathy.

Although Goats aren't excessively sensitive, the 5-9 cord that binds them will allow the Goat to treat the little baby torments and traumas of his Virgo woman with more genuine consideration than is normally his custom. He knows what it's like to endure agonies of guilt and frustration over exaggerated self images of neglecting responsibility. Indeed, the moods of depression with which the kindly, earnest Goat is periodically afflicted, often stem from the same twinges of self-critcism and self-chastisement his Virgo lady suffers. He tends to discipline himself as severely as she does herself, holding his hurt inside, like her, restricting his emotions as she does, seldom allowing them to escape into the freedom of natural expression.

As for those scattered areas of tension between them, they could arise if she's overly critical of his family in any way or nags a bit too much. All Goats tend to balk and butt with their stubborn horns when they're nagged or pushed. Some quarrels could be caused by his refusal to spend enough time talking with her about the hundreds of things she reads and hears that stimulate her active, alert mind. She likes to always be either verbally analyzing something or physically doing something. Idleness bores her and makes her restless, whereas his metabolism and day-to-day behavior are keyed to a much more leisurely, relaxed pace. Then too, there's his self-protective Saturnine selfishness — the Capricorn "me first" attitude he's seldom aware he possesses. Should he take undue advantage of her instinctive *un*selfish urge to serve, their relationship can become lopsided, and she could resent it inwardly for a long time before it spills over into a serious confrontation.

Then she might decide she was right in the first place about a single life being the only sensible and peaceful way to live, pack up her vitamins, her dictionary, her pocket calculator, her toothbrush and other personal belongings — and leave him. The separation may not last long. In a month or so, after she's settled into her bachelor girl's apartment, luxuriating in being a loner again, she'll surprise herself with her own tears some night, in the stillness she thought would be peaceful, but turned out to contain instead only the awful ache of emptiness. She'll realize she misses snuggling in his arms . . . his soft, twinkling Goat's eyes and his shy humor . . . even his occasional gruffness, his grumpy moods and his unthinking selfish moments that hide such a gentle, devoted and loyal heart. As gentle, devoted and loyal as her own.

Is that the doorbell ringing? Yes, it is. Surprise! It's him. He has the *perfect* excuse to stop by and see how she's doing without him. She made a mistake and took *his* toothbrush when she left. He is returning hers, so they can trade. She stares at him for one shocked moment, then exclaims, "But I didn't notice, and I've already been using your toothbrush for nearly a month!" He'll tell her he didn't notice either right away, and *he's* been using *hers*. Then they'll run into each other's arms, because they'll know there's no use fighting it any longer. They love. How could they *possibly* have used each other's toothbrushes if they didn't? They couldn't. For Virgo and

Capricorn, that's the ultimate intimacy, the final proof of destined Oneness. Otherwise, obviously, they would both have surely turned into stone statues as punishment for such an improper trespass against custom, so warned against in childhood as a no-no. Unexpectedly, the two of them feel as free as birds! He drives her back home, so sweetly familiar, but still feeling free, instead of going inside, they race each other into the back yard. He takes off his stuffy tie, and tosses it over the outstretched arms of the nearest tree . . . she removes her uptight Virgo sandals . . . and they dance barefoot in the moonlight, under the surprised stars, the grass tickling their toes deliciously, intoxicated by the heavy fragrance of honeysuckle vines. Finally, they fall down beneath the tree, laughing and crying at the same time . . . and suddenly, without warning, it's silent between them. The only sound is the chirping of crickets. They both know what the silence means. Sometimes, need won't wait. After all, it's their yard, it's surrounded by a high wall, tall spruce and hedges, and the neighbors are asleep. . . . . .

It's about time they broke the chains of restriction, to learn that love will not be imprisoned by anyone's rules. From far away in the distance, Virgo's true ruling planet, Vulcan, thunders approval . . . while in the sky overhead, Saturn weeps with a strange and unaccustomed joy. After a time, a soft, steady rain begins to fall. They don't even notice. His very best tie will surely be ruined. But who cares? His Virgin will knit him a new one, now that she's back home, where she belongs.

That night, of course, there was an earthquake—though not the kind that can be measured on the Richter scale.

☆ ☆ ☆ ☆ ☆ ☆

VIRGO *Man* CAPRICORN *Woman*

◆◀●▶◆

But you simply must fit, and Peter measures you for
your tree as carefully as for a suit of clothes; the only
difference being that the clothes are made to fit you,
while you have to be made to fit the tree. Usually, it
is done quite easily, as by wearing too many garments
or too few; but if you are bumpy in awkward places, or
the only available tree is an odd shape, Peter does some
things to you, and after that you fit. Once you fit,
great care must be taken to go on fitting, and this, as
Wendy was to discover to her delight, keeps a whole
family in perfect condition.

Since Goat Girls prefer to face facts without flinching, the Capricorn female who thinks she can mold the Virgo man she loves into what she considers the proper image of a lover, husband, father and respectable wage earner is hereby astrologically counseled that succeeding in such a goal may not be a piece of cake.

As tough and patient and intractable as her ruling planet, Saturn, may be — Virgo's true ruling planet, the thunderous Vulcan, will also have something quite firm to say about it. Because Vulcan has not yet been discovered and identified (though the event is imminent — see the Virgo-Virgo chapter) the male Virgin remains still partially influenced by his foster ruler, Mercury. This gives him, in addition to Vulcan's distant but determined vibes of resistance, the extra bonus of Mercury's quick intellect and agile mental cleverness, along with Mercury's swift, wing-footed way of escaping uncomfortable situations. Consequently, in the long run, the odds are pretty even that he might end up being the one to cause *her* to fit *his* notions of the way things should be measured instead of the other way around. His notions, at least in the beginning, may not include marriage. It's not just the idea of a long-term commitment that disturbs him. It's the restriction of his freedom. The necessity to harness his personal habits to the strange and unknown personal habits of another. The lack of . . . well, the lack of *privacy* marriage involves. What if she's the kind of person to fill the bathroom medicine cabinet with all her feminine glamour trappings, cosmetics and such, leaving no room for his Milk of Magnesia, Pepto Bismol, Tums, bee pollen, vitamins, Band-Aids, iodine, Roll-Aids, Alka Seltzer, Excedrin, Paba, toe nail clippers and Kelp toothpaste ? She's not. Very, very few Goat girls are addicted to make-up and glamour. Saturn blessed most of them with a flawless skin that only improves with age. Since all Capricorns look younger as they grow older, she doesn't need all that artifice. She thinks it's a big bore, and besides it's expensive. She has no intention of supporting Revlon, so they can buy commercials to annoy her with interruptions when she's watching television.

Well, all right, but she could have a dozen or so other habits that will upset him. For example, he likes his poached eggs cooked a certain way, and it's taken him years to train a certain waiter in his favorite restaurant to fix them just right — how long might it take to train her? She could even be the kind of woman who talks incessantly on the phone, or worse yet, in bed — until he develops those migraine headaches again — or a recurring attack of his intestinal disorder. He just paid two months' salary to a homeopathist to get rid of his asthma and allergies to scented soaps, his headaches and his intestinal disorder (actually, severe constipation) and he's not about to repeat that ordeal if he can help it. He's probably worried about nothing. Being a Cappy, she most likely can handle poached eggs, and she certainly isn't inclined to be a chatterbox on the phone, in bed — or anywhere else.

If he really loves her, he'll have to get it together, take hold of himself and realize what anxieties he's creating in this gentle lady who's really a lady — who is so capable, loyal and appealing — by being so skittish about formalizing and legalizing their love. She wasn't born to carry on an endless love affair. She feels vaguely uncomfortable about flouting convention, she can't bear the disapproval of her family — and she has definite ambitions for the future. To her, both Life and Love must have a clear purpose, a definite direction and goal. Besides, she'd probably like to be a mother someday. Not a whole houseful of children, no. But maybe one. Or possibly two. And she would like them to have a surname, other than her own.

It will take more than a few generations for the Aquarian Age changes to breed out of the Goat Girl her innate reverence for the family circle, her rock-bound conviction that it should be protected as the stronghold of civilization herself. She's right, of course. Capricorns usually are. Saturn, her ruler, symbolizes wisdom gained through experience, faith in the old and dependable over the untried new and doubtful. In the end, Saturn's judgement is always proven to have been sound. Sometimes it takes many years, even centuries of patience, but Saturn itself is never wrong. That's why Cappies can become so depressed at times. They catch it from Saturn, like a disease. Surely it's lonely and depressing to be so enlightened and have to wait so long to share it, while in the meantime, everyone resents you, calls you stuffy and straightlaced. Or worse yet, ridicules you because they don't understand that Father Time will justify your wisdom. That could depress anyone. It's depressed Old Man Saturn (the planetary Master of Karma) for so many eons, it's no wonder that those born under his influence periodically retreat into icy-blue doldrums, just sitting around and brooding for no apparent reason. But there *is* a reason for this woman's silent spells, and now you know what it is — although *she* may *not*. She only knows she feels sometimes an inexplicable sadness and loneliness, a sense of the futility of everything — and while she's feeling it, the greatest good news in the world couldn't jolt her into a joyful smile. Not until the mood has passed. It isn't very helpful of the Virgo man who loves her to add to the Goat Girl's gloomy periods by causing her to become concerned over what people will say if they don't plan to eventually marry. Now and then, it will be Cappy who avoids the altar, because it might interfere with following an ambition or a career, and the Virgo who feels rejected — but not nearly so often as the other way around.

In general, however, their relationship will be rich in mutual affection, and has an excellent chance of becoming permanent. Thanks to the basic harmony of their 5-9 Sun Sign Pattern, their love will be more stable and enduring than most, although there will be occasions when their matching stubbornness causes them to disagree. It probably won't be over financial matters. Allowing for the few exceptions, like a Goat Girl with her Moon or Ascendent in a Fire or Air Sign, or a Virgo man with the same (when hers are *not* — and vice versa) these two will tend to view money in a similar way. To state it bluntly, both Virgo and Capricorn are capable of being as tight as a tick with cash. This is fortunate, because it means he probably won't mind her working, following her own career or profession. Not only because he was born under a Mutable Sign, and is therefore more adaptable than most males, but two jobs mean double income. Double savings. Double investments. Double interest. And only half the time required to accumulate enough security to move to a house in the country, where they'd both prefer to live, if they're typical of their Sun Signs. See? There *are* advantages to being married! Of course, these two may not, in the beginning, be aware of their need to escape into Nature's woodlands. That will come later. For a while, she'll be too busy carving herself a secure position in society, or in some profession where she can quietly and calmly, but surely — lead others (she's Cardinal) or at the very least, be her *own* boss. And he'll be too busy finding a variety of interests that need his alert mind and critical talents, trying a little of this and a little of that, and usually leaving things in a smoother flowing condition than he found them.

One thing that's almost certain to be smooth flowing between them is their sexual chemistry. Earth knows exactly how to bring happiness to Earth. Even with adverse Luminary aspects between their horoscopes (which could cause coldness between them periodically), their trined Suns allow each of them to sense how to give peace and contentment to the other through sexual union. If their Luminaries and Ascendents are trined also (or sextile or conjunct) their passion will be a deep and stirring experience. Sex is often a quiet emotion to Virgo and Capricorn, yet also a powerful magnet that steadily adds strength to their relationship. As with all Earth Sign couples, their closeness will grow with Time. There's a slow sensuality about their lovemaking that makes it rich and meaningful — and since neither the Virgin nor the Goat find it easy to express his or her feelings verbally, this shared silent sensuality gradually becomes a private code between them.

Intimacy is not something this man and woman have to learn, or teach each other, through experience. It was there, trembling between them, when they first met. Reflected in their eyes and their shy, uncertain smiles. Something they recognized without the need for words. They simply knew. As with many 5-9 lovers, Virgo and Capricorn are instantly familiar . . . as the Bible tells, they "*know* one another."

When a man and woman who are influenced by the Earth Element of the 5-9 vibration part for some reason, there's always a feeling of emptiness. And so they hide their naked longing, as Earth Signs will, beneath a detached reserve. But the separation shakes them to their roots, never mind how they try to escape the desolation. The wounds can heal eventually, of course, but it takes a long, long time. (Barbra Streisand is an Earth Sign Taurean, former husband Elliot Gould is a Virgo.) Since parting is so painful for 5-9 guided lovers of the Earth Element, it's worth a lot of effort to compromise their differences. Allowing for the always present exceptions that prove the rule, when Virgo and Capricorn (or any Earthy couples) end their relationship, it's seldom due to the death of love — or the intrusion of a third person. It's almost always ambition, the career or goal of one, that leaves the other behind. This is usually the seed of their problem, though they may hide it, and call it by other names.

The Virgo man and his Goat Girl are both stubborn. They both use coldness as a weapon when they're hurt — to hurt back. They're both reserved, and to each of them — love is a very private thing. But neither will ever let the other down if it can possibly be avoided. They are loyal. And loyalty is the strongest foundation on which an enduring love can be built. Even when love seems to have been destroyed, it can always be reconstructed on the firm foundation of steady loyalty that never cracked through freezing weather, that withstood the fires of anger and the floods of all kinds of temporary emotions. When Cappy and Virgo have had a disagreement, they may pretend the song is over. But it's not. That was just the first verse. There are choruses yet unsung.

Some night they'll run into each other at a party somewhere, each privately hating the crowds and wanting to be elsewhere — anywhere but in the babbling confusion of people talking about nothing. Then she'll realize that the only quiet in the whole room is in his eyes . . . gazing at her softly, but waiting. He'll realize the only stillness and peace in the whole room is in her uncertain smile. She looks even younger now than she did years ago when they met, he notices. (Of course. Cappies grow younger as the years pass, blessed by Saturn's hard-earned gift of age reversal.) She notices how clearly more intelligent, thoughtful and self-contained he is, compared to all the other men with their polished sophistication and aggressive behavior, their tired jokes. Their jaded attitudes. *His* shy humor is so much more perceptive.

After a while, the Virgo man will walk over to his Goat Girl . . . slowly, but very, very surely . . . and say hello again. She'll try to answer him with some reserved, dignified greeting—but the words will unexpectedly become a lump in her throat, so she'll just smile at him, silently. It doesn't matter. Because it's still there. The trembling between them. The knowing. The intimacy. It's time for the second chorus of their song, with the old familiar melody, but new lyrics.

VIRGO

Earth — Mutable — Negative
Ruled by Mercury (also by
the Planet Vulcan)
Symbol: The Virgin
Night Forces — Feminine

AQUARIUS

Air — Fixed — Positive
Ruled by Uranus
Symbol: The Water Bearer
Day Forces — Masculine

The **VIRGO-AQUARIUS** *Relationship*

A Never tree tried hard to grow in
the centre of the room, but every
morning they sawed the trunk through,
level with the floor.

Since Virgo delights in bringing order out of chaos, and Aquarius delights in bringing chaos out of order, these two Sun Signs should represent to one another the ultimate challenge.

Aquarians bounce around making prophecies and predictions as cheerfully as the weatherman (and with a far greater degree of accuracy). They insist on the right to be individualists and refuse to take themselves or anyone else seriously, treating life with a fine and careless detachment. Naturally, all this fascinates the method-minded, order-oriented Virgos, who wouldn't dare to prophesy or predict the future (they're too busy analyzing the past and nit-picking the present), who take themselves and everything else quite seriously — and treat nothing with careless detachment.

Virgos can recite the Gettysburg Address without missing a comma. They keep their checkbooks nicely balanced—and they also understand all about complicated airline schedules and the need to save your ticket stubs at the movies in case you have to go back outside to see if the time has run out on the parking meter. Naturally, all *this* fascinates the absentminded Aquarians, who can never get it straight whether it was Lincoln or Franklin D. Roosevelt who thought this nation of the people, by the people, and for the people should not perish from the Earth (both presidents were Aquarians, so it's easy to get them mixed up); whose checkbooks absolutely refuse to balance; and who are always handing airline stewardesses their movie stubs and handing startled theatre ushers their plane tickets—not to mention being unable to recall where they parked their bicycles or saucers, never mind the meter.

These two like to study one another, preferably at a distance. Neither wants to get too close until he or she has figured out some of the rules to the game the other one plays. They need a little push to get together initially, like an insistent introduction through a mutual friend or the nonoptional fate of being born into the same family circle. However, once they form a relationship, it's seldom a dull one.

Aquarians, ruled by the blitzkrieg planet Uranus, perversely refuse to think, speak, or act like anyone else, yet they want everyone to like them, and they can't seem to understand why they are enigmas to those not tuned in to their zigzag frequency. They are attracted to every concept or idea that blows in front of their noses, until they extract all the truth from it, tire of the game, and move on to the next seductive possibility. What intrigued them yesterday will be erased from the blackboard of the mind tomorrow, wiping it clean for the next new and exciting equation.

An area of mystification between them will be the Virgo's awesome talent for details. Virgo almost never forgets a name, a face, a sum, a date, or an address. Aquarians can forget people, places, pens, pets, umbrellas, and uncles. (Both, however, are unlikely to misplace their billfolds.) The Aquarian penchant for forgetting can be traced to the reluctance of these men and women to clutter their minds with unnecessary data and details when there are so many multitudinous matters to investigate and solve. Gertrude Dial, an Aquarian friend of mine in Cripple Creek, Colorado, always manages to remember both her pocketbook and her burglar alarm (she owns an antique and Indian turquoise jewelry store), but she's been known to be a little fuzzy on some occasions when she's trying to skip down memory lane with a typically vague Uranus road map. I shall always be impressed by the image of the winter day we were chatting in her shop, and a snow-covered man burst through the door, grabbed Gertrude in a polar-bear hug, and cried out, "Gertrude, you sweet potato. How have you been?"

She bear-hugged him right back, answering, "I've been just fine. It sure is good to see you." Then she turned and said to me, "Linda, I want you to meet one of my *oldest* and *very closest* friends. This is... uh... this is... (and she stared at him, her eyes misting with a haze of Uranus confusion). I believe this is... uh... Jim. No, I mean Richard... I mean Tom... uh, that is, uh... what *is* your name anyway?"

It pays to note that this sort of Aquarian mental fuzziness is the stuff of which genius is made. Refusing to bother with the memorization of nonessential data leaves these men and women free to give birth to startlingly original ideas, uncannily accurate hunches, and a lightning grasp of the really important facts of life. So we shouldn't sniff at or put down the absent-mindedness Aquarians exhibit when their thoughts are wandering out there in the clouds. But Virgos will sniff.

They'll sniff and ask, "How in the world can anyone forget the name of a close friend?" Such lack of mental discipline and breach of good manners horrifies the mentally meticulous, carefully courteous Virgo souls. They simply cannot comprehend such intellectual laziness and disorderliness. Shall we tell them that Aquarian Gertrude Dial *can* remember the exact cost of every one of her hundreds of pieces of turquoise jewelry, the year they were made, by which Indian, and precisely how many stones are set in each — with her eyes closed? Yes, let's tell them. Sometimes Virgos need to be tipped off to such non sequitur Uranus behavior, lest they underestimate the unpredictable shrewdness of the Aquarius intuitive intellect and get caught in their own flytraps. Aquarians don't have the time or patience to concern themselves unduly with etiquette-book-type good manners. They have something more important — good hearts.

Virgos are good-hearted and intelligent too, but more timid, less wonder-fully impetuous in demonstrating it than Aquarians. Whereas Aquarius arrives at a gesture of charity or a brilliant intellectual conclusion instinctive-ly, through some sort of invisible telepathic process — Virgo arrives at the same place through painstaking inquiry and analysis — not instantly, like the Water Bearers, but right on time. Right on *what* time? Did someone ask the time?

VIRGO: It's exactly nineteen minutes before six o'clock P.M.
AQUARIUS: The time? What time is it? Uh, well... it's afternoon, isn't it? No, it must be closer to evening. I just noticed the Sun is setting. By the way, why is it that science refers to the Sun setting and rising, when it's the Earth that revolves around the Sun, and not the Sun around the Earth? I mean, why not call it Earthrise and Earthset instead of Sunrise and Sunset?"

Indeed, why not? That will give Virgo something to chew on and analyze for the next fourteen minutes and three seconds at least! Just another carelessly dropped, brilliant observation from an ordinary, garden-variety

Water Bearer, pouring out questions which are really answers, in typical Uranian fashion.

An Aquarian almost never apologizes for his or her shortcomings or eccentricities, whereas the typical Virgo graciously and appealingly says "I'm sorry" every time he or she commits the most minor offense against tradition or popular ideas of behavior. I once saw a Virgo say "I'm sorry" to his elbow after he carelessly bumped it. It's an endearing trait, to be sure. Male or female Virginians will worry-wrinkle their brains and hearts when they think others disapprove of something they've said or done, but Aquarians of either sex hardly even hear the person who repeats gossip to them, especially when the rumors are about themselves. It's in-one-ear-and-out-the-other to an Aquarian, who possesses the helpful wisdom of knowing it's impossible to please *everybody* — so the Water Bearer does his or her own thing and doesn't try to please *anybody*. They love to be liked, and are puzzled and hurt when friends criticize them, but the reaction doesn't last long. Maybe for two or three moments. Then Aquarius happily trots off, whistling a tune backward . . . and tosses some more wishes into penny wells. (No, I didn't mean pennies into wishing wells. I meant wishes into penny wells. You have to learn the knack of upside-down communication if you're ever going to be able to play tic-tac-toe with these people.)

Aquarians are the most curiosity-motivated Earthlings you'll ever meet. Virgos are too, but the latter are often torn between caution and curiosity. They fret and analyze and want to think things over carefully before they act, which deprives them of spontaneity, a quality they can learn from Aquarius, while Aquarius is learning the much-needed lesson of discrimination from Virgo. One thing they usually agree on (relatively) is how to spend money. *Carefully.* However, Virgo may be somewhat more careful than Aquarius, because Virgo believes that if one is to practice generosity, one must first practice thrift. Rams and Lions and Fish and Archers, who go around flinging cash to friends and strangers alike, upset the Virgins, who will caution the extravagant ones against such careless giving by warning that charity begins at home. If that doesn't work, they'll try again with the warning that, "As you grow more wasteful, you must grow less generous."

I'm a Ram, so I don't agree with that philosophy for an instant, but I only report astrological characteristics, I don't endorse them. Anyway, neither Virgo nor Aquarius is likely to squander money, or spend it with a great deal of looseness on himself or herself. However, influenced by a powerful humanitarian urge, Aquarians do worry more than a little about the future of mankind and womankind, about their brothers and sisters who may go hungry and starve, as the Earth faces possible famine. Virgos will worry right along with them. Worrying is Virgo's speciality, they pride themselves in it, and have refined it to an art. Their sympathies, you see, are similar, but their manner of expressing them is somewhat different. Both are sincerely concerned, but Virgo is decidedly more specific about it.

AQUARIUS: Just think how much less food the children of other countries are fed, compared to our American youngsters. It's sad, and it's shocking.

VIRGO: Yes, it is. I wonder if people realize that *exactly thirty* Biafran children, for example, must survive on the same amount of food eaten by only *one* healthy American child. It's really appalling.

AQUARIUS: Do you know that all the fertilizer we use each year for ornamental purposes in this country alone — such as on golf courses, lawns, and flower gardens, all of which could easily do without it for a short while — would mean the difference between life and death to some nations?

VIRGO: That's entirely correct. We know it, but if only there could be a way to make other people in the United States know that by doing without their fertilizer for ornamental purposes for just *twelve months* there would be enough fertilizer to *more than double* the harvest grains of India, where so many millions of people are literally starving to death.

AQUARIUS: I was thinking, it's so costly to convert grain to meat, and if Americans would . . . . .

VIRGO: Exactly! It takes *twenty pounds* of grain to create just *one* pound of beef. Excuse me, please, for interrupting.

AQUARIUS: Sure, that's okay. Like I was saying, if Americans would eat less meat, this would . . . . .

VIRGO: If Americans ate only *10 percent* less meat for only *fifty-two* weeks, or one year, it would free more than *twelve million* tons of grain for people all over the planet whose bellies are bloated from hunger. How can people realize that, and still enjoy their hamburgers and steak? Please forgive me. I didn't mean to interrupt again. I'm sorry.

AQUARIUS: Don't mention it. Listen, I was wondering . . . what would happen if we didn't eat any meat at all?

VIRGO: I'm glad you asked. What would happen is that not only would the world be a happier place to live in, but we'd all be healthier and live longer. Eating the flesh of our brutally murdered, slaughtered animal brothers is what causes nearly all disease. We'll never heal the pain of starvation on this Earth, or heal our own bodies, if we don't stop eating meat. Oh! do you eat meat? I'm sorry, I didn't mean to be rude.

AQUARIUS: Well, I did eat it, but *now* I . . . . say, are you a vegetarian?

VIRGO: Yes, I am. Would you like a glass of carrot and celery juice? If you've never tasted it, it's really delicious.

Not all Virgins eschew meat, of course (although many do), but before long, this particular, courteous, and informed Virgo will convert the curious Aquarian to a meatless diet, through the wise and inborn sense of human health all Virgos possess. Soon, the Water Bearer will be spreading abroad the exciting new discovery, with typical humanitarian enthusiasm — that you can stay well, look young, extend your life span, and simultaneously help those who are starving — simply by treating your body to fresh fruits and veggies, instead of aging and slowly killing it with hamburgers, hot dogs, roast beef, and steak. Then the Water Bearer will investigate further (like a good Aquarian detective) and joyfully pour out the newly discovered knowledge to Virgo that one can become more spiritually enlightened and psychic, as well as prevent and cure one's illnesses, by periodically observing a three-day grape-juice fast, such as every month or two, for which wisdom Virgo will be cheerfully grateful.

Yes, together these two may rescue old Mother Earth and her misguided Earthlings after all. It's the Aquarian Age of brotherhood and sisterhood, so why shouldn't Virgo join the Uranus club too? Virgo cleverness and clear thinking, combined with Aquarian inventiveness and genius, could be just the magical alchemy we need — plus the innate kindness and concern for others which is characteristic of both Sun Signs. Kindness heals all ills.

☆ ☆ ☆ ☆ ☆ ☆

VIRGO *Woman* AQUARIUS *Man*

. . . once she even had to tell him her name.
"I'm Wendy," she said agitatedly.

He was very sorry. "I say, Wendy," he whispered to her,
"always if you see me forgetting you, just keep
on saying 'I'm Wendy,' and then I'll remember."

Of course this was rather unsatisfactory . . . . . .

The Aquarian male's eccentricity often stops just short of the altar. In his choice of a lifetime mate, he tends to be slightly old-fashioned. Maybe that's because there's room for only one cuckoo in a clock.

Since a Virgo female won't compete in the cuckoo clock olympics, you can see that a mating between these two can work out nicely, since sex, to the virgin, is also only one of several interests. She can probably keep his socks washed and matched, the buttons sewed on his ears, remind him of his name and phone number, be a conscientious mother, an intelligent career woman, and a bright conversationalist with his friends — all at the same time. Their relationship contains all the ingredients of success, but they'll have to work at it. Correction: *she'll* have to work at it.

For one thing, she's too discriminating to flip over all the odd, assorted friends he may bring home at various hours. (I know one Virgo wife whose Aquarian husband expected her to play hostess to a snake wrestler from Pakistan for two weeks while he practiced with his reptile in the basement in preparation for the worldwide Python Tournament Match — and that's a *true* story.) For another thing, she's not a torrid sex symbol. But let's face it, he might not know what to do with Raquel Welch if he had her.

It's easy for a Water Bearer to make mistakes handling a Virgin. She has such a large capacity for patient, sympathetic understanding when he's physically ill or emotionally drained, it's a temptation for him to take advantage of her tender consideration. However, just because she often seems willing to out-geisha a geisha girl, doesn't mean her whole purpose in life is to wait breathlessly for his unpredictable arrival each evening — or to faint quietly in his arms when he deigns to notice her by tossing out something like, "You're okay, buddy!" Her ideas of a full love relationship are not quite that skinny.

The reason she fell in love with him was because he saw rainbows no one else knew were out there, and she thought it would be a mad and marvelous thing to chase them with him (since Virgos are never as stuffy as the old astrological textbooks would have you believe, now that their true ruler, the thunderous Vulcan, is so near to being discovered and identified). The reason he made the great sacrifice of allowing her to wash his socks is because she didn't laugh at his rainbows . . . because she had enough sense to see that they were painted in practical colors. But sensible or not, rainbows are rainbows — and they're pretty scarce around washing machines, dust pans, sweepers, or diaper pails. He may neglect her a bit while he's out looking for a purple cow, inventing a bed that walks over to you when you're tired instead of making you walk over to it — or fiddling around with a dozen or so other fascinating projects which engage his hopscotch mind from time to time. If he refuses to allow her to join him in his eternal search for tomorrow, the glue that first stuck these two together may start peeling around the edges.

To be honest (as Virgos insist on being, however painful), any stalemates they face could be more than half her fault. A Virgin has a way of allowing herself to let duty take over, then silently blaming her man for the dusty corners she's swept herself into through her own choice.

She often trudges wearily far beyond the path of duty, then cries because she's lost in the woods of waiting on his whims. It's her ingrained sense of loyalty to the man she's promised to love, honor, and serve, with or without benefit of clergy. And you know how a Virgo is about promises — a regular nut when it comes to integrity. This girl can also be critical on occasion. In fact, she can be critical on lots of occasions. But she does it so sweetly — and the Aquarian male, when he has a mind to, can split a pretty thin hair himself.

The whole thing is that they're both dreamers at heart, never mind how acute their mental capacities may be or how fixed their habits may become. Theirs are not the wispy images of Pisces or the wild goals of Aries. They have more concrete foundations. But still . . . they'll have to hang on to those dreams if they want to hang on to each other.

The oversolicitous Virgin should encourage her Water Bearer to climb his beanstalks alone once in a while. If she persists in enveloping him in her earthy, exaggerated sense of responsibility, he may turn into a sadistic, bullying dictator (especially if he has a Scorpio, Leo, or Aries Moon Sign or Ascendent), or he'll take an extra hour or two in town every chance he gets. Remember that Aquarius is an Air Sign, and all people born in this element need lots of the stuff to breathe — and to wander around in.

There's a kind of secret surprise to their sexual compatibility. A Virgo woman I know (and this is a true incident), who had been widowed a number of years, became lonely. Normally, a Virgo woman would leave well enough alone, since, as you know by now, Virgos of both sexes are basically loners. But this one had a number of Leo planet positions in her birth chart, and therefore she felt the need of romance in her life. So she joined one of those dating services, and for a couple of years she received several mailings per week from them, each containing a half dozen or so photographs of eligible men, along with an analysis of their characters, professions, hobbies, and so forth. She carefully checked them out — one by one — then turned them all down flat. They weren't quite what she was looking for, you see. *Three hundred and twenty-one* men fell short of her expectations and didn't measure up to her image of what she wanted. Think of it. This is why the Aquarian male, with his infinite variety, has a good chance of hitting the right formula with his discriminating and difficult-to-please woman — and that's the secret surprise of their sexual compatibility!

The sexual side of their love, as with all 6-8 Sun Sign Patterns, can be, therefore, unexpectedly rewarding, but for more unique reasons. His Uranus shock treatment and imaginative suprise maneuvers may spark fires in her she didn't know existed before he came along to try to drive her as wonderfully crazy as he is himself. He won't succeed, of course. She's Earth, he's Air. But trying will be stacks of fun for his curious psyche. What he well might succeed in doing is bringing her sexual fulfillment, however. *One* of his many changeable sexual attitudes may be just right — perfect for her requirements. There's an aura of mystery about a Virgin that intrigues the detective in Aquarius. She can keep him guessing for years about her secret self, and guessing is his favorite pastime. Then too, his airy detachment regarding physical intimacy (although it could conceivably be mixed with some far-out experiments at times) will blend rather nicely with her own cool approach to sexual matters, and probably won't disturb her sense of propriety. (Except for those rare, but possible, far-out things, which could be as innocent as his preferring to make love outside in the backyard, in a tent, where he can smell the grass and count the stars.) Passion won't be lacking in their relationship, because she represents the eighth house of the mysteries of sex to him, therefore she may arouse more desire in him than other girls have done in the past — which will flatter her and make her feel needed. You know how happy being needed makes a Virgo, so it could all work out in an unexpectedly satisfactory way for them both.

Aquarians like to tease, but it would be a mistake for him to tease her to the point of tears too often. Virgins are capable of making a decision to cut out and find another man after long deliberation — and of then acting with icy-cold, almost surgical precision. He might also note that her beautiful, clear eyes need a change of scene now and then, as do his — and her lucid mind needs more stimulation than "What's for dinner tonight, buddy?" Granted, she has her own little drawbacks, like picking fuzz off the blankets on a romantic summer night when fuzz-plucking is the very last thing on his mind — or telling him it's freaky to wear brown socks with black shoes (which won't rattle him in the slightest, since he considers freakiness a virtue, except when someone else's interferes with his own fixed personal habits). She may lean a little heavy on the martyr syndrome and fuss too much over punctuality — or worry and fret if he refuses to take a bath in Vick's salve when he sneezes. But these are all symptoms of a Virgo woman who's being taken too much for granted. Serving dinner late in a sloppy kitchen and neglecting to brush her hair one hundred strokes each night (or their equivalents) are her warning signals of boredom.

When she first met him, he used to watch TV standing on his head and munching Goobers peanuts. Now he walks around on two feet like any ordinary, dull Earthling. As soon as that happens, it's time for the Aquarian man to grab his Virgin and charter a plane for Egypt to ponder the puzzles and master the mysteries of the Great Pyramid of Giza — standing on his head, of course, in the king's chamber or the tomb room.

Then they can stroll along the Nile in the moonlight while she whispers softly, "Darling, I have a fantastic idea. Why don't you build an alarm clock into the head of our bed?" — and he can murmur back, "Let's just keep dreaming like this. Who wants to wake up?" — and she can state, Virgo-like, "But we're *already* awake." Then he can feign surprise, Uranus-like, and exclaim, "No kidding? I thought we were here in our astral bodies."

☆ ☆ ☆ ☆ ☆ ☆

VIRGO *Man* AQUARIUS *Woman*

He tried to argue with Tink. "You know you
can't be my fairy, Tink, because I am a
gentleman and you are a lady."
To this Tink replied in these words, "You silly ass,"
and disappeared into the bathroom.

One thing is fairly certain (though few other things are with these two). Virgo
and Aquarius will not keep a lifetime contract unless there's true love
between them, which can be determined from their Moon Signs and other
mutual planetary exchanges in their horoscopes. The rule seldom applies so
frequently to all 6-8 Sun Sign Patterns as to this one, due to the peculiarities
of their natures. Anything less than real and deep love (such as an Aquarian
Age "friendship," with sex thrown in) will never last. No way. You might
say that's true in general of all couples, born under any stars, but you would
be wrong.

Many Sun Sign combinations will remain together through the years, so
long as they share a mutual respect and a comforting empathy, lacking the
energy, desire, or burning need to pursue a deeper relationship with someone
else and settling for what is acceptably nonabrasive, even if not the "grand
passion" dreamed of in youth. Not so Virgo and Aquarius.

Virgos will cut emotional ties (which make them uncomfortable at best)
if they begin to ravel into nothingness. Only a special and meaningful
romance can cause Virgo to become involved in the first place. If he
discovers he's been wrong, he'll retreat into stubborn silence, refusing to
further share his heart—and, not always, but more often than not, remain so
throughout his life. Since Virgo is basically a loner anyway, why should he go
against his nature again? He considers himself lucky to have escaped the first
marital goof. It's safer to live alone, punctuating his bachelorhood with
occasional, lighthearted affairs—than to risk another failure of a shared life,
which would make him vaguely uneasy, even if it worked out. Virgo singer-
entertainer Maurice Chevalier was a perfect example of this astrological
truth. He continued to be, until the very end of his life, a gentle, subtle sex
symbol to women, and he engaged in several flirtations and brief liaisons over
the years—but he wasn't about to make the same mistake twice and allow
himself to be seduced into another permanent tie, after the first one turned
sour in his youth.

When a Virgo man is disillusioned by love, the disenchantment only proves to his analytic mind and heart that he was right in his instinctive, original suspicion that there is no such thing on this planet as even a *near*-perfect relationship, so why court certain and repeated disappointment? He's wrong, of course, but did you ever try to prove a Virgo wrong?

As for Aquarius, the typical Water Bearer (male or female), once a mistake has been recognized, will have no compunction about continuing the love search, discarding old relationships for new until a reasonable facsimile of the first idealized romance of youth is found (which could have been a grade school idyll or a high school puppy love, so stubbornly clung to that it may be the underlying cause why the first real, adult love affair or marriage didn't work. Who wants to share a mate with a ghost?).

Some — not all — but some Aquarian girls are capable of tossing out some pretty salty verbal sallies when they're trying to shock a Virgo male into noticing them or trying to jostle him out of his constant and annoying emotional Declaration of Independence with some unexpected and quite weird behavior. This being the dawning of the far-out Aquarian Age, with the vibes of the unpredictable Uranus blasting all young people in varying degrees, whatever their Sun Signs, I can't say for certain that he'll blush and be romantically rattled by mild profanity from the sex traditionally imaged as "sugar-and-spice-and-everything-nice" — but in the "olden days" before the sexual revolution, Virgo men tended to look askance at ribald language or unconventional behavior from females. Let us not forget that the symbol of Virgo is still the Virgin, representing an innate essence of his inner nature which even the changing times can't completely cancel.

Now, don't jump to the conclusion that I'm accusing the Aquarian girl of being vulgar. I am not. It's just that she's usually more outspoken and frank than her other Sun Sign sisters (except Sagittarius). Not only more outspoken and frank, but also more independent, unconventional, unpredictable, unusual — and just plain more cuckoo and kooky. As an example, the older generation can use cigar-smoking Aquarian, Tallulah Bankhead, who liked to be interviewed by reporters, stark nude in her birthday suit, to test their shock threshold — never mind that her daddy was Congressional Speaker of the House. The younger generation can use Helen Gurley Brown, the sweet-faced, soft-spoken Aquarian female who zigzagged *Cosmopolitan* magazine from red-ink losses into black-ink profits by featuring the first nude male centerfold. Or you might consider one of my very favorite Aquarians, Mia Farrow, a freckled, fresh-faced, and clean-scrubbed Water Bearer, who resembles a faerie-tale princess — the actress who projected such girlish naivete with Frank Sinatra . . . . . . then cut her beautiful long tresses, when Sinatra made her angry, to the same length the nuns used to shear theirs before they entered the convent, causing her to more resemble a sad Easter egg than a princess . . . . then grew her hair long and shining again . . . . was acclaimed for her acting in several pictures . . . . . . was raped by Satan (on film, of course) in *Rosemary's Baby* .... after which she gave birth to twins by composer Andre Previn, sans wedlock (ignoring, Aquarian-like, society's hypocritical standards), marrying him later, almost as a casual afterthought.

But Mia's Uranian intuition appears to have been merrily in tune, for theirs has been, thus far, an uncommonly happy marriage, overflowing with plump, jolly youngsters ...... with everyone seeming to be having a rollicking good time, amid lots of genuine love and laughter.

Aquarian women care nothing for public opinion or gossip, only for their own inner measurement of honesty and decency. To live their lives by the dictates of society would be, to all Water Bearers, the height of hypocrisy. The degree of the strain of Uranian unconventionality varies, but you won't have to look far to find it running through the personal lives of even the most poised, quiet, and conventional-*appearing* Aquarian females. The neighbors are always shocked, along with the relatives, when a quiet, apparently docile Aquarian wife suddenly and unexpectedly leaves her husband to become a dancer, a painter, an actress — or to open a health spa in Siam.

There's this funny thing about a Virgo man. Having been born as what astrology terms one of the "human Sun Signs" (symbolized by the "human" Virgin), he has no animal instinct to guide him when he falls in love, so at first, belonging as he does to the Earth Element, he draws back into the cool woods of his deeper self, until he's had time to analyze these new feelings. It might help the woman who loves him to know that Virgos tend to *fear* and *mistrust* what they most *desire*.

There's this funny thing about an Aquarian woman. Having been born as what astrology terms one of the "human Sun Signs" (symbolized by the "human" Water Bearer), she has no animal instinct to guide her when she falls in love, so at first, belonging as she does to the Air Element, she draws back into the clouds of her deeper self, until she's had time to analyze these new feelings. It might help the man who loves her to know that Aquarians tend to *fear* and *mistrust* what they most *desire*. You can see that this pair is well matched in some respects, at least.

Neither is noted for being intensely matrimony-minded. There are more singles of both sexes among these two Sun Signs than among those born under the influence of the other ten stars. However, once Aquarians have carefully selected the right mate and decided to marry, they usually rush right in, headlong and heart first, which is seldom the Virgo marital pattern — so their romantic timing may be slightly off, and they'll have to synchronize their idiosyncrasies to make it to the altar. Otherwise, they'll just have to share the same sleeping bag, hang up one of those posters that says TARZAN AND JANE ARE LIVING IN SIN, and laugh it off as a fun thing. That is, they'll try to laugh it off, but neither Virgo nor Aquarius is cut out for hilarity when it comes to the serious matter of love — or even the more serious matter (to them) of sharing their sleeping bags, hair brushes, bank accounts, vitamins, wheat germ, and sweet solitude.

Women's lib aside, it has been wisely and correctly stated that a woman's tenderness is scarce in men, but when a man *is* tender, he's more tender than a woman ever could be. In either an illicit or a legally and socially sanctioned union, this is doubly true of the Virgo male. (I didn't say spiritually sanctioned, because all real love is spiritually sanctioned, whether wedlocked or unwedlocked.) This man's tenderness can be almost a tangible thing, touching upon every area of his relationship with the woman he loves temporarily or permanently, including sexual expression. Lots of women would find this a quality to treasure, a precious and comforting trait in a lover or husband. But the Aquarian girl will accept tenderness from a mate in their physical consummation of love with pleasure and gratitude only for a certain length of time. Then she needs a change. She prefers every experience to be fleeting, not too lingering, so she can savor its joy, then pass on to the next experience.

Some experiences, of course, are worth repeating a number of times, and tenderness is undoubtedly among them, but she may expect to share with him this sort of lovemaking only periodically, replaced from time to time with other sexual experiments — from a primal passion or the abandonment of sensual surrender — all the way to the delicate and controlled oriental Tantra method of sexual-spiritual union. (I'm not referring to the degrading aspect of Tantra taught by some lustful gurus, who advocate switching mates if one's partner lacks the proper "aesthetic qualities" for such sensitive coupling, but the pure and true form of Tantra, before it was distorted by these misled and promiscuous disciples.) To keep his Aquarian lady interested and seducible (since the truth of the matter is that she'd just as soon take a hike in the woods and sing along with a chipmunk as indulge in sex merely for the sake of sex anyway), he'll have to remember her basic need for change in all activities. The problem is that the typical Virgo male finds wild caveman abandon-ment — or any kind of abandonment requiring surrender of the total self — difficult to master.

The Aquarian woman shouldn't expect her Virgo man to alternate lovemaking techniques every other night. Every other month or so consti-tutes about the limit of his ability to cope, lest his gentleness become crankiness. She should also never forget that a virginal-type, feminine purity and modesty, in or out of bed, is more likely to turn him on (allowing him to play the alternating roles of jungle man and Tantra guru) than brash expletives, like Tink's "You silly ass!" and similar endearments. Swearing and other freaky habits — like turning cartwheels while she's watching the weather report on radio (that's what I said) are definitely not designed to help him retain his tenderness charisma, which is at the same time, both his most endearing and his most enduring romantic charm — as well as the one she'll eventually find more satisfying and fulfilling herself after they've exper-ienced all the others (including possibly a few tentative and lonely experi-ments with celibacy).

Because all Aquarians are light years ahead of the world, and whole paragraphs ahead of normal discussions and average conversations, she may throw him off balance when he questions her about a small speck he noticed on a cup and saucer she just washed, and she skips merrily ahead with an instant return query about spacecraft. (The word "saucer." That's what tripped her out, you see.) Although it *seems* Aquarians are seeking information when they query, what they're actually doing is trying to discover what *you* know. That's why she always answers his questions with another question. She's an expert at the fine art of sneaky Socratic dialogue (Socrates was definitely an Aquarian), and she may use this disconcerting talent when they've had a quarrel, and have agreed to separate for a time . . . believing, as she uses it, that her estranged Virgo can't see through her game to her real intent. (She hasn't studied her Sun Signs. Virgo can see through anything.)

For example, while they're apart, each thinking it over and trying to decide between a clean, final break and a possible reconciliation attempt — she may write him a tentative letter, closing with one of her clever Socratic questions:

"I hope that, whatever happens, we can still be friends. We *will* always be friends, won't we, darling ?"

Surely a Virgo man is alert enough to recognize that sly Aquarian query for what it really is — a Uranus test of romantic worthiness. If he truly wants her back, he should sock her with her own Socratic subtlety (firmly) when he answers her letter, writing:

"No, we cannot still be friends. Definitely not. It has to be love between us, or nothing. You already know that. You were just trying to find out if I knew it too — *weren't* you, darling ?"

Do you grasp the strategy now ? Just answer her question with another question, the way she does. It will drive her crackers, and teach her a lesson. If she truly wants him back too, she'll call on the phone and tell him he's not such a "silly ass" after all, then dash over to him with a bottle of vitamin C for his sniffles, without stopping to play with any chipmunks along the way. She is being clocked — and this is no time to be late again.

VIRGO

Earth — Mutable — Negative
Ruled by Mercury (also by
  the Planet Vulcan)
Symbol: The Virgin
Night Forces — Feminine

PISCES

Water — Mutable — Negative
Ruled by Neptune
Symbol: The Fish
Night Forces — Feminine

The **VIRGO-PISCES** *Relationship*

..... no one can fly unless the fairy dust
has been sprinkled on him.

*T*he Fish were born under a double feminine influence — the feminine Sun Sign of Pisces, ruled by the also feminine planet, Neptune. The Virgins were likewise born under a double feminine influence (but with a slight difference, as we shall see) for Virgo is also a feminine Sun Sign, whose true ruler is the equally feminine (and powerful) planet, Vulcan — not yet discovered, but soon to be (see Virgo-Virgo chapter). Meanwhile, Virgo is foster-guided by Mercury, a *masculine* planet. Right away, you can see that the Virgins are one up on the Fish, in the sense of active or positive (i.e.: masculine) initiation. Not that Pisceans think they're missing anything, however. All Fish consider active initiation an energy-depleting and tiresome thing at best, and they'd just as soon not be burdened with the astrological necessity to "actively initiate" anything in particular. So they're quite content to leave Mercury's masculine vibes to Virgo.

Still, the Pisceans must keep in mind that Virgos can call on *both* the masculine (Mercury) or feminine (Vulcan) weapons, at will — so they can be tricky. (Admittedly, Pisceans can be more than a little tricky themselves, considering the evasive and elusive influence of Neptune.) The reason I referred to "weapons" is because the Fish and the Virgin represent the 7-7 Sun Sign Pattern of opposition. It's not so much that Pisces and Virgo are at war with one another, but that each of them possesses certain qualities the other (if only on a subconscious level) lacks, envies and would like to acquire.

To begin with, Virgos possess the talent of mental card indexing. They can sort out, efficiently file and quickly locate, when necessary, detailed data on all manner of people, situations, worries, problems and frustrations. Everything is kept neatly recorded. Virgo checkbooks are nearly always properly balanced (allowing for the exceptions that prove the rule, such as those Virgins who have Pisces Moon Signs or Ascendents). Virgo payments of bills are usually made when due, they arrive at work on time, or a few minutes early, obtain the proper number of hours of sleep per night (when they aren't constipated or have insomnia from fretting), write their courteous bread-and-butter letters promptly, keep their clothing and personal possessions in a more or less systematic order — and make sure their cars, their teeth and so on are checked regularly for any possible deficiency. They can spot ring-around-the-collar a block away, and they tend to carefully measure both the bleach and the detergent in the washing machine, therefore avoid using too much or too little. They seldom get parking or speeding tickets — and never spend excessive amounts of energy in counter-productive activities such as daydreaming, wool gathering, relaxing and taking it easy. (Neither are they famous for spending excessive amounts of money.)

The typical Piscean is the veritable opposite of all the foregoing. As far as precise order is concerned, most Piscean personal belongings resemble a Picasso abstract. As for the neatness of their dwellings, whether they live in one room, an apartment, a house or a mansion, the residence of your typical Fish is about as neat as a Salvador Dali canvas — utter chaos. A lovely, charming and rainbow-streaked mess of total confusion. But only in relation to tidiness. Beyond that, there's always a contradictory, yet unmistakable feeling of peace and quiet which is hypnotically inviting, in the very midst of Piscean disorder. Now and then, of course, you'll run across a Neptune person like a male bachelor Fish I know in Colorado, whose house is always ready for the photographers from *Better Homes and Gardens* to pop in the door unannounced — but *he* has several planets in Virgo, and a Virgo Ascendent. Never mind Piscean Dick Johnson, he's one of those rare exceptions; astrology still claims that *most* Pisces homes are like a tangle of colored ribbons — a crazy crochet of warmth, coziness, tea and sympathy, and casual disorder, not carefully dusted in each and every nook and cranny. Who cares about a few specks of dust in nooks and crannies? (The Fish have lots of odd sized secrets tucked away in their nooks and crannies, and may not want them disturbed by Virgo's feather duster.)

Actually, all those Virgo qualities mentioned in the last paragraph are not habits the Fish would care to acquire — *consciously*. Deep down inside, however, they're aware they could benefit by a little less daydreaming and relaxation, a little less procrastination, a little more mental tidiness and emotional neatness — whether involving their cars, their teeth, their check-books or what-have-you. They just don't like to admit it. Nevertheless, they do sense it, which is why the Fish are fascinated by Virgo. That is, they're fascinated by the opposite sex of their opposite Sun Sign of Virgo, but they may feel a little nervous around Virgins of the *same* sex, who seem to project an unspoken challenge of competition with Pisces. There's nothing in this world that makes a Pisces man or woman more fidgety and uncomfortable than to feel that he (or she) is expected, in some manner, to compete with someone. That's an activity *they* happen to feel is "counter-productive," as well as time and energy wasting — competing. Because they were both born under Mutable Signs, Virgo and Pisces often surprise each other by managing to communicate very well together, even when they are competing, despite the vast differences in their polarized personalities. Also, they're both somewhat reticent and reserved with strangers.

It wouldn't be fair (what is Libra doing in here ? Maybe to help us make peace between the Fish and the Virgin ?). As I was saying, it wouldn't be fair (Libra nods, with a beaming smile of approval) to fail to point out that the *Fish* also possess qualities the *Virgins* would benefit by imitating — and it's a safe bet that Virgo, unlike Pisces, is aware of this on a conscious level. Virgo minds are so acute and alert, there's almost nothing left down below in the subconscious. They drag all their thoughts and feelings up from the basement, so to speak, and check them over periodically, to make sure there's nothing being overlooked, neglected or mislaid. So the Virgins are usually painfully conscious, not only of a vague envy they feel around Pisces, but also what *causes* it. It's the Neptune talent for daydreaming and wishing, then making those dreams and wishes *happen* by some sort of strange Neptunian alchemy — from causing a parking space to magically appear at the mall, to becoming happily mated or winning the Nobel Peace Prize, sometimes the Pulitzer. Virgo frowns. Well, but how do they *do* it ? Sprinkle faerie dust on themselves ?

Your guess is right on the button, Virgo — as your estimates frequently are (which the good Lord knows they *should* be, the way you analyze and re-analyze all possibilities before you hazard a guess). The Fish cause their dreams and wishes to manifest into reality by the simple process of continual-ly affirming their faith in the essential goodness of the "all" (the mass, collective subconscious) and in the eternal wisdom of uncomplaining pa-tience. (Virgos are not slouches in the area of patience patterns either, but one wouldn't call it "uncomplaining" patience.) I hate to tell you this, Virgo, but they do it by not fussing and worrying their dreams and wishes into fading away into the shadows of futility. As a matter of fact, these Neptune traits just happen to be the chief ingredients of faerie dust.

Virgo is admiring and interested, but still puzzled. Where may one buy a tad or so of this faerie dust, and is it frightfully expensive ? You just goofed it. Sorry. I know how you hate to goof. But you did. First off, one is either *born* with a supply of faerie dust, or one is *not*. If you are (as Pisces is) you're fortunate — but then it can be unfortunate too, because in possessing an invisible supply of faerie dust, one sends out a certain color in one's aura that's easily detected by the baddies and nasty little entities in the astral, and which invites them to plague you with trillions of all sorts of problems to test your worth. They also keep trying to steal your faerie dust from you. It's the ancient metaphysical law of Light attracting darkness, you see. Second off, if you *weren't* born with it, obviously you'll have to manage to somehow acquire a dram or so of it, at least for emergencies — and the surest way to insure that you *won't* find any to obtain, is to ask the price and worry about the expense. As soon as you start that picky-picky money mantra, the stuff disappears, faerie dust being very contrary (almost as much so as faeries themselves, who can be simply unbelievably contrary when they're in a mood for mischief). The best way to obtain faerie dust is through a close association with a Pisces friend, business associate, relative, lover or mate.

Now, I must be honest and perfectly factual (or Virgo would never forgive me) by confessing that, although the Fish are amply supplied with magical faerie dust, and although they do usually refuse to allow their dreams and wishes to "fade into the shadows of futility," they are at the same time occasionally guilty of submitting to nameless apprehensions, fears and timidity. Don't blame me for confusing you, Virgo. Pisces is a Sun Sign of duality, you know. Oh, one of *those* ? Yes. One of those. Pisces is represented by *two* Fish, not one — and worse yet, the symbolic Fish are swimming in different directions. It's not at all easy to be pulled in different directions simultaneously. It would drive you, as a Virgin, absolutely crackers to be tugged in two directions at once. You wouldn't know which route to analyze first. So you really should give all the Fish you know your sympathy. Goodness knows they're always passing out sympathy to everyone else in such a constant flow, they can certainly use some themselves, to pick up their own spirits now and then. In short, and I hope Virgo forgives our slang, duality can be a drag.

Take, for example, the Piscean sensitivity. The Fish are startlingly perceptive and precognitive. They can read your mind and your heart before you say a single word. Whether you're a friend or a stranger. They pick up your vibes and soak up the emotional joys and sorrows, elations and depressions of everyone within a few feet of them. Taken in one direction, that's a blessing. It makes the Fish compassionate, wise, understanding and psychic. Taken in a different direction, it can be a curse. The ability to be sensitive to the thoughts and feelings of others, whether in the same room or at a distance, brings with it a constant danger, for a sound astrological reason. The gift of being "sensitive" or psychic, is never present (including *all* Sun Sign people who have sensitive planetary configurations in their birth charts) without being accompanied by the twin trait of a vivid imagination — and the potential of exceptional creativity. Even though the latter isn't encouraged in childhood, therefore later grows dormant, it is infallibly latent in the Piscean personality (or in the personality of any sensitive person of whatever Sun Sign). And so the sensitive Fish must always be on guard against allowing the strong imaginations and creative talents they all possess to some degree (whether they're aware of possessing them or not) to distort the "images" they are constantly receiving from others, to cloud their impressions with possibly misleading negative tones and shades. Imagination, like fire, is a "good servant, but a bad master."

There's little chance of Virgo permitting such distortion. Therefore, the Virgins can be very helpful to Pisces, and the opportunity to be helpful is enticing to Virgos, being as it is, their main mission on Earth. They can courteously and gently point out to the Piscean where a certain image, impression or idea may not be quite as negative as the Fish first thought, assisting the Neptune-ruled to bring out all the bright colors of their ideas, after retouching the negative with reality (a reality that's nearly always more hopeful than might appear on the surface). By so doing, the most marvelous thing occurs to Virgos! They come away from a comforting, solacing couch session with a Fish (who needs comfort at times desperately, the same kind Pisces so freely and humbly gives to others) feeling rather happy and cheerful and good inside. Then suddenly, in the middle of the night, Virgo notices that his (or her) hands seem gritty. In fact, the Virgin's whole body, from head to toe, feels . . . well, not quite squeaky-clean and shiny. How could that be, when the nightly shower was taken before climbing in bed? So Virgo hastens into the bathroom to wash his (or her) hands, and lo and behold! A miracle has occurred. The Virgin's hands are covered with a glittery, sparkling, fine substance, like little starflakes. Faerie dust. It rubbed off from the Fish. And it didn't cost a penny. Now Virgo can become a touch magical too, like Pisces — and won't it be grand fun? All because of giving to a sad and lonely Fish just a bit of the same kind of compassion and genuinely interested "listening" the Fish gives so generously to others, and needs so very much himself (or herself). That's how you obtain faerie dust. They don't sell it in stores.

Now that Virgo has his (or her) tad of the mysterious Neptune elixir, it must be remembered what will inevitably happen next. Just as with Pisces, the Virgo aura will instantly be streaked with that strange color which signals to the imps of the astral that here is one who hides a secret stash of faerie dust — and before long, Virgo will face the Piscean kind of testing, becoming, like the Fish, entangled in the skeins of all the various heartaches, intrigues and complex problems of friends, loved ones, neighbors and strangers. Glorious! Pisces could give Virgo no gift more welcome than this. Just *imagine*. A hundred new worries to analyze and solve efficiently, as only a

Virgin can. You see? Virgo has already delightedly danced over to the desk, and is promptly, as usual, writing a bread-and-butter thank you note to Pisces.

Dear Fish . . . . thank you so much for the enchanting F.D. Are you sure I don't owe you something for it? You really musn't give everything away, as you do. It's generous and sweet of you, but remember that "a penny saved is a penny earned." At any rate, I just had to express how grateful I am for all the new problems you've allowed me to share with you and your friends. No one has given me such a marvelous gift since the Christmas I was three years old, and Santa left a huge Tinker Toy set under the tree! It took positively months to figure out exactly where all the pieces fit together. That was the happiest time of my whole life, until now. I do hope you're feeling better since our little talk. I'll drop by in a few days, to see if there's anything you need, any way I might be of further help. Thank you again.

> *Very truly yours*
> *The Virgin*

P.S. I just realized how exciting it was, back then, when I believed in Santa Claus, the Easter Bunny, druids, leprechauns, elves and wishing stars. You've made me remember my old dreams, even made me realize they might actually be worth something, even after all these years. Maybe I'll clean them up a bit. They must have accumulated a dreadful amount of dust all this time in the basement. I hope none of them are broken. Of course, I suppose I could glue them carefully. Do you suppose anyone will notice? I must close now, because it's nearly two and one half minutes till midnight, and I set the alarm for five a.m. since I have to be at work by eight in the morning. Do you know what I might do? I just might take the day off tomorrow, relax and dig into some books I've been wanting to read. My God. That F.D. is powerful. Really quite intoxicating. It's probably healthy too. I'll bet it even aids regularity, and may eliminate my nervous indigestion. You simply must let me pay you something for it, or at least allow me to make a contribution to your favorite charity. I'd feel terribly guilty about accepting it otherwise.

☆ ☆ ☆ ☆ ☆ ☆

VIRGO *Woman* PISCES *Man*

◆◄◆►◆

He would keep no girl in the Neverland
against her will.

I know this sounds weird and unorthodox, but the first thing this man and woman may discuss together when they're initially attracted to each other is . . . well, it's not very romantic, but they may become involved in a thrilling conversation about their feet.

It's an interest they have in common. Their foot problems, their favorite podiatrist and the difficulty of finding the right shoes. At least one or two, if not all three of these topics. Pisces, you see, "rules" the feet. Every Sun Sign is aligned to a particular part of the body, since men and women were formed in the image of our co-Creators (which is, by the way, why medical astrology is so unerringly accurate and helpful, as Hippocrates wisely knew). Because Pisces is associated with the feet, shoes and foot idiosyncrasies are intriguing subjects to the typical Fish. Likewise to the typical Virgin. Her concern with feet and shoes is seeded by several causes, one of them being that her true ruling planet, Vulcan, is the "lame goddess of Thunder" (so called for reasons there isn't space in this book to explain, but they'll be covered in a forthcoming one). Also, most Virgo women have a slight obsession about *practical* shoes.

If you've ever wondered what ever happened to "the little shoemaker" or the cobbler on the corner, he's still there, tapping away with his last and tiny hammer, taking care of his Pisces and Virgo customers (and a smattering of Cappies). Virgos ordinarily do not purchase their footwear casually. They expect the shoes on which they spend their perfectly good money to be serviceable and worthy of repeated repair, not the kind of fragile, fancy booties that fall apart after you've worn them only a decade or so. There are, naturally, some female Virgins who escape this odd Virgo quirk, but most of them have what amounts to a fetish about footwear. They may scrimp and save on clothing, furniture, pleasure, recreation and luxuries, but when it comes to health food, medicine, toilet paper and shoes, they're amazing. Their bathroom cupboards overflow with the softest brand of squeezable toilet tissue (which some of them buy by the case) and Ivory soap galore. The shelves of their medicine chests groan with a drug store-sized inventory of bottles and jars and bandages, their kitchen cabinets are well stocked with vitamins, their refrigerators contain so many boxes of alfalfa and wheat sprouts, they resemble a frozen greenhouse—and their bedroom closets frequently are bulging with shoes. It's not that they're extravagant (Virgo *extravagant?* Heaven forbid!) and it's not that they *buy* that many pairs of shoes, but they *save* them till they accumulate alarmingly, have them repaired and keep them for their children and grandchildren, whose feet they measure carefully every year in the hope their foot size ends up the right size to wear the hand-me-downs.

A Virgo girl will be delighted that the Pisces man is so interested in listening to her Cinderella slipper stories. As for him, he'll be likewise delighted that she's so clearly fascinated by his own foot fables. The Fish is so kind about listening to everyone else, it's a rare treat to discover someone who enjoys listening to *him* for a change. He'll snuggle closer (I told you at the beginning of this chapter that the Neptune-ruled can be sneaky and devious. He has romantic strategies in mind related to more than her toes) . . . so, he'll snuggle closer, unobtrusively, and tell her how, when he walks on the beach barefoot, even in summer, he always has to come in afterwards and warm his feet before a fire, because they're so chilled . . . how humiliated he is sometimes, because his feet are so uncommonly large (or so uncommonly small, for a man—Pisces feet are either huge or tiny, never in-between). She'll sympathize with him charmingly. Then he'll tell her about the time he earned money to pay for his college tuition by posing anonymously as a male model for Dr. Scholl's bunion pads . . . . she'll laugh her silvery bell Mercury laugh . . . he'll move a little nearer, encouraged by the sudden sparkle in her clear Virgo eyes, and confide that his feet always get cold at night, so that sometimes he has to get up out of bed to look for a hot water bottle as a foot warmer, or plug in the heating pad. She murmurs gently, visibly trembling, that it's the same way with her too, sometimes at night, no matter how many blankets and quilts she's sleeping under. "It's a common complaint, I suppose," he says, his voice very gentle and soft now, "of people who sleep alone. I'm sure lovers never have that problem. They keep each other warm all night . . . all over."

That will usually win the first battle for the Fish. Not even a detached, cool Virgin can resist melting at *those* words, despite all her inhibitions and reservations. But only, of course, if by then she's known him and secretly wanted him for a respectable length of time. Never on the first night. Well, almost never. The lure of the male Fish can be unexpectedly seductive, especially to a woman born under the opposite Sun Sign. Their opposed natal Suns do exactly what they are meant to do—attract, in the manner of bar magnets. Buy a pair at any hardware store, try them and see. When you hold them with their two positive or their two negative sides facing, try as you will, they won't go together. Ah! But when you reverse one, so the two bar magnets are facing in polarity or opposition (negative-positive) they join and come together with a powerful rush, no matter how hard you try to prevent it. Actually, buying a pair of bar magnets and experimenting with them in her spare time (of which she has little enough usually) would be a very practical investment for a Virgin in love with a male Fish. It will be a dramatic demonstration to her of what she can most likely expect when she's alone with this man, and they drift into a conversation about feet. It won't protect her from the inevitable, once he's already wrapped himself around her heart—but at least she'll be prepared, and being prepared is only common sense. (Virgos are very big on being sensible.)

The sexual empathy between the Virgin and the Fish is empathetic indeed. These two are natural lovers. Even with an adverse Luminary aspect between their nativities, they certainly won't turn each other off. They'll be more likely to discover that they quarrel about everything *but* lovemaking. Polarity chemistry is potent and powerful. The sheer delicacy of the sexual approach of the Pisces man will cause his Virgo woman to respond fully, as she would never respond to a more aggressive lover or husband. There's something tender and poetic about his Neptune desire that calls irresistibly to the ethereal in her Virgin heart, while her Virgo quietness, combined with her earthy passion and Vulcan's pounding thunder, both surprises and excites the Piscean man, arousing all his secret longings to find, through sexual union with the woman he loves, some beautiful dream of ecstasy he faintly remembers . . . . that's always haunted him, like a familiar melody from the past. They are both instinctively unselfish in making love, so that their sexual blending is seldom a demanding thing, but a gentle giving that's mutually fulfilling and peaceful, supported by a genuine affection and a willingness to consider each other's personal needs concerning intimacy and the physical expression of the depth of their love.

These two may not, however, be quite so empathetic and blissful when it comes to sharing, not just their hearts and bodies—but their money. He likes to share his, she may be reluctant to share hers. Now and then you'll discover a rare stingy Fish or an overly generous, extravagant Virgo, who looks upon finances casually—but the number of these you find won't be staggering. It's possible that she may think he's impossibly immature and careless concerning material matters, and she won't hesitate to criticize him when she believes he's been improvident by wasting cash on ventures that lack, in her opinion, a sound foundation—or simply giving money away to friends, relatives and neighbors who may never be able to pay him back. (He doesn't expect them to, really. Fish seldom loan money—they give it.) He may privately feel that she's overly concerned about money, and her constant worrying about it, nagging him (and herself) about financial security may cause the soft shine in her eyes to disappear for him, her voice will sound less like a silvery chime, more like the tolling of warning bells of a restriction of his freedom to be himself.

The most noticeable flaw in an otherwise nearly perfect Virgo woman is her tendency to be unduly critical, and to nag the man she loves. This is most unfortunate, since the one flaw in the feminine sex this man truly can't bear — is nagging. He's frustrated when he feels he's failed her in some way — in any way at all — and he may be tempted to either retaliate by becoming snappy and cross, constantly irritable — or escape the pain in other ways. Like falling into the habit of stopping in at a bar on the way home, telling his foot fables and other stories to strange but sympathetic ears, then swimming home, because he's not quite steady on his feet. Or he could turn to the dangerous, deadly escape of drugs. Perhaps retreat into daydreams, until the intimate communication they once shared fades into boredom and the silence between them grows into a high wall of mutual bitterness and resentment.

Since the Virgo girl so values common sense, it would be sensible for her to decide, before it's too late, that she fell in love with this man because he had a magic way about him of taking her sailing off to his magical, secret Neverlands, where all kinds of dreams she'd love to dream if she thought they might possibly come true — *do* come true. Or at least, he makes them seem almost as if they really *might*, if they both believed hard enough and long enough. It's not very sensible, she must admit, to unthinkingly, without meaning to do so, kill the very enchantment in him that once moved her to tears of tenderness. Neither the loss of money nor the accumulation of it is worth that. Too much criticism can rob the male Fish of self-respect, always a sad thing to do to Pisces. She should remember all the wonders about him that first made her love him, and forget the rest.

As for him, he'll have to realize that keeping secrets from her can hurt this woman deeply. Earth Signs feel everything deeply. Sometimes, Pisces men keep secrets for no particular reason, except that they get into the habit of doing so with strangers. But she's not a stranger. She's the girl with the clear, sparkling eyes, who understands things about him no one else ever did — and who listens to him with affectionate concern, when no one else will. Most of her worrying is because she wants him to be happy. Besides, when he faces the truth, the Fish must agree that he could benefit from a little looking after by a Virgin who really cares about his future and his peace of mind. He's not very talented at looking after his own best interests, when you really analyze it. It causes her great inner anxiety when a relationship seems to have no clearly defined, purposeful goal. It wouldn't hurt for him to graciously allow her to guide the ship for a while, until they've passed the storms that threaten. Later, she'll be happy to join him in pursuit of Neptune's mysteries and beckoning waterfalls, when she feels safe and secure — but she'd rather they paid cash for their tickets, instead of charging them on a credit card, and going deeper into debt.

Because both Virgo and Pisces are Mutable, they'll enjoy traveling together, talking together — and in general, they'll communicate very well. The chances are they'll talk over their troubles and disagreements, analyze them and find a solution. When everything is smooth and happy between them again, and the old trust has returned, they'll exchange gifts on the anniversary of their first toe talk. She'll give him a pair of sentimental sandals, for walking on the beach in wet sand . . . and he'll give her a couple of bar magnets in a tiny box . . . to remind her, in his subtle Neptune way, of what she'll be missing if he should ever leave her because she feels so restless and unhappy in Neverland with him that it breaks his heart, and he'd rather go away than make her unhappy. She'll probably get the message, as soon as she opens his small gift. After all, she is a Virgo. Her mind is alert and quick. And she's sensible. She knows that a heating pad under the quilts and blankets is a lonely substitute for four warm and cozy feet — and twenty intimate toes, that have grown so close over the years, only a touch is needed . . . . to communicate any wish.

☆ ☆ ☆ ☆ ☆ ☆

VIRGO *Man* PISCES *Woman*

───◄●►───

"Peter," she asked, trying to speak firmly, "what are your exact feelings for me ?"

"Those of a devoted son, Wendy."

"I thought so," she said, and went and sat by herself at the extreme corner of the room.

It's probably a little sneaky of astrology to give away some of Neptune's secrets, but if it helps the Virgo man understand his girl Fish better, they'll both be glad of it someday. You see, this woman who behaves most of the time like an angelic little girl who's afraid of being scolded — and is ever so grateful for the smallest kindness, this woman who's so timid and tentative, so uncertain and dependent, needing his strong shoulder to lean against — knows exactly what she's doing when she thus make-believes. (Pisceans are all quite expert at make-believe, you know.) She is Eve personified, Nature's gift to the male sex, wrapped in an appealingly feminine package, tied with delicate pink ribbons.

She had an excellent reason for moving to the extreme corner of the room in reaction to his detached reply to her question. There's always a method to her madness, a clever strategy behind her sensitivity. We'll explain her secret reason for sitting in the corner like Little Miss Muffet later. It's important to first give the unsuspecting Virgo man some idea what's inside this dainty package, tied with the delicate pink ribbons. That way, he'll be better able to cope with her corner craftiness.

Twelve women. That's what he can expect to find when he cautiously (Virgos do everything cautiously) unties those ribbons. This sweet, deceptively submissive lady is a whole harem, all by herself. If he's been memorizing his astrology lessons, like a proper Virgo, he'll remember that her Pisces Sun Sign carries the seeds of all the other eleven signs around the karmic wheel. That's why she's such an exquisitely fine listener (which, by the way, is how she first enticed him). She listens well because she's wise. She knows. She's been there — karmically — and since all Pisceans are usually in rather intimate contact with their subconscious selves, she remembers well many things she hasn't even come close to actually experiencing in this *present* incarnation. So naturally, she's a good listener. Why shouldn't she be? There's not a single thing anyone on this Earth can nervously confide in her or confess to her sympathetic ear that will cause her to so much as flicker an eyelash in surprise. If one of her twelve karmic memories doesn't comprehend, a couple of the other eleven will.

Pisces men are much the same, but since this is a double feminine influence (feminine Sun Sign, feminine ruler, Neptune) the female of the species is definitely trickier than the male in the technique of employing feminine wiles. That's just good, sound astrological common sense. A Virgo man can surely recognize that, after a bit of meditation. He should also be able to see why it is that she confuses his orderly mind and emotions with her chameleon charisma. When she (rarely) becomes aggressive, and unnaturally (for her) spoiled and demanding, shocking him out of his Earth Sign complacency, it's the small sliver of Aries in her. When she's occasionally being stubborn, and won't budge an inch (even more stubborn than he is, and that's pretty stubborn) it's the strain of Taurus in her nature that's causing her mind to be temporarily set in cement, firmly rejecting all his considerable powers of gentle persuasion. Then, when he finally manages to chip away the cement with his quiet Virgo charm, she turns as flighty as a Gemini butterfly, so changeable, she makes swift, wing-footed Mercury himself (Virgo's foster ruler) seem slow and deliberate. Then she weeps sadly, her tears turning without warning to rich, warm laughter — first snapping at him, then fussing over him like a mother hen — decidedly moody. She's only revealing the Moon Maiden in her soul. (It was likely during her Cancerian phase that he first began thinking of her maternally, so his answer of "a devoted son" to her query about his feelings for her can be excused.)

Also, there was that strange week when she arrogantly expected him to wait on her hand and foot because she'd sprained her ankle, and was too proud to admit the very real pain she was feeling. (She was under her Lioness influence.) Then once, for a whole month, she was simultaneously so humble and courteous, yet so critical of his every word, he felt vaguely as though he was gazing into a mirror of himself. He was. It happened to be the Virgo scene of her twelve-act drama.

When he drove over to show her, with shy pride, the old Model T Ford he'd fixed up like new, after long, weary hours of tinkering with the engine and body work, she couldn't decide if she adored it or hated it. First she wanted to go for a ride in it, then she said it depressed her because it was black, and he should have painted it some cheerful color, like maybe mauve, to match her new dress. (She was feeling a brief breath of her Libra balancing act.) Once when he fell asleep and forgot to call her when he promised he would, she got an unlisted number the next day, and refused to answer her doorbell. She was giving him a small Scorpion sting of retaliation for breaking his word to her. Afterwards, when she forgave him, she gave him such a sensual and lingering goodnight kiss, his knees went weak and he nearly blacked out from the impact of her temporary Scorpio passion.

Then there was the morning she told him abruptly that he needed a haircut so badly, she was thinking of getting him a collar and leash, right in front of his mother and his two best friends. (Just one of the stinging arrows from her karmic bow of Sagittarian truth she shoots only very rarely, when her Archer self emerges.)

For a while after that, she was unaccustomedly reserved and quiet (reminding him of a Capricorn girl he once knew) until finally she told him coldly, without the slightest emotion or sentiment, that she didn't want to get married because she planned to go to Europe to study art, and her career was more important than mere romance — or than him. He was shattered at the hint of icy Saturnine ambition in this normally humble and self-effacing creature he thought he knew so well from having analyzed her so carefully.

Just when he thought things were level again, familiar and comfortable between them, she unexpectedly and suddenly decided to move to a new apartment, within two short days, and forgot to tell him she was moving. She left her new address with the old landlady, but she transposed the street and the number mistakenly, and it took him three months to locate her through her mother, who was in Ohio at the time. When he did locate her, she was dating her yoga teacher. (She was suffering from one of her annual Aquarian lightning bolts of amnesia and eccentricity.)

Eventually — and also essentially — she's her normal, sweet Piscean self. It's just that she has those moments, in twelve varieties. But they're only moments. Most of the time, she's the dearest, most sympathetic, calm and unruffled lady this side of Heaven. Sentimental and sensitive. Serene and dependable. Still, it's best that the Virgo man who loves her knows how many of her he's measuring to see if she fits his idea of a lifelong mate.

Now, would you like to know why she scurried over to the *extreme* corner of the room after she asked him what his exact feelings for her were, and was disappointed in his answer? (Re: Peter Pan verse at the beginning of this section.) Because she was hurt, and went to the corner to cry with a spider? No. Because she was angry, therefore went to the corner to pout and eat some curds and whey, without offering him a bite? Indeed not. She went to the *extreme* corner of the room. Remember, I told you she's wise. She either knew consciously or sensed (same thing to Pisces) about the powerful Sun Sign polarity between them — that their natal Suns were opposed at birth. She knows what that means. After a while, a polarity becomes too magnetic to resist. (Check bar magnet illustration in another portion of this chapter.) So, you see, she knew very well it wouldn't take more than a few minutes for the magnetism of their astrological "opposition" to draw them together, and if she placed herself *physically* in exact or extreme opposition to him — well, things would become "physical" even quicker — and he'd be sure to change his answer to something a little heavier than "a devoted son". She was aware that his actions would soon speak for him and clearly cancel that statement as false. Virgo men tend to rise very early in the morning by nature, but he'll have to rise very early indeed to stay ahead of the girl Fish.

She was right, of course. Her Neptune strategy worked perfectly. As smooth as satin, as pink as ribbons. Within ten (rather silent and uncomfortable) minutes, he behaved in a surprisingly impulsive way (for a Virgo), rushed across the room, swept her into his arms (not with a broom, that was only a metaphor) and actually wept openly, declaring he didn't feel at all like "a devoted son" to her, but more like Alexander the Great, burning to conquer the world — the mysterious world of her. Then, wonder of wonders, he actually proposed marriage to his blushing, once again feminine and submissive girl Fish with the dreamy Neptunian eyes.

Earth and Water Signs nearly always blend sexually in sheer ecstasy, very naturally. The passion between these two is seldom less than deep, enriching their love, in faithful imitation of Nature's own comforting blend of earth and water. She feels safe in his arms, and he feels a new awareness through their lovemaking. Often, a Virgo man loses all his normal self-control with the Pisces girl who's won his heart, and that's the best thing that could happen to him. As for her, she's fulfilled by just the knowing of the peace she brings to him. For he was a man desperately haunted with loneliness until he learned what intensity his imprisoned feelings could contain when he released them with a woman he could trust not to bruise his vulnerability — never to offend his secret image of the purity of sex. Perhaps Virgo and Pisces love so completely because they sense their dreams are warm and safe with each other. And so their bodies respond freely, with a wisdom of their own, to the intimate and the familiar. There shouldn't be many bumpy spots in their 7-7 relationship. He's so clever and she's so wise (there's a dram of difference) that if they really try, they can flatten them into smoothness. They're both Mutable, so it will be easy for them to talk over their problems, and that's always a huge help. She flirts. There's no getting around it, she flirts. She's been doing it since she was six. Men find her magnetically attractive, and she can't help responding affectionately. But he should beware of over-analyzing the catholic compassion and listening ear she gives so freely to friends of both sexes as disloyalty or unfaithfulness. It isn't, and it won't be, unless he should make it so by continually pouting in resentment, thereby causing it to materialize. (That which we fear surely comes upon us.) Nor should she cause him unnecessary tension and worry over her casual attitude about money. She might try a little harder to balance her checkbook, and stop giving away all the cash they saved for their vacation to the first person she thinks might need it. On the other hand, he shouldn't excessively stifle her generous impulses because of his own obsession with thrift, make a genuine effort to be looser, with both his finances and his feelings.

This woman can't remain in love with a man who's stingy, with either his cash or his emotions. She can't respect or warm up to a tight fist, a tight bank balance or an uptight personality. It will gradually turn her frigid (and it can sadly drive some Neptunians to drink, from sheer depression and frustration). If he wants to keep all twelve of her happy, he'll have to learn to relax, take it easy, stop criticizing her when she's trying to please him, be more giving and natural. As for the girl Fish, she's simply going to have to stop hiding his favorite magazines and sweaters behind the davenport when company comes, mismating his socks and forgetting to set his alarm clock.

☆ ☆ ☆ ☆ ☆ ☆

LIBRA

Air — Cardinal — Positive
Ruled by Venus
Symbol: The Scales
Day Forces — Masculine

LIBRA

Air — Cardinal — Positive
Ruled By Venus
Symbol: The Scales
Day Forces — Masculine

The **LIBRA-LIBRA** *Relationship*

*"They live in nests on the tops of trees; and the mauve
ones are boys and the white ones are girls, and the
blue ones are just little sillies who are not sure
what they are."*

The older Librans grow, the wiser they become. After playing both judge and jury, and weighing decisions of yes or no, wrong or right, stop or go, thousands of times, a person gradually begins to have confidence in what he (or she) is doing. It takes practice.

Libra men and women (and children) never pretend to know things they don't know, as some of the other Sun Signs tend to do. They ask. They deliberate. They discuss. If they're in doubt, they'll frankly admit "I'm in doubt." They're obsessed by a moral compulsion to do the fair thing, rather than the unfair thing. To do something they consider morally wrong gravely disturbs their consciences. That's why, when a Libran finally does say something, people believe it's trustworthy — and nine times out of ten, it is.

This is true of the white ones, the mauve ones, and the blue ones.

Incredible as it may seem, a so-called Libran "hit man," one who murders for pay (and a few of them admittedly have been born in October), has what he believes to be just cause for such deplorable professional activities. It would be interesting to know what his justification might be, but you can be certain there's *been* a justification, if he's a Libran — and twisted or not, it's been weighed in the Scales of fairness and morality.

For example, all soldiers and officers in the armed forces who were born under the Sun Sign of Libra sincerely believe they're justified in taking human life, not viewing war as murder, but seeing themselves as patriotic heroes, defending some great cause. Sometimes they're right, sometimes they're wrong, but they always *believe* they're right, arriving at their assessments only after due deliberation.

A Libra porno film actress or *Playboy* model will have gone through the same weighing process as her less exhibitionistic-type Libran sisters, and arrived at what she believes are logical and even moral reasons for her decision to accept money to use her body to deliberately titillate and sexually arouse strangers. She will have considered all sides, and decided that the cash benefits she believes she needs for a private dream somehow balance the abasement of her femininity and her future motherhood. Some of her justifications will contain a modicum of sense, some will be pure self-deception — but you can be sure they'll all have been seriously weighed on Libra's Scales before a decision is made.

This is what makes Libra people so lovable. No matter how major or minor their mistakes in judgment, one always knows they've genuinely tried to do what's right and fair and just — and trying is never less than a virtue when it's sincere, as it invariably is with Libra.

Unfortunately, other people may not see it that way. Librans are always being unfairly labeled by other Sun Signs as unreliable, accused of not following through on Tuesday what they said on Monday last. That's why they often feel more comfortable when they're dealing with one another. At least, two Librans will usually give each other credit for decency of motive, regardless of personal disagreements, and they'll have more than their "fair" share of those. Despite one Libra person's vacillation, the other Libran is sympathetically aware that when his (her) mind is finally made up, there will be a grim determination to follow through that nothing short of a cannon ball could stop. Each Libra knows the other Libra's mind is *firm*, once it's been *firmed*. I mean, really, what could be more logical than that? Before firming, it's like clay, easily changed from one form to another — until the final molding. Then the decision is popped into the potter's oven to be glazed, never failing to come out hard and tough, resistant and enduring.

Two Librans of the same or opposite sexes, adults or children, will spend a great deal of their time together talking. All the subjects will be enthralling because of the logical, intellectual aspect Libra brings to the analysis. Some will concern vital issues of the day involving politics, ecology, and so forth;

some will be petty, inconsequential matters, like what are the best kinds of strings for a guitar or tennis racquet, or whether the window should be closed or open at night when one is sleeping. I'll settle that last argument for them myself. Open. Definitely open. Most especially with Libra, because all Air Signs tend to have poor circulation, and must breathe fresh air while they're sleeping or they'll never achieve stable health and longevity.

But the subject matter isn't what's important in a discussion between these two Venus-ruled people, nor is the question of who wins and who loses important. What's important to Librans is the excitement of a mutually stimulating intellectual debate, which they find mentally energizing, like a tonic. Unlike their debates with other Sun Signs, verbal exchanges between these two usually end in a draw anyway. Each of them starts out choosing a side, and as things progress, they begin taking a different side, then trading sides in the middle, until an onlooker is totally confused. All the while, the two Libra opponents are happily enjoying themselves. As long as these two people are given a reasonable length of time in which to discuss matters with one another and make up their minds, there's no trauma involved. It's when other Sun Signs rush them into decisions that their Scales dip out of balance, causing more mental, emotional, and physical damage than anyone would ever guess — except another Libran. Any Venus-ruled person beset with multiple problems simultaneously, each demanding priority attention, can be pressed beyond endurance, whether it's Libra President Jimmy Carter or your own Libra friend, relative, neighbor, business associate, lover, or mate.

An excellent example of Libra's ability to stick to a decision, once made, is India's Mahatma Gandhi's amazing will power in holding fast to his firm faith in passive nonresistance as the only path to freedom from tyranny and a lasting peace. The caste system of his country was an affront to his Libra sense of justice, dramatically demonstrated by his adoption of the daughter of an "untouchable."

Libra and Libra have more in common than just their mutual dimples and ear-to-ear smiles, their indecisiveness, and their concern for fairness. An office, classroom, store, or home where you see two of them floating on their pink clouds, or hanging around in their helicopters, will probably be tastefully decorated, most likely in pastel shades, or at the very least, in a subdued, matching color scheme, or they won't be there very long. Nor will they be comfortable in the midst of loud noises or jarring sounds. Very few Librans are construction workers, not just because of the ear-splitting offense of riveting and such, but also because the Venus influence causes them to recoil from soiled clothes. All forms of dirt are displeasing to them aesthetically. Ugliness of any kind quickly disturbs the Libra equilibrium. A Libra ambulance driver is certain to be a most unhappy human, considering the shrill scream of the sirens and the nature of the work. Add police and firemen sirens and duties to the list of no-no's for Libra. Any Libran involved in such occupations should already be weighing a change as soon as possible. Whatever the sex, age, or social status, Libra needs to sink back periodically into a pile of plump pillows and listen to music now and then, to restore harmony to the soul.

One of the perplexing problems which will plague two Librans in any kind of an association is the metabolism syndrome. It's like this: When a Libra person is evenly balanced, the life style will consist of equal periods of what some unfair meanies call laziness, but which is really exhaustion *requiring* rest — following exhausting spurts of stamina and energy. Libra will work like a plough horse, feverishly, efficiently, and uncomplainingly for a long while — then suddenly reverse gears into a long spell of trancelike lethargy, during which (believe it or not!) even talking is an effort. It's all Librans can do to keep from taking to their beds at such times. There should be no guilt feelings associated with the Libra lethargic periods, because it simply means the physiological Scales are demanding balance. The batteries must be recharged by complete rest in a tranquil, quiet atmosphere. If a Libra person is unable to do this, but is forced to go to work, mingle with people, and so forth, he (or she) will be so unpleasant, miserable, and just plain nasty, everyone starts to wonder how astrology can possibly be correct in calling these folk peaceful, gentle souls with a smooth temperament and mild manners. Don't blame me, I've always warned you that Librans are regular cross patches when their bodies and minds don't receive the proper rest at the time they need and demand it. I'm the one (as far as I know) who coined the phrase "cranky crocodiles" for Libra, so I haven't led you astray by telling you only about the sweet side of their natures. But the important thing about all this is that, when a couple of Librans get together, they should chart their individual "push-retreat" periods and pray that these occur at different times. Like, when one Libran is weary, dreary, and lethargic, the other one should be in the "manic" stage — peppy enough to wait on, soothe, and pamper the former one. And, naturally, vice versa. If their up-down periods match, maybe one Libra can try to "turn around," so to speak, to counterbalance the other Libran's mood swings — because these two can't expect compatibility unless their metabolisms *are* thus counterbalanced.

Just imagine the scene when two Librans are both in an upswing, furiously writing poems, cleaning out closets, scrubbing floors, walking the dog, waxing the car, bathing the baby every five minutes, their four bare feet happily stomping in washtubs full of grapes, to make wine, singing contin-uously . . . . . smiling those dazzling smiles until there's so much light in the house it fades all the colors in the drapes and furniture (which were already pastel *before* they faded) . . . . . . getting months ahead on any work they do, dancing and prancing, and, in general, carrying on in a veritable frenzy of perfumed, powerful, and vital activity — bicycling, tricycling, jogging, jumping, sun bathing, swimming, winning — sparkling all through the night and leaping all through the day. Just thinking about it is enough to fatigue the faint-hearted.

Next, picture these same two Librans hitting a down-swing together, in unison. There they are, sadly synchronized — walking around like zombies, numb and weak, their four eyes glazed, as irritable as can be, making mistakes in their checkbooks, talking back to the boss at work, dangerously crossing the street without looking, listless, unsmiling, pale and frail and wan — both of them draped across the air-conditioner, or flopped on the floor, in a kind of stupor, unable to move or speak, like helpless puppets whose strings have been abruptly cut. Isn't that a depressing scene to imagine? I paint these pictures with broad strokes of the planetary brush hopefully to startle the two Libra people reading this chapter into realizing how important it is for them to try to polarize their metabolisms if they're going to spend a lot of time hanging around together. That way, they can give each other a helping hand — a kind of buddy-boost to the spirits.

Libra is known to astrology as The Peacemaker, and one of the most beautiful things about two Librans is that they possess the wonderful ability to bring peace into one another's minds and hearts. Both hope and optimism spring eternal in the Venus breast. Sentimental Librans think in terms of poetry, art, and music . . . and so their thoughts have wings, with the power to fly them into ever higher heavens from the darkest hells. Although these people judge themselves harshly, with no allowance for plea bargaining, they won't impose their sense of morality on others.

Libra sternly pronounces the judgment of Truth and Justice, then is counseled gently by Venus to suspend the sentence — to grant to the contrite accused and to the sorrowful guilty their freedom . . . and another chance . . . bringing the faint-remembered echo of someone's compassionate words: *Judge not, that ye be not also judged.* That's how Libra's Scales measure human frailty and mortal yearnings — when they're balanced.

☆ ☆ ☆ ☆ ☆ ☆

LIBRA *Man* LIBRA *Woman*

——— ◆◀◆▶◆ ———

*Tink was not all bad: or, rather, she was all bad
just now, but, on the other hand, sometimes she was
all good . . . .*

*It was a sanguinary affair,
and especially interesting as showing one of Peter's
peculiarities, which was that in the middle of a
fight he would suddenly change sides.*

Ordinarily, in the 1-1 Sun Sign Pattern chapters of this book, when it comes to the male-female section, I place the woman of the Sun Sign first in the title, then the man. After all, that's only fair. Since women have been locked up, put down, kept in virtual slavery, unfairly paid and, in general, unjustly treated by men for so many years, we surely deserve some of what I believe is called "overcompensation." However, I've deliberately listed them in the above order, naming the Libra man ahead of the Libra woman, for a good reason.

Libra is a masculine Sun Sign, ruled by a feminine planet — Venus. This means, quite candidly, that it's the nature of Libra individuals of both sexes to be neither decidedly male nor female, but to partake almost equally of the masculine and feminine qualities, sometimes even in the molding of the physical bodies, often in the voice quality — these being also a bit of each. No offense. Such equal measure merely results in Libra women being unusually handsome creatures of great sentiment — and Libra men being unusually beautiful creatures of great strength — although Libra men are also uncommonly (and appealingly) sentimental, while Libra women are also uncommonly (and admirably) strong. You can see how confusing it becomes. There must be a line drawn somewhere, if one is to make any sense of it at all. The fact that they both possess those powerhouse Venus smiles, which can radiate light for a minimum of one hundred yards, doesn't make matters any easier.

To get directly to the issue of why I listed the Libra man first in the heading, something has to give in this situation, and to be fair, it should be the Libra woman. If she truly loves her Libra man, she'll give him, at the very least, equal billing in their relationship, allowing his masculinity to be unchallenged and unquestioned, so he can appreciate her feminine qualities, and love her as a man loves a woman. To reverse the order of Mother Nature's blueprint is never wise. It's sometimes necessary for the Libra girl, even though she often looks like the seductive personification of every female from Eve to Cleopatra, to remind herself which of the two of them is really the man. The task won't be too difficult for her, once she realizes its importance to their relationship, because this lady is gifted with more natural charm, instinctive tact, and talents of sweet persuasion than she could ever use in just one lifetime. Astrology isn't advising her to demurely acquiesce to his demands, or encourage his male chauvinistic tendencies — only to temper her inner strength with some outward gentleness, and refrain from too frequently demonstrating to him that she's his intellectual equal, if not his superior, in some respects. She should realize that he's also her superior in some respects. Everything comes out even.

Since they're both mental Air Signs, and therefore need constant verbal expression of ideas and opinions, these two will be unable to avoid periodic long discussions — which could grow into serious arguments. Not all, but most of their arguments could be avoided, if they made a pact to discuss only subjects on which there couldn't possibly be any disagreement from any logical thinking person. Then their discussions would be exercises in mutual enlightenment, rather than merely windy verbal excursions that threaten to stir up trouble between them.

It's safer that way, and there are hundreds of subjects from which to choose, topics even the Hatfields and the McCoys or the Capulets and the Montagues would agree upon. For example, there's the despicable action of our government toward the American Indians at Wounded Knee — Ma Bell's strangling dictatorship and potential telephone-tapping possibilities — the unpredictable service of the struggling, overloaded United States Post Office, that falls somewhat short of the speed and reliability of the Pony Express and makes the United Parcel people seem like angels straight from heaven — and many, many others.

With a minimum of effort this man and woman should be able to achieve a mentally stimulating, yet an also peaceful and emotionally secure relationship. Both the Libra man and the Libra woman are usually willing to compromise to obtain harmony. They're cooperative by nature, except when something they feel constitutes a moral or ethical issue is involved. Then they'll each be equally difficult to sway from an opinion. If either feels the other is treating him (or her) unfairly — or if some situation seems to be unjust, the usual Libra "compromise" and "cooperation" may be replaced by tornadoes of temper and hurricanes of anger. Librans are always verbal when they're agitated. Neither he nor she is likely to pout sullenly in the corner or retreat in silence. They'll probably talk about their complaints until they're resolved, one way or the other, even if it takes all night on occasion — which isn't a good idea, because they both need more rest and sleep than most other people, and when they're deprived of it, their normally fine, alert Libra minds become dull and fuzzy. Yes, even illogical.

This kind of Libran debate will have the happy result of deepening the bond between them, not straining it — and maybe helping the rest of us too, since they might decide to do something aggressively positive about the issues they ponder. The next night these two Libran lovers logically discuss the major contribution made to the End of the World by Washington's Atomic Energy Commission, Con Edison, and other nuclear-powered industries who have refused to convert to solar energy for the insane reason that they can't monopolize or make a profit upon it.

Then they can weigh the morality of the American film *Jaws*, that made its producers so wealthy by being directly responsible for the enormous upsurge of shark killings — unleashing such powerful, invisible vibratory waves of human fury and hatred that a group of California thrill seekers, after the film's success, went to Australia, where they amused themselves by feeding sharks punctured cans of Drano — and tossing them hand grenades, wrapped in meat — then watched happily as the animals writhed in agony, delighted with the way their heads were blown off. When one of their grenades blew a hole in their boat, they were forced to swim to shore in water teeming with sharks, yet none of these human beasts were harmed by the animals. Since Libra rules Justice, the two Libran lovers can ponder what cosmic punishment should be meted out to those who spread to millions of people all over the cowardly falsehood that sharks lie in wait to attack humans, when the absolute truth is that sharks have *no* instinct or desire whatsoever to attack humans. When they do bite, rarely, it's a mistake, never intentional — and nearly all these rare occasions are caused by the shedding of blood through spear fishing. They can use their Libra fairness to decide what sort of Galactic Oscar the *Jaws* producers, directors, and actors deserve for the distinction of having now guaranteed the speeded-up extinction of, not only the Great Whites, but also the gentle Grey Nurse sharks, who so vitally insure the ecological balance of our oceans.

They might even turn to a long, compassionate, Venus-inspired discussion of Sheldon Levy, head of New York's *Action Movie News*, who publicly states his approval of his camera crew's urging a lost and lonely, suicidal soul to jump to his death — because "that's the only way we can get salable footage" for the network and local TV news shows. Perhaps our two Librans can offer Mr. Levy the loan of their Scales, so he can weigh common decency against financial greed and contempt for human life.

There are a multitude of subjects two Libra lovers can use to bring them closer together — matters about which any two sane people on Earth would have to be in agreement — without choosing topics certain to lead them into selfish disputes, causing their love to shrink into hurt feelings, then gradually fade into disinterest . . . . . and the emptiness of apathy.

All Libran lovers and mates should be thankful they don't have the pleasant but puzzling problem of a Libra-Libra husband and wife I know in San Diego, California. Librans Darcia and Don (their actual names! Isn't it

Libra-lovely-and-lyrical?) once upon a time were blessed with a couple of baby Crabs, since grown into two lovely Moon Maidens, who have shown a decided and typically Cancerian reluctance to leave their warm home nest for either marriage or a career. Even if daughters Sue and Darlene ever do decide to cut the ties, the odds are strongly in favor of both of them bringing back their husbands to live with Mama and Papa — perhaps even raising their own offspring cozily at home . . . . where childhood dreams still linger, the furniture is comfortably familiar, and the food is guaranteed delicious . . . . where they feel all nice and safe and secure.

Just imagine the trauma of these two doting Libra parents in trying to decide whether to shove their two adored Looney Birds out of the nest, and thus force them to try their wings — or to encourage and protectively permit them to grow at home forever, like cheerful geraniums, with their own families and their Dalmatian dog, Maxwell. Considering such a possible future houseful of people, the second honeymoon all Libran couples desperately need . . . might be a little crowded. And what if the grandchildren should happen to be home-attached Cancerians also?

But there's hope. Daughters Darlene and Sue are now seriously studying astrology, therefore it may yet be these two enlightened Moon Maidens themselves who finally straighten out the family's loving-but-tangled togetherness. How would you like to have the problem of Librans Darcia and Don? See how lucky you are? Be optimistic. Things could always be worse.

It is, to me, one of the most fascinating facets of astrology that Libra lovers and mates who are cosmically drawn together so frequently bear a pair of alliterative names. Like *Don* and *Darcia* Fleury. *Mack* and *Mary* Eaton. *Jim* and *Janet* Jarrett. These are all actual double-Libra couples I know as good friends. I'm so accustomed to finding Libra teams like Don and Darcia, Mack and Mary, Jim and Janet — I would seriously suspect the validity of the October birthdays of any Libra lovers named, for example, Gregg and Melinda. Back to those couples who are friends of mine (or any other Libra man-woman combinations). It's best to remember that they are *equally* as often — only *fairly* called: Darcia and Don, Mary and Mack . . . and Janet and Jim. Don't forget that Libra is a masculine sign, with a feminine ruler, Venus. No fair allowing one sex to take priority of mention over the other. Everything must be nicely balanced. The sense of poetry and beauty and harmony in Librans extends also to the equality of their relationship. It's clearly not "harmonious" to always name the man first — or place the male's wishes ahead of the female's. Just is just. Male chauvinism is so . . . uncoordinated . . . so unpoetic. Don't you think?

Darcia and Mary and Janet think so. Don and Mack and Jim had *better* think so — if they don't want to start one of those long Libra discussions *she* almost always wins. Who can fight an iron fist in a velvet glove and come out victorious? Not even a clever Libra male. After all, whose side would you *expect* Venus to be on? You are right. She is.

As in all 1-1 Sun Sign Pattern relationships, the Libra man and woman must realize that the combining of their similar characters, personalities, and traits imposes an obligation to be alert to the danger of a doubling up of their mutual negative tendencies. Both people influenced by the 1-1 vibration must be more careful with each other than they need be with others—of emphasizing the qualities in themselves they aren't proud to possess. They'll have to beware encouraging in one another the Libra love of parties, which could lead to various forms of overindulgence and dissipation—the Venus love of sweets, which could lead to a double overweight problem (she loves to bake cakes, he loves to eat them, and vice versa) and, as I've already mentioned, the Libra argumentative aspect, which could, if not controlled, its energy rechanneled into positive directions, lead to continual conflict—which will eventually, in turn, lead to anything from an actual physical allergy to each other, to matching nervous breakdowns in His-and-Her beds at the hospital, because continual conflict can be seriously harmful to Libra mental stability and emotional health. Last, but not least, the Venus compulsion for romance can cause the winds of unfaithfulness and jealousy to blow the roof right off the cozy nest of these two lovebirds. If they must be romantic, they should send all their valentines to each other, and confine their flirting to each other too, which will have the exciting result of keeping their love alive and thrilling long after other Sun Sign couples have become emotionally lazy, and therefore, romantically bored.

Of course, there's also the bright side of the penny in a 1-1 relationship—the emphasizing of the good and beneficent Libra qualities. These two will probably never be starved for compliments, they'll usually be graciously considerate of one another's feelings and enjoy many of the same interests, often centering around music and painting, or other art forms, long walks, and lots of reading. A double Libra marriage almost always produces a sizable library and record collection. They'll have a marvelous time going to the movies, and sharing their opinions afterward, of the dialogue, acting, direction, lighting, camera work, and plot. Librans are born critics, especially those who have a Virgo or Gemini Moon Sign or Ascendent. But they should stay away from the refreshment stand in the theatre. Libra is the sign of beauty, and although this means that all Librans are, in some way, strikingly beautiful or handsome, possessing at least one perfect feature—it also means that Libra appreciates beauty in others, and when either or both of them are no longer physically pleasing to gaze upon, they may look elsewhere for beauty. Yet, the Libra man or woman who temporarily strays usually feels uncomfortable. Even mental infidelity subconsciously troubles the Libran sense of morality and fairness—and compels them to return to each other's familiar, intimate smiles and dimples, accompanied by waterfalls of tears. Librans always weep at weddings, and cry over happy endings.

The sexual chemistry of their relationship, if one could analyze it in a laboratory, would reveal itself to be made up of 70 percent mental affinity, 20 percent affection and sentiment — and 10 percent physical passion. Don't be misled. That 10 percent can contain a more powerful potency, by anyone's quantitative analysis, than the same percentage of passion between other men and women. The combined ingredients of mental affinity, affection, and sentiment act as the perfect catalyst in a formula for sexual fulfillment. Libra love always has the magic of imagination through it, and this keeps their physical union open to all kinds of possibilities of change and variety. Their lovemaking will never be dull, never grow stale. It's more likely to suffer from periods of elusiveness and detachment when he smothers himself in a load of work — when she devotes her entire attention to an outside job, or makes a totally time-consuming career of homemaking and motherhood. But the Libra man and woman's desire for each other, however long it's been allowed to lie dormant, is eternally vulnerable to being rekindled by the smallest gesture or incident.

It could be something as fragile as the fragrance of the cologne she used to wear that he's never forgotten, and that she casually sprayed on her hair, because it was a Christmas gift from a neighbor who didn't suspect what an aphrodisiac it would be . . . . a poem one of them comes across in a book, bringing the memory of the night he whispered to her, long ago, when he was selling cars in Pittsburgh to help pay for his tuition at night school to get his law degree . . . . an old love letter, found unexpectedly in a drawer . . . . . . the smell of frost and apples in the air on a golden-blue October day, in football weather . . . . and always, the rush of feeling that never fails to fill their hearts (and bodies) to overflowing, when they hear the music of "their song."

There's not a Libra man and woman anywhere in this solar system who don't adopt a special song, within days of their meeting, which becomes, from that moment forward, a sacred symbol of the thrill they knew when they first loved, increasing its nostalgic power over their emotions with every passing year. Whatever recording artist sang it the night they heard it together will be their heroine or hero, whether it was Frank Sinatra, Bob Dylan, Helen O'Connell, Elvis Presley, Linda Ronstadt, or Ringo Starr. If it was Peggy Lee who first blessed their theme song, they'll follow her concerts and personal appearances to the Moon and back, to relive yesterday. If it was the late Nat "King" Cole, they'll become enthusiastic fans of his daughter, Natalie. Librans are as sentimental as a lavender sachet, tucked away in a trunk in the attic.

The typical Libra man is usually successful in a material sense, either independently following a specialized profession, or securely locked into a position of authority, at the head of some major endeavor. He'll seldom last long, or be completely happy, as an employee, taking orders, for Libra is a Cardinal Sign of leadership, and needs to be in charge. During forced, nonoptional periods of playing the role of employee, he may be super bossy at home, because he must boss *someone*. (But he'll do it sweetly most of the time.)

The typical Libra female is a Wonder Woman as a hostess. Their home won't be a shabby shack or a cluttered cubicle. Her talents and taste will transform it into an oasis of peace and charm, a harmonious haven filled with gracious and beautiful vibrations, soothing to the troubled spirit. She's remarkably cool and calm in a crisis (although afterward, she may collapse in his arms, when the danger's over), fiercely loyal, and cheerfully adaptable to change. His dreams are her dreams, and she's both strong enough and devoted enough to make them come true for this gentle-mannered man she loves, who's so intelligent, often cranky, but always optimistic that tomorrow will be brighter — very much like herself.

She's the kind of woman who will make any sacrifice to help her man graduate from police or plumber's school, obtain his medical or law degree, achieve his goal to be an actor, writer, artist, or musician — become the chief executive of an airline or a lollipop store. Whatever he wants for himself, she wants *for* him, with equal fervor.

He's the kind of man who will romantically give his woman a diamond or a poem (does it really matter which?) because he suddenly realized, one autumn afternoon (flying home to her from a business trip) an unexpected truth — that without his Libra lady's "iron fist in its velvet glove" — he'd still be back in Pittsburgh, selling Buicks.

☆ ☆ ☆ ☆ ☆ ☆

LIBRA

Air — Cardinal — Positive
Ruled by Venus
Symbol: The Scales
Day Forces — Masculine

SCORPIO

Water — Fixed — Negative
Ruled by Pluto
Symbols: Scorpion & Eagle
Night Forces — Feminine

The **LIBRA-SCORPIO** *Relationship*

. . . it's only fair to take this into account.

*L*ibra and Scorpio form a 2-12 Sun Sign Pattern, which means many things, as you will read in the back of this book, but one of the most important of these is Karma's decree to the Libran that there is a mystery to be absorbed from the Scorpion . . . and there is, to be sure. More than one mystery.

The roles of student-teacher will soon emerge, which is only fair. After all, Libra, you play the same instructor role toward Virgo as Scorpio plays toward you, so it all evens out around the wheel. Since Libra represents the twelfth house of the karmic past to Scorpio, the latter will be unusually tolerant of Libra faults and failings, the differences in their individual personalities and dispositions. Scorpio has already passed through Libra's Venus vibration (probably quite recently, relatively speaking) and therefore possesses a strange comprehension of its pitfalls, along with a wistful memory of its joys, yet would prefer not to return there, having moved on to bigger and better problems under the Pluto essence.

"I feel I have something to learn from this person," muses Libra, when exposed to Scorpio's unrelenting gaze. "I somehow understand this person better than anyone else ever will," thinks the Eagle, after studying the Libran carefully.

And so they approach each other, tentatively at first, but with a certain degree of fascination — for the unknown, on the part of Libra — for the known and vulnerable on the part of Scorpio.

This is not, strictly speaking, the same teacher-student vibration of the 4-10 Sun Sign Patterns. Yet the Scorpion has a subconscious recall from some misty past incarnation, of the dreadful disappointments that can follow on the heels of Libra optimism, justice and fairness, and so is sympathetic to Libra's tendency to try to see the positive side of all questions — and is often willing to give a helping hand to this Sun Sign still beset with Venus seductions, this soul experiencing the struggle of trying to balance the Libra Scales.

Libra, keenly sensing the need to benefit from Scorpio's wisdom, is anxious to plumb Pluto's secrets. But Libra is a mental Air Sign, and will not accept every word from Scorpio without a few healthy arguments (Libra calls them discussions) and an occasional mental chess game with teacher.

Whether the relationship is that of friends, parent and child, business associates, mates or lovers, Scorpio soon discovers that Libra is a charmer, pleasant, bright and soothing to be around — on Mondays, Wednesdays and Fridays. On Tuesdays, Thursdays and Saturdays Libra can be a study in contrariness. Sundays depend.

Most Librans do like to talk, especially the females of the Sun Sign. There are also some Libra men who seem shy and reticent, but challenge their sharp wits with an argument or a one-sided statement — and they'll lose their shyness and talk your head off trying to convince you that there are two sides to every question, every problem, every situation. These quiet, untalkative Librans are only remaining silent while they perform their mental convolutions, ready to whip them out to win a victory in the next argument.

Scorpios have decided likes and dislikes. Their preferences are never fuzzy, their opinions often set — as if in cement. The natural *adaptability* of the Scorpio *Water* element seldom wins out over the *Fixity* of the Scorpion Sun Sign nature. Of the three Water Signs, Pisces is far more adaptable than either Scorpio or Cancer, since Pisces is a Mutable Sign, Cancer a Cardinal Sign, and Scorpio an extremely Fixed Sign. Studying such nuances, and recognizing them, helps a lot.

These set opinions, these pronounced likes and dislikes of Scorpio, can cause tension when they offend Libra's innate sense of justice and fair play, and Libra voices disapproval. When this happens, Scorpio will temporarily forget his or her natural tolerance for Libra, and become either mildly frustrated or even secretly bitter over what the Scorp interprets as permissive, lazy thinking — which is a mistake. Libra may be physically lazy periodically, usually following a long surge of incredible vitality (it takes these ups and downs to keep the Libra scales evenly balanced), but there's nothing lazy about the Libra mind. How can a mind grow lazy, with all that hyperactivity or weighing back and forth every decision, from whether it's healthier to eat carob ice cream than to eat none, to whether to vote Democrat or Republican or not vote at all — or to form a new political party? Such continual brain exercise as Libra receives from the trauma of daily and hourly decision making, keeps his or her mental muscles rippling and flexible. Sorry, Scorpio, but calling Libra mentally lazy is an unfair judgment. In the area of permissive thinking, however, you have pretty good grounds for complaint.

A Libran can be amazing in his or her ability to sustain an optimistic "tomorrow will be better" attitude in the face of setbacks, letdowns and catastrophes, which is truly a lovely thing to observe at close hand (or even at a distance), but after a while it begins to chafe. The more cautious, perceptive Scorpion asks himself (or herself) if Libra can possibly be sincere. (Libra is, yes, ever-so-sincere.) How can any human, wonders the Scorp, so eternally continue to see only the good side of everything? *Wait.* Eventually Libra's Scales will tip and they'll be looking on the dark side. If you don't believe me, just say anything at all strongly affirmative to Libra (very aggressively) and watch him (or her) take the opposite stand. Or the middle road. Sometimes, they take both sides at once. Approach a Libran, point your finger and say loudly, "You're a Libran, and that means you like to argue about everything, *right*?"

"Well . . yes and no," answers Libra.

I love to have Libra people approach me to discuss my first book, *Sun Signs,* and spend a half-hour or so telling me why they don't think the Libra chapter fits them. When they're all through, I say sweetly, "But you just proved you're a Libran by arguing about every word I wrote." For a moment, they're silent. Then Libra will continue, "I didn't argue about *every word.* There are *some* things in it that fit me perfectly." "Which ones?" I ask. Then Libra spends *another* half-hour telling me how accurate the description of the Sun Sign was. Afterward, I feel kind of split-down-the-middle, which is the way Librans always leave you feeling. But they're fair!

Scorpios can, surprisingly, rather smoothly handle Librans who are temporarily behaving like cranky crocodiles. It's the 2-12 vibration between them. Scorpio seems to instinctively sense that Libra needs encouragement, that when Libra finds the right outlet for either creative or intellectual expression, he or she will become a most cooperative person — friendly, adaptable and willing to compromise in order to maintain harmony and avoid tension. A little extra patience is worth it to Scorpio to achieve such a desirable goal. A Scorpion always has an excellent reason for every tactic, a hidden motive behind every strategy or course of action in human inter-course. Of course, Scorpio should be warned that the Libra willingness to be friendly, adaptable and cooperative may be, on occasion, merely a weapon to gain what Libra wants, however genuine these virtues are most of the time. Librans are incredibly adept at manipulating situations to their own private ends, with apparent harmless intention and a lack of aggressive attitude, while projecting oozing oodles of charm — so adept that unsuspecting souls are often fooled into doing it Libra's way (oh, that persuasive voice, that heavenly smile!) without fully realizing how they've been programmed to goose-step in the direction Libra had in mind all along.

Scorpio, however, is far from "an unsuspecting soul." Scorpio *invented* the word "suspicious." You don't fool one easily. Governed by the powerfully perceptive Pluto, most Eagles can see straight through the silk and satin of Libra's wiles and seductions. Libra can trick Scorpio only once, if that often. After the first experience, Scorpio will have memorized the Venus strategy of sweet cajoling, and will be armoured against the allurement of such wheedling next time.

LIBRA: (all smiles and dimples) That's a truly excellent letter you wrote, and it reads very smoothly — but do you think it really expresses what you want to say?

SCORPIO: Yes. It expresses exactly what I want to say, which is why I intend to mail it. I'm glad you liked it. Do you have a stamp?

Scorpios are no pushovers for Libra charm. They can be, when they choose, equally as subtle in the strategies of achieving their objectives as the airy, mentally quick and highly intelligent Librans. And far more persistent. Inwardly, the Eagle never admits defeat. But Scorpios are sensitive, and can be quietly hurt when Libra is oblivious to a need. Libra is not a sign noted for in-depth analyzing of human nature. They're better at analyzing stock market reports, legal briefs, color charts, art masterpieces and political polls. Libra may be sweetly sympathetic, for example, to Scorpio's nervousness around kangaroos. But it may not occur to Libra to ask *why*. Scorpio would like to be asked, even *needs* to be asked why. He (or she) may have waited a long, lonely time for someone to care enough to really want to hear the story about that scary trip to the zoo as a child. Speaking of childhood, here's an unpublished Mother Goose rhyme she wrote for the Venus- and Pluto-ruled, while she was shaking out her feathers one day: *Water and air, water and air .. may only reach harmony ..... when Libra treads carefully .. and Scorpio is fair.*

☆ ☆ ☆ ☆ ☆ ☆

LIBRA *Woman* SCORPIO *Man*

*In her dream he had rent the film
that obscures the Neverland. . . .*

*. . . Elation must have been in his heart,
but his face did not reflect it.*

As bright, intelligent and logical as she may be, the Libra woman can spend a lifetime unsuccessfully trying to read the innermost feelings of her Scorpio man from his bland features. She'll never penetrate all the secrets behind his impassive mask. He's a walking enigma that will forever resist a final solution. If he loves her, he'll share more of himself with her than he ever will with anyone else, but this doesn't mean he'll either invite or permit her to wander around in the more private recesses of his mind, heart or soul. These secret compartments are reserved for himself and his Maker — his God.

If he should happen to tell her this, her fine Libra mind will probably find it a good excuse to initiate an argument (excuse me, a discussion) on the subject. "What do you mean, *your* God? Aren't you aware that we have co-Creators, that there is a Mr. and Ms. God, that even your Maker has a female counterpart, as does everything in the entire Universe?" Libra girls are always a trifle Women's Libbish, even when they disguise it with their perfumed femininity and dimpled smiles, but she's on the track to truth when she offers that particular spiritual conjecture. Right on! Libra, and bless your Venus wisdom.

Buried just beneath the surface cool, in even the most evolved of Scorpio men, is the revenge syndrome — so she should beware of driving him into too many inlets of resentment. The retaliatory surprises of a wounded or angered Scorpion can seriously shake her Libran equilibrium. This man is deeply sensitive behind his image of self-sufficiency and confidence. Now, a word of warning to *him*. Despite her soothing voice, beautiful features and sparkling toothpaste smile, Libra is a masculine Sun Sign, also a Cardinal Sun Sign of leadership. A smart Scorpio man knows the Webster definition of both "masculine" and "cardinal." So he should comprehend that this girl, with all her womanly ways, will not become a contented concubine, not even for him. She can, at first, be undeniably convincing in her pose of soft feminine submission, especially if she really loves him. But behind her cheerful countenance and satiny façade, she's miserable unless she's made responsible in some way regarding matters of importance. Brooms, mops, dishwashers and diapers don't fall in that category. I mean, they're important . . but they're not challenging or mentally stimulating, and if she isn't mentally stimulated she'll become a very sad lady. Of course, admittedly, there's nothing more stimulating than trying to capture the love of an Eagle, but once she's won that round, she'll become restless. She's a regular female Ulysses, this girl — with an additional problem Ulysses didn't have when he sailed the seven seas — she needs companionship. She withers when left alone. Libra rules marriage and partnerships. Just imagine what it's like to so need the comfort of a cozy marriage, yet to be constantly longing to dash out and conquer the world at the same time. Do you see why her Scales keep dipping in indecision and frustration?

Because Scorpio is the natural ruler of the eighth astrological house of other people's money (among other things) and, in addition, represents the second house of money and material possessions to Libra, these matters will assume more importance with this couple than with most. The income of either or both will be the subject of much emphasis in their relationship. Whether this financial emphasis is positive or negative will depend on the Sun-Moon aspect they share, and other mutual planetary influences, plus — as always — their own efforts to harmonize in this area of their life together. But they can be certain that money will rear its little (or large) green head as an urgent problem for decision and discussion, not infrequently. Separate checking accounts. I strongly advise separate checking accounts. Actually, that's good counsel for every couple of any Sun-Sign composition, but especially for this one. A Libra woman will not be happy asking her man for a few dollars when she wants to subscribe to *Ms.* magazine or go shopping. Even *Pisces* girls don't do *that* anymore, and Libra women were liberated long before they or you or I ever heard of ERA — when they were born.

If she wants to go to work, he should be enthusiastic. He may as well be because she'll do it anyway. Scorpio can be intimidating, but a Libra woman is not easily intimidated. She'll seesaw back and forth for a while, pretending that her indecision trauma is caused by a concern that her taking a job might upset him or their home life. She's putting him on, using these anxieties as excuses to cover her necessary but frustrating period of Scale balancing. In the end, she'll do exactly as she wishes to do. Whatever that might be. It's hard to guess. But when she does finally decide, she'll be quite firm about it, you can be sure. If it's a job with a title, and relates somehow to the arts, so much the better. She'll be touchingly happy, for Libra must lead in some manner — and to her, anything artistic or beautiful isn't work, it's play. The happiest careers are always those in which we would become involved by choice, even if we weren't paid. To work with love is a holy thing.

In astrology, Libra is closely associated with the law, among other matters. So he shouldn't be surprised if she often sounds like a lawyer when they're debating (I mean discussing) some point of disagreement. Even if he's an attorney himself, she'll rock and sock him now and then with her Libra logic. He may think he's fallen in love with, not a woman, but his old college law professor, and have to look closely to be certain. Those starry eyes and chiseled features and that voluptuous Venus figure should quickly reassure him. Yes, she is a female. Still, her masculine mental processes will give him a start now and then. She'll take turns being sweetly bossy, then docile, which will confuse him, and very few things confuse Scorpio. It can throw him into periods of inexplicable depression, during which he'll ask himself who is *really* in control of the relationship. (It's a valid question.) On the other hand, his habit of silently appraising her virtues, when she needs to hear them praised aloud, of being critical in a detached and unemotional way, can trouble her more than he guesses.

The Libra woman will have to call on all her considerable reserves of charm and tact to learn to be tolerant of this man's dark moods, his long silences. He hasn't left her, he's only swimming out a little further from shore than usual, into the deeper waters of meditation upon life's mysteries, and he doesn't need a bodyguard to float along beside him. He prefers to make such nocturnal excursions alone. Chattering, or insistent questions like "What are you thinking about?" or "Why are you so quiet, sweetheart?" will be answered with a cold stare and more silence. Even the talkier Scorpions with several planets in Gemini, Aries or Leo, will have reclusive moments.

In the beginning, it will cause no small amount of tension between them that he sometimes communicates best with a glance, or perhaps a touch — while she communicates best the way all God's creatures were made to communicate, verbally, with sounds called words. A Scorpion, however gregarious he may be regarding other areas of his life, will never find it easy to be excessively verbal when expressing his emotional or sexual or romantic feelings. If there's a harmonizing Sun-Moon aspect between their birth charts, she'll understand this, begin to measure her words and communicate more often with her dazzling Libra smile — and an eloquent silence.

Should they, however, share a square or opposed Sun-Moon aspect, the prognostications for permanence are not good. If he's one of those Scorps with a weakness for drugs or alcohol, and she's one of those eternal "party girl" Librans, there will be trouble. Libra creates the social atmosphere to tempt Scorpio's latent weaknesses. Her fondness for fun and people and entertaining can be a sticky net for the Scorpion who's easily lured into losing himself through various escapes, from drinking or the temporary high (or low) of grass, to ever more dangerous artificial stimulation. Life is always ready to seduce the Pluto ruled into dark waters, and a dimpled, charming Libra girl can be pretty seductive.

However, an evolved Scorpio male of tenacity and purpose (and there are plenty of these) who can resist such siren songs — and the enlightened, mentally stable, emotionally balanced Libra woman (the kind who far outnumber the Libran party girls) have a solid chance to form a strong association when they fall in love with their heads and hearts in equal measure. He may sometimes suspect she's not completely leveling with him, not saying what she really believes, never mind how many words she uses. Are they reflecting her true feelings? He wonders, for he is suspicious by nature. It's a dual problem, because she'll be troubled by his subtle manner of avoiding an immediate answer to her questions. What lies behind those impassive features? She wonders, for she is curious by nature. There are moments when he'll appear to be more stubborn than he really is, when he insists on a course of action without explaining to her logical mind why he's so set on it, believing she should trust him to have the wisdom to know what he's doing — and he usually does. It's safer for their marriage if she trusts him than if she doubts him. Yes, I said marriage. None of these loose, Aquarian Age live-in plans for the Libra female. She may go along with a live-in arrangement for a while, but eventually she will marry, or leave. Marry her, or you'll lose her — to another man, perhaps — or she'll find a sensational career to wed. Just so she's not alone, and she knows where she's going. Libra women play all games for keeps.

Many Libra females retain their own names when they marry. It's a kind of "thing" with some of them. If a Scorpio man permits this, you can safely wager every penny in your piggy bank that he's one of the very rare, evolved Eagles, and fatten your pig by winning. She may hesitate before deciding, though — what will happen when the children are born? On the other hand, will she miss the warm intimacy of bearing his name while she's keeping intact her independence as an individual? There are actually two sides to it, you see, and . . . .

After a few hours or days or weeks of her weighing the balance, even a stubborn Taurus man might give in, and say, "Do it! *Do* it!" So will the Scorpio man. He'll likewise become weary of her weighing and shout (though he rarely shouts), "DO IT! For %%¢¢&&°° !! sakes, *DO* IT! Like I said when I first suggested it, I think it's a sound idea" (even if he secretly hates the idea).

The funny thing is that the idea itself will probably have originally been hers, not his. She'll sweetly plant it in her lover's mind so subtly and gently, he'll forget where it came from and be innocently convinced it was his suggestion in the first place. That's what astrology means by the female Libran's "iron fist in a velvet glove." When it punches out the perception of a Scorpio, you can be certain it's mighty powerful, however velvety.

These two aren't as emotionally passionate as they are mentally in tune. Sexually, they can anticipate each other's wishes, which is good. But they aren't always aware of how to *satisfy* those wishes, which is bad. The Eagle should study the verse in Ecclesiastes, which states that there is "a time to embrace — and a time to refrain from embracing." One of the latter times is when she's struggling through the throes of some important decision. He may try to relax her, help her unwind with intense lovemaking, then be deeply wounded to discover that his endeavors have only tied her into more pretzels and made her restless, nervous . . . when the act of love should result in peace and contentment. She can be an ideal partner for him when her Scales are balanced, and at these times, their physical Oneness can bring them so spiritually close to each other that tears could fill their eyes at the wonder of love's power to transport the soul into beauty through "becoming one flesh." But when this woman's Scales are tipping, she'll be as pleasant to make love to as the Lady Macbeth.

The Scorpio man will probably satisfy every sensual and erotic longing, every secret need for affection and fierce devotion the Libra girl has ever dreamed about romantically — except one. He definitely will not recite poetry to her in the middle of their mating — nor will he make whispered declarations of his devotion aloud to her during their intimate moments. She'll remind him, perhaps even coach him. He will attempt to comply. But since this sort of thing lacks spontaneity, she'll begin to think he doesn't really love her. He does. But this man is uneasy with open displays of sentiment and romance. He thinks he proves he loves his woman by both his loyalty and his sexual intensity. Why should she need words, to hear him repeat "I love you" constantly? I don't know why, but she does need it. A compromise may be necessary. She should try to be more gentle, less demanding of him . . . . . . and he should realize that this woman doesn't take a crystal ball to bed with her, so how is she to *know* his feelings are as deep and sure as when they first wept together over love's joy, unless he *tells her so*? Using Libra logic, I'll remind the Eagle that a small amount of spoken endearments will prevent a large amount of unreasonable jealousy. Whether his features are plain or handsome, the magnetic force field of Pluto pulses in his aura, and his undeniable magnetism with women can make this lady very jealous. Could Juliet have doubted Romeo, with such constant declaration of his love? Nor did she. Nor will his Libra woman, if she receives her Juliet birthright from him.

Wish them luck in their efforts to blend their vibes. It might be a blessing to us all that they fell in love. She can provide an idealistic outlet for his controlled but driving ambition, helping him guide it into channels that could bring justice to the planet's abused and weary souls. His deeper wisdom will check her airy indecisions, gently molding them into a sensible approach to her daydreams. Her logical mind will help him straighten out the complicated tangles of career, family or personal involvements which are sooner or later faced, to some degree, by every Water Sign, even invincible Scorpio.

The combining of the Eagle's bottomless confidence with his Libra woman's great sense of fairness can be a beneficent thing for everyone within their sphere of influence. Their personal love has an excellent chance to expand outside themselves into a tremendous energy for all mankind and womankind. If the two of them should silently meditate together within the Pyramid or whisper magic mantras in an ancient Incan temple . . . . . what wonders might occur! Our co-Creators would *both* approve.

☆ ☆ ☆ ☆ ☆ ☆

LIBRA *Man* SCORPIO *Woman*

*I know not why it was, perhaps it was because
of the soft beauty of the evening, but there
came over him a desire to confide . . . . .*

Here's an astrological insight about a Libra man his Scorpio woman may already know. He's softer than most men, more gentle, more easily hurt. Just as the female of his Libra Sun Sign is stronger, tougher underneath than most women. It's a contradiction faced by the two sexes of any *masculine* Sun Sign conflictingly ruled by a *feminine* planet. I digress deliberately, for this subject will sooner or later be of vital importance to these particular lovers.

Libra is a *masculine* Sun Sign, ruled by the *feminine* planet Venus. Capricorns, for example, face the same dilemma, Capricorn being a feminine Sun Sign under the control of the masculine planet Saturn. It makes the men of the sign a little more feminine than usual — the women of the sign a little more masculine than usual, which is beneficial in an evolutionary sense. A man is not less macho because he's sensitive enough to weep (Jesus wept), nor is a woman less feminine because she knows her own mind and has the courage of her own convictions.

The problem repeats itself in an even more concentrated way with all the Sun Signs. The *masculine* Sun Signs *also* ruled by a masculine *planet* — Aries, Leo, Sagittarius and Aquarius — make it difficult for females born under their influence to convince their lovers they're really girl-types, longing and needing to be cherished and conquered, never mind how they sometimes behave or how many banners they carry in Women's Lib parades. The *feminine* Sun Signs *also* ruled by a feminine *planet* — Taurus, Cancer, Virgo and Pisces (yes, Virgo's true ruler, Vulcan, is a feminine planet) present the converse problem to males born under their influence, making it difficult for them to project to their ladies that they're really strong, courageous types, longing and needing respect and recognition, never mind that they sometimes behave as if they couldn't care less about such things.

For the foregoing reasons, the both masculine planet-ruled and masculine Sun Signs of Aries, Leo, Sagittarius and Aquarius often produce males who are a shade *too* masculine — while the both feminine planet-ruled and feminine Sun Signs of Taurus, Cancer, Virgo and Pisces often produce females who are a shade *too* feminine. Out of balance, so to speak. (Libra will understand *that* !) These are the girls who infuriate the ERA leaders, the ladies who enjoy being submissive to their husbands, and don't really want their "freedom."

Gemini, we'll skip. Geminis are Twins, and that should be self-explanatory. Gemini's ruling planet, Mercury, is a tricky, double-talking magician, who changes sex when it suits some Mercurial purpose, in the twinkling of an eye.

Is Scorpio one of these sexually upside-down, out-of-balance or overly balanced (sexually) Sun Signs ? Any astrologer who claims an absolute "either-or" answer to that is less cautious than I care to be concerning the mysterious planet Pluto. Scorpio is, of course, indisputably a feminine Sun Sign. But . . Pluto ? Scorpio's ruler ? The awesome force and explosive power of Pluto is that of Mother Nature herself — and has anyone ever dared to call Mother Nature a man ? Yet — force and power of such magnitude as Pluto's are normally associated with the masculine gender.

It bears consideration and meditation. In both natal (birth) aspects and astrological predictive work, through transits and progressions, Pluto likes to hide the truth, to explode the unanticipated, often indicating the opposite polarity of a hidden meaning to disguise a karmic purpose. Would you really like to know the sexual secret of this dark, silent and enigmatic ruler of Scorpio — Pluto ? All right. It's contained within the mystery of the Holy Trinity. An in depth explanation of the sexual identity of the planet Pluto is hidden within "The Twelve Mysteries of Love" in the front of this book, beginning on page 18. I told you Pluto likes to hide things. (Scorpio people even hide things from themselves — and then forget where they hid them.) Pluto doesn't forget. But you certainly couldn't expect the answer to Pluto's secret to be contained within any Scorpio chapter, where you'd be likely to *look*. Like everything else about Pluto (and Scorpios), it will be waiting somewhere inconspicuously, silently . . . for those who care enough to search.

And so, although we know that the Libra man was born under a masculine Sun Sign but is ruled by the ultrafeminine planet Venus — adding an attractive depth to his emotional nature and interesting sensitivity nuances to his personality — we aren't sure about the Scorpio woman. Is she ruled and influenced by masculine or feminine forces? When you discover the answer (in the place where Pluto has hidden it, within this book) you will comprehend the true reason for the *power* behind the minds and wills of Scorpios, including the women born under this Sun Sign.

I introduced this in-depth gender meditation for two excellent reasons — one being to hint to my readers that astrology is very definitely on the side of equality of the sexes — the other being that the subject matter itself will keep Libra and Scorpio busy arguing back and forth with each other for many hours, while we discuss their areas of compatibility and incompatibility. After a time, while the Libra man is still making reasonable, fair and logical points about it, the Scorpio girl will suddenly freeze, stare or glare at him, murmur something like: "I happen to *know*. You do *not*," then lapse into her Fixed Sign silence. That's the way many of the quarrels, discussions or whatever climax between these two, with Libra still pressing arguments for his side — and his Scorpio woman holding tenaciously, intensely to her deep, inner conviction, totally unimpressed with all his logic and charming persuasion.

This should give the Libra man a clear idea of what he's facing with a Scorpio girl. His dimples and charming manners may have other females palpitating the moment he grins and projects his brilliant mind toward them like a romantic laser, but this woman will see through him. She'll know right away whether he's playing a game with her, as Air Signs are wont to do — or seriously attracted to her. In other words, she'll know if his intentions are honorable or not.

I said she would *know* his intentions, not necessarily base her decision on the degree of their honorability. (If there's no such word as "honorability," Webster has goofed, and you may so inform them. It's kind of like "nobility." I just coined it.) Honorability may not be the deciding factor with her. She just likes to *know* things. To Scorpio, knowledge is power. If his initial intentions aren't honorable, she might even be intrigued. Scorpios of both sexes enjoy experimenting with challenging emotional situations. If he's not honorable now, perhaps she can make him honorable later, by the sheer force of her animal magnetism. The Libra male is hereby warned that what begins as a casual flirtation with a lady Scorpion may very well end up being a long-term commitment, and for years he'll wonder how it happened. If their Sun-Moon positions are compatible, he won't really care *how*, he'll just be glad it happened. He'll be happy she "guessed" that his feelings were genuine before he knew it himself. But if their Sun-Moon positions are incompatible, he may later have cause to regret his airy, amusing (he thought) excursion into her deep emotional waters.

It may take Pluto power for the Scorpio woman to enlighten this man to the awareness that he's not flirting, that he really loves her — but it won't be so difficult to make him realize he wants to marry her. If he's a typical Libran, he was born to form a partnership, either business or marital, and his romantic nature prefers the latter. The unhappiest people on the planet are Librans who, for some unique reason, never married. They go around singing the "People" song from *Funny Girl:* "Lovers.. are very special people.. they're the luckiest people in the world.. " — so wistfully they can break your heart. To this man, wedlock can be beautiful. But the trouble with wedlock, as Christopher Morley once observed, is that there's not enough wed — too much lock — and such could become a legitimate complaint of the Libra man married to a Scorp. Because she feels everything so intensely, her possessiveness and jealousy are far more than temporary feelings or passing moods. Her need to know he's faithful to her is a *fierce* need. She can burn with torment if she even suspects otherwise, and she can be the most suspicious of women. The Libra man is so handsome, romantic and gentle (most of the time, when he's not being cranky) that women often are fascinated by him, and some of them will seek excuses to engage him in intellectual conversation — with other things in mind than the intellect. How can he help it if he's so attractive to the female sex ?

He'd *better* help it, if he's made a promise to a Scorpio woman. In his wildest imaginings, he might not be able to image some of her reactions, her ways of getting even, if she's been really hurt, her pride deeply wounded. They will be subtle, perhaps, but they will sting. Libra is known to astrology as "The Peacemaker," but although he may breezily and effortlessly settle disputes between his friends, he may have to call for help in the form of an outside mediator at home when his wounded Scorpion is inwardly boiling in outrage. "Don't try to charm *me*, I *know* you," she'll tell him coldly. This lady may be deceptively sweet and quiet much of the time, but that's just her mask, to hide her inner turmoil. She is no doormat for a philandering male. In no way is she this.

On the brighter side, it's almost certain he'll enjoy making love to her, because her sex drive is as deep and trembling as he'd like his own to be. She'll teach him many lessons of ecstasy. Without her, his attitude toward physical love might have remained somewhat shallow, and he might have searched for a long time for the kind of loving he always believed in but had never found. As a lover, this man is both susceptible and sentimental, both romantic and affectionate, and these qualities will appeal to the Scorpio woman who longs, and truly needs, to possess entirely the man she adores. Initially, she may be the dominant partner in their lovemaking, and this could disturb his sense of balance, but eventually he'll find a tender way to teach her their mating will be more intense if they play an equal role. There's a sweetness to the Scorpio sensuality that almost approaches spirituality, for every Scorpion subconsciously knows that sex and religion are, in some mysterious way, interrelated.. and this will touch his heart in a haunting way. Yes, these two are usually well mated, with much sympathetic magnetism between them physically, assuming there are no severe afflictions between their birth planets or their mutual Suns and Moons.

His sense of fair play will appeal to her own sense of justice and good judgment. Scorpio is loyal and honorable, and so will admire this in others. In most general matters, they'll be in agreement, but in personal matters, he must take care not to injure her dignity. That's always a calamitous mistake with a Scorp. As for his real need to argue or discuss things verbally until a solution is reached, she'll go along with it, even enjoy their private debates — they keep her from being bored — but when one of their discussions has reached a climax, bringing on her silent stare — when she closes up and indicates that the matter, as far as she's concerned, is settled, he'd be wise not to pursue it further.

Although she's capable on rare occasions of exploding into fury, most of the time she possesses the wonderful patience of all Water Signs, and is therefore nicely suited to cope with his changes of mood, when his Scales dip up and down. If any woman knows how to help him become balanced again, through gentle persuasion, it's this one. Call it subtle or call it sneaky, it's her talent. He'll feel that, with her, in some way things always turn rightside up again more easily and quickly than with most other people. He thinks it's some strange, intangible vibration in her aura. No need for him to know it's her power to plant mental suggestion almost hypnotically when he's down, to bring him back up. The result is what counts.

She will be moved by his tenderness and his sentiment. Libra men are so sentimental, they've pretty nearly taught women to be sentimental too. I know it's supposed to be the other way around, but if you believe that, you haven't read the first page or two of this section of this chapter closely enough. Would you care to discuss it? Let's don't. If we do, we'll be in this chapter forever. She won't give in, and he won't give up . . . . . trying to make her give in. You know?

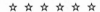

☆ ☆ ☆ ☆ ☆ ☆

LIBRA

Air — Cardinal — Positive
Ruled by Venus
Symbol: The Scales
Day Forces — Masculine

SAGITTARIUS

Fire — Mutable — Positive
Ruled by Jupiter
Symbols: Archer & Centaur
Day Forces — Masculine

The **LIBRA-SAGITTARIUS** *Relationship*

*To describe them all would require a book as large as
an English-Latin, Latin-English Dictionary ...*

ibrans and Sagittarians are sometimes difficult to untangle, especially in bunches. Their astrological passport descriptions can now and then vary as much as those of Gemini and Pisces, since all four Sun Signs are what astrology calls "double signs" or signs of duality. Consequently, there are many Libra and Sagittarian qualities and quirks that defy definition; yet there are also enough familiar stampings of their Sun Signs to make them recognizable in a crowded elevator after a few hours of forced intimacy from being stuck between two floors.

There are the party-loving, playboy and playgirl Librans — the bookish, studious, legal or Judge types of Librans — the scientific, highly intellectual ones — and the artistic, sensitive, floating-on-pink-clouds Librans. Up and down the Scales they go, and where they balance is hard to know. But you can be sure they are *all* incurable optimists who try to be fair. Every last one of them.

As for the Archers, one of the facts we know for certain about them is that they are (and almost always innocently) candid, frank and tactless. They're blissfully unaware that they have just demolished you with a few words, and if that doesn't do it, they'll finish off the demolition with a whole *string* of them that painfully hit the mark. ZINGO! We also know that they're very funny, very intelligent, very idealistic, somewhat clumsy — and even *more* optimistic than Libra. They are inevitably naive in some way. However, in between these reliable signposts of Sagittarian character are miles of short cuts and detours.

There are the owlish, *deceptively* quiet, perceptive Archers, who scowl at you sternly, then suddenly twinkle at you, bounce up and down, knock over the umbrella stand and say something brilliantly funny — or just simply brilliantly brilliant. There are also the Sagittarians who are outwardly conservative and seemingly serious. They go along in this manner for long periods; then, without warning, they pull out Jupiter's bow of truth, aim it skyward and shoot forth shimmering showers of dreams . . . . . so gigantic in scope that only a child would dare to dream them.

Moving right along, there are Archers who do nothing at all but read and think. There are others who spend most of their time singing or dancing and playing practical jokes on their friends. Then there are the Archers who are inspired researchers, authors and scientists — and those who drive their friends, relatives and neighbors crazy with questions, questions, questions. They are all, to some degree, embarrassingly curious. Embarrassing to you, that is, not to them. It is not easy to embarrass Sagittarius. They are not the blushers of the zodiac. There are also Archers who are probably space people. Nothing else could explain their Star-Trekish natures and behavior.

In beginning an attempt to untangle them all, we'll concentrate first on what Libra and Sag have in common, such as — they both like to talk. Yes, talking, very definitely.

In Libra and Sagittarius, mental agility and verbal dexterity are blended in equal parts. The mental agility is always there, even in the more rare, quiet and untalkative Librans and Archers. Instead of expressing their thoughts aloud, they just scribble their philosophies on memo pads, in books, plays or diaries, and keep right on thinking, thinking, thinking. As for the more numerous talkative folk of both Sun Signs, they approach their verbal discourses somewhat differently.

It's like this. Both Libra and Sagittarius are capable of being absolutely charming conversationalists, holding groups of people spellbound for hours. Utterly delightful, they are. But they can both also cause your temper to boil, or send you into frantic frustration when they flip over to their reverse communicative patterns. In this area, Libra prefers to drive you into a nervous breakdown by arguing over every word you speak, back and forth, taking both sides of an issue, and leaving you hanging somewhere in the middle. Worse, they invariably win, one way or another — either through their cool, airy logic, or with the wind-up smile they save till the end, which is so dazzling, you totally forget what it was they said to make you angry — and you smile back. They are deadly debaters for this reason.

The way Sag drives you bananas is slightly different. The Archers, when they're exhibiting their negative conversational traits, do their number on you with tactless, yet honest, observations. In the middle of a discussion of earthquakes in California, or the fluctuating price of gold in Colorado, they'll ask you, point-blank, why you wear a rug, or at what age did your hair begin to fall out. This sort of thing can suddenly short-circuit the chitchat. The reason they ask the second one is because Archers themselves tend to lose their own hair early — not all of them, of course, but an uncommonly large percentage of them — and they are consumed with curiosity about the subject. Paba. Take Paba. Para Amino Benzoic Acid. Get it at the Health Food store, and take 200 to 600 milligrams per day, along with 600 to 1,000 units per day of d-alpha tocopherol (not mixed tocopherols) Vitamin E. You Archers may soon have hair as luxuriant as a Leo's proud mane, and it's also more than slightly possible that the grey hairs, as they fall out naturally, will grow back in their normal color. Now do be still, won't you? And stop asking so many *questions*.

When a typical Libra and Sag get together, there's seldom a still or a silent moment. They'll talk away the hours with zest and vigor, exchanging pure enjoyment of all the mental activity. Libra requires mental stimulation, being a mental Air Sign. Sag requires any sort of stimulation at all, being a Fire Sign. Libra's Air fans the Archer's Fire, and the flames dance merrily. However, if the Archer presses candor too far, the Libra Scales will topple out of balance, and the Air of the Libra person can whip itself into a regular tornado of anger. Since Libra is a Cardinal Sign, Sag a Mutable Sign, Libra will almost always take the lead in the association. Sagittarians seldom resent this, because they much prefer to communicate and wander around, bearing messages of hope (however blunt) and tidings of good cheer, rather than to be stuck with the boring and restrictive responsibilities of leadership, whether it's being in charge of a business, a home or a relationship. When you're bogged down in all that dull and dreary duty, you never get a chance to throw snowballs, ride horseback, rescue dogs and cats from the pound, inspire people with high ideals or travel around the world searching for truth, scooping up excitement along the way. As philosophical as they are, Sagittarians must have fun and changes of scenery. Even Sagittarian nuns and priests are not stuffy sorts. They prefer their missions to be varied and challenging.

That's another of the predictable things about Archers, of all the assorted types mentioned in the beginning of this chapter. They have a thing about religion, as they have a thing about philosophy (nearly synonymous). At one time or another, nearly every Sag will either briefly or permanently contemplate nunhood, priesthood or monkhood. A goodly share of them make the spiritual life a vocation. The ones who don't will spend considerable time arguing with Librans over religion, in debates that range all the way from atheism to Zen — with every shade of Hare Krishna, Mormon, Protestant and Catholic dogma in between.

With few exceptions, despite their good-humored and interesting debates, arguments and discussions, Libra and Sag get along beautifully. Just imagine how the world might have benefited from a teaming up of the combined humanitarianism, friendly candor and energies of Libran Eleanor Roosevelt and Sag Betty Ford — or of Libran actor Charlton Heston (as Moses, Ben-Hur, or just as himself) and wise, jolly, compassionate, outspoken and beloved Sagittarian Pope John XXIII. The Great Justice of a spiritually evolved Libran and the Great Idealism and Honesty of an aware Sagittarian is a combination that can create crescendos of miracles.

Since we no longer have with us Librans Eleanor Roosevelt and Gandhi, or Archers Winston Churchill and Mark Twain, we might image (and pray for) Libran actress Brigitte Bardot and Sag entertainer Frank Sinatra to go together to Libran Prime Minister Trudeau, of Canada, and persuade him to halt the cruel, bloody butchering and skinning alive of the baby seals every spring, causing their terrified mothers to give birth in the icy waters, in a futile attempt to protect their babies from being brutally clubbed and murdered in such agony — only to have them drown, threatening their complete extinction in the alarmingly near future. Bardot has been actively involved in this pursuit of a very holy grail for the longest time, nearly alone among her fellow film stars. She and Sinatra might even convince Libran President Carter to think of a fair way for the United States to offer to substitute some sort of economic benefit to Trudeau to replace the baby seal disgrace, since the financial aspect seems to be the main Canadian concern. Or maybe a group of Archers and Librans could follow the example of actress Terry-Anne Moore, and make a plea on television to all the women who wear sealskin coats, asking them if they realize how sternly their vanity will punish them in their next incarnations. It will be a heavy karmic retribution, from which there is no escape — although it can be negated by a reversal of behavior, and perhaps a generous donation to the Greenpeace environmental group in San Francisco.

"Let the punishment fit the crime, and be meted out accordingly," intones Libra, the judge. "You are all murderers, stained with innocent blood," accuses Sagittarius, Archer of the Truth-that-hurts-but-heals.

Even when they have no Great Cause to pursue, Libra and Sag walk the same path, spreading light in the darkness as best they can, guided by their ruling planets, Venus and Jupiter. Expansive Jupiter, ruler of Sag, takes all the beauty, balance, gentleness and harmony of Venus, the ruler of Libra, and increases it a thousandfold. Sagittarius helps Libra keep those Scales of Justice hanging level — and Libra helps the Archer aim his or her Bow of Truth with a steady hand. These two very naturally need each other, and we all need *them*.

Neither Libra nor Sag will ever bore each other. The Archer is highly intelligent, as inquisitive as a bird dog, alert, bright and anxious to seek all the answers Libra has to offer — which are never less than carefully thought out, and nearly always wise. One of the rare times these two will not get on so well is when one of them has the Moon or Ascendent in an Earth Sign, and throws wet blankets or mounds of earthy stuffiness on the other's need to socialize, because they both love parties, and are, by nature, people-mixers. The Libra half of the team, who has a tendency to lean a little heavily on sweets, must be careful not to gain any extra pounds around his or her Archer friend, who may hand Libra a copy of Bill Dufty's *Sugar Blues* and remark, with cheerful casualness, "You're getting a potbelly, you know. The reason you're so fat is because white sugar is a drug, and you're an addict, and you don't even realize it, because you've become a victim of the sugar pushers." This could be a mite harmful to their harmony. Likewise, Libra can create no small amount of tension in the association by promising Sag to go somewhere or do something, then hedging for hours — or days — weighing the pros and cons of the thing. Finally, Libra says "*Yes*," followed by — "But on the other hand, it might be better not to, because . . . " Or, finally Libra says "*No*," followed by — "But on the other hand, it might be better to go ahead, because . . . ," by which time the Archer has already tuned out and made his or her plans with someone else. It was attending a performance of *Man of La Mancha* that they were discussing, the musical about Don Quixote's impossible dreams and his eternal tilting at windmills. Libra should have gone. He — or she — would have left the theatre with a more comprehensive understanding of the Sagittarian motives and goals.

But don't worry. It will pass. They'll make up, these two, because theirs is a sextile vibration, and in astrology, sextile means opportunity. Libra and Sag will never run short of opportunities for happiness together. If only Sag will learn to count to ten before speaking, and if only Libra will stop deliberating every decision, they can be both cozily and creatively compatible.

☆ ☆ ☆ ☆ ☆ ☆

LIBRA *Woman* SAGITTARIUS *Man*

—◄●►—

"My liking for parties, George."

"My fatal gift of humour, dearest."

The average Sagittarius man is not as marriage-oriented in his youth as he might be, or as the Libra girl would like him to be. She thinks in terms of togetherness in the total sense; so, naturally, if she's in love with him, she images rings and vows. There's nothing wrong with that; in fact, a marriage between them would likely be successful and stimulating. But if this man doesn't work the wanderlust and curiosity out of his system *before* he weds, he may satisfy those powerful Jupiter urges *after* he weds. *Which is preferable?*

Now I've done it. I've given the Libra girl a choice. It will take her a time to sort it all out and make a decision, and we can't just wait around while she's carefully considering all sides of the question, so best to continue with our examination of her relationship with a Sagittarius male. She'll catch up with us later.

Not all, but many male Archers are reluctant to leap into legal liaisons the first moment they're sure it's love. It isn't that this man is against marriage, but he just managed to break loose from his family's smothering hold on his mental, emotional and physical activity, and he needs some time to bask in his freedom, before losing it again. After he's satisfied himself that the world is definitely round, tried on two or three jobs or careers for size, read up a little on Tibetan mysticism, traded in a dozen or so cars, mastered the art of hang-gliding in the Rockies, tried out some cross-country skiing, adopted a score or so of homeless animals, made an attempt to run for political office — and checked out every third girl he sees (at a distance, Libra — stay optimistic!) to confirm his opinion that his own Libra lady is as supremely smooth and superior as he first thought she was — he'll be ready to settle down to a discussion of a long-term commitment.

It seems wiser and safer to allow the Archer to shoot a batch of his arrows into the air first, then have the assurance when he returns that most of his curiosity and some of his longings have been fulfilled, and that he's now anxious to start out on his quest all over again, this time with his woman by his side.

On the other hand, if she lets him go free, and he roams too far, he may forget to return, get lost somewhere out there in his beckoning dreams — whereas, if she'd been firmer from the start, he might still be holding her in his arms, while they listen to the silvery sound of rain on the roof — or holding her hand, as they stroll toward the stables to take a moonlight ride on their horses, smelling the sweet hay . . . . . feeling the cool night air on their cheeks. I just don't know. What do *you* think, Libra? (She's back with us now, and should have decided. No, she hasn't. I can tell by the frown wrinkling her lovely Libra forehead. Well, we won't rush her.)

Naturally, there are exceptions, but whether or not to marry is one of the major problems facing this particular 3-11 Sun Sign Pattern man and woman who are in love. Libra unconsciously feels frustrated unless she's sharing life's ups and downs, joys and sorrows, hopes and hassles — with another person. A Libra woman alone is like a pair of Scales with one tray missing, so you can see how it makes her feel useless. You can't weigh anything into perfect harmony and balance when half your equipment is missing — and the man she loves is the other half of this woman's equilibrium equipment as a total human being. (Unless she's one of those intensely dedicated Libran career women, with a compatible business partner, in which case she'll be content for a reasonable length of time — but not forever — without a mate.)

A Sagittarius male doesn't actually fight togetherness, because he isn't fond of being alone either. He's much happier with a friend beside him as he clowns and bounces and seeks his way along today's trail, leading into tomorrow's highways. If the friend is also beautiful, dimpled, sweet and huggable, that's even better. If she should also be bright enough to match wits with him and exchange philosophies (which this girl surely is, and then some), he has no objection if she grabs her camera, field glasses, pup tent, sleeping bag, canteen and flashlight, and tags along with him. It's only when she starts leading the conversation into dead-end streets like buying property or taking a steady job that he strains at the leash. When he's older, he'll mow his lawn and pay his taxes like any other man, but meanwhile, there are sirens out there, singing to his heart a song more seductive than her Chanel, her charm, her delectable dimples, and sadly . . yes, even more alluring than her soft embrace. Jupiter rules retirement in astrology, and this often causes Jupiter-ruled men to decide to retire first, and work later. They get it backwards.

The Libra girl has stopped frowning. She's smiling now, with that expression of sweet bliss you always see on the composed features of a Libran who's reached a firm and final decision. She's rejected both choices, and settled for one in the middle, to make it come out more nearly even. She won't try to hold him, *nor* will she allow him to go tramping around the town, the state or the world, mailing her cards and letters. She will go *with* him. Good girl! See? I told you she'd catch up with us.

It's an excellent idea for the Libra woman who loves an Archer to go along with him, rather than to try to force him into her mold. However soft, gentle and velvety her manner, he'll sense the danger of being smothered and become restless. She should realize from the beginning that she'll never completely control this Centaur-Clown creature with the sparkling eyes brimming over with dreams. He was born into the vibration of a masculine Sun Sign, also ruled by the masculine planet, Jupiter, and although Libra is a masculine sign, Libra's ruler, Venus, is all feminine. In some ways, this may seem to give her an advantage, because she can think like a man, yet appeal to him in irresistible female ways. It's a powerful combination, but it will never force a double masculine macho vibe such as the Archer's to submit to petticoat persuasion — or if it should, he'll be genuinely miserable within, try as he may to hide it. And the purpose of love is happiness, not misery.

He'll be attracted by her fine mind, and touched by her optimism, so like his own. She looks for the same silver linings as he, behind every cloud. Since she tends to live in a world of her imagination, troubles are never quite real to her. Even those that do manage to penetrate her dreamy consciousness with the sharp stab of reality are normally not allowed by Libra to remain there for long. Her clever mind and talent for logical deduction will usually find a way to solve any problem — or to deliberately discard it, before it grows into a major crisis. She's amazingly capable of turning her back on ugliness, once she's decided there's no way it can be beautified. Sometimes, a Libra woman will solicit admiration, even when she's aware that it's flattery, and to some degree, insincere. She can talk herself into believing anything, true or false, if it makes her feel cherished — one reason why Libra girls marry early and mistakenly. Still, there are those lovely times when her very optimism turns a negative into a real positive, through the sheer steadiness of her faith. It doesn't happen every time, but enough times to convince her it's worth trying, because there's always the chance that maybe tomorrow . . . .

She is, however, sensitive to hurt, and to sharp words. With all her ability to paint rainbows over grey clouds, and despite her natural Libra longing for peace and harmony at any cost, if he pierces her soft heart with too many stinging arrows, she'll weigh him in the cold light of Libra logic, and find his love too lopsided for her. She admires his cleverness and quick wit, but she won't be his pincushion or his dart board.

A Libra woman respects honesty and idealism, because these are qualities she possesses herself. She enjoys parties and people, social gatherings, art and music, as much as she enjoys reading, learning, debate and all forms of mental challenge. The Sagittarius man is molded in just the right shape to fit her needs and desires. The perfect woman for him must be generous, outgoing and gregarious, be his mental equal and his heart's twin. She must believe, as he does, that tomorrow will be a better day, and think it's exciting to do things on the spur-of-the-moment. He needs a woman who never nags him, who believes in his dreams, understands the word "freedom," and who will be kind to his animal friends. A Libra woman is molded in just the right shape for the Archer. She's probably molded in the right shape otherwise too. Being such close relatives of Venus di Milo, most Libra girls inherit her appealing curves, feminine mystique and classic beauty, which is even more effective sculpted in the flesh than it is in marble.

He's quick to sense every unspoken mental, emotional or sensual desire in her, almost before she knows it herself. He's also quick to resent the appeal of his Libra lady to every male within the radius of her completely irresistible Venus smile. They admire her mind, along with her other attributes, and since she so enjoys admiration, she won't discourage them the way he'll expect her to — and will finally demand that she does. She's not as fiery as he, and will probably be more tolerant of the way other women are excited by his contagious enthusiasm. But with both of them so attractive, and exuding such a love of life and people, romantic jealousy can't be ruled out as a danger in their relationship.

Since Air and Fire mix well in sexual compatibility, she can arouse waves of passion in him with the extremes of simply a gentle glance — or a stimulating intellectual debate. The first inspires him to the kind of tender (but also burning) need Romeo felt when he climbed Juliet's balcony. The second causes the same burning need, without the tenderness, because the awareness of a male that a woman is his intellectual equal never fails to stimulate him with the uncontrollable need to answer it as the deep and feral mating challenge it really is on a subconscious level. There's something serene and soothing about her that calms his restless spirit, just as there is something in his physical nearness that excites her imagination — and this causes the sexual union between them to be a happy kind of sharing. There may be times when she seems indefinably elusive to him, as though her body lies within his embrace, but a part of her is elsewhere, and this will trouble him. It shouldn't because it's the nature of air to be elusive, and this is what enchanted him about her in the beginning. The occasional fierceness or demanding aspect of his lovemaking may disturb her more tranquil aura at times, but it shouldn't. It's just another reflection of his enthusiastic, honest and direct emotions that caused her to tremble with the longing for submission when she first knew she loved him. It's the strangest thing, how a man or woman will fall in love with each other for a particular reason, then later fail to recognize some prismed facet of that special quality in the person.

People in love can fall out of love as quickly as they fell into love, when they have only their sexual chemistry to interest each other. There's not much chance of that with Libra and Sagittarius. They'll always have plenty to talk about. She sees the small boy behind his bravado, and would like to spend her whole life educating him. Every Libra woman has a schoolteacher hidden somewhere inside her. He's so curious about everything, understanding how a woman feels and what causes her emotions intrigues him. He has a thousand questions, to which she has at least two thousand answers. He'll teach *her* a lot too, with his quick grasp of what's really important.

"What will I do?" she worries. "I don't know whether we belong together or not. My heart is optimistic about our future, but my mind is pessimistic."

"You can't decide our future by what your intellect tells you alone." (His eyes are saying more intimate things.) "The intellect alone is an unsuitable instrument for accurately measuring an extraordinary emotion like love. The mind is clever, but the heart is wiser. Trust your feelings." He takes her in his arms, holds her very close, then kisses her nose lightly. "Listen to the rain on the roof, like that first night we . . . . . . were together. What do your feelings tell you right this minute, darling?"   (He's quick.)

> WEBSTER: *quick*: sensitive; perceptive
> in a high degree.

☆ ☆ ☆ ☆ ☆ ☆

LIBRA *Man* SAGITTARIUS *Woman*

◆━━◀◆▶━━◆

"See," he said, "the arrow struck against this. It
is the kiss I gave her. It has saved her life."

The Sagittarius woman who has been disillusioned by a Gemini or Virgo man, or has perhaps been deeply wounded by a careless arrow from another Sag, could find the affectionate protectiveness and gentle love of a Libra man a very healing experience. His devotion can remove a lot of remembered pain from her heart, caused by more-callous, less-caring lovers in the past.

But Paradise may be postponed a bit, for the very first problem that often pounds insistently for a solution in a love affair between them is: *How far should it go?* Should it be only a magical moment, destined to fade into memory as a miracle never quite grasped? Is it simply one of those inexplicable excursions into madness, incited by a powerful chemistry? Then comes the terrible double-decision: Should they live together, and wait for Time to determine their feelings, to either deepen them or destroy them, and if so — should they live together secretly — or openly — *which* ?

Or should they just get married right away, and be done with all the deliberation ? The situation can even be more complicated. Perhaps he — or she — is already married, and separated, legally or emotionally, from another mate. Is this mutual need that they feel only a fleeting passion, or is it real enough for them to allow it to break the commitment to the former relationship, which has been in limbo ?

It can be worse. Maybe one or both of them have been divorced for several or even many years, and there's no worry that their love will cause a final break with someone else; there is instead the problem of whether or not one should risk a second marital scene when the first was such a serious and sad mistake, causing misery and unhappiness. When half of a love affair is a Libra, unless these two meet in their teens, chances are that a previous marriage, or more than one, will color the decision of "to love or not to love." Librans almost always marry young, and it works out half of the times — the other half of the times it does not. (Those Libra Scales must balance, even in the area of general statistics.)

She may *not* have already been married when they meet. There are exceptions, of course, always — but normally girl Archers don't rush into legal ties as early as Libra males are wont to do. They're too fond of their freedom. However, if not husbands, it's almost certain she will have had other loves before she meets the soft-spoken Libra man who wraps her up in the feather quilt of his smile (again, unless they're still in high school, and maybe even then, because Sagittarius is as curious and experimental about romance as about every other phase and facet of life). In truth, the Libra man who loves this woman stands a better chance of holding her if they meet after she has emotionally matured. To be her very first love can be a lovely and moving experience, the kind a man may remember for the rest of his life — but it doesn't always accomplish the desired result of permanency. Her heart needs to be seasoned to be able to understand and treasure a lasting love.

Not that she takes love lightly, no matter how many love affairs she might have wandered through with those naïve, trusting eyes, so wide open, yet so blind to the realities of human nature. Because of both the duality and the truth-seeking aspect of the Sun Sign, some Sagittarius females take emotional detours along their searching path, ranging all the way from promiscuity to spinsterhood or the vows of religious sisterhood. But we're discussing, in this chapter, the average, middle-of-the-road Sag, who has her dainty (but slightly clumsy) foot on the Libra man's Scales. (Librans are awfully fond of anything that is middle-of-the-road.) This kind of Sagittarius girl is seldom light or casual concerning love. Each time she loves, she believes with all her heart that this must be the first time two people ever felt such wonder. She sincerely wants love to be real and forever-after, as in the faerie tales she used to read, each time she stumbles over a romantic adventure. In this respect, she differs slightly from the average Sagittarian male, to whom permanency is not a prime priority. (The male Archer has to be seduced into wanting forever things.)

The Libra man in love with this lovely and touching clown of a girl should remember that her Jupiter rulership means she has, symbolically, greasepaint in her blood. Many Archers are professional actors or actresses (just as many Librans are lawyers, judges, policemen, authors or bookstore owners). Even if she's not literally a thespian, she is "of the theatre" and although she doesn't always consciously realize it, she's capable of putting on some Academy Award–winning performances, for which Life never gives her an Oscar. She loves, she trusts, she believes, she tries with all her fiery idealism and determination, then falls into heartbreak with no net to catch her, because Sag would rather gamble on happiness than be burdened with excessive insurance or assurance. It hurts, to fall without a net to break your fall. This woman's heart bears more cuts, bruises and scars than her sunny, optimistic personality ever leads others to suspect, for whether she's a secretary, a scientist or a singer, she make-believes sadness away with her considerable acting talents, aided by her cheerful grin.

When her cheerful Jupiter grin locks into the devastatingly brilliant smile of a Libra man, the room they're in won't need any artificial light. These two will light it up with such candlepower, midnight will seem like noon. This isn't an exaggerated attempt at astrological humor, but quite true. Mixing up the sexes a bit, image the incorrigible sunny grins of Sagittarians like ex-mayor of New York John Lindsay, actress Mary Martin, Sammy Davis, Jr., and entrepreneur-or-whatever David Susskind. Then image the blinding smiles of Dwight Eisenhower, President Jimmy Carter and Eleanor Roosevelt, and you'll see that I am not jesting.

If a Libran and an Archer ever held up a bank (not that they're likely to, because Libra would be unable to decide where to park the getaway car, and Sag would trip over the satchel of money and drop the gun) — but if they did hold up a bank, they'd flash the combination of the Jupiter grin and Venus smile, and the teller would probably hand them the cash, smile back and wave a cheery goodbye to them. They're a contagious, irresistible team. Maybe not *that* irresistible, but almost — and especially so to each other.

Once they've solved all those should-we-or-shouldn't-we, and when-should-we-and-how-should-we problems, this man and woman can draw enough happiness interest from their love so that they won't need to rob a bank — or revert to their search for someone to share their lives. They'll have to work at it, of course, like anyone else, but with much less effort. All the ingredients are there to build romance into a lasting love. They can count on the natural harmonics of human nature to smooth the way for them. Another blessed thing about their relationship, as with all 3-11 vibrations, is that they'll be good friends, as well as lovers. This is what first drew them together — similar goals and sympathies, common ideals and the need for change and excitement. All true lovers are friends, but not all lovers who are friends would *still* be friends if they stopped loving in a romantic sense. Libra and Sagittarius probably would be.

Friendship always adds a rich dimension to the emotional tie between a man and woman, and it never fails to deepen their sexual experience together. For all the Sagittarius woman's impulsive, sometimes careless attitude toward intense emotion, she'll be unusually thoughtful, soft and feminine with her gentle Libra lover or husband. Their strong friendship creates a great deal of real affection between them that makes physical union a happy kind of sharing. It's a nice thing when sex between two people is happy and open and free. Like the clear, cool air of autumn, warmed in the Sun, when the sky is so blue you feel that someone has dropped liquid turquoise in your eyes. The intimacy of physical union with someone you really love, who is also a friend, makes you feel clean and washed and rested — and *good*. Love between Jupiter and Venus is always special in some way. More than most couples, they're *aware* of how the miracle of love makes them both feel extra kind and sweet and generous, able to see their dreams more clearly — the way poets feel when they capture emotion in words. Love does that. It makes a man and woman want to embrace the world, not just each other, to include everyone in their happiness; it makes everything negative just a little more positive, makes fear of tomorrow seem foolish — and almost any wild thing seem possible. Libra and Sagittarius are better able than most to express these kinds of feelings verbally to each other. And expressing them makes them last longer.

These two know how to *talk* together. They may quarrel as much as any other couple, perhaps even more often and more violently, but it's the talking that's important. When they openly discuss their hurts, jealousies, sexual adjustments, financial worries and mutual complaints, they've taken a big step toward solving them . . and sometimes, just the talking them over causes them to disappear. The disagreements of Libra and Sag frequently end in lovemaking and laughter. Self-awareness is less painfully gained when someone who *loves* you is honest enough to hold up the mirror of truth to your faults.

There will be occasions when the blunt way she points out his faults, like working overtime and leaving her alone will sting and anger him enough to make him work even later for a few nights, to teach her who's boss. There will be times when his vacillation will annoy her, because she's more impulsive, quicker to know what she wants. Then she'll tell him to make up his mind, to get his act together, or she'll leave him. He'll tell her she isn't being fair, maybe go to a few parties without her — perhaps drink or eat his troubles away until his Scales are level again. He needs a smoothly run, quiet, peaceful and restful home as he needs the very air to breathe. She despises the drudgery of housework (though she can be a delightful hostess). He may complain that the TV or stereo is too loud, the kitchen is a mess, and the draperies don't match the bedspread, so why did she buy them? She'll retort that, for a neatness nut, he's pretty sloppy himself, and she's not going to spend her life being his maid. But then they'll talk it over, and harmony will hum once more between them.

His physical presence has a wonderfully calming effect on her restlessness, and he'll enjoy teaching her to be more patient when things go wrong. Her physical presence excites him in a way that causes him to forget things, such as his indecisive fretting over trifles, and that's a healthy kind of amnesia. With Libra ruling balanced judgment, and Sagittarius ruling philosophy, a few of their discourses can result in some very sound, Socratic observations on human relationships — as when they're discussing the people they thought they loved before they found each other.

LIBRA: The last man you loved . . . how did he make you feel?

SAG: Somehow, ashamed of my identity. I guess he made me feel confused.

LIBRA: What makes you feel less confused about your own identity?

SAG: You. When I'm with you, I don't mind being myself. He made me feel less me, and you make me feel more me.

LIBRA: That's how you make me feel too. Not less me, like she did — but more me. It's good when someone makes you happy to be yourself, instead of ashamed to be yourself.

SAG: Do you suppose that's what love is?

LIBRA: I'm not sure. But I know that's what *our* love is. I've known that from the beginning.

SAG: Oh, no you haven't! It took you forever to make up your mind about us. I almost went back to Marvin. At least he knows his own mind.

LIBRA: That's not fair of you. I know my own mind perfectly well.

SAG: You're a fine one to talk about being fair. Was it fair of you to keep me dangling while you went off to Tulsa to decide if you wanted to marry me or not?

LIBRA: It wasn't Tulsa. I would never go to Tulsa. It was Coshocton, Ohio.

SAG: I don't care *where* it was, I wish you'd go *back* there, and leave me alone!

It's time to leave them. They're involved in a typical Fire-Air pattern. In an hour or so, they'll be involved in the kind of passionate reconciliation that will make him forget all about the drapes not matching the bedspread. Afterward, he'll help her with the dishes while the stereo plays their favorite song, "You Light Up My Life," . . . . . . a Jupiter-Venus song if there ever was one!

☆ ☆ ☆ ☆ ☆ ☆

LIBRA

Air — Cardinal — Positive
Ruled by Venus
Symbol: The Scales
Day Forces — Masculine

CAPRICORN

Earth — Cardinal — Negative
Ruled by Saturn
Symbol: The Goat
Night Forces — Feminine

The **LIBRA-CAPRICORN** *Relationship*

The pandemonium above has ceased almost as suddenly
as it arose, passed like a fierce gust of wind; but
they know in the passing it has determined their fate.

*T*he challenges thrown in the path of people influenced by *any* of the 4-10 Sun Sign Patterns are considerable. But the soul testing required of a 4-10 relationship in which both people were born under a Cardinal Sign (of leadership) is even more formidable. The 4-10 Cardinal vibrations are: Aries-Cancer, Aries-Capricorn, Cancer-Libra and Libra-Capricorn. (For more information, see special sections in the back of this book.)

When two *Mutable Sign* friends, relatives, business associates, lovers or mates are plagued by the tense 4-10 vibes, they either triumph over their difficulties and claim the rewards in solid (and usually urgently needed) character development — slip away and separate gradually — or lead "double-lives" (meanwhile "communicating" rather noisily when they *do* squabble, for all Mutable Signs are "Communicators").

When two *Fixed Sign* "Organizers" are confronted with the 4-10 influence, they either succeed in achieving harmony through the kind of supreme mutual effort that brings a new inner confidence and satisfaction — stubbornly avoid each other as much as possible — or walk away to "re-organize" their lives, and never return.

However, when two *Cardinal* Sun Sign people enter into the 4-10 competition together, they either settle for a neck and neck finish (a tie) with the dominance of the relationship evenly divided between them — or one "leader" clearly conquers the other "leader" in a sweeping (but unfortunate) victory, leaving the vanquished one sadly defeated. The latter will accept his (or her) fate by eventually becoming an introverted and reluctant follower (always an unnatural situation for a Cardinal person) or finally manages to permanently escape, and in this manner, gain back the self-confidence lost through the relationship. The neck and neck finish is obviously the better goal for Libra and Capricorn, as with all Cardinal combos. It's never easy to make "a tie" hold, of course. Someone is demanding a recount — and the two participants may be forced to go to the polls (the starting gate or whatever) more than once to confirm the votes for their equality of popularity and authority. But it certainly beats the other choices.

It's true that the Masters of Karma require a lot of those who connect their lives through the complicated 4-10 threads. Yet, as I've said before, the rewards of victory are sweeter than those bestowed upon the more "fortu-nate" compatibility combinations. One thing is certain. If you know a 4-10 team, such as Libra and Capricorn, and they tell you their association has been very happy and harmonious for many years, you can be certain of *one* of the following — that (a) the Luminary (Sun and Moon) and Ascendent aspects between their horoscopes are conjunct, sextile or trine (b) that one of them was adopted and given a false birth date *or* (c) that these two Earthlings deserve the kind of respect and admiration usually reserved for heroes and heroines, because they've successfully molded their mutual personalities and characters into the shape of the unselfishness and tolerance needed to adjust to one another's totally different attitudes and motivations — into the blend of self-control and compassion of which sainthood is woven. They may not quite be saints, but they will be nearer that level of self-discipline and genuine inner happiness than are most struggling souls. Submission, humility and selflessness are synonymous with rich peace and other inner and outward serenity, but few believe it till they've tried it — and since they don't believe it, not many try it!

Admittedly, it can be a dull and dreary experiment if only one person is trying, and the other won't cooperate. Martyrdom is dreadfully boring, unless both people sacrifice together. Otherwise it isn't fair, the halo gained feels more like an iron band, and doesn't have much glitter. The wings are rather sparse of feathers too, somewhat skimpy. It's rough to work for the rank of saint or angel all by one's self. Then "sweet humility" can cross over the line into masochism, if one isn't careful. It's a fine line, and masochism is not synonymous with sainthood, never mind what all the Polly Perfects and George Goodies tell you.

Capricorn is a feminine Sun Sign, ruled by a masculine planet (Saturn). Libra is a masculine Sun Sign, ruled by a feminine planet (Venus). This is extremely helpful in assisting the Libra and Capricorn men, women and children to achieve a harmonious blend in their association, since they each possess the blend themselves, and can trade it back and forth. The proper blending of the "feminine" qualities of gentleness, patience and sensitivity and the "masculine" qualities of energy, firmness and idealism.

Now that we have Libra's Scales swinging in the soft breeze of happy balance, all smiles and dimples — and Cappy pleasantly nodding in wise agreement that Peace is better than Conflict — we're off to a good start at post time with these two competitive people. It should be, therefore, a friendlier race to the exciting photo finish. (Libra will want to be sure that he — or she — looks attractive, if there's to be a photographer around, while the Goat will grumble that it doesn't matter, but secretly glance in the mirror to be sure his tie is straight — or that her hair is behaving reasonably.)

The "good start" between these two may not last long, however. They aren't to blame. The "mea culpa" admission rightfully belongs to their ruling planets. How could Libra be unfair? How could Capricorn be unwise or rash in any way? They're both such nice people. No, it's those pesky ruling planets. They cause all the trouble. To be candid, Venus and Saturn are not exactly what an astrologer would call space buddies. Libra's Venus tends toward gentle permissiveness, liberal softness, sometimes excesses of spending and pleasure, and a bit of procrastinating now and then. Cappy's Saturn tends toward stern discipline, conservative hardness and never excesses in anything, especially not for pleasure, definitely leaning more toward economy of the purse, emotions and behavior. As for procrastination (which, to the typical Goat, is synonymous with laziness and the shirking of duty) few Cappies are guilty of postponing until tomorrow what they can force themselves to accomplish today. If circumstances beyond their considerable control should *require* postponement, they won't waste valuable time and energy in arguments, debate, discussion, tears, frustration, indecision or any of those Venus-type strategies and defenses. They'll just resign themselves (temporarily) to Fate, mumbling one of their favorite Saturnine truisms, such as: *"time is on our side"* — *"patience is a virtue"* — *"haste makes waste"* — *"anything worth having is worth waiting for"* — and so on.

Then Libra will add the favorite Venusian truisms, like: *"isn't it a lovely day?"* — *"tomorrow will be better"* — *"everything will be all right"* — *"don't worry about the future"* — *"things are going well"* — *"it will be sure to have a happy ending"* — *"there's a rainbow 'round the bend"* — and last, but not least, Libra's truly-all-time-favorite, *"every cloud has a silver lining."*

These particular Saturnine and Venusian philosophies, at least, are in beautiful harmony, each adding the right amount of light and shadow to make a clear and interesting picture (all pictures are flat when they're painted in one dimension only) and you must admit the foregoing truisms do not conflict with, but rather complement and enrich each other. Although they may appear to reflect different viewpoints they actually reflect the same viewpoint, just expressed in polarized fashion. Sort of like — is the wine flask half-empty or half-full ? Is the end of the day the beginning of night — or is the beginning of night the end of the day ? Is awakening in the morning the beginning of sleep — or is falling asleep at night the beginning of awakening ? When a woman is four-and-a-half months pregnant, is she half-past conception or half-way to delivery ? Do people take vitamins to stay well — or to keep from becoming ill ? It all depends on whether your general outlook is pessimistic (cautious-Capricorn) or optimistic (hope-Libra). If they "half" try, they can probably meet one another smack-dab in the middle of Cappy's caution and Libra's hope.

One nice thing about a linking of these two Cardinal souls is that they certainly do project one huge amount of power as a unit. Make that Power. With a capital "P." They're both iron-determined to get what they want, to arrive where they're going and to bend others to their will. Of course, they go about achieving these goals in markedly different ways, but the bottom line is what counts. (Or is it the top line ?) Once Libra and Cappy have decided to join forces and walk in more or less the same direction, they can accomplish, between them, almost anything they want, whether it's a personal ambition, a mutual private dream — or some blessed mission of mercy to bring happiness to others.

Since Libra is symbolically (and often literally) "the Judge" — and Capricorn astrologically symbolizes Law and Authority, the Wisdom of Age and Experience — these two might laser their combined attention on a multitude of heartbreaking problems on this planet. Only one of many thousands of these is the 1978 law passed in the Bronx, New York, allowing judges to mete out adult sentences to punish youthful criminals between 13 and 16 years old. A 13-year-old child who kills somebody with a gun (and an alarming number of them are doing just that) can now be imprisoned for *life*, with no parole. Unsafe streets and the shocking rise in crime among children must be stopped. No one denies that. But is this the solution to halt it ? How does a 13-year-old obtain a gun ? From adults. Where do children get the idea of violence, of shooting, maiming, killing, crippling ? From television.

To program young minds with vivid images, to set a negative example before impressionable youngsters, who always have (and always shall) *imitate* in order to *learn*, then punish them for being efficient human computers, and reacting precisely to what's been fed into them by their parents and the television networks will never balance out as either "logical" or "fair" on Libra's Scales. Neither will such a solution as life imprisonment be viewed as wise or profound to Capricorn's sensible way of thinking. Perhaps the two of them might call upon the guidance of their ruling planets to suggest a new way to bring light into the darkness, rather than deepening it. Between the merciful justice and compassion of Venus and the "Dispenser-of-Karma" Saturn's unerring instinct for placing the blame infallibly where it belongs, maybe the Bronx — and the world — would be a brighter place in which to live. Not exist. *Live.*

Following Gilbert and Sullivan's counsel to "let the punishment fit the crime," they might begin by lobbying for a law to give life imprisonment, not to children, but to particular television programmers and network chiefs, who are, to a great extent, the cause of the youngsters' crimes — by feigning innocence, claiming their programs have no measurable negative effect on audiences — and refusing to accept the great weight of responsibility for the mass programming of the human mind. Then, with the *real* criminals justly and safely behind bars, the youngsters could all be happily *re*-programmed. Not necessarily with "Andy Hardy," though that wouldn't be a bad place to begin, since "Judge Hardy" was a perfect blend of Libra-Capricorn virtues — but at least with *something* besides cheap comedy, lust, greed, sex, drugs, violence, murder, deadly boring talk and game shows — and an occasional "Roots" and "Holocaust." The computer programming of young minds who will control the future of the planet (if nuclear-powered industries don't succeed in negating a future altogether) is a vital New-Age career Libra and Capricorn might consider engaging in together. It's not an astrological exaggeration to claim that Libra and Capricorn together can create enormous energies and power for the positive, when they choose to combine their vibrations and rise up to (rather than avoid) the 4-10 challenge of their association. The ultimate proof is the September 1978 Summit meeting at Camp David between Capricorn Anwar Sadat, Capricorn Vice-President Walter Mondale, Leo Menachem Begin — and Libran President Jimmy Carter. Whatever occurs or does not occur in the future, the whole Earth brightened a few tones from the great beginning sunrise of that memorable autumn conference of two Goats, a Lion — and the Scales of Balance.

Accused on all sides by angry, disappointed American critics of "constantly changing his mind and his position" had been Libran Carter — who, after all, in being so changeable and having some difficulty in making a decision from time to time, like all Librans, was only being true to his Sun Sign. Until he made (as Librans always *finally* do) a brilliant decision, the most important one of his life. Librans may drive you crazy while they're deciding, but when they balance the golden trays of their Scales and at last make a firm one, they don't fool around. It's never less than profound, and really worth all the seesawing they subject you to beforehand.

In making his decision, Jimmy Carter rose to the heights of his astrological mission of *Libra, the Peacemaker,* faced the 4-10 testing with Capricorn Sadat as coolly as he'd been sailing through it with Capricorn Mondale — glorified his Sun Sign and proved astrology's ancient precepts. Whatever problems arose between the patient and wise, yet sometimes stubborn Goat Sadat and the generous and benevolent but sometimes arrogant Lion Begin, it took a Libran Peacemaker to balance out their differences successfully — to coax them, with his broad Venus smile, to embrace before the world in a display of genuine affection. The entire affair constituted Sun Sign astrology put to its most effective purpose. Cappy "Fritz" Mondale kept Cappy Anwar Sadat cozily comforted, feeling secure and safe (as only two Goats can make each other feel) — while charming, smiling Libran Carter easily smoothed the occasionally ruffled Lion's mane (and mien) of prideful Menachem Begin (easily because Carter and Begin are guided by the sextile 3-11 vibration) — then turned his Venus tranquility upon Saturn-ruled Sadat, and triumphed over the natural 4-10 natal Sun square between them. When all the strain was over, and the Libra happy ending was in sight, Goat Sadat, ever the Capricorn "family man," sent to the Lion Begin autographed pictures of himself, Begin and Carter for Begin's grandchildren. Ever the proud Leo, Menachem royally reciprocated the gift by presenting to Cappy Anwar a medallion by Israeli artist Agam, its theme: *The Dream of Peace.*

The eternal dream of Libra — peace. The eternal grace of Capricorn — patience and wisdom. The eternal blessing of Leo — beneficence, warmth and magnanimous gestures. Everyone behaving in a manner befitting the most positive qualities of his Sun Sign essence . . . and behold what miracles may manifest! Of course, not being there, I can't be sure, but I have a hunch the Libran Carter kept his Venus optimism intact during the dark moments of the Summit meeting by repeating the usual Libra mantras to himself. A bird perched high up in a pine tree outside Carter's window probably heard him sighing more than once to himself that "every cloud has a silver lining" — and sure enough, Libra proved his own truism!

One thing Capricorn and Libra may share is an interest in Art or "the Arts." Not every Goat is an artist, but nearly all Cappies are quietly inspired by paintings, and so are most Librans. They also share an interest in music, these two. Both of them tend more toward "the masters" in all art forms than toward the more modern idiom of artistic expression. There are exceptions, as always, but they are rare. Libra loves fine and elegant furnishings and beautiful objects, whether they're chairs and tables or china and crystal. Capricorn admires craftsmanship — articles which are not only beautiful, but built to last longer than a few months after you bring them home. Somewhere near the center of these two views, Libra the Judge (or Judgess) and the Goat (or the Goat Girl) will meet cheerfully and agreeably. Capricorn will be more interested in the price tag and the practicality of everything, from clothing to carpeting, whereas Libra will be more drawn by the colors and fabric, the overall impression of balance — and the aesthetical-ly pleasing. There are lots of areas where these two can find compatibility rather than conflict when they take the time and trouble to make the distinction.

Capricorn, however, may be unable to hide his (or her) disapproval of Libra's eternal optimism and dances of indecision. And Libra may sometimes feel that hanging out with Cappy is like chumming around with the Warden at Sing Sing or an adult truant officer who turns in guilty adults who occasionally play hooky from the school of life.

But probably, bye and bye, Libra will once more tint the Goat's seriousness with pastel-colored bubbles of hope . . . Capricorn will make Libra feel even-tempered and snugly protected . . they'll both look toward tomor-row, which of course *will* be better . . . realize that time *is* on their side . . . somehow glue their association back together . . . and race for the photo finish again.

☆ ☆ ☆ ☆ ☆ ☆

LIBRA *Woman* CAPRICORN *Man*

━━━◄◆►━━━

. . . and she sat with him on the side of the bed. She also said she would give him a kiss if he liked, but Peter did not know what she meant, and he held out his hand expectantly.

"Surely you know what a kiss is?" she asked, aghast.

"I shall know when you give it to me," he replied stiffly.

In the beginning, the Libra woman will judge the Capricorn man as too stiffly old-fashioned, stuffy, dull and stodgy to fit the rosy-pink image of her dream mate, spun from the silken threads of her rosy-pink imagination.

She'll think he's impossibly conservative, set in his ways, stubborn, prosaic, humorless and depressing. He is also, she decides, unduly pessimistic, opinionated and emotionally cold. After tossing all these assessments into one tray of her Scales, she certainly ought to make an attempt to fill up the opposite tray with a few of his virtues. Otherwise, the Goat, astrology — and

I — will accuse her of being unfair to this man's potential as a lover or husband. You wouldn't want all three of us against you, would you, lovely Libra lady ? All right, then here are some Saturnine virtues for you — to give your analysis of the shy Goat, who's captured at least your attention, if not yet your heart, a little more perspective and balance.

Stubborn he is. We'll give you that one. There's no getting around it. He was born under an Earth Sign, not a mental Air Sign like your own, and can therefore be immovable when he gets a notion into his head. To an extent, old-fashioned too. But in a kind of charming way, don't you think ? It's one of the restful, peaceful things about him. Surely you, as a Libra female, have nothing against restfulness and peace.

Stuffy and conservative ? Well, it depends. One needn't be stuffy just because one is conservative. To be true to your Libra Sun Sign, you'll have to examine your charge more carefully. The meaning of "conservative" is relative. An ordinary mugger is conservative to a big time stock manipulator or clever bank embezzler. The sadistic behavior of Nazi Storm Troopers seems conservative in comparison to the reliable reports of brutal beating, choking and sometimes permanent crippling of helpless victims by particular bullies on the Los Angeles Police Force — and similar "law enforcement" beasts in Chicago, New York and other cities in this land of alleged "liberty and justice for all." Public nudity on beaches is "conservative" to patrons of the new Roman orgy Sex Palaces being built by entrepreneurs like the owner of the Benihana Japanese restaurant chain. A Porsche and a BMW are "conservative" to the owner of a new Ferrari or Lancia. The Beatles are "conservative" to the Rolling Stones, who are likewise to "Kiss" (the rock group so far-out, they returned before they left). Everything is circular, and if you're going to measure a circle's circumference, it really doesn't matter where you begin.

For example, measuring the circle counterclockwise, Lincoln biographer Capricorn Carl Sandburg presents a "conservative" image compared to Capricorn Richard Nixon. Capricorn Howard Hughes is (not was) "conservative" compared to the chaps who run the Summa Corporation. When you check the list carefully, in a circular direction . . . on reflection . . . you might decide to reverse your decision, and classify "conservative" not as "stuffy," but as the lesser degree of Whatever on the Way to Nothing and Nowhere, you know ? So maybe you should change your mind and switch his conservatism over to the Positive tray of your Libra Scales, as a sort of beginning balancer.

Yes, the Goat is definitely opinionated, but you might add to the Positive tray also the reverse, which is that he's not wishy-washy. Emotionally cold he sometimes is, granted, but you can fill up the tray containing his virtues even more by adding the fact that neither is he rash and impulsive, prone to passionate, angry outbrusts (and you know how you recoil in distaste from that kind of thing) unless his birth chart is extremely afflicted, which can happen to any Sun Sign, not just Capricorn. Even Libra. Now, if you don't mind, eliminate from the Negative tray of your Scales the term "humorless." Because you're wrong about that. Wait till you know him better. You'll discover that he has a delightful, whimsical sort of humor that's acutely tuned-in to the vibes of the ridiculous behavior of Earthlings. It's rare and subtle, but his sense of comedy timing is exquisite. He's also gentle and loyal. Dependable and earnest. He's a hard worker, never lazy or shiftless. He possesses an appreciation of art and music he doesn't talk about much. Nor does he rent a billboard to advertise his deep and instinctive wisdom regarding human nature.

How are your Scales balancing him now? Almost even, with his shortcomings on one side and his longcomings on the other? You're still undecided about his pessimism and its depressing effect on you? Well, have you thought of looking at it from the other side — like, *his* side maybe? Which could end up by also being *your* side, when you view it dead-center, because this man secretly wishes he could raise his pessimism a few notches toward your optimism — more than he lets you know. Isn't that your favorite endeavor, cheering the sad and lonely, teaching the futility of futility? He honestly needs the magic touch of your sunny disposition and your airy mental challenge to release him from his inhibitions and to fill the emptiness he often feels, but won't confess, even to himself. He's much too shy to tell you that your smile brings tears to his eyes. Notice him the next time you smile at him the way only a Libra girl can smile, brightening the room like a thousand candles, suddenly flaming all at once. See how he turns his head quickly, pretending he's busy, and you're disturbing his work or his thoughts? When he turns back around, his manner is more crusty than before, his voice gruffer. Self-control does that to a man. Saturn's self-discipline, instilled in him when he was born, blankets him with a chilly charisma that sends people away, never suspecting how much he wants them to stay.

But if you'll take the time and trouble to gaze deeply into his eyes, you'll see hiding there the Goat's soft twinkle of happy, longing to escape and smile with you, if only he could be sure it's safe to trust his feelings. The eyes are the windows of the soul. When you catch him off-guard, you can look through them and see the warm fires inside, behind the frosty winter exterior he sometimes projects.

The sexual compatibility between Libra and Capricorn doesn't always fall into place naturally with the first embrace they share. She may feel hurt and rejected by a certain indefinable coolness in his approach, which she mistakenly interprets as disinterest — and he may also feel that *her* aloof response to *his* advances indicates detachment. Just as the elements of air and earth in Nature are strangers, so are the Air and Earth human natures of

Libra and Capricorn puzzling, each to the other. Gentle and persistent effort can slowly and surely, however, bring an unusual enchantment to their lovemaking. The attraction of the "different" can be a powerful magnet to sexual desire. It's as though they never run out of things to teach one another about themselves. His reticent manner at first disturbs her, then gradually draws her, curiously, with a strange wanting to penetrate his quiet, to fathom its depth. The elusiveness of her airy freedom of behavior and expression holds an intense fascination for him, like the call of a sea gull when you're walking along the shore . . . both tantalizing and haunting. Even if they spend a lifetime together, she'll never completely uncover this man's deeper self — nor will he ever succeed in completely capturing her changing passions.

A desire thus not quite satisfied can take one of two paths. It can intensify their intimacy with a silent challenge that makes their sexual expression always exciting with promise, which can be rekindled and newly aroused even after prolonged periods of mutual withdrawal — or it can cause them to gradually lose interest in lovemaking because of the frustration of being unable to comprehend how to fulfill each other. Which path it takes depends a lot on the aspect between their Suns and Moons in their nativities, also the relationship of their mutual Mars and Venus positions at birth. Even more, it depends on them . . . how much they love.

A Libra woman speaks musically, moves lyrically. She's graceful, tender and sentimental . . . as intoxicating as a fragrant rose. Yet she is also determinedly independent, however well hidden may be her driving ambition and intelligent mind behind the satiny facade of her velvet Venus smile or dimpled grin. She can coax and cajole most any man into willingly (even ecstatically) doing things her way. But the earthbound Goat may resist her charm, when "her way" conflicts with "his way."

Consider Jayne Thompson. She's an Aries woman, but no matter, because both Aries and Libra women are equally free and independent, liberated females by nature. Jayne is the pretty, dark-haired wife of "Big Jim" Thompson, Governor of Illinois — a former public prosecutor (Jayne, not Jim) and an ardent ERA advocate. When they were blessed, in 1978, with the first baby born to an incumbent Illinois Governor in seventy-two years, they gave her the nostalgic name of Samantha, and rocked her in an appropriately old-fashioned, antique cradle — to match her father's old-fashioned ideas about parenthood (never mind Mama's ERA leanings). "This one is going to wear *dresses*," Samantha's father stated firmly in an interview — then glancing at his sleeping infant daughter, "because Daddy is not going to buy you anything *but* dresses." (Samantha being a tiny Lioness, wish him luck!) Although Gov. Thompson is an earthy Taurean, it's all the same. An Earth Sign male is an Earth Sign male. In certain respects, there's not a great deal of difference between a Bull and a Goat (or a conservative Crab, for that matter). The Capricorn man may be funny, lovable, devoted and affectionate (as is "Big Jim," with his warm and friendly ways) but all Goats are a shade chauvinistic about the women in their lives.

Since the Saturn-ruled man can't help being immovable regarding his favorite notions, and since his Libra woman is more flexible, guided by her Air Element, it's easier for her to change her position than for him to do so. Consequently, much of the responsibility for the success of their relationship may fall upon her dainty but strong shoulders. If she really tries, her lovingly grateful Goat should reward her with a romantic honorary degree for the "fine art" of harmonizing her personality to blend with his own, maybe a gold bracelet to encircle her arm, inscribed in Latin sweet talk with: *Artium Elegantium Exquisitariumque Doctoris.* Then she can give him an old-fashioned pocket timepiece, complete with an antique watch fob and chain, to add to his dignified appearance . . . recalling all the sweetness of the past . . . engraved inside the case with the words: *stuffy and conservative equals serene and cozy.* Or maybe a more private code between them, like: *4-10 is the lucky number of the angels.*

☆ ☆ ☆ ☆ ☆ ☆

LIBRA *Man* CAPRICORN *Woman*

◄◄●►►

All he thinks he has a right to, when he comes to
you to be yours, is fairness. After you have been
unfair to him, he will love you again, but he will
never afterwards be quite the same boy.

Oddly and unfortunately or fortunately (I really can't decide which, nor can Libra) this otherwise tense and challenging 4-10 Sun Sign Pattern-influenced relationship is blessed with an inherent positive-plus factor the Libra man and his Goat Girl may not utilize. Taking into account, naturally, the normal number of exceptions that prove the rule, a Libra man is one of the six Sun Sign males — the others being Aries, Gemini, Sag, Aquarius and Pisces — who (if he's not one of the rare, perverse exceptions) is likely to agree with many, if not all, of the platforms proposed by the Women's Liberation Movement. Why not? He's fair. He's just. He's tolerant and adaptable to change, whether within his own personal sphere, or concerning the sweeping changes of social reform. He's thoughtful, logical, reasonable — and pleasantly willing to listen to all opposing sides, including the opposing sides of the Aquarian Age male-female conflict.

On the other swing of the pendulum, the Capricorn woman was born under a Cardinal Sign of leadership (as was he) and she must lead something or someone at sometime — somewhere. She enjoys being in charge of her own life, and of everything and everyone else she can manage to wisely guide and discipline with the "grandma knows best" attitude that hangs over her (which began hanging around her aura when she was approximately six years old). She's marvelously qualified as a Capitalized Career Woman, makes a splendid executive, and is capable of keeping everything serenely functioning in a down-to-earth, sensible way, whether it's the heartbreaking and back-breaking task of holding together a fatherless home in a ghetto, and being the great comforting rock of stability and self-preservation for the whole neigh-borhood — presiding over an antique boutique, a service station (some Goat Girls do) or a trucking company — laying down the rules for a brokerage firm, running a car wash or a finishing school for sheep dogs. With her well-bred voice and manner (whatever her actual background) and her cool common sense, she's exquisitely equipped to be a successful C.W.

Now consider her Libra man — more likely than not to be liberal in his view of his lady working or pursuing a career. Wouldn't you say that was a positive-plus factor between them? The reason they don't always take advantage of it is probably more her fault than his.

Although she needs to lead — being, as noted earlier, Cardinal, like Libra — the typical Capricorn shrinks from the idea of leading out front, in a showy way. The Goat (male or female) prefers to be the "spider" in the corner, who pulls the strings behind-the-scenes and makes it all happen, with no fuss and fanfare. It's difficult for the Goat Girl to find the sort of leadership niche she seeks in the business world. Things haven't yet progressed far enough to create the ideal situation. With extremely rare and fortunate exceptions, the Capricorn woman usually finds but two choices open to her in the success sweepstakes: (a) an underling job at low pay, because she's a female — or (b) a position worthy of her abilities, which can only be attained by advancing herself aggressively and receiving lots of attention from everyone (like *Business Week* and IRS) once she's arrived. Since she refuses to meekly follow orders, to be a small cog in the wheel, and because a pinnacle of power that demands the sacrifice of her personal privacy isn't the kind of leadership she's after — the typical, rather shy Goat Girl either finds her place as a professional in the arts, or some similar "loner" type endeavor — or decides to become the "spider in the corner" at home, contentedly fulfilling her Sun Sign ambitions by weaving her webs of strategy unobtrusively, in the background, "leading" and directing her husband, children, relatives and friends in such a subtle way, they hardly suspect it.

So here they are. A Libra man who's cheerfully willing to have his lady work outside the home — and a Capricorn woman who would just as soon make *him* her career. You know that truism about "behind every successful man there's a woman"? It's often a Capricorn woman. Goats don't waste their valuable time on anything short of success. If this ambitious woman guides her man, she certainly isn't going to guide him toward failure. Whatever she's helping him achieve, her eye is on the most fruitful result. The thing is, he might prefer her to follow her Cardinal instincts outside, rather than inside the home. He adores being the man to whom she's loyal and devoted, the man she loves and cherishes and protects (against himself), but he may rebel at being made her "lifetime career."

He is of the Air Element, and the first lesson an "earthy" female must learn about the "airy" man she loves (especially the *Cardinal* Air Sign) is that "air" seeks freedom of movement, and simply cannot bear restriction — or it becomes stale. Not only that, it will escape the instant the lid is removed. Leave an Air Sign man alone to drift and to dream, to roam mentally, following the breezes of his inclinations, and he'll happily remain more or less nearby. Try to bottle him or box him in, and he'll become "windy," argumentive and resentful — easily stirred into a tornado or hurricane of anger. Then he'll storm away.

If she's genuinely contrite and truly wants him back, he might return. She'll have to be fair enough to acknowledge her mistake and ask for his understanding of her side of the situation. No, let's change that. Acknowledging her mistake and asking for his understanding is fine. He'll probably respond like an absolute angel. But it may not be wise to try to get him to see *her side* of the disagreement — openly, that is. It's always a mistake with a Libran to make a point of defending a particular side of any question, if you expect compromise from him. Enumerate all the positive factors of one side, and this man will instinctively use all his mental energy, deductive reasoning and brilliant logic (with which he is, please believe, more than amply endowed) in making it all balance out even on his Scales by eloquently defending the opposite side — whatever the opposite side may be. Never mind which side he thought his sympathies were with before. He'll change his mind (even a long-held conviction) just to win an interesting debate. Something about the challenge of an argument seems to hypnotize him, until he actually forgets where he stood before the "discussion" began.

This is Libra's Achilles Heel, and few of them realize it. I personally think it's mean and unfair to take advantage of the poor man's Sun Sign weakness, but there could be extenuating circumstances when the end might justify the means. In such a circumstance, the wise Goat Girl will take *his* side all the way, make it clear that she's been completely wrong, recite a sort of monologue (difficult for Cappy, but she can practice by observing his own verbal finesse) containing all the reasons he is right and she is woefully wrong, giving herself not the slightest edge, making it all seem obviously lopsided and unfair to her. It will work like a charm.

He'll be helpless, unable to resist his strong Sun Sign "judgeship" instincts, and begin to point out to her all the flaws in her argument, show her where she's being unfair to herself, offer to take at least half the blame — and end up just where she wants him — making a spoken declaration of his comprehension of the things he's done to hurt and worry her, which caused her to behave as possessively and poutingly as she did. He'll barely know what happened, except that, somehow, he has honestly begun to see where maybe she was justified in her feelings. Soon he'll become his normal sweet and sentimental self again, ask for forgiveness and coax her to have faith in a new beginning. Then he'll smile his outrageous Venus smile. And it happens. The resurrected rush of remembered trembling, the familiar yearning. And sorrow, too. From comprehending the pain caused, that wasn't meant to hurt, but was a reaction *to* hurt — on both sides. Sorrow is always followed by compassion, the overwhelming need to forgive and to be forgiven. A Capricorn woman can resist (if she chooses) any temptation ever conjured to test the human soul. But not even she can long hold out against the blinding brightness of the Libra smile. She'll answer it with her own little shy Goat grin, her eyes and her heart will soften simultaneously . . . . . and roses will bloom again in January's snow.

She may not, however, melt into his arms immediately, if the snowflakes are still falling inside her. He'll have to use all his tenderness and charm to reverse her frigid withdrawal, after he's caused her to feel rejected. Just as she'll have to use all her gentle persuasion to heal the wounds in his optimistic nature she inflicted by her cold, disapproving manner. But this woman can be surprisingly gentle when she trusts the man with whom she's making love. Their sexual harmony will be at times elusive. Nevertheless, it's attainable when both of them unselfishly seek to know what it is the other needs, recognize the differences of desire, and honestly try to bridge them . . . softening the traits that offend and imitating the qualities in each other they individually admire. Saturn's restrictive influence can make her appear too reserved and unresponsive to the romantic and verbally expressive Libra man. Because her approach to sex is one of slow sensuality, his light and airy seeming detachment can leave her feeling empty and yearning for a more tangible passion. But if he tries, he'll be gladdened and amazed by the unsuspected affection and sentiment buried within her, needing only his patience to bring it out. And she'll discover there's much she can teach this man about the deep earthiness of physical union and sexual intimacy that he's touchingly anxious to learn from her. Each of them will benefit by trying to be more like the other. She must try to be more expressive; he must try to be more concentrated during their lovemaking. Then all will be well.

A Libra man contains a bottomless well of sentiment, yet he may not be sensitive enough to his Capricorn woman's silent secrets. Sometimes his logic and clear thinking get in the way of his understanding of the human heart.

He's fair and sympathetic, but often in such a *mental* way that he neglects to comprehend the motives behind what she's doing or saying. Libra isn't noted for a perception of human emotions — more for analyzing the *result* of emotions, their outward manifestation in words and deeds. For all his airy refinement and artistic leanings, his talent for "romance," he can appear "cool" to the Goat Girl, whose own nature is richer with various shades and tones and levels of the heights and depths of all human longings.

They are both moody. He swings from high to low, from cheerful and sweet to cranky and domineering, several times in the course of a week, or even a single day. Her moods are neither as swift nor as multiple. Saturn's depression clouds gather more gradually, over an extended period of time, disturb her more seriously — and last much longer.

She needs his rainbows of hope. He needs her haven of dependability. And someone once wrote that being needed is as good as being loved. Sometimes . . . even better. Because there's a kind of love that blooms too quickly, like a fragile blossom, briefly beautiful, but easily bruised by frost, unable to withstand the first wind of a storm. "Needing" seeds a sturdy, more familiar kind of love, that grows quietly into a strong tree, with roots that remain in Earth, branches that offer shade . . . leaves that sing in the wind a lyric lovely enough for Libra, yet practical enough for Capricorn. Trees don't grow overnight. They must be nurtured throughout the patient waiting of many seasons. But they last. Trees are forever. Libra and Capricorn might meditate on the mysterious truth hidden in Tagore's words, that . . . . . *the faith waiting in the heart of a seed . . . promises a miracle of life which it cannot prove.*"

LIBRA

Air — Cardinal — Positive
Ruled by Venus
Symbol: The Scales
Day Forces — Masculine

AQUARIUS

Air — Fixed — Positive
Ruled by Uranus
Symbol: The Water Bearer
Day Forces — Masculine

The **LIBRA-AQUARIUS** *Relationship*

> *The bubbles of many colours made in rainbow water*
> *they treat as balls, hitting them gaily from one to*
> *another with their tails, and trying to keep them*
> *in the rainbow till they burst.*

Libra is forever blowing bubbles, and Aquarius is forever bursting them. For a while, it's all hysterically funny, full of joy, like a game. But after a time it wears a little thin. Then Libra will become cranky, and Aquarius will be furious over being misunderstood.

Libra will accuse Aquarius of being stubborn. (That's true — Aquarius is a Fixed Sign.) Aquarius will accuse Libra of being bossy. (That's also true, because Libra is a Cardinal Sign of leadership.) After they've told each other the truth, Libra will try to be fair, and admit to a touch of bossiness, apologizing so sweetly the Water Bearer feels mean to keep insisting that he (or she) is not stubborn. Yet Aquarius will go right on being mean in not admitting this character flaw, because people born under a Fixed Sun Sign nearly always find it impossible to see their faults as anything but virtues. Besides, Aquarius thinks such discussions are a waste of time. People either get along or they don't. If they don't, they shouldn't even be talking together. They should wave goodbye, and head on down the road. If they do, they shouldn't be expending energy on fighting. Life is too full of interesting things to do. That's how Aquarius wins arguments. (These people are extremely practical when it comes to wasted motion, and a trifle selfish when it comes to seeing any side but their own.) What I should have said is that's how Aquarius wins arguments with most people. It will not be quite so easy to win when Libra is the other member of the debating team. Very few people top Libra in the argumentive, debating or discussion department.

Aquarians have a way of winning a fight with their hats. They put them on and leave. It's a strategy the Water Bearer may utilize when he (or she) senses Libra is winning through pure logic.

Because both of them belong to the Air or mental element, when they're not involved in a verbal dispute, they'll be sharpening their fine minds with positive conversations, which are never less than stimulating and challenging, all the way from exciting to inspiring. Also, since they're under the influence of the 5-9 Sun Sign Pattern vibration, only rarely will a Libra-Aquarius disagreement be serious or lasting. There will always be an emotional and mental foundation for forgiveness and a new start. Even among those very few Libra-Aquarian people who part and are no longer close friends, who eventually drift away from a day-to-day association for some reason, the chances are that neither will retain any bitterness or speak harshly about the other, for whatever these two may say or do, beneath it all, they understand each other better than they do most other people they both know. Libra and Aquarius often have a common interest in children, animals, higher education, travel to foreign lands, religion, philosophy and the arts. Their Suns are trined, and this gives them intertwined dreams and ideals, regardless of any personal differences they may have from time to time.

Whether the Water Bearer admits it or not, he (or she) recognizes and respects the fact that Libra always tries hard to be fair and impartial. Whether Libra admits it or not, he (or she) recognizes and respects the Aquarian quality of tolerance and the Uranian humanitarian goals. The inescapable admiration and respect are always there between them, even when all that air is being blown around in an intellectual confrontation. The basic compatibility is strong and good, for these two understand each other's motives, however often they may heatedly try to deny it.

There may be occasions when the delicate balance of Libra's Scales is temporarily upset by the eccentric behavior of the Uranus-ruled person. Aquarians tend to behave in an extremely emotional manner when they're angry, and at such times Libra can actually become physically ill from the tension. Venus people require harmony, and tension can affect their nerves to a marked degree. There may be other times when Libra's tendency to always look at both sides of a question will seem like disloyalty to Aquarians, who believe, as I've already mentioned, that there is only one side — their own. The opinions of a Fixed Sign are, quite naturally perhaps, more fixed than flexible. Aquarians are truly totally unprejudiced and tolerant, *except* when it comes to a *personal, emotional* confrontation.

Most Librans, except for those who have heavy afflictions to the natal Sun in their horoscopes, influenced as they are by the gentle planet Venus, possess what Hemingway called "grace under pressure." This will come in handy when Aquarius unpredictably blows a Uranus fuse, for the Water Bearers are susceptible to electrical impulses from the cosmos, and whatever they do, they're likely to do it impulsively and suddenly. The Libra person often brings on the very problems he (or she) wants to avoid by not leaving well enough alone. After a typical electrical outburst of eccentric behavior, Aquarians normally disappear, and refuse to communicate at all for a period of time. If they're left alone, they'll eventually forget what it was that troubled them and become their normal crazy, lovable and fascinating selves. But Libra may keep pressing for an explanation or continue to try to win a decisive victory regarding the disagreement, rather than allowing it to be forgiven and forgotten. Aquarians can't stand being pinned down for an answer. It makes them feel like a butterfly caught in a jar, and that's a mighty uncomfortable feeling. Librans don't mind in the least being pinned down for an answer. It gives them the golden opportunity to weight the pros against the cons, an exercise they find enormously energizing, as long as everyone remains polite and considerate, and no one starts yelling in an uncouth manner. Their individual reactions to conflict and controversy constitute an important basic difference between them, but once they've comprehended this, and made allowances for it, Libra and Aquarius can float around a home, a classroom, a laboratory, a space capsule, an office or a barn on the fluffy clouds of mutual cooperation.

Libra can teach coolness and calm to Aquarius, and the Water Bearer can teach Libra that nothing in this world is black or white, one or the other — everything is grey, a mixture; therefore, tolerance is the only way to balance life on anyone's scales. Aquarius is the inventor of new ideas; Libra is the architect who designs them for practical use.

Libran sensibilities are easily offended; yet the human mind has never conceived of anything capable of offending the Aquarian sensibilities. Absolutely nothing shocks an Aquarian, while any idea, conversation or object that doesn't have flowers painted on it in pastel shades will shock Libra's refined tastes. Being a *Water* Bearer, and also being deeply concerned about the future of the planet, it's only natural that an Aquarian will become enthusiastic over the sound ecological concept of something like the Mullbank waterless toilet. The Water Bearer will excitedly point out to Libra that this is the only way to save all the waters on Earth from fast approaching total pollution, because of the ever-growing population, and the resulting addition- al tons of sewage spilled into our lakes, rivers, streams and oceans each year.

As he (or she) warms to the subject, the Aquarian will expound the theory that the government should pass a law *requiring* every home to use a waterless toilet, allowing the cost to be deducted from the sum of money owed to the IRS that year by each person who installs one to replace the current polluting and water-wasting flush toilet plumbing. "Just think!" exclaims Aquarius, "there's absolutely no odor, and the only waste to be disposed of once a year for a family of six is what would amount to a coffee can of ashes (*also* with no odor) which can be sprinkled on the grass or the garden to make everything grow better and faster!" (See page 1181 for manufacturers' addresses.)

Now, Libra would very much like to espouse anything that guarantees keeping the ecological "balance," but the detailing of anything so scatological concerning the indelicate process of elimination is likely to cause furious blushing, and an expression of extreme distaste, to pass across those beautiful and even Libran features.

"Okay, okay," shrugs Aquarius angrily, "if you'd rather go on drinking and bathing in water polluted by other people's body waste, and insure that your grandchildren, and maybe even yourself and your own children, won't have a drop of pure water to drink in a decade or two, keep flushing your damned toilet, and spraying your bathroom with artificial carnation scents in aerosol cans that are destroying the ozone layer around the Earth, but just remember, you were warned. It's peat moss, compost and manure that are going to save this planet, not perfumed luxury, bubble baths and all your fancy art and music."

Out stalks the Water Bearer in a huff, leaving Libra behind to lie down and recuperate from the ugliness of it all, in a state of near nervous collapse from the ordeal of mentally weighing the trays marked: Survival — and Judgment Day.

A few minutes later, the Aquarian suddenly returns, shouts loudly, "*I SAID MANURE!*" then slams the door and leaves again. Libra's dimples collapse, in a state of shock. That's how Aquarius wins an argument.

Libra's seesaw indecision will cause Aquarius to become rattled, just as the Uranus tendency of Aquarians to pull a complete turnabout, once a decision has already been made (Libra *never* does *that*), will drive the Libra man or woman squirrels. "Make up your mind!" yells Aquarius.

"Well, at least I don't change my mind, once it's made up, the way you're always doing," replies Libra defensively, but softly.

"How would you know?" retorts Aquarius. "You've never made a decision in your life."

Libra smiles radiantly. The room lights up with a thousand candles, a million Suns. "I made the decision to be your friend, didn't I? And I've never regretted it. Other people may think you're crazy, but I think you're a genius. Did I tell you I ordered a waterless toilet?"

Aquarius is shamed into silence. Libra smiles again, dimples winking on and off. "Gee, I'm sorry," finally mumbles the contrite Water Bearer. "Sometimes I say the nuttiest things. I really don't know what I'd do without you." (And *that's* how *Libra* wins arguments.) It requires study.

☆ ☆ ☆ ☆ ☆ ☆

LIBRA *Woman* AQUARIUS *Man*

◄─◄►►─►

"Tink," he rapped out, "if you don't get up and dress at once I will open the curtains, and then we shall all see you in your négligée."

This made her leap to the floor. "Who said I wasn't getting up?" she cried.

Unless they both enjoy having their emotions blown about in continual hurricanes and tornadoes, it will be best to establish in the very beginning who of these two walks in front in the game of follow-the-leader these two play. The Chief walks in front. The Squaw walks a few steps behind. Smoke that in your Peace Pipe, please, for the sake of tranquility.

The Libra girl will simply have to understand that she is the female, the lady, the woman—and he's the masculine half of the duet. He sings baritone, she sings soprano. She might have been born under the influence of a masculine Sun Sign, but she's under the guidance of the gentle feminine planet Venus. No one, not even Bella Abzug, plus the entire staff of *Ms.* magazine, will ever successfully remove the femininity from Venus, with any amount of liberation surgery. This isn't to say that I'm not with you, Bella. I'm with you and Gloria and the others all the way. I'm an Aries Ms., and Rams come kicking and screaming into this world liberated before the umbilical cord has been cut. (I even named my new girl kitty ERA—before I knew for sure she was a girl.) But Truth is Truth, and Venus is Venus. To put it another way, Truth is Beauty, and Beauty is Truth. All those platitudes. L didn't invent the wisdom behind them. Mr. and Ms. God invented it. Our co-Creators. Protest to them, not to me. I'm a mere astrologer, an interpreter of the law, not its architect.

The Aquarian male was born under the influence of a masculine Sun Sign too, but unlike the Libra woman, he is, in addition, under the strong and rather arrogant guidance of the masculine planet Uranus (the male charisma is always a bit arrogant, don't you think?). There are certain astrological birds and bees blueprints that have nothing to do with chauvinism or equality of the sexes, or with any of those transient things. They simply *exist*. Even in the area of the Aquarian-symbolized homosexuality, they exist. That's not to imply that all Aquarians are homosexual, only that the Aquarian *essence* is tolerant of *all* life-styles, representing brotherhood and universal love, un-prejudiced by male-female hang-ups, which sometimes gets translated into the homosexual concept by members of all twelve Sun Signs who become confused by the vibrations of Uranus, even stronger now, in the dawning of the Aquarian Age. It's a simple matter of respecting individuality.

The planetary blueprints exist as unavoidably as the two distinctly different kinds of anatomical design of male and female exist. As free and equal as women ever aspire to be, they will be, for all eternity, designed differently from men, and astrological influences are just as inevitable and unchangeable.

A Libra girl may try to sweetly and softly maneuver for position with her Water Bearer, to manipulate him into her own program and pattern of living, and he'll go along at first, when he's overcome by her dimples and divine charm, not to mention her starburst smile — but there will come the time when he will balk. The stubbornness of a Fixed Aquarian male when he's had enough makes a mule look like the most docile, easily led and persuaded creature in the world. This man won't move a fraction of an inch when he believes he's right. His personal code of manhood and his general public code of morality were delivered to him engraved on a stone tablet, from a hand extended behind a burning bush, maybe belonging to a relative of Moses, who knows? But he remembers the day well. It was before he was born. No influence on this Earth will sway an Aquarian from a course of action he honestly thinks is right and just. You'll notice I said right and just (according to his personal code) — I didn't say anything about fair. Fair is *her* department. And this is what will cause a major portion of the trouble between these two who are basically so truly compatible — the definition of what is fair. I'll give you an example.

A number of years ago in New York, I knew a Libra girl and her Aquarian friend. (I guess they were friends. They didn't say anything about being lovers, but you never know with Aquarius, because this man is unable to distinguish between love and friendship, and if it's the former, he's not the kind to buy a billboard to announce it.) But anyway, the Libra girl gave her Aquarian friend a gift, a fat, chubby St. Bernard puppy. It grew. It grew into a Giant Dog at the same rate the Aquarian man's devotion for his new pet grew. Eventually, the two of them quarreled. (Not the St. Bernard and the Water Bearer, the Libra girl and the Water Bearer.) She weighed the whole situation carefully (and I'm sure sincerely) on her Scales, to try to reach a fair solution. After many traumatic hours of deliberation, she arrived at what she saw as a fair decision.

He had made a promise to always be her friend. Then he started behaving like the Loch Ness monster, completely ignoring his promise, and after all, *he* was the one who kept harping on the holiness, the sacredness of friendship . . . . "If you're really my friend, you'll do this or that" — or — "If you were really my friend, you *wouldn't* do this or that," he was always telling her. She had given him the St. Bernard when she thought they were *friends.* It had been a gift predicated upon the *association,* which no longer was valid. And now she had made up her mind. (Once Librans finally make up their minds, they don't fool around.) She called the sheriff, and insisted that the dog be returned.

The Water Bearer was furious. He considered all manner of things in reaction to this injustice. Maybe even painting her hair green, or tossing a live hornet's nest into her bedroom window. The St. Bernard had become his best friend in all the world, and now she was taking back her gift — kidnapping his buddy ?

The violence of his wounded emotions churned within him, until there was no choice but to leave New York for many months until he cooled off. If this Libra lady had had any hope that her action would bring him to his senses, she had made a dangerous miscalculation of the Uranus vibration. She not only broke his heart, she broke their friendship into a thousand pieces, and that's almost an impossibility with an Aquarian — especially in a relationship with Libra, because their Suns are trined, and the essential understanding of the 5-9 Pattern influence supports almost every difficulty they might encounter. Not this one. You don't separate an Aquarian from his Giant Dog Buddy. It's one of the Uranus laws en*raved* (also engraved) on that stone tablet. And now it has a large crack in it.

A serious mistake, the Libra lady made. She may be able to repair the damage someday, but it will take a lot of patience and humility. If she had just waited a little while longer, he would have stopped behaving like the Loch Ness monster. One has to give Aquarians time to turn around when they're temporarily standing on their heads, contemplating the cosmos and chewing peanut butter balls. Eventually, they'll apologize for whatever outrageously eccentric behavior they exhibited. But they won't be pushed into contrition, especially not by dognapping. It was an educational experience for the Libra girl.

Once these two have reached a comfortable compromise concerning their individual concepts of what is fair, and have developed a slide rule they mutually agree upon to measure justice in a human relationship, they can collect all the rewards and benefits of the 5-9 Sun Sign Pattern influence, and soak in the magical alchemy of the double Air Element, with the music of their trined Suns chiming in the background of all their shared activities. As a matter of fact, music is often the golden cord that draws the Libra woman and the Aquarius man together initially in some manner, either a common interest in it, or the encouragement of one for the other's pursuit of it. Sometimes it's art, sometimes religion, philosophy or travel to foreign countries, higher educational endeavors, children, young people or the theatre in some form . . but there will always be multiple areas they can see as smooth stepping-stones into their garden of compassion and warm compatibility of ideas and ideals.

He thinks she's beautiful, and although love is blind, he's probably right in his image of this Venus lady's pulchritude. Most Libra women do possess an extra abundance of ethereal beauty, and even those who aren't blockbusting beauties have gorgeous smiles that can daze a man's vision and temporarily paralyze his common sense. She thinks he's the most super-smart man she's ever known. Granted, his intelligence is puzzling at times; it turns and twists down some strange detours, with the unconfined imagination of true genius, bubbling into fountains of brilliance, then erupting into tornadoes of illogical reasoning. The occasional lack of logic in his thinking disturbs her a little, but she's mentally alert and clever enough herself to sense the scope of the intellect groping within his unpredictable inspiration for a foothold on reality. He likewise appreciates her fine mind, quickly perceives her ability to converse with him on a variety of topics, and therefore hold his interest with more than her curves and dimples.

Still, on the mental and philosophical level, there may be some sharp disagreements. She enjoys luxury, beauty and comfort. Her optimistic nature causes her to turn in distaste from anything ugly, unhappy or depressing, and this Libran languidness may clash with his great, sweeping humanitarian impulses. He's concerned about the starving children all over the world, the dangerous ecological imbalance, the pollution of our air and water, the plight of the American Indian — all manner of evil and decadence on the human level, and regarding Mother Nature. Her difficulty in coping with the unpleasant will cause him to believe she's guilty of selfishness and self-indulgence, and he'll tell her so bluntly. Libra is deeply concerned with injustice in any form, instinctively desiring to bring about equality and goodness in the world; yet she may, like all Librans, shrink at first from facing the necessary specifics of healing the world's ills because of her natural Venus reluctance to face and accept the negative aspects of Life.

He should lead her more gently into a full realization of her Libra sense of justice, not call her mean things like "lazy," "spoiled brat" and "uncaring" before she's found her way to the light from the torch he carries. As for her, she must learn to change her priorities if she's to live happily with this man, finding ways to make him know that she really does care more about the poverty and misery in the world than the latest fashions, the sleekest cars, parties, good times and culture or the arts. The Libra woman who insists on wearing fur coats, especially sealskin coats, made from the skins of his murdered animal friends, is never going to be adored by an evolved and typical Water Bearer.

Despite these areas of potential tension between them, these two will find calmness and tranquility in their sexual blending. Their hearts and bodies agree with perfect harmony, never mind the occasional confrontations of their minds. And frequently, the joy they feel when they're giving and receiving love through its physical expression has the power to heal, or at least soften the edges of their intellectual differences. For Libra and Aquarius, intimacy of the flesh and emotions is easily attainable, and always results in peace of the spirit. In this facet of their love, they are beautifully in tune, their bodies are in key . . . . . and their passions know the lyric of their lovemaking music by heart. It's as though they've blended in this very way many times before. And they have. For every 5-9 vibration indicates previous incarnations of closeness . . . a mating of the souls and bodies in half-remembered past lives, still possessing the power to haunt them with an indefinable nostalgia, especially during their times of sexual nearness. The first time of their physical union never seems like the "first time." There's something so familiar about the way they feel.

The Libra woman who wants to hold the elusive love of an Aquarian man must allow him to take the lead. There is no other way. Yet it's more than possible that, after all their disagreements and hurts and heartaches and ego battles are over, she will have the last word. If she's patient. Her wisest attitude can be summed up in this verse I hereby dedicate to her, called "Pass the Peace Pipe" or "The Capitulation of a Cardinal Sign."

you want to call the shots ? all right, jump on your horse
and I'll walk three respectful steps behind . . like a proper squaw
you decide the course and byways our stream of madness shall run
how it bends and wanders . . and where and when it flows
                              into the land-of-the-singing-waters
I'll chew my moccasins, and string my wampum
in the pale, new Moon, beside my wickiup
and wait for your bird call, tom-tom beat or smoke puff

but remember, brave Chief Rain-in-the-Heart

while you lead us down this sun-danced warpath
of pride and passion, truth and lie
the spirits of the wind and stars are watching
and it's Manitou who calls the final shots

. . . not you or I °

☆ ☆ ☆ ☆ ☆ ☆

LIBRA *Man* AQUARIUS *Woman*

◆◀●▶◆

. . . there was something in the right-hand corner
of her mouth that wanted her not to call Peter names.

Her name isn't *really* Debra, but let's call her Debra. His name isn't *really* Steve, but let's call him Steve. The names may be fictional, but I assure you that this man and woman are actual, living, breathing human beings. Their natal Suns are trined. Debra is a petite, ponytailed Aquarian Water Bearer, sweetly child-like and feminine (Ha!), who is brilliantly, if at times violently, ruled by the masculine planet Uranus. Steve is a Venus-ruled Libra man, whose intelligence and genius are an equal match for her own. He is sometimes mellow and gentle and kind, at other times just plain mean and despicable, depending a great deal upon how recently she has smashed his delicate Scales out of balance with the sledgehammer of her unpredictable Uranian behavior. They're both working toward their M.D.'s and Ph.D.'s, with a common goal of becoming medical research scientists who will discover something of great benefit to mankind — and womankind. Rather like America's answer to the Curies of France.

Isn't it odd that one always thinks of the latter as Madame Curie and her husband, instead of the other way around? There must be a lesson there. Perhaps the lesson that it doesn't matter which horse wears the garland of posies as long as the wagon gets to town.

We shall use Steve and Debra's relationship as a mirror for all Libra men and Aquarian space women for a few paragraphs. All right, are you all gazing into the mirror? Look closely now.

° *Venus Trines at Midnight*, by Linda Goodman (New York: Taplinger Publishing Company, Inc., 1970. To be republished by Harper and Row, 1979).

He vacillates. He can't decide whether to marry her, live with her, ignore her or leave her. She has no such problem. She knows exactly which of those arrangements she prefers, and her mind is as firm as a rock. On Sundays, she wants to marry him. Every other Tuesday, she's positive they should just live together until they receive their degrees. On certain Uranian-storm-tossed Thursdays, she prefers that he ignore her, which is painfully evident when she leaves the receiver of her phone off the hook and throws the double police lock on her door. On occasional dreary Saturdays, flashed by Uranus lightning, she emphatically wishes him to leave her, a desire she manages to clearly communicate by throwing all his clothes out the upstairs bedroom window, plus his new watch, which unfortunately never seems to survive the fall — and often including his term papers, which of course get blown around in the snow and ice and terribly smudged and therefore must be typed all over again. But let no one accuse her of being impartial.

On such dreary Saturdays she also cuts into confetti the pages of her *own* thesis, on which she has labored long and brain-fatiguing hours, and dramatically flushes them down the toilet, announcing loudly that she's decided to hitchhike across Europe and join a gypsy caravan, and who wants a stuffy old medical degree anyway ?

He can't leave well enough alone, and instead of being happy when she's in a conciliatory mood and invites him over for her special home-baked lasagna, he insists on knowing the *name* of the gypsy who invited her to join his caravan in Europe. He keeps it up. She makes up a name out of her very fertile imagination. He leaves angrily, without eating a bite of the dinner she spent all day cooking for him.

There was a time when he finally decided they should never see each other again. He packed up his dog and his microscope and his sprouts and left her for good, going so far as to move in with a friend in another city, and getting an unlisted phone number. She quickly located both his address and his phone number. (I keep *telling* you Aquarians are born detectives.) A few months later, he was bringing her flowers and poems and stuffed monkeys — and taking her out to dinner by candlelight twice a week. Shortly thereafter, he moved back in with his dog, his microscope, his sprouts and three male friends (to protect him).

The first night, they dismally failed to protect him. Following a rousing quarrel over the fact that he had turned their happy home into a boarding-house, he and his three friends went to sleep on the floor of the den, after carefully locking the door. *He* was locking *her* out ? In a house where she paid *half* the rent ? And he considered himself *fair* ? She wasn't a fledgling scientist for nothing.

It took her until three o'clock in the morning, but eventually she prepared, in the kitchen sink, using some experimental homework test tubes, a dreadful concoction of chemicals with an ammonia base, then carefully poured it into a squirt gun (*yes*, this *really* happened), which she proceeded to squirt under the door to the den, which she had also locked from *her* side. Fortunately, the den had windows, through which the four gasping men escaped the fumes that had awakened them from a sound sleep. They at first thought it was a UFO attack. (It's easy to mistake an Aquarian caper for an interplanetary zapping.) Of course, when they climbed out the windows, they walked all over the Libra man's clothes and his watch, which were strewn around on the ground, waiting for him. Understandably, they were both late for class that day.

Now, I know you aren't going to believe this (unless you're a Libra male or an Aquarian female), but Debra and Steve kissed and made up a few weeks following that Close Encounter, and the last time I heard they were blissfully studying their anatomy and biochemistry together.

They love, you see. They need one another. Because there's no one else who can heal her heart as tenderly as her Libra man, with his sunlit smile — no one else who would ever love him, with all his flaws and vices, as fiercely and loyally and faithfully as his volatile Water Bearer — and certainly there's no one else either of them can intellectually respect as much as they do each other. When she isn't squirting guns under the den door, she's superintelligent, cuddly and affectionate, as dear and desirable as a small puppy. When he isn't being cold and cranky and callous, he's gentle and amusing and clever, and very loving. Then too, there's her home-baked lasagna. And the fact that he's the only man who will ever say "I love you" to her with genuine tears in his eyes, or who would sentimentally wear a smashed wristwatch with the hands permanently set at midnight, because it was a gift from her.

Every time she quarrels with her Libra man, this Aquarian woman phones me around dawn, tearfully, with the same touching words: "He said he was my *friend*. Friends should *understand* each other, shouldn't they ? I don't care about all the rest of it, but he said he was my *friend*."

Aquarians of both sexes place a high value on friendship. You may behave as you like as a lover or husband or wife, but *friend*ship must live up to an inflexible code. There are certain things friends *do*. And there are certain things friends *don't* do. Friends do not talk about you to other people, unless they're saying nice things. Friends do not break promises. Friends accept you with all your faults. Friends are never disloyal — and friends are *there* when you *need* them. Aquarians rarely realize that their definition of friendship is interchangeable with the definition of real love. The Water Bearers never ask for more in friendship than they're willing to give in return. The only difference between the Uranus ideals of friendship and love is the combination of the sexes involved, and in the Aquarian Age, it's difficult to draw the line of distinction.

The Libra man absolutely *must* have peace and harmony in his environment. Without it, he will inevitably become seriously ill physically, mentally, emotionally — or all three. This is an unbreakable law of astrology concerning the Venus-ruled. Consequently, the Aquarian woman who truly loves this man will make a sincere attempt to stifle her eccentricities (except for the stimulating and challenging ones) and exert a strong effort to bring calm and quiet to their relationship. This is not always an easy task for the girl Water Bearer, because a Libra man will perversely create much of his own disharmony by trying too hard to please everyone, working too hard for months on end, until he's on the verge of collapse, and worrying about how to make everyone like him and like each other besides. He either tries to be Henry Kissinger with all his friends, taking on everyone's burdens — or he gives up on trying to make everything come out even, and burns the candle of his creativity at both ends, trying to prove to the world that he, at least, is doing his very best — when the world isn't even aware that he's out there running around in circles to please it.

When he becomes unbearably frustrated, he may turn to drinking and partying to excess, then suffer from pangs of guilt over neglecting his woman, his studies, his work, his physical health, and so forth. Libra men work hard and they play hard. They possess an unerring instinct for compromising disagreements and mediating troublesome situations smoothly and effortlessly. Yet they can't seem to acquire the knack of bringing their own minds and bodies into equilibrium and balance with each other. This man will go like sixty for long periods of time, never relaxing for a moment; then he'll drop in a heap on the bed, and lie there so still for so long, the Aquarian woman who loves him will fear he's slipped into a catatonic trance, or has succumbed to a fatal attack of sleeping sickness. He's only resting. That's all, just resting. Leave him alone, and he'll soon be himself again, once he's recouped his energies and rejuvenated his spirit. If you must join him, play music for him, read softly to him, make sure his room is neat and tidy and bright and cheerful, with lots of fresh air — and *don't* discuss anything negative with him. This is not the time to coax him into agreeing with you, when the poor man is flat on his back. There are more pleasant ways of soothing him during his quiet spells. Venus ways.

Love, in all its variations, certainly not excluding its sexual aspect, is as necessary to the Libra man as breathing. Friendship, in all its variations, is as necessary to the Aquarian woman as breathing. If he'll be her *real* friend, she'll be able to trust him with her heart, which will allow her to be as ardent a sexual and romantic partner as he could possibly desire, even when he's dreaming (and passion is a subject this man dreams about a lot). The reverse is also true.

If she'll be his lace Valentine girl, live up to his glorified image of womanhood (stop threatening him with imaginary gypsies) and respond to his lovemaking with a matching desire—he'll be the most loyal and faithful friend she could possibly hope for (and her hopes are gigantic in the friendship department). It's what you might call an even trade-off, with each giving the other what he or she needs most.

This woman is sexually turned off when her Libra lover or husband has hurt her in some way by breaking her friendship code, however briefly, in however minor a way. Likewise, this man finds it impossible to physically demonstrate his love for her when, a few hours before they embrace at night, she's won an intellectual argument and made him feel foolish in some trifling way. Both of them should apologize for the unintentional wounding of each other—and remember the ancient warning: *Never let the Sun set on anger* (which originated, not with your great-grandmother, but within the mass collective subconscious memory, symbolizing the dreadful twilight when Set murdered his brother, Osiris, causing the Earth's first "Sun-set." How the Earth existed without a sunset before that time we'll discuss in a forthcoming book. Aquarians will be fascinated).

Then the two of them, the Libra man and his Aquarius woman, should simply fall asleep quietly, holding hands, and not pursue love, but allow it to gently surprise them with its depth when they awaken in the morning. Libra and Aquarius will find their sexual love more fulfilling when they approach it lightly and reverently, even poetically, but never aggressively or demandingly. The lovemaking pattern of two Air Signs is very delicate. When their minds are in tune, their bodies will respond, and sing along in beautiful harmony. When their minds are troubled or confused, forcing love will only bruise its fragile loveliness . . . or freeze it into boredom.

These two are bound to hurt each other now and then, because they love so much. But the 5-9 vibration will ever renew their forgiveness, if they give it half a chance. This man can't bear to be alone; he must marry (or live as though he's married) or burn with frustration. The Libran who fights this instinctive urge within himself is a miserable male indeed. Aries, the opposite sign to Libra, vibrates to Sunrise, but Libra vibrates to Sunset.

Sunset is his lonely time, when he's most vulnerable to his Aquarian woman who wants to say "I'm sorry." The golden blaze of light at Sunset, when day is leaving, holds a poignant beauty. No other kind of light can bring so much pain to Libra, when there's no one special to be with, no one who really cares. Enveloped in the darkness of his terrible loneliness, he watches people stream out of office buildings into the day's final brightness, everyone going somewhere but him . . then suddenly he sees *her*, etched in pink-gold, walking toward him, uncertain.

He didn't plan to see her so unexpectedly like this, but he *should* have. Everything about her is unexpected. He hurries to her—and she walks faster too. He can tell she's been crying, because her nose is red. She's carrying a very large box, almost bigger than she is . . . a surprise for him. What could it be ? Believe it or not (*believe* it), it's an electric train set from the F.A.O. Schwarz toy store on Fifth Avenue. That's for "what." As for "why" ? Because he'd stared at it in the window one day for hours, when they were together, and said it was exactly like the one Santa had left under his tree Christmas morning when he was nine years old.

He doesn't know whether to laugh or weep. So he smiles instead. "Do you know you're crazy ?" She nods. She knows. "Can we still be friends ?" she asks him, unsure. He considers. "Only if you promise to come home with me and help me set up the train tracks," he tells her. She smiles back then. They hail a passing yellow-gold taxi, jump in together, close the doors . . . and she leans back against his shoulder at the very moment the Sun disappears from the sky . . . just in time. But it was close.

☆ ☆ ☆ ☆ ☆ ☆

LIBRA

Air — Cardinal — Positive
Ruled by Venus
Symbol: The Scales
Day Forces — Masculine

PISCES

Water — Mutable — Negative
Ruled by Neptune
Symbol: The Fish
Night Forces — Feminine

The **LIBRA-PISCES** *Relationship*

On these magic shores, children at play are forever beaching their coracles. We too have been there; we can still hear the sound of the surf, though we shall land no more.

*B*ecause Pisces is linked with the mystical truth behind all religion — and Libra is linked with the balancing of justice and compassion that equals Peace — this is often (not always, but often) a strangely soothing association. There is sometimes a far-reaching influence over not just the two lives of Libra and Pisces, but over those of others, in various ways, depending on the individual Librans and Fish involved, the way they live, their goals and ambitions . . . their dreams.

In the Libra-Capricorn chapter, we discussed in particular astrology's centuries-old claim that Libra is *The Peacemaker* by using, as only one of countless examples, Libran Jimmy Carter (he, of the flashing smile) and his historic role as Libra "Peacemaker" in the September 1978 Camp David Summit meeting with Israel's Menachem Begin and Egypt's Anwar Sadat.

But in every Libra chapter in this book (and in my first book, *Sun Signs*) is the ancient astrological reminder that all Libran people, every single one of them, possess the dazzling Venus smile, with its awesome ability to melt all opposition. This isn't just an observation of astrological symbolism, but a literal adage regarding the invisible yet powerful stamp of the planets and the Luminaries (Sun and Moon) on the physical appearance (as well as the behavior) of humans — a stamp so unmistakable that even the skeptics who refuse to recognize the holiness of astrology are forced to notice and admit its presence, however grudgingly. Now, they must once again notice.

Like Paul before him, Pope John-Paul, who reigned for a sadly brief span of but 34 days as Catholic Pastor, in the late summer and early autumn of 1978, was a Sun Sign Libran. Among other particular matters, the sign of Libra is traditionally associated with libraries, books and publishing (sharing these with Gemini and Sagittarius, to a lesser degree). Only days after John-Paul was made Pope, he rather timidly released to the world his tiny personal treasures of literature — small, but eloquent, wise and witty letters, addressed to everyone from Mark Twain to the Beatles, Shakespeare and Charles Dickens. Throughout the years of his busy, dedicated life, Libran John-Paul had written these little letters to the achievers of yesterday and today, with the typical Libran love of the literary, and Libra's flair for "belles lettres." I was both touched and amused to see them printed simultaneously with the attainment of his new temporal power over his own affairs, as well as over those of millions, because I knew the joy the Pastor felt (he preferred this title to Pontiff or Pope) as a Libran, to finally be given the opportunity of allowing the public to take a peek at the subtle humor and philosophical observations of his beloved "creative children."

Of course, he never expected his modest letters to constitute a bestseller or anything so grand as that. He was simply as delighted as a boy to see them at last in print, and so widely read — a private dream come true. The release of his letters to the press was very nearly the first thing he did upon becoming Pope, and I'm sure it was with deep inner satisfaction that he saw his humble secret wish granted. Those many Librans of both sexes and all faiths, who secretly write lovely poems or prose, and never have the chance to share them with any wider audience than a few intimates, will understand the gentle John-Paul's shy happiness.

But what touched me even more concerning Libran John-Paul was the first newspaper account I saw of his death, following the sudden heart attack on September 29th, that ended in less than two months, his cheerful, benign reign of goodness, and plans (no doubt) of Venus Peace and Justice. On the front page of the Los Angeles *Times* that day, within the article describing the mourning in Rome, in one column alone there were three clear references to Pope John-Paul's Sun Sign. The *Times* article, in referring to the discovery that the Pope had died in bed the morning after his 11 PM heart attack, said: "The light was on, an opened book of meditation lay nearby, and a senior Cardinal noticed that *his face still bore its usual smile.*"

A few paragraphs further on in the story, readers were informed that: "A tearful woman, who was praying in St. Peter's Basilica, said gently, *his whole life was in his smile.*"

Then, at the close of the article, were the quoted words of Archbishop Aurelio Sabattani, as he told thousands attending the Pontiff's mass in St. Peter's, that: "John-Paul was a man *who carried with him the smile of God . . . . . . his smile will remain like a beam of light.*"

Yes. Libra's Venus smile, its powerful force of energy and light, can be seen by the faithful, the believers and the skeptics alike. No one can resist it. No can deny it. No one can fail to be moved by it. The Venus smile is what made Libran Eleanor Roosevelt a beautiful woman, despite her plain features. It won Libran Eisenhower the Presidency, and also had a great deal to do with the same achievement of Libran Jimmy Carter. It floods and brightens the memories of all those who grieve for the cheerful, kind John-Paul. The Venus smile of Libran Pope John before him was used more sparingly, but was, nevertheless, always there, ready to flash its startling light when it was needed to gently persuade.

The Libra smile . . . and the dreamy Neptune eyes of Pisces, the Fish. Both indications of the indelible stamp of planetary influence upon the features of Earthlings. Speaking of the Fish, in passing, I meant to comment that St. Peter's Cathedral, where Archbishop Sabattani eulogized the late Pontiff's smile, is of course named after the apostle Peter — who (though he was a Sun Sign Aries) is traditionally called *"the Big Fisherman."*

Libra and Pisces form the 6-8 Sun Sign Pattern, which means that neither one has the foggiest idea why the other thinks and acts as he (or she) does. Libra's motives and attitudes, character and personality are totally foreign and perplexing to the Fish — and Pisces, to Libra, is likewise one huge puzzle. As with all other 6-8 influenced people, the Venus-ruled, dimpled Libran and the Neptune-guided, dual-natured Piscean would probably never even get so far as the first "hello" if they weren't somehow brought together by "outside forces" — outside forces being a job or career, a matchmaking friend or relative, the non-optional accident of being born within the same family circle — or the unplanned (consciously) situation of just happening to live near one another as neighbors. All these influences manage to move Libra and Pisces into close enough proximity to be at least introduced. After that, they're on their own. Although they would seldom deliberately choose to form an association, once "fate" has nudged them into a tentative exploration of each other's strange behavior patterns, a fair number of them are so fascinated by the differences between them that they linger awhile, and finally decide to make the investigation of the mystery a permanent hobby.

One of the things responsible for such a decision is that Libra notices rather quickly the willingness of the Fish to serve Libra in some way. Not necessarily as a butler, a maid or a footman, but in some subtle manner, the Pisces will provide a "service" to Libra people, whether actual and tangible, or subtle and invisible. It is distinctly felt — and it's always needed. The "service" syndrome is even stronger between Pisces and Libra than with the other 6-8 combinations, for the simple reason that Pisces, even without the 6-8 influence, is inclined to provide a helpful service to *all* Sun Signs. When the Fish meets Libra, therefore, representing as they do the 6th astrological house to the Venus people, and representing also humility and submission to generally everyone, the tendency to be a helpful and beneficent force in Libra's life is strengthened. But unfortunately, the tendency for a bit of masochism may creep in too — for obvious reasons. Too much of a good thing, you know? And so the Fish must be on guard with the normally kind and fair Librans, lest Libra (unconsciously) takes advantage of this double "service" vibration and keeps the poor Fish swimming around in circles, making Libra's existence a great deal more pleasant and easier perhaps, but ending up on the short end of the wishbone. As I recall, the short end of the wishbone doesn't grant your wish. The one who gets the long end receives first dibs on his (or her) wish, while the one with the short end gets married first.

That isn't fair. Because Libra, not Pisces, is the one who has the burning desire to marry, and balance his or her life with that of another. In fact, Librans rhyme so melodiously with orange blossoms and Lohengrin's "Wedding March" that they suffer from tipped Scales and severe depression if they're forced to live alone for uncommonly long periods. On the other hand, marriage is usually something the typical Fish view as a dangerous, glittering hook to stifle freedom, and they either successfully avoid it — or if not, then manage to slip in and out of the marital net each time they're hooked. Many Pisceans are either unmarried meditative loners (by choice, because both the girl and the boy Fish are alluring to the opposite sex) or instead chalk up an amazing number of multiple ventures into matrimonial waters. It's a rare Piscean who marries only once. They exist, naturally, but they're like the exotic "Butterfly Velvet Crimson" species of Nature fish, as compared to the minnows and trout. Relatively speaking, a once-in-a-lifetime wed Fish is as uncommon as a once-in-a-lifetime wed Gemini. To repeat, so as not to hurt those Pisceans who *are* happily and permanently wed — it happens, but not often.

So here they are, both of them disappointed. Pisces got the short end of the wishbone, Libra got the long end — so it's Pisces who's going to be the *first* one married, which is probably the *last* thing Pisces wants. And it's likely what Libra wished for, but although Libra gets the wish, it won't be first, you see. Libra will have to wait a while longer. Oh, fudge! (Libra is frustrated at having tugged so hard, therefore getting the longer end.) It serves them both right, because neither of them should have been fooling around with a wishbone anyway, since chickens were not placed on this planet for humans to eat. Seeds, nuts, herbs, grains, fruits and vegetables are all for eating. Fish, fowl, birds and animals are not. So it's karmic justice. Although we're being somewhat light, astrology is serious in counseling against the eating of flesh. But matters of sincere concern and serious disagreement will never be solved by everyone crossly scowling at one another. They are better broached with the combination of Piscean compassion, a Libra smile or two, a dash of humor (and maybe a pinch of Aries directness).

The vegetarian controversy is one of the topics these two might choose, now that we've introduced it as a conflict, to become the subject of their next argument (that is, discussion) on Thursday next. It's the perfect platform for this debating team. Pisces can talk about the religious aspects of it, while Libra plays Judge and weighs on the Libra Scales the moral right of fish and fowl, birds and animals to exist without being forced to become part of the food chain, since they aren't necessary to human nutrition. It will be a heavy issue for them to handle. The Piscean religious viewpoint alone contains multiple facets, a dozen controversial pros and cons. Libra's Scales will swing back and forth, trying to sort out all the arguments for and against, to achieve a fair balance—and Pisces will help by adding first a sprinkling of this viewpoint to one tray, then a sprinkling of that to the other tray, assisting the Libran friend, business associate, relative, lover or mate in the task of arriving at a decision. They may *begin* the religious-spiritual-vegetarian discussion on Thursday next, but they may not finish it until a considerable length of time later.

Meanwhile, while they're arguing (discussing) the issue, Libra will win a few strategic points by flashing the dimpled Venus smile, Pisces will make carob fudge balls to renew their energies, serve them to Libra on a delicate, hand-painted china plate, with a sky-blue napkin—and everything will be smooth and harmonious, gentle and soft-spoken. Unless some Taurean friend of the Fish happens to drop by, and innocently suggests that everybody take a break and go out for a steak. The Bull will back off (it takes a lot to cause a Bull to back off) when he sees the shock on the faces of Pisces and Libra. Then Libra will laser Taurus with a Venus grin, the Fish will sweetly offer the Bull a carob fudge ball—and what do you want to bet that, between them, Pisces and Libra will soon be baptizing a new convert?

LIBRA *Woman* PISCES *Man*

*Her romantic mind was like the tiny boxes, one within
the other, that come from the puzzling East. However
many you discover, there is always one more. And her
sweet, mocking mouth had one kiss on it . . . . perfectly conspicuous, in the right-hand corner.*

*. . . . . they were together in the armchair by this time,
and Wendy plied him with more questions. "If you don't
live in Kensington Gardens now . . . ."*

"Sometimes I do still."

"But where do you live mostly now ?"

"With the lost boys . . ."

This thing about the Libra woman's painful difficulty in making up her mind
quickly — best to deal with it in the beginning, don't you think ? Since the
male Fish is not noted for firm, aggressive action in solving a problem, we'll
give him a sure-fire formula for coping with the indecisiveness of the Libra
lady who has lured him into her net. (He didn't resist all that much.)
It's really quite easy, once you get the hang of it. I'll give the Pisces man a
step-by-step illustration of the formula, by way of a true incident.

While writing this book in California, I asked an incredibly talented
artist-designer, a Capricorn Goat Girl, named Sinthia Sullivan, to create for
me a large tapestry, depicting the Egyptian honeymoon scene of two good
friends of mine in New York, who were recently married — as a wedding gift.
(Cappy Sinthia produces these outrageously stunning works of art, not with a
paintbrush, but by using layered, multicolored, multitextured fabrics.) The
bride is a Libra woman, named Susan — dimpled, beautiful, intelligent —
and indecisive. Her groom's name is Arthur, and he's a Scorpio attorney, but
really not vital to the story. I didn't say he wasn't vital. Just not vital to the
story. (One has to be careful with Scorpios.)

So Libran Susan called when the gift arrived, to say, in her musical voice,
that she genuinely adored it — so much, that she simply could *not* make up
her mind whether to hang it in the new apartment she and her equally new
husband just redecorated — or on the wall of her office at the Metropolitan
Opera Guild, where she's Director of Special Events for the Met. Of *course*
she has an office. Of *course* she's an executive. You haven't been listening.

Libra is a Cardinal Sign of leadership. You male Fish must stop dozing off in the middle of your strategy lesson.

Being a Ram myself, therefore overjoyed that she was obviously pleased with her wedding gift, I couldn't bear the vicarious pain of her indecision, so I told her I would order for her, as a celebration gift (celebrating anything at all) a *second* tapestry, depicting her favorite opera — so she could hang the Egyptian pyramid at *home*, and the operatic scene in her *office*. She was thrilled. So was I. (I was thrilled that she was thrilled.) One decision eliminated.

But then, you see, since the Egyptian tapestry so perfectly matched her new evening gown, down to the several shades of mauve and lilac, deep green and gold (with white satin), and since she would soon be attending a formal reception for the Met near the location of her office, where people would be stopping by, perhaps she should hang, instead, the *Pyramid* scene in her *office* — and the *operatic* scene at *home* ? What did I think ? It was, to be sure, an agonizing dilemma. Pay attention, Pisces! Do you know how I neatly solved this first bout of indecision ? Very gently, I led her into *another* decision, which completely blanked out the *first* one. I asked her which was her *favorite* opera, so I could tell Sinthia, the Cappy artist-designer, to begin working on the second tapestry. During the anticipated silence of delibera- tion that followed, I made only one attempt. (It's important to remember never to try more than once to help Libra balance the Scales, or you'll spend a great deal of time, better spent planning the final strategy.) My single attempt was to quickly suggest *Madame Butterfly*. No. That wasn't quite it. (I really hadn't expected it to be.) Then I suggested, cheerfully, that Libra take a couple of days to decide, and let me know her ultimate decision.

That was nearly two weeks ago. No decision yet. And so, today, I mailed the beautiful Libran bride a note, in answer to her own gracious thank-you note. I told her that — this is the vital step in the strategy — I told her in my note that, since she couldn't decide, *I would decide for her* — that I would choose an opera I just *knew* would be one of her favorites — and Cappy would begin work on the tapestry approximately the same day my note was received in New York. Now, shall I tell you what will happen ? I am absolutely guaranteed to receive a telegram or a phone call in a day or two, when Libra Susan reads my note. She will have made her decision. Firmly. And finally. And smoothly. Because, you see, Libra being a Cardinal Sign of leadership, if there's anything Libra women can't stand, it's having the authority of their personal prerogatives delegated to another. It forces them into an amazingly swift decision.

In summary, the strategy, then, is to (1) replace one topic of indecision with another, since the second decision will often cause the first to be no longer important and (2) make only *one* suggestion in helping Libra solve the second decision, *no more* (3) allow a reasonable length of time, since Libra's decisions, once made, are always the very best choice of all possible alterna-

tives, thanks to the Venus wisdom, fairness, justice, logic and exquisite taste —
and finally (4) if no decision is made during the reasonable length of time,
make a decision yourself, and *firmly pretend* you are going to expedite it
immediately, if not sooner. Four simple steps.

The only one Pisces will have trouble with is the fourth. It's never easy
for a Fish to be firm, to expedite — or to do anything "immediately."
Although it must be admitted that the "pretending" part will be duck soup
for the typical Neptune man. He's quite good at make-believing and
pretending. Every Fish is a frustrated actor — or an escaped character who
wandered out from between the covers of a Grimm Brothers *book of Fairy
Tales* one day, to see what was happening out here in this world of illusion
everyone but Pisces calls reality. The Fish knows which is which. He never
gets mixed up enough to believe dreams are unreal, a world of fantasy,
created by the imagination — and Life is the nitty-gritty of it all. No way.
This man knows it's just the opposite. He knows the truth of the matter is that
this is the dream — and the *dream* is where it's all happening for real.

Now we've given these two a subject (dreams versus reality) they can
excitedly discuss for many months, maybe years. A topic so fraught with
controversy, so lacking in any possibility of final proof (of a tangible sort, that
is) it will quickly replace any other arguments the Libra lady and her Pisces
man may have been having up till now. The perfect debate for Venus and
Neptune Lovers. Dreams are closely related to Neptune, naturally, while
Venus adores all things lovely and ethereal . . . anything with a touch of the
imaginative. The Libra logic will be firmly on the side of the "actual," and
the Fish probably won't budge from his defense of the esoteric. But it will be
interesting for him to watch her try to balance the trays of her Scales between
the Libra logic, on the side of reality — and her Venus softness, on the side of
the ethereal and romantic.

In fact, this is the very blend of qualities that caught his dreamy
attention, and lured him into hopelessly loving her, into becoming helplessly
caught up in her net of charm, when he first floated into the sky-blue clouds
of her fragrant presence. The irresistible pattern of her masculine logic and
intelligent reasoning — combined with her Venusian tenderness and romantic
imagination. That seductive Libra mixture of practicality and compassion.
Her compassion nearly (though not quite) equals his own. Her practicality is
something he could most certainly use. The exposure to it will be eventually
beneficial and lasting, even though, at times, uncomfortable.

There's something vaguely Eastern about the Libra woman that intrigues
the Fish. She projects such an essence of autumn-football-weather, apple-
cheeked rosiness and campfire wholesomeness at times. Yet, at other times
there's an elusive air of incense and mantras, and temple bells chiming in the
distance, that makes him think of Tibet, China, or maybe Japan. He's very
sensitive to pick up on this, because the sign of Libra itself astrologically rules
the Orient. She balances the golden-girl-cheerleader image with a mystical

hint of ancient rites in a most unusual fashion — and the Neptune chords in him will silently respond.

Because she was born under a masculine (initiating) Cardinal Sign, and he was born under a feminine (passive) Mutable Sign, however dainty and sweet *she* may be, and however strong and wise *he* may be — his Libra lady will have the last word when it comes to ruling the relationship. But when it comes to the *really* last word — "goodbye" — it could be the Fish who says it. The Pisces man is capable of gradually drifting toward a peaceful pool of tranquility somewhere else, with maybe one of those "Butterfly Velvet Crimson" girl Fish mentioned in the beginning of this chapter, if the Libra woman he loves so deeply becomes too authoritative and demanding, overplaying the Cardinal role in what should be an equal partnership.

He'll be patient with her, though, and struggle less to escape their tightly woven Oneness than he might with another woman — because of the 6-8 influence. He's powerfully attracted to her, both spiritually and physically, and she to him. She magnetizes his desire into a more passionate and uncontrollable need than he ever experienced before — just as she's drawn strangely, against all her logic and reason, into the spell of his pastel rainbow of affection and sensitivity. The Venus vibrations within her soul long for the kind of enchanted ecstasy his haunted, Neptune songs of the sea soothingly promise to fulfill, through memories she sees reflected in his eyes, of a place she's never quite forgotten, and weeps to revisit, yearning . . . . . . a place she knew well when she was about four or so, where she used to search trustingly in the damp, sweet-smelling grass for diamond necklaces, left there carelessly by the elves and fairies who danced there the night before, while she was sound asleep. It broke her heart with a sharpness she still recalls, that spring morning when a cold-voiced adult told her they were only dewdrops, nothing more. Then it suddenly began to rain, soaking her favorite pink-striped pinafore. Now that she's mature and sensible, why does the sharp pain of that morning return to her mind every single time it rains?

Her Pisces man may keep some secrets from her, insisting on the sanctuary of his own inner world of privacy, and that kind of "almost-deception" angers and troubles her. But he would never tell her such a dewdrop lie. He knows all about druid diamonds. She found that out the first night they made love . . . afterwards. He even tried with her, trembling, to pick them up in his hands. When they disappeared at the instant of human contact, he merely kissed her hair, and whispered that they really didn't disappear at all . . . that, through some magic, they were transfigured into a new dimension. "See?" he murmured quietly, comforting, "they didn't go away. Here they are . . . they've turned into tiny raindrops." And he touched gently, then, the tears on her cheek.

Oh, she'll miss him if he should ever leave her! As much as he'll miss the golden dawn of her smile, the way her voice sounds like it's singing a long-ago lullabye he remembers, even when she's speaking only ordinary words . . . or maybe not so ordinary after all . . . "Darling, we really must find some way to add color to this room. It's so monotone and depressing. Why don't you paint a mural for us, on the west wall, where the sunlight will strike it every morning? You can, you know. You can do anything at all you want to do. Never mind that they didn't appreciate you on that last job. Someday, before long, the world will be happier for the things you've worked so hard to accomplish, the beauty you create in your own special way. I've never been so positive of anything in my whole life as I am of that. I *know* you'll be recognized, and finally be able to express everything you've held inside, if you keep trying, and don't give up when your miracle is just around the next corner. You can't see it till you *turn* the corner, so you *can't* stop when you're so close. I'm so sure of your tomorrow. Do you know how *sure* I am?"

Yes, he knows. Despite her sometimes bossy manner and upsetting mood swings, he knows she's the only person who honestly believes in him, and the only one with the right password to suddenly give him the enthusiasm to believe in *himself*. No one else could so gently guide him away from his "what's the use?" response to repeated disappointments. Besides, he's more than a little moody and changeable too. So who is he to judge her? As for his Libra woman, she knows this is maybe the only man who knows the way to that secret, far-off place, where she can refresh herself, shower in cool starlight, and return, feeling stronger than before. The only one who ever was able to tell her where druid diamonds go when they disappear . . . and kiss them into returning.

☆ ☆ ☆ ☆ ☆ ☆

LIBRA *Man* PISCES *Woman*

◆◀◉▶▶

The loveliest tinkle as of golden bells answered him.
It is the fairy language. You ordinary children
can never hear it, but if you were to hear it, you
would know that you had heard it once before.

Ah, yes . . . the tinkle of golden bells. They hear them together, the Libra man and the Pisces girl, when they're cuddling and crooning before a crackling fire on a cold winter night . . . with Jack Frost making beautiful crystal etchings on the window panes . . . while outside, the snow falls silently past the yellow glow of the street light.

It's a cozy canvas of contentment, easily and casually painted by this man and woman, because Pisces and Libra are in no way "ordinary" children of Mother Earth. He's airy and dreamy, faintly scented with the sandalwood of Far Eastern mysteries, yet also touched by familiar apple-pie, swing-on-the-front-porch charm. She's misty and dreamy too, dreamier, even, than he . . . . with the sound of the surf in her eyes, softly foaming against the shore. Yes, I said the *sound* of the surf in her eyes. It's called "poetic license." Every Libran and Piscean owns a poetic license, neatly framed, and hanging on the walls of their romantic minds.

Suddenly, there's a chill in the room. Small icicles form between them, and the warm, peaceful scene turns frosty, as their harmonious conversation hits an unexpected discordant note. Because Pisces is overwhelmingly sympathetic to friends and strangers alike, and Libra is usually well informed on current topics of the day, it was only natural that they drifted into a discussion about the drug problem of some friends. The girl Fish was seriously concerned because one of the friends had been led into the habit of "sniffing" cocaine on a weekend ski trip to Aspen last year. She tried to explain to her how cocaine destroys the nasal tissues and cartilage, about the alarmingly rising numbers of those who use it who've been forced to have plastic surgery . . . and even so, later on the nose simply caves in, leaving the face looking like a grotesque mask. There's little warning. One day, it just happens. The nose collapses, and can never be permanently repaired. Not ever.

She shuddered, leaned closer to her Libra man, and asked, "Isn't that horrible?" He didn't answer her right away, so then she told him how the friend, instead of being grateful for the warning, had just said coldly, "Mind your own business," and how it had hurt her to be so unkindly treated, when she was only trying to help. (The girl Fish spreads so much sympathy around so much of the time, she has every right to occasionally seek a few drops for herself.) She listens for his sympathetic words. He's still silent. But the girl Fish is patient, and she doesn't press him. She waits.

Finally, he sighs, then looks straight into her eyes, as he says sternly, "Why are you so shocked at the horror of collapsed noses in cocaine users? Did you ever stop to think what your lungs look like, struggling with all that black glue of the accumulated tars you clog them with from your cigarettes? When are you going to stop smoking? Lungs are just as important to human health as noses are. You need them *both* to breathe."

It wasn't quite the response she was seeking. How could he be so unfair as to attack one of her few weaknesses, when all she was asking was some understanding from him about something that was troubling her so much?

She drew back then, and as all Pisceans do at times — turned into a "cold Fish."

It reminded her of the week before, when she had enthused for half an hour or so about how much she enjoyed the reincarnation plot of the movie they'd just seen, while they were driving home. *He* had enjoyed it too. She *knew* he had by his behavior in the theatre — the way his fascinated eyes never left the screen, and he didn't make a move to leave his seat until the end of the credits, when the house lights went on. Then when she wanted to share the experience with him, he frowned, "I thought it was a big bore," he told her. "Warren Beatty and Julie Christie were okay, but it never got off the ground, because the plot was too thin, not complex enough. The dialogue was terrible too."

What *is* it with this man? Does he have a doctorate in sadism? Does he lie awake at night, figuring ways to put her down, every single time she tries to be cheerful and positive? *He's* the one who insisted firmly that they stop visiting the friends who introduced the other friend to cocaine. He remarked just yesterday that he had a good notion to punch the husband in the mouth. How can he change his views so drastically for no reason? Maybe he has a touch of schizophrenia, and needs to see a psychiatrist?

She's wrong on all counts. He's not a sadist, he doesn't hate her, and he doesn't lie awake at night figuring out how to cruelly put her down. It makes him ache inside when he knows he's hurt her, so why should he do *that*? Nor is he a schizophrenic. He's a Libran. He's symbolized by the Scales, therefore unconsciously compelled to weigh everything submitted to his ears for judgment. The trays have to be kept even. It isn't fair to hear *one* side of anything, without attempting to balance it out with the *opposite* side.

If she had handled it differently, she would have received the responses she needed from him. If she had mentioned her warning to the friend about cocaine destroying the nose, then sighed and added, "But I have no right to caution *her*, since it looks like I'll *never* give up smoking, and I'm *sure* my lungs are in far worse shape than her nasal tissues," her Libra man would have said something like, "What do you mean 'never'? You stopped once before, darling, and you can do it again. Besides you don't smoke enough cigarettes to cause anywhere *near* the damage cocaine will cause to Cindy's nose in a *much* shorter time period than all the years you've been smoking added together. She was ungrateful to treat you so rudely when you were only trying to help. I'm going to call her and *tell* her so tomorrow."

After the film, in the car, if the girl Fish had remarked, "I don't know why everyone's raving over *Heaven Can Wait*. It's just a re-make of an old movie plot. I didn't see anything so special about it, did you?" — then for the rest of the trip home, Libra would have praised everything about the picture, the acting, directing, plot, color and sound. "What do you mean, there's nothing special about it ? How can you *say* that ? It's been years since I've seen a film I could just relax and enjoy that much. It was *terrific !"*

Now do you see where Librans get their reputations for being "impossible" people, cranky crocodiles, and all that ? They get it, poor dears, from simply trying to be fair and just. Libran film star Charlton Heston personifies every astrological claim ever made about this Sun Sign, every dimple — including that making-you-go-weak-in-the-knees smile, the powerful virility and strength, balanced in equal parts with gentle tenderness — the pulsating masculine macho, blended harmoniously with beautiful sensitivity . . . intelligence, chiseled features . . . the whole Venus rainbow ! The perfectly balanced, gleaming golden Scales — but also, the Libran indecision and struggle for fair judgment that occasionally clouds his noble Moses-Ben Hur brow.

When he was interviewed on television regarding the both criticized and praised behavior of (Aquarian) actress Vanessa Redgrave, in making a political speech when she received her Oscar in 1978, Libran Heston's "noble brow" was clouded. As one reporter asked him if he agreed with Vanessa's critics, he replied (fairly) that "Well, she's always been a very political lady, but she's also a very fine actress, and I don't think people should judge her just because . . ." Suddenly, another reporter's interjection stopped Libra in the middle of his sentence, asking, "Then you are *defending* her ?" upon which Heston continued his sentence in reverse, winding it up with the words . . "but *on the other hand*, I don't think it was fair of her to air her views on such an occasion." Vanessa herself probably still isn't sure what Charlton *really* thought about the incident. I can tell her. If that pesky second reporter hadn't confused him, he would have defended her.

As with all 6-8 Sun Sign Patterns, with the differences between their basic motivations being so pronounced, it's never easy for the girl Fish and the Libra man to fall in love. However, once they do, the differences often blend in a surprisingly satisfactory way, benefiting both of them equally. They share sentiment and sensitivity in common, as well as a love of beauty. Each of them prefers peace and harmony to aggressive behavior and the strain of controversy. (Libran arguing is never "controversy," you see — simply pleasant discussion !) Neither Libra nor Pisces can long endure the sharp reality of tense conflict, and if it should develop because of the severely afflicted horoscope of one of them, the other will soon float away (Libra) or swim away (Pisces) and probably not return. The nice side of it is that the two of them *together* will also float or swim away from *outside* pressures, escaping into the haven of each other's arms for the quiet and peace they need to remain balanced (him) and tranquil (her).

This man and woman can create a romantic bond through their sexual closeness that goes a long way toward smoothing over any difficulties they may have in adjusting their personalities and life-styles. He fills her tender Neptune heart with all the affection she's ever yearned for, instinctively knowing how to demonstrate his love for her physically in the gentle, considerate way she needs, a way that makes her trust him. She brings the same kind of fulfillment to him, sensing his desires almost telepathically. There's a rich passion, interwoven with a dreamy quality, to their lovemaking . . . and perhaps not all the time, but most of the time, it reaches the level of ecstasy poets try to express. These two can express it naturally with each other, composing their own original music and lyrics as they go along . . . never the same, changing with their moods, but always soft with promise.

The two of them may have to be careful that they don't lead one another into procrastination and pleasure seeking, because both are susceptible to nearly any form of seduction, whether it's laziness, drugs, alcohol . . . . or daydreams that never leave the ground. Otherwise, Pisces and Libra can be very happily mated, as their hearts gradually learn to beat to the same rhythm. Her mystical, unswerving faith in him, and his optimistic, cheerful support of her occasional feelings of inadequacy form a strong and beautiful foundation for a lasting kind of love.

She may sometimes complain that he isn't perceptive enough to seek the reasons *behind* the reasons for some of her moods and feelings, that he's often too coldly logical and detached in his approach. But she's perceptive enough herself to realize he's only that way *half* of the time — and if she's patient, if she waits a little while, his compassion will shine through his smile again. He may be disturbed because the house isn't as neat as he'd like, when she casually postpones things he wants her to do, and he may be puzzled by her faraway look when he's trying to explain things to her reasonably. But she'll wrap him in the quilts of emotional peace and coziness he needs, and this will make up for all the rest. She's so innately sympathetic, and he's so innately fair, there's always a way to solve their disagreements.

The Pisces woman and the Libra man are both wise, each with a different kind of wisdom. His is acutely intellectual (despite his sentimental, romantic leanings) and hers is deeply emotional (despite her outward calm, cool poise). It's a magical alchemy, and since they're both usually willing to compromise, they can make each other very happy. But if she smokes, she'll have to give up those cigarettes to prove she loves him. And he'll have to stop being so judgmental. She's not his housekeeper, his laundress or his valet. She's his partner . . . his woman. The sea nymph with the sound of the surf in her eyes, who fits so snugly in his lap, before the fire, when the snow is falling outside. Do you hear the tinkle of golden bells? I believe we've come full circle, back to their beginning.

☆ ☆ ☆ ☆ ☆ ☆

SCORPIO

Water — Fixed — Negative
Ruled by Pluto
Symbols: Scorpion & Eagle
Night Forces — Feminine

SCORPIO

Water — Fixed — Negative
Ruled by Pluto
Symbols: Scorpion & Eagle
Night Forces — Feminine

The **SCORPIO-SCORPIO** *Relationship*

But there was one who did not fear him: there
was one prepared to enter that circle . . .

. . . which will win ? . . .

Putting this combination together is like pairing Merlin and Macbeth to stir a potion of "eye of newt, and toe of frog, wool of bat, and tongue of dog." It's a baffling blend of personalities, as much so to the two Scorpions themselves as to those who watch the contests between them — and oh, there will be contests! You can bet your wool of bat there will be.

Each is cautiously and suspiciously aware of the other's unleashed power, even though both are overjoyed to have finally found someone who really understands them (if "overjoyed" is a word that can be used to describe a reaction from these two poker faces). Just so the understanding isn't carried too far. It's a difficult thing to desire to be understood yet simultaneously and inexplicably be unwilling to allow the one who understands you best to know your innermost secrets. This creates a human pysche game that's thrilling to watch as long as you're on the outside looking in and not personally involved.

I'm pleased that they've found each other, aren't you? But it's disturbing to think of what might occur if one should happen to offend the other — and the offended one decides to get even — then the recipient of the revenge decides to get-even-back — then the first one is compelled to top the revenge action of the second one — and by the time the getting even has become an actual contest . . . one shudders to image the scene. The thing is that Scorpios *must* win. They'll risk anything to win, short of their lives, and some of them will do even that.

If you happen to know a couple of Scorps at the office, in the classroom, in the family circle next door — or down the street (whether children or adults), you'll think I'm making a big mishagosh about nothing. You say they are mild, law-abiding citizens, quiet sorts, soft-spoken, certainly not danger-ous or sinister, and as far as you can tell, not dedicated with fury to winning anything? I see. *Hmmmm.* How well do you know them?

You have to be married to a Scorpio, or be a blood relative of one, to *really* know him — or her. Everyone else receives only the image of the Halloween mask any particular Scorpio has decided to wear to cover Pluto's secret nature. You might start with asking their mothers if they were sweet, quiet, soft-spoken little angels when they were growing up. Go ahead, ask. Ask actress Terry-Anne Moore about her Scorpio son, Grant — how "gentle" he is. (She also has a Leo son, Stuart, but we're not dealing with Lions here — we're in a different part of the zoo. I just didn't want to ignore the Lion, because ignoring Leo is as risky as underestimating a Scorpion.) As a matter of fact, you can even ask me. I have a Scorpio son myself, Michael.

A New York bank recently made the mistake of refusing to allow Mike to open a checking account because he "wasn't old enough." That did it, for all time. He's finished with banks for life. They simply do not exist for him. He is (quite seriously and literally) shopping around for a safe with a combination lock in which to keep his cash in the future. The banks didn't want *him*? Fine. Then he has no use for *them* — now — or ever. That's the way it is, and don't try to seduce him with Christmas Club bonus gifts of electric blankets and egg beaters. When an Eagle has been rejected, he won't forget. Remember that, all you banks. He may possibly give the Colorado Springs National Bank a chance someday, because they've been fair and square with his mother, but they'll have to solicit him with respectful caution if they want *his* business.

A Scorpio, male or female, adult or child, has a long memory. Only Taurus remembers longer. Eagles are quietly outraged when they learn of an injustice suffered by a friend or family member, and they'll attempt *(at-tempt ?)* to see to it that it's not repeated, with a sort of calm "Godfather" undertone. Here's an important meditation exercise for Scorpios (and for all those who deal with them). There are two particular individuals I'm thinking of who have the reputation of successfully attaining their goals by never losing their tempers, consistently remaining cool, poised and collected, and always speaking with a soft voice. A Mafia Godfather. And Jesus, the carpenter. That Great Truth is worth hours of contemplation. Any Eagle understands the message. The key is in the phrase *"attaining their goals."*

When an injustice is committed against Scorpio himself (or herself), retribution is even more certain. It need not be the next moment. As a Water Sign, Scorpio is willing to wait. These people don't need, always, to seek revenge in a tangible way. Just wishing or willing it on a subconscious level often causes it to occur for those ruled by the awesome planet Pluto — also ruler of the underworld, birth, death, the mysteries of sex, reincarnation and regeneration. You can imagine what happens when one Scorpio becomes angry with another. If you can't imagine, I'll tell you. What happens is they'll both learn fast that "getting even" is The Big Boomerang, especially when it's directed against another Pluto person. Negative actions and words inevitably return to the sender, through a law of the Universe not even Scorpio can alter or cancel.

Those times when Scorpio does not seek to even the score, he or she will, at the very least, take care to avoid in the future the person who's caused the unkindness, as if that person didn't exist, until the guilty party begins to feel nervous, not real. He's not, to Scorpio. What the Eagles do not respect, they ignore, with an all-encompassing disdain. It makes the victim want to pinch himself (or herself) to be sure of not being a ghost. Did you ever have a Scorpio stare *through* you, as one stares through a glass window? It's different, somehow even more chilling than when they stare *into* you. There's a decided difference, and the latter is preferable. Once these people have lost faith, it's not an easy thing to earn back their trust and confidence. Yet when one Scorpio has injured another, confidence and trust will usually be restored more quickly. There's more compassion and forgiveness between them than either will ever grant to those outside their Pluto serpent-circle, with the occasional exception of Pisces and Cancer. My literary agent and my editor both being Scorps, PLUS my production editor and my designer at Harper & Row, you can understand that I usually — not *always* but *usually* — tread carefully.

All dangers of a clash of *wills* aside, Scorpio and Scorpio can accomplish many marvels together, considering the immense force resulting from the combining of their latent energies — anything from causing a savings account to grow large enough to purchase their dream home, near the water — producing an award-winning film — to saving the baby seals in Newfoundland from being butchered before their mothers' eyes. Do you happen to know two Scorpions who aren't busy? There's a sad, sick world out there that needs them. Of course, first they'll have to overcome the tendency of all 1-1 Sun Sign Pattern associations to exaggerate the negative qualities of their mutual characteristics. It requires consistent, concerted effort, but if they can cope with keeping this under control, their achievements as a team or a unit can be impressive.

When two Scorps set their minds to anything, be it negative or positive, detouring them from their path would be like — oh, I don't know *what* it would be like — I guess like attempting any other impossible task. Not like landing on Mars. *That's* possible. Not like parting the Red Sea or walking on the water. *They're* possible. Like . . well, like expecting not to become wet when standing in a downpour of rain. How's that for an example of an "impossible" feat? I had to work on it. So few things are really impossible when the Keys of the Kingdom have been found by two Scorpions. Even remaining dry in a cloudburst, perhaps, is then possible — but for now it will suffice as an illustration.

You might have received the impression I'm afraid of Scorpios. *Me*? An Aries, ruled by *Mars*, afraid of Pluto? Or, in Nature-talk, a sturdy Ram afraid of such a simple creature as the Scorpion? To be candid, yes — I am. I'm Fire, Scorpio is Water. As explained elsewhere in this book, Fire is aware that Water can put out its flame. And so, yes. I fear the power of Pluto in Scorpio people. I fear them, but I also respect them — and respect wins over fear every time. I've never yet met a Scorpio who really stung me — who hasn't demonstrated the Eagle's steadfast loyalty and support when I've needed it. Some of them have been quiet (deceptively quiet) and helpful friends, who have treated me gently. A few have amazed me with their intensity of purpose and strength during periods of soul testing in their personal lives — and almost every one I've known has been deeply compassionate when my own spirit has been troubled.

If the two Scorps who are skipping along a sandy beach together in this incarnation share a harmonious Sun-Moon aspect between their nativities, they just might part the Red Sea themselves. It's been done once, why not again? Or perhaps two Scorpios could aspire to somehow prevent the cataclysm predicted for the West Coast, which may be approaching within the next decade, but which *can* be stopped. One way that's been suggested to halt the Earth tremors is through the cessation of nuclear and hydrogen testing beneath the ground. Another way is to speak out against the reign of sexual excesses and financial greed so highly concentrated in California. The planet Pluto governs both the negative and the positive aspects of sex, and is soon to re-enter its own sign of Scorpio, which rules the deeper mysteries of religion. Maybe that's why Scorpio Billy Graham is working on the angle of "speaking out" the truth, as he sees it personally. Since he doesn't believe in astrology, he doesn't know *why* he's so obsessed, so compelled, so intensely determined to *win* his "battle for souls." But we know why, don't we?

The proud Eagle type of Scorpio scorns the meanness and pettiness of revenge, which is sometimes resorted to by the lower-evolved Grey Lizards of this Sun Sign . . . yet even these can rise, like their own symbolic Phoenix, into their full birthright, at any time they choose to do so.

When Pluto power is contained within two ordinary mortals, if both are Grey Lizards, the pitfalls are many. If one is a Grey Lizard type Scorpio, the other an Eagle — the latter has the power and the glory to raise up the "fallen angel" in the former, and this has occurred many times. I've personally observed several occurrences of this sort of miracle, and it's a thrilling kind of magic to see. If both individuals are the evolved Scorpion Eagles, then the heights to which they can fly together cannot be measured. If the harmonious relationship of other mutual planets, especially the Moon, is added to their combined vibration, the influence for great good will be greatly increased. An inspirational and grand friendship or business association may result — an awesome and powerful love affair or marriage may be realized — or a historic spiritual mission on the Earth may be accomplished.

To the two Scorpios reading this: Remember that your ruling planet, Pluto, contains all the power you need to *build* happiness into a tower, or to *destroy* happiness with the energy force of a nuclear blast. Whether or *not* you call upon it, such power of *will* is yours. Used wisely, there is, literally, nothing you dream that cannot manifest for you. Not in the "hereafter," but in the Here and Now.

☆ ☆ ☆ ☆ ☆ ☆

SCORPIO *Woman* SCORPIO *Man*

Not so much as a sorry-to-lose-you between them!
If she did not mind the parting, he was going to
show her . . . that neither did he.

But of course he cared very much.

This man and woman, boy and girl, or whatever the case may be, will wander, hand-in-hand, down essentially the same *intensified* character and personality path as any other 1-1 Sun Sign Pattern couple with conjoined Solar Luminaries, but with a few vital differences. One of these could be termed a lack of the slightest touch of the "casual" in their mutual natures — therefore, in their relationship.

Scorpios unite for keeps. They part for keeps. They reconcile for keeps. Nothing they do is meant to be temporary. At the time the action is taken, the intention is rock-bound permanency. Should something *change the direction* in which they're swimming (which has to be a near Act of God, considering they're both Fixed Signs), the new line of action instantly assumes the permanency of the old or the former.

Now, you're probably asking yourself if I've become confused (and it would be no wonder, with all this complicated mixing and matching of mates) and have made a mistake, allowing a couple of Geminis to hoppity-skip into this Scorpio-Scorpio section. No. I am not confused. I have made no mistake. There are no Geminis within sight. These Scorpio lovers will make a change in their relationship (or anything else) with extreme rarity. I was only attempting to point out that, on those rare occasions when they *do* make a change, the word "permanent" *still* applies — and it's not only well-nigh impossible to swerve them from a declared intention; it is, in addition, dangerous to cause a change in a Pluto heart, because a split will usually be as permanent as the original union was meant to be. Scorpio anger is *also* permanent. There's much less chance of kiss-and-make-up with two Scorpios than with other Sun Sign twosomes. They're both self-protective enough not to want to get stung twice.

There does exist the faint possibility that a couple of Scorps will meet, mate and marry (or meet, marry and mate), then split in divorce, then legally remarry. Very faint. I know of exactly one case in which this occurred between two November lovers, a husband and wife who are now more deeply in love than ever. Divorcing and then remarrying the same person occurs surprisingly often with Sun Signs other than Scorpio, very much more often than few but astrologers realize. Most people would be amazed (and I hope pleased) by the actual statistics of multiple marriages to the same mates, but it's not a pattern that normally fits a man and woman ruled by Pluto. Anything that could cause a change in the affections is carefully considered by each of them, since they're always aware both of their own and of each other's Fixity.

Those other Sun Sign couples just mentioned . . some of them wed, divorce and re-wed up to as many as three and four times, or more. If such a marital double-feature is ever indulged in by Scorpio and Scorpio, *one* such second chance is the absolute ultimate limit they'll grant each other. If you happen to know a couple of Scorpions who've broken that record, you can be sure that there are either heavy Gemini, Pisces or Sagittarius influences in both horoscopes — or they were adopted. The latter is another thing that occurs with far more frequency than people other than astrologers suspect. I've personally stumbled upon a shockingly high number of nativities that reveal, in intricate but unmistakable ways, that they could not possibly be the birth charts of the people they are supposed to represent, resulting in the bringing to light of many secret adoptions, which would otherwise have been buried forever — for at least the life of the unsuspecting adoptee. I happen to be of the opinion that every human being has the inalienable right to be told the absolute truth regarding his or her precise birth data, and never mind the emotional hang-ups of the real and the foster parents.

In astrology the planet Pluto, along with Mercury and Jupiter, governs matters of adoption. This means that there are often reasons why a Scorpio man and a Scorpio woman become involved in the adoption of — or in the giving up for adoption of — children. Naturally, the adoption syndrome doesn't apply to every double Scorpio combination, or even to most, but since it applies to Scorpio with so much more frequency than to other couples, it's a subject worth mentioning here. Since Scorpios tend to believe that keeping personal matters secret is a solid virtue, they need a reminder that children deserve a voice in the matter, especially after they've become adults. More times than not, the tendency of Scorpio to retain secrets, to keep private matters totally private, is a positive thing. In this instance, it is decidedly negative, and this is a good time — and a good way — to remind the Pluto-ruled that there are occasions when complete frankness should be honored over and above the natural Scorpion tendency to be discreet. There are few things on Earth more beautiful and commendable than adoption, than taking a parentless child into one's heart to care for and love. There's no chance that the child itself, when it's old enough to comprehend human emotion, will fail to recognize the unselfish devotion involved in its adoption. But deceiving the child in order to protect the feelings and privacy of adults, is a sad blot upon the beauty and benevolence of the original decision. I pray that this truth is realized by all Sun Signs reading this section, not just Scorpios. For it's time this injustice ended — time we all spoke out honestly concerning a denial of human freedom too long permitted to exist under the protection of the courts.

In addition to ruling childbirth and adoption, Pluto rules death, or what we call death — the transition to another level of awareness — or the moving from one flesh body eventually into another. A chapter written to reveal the areas of harmony and discord between lovers and mates may seem a strange place to find a mention of death. Not when the lovers or mates are both Scorpios. It is a natural subject. It is, in fact, often the very thing that draws them together — or that, if it does not draw them together — causes a deep bond between this man and this woman. They may share highly unique ideas on the subject of death, which others have thought far-out, making them feel lonely and uncertain . . . . . until they found comprehension in each other. Perhaps each has suffered the deep scars of a great bereavement (or more than one) in childhood or youth. One or both might have been married before and is a widow (or widower) at the time they meet. One might have nearly died at one time and feels that he or she was "brought back" for some as yet unsolved purpose. In some way, at some time, death, in its positive as well as its negative aspects, will be a powerful influence in the relationship in some extraordinary way.

In all 1-1 Sun Sign Pattern associations, and especially so in this one, there is an added dimension to love . . . the inexplicable joy of discovering another human being so very much like oneself that there is little need to explain things other people have considered queer or crazy for so long. Someone understands. Someone *sees* — and *knows*! Such timeless moments of trembling joy are rare. The kind of warm "I am home again, at last" feeling experienced when this man and this woman recognize their secret selves behind each other's deep gaze is a beautiful thing, a gift to be treasured, which each can give, one to the other.

Pluto also governs, in astrology, the deeper mysteries of religion and reincarnation. Since all Scorpios are ruled by this silent, powerful planet, many Scorpion men and women experience unusual reincarnational or other religious enlightenment through their love. Some facet of the mystical, the spiritual or the occult is usually woven within the threads of their emotional bond.

Religion leads naturally (for Scorpios) into the subject of sex. Other Sun Sign readers may wonder what on Earth could possibly be the connection between sex and religion. These two will not wonder. For, to them, the physical expression of their love has about it a haunting and indefinable nuance, which may elude them on a conscious level but which mysteriously and beautifully magnetizes their hearts and souls and minds into a rare and singing harmony of Oneness, experienced by too few men and women. The mutual sensitivity and deep wells of need they both possess cause their lovemaking to be an extraordinary source of fulfillment for them. Of course, if there are afflictions between the Sun and Moon, and other planets, in their respective nativities, the sexual compatibility between them may not be so ecstatic. There can be, from powerful Pluto, the extreme problems of frigidity, impotency — or promiscuity. But sex, in all its pure and impure aspects, is an inseparable part of the Scorpion essence; therefore, it will play no small role in the relationship of two Eagles.

One of the most serious threats to happiness for two Scorpios will be the tendency of each to get even when hurt — or worse, to hide his or her true feelings from the other because of false pride and a reluctance to reveal vulnerabilities. This is regrettable, since it only leads them into a series of misunderstandings, like an endless circle going nowhere — or the pain may break out of the circle, and drive them to seek their separate ways, without ever hinting to each other of the mutual need and desire for reconciliation.

For weeks, months, or even years, then, the Eagle and his Pluto lady may contain all their longing within themselves, when all it would take is a confrontation with truth together. Instead, they keep their secret, and speak with each other only astrally, which is far from satisfactory, silently communing . . .

> *the odd-shaped things I save*
> *that smell, and feel of us . . .*
>
> *a crumpled book of matches from the pizza place*
> *some wilted flowers*
> *picked outside the door*
> > *you couldn't enter*
>
> *a bleached and crooked twig*
> *washed ashore at that spot on the sand*
> *where you first said you were lonely*
>
> > *and surprised me into tears*
>
> *a hotel room key*
> *stuffed inside an airline ticket envelope*
>
> *. . . . . . I guess you saved the bird verse*
> *and the memory of my last smile . . .*
>
> *they take so little room in your scrapbook* °

Now, isn't that a sad and unnecessary scene? Two Eagles, pasting their love in a memory book, when they should be exchanging it with each other — in the spirit of regeneration and rebirth represented by the Phoenix rising from its own ashes — which is the higher octave astrological symbol of the Sun Sign of Scorpio.

Pluto's placid mask of indifference is not the entirely safe defense against pain he and she imagine it to be. It can turn Valentine's Day into a very frightening Halloween for them both. The fear of rebuff and rejection is behind the Scorpio pose of "it doesn't bother me at all." But I have a question for both of these intensely emotional lovers. If you can't trust your hearts with each other, then with whom can you trust them? Somehow, someday, someway . . you must trust *someone*. And no one will treat your secret more tenderly, guard it more loyally, than a Scorpio . . . like yourself.

There are the usual number of hidden dangers in this, as in any relationship. With these two Scorpios, such dangers can in some way be related to unfaithfulness (resorted to by the Pluto-ruled only under the most

---

° *Venus Trines at Midnight,* by Linda Goodman (New York: Taplinger Publishing Company, Inc., 1970. To be republished by Harper & Row, 1979).

intense misery and confusion) . . . to hypnosis, mind control, alcohol, drugs . . . and negative facets of the occult.

They are both frequently unnecessarily suspicious, a problem that can be eliminated only by total honesty exchanged between them. They're also both a little selfish — and much more than a little violent, just beneath the surface. These traits are magnified in the Scorpio-Scorpio love vibration, but then, so are the Scorpion courage, durability, gentleness and protectiveness magnified. If they both make a conscious effort to control the negative and stress the positive qualities of their characters and personalities, they can wish on each other, instead of on a star or the new Moon . . and make all their dreams come true.

Forgiveness is the magic key to every Scorpio difficulty. If they can master this greatest of all virtues (for all other virtues are as nothing without it), their love can last as long as all love should last . . . forever-and-a-day.

It's important for both of them to remember this: He is not as self-sufficient, poised and in control of his emotions as he pretends to be. Nor is she as aloof and unmoved as her silences indicate — as her detachment would make her seem. Wearing a mask is such a bother. It may be necessary in public, but when you're in the arms of the one you love, it's time to remove the false face and the dark glasses of pretense . . . . . . to simply be yourself. That's what love really means, you know — acceptance of another person, with all that person's imperfections. In fact, sometimes the imperfections of the one you love make you love him (or her) even more, because they represent the familiar, the intimate . . . . the secret flaws revealed only to someone with whom they can be trusted . . . . someone who won't laugh at them or judge them.

When the Scorpio man and the Scorpio woman have quarreled, and each secretly aches for one more chance to make love return between them, it can be a very sad thing, because neither of them dares to make the first move, to say, "I'm sorry I hurt you." Or, "Please come back." Somehow, they just don't know how. They've practiced self-sufficiency so long with the rest of the world, never admitting dependency. Maybe the wisdom of a child will help.

Once upon an enchanted time, in 1975, a little Scorpio girl then aged eight, who lives in Falls Village, Connecticut, fell in love with a young Scorpio boy — a few years older than she, who lives in New York. Following the Pluto pattern, the "love relationship" between these two young Eagles was shadowed by the consecutive accidental deaths of four of the little Scorpio girl's beloved dogs, within the short period of one year.

For months, the tiny Eagle struggled with her feelings, with her natural Scorpion reticence to reveal them — for fear of rejection or ridicule. Finally, after what must have been much painful soul searching, love won, in a triumph of emotional courage. She sat down and wrote the Scorpio boy a letter. In typical Pluto fashion, it was brief, direct — and to the point. No words wasted.

I've asked her permission (and his) to share it with Scorpio lovers everywhere... and with a touching and beautiful victory over their Sun Sign's innate sense of personal privacy, they have granted it. Both said they didn't mind — and hoped that grown-up Eagles would use it as a guide when there's something heavy in their hearts which they feel will make them burst open if they can't find a way to express it.

Here, then, is her letter — a genuine communication of truth and courage, from Scorpio to Scorpio — in her own words, including even her own spelling.

Dear Mike,

This is going to be a short note ... becase its a short note.

Some of my frends think I am dumb to like you. But that won't ever stop me from loving you. I like you becase we both beleeve in fairees, elvs and druides .. and we both beleeve in magik and the THIRD EYE!!! I gess that means we love each other ... doessnt it ?

Suzanne Chinatti

☆ ☆ ☆ ☆ ☆ ☆

SCORPIO

Water — Fixed — Negative
Ruled by Pluto
Symbols: Scorpion & Eagle
Night Forces — Feminine

SAGITTARIUS

Fire — Mutable — Positive
Ruled by Jupiter
Symbols: Archer & Centaur
Day Forces — Masculine

The SCORPIO-SAGITTARIUS *Relationship*

All are keeping a sharp look-out in front, but none
suspects that the danger may be creeping up from behind.

Everything about Sagittarius is always open, friendly and direct. Everything about Scorpio is *sometimes* open, friendly and direct — on the surface. Don't challenge astrology, please. (Do you hear the noise of all those Archers reading this making a fuss? Questions, questions, questions.) Yes, Archers, there are indeed many Scorpions who, like yourself, may be described as friendly, bright, agreeable and straightforward, whether you realize it or not. Such Scorps as, say, Harold Hern, Dolores Simon, Steve Cook, Kathleen Hyde, Arthur Klebanoff, Lydia Link, Roger Good, Buz Wyeth and Bob Henson. You're not convinced because you've never met these Eagles? Well, *I've* met them — can't you take my word? No, Sagittarians never take *anyone's* word for *anything*, until they've run out of questions. I suppose we'll just have to take the time to prove these claims, so we can get on with it, and have some peace.

All right, Sag, think about the following people, some living, some no longer with us, but all of them who should be well known to you — and all of them Scorpio Sun Signs: Vivien Leigh (alias Scarlett O'Hara, a Scorpio playing an Aries) — Richard Burton (Shakespearean actor and occasional Peck's Bad Boy) — jolly President Teddy Roosevelt (not Franklin, he was an Aquarian) — Marie Antoinette — Prince Charles of England — Princess Grace of Monaco, née Grace Kelly — and actress Katharine Hepburn. Do you wish to argue that these particular Scorpio men and women do not immediately present to the mind an image of open friendliness ? Do you not agree that the whole lot of them could be thought of as bright and agreeable —sometimes— and could be considered to be direct, honest and straightforward sorts ? I hear no objections. Sudden silence from the Sagittarian bleachers. Not a word, not even from Archers Don Gambrill, Marvin Cook, Michel D'Brenovic, David Susskind or William Buckley, Jr. The silence of assent, I trust ? Excellent. When Sagittarians have been silenced (especially those last two), a major victory of logic and intellectual stamina has been achieved.

Now that I've proven my astrological point, and hushed the dissident Archers, we may continue our compatibility analysis, undisturbed and uninterrupted. It's perfectly true that many Scorpios share (on the surface) the bright, agreeable, open and friendly straightforwardness of Sagittarians. The *difference* is — in the words of entertainer Flip Wilson's immortal Geraldine — that when it comes to Sag, "What you see is what you get." But with Scorpio, what you see is definitely *not* what you are going to get. Absolutely never.

It's hard to say exactly what you *will* get. It varies, depending. But you can be sure it won't be what you expected, or what the surface personality of Scorpio might lead you to believe it will be. Every Pluto-ruled man, woman and child wears a false face — from the moment of birth. Every day is Halloween to Scorpio. It's "trick or treat" with these people in their dealings with friends, business associates, relatives, lovers and mates. When you play nasty with them (like hiding in the house with the lights out, pretending not to be home on Spook and Goblin night, or on any night) or are guilty of any similar sort of insult that may justifiably anger the Eagle, the "trick" you get can be as relatively harmless as having the air let out of your tires, so that you face four flats on a snowy morning when you're late for school, the office or the airport, or discovering that the hair dryer you refused to lend Scorp has been carefully hidden, so that it takes you weeks to find it — to slightly more serious retaliations, like being fired when you least expect it, having a bank loan inexplicably refused, having your library card cancelled with no explanation — all the way to the most chilling, fearsome Pluto revenge of all: having a magic spell cast upon you, which makes you totally invisible to the Eagle. You are not heard or seen. The wounded (or angered — same thing) Scorpion will simply walk coldly past you, as if you were a picket fence, a discarded grapefruit rind, an empty trash can (empty, not full), a telephone pole, standing there helpless, feeling twenty feet tall, skinny, lonely and full of splinters—or a teeny-tiny insect, like an ant, so small and insignificant you're in danger of being crushed beneath someone's large boot. (Guess whose boot?)

That's a general idea of the negative side of not getting precisely what you may see from Scorpio. There's a positive and happy side to it too, and the Sagittarian mixed up with an Eagle in this 2-12 Sun Sign Pattern may be on the receiving end of either. But before I describe the positive side of the surprising glimpses behind those Pluto masks, let's switch to Sagittarius for a moment.

The Archers never sneak up on Scorpio from the rear, as the Eagles do to them. There is nothing sneaky about Sag. They're honest enough to kill you right to your face (symbolically, of course) in front of anyone who happens to be standing there . . . or passing by. From Sag, it won't be a retaliatory *act* of revenge the Scorpio is stung with. The sting will be *verbal*. Loud. And clear. Emphatic. And blunt. *Very* blunt. (Or candid, frank, truthful—you may choose your own term.) Since Scorpio is capable of such naughty *actions* when he or she has been hurt or put down or injured in some way emotionally or financially, and Sagittarius stings only with *words* and never ever with underhanded actions, it might seem that Archers are really the least dangerous of the two, all things considered. It might seem so, but it's not necessarily true. Because, you see, the Scorpion only plays "trick or treat" with that Pluto behavior when he or she has been the victim of something negative from Sag—whereas the Archer can shoot those stinging, burning, painful verbal arrows into the Eagle for no reason whatsoever. There need not be a cause. In fact, the happier Sag is, the more likely he (or she) is to aim the bow and shoot. The more bright and cheerful the Archers feel, the more they are apt to feel friendly and talkative—gregarious, as it were.

Sagittarians may not approach from the rear, but Scorpio may wish they would. It would be less public. Not always, but usually, the Archer's zinging darts are well meant, seldom intended to hurt. But for all that, they do. When Sag says to an Eagle, in front of a group of people, including the Eagle's wife: "Hey! Tell everyone that story you told me about that time, last month, when your old girl friend showed up at your office, and coaxed you into taking her out to dinner," the Archer isn't being malicious, he only wants to share a hilarious story with friends. The end of the story is that the Scorpio did *not* take the old flame out to dinner, but his wife might leave the party alone before he can explain this. Facing the Scorpio caper of four flat tires is less traumatic for an Archer than the scene he faces with his wife, later at home, after being the victim of playful, innocent, harmless Sagittarius. Of course, it won't stop there. The following day, poor Sag will become an insect, a splintered telephone pole, grapefruit rind or whatever to the injured

Eagle. Heaven only knows for how long. Probably until Scorpio thinks Sagittarius has suffered for his sins sufficiently, and that can be a long spell, depending on the magnitude of the sin.

I'll give one more example along this line, an event that actually occurred. An Archer and an Eagle I know were sitting in Vince Sardi's in New York in the fall of 1975, having gone there for an after-the-theatre snack. The Eagle had recently gained a few pounds, not many, maybe five or ten, and it was not terribly noticeable, but he was sensitive about it. (Scorps are extremely sensitive about everything.) Sag left the table they were sharing and proceeded to merrily table-hop all over the place, saying hello to friends and so forth . . and after a few minutes, the Archer cheerfully called out across the crowded dining room to Scorpio, "Don't order one of those chocolate parfaits with whipped cream! Remember all that fat you have to lose!"

A sudden silence fell upon the diners. The Scorpio was a famous person everyone knew either personally or by reputation. Approximately ten seconds passed, by the clock. Then the Eagle called out to his Sagittarian friend across the room, in a deep, rich voice, "Shall I tell the waiter to charge both checks on my tab, since your credit has been cut off until you pay your bill?" Every eye in the place turned to the red-faced, humiliated Archer. Ah, yes! "Let the punishment fit the crime" is Scorpio's motto.

As determinedly ruthless as some Scorpios can be when they've really been hurt and feel compelled to teach the guilty a lesson they'll never forget, the Eagles can also be unbelievably loyal and fiercely protective of anyone who has ever been kind to them. That's another surprise the Archer may discover behind Scorpio's Pluto mask — the identity of a warm and loving friend, capable of intense devotion, who will still be there when the fair-weather friends have all flown the coop. The Sagittarian who can learn to keep his or her mouth out of trouble with the Eagle will never find a more secure port in a storm than Scorpio. These people will literally risk their lives for a great cause, or to defend someone they care about from any kind of harm or danger.

But the Archer who can't be still, and who doesn't count to ten (preferably to twenty) before openly blurting out painful observations that cut into Scorpio's poise and self-confidence, will suffer in commensurate measure, or be permanently exiled from Scorpio's magnetic circle. Once a Scorpio has had enough, it's all over. It's the end. Since no one can safely or accurately predict how much it takes to bring an Eagle to that rare, but final, steely-eyed, cold and never retracted decision, Sag should tread carefully and not push his (or her) luck too far. That's the trouble. Archers are always pushing their luck beyond the limit. Often, they win giant jackpots of all kinds by daring to go that last mile. But not with Scorpio.

There are some things these two have in common. Needing to know all the answers is one. With Sagittarius, it's called "inquisitiveness." With Scorpio it's called . . well, simply a burning need to *know*, a compulsion to probe the buried, the hidden and the mysterious, to ferret out secrets. "Curiosity" is too mild a word. As I've said before in this book, and in my book *Sun Signs*, the Eagles are aware that knowledge is Power, and they're after all of *that* they can accumulate. Sagittarians are forever asking blunt, even rude questions, demanding logical answers, wanting to know the "why" of everything, never resting until they've been convinced. Scorpio goes about discovering the truth in a more subtle manner, with equal fervor but with a disguised desire. It's rather amusing to observe the two of them attempting to find out everything about each other. The Archer is determined to strip off Scorpio's protective mask, and Scorpio won't stop until he (or she) has uncovered every last vestige of the Archer's inner character and various thespian roles. Sagittarians do enjoy acting out different parts, from time to time, but only for fun, not for sinister purposes. They'd like to make you guess "Who am I today?" but they're cheerful about dropping hints, and finally confess what they've been up to with their acts.

Both Sag and Scorp usually enjoy competitive sports, if they're typical of their Sun Signs. In this, they are alike, especially the male Archers and Eagles (also many of the females). It's in the losing that they're different. Sagittarius is, admittedly, an admirably good loser, normally brave and optimistic about "winning next time." Scorpio is a very poor loser, frequently saying (and almost meaning) they'd rather die than lose. To the Eagle, not to win is tantamount to a cardinal sin.

These two are influenced in their association by the 2-12 vibration, and so there's no denying that Scorpio has lessons of freedom, optimism, daring and self-honesty to learn from Sag, which the Eagle will actively dislike learning. Yet the situation will be softened somewhat by the Sagittarian's karmic memory tolerance for Scorpio's faults and failings, with the Archer subconsciously remembering what it was like to look upon life so intensely, with such great sensitivity, and dedicated to avoiding such a heavy emotional burden this time 'round . . . which is why Sag is generally so happy-go-lucky, viewing life more casually, taking the time to roll a few hoops, to see as much of the world as possible — refusing to be really serious about anything, except for those occasional Sags who enter the religious life (but seldom before the end of an exciting search). Neither will the average Sag be contentedly tied down, during this incarnation, to the home fires (especially in youth) with the bonds of Scorpio's powerful sense of duty and obligation. Sagittarians want to wander on the wind — to be free to answer the call of wild adventure. Yet they have a genuine compassion for Scorpio's different outlook. The Archers feel, somehow, deeply sympathetic toward the Eagles whose flights are so often grounded, sometimes canceled, by responsibilities, secret fears — and promises to be kept that can't be broken — for the sake of Pluto honor.

But Sagittarians shouldn't blurt out their compassion aloud, making it sound like pity. One doesn't dare say "I feel sorry for you" to a Scorpio. This is a Fire and Water combination, and that sort of mistake could create a lot of steam in the teakettle.

☆ ☆ ☆ ☆ ☆ ☆

SCORPIO *Woman* SAGITTARIUS *Man*

Some of the greatest heroes have confessed that just before
they fell to, they had a sinking. Had it been so
with Peter at that moment I would admit it . . . . But
Peter had no sinking, he had one feeling only, gladness;
and he gnashed his pretty teeth with joy.

Scorpio is Fixed, Sagittarius is Mutable, and Fixed and Mutable are words with totally different meanings. Scorpio is ruled by the Planet Pluto, Sagittarius is ruled by Jupiter. Pluto is secretive and subtle, Jupiter is open and expansive. Scorpio's a Water Sign; Sag is a Fire Sign; and water and fire don't mix easily without some sort of catalyst, such as a great deal of patience or tolerance. Do you think any of these difficulties bother the Archer who's in love with a Scorpio girl? Of course not. These are merely astrological challenges, and Sagittarius eats challenges for breakfast.

The larger the challenge, the brighter the fire that flames in his Jupiter eye. The challenge of a Scorpio female, with its scope, its complications, its intrigue, its depth of mystery or its danger, will surely not discourage the Archer. It will fascinate him.

Because every Sagittarian male, at any given period of his life, is enthusiastically involved with a dog, a horse, a career, a hobby, a dream, a travel plan or a course of study (from religious philosophy to homeopathy or numerology), he'll have lots of things to talk about as icebreakers when he meets a Scorpio girl—and believe me, there's always a substantial amount of ice to be broken in the initial phase of a relationship with any Scorpion.

Unlike many men, he won't be put off or put down by her rather distant manner with strangers. It won't put him off, because it excites him with the possibility of using his charm and persuasion and logic and cheeriness to raise her cool temperature a number of degrees—and it won't put him down because it's next to impossible for Sagittarians to suffer from the pain of a put-down. Mostly for the reason that they don't recognize insults as such. They think *you're* just being honest, the way *they* like to be, and who are they to object to the same sort of honest observations and remarks from others as they pass out themselves?—which is uncommonly decent of them, and I'd say they have a very good point there, wouldn't you? It's difficult to puncture the Sagittarian's Jupiter balloons, filled with the helium of optimism, bless their sunny hearts (and curse their brutal frankness). Unless he suffers from a Scorpio, Capricorn, Taurus, Cancer or Virgo Moon or Ascendent, Sag doesn't often brood very long over a disappointment or a criticism. Normally, the Archer will simply shrug, toss trouble over his shoulder and wait for things to be better. The weather report may say rain, snow and high winds today, but it's sure to be sunny, fair and warm tomorrow. Each sunrise brings to him a new dawn of impossible dreams and an unexpected solution to old problems.

Admittedly, it's a philosophy the Scorpio woman could imitate with great benefit. Let's change "admittedly" to "definitely." If she hears a weather forecast for fair weather, she tends to secretly suspect that the weatherman is deliberately trying to trick her into setting out on a hike just so he can laugh at her when she gets caught in a downpour, and her potato salad gets drenched. Human nature is like that, she tells herself silently. A person can't be too careful. You can't always trust people to be as they appear to be, or to keep the promises they make. You can see how her worldly-wise air and suspicious nature may occasionally clash with the auric colors of the Archer's naivete and blind trust.

She's wrong to suspect this man of being anything other than what he appears to be. Oh, he may symbolically smear on a little greasepaint, now and then, wear a putty nose, dress up like a clown or imagine he's playing some part like *Hamlet* or Jimmy Stewart's role in *Harvey* (he might even play the Rabbit—it's possible), but these are just harmless acts he indulges in, because he has a touch of the theatre in his blood. Usually, he's as delighted as a child when someone guesses the part he's playing, like the game of Twenty Questions. The sort of brief and temporary masque of tragedy-comedy the Archer wears for fleeting moments is easily detected by anyone of normal perception, especially by a Scorpio woman with *her* kind of penetrating perception. No, this man won't deliberately or consciously fool her. God knows he won't lie to her (in fact, she may wish he *would* once in a while, to soften the blows and dull the edges a little).

Whatever flaws he may possess which could cause her grief or worry will probably be painted in vivid colors on his features when she first meets him, or, at the worst, transparently hiding just beneath his cheery grin, and clearly visible to the Scorpio X-ray vision. The Sagittarian man's faults and weak points, just like his virtues and strong points, almost seem to wave at you, after a few hours of conversation, saying: "Hi, there! Recognize me?," completely unafraid that anyone might disapprove. How could anyone disapprove of a few minor faults? Doesn't everybody have them, to some degree? Yes, everybody does have them, to some degree. Thanks to Sag, we are all aware of this great truth. If humanity had not been graced *(graced?)* with the presence of Sagittarians (and Virgos), we would still be blissfully ignorant, for the most part, that we all fall a little short of the angels, now and then.

One of the Archer's flaws that may wave "Hi!" to the Scorpio female when she first meets him, is that he is gregarious concerning girls. He likes females. (He also likes males.) He likes *people.* He likes to play tennis with them, soccer, volleyball, basketball, football (either sex, he's not picky or choosy) — bounce ideas around with them — see plays and films with them — argue with them — question them, about all manner of things — and simply fraternize and co-exist with them. She may frown on the feminine angle, and she won't be overjoyed about the masculine angle either, since it causes him to spend a greater amount of time away from her than she believes ideal. This woman is more than a little jealous and possessive (and suspicious), but she can't hope to hold her Sagittarian man's love unless she cheerfully and trustingly allows him to freely roam when the mood strikes him. She must give him lots of rope, but she can content herself with the certain knowledge that he's sure to eventually hang himself with it. If this man is ever even tempted to be unfaithful, he's not likely to hide behind the mulberry bush. He'll come right out and tell her, if he's a typical Sag, and give her the chance to win him back before he's gone anywhere. So, at least she has the comfort of knowing that "what she doesn't know truly won't hurt her." As long as he comes home each night, kisses her on the nose each morning and makes no confessions, she can be confident that his heart is still hers — and every other part of him, including the most important part, his spirit.

Usually, he'll ask her to go along anyway. He'd much prefer to share his hegiras with a familiar companion than go to the trouble of looking up old friends or tramping around with strangers. If she adapts to his pup tents, road maps and flight schedules happily, he'd rather have her beside him than anyone else.

The compromise, of course, can't be all one-sided. That's not how compromise works. He'll have to give a few inches too, if he wants to be the proud possessor of the deep devotion and thrilling mystery of a Scorpio woman. She greatly admires his honestly, but she is super-ultra-extra-sensitive, and his careless, thoughtless remarks will wound her unexpectedly vulnerable heart more than he'll ever guess, because she keeps her deepest hurt to herself, inside, where it won't show. She'll bear her agony silently for a long, long time. That's the first Pluto stage. Next comes the second stage, when he can expect (but the trouble is, he *won't* expect) the burning sting of Scorpio retaliation. It's impossible to predict what form it will take, but *whatever* the form, he can be sure it will cause him to fumble a few arrows, and he might discover his bow of truth is badly bent for a while. The final stage, if he doesn't wake up and learn to value this woman's rare love, which doesn't grow on every tree, and to appreciate her loyalty and multidimensional emotional challenges — is that she will leave him. And she will not return. Once Scorpio makes a decision, it is seldom, if ever, retracted. Too much agony of soul has gone into the making of it for her to lightly disregard it. A Sagittarian man is, by nature, somewhat impulsive and careless, but to lose what might have been a lasting love is unforgivable carelessness. All it takes is a little more tenderness, a little more consideration of her feelings — and the lost might be found.

Their sexual attitudes are very different, but not incompatible. His lovemaking is passionate, yet just as often touchingly and strangely naive and idealistic. Hers is all-consuming, concentrated — and at certain magical and memorable moments, deep-beyond-deep. It doesn't take astrology to interpret this as a very real opportunity for two people to find a way to blend their physical needs into a deeply fulfilling experience together. One possible area of tension may be her tendency to look upon the act of love as a sacred thing — a silent thing. An unspoken shared ecstasy. He may, at some time, use the opportunity of their intimacy to say something that's been on his mind, and it doesn't occur to him that this could be the wrong moment to say it. However infrequently he makes this blunder, it's too often. Then she may use their lovemaking closeness as a way to get even with him for something he's said or done to hurt her earlier, by deliberately being cold and unresponsive to his embraces, behaving in such a passive manner that his fiery desire is completely extinguished by her Water Element's ability to dampen his feelings and drown his emotions. This is always a danger with a Fire Sign and a Water Sign, in all their areas of adjustment, not just the sexual . . . . . . but they should both be especially ashamed to treat one another any way but tenderly when their hearts and bodies are trying to manifest the miracle of Oneness that is love.

Because this man and woman, whether they realize it or not, are influenced by the 2-12 Sun Sign Pattern, she will sense he knows things she needs to learn, and he will be more tolerant of her different personality than one might expect him to be, because of his karmic memories of the Scorpio essence. If he uses this tolerance, which is there to be brought forth from the subconscious when he calls upon it — and she accepts gracefully that he has things to teach her (such as the foolishness of fear and suspicion, how these emotions bring about the manifestation of misery . . . and how excitement, enthusiasm and optimism are powerful affirmations with the ability to materialize dreams into reality) — they can make their relationship work smoothly and harmoniously. A great deal will depend on whether the

Luminaries between their horoscopes are favorably or unfavorably aspected.

Money is a subject they should agree in the beginning to avoid like the medieval plague. Fortunately, if he's a typical Sag, he won't mind at all if she wants to develop her independence as a woman by following a career. It's one of his more lovable traits—the willingness to grant the woman he loves freedom of expression, without smothering her individuality, which made him fall in love with her in the first place. But since he tends toward extravagance, and she tends toward economy, they should have separate checking accounts, and never question each other over income and outgo.

If he values her love, he'll never be careless of her feelings. For all her gentleness, her apparent poise and calm, sometimes when she's the most silent, the volcano within is the most active. Her secret emotions are powerful. They can incite her to raging anger or cool, premeditated revenge—yet they also make her capable of an enduring devotion that will launch him toward the higher heavens he dreams of reaching, if he *cares* enough to handle her heart tenderly and "speak no evil," like the wise monkey.

As for her, she should treasure his open, honest love, not suffocate it with suspicion and accusation. She must never break his spirit, for this is where his sky-blue dreams, his golden optimism and his starry Jupiter idealism are first born—and later nurtured. When his spirit is broken, he can no longer aim his arrows straight, and he becomes a lost, unhappy Robin Hood, wandering Sherwood Forest without a vision to his name. What a sad thought. Would Maid Marian have so unkindly treated her brave, wistful Archer? Of course not.

☆ ☆ ☆ ☆ ☆ ☆

SCORPIO *Man* SAGITTARIUS *Woman*

----◆◆◆◆----

This dread made her forgetful of what must be Peter's feelings, and she said to him rather sharply, "Peter, will you make the necessary arrangements?"

"If you wish it," he replied, as coolly as if she had asked him to pass the nuts.

I once observed and overheard a meeting between a girl Archer and a man with a Scorpio Ascendent. At the time they were introduced, she was about eighteen, and typically believed she was going to remain in that glowing chronological niche forever. He was soft-spoken and intelligent, perhaps three decades or so her senior. A quiet man, of distinguished appearance, who wore glasses, and whose hairline was slightly receding. He was completely kind and courteous to her when they were introduced, but shortly afterward, she turned to her companion and whispered, "He's really proof of life after death, isn't he?" Then she exploded into peals of laughter, in appreciation of her own cleverness.

Astrology often takes an amused, tolerant view of a Sagittarian's ability to kill with a word, but there are times when the frankness of a Sag exceeds the boundaries of sensitivity and good taste, and can be described as nothing short of inhuman and indecent cruelty. Now and then, these Archers need a slap of truth themselves. A sharp slap.

A female Sagittarian who crosses the boundaries of good taste with a Scorpio male will find that her romance has a miserable ending before the first chapter is even written.

Fortunately, most Sagittarian women are the kind whose Jupiter rulership causes them to spread more joy and sunlight than pain. And it's this type of Sag who can truly bless an Eagle with her holly-berry personality, touching honesty and generosity. Symbolized by the Centaur (half horse, half human), she sometimes stumbles clumsily, sometimes glides gracefully into his life, trailing brightly colored streamers of hope and optimism. Her contagiously cheerful smile flashes into the dark corners of his soul like a remembered song from a happier time, and lights up his buried dreams, resurrecting them with the promise of new life. Unless he locks her out.

As pleasant and mild as he may appear to be on the surface, the Eagle is a man of many brooding moods, inexplicable spells of depression and self-doubt. He may break her heart without meaning to, when he refuses to be caught up in her enthusiasms, because this searching girl needs another human being against whom to bounce her bubbles of happiness, or they simply burst and disappear into the air, just when she thinks she's created them with enough strength to float around for a while, so she can watch their rainbow streaks as they change hues with each new exciting idea. It's not much fun to blow bubbles with someone who won't chase them with you.

The Sagittarian girl requires lots of traveling; she needs lots of pets and people around her. If she's denied a frequent change of scene, or her animal and human companionship, she'll become a restless, dissatisfied woman. Nothing can be sadder than the expansiveness of a Jupiter person being held captive. When the Sagittarian enthusiasm and gregariousness are confined or smothered through circumstances or restriction of any kind, the Archer will sink into severe mental and emotional anguish, leading to despair, a very real danger to these people. Sagittarius must, literally, exist in an atmosphere of hope and happiness, or the spirit will die, and the health will be severely afflicted on all levels. To smack down this girl's friendly, optimistic outlook is an act of great unkindness.

Unlike her, the typical Scorpio man dislikes crowds of people, although he'll usually be kind to animals, barring some Jupiter or Neptune affliction in his nativity. He needs long periods of solitude and quiet, time to meditate and enter into the core of himself. He needs privacy. Naturally, this can cause conflicts between them. It's not, however, an insolvable problem. (No problem is.) He should make a sincere effort to curb his possessive urges and allow her to seek the bright lights, changes of scenery and stimulating conversation she needs, rather than trying to keep her on a leash, as though she were a pet herself. Even real puppy dogs don't like leashes, and Sag is very much like a friendly puppy dog. Of course it makes her happier if he's with her when she's socializing, but if it disturbs his tranquility, it's better that they allow each other the right to retain the earlier individual life-styles without feeling they must force them to overlap. He needn't worry that she's being unfaithful to him when she's out walking the dog, riding her horse, chasing deer with a camera or roaming through the woods alone. A strange peace descends upon her when she's close to Nature, and the solitude he needs so much—that she rejects herself—would be as healing to her spirit as it is to his if she'd allow it to be. (Since Scorps like to meditate mysteries, the Eagle might ponder over the use of the word "nature," as in human nature—the *reason* this is the word used to describe the true inner essence of a person. There's much food for thought in contemplating word games.)

As for other men, the typical Sag isn't likely to carry on a secret affair. Secrecy is Scorpio's department, not hers. If she ever felt she was falling out of love with him and falling in love with someone else, she'd probably pour out her troubled feelings to him before he himself even suspected anything was wrong. Since Scorpios are "by nature" suspicious, also uncannily perceptive—and know nearly everything about everyone close to them before they know it themselves—you can see how quick she can be to speak the truth. It's quite a feat to beat a Scorp to the punch .. of any kind of knowledge.

The one thing that will cause a Sagittarian woman to fall out of love faster than anything else is boredom—whereas the Eagle stops loving only after he's decided his partner is no longer worthy of his devotion, because she has, in some way, not measured up to his ideal of strength of character. Scorpio does not admire weakness, or people who give up easily. He may have compassion for losers, but he respects only the winners.

In the beginning, at least, there should be no boredom between these two during their sharing of physical intimacy. In this respect, her frankness can be a shining virtue, her sexual expression of love as open and honest as such feelings are meant to be — and this is a powerful emotional magnet to a Scorpion. He'll eagerly respond to her fiery passion, just as she'll respond with sincere and flattering interest to the varied facets of his always slightly elusive sexuality, which fluctuates from gentle affection and tenderness to intense sensuality. But if the Luminaries between their birth charts are square or opposed, she may thoughtlessly make a critical remark immediately before, during or just after their physical closeness, which pounds like a hammer on this man's trembling sensitivity. In return, he may retaliate with a sudden coldness and disinterest that cause her to feel both unloved and undesirable, bringing on a scene of tearful reproaches, for she won't hold her frustration inside. As a Fire Sign, she's capable of being consumed by the torturing flames of jealousy, and may angrily accuse him of being in love with someone else when he's hurt her by one of his spells of sexual passivity. Probably not. The sense of honor is as strong in him as the sense of honesty in her, and it's a rare Scorpio who can live a lie.

If they talk it over, they'll uncover the real reason for their tension, and be surprised to discover what a small wound, easily healed, it really is. *She's* always willing to talk it over, but *he* may pout and brood, keeping his feelings bottled up, which is the worst thing he can do with this woman — also the worst thing he can do in relation to the churning and boiling within himself, beneath his mask of indifference.

There's little use to talk, however, regarding money. Let her have her own to spend, then drop the subject. If he wants to save his, and lock it in a safe, fine. If she wants to throw hers away, fine. Unless their Moon Signs and Ascendents soften this area of difficulty, all the talking in the world won't bring their divergent financial outlooks together. They should both handle their own money, as they did before they met.

When they quarrel over anything and stop speaking for a few hours, the situation will be much harder on gregarious Sag than on the Eagle. Scorpios are more or less used to being alone, and you get good at being alone when you've had enough practice. Still, loneliness, even for brief periods, is not a happy feeling. The Sagittarian woman is usually pretty predictable. Her explosions of temper, her impulsive generosity and forgiveness, her serious, philosophical moments . . . . are all easy for the intuitive Eagle to anticipate. But *she* feels far less secure about *his* emotions. Dealing with Pluto is rather like coming to a yellow stoplight when you've been daydreaming, and you try to guess whether it's next going to turn red or green. She'll never fathom his silences completely; his yellow traffic light stages will always puzzle her, for he is Water, she is Fire. But this is a 2-12 vibrational influence, so he will be learning more from her than he'll ever admit, while she finds an unexpected tolerance for his moods eternally springing from somewhere within herself, originating in the deep well of karmic memory.

This is a man who knows how to *will* and image things into existence —if he wants them intensely enough. This is a woman who needs a goal, something to strive for, to look forward to, tomorrow, next week or next year. Her enormous capacity for faith harmonizes beautifully with his vast reserves of will power, so that together, these two can make anything happen they desire deeply enough and long enough — including permanency in their love for each other. Then all lights will be Green for Go.

☆ ☆ ☆ ☆ ☆ ☆

SCORPIO

Water — Mutable — Negative
Ruled by Pluto
Symbols: Scorpion & Eagle
Night Forces — Feminine

CAPRICORN

Earth — Cardinal — Negative
Ruled by Saturn
Symbol: The Goat
Night Forces — Feminine

The **SCORPIO-CAPRICORN** *Relationship*

They left nothing undone that was consistent with the reputation of their tribe.

Neither Scorpio nor Capricorn finds it easy to communicate, but because their association is influenced by the 3-11 Sun Sign Pattern, they'll usually be more conversationally at ease when they're together than when they are with most other people they know. Only with the other 3-11 sextiled vibration of Virgo, and with the trined Sun Signs of Cancer and Pisces, does Scorpio feel as free to be himself — or herself. The same thing is true of Capricorn — with Pisces, Virgo and Taurus. Or with their own Sun Signs in the 1-1 vibrational pattern.

Scorpio and Capricorn will spend most of their time together discussing their individual and mutual hopes, dreams and wishes, and although they'll be in general agreement regarding the nature of their goals in life, they may not be in complete agreement as to the ideal methods of achieving them. They both secretly desire to be respected, they both aspire to a quiet kind of power behind the scenes over their sphere in life, whether it be a home, a classroom, a business or a government (former President Richard Nixon is a Capricorn, former Vice President Spiro Agnew, a Scorpio); yet the Goat may deplore Scorpio's inner intensity, believing it to be a waste of vital energy, while Scorpio may think the Goat lacks sentiment and sensitivity. Still, they're both practical-minded enough to consider their divergent methods of achievement of far less importance than success or failure in the final analysis, and once they decide to trust each other, they can intermingle their abilities to increase their chances of the former.

Fortunately, the Goat will receive the retaliatory sting of the Scorpion somewhat less frequently than others, and will find those few stings easier to shrug off (Cappy tends to shrug off anything that impedes progress or takes up precious time in excessive emotional reacton), while Scorpio is likely to understand and be patient with Capricorn's Saturnine broodings, for Scorpio is also susceptible to spells of inexplicable depression. This sort of astrological sympathy is evident with children of these Sun Signs, as well as with adults. Not always, but almost always, brothers and sisters undergo phases of competitive struggles, ranging from mild disagreement to what temporarily appears to be active dislike. Although Scorpio and Capricorn experience their share of sibling rivalry, these two will normally find a way to work out their difficulties sooner than most, and will usually end up defending each other against outsiders. The same pattern emerges between the Capricorn Goat and the Scorpion Eagle in business, friendship or love relationships. The association may not always be completely harmonious — but there's always a basis for compromise, because of a subconscious comprehension of each other's inner natures.

Although the Scorpion and the Goat are both very private people, the typical Scorpio is apt to do considerably more talking in public than Cappy. But the Scorpion uses words as a smoke screen, verbosity being utilized as a kind of substitute for (or armour against) saying what he or she is actually thinking. Scorpios are fond of all manner of disguises, and talking about everything except what's really important to them is merely one of the many masks Pluto wears to fool the uninitiated. Capricorn recognizes and admires this ability, even envies it, for the Goat is essentially shy. Beneath the surface social nonchalance, Scorpio is also shy, or rather, markedly reserved regarding private feelings and emotions. And so, the Goat's sometimes painful timidity touches Scorpio deeply, and is not frequently the initial basis for sympathy between them.

There are always the exceptions to be considered, of course, always those Scorps and Cappies who are influenced by the Fire or Air elements through the Moon Signs or Ascendents of their horoscopes, but the average or typical Scorpio and Capricorn will place a great deal more emphasis and concentration on getting ahead in life and insuring personal security than on social frivolities and nonproductive activities — often a shade *too* much emphasis and concentration. For man and woman live not by bread alone, and these two would profit immeasurably by adding not only hyacinths for the soul but a little more poetry and magic to their lives. Thanks to Saturn's gift of the reverse aging process to Capricorn (described in detail in the Capricorn-Capricorn chapter), as Scorpio and Capricorn grow older, the Goat is likely to coax the Eagle into more exciting experimentation. One of the dangers of a close and long-continued association between these two Sun Signs is that they could get stuck in the repetitious rut of a monotonous life-style, until Cappy feels that kicking-up-the-heels urge, and wheedles the Eagle into dancing to a more daring tune — the same kind of persuasion used by Scorpio toward Capricorn in the beginning of the relationship. Rather like the rules of American football. It's half-time — change sides!

A somewhat amusing and one might say positive aspect to this combination (depending upon how one views it) is that Scorpio's compulsive secrecy will not normally be a cause of friction between them, for Capricorn is seldom fascinated by anyone's secrets. The Goat is invariably bored by any variation of a guessing game. Unless there's a Cancer or Scorpio Moon Sign or Ascendent, Capricorns will ignore Valentines signed "Guess Who ?" They are not amused by anonymous letters or round robins, and should the Eagle address a remark to Capricorn beginning with the words "Guess what !," the reaction will probably be a polite yawn. The Goat will simply wait until Scorpio gets around to stating *"what."* Cappy is not about to be drawn into such a childish challenge. The typical Saturnine philosophy concerning intrigue is that Time will eventually provide all answers, and those answers not so revealed by Father Time, in all his wisdom, are not worth pursuing (unless it's a Mother Goat who's poking about for information regarding her offspring, in which case she may turn into a rather persistent temporary detective).

Ordinarily, however, Capricorns are not cursed with the torture of a burning curiosity. Let Scorpio follow the starry trail of creatures from outer space, and secretly long for a "close encounter" with alien beings. Cappy considers it risky to fool around with people who might possess the kind of weapons used in the American film *Star Wars*. (The Goat didn't want to go, but the Eagle insisted, with that Scorpion glare, so Cappy gave in and went to see it to keep peace.) Personally and privately, the typical Capricorn feels the whole UFO hoopla is a little silly, because it's based more on fancy than on fact. If such creatures do exist, Capricorn will gladly walk out in the backyard to watch them land in the strawberry patch, but vicarious experience doesn't thrill the Goat. Capricorns have small use for peek-a-boo or hide-and-go-seek, whether as children or adults. If a person has something to say, Earthling or Alien, let it be said now — flat out — instead of all this telekinetic and telepathic beating about the bush.

Most of the time, Capricorn's boredom with curiosity in all its forms will please the Pluto-ruled Scorpions, since nothing makes them angrier than to catch someone snooping in their diaries, checkbooks, sock drawers or private thoughts — until and unless they choose to share their secrets. But now and then, the ultra-sensitive Scorpio man or woman will take offense at Capricorn's refusal to be curious, and interpret it as a lack of interest — which is exactly what it is.

The Goat's lack of interest, however, is not synonymous with a lack of caring. Yet, with Scorpio, a lack of interest *does* indicates a lack of caring, for Scorpios are curious only when they care about something, and when they *don't* care, that thing or person becomes invisible to them. The problem with Scorpio curiosity is that the Eagles tend to stretch it into suspicion. They tell themselves that a little suspicion is a healthy thing, a protection against those who take advantage of the gullible. But suspicion has its negative side too, and can cause Scorpio to suffer many groundless fears. Capricorns, on the other hand, have no need to trouble themselves with undue suspicion, because the Saturnine caution accomplishes the same self-protective purpose with much less wear and tear on the nervous system.

For all their uneasy suspicions, Scorpios are metaphysically and religiously driven; therefore they believe intensely in the power of faith over all manner of failure (even when they don't openly admit such faith), and this is a major difference between the Pluto-ruled Scorps and the Saturn-restricted Cappies. "If you *really* want it," preaches the Eagle to the Goat, *"believe* you'll attain it, and you surely *will."* But Capricorn remains unseduced, unmoved, and replies with one of Saturn's own religious beatitudes: "Blessed are they who expect nothing," preaches Cappy, "for they shall not be disappointed."

Sometimes the philosophical debates between these two do somewhat resemble a church service on a gloomy Sunday, with inspired Scorpio giving the sermon and practical Capricorn passing the collection plate. Yet they're both soul-softened by the sound of the choir and the organ, even when they're singing from different hymnals. Music has a way of filling the space between their attitudes, because music speaks the language they both hear in their hearts but are unable to express in words, and they should not allow themselves to live without its blessing. The finest stereo available would be a sound happiness and harmony investment for this Sun Sign combination. To the Eagle and the Goat: Don't wait for a sale. Buy it *now* — and never mind the cost.

Never mind the cost? !!! Just look at them. Scorpio is frowning, and Capricorn has turned pale. You see? There *are* some things these two have in common.

☆ ☆ ☆ ☆ ☆ ☆

SCORPIO *Woman* CAPRICORN *Man*

For long there was no answer; then again the knock.

"Who are you?"

No answer.

He was thrilled, and he loved being thrilled.

The male Goat is handcuffed by his warden, Saturn, and although he serves his time as a model prisoner in the jail of restricted emotions uncomplainingly, he nevertheless longs for parole.

Anything that promises or threatens a thrill titillates his imagination, and stirs his blood with the call of the wild. This man is more imaginative than you might suspect. Just because he doesn't tell faerie stories in public — or write poetry, then frame it and hang it on the wall of his home, doesn't mean he's not capable of feeling all fresh and rain-washed inside when he smells lilacs or sweet peas in a summer storm. He's not immune to an appeal of the senses.. the scent of grass or freshly turned warm spring earth makes his heart beat faster, and as a boy, he even wished on stars.. when he was sure no one was looking. He enjoys music and art too. Of course, it must be sensible music and classic art. He won't dawdle over the doodles called pop art, and he won't suffer the deafening decibels of punk rock. But try him on "Clair de Lune" or "Rhapsody in Blue," show him a truly lovely sculpture or a beautifully molded piece of turquoise, and you'll see that slow, shy grin appear. Capricorn's grin is incomparable — it makes you feel good inside, just to see it. That may be because it's displayed so rarely, so when you're treated to it, you know it's genuine, not just an empty smile formed by social expediency. The Goat grins when he's happy or amused or when there's something to grin *about*. Wearing a continual "happy face" and smiling just to be polite is, to Capricorns, hypocritical. Perhaps it is, to some extent. But it's also more open, tentatively inviting friendship. Cappy does not invite friendship casually.

This man seldom monopolizes a conversation. He doesn't speak often, but when he does, the Capricorn wit shines through to mix with the Capricorn wisdom, and his rare witty remarks are often the kind you'd like to write down so you can remember them to quote later. Stern wisdom and clever humor make a fascinating blend.

It's no wonder his Saturnine aura magnetizes a Lady Eagle. The Goat is a great deal like herself, and that's why she feels strangely secure when he's near — even across the room, before they really know each other. She won't allow him to be aware of how she feels right away. In fact, she may exert all her considerable self-control to make it appear that she doesn't realize he even exists. He may sense that she's looking at him, but the moment he looks back, her eyes are gazing in another direction, and he believes he only imagined she was looking his way. He didn't imagine it. She *was* looking when she thought he *wasn't* looking. Later, when she's decided she's tortured him long enough, she'll not only look at him, she'll stare at him, with a steady gaze that flusters his poise, and it is not a small thing to possess the ability to fluster a Capricorn's poise. She possesses it.

He is intrigued. Who is this mysterious woman who has such power over his rigidly controlled emotions? Oddly, many men find it difficult to think of this female as a "girl," even when she's in her teens. Something about her seems to fit "woman" more than "girl." Her eyes held whispers of secrets from the time they first opened, after her birth, increasing in depth each year of her life. The imponderable. The unfathomable. It's easy to see why he's thrilled, and feels little shivers in her presence. Not necessarily shivers of fear, or even curiosity . . just shivers.

Capricorns fear nothing, except poverty. And since they are not curious, in the normal sense of the word, if they bump up against a mystery or a secret, they won't pursue it. They'll wait until it unfolds, in its own time. So his shivers are caused by something else. Mostly, from the unexpected knowledge that someone may be about to penetrate *his* secrets, the inner self he guards so well behind his careful composure. He has an idea she may understand that his surface coldness and sternness cover an affectionate nature, and a heart that aches just as painfully as any other heart when it's wounded, maybe more so, even though it never shows. He has the right idea. She *does* understand this.

His first reaction may be to behave in even a more stuffy manner than usual toward her. His innate shyness may deepen, his timidity tremble, and his formal attitude grow even more formal. But gradually, gently and inevitably, he will slowly relax through their unhurried conversations together, and finally risk giving her that special grin. His eyes will shine, saying so much more to her than his spoken words . . and her heart will turn over suddenly. It isn't easy to make a Scorpio's heart turn over, especially suddenly. But this man's soft eyes and shy grin can do it. The quiet wisdom behind his calmness helps too. And this is how the Goat and the Scorpion fall in love. Never noticeably, almost soundlessly.

It takes their friends and family some time to realize what's happening. His normal Saturn allotment of no more than three close friends. And his family. Her family too, but it's *his* family that counts. He won't want to do anything to displease them or make them unhappy — or be forced to spend a lot less time with them just because he fell in love. I mean, they're used to his being around — or at least hearing from him by phone or letter once a week or so. And if they should need his financial assistance from time to time, well . . . .

Yes, this could be one of their problems. The Scorpio woman will find a way to handle it. I shudder to think of the possibilities, but she will find a way. I believe we should say no more about it, now that we've pointed out the potential trouble area, but just let them work it out, won't you ? She'll be sweet and patient for a while, but . . .

The Goat is, by nature, undeniably possessive once a commitment has been made that symbolizes his attempt to make a relationship a permanent thing. The Scorpio woman won't be happy about this, since she's always more or less felt that possessiveness is her own exclusive right. It could be interesting when she discovers it works both ways.

She's probably the one who should make any necessary compromises, however, because a Capricorn man who is really in love with his woman or his wife will seldom demand enough freedom or time away from home to arouse possessiveness in anyone but a woman abnormally possessed of it — and I didn't mean that to be a pun, it just came out that way. Barring a Fire or Air Moon Sign or Ascendent, or an afflicted Mars or Venus in his nativity, the typical Goat won't wander far away from the hearth. He enjoys a quiet evening with the one he loves more than any other activity — besides work. When a Capricorn says he's working late at the office, he is most likely doing just that. If he's one of those sports freaks, involved in politics, is some sort of salesman or travels for a huge corporation, he may be gone from her side often enough to give her good cause for annoyance. But the average Goat won't give her cause. There could be more reason for *him* to be concerned about *her* whereabouts.

This woman will usually insist on leading an independent life. She won't be held under anyone's thumb. It doesn't mean she's not in love with him, or that she's found another man. It's just that she needs the freedom to do things whenever she feels like it, whenever the mood strikes her, without having to account for every minute, to ask permission to visit a friend, go shopping, stop at the library or catch a film by herself, like holding up her hand and asking, "Teacher, may I ?" when she was in school. It's confining.

She should understand that everyone needs this sort of freedom, in varying degrees, whatever his (or her) Sun Sign, and that the way to deal with a possessive person is to make that person *know*, beyond all doubt or speculation, that he (or she) is wholly loved — and to do so frequently. The more frequently, the better. It's really not all that difficult to heal possessiveness and its sibling, called "jealousy." Lots of extra reassurance never fails to do it. It's as simple as that. Anyone who refuses such reassurance to the one who is tortured (and possessiveness or jealousy *is* sheer torture for the person suffering with it) has a sadistic streak hidden somewhere. It's so easy to cure excessive fear, which is exactly what jealousy and possessiveness are made of — fear of losing what is so very much needed, fear of losing love. If you truly love someone, why deny that person a relief of such an awful fear? With enough sincere, loving and affectionate words, and physical touching, the "possessed" person will find that his (or her) desired "freedom" is surprisingly attainable. It's worth the extra time and trouble it takes — and if it *isn't* worth it, the two people don't belong together. To hold the formula of the magic alchemy secret, which can translate sadness into gladness, and not use it, isn't very bright — or very kind. And kindness is what real love is all about.

Sexually, the Scorpio woman will enrich her Capricorn lover or husband's emotional spectrum of awareness. He is stirred into feelings he never experienced before by the depth of her physical need to give — and to receive. And she will feel comfortable with him, in a cozy way. His quiet strength and soothing gentleness calm the unnamed fears that haunt her, and that lie behind all her mystery. She may sometimes wish he would be more imaginative, more verbally expressive in his lovemaking . . . . . . he may sometimes feel she expects too much of him, and this could cause a nameless depression he can't put into words. Being influenced by the 3-11 Sun Sign Pattern as they are, this man and woman are friends, as well as lovers, and so they should talk things over more often, with honesty. It clears the air, and allows them to be themselves with each other. Both of them tend to hide their real selves from the curious and uncaring, but the moment of Oneness is not a time to be anything but real. It's a time to trust all the way, to do — and to say — whatever is true. These two are both experts in self-discipline, self-control, and may need to learn that controlled passion is not the way to discover fulfillment in mating with the one you love. A change of scene, whether it's a new residence or a trip, is often the miracle these lovers need to refresh their emotional energies.

The Scorpio woman and Capricorn man are influenced by Pluto and Saturn through all their love for each other, and this is sure at some time to bring back a chord of music from long ago, connected with death, old memories . . . . relatives or children . . . . . . to touch their hearts with a re-membered sadness that deepens love. There is nearly always a secret they share that intensifies their devotion. It forms a circle of strength around them, helps them to be more patient with each other — and patience is one of love's best friends.

☆ ☆ ☆ ☆ ☆ ☆

SCORPIO *Man* CAPRICORN *Woman*

<hr/>

But unfortunately Mrs. Darling could not leave it
hanging out the window; it looked so like the washing
and lowered the whole tone of the house. She thought
of showing it to Mr. Darling, but he was totting up
winter greatcoats for John and Michael, with a wet towel
round his head to keep his brain clear, and it seemed
a shame to trouble him.

With the rarest of exceptions, when an Eagle and a girl Goat fall in like with each other, then fall in love, they will play it by the rules. They will pay for the license, complaining about inflation, submit stoically to the needle for their Wassermans and seek the benign blessing of a man of the cloth or, at the very least, the respectable approval of a legally authorized Justice of the Peace. They will marry, dear hearts, they will marry. They're certainly not going to carry on an endless love affair. What future is there in that?

Their friends and neighbors will innocently sigh, and remark among themselves that this is surely a union of blissful perfection. Their close relatives will know otherwise. That is, they'll realize that these two are as vulnerable to an occasional problem of adjustment as every other man and woman who struggle to harmonize their natures and habits within the intimate confines of marriage.

The reason Scorp and Cappy's friends and neighbors are fooled is that these two are normally not the kind of couple to wash their dirty linen in public, as the saying goes. Not so much as a hanky of hankering or an old sock in the heart (let alone punch in the nose) would the Goat and the Eagle dream of laundering in public. Nor will they hang their differences out to dry in full view of strangers, neighbors, the postman, the telephone repairman, passing pedestrians and curious joggers. They'll wash out their quarrels behind closed doors, quietly and discreetly, making certain that all spots of hurt are removed, bleaching them relentlessly until they are — and they'll wait more or less patiently until their relationship is thoroughly dry of tears before wearing it again. (Wearing damp differences of opinion can give you an emotional cold, which could develop into flu, and even into pneumonia. Then love can die.)

Capricorn and Scorpio are as practical about love as they are about everything else. Their romance must pass a stern reality check, and score high on a reliability test. Sturdy. Durable. Long lasting. These two insist on receiving their money's worth with furniture, clothing, college degrees, used cars, grapefruit, broccoli, real estate and so forth. They make no exception of their relationship—or the money they laid out for their marriage license, let alone the two dollars he tipped the minister. And when you add the corsage he bought her that day, plus the room at the wedding-night hotel, even though it was a bargain, because they took advantage of the weekend summer rates—one just doesn't permit something that costly to deteriorate without making every effort to save it—in private, of course.

Nor does one allow a small crack in the surface to go unattended until it spreads into a major problem and the ceiling falls in. No, the tiny crack must be plastered and puttied and painted as soon as it's noticed. So it is with the smallest conflict of opinion between Cappy and Scorp. They'll normally repair the damage before it becomes a real threat to their harmony. Such constant watchfulness can be exhausting, unless there's great patience and will power, but this man and woman possess an abundance of both, an ever-flowing supply, from the combined strength of their rulers, Pluto and Saturn.

The Aquarian Age may have zapped society with revolutionary changes, but Scorpio and Capricorn have not been basically affected by the vibrations of Uranus. The conservative natures of Eagles and Goats remain essentially the same at any chronological age—or during any astrological Age. The new social mores might have turned many a Capricorn female into an independent women's libber, but even these emancipated Goats don't flaunt their private lives, or wear their ERA buttons on their sleeves. The new Age may have freed many a man from self-doubt, and allowed him to be more open, but the Scorpio male's inner confidence needed no improving. He does not wish to become "more open," thank you just the same, and if he did, he wouldn't need to seek permission from the Aquarian Age, society or anything else. He has always done pretty much as he liked, and always will, though "Ages" may come and go.

I know a Canadian man with a Scorpio father and a Capricorn mother. As he was beginning his college education, he became romantically involved with a girl, but they weren't sure their feelings about each other represented a forever-type love, so they decided to live together at college in Montreal for a year or so, to test the relationship. The Papa Eagle and Mama Goat were horrified. A family powwow was called, during which the young man and his girl friend were forced to listen respectfully to the parental advice offered. First, the Capricorn mother explained to the girl that she must consider her future. What if she should discover later on that it wasn't really love? Then her reputation would have been permanently damaged, and no decent man would ever marry her. She might spend the rest of her life as a lonely spinster.

"Besides," Mama Goat told her, "since you're both planning to work for your doctorates in zoology, you might both someday achieve the kind of scientific recognition that would qualify you to be listed in *Who's Who*, and if they found out the two of you lived together out of wedlock for a year, you could be blacklisted. They have rules about that kind of thing, you know. I'm *sure* they do. If they don't they *should*."

Then it was the Scorpio father's turn. He had come to the meeting prepared to win, armed with a list of figures he had run up on his calculator the night before. Staring at the two of them, he said: "You see, as a legally married couple, the premiums you pay on your car, life and hospital insurance will be much cheaper. In just one year, you'll save a substantial sum of money on the difference. If you study these figures, you'll see that marriage is the only sensible answer."

The young couple thanked his parents for their concern, and left. They did live together. They did not marry. They finally separated, in friendly fashion. She married a zoologist from France, moved with him to Europe (where no one knew her shady past) and became the mother of several happy children. He managed to avoid poverty, despite paying all those "single man" premium rates for his auto insurance and such—later married a lady lawyer, dropped zoology, switched to archeology and received worldwide acclaim for one of his Egyptian expeditions. *Both* he and his wife were listed in *Who's Who* for their individual accomplishments (the *Who's Who* committee did not blacklist him for his illegal interlude with his college girl friend). Eventually his Scorpio-Capricorn parents recovered from the shock of becoming grandparents of triplets.

Astrologers are always insinuating that Scorpio men are oversexed, passionate male animals, ready to seduce, or even rape, every female they see. I trust this chapter will correct that impression. True, he does have intense inner sexual drives, but "sexual" is a word with more than one meaning, and the Pluto-ruled male can be downright old-fashioned in his ideas of love and marriage. Not every Eagle is Richard Burton. Besides, if you ever lived with this Scorpio Welsh actor, you'd realize he had very sound and practical reasons for buying Liz all those diamonds. They represented a double investment—in career publicity and future financial security for both of them. You'd also quickly learn how he feels about the breath of genuine scandal should it touch his woman. Gossip column lies don't count. I said genuine. Fun is fun, but don't carry it too far with a Scorpion. These men are possessive in love and circumspect regarding their personal lives, and don't you forget it.

Scorpio being a Water Sign, naturally there are male Scorpios with afflicted natal Suns who temporarily slip into the clutches of demon rum or drugs. Even so, the Eagle will never lose control of his dignity, or his sense of right and wrong. This man will never allow himself or any member of his family to play the role of fool. He cares very much what people think about his public image (although he believes his private behavior is none of their business), and so does the girl Goat. Everything she does is done with an eye out for getting ahead in Life, and on her reputation in her community. There may be a few Capricorn females who have loose morals and behave with sybaritic abandon — about twelve, maybe, on the entire planet. But we're not concerned with them. We're discussing the Capricorn woman worthy of the Eagle's intense and loyal devotion, and she will be a lady. Or she can find another man.

The Capricorn woman seldom reveals her inner emotions by her outward manner. Neither are the Scorpio man's innermost feelings imprinted on his features, or exposed by his speech and actions. That's why it's not easy for them to fall in love. Both of them are wearing masks when they meet. It takes a while for these two to trust each other enough to remove them, and even when they do drop their disguises of protective poise long enough to become their real selves — to know and to confess that they love, they won't continue to walk around with their naked emotions showing. They'll embrace, declare their need for one another, marry — then tie their masks right back on for the benefit of the rest of the world, taking them off again only when they're alone together.

There's a strange aspect to the love between this 3-11 Sun Sign Pattern composed of the Water and Earth elements, created by their ruling planets, Saturn (Capricorn) and Pluto (Scorpio). In one way or another, either a heavy or a light influence of death and secrecy will link their hearts. Their life together will be touched by echoes of the past, however faint. This may not occur within the first few years, but the shadow eventually falls . . . . and seems to soften their love in a haunting way. Third house matters of relatives and siblings are often involved, also motherhood. Pluto rules death itself, as a process — also birth, regeneration, reincarnation and sometimes adoption. Saturn rules all matters *pertaining* to the dead themselves, also self-discipline and duty. Obligation. Both planets have a powerful affinity for deeply felt and long-held secrets, and no emotional relationship between these two Sun Signs will escape some trace of such vibrations. Nearly every Goat Girl and her Eagle contain within themselves some unspoken, buried sorrow of the past, mutually experienced, that forms a strong tie of shared memory between them . . . . and somehow draws them closer.

Beneath her air of self-sufficiency, her seemingly cold ambition for herself and her family, and her apparent lack of sentiment, the Capricorn woman's heart aches silently for affection. Her emotions are touched by suffering more than she's able to tell, and she's stirred more than she can show by great music and art. With his penetrating insight, the Scorpio man perceives this, and it arouses in him a fierce desire to love and protect this funny little creature with the droll humor and soft, shining eyes, who is so loyal and dependable and honest.

He's also aroused into deeper desires by her calm manner and gentle ways. The sexual magnetism between Scorpio and Capricorn is clear and uncomplicated. There's an unexpressed loneliness in both of them that calls out to itself, a need to reach for emotional security through companionship. His odd blend of tenderness, mystery and controlled intensity hypnotizes her, and she's able to relax in his arms, welcoming him into the coolness of her quiet waiting. Every part of her Saturnine being is enriched by his more passionate nature. Like all Scorpios, he's conscious of secret longings and vague yearnings he can't define, and these seem to be transmuted into a feeling of peace during their physical togetherness, like coming home from a foreign country, to where everything is once more safe and familiar.

Just so they don't allow familiarity to breed contempt. Scorpio and Capricorn, as a couple, tend to drift into habit patterns over the years that can cause not only their sexual expression but all facets of their love to become stale and uninspired. Like all 3-11 vibrational couples, they will be friends, as well as lovers, and so the natural ease of friendship can be used as a bridge over which they can find their way back to each other when their passions have cooled and their emotions are locked — when long periods of pouting or boredom have separated them by numbing the need they used to feel.

Change is the exhilarating cold shower that will bring love alive again for Scorpio and Capricorn. Travel is a terrific tonic for these two, but even small changes can free them. The Goat and the Eagle may go to bed at night, and awaken in the morning within seconds of the same time for years. They should change their schedule drastically, let the lights burn and hang the electric bill — eat out several nights a week in a Japanese restaurant, sitting on the floor, study Iridology together (look it up, don't be lazy) and give each other some different gifts.

Must she give him a billfold every single Christmas, birthday and anniversary of his life? She can give him a telescope on Guy Fawkes Day. He can bring her a kaleidoscope simply because it's Tuesday. But the Iridology is best. While they're becoming experts in this fascinating, ancient science, on their way to the exciting new joy of being able to help and heal people, they'll need to practice on each other. He'll have to stare deeply and steadily into her eyes for a long time — and you know what *that* means with a Scorpio.

Listen, you know that Scorpio-Capricorn couple who live down the block, in the house where the lights go out after the eleven o'clock news every night, so you can set your clock by them? The ones who *seem* so blissfully happy? Go to a health food store, get an Iridology book by Bernard Jensen and leave it on their front porch some sunrise. Then see if you don't notice something different about them the next time they come outside to sprinkle the hedges. Something about the way they smile at each other . . . . . like a shared secret. After a week or so, you'll notice that she's changed her hair style, he's wearing a bright, rainbow-striped shirt — and you won't be able to set your clock by them anymore. They're free again! And all because of your silent gift. Astrology will send you the Good Neighbor Award for Rejuvenating Love, and that's even more important than winning the Nobel Peace Prize, or being listed in *Who's Who.*

SCORPIO

Water — Fixed — Negative
Ruled by Pluto
Symbols: Scorpion & Eagle
Night Forces — Feminine

AQUARIUS

Air — Fixed — Positive
Ruled by Uranus
Symbol: The Water Bearer
Day Forces — Masculine

The SCORPIO-AQUARIUS *Relationship*

. . . . they are very wild and difficult of approach.

Yes, they are. Both of them. And so, at the outset, I'll say that I am not going to take sides with either of these squared Sun Signs of the 4-10 vibrational pattern. Throughout this chapter, I intend to remain in the middle, neutral, like Canada and Switzerland. On second thought, the literal middle may not be a safe place to be. One is then wide open and exposed to becoming the recipient of whatever these two may fling at each other, like words, baseball bats, boomerangs, yo-yos, hulahoops, Frisbees, insults, compliments, rage, respect — any number of unexpected things.

However, moving right along, and still bravely trying to remain in the middle, it must be admitted that Aquarians are very wild, undeniably — and that Scorpios are difficult of approach, indisputably. Ergo, therefore, i.e.: as a combination, the Water Bearer and the Eagle are indeed very wild and difficult of approach. Separately or together, but *especially* together.

One wonders how these two ever manage to get together in the first place. One also wonders if it is *wise* for these two to get together, in the second place. The square between their Sun Signs admittedly creates a certain amount of tension (like, each thinks the other is playing with half a deck, has bats in the belfry and is completely loco — you get the general idea), but in astrology, tension is synonymous with energy (also in physics; therefore, even more so in *meta*-physics). So let's say that there is a lot of . . . uh, *energy* (we're being tactful) between any 4-10 Sun Sign Pattern like Scorpio-Aquarius. The problem is — no, let's try to be positive — the *question* is: What are the Eagle and the Water Bearer going to do with this tremendous flow of tension (I mean energy) passing back and forth between them? Are they going to channel it into senseless conflict — or into the kind of powerful energy that makes windmills spin, ships sail, trains run, birds fly . . . . and spacecraft break the time barrier?

Just because someone looks upon life through one end of a telescope, and you gaze through the other, is no reason to quarrel and fuss. If it were the same telescope, you'd see that you were both gazing at each other. (Well, hello there! Fancy meeting you, of all people, in the middle of a telescope!) Of course, one pair of eyes would look smaller, the other larger, because that's how telescopes are made, but you are not a telescope. You are an Aquarian, who should not take such a distorted view of all Scorps as sneaky, conservative, ruthless, stingy nasties. And *you* are an Eagle, who must stop taking such a distorted view of all Water Bearers as people who belong in the monkey house in the zoo, except that the monkeys might object. That kind of energy wouldn't power a windmill so much as half a turn, chug a train out of the station or lift a bird from the branch of a tree, wings or no wings.

Those of you in any corner of the world who happened to see the film *Close Encounters of the Third Kind* will recall the trepidation, suspicion and caution with which the Earth scientists and ordinary humans viewed the creatures who (which?) emerged from the Great Mother Ship. To them, they appeared to be strange blobs of jello, weird creatures — perhaps harmless enough, but one couldn't be sure — oddly shaped and possessing any number of possibly freaky philosophies. This is precisely the way the typical Scorpio views the typical Aquarian, whether the Water Bearer has just emerged from the Great Mother Ship, from the apartment next door, Woolworth's, a neighboring barn, a ski lift in Aspen or the Principal's office.

Aquarius takes a similarly tentative view of Scorpio. These people seem relatively mild-mannered and quiet, but you never know quite what they're thinking, and those few, those rare Scorps who are talkative and cheery, are even spookier, because you just *know* that *they* have to be hiding something. Besides, they all have that strange stare that makes you feel that a laser beam is penetrating your Third Eye — to be honest, your entire body. They're always on the defensive, it seems; so sensitive you never know what you may say that could bring on that stare, and you've heard wild stories about the kinds of thing they do to get even if you step on their tails.

No wonder these two approach each other with their safety belts fastened securely, Aquarius packing a parachute, just in case, and Scorpio carrying a hidden water pistol, just in case. It won't do a bit of good. The water pistol. Aquarius is not a Fire Sign you can squirt on and extinguish. Aquarius is an Air Sign, and all your Scorpio Water will not drown this person. Unlike Fire and Water, Water and Air are *not* mutually capable of destroying each other. Actually, Water and Air tend to ignore each other, if anything. Look at the way the air moves around above a stream, a lake, a river, an ocean or a duck pond or a puddle. It doesn't even know the water is down there, nor does it care. Think of the way rain water falls down through the air, right *through* it, if you please, without even asking "May I ?," as if the air didn't even exist. Yet, when the Air and Water elements get together as two Sun Signs, and really work at harmony, the result can be as inspiring, uplifting and intoxicating as the scent of fresh rain, mixed with the air of spring, falling on new-mown hay or grass. Is there any fragrance on this Earth more gorgeous and bursting with miracles than this ? You don't have to live on a farm or in the country to answer in the affirmative. Wet city sidewalks, freshly rained upon, coupled with the warm air of spring, will have the same dizzying effect upon the sensitive soul. Just thinking about it makes me want to leave the typewriter and run somewhere exciting . . . anywhere at all ! But I have at least one planet in Taurus, bless my Faerie Godmother, and so I shall resist the impulse, and remain here in my solitary confinement, pounding the keys. I hope (seriously) that this paragraph has impressed you with the possibilities of beauty in an association between Aquarius and Scorpio when they both work at it. It takes some self-sacrifice, but it's so worthwhile.

Many times, as with 4-10 people of any two Sun Signs, the Water Bearer and the Eagle are brought together in an association involving career or the family circle. Far more often than in friendship or romantic relationships, although the latter, even if less frequent, may also be beneficial, once the edges are smoothed. A 4-10 vibration requires extra effort, and this may be why the combination is so often found in situations where there's not a lot of choice in the matter, such as in business associations and blood relationships — which proves that all of our Higher Selves are wiser in the synchronicity of such matters than we puppets, whose strings they manipulate, not trusting us to always make the correct choice for the good of our souls.

One pastime Scorpio and Aquarius both enjoy (or maybe I should say are unable to resist) when they're together is probing each other's secrets. Both are born detectives, and neither can stand not knowing what makes the other tick. They'll take each other apart, like the works of a clock, Scorpio in a subtle, deceptively casual manner, Aquarius in an occasionally rude and always very direct manner. I'm sure the Aquarians reading this will be protesting that they're not interested in anyone's business, and therefore are *not* snoopy. True, they aren't interested for the purpose of passing on gossip or being judgmental, but they *are* very much interested in checking things out, in accumulating data, so to speak.

The thing is, although both Scorpio and Aquarius would like to learn everything they can about each other, neither wants her (or his) own mysteries unveiled. Obviously, it's a situation fraught with all sorts of possibilities. Each individual association is different, but normally the Scorpion has a slight edge on the Water Bearer when it comes to plumbing the other person's secrets, while managing to keep one's own personal eccentricities and private idiosyncrasies under lock and key. Not always, but most of the time.

Another wee difficulty they'll have to overcome is that both Scorpio and Aquarius are Fixed Signs. Fixed is one degree this side of stubborn. By "this side" I mean on the side of slightly more so. Like, unmoving. Difficult to budge from a position. The problem is, I believe, self-evident. The solution requires one or both of them to have the Moon or Ascendent in a Mutable Sign. This would help a great deal. Very little else will. But the wisdom of the stars will usually ensure that at least one of them is influenced by Mutable planet positions at birth. (Of course, Fixed also means stable and lasting, so, like everything else, it has its positive side.)

One difference between these two is that Scorpio has a long, long memory (only the memory of the Bull is longer, with the Crab running third) — and Aquarius is doing well to recall whether her (or his) car is parked. This absent-mindedness of the Uranus genius does come in handy, however, for forgetting old wounds. The typical Water Bearer will seldom hold a grudge or go out of the way to get even. Scorpio would do well to imitate this Aquarian trait. On the other side of the fence, Scorpio is an expert in the fine art of self-control, not always, but *usually* keeping his (or her) emotions disciplined, and Aquarius would do well to imitate Scorpio's Pluto composure and pose, since the average Water Bearer possesses very little self-control and can flash into a streak of anger as unexpectedly as a lightning bolt (although it normally just as quickly passes).

Scorpio is inclined to spend money at a somewhat slower rate than Aquarius (although there are exceptions), and is usually aware of where and how it's been spent, whereas Aquarius may not remember whether it was spent, stolen or left on a basement shelf by accident. Aquarians are always misplacing their car and house keys, sometimes as frequently as every single day. Scorpio wouldn't dare lose her (or his) key ring often, because there are at least fifty keys hanging on it, including the keys to the refrigerator, the clothes closet and the bathroom. (Scorps adore locking up things against nameless intruders. It makes them feel secure.)

Still, with all their interwoven and tangled qualities and clashing habits, an association between Scorpio and Aquarius is potentially an interesting experiment and experience for each of them, even for the innocent bystanders and onlookers. It's educational . . . enlightening. There's one quality Pluto and Uranus bestow upon both Scorpio and Aquarius — one word that describes the influence of these stars over both their personalities: *"unpredictable."* This same word perfectly sums up all possible scores in any compatibility game between them. But neither Scorpio nor Aquarius would have it any other way. The Eagle and the Water Bearer are not the kind to enjoy making a bet on a sure thing.

☆ ☆ ☆ ☆ ☆ ☆

SCORPIO *Woman* AQUARIUS *Man*

*He would come down laughing over something fear-
fully funny he had been saying to a star, but he
had already forgotten what it was, or he would
come up with mermaid scales still sticking to him,
and yet not be able to say for certain what had
been happening. It was really rather irritating.*

Maybe what he needs is a periscope. It would, at least, be something. When the Aquarian man is helplessly submerged in the Water element of a Scorpio woman, because she's enticed him with the mysteries of her "deep," he can't help but wonder what's happening in the outside world, above and beyond. At first, he may not be sure he really wants to leave behind this thrilling green world of romantic suspense, where he never knows, from one day to the next, if he's going to be treated to the sight of breathtakingly beautiful coral reefs, some incredible buried treasure, glittering and gleaming in the half light, a sudden school of golden fish, playfully swimming by . . . . or will step on a stingray . . . . or get caught up in the tangled seaweed of her dark depressions. He hesitates to float to the surface, lest he be unable to find his way back again. The depths of the Scorpion ocean are always moving, changing, deceptive . . . misleading you with strangeness, just when they seem to be familiar.

Still, he's fairly bursting to know what's occurring to all the birds and sailors and ships up there. A periscope is the only answer during this initial stage of his relationship with a Scorpio female. Having one, he can continue to paddle around in the intense emotional involvement of their love affair, and simultaneously be aware of what's going on in the real world. He can attach it to his shoulders, and the end of it will bob merrily above the waves, while the all-seeing eye of its lens flashes to him a picture of north-south-east-and-west, and he won't feel so left out of everything.

Even with a periscope, however, the Aquarian male who needs an excessive amount of air to breathe (both symbolically and literally, because his physical circulation is poor) may find his tank of patience running short of oxygen. Scorpios tend to be possessive when they love, and Aquarians simply will not be possessed for more than brief periods of time. Yet if he really cares about this intriguing, magnetic girl, he may discover that being possessed is preferable to becoming unpossessed and depossessed at the same time, when he's hurt her by demanding too much freedom. Then she'll no longer care where he goes or what he does, and may even behave as though he's not still among the living. There's no use banging on her door, calling her on the phone or writing her letters, because why should she answer the phone or door to a nonexistent entity — or read letters from an invisible man? The deep freeze of an angry or wounded Scorpion can leave a Water Bearer with a frostbitten heart, and frostbite can be a serious thing. He might wish she'd start being possessive again. It was certainly more pleasant swimming around in her cool, calm "deep" than it is shivering under her disapproval.

Of course, her icy detachment is probably a pretense, her defense against further hurt — her way of teaching him a lesson he'll remember. When other people become invisible to Scorp, they usually remain that way, but when her heart is involved, she may try to pull off the same sort of revenge, then discover she doesn't really mean it, yet not know how to stop, until it grows into a situation of silent desperation, as unpleasant for her as for him. An emotional deadlock. But if anyone can break a deadlock of any kind at all, it's this man. His finest talents lie in breaking things — breaking the orthodox, breaking convention, shocking people with bolts of Uranus lightning and buzz saws of erratic, totally unexpected remarks and behavior. He'll jolt her out of the romantic dead-end they've reached in some eccentric Uranian manner — then they can go swimming together again, more cautiously this time. It's to be hoped that she'll have learned the valuable lesson that he can bear emotional intensity only sparingly. Otherwise, he'll lose his tenuous hold on his self-control. He's not nearly the expert in self-discipline that she is. The lesson we hope *he'll* learn is that, although Scorpio feelings may churn and burn within, the features (except for rare moments of weakness) remain composed and placid. The quieter this woman is, the more upset she feels.

The Water Bearer rejects such disguises. When he's genuinely upset, she won't have to guess. He'll make it abundantly clear. However, while he may not use a mask to cover his more volatile emotions, the Aquarian does enjoy surprising people. He won't always announce his thoughts aloud, and there are a couple of reasons. Sometimes, his thoughts pop into, and right back out of, his mind too quickly for him to remember, let alone to verbalize. At other times, he wisely refrains from voicing what he's thinking, because he senses he'll be changing his mind or idea in a few minutes, so why waste energy expressing something so transient? At still different times, he keeps his thoughts to himself because he secretly thinks it's kicky to see her surprised look, or her shock, when he says or does something special for which no preview has been given. (You can't blame him, nothing is more soul satisfying than forcing a Scorp to show shock.)

She'll complain about the car's shabby looks and performance for weeks, without receiving a single word of sympathy or agreement from him, his blank, faraway gaze indicating he's meditating on a number of other things and hasn't even heard her. Then, PRESTO!—some marvelous upside-down morning she'll glance out the window to check the weather, and a new car will have materialized in the front yard overnight—her favorite color, rich dark wine. When she runs to embrace and thank him, he'll feign innocence, claim no knowledge of how it got there and insist the leprechauns left it.

Some people call Aquarians crazy, but the Scorpio woman who loves her Water Bearer will find it a wonderful kind of craziness that goes a long way toward releasing her spirit for an exciting trip into the kind of freedom of expression she lacks—although an independent character was hers before she met him. Scorps live their personal lives as they like, refusing to conform to anyone's notions of proper behavior in private. Yet Pluto restricts her from displaying her *true* emotions, or verbalizing her *deepest* feelings, while at the same time encouraging her to behave in a markedly individualistic manner, apparently scorning any control over her actions. The latter quality is one of the simpatico things between the Eagle and the Water Bearer. The Uranus-ruled man is likewise contemptuous of society's demands that he live his private life in accordance with other people's opinions. The difference is that his independence has high public visibility and hers is exposed (usually) only behind closed doors. Consequently, most of their disagreements occur over his public capers rather than his private behavior. His eccentric antics acutely embarrass her when they're performed before friends, relatives, neighbors or strangers, but when they're alone together, she beams at him admiringly. It can be confusing, until he gets it straightened out.

The woman's Pluto revenge compulsion to even the score may manifest itself years after the heartache that caused it, because Scorpio is always willing to wait for the right opportunity. I knew a lady Eagle who was justifiably angered and wounded over the way her Aquarian boy friend left her and later fell in love with a Libra girl—right before her eyes. She did nothing then but bravely retreat, in silence. But a couple of years afterward, the chance for sweet revenge presented itself when she ran into the Libra girl, who had just quarreled with the Water Bearer. Scorpio spent the entire day informing the troubled Libran of all the flaws and vices she had observed in the man when he had been *her* lover. The stories were basically true, but she related them cleverly out of context, so they sounded much worse than they actually were. Even though the Aquarian man was unaware of it, the Scorpio stinger had finally stung, like a delayed nuclear reaction. The Libra girl, who once believed her Aquarian to be so kind, so special, was never able to feel quite the same way about him again. This particular Scorpio female is a rather shy, pleasant person, with a great capacity for loyalty; yet Pluto wouldn't allow her to rest until the score of her old love affair had been settled at zero-to-zero, with no one ahead.

The physical chemistry between them may not be what attracts these two when they first meet. It's more likely to be some other sort of bond, an odd and unusual mutual interest, perhaps some duty or obligation they share — or the same kind of work. She'll approve of his humanitarian ideals but may wish he'd spend less time spreading them around with his endless stream of friends and spend more time with her. Gradually, the relationship will grow more emotional in scope, and passion won't be far behind. He should be aware that Scorpio sexuality is deep and intense but not necessarily promiscuous, as he may have heard. A Scorpion who's been hurt may turn to casual affairs, because her initial purity has been shocked by the disloyalty of the man she loved faithfully — or thought she loved. But the typical Scorpio female thinks of sex in a near-religious sense, subconsciously cognizant of its potential power and affinity with spiritual truth, in some indefinable way.

She should be aware that the Aquarian attitude toward the mating of man and woman is one of almost detached curiosity, and this is not a reflection on her personal appeal. Even after gradually increasing familiarity has deepened their mutual need and heightened their physical desire, she'll find that this man is a much more satisfactory lover when she's proven to him she's *really* his *friend* in every other way. Only when friendship has been clearly established will the Water Bearer give his full attention to the physical expression of love; only with a woman he can completely trust is he comfortable enough to give and receive sexual fulfillment.

Home life, the residence, their careers, their individual families — one or all of these are often the most prominent issues for either tension or harmony between Aquarius and Scorpio. The struggle for a peaceful co-existence will be much easier if their natal Luminaries (Sun and Moon) are in positive aspect, considerably more difficult if these are in negative aspect. There may be times when she's inclined to allow the memory of past misfortunes and disappointments to guide her present attitude into the bitter waters of resentment. But he will recall little of the past, even the immediate past, and will have no regret over any mistakes that might have occurred during the yesterdays of his life .... because his course is mapped in the direction of tomorrow. One of the few things he'll remember from long ago, with any clarity, is the poignant memory of the first girl he thought he loved, an idealized image, misty and fragile . . . certainly nothing his Scorpio woman need fear or resent, considering her almost hypnotic ability to make rivals disappear (if she calls upon it, and comprehends that it's there, within her, waiting to be used).

There are some Aquarians, influenced by certain Scorpio planet positions themselves, who will bear grudges now and then, but the typical Water Bearer is too fascinated by the challenges he sees straight ahead to waste energy throwing unforgiving looks back over his shoulder. He'll probably cheerfully allow her plenty of freedom, because he knows its value, being the prized possession it is to him. Since he's not made of stone, he could exhibit an occasional jealous moment, but never without a solid reason, whereas she may need only a hint to arouse her suspicions. She could be suffering for nothing, because the Aquarian who can rely on his wife to also be his best friend will almost never be vulnerable to experimental flirtations, once he's committed. However, if he's repeatedly unjustly accused regarding what are merely platonic friendships, he's not above pretending to be having an affair he's not really having at all, just to show her it's not nice to question his word of honor more than once — one of his Uranian lightning bolts of unexpected response, which is strangely similar to her Pluto sting of revenge.

Within the Scorpio woman is an immeasurable depth of suppressed desire and emotion; within the Aquarian man is an inexhaustible supply of irrepressible excitement and inventive ideas. Yet, as different as they are, they both possess self-confidence and a strong will, which is why they just might decide to hang around together for keeps . . . for where there's enough will, the heart's wisdom can always find a way.

☆ ☆ ☆ ☆ ☆ ☆

SCORPIO *Man* AQUARIUS *Woman*

——◄◗►——

A strange smile was playing about his face, and
Wendy saw it and shuddered.

As intuitive as she is (and she's superbly intuitive), it shouldn't take an Aquarian girl long to catch on to the coded meanings of this man's smiles. His features being under Pluto's iron control, every fleeting expression permitted to pass across his face has a definite purpose. There's never so much as an idle, uncalculated raising of an eyebrow. Every wink, blink and nod is planned for a precise reason. Scorpio almost never frowns. Replacing the frown most people resort to when they're displeased is the Scorpion's blank stare. That is, his *features* stare blankly at you, if you know what I mean, without giving a hint of what's on his mind. His *eyes* contain the secret, but they gaze at you with such hypnotic intensity when his emotions are aroused that, even if they do give you a hint of what's going on within, you're thrown into a trancelike state that causes you to immediately forget what you thought you almost knew.

His smiles are the most complicated code of all, the most difficult to translate for the amateur (slightly easier for the Aquarian woman). There's that heart-tugging grin, containing all the innocent delight of childhood, the one he used to grin when he was a little boy, before he mastered the impassive trick . . . seen so rarely, she's never sure if she really saw it or only dreamed it. (It's real. However rare and fleeting, it's real. She didn't dream it.) Then there's his quick, broad smile (you have to look fast, or you'll miss it) of pleasure, happiness and approval, so seldom bestowed, it's all the more a blessing when it appears. . . . like fasting for many days, and at last being treated to the ecstatic taste of just one delicious raisin, or sip of grape juice, which is tantamount to banquet. And there are his laughs, but the ones that last a while are so soft and modulated, you can barely hear them — and the ones that are loud and merry whiz by in such a few microseconds that the memory finds it hard to retain them, although the haunting, persistent effect lingers on, like that of the subliminal messages sometimes flashed on the screen at a movie theatre which make you go out in the lobby to buy popcorn, even though the naked eye and ear saw or heard nothing — and sometimes, just as potentially dangerous.

Last, but indubitably not least, there is his . . . . well, "*sinister*" is a harsh adjective, and we should apply it only to the unevolved Grey Lizard type of Scorpio male . . . so I'll say, instead, his *warning* smile, the one that says, when you've broken its code: "Look out, little lady. You are very near the precipice of pressing me too far, and that isn't a wise thing to do, for I may have to teach you a lesson, which I'd rather not do, but *will* if I have no choice."

I feel compelled to interrupt myself here and ask the Aquarian girl reading this to turn to the fifth paragraph in the Libra Man–Aquarius Woman segment of the Libra–Aquarius chapter of this book and ask herself what she imagines a Scorpio male might do under the circumstances therein described. It's an excellent meditation in caution for her. I won't go so far as to say it might save her life (though under extreme circumstances it might), but it will save her her romance, love affair or marriage involving an Eagle. So . . read it and *think*. What if a Scorpio man, rather than a Libra man, were the victim of a Uranus caper of this kind? A truly frightening idea, right?

Interestingly, in the eyes department the Aquarian girl sometimes succeeds in confusing even the Eagle, which is a fairly impressive accomplishment. She won't stare at him as he does at her, with a penetrating gaze burning into his very soul. Her trick is different. Aquarian eyes can suddenly, without warning, cloud over with a kind of haze. Like a veil. Or several layers of veils. He can wave his hands in front of her, and she won't blink. He can say, "The building's on fire!" (as a test), and her dreamy look won't change, as though she hadn't heard him. The reason is logical. She *didn't* hear him, literally. When this woman gets that faraway look, not even a Scorpio can follow her to the place reflected in her eyes. She's somewhere high above the Milky Way, beyond all rainbows... perhaps floating on Spica, Arcturus or Uranus, but definitely not on this Earth, not in this world. It will frustrate him, and good enough for him. It's about time he learned what it feels like to be frustrated in a game of peek-a-boo.

After the Eagle carefully studies the Aquarian girl, he'll decide that he admires her independence, her individualism and refusal to conform. These are qualities that match his own. Of course, she displays them more publicly than he's accustomed to doing, with a shameful lack of subtlety and discretion. Still, he secretly respects her for her determination to do her own thing and be her own person, her way of telling the world to go ride its tricycle and let her hopscotch in peace. Even if she's one of the shyer, quieter Aquarians, with a gentle, feminine manner, and a voice like molasses, whispery-soft, you will not push the lady born under this Fixed Sun Sign into doing anything she does not privately really wish to do — nor will you change her behavior one whiffle by warning her that "people are talking." She'll merely shrug daintily and say, "Let them talk. They don't own me. I belong to myself." And so she does.

It's easy to see why her attitude strongly appeals to the Eagle, who likewise belongs to *himself.* On the surface, he may adapt to what people expect of a normal Earthling in a roomful of people, but when he's on his own, in the woods, in his home — or anywhere else — he will do exactly as he pleases, just as he always thinks exactly what he pleases.

Because theirs is a 4-10 Sun Sign Pattern vibration, there may also be other causes for an initial interest between a Scorpio man and an Aquarius woman. Matters related to his or her career, their families — their work — or something strange, unusual, out of the ordinary, like a mutual fascination with astral travel, frogs, elephants or King Tut.

A love affair or a marriage between these two is never going to be anything less than highly instructive, enlightening and interesting. Harmonious it may not be, at least not in the beginning, but harmony can always be attained with the application of astrological wisdom, and the conflicts between them are usually the kind that cause both the feelings and the intellect to stretch and grow.

Aquarius is ahead of Scorpio on the karmic wheel of life; therefore he has lessons in living to learn from her, although he'll never confess it in a billion years. Nevertheless, he's wise enough and perceptive enough to sense this, and will silently imitate her more than he admits, even to himself. Her more casual approach to problems, her ability to forgive and forget, her airy dismissal of misery and bitterness before they've had a chance to carve themselves into her memory bank, the Aquarian detachment that keeps her inner emotions pliable, are all traits Scorpio could profitably acquire.

With all her endearing mannerisms of absentminded genius and her Alice in Wonderland innocent curiosity, this woman has a t-e-m-p-e-r and, at times, it can be as devastating as a tornado. When he's first exposed to it, the Scorpio man may draw back in surprise. (A Scorpio — draw back ? *Yes.*) Not that temper itself shocks him. Hers may be like a tornado, but his own resembles a volcano on those rare occasions when it's activated. But it takes so little to trigger her scenes (which occur as infrequently as his), whereas he always has substantial cause to lose his cool, and then only after a long period of controlling his boiling inner fury. In this respect, *she* might beneficially imitate *him*. All Aquarians could use a shade more control. If she wants to keep his respect, she'll have to put the lid on the tornado episodes and learn to imitate his poise, especially in public.

The sexual dimension of their relationship can be either a constant contest of conflicting desires, or a mellow message of love between them. Much depends on the emotional harmony indicated by the Sun-Moon aspect in their birth charts. If his Sun is in negative aspect to her Moon, or vice versa, her airy response to lovemaking will only skim the surface of his deeper hunger for fulfillment — and his concentrated approach to sexual expression will cause her to feel tense, at a time when she should feel relaxed and happy. If their Luminaries are in positive aspect, however, their lovemaking can be memorable for the renewal of tenderness exchanged between them.

One important difference in their attitudes is that Scorpio tends to be intensely emotionally *involved* in the physical act of loving, while Aquarius never seems to quite lose the Air Sign's sense of emotional *non*-involvement. It's as though part of her is actively and enthusiastically engaged in the physical demonstration of her feelings, while another part of her remains detached and objective. Also, the Aquarian mind is inclined to change levels of awareness more quickly after total togetherness, whereas the Scorpion mind requires a more gradual floating back to Earth from the heights of passion. Obviously, then, it's her responsibility to make a conscious effort to retain the unique kind of spiritual intimacy that follows physical union . . . to match the time period of his need for nearness, not to suddenly "leave," as if she were catching a plane for Alaska, leaving him behind, waving goodbye. Symbolically speaking, of course. There's always the Pluto revenge compulsion to consider. A Scorpio is quite capable of getting even for that kind of romantic desertion by *literally* catching a plane for Alaska some morning after he's been sexually ignored often enough — or, even worse, a slow boat to China. The Aquarian woman who loves him may have to learn the hard way that a little extra compassion and comprehension of her Scorpion's ultra-sensitive emotions and touchy feelings are better than being left alone to commune with herself. How is she ever going to locate him in China? Admittedly, Aquarians are born detectives, but even Sherlock Holmes himself couldn't locate a Scorpio who wants to hide in a pagoda.

The Scorpio man and Aquarian woman who love each other will place his career (and hers) first on their list of goals. Second, always, with these two, will come the security of a home. Third will be the issue of his family and hers. After all these matters, their more personal desires, hopes, dreams and wishes will be given consideration. This is the general pattern followed by all 4-10 Sun Sign couples, whatever their birthdays or Sun Signs, when their association causes the blend of these 4-10 "career-family" vibrations.

An Aquarian woman is always ready with a change of pace, a change of mind or a change of conversation. Scorpio doesn't shift so easily from one gear to another, but he's equipped by Pluto with enough patience and forbearance to successfully tune in to her frequency rate of change, when he makes the effort. (Scorps can do *anything* when they make a Pluto effort.)

The Scorpio man is full of contradictions, mystery and unexpected moods. The feminine Water Bearer is very much like this herself, except for the mystery. The Uranus influence helps her to pick up his vibrations intuitively and almost instantly. And so, they are not so far apart as it may appear at first. The thing they most have to watch is the Fixity they share as Fixed Sins. It's difficult for either of them to apologize. Both tend to show their regret through actions, not words. Scorpio believes, with the poet, that "little said is soonest mended." Nevertheless, when dealing with his Aquarian lady, he would be wise to remember Ben Jonson's warning that "silence in a woman is like speech in a man."

When this girl grows silent, it's time to wonder in which direction those Uranian wheels are spinning, for he can be sure she's up to something unexpected. Like changing her name, painting the house purple, adopting a Vietnamese orphan, enrolling in a computer programming night school course, maybe suggesting that they catch a plane for Alaska or a slow boat to China — together. Why Alaska? Who knows, with Aquarius? It could be she wants to make a wish on the Aurora Borealis, or bask in the Midnight Sun. Why China? She's always wanted to see the pagoda he retreated to when he left her that time they quarreled . . . then enigmatically returned, because he hadn't yet pieced together the jigsaw puzzle of her. Scorpio never gives up until the case has been solved.

☆ ☆ ☆ ☆ ☆ ☆

SCORPIO

Water — Fixed — Negative
Ruled by Pluto
Symbols: Scorpion & Eagle
Night Forces — Feminine

PISCES

Water — Mutable — Negative
Ruled by Neptune
Symbol: The Fish
Night Forces — Feminine

The **SCORPIO-PISCES** *Relationship*

> *The most haunting time at which to see them is*
> *at the turn of the moon, when they utter strange*
> *wailing cries; but the lagoon is dangerous for*
> *mortals then . . . .*

If there were ever creatures more fey than these, who live in a world more ephemeral and haunted with the unspoken than the Fish and the Scorpion, they would exist only in Middle Earth. Indeed, these two (like Pisces and Cancer, and Scorpio and Cancer) do exist in a sort of imaginary Middle Earth of their own — near one of its lagoons, of course. Very few of their friends can understand them completely when they're together, but they do understand each other, deeply . . . and usually divinely.

This is another of the 5-9 Sun Sign Patterns, this particular one vibrating through the Water Element, which is more mystical and mysterious, more intangible and elusive, than the vibes of the Fire, Air or Earth 5-9 Patterns. Pisces and Scorpio are magnetically drawn together by means of a silent and powerful understanding. I know a Fish and a Scorpio Eagle who didn't have this sort of instant empathy when they met, and still do not. But that's because the Eagle's Ascendent and Moon are both in Virgo, opposed to the

Sun of the Fish, and other mutual planets are also in negative aspect between their charts. Still, because of the natural trine between their Sun Signs, the 5-9 influence has caused them to try very hard to comprehend each other. Even when other planetary configurations dilute the trined Suns' positive effect, there will nevertheless be much understanding, some attempt at closeness and almost never enmity or outright disharmony.

Whether the association is that of parent and child, teacher and student, friends, business acquaintances, lovers or mates, Pisces and Scorpio will usually tune in to each other's minds like a couple of short-wave radio sets on the Eternal Now frequency. Normally (which means not always, but usually) there will be amazing telepathic communication between them, once it's established that they are more than mere nodding or casual friends. This will be true whether they're separated by a room or by a continent. Yes, even if they should be separated by dimensional levels, such as what is termed "living" and what is termed "dead." Astral connection of this sort doesn't depend upon distance for its power base, neither Earth distance nor the distance between the third and fourth dimensions of "life" and "death," respectively.

There will be times when the two of them will wander around in a classroom, office or house without an outward sign of the realization of each other's presence. Anyone else in the vicinity may swear the two didn't even notice each other, for often they say very little, back and forth. The typical Fish and Scorpion frequently speak without speaking, because they share a silent sympathetic thought pattern and are therefore able to communicate without verbal contact (words are superfluous), more or less in the telepathic manner of the visitors from space who have been said to communicate with Earthlings — not quite, but with the same conceptual blueprint.

The Scorpio mother frequently knows, without being told, when her Pisces son or daughter is troubled — even why. And vice versa. The Pisces employer comprehends his or her Scorpio employee's tension — and the cause for it. And vice versa. Piscean and Scorpio lovers and mates — or friends — even playmates (children) can sense each other's joys and sorrows. They understand each other's silences more comprehensively than other people understand one another's conversation.

With all this empathy, you'd think these two would have nary a problem area to their names. Unfortunately, this is not the case. Heaven on Earth, although growing ever nearer, has not quite yet been established. The first problem in the relationship between the Fish and the Eagle is that of weakness and strength. Guess who usually wins that battle in the final inning — which is stronger, which is weaker? Don't be afraid to hazard a guess. You know enough about astrology now to be tested.

The Scorpio is stronger, the Piscean weaker? No. It's the other way around. Maybe you didn't notice the structure of the question, which included the phrase "in the *final inning*." Admittedly, Scorpio would seem *at first* to be the stronger of the two. They are both of the Water Element, and since water is the strongest of all the elements, for reasons I've told you elsewhere in this book, this means they both have the strength of endurance. In addition, Scorpio has all that Pluto power I've been writing about — or that you've heard or read about elsewhere. However, Pluto power is based, to a large extent, upon EGO. Human ego. Neptune power (Neptune being the ruler of Pisces) is based upon a force no weapon in Heaven or on Earth, in any solar system, universe or galaxy, can conquer. Its name is . . . humility. You notice I capitalized EGO, and wrote humility in lower case? That's the very reason the latter is more powerful than the former, when all the scores are counted. It has a great deal to do with ". . . many that are first shall be last; and the last shall be first." The message requires meditation.

On a human personality level, the Scorpion who starts out in a relationship with a Piscean believing that he or she can swallow this poor little Fish through the force of a stronger and more intense nature — is going to be surprised. You know how difficult it is to surprise a Scorpion. But it can be done. In a contest of wills or a contest of surprises, the Fish will spring the last surprise. And it will be a real shocker, quite unexpected.

Look at it this way. If you saw a Nature Scorpion in some sort of contest with a Nature fish, which of the two could move faster and more unpredictably? You'd rather use the Scorpio *Eagle* as a symbolic example? Fine. You're on! Which can disappear more quickly, without leaving a sign or a trace — a fish in the water, or an eagle in the sky? Look. The fish is *gone* but the eagle . . . . . well, see that speck over there behind that far cloud? Use your binoculars. Now you see the speck, right? Don't try to use your binoculars to spot the fish. Binoculars don't work in "the Deep."

I hope they don't quarrel about money. But they might. The typical Fish is generous to a fault (if there is such a thing, which I don't believe there is, since no amount of generosity ought to be classed as a fault) and so is the Scorpion, when it comes to close friends, family and what the Pluto-ruled call "the deserving." Scorpio is unstintingly generous with these, but with everyone else the Eagle can be a trifle stingy. Pisces is not really concerned with the beneficiaries of his or her giving. Not all, but most Neptune people unconsciously follow the apple tree philosophy. The apple tree does not ask of those who enjoy its fruit — "Are you deserving? Are you a friend or relative?" then pull back its branches if the correct password is not forthcoming. The apple tree gives to the deserving and to the undeserving alike, for the same reason — without giving, the tree would die. This is somewhat the same way the average Piscean feels. There's something within the Neptune heart which would wither up and die if the boy and girl Fish were not allowed to give freely when the spirit moves either to do so, which can be wonderfully often.

Pisces might help Scorpio comprehend the meaning behind the Naza-rene's words, when he asked, "Why are you so concerned with your riches? O! ye of little faith! You ask, what are we to eat, what are we to wear [where are we to sleep? and so on]..... Seek *first* the Kingdom of Heaven [within yourself] *and all the rest will come to you as well."*

Since Scorpio has a burning desire to prove the truth-*behind*-the-truth of all religious mysteries, any Eagle will benefit profoundly from pondering those words. Only when Scorpio truly comprehends that message, with ultimate compassion, can the Fish and the Eagle travel an enlightened path hand-in-hand and heart-to-heart.... a smooth path, swept clean of the pebbles of disagreements, competition or misunderstandings. Most Pisceans truly take "no thought of the morrow," sincerely believing that "sufficient unto the day is the evil thereof." *More* than sufficient, in the opinion of the majority of Fish, who are forever, it seems, becoming entangled and involved in everyone else's troubles, in addition to their own — including those of the postman, the neighbor's dog or cat, the grocer, the President of the United States, Aunt Samantha, an airline, Muhammad Ali and various assorted friends, relatives and public figures.

Conversely, being a Fixed Sign, Scorpio takes quite a *lot* of "thought for the morrow." It's a compulsion. The Scorpion Fixity pulls on these men and women (and children) to be sure there's something stashed away for lean days — some sort of insurance in case of a blow from Fate or an Act of God (same thing). Scorps tend to look far, far ahead, in order to prepare themselves for whatever calamities might occur in the future. Cancerians do this also, but theirs is not quite the same kind of caution, because the anticipated accumulation of cataclysms, tragedies and emergencies feared by Cancer actually occur only a small percentage of the time, relatively speaking, whereas those that Scorpio precognitively senses nearly always do occur (unfortunately) right on schedule. Noah was probably a Sun Sign Scorp (or had the Moon or Ascendent in Scorpio).

It won't be easy for the also psychic Fish to argue Scorpio out of this point of view. Even a Piscean would have made little impression saying to the Scorpio patriarch prophet, "Listen, Noah — everyone thinks you're me-shugana for making such a big mishagosh about a little puddle of water that will probably dry up by morning......." In truth, although Pisceans are much less inclined to fuss and fret about imagined future troubles than the Pluto-ruled, when it comes to a really strong hunch or intuition, the Fish may lose his or her careless, casual detachment and share the concern of Scorpio. In rare situations, that is. Most of the time, Pisces believes Scorpio stirs up a fine tempest in a teacup. There are, naturally, exceptions, but one might note that Scorpio tends to *silence,* followed by periods of brooding — while Pisces tends to *talking,* followed by périods of brooding. It's the Neptune-Pluto pattern which either begins at *variance*, then trails off and meets in *similarity* somewhere before the end of the path — or which starts in unison (with the brooding) but trails off in a different direction before the end of the path. (This is a deep and vital meditation, worth studying, not just skimming.)

Again allowing for the exceptions; some Scorpios are, generally speaking, a shade more likely to pursue a college degree than Pisces. *"Just think,"* remarks the Eagle, "what Machiavelli might have done under such pressure as I have been subjected to lately, if he had been in my place."

The Fish can't think, because he or she isn't quite sure who Machiavelli was. But Pisces will look it up afterward. When people tell Pisceans something, they like to follow through. Even though a Fish may scoff at college, he (or she) is secretly impressed with what others learn in the halls of ivy. That is, a Fish is impressed until it's discovered that the Scorp with the Bachelor's, Master's or Doctorate can't comprehend how the human voice could have been recorded on a piece of quartz in Atlantis — or even *if* it could have been. "Well," says Pisces, "you see, it works something like this . . . . . "

☆ ☆ ☆ ☆ ☆ ☆

SCORPIO *Woman* PISCES *Man*

——◆◀◉▶◆——

"Spirit that haunts this dark lagoon to-night,"
he cried, "dost hear me ?"

Silly question. Of course she hears him. If the Scorpio woman and Pisces man we're considering are lovers or mates, and not simply friends, she heard him calling many years ago, quite probably when she was a little girl, dreaming about her soul mate . . . who was, she was certain, somewhere on this Earth . . . also dreaming of her. Where would they meet ? When would they meet ? How would they meet ? All these questions concerned her, but never the question of *"if"* they would meet. That she knew, as she has always known many matters of the heart, the spirit and the future.

Faint though the echo might have been, Neptune also whispered into the inner ear of the Pisces man when he was a young boy, that someday, somewhere, somehow . . . he would meet someone who would understand the way he looked at things, who would see things, not as they are in reality, but as they might be and should be . . . as he remembered them to be in some half-forgotten, misty world of long ago, maybe in a dream.

Then he met all those fascinating girls, proper ones, improper ones, the straight and the crooked ones, the shy and the bold ones . . . but they all seemed so shallow compared with the girl in his dreams. Just when he would think he had found her, she would say or do something to make him know she was not the one at all.

You can imagine, then, how he must have felt that soft purple twilight when his eyes first fell upon this strange creature, who seemed so quiet and gentle, yet in some way so strong, but most of all — so deep, not shallow. She gazed at him intently, not seductively or flirtatiously like all the others, but clearly . . . and unafraid . . . until he felt lost in cool, green water. He returned her gaze, and something happened. Later, neither of them was quite sure just what it was. They just knew it had happened.

They were falling in love, of course, in the typical Pisces-Scorpio way — actually, the way most all Water Element people do. Not with skyrocket force and bursting stars like the Fire Sign 5-9 vibration couples, nor floating in clouds as experienced by the Air Elements of this 5-9 influence, nor with the pounding thunder of two Earth Element five-niners, but drowning in mystery, as a Fish and a Scorpion quite naturally should.

Once these two have formally and officially fallen in love, Life will not ever be the same again. Life will have more depth, more meaning, more excitement and wonder than either of them ever dreamed possible, and that's saying a great deal, considering that dreaming might be said to be an area of expertise for both Pisces and Scorpio. But Life will also hold some heartaches, irritations and frustrations. Not even the 5-9 Sun Sign Pattern guarantees absolute harmony every moment — unless they have a single or double Sun-Moon conjunction, sextile or trine between their nativities, then they might achieve something close to perfection.

Otherwise, with all their considerable compatibility — and it *is* considerable — there will be a learning process. He will have to learn, for one thing, the hard way, that the habit he developed over the years before he met her of using his imagination to color the facts — or of elusively avoiding direct questions — spells trouble. First of all, there's no point in telling even the smallest white lie of convenience or courtesy to this woman. She can spot a lie of the tiniest dimension . . . miles away. Light-years away. Secondly, there's nothing that infuriates her more, even though she tries not to show it, than sensing that the man she loves is holding something back from her, keeping a secret, however minor and unimportant. What makes this so frustrating is that she will expect to be able to keep her own secrets when she chooses. It's all right for her to hold back a part of herself, but it's one of the seven deadly sins should he do so. If the Moon was in Libra, or Libra was rising on the eastern horizon when she was born, she might be a little more fair. Otherwise not. Since the typical Pisces male prefers to keep his private affairs to himself, and be somewhat silent about his plans until he's ready to carry them out, you can see the problem.

What kind of plans would a man keep from the woman he loves? He may be thinking of changing jobs, or quitting his steady employment to follow a career dream, but he's not sure yet. Or he may be thinking about becoming a vegetarian, but he's not certain that's what he really wants, mulling over whether or not to go on a diet . . . whether to pull up the chickweed and plant lilac bushes . . . or wondering whether he should join a yoga class. It doesn't have to be anything dark and sinister, or a threat to their relationship. But a Fish can often make it seem that way with his innuendos and evasions.

A Scorpio woman knows what she wants and where she'd like to be going, even though she doesn't announce it to the public or talk about it constantly. She *knows*. And she has the necessary drive to get there — or to help him to get there. She can exhibit amazing stamina toward reaching a certain goal and her efforts can be tireless. It's not a matter of patience and faith. Somehow those words don't describe it. It's better described as a sort of inner intensity that makes her persevere with sheer will to force a particular outcome she desires. Obstacles are as nothing to Scorpio.

The Fish isn't all that intensely determined to get anywhere. He enjoys the trip and the travel too much to be unduly concerned over the destination. He's not too sure that anything in life is worth the kind of effort that drains all one's mental, physical and psychic energy. And so, there are times when he'll procrastinate or move too slowly to please her. A little shaking up of his adrenalin, now and then, would be good for him. And she could stand to be softly persuaded to ease up on the intensity within. It causes ulcers, even in women. (Yes, I know she appears to be Miss Serenity herself on the *surface — that's* the problem.) Her inner turmoil, however outwardly controlled, can also be dreadfully wearing on the man who loves her. Which is preferable, a volcano pouring out boiling lava, which you can at least see and avoid until it quiets down — or a volcano smoldering inside, giving you no hint when it might erupt? Smoldering volcanos make the Fish nervous. He'd just as soon, if he had a choice, avoid any kind of unpleasant situation, whether it be one hinted-to-be-on-the-way, or one already here.

He may not have a choice. As much as she sometimes quietly pressures him, as possessive as she can be on occasion when she feels threatened, as explosive as her temper can be when she's really angry — he loves her. When you really love someone, you don't run from the things that cause the hurt. You find a way to compromise, to work it out somehow. Because you know that the pain of loneliness is even greater, the emptiness of being without that person will be frightening. Nothing could be worse than that — nothing. So you try. And you try again. And you keep on trying. Pisces is very patient. But even the Fish can finally be unable to swim upstream against the current forever, and this man may dive down and disappear without warning. His disappearance (or hers) will only make them both miserable, so it's better to try a little harder.

Lots of love affairs and marriages can't survive storms, but Scorpio is determined to keep the relationship intact, through her incredible will power. Pisces has the same tenacity when he loves, but it's less fierce, more gentle and soothing, and he can think up more imaginative ways to steady the ship against the waves. Oddly, and unfortunately, although both of these people have a sound and sane sense of humor, neither laughs too long or loudly when the joke is on him — or her. The well-known Neptune self-effacement and humility seem to run a little dry occasionally in this area. As for Scorp, when did a lady Scorpion ever roar in amusement when the laughter is directed toward her? *Never.*

The Fish has his own personal and highly individual ideas of how to achieve security for himself and his lady. She may be concerned that he drifts too frequently from one thing to another — or that he doesn't have enough ambition. He will tell her that if he did it by the rules, if he had taken a correspondence course, grabbed a few degrees, read self-improvement books, minded his own business and behaved himself . . . . he might have made it to third assistant manager at a drugstore in a shopping center, without the authority to give change at the cash register.

A Pisces man can talk his way out of just about anything. Except a lady Eagle's disapproval. Therefore, with her he'll try a different Neptune illusion. He'll flatter her, present his side sweetly and tell her how much her opinion means to him. But that won't work either. Eventually, he'll learn that the only effective way to deal with his Pluto-ruled woman is to level at all times — to have the courage of his convictions, yes — but to never try to avoid the issue with charm (or any other Piscean weapon). A Piscean is the kind of man who is offered a job taking tickets at a series of outdoor concerts for one hundred dollars every night it doesn't rain. Then it pours for twenty-three consecutive days. The Fish have that sort of luck. So a Pisces male shouldn't press his luck too far with a female Scorpion. He doesn't have a lot of the stuff to spare.

Sometimes, a Scorpio woman may cry in the middle of physical closeness with her Pisces man. It's because she senses they can never really be completely themselves except during their intimate moments. Away from each other's embrace, there are all sorts of inhibitions and outside influences, but when they're experiencing Oneness, it seems like the answer to everything in the world — in their world, at least. When they're alone together, she knows how much he needs her, she knows she gives him peace . . . . . . and that gives her joy. It's good for a man and woman to know they give each other both peace and joy. He thinks he pursues her in their physical relationship, but she pursues him just as often, although he seldom realizes it. Even when she pretends to be detached, it's so that he will want her all the more.

It's hard for these lovers to be all the way honest with each other. But it doesn't matter. They'll quickly guess each other's games, then pretend they *haven't* guessed. Leaving something unspoken adds a mystical quality to their lovemaking. There's often a silence to the sexual expression of Pisces and Scorpio that allows them to say more to each other than if they spoke a thousand and one words. Water is still and deep . . . . when nothing disturbs it. So is physical love between these two of the Water Element. It may be this quality, or it may be something more inexplicable, but it's very special, whatever it is . . . a quiet passion, with an intensity behind it, waiting to grow . . . as their love grows.

I once heard a physician describe a delicate operation he once watched, on an injured hand. He remarked that the patient wouldn't have to worry about a scar, because the surgeon was painstaking, took his time, and made sure the scar would fall in one of the natural creases of the wrist, where it would never be noticed.

It's sort of like that with the Pisces man and the Scorpio woman when it comes to the normal wounds of any man-woman relationship. There may be some scars in their memories, but they'll be in the natural creases. These two know how to love all the way, and that's the very best way to love. But she must learn from his Neptune wisdom how to forgive. He does it so easily, almost casually. She does it at great cost to her proud spirit. Just as he must learn from her the ability to weather storms, and *know* — not *hope* — that the ship will make it safely to shore.

She can teach him self-confidence, the quality he most needs to master. He can teach her faith and trust, gently lead her to see that suspicion doesn't rhyme with serenity, but with sadness. For whether he ever wins the Pulitzer Prize or not, he is a poet. If she believes in him, he just might win it. Or maybe the Nobel Prize, like Piscean Albert Einstein. Or, best of all, Life's greatest prize — happiness.

☆ ☆ ☆ ☆ ☆ ☆

SCORPIO *Man* PISSES *Woman*

Perhaps it is tell-tale to divulge that for a moment
Hook entranced her, and we tell on her only because
her slip led to strange results. Had she haughtily
unhanded him (and we should have loved to write it of
her), she would have been hurled through the air like
the others.

The strange result the Pisces woman's entrancement with a Scorpio man leads to, more times than not, is love — followed by marriage. If not that, an intense and usually never forgotten affair. At the very least, her submission to that first moment of enchantment will lead to a strong and lasting platonic friendship. Unless, of course, they have severe afflictions between other planets in their horoscopes. It's a rare 5-9 vibration Sun Sign Pattern that ends in either active dislike or coolness. These two were, assuming all other planetary configurations are supportive, made for each other. We needn't consider the platonic friendships between them, for here we're discussing only the Neptune woman and the Pluto man who *love*. The neutral relationship of the Fish and the Scorpion (or Eagle) as it relates to close friends, business associates and relatives, we've already covered at the beginning of this chapter.

If the aspect between their mutual Suns and Moons is a conjunction, a sextile or a trine, their love is potentially a gift from the gods, as with any other 5-9 Sun Sign couple. Yet, sadly, some Pisces and Scorpio men and women who are so blessed allow secret fears or procrastination to dim the glory that could be theirs for the asking. If they don't open their eyes in time, the gods could retract their blessing of grace to these two, and what might have been a beautiful relationship for a lifetime — and beyond — ends in separation. There are several reasons for such a tragedy . . . yes, often a tragedy because, once this man and woman have really loved, in wholeness, the memory of it may linger unto death, and afterward.

One of these reasons is that either or both may be committed to another when they first meet and *know* — therefore, one or both may lack the courage to confess the sudden recognition of their hearts, seen through the windows of their eyes, because of a sense of duty. Sometimes, a mistaken sense, because the mate to whom the loyalty is given is the loser, after all, since to possess someone whose true heart belongs elsewhere is a lonely kind of possession. This is not an advocation for either adultery or divorce; it's an attempt to point out how to avoid both, for men and women do make mistakes, and are ofttimes led astray by their feelings, only to discover later that they should have waited until they felt a deeper passion on all levels of human emotion, rather than having settled for a lesser love of one dimension only. The "old-fashioned" warning that "an ounce of prevention is worth a pound of cure" is not really old-fashioned or outdated, but an eternal, ever-now wisdom. As mentioned elsewhere in this book, "those whom God hath joined together" are not two people who rushed into commitment before they were wise enough to choose. Human relationships are always intricate, especially between Pisces and Scorpio, and often only those directly involved can know the extent of the emotional complications. Outsiders cannot judge the truth of matters as they appear on the surface. Karma is a deep well, which cannot be fathomed at a glance, or in a casual moment of analysis. There is no way to translate even mental unfaithfulness into an act of goodness. It is pure negative. Yet there can be no unfaithfulness where there is truth, for unfaithfulness is dishonesty. Truth can solve any difficulty, when it's faced with openness and compassion.

Sometimes children or other considerations prevent the Pisces man and Scorpion woman from being together, and the tie must be cut. When this happens between a Fish and an Eagle the pain is usually felt deeply, a pain that even Time may never completely heal. It's just this sort of situation in which, for complex astrological and karmic reasons, and certain nuances of character and personality, Pisces and Scorpio lovers frequently become involved. Some solve it through the cauterizing effect of honesty. Some don't.

The girl Fish and the Scorpion who don't face any of these problems (or who solve them together) have an excellent chance for a lasting relationship in which there's seldom a dull or boring moment. However, one additional warning: If the foregoing reasons for disharmony are avoided, these two may still be tested for worthiness by their own Higher Selves or the karmic masters, and may be called upon to overcome powerful temptations toward excesses in various forms, such as drugs, alcohol — unwise involvement in the darker side of the occult — or sexual promiscuity. These are the dark chasms ever waiting to trap the unevolved Neptune- and Pluto-ruled people who have blended their sensitive auras.

Once this man and woman have surmounted such soul testings — or in those cases where none of these obstacles to harmony exist from the start — life is a symphony of serenity and joy, peace and pleasure. There will be, naturally, some percussion in the movement of their romantic concert; not all the passages will be played by flutes and violins. A Scorpio man has a strong will, intense feelings and deep convictions, and will strenuously resist any attempt to lead him anywhere he does not wish to go, both symbolically and literally. He will also be more than a little suspicious. Yet, for all his suspiciousness of her, he'll expect to be trusted implicitly, not just sexually, but in all his judgments of matters pertaining to both of them. It's a bit selfish of him. Actually, it's *very* selfish of him. But the girl Fish won't resent his dominant male double standard as other women might (and probably would). There will be isolated instances where the Pisces female will become a regular Whale-type Piscean, possess these flaws herself, and swallow (or try to) the Eagle who dares to criticize or reform her, but as usual, we're studying the typical or average Neptune-Pluto relationship.

The average Pisces woman won't panic over her Scorpion's occasional manifestations of male macho. She may even be secretly amused, and in any case, she can handle it. All the while he believes he's getting his way, she'll be sweetly and smoothly bringing him closer to capture in Neptune's fragile-strong net. In a far deeper sense than the Libra female, this woman possesses within her every single feminine wile man has feared since Eve, and a few more that are uniquely hers alone. Even the awesome power and penetration of Pluto is faint armour against her Total Womanhood. The Eagle burns to solve every worthwhile mystery he comes across (those that aren't worthwhile, he coldly ignores), but the feminine mystique mystery of the Neptune girl will elude him, always just out of reach... which will chagrin and subconsciously torture him in a large way. (Nothing Scorpio ever experiences is experienced in a small way.) Yet, paradoxically, such is the very lure that magnetizes him toward this creature of many moods, many auric colors and many shades of both sensuality and purity. Although it frustrates and confuses him, nonetheless it draws him ever closer and closer to her, in an attempt to penetrate the depths of her secret self.

One thing about her which may not draw him closer, but may instead drive him into Pluto's dark moods or into a sullen, ominous retreat, is her tendency to nag. Not in a harsh or shrill manner. A girl Fish doesn't do that. She beats you with a feather, nagging softly, almost tenderly, unobtrusively. Unobtrusive, that is, to most males, but the Pluto man's emotions are so finely tuned he can pick up nuances in her wave length of which other men would be blissfully unaware. Like a drop of water, dripping steadily, she can wear down a man's resistance so gradually he'll barely notice. This one, however, will notice. After steady exposure to her drip-drop of subtle suggestion, he may react with the sort of flash flood he's capable of releasing when he loses control over his great self-discipline and poise. It's dangerous to bring on the flood of Pluto anger. It can drown their love. For he will say cuttingly cruel things that tear apart her vulnerable feelings, whereas she can drive him to despair and futility with her excessive tears.. fears.. and elusiveness, despite her seductive mystery charisma. If she's a Whale-type Piscean, and seriously threatens his manhood, he'll leave her, though it tears him in pieces, before he'll sacrifice his integrity as a man or allow his soaring Pluto spirit to be harnessed.

Yet after he's left her, if she learns her lesson, he may return. He might not return to another woman, but this one haunts the wakefulness of his sleep . . . and the sleep of his wakefulness . . . in a way that even he will never completely fathom. As with all 5-9 vibrations, breaking up may mean repeated making up. The time between separation and reconciliation may be measured by the brief span of a few hours or days, sometimes in terms of weeks or months, sometimes years. That's a long time to wait, but both Pisces and Scorpio souls are patient, and inured to the sacrifices necessary to seeking the ultimate. Instinctively, they each sense the magnitude of the rewards for tenacity in the heart's faith.

Whatever disharmony may periodically occur through their emotional chess games, angry spats and pouting silences, the happy times will out-number the unhappy. The combination and ecstasy they exchange in their sexual intimacy welds Pisces and Scorpio together invisibly, but very surely. If there is a Sun-Moon conjunction, sextile or trine between them in addition to their trined Suns, once this man and woman have loved in a physical as well as emotional and mental way, each of them will admit, if they're honest with themselves, that no other experience with anyone else in the past could come near equaling it, nor could any in the future. Ever. That's a pretty good reason for remaining together, when you both already know there could be no greater heights to reach than the heights to which you've already climbed. The silent intensity and complete concentration of his lovemak-ing — the miracle of her willingness to both trust him and surrender her whole self to him — when such magic as this is interwoven into the natural passion between a man and a woman who love each other, desire can travel in no other direction save a circle . . . always returning to its genesis.

When the vibrations of Pluto and Neptune rise to an intensely emotional level, the subject of death may enter the periphery of the relationship. It may touch them closely . . . or distantly . . . maybe manifesting simply in an in-volvement in reincarnational and other various matters generally pertaining to death. Only one example (and there are many) is the powerful bond between actress Elizabeth Taylor and actor Richard Burton, in which the death of Elizabeth's husband, showman Mike Todd, played a major and mystical karmic role of Destiny — a role they have not themselves yet fully realized or comprehended. I say this, not to invade their privacy, for neither of them has ever tried to keep the pride of their passion and the passion of their pride . . . a secret from the public. A streaking comet cannot hide its blazing path from curious galaxies. Naturally, death, in some form, will eventually touch any human association, not just that of Scorpio and Pisces. But the essence of death as created through the haunting and haunted blend of Neptune's and Pluto's combined pulsations is not an ordinary, but an extraordinary, kind of experience. It invariably contains an air of the compellingly mysterious and inexplicable.

The only really important cause for unhappiness between the Neptune woman and her Eagle (all others are trifling) . . . . the only danger that ever threatens these two who should find only supreme fulfillment together . . . is never incompatibility, but the selfish aspect of human emotion lurking behind their devotion to hold them prisoners of their own desire natures. It could be a hasty word, too late regretted, a lack of awareness of each other's carefully hidden yet quivering sensitivity . . . sometimes unjustified suspicion and jealousy . . . . damaging escapes from pain and despair, such as drinking and drugs . . . . or perhaps some mild form of deception or *feigned* disinterest that deeply wounds the other. How sad, that this man and this woman should ever forget the beauty of their love's beginning chords, when the curtain first rose on the drama of their trined and singing Suns.

They might try recalling the prelude carols . . . . the unexpected music of that morning when she fell straight into his eyes, as one tumbles into a deep well, and made no attempt to swim away. The golden afternoon she laughed in delight, like a small girl, when he handed her, not a diamond, but a bouquet of heather, damp with an April rain . . . the first time he touched her, and she trembled, then looked up, startled . . . to find twin tears on his cheek that matched her own. Everything was wild and free and windswept then, like running barefoot through green meadows of sweet grass . . . falcons flying overhead, and a thousand pink-peppermint-striped circus balloons floating all around them . . . when they both knew they could soar around the world in eighty days, as the lark flies . . . measured by a moment in eternity, flashed by lightning . . . . when "home" was the circle of each other's arms. Like all 5-9 Sun-Sign–Patterned lovers everywhere, Pisces and Scorpio, in the beginning, would have sacrificed Kingdoms for their Grand Passion — defied whole Universes to be together.

Whether their names are Smith, Glassberg, Mendenhall, O'Malley, Zopfi, Marshall or Brewster — if only the Fish and the Eagle would allow their karmic memories to write the third act of their play . . . .

PLUTO: Miss Lizzie Schwartzkopf, I believe? Forgive me, but I feel I *know* you from somewhere. Perhaps we met on the Nile . . . or at the Farmer's Market. Could it have been Acapulco?

NEPTUNE: (softly, very softly) Yes. Oh, yes! We must have! Because your eyes . . . are so familiar. I'm trying to recall where . . . . .

PLUTO: Now I remember! It was England . . . in the heath.

NEPTUNE: . . . . and it was raining.

☆ ☆ ☆ ☆ ☆ ☆

SAGITTARIUS   SAGITTARIUS

Fire — Mutable — Positive
Ruled by Jupiter
Symbols: Archer & Centaur
Day Forces — Masculine

Fire — Mutable — Positive
Ruled by Jupiter
Symbols: Archer & Centaur
Day Forces — Masculine

The **SAGITTARIUS-SAGITTARIUS** *Relationship*

There was a fixed rule that they must never hit back at meals . . . .

. . . . . and they would all go chasing each other gaily for miles, parting at last with mutual expressions of good-will.

*L*et's hope we all part with Sagittarian "mutual expressions of good will" at the close of this chapter.

Before a 1-1 Sun Sign Pattern association can be helpfully analyzed, the singular qualities of the Sun Sign itself must be carefully considered and studied, since the 1-1 influence so strongly intensifies everything of both a positive and negative aspect in the character and personality. This particular 1-1 vibrational association needs such a detailed study more than any other, because these two Mutable people contain such an extraordinary potential for communicating messages of either Peace or Conflict to a troubled world. Nothing could be of more vital importance than which of these two messages is communicated. So let's have a *candid* and *vivid* astrology lesson in the Sagittarian style.

There's a solid purpose behind the following several paragraphs, and so you mustn't judge my remarks until the close of the astrology lesson. We'll use a code. When you read the word "Rumpelstiltskin," we will have completed our lesson, and not before. Meanwhile, try to remain alert and dispassionate, whatever your Sun Sign. If you're not a Sag, you're not supposed to be reading this chapter anyway. Our Jupiter astrology lesson may be too blunt for the rest of you, but Archers expect, want and demand the truth, *however* blunt it may be.

Because they're so versatile and multi-talented, Sagittarians follow a great variety of occupations on their quest for truth and self-knowledge. Even when astrology attempts to narrow down their more prevalent and preferred career inclinations, the list is long. A large number of Sagittarian men and women are attracted to the arts, sports, teaching, the stock market, religion, the theatre, the legal and medical professions, the advertising media, publishing and politics.

This is most fortunate, because all these fields and professions would benefit from as many double Archer teams as they could get, bringing the light of some Sagittarius honesty and exposure. At present, they're crammed with corruption, crowded with the criminal element and totally without ethics — except for a rare, precious few of them. The legal and literary professions could clearly use some cleaning up with Jupiter disinfectant. One practically needs a dowsing rod these days to locate an honest, dedicated attorney or publisher. My own attorneys and the publisher of this book are admirable exceptions, but it did take a dowsing rod to locate them. Suddenly, there was a tug on the end of the forked stick, and there they were! Still, it's an unsatisfactory method of discovering legal and literary integrity.

As for the medical trust, if the steadily rising malpractice suits (many of them initiated by idealistic and outraged Sagittarian lawyers with Sagittarian clients) should drive the majority of physicians and surgeons out of business — leaving us with only those few (most of whom are probably Jupiter-ruled) who are sincerely motivated by a desire to prevent and heal illness, we'd all be healthier and live longer.

Politics? Now *there's* a field sorely in need of Sagittarian candor, a field that would be more of a mess than it already is, without the Jupiter influence constantly struggling to mop and scour it. There are so few sincere politicians and elected officials, you could count them all on the fingers of one hand, without using the thumb and ring finger — and many of these have the Sun, Moon or Ascendent in Sag. The rest of them are unabashed liars (as *The New York Times* editorials calmly admit), bribe takers, pitchmen and con artists.

Of course, not even all *Sagittarian* doctors, lawyers, politicians, merchants, Indian Chiefs and Franciscan monks are *perfect*. Archers make mistakes, just like all the rest of us — and when they make them, they're usually whoppers. (Jupiter expansion.) But Sagittarius is never consciously or deliberately hypocritical, and that makes the urgent difference. Sag politician Winston Churchill is a case in point, and you might also meditate upon the refreshing frankness of Sagittarian wives of politicians, such as Mary Todd Lincoln and Betty Ford.

As for organized religion, which is ruled astrologically by Sagittarius and Jupiter (Scorpio rules religious *mystery*, Pisces, religious *mysticism*), it would be even more besmirched than it is now without the periodic benign and benevolent influences of forthright, idealistic Archers, such as beloved Pope John XXIII, and others of his kind, who have taught truth, tolerance and brotherhood, not just within the confines of Catholicism, but also down through the centuries, and even now, as spiritual leaders of people of every faith. Yet regardless of these truly holy ones, every church and denomination, sadly without exception, sells some form of hypocrisy and moral dictatorship.

All religions, including the Protestant varieties, Judaism — and particularly the Roman Catholic and Mormon Power Dogmas, with their delusions of infallibility — appear to spend more time and effort competing with one another in the acquisition of wealth and property than they spend in practicing compassion and forgiveness, or in spreading joy and happiness.

Thank Heaven for the teaming up of Centaurs, and for the fascination of all Jupiter-ruled men and women with religion. Taking into consideration the calendar changes from the Julian to the Gregorian, legend claims that Giovanni Francesco Bernardone — Francis of Assisi — was born in mid-December of 1182, making him also a Sun Sign Sagittarian — an Archer who shocked the hypocritical Roman hierarchy by sticking pins of truth into the balloons of their pompous pretenses. *Pax et Bonum*!

Yet, despite being blessed and graced with such a goodly scattering of integrity-guarding Sagittarians, the major religions of the world still bury their collective heads in the sands of silence, like so many silly ostriches, believing that their bloody, recorded histories of discrimination, persecution and murder are invisible. They refuse to practice what they preach, arrogantly denying their guilt. Nor do they feel any obligation to confess their own past sins, and ask forgiveness for them, in demonstration of that sweet virtue of humility that they extol as a necessity for salvation. Perhaps we shouldn't be surprised, then, that so many young people are either choosing to be "Born-again Christians" through organizations of undeniably well-meaning but misguided pilgrims (so fanatical and prejudiced in subtle, petty ways themselves, they wouldn't recognize the gentle Nazarene if he stood in front of their noses) — or have been forced to turn, in intellectual and spiritual desperation, to a cynical blend of agnostic-atheism. No wonder Satan cults and witch covens are multiplying.

Rumpelstiltskin. End of the candid, vivid astrology lesson. Not all the foregoing remarks reflect my personal views. Many definitely do, some do not. This has been simply an astrological demonstration of the no-holds-barred kind of verbalization that could occur when the painful, absolute truth of Sagittarius, incited by the expansive Jupiter (and *doubled* when two Archers get together), is channeled through the equally honest, and even more direct, essence of a Mars-ruled Aries Ram, like myself.

Two Archers, shooting pointed arrows of truth into each other, can ignite some blazing fires. But should one of them have an Aries Moon Sign or Ascendent, adding the swift and certain penetration of Mars to the frankness of Jupiter, the air will surely be cleared of every trace of misconception, deception and delusion — to say the very least!

If one of the two Sagittarians involved in this 1-1 association does have such a heavy Aries influence in his (or her) horoscope, it would be beneficial if the other had a Capricorn or Pisces influence in the horoscope. This would add the cautionary weight of Saturn, and the softening, compassionate influence of Neptune to the final judgment. In fact, a Sag with an Aries Moon Sign or Ascendent might also need the tempering influence of a Sagittarian friend, relative or mate with some Libra and Aquarius planetary positions in the natal chart, for fairness and tolerance, respectively. Other-wise, those blazing fires might flame into a conflagration of awesome proportions — an example of the possibility of Jupiter honesty creating more trouble than it cures, of two Archers communicating a message of Conflict, rather than Peace, to the world — and to themselves. It's one thing to point out to religious groups, porno or smut peddlers and politicians the error of their ways, but boiling them in oil or burning them at the stake isn't likely to convert them. Nor will, on a personal level, brutal attacks by one Sag on the other create harmony between *them*. They'll only delay the miracles of enlightenment two Archers are capable of accomplishing, when they work together toward a common goal. *The real purpose of the astrology lesson demonstrated here* is to make all double-Sag teams aware of their responsibil-ities, now that *Neptune has moved into the sign of Sagittarius*, and will remain there through 1984. They, as well as the Aquarian Water Bearers, have their missions preordained for them during this crucial period.

Now that we've dealt with the dangers of too much tactlessness and undisciplined frankness exchanged between a couple of Centaurs, it should be noted, with equal honesty, that Sagittarians, as a group, are good-natured sorts. The female Archers are friendly and cheerful, the males are straight-forward and optimistic, the children rather full of vim and vigor — and all of them hop about a lot. There's an unmistakable bounce to the Sagittarian walk. Some of them really do remind you of a rubber ball. At times, they remind you of a race horse, the way they canter around, heads held proud and high, leaping over the fences of society's restrictions and taboos. All Archers are impressively graceful in posture and movement; yet they can't seem to avoid clumsily stumbling, both physically and verbally. This is undoubtedly caused by the Centaur syndrome in every Sag. A symbolic body, with a human on the front end, and a horse on the rear end, trying to balance itself long enough to arch a bow, and shoot an arrow straight, can be awkward. I'm sure if you were to try it yourself, you would see the problem.

But Sag is one of those perplexing signs of duality, and so there's always something contradictory in their natures; therefore we don't really know what sort of team we're analyzing in this chapter. Some Archers are frisky and playful, some are serious and studious. Some are quiet and reflective, quite nearly as "owlish" as Capricorns. The majority of Sagittarians, however, are happy-go-lucky people who adore playing practical jokes and who haven't a worry or a fear to their names — to whom life is one huge gamble or crap game. (I'm sorry to sound vulgar, but there's no sense trying to pull punches with Sag.)

As you might imagine then, when a couple of Archers are thrown together in this 1-1 association, it matters a great deal which types they are. Of one thing we can be certain (and so can they): all Sagittarians, duality aside, are filled with good will and kind intentions. Now and then they'll lose their tempers and say some pretty cruel things. Still, even when they're verbally cutting each other into ribbons with their casual observations or keenly thrust accusations, their motives never stem from malice. They're just calling a shovel a shovel, to paraphrase the "calling a spade a spade" expression. Using a shovel to illustrate a point is just as correct as using a spade, especially when there's no difference in what they're shoveling.

First searching out truth, then recognizing it, and finally being compelled to express it fearlessly is a Jupiter pattern in both the bouncy and the extremely rare quiet and introverted Archers. So is reaching for the brass ring and falling off the horse in the process, wishing on shooting stars and crossing one's fingers and toes for luck. Every Sag is both an idealist and a gambler, in just about equal portions. These people like to sing and draw and dance — play and take chances. They also like to read, study, observe, learn, teach and travel. When two of them are engaged in doing all these things (or even part of them) together, life is never boring. It may be exhausting, but in no way could it be boring.

As with all 1-1 Sun Sign vibrational people, regardless of periodic conflict between Sag and Sag, they'll usually remain friendly, because of a basic sympathy. They almost never become enemies, even after they've exchanged heated words and repeatedly attacked each other's most sensitive spots. Forgiveness is a virtue Sagittarians share equally with the other two Fire Signs, Aries and Leo — and to a somewhat lesser degree, with the three Air Signs. However, forgiveness is one thing — apology is another. Two Archers won't find it any easier to apologize to each other than to anyone else. But they will sense one another's regret, and instead of forcing the issue, they'll simply begin saying nice things back and forth as a sign that there are no hard feelings. Archers never hold grudges. They'll frankly admit they've been wrong (when they really believe they have been), but more often by their actions than in so many words — and by the return of their cheerful grins, inviting you to forget the disagreement and start all over as friends again. Sag finds ways of signaling "I'm sorry" without speaking the actual words. This saves face for both of them, keeps their pride intact and allows the making up of a quarrel to be more or less painless.

At the beginning of this chapter, I mentioned that the theatre — both the "legitimate" stage and the "illegitimate"(?) film beckons to Sagittarius. A great many Archers do follow the footlights in every capacity, from performers, playwrights, producers and directors, to grip men, prop people, costume and scenic designers, light crews and camera men — and women. But even those Jupiter people who enter arenas of endeavor other than the theatre are, nevertheless, what might be termed "of the theatre." They enjoy studying human nature, fully aware that everyone, on occasion, is an actor or an actress, and they take great pleasure in guessing the roles played by their friends. They take even more pleasure in playing parts themselves, especially with one another, whether it's Mary, Queen of Scots, Don Quixote, a circus clown or a bareback rider.

Sagittarians make interesting psychiatrists, whether amateur or professional, when their tactless speech is tempered by a more tactful Moon Sign or Ascendent, such as Libra or Pisces. Two Archers who are associated as business associates, neighbors, friends, kindergarten buddies, playpen pals, relatives, lovers or mates will spend lots of time analyzing each other, and alternating the roles of comedy and tragedy. When one is weeping, the other will turn comedian (or comedienne) to cheer the sad one, which is one of the very nicest things about a double Sag relationship, regardless of the age or sex of the two Centaurs. Having been born under the influence of a Sun Sign of duality, they're eternally aware of the truth of poet Kahlil Gibran's observation that Joy and Sorrow are twins. Each Sag is always ready and willing to remind the other one that, when Failure and Sorrow threaten to dim his (or her) dreams, Joy and Success are waiting in the wings to skip out on stage and do their number — and vice versa. That's why Sagittarians appear to be so incredibly lucky. Luck has nothing to do with it, actually. It's just that Archers are not afraid to gamble for the big stakes, because they know that the odds will eventually catch up to them and make them winners — at least often enough that taking a chance is exciting. The natural Jupiter optimism encourages Sag to believe that all losing streaks are temporary. And so they are.

Considering this instinctive attitude, why shouldn't these two take a chance together, and gamble that they'll succeed in helping each other subdue their mutual vices, and magnify their mutual virtues? It's not at all a bad risk to take — for the venturesome. And Sagittarians are the ones who told Noah Webster the meaning of the word (as usual, without even being invited to do so). "Venturesome," they informed Noah, as he was compiling his first dictionary, "means: daring, bold and fearless, loving adventure, danger and hazard — to have the courage to undertake — to risk or to expose one's self."

"That's us!" the cheery Archers told him. "Be sure to come right out and say so frankly." But Noah Webster omitted their names from the printed dictionary definition, which I think was mean of him. So you may consider this a corrigendum — on behalf of Jupiter.

☆ ☆ ☆ ☆ ☆ ☆

SAGITTARIUS *Woman* SAGITTARIUS *Man*

◆━◆■◆━◆

So they stayed away for years and had a lovely time.

Considering all sorts of things — such as their earnestness, inquisitive natures, candor and independent personalities — and especially considering that this man and woman are both influenced by the Fire element — also both impressed at birth with the stamp of a masculine Sun Sign, their speech and actions likewise ruled by a masculine planet (Jupiter) — their relationship will never be dull.

Double Fire. Double Masculine. And last, but not least, Double Mutable. Which means they're both strongly inclined to frequently practice the verbal art of communication. They'll enjoy playing word games with each other, mostly based on a desire to discover the answer to the question of which of them gets to lead the elephants in the circus parade, and which one has to follow behind with a broom and (very large) dustpan, cleaning up the pachyderm droppings.

Do you find that harmless little allegory in poor taste ? If so, I'm sorry, but after all, this chapter isn't being written for Virgos, Librans, Capricorns and the like. It's meant for Sagittarian men and women, and no Archer would draw back in distaste from a mere mention of pachyderm droppings. Not if they're typical Centaurs. Sagittarius is even more shockproof, if possible, then Aquarius (the elephant Water Bearers). In fact, I have a Sagittarian friend, a girl Archer, whose favorite and frequent expletive when she's annoyed or angry is: "Oh, shut up, and cow flops on your head !" (Sometimes she varies this with: "Oh, shut up, and cow *pies* on your head," depending on her mood.)

The male and female Archer will take turns giving each other lie detector tests, without benefit of a polygraph. Who needs a "Galvanic Skin Response Polygraph Machine?" Jupiter's own gigantic galvanic response is indication enough. They like to test each other with jokes and riddles too, to check out where each other stands, at any given time, morally, ethically, philosophically and intellectually.

HER: Okay, Humphrey, see if you can answer this riddle. A man was driving in a car, with his son. There was an accident, and the father was killed instantly. The boy was taken to the emergency room of a hospital, where it was decided he needed immediate surgery to save his life. He was quickly prepared for the operation, but the resident surgeon came into the room, took one look at the patient, and exclaimed, "I can't operate on this boy! He's my son."

HIM: That's an easy one. The boy was an adopted child, and the man killed in the car was his foster father. The surgeon was his actual father. Right?

HER: Wrong. Guess again, darling. Boy, are you thick-headed.

HIM: Wait, I've got it now! They got the boy mixed up with *another* kid his size and age who was brought into the emergency room at the same time, and the *second* patient *was* actually the surgeon's son.

HER: You might as well give up. You'll never guess it. The surgeon was the boy's *mother*, you male chauvinist hog. It just never occurred to you that women are intelligent enough to be surgeons, did it? You think all women are flea brains. I want a divorce.

HIM: All women may not be flea brains, but you sure act like one sometimes. First off, that's a sick riddle. Second off, I thought you didn't approve of surgeons or surgery. You're always yapping about it. Besides, if you had kept still, I would have guessed. Who can think with you jabbering all the time? Now that you mention it, I think a divorce is a good idea.

HER: You think I talk all the time? Ha! That's really funny, coming from you. And that was not a sick riddle. It was an imaginary situation, so there was nothing negative about it. As for disapproving of surgery, all I've ever said is that about ninety percent of all operations aren't really needed. That doesn't mean I don't realize there are certain human emergencies, like broken bones, a ruptured appendix, and so forth, that require expert surgical attention. I'm only against the sadistic surgeons, who subconsciously enjoy cutting people — and those other ones who pay for their fancy cars and homes with the fat fees they get for performing wholesale and unnecessary appendectomies, tonsillectomies, hysterectomies, and even mastectomies. I'm perfectly aware that our own doctor is an intelligent, sensitive, compassionate man. The trouble is, you never listen to me — you're always interrupting. You've been impossible to live with since you started losing your hair.

HIM: Is that right? Well, you haven't been much fun to live with yourself since you started to get fat last year.

HER: That did it! You have twenty-four hours to pack your clothes and get out of here. And take your dog with you.

HIM: You have it backwards. *You're* the one who has twenty-four hours to pack your clothes and get out. I'm the one who pays the rent on this pup tent, not you. And you can take *your* dog with you when you go.

(Being Sagittarians, they *each* have a dog — maybe also a horse.)

Note to other Sun Sign readers: Don't fret. These two fiery lovers kissed and made up a few hours later, while they were *both* packing their bags (they'd each decided it was more humiliating to be left behind than to leave). He impulsively hugged her, admitted she wasn't fat — told her she had been too thin before, that the few extra pounds she gained in her hips were flattering, and he had been only teasing. (He almost lost the game again when he mentioned her hips, but he managed to get away with it.) She affectionately stroked his hair, told him it was only his imagination that he was losing it, and even if he ever did, it would make him only more handsome. (He squeezed her harder.) Then she went on to remind him that American television star Telly Savalas, as Kojak, is completely bald, like Yul Brynner in *The King and I*, remarking that, in her opinion, both bald and balding men are powerful sex symbols, like that sexy Israeli general and statesman with the eye patch, Moshe Dayan, whose virile image has always simply knocked her out, and made her knees go weak . . . . . (which very nearly started another fight between them).

Often, Sagittarians make matters only worse when they try to patch up a disagreement, by clumsily tripping over a brand-new goof, more awkward than the original one, in their anxiety to make things happy and cheerful again, like exasperating but lovable puppies — or colts. They'll both have to watch the tendency to exaggerate slightly, now and then. Jupiter is the planet of expansion, and his influence sometimes encourages Sagittarians to make everything just a trifle larger than Life. The other two Sun Signs inclined to exaggerate a little are Leo and Gemini (for markedly different reasons), but Sag is far ahead of them in the stretching department. If either the male or female Sag has a Leo or Gemini Moon Sign or Ascendent, things will occasionally grow quite a bit taller in the telling; otherwise, the Archers will keep the urge under control for the most part, but once in a while they must meet this seldom-mentioned Sagittarian test of their ruling planet, Jupiter. It's been kept quiet too long, and that's why I'm bringing it up, for their own good.

Listen, you two — with this big thing you have about telling the truth, don't you think you should be careful that Jupiter doesn't tempt you to tell a little *more* than the truth? That's the astrological test of worthiness, you know, for your particular Sun Sign (every Sun Sign has one) — the test of whether you'll permit your powerful urges involving truth and integrity to be distorted by exaggeration. I'll give you a hint. The temptation always comes in the form of a selfish desire to win a point or an argument *at any cost*. Don't pay the price of your integrity to win.

Nothing these two do will be done faintly or half-heartedly. Their double masculine vibration, channeled through the daring and challenge-loving Sagittarian essence, is bound to result in a close-knit relationship full of good things and bad things . . . . fun and fights and excitement and anger and thrills and laughter and tears and failures and victories. Like a huge, multi-colored afghan of rich experiences. Speaking of thrills (and spills), the girl Archer can expect this man, if he's a typical Centaur, to be the kind who likes to take a chance. Often, the more dangerous it is, the more he likes it. He'll probably enjoy sports with equal relish, whether as participant or spectator — and so, quite possibly, will she. The Jupiter vibration is sometimes so strong, it dominates most all other influences in a horoscope, even occasionally eclipsing other Sun Signs, for brief periods. I'll give her an example. It may not prove anything about her own Archer, but the purpose of an example is to explain things, not prove them. It will, at least, give her more than an inkling of her Jupiter man's daring nature, in case he's been hiding it from her.

Cleve Backster, the fellow who stirred up such a storm of controversy over what science has labeled the "Backster Effect," opening up the vista of primary cell perception — or if you prefer, the Fish who talks to plants via the polygraph, and made it respectable for us all to converse with our green friends — is a Sun Sign Pisces. However, there are several important planet positions in Sagittarius, including the Moon, in Cleve's birth chart. His horoscope also contains two of what in astrology are called Grand Trines: a Grand Trine in Water — and a Grand Trine in Fire. The way it worked out will fascinate any male Sag (or female Sag, for that matter).

Cleve grew up with a dread of drowning, a fear of fire and a terror of great heights. He lived with his trinity of phobias, nurtured by his Pisces Sun Sign. Then one day, when he was seventeen, his multiple Sagittarian planets and Sag Moon took command, bluntly informing his subconscious that the only way to remove his fears was to conquer them by accepting the challenge they offered. And so, his Neptune vibes trembling, but with his Sagittarian planets shoving him from behind, he perfected a thrilling act of daring and endurance at Lake Mohawk, in New Jersey, which he later performed repeatedly, for two summers, before large audiences in the Amphitheatre of Flushing Meadows, New York. Night after night, Cleve ignited his sweat pants, then dove, like a human torch, from seventy-five feet in the air into a pool of water blazing with leaping flames (gasoline had been poured in and lit seconds before the stunt began).

How about that for fulfilling a horoscopic double Grand Trine in Fire and Water! It's also a perfect illustration of the Sagittarian compulsion to take a risk and accept a self-dare. But Cleve's not sure whether his performance was an act of cowardice or bravery (Pisces modesty). For you see, all the audiences required or expected of him was the dive itself, which was certainly thrilling enough. But back in New Jersey, when he was practicing his act, as he was standing up there seventy-five feet in the air, gazing dizzily down at the water and fire below, his Pisces Sun Sign refused to allow him to take the plunge. He was terrified. That's when the idea struck him to *first* spray his sweat pants with gasoline and ignite them. When his rear end caught fire, says Cleve, his reluctance to dive disappeared in an instant. There was nowhere to go but down—and in a hurry! Actually, the idea of setting his backside afire was planted in his mind by the practical-joke-loving influence of his Moon in Sagittarius.

Years later, in 1968, Backster's odd blend of Sag curiosity and Pisces perception caused him to light a more serious fire on what one might term the "backside" of stuffy science. Erudite but dogmatic men, like Taurean Dr. Arthur W. Galston of Yale, are still attempting to delay the detonation of the bomb Cleve rather prankishly dropped into their unprepared laps, a bomb that threatens to explode the revelation of the profound theory of the Oneness of the Universe—and each day, the fuse burns shorter!

The female Archer may as well prepare herself to be the object of a few similar mischievous pranks from her Sag lover or husband, and she'd be wise to leave his sense of fun and games intact.

Unless one or both of them had the Moon or Ascendent in a Water or Earth Element at birth, this man and woman are not what would be called cautious with cash. They'll cheerfully spend it, invest it, lend it and gamble it. As cheerfully as they earn it, for it's a rare Archer, male or female, who will remain in a job or career he or she finds to be distasteful. They're quick to quit a boring occupation and move on to one they find exciting. Sometimes, they'll leave in outrage over some injustice, sometimes because they've been insulted—or because (more likely) they've insulted the boss. Sag doesn't mince words. Yet neither he nor she will be unduly upset over a temporary period of unemployment, or be overly concerned over the risk in changing careers. Both of them are optimistic about the future and seldom gloom around, anticipating a rainy day. Symbolically, Sag expects sunshine, and nearly always gets it.

Both vibrating to the Fire element, these two probably will have few adjustments to make in the achievement of sexual fulfillment. Unless there's a negative aspect between his Sun and her Moon (or the converse), which may create some disharmony, requiring a compromise of sexual attitudes, Sag and Sag will trustingly reach out toward one another, with no fear of rejection, and not be disappointed. They'll feel an instinctive sort of familiarity in their touching, a mutual understanding of each other's desires which doesn't need to be expressed in words. Affectionate bear hugs, laughter and pillow fights are often part of the lovemaking ritual between two playful Centaurs. There's a warmth and spontaneous joy to their passion, and somehow, they feel comfortably "at home" in each other's arms. Their major sexual problem might be jealousy, the hurt or anger felt when one of them discusses an old love affair the other one fears might be renewed in the future. Both of them require and demand freedom as an individual; yet they aren't always willing to return the favor. (It's called selfishness.) Sagittarius isn't normally an overly jealous sign, but when two Archers get together, start asking frank questions, and start receiving equally frank answers, if they allow the inquisition to go too far, the resulting discussions might give even a stone statue a twinge of jealousy.

There could be religious arguments between them, in the beginning, but with a little caution these could bring them both closer to a comprehension of what Life is all about, and gradually closer to each other. Neither of them will stand for being left behind while the other one goes out in search of adventure. And so, they'll have to arrange to do everything together, when possible — even when it's *im*possible. Separate vacations for this man and woman, especially if one or both of them have the Moon or Ascendent in an Air Sign, won't increase the stability of their relationship but may very well have a surprise ending, with one (or both) forgetting to return. As a team, they can feel sure that their intimacy will deepen over the years. But if they take a chance on one of those "open marriages," it could be one of the rare times they lose a gamble.

Traveling somewhere together is always and forever a powerful magic for this couple — even if only overnight, sharing a sleeping bag, deep in a pine forest, near cold, clear rivers . . . . . where the wind smells good and the stars are bright overhead. Or some faraway, unreal place, like Siam or Scotland. (Scotland is unreal if you've never been there. Any place is unreal if you've never visited it, even Brooklyn.) Regular intervals of moving, searching. . . . . . chasing the swallows, and waking at dawn to a coral-streaked sky over a strange, cobblestoned street . . . . is a necessary life-style for two Sagittarian lovers or mates. And if the boss won't say "yes" to a double vacation, when those wings within are beating insistently, then they'll just have to give notice, and quit. Don't worry. Jupiter luck will drop just the right new job or career into their laps when they return. Want to bet?

SAGITTARIUS   CAPRICORN

Fire — Mutable — Positive
Ruled by Jupiter
Symbols: Archer & Centaur
Day Forces — Masculine

Earth — Cardinal — Negative
Ruled by Saturn
Symbol: The Goat
Night Forces — Feminine

The **SAGITTARIUS-CAPRICORN** *Relationship*

> *. . . but truth is best, and I want to tell*
> *only what really happened. Well, not only*
> *could they not understand each other, but*
> *they forgot their manners.*

Sagittarians are droll creatures, sometimes clownish and amusing, sometimes sad and longing. Goats are sensible and surefooted, two knacks the Archers hanker to acquire, since Sagittarians are all a trifle "clumpy" and they trip a lot, over both their feet and their words, bringing an affectionate chuckle from Capricorn. There's undeniably an attraction here, of sorts. Goats know exactly where they're going, and Sag (pronounced to rhyme with badge) finds this an enviable trait, too (if slightly irritating), since Archers would love to have some general idea of where they're going — although, even if they did, it wouldn't be long after they got there till they'd be trotting off somewhere else. With the 2-12 Sun Sign Pattern ruling the association, they'll spend a lot of time learning from and teaching each other. Cappy will do most of the teaching, Sag the learning — reluctantly.

Each possesses a number of qualities which appeal to the other.

Sagittarius, for example, is in absolute awe of Cappy's stoic control in the dental chair. Capricorn secretly envies the Archer's courage in playing the high roller in the game of life, regardless of how the Goat groans and grumbles over such impetuosity (unless the Sagittarian being dealt with is one of those abnormally quiet Centaurs, always traveling and gambling mentally, but because of an overdisciplined childhood, never quite making the leap . . . just dreaming about it). There are other qualities, however, which repel more than they attract — not always, just if they're overdone. For instance, travel could create some clashes between them. While most Archers like to buzz around physically, exploring the world — and canter around mentally, exploring philosophy and religion (they all simply *adore* Don Quixote), Goats become nervous just thinking of such excessive hustling and bustling. The idea of living in an airline terminal, suitcases packed, forever on the ready, freaks them. Nor do they approve of flirting with philosophy and religion. What was good enough for Father (and Mother) is good enough for Cappy. "Give Me That Old-Time Religion," with rare exceptions, is the typical Goat's favorite hymn. The church of childhood is sound and stable, so why question its dogma? As for philosophy, Plato was practical, Socrates was sensible, so why experiment with the new and untried?

"Maybe if you zipped around more," observes the Archer cuttingly, "you'd see how exciting the world of ideas can be! *I'm* searching for truth. Haven't *you* ever searched for truth?"

The Goat yawns. "Searching, searching, searching . . . . and what's to find?" (Note to reader: In ancient astrology legend, Capricorn has always ruled the Hebrew people.) "Running all over the place," continues the Goat sternly, "looking for something you can't even identify is a sinful waste of time. You could be accomplishing something worthwhile with all that energy. I can learn more of real value by following a definite plan than by spinning my wheels as you do, with no sense of direction. I'm not poky. And I'm not stuffy. In fact, I intend to travel to Europe next year to study art. But I know why I'm going, where I'm going, how much it's going to cost — and I have no illusions about what's over there waiting for me. I'm not going to stop in Rome, toss three coins into the Trevi fountain, and make a wish." Not all, but most Capricorns are symbolically (sometimes it seems even literally), firmly centered on the Earth. A few of them are so firmly centered they give the impression that if they stood too long in one place, they'd root in the ground and become ivy, twining their tough tendrils around their ancestral homes for centuries.

The conversational patterns of Goats and Archers don't always mix and match. The occasional quiet, introverted Sagittarians, who are more contemplative types, get along rather well with Capricorns in an average chat together, but most Sagittarians like to talk with more gusto. They're continually asking questions, like friendly puppies, always wanting to know the how and where and why of everything. At first, Cappy won't mind answering the questions. It pleases these sedate souls to impart wisdom to others, but when it becomes obvious after a while that all the Saturn wisdom imparted is being ignored by the independent Sag, the Goat will consider it all a game — and Capricorns don't enjoy wasting valuable time on games. Sag may complain that Cappy is too quiet, and never opens up — Capricorn may complain the Archer is never still, and won't listen.

That's what happens now and then, when idealism and seeking conflict with wisdom and caution. Yet, what would idealism be without wisdom to temper it — or seeking be without caution to guide it? "Scattered," growls the Goat. "More exciting!" retorts the Archer. And so it goes. If the Goats would climb down from that high cliff of know-it-all, and the Archers would stifle their rashness and season their sauce with a little experience, they'd both see what glorious attainment might be possible by blending their polarities of opinions in a cooperative effort, rather than bending them out of shape through constant controversy. What the two of them need is a Lion to give them a good lecture, a Ram to *demand* that they stop fussing, a Libra to listen sympathetically and fairly to both sides of their complaints, and perhaps a Pisces to teach both of them some much needed lessons in humility. Neither counts humility as a great virtue. Sagittarius barely understands the word, and Capricorn only *appears* to be humble. Beneath the apparent Saturnine self-effacement is a certain ingrained sureness on every subject, except perhaps — personal worth. In this area, Cappy can sometimes feel touchingly insecure.

On the positive side of the strict Saturn ledger of accountability in human relationships, the Goat will shyly, if nonverbally, admire and respect the Archer's unquenchable faith — and Sagittarius will know in his or her heart-of-hearts that Cappy is right about looking before soaring. The good Lord knows the Archer has flown into the clouds spontaneously, then fallen to the ground with a thud, enough times to appreciate the Goat's common-sense counsel of waiting a bit to test an idea or an impulse before aiming the bow and arrow.

These two are usually miles apart in their viewpoints concerning money. I'm always prepared to find the exception that proves the rule, but so far, at least, I've yet to meet a Capricorn who doesn't have a savings account, including the youngsters. Many Goats have more than one, in several banks. Sagittarius prefers a personal checking account as a place to sock cash, and there's seldom enough of the stuff left over to save. If you know an accountant, a CPA, or a banker who's a Sag, either that person was adopted, or the Moon Sign or Ascendent will be in an Earth Sign. True, Archers are bright, and they can be quick with figures, but they can be quicker with spending than with saving. There may be a few nontypical Sagittarians who have savings accounts, but even with these, the withdrawals will normally exceed the deposits. Those Archers with the Moon in Taurus, Virgo, or Capricorn — or the Ascendent in one of those signs — will have more harmonious financial vibrations with the Goats. Otherwise, money could turn out to be the "root of all evil" between them.

One happier aspect of their compatibility is that the brutal frankness of Sagittarius — those stinging arrows of honesty — will bounce more easily off the Goat than they'll bounce off less thick-skinned Sun Signs. Most of the time, when a Sagittarian friend, lover, mate, child, relative, or business associate shoots a barbed observation of painful truth toward Capricorn, the Goat simply shrugs. "So *nu* ?" remarks Capricorn. It's not easy to shake these people. Nevertheless, Sag should take it easy. Too many carefree remarks, and the Goat will slap down the Archer with Saturn's own brand of heavy observation of truth, which could cause the happy-go-lucky Sag to brood in a corner for months. Saturn-ruled Capricorns are excellent instructors of necessary lessons to the impulsive and outspoken of this world.

At first glance, Sagittarians do seem to push Capricorns around. At least, that's the way it appears to onlookers. But while all the pushing and bossing is going on, the Goat is quietly and determinedly doing his (or her) own thing, and in the long and short of it, Sag will usually get the short of it. Like all Earth Signs, Cappy only gives in temporarily, to avoid argument. Then, when the Goat's had enough, watch those feet dig into Mother Terra Firma, as the Goat sits there sullenly, a lump of smoldering resentment, those beady eyes daring Sagittarius to push one more inch. Go ahead, *push*. See what happens. Most Archers have the good sense to know when to stop shoving Capricorn. (Before Cappy becomes really angry. *That's* when to stop.)

Sagittarians are, at heart, wistful clowns, bicycling around a three-ring circus, with a generally lighthearted attitude toward life's problems. Undue fretting and worrying distresses them. Their basic natures are sunny and valiantly hopeful, which is why they suffer so dreadfully when they discover the dark side of the rainbow. Capricorn's nature is more somber and restrictive (*self-imposed* restriction), the Goats having been born with a built-in warning signal for excesses and an innate sense of .... well, of surefooted balance on Life's rocky cliffs. When all's said and done, Sag is optimistic, Capricorn is pessimistic. Sagittarian optimism troubles the careful Goat. Capricorn pessimism depresses the Archer's soaring spirit.

Yet, at those times when the happy Sagittarius clown is broken hearted over the cruelty of uncaring souls who didn't share his (or her) gigantic Jupiter faith and generosity, Capricorn is there to heal the hurt with loving tenderness and wisdom — very much in the same way Sag remembers certain beloved grandparents to have behaved in childhood. The Goat may gruffly chide and scold, but no one can be gentler, more affectionate, when Capricorn's Saturnine counsel has been ignored by the careless Archer, bringing all manner of woe down upon his or her idealistic head.

"There, there now," soothes Cappy. "Don't be sad and glum. Everything will turn out all right, sooner or later. The Sun always comes out after the rain. Isn't that what you taught me youself?"

Yes. That happens to be precisely what Sagittarius did teach Capricorn. And the Goat is much wiser for it.

☆ ☆ ☆ ☆ ☆ ☆

SAGITTARIUS *Woman* CAPRICORN *Man*

◄═══•◄█►•═══►

"Don't irritate him unnecessarily."

So you like the truth, no matter how it hurts, is that right, Sag? You believe in honesty, whatever the cost in suffering, correct? All right, steel yourself. You asked for it. You're going to get it. There may be a few Capricorn men on this Earth who were sadly orphaned as infants or small boys (a truly heartbreaking experience for this Sun Sign), and there may also be a few Goats who fiercely resented their parents and ran away from home to join a carnival when they were little shavers. Maybe about half a dozen. On the entire planet. But unless he was born with a powerfully afflicted Moon and Saturn in his birth chart, the average Capricorn man (the kind you're probably in love with) will uphold his family in much the same manner as that statue of Atlas, on Fifth Avenue, in New York, across the street from St. Patrick's, carries the world on his shoulders—with the same resignation, for roughly the same period of time. (Atlas hasn't shrugged the world off his shoulders yet, at least he hadn't when I last passed him.)

Let this be a warning to the cheerful, trusting Sagittarius girl who thinks her Goat loves her above all else in the Universe. He loves her, yes. He may even worship her, bring her a rosebud on their anniversary (when the florist is having a half-price sale), let her drive his car (if he does that, he *really* loves her), but she is not and never will be the most important thing in this Universe to him. His family holds that honor—and they will as long as he draws breath. Whether they're a burden to him because they all get along rather badly or a pleasure because they're all a rolicking fun bunch, *family* is *family*. A Capricorn man who's been irreparably hurt by his siblings or parents may not hang around home forever, but he'll bear the scars for a Lifetime. The Goat won't necessarily cling to the actual house where his parents are residing, like the male Crab. Capricorns will even move out of the city or state where their folks live. Nevertheless, however near or far he may be from them, trying to wean this man away from his family is like trying to unstick that glue that holds a Volkswagen up in the air. Crazy Glue, I think it's called. And crazy is the girl who tries the impossible.

To the girl Archer, families are certainly jolly sorts, and undeniably handy to have around when one needs to borrow an extra few dollars, or needs a place to crash over an occasional weekend, but her individualism probably caused her to cut ties with home early in Life, and rush off to follow the distant calliope music. If this means leaving the family behind and keeping in touch with a picture postcard from time to time, no harm done. Birds are *supposed* to leave the nest, aren't they? As a matter of fact, in Nature, the baby bird is actually *pushed* out of the nest by his anxious parents, so he'll learn to fly and survive. Sag thinks that's both a sensible and an exciting child-rearing theory.

Capricorn thinks it's ghoulish, gruesome, and unfeeling. The very idea turns the Goat pale. What an awful thing to do. Who's going to feed them and take care of them when winter comes? Not the *baby* birds — the *parent* birds. It's Cancer who worries-about-being-worried-about. Capricorn is concerned about his family, not because *he* needs protection, but because the Goat thinks *they* need protection. It's different. The end result is the same — both Cancer and Capricorn are difficult to separate from their families. But the motive is anything but the same, and motives are what matter.

Can you imagine what happens with a Capricorn parent and a Cancer child — or vice versa? It's frightening, really frightening. Read the Cancer-Capricorn section and see. But not yet. We still haven't rescued that poor girl Archer from her romantic notions about the Goat she loves.

The Capricorn male is not the aggressive type. Most of them are touchingly old-fashioned and gallant. This is not a man who will swoop her off her feet with a Tarzan yell and head for the jungle to woo her near a sleepy lagoon in the moonlight. What if Boy should be looking — or a strange gorilla should happen to pass by, out for a midnight stroll? Capricorns are quite proper and circumspect, always concerned — to some degree, at least — about "what people will think." This doesn't mean he's unromantic. It only means that his romancing (in the early stages) might be tinged with timidity. But to the Sagittarian woman who loves him, when he ventures a shy grin . . . when his quiet eyes twinkle as he says something intimate in a coded way only the two of them understand, he'll bear a remarkable resemblance to a jungle hero, even if he doesn't swing on a vine while he's saying it. All the other men in her life will seem like apes—gauche and brassy, pushy and immature. If there's anything a Capricorn male is *not*, it's immature. His emotional maturity is, in fact, the thing she needs most from him, and give her credit for sensing this.

Male Goats seldom behave like little boys, even when they are chronologically little boys. Those few Capricorns who drink or take drugs to excess— or allow their emotions to spill over in public—have extremely afflicted birth charts, and should be pitied, not censured. Such behavior troubles their own consciences more than it could possibly trouble those around them, because it's foreign to their very natures. It's like being bottled up inside a body which behaves in a way so unlike yourself, it's truly scary and tragic. Not being true to one's own Sun Sign essence is a warning signal of serious dimensions. A lazy Virgo, a timid Leo, a pushy Pisces...an extravagant Taurus... and so on... can be headed in the wrong direction, with much sadness in store.

If the girl Archer has complaints to register with her Capricorn lover or husband concerning his disposition at times, she should curb her natural instinct for candor and bluntness. She can save his feelings—and their relationship—by studying a thesaurus and using her head. It will save lots of wear and tear on her heart in the long run if she'll play a kind of synonym game when she's angry. Here's an example. What's another way to say selfish? Self-indulgent. Another way to say cold and heartless? How about sensible, but insensitive? Stingy is a harsh word. Economical or thrifty is kinder. Instead of stuffy, how about careful and respectable? And like that.

If she yells at him: "You're selfish! You're cold and heartless! Besides all that, you're stingy and stuffy!"—she'll lose him (and also lose her chance to mature under his firm, patient guidance). It's softer, less raw and stinging, if she simply says, calmly: "You're very self-indulgent, you know, at times. You're also a little too practical, economical, and careful. Do you realize that?" (Even if she's calling him a stingy, selfish, cold-hearted monster under her breath.) When she expresses her complaints like this, he'll probably make a mental note that he should soften his edges a little, and he may even smile. Yes, smile.

It's amazing how people are pleased to hear a dubious quality of their Sun Sign described (if the harsh word for it is avoided), even though that quality may be what others consider negative. Tell a Taurus he's impulsive, he'll frown. The same word will utterly delight an Aries. Tell a Leo he's proud, he'll beam. The same word will offend a Virgo. Tell a Gemini he's changeable, he'll grin in assent. The same word will bring you a sting of resentment from a Scorpion. *Him* changeable? No way. Tell a Cancerian he's conservative, he'll take it as a compliment to his cautious nature—but tell a Sag she's conservative, and she'll tell you to go sit on a cow pie. And so on. What is one person's fault in the eyes of others, is to his (or her) way of viewing it, a virtue. It's a good thing it works out that way, otherwise none of us could live with ourselves, right? *Right!* (Aries is always right, never wrong. Do you think that's self-centered? I'm an Aries, and I think it's a *splendid* quality! If you think it's negative, it's just because you're jealous.)

There's not doubt that a Capricorn male can appear to be cold, because he's afraid to show his emotions too openly, lest they be trampled upon (and a Sagittarius woman can walk pretty heavily over the heart sometimes). But he's not totally selfish. It's true he can be most considerate of himself, but constantly telling him he's selfish will only cause him to eventually live up to the image. The person you love gradually grows into the image you hold of him (or her) in your mind and heart. Didn't you know that? It's true. It's an inviolate metaphysical law regarding the interreaction of human emotions within the powerful vibratory sphere of love.

Speaking of love, that leads us to sex, since the two matters can't be separated with success in an emotional relationship between a man and woman. Sex alone leads to sickness of the spirit and deadly emptiness. Love alone, without sex, is unfulfilling and lonely — for love and sex are twins. The sexual compatibility of this 2-12 Sun Pattern, made of Earth and Fire, will be as good or as bad as their adjustment in other facets of their personalities cause it to be. In the beginning, there's a compulsion to touch, a powerful sense of curiosity on the part of each, which adds much magnetism to the chemistry between them. He is so ... different; what is he like as a lover? (Different from her, she means.) She is so ... different; what would it be like to totally possess her? (Different from him, he means.)

Undeniably, such strong mutual curiosity creates a powerful sexual attraction between them. It's only later, when their love has passed the new stage and entered into the familiar, that the physical aspect of their relationship may begin to lose its appeal. Satisfied curiosity takes the edge off the trembling anticipation. But with a little more imagination from him ... a little more patience from her ... they'll learn that familiarity need not breed contempt. Familiarity can bring a rare kind of warm affection and deep passion that mere curiosity for the strange can't touch. He must guard against the emotional clumsiness of making love then quickly falling asleep — or of sexual blending without endearments. She must watch her tendency to verbal clumsiness, like zapping him with an arrow of hurtful truth a second or two before he reaches out to embrace her. Then she'll complain about his "coldness," when she's the one who doused his erotic intentions with ice water.

Their ruling planets tell the story. His is Saturn, and Saturn can be unduly restrictive. Hers is Jupiter, and Jupiter can be excessive and overwhelming. When Saturn and Jupiter blend their vibrations, these two planets can (literally, in astrology) create earthquakes. Each planet possesses a different kind of power — but neither planet is bland nor boring. Taking a planetary hint, he should make an attempt to mature her impulsively passionate nature into a deeper, more satisfying ecstasy, taking care not to freeze her desire in the process. She should realize how achingly he longs for someone to unlock the key of his Saturnine prison of caution . . . someone like her to set him free emotionally, so he can abandon his caution and enjoy the passion he feels more strongly than she knows . . . deep within.

This is a man who is more at home perched high on a mountain top alone (or with her) than walking the noisy, crowded highways of Life. He requires some degree of fame and wordly success. (As long as he doesn't have to sign autographs. He'd hate that.) To the extent this is denied him, he needs from his woman an equal measure of respectful recognition of both his public and private achievements. It's a vital need, and can't be stressed too much. He admires and envies the famous, the successful, and therefore feels he's failed if he hasn't made it to the top of at least a modest hill. It needn't be Pike's Peak. The key to his moods is his disappointment in himself, in his level of attainment — the distance between his actual record and his inner goal.

The Sagittarian woman doesn't share his quiet and controlled, yet desperate, need to reach the mountain top, but she does need to know that the arrows of shining hope she shoots from her Jupiter bow of faith and idealism occasionally hit their mark. Her seeking heart needs a miraculous bull's-eye now and then, or her fiery spirit will leave her. And what is a Sag without fire and spirit? A very sad girl clown. There's nothing sadder than a clown whose bright, brave greasepaint is smeared with tears.

When he's grumpy because his success is still hiding in the mist . . . and she's blue because her dreams are so slow and poky coming true . . . they should catch a flight to some faraway, exotic place where there's a touch of magic in the air. It sometimes happens that a trip together will bring out the wishing stars again for a Goat and an Archer who have stopped kissing each other goodnight.

☆ ☆ ☆ ☆ ☆ ☆

SAGITTARIUS *Man* CAPRICORN *Woman*

◄─◄◉►─►

Peter's heart bobbed up and down as he listened.
Wendy bound, and on the pirate ship; she who
loved everything to be just so!

"I'll rescue her," he cried, leaping at his weapons. As he
leapt he thought of something he could do to
please her. He could take his medicine.

Here is this enchanting female creature, who seems to know exactly what she wants from life, and how to set about getting it. The Archer senses the Capricorn girl's goals are not small ones, but may even be as gigantic as his own, and it thrills him. She's quiet and modest, she doesn't interrupt him when he's talking about his ideas and dreams, and that stamps her as a very special lady indeed. She appears to him to be a gentle, docile, girl-type girl. Feminine and appealing.

He is making a sizable mistake. She may have been born under a feminine Sun Sign, but her nature is ruled by the masculine planet Saturn, and planets don't get much more masculine than Saturn. Although she may have gentle manners, she's anything but docile. Appealing she may be, but he shouldn't image her twirling a lace-trimmed parasol, tip-toeing around in a hoopskirt under the apple tree in the backyard, dropping a fragrant hanky to tease him. This girl is tough.

After all, she is a mountain Goat, never mind her sex. She'll digest anything to get where she's going, except the one food that upsets her, which comes in a can labeled: *Foolishness*. To Cappy, "foolish" is defined as anything that wastes her time and doesn't have a concrete purpose. This definitely includes idle flirting and casual affairs. Note that I didn't say she's against flirting, only *idle* flirting. I didn't say she's against affairs, only *casual* ones. The distinction may prove to be important, sooner or later. The thing is, a Capricorn girl wants to know what your intentions are before you have any. Or shall I say before the Sagittarius man has thought over what his intentions might be toward her. They had better not be what they are toward most women, or he can forget it. Male Archers are typically rather romantically promiscuous, not the most faithful types in the world, at least not while they're searching and seeking and investigating the scene. After he's found Lady Guinevere, Maid Marian—or whomever, the Jupiter-ruled knight (who views himself as both Robin Hood and Lancelot) is capable of Camelot-pure devotion and loyalty. But while he's riding around through Sherwood on his white horse looking, his shining armour can become a trifle tarnished. Of course, love — true love — can polish it right up again.

Tarnished armour won't deter this woman. She is as practical in love as in everything else. If armour is rusty, it can be scrubbed clean and shiny, like new — and no one will ever know the difference. A little tarnish is nothing to fuss about, if it can be removed. Yesterday is gone, today is here. Just watch out for tomorrow. She may forgive her Archer for past transgressions, and she's sensible and emotionally secure enough to trust him today — but she will not put up with any monkey business in the future, or he'll be dumped into her past, with barely a flick of her long, feminine eyelashes, to join the memories of the few mistakes she's made throughout her life (and you can count those on one hand with cautious Cappy).

Her toughness won't stop the Archer immediately. Remember he was born under a masculine Sun Sign, and he's ruled by the masculine Jupiter as well. A double macho vibe. So he's not likely to run from her challenge. This girl is not for the fainthearted lover to subdue, but a Sagittarian male is not fainthearted. He's just a little awkward in the finesse department. He may blurt out some candid observation that offends her dignity, without thinking. (Goat Girls are terribly dignified, especially in public.) It's not that she doesn't appreciate wit, she has a whimsical, delightful sense of humor herself, but she'll frown at shaggy-dog stories without a punch line, rude manners turn her off — and she will not like hearing her faults candidly analyzed in front of others, which is one of the Archer's more obvious talents. (I am being kind to call it a talent.)

She will, however, appreciate his honesty. And he, conversely, will admire hers. In this area they'll get along famously. She's sensible and practical, not inclined to paint things rosier than they actually are — and he calls the shots as he sees them, refusing to dress up the truth in fancy language. The direct approach appeals to both of them, and this will be a shared quality that forms a strong basis for empathy between them, even though it may be hard on their friends. If you're visiting this couple in their home, and they have to rise early to go to work or catch a plane or whatever, you'll be firmly reminded of the lateness, should you remain past their pumpkin hour — in a nice, genteel, courteous manner from Cappy, with open, friendly frankness by Sag. But you will be told. You will know you have overstayed your visit. They won't actually pull the welcome mat out from under your feet as you leave, but you'll definitely get the message.

These two may have a mutual interest in music or art, the law or religion, and he gets the impression she'll sacrifice anything for her heart's desire. He's right. If she's living in a small town, for example, and attending a high school where she can't get all the art courses she needs, she'll take a job in a service station, filling gas tanks, scrubbing windshields — "Check your oil, sir ?"—to save enough money to go to New York where they teach what she wants to learn. Still, one way or the other, Cappy will usually manage to live with her family while she's getting her education—and will leave their home reluctantly to strike out on her own. The Archer can understand her fierce dedication to her goal. He possesses great bushels of such dedication himself. But his route to the Emerald City is somewhat different. A Sagittarius man is always ready to strike out for Oz or Shangrila with a turtleneck tucked under his arm and a toothbrush in his pocket.

She won't go with him. She has a million excuses. "No planning," she says. "More fun!" he replies. She frowns. He coaxes. She is firm. It's about at this point when he begins to think she's stuffy. Then she'll twinkle that shy Saturn smile at him, he'll melt and approach her again, with a light, optimistic heart, thinking there must be a way to win her over. There is. Just prove you're serious—not only about loving her—but about what you expect to contribute to this world—and what you expect to receive in compensation for your efforts. A Sagittarius man is brimming over with daydreams (until they're smothered by life's disappointments). He offers her a basketful of them, and her heart is touched, but she waits. A daydream is fine with her, but where is the blueprint for it ? You can't build a house without one—you can't build a dream without one. "Wishing will make it so!" whistles the Archer, arguing with her. "That's just a Disney double-dip ice-cream cone of delusion," retorts Cappy. "It takes more than wishing. So, all right, if wishes are the dreams we dream when we're awake, like your song says—even wishes need a blueprint. If things don't work out the way you think they will, if we were married and neither of us had a job—what would we eat, what would we wear, how would we pay the rent ?"

"Oh, ye of little faith !" answers the Archer. It may soften her. He can try. Sagittarius (like Scorpio) often quotes the Bible to make a point. It properly impresses most people, but Cappy would demand proof from God Himself that He knows where He's going. Considering the condition of the world today, it's a sensible, Saturnine sort of question. "*We* cause these cataclysms and tragedies, poverty and misery, on Earth, not God," explains the Archer. "And as for astrology, how do we know the *planets* cause *our* actions ? Maybe, by our actions, *we* cause the course and direction of the *planets*." (She may think that one over for a while.)

The older the Capricorn woman becomes, the more likely she is to enjoy traversing the planet with her Sagittarian lover or husband. She missed that sort of bounding joy and freedom as a child, since she was born at age one hundred and five, give or take a few years . . . and her practical, yet secretly yearning, heart beats a little faster at the thought of experiencing it with the man she loves. The key to her heart is patience. But all the advice can't be one-sided. She may need a blueprint for happiness herself, once the Archer has conquered her emotionally. He puzzles her, and sometimes he hurts her — deeply — with his blunt speech. She should try to understand that he doesn't really mean to be unkind. His candid speech is spontaneous, springing from a sort of instantaneous compulsion to express truth. Actually, when he said the picture she painted of an ancient druid looked like a potbellied stove — when he remarked that her nose was a little crooked, her hair would look better short than long — and her best girlfriend was a dingbat — it was only proof that he really meant it when he said "I love you." This man couldn't lie if he tried. When you look at it that way, being loved by the Archer can be like a romantic insurance policy. You're secure until he says he doesn't love you. At least with him, you *know*. That's sort of like having a blueprint, isn't it? A Sagittarius man who's been rejected by the woman he loves may become a Franciscan monk or join the Merchant Marines — but he won't be dishonest with himself — or with her. If he ever lies, he's convinced *himself* it's truth, and that's rare because . . . well, did you ever try to convince him of anything? It's not easy, even when it's himself trying to win an argument with himself. It's not that he's stubborn (*she's* stubborn), it's just that he can always think of another point to make, a new idea, to change the entire initial concept of the situation.

The sexual compatibility of these two Sun Signs will suffer from only two things — which can be brought under control if they wish. They are: his tendency to thoughtlessly say something that causes her emotions to freeze, then to expect her to melt in his arms a few hours (or minutes) later — and her tendency to classify their lovemaking as an enjoyable necessity, which should conform to their schedule, but never interfere with it, combined with her fear of allowing passion to control reason. Her sexual responses may seem too disciplined to him, as though she really isn't submitting to love's mysteries, only tolerating her body's needs as a practical matter. But she will never be able to find joy in their Oneness until he gently, tenderly helps her to learn to trust his embrace, until she's sure such abandon of her inner self is *safe*. Just when she starts to trust him, he shoots an unnecessary arrow of painful truth into her heart, something which would have been better left unspoken. When a Saturn heart is wounded, it takes longer to heal than other hearts. Much longer.

She may seem to shrug off his cruel words, even the kind and complimentary ones, as though she couldn't care less, either way. Oh, but she does care. She cares deeply. The unkind words will leave scars she'll never show. The kind ones will cause her to grin shyly, and breathe a little sigh of happiness, when she's sure he's not looking or listening. The outward coolness of this lovely, serious, and self-contained girl hides a depth of loneliness inside she can never express. This is a woman who needs so very much . . . kindness. To be told she's pretty, to be appreciated verbally, will bring more brightness into her life — more than this man who loves her may realize. Never mind that her verbal response is: "What mushy sentiment!" Don't you believe it. Saturn restricts her from demonstrating her gratitude, from showing her tenderness, but it's there—just as *she's* always there, when he needs her. Her love is steady and dependable, like a grandfather clock, ticking away forever (unless he insults her family, then the chimes may stop).

Still, for all the growing pains of their love, the Sagittarian man's soaring ideals will teach the Goat Girl's mind to fly higher into the realms of Life's meaning than she ever dared venture before he came along to take her by the hand, and race her to Sirius and back.

He has a truly magical way of lifting her out of her inky-blue spells of Saturn depression, with a bright sunbeam thought that turns her eyes and her spirit toward the sky, where his ruling star, Jupiter, twinkles all his riddles of existence. One gloomy Sunday, when she's unable to respond to his cheerful optimism, and his bright faith in a Higher Power solving all their problems, she may tell him that she doesn't believe he should count so much on God— and miracles.

"Maybe you're right," he'll reply then, Jupiter-like. "Maybe we shouldn't count on Him. Maybe the real truth is that *He's* depending on *us* . . . for some sort of ultimate miracle."

His logic touches her, and she answers, slowly, "I never thought of it that way." For a moment longer, she's silent. Perhaps God, too, is lonely and uncertain. The loneliest One of all. For, *who* and *what* may a Supreme Power count on, lean on? Yes, he'll stretch her Saturn-bound soul, this Sagittarian man of the impossible dreams and endless queries. To be depended upon, counted upon by a trusting Divinity . . . is a lovely new concept to responsible Cappy. And so much truer than she knows . . . truer than even her searching Archer guesses.

His love can be an experience in both heartache and ecstasy for her, but if she'll turn over the comic valentine her Centaur clumsily offers her, she'll see that he's drawn a heart on the back—his own. The one he offers her so honestly, with such faith she'll never break it, like an awkward boy in a schoolyard, whatever his chronological age. I can hear her words as she reads this, can't you? "Mush, mush, mush!" as she turns away with a shrug of dismissal. But watch her closely. See her Mona Lisa smile?

☆ ☆ ☆ ☆ ☆ ☆

SAGITTARIUS

Fire—Mutable—Positive
Ruled by Jupiter
Symbols: Archer & Centaur
Day Forces—Masculine

AQUARIUS

Air—Fixed—Positive
Ruled by Uranus
Symbol: The Water Bearer
Day Forces—Masculine

The SAGITTARIUS-AQUARIUS Relationship

◄◄►—►◄►►

*...sitting on stools, flinging balls in the air, pushing
each other, going out for walks and coming back...*

The Centaur and the Water Bearer dance to the lively drum beat of the
friendly and karmic 3-11 Big Band Sound (Sun Sign Pattern). They
vibrate together sometimes noisily, a little strangely, but excitingly, as
Fire and Air are wont to do—generating sparks of ideas, flurries of fabulous
freakishness, at times scintillating each other's sauciness, at other times
blunting each other's edges a bit—and at all times baffling the rest of us.

Sagittarians can't help being basically cheerful, because they're born
optimists. Yet they are also born skeptics. It's a tricky balancing act to juggle
the contradictory qualities of optimism and skepticism simultaneously, but
the Centaurs manage to do it. That's the way it is with what astrology calls
the "double" signs—or the Sun Signs of "duality". Sagittarius being half
horse, half human Archer, Sagittarians are therefore, half happy, half sad.
Half frivolous, half serious. Half foolish, half wise. Half clown and half
philosopher. They're not quite the human clones that Geminis are; nevertheless, they are dual.

Aquarius is *not* an astrological sign of duality, consequently the Water Bearers were not, like Sag, born under the influence of a "double" sign, although they're sometimes even more contrary and contradictory than the Archers. Two sides aren't really enough for the Uranus-ruled men and women. It's easy to become bored, just knocking around with two of yourself. The typical Aquarian has a dozen or so personalities. It would be mundane to possess only a couple, and Aquarius is a sign which is in no way related to the mundane. Water Bearers defy mediocrity (and hate hypocrisy), being more closely related to the marvelous, to all magic and madness. They are, in a word, *different*.

Combining the essence of Jupiter's bluntness (Sag) and the unpredictable quality of Uranus (Aquarius) can create some unexpected expectancies. Like, you know how I'm always telling you that Aquarians love to surprise you, and seldom tell you what they're up to, because they'd rather spring it on you unawares? Well, that's true. Aquarians do adore surprising people. But they tend to spoil surprises others would like to stage. (If *they* can't surprise you, they'll see that no one *else* does!) In the late summer of 1978, a California lady, for many weeks ahead, made careful, intricate plans to throw a surprise birthday party for a close friend. All of his dear friends and Hollywood intimates had been invited, and the whole affair had been kept successfully hush-hush, entre nous — until the innocent honor guest's phone rang a couple of days before the affair. It was Hungarian-American film actress Zsa Zsa Gabor (Zsa Zsa is an Aquarian, with heavy Sagittarian positions in her horoscope). "Darling!" the Hungarian Water Bearer blurted out, "I'm so terribly sorry I'll be out of town and won't be able to come to your surprise party Saturday night!" The hostess could have cheerfully strangled the lovable, glamorous Gabor. Understandably.

What is *not* understandable, however, is how one lone Virgo lady managed to raise three Aquarian daughters. But I'm getting it backwards, Uranus-like. What I meant was that Zsa Zsa and her two sisters, Eva and Magda Gabor, are *all three* pixilated but brilliant, nitzie but magical female Water Bearers! Their mother, Jolie Gabor, is a Virgo. We should all send Jolie sympathy cards. At least, mental sympathy cards. Tons of them. Can you believe it? They should award medals to women like that — to mothers born under any sign whatsoever, who manage to raise three Aquarians under the same roof, especially of the female sex. Actually, coping with any mix of boys and girls ruled by Uranus would be sufficient challenge to deserve at least a small blue ribbon for valor. Particularly when one of them is a mixture of Aquarius and Sagittarius. One would hardly know what to expect next, except more shocks. (Did you ever notice that, by just moving around the "p" and the "c", "expect" becomes "except"? Aquarians have. They *notice* things like that.)

If an astrologer could sum up planetary wisdom in one brief phrase, for counseling Sag and Aquarius concerning the achievement of a smooth association together, it would be to advise both of them to make one powerful effort (not just think about it, and agree in principle, but DO IT) to remain *calm, cool* and *collected*, under any and all circumstances. Such a few words. But so vitally important to these two Earthlings. Sagittarius is a Fire Sign, therefore extremely volatile. Perhaps not as easily incited into combustion as Aries, but nevertheless volatile. When the Water Bearer (Aquarius is an Air Sign, remember) becomes a little windy and fans the Archer's fiery nature into flames — the resultant conflagration will whip the Aquarius Air into a regular tornado of fury. Anyone with good ears who happens to be hanging around within a few blocks of the conflict will think the UFO's have landed, prepared to launch an attack. The close encounters between these two will admittedly, at times, resemble full scale war. Or invasion.

Normally, the male or female Water Bearer is a good natured, tolerant soul, happily tinkering with nonsense and genius, willing to live and let live, bothering no one and behaving in a charming, agreeable, even fascinating manner. Normally, the male or female Archer is a happy-go-lucky soul, cheerful and friendly, equally tolerant of everyone and everything, bouncing around like a basketball or a hula hoop, grinning and likeable. When they bump into one another on their way to the Farmers Market, the ASPCA or a Greenpeace meeting, they become even more cheerful, bouncy, and friendly. Most of the time, their association is lilting and full of likability. It's just those times when the Aquarius Air happens to fan the Sag Fire a bit too much, and the Sag Fire whips the Aquarius Air into a frenzied reaction. These are rare occasions, not the rule. But it's best to be warned.

Generally speaking, the 3-11 vibration graces the Archer and the Water Bearer with a foundation of real friendship beneath whatever is the outward reason for their relationship, whether they're simply friends (in which case they'll be *very* good friends), relatives, business associates, lovers or mates. Being a sextile vibe, it also presents them with lots of opportunities to make up and start all over those times when they do quarrel, with little or no bitterness over past mutual resentment. They usually do reconcile eventually, these two, because of the karmic implications of the 3-11 Sun Sign Pattern (see Sun Sign Pattern section in the back of this book).

One nice thing about their togetherness is that the Archer's blunt arrows of truth seem to be rubber tipped when they're shot toward the Aquarian. Even if they're sharp, they *seem* soft-tipped. Because the typical Water Bearer doesn't really mind the truth all that much. It doesn't hurt or fluster them the way it does with most Sun Signs. They just shrug, wiggle their ears and agree, surprising the Archers, who are accustomed to taking it on the chin from others after they've unintentionally stuck the rather large Jupiter foot in their mouths. Besides, since Aquarians frequently see Life in a kind of upside-down or backwards fashion (the Present always confuses them, since they live in the Future) and since they tend to laugh when they're sad, and weep when they're joyous — they also tend to view an insult as a compliment.

However, conversely, they do not take kindly to certain compliments to which they might apply their reverse trick and turn into an insult. That's when the Uranus hurricane picks up velocity and could blow the Sag fires into flaming response. These are their Red Alert moments of too-close-for-comfort encounters, forest fires and such, when they should be following the earlier given Smokey the Bear astrological advice about remaining cool, calm and collected.

Both Sag and Aquarius are essentially humanitarians, both easily persuaded to join causes that promote brotherhood and sisterhood — and animal-hood. They both enjoy, if they're typical of their Sun Signs, camping and hiking, being close friends with Mother Nature. They both like fun and parties and people. They both have bushel baskets full of friends. Neither could be called a loner. But the Archers are more adaptable in their life styles than the Aquarians, who are more or less Fixed about their private lives and habit patterns, while advocating sweeping changes for the rest of the world. This could occasionally cause a donnybrook between them.

Sag is Mutable and Aquarius is Fixed. Mutable means that the Centaurs like to communicate a lot, and aren't terribly bossy or domineering. Although they do kind of like to have their own way. I know it's a fine line, but there *is* a difference. They certainly don't like to be bossed around with too heavy a hand — told what to do — or suspected of dishonesty. Then they become slightly outraged, if there is such a thing as "slightly" outraged. And Fixed means that Aquarians are just a tad this side of stubborn now and then, somewhat immutable — which is, as you know, the very *opposite* of Mutable. Neither do the Water Bearers demand dominance, but on the other hand, they don't like to be pushed around or shoved into things they don't want to do any more than Sag does.

The eccentric and unconventional behavior of Aquarius is more likely to delight than to annoy the Archers, just as the Sagittarian love of travel, freedom and frankness will please the Aquarians. Right away the Water Bearer can see that Sag is anything but a hypocrite, and that qualifies the Centaur as a lifetime friend to the Uranus person, who despises any thing resembling pretense. "Be what you are, do what you feel and say what you think" — is a motto Jupiter and Uranus espouse with equal enthusiasm.

The Aquarian involved in an association with Sagittarius will soon enough learn what it's like to have to swallow an occasional dose of his (or her) own curiosity medicine. Sag will toss many a question into the Water Bearer's little brown jug of knowledge, and probably receive only another question in reply. (All Air Signs tend to use the technique.) It won't take the Archer long to answer.

SAG: Why are you so quiet?

AQUARIUS: Why haven't you mentioned my new haircut?
SAG: I was just about to say that it makes it more visible. Now there's no problem guessing which one of them.
AQUARIUS: Makes *what* more visible? Who is *them*?
SAG: The Seven Dwarfs. Your ears stick out like Dopey's, and that haircut really sets them off!

The wise Water Bearer, with the sudden, flashing intuition of Uranus, ought to know that Dopey is the Archer's all-time-favorite character. A little later, Sag will merrily toss the Aquarian another knuckle ball compliment.

SAG: Your eyes remind me of Dopey too. They have that same kind of blank expression. Sort of dazed all the time. But your disposition is more like Grumpy's. And your hay fever makes me think of Sneezy. God knows you're not Bashful.
AQUARIUS: Do you know why *you* could *never* remind anyone of Dopey?
SAG: Why?
AQUARIUS: Wasn't Dopey the dwarf who never spoke, and kept his mouth shut all the time?
SAG: Yes, but he didn't need to talk. He spoke with his eyes.
AQUARIUS: Smart dwarf.
SAG: Okay, Happy, I get the message. Touché!

It's that 3-11 friendship vibration of inexplicable empathy. Anyone else the Archer would have belted. But the Water Bearer gets away with it. Sometimes.

☆ ☆ ☆ ☆ ☆

SAGITTARIUS *Woman* AQUARIUS *Man*

◆━◆▶━◆

For a moment, the circle of light was broken, and something gave Peter a loving little pinch.

Let's lead off with Uranus. His ruler. It's not by any means a stronger or swifter orbiting planet than Jupiter (her ruler) but *quicker*. Uranus rules electricity and lightning, which is quicker than almost anything you can think of (except perhaps the Sagittarian temper). The Aquarian man has a persistent scientific bent, wherever he works, whatever he does. If he's a gardener, he'll design hanging gardens. Hanging from unexpected places. Like the chandelier in the living room. If he's a plumber, he'll figure out a way to wire the dishwasher drain to the television, so one can watch Tom Snyder on Tomororow while stacking the dishes tonight because one felt lazy yesterday. If he works in a library, he'll scientifically design the book shelves so that all the titles can be nicely read upside down, the way *he* reads them, and probably categorize them in a peculiar (but to him a sensible) manner. Like the love stories under "M" for Mush, the Tolkien books filed in the aisle marked "S" for Super-Superlative, and the books about spacecraft and UFO sightings on the shelf labeled "W" for When? or Wow! or possibly "T" for Terrific. Louisa May Alcott's "Little Women" he'll file under "P" for Pornographic. Maybe "E" for ERA. It's hard to tell. And like that. (Aquarian actor, Telly Savalas, invented the phrase *"and like that,"* you know. You didn't? Now you do.)

There was this radio station where I used to write continuity, in Johnstown, Pennsylvania. One night the announcer who read the eleven o'clock sportscast was desperate. He couldn't find the theme music for his ten minutes sports show. The station's Aquarian record librarian had absent-mindedly filed it away and gone home for the day. Panic and pandemoni-um! The turntable was spinning, and it was 30 seconds before air time. No theme record. Since the name of the theme was *The Notre Dame Victory March*, naturally, the announcer looked under "N" (Notre Dame) for the missing disc. Not there. Frantically, he looked under "V" for *Victory March*, then under "M" for maybe *Marches*. No luck. I will never forget as long as I live the expression of pathetic gratitude on that poor perspiring announcer's face when I rushed into the control room exactly one second before air time, and handed him the theme record I'd miraculously managed to find for him. On a crazy hunch, I had checked the "F" drawer. Sure enough, there it was! Filed under *Fighting Irish*. The next day the Aquarian record librarian couldn't understand all the mishagosh. Where else could anyone file it? Wasn't that the most logical place?

Aquarians are closet humanitarians, along with being ecologically in-clined. I (seriously) know a biology major at San Diego State University, who plans, after he gets his degree as a biologist, to enter law school, take the Bar and become a practicing attorney, so he can file Class A Action lawsuits on behalf of green plants and animals. (True, not make-believe.)

The Uranus-ruled man is uncommonly inventive, and is always popping up (not coming up—popping up) with some new idea no one has ever thought of before (in this particular solar system, that is). His mind is both brilliant and wayward, his mental process highly original. Unique, one might call it. Fruity and off the wall the girl Archer might call it, in her "charmingly tactful" manner, when she happens to be temporarily furious with him. Yet the Aquarian man's scientific nature isn't motivated by the attitudes and methodology of science today. Naturally. Aquarius lives in tomorrow, so why should he care a pickle about the rules of today ? It has a certain ring of logic, you must admit. Today's scientists insist on having everything properly proven and substantiated by hard facts before they'll deign to even listen to a new idea, let alone consider it. The Water Bearer knows instinctively that mankind would never advance (neither would womankind, but he's hardly aware of the difference between the two) unless people are willing to *first* dream, however wild the dream, *then* set about proving it — rather than the other way around, which to him, is clearly viewing the process of discovery in the exact reverse of the way it should be, in his opinion, viewed.

Many of the great minds responsible for the leaps and strides of knowledge in every area have been ruled by the progressive planet, Uranus. Fortunately for the planet Earth, we've been blessed with a fair number of Uranus-guided Aquarian births, of the male and female and combined gender (Aquarius is the sign of the uni-sex, so they're all a little of this and a little of that, which is why they're so fascinating) or we might not have progressed beyond the cave dweller stage.

Enter now the Sagittarius girl (stumbling over the Water Bearer's rock garden in the hallway) and already we have a slight problem. She may think (at least occasionally) that the Aquarian man she loves and hates with equal purple passion belongs exactly there, and nowhere else. In a cave. As a cave dweller. Preferably one at the zoo, with a fence around it, so he can't escape. Secretly, of course, she adores his unconventional ideas and wierdo behavior. His very unpredictability is what drew her heart to skip over and wave hello to his when she first met him — the day he offered her his umbrella in the rain, and she grinned a grateful thanks, until she discovered it was full of holes because he likes to walk in a bit of a shower, but not a downpour. "A *little* rain is refreshing and exciting," he told her, "but too much is a real drag. Don't you think ?"

She wasn't sure. She nodded. But it was a long time before she was *sure*. When she was, she punched tiny holes in her own umbrella — the one she saved up for a month to buy on sale at Saks. By then, as you've probably gathered, she had caught his craziness. It's very contagious, and the worst of it is that there's no immunity serum available. (No way for the unsuspecting, trusting girl Archer to seek immunization from the lightning bolts of her Uranus man either. But later for that.)

There will be moments when she forgets that she once thought his odd-ball antics were the most virtuous of all virtues, and see them as the viceiest of all vices. At such times, her Jupiter expansiveness can cause her to expand her annoyance into a volley of stinging arrows of truth (or truth as she sees it at that particular moment) that she'll regret later and probably apologize for profusely, when she's had a chance to think it over and decide she's been too hasty. She's sorry she told him he needed to have his head candled and was missing more than a couple of his marbles upstairs. He'll most likely forgive her — he may even shock her by being puzzled because he's forgotten she ever said those things. He *forgot*? When he was so angry at the time he emptied a bottle of glue in her hair? How could he have forgotten? Never mind how. He forgot. Aquarians don't clutter their craniums with unnecessary data when it's no longer relevant. It leaves less room for their inventive ideas and zig-zag thoughts about things that really matter.

There's something bright and brave and honest about the Sagittarian woman that makes the Aquarian man's heart do funny cartwheels. He's genuinely touched by her obvious lack of pretentiousness, her open, friendly manner — and her also obvious integrity. So she says a few brutally blunt things once in a while. At least she doesn't lie or pretend to be someone or something she isn't. She's herself. She's real, not phony. The kind of person he likes best. He asked her to be his friend, then — and hopefully she realized it as the most sincere invitation she ever received from a male. Because to an Aquarian, friendship is never taken (or given) lightly. Aquarians place a higher value on friendship than the majority of people nowadays place on love. And so, to be invited to be his friend could be near the equivalent of a proposal of marriage from other Sun Sign males. Maybe even better. It's simply great when lovers and mates can also be real friends. A rare romantic bonus. This man and woman have a better chance to achieve that kind of desirable blend in their relationship than lots of other couples, thanks to their 3-11 karmic friendship vibratory pattern.

Because the Sagittarius girl is a friendly person herself, she trusts most everyone she meets to share her own open and frank way of communicating and expressing her feelings on all subjects, romantic or platonic. Repeatedly, human nature being as varied and fickle as it is, she's disappointed. Her negative experiences seldom turn her bitter, or drown her innate Jupiter enthusiasm and optimistic outlook, but they can cause her to become a trifle skeptical. The dictionary interprets *bitter* as "characterized by hatred and resentment" — and *skeptical* as "not easily convinced, doubting or questioning." However heartbreaking and tragic some of her emotional memories may be, this is not a woman you could label as "characterized by hatred and resentment" (barring unusually severe planetary afflictions in her birth chart). But this *is* definitely a woman who's not easily convinced, who sometimes doubts until she's sure — and assuredly a female who is "questioning." She's spilling over with questions. From the time she was small, she began asking the world what it was up to, spinning around and going nowhere but back to the beginning. She more than questions love. She has her doubts and curiosity about politics, architecture, films, books, advertising, biology, zoology, ecology — and most of all, religion. She swings from being devoutly spiritual to stark atheism, and back again ... forever searching ... seeking truth. She possesses a talent for prophecy too, of which she's probably blissfully unaware, and she's a gay philosopher at heart. Most of the conclusions she reaches, after giving relatives, friends and strangers her Jupiter third degree, are happy ones, in the final analysis, containing a positive note about the future, rainbow-hued with hope. It's just that she doesn't like to fool anyone, or be fooled herself. For all her shining idealism, she'd still much rather hear it like it is, so she can deal with the realities, not illusions. Because she was born under a sign of duality, she can be a puzzling contradiction, even to a Water Bearer, and that's saying a lot!

The Aquarian man will agree with her viewpoints more often than not. He, too, seeks reality, not illusions. The difference is that he realizes, perhaps sooner than she, that reality itself may be an illusion — and what others have called illusions may be the true reality. The theory itself will fascinate her. She'll ask him a thousand questions, excitedly, far into the night .... her curious, alert mind, as always, stimulated by a new concept.

He may also be stimulated during their "far-into-the-night" philosophical rap sessions, but by something more than a new concept. Aquarian males don't normally concentrate unduly on the sexual side of a human relationship. But once a sensual or an erotic thought has been accidently planted in his Uranian mind, it will grow and sprout like any other seed in his busy mental bean bag — swiftly, and in an odd variety. But beautiful. Like wildflowers.

The Sagittarian woman is easily bored almost literally to tears by unimaginative, uninspired, ordinary and mundane lovemaking. Her Water Bearer will surely not let her down when it comes (finally) to the physical expression of his love for her — or his friendship offer — same thing to him. Sometimes he'll cause her heart to turn over with his gentleness and tender touch. Other times, he'll make her laugh till she cries with his awkward, clumsy, nighttime surprises — like crawling in bed wearing his ear muffs, reciting a poem to the small toe on her left foot ... maybe whispering a confession to her just before he kisses her in the darkness, that he hopes she won't hate him, but he's been having an affair with another woman. Just one of those things. Uncontrollable. It happened so suddenly, so unexpectedly, and he was seduced before he realized he was being unfaithful to her. She'll snap on the lights then, throw a pillow (or something more substantial) across the room, and demand to know her name, trembling. He'll offer to show her a picture of her rival ... walk over to his favorite, baggy sweater, dejectedly, guiltily pull out a snapshot from the frayed pocket, and hand it to her, begging her to forgive him. She'll grab it from him, saying something like, ¢¢&&°°°!!##$$%°!!.

"Isn't she beautiful?" he'll ask her, softly. "She looks a lot like you. Maybe that's why I couldn't help myself."

She'll gather all her courage, her heart pounding, and gaze at the picture. It is a photo of the new baby girl walrus at Sea World, with dainty whiskers and small, round, eloquent eyes. The lights go out again almost instantly, and he'll murmur against her ear, in the purple darkness.... "Now, where were we? Oh, now I remember! I was kissing you Good Morning..." She'll remind him that it isn't morning, just a little past midnight. He'll hold her closer, and ask, very quietly... "Then why did I see sunrise in your eyes a few minutes ago?"

No. Making love will never be mundane between the Centaur and the Water Bearer. Air fans Fire into passion, sometimes with the slightest breath. And her Fire will warm his airy nonchalance into a depth of desire and a steady need few other women could arouse in him. They respond affectionately to the soaring spirit in one another, this man and this woman. Because they both know that sex can be funny... and sublime. Their intimacies are as unpredictable as a playful breeze..... now and then, as softly silent as a snowfall in a deep forest. Still and peaceful. Suddenly, she'll become a clown — and he'll become a complete circus, monkeys, trapezes, peanuts, elephants and all. With three rings. Then back to snowflakes. And Good Morning embraces at midnight.

There will be moments when his irrational Air Sign anger will strike like a bolt of lightning, out of the blue. There will be other moments when her Jupiter temper will swell into a fury, and she'll hailstone cold accusations across the room in his general direction. But he'll just put on his ear muffs, and scribble her a note on her new T shirt with a crayon. "Now it's *really* midnight." She'll melt, pack a picnic basket.. and off they'll go to find a gurgling stream in the woods together... build a campfire and tell each other ghost stories in the twilight, leaning against a surprised tree, munching Triscuits.

☆ ☆ ☆ ☆ ☆ ☆

SAGITTARIUS *Man* AQUARIUS *Woman*

◆━◖●◗━◆

Novelty was beckoning to them again, as usual . . .

So you are a Sagittarian man, and you like to face the truth straight-on. No shilly-shallying around. You're brave enough to handle it, and you much prefer it to pretense. Excellent. This is wiser of you than you realize, when it comes to coping with the Aquarian girl you've just joyously bounced in love with because she's so feminine, so fragile, so free and so fey.

Fey she is. No doubt of it. But since love has a way of shading the unvarnished truth with a tone or two of rosewood, perhaps best that we open your eyes fully to what you might be facing in a relationship with the "feminine," fragile and free lady Water Bearer, who's uncontrollably guided by Uranus. (Never ruled. She can't be ruled, because she doesn't measure to any yardstick ever invented.) Of course, I'll grant you that every Aquarian girl is different (oh, are they different!) so you can't always judge one by another. Still, it helps to be aware of all the possible detours. I'm always telling you that Aquarians are a touch absent-minded now and then, and you may believe I exaggerate to make astrology more fun. I've no objection to astrology being fun, but I do not exaggerate. Especially not when I tell you Aquarians are sometimes a little forgetful. In fact, my illustrations of this particular Uranus trait, sprinkled throughout all the Aquarian chapters in this book, may be somewhat under-played, de-emphasized, so to speak. Milder than the truth. Colored with tones of rosewood. And so forth.

I can see you doubt my veracity. Your Archer's eyebrows are already assuming the Jupiter bow's skeptical curve. You Sag creatures never believe anything without asking a couple of dozen questions first. All right, Centaur, stifle your questions for a moment, and see if I can telepathically answer them before you ask them. You want proof that she's as absent-minded as I claim. Not heresay. Not second or third handed. The unqualified truth about her, you're thinking, straight from the horse's mouth, right? Well, *she's* not a horse. *You* are. At least, half of you is a horse (the other half is a prophetic, prognosticating philosopher) but never mind, I know what you mean. Here goes.

You have, naturally, heard of the Hungarian Aquarian, actress Zsa Zsa Gabor? If you haven't, you undoubtedly live in Tibet or Pago-Pago, and you aren't even reading this book, because my publishers, as far as I know, do not plan a Tibetan or Pagoan translation, at least not of the first edition. Everyone *else* on this planet has indisputably heard of Zsa Zsa — even some

Tibetan monks, I imagine, but they're not planning to marry one (an Aquarian, that is) having taken a vow of chastity, blessedly protecting them from experiences like wedlock with a Water Bearer. I mentioned the glamorous Gabor briefly at the beginning of this chapter, but I saved the good stuff till now, where it would be more effective — where you, poor unsuspecting Archer, will find it more useful.

First off, Zsa Zsa has been married no less than 7 times. Aquarians change their minds a lot, sort of like Libra and Gemini women — and a smattering of Sagittarians too, like yourself. It's not that you Archers are promiscuous, but you do like to flirt a lot, and sometimes get caught in your own blarney. I hope that doesn't offend you. After all, you can't help it if you're often dumb-dumb romantically. (I sound like a Sag, don't I ? But I'm really not, I'm a Ram, only pretending to be a Sag, to show you what it's like to be on the receiving end of your Jupiter-type, cheerful but candid, casual observations.)

Well, anyway, Zsa Zsa's 4th Uranus lightning bolt marriage was to an industrialist named Herbert Hutner. Remember his name, please. It's important. *Herbert Hutner.* You have that ? Good. Remember it. Aquarian Gabor thought he was, in her own words, "a really darling guy, but too good a husband. *There was no challenge.*" Are you picking up points, Sag man ? Keep listening. Since you like guessing games, would you like to guess what happened on Zsa Zsa and Herbert's honeymoon ? You give up ? Smart fellow. As imaginative as you are, you'd still never guess. So I'll tell you. Three days after her lovely, traditional wedding to Herbert, Zsa Zsa *herself,* mind you, confesses that an odd thing occurred when her groom left her in the wedding suite and went out to tend to some business. (Industrialists are always running around here and there, attending to business.) While he was gone, he missed his charming, lovable, sweetly-scented, pretty-butterfly-bride, as all lovers since Romeo are wont to do, so he phoned their honeymoon hotel to speak with her.

"Tell Mr. Hutner I *never* accept calls from strangers," Zsa Zsa icily informed the shocked hotel switchboard operator, then firmly but daintily replaced the soft rosewood receiver, and returned to her fragrant rosewood bubble bath, humming a happy little Hungarian tune. No. They hadn't quarreled. She *had forgotten her new husband's name.* After all, he'd been gone a whole day, and she had a lot on her mind.

Now, do you believe me ? You wanted the truth, and you got it. If you don't believe me, ask Zsa Zsa. Or Herbert Hutner. It might be kinder to ask Zsa Zsa. Mr. Hutner may find other subjects more pleasant to discuss. But, being a Sag, I suppose if you ever run into him when he's out industrializing somewhere, you'll ask him bluntly anyway. Better be cautious. He could take a swing at you. He might be a Sagittarian like yourself — and you know what a quick temper *you* have, right ? I'm sorry I don't actually know Herbert's Sun Sign. I was kind of scared to find out. But if he should happen to also be a Water Bearer, he won't have the slightest idea what you're talking about. By this time, he'll have forgotten the hotel, the phone call — and possibly also the marriage. Except when his nose catches a whiff of rosewood. Ah, memories . . .

I assume you Aquarian women have also picked up a few points about the Archer you love by now. In case you did, but have already forgotten, I'll remind you. He's a walking, talking question box. He's honest and forthright, like you. He's an idealist, like you. He likes the truth, however painful. He likes girls. But mostly to pal around with, although he's incurably romantic and multiple-minded until he falls in love for keeps. Then he's a sentimentalist. He won't be deceptively unfaithful. He'll tell you first. He has the temper of Jupiter. (Jupiter rules all *large* things.) He's fond of animals, and may give you a horse or a dog for your birthday. Never mind if you don't remember that about him. Actually, you didn't forget, because this is the first time I've told you. (In this chapter.) Sometimes he's a clown, and he'll amuse you marvelously. At other times, he's a veritable and venerable sage, a fountain of intellectualism, philosophy and wit.

He has this kind of religious-spiritual charisma that permeates his aura. He could be anything from a Born Again Christian (who'd like to return and be re-conceived) to a garlanded guru, who sits in the lotus position on a lotus, chewing an alfalfa sprout and meditating upon the navel of a turtle. He could be a harried Krishna, complete with clanging cymbals and chanting pigtail, mumbling melodious mantras — or a total atheist. He probably won't be a plain garden variety Protestant (though he does enjoy protesting). Not enough challenge. You see. He *is* a lot like you! He adores excitement, the unusual and the thrilling, even if his outward mien is that of a scholarly bookworm or a bored litigation lawyer. (Nothing could be more boring than litigation.) Pay no heed to his quiet surface personality — he's dual. He could be an explorer, because he thrives on suspense and danger. He loves to play games and gamble (*that's* pretty dangerous, especially in Vegas) and he especially loves to travel. He may take off to Macchu Picchu and forget to tell you he left. (See how it feels?) But he'll call you from darkest Peru, like a Postscript, and ask you to join him poking and perusing around in the ancient ruins. You'll most likely go. Take your checkerboard. And maybe a basketball. He also likes sports. Indoor and outdoor.

The lovemaking game between the Archer and the lady Water Bearer can be something like touch football. He touches her foot with his toe, she touches his cheek tenderly with his hand, and her airy essence fans his fiery essence into a sizable amount of expanded Jupiter passion. Desire is truly like a game they play together, sometimes energetically . . . sometimes gently, restfully, just exchanging affection and warmth between them. Like all 3-11 Sun Sign Pattern mates, the sexual facet of their love is friendly and giving. Neither of them are in the least bit possessive, but they're both very jealous. That means they'll usually be willing to give each other miles of freedom to be an individual, but they also like what is theirs to be theirs—such as one another. Neither will object to the other sharing his or her mind with anyone at all, but they'll draw the line (if they're typical of their Sun Signs) at sharing bodies. Which is nice, because they're also both essentially idealists, and ideals become them beautifully. When either Sagittarius or Aquarius makes a mistake impulsively, their ideals become tarnished, and a tarnished ideal to an astrological idealist can be sadly tormenting to the heart and soul.

She'll have oodles of friends of every rank and file, and let's hope he likes them, since, if he doesn't he will almost surely make it painfully clear to her (and to them) that he doesn't. Well, she wanted an honest man, this woman—she's searched for one in and out of her dreams ever since she was the age of Juliet. In the Archer, she's found one, and telling the truth is a part of being honest. Even when the truth stings a little. A brief sting isn't as bad as the deeper cut of deception and lies that can create wounds which never heal. These two may quarrel frequently, but they'll forgive and forget, kiss and make up quickly. Forgetting injuries without holding bitterness is the nicest kind of absent-mindedness, and they both are blessed, to a large degree, with this quality. His anger flares swiftly, hers zig-zags like a lightning flash, but both soon fade into laughter and loving again.

The main thing to remember is that she was born under a Fixed Air Sign (stubbornly changeable or changeably stubborn, take your choice) as well as a masculine Sun Sign (her "femininity" is *not* fragile) and is also ruled by a masculine planet. Double masculine Fixed. Likewise, *he* was born under a masculine Sun Sign, so he's aggressive and tough, therefore will balk at being bossed—and *he's* ruled, too, by a masculine planet. But he is not Fixed. He's Mutable Fire. Double masculine Mutable. Therefore, his mutability and her airy adaptability to change (except when she's being Fixed and stubborn) will allow them to handle the various emotional fluctuations of a relationship rather well, between them. He's somewhat hot-headed. She's more or less cool-headed, logical and detached (which may be what brings on some of his hot-headedness). But she's also soothing enough to cool his fevered brow at such times with her light touch. So it works out quite magically, when they really love each other.

Just so the Archer doesn't forget the sage advice of marriage counselor, Z. Z. Gabor, Phd. (Pretty-Hungarian-Damsel) who sighed sadly and daintily, "Darling, there was no *challenge*." As for the Uranus lady, it would help if she'd remember to be maybe a little less fey. Still, while she might forget his name now and then, she'll never forget his soft, puppy-dog eyes, his cheerful grin . . . the superb ways he plays touch football at night. She'd know him anywhere. Because the Aquarian women always remembers her dreams. And that's where she first met him . . . a long, long time ago.

☆ ☆ ☆ ☆ ☆ ☆

SAGITTARIUS

Fire — Mutable — Positive
Ruled by Jupiter
Symbols: Archer & Centaur
Day Forces — Masculine

PISCES

Water — Mutable — Negative
Ruled by Neptune
Symbol: The Fish
Night Forces — Feminine

The **SAGITTARIUS-PISCES** *Relationship*

> . . . . . *the night was peppered with stars . . . . they*
> *were crowding round the house, as if curious to see*
> *what was to take place there . . . . .*

As you may have already surmised from the title, this is one of those "challenging" (is that the tactful word?) 4-10 Sun Sign Pattern associations. The natal Suns of the Archer and the Fish are squared. In astrology, the square is an aspect of tension. However, tension can be transmuted *at will* into energy, and indeed, tension is absolutely necessary for energy to "become" — whether it's in a physics lab or between two people. A touch of tension can be a mighty healthy thing in human communication. *Please,* I said a *touch*! Obviously, a lot of it brings quite different results — less beneficial, though perhaps equally stimulating.

One never knows what an overload of energy might cause. It can surely explode test tubes — and Heaven forbid, even Mother Earth — if the governments of the world and America's Atomic Energy Commission continue to have their mad way. It can also explode a friendship. Ergo, if Sag and Pisces expect to achieve serenity together, they'll have to cool it when tension begins to mount. Should they accomplish this, they'll both be rewarded with a glittering gold star on their karmic records, like the kind you used to get in Sunday School — or anyway, like the kind I used to get in Sunday School in West Virginia (when I was very good). Maybe even a whole row of them. Oh, Joy-and-Wonder-Never-Ending!

How do we begin this attempt to tighten the cord of compatibility between Pisces and Sagittarius? With some positive note, naturally, but played in what key? When one meditates on their ruling planets, Neptune (Pisces) and Jupiter (Sagittarius), one realizes that these two do have some solid positive factors linking them in agreement. The planets themselves have a lot in common. (In fact, Jupiter was at one time the ruler of Pisces, before Neptune was discovered.) Whether this 4-10 vibrational combination consists of children or adults, whether it involves two men, two women, or one of each sex — whether the Fish and the Archer struggle for harmony in school, in an office, a laboratory, or a home — they'll save themselves a great deal of grief and aggravation by the simple decision to concentrate on those qualities with which each is blessed that the other can openly respect and admire — and de-emphasize their differences. For instance, the typical Piscean can surely find it in her (or his) gentle heart to respect and admire the Sagittarian's pure streak of shining idealism. The Fish's Neptunian compassion should be deeply touched by this trait in the Archer that covers such a multitude of Sagittarian sins. Of course, when Sag impulsively and playfully arches the Bow of Jupiter's giant idealism, these people being as blunt as they are, their humor being as whimsical as it is, the archery demonstration is sometimes highly individualistic, to state it mildly.

Another positive factor between Pisces and Sag is their mutual fascination with what is not very definitively called "religion." A strikingly large percentage of nuns, priests, rabbis, monks, and ministers are Sagittarius or Pisces Sun Signs. A Fish is drawn into the mystical waters because of Neptune's influence of humility and sacrifice — the Archer because Sagittarians are consumed by curiosity concerning spiritual truth, with results ranging all the way from agnosticism or stark atheism to meditative seclusion in a convent or monastery. Still, those Fish and Archers involved in a religious life-style (or atheism) never lose their sense of humor.

We may need a case in point, so I'll share with you a story of one Archer's final, whimsical resolution of the religious-moral issues that plague Sagittarians and Pisceans alike. It's the ultimate example — the perfect illustration of Sagittarian humor, honesty, and idealism — and 100 percent true. I wouldn't dare relate anything but a true example in a chapter dealing with the brutally frank Sagittarians, who class Truth as the Highest of All Virtues — which it likely is, next to Forgiveness — and who are always quoting to you (like Scorpios) their favorite phrase from the Bible: *Great is truth, and mighty above all things.*

Pisces has nothing against truth either, but the Fish do like to squeeze it, stretch it, shrink it, throw a few garlands of pussy willows round its neck, dress it up a little, because the unvarnished truth is so stodgy, you know? But we'll get to the Neptune Truth Trip later on. Let's move along to our example of the shining idealism, truth, and whimsical humor of Sagittarius. The sex of the Archer is incidental to the character of Jupiter. In this story, the Sagittarian is a man, but our hero might just as well have been a girl Centaur.

To prove to the Fish and Archers that this incident is true, the Sagittarian man's name is Dan Williams — and the source of the incident is his daughter, whose name is Mary Ann Williams Henson, currently residing on the West Coast. That's not specific enough proof for you inquisitive Archers and skeptical Fish? All right then, you may write (to verify or to congratulate) Mary Ann Henson at 861 Sixth Avenue, Suite 219, San Diego, California, 92101. Although Mary Ann's Jupiter-ruled father passed away more than twenty years ago in her hometown of Elizabeth, North Carolina (it's interesting to note that North Carolina is a Sagittarian Sun Sign state), she still remembers his sunny personality with affection — and his fiery idealism with pride. Now you too will always remember Dan Williams with fond affection, I trust, whatever your Sun Sign, but especially if you're a Pisces, whose heart is filled with Neptune's sympathy for the weary and downtrodden (and who also enjoys, like the Archer, seeing snobbish, stuffy people deservedly stifled). For you, dear Fish, and for all of us, Dan Williams struck a ringing blow for Truth which should be emblazoned on a marble monument somewhere, but for the moment, will at least be resurrected in these pages.

All through his Life, Sagittarian Dan aimed his arrows of Jupiter Truth straight to the mark (admittedly sometimes painfully), but his finest bull's-eye arrow was shot forth toward the blue skies of freedom on the unlikely occasion of his death, for Dan's last will and testament contained a most unusual clause. At that time, it was the accepted, woeful wont of the Christ Episcopal Church fathers, in Elizabeth, North Carolina, to conduct their Sunday services with the town's socially prominent and politically powerful *white* parishioners seated in the downstairs pews — and the *black* parishioners safely tucked away out of sight in the balcony pews.

But Dan's will stated, quite candidly and bluntly, that those who desired to pay their last respects to him upon the occasion of his death would have to obey his wishes. (Dan himself was a white man, although this is also incidental.) The directive clause in his will was as follows: Everyone attending his funeral services at the Christ Episcopal Church, where he would be formally receiving the bereaved from his casket — silently, but oh! so eloquently — would be required to observe a new seating arrangement on that day. His *black* friends (who made up nearly the entire Negro population of the community) must be seated in the prestigious and coveted downstairs pews, before the altar — the white mourners seated only in the uncomfortable, tucked-away-out-of-sight balcony pews. It was, in Dan's view, a clear issue of priorities.

On the morning of the funeral services for Dan Williams, the church was filled to overflowing, the seating arrangement dictated by his will adhered to strictly, according to Dan's dying wishes — and the shock of surprise on the humiliated faces of those who were ushered firmly to the balcony pews was something to forever remember. Throughout the services they sat there, ramrod straight and red-faced, in barely suppressed resentment. The Archer had the last word, all the way.

I am certain that somewhere in this place of worship on that miracled May morning, probably over near the stained-glass window through which the Sun was streaming the brightest ever, stood the astral figure of the honor guest, fully cognizant of the scene before him (as all souls who have recently made transition from this dimension to the next always are), with an enormous grin on his face, like a mischievous boy. His widow, his children, and his friends were all smiling too, through their tears, in sheer delight, which lightened the sorrowful burden of their loss that day in the Christ Episcopal Church. And Christ was smiling with them — also Jesus, the carpenter. Dan's Scorpio wife, Nettie (who was secretly proud of his gesture), was to later remark that, although the whole affair embarrassed her dreadfully, she was nevertheless grateful that Dan had decided to play the last of his infernal practical jokes on someone besides her for a change. (But Nettie Williams' Pisces Ascendent was pleased.)

When I heard this true story, my joy was interrupted for an instant by a puzzling question. "How was it," I asked Mary Ann, "that Dan was so sure he'd be able to pull off his glorious Jupiter caper, his thundering chord of Truth? After all, the offended whites might have turned at the door, and left, in a fury. The deacons of the church could have refused to honor his final request, and tactfully suggested that the services be held at home, or in the local funeral parlor. Your father must have been someone important in that southern community. What was his profession, his occupation?" Her answer is the most delicious part of the story.

"He was," Mary Ann twinkled, with a trace of her dad's mischievous grin, "the Democratic ward leader — and the Chief of Police."

Is the magic working? Has it reached all those Pisceans who dream of the Neverland of Brotherhood and Sisterhood, and who are therefore nearer to the Sagittarian ideal than they think? Are you Fish and Archers hopefully grinning at each other now? Do you Pisceans admit that the Sagittarians who bug you are just the type to pull off such a prank, and if you thought you could get away with it, you'd join them? Fantastic! We're making progress.

Just as the frequently cleansing (but also sometimes rude and unnecessary) Sagittarian habit of slinging the awful truth in the face of friend and stranger alike wounds and annoys Pisces, the Fish's habit of playing subtle games with truth hurts and infuriates the Archers, who often angrily accuse the Fish of being outright liars. That's not fair, Sag. Pisces people don't lie. They just now and then avoid the truth. Think about it, and you'll see it's not the same thing. Have you thought about it? Good. Now, think about this. Pisceans have only two reasons for avoiding the truth, on those occasions when they do it. They swim away from an explicit answer or statement of fact either because it (1) involves something very intimate and personal about their own private lives, in which case it's none of your business, or anyone else's (will you please admit that?); or because (2) it might possibly, in the Fish's compassionately considered opinion, be hurtful to someone, and therefore would serve no useful purpose—in which case, you must recognize this as an ethic somewhat less abrasive than your own. Right? Your Jupiter ethic is honesty, whatever the cost or the damage. Their Neptune ethic is evasiveness, to avoid the emotional drain of conflict (for themselves and others) whenever possible. But an ethic is an ethic, whatever form it takes. Correct?

As for you Pisceans, try to be more sympathetic to the *purpose* of those burning barbs of the Archer you'd like to bop over the head with his (or her) own Jupiter Bow. By now, you should realize that the purpose is always integrity, an uncontrollable urge to search for and express the truth. Since all that really matters in any sort of human speech or action is the motive behind it, can you see that the Sagittarian intention, at least, is honorable? True, they say Hell is paved with good intentions, but I rather think that Heaven may be too.

The Archers are free and easygoing as they trot along the pathway of Life, completely independent, scorning self-pity—yet they often neglect duty and responsibility if it interferes with their exciting search for themselves or stands in the way of their goals and wanderlust—and this brings disapproval from Pisces, who can't conceive of placing one's own desires before dutiful service to others who might need them. The kindly, gentle Fish are only rarely irritable as they float calmly around obstacles, unobtrusively charting their patient course upstream, sometimes pausing to linger in the cool stillness behind a waterfall .... making little effort to escape the entanglements of people who need their sympathetic listening ears (or money), even when it creates a detour, or a delay in their long-range plans. They're exasperatingly changeable, first following half a dozen dreams at once, refusing to settle down to the practical pursuit of just one—then deciding to lazily procrastinate for a while, allowing solid opportunities to glide past them, which causes the Fish to merely shrug—but brings an angry scolding from the Archer.

Sag must stop trying to coax Pisces out of the temporary ponds where he (or she) feels fleetingly serene and secure. And Pisces must stop projecting the Neptunian silent doubt that holds Sag back from aggressively following tomorrow's promise. Instead of such futile confrontations, Sagittarius might try to keep those optimistic promises by traveling to the Moon or China, and returning with a handful of stardust to sprinkle on Pisces to prove there do exist out there new worlds to conquer, for those who have the audacity to pursue them — then grin, and say, "See? I told you if you trusted me, I wouldn't let you down." That's the most effective way to lure a reluctant Fish to come out of the water and play leap frog.

In closing, I have saved, to share with you, the very last codicil in Archer Dan Williams' will. He was rumored to have died, perhaps not a wealthy man, yet rather comfortably fixed financially. But alas, Sagittarian Dan had loaned all his money to those in need, over the years. There wasn't a penny left. And so, his bequest to his family was, in his own, beautifully typical Jupiter words, in the last paragraph of his will: *I leave to my wife and children the whole wide world — in which to earn a living!*

Although Pisceans can certainly empathize with Dan's compassionate charity, a Neptune last will and testament would never contain such an inheritance. The modest and humble Fish wouldn't dream of presuming to have the right to give away the whole wide world — for it doesn't belong to them. But there's a deep wisdom in the Sag philosophy.

PISCES: Do you Sagittarians really believe you own the world?

SAG: Of course! *Doesn't everyone?*

☆ ☆ ☆ ☆ ☆ ☆

SAGITTARIUS *Woman* PISCES *Man*

She did not understand, even now. "We must go,"
she said, almost brightly.

"Yes," he answered, faintly.

There will be times when the perplexed girl Archer wonders if she's fallen in love with a Gemini, instead of a Pisces. She's absolutely justified in her perplexity. Pisces and Gemini are both Sun Signs of duality, and in respect of their ability to change dreams and goals in midcourse, for some inexplicable inclination, the Fish and the Gemini Twins are amazingly alike. (Their differences lie in other areas.) But she was also born under the influence of a Sun Sign of duality, the Sagittarius Archer actually being a Centaur, you see — half-horse, half-human. So who is she to question his changeability? She is a Sag, that's who, and Sagittarius can't help questioning everything and anything. This man will give her lots of room for exercising her Jupiter proclivity.

There are, naturally, some Pisces men whose careers and occupations remain relatively stable throughout the years, but they're definitely in the minority. Most Fish are forever fascinated by Life's multiple choices. Sometimes the changes they make are nothing less than startling. I'll give the girl Archer some examples from Life (which is, after all, the logical place to find examples for those living it).

Cripple-Creek raised, but Denver-based (at least, at the moment), Piscean Mike Thornton once dabbled with the possibilities of becoming a gold miner, a horse breeder, a writer, and an artist. Then he switched into a career as a professional landscaper of lawns and gardens, after which he experimented with raising night crawlers. Following this venture, he began an apprenticeship to an electrician, and became an expert in the art of rewiring homes and office buildings. Last week he called me, wondering if his horoscope was favorable to his opening a canteen-discotheque-type operation for *human* night crawlers, complete with pinball games, also maybe dancing, checkers, and chess.

If you Sagittarian girls are feeling a little jittery reading this, you can just imagine the effect on his patient, pretty Taurus wife, Carolyn. She smiles sweetly, lovingly, always supportively, but her fingernails grow shorter every day, from private nibbling. Now Carolyn and Mike have a beautiful, dimpled, new baby daughter, Mandy, a *Libra* child, who is simply *never* going to be able to make up her mind what she wants to do when she grows up, and is positively guaranteed to top her Pisces dad in the quick-change department. Please send your prayers to poor Taurean Carolyn. After all, you women who are trying to keep up with the backflips, jackknives, swan dives, and belly smackers of a male Fish influenced by the elusive Water Element have to stick together, *whatever* your Sun Signs.

There's another Pisces man of whom the Sagittarian girl should be made aware. Mark Shaw. He's a Piscean who graduated from Indiana University Law School, then spent a thriving five years in Aspen, Colorado, as a busy and brilliant attorney, totally engrossed in the practice of his legal profession, apparently quite contented and successful. In the spring of 1978, Mark decided to completely chuck his law practice and toss his shingle in the attic — donned his bright-red "lucky tennis cap" (he has a couple of planets in Aries) and flew to New York to accept a full-time position with the ABC "Good Morning America" show, where he immediately began floating around all over the country, filming special subjects for the program, as producer, director, and writer of these segments — and he appears on camera in them, too! But you'll have to catch him quickly on your television set if you want to see what this Fish looks like. By the time this book is printed he may be leading an expedition to the South Pole, to discover the inner Earth.

These are all the sorts of surprises a Sagittarian girl in love with a Pisces man must prepare herself to experience at various times in their relationship. At first, she won't mind it awfully much. She'll even find it exciting, especially if the changing pursuits of her Fish involve a lot of traveling. She was infected with an incurable case of wanderlust when she was about fourteen, the age at which the typical Archer of either sex leaves home (though some of them leave a few years earlier, at ten or twelve). So in the beginning, she'll cheerfully pack their luggage and optimistically trot along beside him as he follows all those circus parades, trades his drums for a clarinet, or gives up his dental practice to become a computer programmer. In the beginning, she will.

Later . . . . well, later, she may put her fiery foot down — hard. She may glare at him, and say something tactful, like: "Look, dingbat" (you thought only *females* could be called dingbats? Good grief, what a revealing chauvinistic attitude!). Now my concentration has been interrupted. I'll have to begin again. She may glare at him, and say something tactful, like: "Look, dingbat — I'm sick and tired of playing gypsy with you. You've changed careers so many times, even I can't remember whether you wanted to run for congress, open a Japanese tea house, or sell beanbags. You either straighten up and settle down, or I'm going to see how much they'll offer me for you at the zoo. You need a shrink; your head is screwed on backward."

After a few verbal blasts along that line, the sensitive Fish may literally dematerialize from shock. One way or the other, he'll disappear. The next time she sees his face may be in the newspaper, when he's been elected congressman, posing with his new lady friend beside him as a subtle hint to Sag that he's filed for divorce. With American politics the way they are today, that's an entirely plausible situation. Attorney Generals and Presidential advisors go to jail, the brothers of Presidents cheerfully plug booze and judge beauty contests — and ex-Jesuit priest-in-training, California's own Jerry Brown, is rumored to perhaps be considering making rock singing-star Linda Ronstadt his bride. They're probably only good friends, but on the off chance the rumor should ever prove to be true (considering his political aspirations), Linda could be residing in the White House as First Lady of the Land, with the Jefferson Starship and Fleetwood Mac alternating at the Inaugural Ball — and Bob Dylan or Alice Cooper as Secretary of State. So let's face it, anything can happen in the Aquarian Age. Don't misunderstand,

I think the Uranus fresh winds of change are exhilarating and commendable, for the most part — and I'm sure Linda Ronstadt is a sincere and enlightened girl. I'm just emphasizing that my illustrative anecdotes are both reasonable and feasible, in view of current happenings.

Naturally, not every Sagittarian woman is as brutally blunt as the one in our example. Some female Archers are the softer-spoken, more quiet types, and far less expressive, but even they are unexpectedly candid on occasion, and would never win First Prize for Tact. The point is, the Sagittarian girl who impulsively and warmly loves a Pisces man must soften her approach, or she could carelessly and unintentionally break both his spirit and his heart, not to mention lose his rare kind of affection and devotion. And *he* must not be so thin-skinned that he winces every time this lady speaks the truth. She can't help her compulsion to be honest, and she nearly always means well. He'll have to tenderly explain to her how much it hurts. Her Jupiter emotions will be stirred then, probably causing her to be contrite, apologize — and genuinely try to think before she speaks in the future. (However, it's also probable that she'll need periodic reminders.)

The first thing this happy-hearted, well-intentioned Sagittarian girl may want to do, if she's considering raising a school of small minnows, and in general, clowning around on a permanent basis with a Neptune-ruled man, is to determine which kind of Fish he is, for there are two kinds of Pisceans born under this dual Sun Sign. There are those who swim upstream toward success and personal fulfillment and those who float downstream toward failure, their dreams engulfed in waves of misfortune — and end up as beachcombers.

Now, a beachcomber on a beach isn't necessarily a bad risk in "happy" for a curious, adventuresome, female Sag who likes to go barefoot in the sand and eat berries. But the beachcomber who sadly combs and wanders the "beaches" of city streets, heartbreakingly scavenging for self-respect, is another matter. Actually, this may be the very Fish who needs her faith and courage, and I'm not saying she should avoid him. Nothing could be more beautiful than a Jupiter miracle which might save such a lost soul from despair. I'm just saying she should at least initially be aware of which type of Fish with whom she's coping.

A good friend of mine, a Pisces man who lives in Manhattan and often strolls Times Square to check out the passing scene and analyze the colorful human species drifting by, told me about a certain night he stopped in Nathan's, a Broadway landmark, for a midnight snack. Since Nathan's is not exactly a place where the tables are reserved (you pay your quarter, grab your mustard jar, and take your choice), he found himself sitting across from a rather talkative table mate. His clothes were somewhat shabby, in addition to being a couple of sizes too large, and a half-empty wine bottle was tucked into the waistline of his baggy trousers. Still, the general appearance, when you didn't look too closely, was rather dapper — and his personality was undeniably chipper. As they sat there across from each other, passing the napkins and drinking black coffee, this Manhattan beachcomber found my Pisces friend to be a typically Neptune interested and sympathetic listener — so he confided in him his occupation. He sold what he called "hot jewelry." After a furtive glance around to make sure the place was "clean" of night-shift cops at that particular moment, he treated him to a brief peek at his merchandise (rhinestone bracelets and pins and such, which he claimed were diamonds) and did his darnedest to make a quick sale — unsuccessfully, since my New York street-wise friend takes only small change with him on his Broadway night tours. After tactfully explaining his "tap city" financial position, my Fish friend asked the man what his Sun Sign was. With a merry twinkle, this gentle-spoken but spunky lost soul replied, "Who, me? Oh, I'm one of them Pisces characters." But he pronounced the word with a distinct twist, to rhyme with *Hiss*-eez or Ulysses. "Yep," he repeated jovially, "I'm a *Piss*-eez."

My Piscean friend says that, from that moment, he's always thought of a Fish swimming *up*stream as a *Pisces* (pronounced to rhyme with *Pie*-sees) and a Fish swimming *down*stream as a *Piss*-eez. He finds it a helpful distinction. I pass along this observation to the Sagittarius girl, to use in measuring the potential of her Neptune man. Like, for instance, Albert Einstein was clearly a *Pie*-sees.

Because this is a 4-10 Sun Sign Pattern vibration, the Sagittarian woman and Pisces man must expect a certain amount of tension from the occasional clashing of their divergent personalities. His tendency toward self-pity, and her tendency toward self-willfulness, obviously won't make their challenges easier to face, but will only deepen their problems. It's not likely, however, that jealousy and possessiveness will be a major issue of discontent between Pisces and Sag, because neither is really possessive by nature, and both enjoy their freedom too much to deny it to the other (unless an Ascendent or Moon Sign stirs up trouble in this area). Generally and typically, these two are willing to allow themselves space in their togetherness. If there are any minor flare-ups of the little green monsters (or giant green monsters), the chances are greater they will initiate with her. There are some Sagittarian women who are, upon provocation, a touch jealous, though seldom unduly so. When they are, their tempers will blaze quickly. But the typical Sag won't feel the tug of the possessive urge, as the term is commonly interpreted. And there's a difference between "Jealous" and "Possessive."

Sexually, Pisces being a feminine sign, ruled by the also feminine planet Neptune, the Piscean man, to achieve physical harmony with the Sagittarian woman, should make a conscious effort to be less passive and casual, more active and enthusiastic. Yet the same influence makes him a tender and intuitive lover for this woman . . . gentle and imaginative. Sagittarius being a masculine sign, ruled by the also masculine planet Jupiter, she'll have to be careful of his feelings, less impulsive and outspoken. Otherwise, her fiery emotions could discourage his confidence in his ability to bring her fulfill-ment. Yet this same masculine-positive vibration in her auric field also has the power to increase his desire and arouse in him the latent passion of the Water Element. But frequent emotional conflict and tension, while it may stimulate her, will freeze his desire, just as a lack of enthusiastic response, or being ignored, will freeze hers.

So few people ever comprehend the great secret of joyful sexual expression, which is simply that repeated words and acts of genuine *kindness* kindle tiny flames in the heart. These gradually grow into a larger fire, which eventually leads to an ecstatic consummation of the physical need thus awakened. Sex with those who love is basically a gesture of mutual gratitude, not merely the satisfaction of two separate, selfish urges, but a shared awareness of the magnitude of the gift of wholeness. Sex, like everything else, is inescapably governed by the Golden Rule. Otherwise, physical union only leaves both partners with a stronger sense of separateness than ever, feeling even more alone and restless than before.

There are many ties of tenderness and bonds of sympathy between the planets Jupiter and Neptune. Before Neptune was "discovered," Jupiter was the astrological (and astronomical) ruler of both Sagittarius and Pisces, meaning that its influence impressed a similar pattern on Fish and Archers alike. (George Washington, for example, was a more aggressive, Jupiter-guided Piscean.) This kindred empathy of their ruling planets binds the Sagittarian woman and the Pisces man closer than they may realize. They're both compassionate and idealistic. Both of them are tolerant — and normally unshockable. But there are also ways in which the giant Jupiter and the elusive Neptune influences clash. The Jupiter essence despises any trace of Neptunian secrecy, double-talk, or deception, while the Neptune essence is deeply disturbed by the Jupiter kind of honesty that wounds more than it heals — and is repelled by careless, excessive emotions.

But if they love enough, the Sagittarian woman and Pisces man can find a way to dissolve their differences. She must try to be a little more tactful, thoughtful, and gentle, without sacrificing the integrity and independence of the Fire Element in her nature. He must try to be a little more open, direct, and expressive, without sacrificing the spiritual privacy and inner tranquility of the Water Element in his nature. Then they can reflect each other's stars, yet still remain themselves.

☆ ☆ ☆ ☆ ☆ ☆

SAGITTARIUS *Man* PISCES *Woman*

------◆◀◉▶◆------

As they lay side by side, a mermaid caught Wendy
by the feet, and began pulling her softly into
the water. Peter, feeling her slip from him,
woke with a start, and was just in time to draw
her back. But he had to tell her the truth.

Some Pisces girls talk quite a bit, some are quiet and seldom initiate a conversation (although once someone else initiates it, they usually won't be at a loss for words, however shy they may be at first). But the important thing is that, in addition to being interesting conversationalists, *both* kinds of girl Fish are great listeners. I mean, *really* great listeners. So far, wonderful, because the Sagittarius man enjoys talking to someone who pays rapt attention to what he's saying, equally as much as a Leo or an Aries man — and you know how *those* two adore an attentive audience. So that should give you an idea how strongly this girl will appeal to the Archer. Of course, in the middle of one of her listening sessions, he's sure to feel compelled, at one time or another, to make a truthful remark of some sort. If the truth is too blunt, she may stop listening. Pisces women are uncommonly sensitive to hurt — neither do they pursue the unvarnished truth with much energy. This lady prefers truth to be draped in the gossamer veils of "maybe" and "it might have been" or "it could be." No Fish likes her truth served straight on the rocks, the way Sag likes to belt it. Then he'll lose her dainty feminine ear, and he'll wish he hadn't stuck his clumsy foot in his mouth. A bit of warning is helpful. Now he may consider himself warned.

Few people realize that listening is truly an art, difficult to acquire, because most good listeners are born, not made. It requires an unusually sympathetic and unselfish nature, because a good listener is genuinely interested in hearing about people and events outside the *self*, not simply keeping quiet until there's an opportunity to interrupt the speaker. The girl Fish is able, through some sort of Neptune alchemy, to project herself into the situation being verbally described and become as fascinated by it as she would be by any personal situation. She makes what she's hearing into her own vicarious experience, melts into it, is actually part of it, and the Archer knows by her eyes, her expression, her very attitude . . . . that she's not just pretending to be polite. No, what he's saying really matters to this woman. There's no more soul-satisfying feeling in the world than truly being listened to by someone who clearly cares. Every human being needs the lift of such a therapeutic feeling now and then — the Sagittarian man more often. And since it's of such value to him, he should try as best he can to avoid shattering this rare gift the girl Fish offers him, which is one of the loveliest parts of her nature.

Despite the fact that this man and woman must face many tensions and testings of their tolerance and patience within the difficult 4-10 vibration that influences the relationship, if he happens to be one of those occasional Sagittarian males who's often quiet, she'll have a pronounced beneficial effect upon him. We must remember that this kind of Archer isn't quiet *all* the time (no Sag ever born is *that*), but if he's one of the less talkative types — meaning he doesn't talk constantly, but when he's decided to do so, he does rather well — no one can draw out his thoughts with more success than a Pisces woman. She's so good at persuading him to express himself, she makes you wonder why she doesn't become a psychiatrist and be done with it. Some Fish do choose psychiatry as a profession, but the majority of them do not. That's because the typical Piscean hates the concept of prying into other people's secrets (barring an afflicted natal Sun, which can cause the Fish so influenced to become quite gossip-minded). Mostly, Pisces hates the concept of someone delving into their *own* privacy. And since the Fish are so naturally inclined to put themselves in the other person's place, they are reluctant to do unto others what they most definitely do not want others to do unto them.

Nevertheless, without making any particular conscious effort to probe, even in the beginning the Pisces woman will learn a great deal about the Sagittarian man he seldom guesses she's learning. This lady is powerfully perceptive. She'll discover things about him he thinks no one knows (or would be able to perceive), without even trying. She can't help it. It's instinctive with her to "sense" and to "know" what another person is holding back, especially in a love relationship. It isn't that she tried to find out. It's just there for her to read and interpret — as though he might be a human crystal ball she's gazing into. It probably won't make him feel uncomfortable, however, because her talent for penetrating private feelings and intentions is such a subtle, graceful art, never pushy or overtly pressing, as a rule, no one ever suspects it's happening (sometimes not even the girl Fish herself). In fact, if the truth were told, she'd just as soon not possess this aptitude. To her, it's an unwelcome ability. It troubles her mind to sense so many things about people. She has enough of her own worries without adding to them by being unable to prevent the unbidden passing through her consciousness of all those uninvited images belonging to others. Nevertheless, she's fated, it seems, to continually become involuntarily involved in the complications of other people's lives. It's her Neptune twelfth-house Kismet, and one must admit, she accepts it in good grace, with minimal complaining. The gentle art of submission to the inevitable is one of her enviable traits of character.

Not that the Archer will mind her knowing most of his inner thoughts. This is not a man who makes a big thing out of secrecy. Most Sagittarian men don't have a secretive bone in their bodies (unless there's a Scorpio, Pisces, or Cancer Ascendent or Moon Sign). The typical Sag will cheerfully confess anything you'd like to know about him — often more than the Pisces woman would like to hear. He has little or nothing to hide. Just ask him and he'll tell you straight out. If he's broke, he'll say so. If he's worried about his hairline or his boss, he'll tell you. He believes in truth, not evasion. And he thinks everyone should follow his example, in particular the woman he loves. Since some form or degree of evasiveness is part of her Neptunian essence, they may have more than a few quarrels initiated by the various levels of their different approach to honesty, having to do with his definition of hypocrisy — and her definition of the cruelty of unnecessary candor, impatience, rash speech, and impulsive action. Their attitudes toward all these matters may differ somewhat, to state it mildly.

Sexually, the double masculine-influenced Archer will find the double feminine-influenced girl Fish seductively alluring. Nature smilingly cooperates with the physical blending of this man and woman. If only *they* would cooperate. After the initial allurement, the Archer may accuse his Pisces woman of being too cool to his advances, her responses not enthusiastic or spontaneous enough to match the ardor of his own desire. There may be more than a grain of Jupiter truth in his analysis. Unless the Moon or Ascendent of the girl Fish was contained in one of the three Fire elements at her birth, she may indeed be emotionally "cooler" and more detached concerning sexual passion than he could possibly ever be — even if he tried (which he's not about to do). This means it's her responsibility to do the trying (isn't everything always with Pisces?). She's the one who will have to make a conscious effort to match his sudden urges of desire with the same *visibly demonstrated* depth of need. He'll enjoy her sensitive feminine approach to their sexual union — but he'll nevertheless be very hurt by her periodic coolness. The problem seems to be a very clear one. Once it's been analyzed and pointed out, Neptune should instruct her in the ways to solve it.

As for him, he must beware of causing her to think his need for her is concentrated unduly upon the physical aspect of love, and be sure to show his feeling for her in ways other than sexual — which will have the nice round robin effect of eliciting from her a more enthusiastic response to his lovemaking. So he has a few responsibilities too. It's not entirely one-sided.

The Pisces woman needs much gentleness from the man she loves, a whole lot of tenderness. She flowers under imaginative or creative interests, which have the power to enchant her. She blooms visibly when he suggests a trip or change of scene (and so does he). But she wilts into depression when she's subjected to harshness or tactlessness. Her feelings can be wounded repeatedly before he's even aware it's happening, for this woman won't usually show her hurt the first few times. She'll try to hide it or subdue it—to either accept it or forget it. But after a time, it will show. This is his warning signal to soften his attitudes (especially his speech) and realize that his powerful "Fire" may be slowly but surely dehydrating her still "Water."

Of course, it can also work the other way, if she should be one of the Whale-type Pisceans. Then her stronger Water nature can drown his natural Jupiter optimism. And that's equally as sad a fate for a Fire-Water blended pair of lovers or mates who don't try hard enough to overcome the problems of their divergent outlooks, attitudes, and motivations. After a while, they may give up on confrontation, and simply drift further and further apart, until they become total strangers living together under the same roof.

There are only two possible ways of dealing with such a situation. Each of them can decide this "stranger" is not the kind of person he or she would like to get to know better—and they can part as friendly acquaintances, rather than allow their relationship to turn them into bitter intimates. Or they can choose the other attitude one sometimes takes with a stranger. Each of them could decide this is an interesting person he or she would like to get to know better—and begin to become re-acquainted all over again, with both of them wise enough the second time around to know that two people needn't be exactly alike and always agreeing in order to be happy—as long as each respects the other's different viewpoint. Differences can add sparkle to a relationship—or dull it. Which shall it be? It's really their move. So let's leave them alone, pondering their chess pieces. Especially the knight and the pawn. The strategy of love is a very private thing.

Sometimes, that's the major problem. This man and woman may lack as much privacy as their relationship needs to protect it from outside destructive forces. So they should fly away somewhere together and discover the power of a simple thing like privacy to heal broken hearts between two "strangers" who once loved so much. It's often amazing. They can leave the chess board behind, and pick up the game where they left it when they return. Or they can promise to stop playing games with each other permanently. That would be even better—and much luckier for the future of their love affair or marriage. There are some games that no one wins. Not even the high rollers.

CAPRICORN   CAPRICORN

Earth — Cardinal — Negative
Ruled by Saturn
Symbol: The Goat
Night Forces — Feminine

Earth — Cardinal — Negative
Ruled by Saturn
Symbol: The Goat
Night Forces — Feminine

The CAPRICORN-CAPRICORN *Relationship*

◆━◗◆◗━◆

> *It is sad to have to say that the power to fly gradually left*
> *them . . . . In time, they could not even fly after their*
> *hats. Want of practice, they called it; but what it*
> *really meant was that they no longer believed.*

Most children remember how to fly (astral travel) and all sorts of other grand things for some years, a decade or a dozen, say, after their entrance into this stodgy world. But Capricorn children forget quite rapidly. It takes most small Goats only a few months or so to lose all memory of where they came from . . . and what wondrous powers they possessed. By the time they've passed their six-month birthdays they are seldom able to any longer see the druids dancing in the moonlight, under the oak tree, on Twelfth Night Solstice . . . although I know of one small Capricorn girl named Jill, and another named Lael, who remembered them well enough to draw rather charming sketches of them years later.

However, we mustn't sniffle over them in sympathetic sentimentality, because (as I've told you in other Capricorn chapters, and also in my first book, *Sun Signs*) the Goats are chronological miracles. As they grow older, they grow younger. After normal children have long since become boring adults, trotting off to work, their briefcases under their arms, Capricorns — who were all born looking and behaving like their own great-grandparents — will be starting to reverse gears and travel backward toward the blooming cheeks, light hearts and merry, twinkling eyes of true children.

It's Mother Nature's magical gift to the Saturnine Goats. Assisted by old Father Time Saturn, himself, she allows Cappies to begin — slowly and gradually, the way they do everything — to recapture the faith and wonder of their lost youth, when the years of responsibilities have passed. Better late than never. In fact, it may be better, even, than sooner — when you really think about it. The exact calendar age when this miracle occurs is individual with each Goat, but happen it will.

How very perceptive of these people to teach us the valuable lesson that we contained the wisdom of how to be happy when we were born into this earthly existence, then threw it all away, but if we wish, we can make up for our foolishness later, and laugh at arbitrary life spans, even laugh at the false propaganda that the process of death and decay is unavoidable. Trust Saturn, the ruling planet of Capricorn, to teach that sort of lesson. Saturn's tests for the soul are wearying and severe, but his rewards never fail to be solid gold, and lasting.

The way it works out with a pair of Goats is that they may have a somewhat smothering and restrictive influence on each other when they're young, but together they'll have more fun than a whole cageful of baboons later on. Of course, when they're younger, they make up for their precocious maturity and stifling caution by sharing their shy sweetness and cozy dependability. Admittedly, with some Capricorns — though not all — this may be soured a bit at times by gruffness and sternness. Nevertheless, the qualities of sweetness, coziness and dependability are worth a little mutual crankiness. It's comforting to a Goat to have another Goat around, someone who is reliable — someone who will still mean on Tuesday week exactly what he or she said on Saturday last. Especially if you've been hanging around with a bunch of Geminis, Librans or Aquarians. It can be a blessed relief.

When two Capricorns toss in their lots together — no, that doesn't sound right, Cappies never toss anything. When two Capricorns carefully enter an office, home, classroom or bank together, they communicate with one another much in the same manner as busy ants, with their antennas wiggling silently, bustling away in perfect coordination and understanding. Whatever they do, they will be working admirably hard at doing it. Even if they are only talking together, they work hard at saying things that matter, that *mean* something, rather than just exchanging silly superficialities. Capricorns absolutely *never* exchange silly superficialities. If you'll picture Capricorns Howard Hughes, Carl Sandburg, Gary Cooper, Richard Nixon, Humphrey Bogart, J. Edgar Hoover and novelist Henry Miller sitting around together having a fireside chat, discussing matters of mutual concern and interest with Capricorns Jill Kemery Goodman, Steve Mackin, Lael Weisman, Royce King, Sinthia Sullivan, Lennart Mucke, Evelyn Brewer and Rachael Fallon, you will not expect the conversation to consist of silly superficialities or expect them to be wasting their time in inconsequential chitchat and meandering minutiae.

Now, you might say, "I don't know Jill Kemery Goodman, Steve Mackin, Lael Weisman, Royce King, Sinthia Sullivan, Lennart Mucke, Evelyn Brewer or Rachael Fallon, so how can I picture such a scene ?" You are wrong. You *do* know them, because I've told you their Sun Signs; therefore, you know them as well as I, or at least well enough to picture them. Astrology is that reliable, especially when it comes to Goats. Other Sun Signs may deviate and differ here and there in their Sun Sign attributes, due to additional planet positions at their birth, but Cappies almost never deviate or differ in the basic Sun Sign essence, despite their other planetary positions. They root into the Earth and behave with nearly perfect predictability, bless their hearts. Whether they are naughty or nice, they are predictable. You can see why they like to flock together. They know they can trust one another. (And while they are trusting one another, they keep one eye open for any monkey business.) Did I say "flock together" ? I'd like to retract that descriptive phrase. Most Goats are loners — or they have just one very good chum for a lifetime of chumming. Never more than three. That's a rule written into the Saturn Constitution, called the Third Saturnine Amendment. When it comes to people picking, a Capricorn's first choice for good company is often another Goat. If not, then some other Earth Sign, followed in preference by a Water Sign. Most of them tend to be extremely wary of Fire and Air Signs, and this may be one of their few misjudgments, because life requires a mixture of personalities to be interesting.

A Capricorn seldom complains about another Capricorn's faults and failings, which is quite sensible of them, because they have the same faults and failings. It's like criticizing yourself. They also benignly smile upon each other's virtues, which, again, is only natural. Like all other Sun Signs, most Goats think their faults are great strengths, and so when they see them reflected in another Saturn person, they approve.

Almost every Capricorn is devoted to relatives and family, sometimes grudgingly, and with a sigh of resignation, but nevertheless, devoted. Once in a while one of these typical family-worshiping Cappies enters an association or relationship with the rare kind of Goat who has, for heavy and soul-wrenching reasons, cut ties with his or her family. The first or typical Cappy will deeply sympathize with such a situation, and have the good sense not to nag the other about it, but he or she will be secretly very deeply affected and will treat the Goat who is separated from "family" with unusual gentleness and compassion.

From youth through adulthood, until the reverse aging syndrome begins, Capricorns are dyed-in-the-wool realists. They face life squarely, without flinching. When life socks it to them, they don't whine, complain or try to pin the blame on someone else. They simply get up, dust themselves off and make a practical decision about how to turn their failure into at least a semblance of success. These people will figure the most deviously deliberate ways to attempt to salvage something of value from any kind of wreckage of their plans. When I said they won't try to pin the blame on anyone else, I should have added that they also dislike to shoulder the blame themselves. That's because they never make mistakes. Or if they do, they are not enthusiastic about admitting these rare slip-ups. They may glance around a little nervously, chastise themselves privately with great severity, but they will seldom publicly say "I'm sorry — I was wrong — forgive me." Capricorns feel that the best way to handle a goof is to bury it, make a firm mental note never to allow it to occur again, and do nothing to call undue attention to it. After burying a mistake, the Goat will not set up a road sign with an arrow pointing to the spot. Only now and then will a Capricorn with an afflicted Sun or Ascendent say or do something against his or her own nature. Most of the time the Goats will take a rusty failure, the nails and broken glass of defeat or ridicule, and do their darnedest to Scotch-tape or glue them together into something *usable*. They don't always succeed, of course, but they are determined, and they usually won't back down unless they see a steamroller headed toward them. Then Cappy will move. For these people are, to repeat — practical. They're extremely shrewd at estimating the extent of their difficulties and the basics of the situation, whatever it may be. Note that I said "estimating," not guessing. Capricorns never guess. They estimate. There's a difference. The former is chancy, the latter is based on data and deduction.

Unlike Taurus people, who will shove despite all obstacles, and who sit obstinately while the steamroller runs right over them, Capricorn is level-headed and wise enough to know when retreat is the only solution short of total disaster. If there's one thing Goats try to avoid at all cost, it's total disaster. They'll utilize every aspect of disappointment, every twist and turn of fate to some sort of advantage before discarding it — as Nature's billy goats will find something of nutritional value or chewing pleasure in whatever you offer them.

This is why, when two Capricorns get together, they can make gigantic successes from only small scraps of possibilities. They plod along, side by side, not wasting any more time speculating than absolutely necessary, getting things in the proper perspective and paying strict attention to priorities. After a reasonable length of time, they reach their combined goals — and no one deserves an achievement more. They worked for it, earned it and waited for it. It's hard to resent a Capricorn team's success or begrudge them their security, because you know they paid their dues to get there (but not a penny more!). Goats are not really stingy, they're genuinely generous with their real friends (all three of them) and their families — just a little reserved with the cash when it comes to anyone else.

The association of two Capricorns is not all seriousness and sacrifice. Only about three fourths of the time. But, during that remaining fourth, these two can enjoy life more than others ever suspect. For the Goat finds deep pleasure and satisfaction in Nature, art, music . . and improving the mind. Cappies can find happiness and excitement in anything that makes good sense, and that includes a lot of things. Tinkering with cars or engines, building or constructing, gardening, reading, creating beauty from the plain and ugly, watching the interest grow in their savings accounts — challenge and inspire the Goats. To be able to remodel an old shirt into wearability, or to mend the broken washing machine so it agitates like new, thrills them. The women darn socks and patch the dish towels; the men putty up the cracks and turn old glass bottles into lamps. It seldom bothers two Capricorns to be snowed in during a blizzardy winter. They have, literally, a thousand and one things to keep them busy and contented.

Most Cappies are unusually kind to pets. They'll never spoil an animal, fuss over it or allow it to get hairs all over their navy-blue sweaters, but they will be good to it. They also love babies, the small and teeny-tiny human infants and animal kingdom babies equally (secretly they adore them), but they will never be found "kitchy-cooing" them. At least one Goat I know, Royce King (the one you said you didn't know, but you really *do*), keeps the symbol of his Sun Sign, a pet Goat named Gomer, right in his front yard in Cripple Creek, Colorado. Gomer is not allowed by Cappy and his Virgo wife, Laverne, to come in the house and eat dinner at the table, but aside from that, he is definitely a "member of the family." No Goat ever had it so good, because you know how Capricorns are about "family." If you want to see a Capricorn's hard heart go suddenly soft, try as he or she will to disguise it, just show the Goat an appealing kitten or puppy or cuddly baby — including a baby porcupine. These folk, who spurn any sort of "mushy" talk or overt sentiment, verbally or otherwise, will see a two-month-old puppy and exclaim, involuntarily, "Oh, the adorable thing! Look at his fat little paws, and his plump little tummy, and his soft little eyes." Then they'll blush furiously, compose their features and remain silent for an hour or so to punish themselves for capitulating to an open display of emotion.

Capricorns are greater secret-keepers than either Cancer or Scorpio, and the deepest secret they keep (from everyone but each other) is their sentiment, buried beneath Saturn's strict composure and self-control, all the more intense for being so suppressed. Once two Capricorns reach within to strike that chord in each other's hearts, the music of their mutual vulnerability will move them to the kind of recognition that brings unwonted tears to their eyes.

Capricorn Howard Hughes is the ultimate example of the Saturn nature.

Yes, you read the verb correctly, I said *is* — not *was*. He exemplifies the pure strain of Saturnine responsibility, seriousness and dogged determination to climb to the mountain peak. He's a loner, with Saturn's preoccupation with the mechanical — and the great, sweeping vision of Capricorn for practical, not frivolous, miracles. He possesses (no, not possessed, but possesses — *present* tense) the intense Capricorn ambition, the wisdom to keep his own counsel, Saturn's brooding silences and inky spells of depression and futility — also Capricorn's innate shyness and rigid self-discipline, plus the insistence that his associates and few friends (the normal Cappy quota of three) be as sensible, efficient and loyal as he is himself. Beneath all his hardness and firmness of purpose lies a softness and sentimentality, a gentleness and tenderness only a very few would ever guess were there — and even fewer have ever glimpsed. Then too, there's the matter of Capricorn's longevity (don't forget the magical reverse-aging process either), and Hughes fits also these Saturnine nuances. Astrologically and historically, the planet Saturn is synonymous with the cold and the north, which is why the Goat is more content living in sub-zero temperatures than most of the rest of us. (Neither is Hughes an exception to this rule of Capricorn.) Since Saturn keeps secrets so well, it's both appropriate and proper that a great secret is contained within this chapter, to be revealed sooner, perhaps, than anyone knows. Except, of course, the Goat. You can be sure the sensible time for revelation will be chosen. Capricorn never rushes things, and instinctively avoids the premature. One might also add that the Capricorn sense of humor and sense of timing are both exquisite. This, also, fits the picture of the aforementioned secret. It seems almost superfluous to add that Saturn, in astrology, has domain over wills, as in "last will and testament." When dealing with any Capricorn, especially *this* one, it's well to remember that sense of humor.

Two Goats frolicking (they do sometimes frolic) together can result in a beneficent scene for both. Even as children, these two normally get along remarkably well, quietly using their Crayolas, taking turns placing pennies in their piggy banks and, on the whole, having a gently jolly time of it. As adults, they may have some differences, and since Capricorn is a Cardinal Sign of leadership, there could be a taffy pull now and then over who is really in charge of the association or relationship, but they are less wearing on each other's nerves than other 1-1 Sun Sign Patterns frequently are. They are, of a certainty, less shy with each other than they are with others, more relaxed.

The typical Capricorn has a kind of blanket rule about everything: *Whenever you're in doubt about something, don't do it, because it's likely to be wrong.* And another rule: *Don't rush into things. Time is always on your side.* Wouldn't you just know that Cappy would consider Time (ruled by Saturn) a good friend, rather than an enemy? When a couple of compatible Goats join their industrious hands, hard heads — and most important, their gentle hearts — they're guaranteed of doubling their already impressive individual potentials for solid achievement, financial security and emotional serenity, and what could be more sensible, more practical than that ? The last sentence contains a *"drawoh-drabor"* twin riddle. Don't try to guess it. The answer is too mind-boggling, unless your mind does not boggle easily. Saturn minds do *not*.

☆ ☆ ☆ ☆ ☆ ☆

CAPRICORN *Woman* CAPRICORN *Man*

◄◆►

[Him:] "Fame, fame, that glittering bauble, it is mine,"
he cried. . . . "Is it quite good form to be distinguished
at anything ?" the tap-tap from his school replied.
. . . . Most disquieting reflection of all, was it not
bad form to think about good form ?

[Her:] Wendy was grown up. You need not be sorry for her.
She was one of the kind that likes to grow up. In
the end she grew up of her own free will a day quicker
than other girls.

When a Capricorn man receives a gift, although he'll be shyly and secretly pleased, he will, nonetheless, accept it with some slight suspicion and examine it with caution — including the gift of love.

And so, if the Goat appears to treat the Capricorn girl's gift of love a little suspiciously, and examines it with great care, before accepting her devotion and returning to her his own total commitment, she really has no right to become unduly upset. This happens to be exactly the way she handles his gift of love to her. It's a matter of who capitulates and gives whose heart to whom first. Whichever one takes the lead in this 1-1 vibration must suffer the penalty of cautious acceptance from the other. But *somebody* has to make a move *sometime*. A man and woman who are powerfully attracted can't go on silently stalking out each other forever.

Seldom do Cappies fall in love at first sight, or overnight — or even after a few days, weeks or months. It can happen, of course; anything can happen when the element of human nature is awash in romance, but it normally takes a respectable length of time for both the boy and the girl Goats to admit they've lost their self-control to the extent of needing another person, that they've permitted themselves to place personal happiness within another's power to bestow — or to refuse to bestow, as the case may be. Cappy does not usually release the reins of power, without a long, hard struggle. A Capricorn does not like to *need*. The Goat believes that "needing" is a synonym for "weakness."

With all their wisdom and good sense, the Capricorn man and Capricorn woman could use a few lessons in the subject of human emotions. They have to learn to recognize the great role "need" plays in real love. It may seem presumptuous of a mere Ram to attempt to teach anything to Saturn people, but even they can stand an occasional refresher course in the intangibles of the heart.

To love, and know that we are loved in return, allows us to approach gloriously near the higher levels of happiness of our aptly named Higher Selves. To love is not, by itself, enough. Nor is it sufficient to simply *be* loved. *Reciprocity* is the necessary ingredient for any romantic recipe, the yeast, the leavening — without which the emotions will starve for the lack of complete nourishment.

Another way to say "to love, and be loved in return" — is: "to *need*, and be *needed* in return." No matter how desperately the Saturnine man and woman's pride in their self-sufficiency may struggle against the knowledge, love and need are identical twins — though not in the context of a need for material things. Everyone, especially Capricorn, knows that one doesn't have to *love* one's banker, although one surely does *need* one's banker, from time to time. Or one's dentist. Or auto mechanic. Or the telephone company. Admittedly, we desperately *need* Ma Bell, but I know of no one who really *loves* the greedy, Midas-wealthy, domineering, monopoly-minded Matriarch (and never mind her Public Relations sweet-talk). When I say that "need" is synonymous with "love," I'm speaking of needing in an emotional sense, in the context of needing something related to the *heart*, not related to things of intrinsic value. However, under the law of the macrocosm-microcosm (as above, so below), the material type of need is what makes the pairs called "strange bedfellows," in politics and other areas of life.

You Capricorns must remember that, in order for you to be able to *love*, the one you love must be vulnerable in some way, must have some weakness that only your strength can support, only your compassion can overlook — in short, must *need* you. In order to *be* loved, you must, yourself, be in some way vulnerable, possess some weakness, which only the strength of the one you love can support, only his or her compassion can overlook — and love you anyway — in short, you must *need* that person, just as that person must need *you*. Only when need is thus *mutually* experienced and exchanged by both partners, does love begin to grow.

Such a delicate miracle as love can be so easily overbalanced, on one side or the other. It's impossible to love when all we feel is respect and admiration for someone, yet can find no vulnerabilities in him — or in her — which cause that person to *need* us, therefore causing *us* to feel *needed*. Conversely, it's *equally* impossible to love when all we feel is sympathy or compassion for another person, yet can find nothing in him — or in her — to respect or admire, nothing that causes us to *need* the other person in order to make our *own* happiness complete. This sort of interchange of need is why love must be a two-way street — or be simply unrequited infatuation, on the part of the man or the woman. End of the Ram's lecture to the Goat.

Now that we've established, I hope, the necessity of need, we've removed the largest boulder in the path of the Capricorn man and woman who genuinely care about each other. Once they've learned that mutual need is permissible, even desirable, they'll be ready and willing to make an also mutual confession that they've fallen in love. The next obstacle, which is a rather sizable rock, although nowhere near the immensity of the first, is the sticky situation that occurs should their families not happen to get along together. This is a tough one.

Here he is, ready to accept her Capricorn gift of love, having carefully inspected it for endurability — and his contrary cousin Horace refuses to join them for Thanksgiving dinner because he's not speaking to *her* trigger-tempered Uncle Tony, who was invited as long ago as last Easter. Here *she* is, ready to commit herself to her Goat for a lifetime, having assured herself that he'll be a faithful husband, earn enough money to keep their heads above water and be a good father, who will make sure the children have braces, the proper vitamins and go to a good college — and *his* family is threatening to spoil it all by this emotionally immature attitude toward *her* family. If his cousin Horace and her Uncle Tony refuse to call a truce, the two Cappies may not break off their marriage plans over it, perhaps — but they might do something that tragic and drastic if the antagonists are closer relatives, like siblings, Mama or Papa. It's advisable for the male and female Goats to test the compatibility of their mutual families before things get serious, if they want their relationship to remain stable and trouble-free.

It's seldom that a Capricorn man and woman in love will find discussions of money a troublesome aspect of their union. If they're typical Goats, about the only quarrels they'll have over money are which would be the safest bank to salt it away in, and which interest plan is the soundest in the long run (unless the Moon or Ascendent of one or both should be in a Fire or Air element; then there might be some scattered disagreements).

The reason the typical Capricorn woman is so cozily compatible with a

Capricorn man is that, not only is he as quietly ambitious as she, but he may be the only male prepared to face her outward toughness head-on, yet still be able to sense her hidden softness, and appreciate her as a woman. The Goat Girl is amazingly self-sufficient, and that puts off men who view it as a threat to their delusion of women being the weaker sex. Not so this man. He admires her toughness and her strength, her refusal to allow sentiment to rule her decisions or her life, and the fact that she looks for happiness in the same location where he digs for it — on solid, secure ground. A Goat Girl seldom indulges herself in ultra-feminine, excessive sentimental behavior, unless her heart happens to catch her when she's not looking.

That's just what the male Goat may do, if her heart doesn't do it — catch her when she's not looking. The average Saturn-ruled male underplays his emotions so instinctively, possesses such a great sense of romantic timing, is so patient and so willing to wait for the right opportunity, that she may allow him to become an integral part of her life, thinking they're only friends — until she suddenly realizes he means much more to her than just another Capricorn chum, with whom she can discuss her practical dreams. But dreams are dreams, practical or not, with a powerful hold over the emotions. And when she finds someone whose aspirations are as high as her own, who smiles with her gently when something's really amusing, rather than laughing loudly over nonsense, who never lies to her, and has a way of looking into her eyes calmly, with his own quiet ones . . someone who can be tender, without being embarrassingly emotional, who's kind to her family (and his), knows how to fix his own car (and hers) when it breaks down, and has a respectable bank balance attached to his plans for tomorrow . . . some bright afternoon when he's mending her clutter boots, she will recognize him as one of those practical dreams, maybe even the most important one.

Chances are, by the time her slow awakening to the truth of the matter occurs, he will already have selected her — privately — as the woman he wants as the mother of his children, the custodian of his home (the one he's going to build that's on his carefully calculated schedule for the future) — and the only girl he would ever permit to use his treasured chain saw to cut wood. He will be prepared for her realization that she loves him, and will have been long expecting the new light in her eyes. He'll know exactly what it means. Furthermore, he'll know exactly what to do about it. All the while he's been waiting, he's been planning this moment, so there's no chance he'll fumble it. Everything he says — and does — will be just right.

One thing with an excellent chance of being "just right" between them will be the physical aspect of their love. It can be an earthquaking expression of deep feeling, a way to release all the emotion they both keep under such strict control in other facets of their lives — with other people. The joyous discovery that they can allow their emotions full scope in the privacy of their intimate sexual relationship can be compared with the thrill

Columbus must have felt when he first sighted land. To be able to free your inner and controlled, but insistent desires with someone you trust, someone who understands you totally, brings peace and contentment to both the mind and the body.

This sort of fulfillment from the physical demonstration of their love may not be discovered overnight. Neither did Columbus discover America overnight. The first sure sign that his dream would come true was when he saw the floating twigs and soaring birds that meant land was just beyond the horizon. So it is with this man and woman, when they see the first signs of gentleness and affection from each other. Patience and tenderness are strong building blocks for passion.

Very few male or female Goats are jealous by nature, but they *are* often possessive. There is a difference. If they're not alert to the potential problem, they may gradually grow to possess each other to the exclusion of missing the benefits of individual freedom. When I use the term "individual freedom," in no way do I intend to convey the permissive individual freedom theories promoted by the "open marriage" fanatics. Individual freedom need not be the freedom to indulge in sexual experimentation with multiple partners. An emotional commitment between two people that includes this sort of "freedom" is not a commitment at all, but self-delusion. What I mean by individual freedom is the wisdom that allows both partners in a relationship to be themselves, since that's the only way they can remain exciting, interesting and challenging to each other. The Capricorn man and woman who tend to smother each other should hang one of those posters over the fireplace that says: *If you love something very, very much, let it go free. If it does not return, it was never meant to be yours. If it does, cherish it forever!*

All 1-1 Sun Sign Patterns create an over-emphasis on both the positive and negative qualities of the sign, and so Cappy and Cappy will have to realize that too much of a good thing can be a bad thing. The "good thing" of their caution, when doubled in intensity between them, can become a dangerous restriction that could slowly but surely bury their dreams beneath tons of earth. Their mutual innate reserve with strangers, if overdone, can cause them to appear to be a cold couple indeed to those who could become richly rewarding friends. The combining of their natural Saturn economical tendencies can stifle any chance they have of reaching the top of the mountain, sort of boomeranging back upon their shared ambition — and delaying their goals. Taking a chance, now and then, whatever the odds, would be a very healthy thing in this relationship. Capricorns tend to seek the "glittering bauble" of Fame persistently, then reject it for fear it may burst. This sort of self-imposed restriction buries many of their most shining daydreams beneath mountains of unnecessary caution.

It's no use asking the Cappy man and woman to take a chance on Life to the extent of cashing in their insurance policies, and recognizing that these indicate a fear of the future, rather than confidence. There's hardly a Capricorn on the face of the Earth who doesn't own a paid-up insurance policy on his own life, his wife and children's lives, their home, their health, their cars, his chain saw, her sewing machine or artist's drawing board, the silver-framed group photo of their families, the oil paintings of their great-grandparents — and everything else of a material value it's possible to guarantee against loss or theft. We'd get nowhere trying to convince this man and woman to trust in tomorrow or reminding them that the most effective way to insure and guarantee that something negative does occur is to expect or to fear that it *will* occur — and the most reliable insurance that anything negative will *never* happen is the inner security of *knowing* it *won't* — because the typical Saturn-ruled Goats wouldn't comprehend this sort of spiritual advice. (Neither would a lot of Cancerian Crabs, Taureans or Scorpions.)

And so, instead, I'll remind them that none of the insurance companies that have become fat corporate cats through providing people with a sense of security by anticipating every major and minor worry of which the human mind can conceive, have ever been able to figure out a way to make a profit from offering an insurance policy on love. Because the lovers themselves are in control of the destiny of their love, the human element makes it too risky a venture. There are no money-back guarantees attached to love — no large cash pay-offs in case of loss, theft, accident or death-of-the-relationship.

I'll bet you never thought of that, did you, Cappy? Just imagine. The absolutely most valuable, precious thing you own in all the world . . . uninsur-able. A true tragedy. But not unless you allow it to be. Actually, your love is as easy to guarantee against future damage as everything else you've both always sought to insure — including your health, your property and your life. No monthly premium payments required. The name of the policy is: *Faith*. You won't find it listed in the Yellow Pages of your phone directory, but you'll find it if you look inside your hearts, under "M" . . for Miracle.

☆ ☆ ☆ ☆ ☆ ☆

CAPRICORN

Earth — Cardinal — Negative
Ruled by Saturn
Symbol: The Goat
Night Forces — Feminine

AQUARIUS

Air — Fixed — Positive
Ruled by Uranus
Symbol: The Water Bearer
Day Forces — Masculine

The CAPRICORN-AQUARIUS *Relationship*

> *The extraordinary upshot of this adventure*
> *was . . . but we have not decided yet that this*
> *is the adventure we are to narrate.*

Picture Old Man Saturn, with his lined face and beard, scythe and sickle — stern-looking, severe, strict but kindly. Now picture wild Uranus, thundering riddles in a booming voice, flashing lightning from his eyes, wearing daffodils in his hair, and playing with a yo-yo. Can you see any similarity or grounds for intimacy? Well, there are some but . . . .

It's extremely difficult to predict the outcome of any kind of getting together of these two Sun Signs. Mostly, it will depend on the Moon Signs, Ascendents, and such. It may also depend on how tolerant Capricorn can be of the slightly pixilated Aquarian personality. Or how quickly Aquarius gets bored by the Goat's eternal insistence on the status quo, when the Water Bearer's whole purpose on this planet is to shake up the status quo. Being a 2-12 Sun Sign Pattern, Capricorn dimly senses some intriguing lesson to be learned from Aquarius, the sign ahead of the Goat on the karmic wheel of

Life — and Aquarius tends to be more sympathetic toward Cappy's little flaws and compulsions than of the peculiarities of the other eleven signs. Aquarius has already been there, has lived through the Saturn experience during at least one past incarnation, and therefore tends to understand the Goat's hang-ups regarding duty, responsibility, and tradition. But this time around, he (or she) is here to break with tradition — even though Aquarius still recalls how it was during that lifetime when such things assumed great importance, remembering it all subconsciously.

Despite the rare occasions when Capricorns exhibit a quiet and delightful humor, they are essentially serious-minded folk. Their Saturnine dry humor, accompanied by twinkling eyes and a shy little smile, is mostly tongue-in-cheek. Along with their basically sedate dispositions, Goats have a strong sense of the practical, which is usually more visible than their humor. Although Aquarius is a Fixed Sign and Aquarians can therefore be quite determined and purposeful, these men, women, and children are not anywhere near as serious as Capricorn. Aquarius, in fact, enjoys toppling the sedateness of other signs — in particular, Capricorn's. The Water Bearer will inevitably shock the Goat in various major and minor ways when Capricorn least expects it. Aquarius does everything when people least expect it. That's the whole point of shocking. If people expect it, there's no surprise element — and Aquarius simply adores being the bearer of surprises.

A Capricorn associated with the Water Bearer may read these words, murmuring . . . "I've never been surprised or shocked by this person I know so well." The Goat should say "this person I *think* I know so well." Because one fine day Capricorn will find a Brussels sprout in the toothpaste glass that hangs over the bathroom sink — and do a double take. Aquarius will wonder what all the fuss is about. What difference does it make anyway? I mean, didn't you ever get to wondering if a Brussels sprout would sprout in a glass of water, like other plants do — and get curious about the same time you started to take a shower? Doesn't everyone?

No. Everyone does *not.* Capricorn, especially, never wonders about anything that isn't practical. The Goat is unconcerned about whether Brussels sprouts will sprout in water, or whether cauliflower will flower, for that matter — unless he (or she) is a gardener by profession or owns a vegetable market. Even then, Cappy's most consuming interest will be profit and loss. Capricorns of both sexes need the security quilt of a reasonable bank balance to avoid breaking out in a rash, with their ultra-sensitive but often lovely and translucent skins. Not as large a bank balance as Cancer needs to prevent trembling in terror of poverty, but reasonable.

Aquarius seldom does anything reasonable by Saturn standards. To Aquarius, a thing is reasonable if it adds to the knowledge of the world and what makes it spin on its axis. Never mind what other people think. What other people think is the last thing Aquarius worries about. The very *last.* The next-to-the-last thing these Water Bearers worry about would be, let's see . . . social customs and personal appearance. Typical Aquarians make their *own* social customs, set their *own* rules. As for the Uranian appearance, these people sometimes look so strange and unreal in their choice of threads and hair styles (weird is actually the more fitting word) that you'd be surprised how many of them are mistaken for immigrants from an errant UFO. This studied carelessness and originality of dress, manners, and public opinion naturally mortifies and distresses Capricorn, to whom the most important thing in Life is to be well thought of by one's neighbors. No, *first* by the members of one's family. *Then* the neighbors. After that — friends, acquaintances, and business associates. On reflection, perhaps best to reverse the order, and place business associates first. And finally . . . . the whole world. It would disturb the typical Cappy if some stranger in Scotland didn't approve of his (or her) shoes, and the Goat somehow got wind of this humiliation. That's another thing. Along with Pisces and Virgo, Capricorns are all uncommonly interested in their booties. Their footwear is a major concern — and the purchase of new shoes or boots is a matter to be considered carefully, from all angles, with the cost, the proper fit, and the serviceability of equal importance.

There are, however, some ways in which these two are alike. One of them is that the judgments made by Aquarians are based on firm principles and rockbound facts (something most people don't realize). These always determine the final decisions of both Sun Signs. But Uranus bestows upon Aquarius flashing streaks of intuition, enabling Water Bearers to skip over all the *useless* principles and rockbound facts to the real truth, somewhere beyond. Still, he or she *began* the judgment with principles and rockbound facts. I know it's a little confusing, but "confusing" is a word invented by Uranus people. Aquarians think and plan so far ahead, with such an odd mixture of practicality and vision, their ideas and ideals may not manifest for many years — so they appear to be dreamers to the average mind, particularly to the level-headed Capricorn. You must always remember that Aquarius is the sign of genius and insanity, in just about equal proportions. The Goat sympathizes with neither. In fact, to most Capricorns, the two words are synonymous (which they are, in an intricate way). So there could be problems of communication.

It's usually difficult for Capricorn to believe in the illogical, the unreasonable, the impractical, or the nonfactual. To Aquarius, there is no such word as impossible in the Uranus dictionary, and the Water Bearers believe it should also be stricken from every thesaurus, unless it's defined as a word describing an attitude that should be avoided. Aquarians all have in common a most curious, inquiring nature. They're unusually susceptible to the illumination of inspiration, having few or no prejudices — and this includes prejudice against facts. Aquarius has nothing against a theory with facts to support it — any more than he or she has anything against a theory *without* facts to support it. The Uranus-ruled mind is so wide open you'd think their brain cells would catch their death of pneumonia. But they seem to thrive on it, like the Eskimos thrive on the ice floes. Brain cells, being electronic, are very Aquarian-like themselves. Even Saturn brain cells — if Cappy would give them a chance to leap around on the trampoline of the imagination more often.

I have known, admittedly, Capricorns who are deeply involved and interested in matters such as UFO research, astrology, reincarnation, and metaphysics — but not many. And those who are have other planetary configurations in their horoscopes, giving them more daring instincts of imagery, more simple faith in the unseen, more childlike trust. The typical Goat is anything but childlike. The closest most of them get to childlike innocence is during the second half of Life, when they at last begin to enjoy the carefree abandon they missed as youngsters — about the same time Aquarius is cartwheeling through the marvelous Uranus brand of "second childhood" (unkindly and very falsely called by some "senility"). So one might say that these two get along famously when they're both older — but the younger they are, the more they'll be inclined to think each other's personalities and habits are freaky.

Capricorn novelist Henry Miller is an archetype example of the glorious freedom and childlike glee the Goats experience after they've released themselves from Saturn's prison. The older Cappy Henry gets, the brighter the twinkle in his eyes, the younger he looks, and the more outrageously he behaves.

When one of Henry's ex-wives left him, she took all the furniture and furnishings along with her, leaving Henry sitting there on the floor, literally. The first thing the Goat did was quite properly Saturnine, practical, and economical. He got boxes from the grocery store to sit on and eat on. Made a dining room table out of them too. After a while, he says, "I got this sudden idea. I said to myself, Henry, goddamn it, why don't you get a pair of roller skates and go roller skating through the rooms here? I had a marvelous time!"

You see? As soon as Henry was paroled (as all Cappies are, at various individual ages past thirty or so) from Saturn's stern grip of propriety, an onlooker couldn't outwardly tell the difference between this Goat and a Water Bearer. But a Capricorn is still a Capricorn at heart, paroled or not. Only recently, as I write this in 1978, the Saturn-ruled novelist criticized the student protests of the sixties by remarking that their protesting was too feeble. "You don't do it by getting drunk and insane," he intoned. "You've got to have all your wits, to be more clever than the man you want to beat." Pure Saturnine philosophy.

A Goat is a Goat, even taking into account Capricorn's reverse aging process, but I'm sure Henry wouldn't be above wearing a garland of daffodils when the mood hits him — and if a yo-yo happened to be handy, he'd have it spinning like a champion. The young at heart and otherwise youthful Goats reading this might want to send Henry a yo-yo as a kind of code between them . . . . and the Water Bearers could send him some daffodils (which he'd promptly paint — painting being his newest hobby, proving he's as talented an artist as a writer). Pacific Palisades, California, will reach him. He'd be delighted.

While the Goats are still trying to reach the mountain peak of their ambitions, however, they frown on foolishness and frivolity of all kinds. The Aquarian who has such a simple, merry knack for stringing together fascinating words that make no sense . . . . who is touched by the wonderful madness of genius . . . . tosses stars into wishing wells and dreams of pink frogs . . . . can appear to be strange indeed to the earthy Capricorn, who believes in working to make wishes come true. Goats normally speak only words of common sense, so naturally the Uranus natives may sometimes seem to them like creatures from another world, not sensible, ordinary, day-to-day Earthlings. How can frogs be pink, and moreover, why should they be? Green is a perfectly good, satisfactory color for frogs.

I can attest to this Saturn reaction to Uranus. On my mind's canvas will always be painted the clear image of the look of utter puzzlement and annoyance in the chocolate-brown, steady eyes of my Capricorn daughter, Jill, when her dreamy-eyed, slightly pixilated, Aquarian brother, Bill, walks into the room — dangling weird sentences, wearing a hairstyle like no other human has ever worn, his feet sporting one red sock and one yellow sock, carefully hiding his genius IQ beneath mumbles of, "Cool, man, cool."

To give Capricorn credit, after Aquarius blazes the pathway to new inventions and discoveries, the Goats come plodding along to guard the wonders and the miracles — to make them practical enough to eventually benefit us and keep the planet spinning on course. One of the areas of dissension between these two is that Cappies will accept nothing without rigid scrutiny, often through negative criticism. They allow no fallacy or incoherence to cause them to believe the unbelievable. Normally, the Goat will insist on having the meaning of every word they speak clearly understood before they utter it, the meaning of every idea or proposition clarified in their own minds before presentation. Suggestions that don't meet these strict standards are frequently discarded or deliberately stifled, whereas Aquarius questions all things with two eyes — the cold eye of scientific dissection and the perceptive eye of lightning intuition. The true Water Bearer isn't sure the idea Capricorn is trying to stifle is a false one, and even if it were, the Uranus-ruled believe that stifling it would be an evil in itself. "Live and let live" is the Aquarian motto. "Get rid of the dead wood, and save only what is useful" is the Capricorn motto. "Save everything, because eventually *all* will be useful in the light of new understanding" argues back Aquarius. I have no intention of entering their argument. So we'll leave them here, with only the suggestion that Aquarians might do well to pull up their socks—and the Goats might have more fun if they learned to play with a yo-yo.

☆ ☆ ☆ ☆ ☆ ☆

CAPRICORN *Woman* AQUARIUS *Man*

◄─◄●►─►

"Let me go!" she ordered him.

"Wendy, come with me and tell the other boys." Of course, she was very pleased to be asked, but she said, "Oh, dear, I can't. Think of Mummy!"

There they are in Manhattan's Central Park—or in London's Kensington Gardens, for that matter—listening to a band concert together. Or rather, *he* is listening to a band concert—and she is sketching the scene in pastels. Doesn't it sound romantic, lovely, beautiful, harmonious? It would be all those things except for one small flaw. There is no band. The concert he is hearing is in his head. Therefore, when he starts waving his arms in the air in rhythm to the percussion, nods his head back and forth to the tune of the fiddles, taps his feet in tempo and hums the melody, all at the same time, he—well, he looks a little odd to her.

To be perfectly honest, she thinks he's as crazy as a loon. But being a Capricorn female, with graceful manners in the Bryn Mawr tradition (also Vassar, my dear, whether she went there or not), she will blush slightly, concentrate harder on her drawing, and pretend not to notice. It's only if he invites her to sing along or asks her what she thinks of the drummer that she'll get jittery. Capricorns do not get jittery all that easily. It takes something really monumental.

The Aquarian man can very well be that monumental. His strangeness can be gigantic, especially when viewed through the quiet, steady eyes of a Capricorn girl's sedate nature and proper behavior pattern. I realize someone might point out I wrote in the "Capricorn Woman" section of my first book, *Sun Signs*, that this is the only girl who can look at an ugly frog and know he's actually a prince in disguise—or something like that. So I must admit that if she can have that sort of love and faith, I suppose she could also decide this freaked-out character might somehow be salvaged into a creature more resembling the kind of husband and father mold she insists a man fit into if he's going to be worth her time and trouble. Assuming he has enough other solid virtues, she could even break down and pretend she hears the drummer — and sing along with him, to humor him temporarily. Just until she has a chance to change him and gently point out that *she* understands his eccentricities, but it's a matter of what *other* people think. I mean, you have to keep your image respectable in front of strangers. Everybody, but simply everybody, knows it's important to be respected — and how can a dodo bird be respected? Loved, yes, but respected?

She is wrong. Woefully wrong. This man cares not a fig about being respected. He has nothing against it, mind you, but it carries no weight with him. And this will be, from time to time, a rather large bone of contention between them. The Aquarian male is highly individualistic, with some really far-out opinions and ideas. The Capricorn female can also be highly individualistic, with some very far-out opinions and ideas. The difference is, she keeps them to herself, to avoid ridicule and harsh judgment from others, while he has no qualms about advertising his eccentricity. Since they both have their little idiosyncrasies, they can empathize with each other's. It's how they handle them that creates the tension.

Her world, unlike his, is not invented. It's a realistic place, purified by peaceful and practical peripheries, sometimes refined by art (many Cappys are artistically inclined), peopled by puppy dogs, dreams of warm kitchens, families singing carols together, maybe an apple tree with a proper swing attached, on which she might soar out only far enough to achieve modest success through hard work. Capricorn yearnings never exceed what may be deserved. Her Water Bearer's world can be both inventive and invented, unreal — and clogged with sudden shortcuts to magnificent waterfalls; a place where the unusual can happen, and usually does, peopled by all kinds of characters in all shapes and sizes. This is a man with friends of every type and description, who will shuttle back and forth, in and out of both his dream world and the real world — among the daffodils, dinosaurs, waterwings, and Wassermans.

She'll have to enjoy his friends. That's a must for a woman in love with an Aquarian man. He has an almost unearthly loyalty and devotion to them, and you have to remember too, that he can call a doorman he's met only once "friend." Aquarians have a very loose definition of the word. Sometimes he'll even get absentminded and introduce his wife as, "my good friend, Eloise . . . ."

Since Capricorn girls, as a rule, make quiet, unobtrusive wives who are not especially snoopy, curious, or demanding, it's easy to see why the Uranus man is attracted to this woman. Just so she doesn't become so quiet, unobtrusive and undemanding that he forgets she's there. Aquarian men have been known to do that, you know — forget they have wives altogether, and have to be reminded now and then. The problem usually isn't unfaithfulness, just amazement at realizing he's had a weak moment and actually made a forever promise.

This man, I'll tell you right now, has a thing about promises. Not *for* them — *against* them. It's the strange blend of Uranus integrity. He thinks it's both wrong and ridiculous to say something you're not sure you'll mean a week or a month or a year later. No one can be sure he won't change (especially Aquarians, who are *always* changing), so why mislead anyone? Most people born under this sign can't stand being accused of breaking a vow or letting a friend down, so they just do the best they can without making what to them might be a false commitment. Who knows how a person will feel tomorrow about what he said yesterday? Not an Aquarian, that's certain. This doesn't mean there aren't many Aquarian men who keep their marriage vows and remain with one woman for a lifetime. There are. Some of them are deeply in love; but even those who aren't are reluctant to go to the trouble of seeking a divorce. It's seldom "another woman" the wife of an Aquarian faces as a problem. Not in the accepted sense of the term. Women interest this man for what to him is a very sound reason. They make up roughly half of the human race — and Aquarius is intensely concerned with the various problems of the human race. The fact that women are members of the opposite sex, with a magnetic, masculine appeal (the birds and bees bit), may escape his notice at first. He's not unaware of sex by any means, but it's of secondary importance — secondary to his flights of fancy, his haunting dreams, visions, self-absorption, dedication to his work or career — and always and eternally, his Friends. I used the capital letter deliberately. Nonetheless, if a woman makes even a mediocre effort to love this man, she will, in most cases (not all but most), be rewarded by a faithful lover or husband who provides plenty of variety, interest, fascination, unexpected surprises, and excitement. A Capricorn woman should make *more* than a mediocre effort, since this girl has been the type, since childhood, to follow the precept that anything worth doing at all is worth doing well.

Oddly enough (or on second thought, perhaps not oddly at all), an Aquarian male often arouses unreasonable jealousy in his woman — even when she's a normally cool, placid Goat Girl. Since he can be intellectually attracted to a stranger at first glance, let alone first meeting, he may treat the stranger as an intimate friend. If the stranger is female, his Capricorn wife, or whatever, may fail to realize it probably means nothing. She'll have to remember that this man is inclined to divorce love from physical passion; and therefore can "love" his friends, while sharing sexual union only with her. Actually, a Capricorn is better equipped to tolerate this than most other Sun Signs. Even so, it can be upsetting. She'll just have to keep in mind that once he has given himself completely to her on a physical plane, he sees no reason why he can't continue to have warm, intellectual friendships with other women. An Aries or Leo woman could show him plenty of reasons why he shouldn't — and *couldn't* — after giving him back his friendship ring (or throwing it at him), but a Saturn-ruled female can understand it all, if she half tries.

The physical side of their relationship may be changing and unpredictable. *Everything* with Aquarius is changing and unpredictable. His attitude toward sex can range from intense curiosity to detached acceptance. Hers can range from a sense of mating as a duty of love — expected, therefore indulged in — to a deep and wholesome enjoyment of their intimacy with no false modesty or pretense. Neither of them is likely to either underrate or overrate sex. Both are inclined to accept it for what it is, no more, no less — and are capable of experiencing it without excessive passion or emotional storms — although some Aquarian males do bring a tone of dreamlike unreality to physical mating, an air of titillating suspense to courtship and preliminary lovemaking. And some Capricorn females blush, with a rising pulse, regarding the subject of sexuality, all of their lives. He may fantasize somewhat in the area of lovemaking, which she will find mystifying, even disturbing, but if they are emotionally and mentally in love, these two can surmount any minor problems of sexual adjustment.

If one of them has the Moon in harmonious aspect to the other's Sun, their physical union will be more than satisfactory. With a square or opposition between their mutual Sun and Moon, fulfillment may be elusive. In either case, there may not be the overwhelming soul-hunger attached . . . . of the type poets write about. Capricorn girls are frequently quite slow in developing the sexual instinct, and so are many, but not all, Aquarian males — so the later they marry, the better chance they have of making a success of it.

Grounds for dispute may arise over her exaggerated devotion to her family, or his refusal to cooperate with her in keeping up appearances with neighbors and relatives. But they should concentrate on each other's virtues and forget petty annoyances and differences. A Capricorn woman can be surprisingly affectionate, emotionally stable, and loyal — with a strong sense of moral responsibility. She'll seldom do anything to cause him pain or embarrassment. This is true of all except the rare coldhearted Goat, who takes the wrong path in childhood and has no capacity whatsoever for romantic love, while accepting sexual love as matter-of-factly as a handshake. But we are assuming the Cappy or the Water Bearer is reading this section to better understand, and doesn't fall into that unfortunate category.

As for the virtues of an Aquarian lover or husband, no man can keep an intellectual challenge going as long as he can — and love does begin in the mind. Correction: It begins in the minds of those born in the Air Element, like Aquarius. To those born in the Earth Element, like Capricorn, love begins with emotional security. This man is a little short on reliability and emotional security. But with enough tolerance and patience from his mate, he can learn. A Capricorn girl who can look upon an ugly frog and see a handsome prince should be able to handle that.

He would like to discover a world where leaves never fall — and the Sun never sets. She is sure there is no such world. If they expect to achieve contentment together, she'll have to help him search for it anyway. And who knows? Maybe he'll surprise her and find it . . . . if she'll open her mind, unlock her heart, and discard that word "impossible" from her vocabulary . . . . as he did the first time he ever heard it.

☆ ☆ ☆ ☆ ☆ ☆

CAPRICORN *Man* AQUARIUS *Woman*

"Tink, where are you?"

She was in a jug for the moment, and liking it extremely. She had never been in a jug before.

A love relationship between this man and woman can run smoothly on course for long periods of time, until she pops up with some humiliating and incomprehensible remark in front of a group of friends or his holy (genuflect please) family — or suddenly decides to turn upside down because of a change of opinion or plans. Then the Capricorn man will become slightly nervous — a very rare situation, since Goats are hardly ever nervous, as you know by now. When they do get upset, they bite their nails and break out in boils or warts. (I know one Colorado-planted Capricorn man who goes off by himself and sets off dynamite caps when he's nervous, but he has the Moon in Aries.) When an Aquarian girl gets nervous, which is quite likely after being subjected to unrelieved periods of Saturnine discipline and drabness, she may stand on her head or wiggle her ears anxiously, as a Uranian flash signal that she's disturbed and restless.

The very first thing she has to learn when she becomes involved with this man is to love and respect his family as her own; even more than her own. This is a necessity, whether his family resembles a Norman Rockwell painting or the Borgias. He's not blind to their flaws, defects, and vices, but no matter. A Capricorn man will feel obligated to worship his parents and insist that everyone else in his presence worship them, despite any failings they may have. Otherwise, he suffers from the guilties. His family's shortcomings are either rationalized or overlooked. They had better also be overlooked by the woman who expects to be invited into his heart. He may occasionally be forced to honestly find fault with them, but he prefers the criticism to come from himself — not from "outsiders." Of course, there's no denying that such filial loyalty is admirable, especially since it gives a hint as to his future attitude toward her and their own children. I won't keep you in suspense. It will be the same unswerving devotion, unless he should happen to have an afflicted Venus, in which case this man can become, not only a cold tyrant, but even occasionally promiscuous — in a peculiar, quiet sort of way. Aquarian girls can take heart, however, because very few Capricorn males have afflicted Venuses, and even those who were cursed with such a planetary flaw at birth usually manage to control it with the help of Saturn's iron self-discipline.

Because this is a 2-12 Sun Sign Pattern, a strong mutual interest in money or financial security, plus self-sacrifice, will enter into the relationship in some form. Also, he will secretly look up to her, sensing she has some indefinable wisdom to teach him which he has not yet learned (and she does, oh! she does!), while she will be gently tolerant of his occasional, inexplicable depressions and indigo moods — his now-and-then prudish, stuffy spells — because of her own soul memory of having lived through the Saturn experience in a past lifetime. Still, she has no intentions of spending her present existence bound by such stifling ties of caution. This is her lifetime to experiment with the wonders of the world — and every Aquarian girl has this yearning within her heart, even if she only pursues it astrally at night — when she's pretending to sleep.

He is Earth and she is Air, so their basic motivations have little in common. Often, these two will make a mutual business endeavor — or hearth, home, and family will be the focal point of their relationship, and once in love, they'll both try to overlook the obvious differences in their natures and personalities. If one is to mold the other, it will be more likely she who is molded than the Goat. Not always, but most likely. Capricorns are already pretty much set in their earthly sameness clay at a very young age. Aquarius, being of the Air Element, is more pliable, more adaptable to circumstances — more moldable. (Still, she was born under a Fixed Sign, and may, at some time, demonstrate an unexpected stubbornness.) But normally, if she must change to keep his love, then change she will, although change comes so easily to Aquarians that we need not excessively extol her character for doing so. It's a natural process to this woman. Change is not a natural process for the Goat. He dreads major changes of occupation (career or profession), residence, and friendships. While she longs to meet new people and is happily at home among all types, he's reluctant to submit himself to communicating with any but his immediate family, or within the tight circle of his few close friendships, most of which were formed in childhood. Consequently, their social life may be somewhat subdued—and there's always the possibility that she will be haunted by a feeling that something is missing.

Now, I did say that she would most likely be the one to change to fit his mold. That's true. I do not retract it. But I've also warned you that Aquarius is a Fixed Sign. So there will be ways she will discover to manage and manipulate him, while sweetly appearing to conform to his every wish. A little sneaky? No, just the Uranus talent for fitting square pegs into round holes and round pegs into square holes in a rather charming, confusing way, quite subtle—and generally not even noticeable on the surface.

After she chains her dreams to his more mundane habits and desires, she may not at first recognize her own restlessness. Later it will begin to show in a variety of ways.... by going back to school to get a degree, visiting her home town alone for longer and longer periods, taking up a hobby like music, singing, dancing, or astrology to absorb some of her unused energy—or in becoming insistently anxious to have a baby. These are all changes. And Aquarius has faith in change. To the Water Bearer, the right change at the right time can solve simply anything.

What brings them together in the first place is frequently the invisible vibration of integrity she sends out, like a radio signal. Capricorn men can't stand flighty, promiscuous, vulgar, aggressive, or basically dishonest women. So he picks up this signal, investigates, finally decides she is steeped in the same qualities of truth and honesty as he and—after a decent interval— proposes. Whatever he proposes (and it will usually be a business partnership or marriage—or both), it will always be a decent interval. Goats do not leap into things.

What he fails to realize is that, although she does have integrity, it is her own individualistic brand of the stuff. Aquarians are, above all, true to themselves (also honest with themselves), ever true to what they believe truth to be—but that's not quite the same thing as the Saturn brand of integrity and traditional custom of honesty. Capricorn lives by the rules. So does Aquarius, granted, but they are her own private and individual set of rules.

Another thing that probably brought them together initially is her beauty. All Uranus-vibrating females have an unearthly, fragile beauty, like a morning mist or a summer rainbow.... first here, then invisible.... now returning; along with clearly defined features, faintly reminiscent of Greek goddesses. Her eyes probably magnetized him too. There are no eyes quite like Aquarian eyes.... dreamy, mysterious, always with that faraway and long-ago-in-tomorrow look. (Yes, I meant to say "long-ago-in-tomorrow." It's a time thing. All Aquarians understand the Einstein time thing.) *His* eyes are strictly focused on (and in) today—guileless and earnest, much different from hers. The difference attracts.

One thing that could conceivably cause trouble between these two (unless the Aquarian girl's Moon or Ascendent is in an Earth Sign, to match the Goat's more sedate image) is the typical Capricorn male's neurotic ideas about "his woman" working. Most Goats frown on career women. Some of them do more than frown, they straight out forbid it, with the one exception of allowing the "little woman" to work in the family business. Some Capricorns are so oriented to masculine-feminine stereotypes, they're firmly convinced that any man who marries a successful career woman just has to be marrying her for her money — however obvious it may be that the love between them is clearly reciprocal. This type of Goat is stubbornly certain any such man is only pretending to care. It has to be the cash. Even if he himself ever sincerely loved a successful career woman, he'd be equally convinced that his own motive was ambition — no matter how beautiful, desirable, or intelligent she might be, or how deeply he cared about her. Sadly, an occasional Goat will display this odd Saturnine quirk, which makes it impossible for him to believe in man-woman love unless it fits a preconceived pattern, dating back, roughly, to the Dinosaur Age.

Unless her Capricorn man has a real hang-up about forbidding a woman's independence, the female Water Bearer (born under a Fixed Sign, remember) may strangely admire his somewhat old-fashioned viewpoints. After all, she fell in love with him because he was a man she could count on to be in the same place most of the time, unlike all the other men she knows, who are as unpredictable as — well, as she is herself (or *was* herself, before the Goat molded her more into his own image). With all her own chameleon qualities of suspense and intuitive hunches and kooky, upside-down thought processes, the Aquarian woman often seeks in a mate the dependable, the reliable, and the secure. It's a non sequitur, but as I've pointed out repeatedly (in other sections of this book), Water Bearers are all living non sequiturs. Maybe they're attracted to stability because of the basic Fixity of Aquarius. Fixed, after all, is *Fixed* — even though you'd never guess it by their vague speech and abstract behavior, which is rather like seesawing at the time you're traveling in a circle on a Ferris Wheel.

Their quarrels will usually be about outside situations — incidents or people she tends to be tolerant of — and he tends to be rigid about. Yet, mold her as he may, she will nevertheless rule the roost when they go to the post to argue, with her gently persuasive, Air Element charm — by appearing to *suggest*. In this manner, the Aquarius woman, in the end, wins nearly every quarrel or confrontation with the stubborn, earthy Goat, perhaps because she amuses and confuses — and does it all so effortlessly, never demanding, only suggesting when others can't hear her. No wonder everyone *thinks* he's the real boss. If their Suns and Moons are opposed or square, he might wake up some rainy morning and finally realize he's being delicately manipulated, reject such an unmanly role — and ponder a separation. He'll ponder it for a long, long time. A Capricorn man never does anything hastily, especially break up a home, which tears him apart. A separation or divorce will hurt her too. Nevertheless, an Aquarian girl adjusts to a broken relationship in the long run more quickly and easily than any other sign except Gemini, Pisces, or Sag. Divorce, like marriage, is essentially a change — and change never frightens this girl as it does others.

Sexually, the union of Capricorn and Aquarius may leave something to be desired. Not always. Just sometimes. Aquarius is a masculine sign, ruled also by the masculine planet, Uranus — never mind how soft-spoken she may be. The changing moods of her undeniably feminine mystique, with its contradictory masculine vibrations, at first excites the Capricorn man, but later may merely irritate him. Somehow, her real essence eludes him. As for him, well . . . . his earthy sensuality draws her irresistibly at the beginning of the romance, then later could become a heavy thing to bear — since her ideal of sexual expression is far more ethereal, requiring imaginative, preliminary, mental preparation to actual lovemaking. But love, of course, can turn every gravel alley into a Yellow Brick Road. All it takes is a little magic. So, if they really try, these obstacles can be overcome, as each fulfills the other's very different needs through the Goat's capacity for patient, gentle affection — and the Aquarian capacity for tolerant understanding of human nature, especially his.

Assuming their Sun-Moon aspects are harmonious, the relationship will deepen through the years until gradually, each will supply what the other lacks. She'll become more secure and settled . . . . less restless and yearning. He'll become less rigid-frigid, more free and open. They'll become less and less like themselves . . . . more and more like each other . . . . blending into such unity that their friends begin to think of them as one person, one unit of measurement, not two individuals. Obviously that's not a natural state for Aquarius, but if carefully balanced, it can work beautifully. Most people forget how desperately the Goat secretly and silently longs to romp and frolic. Only stern Saturn holds him back.

I once knew a Capricorn man named Roy, from Oklahoma, who used to visit Colorado every summer, where he felt free to break Saturn's restrictive bonds and just be himself — in the clean, fresh, mountain air that always acts as an exhilarating tonic to Goats. After all, they are mountain climbers, at home in high altitudes. Ten thousand feet above sea level, in Cripple Creek, Colorado, this Cappy frolicked like an elf or a druid of old. He discarded his proper Oklahoma business clothing and wore whatever he pleased. Some of his outfits would have made Elvis Presley (also a Goat, by the way) seem conservatively dressed. But he looked marvelous! One day he merrily left his house at the break of dawn, wearing nothing but a pair of bright red and yellow swim trunks . . . . to pick wildflowers. Another time, he burst through my front door during a violent summer electrical storm, with "T" (as he affectionately called her) somersaulting along beside him — the bright-faced, delightful, and unpredictable Aquarian woman who was his dearest friend as well as his business partner (antiques, what else? Capricorn's favorite career)....... and handed me an unexpected bouquet of sweet peas, drenched with rain.... smelling exactly the way I'm positive Heaven must smell. He had spent the entire morning driving down rain-soaked country roads with "T," the two of them rejoicing in every Uranus thunder clap and flash of lightning.... just to find them for me.

This Goat's sense of fun and laughter, his beautiful sensitivity and psychic perception, were illuminated with a loving heart that so very much longed to be free. Nevertheless, he suffered from the usual Saturnine shy and bashful spells — and there were days when he brooded in bleak melancholy, approaching despair, for no apparent reason. But Aquarian "T" was exquisitely patient as she waited for the gentle rainbow she *knew* would soon sparkle again in his aura — and it always reappeared.

The Aquarian woman who loves a Capricorn man should handcuff the Saturn in him now and then, grab his hand, and throw him a challenge: "Hey, funnyface! Want to go wade in a puddle, play tag with some turtles, build a house with no walls... and laugh at nothing?" The shy Goat may surprise himself, and skip right along beside her. But if he should ask, "How can you build a house with no walls?" the honeymoon is over — and so is love.

Even so, it can be miraculously reborn. And isn't that what Aquarians do best — make miracles?

CAPRICORN   PISCES

Earth — Cardinal — Negative   *Water — Mutable — Negative*
Ruled by Saturn   *Ruled by Neptune*
Symbol: The Goat   *Symbol: The Fish*
Night Forces — Feminine   *Night Forces — Feminine*

The CAPRICORN-PISCES *Relationship*

*Strange to say, they all recognized it at once, and until
fear fell upon them they hailed it, not as something long
dreamt of and seen at last, but as a familiar friend to
whom they were returning home for the holidays.*

In the calm presence of Capricorn, the Piscean Fish often feel cozy and snuggly-secure, rather like baby bears when they're tucked into their winter logs for a nap. It may seem odd to think of the Fish as a bear, but Capricorn's ruling planet, Saturn, has that effect on Pisces. Because they're ruled by the slippery, subtle, and elusive planet Neptune, Pisceans find the solid stability of Saturn so comforting, it makes them *feel* like baby bears — (or Mama or Papa bears).

Conversely, in the serene presence of Pisces, the Capricorn Goats often feel a light-hearted, floating sensation .... like bubbles, when they're released, shimmering, into the air. It may seem odd to think of the Goat as a bubble, but the Pisces ruling planet, Neptune, has that effect on Capricorn. Because they're ruled by the stern, demanding discipline of Saturn, the Goats find the dreamy, relaxed looseness of Neptune so fascinating and so full of the promise of freedom, it makes them *feel* like bubbles.

So, here they are, a Fish and a Goat, magically transformed by each other's proximity into a bear and a bubble. It's really quite beautiful, don't you think? All Pisces and Capricorn people should ponder the previous two paragraphs for a while, until they're permanently impressed by all the good things they can derive from their association, and realize the great value of the intangible, but precious, gifts they can exchange. The thought will bring them smoothly through the problem periods they'll experience, from time to time. But let's stay with their positive points of compatibility a bit longer, before deliberating on the dangers they must guard against.

There's often a marvelous serene sympatico inherent in this 3-11 Sun Sign Pattern, because it vibrates through the Earth and Water elements. Their association causes Capricorn's Earth essence to be greatly enriched, and the Piscean Water essence to find a secure place in which to flow. In these dual rewards, it's similar to the 3-11 Sun Sign Pattern influence of Earth and Water also experienced by Pisces-Taurus, Taurus-Cancer, Cancer-Virgo, Virgo-Scorpio, and Scorpio-Capricorn.

Goats feel somehow safer with a Fish than with most Sun Signs, other than Scorpio, in kicking up their heels defiantly against the natural Capricorn restrictive behavior. Although the Goats also get along smoothly with Taurus and Virgo, they may feel considerably less inclined to kick over the traces with the Bulls and Virgins than with Pisces. Contrariwise, the Fish, somehow, feel more protected with a Goat than with most Sun Signs, other than Taurus, from life's harsh, abrasive experiences — more courageous in overcoming the natural Piscean introverted behavior. Although the Fish also get along smoothly with Scorpio and Cancer, they may feel somewhat less protected, as well as less courageous, with the Scorpions and Crabs than with the Goat. In many ways, therefore, Capricorn and Pisces were made for each other. If one of them has a Moon Sign or Ascendent in conflict with the other, they'll sputter and spat back and forth occasionally. Otherwise, these two will be far happier and more harmonious together than uptight and tense.

Because Pisces and Capricorn feel alike and think alike about most major issues, their differences of opinion are relatively less frequent than their times of agreeable, almost effortless, cooperation and compromise. Even in those areas where they differ and disagree, they'll take turns carefully convincing each other to come around to the other side of whatever question caused the friction. Sometimes it's the Goat who manages to straighten out the confused or muddled thinking of the Fish; at other times, it's the Fish who manages to soften the Goat's firm stand. For example, if they should become involved in a discussion of controversial subjects like astrology and religion, they probably won't be able to avoid clashing in principle, because Cappy is so big on tradition and authority — suspicious of the abstract — and less instinctively compassionate and perceptive than Pisces. In this case, it will usually be the Fish who gently turns around the Goat's wrong thinking — although on other subjects, an equal number of times, it's the Goat who determinedly switches the Fish's viewpoint to his (or her) own.

Actually, these two subjects are nearly certain to be debated at some time between the two of them, since Saturn is the defender of the status quo, and Neptune (along with Pluto) governs both astrology and religion. (Jupiter is involved chiefly with the philosophy of religion, Pluto with its mystery, Neptune with its mysticism.) Therefore, it's reasonable to suppose that this Saturn- and Neptune-influenced association will contain its share of disagreements in these departments, which Pisces will nearly always win.

PISCES: Don't you believe religion is failing people, by not giving them a sense of the continuation of individual consciousness?

CAPRICORN: What is *that* supposed to mean? Sometimes you get too abstract for me to follow. Why can't you speak in *plain* and *simple* terms an ordinary person can understand?

PISCES: I'll try. What I meant was that reincarnation, which is the foundation of astrology, is the real truth of existence, and all the churches have removed this wisdom from their teachings. That's as plain and simple as I can say it.

CAPRICORN: Reincarnation? I won't even discuss it with you. It's too ridiculous to even be considered.

PISCES: (only *pretending* to back down — sneaky Neptune!) All right. We can always discuss reincarnation some other time, and when we do, I'll tell you some things I'm sure will change your mind, but right now let's just talk about religion and astrology.

CAPRICORN: That's almost as bad. Astrology. Maybe even worse.

PISCES: (ignoring Cappy, as though he — or she — hadn't heard) Do you know that nearly every religious faith teaches that astrology is a sin, and won't permit their members to even investigate it?

CAPRICORN: They're certainly justified in taking that position, if you ask me, considering all the quackery associated with it. I don't blame them. Astrology has such a bad name, the Catholic Church requires formal confession from Catholics who have been contaminated by having anything to do with it, before they're allowed to take communion.

PISCES: Every art and science has quackery associated with it, not just astrology, so that doesn't prove anything, either way. But I'm glad you mentioned communion. That's the ritual of swallowing a wafer symbolizing the body and blood of a simple carpenter — who was himself an astrologer — as were his teachers, the Essenes, where he spent the eighteen "lost years" of his life, which were conveniently removed from the scriptures.

CAPRICORN: How could someone like Jesus have practiced astrology, when the Catholic Church, and every other faith, has defined it as a dangerous belief in the control of stars and planets over human destiny?

PISCES: (smiling softly) I see. So only church dogma should be allowed to control human destiny? You probably don't realize that the Church Fathers themselves are well aware that the purpose of studying astrology is just the opposite — to teach us that the only way to *escape* the control of the stars is by understanding their powerful influence, so we can then use our own free choice to guide our own destinies. A knowledge of astrology *releases* us from planetary control — but it also releases us from church dogma's moral dictatorship, and that's the *real* reason the definition of astrology has been deliberately distorted and maligned.

CAPRICORN: The trouble is, you're just anti-Catholic. You're prejudiced against Protestant denominations too.

PISCES: (softly, not antagonistically) Not at all. The Catholics and Protestants aren't the only ones who cause their followers to believe untrue things about astrology — or who suppress the facts. Judaism has also denied its own roots in the Hebrew Qabbalah, which is one of the deepest sources of both astrological and numerological wisdom. And the Mormon church calls astrology "the work of the devil."

CAPRICORN: You just lost the argument. All those Mormons are so polite and neat and well scrubbed — decent, law-abiding people. They believe in the sanctity of the *family,* and *so do I.*

PISCES: (again smiling gently) Outside appearances are sometimes deceptive. Is being clean-shaven, then, a necessity for illumination and salvation? That removes Lincoln, Moses, Jesus, the Apostles, and countless others from the list of the virtuous. You're right about the Mormon reverence for the family circle, but did you know that their founder, Joseph Smith, claimed he had a vision which told him that *all* religions other than the Mormon religion are "an abomination" to the Lord?

Now Cappy is silent — and the Fish calmly continues.

PISCES: Only since 1978 has the Mormon church allowed blacks to be priests. Before that, the Mormons taught that "Africans are unworthy," their darker skin tones a sign of God's disfavor.

CAPRICORN: Well, at least they finally admitted their mistakes.

PISCES: Yes, they did. One of them, at least. Mormon President Spencer Kimball has taken many great strides toward truth and tolerance. Still, even he currently states firmly that it's "absolutely impossible" for women to ever be permitted to teach or preach in the church. But I believe he's trying . . and someday that belief will be softened too. There are many good and positive things about Mormonism. Many more than the negative attitudes. Most of their principles are sound and sensible.

CAPRICORN: Listen . . I've decided you aren't prejudiced after all. Tell me some more about astrology and reincarnation.

And Pisces wins the discussion, as he or she almost always does. The Fish made a solid impression on the Goat's normally inflexible mind by exhibiting the typical Neptune tolerance and compassion — by refraining from an offensive or emotional attack — and especially by winding up the talk between them with the words "sound" and "sensible" (two of Cappy's all-time favorite words, that bring to the Saturn-ruled a subconscious sense of security). It takes patience to bring the stubborn Goat to a change of views, but Pisces is endowed with lots of patience, plus an ample supply of the persuasive charm and gentleness necessary to move an Earth Sign from a long-held conviction.

There's no doubt that the Neptune Fish of either sex and any age tends to procrastinate and to be, at times, too flexible. This sort of attitude will deeply disturb the typical Goat, who almost never procrastinates on either minor or major matters, and is frequently too *inflexible*. It's easy for an outsider to see how they'd both benefit from each adopting part of the other's nature, yet it's not so easy for Pisces and Capricorn to realize the obvious. If the Piscean is the rare Whale-type man or woman, he (or she) could overpower the Goat, until Capricorn frantically feels the panic of one who can't swim, going under for the last time, unable to cope with being in such elusive, changeable territory as the Goat has been deceived into entering by the Whale Piscean, with nothing solid to cling to, and no foothold in sight . . . nothing underneath but treacherous quicksand.

But if the Fish is a typical Piscean, the danger is different. Then there's always the possibility that the stronger Goat will so control and dominate the Neptune person that the Piscean becomes only a shadow of Capricorn, suffering silently from a frightening loss of personal identity. A frightened Fish can turn to lying, drugs, or alcohol . . . or simply disappear, quietly, without a word of warning . . . because the Neptune-ruled will eventually escape imprisonment of the spirit, one way or the other. It's inevitable. And none of the possible escape routes are pleasant or desirable.

But these are the extremes of unfortunate Neptune-Saturn associations, which occur only when other planetary positions between the natal charts are negative. Far more often, Pisces and Cappy become lasting friends (especially if their Luminaries were harmonious at birth), whether they're classmates, lovers, neighbors, coworkers, or relatives. They're alike in many more ways than they're different — and even in those ways that they're not alike, their differences usually complement each other nicely. Normally, they'll enjoy the same music and laugh at the same jokes. Cappy's humor is subtle and gentle, and nearly always brings a smile to the expressive features of the Fish.

"Do you know what a Naptune is?" asks the Goat.

"You mean Neptune, don't you?" politely corrects the Fish.

"No, I mean N–a–p–t–u–n–e," repeats the Goat. "What is a Naptune?"

"I give up," sighs Pisces. "What's a Naptune?"

Capricorn grins shyly. "A Nap-tune is a Pisces lullaby." Suddenly, the magic sparkles between them again, as the Fish becomes a bear — and the Goat becomes a bubble — each of them once more snug and serene. Let's leave them there, shall we? Crowds make both Cappy and Pisces nervous. They're more comfortable with a few close friends, and a quiet dinner at home.

☆ ☆ ☆ ☆ ☆ ☆

CAPRICORN *Woman* PISCES *Man*

"I can't fly."
"I'll teach you."
"Oh, how lovely to fly!"
"I'll teach you how to jump on the wind's back, and then away we go!"
"Oo!" she exclaimed rapturously.

Yes, I know Pisces is a Water Sign, not an Air Sign, but have you never heard of a flying fish? Before these two get carried away with the idea of flying anywhere together, they'd best synchronize their propellers and adapt themselves to each other's decidedly different mores. Although it's true that they frequently mix and match traits very well, they are not cut from quite the same pattern. For instance, very few Fish are formal.

The typical Pisces male cruises through Life, taking little or nothing seriously, including himself — least of all custom and tradition. He's as informal as can be.

Conversely, all Capricorns *are* formal. As formal as can be. The girl Goat projects an image of "class" and "quality," whether she lives in a railroad car down by the depot (where she won't remain long) or in the governor's mansion — whether she spends her time signing up for food stamps (which she won't do for long) or shuffling her stock certificates. Everything this girl does is formal and formalized — even breathing. She inhales and exhales correctly. She also brushes her teeth carefully and thoroughly, in the right direction, and even gargles discreetly. You may wonder how one manages to brush one's teeth and gargle in a well-bred manner, but this female has the hang of it.

An acquaintance of mine in San Diego, California, has a neighbor, a Capricorn girl named Laurie, who works in a topless bar. Now, that's a comparatively rare occupation for the normally shy and reticent (on the surface) Saturn-ruled female. But now and then it happens to even reputation-conscious Cappy. Nevertheless, despite the fact that she's temporarily employed in such an untypical Capricorn manner, she never forgets or neglects her Saturnine sense of status and style. Along with the group of three or four girls she works with, Laurie is naked above the waist, as she performs her acrobatic dances on the barstage, turning miniature cartwheels and the like, to the beat of rock records from overhead speakers. Yet, Capricorn Laurie stands out from the rest. That is, one notices her. There's something that sets her apart. Whereas the other girls are totally topless — above Laurie's twisting and turning nude torso, around her neck, Laurie wears a modest white collar, demurely fastened with a black bow tie.

At the sound of the music that signals her entrance cue, Cappy calmly adjusts her collar and bow tie, then prances out before the customers with her dignity intact, secure in the knowledge that she's dressed formally and appropriately — relatively speaking. If the owner of the bar should ever demand that Laurie remove her "costume" to match the appearance of the other girls, I guarantee you Cappy would coldly resign before she'd comply. After all, a lady is a lady, and anyone with true class and breeding dresses correctly for all occasions. (Obviously, Capricorn Laurie considers her appearance in the bar to be a "black-tie affair," not one of those ill-bred come-as-you-are-when-invited parties.) She won't be there much longer anyway. Laurie is moving to Las Vegas soon. A girl has to think of her future and make plans to advance herself. After Vegas, perhaps Broadway or Hollywood, and a starring role in which she'll dance fully — but still formally — clothed. Capricorn Laurie, you see, thinks of herself not as a topless dancer (that's merely a practical expediency of the moment), but as the new Ginger Rogers or Ann-Margret. Considering Capricorn's patient and plodding, yet nearly always successful, trek to the top of the mountain, it's quite possible that she is.

Laurie may not be aware of it, but she's following a solid, well-marked path up the moutainside. Everyone's favorite ecdysiast, Gypsy Rose Lee, was also a Capricorn. Like Laurie, Gypsy had her own, personal sense of Saturnine dignity. Disdainfully refusing to imitate the other burlesque queens of her day, Gypsy never exposed her totally nude body. With carefully designed costumes, featuring strategically placed zippers, she revealed just enough to intrigue, but never enough to be vulgar — and consequently, made more money and achieved a more lasting fame than today's centerfold girls could ever hope to realize. The most popular and unique part of her performance was her wry Capricorn humor.

One of her closest and most trusted friends was showman Mike Todd, who used to take the "the Gyp" to art galleries (when he was in the chips) to thank her for making one of his Broadway musicals a hit. "Take your choice," he'd tell her, chomping on his cigar, "pick a painting, and whatever it costs, it's yours."

Capricorn Gypsy never failed to select the most expensive painting of the lot — usually in the $4,000 price range (quadruple the sum for today's inflation), and they all greatly increased in value over the years — according to Mike Todd's sensitive, perceptive biographer, Art Cohen, who was tragically killed in the plane crash that ended Todd's life. Also according to Cohen, when Gypsy hit the jackpot, playing the lead in Mike's hit show *Star and Garter*, she sensibly purchased the three-story, twenty-six-room town house built by Anne Vanderbilt, on East Sixty-third Street, in Manhattan — and "its five thousand dollar marble floor, fountained patio, seven baths, and elevator were a considerable improvement over her thirty dollar a month flat." Later, the town house was worth ten times what Cappy paid for it. Like Laurie, Gypsy was a practical lady, whose modesty was equalled only by her common sense and ambition.

I relate these little stories as a hint to the Pisces male that not every Capricorn woman is a schoolteacher or librarian, which brings us to the second thing the male Fish should know about this usually soft-spoken, always hard-headed lady. Not only will she frown on informality, sloppiness, and improper behavior (especially in public), she'll also disapprove of a lack of ambition in a man — or in a woman, including herself.

A Goat Girl is amazingly surefooted when she's climbing a ladder. Not a stepladder — the ladder to the success and recognition that bring her a sense of self-esteem. If not public achievement, then at the very least, her grimly determined goal will be to gain the respect and admiration of her friends, neighbors, and relatives. Especially her relatives. She probably only has one or two close friends, three at most, from grade-school days. As for neighbors, if she lives in the country, they're a far piece down the road, and if she lives in the city, well.... metropolis cave dwellers aren't very chummy. So actually, it's her own family she needs to impress, in a quiet way, if she's not the kind of Goat Girl to pursue a wider fame. Cappy will rise to the "best of the breed," in however large or small a circle. She'll sell the most Avon products in her district, have the cleanest house on the block — or be acknowledged as a chef supreme for her Thanksgiving and other holiday family dinners. Status is status, whatever form it takes.

Unless she was orphaned as an infant or small child, this girl will stick to her family like a persistent burr. If she was orphaned, she'll transfer her frustrated and detoured sibling-parent loyalty to her own immediate family, children, and grandchildren — or she'll attempt to encompass *both* family circles with Saturn's compulsive, devoted duty. It's a lovely quality, one of her most endearing character traits. But the Fish should be aware that he'll always rank second to her family with her, not in love or affection, but in the areas of her prime concern and attention.

Actually, the Pisces man will probably adjust contentedly to her family fetish. Unless his birth chart contains afflicted planets in Gemini, Aquarius, or Sagittarius, he'll enjoy being made an honorary member of her family, and love her all the more for her devotion to them. It proves she's reliable, dependable.... words which have a strong appeal to his Neptune subconscious, though he may fight it. He's more relaxed, less restless, when he feels a sense of emotional security in a relationship. Families are stable. (Naturally, there are some Cappies who, for one sad reason or another, are without any family ties, but it's extremely rare.) Yet, regardless of his need for stability, if the family togetherness is overdone, it could create a problem. When a Pisces man begins to feel someone's constantly looking over his shoulder, and discussing the pros and cons of every move he makes, he'll begin having nightmares about the Great Inquisition (as he did when he studied it in history class, in school). All Pisceans have a thing about personal privacy — and freedom. Freedom of *thought, action,* and *movement.* Any sort of confinement (mental, emotional, or physical), whether actual or merely implied, will cause him to become restless and irritable. The Goat Girl should remember that a Fish needs to know he's swimming in a large body of water. Like the Nature fish, it's unkind to confine a male Pisces in a small tank, where all he can do is swim eternally in circles, never straight ahead — to explore. Never mind all the pretty, decorative shells at the bottom of the tank, it's both cruel and boring, and causes both kinds of poor fish to become neurotic. Like the unkindness of keeping a bird in a cage. Or tying a goat to a fence post. How would *she* like to be tied to a fence post, and have to depend on someone to toss her a few crumbs, now and then ?

Although the Capricorn woman can be silently possessive, unmistakably indicating her disapproval by an icy look, or a refusal to communicate, she's not likely to subject her Fish to stormy, emotional scenes of angry, tearful jealousy — and he just might be so grateful, he'll stay away less and less frequently, until he's nearly as rooted as she. (Roots are what he's really seeking, but he doesn't know it.) All Pisces men are alike in this way. When they're cheerfully given all the freedom they need, they seldom roam far, and are nearly always faithful lovers and loyal husbands. But when their freedom is smothered, they'll feel nervous and restless, and begin to slip and slide out of the grasp of unfounded jealousy, until they become unwilling channels to prove the wisdom of the old rule that a person will become what the one he loves and who loves him expects and believes him to be.

The moral of the story is that the quickest way to insure a Pisces male's being unfaithful is to expect him to be, and let him know your suspicions — while the most reliable way to insure he'll never be disloyal is to have complete faith in his integrity, to let him know his love and his support is needed and appreciated. More than most Sun Sign males (except maybe Gemini and Sag), this man is strangely vulnerable to being completely trusted. Somehow, it makes him ashamed to betray that trust. Yet (also like Gemini and Sag), if he's doubted, the doubt itself (although he may not consciously realize it) weakens his will, at the same time that it strengthens the darker side of his curious nature, creating the necessary excuse for an inclination toward variety and multiple experience.

No one, man or woman, really *wants* to be unfaithful to love. Unfaithfulness inevitably brings only the sharp pain of guilt and tangled emotions, never joy. But some men must have a constantly changing challenge, varied forms of excitement (not necessarily sexual), or become deadly bored and depressed. The wise Goat Girl who loves a Fish will understand this, and provide him with so much brightness and lightness and unexpected surprises within their own relationship, that he finds the kaleidoscopic interests he needs — with her. That's truly the way he'd so much rather have it, in his secret heart.

It may sound strange, but there's much that is practical in the way the Pisces man and Capricorn woman approach their sexual relationship. She may be, at first, more than a little shy — but by "at first," I mean before she's ever been embraced by a male, before her first goodnight kiss. Once initiated, this woman isn't the kind to be coy or play romantic games. Her sexual expression is as direct as everything else about her — and, of course, also like everything else, practical. As for him, he is, like all the Neptune-ruled, completely shockproof in all things, including the area of his own lovemaking experience. Added to these individual and mutual qualities of the Fish and the Goat is the fact that the Earth and Water elements are represented in their passion, which adds both depth and imagination to their sexual union, causing it to be a many-faceted rediscovery of themselves, especially if there's a single or double conjunction, sextile, or trine between the Sun and Moon in their birth charts.

If there's disharmony between his Sun and her Moon, or vice versa, her approach to sex may not be romantic enough to fulfill him, and might leave him still vaguely yearning — while his approach may seem to her to be too light and fleeting, not deep enough to satisfy her inner longings. But even so, the foundation of friendship these two share because of the 3-11 Sun Sign Pattern vibration — and the easy communication usually achieved through the 3-11 influence — will probably be sufficient to enable them to smooth out any problems, after a while. Often, the understanding achieved after trust has inspired confession deepens desire in a startling way.

It's not that she wants to deny him. Her first instinct is to provide the man she loves with anything she knows will give him the warm feeling of security, on every level. But she often thinks the only way to do this is to be a rock herself — for him to lean on in every storm. That's fine, it's wonderful, but it's not quite enough. She'll have to be his rock (for he does need that kind of security), yet *also* somehow manage to match his own personality and desires, which are so much more peripatetic than hers. It won't be easy for her to make a deliberate effort to be looser, more willing to fly in the wind and take chances, more adaptable and less cautious. But if she really wants to keep him near her, and mold love into a forever shape, she can always call on Saturn to firm her resolve. Whatever a Capricorn woman wants intensely enough, she has the strength within her to make happen. She can do anything she really *wants* to do, anything at all. Her patience and her instinctive wisdom are a formidable combination. In the final analysis, Neptune can always be conquered by Saturn, when Saturn chooses to take the time and trouble to be victorious.

The greatest gift a Goat Girl brings to her gentle Fish is the warm comfort of her dependability. He knows he can depend on her steady faith in him, when he's discouraged from repeated disappointments, weary and soul-wounded from the rejection of his dreams by a cold, uncaring world. The greatest gift he brings to her is his marvelous Neptune imagination.

He'll tell her she has skin like a lotus petal (he's never seen a lotus) — hair as golden as a sunset over the Swiss Alps, or as shiny black as a raven's wing (he's never been to Switzerland, and the only raven he knows of, firsthand, is the one in Poe's verse) — and eyes like sapphires (even if he's never seen such a gem, and couldn't distinguish a sapphire from a piece of blue glass).

When he tells her she reminds him of the Mona Lisa, neither will he need to have viewed da Vinci's original masterpiece to be unerringly right in his comparison. Every Cappy's smile is hauntingly reminiscent of Mona Lisa, because the girl who posed for the painting was a Capricorn herself . . . . . rumored by several historians to have been a direct descendent of Anne, mother of the girl called Mary, who was the wife of Joseph, the carpenter — and it was the mystery of the woman Anne that da Vinci was attempting to capture through the expression of holy secrets in Mona's Saturn eyes. Only a Pisces man would sense that truth without ever having read it anywhere.

☆ ☆ ☆ ☆ ☆ ☆

CAPRICORN *Man* PISCES *Woman*

"She thinks we have lost the way," he replied stiffly,
"and she is rather frightened. You don't think I would
send her away all by herself when she is frightened?"

Not all male Goats are male chauvinist pigs. Just most of them. Before we discuss the kind who are not, let's analyze both the problems and the blessings a Pisces woman faces with the kind who are.

The most vivid and all-encompassing example of the latter is Cappy Muhammed Ali, the generous-hearted, funny, tough-as-nails powerhouse Goat who's achieved such fame he needn't be identified beyond his name alone. Hint to any hermits who may be reading this, who haven't seen a newspaper for decades: Ali is the Champ, man, the Champ. I mean, he is the Greatest. Champ of what? Whadda ya mean *what*, ya bum? Ali is Champ of *everything*—of anything you can think of—*that's* what. (I'm writing these words, dear reader, in August of 1978, several weeks *before* his scheduled attempt to *regain* his title from Leon Spinks next month, in September!)

Does it surprise you to learn the Champ is a Goat? Did you think his lightning-fast repartee and quick, clever wit stamped him as an Air Sign? You're going to have to brush up on your astrology lessons. How could such an Immovable Force and Irresistible Object be anything but Cardinal Earth? If you're still wondering about his glibness, Ali's inventive verbal surprises, such as "float like a butterfly, sting like a bee," explode spontaneously, geniuslike, from his well-aspected Moon in Aquarius (an Air Sign). But he is a Sun Sign Cappy. For sure and certain. Haven't you noticed his Saturn reverse-aging twist, his knack of looking younger and more handsome as he grows older? In brief, dig it.

Throughout the several lengthy magazine interviews Goat Ali has given on the subject of women in general—and *his* woman in particular—he's pulled no verbal punches. When the Champ discusses his wife, he's as chauvinistic as they make them. Which wife? (He's had two.) It doesn't make a particle of difference, because his total attitude toward the rights and freedom of either or both is identical. (Are you Pisces women paying close attention, whether the Goat you love is a public or a private champ? Good. Stay with us. You'll be learning.)

Not only does Ali continually repeat to reporters variations of those familiar and these days nearly archaic themes, like: A woman's place is in the kitchen and the bedroom, taking care of business at home, lovingly looking out for her man's needs, patty-caking with the children, etc., and so on — but he becomes firmer, louder, even more adamant and emphatic when he's asked if he'd consider allowing his wife to work, or to pursue a career. *"My woman? Go to work?* No woman of *mine* is gonna work, *no way.* In the first place, she wouldn't need to, 'cause I make enough bread for both of us" (and in the second place, if she did, she would probably come home to find the door locked). "She'd better be a *lady.* And she'd better not be comin' on and flirtin' with guys either, if she knows what's good for her. Me? Well, now, that's my business, not yours — but a man, you see, he's different, and if he wants to rap with some chick, there's nothin' wrong with that." (Ali believes the double standard is a Divine Command from Above.) "Men and women are different," he says, "and there's no gettin' around it. The Almighty Himself made 'em that way, and He sure enough knew what He was doin'."

Yes, Ali is a Capricorn male, all the way. Along with his inflexible code and stern discipline of "his woman," he's unquestionably kind, gentle, and protective of her. Never has he spoken any but old-fashioned and gallant words about his first wife, even during their rather unpleasant divorce proceedings, nor has he never said anything disrespectful about his present mate, Veronique — or for that matter, about any female. To Ali, all women are ladies, until they prove otherwise — and even then, he'd never seriously insult or berate them, publicly or privately.

His iron self-discipline is legendary, nothing less than incredible — a direct inheritance from Saturn. He's also possessed of the Saturnine horror of scandal, and is constantly concerned for his reputation, which he intensely desires to be as spotless as it's humanly possible for him to make it. His hilarious (and carefully calculated) image of the clown is not accidental, but deliberate. His genuinely funny remarks are a far-out blend of his Moon-in-Aquarius original, unconventional sense of the ridiculous — and his Capricorn dry sense of humor. But all the fun and games aside, his public image is not only exemplary, it's far more dignified and commendable than that of many of our highest political leaders and socially prominent citizens. As a living legend, Ali's always been aware of his responsibility to set a good example for the young people who worship him and try to imitate him. He is, in the truest sense of the word, a *gentleman.*

And let no one say that this Goat isn't ambitious. He climbed the Capricorn mountain with steely determination, and made it all the way to the top peak, where he most definitely intends to remain, one way or the other, by effecting, at the proper time a judicious and gradual change of careers. Then too, there's Ali's generosity. Subconsciously obeying the dictate of Saturn, his frequent and large gifts of cash to his people, his friends, and his community are given in the biblical sense with "the right hand unaware of what the left hand is doing." For all his bragging, never once has

Mohammed Ali bragged about his charity, which is more extensive and continual than anyone but the grateful recipients of it is ever likely to know. Allowing for the normal percentage of human errors and failings, Ali is the perfect picture of the higher-type evolved Capricorn man. *But he is also a male chauvinist pig.*

The Pisces woman who loves a Goat can find no more complete character analysis of the Saturn syndrome to meditate upon than the foregoing. It should help her decide if the blessings are worth the put-downs.

Naturally, not all male Capricorns have such fixations about their women working. There are plenty of the other kind of Saturn men, who think it's just peachy-dandy for their ladies to be busy, and to be gainfully employed. They don't object at all. I know a Capricorn milkman, named Charlie Dorfman, who services a rural delivery route just outside Marietta, Ohio, and cheerfully allows his wife to work — right along beside him in the dairy truck. He keeps the engine from stalling, while she lugs the milk jugs to the farmhouses, through sunshine, rain, sleet, and hip-deep snowbanks. Then, of course, there's the well-known Goat who made everything "perfect-ly clear" regarding his feminist views — and who broadmindedly permitted his Pisces wife, Patricia, to work as much as she liked in the business he ran for a few years. He even allowed her to "watch the store" for him occasionally in the White House. So it's not really fair to claim that all Capricorn men refuse to allow their women to work.

However, it is fair to claim that nearly all Capricorn men who agree with their wives' working because of financial necessity do so reluctantly, while inwardly anticipating a time when circumstances will remove the need for the women they love to work outside the home. There are exceptions of course, as always, but few male Goats are genuinely overjoyed by the thought of their wives' jobs or careers — if they're honest with themselves. And once they become honest with themselves, they might see the light and change their attitudes permanently, from within — with happier emotions on both sides.

The Pisces woman will resent her Capricorn man's attitudes less than most other women would. She's tolerant and sensitive enough to comprehend that the very instincts which cause his inflexibility also create the qualities in him that attract her. From the same source springs the Goat's protectiveness and dependability, his kindness toward her — and his unswerving loyalty and devotion to those he loves. His stability calms her own restless spirit. His confidence gentles her own uncertainties. She's touched by his formal manners, moved by the loneliness that hangs over him. She sees behind the defense of his outward sternness to the sadness and longing it attempts to hide. Beautifully, a Neptune-guided woman can sense that only a great heart would — or could — permit a man to set himself such difficult goals — only great strength and determination would — or could — aspire to the self-mastery a Saturn-ruled man is dedicated to attain. His spells of depression and silence don't trouble her as they would another, but instead, cause her love for him to grow, as she's challenged to find ways to smile and tease and brighten him out of his moods with the softness of her ways . . . . . . her graceful acceptance of his Saturnine nature . . . . . . and her obvious respect for his virtues (which almost always exceed those of most other men).

Piscean love is tempered with mercy and the deeper wisdom of the nonjudgmental. After a while, she'll change him, ever so gradually, until he grows to realize and know that he can relax the strict rules he sets for himself (and sometimes others), and no one will criticize him for doing so. By then, he'll have entered the typical Capricorn age-reversal period of his Life, and begin to open up both his heart and his mind to the possibilities of all kinds of freedom — of the spirit — and of his own behavior. He'll be willing to travel with her, to be more careless and casual . . . to take the time to smell flowers and chase the wind . . . . . . allow an excitement for adventure and new horizons to peek through. Goats become absolutely charming and delightful when Saturn eases the restriction of discipline over them and they become their true gentle selves — once they've escaped their self-imposed habit patterns.

As with all Earth and Water combinations, the physical love between the girl Fish and the Goat can be a deep and enriching experience for both of them. Somehow, a Capricorn man is refreshed after the fulfillment of sexual union with the Pisces woman he's learned to trust. The sudden sense of happiness he feels after they've shared intimacy is obvious in the lightness of his manner, the visible sparkle in his eyes, as though he had just rediscovered innocence and pleasure, unburdened by worry and guilt. She's happy too, because to the Pisces woman, happiness is always defined by the amount of happiness she's able to give to others. Silence is nearly always the foundation of lovemaking between Pisces and Capricorn — an eloquent silence made of understanding and a depth of feeling impossible to express in words. These two reach out to one another with a kind of natural and wholesome sureness, causing their bodies and minds to blend in a quiet song of peace, contentment, and restful stillness.

If there's a disharmonious aspect between the Suns, Moons, and Ascendents of both their charts, their sexual compatibility will still be more positive than negative, although the "stillness" and "quiet" between them during their physical expression of love may turn to the polarities of coolness and bored disinterest at times. When this occurs, it's because he has placed physical desire above consideration for her more romantic needs — or because she has refused to respond with enough intensity to his earthier nature. But if they try, these two lovers, influenced as they are by the 3-11 vibration of friendship and easy communication, can talk it over, with the happy result of more consideration and comprehension of each other's different requirements. To honestly discuss what the other person really expects to accomplish in relation to the completeness of love can clear up problems like these in a surprisingly effortless manner.

The most frequent area of tension between Pisces and Capricorn lovers or mates will be her tendency to be sensitive — and his tendency to be insensitive. She may find him too cold and unsympathetic, whereas he may find her too elusive, secretive, and emotionally vulnerable — which makes him nervous and apprehensive, afraid to be himself for fear of hurting her feelings. They'll have to solve these conflicts when they first appear, not allow them to compound themselves into a barrier that causes a gradual withdrawal from candid discussion between them. For, when Pisces feels frustrated, the Fish will often be tempted to turn to drugs, alcohol, or daydreams — or the more direct "escape" of divorce. And when a Goat is deeply perplexed, he may be tempted to turn to a stubborn and icy disapproval that's cruelly apparent in his words and actions, and which only makes matters worse.

Many of their emotional problem areas will be lightened by the position of their Moons and Ascendents in their horoscopes. If the Goat's Moon or Ascendent is in Virgo, for example, instead of resenting his Pisces woman's desire to hold down a job, he'll be more likely to consider working a great privilege for *either* sex. If his Moon or Ascendent is in Libra or Aquarius, he'll be substantially more jolly and generous about his Neptune lady's career, maybe going so far as to approve, even if her chosen profession should require her to travel now and then. These are the exceptional Capricorn men, but there are a fair number of them around.

The Goat who loves a girl Fish can be easily misled by her soft femininity. There are other things about this female he should know. For one thing, she's of the Water Element and that means she's capable of wearing down the Goat's determination, not by violent emotional demands, but by the invisible pressure of insistent and consistent persuasion and subtle suggestion. Water is the toughest of all the elements, simply because of its passivity, which eventually wears down all forms of resistance. She can also be cranky and irritable, though seldom or never aggressive. He won't find it easy to pin her down to a direct answer when he wants to know what she's really thinking and feeling. The tactic of evasiveness is refined to a rare art by Neptune people, since it's one of the few defenses they have against an intrusion of their privacy. There are times when he'll feel she's trying to avoid the issue — or him. Just as there'll be times she'll think he's too possessive and smothering, not allowing her the freedom of her own opinions.

But these are only passing clouds, not permanent darkness. Like an occasional shower, quarrels between this man and woman, who are guided by the 3-11 harmonic vibration, can always be followed by the rainbow of reconciliation — if they'll remember to look up toward forgiveness and not down toward futility. No one ever saw a rainbow on the ground. They appear in the sky . . . . . . the place where balloons, birds, and dreams fly free . . . . . unhampered by the chains of self-pity, fear, and dogmatic thinking. Flying is such a lovely feeling. Both the Fish and Goat would find it an exhilarating experience if they'd try it. Together. It's lonely flying alone. Everyone needs a space buddy.

AQUARIUS

Air — Fixed — Positive
Ruled by Uranus
Symbol: The Water Bearer
Day Forces — Masculine

AQUARIUS

Air — Fixed — Positive
Ruled by Uranus
Symbol: The Water Bearer
Day Forces — Masculine

The **AQUARIUS-AQUARIUS** *Relationship*

Odd things happen to all of us on our way through
life without our noticing for a time that they
have happened.

Yes. This is truth. Odd things do happen to all of us, every few years or so, and we don't notice right away that they have happened; we only notice the oddity of the incident or event later on.

However, odd things happen to Aquarians on the average of once a day or more, and the Water Bearers *never* notice what happens. Why should an Aquarian notice close encounters of the first, second, third, fourth, fifth or one hundred and sixty-sixth kind as unusual in any way? To Aquarius, odd is normal. *Normal* is odd.

When two of them link their auric patterns in a 1-1 Sun Sign relationship in any manner — at school, in an office, at home, in a space capsule, on a Ferris Wheel, or in a rowboat — Life becomes very odd to be sure, sort of upside-down pineapple-prune cake, zircle-and-zebra, Hobbity indeed, and Mad-Hatter-through-the-croquet-hoops. I will level with you. An Aquarian is as dingbatty, brilliant, genius-oriented, and patty-cake as they come. Two

Aquarians together are exactly twice as dingbatty, brilliant, genius-oriented, and patty-cake as they come. Now you get the picture — the kind of picture you get when you gaze into one of those loopy mirrors in a carnival fun house. For, as I've written before, both in this book and in *Sun Signs*, Aquarius is the sign of genius and insanity, and it's often difficult to draw a fine line between these two virtues.

You may place the entire basket of blame for this freaked-out age we're living in right on their doorsteps. Of course, if you do, they will merely walk out each morning on their way to Disneyland, leap over the basket without even noticing it, then absentmindedly proceed to go about their business. Yes, Aquarians *do* tend to business, they believe in TCB (taking care of business). They mind their own and they fully expect you to mind yours. And so they will leap over the basket, without even noticing it, each morning of their lives. It might be a baby someone left on their doorstep. If so, it would have to cry out loudly if it expected an Aquarian to glance down and see it. These people are forever looking skyward, to the back of their heads and to the sides, but they never look down. That's why they're so seldom aware of any particular terrain they may be trespassing across and through. You might say they see it only with peripheral vision. But somehow, these two manage to find one another. I believe they may use radar. They don't have to go into a store and *buy* a bottle or a carton of the stuff, mind you — they have it built into their Third Eye.

Aquarians are not to be insulted by all this, and they are not to parachute to the conclusion that I am putting them down. In fact (truthfully and sincerely) Aquarius just happens to be my personal favorite Sun Sign, next to Leo — and Aries, of course. A fine astrologer I once knew in New York called you Aquarians "the torch bearers of human dignity." (That really startled me, because how can one associate anything dignified with people who go around standing on their heads all the time?) The very wise ancients called you "the humanitarians of the planet Earth." At least one writer has called you "the last hope for the human race." You are called "brilliant and precognitive, inventive geniuses" by most everyone who studies astrology. And you have also aptly been called "the Leaders of the New Golden Age." Never mind all that. I call you nitzie, cuckoo, as unpredictable as a comic valentine sent to Quasimodo in the tower room of Notre Dame — with one foot in Heaven, one on Earth, your head in the clouds, and your ears fastened on the wrong way. In other words, *weird*. In addition, you are forever losing your contact lenses in the ice-cube tray of the refrigerator.

Aside to readers: Don't worry, Aquarians are immensely flattered by having the foregoing qualities attributed to them. Strange? Not really. You see, Capricorns feel as though you've awarded them a Nobel Prize when you tell them straight out that they're stuffy. Taurus folk swell up in pride when you tell them they're as stubborn as glue — Leos smile benignly when you level with them about their insufferable arrogance, and . . . say, you know what ? *Everyone* is weird. I mean, but EVERYONE ! It must depend on the theory of relativity or something. There are, evidently, twelve groups of us here on this spinning ball, looking at life in twelve different ways. (Do you suppose *that's* the tolerance lesson the Water Bearers are here to teach us ?) Of course, the only sensible and true way to look at life is the Mars-Aries way. Someday that will be proven to be indisputably correct. Meanwhile, as a Ram myself, I refuse to argue the subject further.

Many people have written to me to ask why Aquarius is an Air Sign, and yet Aquarius is symbolized by the Water Bearer. They want to know specifically how a *Water* Bearer can be said to belong to the *Air* Element. I would like to take this opportunity to answer them.

I don't know.

Why are you complaining ? That's a typical Aquarian explanation. As clear as the smog over Los Angeles. Mixing up the Air and Water elements doesn't surprise me in the least, as an astrologer. And as you learn more about these off-beat, star-crossed creatures of creative confusion, it won't surprise you either. Hopefully, the knowledge of the stars and planets will stop you all from writing in to ask something so foolish as an explanation of the *why* of anything related to the February-born. (Some Aquarians are born in late January, but most are born during the month of the groundhog . . which figures.)

Now, just image this. Two Water Bearers have discovered one another, in the playpen, in college, on a basketball team, in a hangar at TWA, or in the audience watching *Star Wars*. They are reading this book together. That is, one of them (excluding the playpen tots) is reading it aloud to the other, who is wandering around the room, watering and talking to the plants (but *listening*). The reader stops, about here . . . turns to the Aquarian with the sprinkling can, wearing the jump suit, and says: "What in the world does this author mean ? Is there something unusual about us ? You have a Ph.D. in nuclear physics, I'm a brigadier general in the Salvation Army, we are clearly both intelligent, normal, unobtrusive, quiet people. This book insinuates that we are, in some way, 'queer.' Astrology can't be accurate if it implies such a thing as that, don't you agree ?"

The second Aquarian stops near the African violets, contemplates carefully, in an attempt to correctly analyze the question, then gazes at the other Aquarian, with a dreamy look, and answers: "All the world is queer, save for me and thee . . . and sometimes . ." (trailing off).

The first Aquarian interrupts, dreamily too: ". . . . and sometimes thou art a little freaked . . . . ." (completing the quote).

"Thanks, buddy, for helping me out ! I had forgotten the last line. You took the words right out of my subconscious," remarks the second Aquarian. "I'm so absentminded sometimes."

FIRST AQUARIAN: We do seem to read each other's minds a lot, don't we? Maybe we should take a course in ESP or something, so we can understand why we understand so much.

SECOND AQUARIAN: I don't think so. That wouldn't excite me. Why don't we buy a book on picking up voices of the dead, instead? There's a book called *Breakthrough*, published by Taplinger, or someone, that explains how we can pick up anyone's voice, living or dead, with an ordinary tape recorder. They've already found it works at several major universities. Listen, did you see what I did with my watering can?

FIRST AQUARIAN: You just put it in the bureau drawer. Was it empty?

SECOND AQUARIAN: Oh, my gawd! It was still half full. Just look at my sweaters! They're sopping wet.

SECOND AQUARIAN: That's *my* bureau drawer, and those aren't sweaters, they're my kittens.

FIRST AQUARIAN: Well, I'm so sorry .... but what are your kittens doing in the bureau drawer?

SECOND AQUARIAN: They always take their nap in there, because they like the smell of cedar. Don't you remember?

FIRST AQUARIAN: That's right. I had forgotten. May I borrow your blow dryer to dry them off? Poor things.

SECOND AQUARIAN: Never mind, I'll dry them. You run down to the library and get *Breakthrough*. You can use my bicycle. But be careful. The rear wheel is missing. Just try to avoid heavy traffic.

Do you see what I mean? The outcome of any sort of association, lasting from fifteen minutes to a couple of decades or to a lifetime, between two Aquarian individuals of any of the three or four sexes — is totally unpredictable. The only thing predictable about their relationship, whatever their age, weight, height, Social Security numbers, and previous references, is that they will immediately understand each other. That alone is a glorious miracle. A meeting between two people ruled by Uranus often (literally and seriously) brings tears to the eyes of each. It's like that, when you've been thinking no one in the entire world will *ever* feel as you do about *anything*, or ever understand *why* you feel as you do about *everything* .... to find someone who smiles in recognition is a day to be marked on your Tolkien calendar as a RED LETTER DAY of unexpected, but warmly welcomed, peace and joy and good.

At long last, there's another human being who will silently hike through the hills to hunt mushrooms with you, and not chatter every minute about matters of no consequence. Someone who knows where to look for Regulus and Spica on a starry summer night in the mountains, and can point out Arcturus too . . someone who has read *Walden*, by Thoreau, exactly twenty-three times, as you have . . . someone who is willing to punch every member of Congress in their windbags for refusing to honor and treat the American Indians with the enormous reverence and respect they deserve, let alone refusing to apologize to them for the theft of their land and their country. Someone who knows what a quark is, why the number nine is the Universal solvent, and also the Red Dragon of alchemy . . . . someone who's aware that it's time to either heal this planet or say a farewell to it . . . . someone who's dedicated to waterless toilets, as the great hope for our future, which could bring the double blessing of once-more rich, fertile soil and pure, unpolluted waters on the Earth . . . . someone who wants to swim rivers, climb trees . . . . to be free . . . . rather than spend a lifetime in this loveless toil we fill our days with . . . . who believes in homeopathy and radionics because they *work* . . . someone who is at war with those who carve up the Earth and call it "subdivision" . . . . who is determined to halt the unnecessary medical and scientific slaughter of our living, terrified, animal brothers . . . . someone who is, in a word — *sane*.

Now you comprehend (I hope) what I meant by the nineteenth and twenty-first words of the sixth sentence in the third paragraph, at the beginning of this chapter. Let's all say a silent and reverent prayer that more Aquarians find one another during this, their own age, which is now dawning. As we pray, we'll be joined by Water Bearers Abraham Lincoln, Joanne Woodward, Paul Newman, Adlai Stevenson, Lewis Carroll, Mia Farrow Previn, Franklin D. Roosevelt, Professor Ray Neff . . . Jimmy Hoffa, Bill Snyder, Edith Bunker, George Jefferson alias Sherman Hemsley, Pearl Burt, and Thomas Edison . . . . by all the helpless plants and animals and sea life . . . . the baby seals and their mothers . . . . the butchered cows and pigs and leopards . . . . Aquarians Charles Lindbergh, Vanessa Redgrave . . . . the Coyote tribe of Hopis . . . . Tom Banyaca . . . . Craig . . . . Joel Cohen, Debra Hayek . . . . Goldfield Druid, Nona Stodart . . . . Claudine Longet . . . . Alfred E. Neuman . . . . Ruth Edwards . . . . and Bilbo Baggins.

> . . . also *honorary* Water Bearers Claire Faverone
> and Francesco Bernardone, of Assisi
> . . . Jesus, the carpenter, and Mary Magdalene.

☆ ☆ ☆ ☆ ☆ ☆

AQUARIUS *Woman* AQUARIUS *Man*

―――――――◆‑◀◉▶‑◆―――――――

*"What nonsense you talk, precious. No one can
get into the house without knocking."*

"I think he comes in by the window," she said.

"My love, it is three floors up."

. . . . oh, surely she must have been dreaming.

No. She is definitely not dreaming. Aquarian men do enter a room in a
unique and unusual manner, like everything else they do. In fact, to enter a
house, a classroom, a theatre, a stadium, a church, or a chicken coop via a
window would be disappointingly mundane of a Water Bearer. He could
clop in the door wearing water skis or snowshoes. I know an Aquarian (a
grown-up one) whose hobby is walking on stilts — the kind I used to hobble
on down the back alley when I was a child. He is the stilt champion of his
neighborhood. Truthfully. Made his own stilts too. Another Water Bearer I
know, named Bernie, skate-boards around the block in the Bronx, near
Decatur Avenue, checking on the scores of the local stickball games, the
absolutely brilliant song lyrics he writes tucked under his arm, a tattoo of his
favorite singer, Frank Sinatra, somewhere behind his left ear, nibbling on a
kosher dill pickle and a freshly baked bagel — wearing a blue-and-white
badge printed with the words: *May the Force Be with You.*

These male Water Bearers are, every last one of them, from outer space,
which is their very logical excuse for being so spaced-out. I have an Aquarian
friend whose initials are J. C. (no, not the Peanut King — and not that other
one, although my friend is also of Hebrew descent. But he's from Wantagh,
New York, not Jerusalem). Anyway, Joel Cohen visited me recently. Before
he arrived, he phoned and made an appointment with me for eleven o'clock
A.M. When I asked him why he couldn't come earlier, so we could have
breakfast, he replied that he didn't want to be committed to any earlier hour
because he wanted to allow enough time for getting lost in trying to locate the
meeting place. I found that quite sensible of him. Aquarians frequently get
lost on the subway, on the freeway, at airports . . . . and sometimes, in their
own homes.

In whatever manner the male Water Bearer may choose to enter a room,
once he has entered, if there should be an Aquarian female present, their eyes
will grin at each other immediately, then blink a few times, then wander to

the ceiling. (Aquarian eyes are hard to pin down. So are Aquarians themselves.) If either of these two Water Bearers happen to be already committed, attached to someone else, engaged, involved in a romance, or legally wed, neither would dream of attempting to become more intimate emotionally. Infidelity is not part of the code of the typical Aquarian. (I can't speak for the untypical ones, except to say that, if they morally transgress, there will be a good and logical reason, which may not make sense to anyone else, but will make perfect sense to them.) And so, should one or both of our typical Aquarians belong to someone else (be previously romantically committed), they will not fall madly in love, arrange a secret tryst, or break the rules in any way. Instead, they will just become close, platonic friends.

If they happen to both be *un*involved with others, and therefore technically free to search for true love at the time of their meeting, exactly the same thing will occur. They will become close, platonic friends. Often, for a fairly long period of time, considering that they are members of the opposite sex. Aquarians, both the girl and boy Water Bearers, think far more highly of friendship than they do of love. Friendship is their great goal in life — to be friends with every king, queen, prime minister, ambassador, peasant, beggar, chooser, fakir, baker, and candlestick maker .... every dog, cat, mule, rose bush, swallow, thrush, child, baby, president, ant, fly, horse, anteater, singer, dancer, clown, and elephant on this planet. Naturally, they don't achieve this goal entirely. But they come surprisingly close.

Friendship, you see, they trust. But romance .. love .. represents to the Water Bearers a state of mind of which to be suspicious. Those few Aquarians whose Suns were extremely afflicted at birth by malefic planets from the fifth or eighth houses in their horoscopes, may lead shockingly unorthodox and promiscuous sex lives. But the majority of Aquarian men and women have this attitude in common — they think thusly: Romance leads to Love. Love leads to Sex. Sex is, quite simply, the study of two distinctly different types of plumbing. Once this difference has been discovered, established, and carefully tested a few times, to continue the research project indefinitely is a waste of time. There are too many fascinating subjects in the world to investigate for a person to spend all his (or her) time with just one.

Even Leo and Scorpio lovers must admit the Water Bearers do have a point there, theoretically, at least. Everything these Uranus-ruled people think, say, or do is theoretical — abstract or academic. Including falling in love, when they've decided it's safe and sensible, but mostly because they are curious, and they can't stand the mystery any longer .. the mystery of Him .. the mystery of Her.

The Aquarian male will require the woman he finally chooses as "his very-own-to-pal-around-with-him-on-his-grand-tour-of-Life," to be more than just a wife, a mistress, a mother, and a maid. He will expect her to be a geisha girl, his confidante, his secretary, his confessor, his very-best-friend-in-all-the-world, his buddy, his partner in all his crazy, far-out, magical, and impossible schemes. She will also have to be fond of the rest of his friends (which could be a sizable group), be pretty good at doing math in her head, be able to tell the difference between Uriah Heep and Ophelia, and to have read and be able to intelligently discuss whether Sherlock Holmes was killed by Professor Moriarty or vice versa. (She doesn't have to know the *answer*, just have an interesting *opinion*.) If the Aquarian girl he loves can manage all that, he might be able to manage a few miracles for her.

Of course, the Aquarian female will require essentially the same magic tricks from him. She'll expect him to be far more than just a good breadwinner, husband, father, lover, and so on. He'll have to be her guru, her judo instructor, her father, brother, very-best-friend-in-all-the-world, her Tibetan monk, her Romeo, her Valentino, her Cleveland Amory (referring to the latter's notable crusade for the rights of animals), and definitely her Ralph Nader and her Amory Lovins (the Pied Piper of solar and other alternative energies).

He must, in all the important ways, remind her of the boy she first loved, the one who handed her a raggedy daisy behind the teacher's back in algebra class . . . . just as *she* must, in all the important ways, strongly resemble the girl *he* first loved, the one with one blue eye and one brown eye, who was the most beautiful girl in his geometry class, to whom he loaned his handkerchief one afternoon when she was weeping inconsolably because she goofed her equilateral triangles.

You see, the requirements for forever-after love are so heavy with Aquarians, it's little wonder lots of them never marry. You need a considerable amount of in-the-field experience to qualify for the job of his wife — or her husband. Not experience in the fields of love or sex or any of that nonsense, but in the field of ordinary living. Scratch that. Make it "extraordinary" living.

Once they've met each other's delicate, complex, convex, and convoluted qualifications, and passed with an A-plus, this man and this woman will stand an excellent chance of achieving sexual harmony together. Both he and she instinctively know one of sexual love's greatest secrets — that rarity makes anything in the Universe more exquisite, and lovemaking is no exception. Not that they will live platonically as brother and sister — no, far from that — but they will not, if they are typical Water Bearers, satiate their bodies with mating for the sake of mating alone. When they express their love physically, there will usually have been a gradual build-up of desire, beginning with their eyes grinning at one another over dinner or breakfast. I said "usually." At other times (not often, but frequently enough) physical love between them will be sudden, unexpected, and explosive, with not a nuance of warning from either. Just instant need, followed by silent and instant fulfillment. It's just possible that the Uranus boredom with over-experimentation in the area of sexual plumbing they both felt individually before they met wouldn't be such a bad school of erotic research for lovers of all Sun Signs to attend, considering the value of its diploma.

If the Moon Signs and Ascendents of this 1-1 Sun Sign Pattern couple are harmonious, their potential for rainbows and leprechauns are as bell-ringing as they could hope for . . but if their Lunar-Solar positions or Ascendents are in conflicting aspect in the mutual nativities, there could be too much of a similar good thing (or weird thing) in their natures, and they'll have to make some serious adjustments if they expect to be able to live together in peace.

For one thing, they may like one another's friends *too* much. Most couples have problems because one or the other of them can't get along with the other's friends. Not this couple. Because they'll be so curious and fascinated with their mutual friends, they may completely forget about their curiosity and fascination for each other, and wander off some night with one of the friends . . . not necessarily to have an affair, perhaps to discuss starting a discotheque for UFO pilots or opening a health food store for giraffes. Maybe to discuss the possibility of the Aquarian himself (or herself) running for President. It's hard to keep romance alive when the kitchen is crowded with friends, the living room is crowded with friends — and the bed is piled high with the coats and scarves and sweaters of their continual flow of . . . . friends.

Another trait which can be a troublemaker if it's overemphasized, for the reason that both Aquarians share it, is their mutual Fixity. Fixity is stubbornness, only a bit more so. In the Uranus-ruled man and woman, it's woven through with their unpredictable behavior, so you might say that these two double up on the syndrome of inventive, unconventional stubbornness. Like, he will be *adamant* about allowing his dog, Jeep, to sleep with them every single night, curled under his chin. It's difficult and slightly unaesthetic to kiss a man goodnight who is wearing a Labrador retriever puppy around his neck. You never know whether it's the man you love or the dog kissing you on the nose. That can be disconcerting to a girl who wants to be loved to sleep. Or . . . *she* may be adamant about insisting on the right to drive his car, even though she pretzeled it around a mailbox two times in one week, and has a collection of parking and speeding tickets that fill up the glove compartment. That can be frustrating to a man who would like to be able to be assured of transportation on a fairly regular basis. It's *almost* impossible to wheedle an Aquarian into changing his or her mind (and it's *totally* impossible to *make* them do it) about anything whatsoever.

Fortunately, even the Aquarian man and woman who have negative aspects between their Suns and Moons have an easy solution to their areas of tension. They can concentrate on mutual — or even separate — goals of humanitarianism or scientific research. That way, they won't have as much time to argue with each other's Fixity. It's a fact that many missionary couples, explorer man-and-wife teams, and scientific researchers, collaborating authors, and so on ... belong to this double Aquarian 1-1 Sun Sign Pattern. The two of them can always lose *themselves* together in dedication to an idealistic goal and, therefore, run less risk of losing *each other* through discontent and restlessness. They don't have to go on safari together in Africa, climb the Himalayas in search of the High Lama, or work in a chrome-plated laboratory as a team. They can involve themselves in more normal, mundane teamwork, like training baby gorillas, starting a unicycle repair shop, testing faulty parachutes, researching out-of-the-body experience through catatonic trance in the Cheops pyramid in Egypt, or writing a book which explains that Cheops did not build the Giza Pyramid, and reveals who actually did build it .... in contented togetherness. Yes, I know these double career suggestions are not "normal and mundane" to you and me, but to the Aquarian man and woman they are not in any way abnormally far-out or freakish.

As I've mentioned before in this book, and also in *Sun Signs*, the Uranus-ruled man and woman believe in *change* — except as it relates to themselves. He may tend to believe everything and everyone in the world should change, including her (his buddy), but he refuses to make the slightest change in his own personal pattern of habits. She may tend to believe — and to refuse — likewise. Obviously, one of them will have to see the error of this sort of blindfolded thinking. Preferably both of them.

Their happier moments together will be when they spring surprises on each other. Aquarians love to both give and receive surprises. These two will seldom hint about their individual plans before they carry them out. The old Model T Ford he gives her for Christmas will be completely unexpected. The doghouse she builds for him, attached to their bed, where Jeep can sleep every other Tuesday night, will not be announced, but just be there, to shock him some morning when he awakens to think it's Jeep kissing his nose, and finds out the puppy is snoring contentedly in his new home a few feet away — and it's really his buddy who's kissing him. His good old buddy, his best friend, the girl who looks so much like his first love, she's made him forget her name. Whose name ? The old flame's name, I meant. But it's also entirely possible for an Aquarian male to forget his wife's name. Names are unimportant. He remembers the important things about her, like the way she looks when her hair is wet, after a swim or a shower .. the way her voices soothe his spirit when she reads him Tolkien bedtime stories at night .... and the way she fixes his spinach soufflé and prune whip every morning.

The Aquarian woman is absentminded too. She may forget her lover's or husband's name now and then, when she's busy doing other things, like sawing the wood for his doghouse, or writing her thesis on the development of a camera to photograph scenes of the past, using quartz crystals in the lens .. but she'll remember what really matters. She'll remember how he was the first man who was able to point out Sirius and Orion to her in the sky .. who explained to her how the common usage of a waterless toilet might actually save the planet .. who gave her a subscription to *National Geographic* as a wedding gift, and a set of tools for tuning the car on her birthday. Then, of course, there are those moments of . . . instant need . . . and instant fulfillment . . . unexpectedly . . . and the way his eyes grin at her, afterward. These things she will remember forever, because they are matters of consequence.

AQUARIUS

Air — Fixed — Positive
Ruled by Uranus
Symbol: The Water Bearer
Day Forces — Masculine

PISCES

Water — Mutable — Negative
Ruled by Neptune
Symbol: The Fish
Night Forces — Feminine

The **AQUARIUS-PISCES** *Relationship*

*With a blow of their fists they made windows, and
large yellow leaves were the blinds. But roses — ?*

"Roses," cried Peter sternly.

*Quickly they made-believe to grow the loveliest roses
up the walls.*

Roses? Certainly. Why not? A whole field of Dutch tulips, waving in the wind, if you like. These two can make believe, and eventually manifest, just about anything they should happen to choose. Uranus, the ruling planet of Aquarius, is called in astrology "the Alchemist," and it's true that most Water Bearers are inventive, mad, and miracle-minded. Only now and then does the Fixity of this particular Air Sign hamper the Uranian lightning flashes of the far-out, causing a few Aquarians to live like regular stick-in-the-muds, all unmindful of the glorious insanity (and genius) struggling to shimmer just beneath the surface of their Fixed habits and opinions, their somewhat monotonous life-styles. I speak now, mind you, of the minority.

Ah! but when the Mutable Fish enters the abracadabra scene with Aquarius, the Fixity of even these rare Water Bearers is considerably gentled by the Pisces Water Element, and the Uranus essence is free then to break through. Of course, with the *average* Aquarian, nothing additional is needed for the baffling to break through. The Fish merely adds an extra dimension of madness and magic.

In nature, water softens air, creating a moist fog, just the right atmosphere for the mysterious alchemy capable of transmuting wishes and dreams into rainbow-streaked realities. In plainer talk, the Fish and the Water Bearer are good for one another, and also for this weary old world. There's no end to the wonders and marvels they might conceive and create together. The list is long and varied. They could team up as archaeologists, and successfully dig for a trove of Tutankhamen-type treasures in the silent sands of Egypt . . . . . become missionaries at Broadway and Forty-second Street or on Eighth Avenue, in Manhattan (much more dangerous than the wilds of Africa or Borneo) . . . . . develop a communications system with whales and dolphins, so these splendid ones could be warned when the murderous whale boats are approaching . . . . invent a camera that photographs yesterday in color and tomorrow in stereophonic sound . . . . . open a shop to repair guitars, tennis shoes, and spinning wheels . . . . . or any number of marvelous things, just so they aren't musty and mundane.

The two of them would make a terrific detective team, with the Water Bearer as Sherlock Holmes, complete with spyglass, silly hat, and erratic habits, probing for precise facts and scientific clues — and the Fish as a far more sensitive, precognitive, and clever Dr. Watson than Sir Arthur Conan Doyle's character. The moist fog of London, by the way, typifies the Water-Air blend I just mentioned, so it was an excellent and appropriate setting for the Holmes mysteries. With the unconventional, yet ultramethodical, Aquarian following the Piscean's Neptune hunches, solving the "Great Train Robbery," the "Great Jewel Theft," or the "Secret of Goldenrod Lane" . . . . would be a piece of cake. It doesn't matter whether the Pisces is a male, the Aquarian a female — or vice versa. Neither the age nor the sex of this team changes the potential for penetrating the unknown.

I know an Aquarian-Pisces couple who are a sort of private man-and-wife detective team, in a sense. Ray is a Ph.D. toxicologist, a professor at Indiana State University, and also one of the world's foremost Lincoln scholars — an Aquarian who walks around with a microscope under one arm and a test tube tucked under the other, always misplacing his pencil behind his ear. She's a gentle, very pretty girl Fish, named Gus (for Augusta). Aquarian males often nickname their females with tags like George or Sam (makes them seem more like "buddies"), but this one's nickname is for real.

Her sensitive feelings and uncanny perceptions blend beautifully with his disciplined attention to detail and his undisciplined flashes of intuition. When these two clink their heads together, they can find an answer to most anything that's puzzling to ordinary mortals. Sometimes their everyday magic stretches into a miracle, like the time they helped locate a missing child, alleged to be dead, for a close friend.

When the Fish and the Water Bearer get together in a mixture of boy-boy, girl-girl, boy-girl, or any other combination (Aquarius being the astrological sign of the unisex), they will deviate slightly from the normal in their behavior with one another, not to mention in their combined behavior toward others. Whether they're found soaring and swimming around in an office, a church, a museum, a home, or a classroom, these two are really something to behold.

Stamped with the 2-12 Sun Sign Pattern, Aquarius should sense there's something she or he should learn from Pisces, but Aquarians, you see, usually believe they already know most everything. The Water Bearer could, however, benefit from imitating the patience possessed by the typical Fish, since Aquarius has very little of the stuff. Pisces should react to the 2-12 vibration of their association with a sympathetic tolerance for the fancies and foibles, the eccentricities of Aquarius, and most Fish do — but some of them may react with nervousness to the Uranus disregard for public opinion. By nature, Pisceans tend to go out of their way to try to please people, whereas Aquarians are not bothered in the least if they please absolutely no one.

One matter which may be difficult to harmonize is the Neptunian tendency to be secretive, always keeping back a little something. This can drive the average Aquarian right up the curtains. Ordinarily, a Water Bearer is not interested in other people's personal or private lives, Aquarius being the least likely of all Sun Signs to gossip, barring an afflicted Mercury in the horoscope. Under average conditions, these people are not super snoopy. But this man or woman is tempted and tantalized by deliberate elusiveness, and should this occur, out will come the spyglass, and the secret will be both perused and pursued. Aquarius simply cannot stand for Pandora's Box to remain locked — once the Water Bearer has *noticed* it's locked.

When it comes to the riddles or puzzles of life in general (or of people in particular), the Fish and the Water Bearer will delight in guessing the answers together, whether it's why a fly must buzz in circles before it's able to take off and fly in a straight line (a secret of energy, which hides a mystery of human emotion within it) . . . . or why those people across town are building a house in the shape of a pyramid. Aquarius will pop his or her head right in the window and ask. Pisces will hang back a few paces (the typical Fish wouldn't dare intrude in such a manner with strangers) but be filled with curiosity and excitement to learn what the Water Bearer has discovered through the Uranian casual, yet direct, approach. These Aquarians will walk right up to people and ask the most astounding questions. They're not intentionally rude — they simply want to know. Quite often, they find out because most of us are so surprised to be asked something like, "Did you ever fill balloons with water and drop them out the window when you were small?" that we answer immediately, without thinking twice. Only Sagittarius has more curiosity than Aquarius. (Leo and Scorpio are curious too, but it's a more controlled kind of curiosity.) There's a difference between "gossip" or "snooping" (as I mentioned a couple of paragraphs back) and the Uranus curiosity. An Aquarian won't give two safety pins about why a neighbor has been married six times or what his bank balance may be — but she or he will unexpectedly ask why he painted his house pink, if he ever kept a pet snake, what he thinks about cloning, or if he ever earned a free ticket to the circus by carrying water to the elephants. It's difficult to define.

Most Pisces don't ask outright questions. Their guesses and psychic perceptions are usually so revealing they don't need to query much. The Uranian hunches and natural intuition should allow the Water Bearer to guess just as effectively as Pisces, in silence, but Aquarians like to cover their bets and submit everything, including their own estimates, to a blue litmus-paper test. The Aquarian Fixity again, you see. They need to be sure that what they feel or sense is reliable — so they test it by asking.

There are many quirks and qualities Aquarius and Pisces have in common. Yet, there are also a few marked differences. Neptune folk are, for example, dreamy. Uranus folk dream too, but in a wilder, more crisscross pattern. The Fish likes art, music, and poetry, or most of them do. The Water Bearer likes these things too, but may prefer graphics or graffiti to a Goya, a xylophone or a hand organ, complete with monkey, to an ordinary piano — and the limericks of Lear or the fanciful trips of e. e. cummings to heavies like Wordsworth or sentimentalists like Browning.

These two will also probably lose their tempers differently. When Pisces becomes angry, he or she either spills out a stream of irritable words — or measures out a few soft-spoken, but clearly disapproving, sentences, then retreats in watery silence to the ocean floor, which frustrates the Aquarian, who can't understand this way of coping with a disagreement. The Uranus way of meeting a misunderstanding is to explode quickly (and unpredictably) a few flashes of lightning and claps of thunder, expecting the storm to clear the air, then be forgotten. But Pisces remembers unpleasantness a bit longer than a few moments, and needs a time to meditate alone before swimming back out from behind the coral reefs.

On the subject of money, they are more or less alike. Some Aquarians carefully count every single penny they earn or spend — then promptly proceed to forget the total. Pisces is equally confused about cash. The Fish frequently keeps a bank balance in his (or her) head, on the back of an envelope — or on the wall, near the telephone. However, if they both should have the Moon or Ascendent in Virgo, they'll behave like regular human calculators, these two. Of course, we're studying the average or typical Water Bearer and Fish, as with all the Sun Signs, but I feel I should keep reminding you of the exceptions, whose other planetary positions dilute the Sun Sign qualities either a little or a lot. There won't be as many of these as there are of the typical ones, but you'll come across them, scattered here and there. Still, when you scratch the surface, you'll find the basic qualities described pertaining to their Sun Signs, in one form or another, stamped upon the subconscious if not on the conscious level.

In helping Aquarius understand how to comprehend and cope with the Fish, astrology would counsel great amounts of gentleness, peace, and quiet. And imagination. The Neptune-ruled are easily made nervous by a lack of tranquility, and they need also constant abstract mental stimulation. A check of Webster's definition of "abstract" would be constructive.

In helping Pisces understand how to comprehend and cope with Aquarius, I would personally advise memorization of an observation by Aquarian Abraham Lincoln.... "they do what they do because they are what they are." No one could possibly sum up the Uranus nature more succinctly. It takes one to know one.

☆ ☆ ☆ ☆ ☆

AQUARIUS *Woman* PISCES *Man*

———◄◆►———

If he thought at all, but I don't believe he ever thought, it was that he and his shadow, when brought near each other, would join like drops of water; and when they did not he was appalled.

..... his sobs woke Wendy, and she sat up in bed. She was not alarmed to see a stranger crying .... she was only pleasantly interested.

Aquarian girls are not easy to shock or alarm, even less easy to surprise. The shocks, alarms, and surprises are mostly on their side of the fence. This female likes to keep her man in suspense by such picaroonish peccadilloes as suddenly appearing before him wearing brown-tinted contact lenses, and saying sweetly: "Whatever gave you the idea I had blue eyes, darling?" — phoning him on his lunch hour with the cheerful message: "I became restless hanging around the house, so I decided to fly to Mexico and go surfing. Could you catch a plane after work and join me?" — using his hairbrush to comb out the silken strands of her Oriental rug — or perhaps waking him in the middle of the night with the sound of another man's sensual voice in his ear. (It's only a small tape recorder under her pillow, so she can learn the Italian language while she sleeps, but she forgot to tell him. Well, how could she tell him, for gosh sakes, when he came home and ate dinner and then went right to bed without even saying goodnight?)

Rule Number One. Don't bore this girl. Her boredom threshold is extremely low.

Of course, the Fish, although he doesn't have a habit of shocking people himself, is almost as hard to surprise as she is, so he may not be unduly shaken over her antics, such as a Taurus, Virgo, or Capricorn man might be. Pisces understands human nature, even freaky human nature. It's all part of being resigned to having been born into a world of misfits, which takes in not just Aquarians but the entire population of the planet. The Neptune-ruled are enormously tolerant of behavioral oddities. All Pisces men contain a trace of the confessional priest or the contemplative monk. They also have hiding somewhere within them an Einsteinish sort of abstract reasoning . . . and a playful dolphin. They can be regular geniuses in things like mathematics and mechanics, but they also like to walk in the rain and pick daffodils, sleep outdoors and watch the Milky Way twinkling at Regulus on a summer night . . . . . and make dandelion rings. I guess, when you ponder it profoundly, a Pisces man definitely possesses enough curious charisma to keep an Aquarian girl from becoming bored.

Most Pisces males are, except during their rare moments of crankiness (always for good reason), on the whole, considerate and thoughtful fellows, with rather shy, gentle, and benevolent dispositions. The Fish will usually give his family — or the woman he loves — everything he owns. Of course, if he's a certain kind of Piscean, he may not own much of a material nature to give. For one thing, others may have borrowed or taken it from him already. For another, he tends to procrastinate, to put off his dreams for another day . . . which can stretch into years. Pisces often turns away from facing the cold, hard demands Life makes upon those who aspire to substantial worldly success.

If he's the opposite kind of Fish, he has enough talents, and is gifted with sufficient direction to achieve both recognition and financial compensation in nearly any endeavor he might wish to undertake. He will enjoy the finer things of Life and will be well fitted to purposefully pursue the material pattern necessary to attain them. These are the Pisceans astrology refers to as "Whales" — still gentle, still playful, psychic and benevolent — but with far more power and aggressive drive than the Neptune dreamers. Whichever kind of Fish the Aquarian girl loves, she won't count the cost of the material things he gives her, for he's just as willing to give her the intangibles . . . his thoughts and dreams . . . his ideas and ideals . . . his visions and perceptions . . . and his vulnerable heart.

All those things are worth far more than electric organs, Haviland china, car ports, expensive gifts, and household trinkets. They should certainly be worth more to the Aquarian woman, whose sense of values is normally tuned in to the true and genuine. Unless she was born with a more materialistically oriented Moon Sign or Ascendent, the typical Water Bearer of the female gender is able to discriminate between the real and the phony with little effort. She understands that the intangible is often what is real . . . . and treasures things that can't be perceived by the senses.

The Fish who loves her may expect always the unexpected from this lady. Unconventional behavior, however mildly unconventional, is the mold into which she was poured in the womb. Her name may be Leslie, the ballerina, or Broomhilda. Her job may be sweeping chimneys — or she may have an ordinary name, like Ruth Edwards, and be a bank teller. But she will be, to repeat, at the very *least*, mildly unconventional. Aquarian women can be surprisingly practical in day-to-day matters like banking and such (some of them are brilliant with math, and able to add whole columns of figures in their heads). Nonetheless, they are . . *different* in some way. If you meet a nice, quiet, conservative bank teller named Ruth, who was born in February, don't form a judgment without first asking her fellow employees, her husband, or her family a few discreet questions. You may be in for a jolt. She might drive a tractor to work on snowy days, tote her lunch in a gym bag, wear snowshoes behind the counter, have a hobby of checking Russian timetables to see how often their trains are late, use a genuine antique quill pen from the desk of Abe Lincoln to write out a wire transfer — or secretly collect Andy Gump and Tillie the Toiler comic books. And . . . did you notice that tiny tattoo of the Wizard of Oz just above her right elbow? *She is . . . somehow . . . different.*

The Aquarian girl's love for humanity and her innate kindness shine through everything she says or does. However, her love for humanity is no barrier to her lack of concern regarding what people think. Her Pisces lover or husband may have more than one cause to blush over her refusal to live her life to please the folks next door. Not that she'll do anything really dreadful, but it could be a mite embarrassing if she decides to keep a chicken coop on the front porch, sings ancient Incan mantras in the backyard, in the moonlight, or runs the electric lawnmower about five A.M., just before sunrise, wearing her trainman's hat and overalls, shouting "ALL ABO—A—RD !" because she has this nostalgic thing about the trains she rode as a child. People don't always understand.

The Aquarian woman and the Pisces man have similar ideas about promises. They both mistrust them, and dislike to make them — to one another or to anyone else. The Fish will occasionally break his own rule and make a promise, only to slide away from it later, should changing circumstances prevent him from keeping it. An Aquarian woman will tell you right out that she doesn't like to make a promise, because she might have to break it. It's a unique form of Uranus integrity. No one should make promises or swear on things, believes Aquarius, for the sensible reason that no one can predict with certainty what might happen. Usually, all you can persuade this woman to say is that she'll try as best she can to do tomorrow what she believes she wants to do today. That's about as far as she'll go. Promises are for those who like to fool themselves, and others, into thinking they totally control their own future feelings.

The very first thing the Uranus-ruled woman is likely to do when she falls in love with a Pisces man is to tell him her problems, ideas, thoughts, and theories, to see what he thinks of them. She won't use him as a shoulder to cry upon as much as a sounding board for projected action. Strangely, she will listen to much of his advice. But in a few matters, she'll go her merry way, despite his wiser counsel. Then, when she stumbles, he will tenderly pick her up and comfort her. She reaches for his hand, and it's always there. Even for an unpredictable Aquarian woman, that's a nice, cozy feeling.

Well, to be honest, sometimes he may *not* be there. He's capable of suddenly disappearing — or perhaps not suddenly, but gradually. Normally, the Fish is emotionally dependable. He'll take a great deal before his limit is reached. But when he can no longer bear the hurt and the pain, in whatever form it takes, he will swim softly away, rather than face the continual wear and tear of confrontation.

The Aquarian woman is capable of the same sort of disappearance, except that her vanishing act is the kind you see on a stage, with a magician. Presto! Now you see her — now you don't. She fades into memory, like the magician's brightly colored silk scarves and fluffy white rabbits. Like the Pisces male, she, too, can bear only a certain amount of growing tension before deciding to release *herself* from an emotional prison. Unlike many others, this woman catches on early in life to the esoteric truth that she is her own jailer and warden, that she herself, and no one else, holds the key to her own freedom.

The sexual relationship of the Fish and Water Bearer is often more of an experiment than an experience, at least in the beginning. Each is a degree dubious about the wisdom of submitting one's whole *self* to another. Bodies are less important. These two lovers will go through all the motions of lovemaking, and yet not be certain this is a total union, until the spirit catches up with the desire and need of the flesh. When this does occur, the physical demonstration of their love is, for him — the realization of a long-cherished dream; for her — another of life's ecstatic joys. Not the *only* one — but a very special, enchanted one. For, in truth, she loves Life itself, with all its varied surprises, far too much to ever place all her hopes in only one of its miracles. Still, these two can discover more poetic meaning to the naturalness of their physical intimacies than many other couples suspect can be attained.

First and foremost, however, before this woman will totally commit herself to the man she loves, he must prove to her that he is her friend — her *real* friend — that he desires not just to possess her heart and her body, but to blend their minds as well. The barest hint of disloyalty on the friendship level, and she'll turn as cold as the first frost of winter. Friendship comes first to Aquarius, love second — and sex is an enjoyable, but not-to-be-overrated third. This is not to say she isn't passionate, for she is. It depends upon your definition of passion. Mental affinity, mental intercourse, if you will, in its *purest* meaning, adds a deeper dimension to passion, always. The Uranus-ruled sense this truth within themselves, long before others ever learn it.

The greatest weakness of a Pisces man is the possibility that he may neglect his personal welfare, and carelessly disregard his own needs and rights, because of his tendency to give both his time and his money to those who need his help. But to his Aquarian woman, self-sacrifice is not a weakness. It's a strength, without which a man is not really a man — let alone qualified to be her *friend*.

The greatest character flaw in the Aquarian woman is her Fixed refusal to conform, her thirst for change, and her hunger for adventure. But to her Pisces man, unconventionality is not a flaw. It's what made him love her in the first place, because it's so much like his own. Being just a little crazy together is the stuff from which their magic is made.

Yes, they will argue, even frequently. But it's a funny thing about arguments between a man and woman who love each other. You imagine that you're quarreling about this or that, when what you both really mean is — I want you. After all her Uranus guessing games are over, after all his Neptune evasions fade away, that's what matters.

☆ ☆ ☆ ☆ ☆ ☆

AQUARIUS *Man* PISCES *Woman*

———◄◄◈►►———

In her extremity an instinct told her to which
of them to turn.

"Tootles," she cried, "I appeal to you."

Was it not strange ? She appealed to Tootles,
quite the silliest one.

Grandly, however, did
Tootles respond. For that one moment he dropped
his silliness, and spoke with dignity.

"I am just Tootles," he said, "and nobody minds
me. But the first who does not behave to Wendy
like an English gentleman I will bloody him severely."

Trust a Pisces girl to know instinctively what less sensitive, less perceptive maidens often miss. Despite his strangeness, his undeniably odd behavior, the curious way his ears wiggle; despite his absentmindedness, and the faraway look in his eyes — this man was born under the influence of a masculine sign, and he is, in addition, ruled by a masculine planet. Besides all that, he is an idealist, protector of the weak. No one is more suited to play the role of male animal than the Aquarius man. He can be unexpectedly Flash Gordon-like, or Clark Kent-like, capable of great courage in the clutch of calamity, and therefore, totally equipped to defend his lady against danger at all times. A magnificent macho hides behind his freaky facade. He's a man's man, the kind who used to make women faint in the movies. Actor Clark Gable, who played Rhett Butler in *Gone With The Wind*, was a Sun Sign Aquarian.

This works out rather nicely when his faraway look accidentally lights upon a Neptune girl. In beautiful and marked contrast to his maleness, is her femininity. Pisces, remember, is a feminine sign, and she is also ruled by a feminine planet. Talk about polarities, about opposites attracting! These two will usually feel the pull of Nature's basic magnetism within minutes after they meet. If there's any female who can turn a Water Bearer's interest away from his hobby of people-watching and all forms of investigation, to research of a more personal nature, on a more intimate level, it's a girl Fish.

Aquarian men are, as I've pointed out elsewhere in this book (and also in my first book, *Sun Signs*), as a rule, not terrifically hung up on the attraction between the sexes. Yet, when he meets a Pisces girl, the Water Bearer may suddenly become acutely aware of his sexuality (not to mention hers), causing him to behave in a very strange manner. That is, stranger than his *normal* manner, and this could be very strange *indeed*. It might make her believe he actively dislikes her.

She should not allow herself to be so misled, just because: when she drops her white angora sweater, he walks on it with his muddy boots — he takes her to the theatre, then wanders up to the balcony to munch his popcorn alone (because he's forgotten where they were sitting) — he calls her up and asks if he can borrow her dog to take for a walk, without asking her to go along — or he blows up a paper bag and pops it near her ear, then laughs hysterically, when she's wondering if he noticed her new perfume. He *has* noticed it. He has, he has! That's why he blew up the paper sack and popped it. It kept his hands busy, when they were straining to reach out and gently touch her cheek. Only sissies behave like *that*. And he is no sissy. What will his pals, his buddies, all his friends think? That kind of nonsense is for romantic sentimentalists, not for him. Wait. He'll come around.

The Pisces lady who weeps herself to sleep because the Aquarian man she's fallen in love with has been treating her with (calculated) detachment, as though she totally turns him off (when he's actually so turned on by her he's forgotten what year it is), should memorize these few lines from a poem I once wrote to expose this sort of situation.

> *I must go now . . .*
> *don't hold me with your eyes*
> *and reach your heart across the room like that*
> *or my own will break*
>
> *love you? of course I love you*
> *that's why I have to go . . . before you know*
> *how much*°

These two will make love on a mental level rather nicely. In fact, on their honeymoon. Yes, they got as far as the honeymoon. Once a Neptune girl has caught on to this man's romantic pretenses, stops crying, and starts seducing, he hasn't a chance. On their honeymoon, they could spend lots of hours trying to figure out the answers to nutty questions, like: If their two Mickey Mouse watches keep ticking the time farther and farther apart from each other, at a definite rate, how long would it be before both of their watches tell the same time? *He'll* try algebra, *she'll* try meditating. In her confused Neptune way, she'll remark that it couldn't happen, because her grandma taught her that two wrongs never make a right. He will not hear

---

° *Venus Trines at Midnight,* by Linda Goodman (New York: Taplinger Publishing Company, Inc., 1970. To be republished by Harper & Row, 1979).

her. He is busy figuring. Then, in her "confused Neptune way," she'll ask him if the answer is supposed to be: When will both of their watches tell the *same* time — or the *correct* time ? This sort of question will, of course, negate all his careful calculations, causing him to throw his pencil sharpener across the floor in a sudden Uranus fit of frustration. She will remain as calm as can be, and in her "confused Neptune way," she'll smile at him dreamily, then murmur that, as far as making love is concerned, "any time is the right time." His ears will turn red, he will grin, remove his Mickey Mouse watch . . . . the lights in their room will go off . . . . and . . .

I usually don't describe the physical relationship between couples of the various Sun Sign Patterns this soon into the section, but with a man who is all man, and a woman who is all woman, this kind of thing begins early. There's really no need to cause them to blush (both blush easily) by detailing the joys of their sexual compatibility. Everything is as Nature intended it to be, and this means a smooth and harmonious blending of two separate individuals into the explosive Oneness of mating. Only if there is an aspect of tension between their Luminaries (Sun and Moon), or otherwise negative mutual planet positions in their nativities, will this man and woman have any difficulty achieving real happiness through the closeness of their physical union. I believe we'd best leave it at that, since both Pisces and Aquarius resent even the slightest invasion of their personal privacy, from Big Brother — or Big Sister.

Of course, this isn't altogether fair of either of them, since she's so adept at psychically knowing so much about everyone she meets, and he's able to investigate every "hello" from his friends (and even strangers) and come up with practically their entire life history from this one clue.

Now and then, not being perfect, the Pisces woman will unintentionally do something to trigger her Water Bearer's unpredictable temper. All Aquarians have a problem leaving well enough alone. Instead of ignoring any angry incidents between them, as he should, considering this woman's ultrasensitive feelings, he's tempted to leave no stone unturned to prove he's right, and she's wrong. Let's say, for an example, that they live in the country and have a large vegetable garden. One day, he'll plant some flower seeds near the cabbages and tomatoes, carrying out some complicated green-thumb idea he hasn't bothered to mention to her. She'll be watering the cabbages someday, notice them, and pull them up, thinking they're stinkweeds. He'll erupt into one of his Uranian electrical storms, causing her to retreat into wounded silence, her eyes misting, her hands trembling. If she makes the mistake of insisting they're weeds, to defend her action, he'll sure enough take one of the seedlings she pulled up and plant it in a brass spittoon. He'll nurse it secretly, talk to it, sing it the "Flower Drum Song," sprinkle it with plant food . . . . and when it blooms into a beautiful, velvety-petaled, yellow and purple pansy, plunk it down in front of her granola on the kitchen table some sunny noontime, and say triumphantly, "Here's one of the stinkweeds you missed in your purge." She'll run upstairs, slam the bedroom door, and weep, because he's gone to so much trouble to prove she was wrong — and he'll probably not have any idea why she's so upset. In such manner does the disruptive influence of Uranus sometimes disturb the delicacy of the Neptune vibration. After a few years together, he'll learn to tread more softly on her tender heart, and she'll learn he doesn't love her any the less just because he's so dead set on proving himself to be right in every minor and major matter. But before they both learn, there will be some pain.

As with all 2-12 Sun Sign Patterns, she's more tolerant of him than others may be, because he represents to her the twelfth house of Karma, where she has resided more recently than she likes to even subconsciously recall. She doesn't want to return to such concentration on investigation and curiosity, because she's advanced in her present existence to accepting many things on faith alone, but she remembers the pitfalls of the Uranus experience, and sympathizes, because they're familiar to her Higher Self. She represents to him the next lesson he has to learn in human evolvement, and he's not certain he wants to enroll in the course. But he peeks at the textbook now and then, through her eyes . . . . and learns a great deal through her example.

Unless Venus was afflicted at her birth, the typical Pisces woman is spared the torture of jealousy that plagues some of her other astrological sisters. She will seldom suspect him of unfaithfulness, and that alone smooths out a lot of the wrinkles in their relationship. There's not a whole lot to suspect this man of anyway (barring, of course, an afflicted Venus or Mars in *his* horoscope, which happens once in a while), because the typical Aquarian man finds quite enough emphasis on the man-woman relationship with one female without running around looking for complications. Romance and physical passion are very nice, he has nothing against either or both, in fact, he's investigated them and found them to be surprisingly satisfying in every possible way — but there's little danger that he'll concentrate on this to the exclusion of all the other fun they have together, and practically no danger that he'll flirt with the neighbor, even if she comes to the door in a bikini to borrow his hedge clippers. He may enjoy the view, and tease his Pisces woman a little after the neighbor leaves, but then he'll get right back to his latest interest, whether it's running for governor of the state, reading his Sherlock Holmes book, working on the plans for their new solar-heated house, or feeding his parakeet.

She'll smile, and busy herself too, helping him when he needs her, but otherwise leaving him alone to putter around in his mind. It's rather wonderful to be in love with — and be loved by — a genius. Life may be a little mad, but it's never monotonous. She never knows what to expect next. Like just now, he told her to look in the bottom desk drawer. Wondering, she did, and there was a white angora tam, with a scarf to match.. "Surprise!" he says, and winks at her. "It's lovely," she replies, "but what's the occasion for the gift?"

AQUARIUS: No occasion. It's no special day or anything. I was just remembering yesterday, about that time I walked on your white angora sweater with my muddy boots, seven or eight years ago, and how you didn't even mention it.

PISCES: But that was so long ago. How sweet of you to think about it, after all this time on an ordinary day, for no special reason. Thank you! It's really beautiful. A lovely Wednesday morning surprise.

Actually, today is their wedding anniversary, and he hasn't the foggiest notion of it (on a conscious level). But she won't say a word. She'll just smile, blow him a gentle kiss . . . . and water the purple pansies on the windowsill.

☆ ☆ ☆ ☆ ☆ ☆

PISCES

Water—Mutable—Negative
Ruled by Neptune
Symbol: The Fish
Night Forces—Feminine

PISCES

Water—Mutable—Negative
Ruled by Neptune
Symbol: The Fish
Night Forces—Feminine

The **PISCES-PISCES** *Relationship*

> *They gathered round him; all eyes averted from the*
> *thing that was coming aboard. They had no thought*
> *of fighting it. It was Fate.*

Four Fish, when they're involved in any sort of an association together (each Pisces person represents two Fish, you see, swimming in opposite directions), have several choices of behavior open to them. They can both get lost in the euphoric escape of drugs or alcohol . . . . . become exquisitely creative in many forms of mutual endeavor, from the arts to architecture . . . . . explore places like Oz and Wonderland . . . . . team up to teach schools of small minnows, patiently and perceptively . . . . or just swim and pal around together, avoiding the seaweed, making friends with the sharks, talking to the dolphins, waving cheerfully to the sea gulls overhead, frolicking through the waves, and playing tag with each other. The choices are much the same, in general, as when the other two Water Signs are involved in the same sort of 1-1 Sun Sign Pattern influence, although normally not quite so intense as the double Scorpion vibration — nor quite so materially oriented and possessive as the double Cancerian vibration.

There's a certain softness and placidity inherent in the Pisces Sun Sign, which may, in varying degrees, diminish vitality of motivation and consequent action. Pisces people are usually extraordinarily sensitive or "psychic," although the quality often manifests itself in a passive way, the Fish depending upon dreams, intuition, and instant impressions in his (or her) daily, personal life. The drive and forcefulness that creates mystics who are also great leaders is sometimes lacking, Pisces preferring to spread their light quietly, behind the scenes.

Albert Einstein and Rudolph Steiner, both Pisceans, had other powerful planetary configurations present at their births which considerably diluted the dreamlike, procrastinating quality of the Sun Sign and made them *practical* visionaries.

Two Pisceans must always be aware of the various aspects of the negative polarity of Neptune's psychic bequest to them: delusions, false illusions, idle daydreams, and self-deception, as well as the subtle temptation to mislead others in some way. Much will depend upon the Moon Signs of the two Fish, as to their individual destinies and the fate of their 1-1 association. If the Sun-Moon exchange between the two nativities is favorable, harmony will be easy. If not, much watchfulness will be required, lest they drown one another's initiative and ambition.

There's a good chance that there'll be a scattering of petty bickering, crossness, and irritability between them now and then, but generally, they won't face the kind of difficulty understanding one another's basic natures they experience with other Sun Signs, such as Gemini and Sagittarius, for example. The Neptune-ruled not only easily comprehend each other's secrets and elusive personalities — they also possess an instinctive sympathy for one another's woes and sorrows. It's rare for two Fish to meet and not almost immediately sense this empathy, never mind the other planetary positions in their birth charts. All 1-1 associations feel the same mutual familiarity, but none of them sense it so quickly and so deeply as Pisces and Pisces (with the possible exception of a couple of Scorps).

These two gravitate toward each other naturally and smoothly. Often, they'll meet at the seaside, or over a drink, whether it's a glass of Perrier water, or something stronger. They can, of course, also meet in a concert hall, in the park, in a hospital, newspaper office, the theatre, a convent, a monastery, or a science lab . . . . . involved in any sort of occupation or career that allows Pisces to provide some kind of creative "service" to others (if only to entertain them) with minimum authority required — and maximum freedom permitted.

Pisceans are ordinarily outwardly gentle, soft-spoken, and accommodating. They're not perfect, they have their naughty moments, but the Fish aren't usually inclined to make a major issue out of a minor slight. They bear their troubles rather lightly and casually, and when the burden becomes too heavy, the Fish are more apt to simply drop the problem and walk away from it than to struggle in futile fashion, fighting fate — or what they view as the inevitable.

To illustrate the quality of accommodation, which is so ingrained in the Neptune nature, check the table of contents in this book. You'll notice that all the other Sun Signs are listed in columns of gradually diminishing length. Since Pisces is the last sign covered in the compatibility analysis of each of the previous associations, by the time I reached the *Pisces* compatibilities (while blocking out titles), it was clear that it could contain only one chapter — that of "Pisces-Pisces" — all other Pisces relationships having already been discussed at the end of each of the other eleven Sun Sign sections preceding the Piscean one. Not wanting to slight my Neptune readers, I tried several variations of format, to rectify this seeming ill-treatment of the poor Fish. But each change I tried was confusing in relation to all twelve Sun Signs. Finally, I decided to leave matters in their natural astrological order, realizing it wouldn't make a particle of difference to Pisceans. Your average gentle Pisces soul *expects* to be last, to have least, to end up with the smallest piece of fudge cake, and to be the one head in the crowd most favored by a low-flying flock of pigeons. Believe me, Pisces folk might be nervous if they saw an entire section of twelve chapters devoted exclusively to them.

The Fish will feel more secure when they discover themselves hiding, as usual, in among the other Sun Signs, making their own individual compatibility associations with other signs difficult for the rest of the readers to find. They like it that way. All their friends will have trouble locating them and learning how they get along with people, isn't that right, Pisces? But you'll know where to look for yourselves, even though you may be overlooked by everyone else. (Aren't you always?) It doesn't ruffle your calm to be "last, with the least" instead of "first, with the most" — because you remember the biblical warning that "he who is first shall be last and he who is last shall be first." (To be fair to women's lib, we'd best say "he-she who is first shall be last, and she-he who is last shall be first.") And what was that other Pisces promo in the New Testament? "Blessed are the meek: for they shall inherit the earth"? Poor Neptune souls. If they ever did inherit the Earth, the inheritance taxes would probably shrink it so they'd be left with only the Bronx — and maybe a small slice of Siberia.

There's this medium-famous Pisces rock singer from Indiana (I won't embarrass him by using his name, he has enough problems), but during his very first television appearance, after the big build-up by the announcer and cheers from the studio audience, he began to play and sing his hit record — and after just two bars, he dropped his guitar pick down inside the hole in the instrument. Fortunately, the show was taped. That sort of thing frequently happens to the Fish.

Pisces men, women, and children are always being overlooked by friends, neighbors, relatives, and business associates — sometimes even by their own lovers or mates. But you needn't feel sorry for them, truly. Actually, they prefer to enjoy the passing scene around them while being unobserved themselves. Pisces is *deliberately* unobtrusive. These two aren't in the habit of carrying large banners, spelling out HERE I AM ! in bright red and yellow lettering (they hate wearing name tags at conventions), and so, a couple of Fish can easily pass, almost completely unnoticed, in a crowded room — unless, of course, one of them should happen to become tipsy from too much tequila and knock over the aquarium or the potted ferns, which would cause the unfortunate Fish to blush, and suffer acute shame, not because of being tipsy or clumsy, but because of attracting so much unwelcome attention. There are a fair number of Pisceans who are in the public eye, through their choice of profession, but they never really *enjoy* it, and I never knew a Fish who complained about *not* being in the public eye. You must always think of the symbol of the sign, in the case of Pisces, the Nature fish. Would you say that trout, salmon, or any other kind of fish are apt to leap up out of the water, just to be noticed ?

It's no wonder they hide, with all those fishermen out to hook them painfully in the mouth, then leave them to die slowly in a basket, gasping for breath, telling you that it doesn't matter, because the fish "is a cold-blooded animal." Anyone who's watched a fish thrashing about in agony wonders at the kind of intellect that claims this creature feels no pain or terror. The cold-blooded animal is the fisherman, though he may have no deliberate intention of unkindness. Not every nervous system in nature is identical, but the will to live is equal in all, through a kind of consciousness unknown to humans — yet as to its level of awareness, perhaps very akin, who knows ? Certainly not insensitive scientists, hunters, or fishermen.

Since Pisces, along with Scorpio and Sagittarius, is astrologically inseparably linked to "religion" (or more accurately, to spiritual truth), this Pisces-Pisces chapter of *Love Signs* is an appropriate place to remind the reader that Jesus was not, as some people falsely believe, a fisherman. Jesus, like his father, Joseph, was a carpenter by trade. In fact, not fiction, he drew most of his disciples *away* from their occupation of fishing, promising to make them, instead, "fishers of men" (and of women too, of course, but the Bible is full of male chauvinism). The Nazarene was not by any means a chauvinist, but he had no control over those who wrote about him (especially not those who tampered with the various accounts of his ministry in later centuries). As supported by both the protests of the prophets — and the more recently discovered and translated Dead Sea Scrolls — Jesus not only was well versed in astrology, but he said: "Seek not the law in your scriptures, for law is *life*, whereas the scripture is dead. I tell you truly, Moses received not his laws from God in writing, but through the *living* word."

Also contained within little-known New Testament manuscripts which exist in the library of the Vatican, in Rome, are some texts dating from early Christian centuries, containing writings which refer to otherwise inaccessible words of Jesus, such as: "For I tell you truly, from one mother proceeds all that lives upon the earth. Therefore, who kills, kills his brother. And from him will the Earthly Mother turn away, and will pluck him from her quickening breasts . . . . . kill not, neither eat the flesh of your innocent prey . . . . for that is the path of suffering, and it leads to death. But do the will of God, that His angels may serve you on the way of *life*. Obey, therefore, the words of God: Behold! I have given you every herb bearing seed in which is the fruit of a tree, yielding seed; to you it shall be for meat."

One wonders at all the great truth and wisdom contained within the Vatican library, yet not spread to the multitudes who spiritually hunger and thirst for it. But one must be grateful, at least, for the access to truth permitted searching scholars. In this respect, the Catholic Church deserves a bright, shiny, gold star. It seems a non sequitur to teach falsehood (interspersed with truth) while at the same time allowing suppressed truth to be researched. Yet, let us not question, but rather be grateful for such blessings, lest even these be denied us.

The alleged instances of Jesus, who ushered in the Piscean Age of the Fish, partaking in the eating of flesh, including the flesh of fish, is nothing short of blasphemy upon his actual teachings of *love* and *life*. The false stories spread by the gospel "correctors" down through the centuries have too-long profaned the message of the simple carpenter. Certainly the ethics of the Galilean were not less righteous and compassionate than those of his fellow Essenes, the very ones who "prepared him for his mission" (whose own written records have *not* been so tampered with and profaned), who clearly both respected and practiced astrology — and sternly opposed the sacrifice and eating of the lamb, as well as fish, and all flesh.

There was no blood spilled in Eden. It was only later that man became a flesh eater — "and the fear of him, and the dread of him was upon *every* living thing, *even the fish in the sea.*" And the fear of *her*. The women flesh eaters. This ringing truth may be heard echoed today by the faint, sad voices of the whales, dolphins, and baby seals, foxes, and deer . . . . if one listens with the Neptune-guided heart. The carpenter came (and shall again, unsuspectedly soon) to teach us how to regain our lost manhood and womanhood, how to return to that Golden Age when . . . "*there shall be no more harm or hurt upon my holy mountain*" . . . and this time, he will once more, quietly . . . and perhaps as before, nearly unnoticed, try again to bring about, in the new Golden Aquarian Age, the realization of "Thy will be done on *Earth*, even as it is in *Heaven*."

A rather simple rule for truth and kindness, for those Pisceans who would follow the true teachings of the carpenter, not the distortions of his message, and therefore be gratefully recognized by him *this time,* is: avoid eating the flesh of your animal brothers and sisters, who bear their own young — or any creature who has eyes with which to look back at you. As noted by the clear-eyed, clear-minded, New Age apostle, Upton Ewing, a return to a condition of Life before the first blood was let in Eden, when men and women, and all living creatures, lived in peace upon the fruits of the soil — would truly be proclaiming an acceptable year of the Lord.

I don't know whether or not the foregoing true-to-the-Pisces-Sun-Sign Essence dissertation has in some way planted seeds for someday soon easing the sad Karma of the Pisces symbol of the fish and all manner of creatures who live in our seas — although one hopes it may have shed a small ray of light. But I do know that it's undoubtedly destined to cause annoyance to a lot of fishermen, some of whom are very close relatives, others who are dear friends of mine, and sincerely wonderful human beings. I'm genuinely sorry about that. But this is not a book which intends to tread softly for fear of offending. In view of the greatly increasing wholesale slaughter of our animal friends in the woods, the seas, and the air — and through the torture and horrors of vivisection — there is no longer time for politeness. It's time to face the facts of the degeneration of compassion, on all levels.

If Man and Woman do not soon heed the music of their own souls, and turn their eyes toward the remembered Light of Eden, there will be a time on Earth when all music shall be stilled in wells of absolute silence, and there shall be nothing to see but total darkness. The shadows are lengthening, and such a time is drawing so near — it must now be measured by the year, instead of by the century. This is the hour of self-honesty, and the facing of truth, not evasion . . . . . . a time for uplifting, not further sinking into shadows, deepened by cruelty. Killers are killers, whether, in their present stage of awareness, they comprehend that they are or are not — and calling themselves "sportsmen" doesn't change Universal Law.

Sometimes truth may be whispered gently, sometimes it needs to be stated in a more thunderous manner. But it may never be suppressed. It's against the nature of truth to suffer suppression forever, especially not by a "sacrificial Ram" in writing about the "persecuted Fish." (For more detailed information concerning all of the various, what might be termed "controversial," matters within the pages of all seventy-eight of these *Love Signs* combinations, see the recommended list of books that follows this chapter, titled "For the Pilgrim's Progress.")

Thanks to their mystical inheritance from the Nature fish, which symbolizes the inner nature of Pisceans (as the inner nature of all twelve Sun Signs may be found within the symbol of each), those ruled by Neptune are not driven to seek self glory aggressively. If glory should decide on its own, so to speak, to descend upon them, they'll resign themselves to wearing its

mantel, uncomfortably, at best. The typical Piscean will never enthusiastically pursue fame. He or she merely bears it, as another of life's many burdens.
For example, neither did Pisces actress Elizabeth Taylor *willingly* pursue it
(then or now), as she's the first to profess, confess, and freely admit.

Such humbleness is a fine and spiritual thing, but as all qualities of the
Sun Sign are intensified and sometimes overbalanced in all 1-1 Pattern
vibrations, the double Pisces association must be careful that this normally
admirable trait doesn't cause them, when they exaggerate it in Neptunian
unison together, to lose all incentive for actively participating in the life
stream. The richness of their creative and other contributions is sorely
needed by a jaded, glutted world.

Whatever their other planetary positions in their birth charts may be,
any two Pisceans who are brought into close contact will never fail to be
aware of the amazing depth of the ESP channel between them. In illustration
of this mystical Neptune link of extrasensory perception between Pisceans, I'll
share with you its manifestation between my Pisces next-door neighbor and
close friend in Cripple Creek, Colorado, Ruth Cook, and her son, Mike, who's
also a Pisces Sun Sign.

When Mike was a teenager, and was sometimes late getting home at
night (as youngsters are, whether they live in a tiny town, high up in the
Rockies, or in a major city), because he was involved in the excitement of the
various festivities of his local group of buddies, like basketball games, shooting
pool, hiking, and such — Ruth worried. Not *much*, being a typically tranquil
girl Fish, but she worried. Since she and her husband, Lowell, didn't have a
telephone at the time, there was no way for her to get in touch with him. No
electronic way, that is. But between two Fish, such problems of communication are easily solved.

Piscean Ruth merely sat down in a chair in the front room, closed her
eyes, and quietly meditated, imaging her son's face and flashing him the
telepathic message: "Mike, it's too late for you to be out on a school night, and
I'm concerned about you. Get yourself home right away."

Over and over again, repeatedly it happened. Wherever he was,
whatever he was doing, her Piscean son would invariably stop talking,
suddenly, in the middle of a conversation with his friends, his eyes misting
with a faraway look (which was more than a little odd on certain of those
nights when he was maternally telepathed while he was in the Cottage Inn,
chalking his cue stick, as the band was playing loudly a popular Norbie
Larson tune). Finally he would mumble, in a trancelike daze: "Say . . . . uh,
look, I think my Mom needs me for something. I'll see you later." Then he'd
leave, rush home, open the door, and he and his mother would exchange a
deep, knowing Neptune smile, as she said softly, "Well, it's about time you
got here."

This bit of Pisces magic always worked within five minutes, or less, between them. Now that Mike's married and lives in Denver, it takes a little longer for Ruth to telegram him to phone her — like maybe ten minutes or so. The Fish save lots of money that way, on their telephone bills. And it's faster . than Western Union, certainly swifter than the snail delivery of the present-day U.S. Postal Service.

It should be noted that all is not sweetness and serenity between two people ruled by Neptune. If one has a conflicting Moon Sign, like Gemini or Sag, a gulf can develop, which is not so easily bridged. Such Luminary inharmony between their mutual Suns and Moons can cause them to get caught in the cross-currents, and chill each other occasionally with silent accusation (the worst kind), sullen detachment, or deceptive answers. But when the Moon of either is deposited in a sign of the Water Element or the Earth Element, the harmony of their relationship will usually be marked and extraordinary . . . as well as their mutual mental telepathy.

Both Fish understand the crosses Neptune people are called upon to bear, like the unjust attitudes of people not similarly motivated, who are overly anxious to accuse the Fish of being sneaky, or lying. This occurs because of the sometimes extreme contrast between the idealistic and altruistic motives of Pisces — and the devious and detoured routes they occasionally follow to achieve a desired goal. Not all, but many Piscean people are guilty of the frustrating habit of avoiding total truth, to a lesser or larger extent, but the underlying reason is the same which lies behind all Pisces attitudes and actions — to avoid outright abrasive confrontation, which would serve no purpose and only wound unnecessarily.

The Fish shrink from stormy emotional scenes and ugly personal vendettas. They'd rather lie by omission than hurt — or be hurt. Yet one Piscean will normally be more likely to level with another Fish than with any of the other Sun Signs, probably because they realize the futility of trying to fool each other. Consequently, two Fish will often speak the whole truth, no matter how unpleasant it may be, when the discussion is between them alone. They can trust one another, you see, not to cause a loud, abrasive, ugly scene.

For all of their virtues of humility, patience, and unselfishness, two Pisceans aren't unduly demonstrative in displaying their respect, regard, or affection for each other. Understanding and sympathy may flow freely between them, but it isn't always expressed in visible, tangible ways, so they'll both have to work on this "cold fish" quality they each project and readily recognize in one another — but seldom in themselves.

There's a beautiful part of the Pisces nature two Fish can magnify when they're together, to the benefit of both themselves and all the rest of us, who so need their calm tranquility and compassionate, listening ear. They possess the rare grace to accept negative or upsetting people and situations —

including their own mutual problems — with a kind of gentle resignation. They both comprehend that their human weaknesses (and those of others) are always entwined, somehow, with good intent — and Neptune softly whispers to them that resisting evil only gives it more strength. The Pisces ability to shrug complacently when things go wrong, refuse to make mountains out of molehills, stir up a storm in a teakettle, or cut down a beanstalk for no reason . . . leaving poor Jack to fall to the ground with a thud . . . is such a lovely thing. So, there's a giant at the top of the beanstalk. So what ? A giant has no power over "four" Fish who can, the two of them together, abracadabra him into a docile creature who will invite them to his castle to listen to him play and sing jolly giant songs.

That's the Piscean formula for magic. Love and mercy. It works every time — and how much more so when the Fish splash it on one another, along with a few sprinkles of the marvelous Neptune humor that allows typical Fish to laugh at themselves, without the burden of false pride restricting their laughter. That's a talent few possess, which constitutes part of the great golden treasure of those who may *appear* to be "last with the least" — but who were born wealthy with wisdom, and generously endowed with the fabulous riches of inner serendipity. King Midas himself should have been so lucky !

☆ ☆ ☆ ☆ ☆ ☆

PISCES *Woman* PISCES *Man*

*"Oh no, he isn't grown up," Wendy assured her
confidently, "and he is just my size." She meant
that he was her size in both mind and body; she
didn't know how she knew it, she just knew it.*

Gently floating around in the sometimes serene and placid, sometimes choppy and churning, atmosphere of the Bronx in New York, is the dearest, nicest, spunkiest, wisest, and most patient girl Fish in this or any other ocean. Her name is Pauline Hoffenberg Goodman.

Any Pisces female who imitates petite Pauline's winsome ways can count on charming her boy Fish into the net of romance without the slightest trouble. Pauline is the epitome of Piscean grace, humor, and feminine glamour — and the astrological counsel given to lady Pisceans within these pages reflects her personal, unerring instinct for delicately weaving those subtle Neptune nuances which make the Pisces woman the secret ideal of every male Fish in the world. Besides all that, she's a delicious and delectable cook. What more could a male Piscean dreamer ask? Poetry? Pauline is also poetic . . . and as pretty as a pink geranium.

Actually, every Pisces girl possesses a satisfactory share of Pauline Hoffenberg Goodman's qualities, traits, and talents — so it's no wonder the Pisces man who's in love with a Neptune lady feels he's finally managed to swim past all the dangerous, dangling hooks of the aggressive females who are trying to land him . . . into the cool, clear waters of the kind of love he's been searching for ever since he was hatched near the beautiful waterfall of tears he subconsciously recalls. He remembers thinking, as a tiny tadpole, that teardrops are lovely things, crystal-prismed and rainbow-hued, when the Sun shines through them. Then he grew up, and one bright, miracled, many-faceted morning, he realized, with a ripple of joy, the answer to his tender tadpole riddle. Suddenly, he knew that *love* was the sunbeam which could shine through the tears of his silent sadness . . . and transmute them into sparkling spectrums of light.

The waterfall memories of the girl Fish are exactly like his. She too recalls the wistfulness of her own genesis moments, when there was a dream too lovely to describe, gently wafting over her heart like a mist . . . faintly promising a tomorrow as free and faerie-like as yesterday's forgotten Eden. All her life she's wondered, secretly and silently, if that dream was real . . . or only an imaginary fragment of happiness and serenity. She's quietly and patiently waited for it to reappear, to manifest from the mist of memory . . . and the times when she's been disappointed — just when she thought it was about to envelop her heart again — are countless.

Then she looked into *his* eyes — and wonder of wonders? She saw her dream reflected there, as in the still pool of a pine-scented green wood . . . smiling back at her in beautiful recognition. She saw herself in his eyes. Just as he saw himself in hers.

It would be divine if we could sign off right here, with the wonted faerie tale ending of "they-lived-happily-ever-after." But that's not allowed. One must first pass through the Black Forest and fight off all those lurking dragons, witches, ugly toads, and Incredible Hulks who loom and lurk in the lagoons, waiting to capture these Pisces lovers, then separate them and drop them down into the terrible well of loneliness — KERPLUNK!

I do so hate to switch from the poetic to the prosaic (as does every Fish ever born, in every way), but we must move along to the more mundane matters of Neptune compatibility before we enjoy the rewards of solving the tender tadpole riddle.

As with other doubled-up 1-1 Sun Sign Pattern lovers, two people ruled by the same planet (in this instance, of course, Neptune) must face the certain increase and intensification of both the positive and the negative aspects of their own personalities. With the Pisces-Pisces couple, the positive qualities they share and therefore will find easy to multiply together are: gentleness, sensitivity, imagination, creativity, compassion, perception — and a great deal of cleverness and wit — plus the good sense not to stand in each other's light . . . or shadow.

The negative Piscean weeds they'll have to prune (perhaps even stomp on) lest they choke and strangle the lovely flowers of their romance are: too much daydreaming, idleness, laziness, confusion, untidiness and chaos, procrastination, fears, phobias, and various forms of neurosis, the temptation to tell fibs — and the odd habit they might drift into of playing doormat to each other.

These two assuredly do have a sizable number of dragons, polliwogs, witches, and such to fight off as they tremble through the dark forest, don't they? Never mind. They have all sorts of magic to use to banish the goblins who threaten their happiness. And as everyone knows (or should know), even the most TERRIBLE trolls and trogs (not frogs, they're nice — trogs) are terrified of magic.

The private anxieties of Pisces are also doubled (even quadrupled, considering that there are "four" Fish between the two of them) when these lovers plunge into an emotional relationship. If one of them has a strong Moon Sign or Ascendent, preferably in the Earth Element, he or she can be a veritable anchor of stability for the other. (A Water Element Moon Sign or Ascendent is lovely for harmony, but we're talking about protective stability.) Without such support from their mutual Luminaries and Ascendents at birth, these two face the danger of either fretting themselves into fantasies of fears — or gliding casually through a love affair or a marriage which is too fragile to be lasting.

There are Pisceans who are afraid of their own shadows. There are others (called "Whales") who fear neither man nor beast. At least, they claim they don't. It's always good to remember that what Pisces says is not necessarily what Pisces means, at all times. Some Fish fear themselves, rather than outside circumstances or people, never pushing ahead, and therefore missing opportunities for anything they really want to do. Then too, there are the playful, perceptive, and absolutely brilliant Dolphin types.

The peculiarly sympathetic nature of the Pisces woman and the Pisces man can cause them to be ultrasensitive to sense impressions, which are sometimes misleading. If the birth chart of one of them contains more planets in Earth than that of the other, the more "earthy" Piscean might accuse the less practical one of refusing to face facts, of viewing things through such pastel-tinted glasses that dangers are not recognized because every potentially serious situation seems to be bathed in a luminous veil of beauty, which is but a seductive illusion. This is actually the germ for all Neptune fears and phobias — the memory of having such a golden haze fade into a shrouded grey cloud of fog too many times. Yet, one of the two Pisceans in the relationship may cling to the "illusion," knowing it's more real than what *appears* to be the truth — and surprisingly often, through sheer persistence of faith, even proving it's so. When that happens, it's called a miracle. It's no accident that so many of the saints were born under the sign of the Fish.

It's possible that either he or she is a Fish swimming in the wrong direction, behaving as though life itself is a dream, and that's a bit too much Neptunian make-believe for the other. Or, one of them could be the Whale-type Piscean, who scoffs at the esoteric, ignores all spiritual truth, is loud, talky, pushy, and aggressive. When these Whale Pisceans behave in such a manner, diametrically opposed to his or her natural Sun Sign qualities, as I've stated elsewhere in this book, it's symptomatic of some form of neurosis of the heart, mind, or soul. A bashful Ram, an impulsive Bull, a careless and carefree Crab — like a brash, markedly extroverted Whale — are all inwardly unhappy people denying their own essences.

By the way, when you remove the letter "c" for Christ, from the word "essence," what you have left is the word "Essene" — the name of the metaphysical sect of people who taught Jesus, the man, up in the mountains, during his "lost years" (eighteen of them), during which there's no mention of his activities in the scriptures. These are the kind of word games Pisces people like to play. Gliding gently back to the subject, for a Capricorn to be staid and stable is natural — for a Piscean, it is not. Each sign must do what comes naturally, in general, to achieve harmony in each incarnation, by learning well the lessons of the sign he or she was born under.

Either the male or female half of this Neptune team might be a domineering Whale or an embittered Fish, who has seen too much of life's ugliness, and has retreated into romantic promiscuity or cutting speech to hide a broken heart, stemming from a crushed faith. If so, the stronger Piscean will need to handle the other with much compassion. It takes unending patience to rescue such a Whale — or Fish — who is floundering in his or her murky waters of disillusionment, and swimming upstream, against the true current of Pisces experience.

A Pisces woman is well qualified to snare a male Fish in a net of love, and keep him there. She'll intuitively sense that he doesn't like probing into his private thoughts. A bossy mate would never to able to hold this man, and the girl Fish, if she's a typical Piscean female, is submissive without being masochistic. She's intelligent, even wise, yet still vulnerable enough to appeal to the sense of masculine protectiveness within him he so needs to have nurtured. Conversely, she needs a mate who is tender enough to handle her own extrasensitive feelings with consideration, and no one can do that better than a Pisces man.

Their physical union will seldom be unduly passionate and demanding, but then, not everyone needs wild jungle thrills every night. This doesn't mean they'll lead a sterile sexual life. In fact, the sexual experience between two Pisceans can be deeply intimate, in the *true* sense of intimacy. They can escape into their man-woman love from the dark, dreary, mundane drabness of the material world around them, as Nature fish escape from the stale inlets and bays into the cool, green ocean, sparkling in the sunlight, soothing the shore with soft, splashing waves in the moonlight. Sex between these two can be exactly like that—clean, fresh, free—and continually flowing with the mystical poetry of romance. The knights of the medieval days and their ladies fair must have known similar physical expression of their love.

If a Pisces woman notices that the male Fish is somehow dissatisfied and unhappy with his work, despondent around the house, and appears to be increasingly secretive, withdrawn, and cool . . . she might try listening more carefully to his song of lonely. If she tries, she's the one woman who can explain the lyrics to him, since Pisceans are very seldom *self*-analytical, for all their intuitive sense of the feelings of others. He was born under the vibrations of Neptune, and so he instinctively knows that man is a spirit—he has a *soul*—and this is what he longs to recapture, his soul! His secret dream is to stride mountains, swim rivers, climb trees, run through the grass in the rain—barefoot, without shoes—to live his nights and days unburdened by possessions, unrestricted by society's hypocritical dictates. Like Francesco de Bernardone, of Assisi, the Pisces man is at heart a spiritual beggar, yearning privately to follow the bright song of the meadowlark, wherever it may take him. But the modern-day materialistic world permits him neither to confess nor to express his inner longings.

Unless he finds a way to aggressively pursue his real goal, the male Fish can drown in frustration, sometimes sadly turning, in quiet desperation, to the release of disappointment, through the escape of aimless wandering . . . . alcohol, or drugs. He needs a woman who can understand, who won't bind him by the chains of her fears—or condemn him for the passion of his spirit.

As for the girl Fish, her changing moods and periodic teardrops, her long spells of silence . . . nearly always mean that she, too, wishes they could leave behind them the confining aquarium of their existence and swim into wider vistas of wonder and excitement . . . to rest awhile on calm and peaceful lakes of placidity . . . then travel on to beckoning mysteries beyond the faraway horizons. As patient as she is, the Pisces woman gets weary of reading about the adventures of others who dare to drop responsibility and chase the wilder winds out yonder . . . so weary that, after a while, like the Gaelic "Kathleen," even her voice is "sad when ere it speaks."

All she seeks is a light touch on her hand, some sign, some answering light in the eyes of her Pisces lover or husband that says he does — oh! yes, he *does* know how wistfully, yet urgently, she wants to trade security for freedom. Then they can leave together, never mind whether or not it's time for a vacation. Neptune's insistent alarm clock is ringing, telling them both it *is* time to follow their dreams — now or never.

That's when they should run right out and buy a couple of tickets for Ireland, Scotland, Wales, Switzerland, or Tibet. Money? All they need is enough cash for the transportation. Food and shelter will be provided in all sorts of mysterious and unexpected ways by Providence, as surely as with the birds in the sky and the lilies of the field. This Neptune-haunted man and woman know that better than anyone, but they tend to forget it from time to time, when they allow concern for the morrow to take over and smother them. For, when a Pisces man or woman is working at something he or she enjoys, the channels for material security are thrown wide open — like a window to the future.

When they allow themselves to live and love freely, two Fish can become Dolphins, playing happily and wisely together in perfect peace and contentment. And there will be less chance that the fishermen of the cold, hard world, who dangle their sharp hooks in the water to catch the Fish unaware, will be successful. One can warn the other to avoid the tempting bait.

But if they fall into stale habit patterns, allowing all their golden chances to pass them by . . . after a time, they'll begin to deceive each other, to avoid the energy and commitment of emotional confrontation, retreating further and further into themselves. Do you know what that is? It's lazy. And it's a most unhappy ending to a story of enchantment. Why let the trogs and trolls win? That's no way to solve the tender tadpole riddle . . . or learn the lyrics to the love songs of the frogs.

☆ ☆ ☆ ☆ ☆ ☆

Apologia

I regretfully confess that, in 1968, I unintentionally planted a baobab seed of confusion in the Foreword of my book *Sun Signs*. In atonement, I would like to here inform my readers of my awareness of this mistake. In giving an example of the various planet positions of a typical horoscope, a Gemini Sun Sign birthday is presented. The text mentions that, in such a nativity, Mercury might be in Scorpio, giving the person a Scorpion mental process, since Mercury rules the mind, etc. In fact, Mercury could not be in Scorpio when the Sun is in Gemini. Mercury is always located in the same sign as the Sun, or in the sign immediately behind or ahead of the Sun Sign. Therefore, when the Sun is in Gemini, Mercury could only be in Gemini, Taurus or Cancer. In any horoscope at any time.

In self defense, I must explain that the reason this mistake occurred is because I had first written a Libra Sun Sign in my original manuscript as my Sun Sign example of a "typical nativity" — in which Mercury would correctly be in Scorpio. However, as often happens, the Libran "indecision" essence was contagious, and I changed my mind, telling the editor to switch Libra to Gemini, neglecting to also direct the changing of Mercury to Cancer. Perhaps I was subconsciously following the concept of the Persian rug makers, who traditionally leave one tiny flaw in their carpets, so as not to offend Divinity by the presumption of "perfection" in a humble servant of Allah. Perhaps Allah was pleased by Mercury's incorrect placement in Scorpio in the printed text. But I'm sure a rectification of the mistake will leave my writing with sufficient "imperfection" to still appease the supremacy and superiority of Divinity.

As for all the observant readers who have quite properly written to remind me of this error, I'd like to (a) apologize for my own original carelessness which led to a mistake that could be seriously misleading to a student of astrology, (b) thank them for their understanding of the occasional amnesia of the fallible human mind, (c) sincerely and even urgently request that they write, not to me, but to the publishers of *Sun Signs*, Taplinger (hardcover) and Bantam Books (paperback) who are the only ones empowered to rectify the mistake in future printings. Perhaps multiple requests from the public, rather than a repeated single request from one lone author, will at last have the long-desired effect of placing either Mercury or the Sun where it belongs. Meanwhile, I trust this explanation will clarify the Mercurial confusion. The Future is in the hands of those of you who can persuade the book's publishers to consider this more than a minor matter. Thank you for your help in accomplishing this, and for your patience during the last decade. You've been wonderful!

Famous Sun Sign Personalities

Aries, the Ram

1964 Alaskan Earthquake
Hans Christian Andersen
Desi Arnaz
Richard Alpert
   (Baba Ram Dass)
Anita Bryant
Marlon Brando
Bismarck
Chaeli Layne Boken
Jerry Brown
Pearl Bailey
Wernher von Braun
Warren Beatty
Julie Christie
Charles Chaplin
Casanova
Theodore Chapman
Joan Crawford
Stuart Cramer III
Karen Chinatti
Canada/The Civil War
Bette Davis
Denmark
Doris Chase Doane
Thomas E. Dewey
Doris Day
Clarence Darrow
Barbara Doop
Wally Eckert
England
Robert Frost
David Frost
Aretha Franklin
Alec Guinness
Danny Griffith
Vincent van Gogh
Germany

Merle Haggard
Harry Houdini
Mary Ann Henson
William Holden
Billie Holiday
Iceland
   Aries Fire is less
   dangerous than
   Aries Ice.
Henry James
William Lester Jacobs
Linda Janklow
George Jessel
Thomas Jefferson
James Keener
Nikita Khrushchev
William E. Kemery III
Ethel Kennedy
Henry Luce
Clare Boothe Luce
Edmund Muskie
Marsha Mason
Steve McQueen
Ali McGraw
Jim Minow
Myke Minow
Wayne Mackin
Gail Maninna
Wayne Newton
Fr. Anselm Ober O.S.B.
Scarlett O'Hara
Andre Previn
Gen. George S. Patton
Anthony Perkins
Norman Porter
Gregory Peck
Wilhelm Reich

Dane Rudhyar
Diana Ross
Harry Reasoner
Debbie Reynolds
Paul Robeson
Carol Roberts
Gloria Swanson
Gari Lou Cook Schwab
Robert Slatzer
Rod Steiger
Leopold Stokowski
Daniel Schorr
Allison Saul
Omar Sharif
Bessie Smith
Simone Signoret
Spencer Tracy
Lowell Thomas
Evelyn Tucker
Arturo Toscanini
Peter Ustinov
Bobby Vinton
Wilbur Wright
F. W. Woolworth
   Some Rams do
   take care of
   business!
World War I
Thelma Williams
Debbie Williams
Kim Weis
Walter Winchell
Tennessee Williams
Christian Williams
Julie Yarbrough
Fred Zopfi
Alfred E. Neuman

Since not a single one of the fifty states in the USA is an Aries state, we Rams all hereby petition the Government — no, we Rams all hereby *order* the Government to grant statehood to Puerto Rico, and demand that it be accepted into the Union of these United States in April. Any April will do.

Taurus, the Bull

Cher Bono Allman
Fred Astaire
Debbie Atwell
James M. Barrie (author
    of *Peter Pan*)
        Who says the Bull
        has no
        imagination ?
Johannes Brahms
Charlotte Brontë
Archie Bunker
        Carrol O'Connor is
        a Leo, but Archie
        is a Bull.
Robert Browning
Shirley Temple Black
Your Friendly Banker
Lionel Barrymore
Carol Burnett
        Slapstick, slapstick !
Oliver Cromwell
Jacque Cook
Earl Cunningham
Sue Cook
Gary Cooper
Howard C. Chinatti
Glen Campbell
Joseph Cotten
Scott Carpenter
Judy Collins
Bing Crosby
Pierre Curie
Salvador Dali
Thelma V. Dunlap
Queen Elizabeth II
Glenn Ford
Cynthia Hayward Ford
Margot Fonteyn
Barry Farber

Henry Fonda
Patrick Ferguson
Ella Fitzgerald
Jim Fox
Herr Sigmund Freud
Ulysses S. Grant
        "I propose to fight
        it out on this line
        if it takes all
        summer."
        (Spoken by Grant
        during the Civil
        War)

Sam O. Goodman
Greenland
Brian Gravestock
Greece
Adolf Hitler
Audrey Hepburn
Wm. Randolph Hearst
The State of Israel
        "and so they made
        a garden in the
        desert . . ."
Iraq
Coretta King
Mazie McBee Kemery
Henry J. Kaiser
Randy King
Catherine, the Great
Lamarr Koford
Liberace
        (music in his soul !)
Joe Louis
Louisiana
Nikolai Lenin
Gail Scott Longshore
Ho Chi Minh

Karl Marx
        I have no idea
        why people claim
        Bulls are stubborn,
        have you ?

Golda Meir
Richard R. Mertens
        Vice Pres.
        Colorado Springs
        National Bank

Machiavelli
Henry Morgenthau
Minnesota
Dr. Charles A. Musès
Christiane Musès
Jeff Mackin
Ted Mueller
Maryland
Rod McKuen
Willy Mays
Shirley MacLaine
James Mason
Ricky Nelson
Persia
Tyrone Power
Anthony Quinn
Madame Olga Ryss
Sugar Ray Robinson
Robespierre
John Simon
Socrates
Phil Sylvia
Dr. Benjamin Spock
William Shakespeare
William "Bill" Scheffer
Barbra Streisand
Tom Snyder — NBC

Spanish-American War
James Stewart
Bill Smith
Clyde Timmons
Peter Tompkins
Tchaikovsky
Carolyn Thornton

Harry S Truman
Leslie Uggams
Rudolph Valentino
  Never
  underestimate the
  sensuality of the
  male Bull.

Leonardo da Vinci
Mike Wallace
Orson Welles
Gene Williams
Alfred E. Neuman

Gemini, the Twins

Arkansas
The Ascendent of the
  United States
Linda Bailey
F. Lee Bailey
Frank Blair — NBC
Pat Boone
Stephanie Blank
Martin C. Carney
Arlene Cohen
Your Favorite Clone
Rachel Carson
Tony Curtis
Roland Chinatti, Sr.
Judith Crist
Bennett Cerf
Lowell Cook
John Dillinger
Bill Dufty
Florence Dessart
Arthur Conan Doyle
Jefferson Davis
Bob Dylan
William "Bill" Elliott
Sir Anthony Eden
Egypt
Ian Fleming
Errol Flynn
Paul di Franco
Hank Fort
Judy Garland
Flo Gaffney
Avrumele Hirsch
  Goldboggen
Helen Hall
Lillian Hellman
Bob Hope

Hubert Humphrey
Lodi Hern
Jackie Habeggar
Burl Ives
Angela Janklow
Al Jolson
Dr. Jekyll and Mr. Hyde
  (See also Scorpio.)
Morton Janklow
John Fitzgerald Kennedy
Kentucky
Henry Kissinger
T. Bertram "Bert" Lance
  . . . and you say
  you don't believe
  in astrology ?

Paul Lynde
Stan Laurel
  (Laurel & Hardy)
Peggy Lee
Beatrice Lillie
Grant Lewi
Norbie Larsen
Dorothy McGuire
Paul McCartney
Katie Mead
Dean Martin
Joe Namath
Charles Frederick Neff
Robert Preston
  (The Music Man)
  "I tell you there's
  trouble, yes,
  trouble—right
  here in River
  City . . ."

Rodney Proffitt
Your Favorite Polygraph
  Examiner
Vincent Price
Norman Vincent Peale
Prince Philip, Duke of
  Edinburgh
Cole Porter
Vance Packard
Rosalind Russell
Jane Russell
Jill Schary Robinson
Basil Rathbone
Nomi Rubel
Rhode Island
Nancy Sinatra
William H. Snyder
South Carolina
Wally Simpson
Tennessee
Mike Todd
Mo Udall
Your Friendly Used Car
  Salesman
Queen Victoria
Walt Whitman
John Wayne
Wisconsin
Johnny Weissmuller
Wales
The War of 1812
Brigham Young
  Gemini people
  must own two of
  everything — or
  more.
Alfred E. Neuman

Cancer, the Crab

John Armstrong, Sr.
    Chairman of the
    Board
    Colorado Springs
    National Bank
John Armstrong, Jr.
    Loan Officer
    Colorado Springs
    National Bank
John Quincy Adams
Louis Armstrong
Your Friendly Banker
Milton Berle
Orson Bean
Ralph Bergstresser
Ingmar Bergman
Saul Bellow
Nancy Lee Boken
Yul Brynner
Pearl S. Buck
Captain Kangaroo
Mark Cohen
Glen Cohen
Julius Caesar
Calvin Coolidge
George M. Cohan
    "It's a Grand Old
    Flag!"
James Cagney
    who played George
    M. Cohan, naturally.
Bob Cortez
John Calvin
Marc Chagall
Dorothy Chinatti
Marvin Cook (Sr.)
John Chancellor
Diahann Carroll
Bill Cosby
Cathy Dressel
Olivia De Havilland
Phyllis Diller
Mary Baker Eddy
Glen Evelyn Fuller
Elias Santillames
Lori Ferguson

Cathy Fenton
Tillie Friedman
Stephen Foster
Gerald Ford
Darlene Fleury
Sue Fleury
Ilene Goldman
Merv Griffin
John Glenn
Erwin Glikes
King Henry VIII
    Watch your
    waistline, Henry!

Ernest Hemingway
Richard "Hap" Housman
Teddy Hayek
Lena Horne
Holland
Hermann Hesse
Oscar Hammerstein II
John Handrock
Your Friendly Insurance
    Salesman
Idaho
Alix Jeffry
Elisabeth Jakab
Dorothy Kilgallen
Rose Kennedy
    (Mother of
    Mothers)
The Korean War
Donald Katz
Victor Kupelian
Helen Keller
Steve Lawrence
Art Linkletter
Ann Landers
Liberia
Charles Laughton
Gina Lollobrigida
Anne Morrow Lindbergh
Dorothy Mackin
George McGovern
Joseph Montebello
The Moon Landing
New Hampshire

New York City
    Come on now,
    confess your secret.
    You're not really
    broke — you have a
    little something
    tucked away you're
    saving for a real
    emergency, right?

Lloyd Ostendorf
George Orwell
W. V. Quine
Rembrandt
John D. Rockefeller
Nelson Rockefeller
Della Reese
Ginger Rogers
Linda Ronstadt
Richard Rodgers
Jason Robards
Red Skelton
George Sanders
Jennifer Smith
Scotland
Ringo Starr
Neil Simon
Henry David Thoreau
Nikola Tesla
Lynda Sturner Traum
The United States
Virginia — West Virginia
    I know the two of
    you quarreled over
    the Mason-Dixon
    line, but tell the
    truth now, you're
    homesick for
    Mama, right?

Joe Vetter
Abigail Van Buren
The Duke of Windsor
Philip Willas
Tim Williams
Andrew Wyeth
Alfred E. Neuman

Leo, the Lion

Neil Armstrong
Gracie Allen
Tara Andromeda
Peter Alfano
Robert A. Brewer
Eleanor Boardman
Ray Bradbury
Bill "Count" Basie
John Bowman
Lucille Ball
Ethel Barrymore
James Baldwin
Helena Blavatsky
Emily Brontë
Robert Burns
Bernard Baruch
Napoleon Bonaparte
Stuart Cramer III
Fidel Castro
Rosalynn Carter
Colorado
Roland Chinatti, Jr.
Tyrone Culbreath
Denver Dressel
Alexandre Dumas
Cecil B. De Mille
Paula Diamond
Amelia Earhart
Richard Finch
Philip de Franco
Dr. Rosemary Felton
Eddie Fisher
Henry Ford, Sr.
Florence Goldstein
Samuel Goldwyn
Goober

William Goldman
Ed Gilbert
Hugh Guinn
Alfred Hitchcock
Valerie Harper
Hawaii
Isabelle Hickey
Aldous Huxley
Hollywood
Ed Hall
"June" Hack
Italy — and Texas
Carl Jung
Bill Janson
Gene Kelly
Luella Koford
Robert Stratton Kemery
B. N. Kljunak
Your Favorite King
Los Angeles
Alan Leo
Bert Lahr
Princess Margaret Rose
Benito Mussolini
Missouri
Mata Hari
Robert Mitchum
George Meany
Ogden Nash
New York State
Carroll O'Connor
    (but Archie Bunker
    is a Taurus)
Jacqueline Kennedy
    Onassis
Sydney Omarr

Rita Ostendorf
Carol Peel
Your Favorite Queen
Pres. Richard Nixon's
    resignation
Henry Rothblatt
Rome
    Home of the
    romantic Italian
    lovers.

Robert Redford
Pat Sawyer
David Steinberg
Yves Saint-Laurent
Sally Struthers
George Bernard Shaw
James Songer
Superman
Robert Taylor
Teddy Traum
Rudy Vallee
Orville Wright
Paul Weis
Carroll Weis
William Webb
Natalie Wood
Shelley Winters
Mae West
Geoffrey Whitney
Andy Warhol
Bobby Williams
Mike Williams
Whitney Young
Alfred E. Neuman

Virgo, the Virgin

Eddie "Rochester"
    Anderson
Cleveland Amory
Geof Andromeda
Athens, Greece
Prince Albert

Anne Bancroft
Donna Blank
Sheila Barry
Boston, Mass.
    Wouldn't you just
    know ?

Your Favorite CPA
Ingrid Bergman
    (cusp Leo)
Lauren Bacall
Leonard Bernstein
Charles Boyer

Betty Burton
Miriam Birmingham
Olive Carney
Lloyd Cope
California
  Living down Leo
  Hollywood is so
  humiliating.

Maurice Chevalier
Taylor Caldwell
Charles Edison Cameron
Your Favorite Computer
Ray Charles
Sid Caesar
Queen Elizabeth I
Henry Ford II
Peter Falk
Elliott Gould
Greta Garbo
Arthur Godfrey
Jesse James
  Well, after all, he
  was a loner.

Lyndon Baines Johnson

Laverne King
Virgie Kistler
Joseph Kennedy, Sr.
Annette Kemery
Elia Kazan
Shelley King
Ira Levin
Peter Lawford
D. H. Lawrence
Alan Ladd, Sr.
Sophia Loren
Eve Leonard
George Montgomery
Grandma Moses
Martha Mitchell
John Mitchell
H. L. Mencken
Joyce Mueller
Mickey Mouse
Robert Allen Neff
O. Henry
J. C. Penney
Jack Provenzano
Paris, France
Cardinal Richelieu
Walter Reuther

Adel Ramadan
William Saroyan
Wallace Seawell
Peter Sellers
Your Favorite Scrub
  Brush
Twiggy — Leslie Hornby
Teddy Traum
Turkey
Robert Taft
Leo Tolstoy
Wm. Howard Taft
Margaret Trudeau
Cornelius Vanderbilt
Nancy Wyeth
Andy Weis
George C. Wallace
Anne Williams
Hank Williams
H. G. Wells
Washington, D.C.
Roy Wilkins
Sheila Barry Weisman
Darryl F. Zanuck
Alfred E. Neuman

Libra, the Scales

Julie Andrews
Jack Anderson
Margaret Kemery Bolden
Rona Barrett
  She does try to be fair,
  Frank.

Markell "Binky" Brooks
Art Buchwald
Charles Boyer
Charlie Brown — Peanuts
Faith Baldwin
Sarah Bernhardt
Brigitte Bardot
China
Al Capp
Diane Chinatti
Truman Capote
Montgomery Clift

Gladys Cunningham
Johnny Carson
Jimmy Carter
Mary Eaton
Mack Eaton
Dwight Eisenhower
F. Scott Fitzgerald
Don Fleury
Darcia Fleury
Arlene Francis
George Gershwin
Mahatma Gandhi
David Ben Gurion
John Gaffney
Dan Gravestock
Helen Hayes
Charlton Heston
Susan Hirschhorn
Rita Hayworth

Charles Jayne
Marc Edmund Jones
Your Favorite Judge
George King
Deborah Kerr
Stanley Kramer
Buster Keaton
  Well, he did display
  great Libra BALANCE
  in his pratfalls, even if
  he wasn't dimpled.

Latvia
Timothy Leary
John Lennon
Franz Liszt
Carole Lombard
Connie Larsen

Groucho Marx	Mickey Rooney	Tibet
Argue, argue, argue !	Marriage is a "must"	Amanda Thornton
	for Libra.	Vienna, Austria
Yves Montand		Gore Vidal
Marcello Mastroianni	Eleanor Roosevelt	Shame on you, Gore.
Walter Matthau	Mary Alice Robinson	You and Aquarian
Jayne Meadows	George Redfield	Mailer are Trine.
Mickey Mantle	Mary Redfield	
Mary Alice Morris	Steve Stutman	Oscar Wilde
Arthur Miller	Ed Sullivan	Dee Watson
Eugene O'Neill	George C. Scott	Barbara Walters
Carol Peel	Marc Salinger	Margaret Whitney
Emily Post	Pierre Trudeau	Thomas Wolfe
George Peppard	Kenneth Traudt	Noelle Williams
	Michael Todd, Jr.	Alfred E. Neuman
	Jerome Traum	

Among the fifty states, there are only two Sun Signs not represented. Aries and Libra. There are no Aries states and no Libra states in this country. We Rams have already ordered Washington to take Puerto Rico into the Union in April. (Any April.) But when Puerto Rico becomes the fifty-first State, and the first Aries state, we're still facing the problem of having no Libra State. What sort of nation will this be in the future with no Balance, no Justice, no Fairness — no Libra influence ?

It's really time to make a firm decision. I suggest that all Librans now write to their congressmen and inform them (pleasantly and charmingly) that we insist that our Government invite and accept the Hopi Indian Nation into the Union of these United States, and that the Hopis should be granted statehood in October. (Any October, but preferably soon.) Considering the unjust way our Government has treated the True Owners of this country in the past, it's the only *fair* thing to do, to balance the crimes of yesterday.

Still, when you look at the *other side*, you have to consider the possibility that the Hopi Nation might refuse the invitation to statehood. The Hopis may not want to become part of the USA, and who could blame them ? So, it would be more *fair* to ask the opinion of the Hopis first, don't you agree ? It may even be a better idea to incorporate all American Indians into the fifty-second State of the Union—or maybe incorporate each still-existing Indian tribe as one State each (split between Aries and Libra, incorporating all of them in either April or October). *What do you think ?*

Scorpio, the Scorpion
with some scattered Grey Lizards and Eagles

Charles Atlas
John Adams
Saint Augustine
Spiro Agnew
Dan Blank
Brazil
William S. Bolden
Daniel Boone
Pamela Lynn Boken
Richard Burton
Bradley Brewer
Steve Cook
Chiang Kaishek
Walter Cronkite
Grant Cramer
Prince Charles
Dick Cavett (surprise!)
Suzanne Chinatti
Marie Curie
Art Carney (surprise!)
Count Dracula
Charles de Gaulle
Richard Dreyfuss
Lois McAtee Earley
Mamie Eisenhower
Herbert Elliott
Phyllis Finkel
Frankenstein (See also
    Sagittarius.)

Sally Field
Elmer Gantry
HRH Princess Grace of
    Monaco
Ann Guinn
Herbert Goodman
Donna Goodman
Chester Gould
    Therefore, also
    Dick Tracy.
Michael Aaron Goodman
Art Garfunkel
    "Sounds of
    Silence" — shhh!

Indira Gandhi
Roger Good
Billy Graham
Kathleen Hyde
Margaret Mary Hack
Goldie Hawn
    "You never know,
    with Scorpio."

Harold Hern
Katharine Hepburn
Your Favorite Hypnotist
Rock Hudson
Warren G. Harding
Anna House
Robert Henson
W. Averell Harriman
The Incredible Hulk
Mahalia Jackson
Dr. Jekyll and Mr. Hyde
    (See also Gemini.)

James Jones
Robert Kennedy
Arthur Klebanoff
King Kong
Robert Keller
Hedy Lamarr
Lydia Link
Martin Luther
Vivien Leigh
Elsa Lanchester
Alan Ladd, Jr.
Burt Lancaster (Elmer
    Gantry)
Moe — New York
Marie Antoinette
Burgess Meredith
Montana
Don Mabry
Margaret Mitchell
Jawaharlal Nehru
Mike Nichols
Norway

Ernest Nagel
North Dakota
Oklahoma
Your Friendly
    Psychiatrist
Panama
Pablo Picasso
Rose Rankin
Theodore Roosevelt
Will Rogers
Sheila Ray — just
    received
    her Eagle
    wings in
    Detroit.

Skip Reagan
South Dakota
Dolores Simon
Carl Sagan
Gracie Slick
Jonas Salk
June Simpson
Stock Market Crash
    of '29
Soviet Union — U.S.S.R.
    Trick or Treat!

Sicily (ditto)
Bud Saunders
Billy Sunday
Cody John Schwab
Leon Trotsky
Dylan Thomas
The United Nations
Kurt Vonnegut, Jr.
Voltaire
Washington State
Barbara Weis
Buz Wyeth
Dale Weis
Jonathan Winters
Ort "Zeke" Yeager
Alfred E. Neuman

Sagittarius, the Archer

Australia
Alabama
Louisa May Alcott
Wm. F. Buckley, Jr.
Billy the Kid
Leonid Brezhnev
Beethoven
William Blake
Dolly Brown
Andrew Carnegie
Maria Callas
Marvin Cook
Dale Carnegie
Winston Churchill
Chile
Noël Coward
Suzy Chaffee
Kirk Douglas
Patty Duke
Winston Davis
Sammy Davis, Jr.
Benjamin Disraeli
Walt Disney
Donald Duck
L. Sprague de Camp
Joe DiMaggio
Delaware
Joanna Ellison
Betty Ford
Carolyn Finch
Douglas Fairbanks, Jr.
Finland
Jane Fonda

Aaron Goldblatt
Julie Harris
Hungary
Paul H. House
Sydney Hook
Indiana
Illinois
Pope John XXIII
Emmett Kelly, clown
Boris Karloff
   (See also Scorpio.)

Wally Koford
Jay King
Jackie King
Jeff King
Mary Todd Lincoln
The Louisiana Purchase
John Lindsay
John Mayall
Monaco
The Monroe Doctrine
John Milton
Harpo Marx
Agnes Moorehead
Mary Martin
Mississippi
New Jersey
Neil Neff
Betty Neff
North Carolina
Michel d 'Obrenovic

Otto Preminger
Pennsylvania
Adam Clayton Powell, Jr.
Eleanor Roosevelt
Lee Remick
George Segal
Sally Snyder
Charles Schultz
Bill Swain
Ruby Swain
Frank Sinatra
Spain
Siam
David Susskind
Betty Scheffer
James Thurber
Toulouse-Lautrec
Mark Twain
Cal Worthington
   "Go see Cal."
   But watch that
   Moon-in-Gemini.

Mark Weisman
   who saw the rings
   around Saturn

Dionne Warwicke
Andy Williams
World War II
Virginia Zitnik
Alfred E. Neuman

Capricorn, the Goat

Alaska
Afghanistan
Konrad Adenauer
Isaac Asimov
Steve Atwell
Steve Allen
Muhammed Ali
Horatio Alger

Your Friendly Banker
Julian Bond
Louis Braille
Ray Bolger
George Burns
   (cusp Aquarius)
   played title role of God
   in *Oh, God!*

Clara Barton
Humphrey Bogart
Pablo Casals
Molly Malone Cook
Nat "King" Cole
Al Capone
Doris Cooper
Jay Cheda, M.D.

Marlene Dietrich
John Denver
Federico Fellini
Benjamin Franklin
Rachel Fallon
Francis Gunn
Henry Gine
Georgia
Eydie Gormé
David Lloyd George
Jill Kemery Goodman
Barry Goldwater
Ava Gardner
Cary Grant
Gold discovered in
    California
Howard Hughes
    Jan. 9, 1907 (not
    12–24–'05)
    morning hours

Robard Hughes
    Jan. 9, 1907 (not
    12–24–'05)
    afternoon hours

Alexander Hamilton
J. Edgar Hoover
Oliver Hardy
    "Okay, now stop
    the foolishness,
    Stan."

Ann Hayek
Iowa
India
Joan of Arc
James Earl Jones
Diane Keaton
Royce King
Alan King
Danny Kaye
Rudyard Kipling
Martin Luther King
General Robert E. Lee
Gypsy Rose Lee
Shari Lewis
David Nathaniel Moore
Terry Moore
Steve Mackin
Henry Miller
Zoltan Mason
James Mendenhall
Ethel Merman
Sal Mineo
Mexico — New Mexico
Mao Tse-tung
Nostradamus
Patricia Neal
Richard Nixon
Sir Isaac Newton
Aristotle Socrates
    Onassis
Louis Pasteur

Kay Powers
Bobbs Pinkerton
Elvis Presley
Edgar Allan Poe
Roy Rogers (Tulsa, not
    Hollywood)

Helena Rubenstein
Rod Serling
Jack Schwab
Carl Sandberg
Robert Stack
Comrade Joseph Stalin
Anwar el-Sadat
Jean Stapleton (See
    Aquarius.)
Albert Schweitzer
Danny Thomas
Utah
Darth Vader —
    (Star Wars)

Edward Watson
Woodrow Wilson
Lael Weisman
Daniel Webster
Alan Watts
Jane Wyman
"Doc" Yarbrough
Loretta Young
Alfred E. Neuman

Aquarius, the Water Bearer

Arizona
Evangeline Adams
The Abominable
    Snowman
Big Foot — Sasquatch
Kelley Blank
Tallulah Bankhead
Jack Benny
Robert Burns
Pearl Burt
Sonny Bono
Jim Brown

Helen Gurley Brown
    "Listen, Burt, I
    have this
    absolutely unique
    concept for a
    Cosmo
    centerfold . . . . . ."
Burt Reynolds
    "Helen, that's a
    really wild idea !
    Let's shock 'em !"

Ernest Borgnine
Shelley Berman
Francis Bacon
John Barrymore
Edith Bunker (See
    Capricorn.)
Lewis Carroll
Joel Cohen
Carol Channing
Paddy Chayefsky
Pat Caps

Anton Chekhov
Gus Carlson
Gertrude Dial
James Dean
Jimmy Durante
Charles Darwin
Ruth Edwards
Richard Ellsberry
Thomas Edison
Jules Feiffer
Bernard Friedman
W. C. Fields
Galileo
Kathryn Grayson
Clark Gable
Eva Gabor
Zsa Zsa Gabor
Thelma Guinn
Mother Goose
Ann Hayek
Debra Hayek
Sherman Hemsley
Hans Holzer
Langston Hughes
Sherlock Holmes (See also
    Gemini.)
James Riddle Hoffa
Harvey, the Rabbit
James Joyce
George Jefferson
Kansas
Ron Kistler

Vickie King
Liechtenstein
Abraham Lincoln
Charles Lindbergh
Jack Lemmon
The Loch Ness Monster
Claudine Longet
Edward Mannina
Wolfgang Mozart
Massachusetts
Lee Marvin
Norman Mailer
Leslie McKetchnie
    —an Aquarian
    toe dancer with
    flexible arches
    whose sister starred
    in *Chorus Line* on
    Broadway

General Douglas
    MacArthur (cusp)
Michigan
Bonnie Mackin
The Mad Hatter
Somerset Maugham
Ray Neff
Kim Novak
Paul Newman
Joanne Woodward
Oregon
Yoko Ono

Leontyne Price
Mia Farrow Previn
Princess Caroline of
    Monaco
Carroll Righter
Norman Rockwell
Vanessa Redgrave
Franklin D. Roosevelt
Bill Robinson
Ronald Reagan
Ayn Rand
Nona Stodart
Erika Songer
Telly Savalas
Wm. Dana Snyder
Adlai Stevenson
Gertrude Stein
Bobby Smith
Saint Subber
Franz Schubert
Sweden
John Travolta
Lana Turner
Fern Vetter
    (cusp Cappy)
Jules Verne
Paul Weisman
Robert Wagner
Virginia Woolf
John Warner
Alfred E. Neuman

Pisces, the Fish

Edward Albee
Ron Austin
George Abell
Alexander Graham Bell
    (no relation to
    Ma Bell)
Joan Bennett
Elizabeth Barrett
    Browning
Dr. Floyd R. Banks, Jr.
Harry Belafonte

Luther Burbank
William Bairn
Way Bandy
Frank Borman
Cleve Backster
Grover Cleveland
Johnny Cash
Godfrey Cambridge
Amy Cohen
Shannon Chinatti
Fréderic Chopin

Barbara Cook
Enrico Caruso
Ruth Cook
Edgar Cayce
Sandy Duncan
Winston Davis
John Foster Dulles
Julian E. Davis
J. Fred Earley
Sue Snyder Elliott
Leroy Davis

Albert Einstein
Florida
Peter Fonda
Leland Feitz
Nina Greenhouse
Jackie Gleason
John Kevin Gaffney
Pauline Goodman
Milton Green
Patricia Hearst
Manly P. Hall
Ruth Henderson
Jean Harlow
Victor Hugo
Rex Harrison
Handel
Annelore Hall
George Harrison
Dick Johnson
Lord Snowden
Ted Kennedy
Sybil Leek
Jerry Lewis
Mike Mansfield

Zero Mostel
Pamela Mason
Michelangelo
James Madison
Liza Minnelli
Maine
Helen Mason
Patrick Moynihan
Nebraska
Rudolf Nureyev
Ralph Nader
Augusta Neff
Waslaw Nijinsky
David Niven
Patricia Nixon
Ohio
Portugal
Sidney Poitier
Lois Proffitt
Charles Ruffing
Michael Redgrave
Lynn Redgrave
Auguste Renoir
Lee Radziwill

Carl Reiner
Rimski-Korsakov
Rudolph Steiner
Dale Simpson
Buffy Saint Marie
David Sarnoff
John Sporing
Dinah Shore
John Steinbeck
Svetlana Stalin
South Africa
Mike Thornton
Vermont
Elizabeth Taylor
Thomas Wolfe
Danny Weis
Lawrence Welk
      Mister Bubbles!
George Washington
Harold Wilson
Robert Young
Maude Zopfi
Alfred E. Neuman

Note: Not all, but most of the Sun Signs of the cities, states and countries in the foregoing lists were kindly contributed by the distinguished astrologer Manly P. Hall.

Personality Types

CARDINAL SIGNS	FIXED SIGNS	MUTABLE SIGNS
(leaders)	(organizers)	(communicators)
Aries	Taurus	Gemini
Cancer	Leo	Virgo
Libra	Scorpio	Sagittarius
Capricorn	Aquarius	Pisces

POSITIVE (MASCULINE) SIGNS	NEGATIVE (FEMININE) SIGNS
(aggressive, dynamic idealists)	(secretive, reflective strategists)
Aries	Taurus
Gemini	Cancer
Leo	Virgo
Libra	Scorpio
Sagittarius	Capricorn
Aquarius	Pisces

FIRE SIGNS	AIR SIGNS
(inspirational)	(mental)
Aries — Cardinal Fire	Libra — Cardinal Air
Leo — Fixed Fire	Aquarius — Fixed Air
Sagittarius — Mutable Fire	Gemini — Mutable Air

EARTH SIGNS	WATER SIGNS
(material)	(sensitive)
Capricorn — Cardinal Earth	Cancer — Cardinal Water
Taurus — Fixed Earth	Scorpio — Fixed Water
Virgo — Mutable Earth	Pisces — Mutable Water

ARIES:	Fire-Positive-Masculine-Cardinal
	Inspirational, aggressive, dynamic, idealistic *Leader*
LEO:	Fire-Positive-Masculine-Fixed
	Inspirational, aggressive, dynamic, idealistic *Organizer*
SAGITTARIUS:	Fire-Positive-Masculine-Mutable
	Inspirational, aggressive, dynamic, idealistic *Communicator*

CAPRICORN:	Earth-Negative-Feminine-Cardinal
	Secretive, reflective, strategist *Leader*
TAURUS:	Earth-Negative-Feminine-Fixed
	Secretive, reflective strategist *Organizer*
VIRGO:	Earth-Negative-Feminine-Mutable
	Secretive, reflective, strategist *Communicator*

LIBRA:	Air-Positive-Masculine-Cardinal
	Mental, aggressive, dynamic, idealistic *Leader*
AQUARIUS:	Air-Positive-Masculine-Fixed
	Mental, aggressive, dynamic, idealistic *Organizer*
GEMINI:	Air-Positive-Masculine-Mutable
	Mental, aggressive, dynamic, idealistic *Communicator*

CANCER:	Water-Negative-Feminine-Cardinal
	Sensitive, secretive, reflective, strategist *Leader*
SCORPIO:	Water-Negative-Feminine-Fixed
	Sensitive, secretive, reflective, strategist *Organizer*
PISCES:	Water-Negative-Feminine-Mutable
	Sensitive, secretive, reflective, strategist *Communicator*

The Karmic Mission of the Twelve Sun Signs

ARIES:	to LEAD — in an *inspirational*, aggressive, dynamic and idealistic manner.
LIBRA:	to LEAD — in a *mental*, aggressive, dynamic and idealistic manner.
CAPRICORN:	to LEAD — in a *material*, secretive, reflective and strategic manner.
CANCER:	to LEAD — in a *sensitive*, secretive, reflective and strategic manner.
LEO:	to ORGANIZE — in an *inspirational*, aggressive, dynamic and idealistic manner.
AQUARIUS:	to ORGANIZE — in a *mental*, aggressive, dynamic and idealistic manner.
TAURUS:	to ORGANIZE — in a *material*, secretive, reflective and strategic manner.

SCORPIO:	to ORGANIZE — in a *sensitive*, secretive, reflective and strategic manner.
SAGITTARIUS:	to COMMUNICATE — in an *inspirational*, aggressive, dynamic and idealistic manner.
GEMINI:	to COMMUNICATE — in a *mental*, aggressive dynamic, and idealistic manner.
VIRGO:	to COMMUNICATE — in a *material*, secretive, reflective and strategic manner.
PISCES:	to COMMUNICATE — in a *sensitive*, secretive, reflective and strategic manner.

And so, the Holy Mission with which each man and woman is charged, is to personify the blessed birthright of the individual Sun Sign.

This is the wise and loving message from our co-Creators, channeled through Their messengers and interpreters, the stars, planets and Luminaries — through everything Solar, everything Lunar and everything Stellar — to all men and women everywhere.

Only in being true, each to his or her own holy Sun Sign mission, may unity and harmony be created out of chaos and confusion, to bring about that day when Their Will *shall* be done on Earth, as it is in Heaven.

In the beautiful synchronicity of astrological balance, our co-Creators arranged that all four Cardinal Signs (Leaders) be made up of equal parts of the positive-masculine and the negative-feminine essence, and also of equal parts of the four elements, of Fire, Earth, Air and Water.

The same perfect balance and harmony exist within the ranks of the four Fixed Organizers, and the four Mutable Communicators.

Each part of the whole is different, with the result that all are the same — which is the Great Cosmic Riddle of Wisdom and Truth. The first step toward solving it — and it is only the first step, for there are many more — is that *Imperfection* equals *Perfection*. This first step toward enlightenment is detailed in "The Twelve Mysteries of Love" in the beginning of this book.

The Blending of the Elements

FIRE SIGNS

Aries
Leo
Sagittarius

Fire blends easily with Fire and Air but requires tolerance to blend with Earth and Water.

AIR SIGNS

Libra
Aquarius
Gemini

Air blends easily with Air and Fire but requires tolerance to blend with Earth and Water.

EARTH SIGNS

Capricorn
Taurus
Virgo

Earth blends easily with Earth and Water but requires tolerance to blend with Fire and Air.

WATER SIGNS

Cancer
Scorpio
Pisces

Water blends easily with Water and Earth but requires tolerance to blend with Fire and Air.

FIRE and FIRE

When Fire meets Fire, the resulting higher and hotter flames may create a conflagration, which will either consume itself, and burn out — or light the darkness, and melt the ice and fear of negative thinking. The choice lies equally with both individuals.

AIR and AIR

When Air meets Air, there is complete freedom of movement, little or no restriction. This blend can result in a glorious mental, emotional and spiritual uplifting. But Air becomes stale and polluted without the winds of change, and Air can be whipped into the frenzy of a tornado under certain conditions. The choice lies equally with both individuals.

EARTH and EARTH

When Earth meets Earth, this blend can build itself into a tall mountain of faith and strength — or can instead become a dry desert, depending on which direction it takes. When agitated, the result can be an earthquake, with volcanic repercussions. The choice lies equally with both individuals.

WATER and WATER

When Water meets Water, there is no resistance, resulting in a continual stream of inspiration, flowing eventually into a greater ocean of enlightenment — or on the negative side, it may trickle into a stagnant inlet, where there is no escape. Water cools the thirst but, when out of control, brings destructive floods. The choice lies equally with both individuals.

FIRE and AIR

Air fans Fire, and causes it to burn more brightly, stimulating enthusiasm and excitement — or inciting passion and anger. Too much Fire can burn up the oxygen in Air, making it difficult to breathe — and too much Air, such as a strong wind, can cause a flame to flicker ever more dimly. The choice lies equally with both individuals.

FIRE and EARTH

It is always obvious which is the stronger and more enduring of the two elements. Earth remains where it is, unless moved by inner explosion, or through outside forces. Fire charts its own course, ever reaching toward the heavens. Fire can scorch Earth but never completely destroy it. Earth will support Fire, forming a stable foundation for its flames; yet too much Earth can bury the brightest Fire. The choice lies equally with both individuals.

FIRE and WATER

A large Fire can dehydrate or dry out a small amount of Water, with excessive heat. On the other hand, large quantities of Water can extinguish Fire, put out its flames. Therefore, Fire instinctively either fears or respects Water, and vice versa. Both subconsciously sense the danger — that each is capable of completely destroying the other. The choice lies equally with both individuals.

EARTH and AIR

Earth contains Air and needs it, but Air neither contains Earth nor needs it. Earth is obligated to remain where it is, moving only through earthquake, volcanic or outside forces. Air has freed itself from such restrictions, moving above the Earth at whim, neither changing Earth nor long remaining. Earth is detached from Air, seemingly unaware of its existence, until strong winds disturb the plants and flowers growing on its surface, rooted in its bosom. The outcome is determined by choice, which lies equally with both individuals.

EARTH and WATER

Water seeks a home, which it finds within the Earth, penetrating Earth and moistening it, which is a blessing to the Earth — for it is Water's penetration alone that allows Earth to "mother" all forms of living plants, trees and flowers. Without the *enrichment* of Water, Earth is dry and useless. Without the Earth to moisten, Water's course is aimless and equally useless. These two elements were designed each to need the other. But too much Water can turn Earth into mud or quicksand — and too little Water can be lost, can disappear within the mountainous masses of Earth. The outcome is determined by choice, which lies equally with both individuals.

AIR and WATER

Air penetrates Water . . . stirs it, churns it into lashing waves . . . then moves away . . . an infiltration or attack over which Water has no control. When Water penetrates Air in the form of moisture, it causes Air to be heavy. But, in the process, it also brings to all of Nature the blessed relief of rain, magically changing Air *into its own element*, a transmutation over which Air has no control. In the final analysis, there is no choice of outcome for *either* individual — only through Destiny's Higher Will.

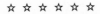

☆ ☆ ☆ ☆ ☆ ☆

Sun Sign Patterns

1-1 Sun Sign Pattern

Aries — Aries
Taurus — Taurus
Gemini — Gemini
Cancer — Cancer
Leo — Leo
Virgo — Virgo
Libra — Libra
Scorpio — Scorpio
Sagittarius — Sagittarius
Capricorn — Capricorn
Aquarius — Aquarius
Pisces — Pisces

2-12 Sun Sign Pattern

Aries — Pisces
Taurus — Aries
Gemini — Taurus
Cancer — Gemini
Leo — Cancer
Virgo — Leo
Libra — Virgo
Scorpio — Libra
Sagittarius — Scorpio
Capricorn — Sagittarius
Aquarius — Capricorn
Pisces — Aquarius

3-11 Sun Sign Pattern

Aries — Gemini
Aries — Aquarius
Taurus — Cancer
Taurus — Pisces
Gemini — Leo
Cancer — Virgo
Leo — Libra
Virgo — Scorpio
Libra — Sagittarius
Scorpio — Capricorn
Sagittarius — Aquarius
Capricorn — Pisces

4-10 Sun Sign Pattern

Aries — Cancer
Aries — Capricorn
Taurus — Leo
Taurus — Aquarius
Gemini — Virgo
Gemini — Pisces
Cancer — Libra
Leo — Scorpio
Virgo — Sagittarius
Libra — Capricorn
Scorpio — Aquarius
Sagittarius — Pisces

5-9 Sun Sign Pattern

Aries — Leo
Aries — Sagittarius
Taurus — Virgo
Taurus — Capricorn
Gemini — Libra
Gemini — Aquarius
Cancer — Scorpio
Cancer — Pisces
Leo — Sagittarius
Virgo — Capricorn
Libra — Aquarius
Scorpio — Pisces

6-8 Sun Sign Pattern

Aries — Virgo
Aries — Scorpio
Taurus — Libra
Taurus — Sagittarius
Gemini — Scorpio
Gemini — Capricorn
Cancer — Sagittarius
Cancer — Aquarius
Leo — Capricorn
Leo — Pisces
Virgo — Aquarius
Libra — Pisces

7-7 Sun Sign Pattern

Aries — Libra
Taurus — Scorpio
Gemini — Sagittarius
Cancer — Capricorn
Leo — Aquarius
Virgo — Pisces

THE KARMIC WHEEL OF LIFE

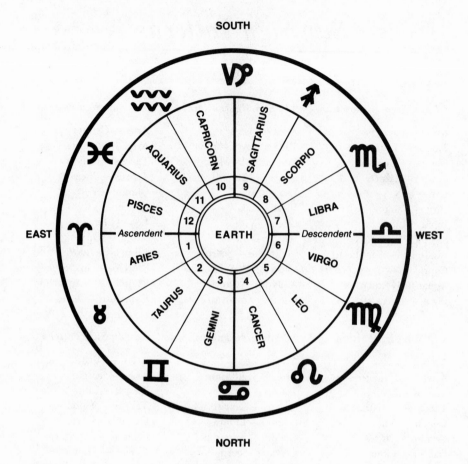

THE SYMBOLS

Aries	♈	Libra	♎	Mars	♂	Pluto	♇
Taurus	♉	Scorpio	♏	Venus	♀	Jupiter	♃
Gemini	♊	Sagittarius	♐	Mercury	☿	Saturn	♄
Cancer	♋	Capricorn	♑	Moon	☽	Uranus	♅
Leo	♌	Aquarius	♒	Sun	☉	Neptune	♆
Virgo	♍	Pisces	♓				

As you will see from the Karmic Wheel of Life on the opposite page, the Sun Sign Patterns are derived as follows: Counting each Sun Sign itself as Number One, Aries is the ninth house from Leo and Leo is the fifth house from Aries (always counting counterclockwise). Therefore, Aries-Leo is a 5-9 Sun Sign Pattern.

Taurus is the ninth house from Virgo — and Virgo is the fifth house from Taurus. Therefore, Taurus-Virgo is also a 5-9 Sun Sign Pattern. Likewise — Taurus-Capricorn and Virgo-Capricorn. The same method may be used to locate all the various Sun Sign Patterns.

You will notice that the numbers of all Sun Sign Patterns add to the double number 14. All except the 1-1 Sun Sign Pattern. This contains a deep mystery, and represents an important mystical symbolism of the Male-Female principle, related to Twin Souls.

The number 14 symbolizes the fourteen pieces of Osiris, who was slain by his brother, Set — his body then cut into fourteen pieces and his soul simultaneously separated into fourteen pieces. It has been the task of the Twin Soul of Osiris — Isis — to search for these fourteen pieces of her mate, throughout many weary eons of time. Legend states that, in the Aquarian Age, the fourteen pieces of Osiris will come together in one man — *"with all his scattered pieces whole"* — and he will be re-united with his Twin Soul, Isis. (Note that the name Osiris contains within it the name of Isis.)

All Sun Sign Patterns add to the mystical Isis-Osiris number of Fourteen allowing each Sun Sign combination to search for unity, each within his or her own vibratory pattern. The only way lovers or mates who are influenced by the 1-1 Sun Sign Pattern vibration may recognize one another as Twin Souls — and satisfy their Karma — is for one of them to be sufficiently spiritually evolved to "vibrate" to the Higher Octave number of the "1" — which is thirteen. When added to the "1" of the other person, this combination then adds to the mystical Isis-Osiris Twin Soul number of fourteen. If both people under the 1-1 Sun Sign Pattern influence vibrate to the Higher Octave of "1," which is the number 13 — then the two of them will be under the vibratory influence of the number Eight (8). (Two times 13 equals 26, which, when its two numbers are added together, becomes the single number eight.) The number eight represents the DOUBLE Serpent Circle Mystery of Love. Two circles or Zeros, one on top of the other. (See "The Twelve Mysteries of Love" section in the front of this book.) Therefore, when the two persons involved in a 1-1 Sun Sign Pattern are spiritually advanced in equal measure, they may experience the "Thunderbolt Path" of Karma (along with certain others, under different particular circumstances) and reach enlightenment swiftly together . . . though this is a rare mystical achievement.

☆ ☆ ☆ ☆ ☆ ☆

Mutual Aspects

A reference guide for the
following Sun Sign Compatibilities

Sun Signs, *Moon Signs* and *Ascendents* that are TRINE (positive or harmonious) to
each other

Aries — Leo	Gemini — Libra	Leo — Sagittarius
Aries — Sagittarius	Gemini — Aquarius	Virgo — Capricorn
Taurus — Virgo	Cancer — Scorpio	Libra — Aquarius
Taurus — Capricorn	Cancer — Pisces	Scorpio — Pisces

Sun Signs, *Moon Signs* and *Ascendents* that are SEXTILE (positive or harmonious)
to each other

Aries — Gemini	Gemini — Leo	Libra — Sagittarius
Aries — Aquarius	Cancer — Virgo	Scorpio — Capricorn
Taurus — Cancer	Leo — Libra	Sagittarius — Aquarius
Taurus — Pisces	Virgo — Scorpio	Capricorn — Pisces

Sun Signs, *Moon Signs* and *Ascendents* that are CONJUNCT (positive or
harmonious) or CONJOINED with each other

Aries — Aries	Leo — Leo	Sagittarius — Sagittarius
Taurus — Taurus	Virgo — Virgo	Capricorn — Capricorn
Gemini — Gemini	Libra — Libra	Aquarius — Aquarius
Cancer — Cancer	Scorpio — Scorpio	Pisces — Pisces

Sun Signs, *Moon Signs* and *Ascendents* that are SQUARE (negative or
inharmonious) with each other

Aries — Cancer	Gemini — Virgo	Virgo — Sagittarius
Aries — Capricorn	Gemini — Pisces	Libra — Capricorn
Taurus — Leo	Cancer — Libra	Scorpio — Aquarius
Taurus — Aquarius	Leo — Scorpio	Sagittarius — Pisces

Sun Signs, *Moon Signs* and *Ascendents* that are OPPOSED (negative or
disharmonious) or in OPPOSITION to each other

Aries — Libra	Cancer — Capricorn
Taurus — Scorpio	Leo — Aquarius
Gemini — Sagittarius	Virgo — Pisces

Sun Sign Compatibilities

1-1 Sun Sign Pattern

If your own Sun Sign is:

Aries	....	Aries
Taurus	....	Taurus
Gemini	....	Gemini
Cancer	....	Cancer
Leo	....	Leo
Virgo	....	Virgo
Libra	....	Libra
Scorpio	....	Scorpio
Sagittarius	....	Sagittarius
Capricorn	....	Capricorn
Aquarius	....	Aquarius
Pisces	....	Pisces

You are influenced by the 1-1 Sun Sign Pattern with the signs listed here opposite your own — in friendship, business, family or love relationships.

In your associations with these people born under your own Sun Sign, you will each be tempted to magnify your own virtues and failings. All the positive personality and character traits in both of you will increase in their intensity — as will the negative traits. A constant effort should be made to encourage in one another the "good" qualities of the Sun Sign you both share — and to discourage and be tolerant of the "bad" qualities of the Sun Sign you both share.

° Mutual aspects between the other planets, the Moons and the Ascendents of the two horoscopes will somewhat modify the description of the relationship given above (in either a positive or negative way) but will not basically alter the foundation of the 1-1 Sun Sign Pattern interchange as described.

2-12 Sun Sign Pattern

If your own Sun Sign is:

Aries	Aries has lessons to learn from Taurus — Taurus is tolerant of Aries shortcomings and different outlook.	Taurus
Taurus	Taurus has lessons to learn from Gemini — Gemini is tolerant of Taurus shortcomings and different outlook.	Gemini
Gemini	Gemini has lessons to learn from Cancer — Cancer is tolerant of Gemini shortcomings and different outlook.	Cancer
Cancer	Cancer has lessons to learn from Leo — Leo is tolerant of Cancer shortcomings and different outlook.	Leo
Leo	Leo has lessons to learn from Virgo — Virgo is tolerant of Leo shortcomings and different outlook.	Virgo
Virgo	Virgo has lessons to learn from Libra — Libra is tolerant of Virgo shortcomings and different outlook.	Libra
Libra	Libra has lessons to learn from Scorpio — Scorpio is tolerant of Libra shortcomings and different outlook.	Scorpio
Scorpio	Scorpio has lessons to learn from Sagittarius — Sagittarius is tolerant of Scorpio shortcomings and different outlook.	Sagittarius
Sagittarius	Sagittarius has lessons to learn from Capricorn — Capricorn is tolerant of Sagittarius shortcomings and different outlook.	Capricorn
Capricorn	Capricorn has lessons to learn from Aquarius — Aquarius is tolerant of Capricorn shortcomings and different outlook.	Aquarius
Aquarius	Aquarius has lessons to learn from Pisces — Pisces is tolerant of Aquarius shortcomings and different outlook.	Pisces
Pisces	Pisces has lessons to learn from Aries — Aries is tolerant of Pisces shortcomings and different outlook.	Aries

You are influenced by the 2-12 Sun Sign Pattern with the signs listed here opposite your own — in friendship, business, family or love relationships.

In your associations with these people, one of you will feel that he (or she) has many lessons to learn from the other. The one who has lessons to teach will feel an inexplicable compassion for the weaknesses and mistakes of the other person, strangely understanding the other's markedly different motives and behavior.

° Mutual aspects between the other planets, the Moons and the Ascendents of the two horoscopes will somewhat modify the description of the relationship given above (in a positive or negative way) but will not basically alter the foundation of the 2-12 Sun Sign Pattern interchange as described.

3-11 Sun Sign Pattern

If your own Sun Sign is:

Aries	....	Gemini and Aquarius
Taurus	....	Cancer and Pisces
Gemini	....	Aries and Leo
Cancer	....	Taurus and Virgo
Leo	....	Gemini and Libra
Virgo	....	Cancer and Scorpio
Libra	....	Leo and Sagittarius
Scorpio	....	Virgo and Capricorn
Sagittarius	....	Libra and Aquarius
Capricorn	....	Scorpio and Pisces
Aquarius	....	Aries and Sagittarius
Pisces	....	Taurus and Capricorn

You are involved in a 3-11 Sun Sign vibration pattern with the signs listed here opposite your own — in friendship, business, family or love relationships.

You'll feel a strong tie of friendship, whatever the association you share with these individuals. There will be mutual trust, and much ease of communication, back and forth. You are very different; yet these differences have little or no effect on your regard for each other. There could be a sense of responsibility, some sort of inescapable duty, that brings you together, and strengthens the bond between you. You'll find these individuals easy to talk with, and you'll constantly stimulate each other into changing habits and existing situations.

You'll probably form very close friendships with these people, and remain friendly always. Any quarrels will usually be quickly resolved, forgiven and forgotten. You may bicker and disagree frequently, and be annoyed by some mutual obligation that ties you together, yet be unable to avoid it — and even when the association seems to be a closed chapter — it will reappear months or years later, to be once more resumed.

° Mutual aspects between the other planets, the Moons and the Ascendents of the two horoscopes will somewhat modify the description of the relationship given above (in either a positive or negative way) but will not basically alter the foundation of the 3-11 Sun Sign Pattern interchange as described.

4-10 Sun Sign Pattern

If your own Sun Sign is:

Aries	.... Cancer and Capricorn
Taurus	.... Leo and Aquarius
Gemini	.... Virgo and Pisces
Cancer	.... Libra and Aries
Leo	.... Taurus and Scorpio
Virgo	.... Gemini and Sagittarius
Libra	.... Cancer and Capricorn
Scorpio	.... Leo and Aquarius
Sagittarius	.... Virgo and Pisces
Capricorn	.... Aries and Libra
Aquarius	.... Taurus and Scorpio
Pisces	.... Gemini and Sagittarius

You are influenced by the 4-10 Sun Sign Pattern with the signs listed here opposite your own — in friendship, business, family or love relationships.

Not always, but surprisingly often, you'll feel a noticeable tension or conflict of personality in the presence of those born under the Sun Signs listed here opposite your own — either disapproving of them, or sensing that they disapprove of you in some way. One person may grow restless because of the strict disciplinary attempts of the other. There will always be some degree of mental and emotional restriction, for various reasons.

° If other planets between the two horoscopes (especially the Moons and Ascendents) are in harmonious (conjunction, sextile or trine) mutual aspect, an intense devotion, loyalty and respect will be exchanged between you and these people — causing the undeniable basic differences of motivation and personality to be less frustrating, less irritating — although these major differences of outlook and goals will always remain.

° If the other planets between the two horoscopes (especially the Moons and Ascendents) are in square or opposed (negative) aspect, your relationships with these people will be tense and difficult indeed, and will require nearly the patience of sainthood to be overcome — although the rewards of such overcoming will be great.

5-9 Sun Sign Pattern

Aries	....	Leo and Sagittarius
Taurus	....	Virgo and Capricorn
Gemini	....	Libra and Aquarius
Cancer	....	Scorpio and Pisces
Leo	....	Aries and Sagittarius
Virgo	....	Taurus and Capricorn
Libra	....	Gemini and Aquarius
Scorpio	....	Cancer and Pisces
Sagittarius	....	Aries and Leo
Capricorn	....	Taurus and Virgo
Aquarius	....	Gemini and Libra
Pisces	....	Cancer and Scorpio

You are influenced by the 5-9 Sun Sign Pattern with the signs listed here opposite your own — in friendship, business, family or love relationships.

Not always, but surprisingly often, you'll find easy empathy, mental stimulation, emotional affinity (or romantic fulfillment) with these people.

There will be strong sympathy between you, and misunderstandings will usually not be severe or lasting. The chances for harmony are excellent, and a happy relationship on a permanent basis is more effortlessly achieved than with any other Sun Sign.

° If other planets (especially the Moons and Ascendents) between the two horoscopes are in square or opposed (negative) mutual aspect, there will be some personality clashes and tensions between you and these people — causing the compatibility you share to rock and waver from time to time — although the basic empathy and understanding will always remain.

° If other planets between the two horoscopes (especially the Moons and Ascendents) are in harmonious aspect (conjunct, sextile or trine), your relationships with these people will be most extraordinarily happy, smooth and sympathetic.

6-8 Sun Sign Pattern

Aries	...	Virgo and Scorpio
Taurus	...	Libra and Sagittarius
Gemini	...	Scorpio and Capricorn
Cancer	...	Sagittarius and Aquarius
Leo	...	Capricorn and Pisces
Virgo	...	Aries and Aquarius
Libra	...	Taurus and Pisces
Scorpio	...	Aries and Gemini
Sagittarius	...	Taurus and Cancer
Capricorn	...	Gemini and Leo
Aquarius	...	Cancer and Virgo
Pisces	...	Leo and Libra

You are involved in a 6-8 Sun Sign vibration pattern with the signs listed here opposite your own — in friendship, business, family or love relationships.

You will have some problem in communicating with these individuals. Yet, you'll be oddly intrigued by the puzzling charisma, and powerfully drawn into its spell. If the tie between you is a love relationship, you'll feel an irresistible sexual attraction toward the individual.

If the relationship is not love, but is one of friendship, or a business or family association, then the person will draw you, not through sexual chemistry, but through some shared interest in the supernatural — death, birth, reincarnation, adoption, and all spiritual matters — or situations involving money which belongs to neither of you — i.e.: other people's money. There may be times when this person will seem unnecessarily secretive in your association.

In some way, these individuals will have a desire to help you, and you'll feel an urge to help them. One or both of you, will serve the other willingly, with little or no resentment — and one will often protect the other from those who attempt to harm her — or him. There may be times when the favors extended are resented; yet there will be no choice in the matter. Under this vibrational pattern, service given will always be repaid by the fascination of the association itself. In some way, a great benefit will come from one to the other through the relationship, and the one who serves will usually remain loyal.

° Mutual aspects between the other planets, the Moons and the Ascendents of the two horoscopes will somewhat magnify the description of the relationship given above (in either a positive or negative way) but will not basically alter the foundation of the 6-8 Sun Sign Pattern interchange as described.

7-7 Sun Sign Pattern

If your own Sun Sign is:

Aries	....	Libra
Taurus	....	Scorpio
Gemini	....	Sagittarius
Cancer	....	Capricorn
Leo	....	Aquarius
Virgo	....	Pisces
Libra	....	Aries
Scorpio	....	Taurus
Sagittarius	....	Gemini
Capricorn	....	Cancer
Aquarius	....	Leo
Pisces	....	Virgo

You are involved in a 7-7 Sun Sign pattern with the sign listed here opposite your own — in friendship, business, family or love relationships.

Not always, but frequently, you will be either physically attracted to — or secretly admire and respect — those of the *opposite sex* born under the Sun Sign listed here opposite your own (and also opposed to your own on the Karmic Wheel) because these individuals possess the qualities of character and personality traits you yourself lack. The attraction and the urge to imitate will be strong.

However, you may feel uneasy, envious of — or strongly competitive with those individuals of *your own sex* who were born under this Sun Sign.

° Mutual aspects between the other planets, the Moons and the Ascendents of the two horoscopes will somewhat modify the basic description of the relationship given above (in either a positive or negative way) but will not basically alter the foundation of the 7-7 Sun Sign Pattern interchange as described.

A Time to Embrace

Astrology's answer to Birth Control
and Abortion

". . . . . . flesh of our flesh, joy of our joy, Life of our Love"

*To everything there is a season, and a time for
every purpose under the heaven . . . . . . a time to be
born . . . . a time to cast away stones, and a
time to gather stones together . . . . . . a time to
embrace, and a time to refrain from embracing . . .*

ECCLESIASTES 3:1–5

The Biblical verses from which the above words are taken contain some of the few references to astrology that still remain in the scriptures for our enlightenment. Originally, there were many references to both astrology and reincarnation. But this was before particular religious groups and individuals that found cause to hide these truths from the masses committed their spiritual surgery upon the holy works. Thankfully, they missed a few in their various purges — and this quotation is one of several overlooked until it was too late to remove it. Too late because too many followers would have questioned its disappearance after the advent of the printing press, which made mass distribution of the Bible possible, enabling it to become well known and widely quoted.

The entire verse from Ecclesiastes (quoted only partially here) refers to the synchronizing of events on Earth to planetary movements and configurations — and the need for men and women to learn the expediency of timing their important actions to *harmonize* with the flow of cosmic currents, rather than timing them to *oppose* these powerful forces. What could be more natural, more sensible than that ?

The reference to *"a time to embrace, and a time to refrain from embracing"* concerns a specific knowledge possessed by the Temple High Priests. These men, who, during the ministry of Jesus of Nazareth, were all competent astrologers (as was Jesus himself, having been trained and taught by the Essenes), had prostituted the basic spiritual aspects of astrology all the way to teaching that "God" demanded the bloody sacrifice and "burnt offering" of helpless animals and birds. These same High Priests forced worshipers to pay a steep price for their pathetic victims at the very doors of their places of worship—which so incensed even the gentle Galilean that, in outrage, he lashed these greedy money changers with a whip.

One of the specific bits of wisdom known to the Temple High Priests was that which "a time to embrace" makes reference to, as well as "a time *not* to embrace." The words concerned (and still do today) the planning of "fortunate" conceptions—and the avoiding of conception (of human life).

Things haven't changed much since the "inner circle" of religious adepts (who were, every single one of them, astrologers) kept helpful knowledge exclusively among themselves to give them more "mysterious power" over the people—or since the time when either the discussion of such knowledge was sternly forbidden—or the matters themselves were simply removed from the scriptures. The suppression of vital facets of astrological truth continues today, to the serious detriment of progress in all walks of Life. Such as "the time to embrace"—or *not* to embrace.

Love Signs is a book concerned with love and harmony, and this leads naturally into the mystery of birth in all of Nature. To a man and woman who love, who are happily and harmoniously mated, the child they create together in their own likeness (as their co-Creators conceived *them*) is a very special miracle. "Flesh of our flesh, joy of our joy, *Life* of our love." There is no magic so deep as that which allows us to become creators ourselves. Yet, to possess the power of such magic and mystery is to be burdened with the *responsibilities* of wisdom. All power, whether temporal or spiritual, brings with it the obligation to exercise it with compassion—and wisdom.

It was predestined that the Aquarian Age should explode the controversy of abortion upon us and *demand* a solution. Each man and each woman holds an opinion, highly individual, regarding this vital matter of life and death. But whether abortion is right or wrong is not the true Aquarian issue. Our concentrated efforts in the New Age should not be directed toward judging the guilt or innocence involved in either the acceptance or the rejection of abortion, but toward the problem that *causes* the agonizing choice—unwanted pregnancy. Right *or* wrong, abortion would not be necessary if all babies were desired, and none unwelcomed. And so, the real problem, the true issue, is not one of abortion, but of how to eliminate all unwanted conceptions.

The Catholic Church has taken the view that abortion is an act against Nature and against spiritual Wholeness. The Catholic view is correct. Abortion is precisely that. I'm sorry, ERA ladies, but honesty forces me to point this out as a basic law of biology. Never mind the accusations of anti-Catholics, who claim the Catholic abortion stand is taken "so there will be more Catholics in the world." That's beginning to be a worn and weary claim, whether it's true *or* false. The fact is that abortion *is* an act against Nature. The motive of the Catholic Church Fathers in so decreeing is not important — only the validity or nonvalidity of the stand itself. The Catholic Church and all other orthodox and unorthodox religions, like everything else (and like every individual — except Virgos, or course), are imperfect in some ways and perfect in others. Even the suppression of astrology by the Church *in the beginning* was wisely and properly motivated (before it was later distorted). It's true that astrology is knowledge — knowledge is power — and power can most certainly corrupt. Especially when scattered to the masses without discrimination.

Human nature being what it is, there are bound to be those uninitiated, material-minded people who abuse and disuse astrology for selfish purposes, who "abort" (pardon the word) and prostitute this ancient art and science for worldly gain — or even for dark and sinister purposes. (Hitler was one.) The proof of this particular pudding lies all around us today. There are thousands of people who practice astrology as some sort of corny fortune-telling device, commercializing it for financial profit and treating it as merely an entertaining party pastime.

Because the Catholic Church has taken the view it has concerning abortion, sincere Catholics have available to them only the "rhythm method" of controlling birth, which fails substantially more often than it succeeds — quite naturally, since its "successes" are pure accident, being rather like spinning the "Wheel of Fortune." Episcopal Bishop James Pike aptly termed it "Vatican Roulette."

As for men and women who are not bound morally by the Catholic view, they've already investigated, discussed or personally experimented with other various birth control methods, from the dangerous coil and even more dangerous "pill," to all the rest of the several remaining artificial methods and devices for circumventing conception, and have found them all to be far less than ideal. Some are ineffective and unreliable, some harmful to the body, some offend human sensitivity and remove all beauty from the physical expression of love — while others are emotionally upsetting and mentally disturbing for both men and women — and still others are depressingly final, removing all possibility of a future change of mind regarding parenthood.

Consequently, we're left with the same problem, which continues to trouble all men and women greatly — and deeply. Children are a blessing, representing the continuation of human life; yet no useful Heavenly or otherwise purpose is served by bringing *unwanted* babies into a world already trembling with the fast approaching tragedy of over-population, conjuring the spectre of the Apocalypse Horsemen of Famine and Starvation. There must be a way of controlling birth that's not harmful to health, is both religiously and aesthetically acceptable, costs nothing and is 100 percent dependable.

There is. It's called "astrobiology," and it works like this. As the ancients who planned the conception of Kings knew well, a woman can conceive *only* during a certain approximately two-hour period of each Lunar month, when the Sun and the Moon are exactly the same number of degrees apart as they were at the moment of the woman's first breath at birth — which may be discovered simply from the planetary positions (astronomically calculated) contained in any ephemeris. Without exception, a woman can conceive at no other time than this approximately two-hour period, easily determined if her birth data are known. Each individual woman's "cycle" is different, bearing no relation to the generalized, and consequently inaccurate, so-called "rhythm method." It's absolutely foolproof. And awesomely profound.

Assuming the birth data given by the woman's parents to her (and by her to the astrologer) is *correct* — and barring all the deplorable deceptions practiced in legal adoption — a woman doesn't even need to know the hour of her birth. Simply the *correct* month, day and year will suffice to allow the professional astrologer (who should, of course, be chosen with great care, as to both efficiency and ethics) to present her with the gift of this totally reliable, absolutely harmless and spiritually acceptable "period of abstinence." For it falls on a certain day, different each Lunar month, as well as different for each woman. If a day or two are added as a safety margin on either side of the day within which the two "fertile hours" fall — lovers and mates will need to *"refrain from embracing"* only five days per month.

In addition to the men and women who don't desire to create a child or children, whatever their personal reasons, there are those many thousands of heartbroken, yearning couples who desperately want a child but who have been unable to create one, for various, frequently incorrectly diagnosed reasons — and to these Sun Sign lovers, astrobiology can truly be the greatest of blessings.

When a man or woman believes (usually mistakenly) that he or she is sterile or barren, the solution need not (and should not) be a "test tube" baby. For complex metaphysical reasons, the test tube creation of life can be a serious danger to human evolvement. There's no space to explore these reasons here, but I'll discuss such dangers in detail in a forthcoming book. The point is that couples who have been medically told they can't create a baby — and who sincerely long for one — have two choices open to them, both of which can bestow happiness — and neither of which will bring the possible negative future results of test tube conceptions (negative for the entire planet, not just for the individuals directly involved).

The first choice is the adoption of one of the millions of babies and children all over the world who so very much need love and care. According to obstetricians, it's a strange and statistically supported phenomenon that more than 70 percent of women who have adopted babies because they've been told they are "barren" by doctors (or believe they are) or have been told their husbands are "sterile" (because of a low sperm count, which can *also* be remedied through the use of the man's birth data) have "miraculously" conceived their own child *after* having adopted one — and *after* having been told they could never bear an infant of their own. There's really nothing "miraculous" about this frequent phenomenon. It simply follows the basic law of Karma and Reincarnational precepts. The woman's (or man's) inability to create a child stems from karmic causes, in former incarnations, and these karmic obligations are often erased (or fulfilled) by the act of taking in a homeless child to love and protect — the child of another. Such an act of love and compassion has the energy and power to cancel most karmic debts of "childlessness," unless they are too heavy for such a "reprieve" to occur in the present lifetime, and must wait for the next. But such latter instances are rare. This is an oversimplification of the Law of Karma, but a more detailed explanation must wait for the aforementioned forthcoming book.

Perhaps some couples who have chosen to avoid the responsibilities of parenthood (which is their undeniable right and privilege) could devote a little of their free time (free from the task of raising a family) to helping those who do want children — by making an effort to assist in untangling the red tape, the illogical, irrational and outdated adoption requirements that cruelly separate so many worthy couples from the homeless infants and children who need their love and devotion. The desire to adopt is repeatedly and sadly thwarted by archaic laws and intimidating procedures every hour of every day. We should all try to help one another, instead of labeling and attacking one another. That's what the Aquarian Age is all about. And love, too. And harmony. And Peace. All those good things.

The second option open to those couples who wish to conceive a child rather than to prevent conception, is astrobiology — which they may use with the same kind of success as those who seek prevention. The only difference is that when astrobiology is used for *prevention* of conception — the hour and minute and location of the woman's birth are not needed. As I mentioned earlier, only the *correct* month, day and year are necessary. But when astrobiology is utilized for a *wanted* conception, in order to guarantee success, the precise two-hour fertile period must be known, which requires, in addition to the *correct* month, day and year of the woman's birth — also the hour and minute she drew her first breath — and the longitude-latitude of her birthplace.

The concept of astrobiology has been meticulously researched, in scientifically controlled tests with thousands of women, by scientists of impeccable reputation, such as medical-astrological pioneer Dr. Eugene Jonas of Czechoslovakia. Dr. Jonas' work also has been confirmed by Dr. Karl Rechnitz, a professor of gynecology, in Budapest. All medical testing has resulted in a consistent record of 98 to 99 percent accuracy.

Yet astrologers know that the 98 to 99 percent record is misleading. Astrobiology must be 100 percent reliable, because the planets and the Luminaries are precise in their movements. Astrology is a mathematical science, and when applied to such instances, cannot be wrong, even two percent of the time. (Astrobiology is unrelated to either the character analysis or the predictive aspects of astrology. It is not an "interpretive" process. It is pure math.)

The 98 to 99 percentage results achieved by Dr. Jonas and Dr. Rechnitz, startling and miraculous as they are by comparison with other birth control methods, have undoubtedly failed of 100 percent reliability for reasons that all professional astrologers are familiar with — that adopted women's foster parents have given them false birth dates — or that, in large part, women have been reluctant to admit they cheated on the abstinence period assigned to them by the calculations made in Dr. Jonas' clinic. After all, he did not accompany them home or station an observer outside their bedroom doors. It would be nice to know for a certain fact that human nature has so evolved as to be incapable of deception, but let's be realistic.

I attempted to discuss this during an exceptionally enlightening conversation with Dr. Jonas himself, on an overseas phone call in 1970. But we were somewhat hampered by the necessity of using an interpreter — and by his being unable to meet with a group of intensely interested medical people and myself here in America because of government restrictions over his movements — which still exist, but which may someday soon be lifted, in a spirit of international trust and cooperation toward a common goal for the benefit of all people of all countries.

You see? All this fussing and fighting over the subjects of abortion and birth control, when astrology could solve it all, and keep everyone on both sides of the issue happy — even the immovable Vatican — not to mention the infants themselves, who would so much rather be warmly welcomed into this world with love . . . . . . than to be coldly rejected.

It's surely time for all of us to *demand* of the scientific community and government agencies that they begin to exhibit some Capricorn common sense regarding astrobiology — that they display some Aquarian Age vision — or at least curiosity — concerning these matters they've so long stubbornly refused to investigate, or to even seriously consider, because certain dogmatic astronomers and the like have insisted on petulantly dismissing astrology as childish superstition. *They* are the childish ones. *They* are the superstition-governed ones. Not astrologers.

When scientists finally get around to seriously and open-mindedly investigating and researching astrobiology, they'll find the simplest and most dependable way to prove its reliability is to work backward through what the astrologers call "the pre-natal epoch," which is merely an astrological method of counting back from the exact birth time of a test group or perhaps a thousand infants to the true and precise time of conception — which will invariably and infallibly reveal a Sun-Moon relationship to match that of the mother's at her birth — and will also match the sex of the infant by the "sex" of the astrological sign in which the moon was deposited at that time. A computer could easily be programmed to accomplish this.

Meanwhile, the abortion controversy rages on — and because of the blindness of scientists who wear the dark glasses of dogma, the entire planet faces the possibility of over-population, which will bring the certain results of famine, hunger and death-by-starvation of every-hour-increasing-millions-upon-millions of men, women and children all over the world.

It could mean the destruction of all we hold dear that medicine, government, religion — and yes, even the Women's Liberation Movement itself — have all been so brain-washed and soul-washed by groups of misguided astronomers and other scientists who haven't the slightest idea whereof they speak regarding planetary matters. To these critics who seem never to halt their intense campaign to discredit astrology, one can only repeat Isaac Newton's answer to the astronomer Halley, when the latter scoffed at astrology: "Sir, I have *studied* the matter. *You have not.*"

Unfortunately, as the brilliant Gemini astrologer Grant Lewi once noted: astrology is believed in by a lot of people who know practically nothing about it — and *dis*believed in by even more who know *absolutely* nothing about it. The skeptics who continue to attempt to crucify this ancient art and science seem to be driven by some obsession they can't explain in any rational fashion. Pathetically, the ones who are suffering from their obsession are the unhappy and unfulfilled childless couples, who long for a family — and those who would like to avoid both abortion and the defiance of their own religious faith through using "forbidden" and dangerous birth control methods — plus those of us who would like to save this planet from the future nightmare of all manner of unnecessary human misery.

Astrology is a Science of Time. This is the basis of all its precepts (including astrological character analysis, which is itself based on the *time* of birth). Astrology is concerned with all human events and destiny, as well as with the twelve basic personality types that encompass all of mankind and womankind. Time is an essential astrological factor of our lives, because we are completely and eternally dependent upon the world around us, dependent upon the synchronicity of the Universe and the cosmic currents for the very air we breathe, the food that nourishes us, the water we drink, the Light that illuminates our existence . . . and even the thoughts and ideas that are seeded into our minds to finally grow into manifested forms in the material world.

Time is Life itself, actively engaged in *being*. Time is the constantly flowing stream of circular motion that represents and *manifests* the consciousness of our co-Creators throughout all the Solar Systems, Universes and Galaxies of Their creation. It's only intelligent then, to place ourselves, as individuals, in harmony with other people, and with our surrounding environment — which we can do only by cooperating with the vibratory influences of the planets and the Luminaries (the Sun and Moon), which are themselves *governed and directed* by our co-Creators. What matter if They are called by the name of "God," "Divinity," "Allah," the "Almighty" or the

"Supreme Being"? Just as "a rose by any other name" is still a rose, so is a Higher Intelligence by any other name still a Higher Intelligence. To align ourselves *against* rather than *with* a Higher Intelligence is futile, although perhaps clearly the proof of our own *lower* intelligence — which, as it rises in awareness, brings us ever closer to recognizing our Makers and to *being able to effectively communicate with them.* No mere mortal can possibly imagine the depth of longing with which *They* pray for such communion ... such eons-awaited reunion. As even Earth parents dream achingly of the return of their own children ... in their *first state of innocence,* so swiftly gone ... so do God and His Mate dream achingly of the return, in original innocence, of Their own angels, as they were before they "fell" and forgot the beauty and wonder of cosmic joy. Jesus tried to convey the pathos of this Divine Desire by saying, "Except as ye become as little children, ye cannot enter the Kingdom." But his words fell, for the most part, on deaf ears ... upon hearts too hardened to be able to comprehend their sheer simplicity.

Although Time (which astrology *alone,* among all sciences, allows us to control, channel and synchronize) is an urgent factor in our very existence, it is not always the single factor of human success and happiness on Earth. There are situations that require the additional factors of our divine gifts of choice and reason. Therefore, the timing of astrology is, upon occasion, effectively used only in connection with the individual's choice of attitude and reasoning ability. A farmer, for example, may choose exactly the *right* planetary Time to plant his corn. Yet if he exercises poor judgment in the selection of his seed, or plants his seed in rocky, barren soil — he will achieve negative results. Conversely, he can plant good and fertile seed in rich, nourishing soil at the *wrong* planetary Time — and achieve the same negative results. It's a matter of harmony and balance. The planets are not in *full* control of our destiny. *Nor are we.* But when we join forces with astrology's infallible "timing," we are then (and *only* then) undefeatable and guaranteed victorious.

One aspect of astrological "timing," however, is always dependable, with or without the human factor of choice and reason (once the decision to use it has been made). Astrobiology. The Timing of the creation of Human Life, over which our co-Creators have wisely retained absolute and ultimate control. They share the power over Life with us only when we submit to Their own more perceptive Timing Wisdom — which is too complex for us to calculate alone. Nor is our mortality capable of comprehending and analyzing the reasons for its inflexible structure. This offer of sharing control over such urgent matters as conception and birth is a sacred gift from Them ...... to those of Their own children who are spiritually mature enough to understand it.

Only a few short weeks before his death in the summer of 1978, Pope Paul VI unexpectedly, and somewhat inexplicably, made a touching public appeal through the news media all over the world — a moving plea for scientifically minded people of integrity and compassion to *strive harder* to find some solution to the birth control problem that lies at the bottom of the agonizing abortion dilemma. A solution that would be safe, effective — and of which the Church could also morally approve. (It was more than coincidental that his appeal was made shortly before the announcement of the birth of the first test tube baby.)

Like his namesake, Paul, before him, he faced a nearly impossible task. As mentioned elsewhere in a Gemini chapter of this book, the earlier Paul was faced with the challenge of telling the Gentiles they could be "saved" *without* circumcision, when the Jews had already decreed that circumcision was a *necessity* of salvation. With Gemini mental brilliance and verbal adroitness (for Paul was surely born under the Sun Sign of the Twins) he managed to pull off this miracle of persuasion and apparent contradiction in a manner acceptable to both sides. A major spiritual and intellectual triumph.

In a similar manner was Pope Paul VI forced to combine his wits, his compassion and his fair Libran judgment to try to encourage and bring about a sensible solution to the pressing and inseparably linked problems of birth control and abortion. The Church Fathers in Rome, the Pope himself included, of course, are a group of learned, astute, exquisitely educated and informed men — who are presently and always have been fully aware of the concept of astrobiology. For the simple reason that they are fully aware of *all* aspects of astrology. (The largest astrological library in the world is in the Vatican, and the Pope's bathtub itself is inscribed with the twelve Sun Signs of the zodiac. Although these facts are not sent forth as news releases, neither are they suppressed.) Yet despite the extent of his awareness, Libran Pope Paul was faced with the certain knowledge that he could not dare take such a giant step as to encourage a belief in astrology, so long formally condemned by the Roman Church, whatever his personal views might or might not have been as to the reliability of all or partial planetary matters. He surely could not "commission" or ask directly for such an astrological study as that of Dr. Jonas — although you can be absolutely positive that he knew, that he was aware of Dr. Jonas' work. (The Vatican is aware of simply everything.)

But . . . if perchance someone *else* should seriously investigate astrobiology, prove its validity — and Catholic women should begin to use this safe and sure method of birth control — the Church would then be asked publicly to either approve or disapprove. Just as the Church approved of the unreliable "rhythm method" of birth control because it offended no spiritual principles, so would the Church (by *fairly* applying the identical requirements) be forced to approve of astrobiology, if queried, for the same reason. However, for Rome to pronounce that astrobiology "offends no spiritual principles," some prudent "religious deception" and "looking the other way" might be a required expediency, such as calling the process by another name, perhaps linking it to astronomy or some other "respectable" science. But a rose by any name . . . . as we know . . . is still a rose. Few people know that astrology is the mother of astronomy, not the other way around. The great astrologers of the past whom modern scientists now term "astronomers" would be amazed to hear themselves so described, for the term "astronomy" itself is very new, compared with "astrology." The true reason behind the coining of the term "astronomy" is fascinating . . . but more about that in a later book.

If Paul's impassioned appeal should bring about an honest investigation of astrobiology, and such research should prove successful, the Catholic Church might then give this solution its Papal blessing, without appearing to endorse astrology itself. A happy, typically Libra-conceived ending for everyone. I can't speak for Pope Paul's inner, secret motives in making this strangely intense plea at a time when he knew his weary days of duty were numbered. But I can guess. We all have the right to hold a personal, individual opinion or conviction. It's called freedom of thought.

Until Pope Paul's plea is answered by the scientific community to which he so eloquently and directly appealed, there may yet be a way to bring Light to the birth control–abortion controversy — through women themselves, individually. And in a manner in which they need not be troubled by the very real difficulty of finding an ethical, competent and reliable astrologer. I take great pleasure in mentioning such a possibility in *Love Signs*, since this is a book concerned with love in *all* its forms . . . including human birth and human survival.

A concerned friend and astrological associate of mine will be, within the very, very near future, authoring a book on this subject. The authorship will be initialed R. C. (and no, the letters don't stand for Roman Catholic — not yet. Such religious conversion to the holiness of astrology is not quite *that* near). It will be a book that will teach women of all twelve Sun Signs how to easily calculate their own astrobiology dates, thus circumventing all the stubborn blindness and ignorance around them. So hang in there, Earthlings! Rescue from the stars is on the way. Just make sure your parents told you the true date of your birth, be prepared to respect the wise counsel of Ecclesiastes regarding *"a time to embrace, and a time to refrain from embracing"* . . . and be patient just a little while longer.

Meanwhile, there are lots of homeless babies and children of all ages out there, all over the world . . . who would like to light up your life while you're waiting . . . if you'll just open your hearts and allow them to dance in, trailing sunbeams and songs to brighten the darkness, through the magic of loving . . and being loved in return. You don't need astrology to calculate the right "time to embrace" the lost and lonely. Any time is the right time for bear hugs . . . and the carols of children's laughter. Any time *you* choose.

☆ ☆ ☆ ☆ ☆ ☆

For the Pilgrim's Progress

Recommended Reading List

Over the years, I've received such a blizzard of letters asking me to recommend books for the fledgling astrologer and the occult beginner, I'm offering here some suggestions for further study—these all being either my past and current personal astrological "bibles"—or books that have expanded my own awareness in the myriad metaphysical fields, at various times.

There are many hundreds of astrology textbooks published, most of them repetitious, some of them of no help whatsoever—and only a very few of them of any real value to the serious, esoteric professional. One can waste a good deal of money, since astrology books are so expensive, using the slow process of trial and error. I don't claim that these are the only valid textbooks. There are a number of other fine ones. But these, in my own opinion, constitute a *required* library for the sincere student of astrology. They are basic. After these books have been acquired, others may be added according to personal preference.

Also, in answer to those many who have written to ask, I use the Equal House system of the ancients in calculating a horoscope myself, having tested and found the modern Placidian system not nearly so dependable or revealing. In my own experience, the Placidian "intercepted houses," which claim to give more depth to astrological interpretation of the nativity, only serve to cloud the issues and to create ambivalence. Human nature is strange. People always tend to lean toward the more "complicated" methods in any field, rejecting the simplistic—when the fact is that "truth" invariably is hidden within simplicity. To each his own, of course. And to each *her* own. The catholic-minded student should learn all the common systems, and then decide for himself or herself. I merely state here my personal faith in the decided superiority of the Equal House system of the ancients for those who have inquired, and who have expressed an interest in my private preference. For me, the Placidian system results in many inaccuracies of interpretation. But if it works for you, by all means use it. The very finest technical explanation of why the Equal House system is the more accurate and reliable is contained in the front section of Sydney Omarr's excellent book, *My World of Astrology.*

The following astrology textbooks are listed in order of importance to the novice in the beginning stages of learning to calculate a nativity (natal chart or horoscope). If possible, it's desirable to purchase at the start all the books listed. If you can afford only a few at a time, my recommendation is that they be purchased in the order in which they're given here.

In answer to the many requests for recommended reading in the entire occult or esoteric-spiritual field (supplementary to astrology itself) I've also listed here the books I've personally found the most inspiring and enlightening for the beginner. This is by no means a complete list. There are many others. But these are the ones that bestow a more comprehensive "awakening," and which I therefore believe should be read *first*. This second list of recommended books is not given in any particular order of importance. If I were pressed to advise which of the books among these should constitute the *initial* introduction to these matters, I would say *There Is a River*, by Thomas Sugrue, because this book is a sound general preparation for the wisdom to be found in all the others and holds the reader's interest completely, whether a believer or a disbeliever. It is a good place to begin.

Not all but some titles are annotated for the reader's greater convenience.

TO LEARN TO CALCULATE AND INTERPRET A HOROSCOPE

Ephemeriden 1890-1950 (Zurich), calculated for noon GMT (Greenwich Mean Time)

or

The Complete Planetary Ephemeris, calculated for midnight GMT for 1950 to 2,000 A.D.

If the Zurich ephemeris is used, the student will also need *Die Deutsche Ephemeride* (calculated for midnight GMT) for any ten-year period after 1950, such as the current one for the years 1971 through 1980, inclusive.

The Rosicrucian Tables of Houses

This contains, in addition to the necessary information for locating the Ascendent and MidHeaven of a nativity, a surprisingly comprehensive listing of the latitudes and longitudes of both American and foreign cities. (When such a list contains Cripple Creek, Colorado — *that's* comprehensive!)

Time in the U.S.A. Compiled by Doris Chase Doan.

This is a "must" for accurate calculation and for birth hour rectification. It contains the very necessary Daylight Savings Time information, which cannot be found in any other book. This is the best book of its kind — and since a chart is not accurate if you don't know the facts about DST in various places at various times, it is vital. For many decades in the U.S.A., each state and town and city has had an individual rule about DST, rather like the Mad Hatter's Tea Party. The only time the entire nation was on DST simultaneously was during the years of World War II, when it was called War Time — and it lasted consecutively all year long, every year, during the period of the war. *Time in the U.S.A* explains War Time, gives the period when it was in effect — and also gives the DST of other years for different hamlets, cities and towns within the States, for which there is considerable variation.

My World of Astrology, by Sydney Omarr. New York: Fleet Publishing Company, 1965.

No published astrological textbook so clearly and definitively demonstrates the CORRECT WAY to cast a chart. All other books written on the subject are to some degree confusing and misleading. Sydney's book is the only one that explains (or at least the only one that makes it CLEAR to a beginner) the URGENT IMPORTANCE of the position of the SUN in a horoscope. The Sun MUST fall at the right "Time" in the chart. Otherwise, you can be sure that you've either made a mistake in your math calculations—or that NO BABY could have been born on that particular day, month and year—at that particular time, in that particular longitude-latitude.

This constitutes the greatest proof of the validity of astrology. It's also an enormous help in the rectification of the true birth time. (Mother's memory and the Nurse's accuracy are both less than ideal.)

The World-Breath has definite and periodic pulsations — a systole and diastole action — whereby birth is controlled. Nature's infinite periodicity may not be altered nor disputed. Births may take place in respect to any single locality and date *only* at intervals that are in accordance with certain Lunar motion. Only particular conditions involving the World-Breath PERMIT BIRTH to occur in a given location, at a specific moment in Time.

Repeatedly, I and others have challenged skeptical astronomers and scientists to allow us to prove this profound proof of the holiness of astrology — to no avail.

Omarr's book also contains fascinating accounts of the author's several successful debates with various "erudite" critics of astrology — and a wealth of other assorted natal and esoteric information.

The Manual of Astrology, by Sepharial. London: W. Foulsham and Company, Ltd., 1962.

This is perhaps the one book I would place at the very top of the list of absolutely indispensable interpretive textbooks. This book alone can make anyone who has a natural aptitude for such work a competent astrologer of natal science.

The Complete Method of Prediction, by Robert de Luce. New York, N.Y. 10016: ASI Publishers, Inc. 127 Madison Ave., 1978.

An exceptional and extraordinary interpretive guide on a level with the Sepharial textbook. In particular, this is a fine book regarding transits and progressions in *predictive* work; whereas the Sepharial book is more helpful concerning the interpretation of the natal horoscope (character and potential, etc.).

Heaven Knows What, by Grant Lewi. St. Paul, Minn. 55165: Llewellyn Publications, P.O. Box 3383, 1962.

A classic, and deservedly so. This book can bring a quick comprehension of astrology to even the amateur, and is written in Gemini Lewi's wonderfully readable and witty style, without his sacrifice of a single thread of the scientific foundation of astrology. Lewi was a mathematical genius, as well as a fine creative writer, a rare combination. This book is concerned mainly with character analysis and potential, on the basis of the Luminary (Sun-Moon) positions and other planetary aspects in the birth chart — and the reader doesn't have to know how to calculate a horoscope to find it useful and amazingly reliable as a measurement of character and personality on the basis of more than the Sun Sign alone. Charts in the back allow the reader to look up the natal aspects of any birthday. But caution should be used in relation to the MOON SIGN. It's best to have this particular position calculated *exactly.*

Astrology for the Millions, by Grant Lewi. St. Paul, Minn.: Llewellyn Publications, 1975.

The same kind of classic as the above book, except that this one deals mostly with the predictive facet of astrology for the amateur and professional alike. Both books contain a wealth of additional reading material regarding the entire field of astrology, easily understood by those who know nothing about this art and science whatsoever — and are useful as well for the serious student of astrology.

Astrology and the Human Sex Life, by Vivian Robson. London: W. Foulsham and
Company, Ltd., 1963.

An excellent book for the purpose of comparing two horoscopes in detailed
compatibility work.

How to Handle Your Human Relations, by Lois Haines Sargent. Washington, D.C.:
American Federation of Astrologers, 1958.

A most reliable guide concerning compatibility aspects between horoscopes,
on the same level as the above book but not quite so in-depth regarding this
particular branch of astrology.

Aspects, by Charles Carter. London: L. N. Fowler & Co. Ltd.

Any book at all by Alan Leo.

Any book at all by Manly P. Hall.

The Dictionary of Astrology, by James Wilson. New York: Samuel Weiser Publications, 1974.

This an indispensable book for the student who intends to make a serious
study of astrology — or to become a professional astrologer. A really urgent guide
for all manner of astrological terminologies and methods.

Horary Astrology, by Robert de Luce.

Horary Astrology, by Geraldine Davis. N. Hollywood, Cal. 91607: Symbols and Signs,
P.O. Box 4536.

Linda Goodman's Sun Signs. New York: Taplinger, 1968.

Any good Pluto ephemeris.

Showing the "movements" or the sign positions of the planet Pluto over the
years — and giving an interpretation of Pluto's natal aspects in the birth
horoscope (potential) as well as the meaning of Pluto's transiting and progressed
aspects in predictive work. The German books concerning Pluto are the most
definitive and reliable.

The Technique of Prediction, by Ronald Carlyle Davison. London: L. N. Fowler &
Co., Ltd., 1971.

One of the finest textbooks available concerning the interpretation of
transiting planets and progressions.

Lectures on Medical Astrology, by Davidson, M.D.

You'll be extremely fortunate to locate and possess this series of lectures by
Dr. Davidson on Medical Astrology. It is not easily available. At one time it was
printed by astrologer Charles Jayne, of New York. This is, without question, the
most accurate, perceptive and comprehensive study of medical astrology thus far
published, to my knowledge.

Any book by Margaret Hone.

Any book by or about Evangeline Adams.

The Astrology Annual Reference Book. Symbols & Signs — Hollywood, Cal.

This reference guide has been compiled with loving care and rare integrity
as a quick and easy, reliable source for a multitude of purposes, and is
republished and re-created every year — with many new astrological concepts for
study, which the editors neither endorse nor condemn but offer for consideration
and research.

Reincarnation in World Thought, edited by S. L. Cranston & Joseph Head. New York: Julian Press, Crown Publishers, Inc.

    This is an excellent and incredibly detailed book concerning the vast subject of reincarnation, even giving the private experiences of many famous people regarding *déjà vu.* It is scholarly and utterly fascinating, and would prove for the most skeptical the sound common sense of this basic truth of all Life — the original foundation of all religion.

Reincarnation, The Phoenix Fire Mystery edited by S. L. Cranston & Joseph Head. New York: Julian Press, Crown Publishers, Inc., 1978.

    This book is interesting and informative for anyone who wishes to pursue the subject of reincarnation, but the above book edited by the same people is far more helpful and enlightening.

The Search for the Girl with the Blue Eyes, by Jess Stern. New York: Doubleday & Co.

The Game of Life, by Florence Shinn. Marina Del Rey, Cal.: De Vorss & Co.

You Forever, by Lobsang Rampa. London: Corgi Books, 1965.

    Other Rampa books are fascinating, but not nearly so helpful and enlightening as this one.

There Is a River, by Thomas Sugrue. New York: Henry Holt & Co., 1942.

    Or, The Association For Research and Enlightenment, Virginia Beach, Va.

Any book about Edgar Cayce.

    Any book published by the A.R.E (Association For Research and Enlightenment) Virginia Beach, Va.

Any book by Hugh Lynn Cayce.

The Sexuality of Jesus, by Rev. William Phipps. New York: Harper & Row, 1979.

    To be republished by H & R under the title *Did Jesus Love?*

Any book by Rev. William Phipps.

The Aquarian Gospel, by Levi. Marina Del Ray, Cal.: De Vorss & Company, 1964.

    A truly necessary classic.

The Essene Gospel of Peace.

    Available only through Academy Books, 3085 Reynard Way, San Diego, Cal. Any book at all published by Academy Books, above address. They will send you a complete list of titles and content.

Astrology, the Space Age Science, by Joseph F. Goodavage. New York: New American Library, W. W. Norton & Co., Inc. 1967.

    This book should be required reading for all schools.

The Secret Life of Plants, by Peter Tompkins and Christopher Bird. New York: Harper & Row, 1973.

The Secrets of the Great Pyramid, by Peter Tompkins. New York: Harper & Row, 1971.

The Mysteries of the Mexican Pyramids, by Peter Tompkins. New York: Harper & Row, 1976.

Cheiro's Book of Numbers, by Cheiro. New York: Arc Books, 1964.

The Kabala of Numbers. New York: Samuel Weiser Publishers, 1913.

>One of the finest, if not *the* finest book in the field of spiritual numerology, closely aligned with astrology. Extremely enlightening and awakening.

Psychic Discoveries Behind the Iron Curtain, by Shelia Ostrander and Lynn Schroeder. New York: Bantam Books, 1971; Englewood Cliffs, N.J.: Prentice-Hall, Inc., 1970.

>This should be purchased in hardcover if possible. A superlative basic book regarding the entire occult field of worldwide scientific investigation of the metaphysical.

Health and Light, by John N. Ott. New York: Pocketbooks, 1976.

The Life Everlasting, by Marie Corelli. Borden Publishing Co., 1855 West Main St., Alhambra, Cal. 91801.

Ardath and *Romance of Two Worlds,* by Marie Corelli. Try used bookstores.

>The above books are classics concerning Twin Souls and mystical awareness. Other Corelli books not so helpful, but always interesting. Corelli's writing is inspired and will be extremely enlightening for those curious to learn more about "Twin Souls." Her spiritual revelations are reliable and follow all the higher precepts of metaphysics, with the single exception that the author, at the time she wrote these books, had not yet been illuminated regarding the falsehood of the "Divinity" of Jesus — that he was an exceptional and extraordinary human, but only a man and not Divine. Other than this one misleading factor, the Corelli books are flawless regarding all occult matters.

A Dweller on Two Planets, by Phylos. Borden Publishing Co., 1855 West Main St., Alhambra, Cal. 91801.

>For the advanced student of the occult.

Any book by Dion Fortune. St. Paul, Minn.: Llewellyn Publications, or secondhand bookstores.

>Dion Fortune books are only for the *very* advanced initiate.

Consciousness and Reality, by Dr. Charles Musès.

>Soon to be republished. Check with your local bookstore in 1979–80.

The Essene Christ, by Upton C. Ewing. The Edenite Society, Inc. P.O. Box 115, Imlayston, N.J. 08526.

The Prophet of the Dead Sea Scrolls, by Upton C. Ewing. The Edenite Society.

>These two Ewing books should also be required reading in schools, for the awakening of all the children of the Aquarian Age.

A Time For Astrology, by Jess Stearn. New York: New American Library, W. W. Norton & Co., Inc., 1972 East Rutherford, N.J.: Coward, McCann & Geoghegan, Inc., 1971.

Design for Destiny, by Edward W. Russell. New York: Ballantine Books, Inc., Division of Random House, Inc., 1973.

>A most important book, containing serious answers to those who are skeptical of all spiritual phenomena.

The Last Days of the Late Great State of California, by Kurt Gentry. New York: G. P. Putnam's Sons, 1968 (probably available only through secondhand bookstores).

A Wrinkle in Time, by Madeleine L'Engle. New York: Dell Publishing Co., Inc.

Any book by George Hunt Williamson.

Any book by Michel D'Obrenovich.

The Little Prince, by Antoine de Saint-Exupéry.   New York: Harcourt Brace Jovanovich, 1943.

The Spear of Destiny, by Trevor Ravenscroft. New York: G. P. Putnam's Sons, 1973.

The Gospel of St. John, by Rudolph Steiner.   Spring Valley, N.Y.: The Anthroposophic Press, Inc., 1940.

> From a cycle of twelve lectures given by Steiner at Hamburg, Germany, in May of 1908.

Any book by Rudolph Steiner.

> For a list of all books by Steiner, check with the Goethe Society, New York. Rudolph Steiner was a metaphysician unequaled before or since his time regarding all spiritual writings.

Four Arguments for the Elimination of Television, by Jerry Mander.   New York: William Morrow & Co., Inc., 1978.

> The subject matter concerns far more than television itself. It concerns your literal survival, and is one of the most important books of the dawning Aquarian Age. It should be required reading in schools, but probably won't be because it offends those who make large fortunes from activities that harm us all.

A Tree Grows in Brooklyn, by Betty Smith.   New York: Harper & Row, 1947.

> A book about metaphysical truth, and all forms of love, disguised as everyday living. My personal favorite of all books written during this century. It will carry an open mind wherever it wishes to go, especially inside itself. Reading it for the first time is like finding an old friend you thought you'd lost a long time ago, even if you're not from Brooklyn! You're as much in need of its wisdom and promise for tomorrow as was the generation of the forties. Maybe more.

The French Lieutenant's Woman, by John Fowles. Boston: Little Brown, 1969.

> This is a Scorpio tale of strangeness, holding a truth as old as Eve and Adam. The ultimate in the often forgotten quality of miracles, which is the unexpected. It emphasizes the vast gulf between the feminine and the masculine principles and the mystery of the silent power that brings the oppposed into unity. Many secrets sleep between the lines for the perceptive. Not a metaphysical work in any sense, this book nevertheless demonstrates impeccably the strength of the cord that binds Twin Souls — a cord no force can break — even allowing you, the reader, to participate in the final karmic solution. Not for the casual or the impatient seekers, but a secret treasure for the wiser pilgrim.

A few of these books may only be obtained as indicated. If your local occult bookstore doesn't carry any of the others, most of them may be obtained by writing to:

> B. Dalton (Pickwick Books), 6743 Hollywood Blvd., L.A., Cal. 90028
> Gilbert's Bookshop, 6278 Hollywood Blvd., L.A., Cal. 90028
> Samuel Weiser Bookshop, 734 Broadway, New York, N.Y. 10003
> Zoltan Mason Bookstore, 789 Lexington Ave., New York, N.Y. 10021
> Chinook Bookstore, 210 North Tejon, Colorado Springs, Co. 80903. (they will order any of these books for you).

If any of these fine books, which should be always available to the public, happen to be "out of print," I suggest that you write to the publisher and strongly urge republication. Publishers have no right to withhold from you books which could so benefit your lives, which perhaps did not sell as quickly as their publishers would like — for the good reason that they were not properly promoted and advertised.

For more information about Waterless Toilets

Clivus Multrum, 14A Eliot St., Cambridge, MA. 02138. (617) 491-5820.

Enviroscope Inc., 2855 E. Pacific Coast Highway, Corona del Mar, CA. 92625. (714) 673-7774

Recreation Ecology Conservation of United States, Inc., 9800 Bluemound Rd., Milwaukee, WI. 53226.

Acknowledgments

MERCI BEAUCOUP . . . TANTE GRAZIE . . . DANKE SCHÖN . . . ARIGATO GOZAIMASU . . . TACK   KÖSZÖNÖM . . . MAHALO . . . SHUKRAN . . . ASHANTE . . . DANK U . . . TAKKE . . . DIK . . . ZAHVALA   DZIEKI . . . DIOLCH . . . PÁRIKARÓVA . . . PODZIEKOWAME . . . GRACIAS . . . EUCHARISTO

THANK YOU !

Any book requires more than its writer and creator to bring it into final form, as most authors readily admit in their pages of acknowledgments — especially a book of the sheer length and magnitude of this one, which attempts the enormous task of covering astrological compatibilities in depth in 78 chapters and 168 separate sections, plus assorted material of a metaphysical and mystical nature.

As the author of *Love Signs* then, I'd like to express my warm gratitude to the following people who aided me in the gigantic undertaking of the completion of this work. It seems appropriate to say "thank you" to them at the end, rather than at the beginning, because it is actually the Omega of the book which they helped to bring about.

My abiding friend and editor, Dr. Charles Musès, who performed the repeated wizardry of refining each chapter with his wonted scholarly and literary excellence . . .

Dolores Simon, Kathleen Hyde and Lydia Link, the three Scorpion Eagles in the Harper & Row copy editing and design departments, who kept me from dangling my participles and splitting my infinitives . . .

Joe Montebello, the gentle Crab who heads the Harper & Row art department, whose artistic sensitivity to color and design kept the aura of the book in harmony with its concept, from jacket and binding to endpapers and art work . . .

Lioness Paula Diamond, the magical lady at Harper & Row who sunbeamed the book toward the public in her usual miraculous manner . . .

Cleve Backster, the Fish who kept my often bruised nose to the grindstone, through an odd combination of teasing, threat, praise and promise — when I was discouraged, which was frequently . . .

J. B. Handelsman, the perceptive, witty and clever *New Yorker* artist, who conjured and designed the eloquent sketches of the Twelve Sun Signs displaying their astrological vices and virtues in the front and back of the book . . .

The relatives and friends who kindly allowed me to relate their intimate, personal experiences to make astrological compatibility come alive for my readers . . .

and finally . . .

Bob Brewer, who created the Twin Soul logo for *Love Signs* and who, as my mentor for "controversial" passages, exercised a wise control over some — inspired me with his wholehearted support of others — and continually guided my statements on urgent issues with his own compassionate viewpoint and deep insights . . . as always.

To All Those Who Love . . .
Expect a Miracle!

Miracles *are* possible. Miracles *do* happen. They are not "interruptions" of the laws of physics. They are not "violations" of the laws of Nature. They are confirmations of the laws of *Meta*-physics (beyond physics) and affirmations of the *deeper depths* of Nature's law. Only the Spirit, the Higher Angel of yourself, controls these deeper depths — which have not yet been discovered even by the most searching, seeking scientists. But this does not negate their existence, for they *shall* be discovered in the New Age!

Science is presently concerned only with the material forces, failing to recognize the Spiritual Forces. Yet, what is material force but the visible manifestation of the Spiritual Force behind it? To accept the material manifestation and deny the Spiritual Force that creates and controls it is to place yourself in the illogical position of accepting an effect — and denying its cause.

Once you have accepted the Spiritual Force *cause* and the material force *effect* as a perfect unity, then how can you dare presume to set a limit to the manifestations of either of these forces . . . especially to the Power of the cause and the effect combined? You — and your Supraconscious — control your miracles. All that's needed to produce them is the marriage of Truth and Faith.

Pax et Bonum = Verum et Unum : "Seek the Truth, and it shall set you free!"

Before

LOVE SIGNS